Migrant Support Handbook

Connor Johnston is a barrister at Garden Court Chambers who specialises in housing, homelessness, community care and public law. A significant proportion of his work over the last 10 years has been in the field of migrant support, with a focus on ensuring his clients have access to safe, suitable accommodation and financial support. As part of this, he has volunteered with the Asylum Support Appeals Project providing pro bono support at the Asylum Support Tribunal since 2017. He is recognised in the legal directories for his expertise, is a member of the EHRC panel of approved counsel and a former Legal Aid Lawyer of the Year. He has been a regular contributor to *Legal Action* magazine and a speaker at Legal Action Group events, and is a co-author of *Housing allocation and homelessness,*[1] one of the leading textbooks on homelessness.

Shu Shin Luh is a barrister at Doughty Street Chambers. Her practice has a strong human rights, civil liberties and anti-discrimination focus. Her expertise covers a broad range of subject matters including community care, mental health and mental capacity, healthcare, education, housing and welfare benefits, human trafficking, immigration and asylum, and deprivation of liberty. She pursues significant public interest litigation on behalf of individuals and organisations and is recognised for her particular expertise in children's and migrants' rights and has appeared in many of the leading cases in these areas. She received the Young Legal Aid Lawyer of the Year award in 2012, Advocate's Junior Pro Bono Barrister of the Year in 2019, and Chambers and Partners' Human Rights and Public Law Junior of the Year in 2021.

The Legal Action Group is a national, independent charity which campaigns for equal access to justice for all members of society.

Legal Action Group:

- Strengthens the voice of people and communities denied access to justice
- Supports frontline charities, lawyers and advisers to deliver access to justice
- Influences law and policy to improve access to justice and create a fair legal system for all

1 *Housing allocation and homelessness: Law and practice* HHJ Jan Luba KC, Liz Davies, Connor Johnston and Tessa Buchanan, LexisNexis, 6th edn, 2022.

Migrant Support Handbook

Shu Shin Luh
Connor Johnston

LAG Legal Action Group
2023

This edition published in Great Britain 2023
by LAG Education and Service Trust Limited
Gatehouse Chambers, 1 Lady Hale Gate, London WC1X 8BS
www.lag.org.uk

British Library Cataloguing in Publication Data
a CIP catalogue record for this book is available from the British Library.

FSC www.fsc.org MIX Paper from responsible sources FSC® C020438

This book has been produced using Forest Stewardship Council (FSC) certified paper. The wood used to produce FSC certified products with a 'Mixed Sources' label comes from FSC certified well-managed forests, controlled sources and/or recycled material.

print ISBN 978-1-913648-53-4
eBook ISBN 978-1-913648-54-1
bundle (print and ebook) 978-1-913648-55-8

Typeset by Refinecatch Limited, Bungay, Suffolk
Printed in Great Britain by Hobbs the Printers, Totton, Hampshire

Contents

Foreword

In 2001, the late, great Helen Bamber wrote in the foreword to LAG's first asylum support handbook that it was needed to both understand and challenge the muddle and misery of support for asylum-seekers.

Since then, as the authors' introduction helpfully describes, there has been a mountain of legal reforms, aptly described by the Court of Appeal as 'destitution by design'.

In the face of a relatively new and niche area of law, activist and non-activist lawyers and judges have relied on LAG's reliable guide through the law, policy and procedure to enable those seeking asylum in the UK to access a minimum standard of support. Contractors, social workers, researchers, medics, faith workers, trade unionists, advice-workers, campaigners and just ordinary members of the public have also depended on it as a guide through the system.

I continue to be inspired by the alliances formed between indefatigable lawyers and non-lawyers, supported by NGOs, to improve the treatment of asylum-seekers. In the past 20 years, there have been countless court judgments upholding fundamental rights, from ending the use of vouchers, to defeating the 'section 55' policy which refused support to those who had not claimed asylum promptly on arrival in the UK. This handbook explains the law clearly in LAG's accessible style and provides the foundation for both individual advice and systemic challenges. The authors' combined expertise in immigration and social welfare law is invaluable in unpicking the intersection between the different legal specialisms at play in migrant support law.

At the end of June 2023, there was a record number of 117,450 individuals in receipt of asylum support, mostly due to the Home Office's failure to promptly process asylum claims. Because the Home Office has failed to contract sufficient accommodation, asylum-seekers, including survivors of torture or trafficking, face years housed in unsuitable hotels, military bases and now barges, or even detention centres. So this book could not be more timely.

The asylum/asylum support system is operated in a way which aims to distance migrants from the rule of law and access to justice. This can be seen graphically in the current provision of accommodation on barges and military bases, segregating them from the rest of society. The purpose of this book is to help its readers reunite them.

In the words of Lord Hoffmann: 'Human rights are the rights essential to the life and dignity of the individual in a democratic society . . . I think it is well arguable that human rights include the right to a minimum standard of living, without which many of the other rights would be a mockery.'[1]

It is a privilege to introduce such a desperately needed compass in migrant access to the fundamental right to food, shelter, and other necessities.

Sue Willman
September 2023

1 *Matthews v Ministry of Defence* [2003] UKHL 4.1

Authors' note

This book started off as a suggestion made by Esther Pilger at a conference in late 2017 that we might like to think about working on a text to take the place of the inestimably valuable *Support for asylum-seekers and other migrants*, by Sue Willman and the late Steve Knafler QC.[2] 'Easy', we thought. 'We'll have that done in six-months . . .' Nearly six years on and it is a little difficult to say exactly where the time has gone. But there are three stand-out factors that account for much of it.

The first, of course, is our naively optimistic miscalculation of how much time is actually required to write a specialist textbook from scratch. The inability of barristers to correctly estimate how much time they need to say or do anything is a phenomenon familiar to solicitors and judges across the land and our time estimate in this case might be regarded as a classic of the genre.

The second – much more seriously – is that we are trying to replace the irreplaceable. *Support for asylum-seekers and other migrants* was written by two pioneers in the field and for many years was the go-to resource for advisers, providing a comprehensive, insightful and accessible resource. Trying to emulate this to some degree has been a gargantuan task which has only served to emphasise the huge contribution made by Steve to the law, and how keenly his loss continues to be felt. We owe a debt of gratitude to Sue and Steve not only for providing a template, inspiration and reference material for this text but also for their work, and the work of their colleagues, in creating the specialism of migrant support in the first place.

The third has been the constant and pernicious stream of legislative and policy changes that have made, and continue to make, it harder and more complex for those seeking sanctuary, or to make a new life, in the UK to access ever-diminishing levels and standards of support. Things that might have been unthinkable even a few

2 *Support for asylum-seekers and other migrants: A guide to legal and welfare rights* Sue Willman and Steve Knafler QC, Legal Action Group, 3rd edn, 2009.

years ago – the UK's exit from the European Union, the forced removal of asylum-seekers to Rwanda or making them live on a barge with more than a passing resemblance to a prison ship – are close to becoming a reality. Trying to produce a text in this everchanging landscape has not been an easy task, and has necessitated numerous revisions and rewrites. We have made the decision to publish the text now, notwithstanding the looming spectre of the Illegal Migration Act 2023 which will bring further flux to the law, precisely because the landscape is ever changing and the need for some kind of guide to navigate this landscape has become so acute. Hence, we feel that we must draw the line somewhere and have chosen to do so here. We have endeavoured to state the law as of May 2023.

The subject matter of this book is, of course, an incredibly complex one. We do not pretend or imagine that we have covered every detail or that we have done so without making errors, particularly as this is a first edition. But one of the most heartening things about working in migrant support is the spirit of collaboration in the sector and the sharing of information and ideas for the common good. With that in mind, we will gratefully receive thoughts and constructive feedback on this edition in the hope of developing the text in years to come.

Professionally, we would like to thank Esther Pilger, who saw the need for this book and started us on the project, and Jen Cowan and Elisabeth Doyle for the editorial work on the text as it evolved. We could not have completed this project without the generous time, expertise and insights that the contributors have offered up. Many of our colleagues have also given up time to review and comment on draft chapters of the book. They know who they are and we are grateful to each of them. In particular, we would like to thank Marie-Anne Fishwick and Deborah Gellner for their comments on early drafts of the asylum support chapters.

A book does not come together without a publisher. We are grateful to Legal Action Group for giving us the opportunity, for supporting us to see this project through and for patiently forgiving us for every missed deadline we ever agreed to.

Finally, we would also like to extend thanks to our families who have been so patient with us and supported us throughout, and are bored of us talking about 'the book' and it taking up family time. Particular thanks are owed by Connor to Rebecca Omonira for her tolerance, encouragement and inspiration.

Shu Shin Luh and Connor Johnston
16 August 2023

List of contributors

Tessa Buchanan, Garden Court Chambers
Emma Fitzsimons, Garden Court Chambers
Helen Foot, Garden Court Chambers
Louise Hooper, Garden Court Chambers
Maria Moodie, Garden Court Chambers
Oliver Persey, Garden Court Chambers
Tom Royston, Garden Court North Chambers
Irena Sabic KC, Garden Court Chambers
Anthony Vaughan, Doughty Street Chambers

Stop press

Since the final draft of this text was prepared there have been several important legal and policy developments which impact on the content that follows. In particular:

- The Illegal Migration Bill is now the Illegal Migration Act 2023. Chapters 3, 5, 6, 9 and 11 need to be read in light of this. Although migrant support is not the primary focus of the Act, the Act will have ramifications in this field, for example, the increased use of declarations of inadmissibility, discussed at paras 3.131–3.142, in respect of persons seeking asylum in the UK will impact on the eligibility of such persons for asylum support, as discussed at paras 5.39–5.44. The Act, as foreshadowed at para 9.5, also paves the way for significant changes to support for unaccompanied children, albeit the nature and extent of those changes is still not known.
- The Retained EU Law (Revocation and Reform) Bill is now the Retained EU Law (Revocation and Reform) Act 2023. Paragraphs 2.25–2.29 should be read in light of this.
- Judgment has been handed down by the Court of Appeal in *R (AAA (Syria)) v SSHD*[3] (the Rwanda case) overturning the decision of the Divisional Court. Paragraphs 3.19, 3.131–3.142 and 5.39–5.44 should be read in light of this.
- The classes of person eligible for social housing, homelessness assistance and welfare benefits have been expanded to include certain Sudanese nationals.[4] Chapters 4 and 7 should be read in light of this.

3 [2023] EWCA Civ 745.

4 Allocation of Housing and Homelessness (Eligibility) (England) and Persons Subject to Immigration Control (Housing Authority Accommodation and Homelessness) (Amendment) Regulations 2023 SI No 530; Social Security (Habitual Residence and Past Presence) (Amendment) Regulations 2023 SI No 532.

- On 25 May 2023, the Court of Appeal allowed an appeal in *R (Bui) v SSWP*,[5] finding the Secretary of State for Work and Pensions' blanket policy of not making payments of universal credit until applicants have been allocated national insurance numbers to be unlawful. See para 4.113.
- On 17 July 2023, asylum support rates were increased from £45 to £47.39 for those in self-catered accommodation and from £9.10 to £9.58 per week for those in catered accommodation. Chapters 5 and 6 should be read in light of this.
- On 27 July 2023, the High Court handed down judgment in *R (ECPAT UK (Every Child Protected against Trafficking)) v Kent CC and SSHD*[6] in which it found that Kent County Council had acted unlawfully in refusing to receive all unaccompanied children arriving in its area into its care under the Children Act 1989, and the Secretary of State for the Home Department's solution of housing these children in unregulated hotels was unlawful. The High Court also found that the two public authorities acted unlawfully in entering into an agreement that would cap the number of unaccompanied children that Kent County Council has to accommodate and look after at any given time. Both public authorities have been ordered by the High Court to take remedial steps in the light of the judgment, the effect of which is not yet fully known.
- The Bibby Stockholm barge has arrived in Portland for use as asylum support accommodation. The *Allocation of accommodation policy*[7] has been updated to include eligibility criteria for accommodation on the barge. Paragraphs 5.169–5.184 should be read in light of this.
- Litigation concerning the legality of the government's scheme to remove asylum-seekers to Rwanda for the examination of their asylum claims has yet to conclude and is likely to have an impact on the implementation of the Illegal Migration Act 2023.

5 [2023] EWCA Civ 566.
6 [2023] EWHC 1953 (Admin).
7 V9.0, Home Office, July 2023.

Table of cases

MK v Secretary of State for the Home Department [2012] EWHC 1896 (Admin), [2012] 7 WLUK 224 — 5.246
MMA v Secretary of State for the Home Department AS/11/06/26857, 24 August 2011, FTT (Asylum Support) — 6.130
MN v Secretary of State for the Home Department AS/15/05/33235, 12 June 2015, FTT (Asylum Support) — 6.77
MN and IXU v Secretary of State for the Home Department [2020] EWCA Civ 1746, [2021] 1 WLR 1956, [2020] 12 WLUK 350, [2021] HRLR 2, (2021) Times, February 2 — 11.178, 11.190–11.192
MS v Secretary of State for the Home Department AST/07/04/15053, 24 April 2007, FTT (Asylum Support) — 6.135
MS (British citizenship: EEA appeals: Belgium), Re [2019] UKUT 356 (IAC), [2019] 10 WLUK 834, [2020] INLR 226 — 2.7
MS (Ivory Coast) v Secretary of State for the Home Department [2007] EWCA Civ 133, [2007] 2 WLUK 547, [2007] Imm AR 538, [2007] INLR 513, (2007) 104(10) LSG 28, (2007) Times, March 27 — 6.135
MS (Pakistan) v Secretary of State for the Home Department [2020] UKSC 9, [2020] 1 WLR 1373, [2020] 3 All ER 733, [2020] 3 WLUK 246, [2020] Imm AR 967, [2020] INLR 460, (2020) Times, March 24; *Reversing* [2018] EWCA Civ 594, [2018] 4 WLR 63, [2018] 3 WLUK 583, [2018] Imm AR 1055, [2018] INLR 516, (2018) Times, April 11 — 3.61, 3.62, 3.63, 3.64
MSM v Secretary of State for the Home Department CO/4687/2018 — 6.255
MVN v Greenwich LBC [2015] EWHC 1942 (Admin), [2015] 7 WLUK 321, (2015) 18 CCLR 645, [2015] ACD 141 — 11.37
MYA v Secretary of State for the Home Department AS/19/02/39259, 5 March 2019, FTT (Asylum Support) — 5.81
Maaouia v France App No 39652/98 [2000] 10 WLUK 172, (2001) 33 EHRR 42, 9 BHRC 205, ECtHR — 6.134
McFaddens (a firm) v Platford [2009] EWHC 126 (TCC), [2009] 1 WLUK 579, [2009] PNLR 26, (2009) 159 NLJ 198 — 10.157
Mahmud's application for judicial review, Re [2021] NIQB 6, [2021] 1 WLUK 558 — 5.128, 5.146, 5.225
Mahmud's application for judicial review, Re [2021] NIQB 37, [2021] 3 WLUK 770 — 5.128, 6.9, 6.200
Mandalia v Secretary of State for the Home Department [2015] UKSC 59, [2015] 1 WLR 4546, [2016] 4 All ER 189, [2015] 10 WLUK 352, [2016] Imm AR 180, [2016] INLR 184, (2015) Times, October 26 — 1.18
Masterman-Lister v Brutton & Co [2002] EWCA Civ 1889, [2003] 1 WLR 1511, [2003] 3 All ER 162, [2002] 12 WLUK 600, [2003] CP Rep 29, (2004) 7 CCLR 5, [2003] PIQR P20, [2003] Lloyd's Rep Med 244, (2003) 73 BMLR 1, [2003] MHLR 166, [2003] WTLR 259, (2003) 147 SJLB 60, (2002) Times, December 28 — 10.159

Patel v Secretary of State for the Home Department [2012] EWCA Civ 741, [2013] 1 WLR 63, [2012] 4 All ER 94, [2012] 6 WLUK 53, [2012] Imm AR 898, [2012] INLR 485, (2012) Times, August 30 — 1.1

Patel v Secretary of State for the Home Department; Secretary of State for the Home Department v Shah [2019] UKSC 59, [2020] 1 WLR 228, [2020] 2 All ER 557, [2019] 12 WLUK 196, [2020] 2 CMLR 12, [2020] Imm AR 600, [2020] INLR 350 — 2.94–2.97

Pirzada (deprivation of citizenship: general principles) [2017] UKUT 196 (IAC), [2017] 4 WLUK 369, [2017] Imm AR 1257 — 1.74

Poshteh v Kensington and Chelsea RLBC [2017] UKSC 36, [2017] AC 624, [2017] 2 WLR 1417, [2017] 3 All ER 1065, [2017] 5 WLUK 211, [2017] HLR 28, (2017) Times, May 16; *Affirming* [2015] EWCA Civ 711, [2015] 7 WLUK 235, [2015] HLR 36 — 7.252, 9.46

Practice Direction (UT: First-tier and Upper Tribunals: child, vulnerable adult and sensitive witnesses) [2009] 1 WLR 332, [2009] PTSR 331, [2008] 10 WLUK 798 — 3.101

Pretty v United Kingdom App No 2346/02 [2002] 4 WLUK 606, [2002] 2 FLR 45, [2002] 2 FCR 97, (2002) 35 EHRR 1, 12 BHRC 149, (2002) 66 BMLR 147, [2002] Fam Law 588, (2002) 152 NLJ 707, ECtHR — 3.45, 6.70

R (A) v Coventry City Council [2009] EWHC 34 (Admin), [2009] 1 WLUK 363, [2009] 1 FLR 1202, [2009] 1 FCR 501, [2009] BLGR 486, [2009] Fam Law 289 — 9.112

R (A) v Croydon LBC [2009] UKSC 8, [2009] 1 WLR 2557, [2010] 1 All ER 469, [2010] PTSR 106, [2009] 11 WLUK 652, [2010] 1 FLR 959, [2009] 3 FCR 607, [2010] HRLR 9, [2010] UKHRR 63, [2010] BLGR 183, (2009) 12 CCLR 552, [2010] Fam Law 137, (2009) 159 NLJ 1701, (2009) 153(46) SJLB 34, (2009) Times, November 30; *Reversing* [2008] EWCA Civ 1445, [2009] PTSR 1011, [2008] 12 WLUK 537, [2009] 1 FLR 1325, [2009] 1 FCR 317, [2009] BLGR 24, [2009] ACD 17, [2009] Fam Law 290 — 9.81, 11.34

R (A) v Croydon LBC [2015] UKUT 168 (IAC) — 11.35

R (A) v Enfield LBC [2016] EWHC 567 (Admin), [2016] 3 WLUK 459, [2017] 1 FLR 203, [2016] HLR 33, (2016) 19 CCLR 236, [2016] ACD 89, [2016] Fam Law 688 — 9.81, 9.191

R (A) v Lambeth LBC [2010] EWHC 1652 (Admin), [2010] 7 WLUK 192, [2010] 2 FCR 539 — 9.133, 9.135, 9.147

R (A) v Lambeth LBC [2010] EWHC 2439 (Admin), [2010] 10 WLUK 110 — 9.133, 9.147

R (A) v Lewisham LBC, 5 May 2016, Admin Ct — 9.46

R (A) v Liverpool City Council [2007] EWHC 1477 (Admin), [2007] 6 WLUK 593, (2007) 10 CCLR 716, (2007) Times, August 1 — 11.35

Table of statutes

s23C(5C)	9.160
s23C(6)–(7)	9.163
s23C(6)	7.316
s23C(7)	7.316
s23C(8)	9.163
s23C(9)	9.160
s23C(10)	9.161
s23CZB	9.172, 9.174, 9.196,
s23CZB(1)–(2)	9.169
s23CZB(3)–(6)	9.169, 9.170
s23CZB(3)	9.170
s23CZB(4)(a)	9.170
s23CZB(4)(b)	9.170
s23CZB(5)	9.171
s23CZB(6)	9.173
s23CZB(7)	9.174
s23CA	9.167, 9.168, 9.196
s23CA(1)–(5)	9.165
s23CA(2)	9.165
s23CA(3)(a)	9.165
s23CA(3)(b)	9.165
s23CA(4)–(7)	9.165
s23CA(6)	9.168
s23CA(7)	9.168
s23CA(8)	9.165
s23CA(9)	9.165
s23CA(11)	9.165
s23D(2)	9.172
s23E(1)(aa)	9.170
s23E(1)(b)	9.138, 9.145, 9.165
s23E(1B)	9.172
s24	9.176
s24(1)–(1B)	9.120, 9.177
s24(1A)	7.146, 9.177
s24(1B)	9.177
s24(2)	7.138, 7.144, 9.177
s24(2)(a)	7.146
s24(4)	9.179
s24(5)(za)–(a)	9.178
s24(5)(b)	9.178
s24A	9.178, 9.196
s24A(1)–(2)	9.180
s24A(3)(a)	9.181
s24A(3)(b)	9.181
s24A(4)	9.181
s24A(5)	9.181
s24A(6)	9.181
s24B	7.145, 9.85, 9.178, 9.196, 11.118
s24B(1)	9.160, 9.183
s24B(2)	9.160, 9.184, 11.120

Table of statutory instruments

Asylum Support (Interim Provisions) Regulations 1999 SI No 3056	5.50, 5.119, 6.94, 7.314
Asylum Support Regulations ('AS Regs') 2000 SI No 704	5.53, 5.56, 5.73, 5.200, 5.202, 5.203, 5.204, 5.233, 5.239, 6.41
reg 2	5.50, 5.56
reg 2(1)	5.50, 5.54, 5.296
reg 2(2)	5.30, 5.37, 5.43, 6.145
reg 2(2A)	5.36, 5.37, 6.145
reg 2(2A)(a)	5.30
reg 2(2A)(b)	5.30
reg 2(2A)(c)	5.30
reg 2(4)	5.50, 5.51, 11.253
reg 2(4)(a)	5.50
reg 2(4)(b)	5.50
reg 2(4)(c)	5.50
reg 2(4)(d)	5.50, 5.52
reg 2(4)(e)	5.50
reg 2(4)(f)	5.50
reg 2(4)(g)	5.50
reg 2(4)(h)	5.50
reg 2(4)(i)	5.50
reg 2(5)	5.51, 5.52
reg 2(6)	5.53
reg 2(7)	5.50
reg 3	5.221, 6.178
reg 3(1)	5.52, 5.221
reg 3(2)	5.52
reg 3(3)	5.221
reg 3(4)	5.139, 5.222, 6.179
reg 3(4)(a)	5.317
reg 3(4)(b)	5.317
reg 3(5)	5.222
reg 3(5A)	5.223
reg 3(5B)	5.223
reg 3(5C)	5.223, 5.283, 5.299
reg 3(6)	5.221, 5.222
reg 3(7)	5.223
reg 4	5.119–5.121, 5.319
reg 4(1)	5.319
reg 4(2)	5.120
reg 4(3)	5.120
reg 4(4)	5.119
reg 4(4)(a)	5.119
reg 4(4)(b)	5.119
reg 4(4)(c)	5.119
reg 4(8)–(9)	5.283
reg 5	5.52, 5.58
reg 6	5.64, 5.68
reg 6(3)–(4)	5.70

Housing Benefit (Persons who have attained the qualifying age for state pension credit) Regulations 2006 SI No 214	4.11
reg 4	4.109
reg 7	4.88
reg 10	4.51, 4.66, 4.84
reg 21	4.94
reg 51	4.18
reg 74	4.140
Housing Benefit Regulations 2006 SI No 213—	
reg 49	5.70
Immigration (Citizens' Rights Appeals) (EU Exit) Regulations 2020 SI No 61	2.174, 2.220, 2.228
reg 3	2.221
reg 3(2)	2.220
reg 4	2.221
reg 5	2.221
reg 6	2.221
regs 6A–6E	2.221
regs 6G–6J	2.221
reg 7	2.222
reg 8	2.223
reg 9(4)–(5)	2.223
reg 12	2.226
reg 13(5)	2.224
reg 14	2.224
reg 15	2.227
reg 16(3)	2.225
Sch 1	2.222
Sch 3 para 1	2.226
Immigration (Citizens' Rights etc) (EU Exit) Regulations 2020 SI No 1372	2.220
Immigration (European Economic Area) (Amendment) Regulations 2019 SI No 1155—	
reg 2(9)(a)(iii)	2.122
Immigration (European Economic Area) Regulations 2006 SI No 1003	2.39, 2.118, 2.120
reg 8(2)	2.118
reg 8(3)	2.118
Immigration (European Economic Area) Regulations ('EEA Regs') 2016 SI No 1052	2.6, 2.14, 2.39, 2.40, 2.41–2.137, 2.141, 2.144, 2.149, 2.153, 2.162, 2.191, 2.205, 2.206–2.218, 2.226, 4.46, 4.69, 4.81, 4.83, 7.19, 7.22, 7.24, 7.26, 7.404
reg 2	2.17, 2.122, 2.191, 2.207
reg 2(1)	4.46
reg 4	7.25

Table of Immigration Rules

Table of European and international legislation

EU legislation

Treaties, conventions and charters

Agreement between the United Kingdom of Great Britain and Northern Ireland and the Swiss Confederation on citizens' rights following the withdrawal of the United Kingdom from the European Union and the free movement of persons agreement ('Swiss Citizens' Rights Agreement')	2.12
Art 16	2.18
Art 17	2.196
Art 20(3)	2.196
Agreement on arrangements between Iceland, the Principality of Liechtenstein, the Kingdom of Norway and the United Kingdom of Great Britain and Northern Ireland following the withdrawal of the United Kingdom from the European Union, the EEA Agreement and other agreements applicable between the United Kingdom and the EEA EFTA States by virtue of the United Kingdom's membership of the European Union 2018 ('EEA EFTA Separation Agreement')	2.12
Art 17	2.18
Art 19	2.196
Agreement on the withdrawal of the United Kingdom of Great Britain and Northern Ireland from the European Union and the European Atomic Energy Community 2020 ('Withdrawal Agreement')	2.8, 2.10, 2.13, 2.15, 2.16, 2.18, 2.19, 2.20, 2.117, 2.138, 2.223, 4.82, 7.20, 7.404

Regulations

Directives

International legislation

Council of Europe

Protocol 1 Arts 1–3	6.90, 9.212
Protocol 1 Art 1	9.212, 9.217
Protocol 1 Art 2	11.115, 11.124
Protocol 13 Art 1	6.90, 9.212
Protocol 13 Ars 16–18	6.90, 9.212
European Social Charter 1961 (CESC)	4.34, 5.119

League of Nations

Convention to Suppress the Slave Trade and Slavery ('Slavery Convention') 1926	11.133

Miscellaneous

Good Friday Agreement (Belfast Agreement) 1998	2.184, 7.55
Constitutional Issues, Art 1(vi)	7.55
Sangatte Protocol (Protocol between the government of the United Kingdom of Great Britain and Northern Ireland and the government of the French Republic concerning frontier controls and policing, co-operation in criminal justice, public safety and mutual assistance relating to the Channel fixed link 1993)	1.79
Sino-British Joint Declaration on the Question of Hong Kong 1984	7.44

United Nations

Convention against Torture and Other Cruel, Inhuman or Degrading Treatment or Punishment 1987 (UNCAT)	1.21
Art 1(1)	10.69
Convention Against Transnational Organised Crime 2000	1.21
Protocol to Prevent, Suppress and Punish Trafficking In Persons, Especially Women and Children 2000	1.21
Convention on the Elimination of all Forms of Discrimination against Women 1979 (CEDAW)	11.226, 11.227–11.232
Art 1	11.227
Art 13	11.229
Convention on the Rights of Persons with Disabilities 2006	8.24, 11.232
Art 19	8.24
Convention on the Rights of the Child 1989 (UNCRC)	1.21, 1.24, 5.306, 11.7, 11.8, 11.10–11.23, 11.27, 11.115, 11.232, 11.248
Art 2	11.10
Art 3	9.26, 9.223, 9.224, 11.15

Introduction

Connor Johnston

This book is about migrant support. That is, the rights and entitlements of persons from abroad to access state support,[1] on the grounds of poverty, vulnerability, age or ill-health. At a time when the UK is grappling with the consequences of its departure from the European Union (EU), in the aftermath of the Windrush scandal which brought the 'hostile environment'[2] to the attention of the public at large, and in the midst of daily headlines about refugees attempting the dangerous journey from France to the UK by boat across the English Channel, it perhaps goes without saying that the topic of migrant support is an intensely politicised one. This has always been the case, and indeed a number of parallels may be drawn between current issues in the field of migrant support and those that have arisen in centuries gone by.

The relief of the poor in mediaeval England largely fell to the Church. However, the dissolution of the Monasteries by Henry VIII removed one of the main sources of alms for the poor. This caused the state to intervene by way of legislation, enacted in 1531, described as 'the first tentative step towards a national poor law'.[3] Under that legislation, any vagrant apprehended by the state was to be whipped 'til his body be bloody by reason of such whipping' and thereafter to be sent back 'to the place where he was born, of where he last dwelled the space of three years, and there put himself to labour as a true man oweth to do'.[4] This Tudor-era legislation embodies a number of concepts that will be familiar to those working in the field of immigration or migrant support today: the claimed injustice of a place having

1 In England and Wales.

2 See paras 1.2–1.4.

3 B Inglis *Poverty and the Industrial Revolution*, Panther, 1972, p43.

4 B Inglis *Poverty and the Industrial Revolution*, Panther, 1972, p43.

to take responsibility for supporting newly arrived travellers; the idea of sending those travellers back to where they came from; and the idea of discouraging people from travelling in the first place by making life more difficult for them at their destination. Today, these ideas find popular expression in newspaper headlines about 'benefits tourism'.[5] And they are given legal voice through legislative and policy measures such as the exclusions from benefits that apply to those of irregular immigration status contained in Nationality, Immigration and Asylum Act (NIAA) 2002 Sch 3,[6] the Home Office policy on the dispersal of asylum-seekers around the UK[7] and in the 'hostile environment' measures contained in the Immigration Acts of 2014 and 2016.[8]

Other legislation enacted under Henry VIII finds its modern parallel in the 'right to rent',[9] introduced under the Immigration Act (IA) 2014, which restricts the ability of certain migrants to access accommodation in the private rented sector, by preventing landlords from renting to them. A policy which bears more than a passing resemblance to a statute enacted in the 32nd year of Henry's reign,[10] described in the 10th edition of *The Law-dictionary*[11] published in 1797, as 'prohibiting alien artificers to work for themselves in this kingdom, and making void all leases of houses or shops to aliens'.

The inevitable consequence of legislative measures which made it harder for travellers and 'aliens' to settle in new areas, was to generate legal disputes as to which parish, if any, should take responsibility for supporting newcomers. These 'settlement' disputes, as they were known, find their modern-day counterpart in disputes between social services departments as to who should take responsibility for helping homeless migrant families under Children Act 1989 s17(1),[12] or the disputes that arise between local housing authorities as to which area a homeless household has a 'local connection' with.[13] Commenting, in 1981, on the similarity between the latter type of dispute and the old settlement disputes Lord Denning MR observed that:

5 G Owen 'Tories to get tough on post Brexit migrants: New government promises to crack down on health tourism that is draining the NHS and benefits for foreign children living abroad' *Daily Mail online*, 16 November 2019.
6 See paras 5.122–5.131 and 9.195–9.217.
7 See paras 5.169–5.184.
8 See paras 1.2–1.4 and 1.32–1.35.
9 See paras 7.389–7.434.
10 32 H8 c16.
11 TE Tomlins *The Law dictionary: Explaining the rise, progress, and present state of the English law*, Strahan, 10th edn, 1797.
12 See paras 9.12–9.69.
13 See paras 7.307–7.317.

> One or other local authority is bound to house him. Which is it? To us old folk this is a repeat performance of the disputes under the poor law 200 years ago. In those days each parish was responsible for the relief of those who were poor and unable to work. When a poor man moved from one parish to another, the question arose: which parish was responsible? The disputes, Blackstone tells us, 'created an infinity of expensive lawsuits between contending neighbourhoods, concerning those settlements and removals': see Blackstone's Commentaries, 17th ed (1830), vol I, p361.[14]

One such dispute arose in 1714, under the reign of George I, between the parishes of St Giles and Westminster. The legal issue that fell to be determined by the Court of the Kings Bench was which of those two parishes should take responsibility for a woman who 'having gained a settlement marrie[d] a foreigner', following the death of her husband. Although the case concerned support for the English widow, the Law Report records that in giving judgment the Chief Justice, Lord Holt, made what might be the first legal reference to migrant support, questioning the very idea that a 'foreigner' had any 'right to be maintained in any place to which he came' suggesting rather that the parish 'might let him starve' instead.[15]

Giving judgment in a case nearly ninety years later, in 1803, the Chief Justice of the day Lord Ellenborough expressed disbelief that his predecessor could have reached such a conclusion: 'We owe it to the memory of Lord CJ Holt to believe that he never uttered such a sentiment.' The question raised in the case before Lord Ellenborough was whether the Poor Laws 'which give a benefit and interest to the poor in a certain fund for their support are applicable to foreigners?' He held that they were, and that John Borchert, a baker from Germany whose trade had declined, was entitled to relief in the parish of Seaford together with his wife Anne and their four children. 'The law of humanity', the Chief Justice reasoned, 'which is anterior to all positive laws, obliges us to afford them relief to save them from starving'.[16] However, in reaching this obviously humane decision, Lord Ellenborough was influenced by the fact that 'this man was not an alien enemy, but a German by birth, an alien amy [friend]'. This is perhaps the first legal reference to the dichotomy between the 'good' and the 'bad' immigrant that permeates present day discussions on immigration that can be seen in the varying degrees of access which different migrants are granted to state support. A dicho-

14 *R v Slough BC ex p Ealing LBC* [1981] QB 801, CA at p808.

15 *St Giles's v St Margaret's Westminster* 93 ER 31, Court of King's Bench.

16 *R v The Inhabitants of Eastbourne* 102 ER 769, Court of King's Bench at p770.

tomy reflected in the sentiment expressed by the writer Musa Okwonga whose parents fled to the suburbs of West London from Idi Amin's Uganda in the 1970s, that:

> . . . the biggest burden facing people of colour in this country, is that society deems us bad immigrants – job stealers, benefit scroungers, girlfriend-thieves, refugees – until we cross over in their consciousness, through popular culture, winning races, baking good cakes, being conscientious doctors, to become good immigrants.[17]

Putting aside these few intriguing historical examples, it has to be acknowledged that 'migrant support', as a distinct set of legal rules and policies, is a relatively recent development. In considering our current system, how we arrived at it and the political context in which it operates, it is convenient to start in the years following the Second World War:

> There was a time when the welfare state did not look at your passport or ask why you were here . . . immigration status was a matter between you and the Home Office, not the concern of the social security system. As immigration became a political issue, this changed.[18]

As Lord Hoffmann observed, in the opening decades of the welfare state, immigration status had little relevance to the question of whether or not those who were homeless or destitute were entitled to assistance from the state. In terms of financial support, following the repeal of the Poor Laws,[19] the post-War 'safety net for those who were not covered by social insurance'[20] was national assistance under National Assistance Act (NAA) 1948 Part II which was provided by the National Assistance Board. So long as the applicant was within Great Britain, eligibility for assistance was, in simple terms, a question of need rather than nationality or immigration status.[21]

In time, national assistance came to be replaced by supplementary benefit[22] which, in its turn, came to be superseded by income

17 N Shukla et al *The Good Immigrant*, Unbound, 2016.

18 *R (Westminster City Council) v National Asylum Support Service* [2002] UKHL 38, [2002] 1 WLR 2956 at paras 19–20 per Lord Hoffmann.

19 Repealed by NAA 1948 s1.

20 *R v Wandsworth LBC ex p O* [2000] 1 WLR 2539, CA at p2554G per Hale LJ.

21 See, for example, NAA 1948 s4: 'It shall be the duty of the Board in accordance with the following provisions of this Part of this Act to assist persons in Great Britain who are without resources to meet their requirements . . .'

22 Under Supplementary Benefits Act 1976 Part I.

support,[23] which still exists in modified form to this day, albeit it is being gradually subsumed and replaced by universal credit. It was in relation to entitlement to such benefits that immigration status came to be a feature during the 1980s. For example, regulations enacted in 1980, specifically linked entitlement to supplementary benefit to the question of whether or not the applicant had leave to enter or remain in the UK.[24] By the end of the 1980s the position was that asylum-seekers were still potentially eligible for income support while their claims were determined, but at the rate of 90 per cent of the standard entitlement.[25] This had the consequence that they were also eligible for housing benefit to pay toward the cost of their accommodation.[26] Illegal entrants and overstayers, on the other hand, had no such entitlement.

Entitlement to accommodation followed a similar course. Initially, temporary accommodation was potentially available to those in 'urgent need' among others, with no regard given to immigration status, under NAA 1948 s21(1)(b). The provision of such accommodation fell to local authorities and entailed a wide degree of discretion,[27] meaning, in practical terms, that entitlement was limited.[28] In the words of Baroness Hale, 'paragraph (b) was used to house those homeless people who qualified for help. The post-World War II welfare state never purported to provide housing, as opposed to the means of obtaining it, for all'.[29] The flagship Housing (Homeless Persons) Act 1977, the progenitor of the modern homelessness legislation,[30] elevated the provision of accommodation to the homeless to a more solid footing while remaining silent on the relevance of

23 Introduced by Social Security Act 1986 Part II and now available under Social Security Contributions and Benefits Act 1992 Part VII.

24 Supplementary Benefit (Aggregation, Requirements and Resources) Amendment Regulations 1980 SI No 1774 reg 3 and Sch 1 para 16 amending the Supplementary Benefit (Requirements) Regulations 1980 SI No 1299.

25 Income Support General Regulations 1987 SI No 1967 regs 21, 70 and 71 and Sch 7.

26 See *R v Secretary of State for Social Security ex p Joint Council for the Welfare of Immigrants* [1997] 1 WLR 275, CA at p285D per Simon Brown LJ.

27 See *R v Hammersmith and Fulham LBC ex p M* (1998) 30 HLR 10, CA at p18 per Lord Woolf MR.

28 See *Southwark LBC v Williams* [1971] Ch 734, CA for, what was referred to by Carnwath LJ at para 19 of *R (O) v Haringey LBC* [2004] EWCA Civ 535, [2004] 2 FLR 476 as, a failed attempt to 'press' the NAA 1948 'into service to meet the needs of the homeless'.

29 *R (M) v Slough BC* [2008] UKHL 52, [2008] 1 WLR 1808 at para 8.

30 Contained in Housing Act 1996 Part VII as amended by the Homelessness Reduction Act 2017.

immigration status. It fell to the courts to regulate the position, with the Court of Appeal taking the view that asylum-seekers were eligible for assistance but that, implicitly, illegal entrants and overstayers were not.[31] This approach survived the replacement of the Housing (Homeless Persons) Act 1977 by Housing Act 1985 Part III, though became subject to an additional limitation imposed by parliament in 1993, prohibiting local authorities from providing accommodation to any asylum-seeker or dependant of any asylum-seeker who had available for their occupation 'any accommodation however temporary, which it would be reasonable for him to occupy'.[32]

In broad terms, it can be seen that from a post-War starting point of eligibility for all irrespective of immigration status, by the mid-1990s the law had developed to a point where asylum-seekers were still eligible to access mainstream welfare benefits and homelessness accommodation, but on a somewhat less generous basis than the public at large, and those who were in the country unlawfully were not intended to be eligible for support at all. All of this was to change quite significantly in 1996 and the years following, by means of a series of measures first restricting the rights and entitlements of asylum-seekers to access mainstream support and then, latterly, diverting responsibility for supporting and accommodating them from local authorities to the Home Office.

The foundations of this modern regime were laid by the Social Security (Persons from Abroad) Miscellaneous Amendments Regulations 1996.[33] These regulations had the effect that asylum-seekers who had not immediately claimed asylum 'on arrival' in the UK, or who were seeking to appeal against the rejection of their asylum claim, were no longer entitled to income support or housing benefit.[34] The regulations were based on the Conservative government's politically charged view that many of those claiming asylum in the UK were actually 'economic migrants . . . influenced by the ready availability of benefits',[35] and were intended to deter such

31 See *R v Hillingdon LBC ex p Streeting (No 2)* [1980] 1 WLR 1425, CA at pp1434C–1434D per Lord Denning MR.

32 See Asylum and Immigration and Appeals Act 1993 s4.

33 SI No 30.

34 Social Security (Persons from Abroad) Miscellaneous Amendments Regulations 1996 regs 7–8.

35 See the statement of the secretary of state made to the Social Security Advisory Committee at the time, referred to in *R v Secretary of State for Social Security ex p Joint Council for the Welfare of Immigrants* [1997] 1 WLR 275, CA at pp280A–281A per Neill LJ.

applicants. The view was that 'bona fide asylum-seekers could be expected to declare themselves as such when they arrived' and that failing to do so 'was the badge of an economic migrant'.[36]

Some of those affected turned to the housing departments of their local authorities for assistance and in *R v Kensington and Chelsea RLBC ex p Kihara*[37] the Court of Appeal recognised the principle that 'the utter poverty and resourcelessness afflicting certain asylum-seekers . . . now deprived of all benefits' was 'in law capable of constituting them "vulnerable as a result of . . . other special reason" '. There was no reason, Simon Brown LJ explained, why a person likely to suffer injury or detriment 'through a total inability to clothe, feed or shelter himself should be any less entitled to priority housing than someone vulnerable through age or disablement'.[38] The effect of this decision, upending the orthodox view shared by a number of local authorities at that time, was that a destitute asylum-seeker could potentially establish a 'priority need',[39] and thereby qualify for accommodation as a homeless person under Housing Act 1985 Part III, simply by virtue of their destitution, rather than having to establish a priority need by reason of any physical disability, mental health condition or the like.

Others affected went further and sought to challenge the legality of the Social Security (Persons from Abroad) Miscellaneous Amendments Regulations 1996 and in *R v Secretary of State for Social Security ex p Joint Council for the Welfare of Immigrants*[40] the Court of Appeal found the regulations to be unlawful, in that they affected a significant number of genuine asylum-seekers, forcing them to abandon their claims or 'maintain them as best they can but in a state of utter destitution',[41] thereby conflicting with their statutory right to remain in the UK while their claims, and any appeals, were considered.

Victory, however, was short-lived. Parliament responded by means of the Asylum and Immigration Act (AIA) 1996, not only reinstating

36 *R (Westminster City Council) v National Asylum Support Service* [2002] UKHL 38, [2002] 1 WLR 2956 at para 22 per Lord Hoffmann.

37 (1997) 29 HLR 147, CA.

38 *R v Kensington and Chelsea RLBC ex p Kihara* (1997) 29 HLR 147, CA at pp159–160 per Simon Brown LJ.

39 A precedent condition for the provision of accommodation under the homelessness legislation. See Housing Act 1985 ss59 and 65.

40 [1997] 1 WLR 275, CA.

41 *R v Secretary of State for Social Security ex p Joint Council for the Welfare of Immigrants* [1997] 1 WLR 275, CA at p293 per Simon Brown LJ.

the impugned regulations[42] but going further by prohibiting the same cohort of asylum-seekers from accessing homelessness assistance under Housing Act 1985 Part III,[43] thereby reversing the effect of the decision in *R v Kensington and Chelsea RLBC ex p Kihara*.[44]

In these circumstances, deprived of access to income support, housing benefit and homelessness assistance, it was perhaps no surprise that 'homeless and destitute asylum-seekers were thus driven to seek social services to meet their basic needs'[45] under NAA 1948 s21(1)(a). However, this new trend of destitute, able-bodied asylum-seekers, seeking support under a legal provision that had generally been assumed to be the preserve of the elderly and the infirm, did not sit well with local authorities. The refusal by several such local authorities to provide accommodation and support to four destitute asylum-seekers who had claimed asylum subsequent to their entry into the UK fell for consideration by the Court of Appeal in *R v Hammersmith and Fulham LBC ex p M*.[46] The unanimous view of the court was that the consequence of the AIA 1996 was to shift the financial burden of supporting such applicants from central to local government and that destitute asylum-seekers who were in need of care and attention by reason of 'the problems under which they are labouring' such as 'the lack of food and accommodation . . . their inability to speak the language, their ignorance of this country and the fact they have been subject to the stress of coming to this country in circumstances which at least involve their contending to be refugees' should be supported under NAA 1948 s21(1)(a).[47]

As Lord Hoffmann would later observe, 'the stark facts of that case – able bodied asylum-seekers having to be accommodated by social services – caused consternation'.[48] It was against this political

42 AIA 1996 s11 and Sch 1 paras 2–3.

43 AIA 1996 s9 and Sch 1 paras 2–3; and Housing Accommodation and Homelessness (Persons Subject to Immigration Control) Order 1996 SI No 1982 art 4. Similar restrictions were maintained in subsequent homelessness legislation until April 2000. See Housing Act 1996 ss185–186; Homelessness Regulations 1996 SI No 2754 reg 3; Homelessness (England) Regulations 2000 SI No 701 regs 2–3; and Allocation of Housing and Homelessness (Eligibility) (England) Regulations 2006 SI No 1294 reg 5.

44 (1997) 29 HLR 147, CA.

45 *R v Wandsworth LBC ex p O* [2000] 1 WLR 2539, CA at p2555D per Hale LJ.

46 (1998) 30 HLR 10, CA.

47 *R v Hammersmith and Fulham LBC ex p M* (1998) 30 HLR 10, CA at p20 per Lord Woolf MR.

48 *R (Westminster City Council) v National Asylum Support Service* [2002] UKHL 38, [2002] 1 WLR 2956 at para 28.

backdrop that the modern legislative framework for supporting asylum-seekers was conceived. In the 1998 white paper *Fairer, faster and firmer – a modern approach to immigration and asylum*[49] in order to deal with what was seen as the 'inappropriate' burden that had fallen on local authorities as a result of the decision in *R v Hammersmith and Fulham LBC ex p M*,[50] the new Labour government proposed the creation of an entirely new support scheme. The idea was that, under this scheme, asylum-seekers would be catered for outside of the mainstream welfare benefits system and that accommodation (offered on a no-choice basis) and financial support to meet only basic needs would be made available by way of a last resort to those who had no access to other forms of support. The new scheme was to be administered and operated by the Home Office. To facilitate this, the NAA 1948 was to be amended to 'make clear that social services departments should not carry the burden of looking after healthy and able-bodied asylum-seekers'.[51]

So it was that the Immigration and Asylum Act (IAA) 1999 came into force, creating for the first time a distinct national scheme for supporting and accommodating destitute asylum-seekers, to be administered by the National Asylum Support Service. In addition, the new legislative framework excluded 'persons subject to immigration control' from mainstream welfare benefits such as income support and housing benefit,[52] and from accessing support from social services in cases where their need for care and attention had arisen 'solely' from the fact they were destitute.[53] Associated amendments were also made to the Housing Act 1996 restricting the access to social housing and homelessness assistance by those subject to immigration control.[54]

Unsurprisingly, the introduction of this complex new regime did not put an end to disputes between destitute migrants, local authorities and central government as to who was entitled to what support and from whom. The first major dispute to come before the Court of Appeal was *R v Wandsworth LBC ex p O*,[55] which involved a destitute Nigerian overstayer with chronic and relapsing psychiatric problems.

49 Cm 4018, Home Office, 1998.

50 (1998) 30 HLR 10, CA.

51 *Fairer, faster and firmer – a modern approach to immigration and asylum*, Cm 4018, Home Office, 1998, at paras 8.12–8.26.

52 IAA 1999 s115.

53 IA 1999 s116 amending NAA 1948 s21.

54 Housing Act 1996 ss161(2A) and 185(2A), inserted by IAA 1999 s117(3)–(4).

55 [2000] 1 WLR 2539, CA at pp2553G–2558A per Hale LJ.

The case concerned the scope of the exclusion introduced by IAA 1999 s116 and the question of whether or not persons in the country unlawfully were entitled to accommodation under NAA 1948 s21. The court held that accommodation under NAA 1948 s21 was not restricted to those who were lawfully resident in the country and that a person subject to immigration control, within the meaning of IAA 1999 s115, would be eligible for accommodation under this provision provided that their need for care and attention was to any material extent made more acute by some circumstance other than the mere lack of accommodation and money. 'If there are to be immigrant beggars on out streets', Simon Brown LJ reasoned, 'then at least let them not be ill, old or disabled'.[56]

This decision then led to what has been described as an 'inverted and unseemly turf war between local and national government'[57] as to where the responsibility lay, for accommodating 'infirm destitute' asylum-seekers. Were they, like the applicant in *R v Wandsworth LBC ex p O*,[58] the responsibility of social services under NAA 1948 s21? Or were they the responsibility of the Home Office under IAA 1999 s95? The answer, according to the House of Lords, was the former. The new regime for supporting asylum-seekers under IAA 1999 Part VI endowed the secretary of state with residual powers to accommodate asylum-seekers, available only where no other support was available. The effect of the new NAA 1948 s21(1A) had only been to exclude the able-bodied destitute from local authority support. The infirm destitute remained the responsibility of social services,[59] and continue to be so to this day.[60] The same approach has been taken to apply to failed asylum-seekers also.[61]

56 *R v Wandsworth LBC ex p O* [2000] 1 WLR 2539, CA at pp2548F–2548H per Simon Brown LJ.

57 J Sweeney 'The human rights of failed asylum-seekers in the United Kingdom' [2008] PL 277, 285, cited in *R (M) v Slough BC* [2008] UKHL 52, [2008] 1 WLR 1808 at para 28 per Baroness Hale.

58 [2000] 1 WLR 2539, CA at pp2553G–2558A per Hale LJ.

59 *R (Westminster City Council) v National Asylum Support Service* [2002] UKHL 38, [2002] 1 WLR 2956.

60 See *R (SG) v Haringey LBC* [2015] EWHC 2579 (Admin), (2015) 18 CCLR 444 at para 12 dealing with the analogous provisions of the Care Act 2014 which have superseded NAA 1948 Part III. See paras 5.94–5.102.

61 *R (AW) v Croydon LBC* [2007] EWCA Civ 266, [2007] 1 WLR 3168; *R (SL) v Westminster City Council* [2013] UKSC 27, [2013] 1 WLR 1445. See paras 6.139–6.140.

The next significant upheaval to the migrant support regime came in the form of the NIAA 2002.[62] This piece of legislation imposed a number of significant restrictions on the ability of migrants to access state support, some of which had not been contemplated in the white paper that preceded the legislation[63] and were introduced into the bill by the government late in the parliamentary process thereby receiving relatively little scrutiny.[64]

The first notable restriction was contained in NIAA 2002 s54 and Sch 3[65] which, subject to certain caveats,[66] prohibits those of irregular immigration status from accessing state support.

The second notable restriction was contained in NIAA 2002 s55(1), which prohibits the Home Office from providing asylum support to an applicant in circumstances where 'the Secretary of State is not satisfied that the claim was made as soon as reasonably practicable after the person's arrival in the United Kingdom', subject only to the caveat that support could be provided where necessary in order to avoid a breach of the individual's rights under the European Convention on Human Rights (ECHR).[67] The similarity between this restriction and between those introduced six years previously in the Social Security (Persons from Abroad) Miscellaneous Amendments Regulations 1996 will be readily apparent. Indeed, the political motivation underpinning the restriction was identical: a perception that those asylum-seekers who did not lodge their claim immediately were not 'genuine cases' and that by denying them support, they would be forced to return home.[68]

The potential for hardship caused by this second restriction is well illustrated by the facts of *R (Limbuela) v SSHD*,[69] the leading case on the application of NIAA 2002 s55. Each of the three applicants in that case – Mr Limbuela, Mr Tesema and Mr Adam – made

62 Further changes to the regime are contained within the IA 2016. However, it is not clear if or when these changes will come into force. See paras 5.7–5.8.

63 *Secure borders, safe haven integration with diversity in modern Britain*, Cm 5387, Home Office, 2002.

64 See Hansard HL Debs col 1011, 15 July 2002 and cols 975–976, 17 October 2002. See further, D Stevens *UK asylum law and policy historical and contemporary perspectives*, Thompson Sweet & Maxwell, 2004, pp192–195.

65 See paras 5.122–5.131 and 9.195–9.217.

66 Contained in NIAA 2002 Sch 3 paras 2–3.

67 NIAA 2002 s55(5). See paras 5.132–5.136.

68 See Hansard HL Debs cols 978–979, 17 October 2002.

69 [2005] UKHL 66, [2006] 1 AC 396. See further paras 5.127–5.131 and 9.203–9.217.

claims for asylum which were recorded on the day of their arrival in the UK or the day after. In each case the secretary of state adjudged that their claim had not been made 'as soon as reasonably practicable' and so they were refused support. Mr Limbuela and Mr Adam were both forced to sleep rough as a result, for several days and a month respectively. During that time Mr Limbuela was without money, access to food or washing facilities, or even a blanket. Mr Adam for his part was able to wash himself and have the occasional meal at the offices of the Refugee Council, but was exposed to the elements and to abuse at night when sleeping outside in the car park. The House of Lords held that the regime that the government had constructed which precluded the provision of support to asylum-seekers like the applicants but also prevented them from working to support themselves, amounted to 'treatment' within the meaning of ECHR Article 3. Where such treatment resulted, as in the present cases, in an applicant facing 'an imminent prospect of serious suffering caused or materially aggravated by denial of shelter, food or the most basic necessities of life' then it would be regarded as 'inhuman or degrading' and in breach of Article 3.[70] For an applicant to qualify for support, Lord Bingham noted, there was no need for the secretary of state's treatment of them to 'merit the description used, in an immigration context, by Shakespeare and others in Sir Thomas More when they referred to "your mountainish inhumanity" '.[71]

More recent changes to the migrant support system have been a direct or indirect consequence of, what has become known as, the 'hostile environment' policy. In the words of Theresa May, then Home Secretary, the plan was to 'create a really hostile environment for illegal migrants'[72] by means of 'measures to limit access to work, housing, healthcare, and bank accounts, to revoke driving licences and to reduce and restrict rights of appeal against Home Office decisions'.[73] Elements of this policy were given legal effect by the IA 2014 and then supplemented and reinforced by the IA 2016.

70 See *R (Limbuela) v SSHD* [2005] UKHL 66, [2006] 1 AC 396 at paras 6–9 per Lord Bingham, paras 56–63 per Lord Hope and para 78 per Baroness Hale.

71 *R (Limbuela) v SSHD* [2005] UKHL 66, [2006] 1 AC 396 at para 7 per Lord Bingham.

72 A Travis 'Immigration bill: Theresa May defends plans to create "hostile environment" ' *Guardian*, 10 October 2013.

73 House of Commons Home Affairs Committee, *Immigration Policy: Basis for Building Consensus*, 15 January 2018, HC 500 of session 2017–19, p20. See further paras 1.2–1.4.

The elements of this policy which impact directly on migrant support consist of significant changes to the regime for supporting asylum-seekers[74] and failed asylum-seekers, as well as new restrictions on the support currently available to migrant families and care leavers under the Children Act 1989.[75] These changes are, for the most part, not yet in force and there is currently no indication of when, if at all, they will come into effect.

The elements of the policy which impact indirectly on migrant support consist of those measures which, in the words of journalist Maya Goodfellow, had the consequence that 'a whole host of professionals – from landlords and letting agents to doctors and nurses – were turned into border guards'.[76] For example, the restrictions on the opening and holding of bank accounts have the consequence that it is more difficult for destitute migrant families to prove that they are destitute and thereby eligible for support from social services.[77] While the restrictions on the right to rent[78] have the perverse consequence that migrant households who have the funds to support themselves without placing any burden on the state may now need to seek state support because they cannot find a private landlord willing to rent to them.

At the time of writing, the dust is still settling on the UK's departure from the EU. The long-term ramifications of this, in the context of migrant support, remain to be fully appreciated. However, given that opposition to immigration was a significant factor for many in the decision to vote leave,[79] and given that the legal task of extricating domestic law from EU law is an exceedingly complex one, it seemed probable from the outset that in the next decade the rules governing migrant support would become more restrictive and complex, and not less. This is already playing out in the series of legal and policy developments that have been announced and introduced in the duration of the writing of this book between 2020 and 2023, including: the introduction of 'new asylum reception centres' to accommodate new arrivals seeking sanctuary in the UK,[80] the controversy over the

74 See paras 5.7–5.8.

75 See paras 9.5–9.6.

76 M Goodfellow *The Hostile Environment*, Verso, 2019, p2.

77 See paras 9.44–9.48.

78 See paras 7.389–7.434.

79 'How the UK voted on Brexit, and why – a refresher', Lord Ashcroft Polls, 4 February 2019.

80 *New Plan for Immigration Policy Statement*, HM Government, March 2021, pp19–20.

inhuman and degrading conditions in which asylum-seekers, including women and children, were kept at Manston Baracks, the coming into force of the Nationality and Borders Act 2022, the provisions of which curtail the rights of asylum-seekers, victims of modern slavery and human trafficking, and unaccompanied asylum-seeking children,[81] coupled with the highly politicised 'Rwanda' scheme to relocate asylum-seekers to Rwanda for the examination of their asylum claims. Building on this, at the time of writing, the Illegal Migration Act 2023 – which will dramatically undermine the right to seek asylum in the UK – has received Royal Assent, and a barge, intended to warehouse new arrivals off-shore, is making its way from the Netherlands to Portland. Such measures have knock-on effects on the entitlements of new arrivals to state support. Alongside these policy and legislative developments, the language used to describe the plight of asylum-seekers, refugees and migrants has become increasingly highly charged, dehumanising and predicated on the othering of people seen not to be deserving of entry or residence in the UK.

The purpose of this introduction is not to cover every such case, development and restriction in the field of migrant support. Rather it is to give readers a flavour of how it was that the complex set of laws and policies on migrant support which we currently have, came to exist and the political context in which they operate. It should be clear from the foregoing that, as Lord Hope observed in *R (Limbuela) v SSHD*,[82] 'the question whether, and if so in what circumstances, support should be given at the expense of the state to asylum-seekers is . . . an intensely political issue' and the same applies with equal force today, and to other migrants, whatever their immigration status.

The laws and policies which migrants to the UK who are in need of assistance from the state must seek to navigate are labyrinthine. The conditions which an applicant must satisfy to qualify for support are tightly drawn. Refusals of support are common. And the consequences of a refusal of support are invariably severe. This makes it all the more important that those providing advice in this area have a thorough grounding in the relevant legal principles. It is hoped that this book will assist in this task.

81 See paras 3.131–3.142, 5.7–5.8, 5.39–5.44, 11.58–11.59 and 11.193–11.194.

82 [2005] UKHL 66, [2006] 1 AC 396 at para 13 per Lord Hope.

CHAPTER 1

An overview of nationality and immigration law

Shu Shin Luh
with Louise Hooper and Helen Foot

continued

Key points

- Whether a person is eligible for and able to access a specified kind of support in the UK is heavily dependent on the nature and extent of their right to reside in the UK.
- The main sources of such rights include a plethora of primary legislation beginning with the Immigration Act 1971, the Immigration Rules and executive policy, which may be influenced by, or need to be interpreted in light of, various international treaties.[1]
- British citizenship carries with it the right to live in, and come and go from, the UK without 'let or hindrance'. It may be acquired automatically, by registration or by naturalisation.[2]
- As a general rule,[3] any person who is not a British citizen requires leave to enter or remain in the UK. The various categories of leave to enter or remain of principal relevance in the field of migrant support are discussed at paras 1.75–1.139.
- The application process for obtaining leave to enter or remain, including the common grounds on which applications may be refused, are discussed at paras 1.140–1.164.
- Leave to enter or remain may be granted subject to conditions, including (infamously) that leave shall be granted with no recourse to public funds.[4]
- The secretary of state has various powers to remove, deport and detain (or release on bail) persons who require leave to enter or remain in the UK but do not have it, and persons whose presence is not conducive to the public good, among others.[5]
- Remedies against adverse immigration decisions include statutory appeals, administrative review and judicial review.[6]

1 See paras 1.9–1.35.
2 See paras 1.36–1.74.
3 See chapter 2 for the position in relation to EEA nationals.
4 See paras 1.165–1.172.
5 See paras 1.173–1.218.
6 See paras 1.219–1.236.

Introduction

1.1 Whether a person is eligible for and able to access a specified kind of support in the UK is heavily dependent on the nature and extent of their right to reside in the UK. The structure of both primary and secondary legislation governing this important question is hugely complex, supplemented by an ever-growing body of case-law as an aid to interpretation. It is no surprise that judges in the Supreme Court and the Court of Appeal have consistently criticised immigration legislation, rules and policies as incomprehensible, with the Master of the Rolls describing it as 'an impenetrable jungle of intertwined statutory provisions and judicial decisions',[7] and Lord Lloyd Jones, a Supreme Court justice, calling for an urgent review of the immigration laws to 'make the law and procedure clear and comprehensible'.[8] There is no single document where all the applicable rules and criteria for obtaining leave are set out. As was observed by Beatson LJ in *Hossain and others v SSHD*:

> . . . the detail, the number of documents that have to be consulted, the number of changes in rules and policy guidance, and the difficulty advisers face in ascertaining which previous version of the rule or guidance applies and obtaining it are real obstacles to achieving predictable consistency and restoring public trust in the system, particularly in an area of law that lay people and people whose first language is not English need to understand.[9]

1.2 This has only become more complex since 2012, when a series of legislative and policy measures were introduced under what is now commonly known as the 'hostile environment' policy,[10] the aim of which was to identify and remove migrants in the UK with no right to remain and to deter others without permission from entering or remaining in the UK. Ministers expressly stated that the aim of the measures was to 'create a really hostile environment for illegal migrants'.[11] The measures comprised more stringent Immigration

7 Per Lord Neuberger, the Master of the Rolls in *Patel v SSHD* [2012] EWCA Civ 741, [2013] 1 WLR 63 at para 40.

8 Per Lord Lloyd Jones in *R (Robinson) v SSHD* [2019] UKSC 11, [2019] 2 WLR 897 at para 66.

9 [2015] EWCA Civ 207 at para 30.

10 See further paras 1.32–1.35 and House of Commons Home Affairs Committee, *Immigration policy: basis for building consensus*, HC 500 of session 2017–19, 15 January 2018, p20.

11 Alan Travis 'Immigration bill: Theresa May defends plans to create hostile environment' *Guardian*, 10 October 2013.

Rules (HC 395), the removal of appeal rights and an embedded network of immigration controls throughout society which seek to limit people's access to housing,[12] healthcare,[13] education,[14] work, bank accounts, benefits and driving licences.[15] Often the measures require members of the public to act as unofficial immigration officers or otherwise risk sanctions themselves. The majority of these proposals became law via the Immigration Act (IA) 2014 and were subsequently tightened or expanded under the Immigration Act (IA) 2016. The limiting measures function alongside a system of civil and criminal penalties which are now applied to people without leave to remain, those who provide services to such migrants and, very often, members of the public who are their family or friends.

1.3 Although there was a brief attempt in 2018 to re-brand the 'hostile environment' policy as a 'compliant environment' policy,[16] it did not alter the substantive effect of the policy, some of which has been challenged.[17] In 2021 and 2022, further to the UK's exit from the European Union (EU), further hostile environment policies were introduced through the Nationality and Borders Act (NBA) 2022. For the first time, primary legislation sought to curtail protection for certain categories of asylum-seekers, unaccompanied asylum-seeking children and victims of trafficking, three groups of vulnerable people who had not been the subjects targeted by previous 'hostile environment' policies. At the writing of this chapter in May 2023, further primary legislation is going through parliament with the intention of further curtailing rights to claim asylum, to access protection as

12 The 'right to rent' provisions require landlords to conduct checks on the immigration status of potential tenants in order to avoid potential fines of up to £3,000 or the commission of a criminal offence: IA 2014 ss21, 23(1)–(2), 33A–33C and Sch 3. See paras 7.389–7.434.

13 Measures restricting access to healthcare are addressed at chapter 10.

14 Access to higher education and student finance for migrant young adults is addressed in paras 11.124–11.126.

15 For example, it is now a criminal offence for a person to drive in the UK if they do not have leave to remain: IA 1971 s24C. See also IA 2016 Schs 4 and 5 (in relation to licencing) and IA 2014 ss40, 40A–40H in relation to the duties of banks to conduct immigration checks on account holders. Under the provisions, the secretary of state has the power to apply to the magistrates' court for a freezing order if the account holder does not have leave to remain.

16 Alan Travis 'Post-Brexit immigration white paper delayed until late autumn' *Guardian*, 2 October 2017. See also Steven Poole 'Compliant environment: is this really what the Windrush generation needs?' *Guardian*, 3 May 2018.

17 See, for example, *R (Joint Council for the Welfare of Immigrants) v SSHD* [2020] EWCA Civ 542. See also Denis Campbell 'NHS will no longer have to share immigrants' data with Home Office' *Guardian*, 9 May 2018.

unaccompanied and accompanied children, to obtain leave to remain in the UK, to naturalise, and to reunite with family in the UK.

1.4 Although the 'hostile environment' policy was directed at those who require permission to remain in the UK and do not have it, the policy has had far-reaching and, at times, unintended consequences for other groups of migrants who are not the intended targets. In particular it has included those who may have a right to reside in the UK but who are unable to produce documentary proof of their entitlements to be here. This unintended consequence garnered increased attention following press reports of the barriers faced by citizens of Commonwealth countries, many of whom arrived in the UK as children prior to 1973, many from Caribbean countries (although not exclusively so). This is now well known as the 'Windrush scandal'. Although most, if not all, of those in the 'Windrush generation' had entitlements to remain in the UK, many were without documentary proof of their right to be in the UK and consequently found themselves denied healthcare, pensions and jobs under the 'hostile environment' policy. People eligible to access services were not able to prove their entitlement. Some have struggled to provide the evidence and associated fees that the Home Office has required to issue status confirmation documents.

1.5 The UK's exit from the EU on 31 January 2020 created significant new concerns for EU nationals unable to secure clarity over their residence status in the UK through the government's EU Settlement Scheme[18] and to obtain documents to demonstrate their entitlement to remain in the UK at the end of the transition period which ended on 31 December 2020.

1.6 With this context in mind, this and the next two chapters provide an outline of key aspects of the complex and developing area of immigration, nationality and asylum law so far as it is relevant to individuals' ability to access support. The information contained in these first three chapters of this handbook are intended as reference only to signpost readers to the issues that may affect access to support for people affected by immigration control measures. There is a wealth of other published material which provide more comprehensive information about the changing landscape of immigration, nationality and asylum law and to which readers are directed for specialist analysis of the subject matter. Given the complexity of immigration, nationality and asylum law, it is advisable to seek legal advice on individuals' personal circumstances.

18 Discussed in detail in chapter 2.

1.7 This chapter will deal with nationality and forms of leave to enter and remain for those who are not European Economic Area (EEA) nationals and who are outside the asylum and international protection framework. By way of an outline, this chapter considers:

- the main sources of immigration law;
- British citizenship and the right of abode;
- the concepts of leave to enter and remain;
- common types of application for leave to remain and how to make them;
- grounds for refusal of leave to remain;
- removal and deportation;
- immigration bail and detention;
- remedies, including appeals and administrative review.

1.8 Chapter 2 deals specifically with EEA nationals, and chapter 3 addresses asylum and international protection.[19]

Structure and sources of immigration and nationality law

1.9 The structure of immigration and nationality law is an interwoven web of 1) primary legislation; 2) secondary legislation, including the Immigration Rules; 3) executive policy; and 4) international law. There is no one piece of law containing all of the hostile environment measures. They are embedded in all of these layers of immigration and nationality law as well as in legislation and policy concerning specific welfare provisions.

Primary legislation

1.10 Primary legislation provides the legal skeletal structure. The key primary legislation includes:

- Immigration Act (IA) 1971;
- British Nationality Act (BNA) 1981;
- Immigration and Asylum Act (IAA) 1999;
- Nationality, Immigration and Asylum Act (NIAA) 2002;

19 There are established practitioners' handbooks which focus on a detailed examination of immigration law and practice. The purpose of this chapter and chapters 2 and 3 is to provide an overview for the purposes of aiding understanding of the impact of immigration law on access to and provision of support to those who are subject to immigration control.

- Asylum and Immigration (Treatment of Claimants, etc) Act (AITCA) 2004;
- UK Borders Act (UKBA) 2007;
- Borders, Citizenship and Immigration Act (BCIA) 2009;
- IA 2014;
- IA 2016;
- NBA 2022.

1.11 The IA 1971 still contains the power to make Immigration Rules,[20] although appeal rights and other statutory provisions have been introduced through subsequent primary legislation. The successive statutes all provide for implementing orders and regulations, usually to be made by statutory instrument, sometimes by Order in Council. The IAA 1999, for example, has 12 instances of powers to make Orders by statutory instrument; 26 for Regulations; seven for rules; seven codes of practice will apply; two sets of directions; one Order in Council; and one set of arrangements. Not all these powers have been used, but the list of Orders and Regulations, covering a very wide span, is formidable. All are subject to change. All are now available on the internet to check the up-to-date position. This further complicates the web of interacting immigration laws.

The Immigration Rules

1.12 The key rules are the Statement of Immigration Rules, made under IA 1971 s3(2) and usually published as a House of Commons paper (currently HC 395, as amended many times), setting out the criteria for entry and stay in the various immigration categories. Examples include: as the partner of a British citizen; as a student or entrepreneur under the points-based system; as a parent of a child who is settled in the UK or has British nationality or on the basis of long residence. A consolidated version of the current Immigration Rules is available on the Home Office website[21] and the most recent Statement of Changes is also available separately.

1.13 The Immigration Rules have a 'unique' and 'quasi-legal' status.[22] They are not delegated legislation. While the IA 1971 makes provision about what the rules must contain,[23] and about how parliamentary

20 IA 1971 s3(2).
21 See: www.gov.uk/topic/immigration-operational-guidance/immigration-rules.
22 *SSHD v Pankina* [2010] EWCA Civ 719, [2011] 1 QB 376.
23 IA 1971 s1(4).

approval of the rules is to be obtained,[24] the rules are not themselves derived from any empowering legislation. The rules are not law but rather a statement of the Home Secretary's administrative practice.[25] They do not therefore possess the same degree of democratic legitimacy as legislation made by parliament.[26] As an appellate body, the appeal tribunal's decision-making process is not governed by the rules, but the tribunal is expected, nevertheless, to consider the rules and the criteria set down within. Where an immigration appeal concerns European Convention on Human Rights (ECHR) Article 8, and involves consideration of what outcome would be proportionate to the qualified protection under Article 8, the appeal tribunal will take account of the Home Office's assessment but must make its own assessment of the proportionality of the outcome, such as deportation or administrative removal, on the evidence available to the tribunal. Where the Home Office has adopted a policy in relation to the assessment of proportionality, set out in the rules and endorsed by parliament, the appeal tribunal should give considerable weight to that policy,[27] but still needs to carry out its own assessment.

1.14 Normally the Home Secretary must abide by the Immigration Rules, but they may depart from the rules by making a decision more beneficial to an applicant, by overruling an immigration official, granting someone discretionary leave to remain outside of the Immigration Rules, or adopting a policy that people of a particular class or nationality should get leave outside the Immigration Rules, or granting a general amnesty. This discretion derives from IA 1971 s4(1), and is a very broad discretion, not constrained by the Immigration Rules. The Home Secretary can, therefore, waive a requirement of the rules in an individual case as a matter of statutory discretion.[28]

Executive policy

1.15 The Immigration Rules are not a comprehensive code of all the practices regulating entry into the UK. The next level down in the immigration law framework is the suite of executive policy, whose purpose is

24 IA 1971 s3(2).

25 *Hesham Ali v SSHD* [2016] UKSC 60, [2016] 1 WLR 4799 at para 17. 'Secretary of state' refers to the Secretary of State for the Home Department (SSHD), ie the Home Secretary.

26 *Hesham Ali v SSHD* at para 17.

27 *Hesham Ali v SSHD* at para 46.

28 *R (Alvi) v SSHD* [2012] UKSC 33, [2012] 1 WLR 2208 at para 31.

to provide further guidance to those making decisions on behalf of the secretary of state on a range of matters relating to immigration control. These are available on the Home Office website. Note that they differ in content to the guidance issued to applicants that accompanies application forms. Executive policies are amended from time to time, and the wording of aspects of the relevant policy may change as a result. This chapter refers to the relevant version of the policy as at May 2023.

1.16 Executive policies provide explanation on the content of the criteria for entry, leave to remain, administrative removal and deportation. They also fill in the gaps on details regarding procedure and practice and are, in that way, a necessary extension to the system of immigration control. The issues addressed in detail by policy range from the criteria applied to decisions on a person's eligibility for leave to enter or remain under the Immigration Rules, the content and balance of the 'public interest' in human rights and deportation cases, and the approach to assessments of credibility in certain immigration decisions, such as asylum and international protection claims and in respect of all aspects of decisions to remove, deport and detain individuals.

1.17 Policies, unlike Immigration Rules, are not part of any statute or statutory instrument and do not form part of the Immigration Rules. They therefore do not attract parliamentary scrutiny. That said, the secretary of state is not entitled, by guidance or instructions to their officers, to restrict the rights which would otherwise exist under legislation and the Immigration Rules. Generally, guidance cannot be relied on to interpret the Immigration Rules, but they may explain the purpose of the rule and the context in which it is intended to operate.[29] Policies applicable to immigration and asylum decisions must be published.[30]

1.18 A failure to take such a practice or policy into account, or a misinterpretation or misapplication, might well open the decision to a successful challenge on appeal although this is limited to human rights appeals following *Re Charles (human rights appeal: scope)*.[31] A decision may also be challenged by way of judicial review on the grounds that the secretary of state has failed to follow policy; an error of law in its

29 *ZT (Kosovo) v SSHD* [2009] UKHL 6, [2009] 1 WLR 348 at para 31 per Lord Hope.

30 *R (Lumba) v SSHD* (also known as *R (WL (Congo)) v SSHD*) [2011] UKSC 12, [2012] 1 AC 245 at paras 34–39, 170, 206, 221, 247.

31 [2018] UKUT 89 (IAC).

own right.[32] In *R (Lumba) v SSHD*[33] it was held that the secretary of state was liable for the false imprisonment of two foreign national prisoners pending their deportation, as she had applied an unlawful and unpublished policy when exercising her power of detention.

Applicability of international law

Overview

1.19 International law plays an important role in the UK's domestic immigration law framework, and many of the key principles contained in international treaties are directly enforceable as a consequence of being incorporated into domestic law.

1.20 The most-used international human rights treaty in the immigration law context is the European Convention on Human Rights (ECHR), which has been incorporated into domestic law via the Human Rights Act (HRA) 1998. Consistent with the jurisprudence of the European Court of Human Rights (ECtHR), the articles under the ECHR, as incorporated into HRA 1998 Sch 1, are construed in the light of relevant international law, particularly more specialist regional or global instruments.[34]

1.21 Through this route of interpretation, other international human rights treaties, which the UK government has ratified, have acted as an interpretative aid to the scope and content of the ECHR and its application to immigration law. This has included:

- the UN Convention against Torture and Other Cruel, Inhuman or Degrading Treatment or Punishment;[35]
- the UN Convention on the Rights of the Child (UNCRC);[36]
- the Protocol to Prevent, Suppress and Punish Trafficking In Persons, Especially Women and Children, supplementing the UN Convention Against Transnational Organised Crime; and

32 See *Mandalia v SSHD* [2015] UKSC 59, [2015] 1 WLR 4546 at paras 29–30 per Lord Wilson, citing *Lumba* at para 35 per Lord Dyson.

33 [2011] UKSC 12, [2012] 1 AC 245.

34 *Demir and Bavkara v Turkey* App No 34503/97 (2009) 48 EHRR 54, ECtHR at para 69: 'The precise obligations that the substantive provisions of the Convention impose on Contracting States may be interpreted, firstly, in the light of relevant international treaties that are applicable in the particular sphere.'

35 *A and others v SSHD (No 2)* [2005] UKHL 71, [2006] 2 AC 221.

36 See paras 1.24–1.31 and 11.10–11.23 for further detail on the UNCRC and its application in domestic law in the context of support for children affected by or subject to immigration control.

- the Council of Europe Convention on Action against the Trafficking in Human Beings (ECAT).[37]

1.22 Additionally, the Convention Relating to the Status of Refugees (Geneva, 1951) and its 1967 Protocol ('the Refugee Convention') are incorporated into domestic law through the Immigration Rules such that leave to remain should be granted if it is accepted that a claimant for asylum meets the definition.[38]

1.23 On an appeal, the statutory role of an immigration judge[39] is to determine whether the removal of a person who has made a protection claim either as a refugee or on human rights grounds or both would breach the UK's obligations under those conventions.

Borders, Citizenship and Immigration Act 2009 s55[40]

1.24 Further to the UK government withdrawing the reservation placed on the UNCRC in respect of immigration matters, parliament introduced BCIA 2009 s55. This provision in its language and structure mirrors the pre-existing Children Act 2004 s11 which applies to all local authorities and certain specific public authorities, including the police, prisons, probation and youth offending teams and schools and colleges.[41]

1.25 BCIA 2009 s55 places a duty on the secretary of state to make arrangements for ensuring that immigration, asylum, and nationality functions are discharged having regard to the need to safeguard and promote the welfare of children in the UK. The functions referred to in section 55 include any function of the secretary of state in relation to immigration, asylum or nationality and any function under the Immigration Acts.

1.26 Statutory guidance has been issued by the secretary of state under BCIA 2009 s55(3), entitled *Every child matters: change for children.*[42] Paragraph 1.4 identifies the ambit of the section 55 duty as:

- protecting children from maltreatment;

37 The enforcement of the rights of victims of trafficking is a fast-developing area of law which is considered separately in chapter 11.

38 Chapter 3 provides an overview of the asylum law structure.

39 NIAA 2002 s82.

40 See further paras 5.302–5.309.

41 For further discussion on Children Act 2004 s11, see paras 9.25–9.27.

42 *Statutory guidance to the UK Border Agency on making arrangements to safeguard and promote the welfare of children Issued under section 55 of the Borders, Citizenship and Immigration Act 2009*, November 2009, available at: www.gov.uk/government/publications/every-child-matters-statutory-guidance.

- preventing impairment of children's health and development (where health means 'physical or mental health' and development means 'physical, intellectual, emotional, social or behavioural development');
- ensuring that children are growing up in circumstances consistent with the provision of safe and effective care;
- undertaking that role so as to enable children to have optimum life chances and to enter adulthood successfully.

1.27 Paragraph 2.7 of the statutory guidance requires that children be consulted, and their wishes and feelings taken into account wherever practicable when decisions affecting them are made, albeit it will not always be possible to reach decisions with which the child will agree.

1.28 The guidance places emphasis throughout on the importance of effective inter-agency working, especially with public bodies qualified to plan for children's futures, such as local authorities: see paras 1.9(g) and 1.17. Paragraph 1.5 states that the overall framework require all agencies to 'take all reasonable measures to ensure that the risks of harm to children's welfare are minimised'. The statutory guidance specifically refers to the context of detention and removal as well as prompt decision-making in this context.

1.29 BCIA 2009 s55 may be relied on in several contexts in immigration law. As a general rule, it is more likely to be relevant to decisions which involve the exercise of discretion or an evaluative judgment.[43] For example:

- **When resisting a parent's removal or deportation from the UK.** In *ZH (Tanzania) v SSHD*,[44] a landmark case on section 55, the Supreme Court held that when assessing whether removal or deportation is proportionate with reference to ECHR Article 8, the best interests of the child should be *the primary consideration*. In other words, they must be considered first, albeit that they may be outweighed by the cumulative effect of countervailing considerations, for example, a parent's poor immigration history.[45] Where a child is British, this will be of particular importance in determining best interests, albeit that it is not a trump card.[46]

43 As opposed to 'binary' decisions such as entitlement to nationality or length of residence: See Lady Hale in *Nzolameso v Westminster City Council* [2015] UKSC 22, [2015] HLR 22 at para 25, there with reference to a similar provision in Children Act 2004 s11(2).

44 [2011] UKSC 4, [2011] 2 AC 166.

45 At para 33 per Lady Hale; at para 46 per Lord Kerr.

46 At para 30 per Lady Hale; at para 47 per Lord Kerr.

These are critical principles which should be relied on in any application or appeal concerning a child.

- **When considering the grant or duration of leave to remain.** In *R (SM) v SSHD*,[47] it was established that when considering not only whether to grant leave, but if so for what period, the decision-maker must comply with the section 55 duty to promote and safeguard the welfare of the child, taking into account his or her interests as a primary consideration.[48]
- **When resisting family separation caused by detention.** In *R (NXT and others) v SSHD*,[49] the Administrative Court found that once the Children's Champion had recommended release on the basis that a parenting assessment was required before the parent could be deported without their children, there came a point in time where the secretary of state could not effect deportation within a reasonable timescale. The parent's detention was held to be unlawful. In the similar case of *R (AJS and AJU) v SSHD*, the Home Office accepted that a father's detention, which separated him from his daughter and may have caused her to have to be adopted if he were not released within a certain timeframe, was unlawful.[50]

1.30 Its relevance in the context of the provision of support by the Home Office under the IAA 1999 and IA 2016 Sch 10 are discussed in further detail in chapters 5 and 6.

1.31 In any case concerning or affecting children, whether at the initial application stage or on appeal, it is important to adduce evidence as to the child's best interests in order to make full use of these principles to the advantage of the applicant or appellant. This is relevant not only to cases where the child is a direct applicant or dependant on the applicant, but also where the child's best interests, welfare and family life may be impacted by a decision made in respect of another person. For example, this may arise where the parent is being considered for deportation, which would occasion a long-term or permanent separation of the family, as was the case in *ZH (Tanzania)*.[51] Evidence from professionals who have contact with the child – for example, through

47 [2013] EWHC 1144 (Admin).

48 At paras 35–37 per Holman J. See also *R (Alladin and Wadhwa) v SSHD* [2014] EWCA Civ 1334 and the discussion below at paras 1.89–1.91.

49 [2011] EWHC 969 (Admin).

50 CO/88/2018, reported on the Bhatt Murphy Solicitors' website, https://bhattmurphy.co.uk/. See further below at paras 1.205–1.209.

51 [2011] UKSC 4, [2011] 2 AC 166.

school, extra-curricular activities, or as the result of health problems or special educational needs – will be useful to demonstrate in detail the child's individual needs and circumstances, and any vulnerabilities. A report from an independent social worker, or child psychologist, setting out in detail what a child's best interests require, can be especially helpful. Such a report can assess the impact on the child on separation from a parent in the event of removal or deportation, and may be relied on to argue, for example, that it would be unreasonable to require the child to leave the UK, or that the effect of deportation on a child would be 'unduly harsh'.[52] Many cases engaging ECHR Article 8 will turn on these issues.

Hostile environment measures

1.32 The IAs of 2014 and 2016 are the two key pieces of primary legislation underpinning the 'hostile environment' and directed at tackling the number of migrants in the UK who are unlawfully present – ie those who require leave but do not have it. The NBA 2022 extends certain hostile environment measures to asylum-seekers, unaccompanied asylum-seeking children (UASC) and victims of trafficking. They are accompanied by guidance on implementation of the measures.

1.33 IA 2014, which received royal assent on 14 May 2014, contained the following measures:

- extending authorities' powers to try to identify migrants unlawfully present in the UK (including those relating to the search of premises for documentation and the use of biometrics, such as fingerprints);[53]
- simplifying the removal of unlawfully present migrants, and limiting individuals' rights of appeal and access to bail;[54]
- prescribing in statute the government's view of how the balance between the right to respect for private and family life under ECHR Article 8 and the public interest should be struck.[55] The prescribed considerations operate as a direction to courts and

52 See below at paras 1.111–1.117 and 1.222.

53 IA 2014 Schs 1 and 2.

54 IA 2014 s1, substituting a new section 10 into IA 1999; IA 2014 s7, amending IA 1971 Sch 2 in respect of bail; IA 2014 s15, substituting a new NIAA 2002 s82, in respect of appeals to the First-tier Tribunal. Bail is discussed further at paras 1.188–1.197 and 6.201–6.220.

55 The IA 2014 introduced a new Part 5A into the NIAA 2002. See in particular NIAA 2002 ss117B–117D.

tribunals, which must follow and apply those considerations. This includes the 'precarious nature' of an appellant's immigration status and the public interest in migrants being able to speak English and be 'financially independent';[56]
- requiring landlords and banks to check the immigration status of their tenants/clients, and prohibiting them from providing such services to those who are unlawfully present in the UK;[57]
- refusing and revoking UK driving licences for those living in the UK who require leave to remain but do not have it;[58]
- giving greater powers to the Home Office to investigate suspected 'sham marriages' involving non-EEA nationals subject to immigration control;[59]
- giving further powers to require non-EEA nationals (subject to certain exemptions) who already were or were planning to stay in the UK for longer than six months to pay an annual health surcharge.[60]

1.34 The IA 2016 built upon the powers contained in the IA 2014 and introduced increased civil and criminal sanctions as follows:
- stronger criminal sanctions to deter 'illegal working' (ie the employment of migrants who are disqualified from working owing to their immigration status), targeted at both employers and employees, and powers to close premises;[61]
- new criminal offences aimed at landlords (and letting agents) who know, or reasonably suspect, that migrants who are disqualified from doing so are occupying or renting their property;[62]
- new powers for landlords to obtain possession of their property where a tenant or other occupier no longer has a right to rent under the IA 2014;[63]
- a new offence of driving when unlawfully in the UK, and new powers for police and immigration officers to search individuals

56 See, for example, *Rhuppiah v SSHD* [2018] UKSC 58, 1 WLR 5536.
57 IA 2014 ss20–33 (landlords) and 40–43 (banks). The operation of the 'right to rent' scheme is discussed at paras 7.389–7.434.
58 IA 2014 s47.
59 IA 2014 ss48–52 and Sch 4.
60 Immigration (Health Charge) Order 2015 SI No 792 arts 38–39. See further paras 10.32–10.113.
61 IA 2016 ss34–38.
62 IA 2016 s39.
63 IA 2016 ss40–42.

or premises where they have reasonable grounds to suspect a person who is unlawfully present has a driving licence;[64]

- amendments to the IA 2014 requirements for banks and building societies to periodically review existing accounts and to notify the Home Office if an account is found to be held by a person disqualified due to their immigration status. Subsequent statutory instruments provided for the checks to be carried out on a quarterly basis and for the information to be provided to the Home Office. Subject to conditions, the Home Office can then order the accounts to be frozen or closed;[65]
- increased powers for immigration officers and custody officers to search for and retain individuals' nationality documents, and for immigration officers to search premises for documents which might assist in the imposition of civil penalties relating to renting property to or employing migrants who do not have permission to work;[66]
- statutory authority for a wider range of public authorities to share information for immigration purposes, and a statutory duty for specified bodies (such as local councils and NHS trusts) to supply nationality documents to immigration officers upon their request, if they already hold that information (ie it does not require these bodies to 'collect' the information, just to pass it on if they do have it).[67]

1.35 The NBA 2022 contains provisions to disqualify asylum-seekers and victims of trafficking from accessing support if certain criteria are met, and prescribes approaches to resolving age disputes concerning unaccompanied asylum-seeking young people who claim to be under 18 on arrival but whose age and date of birth are disputed. The NBA 2022 provisions as they pertain to unaccompanied asylum-seeking children and disputes over their age are addressed in outline form in chapter 11 concerning special cases. The NBA 2022 provisions pertaining to victims of trafficking and their entitlement to support and protection from removal pending the resolution of their victim status are also addressed in chapter 11. The effect of the NBA 2022 on recognised victims' eligibility for leave to remain on the basis of their status and associated needs is addressed in chapter 3 alongside

64 IA 2016 ss43–44, not fully in force at time of writing. For further discussion on the 'right to rent' scheme, see paras 7.389–7.434.

65 IA 2016 s45 and Sch 7.

66 IA 2016 ss46–58.

67 IA 2016 s55, which also inserts new ss20A, 166(5A) and 166(6)(ab) and Sch A1 into IAA 1999.

the discussion about the effect of the same on protection claims under the Refugee Convention and human rights conventions.

Citizenship and the right of abode

Introduction

1.36 Having British citizenship is not the same as being in possession of a passport – a passport is rebuttable evidence of citizenship, which is acquired by strict application of nationality law, determined by the BNA 1981.

1.37 The 'right of abode' refers to all those who 'shall be free to live in, and to come and go into and from, the United Kingdom without let or hindrance'.[68] Although historically this was an important right held by some Commonwealth citizens[69] as well as British citizens, nowadays it is only likely to apply to those who are British citizens. The right of abode is to be distinguished from free movement rights under EU law, exceptions from immigration control conferred on diplomats and others, free movement within the Common Travel Area (CTA)[70] and settlement or indefinite leave to remain (ILR). Although these distinctions may make little difference for the practical purpose of entering the UK, they are important for the purpose of immigration control, ie what may happen to them following entry. Anyone with the right of abode is not subject to immigration control and cannot be deported or removed unless they are unable to prove their status or their right is taken away by the deprivation of British citizenship.

1.38 A person is or can become British through:

- automatic acquisition;
- registration by entitlement or discretion;
- naturalisation.

68 This is defined in IA 1971 s1(1), 'except such as may be required under and in accordance with this Act to enable their right to be established or as may be otherwise lawfully imposed on any person'. This refers to the power of immigration officers to inspect the passports of British citizens on entry to the UK.

69 IA 1971 s2(1)(b), broadly some Commonwealth citizens who, prior to 1983, either had a parent born in the UK or were women married to another Commonwealth citizen who was born, adopted, registered or naturalised in the UK.

70 The CTA refers to movement within the UK, Channel Islands, Isle of Man and the Republic of Ireland. See IA 1971 ss1(3), 11(4) and 33(1).

1.39 Nationality law is complex and will often require advice from a specialist practitioner. The following is an overview of the key provisions affecting those seeking support, including 1) the three pathways listed above; 2) the 'good character' requirement; and 3) the deprivation of citizenship.

Automatic acquisition

1.40 The BNA 1981 abolished automatic acquisition of citizenship solely by birth in the UK. Whether or not a child is entitled to citizenship, or may apply to be registered as a citizen, depends on a variety of factors relating to their parentage or their length of residence.

Children born in the UK

1.41 BNA 1981 s1(1) provides that the child automatically acquires citizenship at birth where the child is born in the UK to a mother or father who at the time is a British citizen or had ILR.[71] 'Father' is defined for these purposes as the husband of the woman who gives birth to the child, or a person who meets 'prescribed requirements' as to proof of paternity (by which it is no longer sufficient to be named as the father on the child's birth certificate).[72]

1.42 BNA 1981 s1(3) provides that if a UK-born child has a mother or father who becomes a British citizen or obtains ILR during the child's minority, the child is entitled to be registered as a British citizen on application to the secretary of state so long as the application is submitted while the child is still under 18. The right to register is also extended under BNA 1981 s1(3A) to those who are born in the UK where, during the child's minority, their father or mother becomes a member of the armed forces.

1.43 Under BNA 1981 s1(4), a UK-born child who has resided in the UK for ten years is also entitled to citizenship by registration, so long as they have not been absent from the UK for more than 90 days during any of the first ten years of their life.[73] There is a discretion to waive these absences in certain circumstances under

71 BNA 1981 s1(1).

72 BNA 1981 s50(9A); British Nationality (Proof of Paternity) Regulations 2006 SI No 1496 (as amended).

73 BNA 1981 s1(4).

Home Office policy.[74] Applications under section 1(4) can be made at any time after the child reaches the age of ten, even after they have become an adult.

1.44 NBA 2022 s7 amends various provisions of the BNA 1981 to provide an entitlement to British citizenship for individuals who were previously unable to acquire it because their mother was married to someone other than their biological British citizen father at the time of their birth. This addresses the decision in the case of *R (K (a child)) v SSHD*,[75] which found that in these circumstances, the definition of father in BNA 1981 was incompatible with ECHR Article 8, read with Article 14.

Children born outside the UK

1.45 As to children born outside the UK, the criteria are more complicated. If the child's mother or father was a British citizen 'otherwise than by descent'[76] at the time of birth, the child automatically acquires British citizenship by descent under BNA 1981 s2(1). This applies to all mothers and fathers who were themselves citizens through birth in the UK, registration (if not by descent) or naturalisation. For non-UK born children with a parent who is a British citizen by descent, there is an entitlement to citizenship by registration under BNA 1981 s3 if certain residence conditions are met.[77] Finally, the Home Secretary has a general discretion to register any child as a British citizen, on application, if they 'see fit'.[78] The Home Office guidance sets out the circumstances in which an application will normally be successful, for example where a child is born and adopted abroad and the adoption procedures of the country in question are recognised by the UK.[79]

74 *Registration as a British citizen: children*, v10.0, 16 September 2022, www.gov.uk/government/publications/children-nationality-policy-guidance.

75 [2018] EWHC 1834 (Admin), [2018] 1 WLR 6000.

76 BNA 1981 s14 provides an exhaustive definition of a British citizen 'by descent'. Hence anyone not in the list is by definition a British citizen 'otherwise by descent'. As s14 makes clear, determining whether or not a person is a British citizen by descent is not always a straightforward matter.

77 See BNA 1981 s3(2) and (5) which provide two different routes to registration, depending on whether the child has a grandparent who was a citizen otherwise than by descent at the time of the parent's birth.

78 BNA 1981 s3(1).

79 *Registration as a British citizen: children*, v10.0, pp19–22.

Registration

1.46 The BNA 1981 (as amended) provides for certain categories of people to be registered as British, either through entitlement or, if the specified conditions are not met, at the discretion of the secretary of state.

1.47 BNA 1981 s3 provides a general discretion for the Home Secretary to register any child as British where an application is made whilst that child is under the age of 18. This provision can be particularly important for children in the care of the local authority where it is clear their future lies in the UK.

1.48 A further set of provisions is intended to remedy historic discrimination against the children of unmarried mothers in previous legislation, to adequately cover the situation for British Overseas Territories citizens, British Nationals (Overseas), British Overseas Citizens, British subjects and British protected persons and to ensure that stateless nationals obtain citizenship. Detailed provision is found in the BNA 1981 at ss4–4I.

1.49 NBA 2022 s1 inserted into BNA 1981 a new section 17A which permits certain adult children of British Overseas Territories Citizen mothers to acquire British Overseas Territories citizenship. New BNA 1981 ss17B–17G, inserted by NBA 2022 s2, provide a route for adult children of unmarried fathers who are British Overseas Territories citizens to do the same. NBA 2022 s3 inserted into BNA 1981 a new section 17H, which allows direct descendants of Chagos Islanders to make an application to be registered as British Overseas Territories citizens where certain conditions set out in the provision are met. This has not yet come into force.

1.50 Those who are able to register as a British Overseas Territories citizen under amendments inserted into the BNA 1981 by NBA 2022 ss1–3 are also able to seek registration as British citizens under the new provision, section 4K under the BNA 1981.

Naturalisation

1.51 One of the provisions of BNA 1981 most likely to affect migrants who were not born in the UK and do not have UK parentage is section 6(1), which determines citizenship by naturalisation. Section 6(2) is a similar provision applying to those who are married to, or civil partners of, British citizens. In order to meet the criteria for naturalisation, applicants must first meet the residence conditions set out in BNA 1981 Sch 1, which applies in the following ways:

- For BNA 1981 s6(1) cases, an applicant must have been in the UK at the beginning of the period of five years ending with the date of application and have been absent fewer than 450 days within that period and fewer than 90 days in the 12 months preceding the application.[80]
- For spouses and civil partners, the applicant must have been in the UK at the beginning of the period of three years ending with the date of the application and have been absent fewer than 270 days and fewer than 90 days in 12 months preceding the application.[81]
- There is no discretion to waive the requirement to be 'in' the UK at the beginning of the relevant period unless the absence was due to serving in HM Forces (including civilian services) and those who are 'technically absent' from the UK such as diplomats.[82]
- Absences in excess of the permitted limits during either the previous 12-month or five-year periods can, however, be overlooked at the discretion of the secretary of state.[83]
- Applicants must also not be in breach of the immigration laws during either residence period,[84] and must be free from any time restrictions on their length of stay in the UK during the 12-month period.[85]
- For spouses or partners applying under BNA 1981 s6(2), they may apply for citizenship immediately after acquiring ILR (or permanent residence). Generally, they will have to have had five years leave to remain before qualifying for ILR in any event. Other applicants must have had no time restriction on their stay for at least 12 months prior to the application.[86]
- Applicants for naturalisation must demonstrate sufficient knowledge of English (or Welsh or Scottish Gaelic) and life in the UK.[87]

80 BNA 1981 Sch 1 para 1(2)(a)–(b).

81 BNA 1981 Sch 1 para 3(a)–(b).

82 BNA 1981 Sch 1 para 2(2)–(3).

83 BNA 1981 Sch 1 paras 1(2)(a), 2(1)(a), 3(a) and 4(b). See also detailed policy guidance in *Nationality policy: naturalisation as a British citizen by discretion*, v11, 1 November 2022, www.gov.uk/government/publications/naturalisation-as-a-british-citizen-by-discretion-nationality-policy-guidance.

84 BNA 1981 Sch 1 para 1(2)(d). Although some breaches can be overlooked, depending on the circumstances: see Sch 1 paras 2(1)(d) and 4(b).

85 BNA 1981 Sch 1 para 1(2)(c).

86 BNA 1981 Sch 1 para 1(2)(c).

87 BNA 1981 Sch 1 para 1(1)(c) and (ca).

1.52 Certain requirements for naturalisation, concerning a person's presence in the UK or British Overseas Territory, may be waived by the Home Secretary if certain requirements are met under NBA 2022 ss8 and 9.

The 'good character' requirement

Overview

1.53 Applicants for naturalisation and all applications for registration of any adult or young person over the age of ten by discretion (rather than entitlement)[88] must be of 'good character'.[89]

1.54 'Good character' is not defined in the BNA 1981, but there is detailed policy guidance available from the Home Office as to what is likely to be considered behaviour that indicates a person is not 'of good character': *Nationality: good character requirement.*[90] The policy runs to 53 pages and includes a long, non-exhaustive, list of issues which would, in the secretary of state's view, indicate that a person is not of good character and would therefore lead to refusal. The list includes issues which may be to be expected, such as war crimes and terrorism. It also includes more controversial and subjective factors when it comes to deciding whether a person is of 'good character' for the purposes of nationality, including issues of bankruptcy and liquidation.

1.55 There is no specific Home Office policy in relation to good character for children, save that decision-makers are required to 'take into account the standards of character required for the grant of citizenship to an adult at the secretary of state's discretion'.[91] All applications must of course take into account the need to safeguard and promote the welfare of children under BCIA 2009 s55.[92]

88 Applications for registration by entitlement (rather than by discretion) refer to applications where, if the statutory conditions are met, the person is a British citizen and the application is not subject to discretion on the part of the secretary of state. Examples are BNA 1981 s4B (entitlement to registration for certain persons without citizenship) and s4C (entitlement to registration for certain persons who would have become British citizens on commencement of the BNA 1981 but for sex discrimination in the historic legislation).

89 BNA 1981 s41A and Sch 1 para 1(1)(b).

90 V3.0, Home Office, 8 September 2022, www.gov.uk/government/publications/good-character-nationality-policy-guidance.

91 *Registration as British citizen: children*, v10, p35.

92 See paras 1.24–1.30.

1.56 Following the Supreme Court decision in *R (Johnson) v SSHD*,[93] an individual who would automatically have been born British before 1 July 2006 but for the fact their parents were unmarried and it was their father, rather than their mother, who was British, is also exempt from the good character requirement. The Supreme Court held that those who had been denied British citizenship by this historic legislative bias were entitled to register as British even if they were of bad character. This has now been extended to other categories of people who experienced historic unfairness in respect of citizenship. As a result, most applications for registration by entitlement under the BNA 1981 are exempt from the good character requirement following amendments made by the British Nationality Act 1981 (Remedial) Order 2019.[94]

Matters relevant to character

1.57 Matters relevant to character include:

- criminal convictions;
- financial conduct;
- deception and dishonesty;
- past immigration breaches.

Criminal convictions

1.58 Unsurprisingly, previous criminal convictions will often lead to an application for naturalisation or registration being refused on good character grounds. A series of 'tariffs' or periods of exclusion from qualifying for British citizenship are set out in the *Nationality: good character requirement* guidance. Criminal convictions attracting a sentence of imprisonment of four years or more, will normally be refused, regardless of when the conviction occurred. As for convictions attracting less than four years' imprisonment, applications will normally be refused unless there has been a sufficient passage of time between the conviction and the application. For sentences between 12 months and four years, a sufficient passage of time is 15 years; for sentences under 12 months, it is ten years. A non-custodial sentence or other out of court disposal that is recorded on a person's criminal record will normally lead to a refusal if the conviction occurred in the last three years.[95]

93 [2016] UKSC 56, [2017] AC 365.

94 SI No 1164.

95 *Nationality: good character requirement*, v3.0, pp11–12.

1.59 It is the entire sentence imposed on an individual which will be looked at, not the actual time spent in prison. A suspended prison sentence will be treated as a 'non-custodial offence or other out of court disposal that is recorded on a person's criminal record', unless the sentence is subsequently 'activated'. The guidance also contains detailed information as to what constitutes 'out of court disposals'. They include cautions, warnings, community sentences, hospital orders and fines. They do not include fixed penalty charges (for example, for traffic violations). However, these may be relevant when making the overall assessment as to whether a person is of 'good character'.[96] While they will not normally result in refusal of an application, receiving multiple notices over a short period of time 'could demonstrate a disregard for the law and therefore demonstrate that someone is not of good character'.[97]

1.60 The 'tariff' table is not the be-all and end-all when it comes to assessing good character. The decision-maker is expected to make an overall assessment as to the character of the applicant. This includes consideration of persistent offenders and means that, in some cases, the 'overall pattern of behaviour *may justify refusing an application, even if the individual sentences imposed would not normally in themselves be a reason for refusal*'.[98] The decision-maker will take into account factors such as the number of offences, the time period over which those offences were committed, the impact on the public, and whether there has been an escalation in the seriousness of the offences. In some cases, an applicant may be refused even when they have never been charged or convicted if there is 'firm and convincing information to suggest that a person is a knowing and active participant in serious crime, for example drug trafficking'.[99] The decision should give careful consideration to the nature of the information and the reliability of the source in such cases.[100]

1.61 Under the Rehabilitation of Offenders Act 1974, some criminal convictions become 'spent' after a certain period of time. This means that the offence does not have to be declared for most purposes, for example, when applying for employment or insurance. The period of time before an offence is spent varies with the seriousness of the offence. However, criminal offences never become spent for the

96 *Nationality: good character requirement*, v3.0, p17.
97 *Nationality: good character requirement*, v3.0, p18.
98 *Nationality: good character requirement*, v3.0, p14 (emphasis added).
99 *Nationality: good character requirement*, v3.0, p27.
100 *Nationality: good character requirement*, v3.0, pp17–28.

purposes of immigration and nationality law. The law on rehabilitation for immigration and nationality purposes was changed by Legal Aid, Sentencing and Punishment of Offenders Act 2012 s140 with effect from 1 October 2012. This means that all convictions, including spent convictions, have to be declared in an application for naturalisation.[101]

Financial conduct

1.62 When deciding on an applicant's good character, the Home Office may also look at their 'financial soundness', which includes bankruptcy; liquidation of a company of which the applicant was a director; debt; and non-payment of council tax (where the person unreasonably failed to pay or committed fraud in an attempt to pay less).[102]

1.63 Bankruptcy or liquidation will not be automatic reasons for refusal, except where fraud has occurred. In all other cases, the decision-maker will look at the level of culpability of the applicant in the events which led to bankruptcy or liquidation and the timing of the bankruptcy or liquidation. Similarly, debt in itself will not normally be a reason for refusal. However, where a person deliberately and recklessly builds up debts and there is no evidence of a serious intention to pay them off, the decision-maker will normally refuse the application.

Deception and dishonesty

1.64 Present or past alleged deception or dishonesty by an applicant is one of the most common reasons for refusal on good character grounds.[103] The deception or dishonesty is not limited to use in the person's application for British citizenship or previous immigration application. It can also include deception in their dealings with other departments of the government, including in relation to benefits.

1.65 Where deception was used in a previous immigration application, it does not matter whether the deception was material to the grant of leave or not. Even if the deception was not relevant, a later application for naturalisation will still normally be refused. The consequence of using deception in connection with a previous immigration application is that any application for British citizenship will normally be refused for a period of ten years starting with the date on which that

101 This is not the case for applicants who reside in Northern Ireland who are only required to disclose unspent convictions as defined in the Rehabilitation of Offenders (Northern Ireland) Order 1978 SI No 1908 (NI 27).

102 *Nationality: good character requirement*, v3.0, p38.

103 *Nationality: good character requirement*, v3.0, pp41–42.

deception was discovered or admitted. When the deception relates to the current application for citizenship, any subsequent application for citizenship will be normally be refused if it is made within ten years from the date of the refusal unless the failure to disclose was unintentional and a genuine error. Where deception is committed in an application for naturalisation or registration and is not uncovered at the time of the application, the Home Office has a power under BNA 1981 s40 to later deprive a person of their British citizenship.[104] This has occurred in some cases involving, for example, successful false asylum claims leading to a grant of a settlement and eventually to naturalisation.[105]

Past immigration breaches

1.66 Following the introduction of the new guidance on good character in January 2019, the Home Office started refusing naturalisation applications on the basis of previous non-compliance with immigration law.[106] This is now one common reason for refusal on the basis of good character. Under this amended guidance, a decision-maker will normally refuse an application if, in the ten years prior to the application, an applicant:

- entered into a false marriage or marriage of convenience. The ten years will start running from when the deception is discovered or admitted;
- cheated in a 'Knowledge of life in the UK' test, or an English language test. Again, the ten years start running when the deception is discovered or admitted;
- was prosecuted for making a false statement in an application;
- was complicit in deception on the part of referees;
- entered the UK without being granted leave to enter, but the policy makes clear that refugees are not to be penalised for entering unlawfully provided they claim asylum soon after arrival.[107] The ten-year period starts running from the date of entry if

104 See below at paras 1.71–1.74.

105 See *R (Hysaj and others) v SSHD* [2017] UKSC 82, [2018] 2 All ER 471, concerning Albanian citizens who falsely claimed to be Kosovans on order to be granted asylum on arrival in the UK in the late 1990s.

106 Referred to in the guidance as 'Immigration related issues' See *Nationality: good character requirement*, v3.0, pp43–45.

107 *Nationality: good character requirement*, v3.0, pp46–48. But see also NBA 2022 s12 in respect of the differential treatment of refugees depending on whether they enter the UK unlawfully.

known, or otherwise the date the applicant brought themself or came to the attention of the Home Office;
- evaded immigration control in the last ten years, including but not limited to having failed to report or comply with any conditions imposed under the Immigration Acts, been detected working in the UK without permission;
- absconded, ie failed to report when granted immigration bail;
- assisted a person to evade immigration control, for example, assisting someone to enter the UK in order to enter into a sham marriage. In such cases refusal will normally be indefinite;
- employed an 'illegal worker', ie a person who does not have permission to work from the Home Office;
- was deprived of their citizenship because of fraud, false representation or the concealment of material fact. The ten-year period will start running from the date the deprivation order was issued.

1.67 Not every past breach of immigration law triggers a refusal. The Home Office guidance contains a detailed section on overstaying. While overstaying in the past ten years is a potential ground for refusal, it can be disregarded if it is the sole reason for refusal and falls within certain timelines.

Decision-making on citizenship applications

1.68 The refusal of an application for British citizenship does not by itself prejudice an applicant's current immigration status or future applications for British citizenship. In other words, an applicant who submits an application for British citizenship which is refused will retain their current immigration status. They will also be free to submit a new application for British citizenship in the future, if or when they meet the good character requirement. The exception to this rule is where the reason for refusal is that the applicant has used deception in the current application. In this case, any new application will be refused for a period of ten years.

1.69 According to the Home Office policy, an application for British citizenship will only be granted in 'exceptional circumstances' when there are factors which would normally lead to the application being refused. Examples given in the policy include where the person's criminal conviction is for an offence which is not recognised in the UK or there is no comparable offence (for example, homosexuality or membership of a trade union); the person has one single non-custodial sentence for an offence which occurred within the first two years of the preceding three, and there are strong factors which suggest the person is of good character in all other regards so the decision to refuse would be disproportionate; or the applicant has one single conviction but has lived in the UK all their life or since a very young age and the conviction was many years ago, This suggests a very strict interpretation of the guidance. However, judges have suggested that the Home Secretary should apply the policy in a more flexible way.[108]

1.70 If an application for citizenship is refused, the applicant can bring a judicial review against the refusal on traditional public law grounds.

Deprivation of citizenship

1.71 Where citizenship obtained by naturalisation or registration has been procured by means of fraud,[109] the Home Secretary has the power to deprive a person of their citizenship under BNA 1981 s40(3). A similar power exists under BNA 1981 s40(2), whereby the Home Secretary may deprive a person of their citizenship if satisfied that deprivation is 'conducive to the public good', so long as deprivation would not render the person stateless.[110] The 'conducive' power is not limited to citizenship obtained by registration or naturalisation, and applies to all categories of citizenship including citizenship acquired by birth. There is no published policy on when and how the section 40(2) power is to be used, and decisions are taken by the Home Secretary individually. Section 40(2) cases tend to involve very serious crime and/or or allegations of terrorism.[111]

1.72 NBA 2022 s10 amends BNA 1981 s40 to insert subsections (5A)–(5E), which allow a decision to deprive a person of British citizenship to be made in the absence of contact with the person and to ensure that the associated deprivation order is valid. There is an obligation on the Home Secretary to give the affected person written notice that the Home Secretary has made the order, the reasons for the order and the person's right of appeal against the order where the person

108 See, for example, *Hiri v SSHD* [2014] EWHC 254 (Admin).

109 Specifically, fraud, false representation or concealment of a material fact: BNA 1981 s40(3).

110 Unless certain conditions apply, namely that the citizenship was obtained by naturalisation, the secretary of state believes that the person has conducted themself in a manner seriously prejudicial to the UK, and has reasonable grounds to believe that the person is able to become a citizen of another country: section 40(4) and (4A).

111 See, for example, *Aziz v SSHD* [2018] EWCA Civ 1884, [2019] WLR 266, concerning those convicted of the sexual abuse and trafficking of children in Rochdale.

makes contact with the Home Secretary. Those people who were not given notice before a deprivation order is made still have a right to appeal against the decision, with time not starting to run for an appeal unless and until the person is given notice of the fact that the order has been made.[112]

1.73 There is a right of appeal to the First-tier Tribunal (Immigration and Asylum Chamber) (FTT) against a decision to deprive a person of their citizenship,[113] unless the decision is certified by the Home Secretary based on information which in the Home Secretary's opinion should not be made public, including in the interest of national security, in which case the right of appeal lies to the Special Immigration Appeals Commission (SIAC).[114]

1.74 In *R (Begum) v SSHD*,[115] the Supreme Court held that in a SIAC appeal against a deprivation decision, SIAC is not entitled to reconsider the Home Secretary's exercise of their discretion to deprive citizenship for itself. Instead, SIAC is confined to reviewing the decision on convention public law principles, unless there is an issue as to whether or not there has been a breach of the person's human rights under the ECHR, in which case SIAC must decide the matter for itself on the merits.[116] The Supreme Court did not explicitly state that the same approach applies to the FTT, but stated *obiter* that previous case-law, holding that the FTT can reconsider the exercise of the Home Secretary's discretion for itself, had been wrongly decided.[117]

112 BNA 1981 s40A(1) and (2A) as inserted by NBA 2022 s10(3).
113 BNA 1981 s40A.
114 BNA 1981 s40A(2).
115 [2021] UKSC 7, [2021] AC 765.
116 Lord Reed at paras 68–71, 118–119.
117 Lord Reed at paras 41–44, suggesting *Deliallisi (British citizen: deprivation appeal: scope)* [2013] UKUT 439 (IAC) is wrongly decided, but that Mr Ockleton's approach in *Pirzada (deprivation of citizenship: general principles)* [2017] UKUT 196 (IAC) is correct. *Pirzada* held that the tribunal cannot exercise the secretary of state's discretion for itself. See also *Laci v SSHD* [2021] EWCA Civ 769, [2021] 4 WLR 86.

Control of the border: leave to enter and remain

1.75 As a general rule, any person who is not a British citizen requires *leave to enter or remain* in the UK.[118] The general power to control entry to and stay in the UK derives from IA 1971 s3(1), which gives the secretary of state the power to grant leave to enter or remain for a limited or an indefinite period. The enforcement of these powers is generally conducted by immigration officers acting on behalf of the secretary of state.

1.76 Control can take place: 1) before entry; 2) on entry; and 3) after entry. These are discussed below, along with categories of applications for leave to remain.

Control before entry

1.77 In many cases, leave to enter will be granted in the country of departure, before a person travels to the UK. This is known as 'entry clearance', or, in ordinary language, obtaining a visa. It normally takes the form of a sticker or 'vignette' contained in a passport or travel document, which will state for how long leave to enter is granted. Decisions on entry clearance are generally given by entry clearance officers at British embassies based abroad.

1.78 In general, anyone who is a 'visa national' requires entry clearance to enter the UK. The list of 'visa national' countries is defined in the Immigration Rules.[119] As a rule of thumb it includes most African, Asian and Middle Eastern countries but not North America, Australia or New Zealand. Non-visa nationals, who are not also EEA citizens, may enter the UK for a period of up to six months for the purposes of a visit, so long as the purpose of the visit is not to marry or form a civil partnership.[120] In practice then, a non-visa national who wishes to visit the UK for a period of up to six months may simply arrive in the UK with their passport and 'apply' for leave to enter at the border, which will be granted by an immigration officer

118 At the time of writing, EEA citizens are in a different category; see chapter 2. In addition, there is a limited category of non-EEA non-British citizens who do not require leave to enter or remain, namely Commonwealth citizens with a right of abode, persons arriving from Ireland, as well as diplomats and the crew members of planes, ships and international trains (who do not require leave to enter, at least for a limited period). These exceptions to the general rule are beyond the scope of this book.

119 Currently in the Immigration Rules Appendix V: Visitor: Visa national list.

120 Immigration Rules Appendix V: Visitor paras V1.4–1.5.

in the form of a stamp in their passport stating that they have leave to enter until a date six months after the date of entry. However, just as with visa nationals, non-visa nationals need to obtain prior entry clearance if they wish to enter the UK for any purpose other than visiting.

Control on entry

1.79 When a person who is not a British citizen arrives at the UK border (an airport or a control area in a Eurostar terminal or ferry embarkation point in Europe[121]), it will be an immigration officer who grants leave to enter. In most cases, a prior grant of entry clearance operates as leave to enter, such that the immigration officer is simply checking the vignette in the person's passport. However, that is not the end of the matter, since an immigration officer on entry has the power to cancel leave to enter already granted, for example, if entry is being sought for a different purpose to that for which entry clearance was granted. Moreover, immigration officers may conduct entry checks on any person to establish whether that person:

- is a British citizen;
- may enter the UK without leave;
- has leave to enter or remain still in force;
- if not whether they should be granted or refused such leave;
- whether any conditions should be imposed on their leave; and if so
- whether it should be cancelled.[122]

It is for this reason that even British citizens are required to show their passport at the border when re-entering the UK. The power to cancel or curtail leave, however, needs to be read with the grounds on which leave can be curtailed or cancelled under Part 9 of the Immigration Rules.

121 There are reciprocal agreements on border control with European countries where ferry and train terminals from which ferries and trains going directly to the UK depart from. For example, the Sangatte Protocol sets out arrangements which provide UK border officials authority to exercise powers under the IA 1971 within control zones in the European countries set up under the agreement. There is a control zone, for example, at Paris Gare du Nord, set up pursuant to the Channel Tunnel (International Arrangements) Order 1993 SI No 1813 as amended by the Channel Tunnel (International Arrangements) (Amendment No 3) Order 2001 SI No 1544.

122 IA 1971 Sch 2 paras 2–2A.

1.80 Immigration officers also have the power to require a person to submit to medical examinations or further examination by an immigration officer.[123] These powers are accompanied with a power to detain pending a decision to grant, refuse or cancel leave to enter.[124] Further examination often arises where there has been a change of circumstances known to or declared to the Home Office since the grant of entry clearance or leave to remain. For example, where there is evidence or suspicion of fraud or misrepresentation (particularly important in cases where the person may have been embroiled in the English language testing scandal[125]) or an unpaid NHS debt. Particular abuses can occur where a wife is 'tricked' into leaving the UK and then stranded abroad. An abusive husband then informs the Home Office that his marriage has broken down to prevent the wife returning to the UK, resulting in either a separation of mother from children or British citizen children being stranded abroad.

Control after entry

1.81 Under the IA 1971, leave to remain (and indeed leave to enter) may be granted for a limited or unlimited period.[126] Any person wishing to extend their stay in the UK beyond the period for which they were initially granted leave to enter, or change the basis on which they were originally granted it, must apply for leave to remain. Applications for leave to remain are handled generally handled by UK Visas and Immigration (UKVI), a department of the Home Office and therefore the Home Secretary for the purposes of litigation.

Categories of applications for leave to remain

1.82 The categories in which a person can apply for further or different leave to remain without leaving the country are limited. Given the complex and evolving nature of immigration legislation and rules, it is not possible in the context of this overview to set out in any comprehensive manner the types of applications for leave to remain which such individuals may pursue. However, the section below deals with the following common categories of immigration applications which

123 IA 1971 Sch 2 paras 2–2A.
124 IA 1971 Sch 2 para 16.
125 See, for example, A Gentleman 'MPs to question Home Office officials over English test scandal' *Guardian*, 9 July 2019.
126 IA 1971 s3(1)(b).

are most likely to arise outside the asylum and EU law contexts which bear on questions of eligibility for and access to support:

- human rights and protection claims;
- leave to remain 'outside the Rules';
- leave to remain on family life grounds;
- leave to remain on private life grounds;
- leave to remain as a domestic violence victim;
- leave to remain as a trafficking victim;
- leave to remain for the 'Windrush generation'.

Human rights and protection claims

1.83 Whether a claim is a human rights or protection claim has become an important issue since the IA 2014 removed all rights of appeal in respect of immigration decisions save for those which constitute the refusal of protection or human rights claims.[127]

1.84 For the purposes of appeal rights only, a 'protection claim' is defined as a claim that removal of a person from the UK would breach the UK's obligations under the Refugee Convention or the UK's obligations in relation to persons eligible for a grant of humanitarian protection.[128] This is discussed in detail in chapter 3.[129]

1.85 A 'human rights claim' is defined as a claim made by a person to the Home Secretary at a place designated by the Home Secretary that to remove the person from or require them to leave the UK would be unlawful under HRA 1998 s6.[130] This includes non-protection based human rights claims made following a failed asylum claim.[131] The definition of a 'human rights claim' also applies to those outside the UK who have applied for entry clearance, raising human rights in their application, but have had the application refused.[132]

1.86 The Home Secretary has never specified a particular place or defined what a 'designated place' for the purposes of making a

127 IA 2014 s15, which rewrote NIAA 2002 s82.

128 NIAA 2002 s82(2).

129 NIAA 2002 s82.

130 NIAA 200 s113.

131 *Further submissions*, v10.0, 28 June 2022, p20, www.gov.uk/government/publications/further-submissions.

132 *Baihinga (r22; human rights appeal: requirements: Sierra Leone)* [2018] UKUT 90 (IAC).

human rights claim, although has a detailed policy on assessing whether the claim has been made.[133]

1.87 The onus is on the Home Secretary to identify whether a 'human rights claim' has been made. The Home Office guidance lists various applications under the Immigration Rules which, if made, are deemed to constitute a human rights claim.[134] This includes most applications based on long residence in the UK and those made on grounds of family life under Appendix FM, as discussed below, except for bereaved partners or applications for ILR for victims of domestic violence (DVILR).[135] This does not mean that only applications on the Home Office list will constitute a human rights claim generating a right of appeal on refusal. In reality, the litmus test is the substance of the application and whether it engages a right under the ECHR. The FTT (IAC) has determined that:

> . . . an application will constitute a human rights claim if, on the totality of the information supplied, the applicant is advancing a case which requires the caseworker to consider whether a discretionary decision under the rules needs to be taken by reference to ECHR issues (eg Article 8) or requires the caseworker to look beyond the rules and decide, if they are not satisfied, whether an Article 8 case is nevertheless being advanced.[136]

1.88 There are still several important categories of human rights claims that are dealt with under policy rather than through the Immigration Rules, including those seeking to remain to take part in criminal, civil or family court proceedings which may engage rights under ECHR Articles 6 and/or 8.[137]

133 *Rights of appeal*, v13.0, 22 September 2022, https://assets.publishing.service.gov.uk/government/uploads/system/uploads/attachment_data/file/1106091/Current_rights_of_appeal.pdf.

134 *Rights of appeal*, v13.0, pp12–16.

135 Although note individuals in both categories may well have ECHR Article 8 grounds on which they seek to remain in the UK such as length of residence, private life or existence of children.

136 *Baihinga (r22: human rights appeal: requirements: Sierra Leone)* [2018] UKUT 90 (IAC) at para 2.

137 See, for example, *Re MH (pending family proceedings: discretionary leave: Morocco)* [2010] UKUT 439 (IAC), which describes the Home Office policy of not removing or deporting parents or others who are parties to pending family court proceedings. See also *Rights of appeal*, v13.0.

Leave to remain 'outside the Rules'

1.89 As indicated above, the Home Secretary has a general discretion under IA 1971 s4(1) to grant leave to remain outside the Immigration Rules, where the requirements of the rules are not met. There is also discretion to grant leave for a limited or an indefinite period,[138] such that, for example, even if the requirements of the Immigration Rules for ILR are not met in an individual case, the decision-maker must not fetter their discretion to consider whether indefinite (rather than limited leave) should be granted if the application clearly requests it.[139] Where an application concerns a child, the decision-maker must comply with the BCIA 2009 s55 duty to promote and safeguard their welfare, and consider their best interests as a primary consideration, when considering whether to grant leave for a longer period than is specified in the rules.[140]

1.90 The Home Office has issued policy guidance on leave outside the rules (LOTR),[141] which aims to cover those cases where leave to remain should be granted on 'compelling, compassionate grounds' other than on Article 8 grounds, Article 3 (medical) grounds or asylum/humanitarian protection grounds. These cases are covered by separate guidance: for example, Article 8 cases which do not meet the requirements of Appendix FM (family life) or the Immigration Rules on private life but which may justify a grant of leave for a limited or indefinite period are covered in the policy on Appendix FM and long residence.[142]

1.91 The general LOTR guidance specifies that applications must be supported by documentary evidence and be made using the specified form which most closely matches the applicant's circumstances, with the requisite fee paid unless the applicant qualifies for a fee waiver.[143]

138 IA 1971 s31(b).

139 See, *R (Alladin and Wadhwa) v SSHD* [2014] EWCA Civ 1334, in the context of applications concerning children.

140 *R (SM and others) v SSHD* [2013] EWHC 1144 (Admin). See paras 1.24–1.31.

141 *Leave outside the Immigration Rules*, v2.0, Home Office, 9 March 2022, www.gov.uk/government/publications/chapter-1-section-14-leave-outside-the-immigration-rules.

142 *Family policy: family life (as a partner or parent), private life and exceptional circumstances*, v18.0, 11 August 2022, p70, www.gov.uk/government/publications/family-life-as-a-partner-or-parent-private-life-and-exceptional-circumstance

143 See below at paras 1.155–1.156.

Leave to remain on family life grounds

1.92 Appendix FM of the Immigration Rules sets out the various routes to leave to enter or remain based on family life with a person who is a British citizen, settled in the UK, or in the UK with limited leave as the result of being a refugee or a person granted humanitarian protection. In addition to the domestic violence route discussed below,[144] the routes are as follows:

- family life with a partner;
- family life with a parent of a child in the UK;
- family life as a child with a person with limited leave as a partner or parent;
- adult dependent relatives;
- bereaved partners.

1.93 Each route follows a similar structure within Appendix FM, setting out 'eligibility requirements' and 'suitability requirements' which need to be met in order to qualify for leave to enter or remain under that route. The eligibility requirements are broken down into relationship requirements, financial requirements, immigration status requirements and English language requirements.

1.94 Appendix FM itself is lengthy and difficult to navigate. The following sections discuss, in broad terms, the relationship and financial requirements for the partner and parent routes, as well as the 'exception' provision EX.1, which, if it applies, exempts the applicant from having to meet certain eligibility requirements for leave to remain as a partner or parent.

Appendix FM partners[145]

1.95 In order to meet the relationship requirements for this route, the applicant's partner must be a British citizen or present and settled in the UK, or in the UK with leave to remain as a refugee or a person with humanitarian protection.[146] Both applicant and partner must be 18 or over, have met in person, be in a genuine and subsisting

144 See paras 1.118–1.125.

145 A 'partner' for these purposes is defined as a spouse, civil partner, fiancé or proposed civil partner, or a person who has been living together with the applicant in a relationship akin to marriage or civil partnership for at least two years prior to the application: Immigration Rules Appendix FM Gen 1.2.

146 Immigration Rules para E-LTRP 1.2 for the leave to remain route. Analogous requirements for applications for entry clearance and ILR are set out at sections E-ECP and E-ILRP of Appendix FM respectively.

relationship, and 'not within the prohibited degree of relationship'.[147] Any marriage or civil partnership between the applicant and their partner must be valid,[148] any previous relationship they may have had must have broken down permanently,[149] and the couple must intend to live together permanently in the UK.[150] If the applicant is in the UK with leave as a fiancé(e) or proposed civil partner, and the marriage or partnership did not take place during that period of leave, there must be good reason why and evidence that it will take place within the next six months.[151]

1.96 One of the most challenging aspects of Appendix FM for applicants under the partner route is the 'minimum income rule', according to which the applicant must provide specified evidence of a gross annual income of at least £18,600, from sources which are specified elsewhere in the Rules.[152] If the couple has children, this rises to an additional £3,800 for a first child and an additional £2,400 for each additional child. The requirement can be met with this figure alone or in combination with savings above £16,000.[153] Appendix FM-SE sets out detailed rules specifying the type of evidence which must be provided in order to demonstrate that the financial requirement is met. While the rules appear onerous, decision-makers are given some flexibility as to how they approach the evidence, for example, by contacting applicants to give them the opportunity to rectify a documentary error or provide a missing document in a sequence.[154]

1.97 Applicants must also provide evidence that there will be adequate accommodation, without recourse to public funds, for the family, including other family members who are not included in the application but who live in the same household, which the family own or occupy exclusively. This requirement is waived if the exception in

147 Immigration Rules paras E-LTRP 1.3–1.7. This term is defined by the Marriage Act 1949 and related legislation prohibiting marriage between certain family members including parents and children, and siblings.

148 Immigration Rules para E-LTRP 1.8.

149 Immigration Rules para E-LTRP 1.9.

150 Immigration Rules para E-LTRP 1.10.

151 Immigration Rules para E-LTRP 1.11.

152 Appendix FM-SE and the IDI *Family migration: Appendix FM section 1.7*, v8, 7 December 2021 provide detailed requirements as to the permitted financial sources for the income (for example, salaried employment of the partner or applicant, income from property rental, self-employment, or cash savings etc).

153 Immigration Rules para E-LTRP 3.1.

154 Immigration Rules Appendix FM-SE para D.

para EX.1 applies.[155] Accommodation is not deemed adequate if it is overcrowded or contravenes public health regulations.

1.98 In R (*MM (Lebanon)) v SSHD*,[156] the Supreme Court upheld the minimum income requirement in principle, but held that Appendix FM needed to take proper account of the duty under BCIA 2009 s55 to promote and safeguard the welfare of children and consider alternative sources of income for enabling applicants to meet the financial requirements of the rules. Appendix FM was amended accordingly.[157] The amended rules also expressly require decision-makers to consider whether, if any of the requirements of Appendix FM are not met, there are 'exceptional circumstances' which mean that refusal of the application would result in 'unjustifiably harsh consequences' for the applicant, a partner or a child such that entry clearance of leave should nevertheless be granted on the basis of ECHR Article 8.[158]

Appendix FM parents[159]

1.99 This route is aimed at parents who have responsibility for or access to a child following the breakdown of their relationship with the child's other parent. Eligibility for leave to enter requires the child of the applicant to be under the age of 18 at the date of the application, living in the UK, and either a British citizen or settled.[160] Where an application is for leave to remain, in the alternative to the child being British or settled, the relationship requirements will be met if the child has lived in the UK for at least a seven-year period preceding the date of the application, where the exception EX.1 also applies.[161] It is important to note, therefore, that when an application for leave to remain relies on a child who has lived in the UK for seven years, rather than a child who is settled or British, the additional requirements of para EX.1 must also be met.[162] Where an application is for leave to remain, it will not be refused if the child has turned 18 since

155 Immigration Rules para E-LTRP 3.4. See paras 1.103–1.106.

156 [2017] UKSC 10, [2017] 1 WLR 771.

157 With effect from 10 August 2017: *Statement of changes in Immigration Rules*, HC 290, 20 July 2017.

158 Immigration Rules para GEN 3.2.

159 'Parent' in this context includes step-parents where the biological parent is decease, adopted parents, and fathers of 'illegitimate children': see Immigration Rules para 6.

160 Immigration Rules para E-ECPT 2.2.

161 Immigration Rules para E-LTRPT 2.2(d).

162 See paras 1.103–1.106.

the parent was first granted entry clearance or leave to remain, so long as the child has not formed an independent family unit or is leading an independent life.[163]

1.100 For entry clearance applications, the applicant parent must provide evidence that they have sole parental responsibility for the child, or direct access to the child (as agreed with the parent or carer with whom the child normally lives or as ordered by a UK court). The person with whom the child lives must be a British citizen or settled and not the partner of the applicant.[164] In all cases, the applicant must demonstrate that they are taking and intend to continue to take an active role in the child's upbringing. 'Sole parental responsibility' refers to the situation where one parent takes primary parental responsibility for decisions relating to the child's upbringing.[165]

1.101 For leave to remain applications, the applicant parent must show that they have sole parental responsibility for the child, or that the child lives normally lives with them and not their other parent (where that parent is a British citizen or settled), or that they have direct access to the child as agreed by the courts or the other parent.[166] Whether the child lives with the applicant or their other parent, the other parent cannot be the partner of the applicant and the applicant cannot be eligible to apply for leave to remain under the partner route.[167] In all cases, the parent must show an active role in the child's upbringing.

1.102 The financial requirements under this route are that the applicant can maintain themself and any dependence without recourse to public funds and access adequate accommodation.[168] Applicants for leave to remain are exempt from these requirements if the exception EX.1 applies.

163 Immigration Rules para E-LTRPT 2.2(a).

164 Immigration Rules para E-ECPT 2.3.

165 *Re TD (paragraph 297(i)(e): sole responsibility: Yemen)* [2006] UKAIT 49; *Buydov v Entry Clearance Officer, Moscow* [2012] EWCA Civ 1739. Further guidance is set out in *Family policy: family life (as a partner or parent), private life and exceptional circumstances*, v18.0.

166 Immigration Rules para E-LTRPT 2.4. Guidance on the meaning of 'normally lives with' and evidence of direct access is set out in *Family policy: family life (as a partner or parent), private life and exceptional circumstances*, v18.0, pp38–40.

167 Immigration Rules para E-LTRPT 2.3.

168 Immigration Rules paras E-ECPT 3.1–3.2.

The exception

1.103 Paragraph EX.1 applies to parents if the applicant has a genuine and subsisting parental relationship with a child who:

- is under the age of 18 years, or was under the age of 18 years when the applicant was first granted leave on the basis that this paragraph applied;
- is in the UK;
- is a British citizen or has lived in the UK continuously for at least the seven years immediately preceding the date of application; and
- taking into account their best interests as a primary consideration, it would not be reasonable to expect the child to leave the UK.

1.104 For parental applications then, the key question is whether it would be 'reasonable' to expect the child to leave the UK. The Home Office policy[169] sets out relevant factors for caseworkers making the decision as to whether it would be reasonable to expect the child to relocate abroad. These include:

- whether the child would be leaving the UK with their parent(s) – 'it is generally the case that it is in a child's best interests to remain with their parent(s)';
- the extent of wider family ties in the UK;
- whether the child is likely to be able to (re)integrate readily into life in another country, relevant factors including the extent of any social, cultural, linguistic ties, access to citizenship, and whether the child has ever attended school in that country;
- whether removal would give rise to a significant risk to the child's health;
- country-specific information.

1.105 Paragraph EX.1 applies to partners where the applicant has a genuine and subsisting relationship with a partner who is in the UK and is a British citizen, settled in the UK or in the UK with refugee leave or humanitarian protection, and there are insurmountable obstacles to family life with that partner continuing outside the UK. The term 'insurmountable obstacles' is defined in para EX.1 as meaning 'the very significant difficulties which would be faced by the applicant or their partner in continuing their family life together outside the UK

169 *Family life (as a partner or parent), private life and exceptional circumstances*, v18.0, p47.

and which could not be overcome or would entail very serious hardship for the applicant or their partner'.

1.106 The requirement for 'insurmountable obstacles' is to be distinguished from the less stringent requirement for 'very significant obstacles', found elsewhere in the Immigration Rules.[170] Current Home Office policy provides that in assessing insurmountable obstacles, the factors to be taken into account include:

- the family's ability lawfully to enter and stay in another country (for example, where the UK partner is settled as the result of previous refugee status and the partner is of the same nationality);
- serious cultural barriers to relocation overseas (for example, being in a same-sex relationship where there is a risk of prosecution or serious harm);
- the impact of a mental or physical disability or serious illness requiring ongoing medical treatment;
- the absence of governance or security in the country of origin.

Suitability, English language and immigration status requirements

1.107 These requirements are common to the parent and partner routes. An applicant will not be eligible for leave to remain on family life grounds where they were previously granted leave as a visitor or for six months or less; or, where they are on immigration bail or in the UK in breach of immigration laws, unless the exception EX.1 applies.[171]

1.108 The English language requirements specify that applicants must demonstrate a minimum level of English, unless they are from a majority English-speaking country; have a qualification taught in English; or are exempt on the basis of age, disability or other exceptional circumstances.[172]

1.109 Finally, all applications under the parent and partner routes are subject to the suitability requirements. These prohibit, for example, leave to enter or remain being granted where the applicant is the subject of a deportation order or their presence in the UK is not conducive to the public good as the result of a criminal conviction.[173] Some of the requirements amount to discretionary, rather than mandatory, grounds of refusal, for example, where the applicant

170 For example, para 276ADE(1)(vi), see below at paras 1.111–1.117.
171 Immigration Rules paras E-LTRP 2.1 and E-LTRPT 3.1.
172 Immigration Rules paras E-LTRP 4.1–4.2 and E-LTRPT 5.1–5.2.
173 Immigration Rules paras S-LTR 1.1–4.5.

owes a litigation debt to the Home Office. The suitability requirements are similar to the general grounds for refusal for applications made outside Appendix FM.[174]

Routes to settlement under Appendix FM

1.110 Leave to enter or remain as a partner or parent is granted for 30 months. There are two routes to ILR (or 'settlement') under Appendix FM, the five-year and the ten-year routes. Where a partner or parent meets all the requirements of the Rules, they are eligible for settlement after five years. The ten-year route is for applicants who meet all of the suitability requirements and the exception EX.1 but are unable to meet certain financial requirements (including the minimum income requirements under the partner route).[175]

Leave to remain on private life grounds

1.111 The Immigration Rules aim to set out when long residence will result in a person qualifying for leave to remain. These categories include a person who is:

- a child under 18 at the date of application who has lived in the UK for seven years – such a person may qualify for limited leave to remain on the basis of their ECHR Article 8 private life, if they can show that it would not be 'reasonable' for them to relocate abroad;[176]
- aged 18 years or above but under 25 years old and has spent at least half of their life living continuously in the UK (discounting any period of imprisonment);[177]
- aged 18 or above and has lived continuously in the UK for less than 20 years but there would be very significant obstacles to the applicant's integration into the country to which they would have to go if required to leave the UK.[178]

1.112 These rules create bright lines so that many people who fall outside the very specific rules may have found themselves missing requirements by mere days or weeks for reasons that are often not within their control. For example:

174 See paras 1.160–1.164.
175 See, for example, the broad requirements under para R-LTRP 1.1(6).
176 Immigration Rules para 276ADE(1)(iv).
177 Immigration Rules para 276ADE(1)(v).
178 Immigration Rules para 276ADE(1)(vi).

- Young people brought to the UK as children at the age of 12½ and older will be unable to meet the criteria under paras 276ADE(1)(v) and 276ADE(1)(iv) due to their age at date of entry. Although they will have been in the UK for a significant part of their childhood, they will only qualify for limited leave to remain on a private life basis if they can show that they will be face 'very significant obstacles' to re-integration into their country of origin.
- Another example highlighting the realities of this bright-line approach to private life is the group of children who enter the UK between ages of 11 and 12½. They will never qualify under para 276ADE(1)(iv), as they are already over 18 when they reach the seven-year residence requirement. They will be stuck in limbo until they reach the half-life point (at the earliest, aged 22) where their private life will suddenly be considered as sufficient; the only determining factor being their age and their length of residence, with no further test required.

1.113 On 15 March 2022, the Home Office published a *Statement of changes in Immigration Rules* which introduced a new Appendix Private Life, replacing paras 276ADE–276DH. This took effect on 20 June 2022 and applies only to applications made on or after that date. Applications made before 20 June 2022 will still be considered under the rules in force on 19 June 2022. By and large, for children, the new Appendix Private Life requirements mirror those under para 276ADE(1)(iii)–(vi). Applications still need to be made by a specified online form to be valid, and applicants still need to pay the application fee and the Immigration Health Charge. The first and third of these requirements will be waived if a private life claim is made under ECHR Article 8 at the same time as a protection claim or further submissions following the refusal of a protection claim, when the applicant is in detention or during an appeal.

1.114 The new Appendix Private Life still maintains the bright-line approach under Immigration Rules para 276ADE(1), which had been criticised by the appellate courts in the past.[179] As the House of Lords held in *EB (Kosovo) v SSHD*:

> . . . 'Firm immigration control requires consistency of treatment between one aspiring immigrant and another'. In a complex and overloaded system perfect equality of treatment between applicants simil-

179 The so-called '18th birthday point'. See, in the context of risks on return for refugees, *KA (Afghanistan) v SSHD* [2012] EWCA Civ 1014, [2013] 1 WLR 615 at para 18 per Maurice-Kay LJ; *DS (Afghanistan) v SSHD* [2011] EWCA Civ 305, [2011] INLR 389 at para 54 per Pill LJ.

> arly placed will be impossible to achieve, but startling differences of treatment between such applicants, or anything suggestive of randomness or caprice in decision-making, must necessarily give grounds for concern.[180]

In this context, 'the search for a hard-edged or bright-line rule to be applied to the generality of cases is incompatible with the difficult evaluative exercise which Article 8 requires'.[181]

1.115 The Home Office guidance on what will constitute very significant obstacles to integration[182] requires an applicant to show that they are unable to establish a private life in the country of return (within a reasonable period of time) or that establishing that private life would entail very serious hardship for the applicant. Country evidence of relevant national laws, attitudes and the general situation should be considered. Where an applicant would be at risk of prosecution, harassment or discrimination as a result of their sexual or political orientation or faith or gender, or where their rights and freedoms would otherwise be so severely restricted as to affect their fundamental rights, the test would be met. Individual factors including the applicant's cultural background, length of time spent in the country of return and existing family, friends and social network must also be considered. These matters must be considered cumulatively and not in isolation. Although private life formed in the UK will not be relevant to an application under para 276ADE, it will be relevant to considering ECHR Article 8 outside the Immigration Rules.

1.116 Where leave to remain is granted, it will ordinarily be for a period of 30 months and subsequent applications will also attract periods of 30 months. When a person has accrued 120 months (ten years), they will be eligible for ILR.

1.117 The parent of a child granted leave to remain under para 276ADE should be able to make an application to remain in the UK under Appendix FM, discussed at paras 1.99–1.102 above.

Leave to remain as a domestic violence victim

1.118 The domestic immigration provisions are set out under section DVILR of Appendix FM and Part 6 of the Appendix Armed Forces. They apply to applicants who have previously been granted leave to

180 [2008] UKHL 41, [2009] 1 AC 1159 at para 10.

181 *EB (Kosovo)* at para 12.

182 *Private Life*, v1.0, 20 June 2022, https://assets.publishing.service.gov.uk/government/uploads/system/uploads/attachment_data/file/1083717/Private_life.pdf.

enter or remain as the spouse, civil partner, unmarried or same-sex partner of a British citizen, settled person, a person with refugee leave or a member of the HM Forces who has served for at least four years.

1.119 Fiancés or proposed civil partners of British citizens, settled persons or members of the HM Forces are not treated the same and are not eligible for the domestic violence provisions. Nor are partners of asylum-seekers, those with humanitarian protection leave, or those with limited leave to remain. Those with leave as a parent of a child settled in the UK or with seven years' continuous leave or exercising EU Treaty rights are also excluded. However, there are separate provisions relating to EEA nationals under Appendix EU which are not discussed here.[183]

1.120 The policy justification for this approach is that a partner of a person who is neither British nor already has ILR should have no expectation of remaining in the UK outside that relationship. This is of some concern, since it may lead to individuals within these groups remaining in violent or abusive relationships owing to their immigration status. Moreover, at least historically, some visa routes were designed to enable the migrant and their dependant spouse to qualify for settlement providing certain conditions were met and thus the expectation that the family were on a pathway to settlement would have been the same for them as an individual arriving on a spouse/partnership visa. It is important to note that the Home Secretary still retains an overarching discretion in respect of these groups and there are sometimes alternative routes available under Appendix FM to enable individuals to leave the relationship and obtain status in their own right.

1.121 The applicant is expected to prove the domestic violence took place on the balance of probabilities through submission of evidence. Guidance explains what weight will be given to that evidence.[184]

1.122 Although there is no requirement in DVILR for the applicant to hold current leave to remain for an application to be valid, where an applicant does have leave to remain it is important to make an application either under the 'destitute domestic violence concession' (see below) or DVILR in time as otherwise the individual becomes an overstayer and subject to the hostile environment provisions.

183 See chapter 3.

184 *Victims of domestic violence and abuse*, v15, 24 November 2021, www.gov.uk/government/publications/victims-of-domestic-violence.

1.123 The 'destitute domestic violence concession' (DDVC) applies to those who intend to apply for ILR under the domestic violence rules (DVILR) and who need access to public funds in order to leave the relationship.[185] It is a particularly important provision for women without recourse to public funds who require access to a woman's refuge or other form of safe house. An individual migrant woman eligible for the DDVC will be granted three months' leave to remain outside the Immigration Rules with a condition that does not restrict access to public funds. The expectation is that they will make an application for ILR under the domestic violence provisions before their leave under the concession expires as the applicant's period of leave under the DDVC will be treated as extended under IA 1971 s3C ('section 3C leave') which ensures continued access to public funds whilst the application is determined. If the applicant has leave under the DDVC and the application is not made within the three months, they will lose their entitlement to public funds, become an overstayer and become subject to removal.

1.124 The Home Office's policy makes explicit that there is no guarantee that a woman granted leave outside the rules under the DDVC would subsequently secure leave under the domestic violence provisions.

1.125 Partners with retained status under the EEA regulations do not benefit from the DDVC concession. They therefore have no guarantee of a bridging period of three months' leave outside the rules to gather all relevant evidence to support an ILR application.

Leave to remain as a trafficking victim

1.126 The Council of Europe Convention on Action against the Trafficking in Human Beings (ECAT)[186] provides for the grant of a residence permit to a victim of trafficking if either the victim's stay is necessary owing to their person situation and/or co-operation with an investigation or criminal proceedings. The UK signed the convention on 23

185 *Destitute domestic violence (DDV) concession*, v1.0, 5 February 2018, https://assets.publishing.service.gov.uk/government/uploads/system/uploads/attachment_data/file/679269/victims-of-domestic-violence-and-abuse-DDV-concession-v1_0.pdf. See also *Apply for destitution domestic violence (DDV) concession*, 2019, www.gov.uk/government/publications/application-for-benefits-for-visa-holder-domestic-violence.

186 ECAT Article 14(1), Council of Europe, CETS No 197.

March 2007 and ratified it on 17 December 2008.[187] ECAT Article 14 provides that state parties 'shall issue' a renewable residence permit to victims in one or other of the two following situations or in both:

a) the competent authority considers that their stay is necessary owing to their personal situation;
b) the competent authority considers that their stay is necessary for the purpose of their co-operation with the competent authorities in investigation or criminal proceedings.

1.127 This provision for granting a residence permit has been incorporated into domestic law via Home Office executive policy[188] for those recognised in England and Wales as victims of trafficking under the National Referral Mechanism (NRM),[189] the UK's formal mechanism for identifying people who are victims of trafficking or modern slavery.

1.128 Consideration of whether a victim will be granted a residence permit will only be addressed at the conclusion of the NRM identification process, and only if a person receives a positive 'conclusive grounds' decision that on a balance of probabilities they are a victim of trafficking. No application for a residence permit is required. The consideration automatically follows from the conclusion of the NRM.

1.129 In *R (EOG and KTT) v SSHD*[190] the Court of Appeal found that there was no requirement on the Home Secretary to grant individuals leave during the period between a positive decision that there are reasonable grounds to believe that they are a victim of trafficking and the conclusive grounds decision. In KTT's case, on the facts, she had an asylum claim which related to her situation as a victim of trafficking because it was based on the risk of her being re-trafficked if she were returned to Vietnam. She said it was necessary for her to stay in the UK in order to pursue that claim. The Court of Appeal found that this situation fell within ECAT Article 14(1)(a), that is the duty to issue a residence permit where the competent authority considers that their stay is necessary owing to their personal situation at the

187 For a more detailed discussion of the obligations that the UK owes to victims and potential victims of trafficking under international law and as implemented in domestic law, see chapter 11.

188 *Discretionary leave considerations for victims of modern slavery*, v5.0, 10 December 2021, www.gov.uk/government/publications/interim-operation-guidance-discretionary-leave-for-victims-of-modern-slavery.

189 For a description of the NRM and more detail on the UK's trafficking obligations, see further chapter 11.

190 [2022] EWCA Civ 307, [2023] QB 351.

stage of the individual having a positive reasonable grounds decision and the NRM process having not yet been concluded. The court found that the secretary of state's policy intended to but did not properly reflect this requirement of the ECAT. The secretary of state sought permission to appeal to the Supreme Court in respect of this judgment but was refused permission. The basis for obtaining temporary leave to remain has in any event fallen away in the light of NBA 2022 s65 coming into force on 30 January 2023.[191]

1.130 The right to be considered for a residence permit is in addition to, and without prejudice to,[192] other entitlement to leave to remain under domestic law as the result of a successful human rights or asylum claim. Thus, it would be unlawful for the Home Office to postpone consideration of a recognised victim's entitlement of a residence permit until the asylum claim has been determined. The High Court in *R (JP and BS) v SSHD*[193] found the Home Office's policy of routinely deferring the consideration of an asylum-seeking victim's entitlement to a residence permit until after the asylum claim discriminated against asylum-seeking victims of trafficking in breach of ECHR Article 14 read with ECHR Article 4.

1.131 Because the grant of a renewable residence permit to victims of trafficking is not provided for under the Immigration Rules, the leave granted will be discretionary leave granted outside the Immigration Rules.[194]

1.132 Relevant factors to inform whether it is necessary to grant a period of leave to remain because of a victim's personal situations include:

- the victim's mental and physical health and need for treatment;
- any risks to the person on return and likely availability of protection;
- whether or not the victim needs to remain in the UK to pursue a claim for compensation or assist with police inquiries into the victim's trafficking.

These factors will also be relevant to the duration of leave to be granted to a victim, although the standard duration according to Home Office policy is normally 30 months.

191 See para 1.133 below.

192 See ECAT Article 14(5).

193 [2019] EWHC 3346 (Admin), [2020] 1WLR 918.

194 This means leave granted at the discretion of the decision-maker, acting on behalf of the secretary of state, pursuant to the general power to grant leave under IA 1971 s3(1)(b).

1.133 NBA 2022 s65 puts the criteria for the grant of a residence permit to victims of trafficking on a statutory basis. It came into force on 30 January 2023.[195] Section 65(2) provides that the Home Secretary 'must grant' the person limited leave to remain in the UK if the Home Secretary considers it is 'necessary' for the purposes of:

a) assisting the person in their recovery from any physical or psychological harm arising from the relevant exploitation;
b) assisting the person to seek compensation in respect of the relevant exploitation; or
c) assisting the person to co-operate with a public authority in connection with an investigation or criminal proceedings in respect of the relevant exploitation.

It is relevant to note that NBA 2022 s65(2)(a) represents a narrower basis for the grant of leave to a confirmed victim than under Article 14(1)(a) (ie necessary on grounds of the victim's 'personal situation'). This appears to be a deliberate policy choice of the Home Secretary and is a fundamental departure from the Home Secretary's previous policy approach which accepted that her policy concerning trafficking leave expressly implemented Article 14 ECAT to its full extent. This is confirmed in new guidance issued in respect of the implementation of section 65, entitled *Temporary Permission to Stay considerations for Victims of Human Trafficking or Slavery*.[196] In the policy, the secretary of state has stated that she will grant a victim of trafficking leave to remain in the circumstances described in Article 14(1)(b), concerning the need to grant leave to remain to assist a person to co-operate with a criminal investigation or proceedings concerning their exploitation. However, the secretary of state has said that in respect of Article 14(1)(a), this will only be granted to the extent required under NBA 2022 s65.

1.134 Under NBA 2022 s65(4), leave to remain is not treated as 'necessary' if the Home Secretary considers the victim's need for assistance is capable of being met in their country of origin or in another country where they may be removed by an agreement with the UK. NBA 2022 s65(5)(b) defines such a 'country' referred to in section 65(4)(a), (b) as including '*one to which the person may be removed in accordance with an agreement between that country or territory and the United Kingdom*'; that agreement does not need to be one contemplated

195 See Nationality and Borders Act 2022 (Commencement No 4 and Transitional Provision) Regulations 2023 SI No 33 reg 3(f).
196 V2.0, 2 February 2023.

under the ECAT. The Migration, Economic and Development Partnership ('MEDP') agreement between the UK and Rwanda would clearly be an agreement falling within section 65(5)(b). Of particular note is that NBA 2022 s65 applies to any confirmed victim of trafficking irrespective of whether they are an asylum claimant. It is triggered at the end of the NRM process, at the point at which the individual receives a positive Conclusive Grounds decision. NBA 2022 s65 presents a separate route by which the secretary of state may seek to relocate an individual – specifically a confirmed victim of trafficking – to Rwanda. For further discussion about the MEDP agreement between the UK and Rwanda and its interrelationship with NBA 2022 s65, see paras 3.131–3.142.

1.135 Furthermore, by section 65(3) read with section 63(2), a person is disqualified from a grant of a residence permit where the Home Secretary is satisfied that the person is either a) a threat to public order, or b) has claimed to be a victim of slavery or human trafficking in bad faith. The circumstances in which a person is a threat to public order includes circumstances identified at section 63(3).

1.136 As for the duration of leave, the reference in the NBA 2022 to 'limited leave to remain' suggests that the duration is likely to remain 30 months consistent with the current practice. However, section 65 still leaves open the wide discretion that the Home Secretary has under IA 1971 s4(1), and in a case with the right facts and evidence in support, it is arguable that the duration of leave should be longer than the normal grant.

Leave to remain for the 'Windrush generation'

1.137 In general terms, the 'Windrush generation' refers to those who migrated to the UK from former UK colonies between the late 1940s, when the former colonies started to become independent, and the 1970s. Many of them will have had ILR on arrival or have been entitled to citizenship, owing to the operation of nationality law at the time. However, on account of being unable to document their leave to remain or right of abode, and in many cases, the destruction of documents by the Home Office, many were wrongly detained, threatened with removal, or even removed.

1.138 In response to the scandal, the Home Office has set up a 'Windrush Scheme', whereby Commonwealth citizens who settled in the UK before 1 January 1973,[197] or their children born in the UK or

197 When the IA 1971, and the provisions on right of abode, first came into force.

who arrived as children, or citizens of any nationality who settled before 31 December 1998, may apply for documentation to prove their status. At the time of writing, the 'Windrush Scheme' is published on ww.gov.uk,[198] but from time to time the government websites are rearranged so that it may appear on the departmental website in future. Please check the website at the relevant time when an application is contemplated.

1.139 Financial compensation is available under the scheme for those who suffered loss as the result of being unable to prove their status, including being unable to access work, benefits or other services. The compensation scheme is open to a wider category of persons including the children, grandchildren and close family members of Commonwealth and other citizens in certain circumstances, and the estates of those deceased but who would otherwise been eligible for compensation. Again, the compensation scheme is published on the www.gov.uk website, but please check the website at the relevant time when an application is contemplated.

Applications to the secretary of state

Introduction

1.140 As indicated above at para 1.81, except for applications for entry clearance, which are made to entry clearance officers, all applications for leave to remain are made to UKVI. Some applications can be made online, though in general such applications are required also to be posted to the relevant department of the Home Office within a specified period of online submission. It is also possible, in certain circumstances, on payment of an additional fee, to have an application expedited by submitting a paper or online application form at a Home Office 'premium service' centre. Immigration legal representatives should be in a position to provide advice on the appropriate routes and requirements to make an application.

1.141 This section will cover the timing of application; application forms and multiple claims; and application fees.

198 *Windrush Compensation Scheme Rules*, November 2022, www.gov.uk/government/publications/windrush-compensation-scheme-full-rules.

Timing of application

1.142 It is essential that where a person has leave to enter or remain, a valid application is made before the existing grant of leave to enter or remain expires – otherwise the person will become an 'overstayer', defined as a person who remains in the UK without leave after the date on which their limited leave expires. An overstayer is liable to immigration detention and removal and will be subject to the host of 'hostile environment' measures as outlined at paras 1.32–1.35 above.

1.143 There are no set waiting times for immigration applications. They depend on the type of application and the applicant's individual circumstances. Whereas the Home Office publishes waiting times for visa applications made in the UK – such as for student visas and work or family visit extensions – it does not publish waiting times for other categories of immigration applications, such as application on grounds of family or private life under Appendix FM or Appendix Private Life. There used to be a service standard for asylum claims of six months, but this was scrapped in 2019. The harsh reality is that an immigration decision can be pending for months or, in many cases, years.

1.144 Providing that the application for an extension of leave to remain or for leave to remain on a different permitted basis is made before the person's current grant of leave expires, IA 1971 s3C operates to protect the applicant from becoming an overstayer by deeming the existing leave to be extended (along with any conditions attached to it) while the new application is pending. IA 1971 s3C does this by extending the leave and conditions of leave that the applicant had prior to making the application to extend or vary their leave. The leave is further treated as extended during the period within which any appeal to the FTT (IAC) could be brought,[199] and while any such appeal is pending.[200] Leave is also extended by section 3C where an

199 IA 1971 s3C(2)(b). This is a period of 14 days from the date on which the decision was sent (if the person who applied for further leave is in the UK) within which the person may appeal to the FTT. See Tribunal Procedure (First-tier Tribunal) (Immigration and Asylum Chamber) Rules 2014 SI No 2604 r19.

200 An appeal is pending until it is finally determined, withdrawn or abandoned. See IA 1971 s3C(2)(c); NIAA 2002 s104.

administrative review could be sought or is pending.[201] Where a decision to refuse is maintained following an administrative review, there is no right to request an additional administrative review,[202] hence section 3C leave ends on the date of determination of the review. Where an in-time application is refused but the result of administrative review is that the decision is withdrawn to be reconsidered, section 3C leave will continue as if the original decision were yet to be decided.[203] This protection under section 3C cannot be underestimated. It allows an applicant to preserve the status quo of their existence in the UK, including their right to work, and any rights to access mainstream benefits, if they had not been subject to a condition of no recourse to public funds (NRPF).[204] It does not, however, apply during any subsequent period in which any judicial review is brought or pending challenging the refusal of an application for immigration leave. This can cause obvious and real difficulties for individuals seeking to challenge a decision that does not attract the right of appeal because at the point when the administrative review process concludes, they will no longer have the protection afforded under section 3C.

1.145 The date of application is also relevant to assessing whether documents sent in support of the application are up to date. For example, for applications for leave to remain as a partner under Appendix FM of the Immigration Rules, bank statements and other documents must end no earlier than 28 days before the date of the application. For this reason it is often advisable not to submit an application earlier than 28 days before expiry of the leave.[205]

201 IA 1971 s3C(2)(d). The period within which a review 'could be sought' is discussed below at paras 1.233–1.235. An administrative review is 'pending' until it is withdrawn, determined, or a fresh application is made which brings section 3C to an end. See *Leave extended by section 3C (and leave extended by section 3D in transitional cases)*, v11.0, October 2021, www.gov.uk/government/publications/3c-and-3d-leave. Also see further below for a discussion of appeal and administrative review procedure.

202 *Administrative review*, Home Office, v12.0, 3 September 2021, p59, www.gov.uk/government/publications/administrative-review.

203 *Administrative review*, v10, p57.

204 See further on NRPF at paras 1.166–1.172 below.

205 Albeit there is no *general* prohibition on applying for further leave to remain more than 28 days before leave is due to expire, there are other examples of this 28-day policy, for example, those on a five-year route to ILR may submit an application up to 28 days before they reach the end of the five-year policy. See, for example, *Indefinite leave to remain: calculating continuous period in UK*, v22.0, 1 December 2020, p10, www.gov.uk/government/publications/indefinite-leave-to-remain-calculating-continuous-period-in-uk.

1.146 The Immigration Rules define the day on which an application is deemed to be made and this depends on the method of application. For example: for online applications it is the date on which the application is submitted; for postal applications via the Royal Mail it is the date of posting according to tracking information; for paper applications submitted in person at a Home Office premium service centre, it is the date of receipt at the service centre.[206]

1.147 The difficulty that arises, even with IA 1971 s3C acting as a bridge between the expiry of the previous visa and a decision on an in-time application for further leave, is the lack of any formal document explaining the effect of section 3C to a layperson, such as an employer, a benefits agency, a landlord or a bank. Applicants will either receive a confirmation on the website if the application is submitted online, or a letter in the post confirming the submission of the application. However, that confirmation does not mention anything about IA 1971 s3C applying on submission of an in-time application or the effect of submitting an application in-time in respect of a person's leave to remain in the UK. Whereas asylum-seekers are given an 'asylum registration card', there is no equivalent identity or status document issued to someone in that in-between period between the expiry of existing leave and a decision on the in-time application for an extension of leave. The Home Office's internal systems are not always updated in real time so whether a person has made an in-time application for further leave may not registered in a way that could be obtained from landlord and employment checking services. Research published by RAMFEL[207] in September 2022 found that one in three of its clients with leave extended under IA 1971 s3C were affected by hostile environment measures because they were unable to demonstrate their continued lawful immigration status. Their biometric residence permit contained the date of expiry of their previous leave but did not reflect any updated status conferred under section 3C. Many were suspended from their jobs or from receiving welfare benefits because they could not prove their continued lawful immigration status. RAMFEL found their experiences echoed those of people of the Windrush generation.

206 Immigration Rules para 34G.

207 RAMFEL, 'The Hostile Environment Remains in Place', September 2022: http://www.ramfel.org.uk/reportonhstileenvironment.html.

Application forms and multiple claims

1.148 In most cases, and for all applications for leave to remain under specified categories of the Immigration Rules (for example, leave to remain as a partner or parent under Appendix FM or leave to remain under the points based system), it is compulsory to complete a specified form and pay a specified fee in order for the application to be valid.[208] A form is defined as 'specified' when it is a form which is posted on the Home Office website[209] and for this reason it is essential to check the Home Office website shortly prior to submitting an application, since the application forms change regularly.[210] All mandatory parts of the form must be completed and proof of identity provided.[211] Most categories of applications require understanding of a system so complex the Court of Appeal has repeatedly described it as 'Byzantine'.[212] There are also a myriad of guidance notes to the forms, which are not always accurate, may mislead or contradict the rules and policies. It is therefore vital to check the primary source rules and policies rather than rely solely on the guidance notes to the form.

1.149 The IAA 1999 introduced a comprehensive 'one stop' appeals process,[213] which replaced the previous system of multiple appeals. Applicants were required to state all the reasons, outside the scope of the original application, why they wished to enter or remain in the UK. An applicant could make only one application. Anything they said to add to it or change it, prior to a decision being made, was a variation of that application such that there was only one decision and therefore just one appeal. The NIAA 2002 built upon the 'one-stop' system of the IAA 1999, with a single right of appeal which could be brought on one or more well-known grounds restated in NIAA 2002 s84. As previously, an appellant could raise further grounds of appeal in a 'one-stop', statement which an adjudicator would consider on appeal.

208 See generally *Validation, variation and withdrawal of applications [for leave to remain in the UK]*, v4.0, 15 October 2021, www.gov.uk/government/publications/specified-application-forms-and-procedures.

209 Immigration Rules para 34.

210 There is a limited exception to this rule: an applicant may rely on a previous version of the form so long as it is 'no more than 21 days out of date', Immigration Rules para 31(1)(c).

211 Immigration Rules para 34.

212 *R (Firdaws) v First Tier Tribunal (Immigration and Asylum Chamber) and SSHD* [2019] EWCA Civ 1310 at para 14 per Irwin LJ.

213 IAA 1999 s74.

1.150 This, however, changed when appeal rights were reduced by the IA 2014.[214] Under the new regime, only decisions which constitute a refusal of a human rights or protection claim, or a decision to revoke protection status, generate a right of appeal. Current Home Office policy is to require a separate paid application for each category of application an individual may wish to make. However, it is not permitted to make more than one application at a time.[215] Any other grounds on which a person wishes to remain, for example, human rights grounds, must still be identified and put forward on the initial application if it includes a 'one stop' notice.[216] If there is a 'one stop' notice, and the applicant does not set out all of the grounds on which they may wish to remain in the UK, it may not be possible to appeal on such grounds if a similar application is refused in the future.[217]

1.151 The upshot of the regime under the IA 2014 is that applicants are forced into the unfortunate position of having to decide which application to pursue, albeit that they are required to raise all grounds in their application. The difficulty arises because only those applications giving rise to a decision on a human rights or protection claim will attract a right of appeal A person may, however, be entitled to make another type of immigration application that, if successful, results in a longer duration of leave or settlement but does this at the risk of being refused and having no right to appeal against the decision. The applicant in this situation would then fall outside the protection of IA 1971 s3C, become an overstayer and lose any existing entitlements to mainstream support and benefits as well as become subject to more restrictive immigration control measures on their housing, access to social security, health and support. This may arise even though an applicant has additional, often legitimate, grounds to remain in the UK but which can only be made by way of a second application, made at a time when the applicant is likely to have become an overstayer.

1.152 By way of an example, if a person wishes to apply for ILR on the basis of a marriage breakdown due to domestic violence and as the parent of a British child, they have to choose to apply either under DVILR (the rule for ILR as a victim of domestic violence) or limited leave to remain as a parent (LTRPT) because each application

214 IA 2014 s15, repealing the former NIAA 2002 s82 and in force as of 20 October 2014.

215 Immigration Rules para 34BB; *Validation, variation and withdrawal of applications [for leave to remain in the UK]*, v4.0, p18.

216 IAA 1999 s120.

217 NIAA 2002 s96.

requires a different form and different fee. If they apply for ILR as a victim of domestic violence and are refused, the Home Secretary will often not consider whether they should be allowed to remain in the UK as a parent, and there is no right of appeal against the refusal of ILR. Following *R (AT) v SSHD*,[218] it was expected that the application form would be amended to enable a human rights claim to be raised when applying for ILR, but at the time of writing that change has not yet been effected. The High Court had found that where a victim of domestic abuse, in the application for ILR raises a human rights claim, the Home Secretary cannot remove the victim's right to appeal, in reliance on the general rule that only one application can be made.

Application fees

Overview

1.153 The fee for each application is specified on the application form and a list of current fees can be found on the Home Office website.[219] Fees are prescribed by regulations made under IA 2014 s68. Where a form changes, even if the old form remains valid, the fee may have increased and it is the new fee that must be paid. If in doubt, check before sending. Fees can be very expensive; for example, at the time of writing the fee for an application for ILR made within the UK is £2,404.

1.154 Where the correct fee is not paid, the application is deemed to be invalid. This is distinct from substantive rejection of the application, and has the consequence that any previous leave is not extended by IA 1971 s3C while the application is being considered.

Fee waivers

1.155 It is possible to request a fee waiver for certain specified applications. The most obvious category of candidates for a fee waiver relate to those who make certain specified human rights applications where to require payment of the fee before deciding the application would be incompatible with a person's human rights.[220]

218 [2017] EWHC 2589 (Admin).

219 See *Home Office immigration and nationality fees* at: www.gov.uk/government/publications/visa-regulations-revised-table.

220 See *R (Omar) v SSHD* [2012] EWHC 3448 (Admin) and *R (Carter) v SSHD* [2014] EWHC 2603 (Admin).

1.156 Fee waiver requests must be done online.[221] In broad terms, a fee waiver will be granted if the applicant can demonstrate by way of evidence that they are destitute, or would be rendered destitute by payment of the application fee, or has provided evidence that, though the destitution criteria do not apply, there are exceptional circumstances justifying the grant of a fee waiver.[222] Applications for leave to remain based on ECHR Article 3 (as well as asylum claims) do not require a fee to be paid.

Grant of leave and duration

1.157 The duration of leave to remain or enter granted following a successful application depends on the category of leave applied for:

- For applications on asylum or humanitarian protection grounds,[223] leave is normally granted for five years,[224] with ILR normally granted at the end of the five-year period so long as the person continues to require protection as a refugee or person in need of humanitarian protection.[225]
- For human rights applications on the grounds of family or private life under ECHR Article 8,[226] leave is normally granted for 30 months, with eligibility for the person to be granted ILR after ten years.
- For applications under Appendix FM on the grounds of family life, there is a ten-year and a five-year route to ILR, to be accrued via successive grants of leave of 30 months' duration. Whether a person qualifies for the ten- or five-year route depends on whether they can meet all of the requirements of Appendix FM.[227]
- Leave 'outside the Rules' on human rights or other grounds is normally granted for 30 months.

1.158 It is important to remember, however, that the Home Secretary has a general discretion to grant leave for a shorter or longer period than

221 As of 4 January 2019.

222 See the Home Office policy on *Fee waiver: human rights-based and other specified applications*, v6.0, 8 April 2022, www.gov.uk/government/publications/applications-for-a-fee-waiver-and-refunds.

223 Discussed in detail in chapter 3.

224 Immigration Rules para 399Q(i) and (ii).

225 Immigration Rules paras 339R, 339A and 339G.

226 See above at paras 1.111–1.117.

227 See above at para 1.110.

the default position as set out in the relevant immigration rule, including a discretion to grant ILR.

1.159 Where an application concerns a child, the decision-maker is duty-bound under BCIA 2009 s55 to consider what a child's best interests require, not only when deciding whether to grant leave but when deciding the duration of leave to be granted.[228]

General grounds for refusal of an immigration application

1.160 An application for leave to enter or remain may be refused because the applicant does not meet the requirements of the relevant part of the Immigration Rules, or it may be refused on 'general grounds'. The general grounds are set out in the Immigration Rules,[229] which contain both mandatory and discretionary grounds for refusal. These general grounds are complex and can be different for different applications for leave to enter and remain. Generally, applications for entry clearance or leave to enter or remain on family and private life grounds are not caught by the general grounds for refusal except for the requirement to produce a passport and in circumstances where the applicant has previously contrived in a significant way to frustrate the intention of the Rules.[230]

1.161 The mandatory refusal grounds include circumstances where an applicant has made false representations, submitted false documents, or failed to disclose material facts in the application. Following *Balajigari v SSHD*[231] the Home Office produced detailed guidance[232] in respect of dishonesty. This guidance recognises that the dishonesty must be sufficiently serious to justify refusal and makes explicit that an honest mistake is insufficient. Very importantly, where the secretary of state is considering refusing an application, or curtailing

228 See *R (SM and others) v SSHD* [2013] EWHC 1144 (Admin). See also the Home Office guidance, *Discretionary leave*, v9.0, 16 December 2021, www.gov.uk/government/publications/granting-discretionary-leave.

229 Immigration Rules paras 320–322.

230 Immigration Rules para 320(3) and (10)–(11). However, the suitability requirements contained in Appendix FM provide similar restrictions in family cases. See above at paras 1.107–1.109.

231 [2019] EWCA Civ 673, [2019] WLR 4647.

232 *Suitability: false representations, deception, false documents, non-disclosure of relevant facts*, v2.0, 22 December 2020, www.gov.uk/government/publications/suitability-false-representations-immigration-staff-guidance.

leave, on the basis of false representation, the applicant must be given an opportunity to address that allegation before a decision is made. This will be done through a 'minded to refuse' procedure.[233]

1.162 The discretionary grounds, expressed in terms of when leave to remain or enter should 'normally' be refused, include circumstances where any of the mandatory grounds applied to a previous application[234] and, for example, failure by the applicant to pay accrued NHS charges over a certain limit (set under the Immigration Rules), in accordance with the relevant NHS regulations on charges to overseas visitors.[235] Leave may also be refused where the applicant has failed to pay costs awarded against them to the Home Office in previous litigation.[236]

1.163 As a result of these provisions, for many migrants the risk of litigation against the Home Office can have far-reaching consequences for their future immigration status. For example, if a migrant unsuccessfully challenges the Home Secretary in judicial review proceedings or in a civil claim for damages and is subsequently removed and fails to pay costs, this can result in a barrier to re-entry to the UK in the future. The possibility of accrual of litigation debt should not, however, deter people from bringing meritorious applications for judicial review. Current Home Office policy indicates that when considering whether to refuse an application based on litigation debt, decision-makers must consider all relevant factors, including how the debt was accrued and the conduct of the applicant in bringing the litigation; the extent to which the applicant has co-operated with the Home Office in attempts to recover the debt; the purpose of the application and whether it raises exceptional circumstances; the applicant's ability to pay; and the amount and age of the debt.[237]

1.164 Following the case of *Ahsan and others v SSHD*,[238] where an application is refused under the general grounds provisions this may give rise to an appeal on human rights grounds in reliance on ECHR Article 8.

233 *Suitability: false representations, deception, false documents, non-disclosure of relevant facts*, v2.0.

234 Immigration Rules paras 320(11), 322(2)–(2A).

235 Immigration Rules paras 320(22) and 322(12). See further chapter 10 in respect of NHS charging for overseas visitors.

236 Immigration Rules paras 320(23) and 322(13).

237 *Suitability: unpaid litigation costs*, v5.0, 11 October 2021, www.gov.uk/government/publications/litigation-debt.

238 [2017] EWCA Civ 2009, [2018] HLR 5.

Conditions on leave

1.165 Leave to enter or remain may be granted subject to conditions. These include:

- a restriction on employment or occupation in the UK;
- a restriction on studies;
- a condition requiring the person concerned to accommodate themself without recourse to public funds, or to register with the police, or to report to an immigration officer or the secretary of state; or
- a condition about residence.[239]

Where leave is extended by IA 1971 s3C, the leave remains subject to the same conditions. Conditions may only be imposed on limited leave to remain, so if an individual is granted ILR, the conditions automatically cease.[240]

1.166 The Home Office frequently imposes a condition of 'no recourse to public funds' (NRPF) when granting limited leave to remain.[241] Persons with a NPRF condition attached to their leave will be in breach of a condition of their leave (and therefore committing a criminal offence)[242] if they claim certain welfare benefits or support known as 'public funds'. Public funds are defined by the list in para 6 of the Immigration Rules[243] which at the time of writing comprises: allocation of local authority housing, local authority homelessness assistance, attendance allowance, carer's allowance, child benefit, child tax credit, council tax reduction, council tax benefit, disability living allowance, income-related employment and support allowance, housing benefit, income-based jobseeker's allowance, income support, pension credit, personal independence payment, service disablement allowance, social fund payments, working tax credit and universal credit.[244]

1.167 The government's policy rationale for imposing NRPF restrictions is based on the view that those seeking to establish their family life in the UK must do so on a basis that prevents burdens on the

239 IA 1971 s3(1)(c).
240 IA 1971 s3(3)(a).
241 See further paras 4.35–4.41 and 4.153–4.158.
242 IA 1971 s24(1)(b)(ii).
243 Immigration Rules para 6.
244 Eligibility criteria for social security benefits are set out in chapter 4.

taxpayer and promotes integration. This is said to be a legitimate aim in the balancing exercise under ECHR Article 8.[245]

1.168 The *Family life (as a partner or parent) and exceptional circumstances* policy confirms that those who have been granted leave to remain in the UK on the grounds of long residence, private life or other ECHR Article 8 grounds may make a request to have the NRPF condition lifted on one of the following grounds:[246]

a) The person has provided satisfactory evidence that they are destitute (homeless or unable to meet essential living needs). The 'destitution' definition under IAA 1999 s95 is used here.[247] Generally those in receipt of support from the local authority under Children Act 1989 s17 will satisfy this exemption if they are able to produce evidence that the support is provided to avoid destitution.
b) The person has provided satisfactory evidence that there are particularly compelling reasons relating to the welfare of a child on account of the parent's very low income.
c) The person has established exceptional circumstances relating to their financial circumstances.

1.169 The Home Office's policy on imposition of NRPF restrictions has come under challenge in several High Court cases.[248]

1.170 In *R (W (a child)) v SSHD*,[249] the High Court found the Home Office's policy on imposing NRPF restrictions on people on a ten-year route to settlement on grounds of family or private life was unlawful. This affected many parents of children who have British citizenship or are settled in the UK. The court held that a person does not have to be already destitute for the NRPF condition to be lifted or not be imposed in the first place. The question a caseworker should consider is whether the person is at imminent risk of destitution without recourse to public funds. The *Family life (as a partner or parent) and exceptional circumstances* policy was amended to reflect this.

245 See *Family policy: family life (as a partner or parent) and exceptional circumstances*, v18.0, 11 August 2022, p77, www.gov.uk/government/publications/family-life-as-a-partner-or-parent-private-life-and-exceptional-circumstance.

246 *Family policy: Family life (as a partner or parent) and exceptional circumstances*, v18.0.

247 For a more detailed explanation of destitution under IAA 1999 s95, see paras 5.57–5.90.

248 See further paras 4.153–4.158.

249 [2020] EWHC 1299 (Admin), (2020) 23 CCLR 673.

1.171 In *ST (a child, by his litigation friend VW) v SSHD*,[250] the claim focused specifically on the approach to NRPF in Appendix FM, the section of the Immigration Rules applicable to family members of British citizens and those with long-term residence. The claimants advanced three arguments as to why the NRPF scheme was unlawful as applied to family members in this context.

1) The first argument – that it deprives British children of benefits to which they are entitled by law – was rejected as IAA 1999 s115 expressly excludes people subject to immigration control from 'entitlement' to mainstream state benefits.
2) The second argument was, broadly, that the policy was discriminatory on grounds of race it was likely to have a greater impact on Black British children than white British children. The court considered that the wrong comparator was chosen. While it was true that non-white British children were more likely to be affected than white British children, around 80 per cent of applicants in this visa category were families from Africa or Asia. The claimants' position was therefore not disadvantaged because of their colour, but because of their immigration status.
3) The third argument – that the NRPF provisions in Appendix FM and its associated guidance were in breach of BCIA 2009 s55 – succeeded. There is an assertion in para Gen 1.1 that Appendix FM had taken into account the duty to safeguard and promote children's welfare 'in line with' section 55. However, the High Court said that did not sufficiently state what was required of the duty. The High Court noted that para Gen 1.11A did not make any reference to the best interests of a child. The wording actually produced the opposite effect, imposing a more stringent test than that set out in BCIA 2009 s55. Paragraph Gen 1.11A referred to 'particularly compelling reasons relating to the welfare of a child of a parent in receipt of a very low income' – in contrast to the section 55 obligation to simply 'safeguard and promote' the welfare of children.

The court then considered whether the caseworker guidance fixed the issue, and concluded that it did not. While acknowledging that the guidance demonstrated an understanding of the approach required under BCIA 2009 s55, the guidance was only directed at the approach to be taken to grant a visa, but not in the context of whether to lift or not impose an NRPF condition. Paragraph Gen 1.11A was amended

250 [2021] EWHC 1085 (Admin), [2021] 1 WLR 6047.

in March 2022 so that the phrase 'particularly compelling reasons relating to the welfare of a child' has been replaced with 'there are reasons relating to the welfare of a relevant child which outweigh the considerations for imposing or maintaining the condition (treating the best interests of a relevant child as a primary consideration)'. This amendment took effect on 20 June 2022.

1.172 In a further judgment, *R (AB and others) v SSHD*,[251] the claimants challenged the wording of Gen 1.11A, which had not, at the time of the decisions affecting them, been changed in the light of *ST v SSHD*. The claimants also challenged the guidance as being in breach of BCIA 2009 s55. This was on the basis that, in addition to considering the best interests of the child, caseworkers are directed to consider whether the NRPF restriction 'would significantly impact on a child's particular and essential needs'.[252] This was held to be unlawful because this wording of the guidance does not reflect what is required for a structured consideration of best interests of a child. In a further, more recent case, the Home Office conceded that the current guidance and rules fail to comply with the Equality Act 2010.[253]

Removal and deportation

1.173 Although 'deportation' is often used in everyday language to refer in general to the process of enforced removal from the UK, 'deportation' and 'removal' are terms of art in immigration law and they have distinct meanings.

Removal

1.174 Under IAA 1999 s10 (as amended),[254] the Home Secretary has the power to remove any migrant 'who requires leave to enter or remain in the United Kingdom but does not have it'. Since anyone who is not a British citizen requires leave to enter or remain,[255] this applies to non-British citizens who are either overstayers (ie those who have

251 [2022] EWHC 1524 (Admin), [2022] 1 WLR 5341.

252 *R (AB and others) v SSHD* at para 34.

253 See https://dpglaw.co.uk/home-offices-no-recourse-to-public-funds-nrpf-policy-found-unlawful-for-the-fifth-time-in-five-years/

254 This was substantially amended by the IA 2014.

255 Save for the limited category of persons referred to in fn 118 above.

remained in the UK beyond the expiry of their leave) or 'illegal entrants'. 'Illegal entrants' are defined as those who have entered or sought to enter the UK in breach of immigration law (ie without prior leave to enter or entry clearance) or who have entered or sought to enter by means including deception.[256] The section 10 power also enables the family members of those without leave to enter or remain to be removed, if certain conditions are met and written notice is given.[257] This is even if the family members have valid leave to remain in the UK, including citizenship or settled status.

1.175 Unlike their family members, those without leave to enter or remain are not required to be given written notice of removal under IA 1971 s10. The Home Office has operated a policy, since 2015, of issuing a 'notice of removal window', which provides notification of removal taking place within a three-month or 21-day 'window' after a 72-hour notice window.[258] This is in contrast to the issuing of 'removal directions', which is increasingly used as an exception rather than a norm, whereby the person is given notice of the date and time of their flight back to their country of origin. Notice of removal and removal directions do not generate a right of appeal, but may be challenged by way of an urgent application for an injunction deferring removal, as part of a judicial review, for example, if the proposed removal will breach a person's rights under the ECHR or Refugee Convention.

1.176 The 'notice of removal window' policy was subject to legal challenge in two claims on grounds of procedural unfairness and barriers to effective access to legal advice and representation.[259] The operation of this removal window policy was suspended on 14 March 2019 further to a successful injunction application made by Medical Justice in its challenge to the policy.[260] The two claims were both unsuccessful in the lower court (the Upper Tribunal in *R (FB) v SSHD (removal window policy)*[261] and the High Court in *R (Medical Justice) v SSHD*[262]). On appeal, however, the Court of Appeal[263] held

256 IA 1971 s33(1).
257 IAA 1999 s10.
258 *Judicial reviews and injunctions*, v23.0, 21 October 2022, www.gov.uk/government/publications/returns-preparation.
259 *R (FB and another) v SSHD (removal window policy)* [2018] UKUT 428 (IAC); *R (Medical Justice) v SSHD* [2019] EWHC 2391 (Admin).
260 The judgment of the full claim is at [2019] EWHC 2391 (Admin).
261 [2018] UKUT 428 (IAC).
262 [2019] EWHC 2391 (Admin).
263 *R (FB (Afghanistan) and another) v SSHD* [2020] EWCA Civ 1338, [2022] QB 185.

that whilst the concept of a removal window is not inherently unlawful, the way the policy was being operated by the Home Office was unlawful.

1.177 This was because although the person facing removal could in theory make an immigration or asylum application during the notice period, there was a variety of reasons why they may not be able to do so, such as difficulties in accessing legal advice and assistance. Even if a person was able to make an application with legal advice and assistance, that person may not necessarily have a chance to challenge any refusal in the courts prior to removal, especially if the refusal decision is provided after the notice period. Because of this timing, the person might potentially be removed immediately after being refused without a chance to bring a challenge in court. The Court of Appeal found that there was a real risk of denial of access to justice and this was sufficient to render the policy unlawful. The Court of Appeal, however, did not say that the removal window policy could not be introduced and did not comment on what would be an appropriate notice period. It could if it is done in a way which properly protects the right of access to a court. It has since been re-introduced, and the structure of the removal window is the same. It remains to be seen whether the evidence on the ground demonstrates that the risks of unfairness have been properly addressed.

1.178 Unlike deportation, removal does not operate under the IA 1971 as a formal ban on return to the UK, although the Immigration Rules impose a re-entry ban of up to ten years unless a person issued with notice of removal avoids enforced removal by departing the UK voluntarily (in which case they may re-enter after two or five years, or 12 months if they depart voluntarily at their own expense).[264]

Deportation

1.179 Deportation is a more draconian form of removal applicable to non-British citizens (and their family members) whose presence in the UK is deemed generally not conducive to the public good,[265] or more often because they have committed a criminal offence or offences.[266] Deportation powers can be used against individuals born in the UK or who have lived in the UK lawfully all their lives, including those

264 Immigration Rules para 320(7B). See paras 1.185–1.187.

265 IA 1971 s3(5).

266 IA 1971 s3(6); see also UKBA 2007 ss32–38 on automatic deportation for those foreign nationals sentenced to at least 12 months' imprisonment.

who have ILR. A deportation order automatically invalidates any leave to remain the deportee may have had at the time the order is signed.[267]

1.180 Unlike removal, deportation operates as an automatic and permanent ban on re-entry to the UK and until and unless it is revoked the order invalidates any leave granted before it was made or while it is in force.[268] It is therefore necessary to apply to revoke the deportation order prior to seeking re-admission or, if not already deported, leave to remain.

1.181 Under the Immigration Rules, there is a presumption against revocation of the order in criminal cases for at least ten years where the deportee has been sentenced to a period of imprisonment of less than four years[269] and indefinitely for sentences of more than four years.[270] In either case, an applicant for revocation must demonstrate that continuation of the deportation order would breach their rights under the ECHR or there are exceptional circumstances. In all other circumstances a material change in circumstances is required before revocation is warranted. Revocation of the order does not entitle the person to re-enter the UK, rather it enables the person eligible to apply for admission under the Immigration Rules.[271]

1.182 In this context, the mandatory grounds of refusal discussed above[272] require any such application for entry clearance or leave to enter to be refused if a deportation order has been made in the last ten years unless applying to return to the UK on the grounds of family relationships or private life, rules relating to the armed forces or domestic law provisions relating to EU nationals and their family members.

1.183 A person who is not a British citizen may be deported in the following circumstances:

- following conviction for a criminal offence attracting at least one single sentence of imprisonment of 12 months or more;[273]
- where the secretary of state deems their deportation to be conducive to the public good;[274]

267 IA 1971 s5(1).
268 IA 1971 s5(1).
269 Immigration Rules para 391(a).
270 Immigration Rules para 391(b).
271 Immigration Rules 392.
272 See paras 1.160–1.164 above.
273 UKBA 2007 s32.
274 IA 1971 s3(5)(a).

- where a criminal court recommends deportation in the case of a person over 17 years of age following conviction of an offence punishable by imprisonment;[275]
- another member of the family to which they belong is deported.[276]

1.184 There is no appeal against a decision to deport or a deportation order, but in many cases a deportee will make a human rights or protection claim which if refused will give rise to a right of appeal to the FTT.[277]

Re-entry bans

1.185 The Immigration Rules prohibit individuals from returning to the UK in certain categories other than as family members, private life provisions or as EEA family members[278] where they have previously:

- breached immigration law by overstaying;
- breached a condition attached to their leave;
- been an illegal entrant; or
- used deception in an application for entry clearance, leave to enter or leave to remain.[279]

1.186 The time-bar on re-entry depends on the circumstances of the case. Periods of overstaying do not count if the person left the UK voluntarily not at the expense (directly or indirectly) of the secretary of state and either the period of overstay was 90 days or less (if it began before 6 April 2017) or 30 days or less (if it began after 6 April 2017).[280] If a person used deception in a previous application or was previously deported or forcibly removed, the time-bar is ten years.[281] For cases not involving deception or deportation/forcible removal, the time-bar is:

- 12 months if the person left the UK voluntarily and not at public expense;[282]

275 IA 1971 s3(6).
276 IA 1971 s3(5)(b).
277 See further paras 1.220–1.232 below on appeals.
278 See Immigration Rules paras A320–E320 but note EEA provisions are complex and outside the scope of this text.
279 Immigration Rules para 320(7B).
280 Immigration Rules para 320(7B)(i).
281 Immigration Rules para 320(7B)(ii) and (vi).
282 Immigration Rules para 320(7B).

- two years if the voluntary departure at public expense occurred within six months of the date on which either notice of removal was given, or the person no longer had a pending appeal, whichever is later;[283] or
- five years if the person left voluntarily at public expense.

1.187 Accordingly, those given notice of removal may reduce the ten-year re-entry ban to two or five years if they avoid enforced removal by leaving the UK voluntarily, and to 12 months if they do so at their own expense.

Immigration bail

1.188 Prior to the coming into force of the immigration bail provisions in IA 2016 Sch 10 on 15 January 2018, the immigration control rules distinguished between those who were granted temporary admission pending examination of their status or removal from the UK[284] and those who were subject to immigration bail, most frequently if they had criminal convictions and were released from immigration detention by the grant of bail. Those who were liable to detention under IA 1971 Sch 2 para 16 were normally granted temporary admission to be in the UK pending the examination of any immigration application. There was no attendant power to re-detain attached to the power to grant temporary admission, as opposed to a breach of immigration bail conditions which may give rise to consequences of re-detention, subject to there being a realistic prospect of removal.[285] However, temporary admission was distinct from leave to remain or enter, and was in essence a practical measure to avoid detaining all persons in relation to whom a decision on whether to grant them leave to enter or remain, or to remove them, was pending.

1.189 This changed with the implementation of IA 2016 Sch 10 which repealed the powers to grant temporary admission. Instead, everyone who is liable to detention[286] will be subject to immigration bail if they are not detained. Bail must be granted subject to one or more conditions, but there is no requirement of more than one condition. The list of potential conditions is given at IA 2016 Sch 10 para 2 and includes: a condition requiring the person to appeal before an

283 Immigration Rules para 320(7B)(iv) and (v).
284 IA 1971 Sch 2 para 22, which was repealed on 15 January 2019.
285 *B (Algeria) v SSHD* [2018] UKSC 5, [2018] AC 418.
286 See below at paras 1.198–1.218.

immigration officer or the First-tier Tribunal at a specified time or place; a condition restricting the person's work, occupation or studies; a residence condition; a condition requiring reporting before an immigration officer; an electronic monitoring condition; and such other conditions as the person granting immigration bail thinks fit.[287]

1.190 In respect of electronic monitoring, IA 2016 Sch 10 para 2(2) and (3) came into force on 31 August 2021. It requires the Home Office to impose an electronic monitoring condition on anyone subject to immigration bail who is liable to be deported, is subject to deportation proceedings or is under a deportation order unless the defendant considers that doing so a) would be impractical (para 2(5)(a) or (b)) would be contrary to the person's ECHR rights (para 2(5)(b)). Under the *Immigration bail* policy,[288] the secretary of state has also identified two further policy exceptions to the requirement to impose electronic monitoring on a person subject to deportation, where: a) the person is under the age of 18; or b) the person remains subject to a supervision order following discharge from mental health detention under Mental Health Act 1983 s37 or s41.

1.191 IA 2016 Sch 10 para 4(1) explains the 'electronic monitoring condition' as requiring a person to:

> ... co-operate with such arrangements as the secretary of state may specify for detecting and recording by electronic means one or more of the following–
> (a) [the person's] location at specified times, during specified periods of time **or** while the arrangements are in place;
> (b) [the person's] presence in a location at specified times, during specified periods of time **or** while the arrangements are in place;
> (c) [the person's] absence from a location at specified times, during specified periods of time **or** while the arrangements are in place [emphasis added].

Schedule 10 para 4(2) sets out other requirements that the Home Office may impose on someone subject to electronic monitoring.

1.192 The list of conditions that can be imposed under the new immigration bail regime is different to the conditions of temporary admission. To the list of conditions that can be imposed, the IA 2016 added restriction on studies as a possibility. However, in deciding what conditions to impose, the Home Secretary must have regard to the

287 IA 2016 Sch 10 para 2.

288 V13.0, 30 August 2022, pp28–29. https://assets.publishing.service.gov.uk/government/uploads/system/uploads/attachment_data/file/1132640/Immigration_bail.pdf.

objectives to be achieved by bail, which are centrally to do with ensuring that the individual remains in contact with the Home Office and to impose restrictions that would reduce the risk of offences being committed while in the community, as is clear from the statutory considerations set out in IA 2016 Sch 10 para 3. The approach to be taken by the Home Secretary is elaborated upon in the *Immigration bail* policy.[289]

1.193 Although the bail powers make clear, at IA 2016 Sch 10 para 2, that there is no requirement to impose more than one bail condition, there have been concerns that the bail powers have resulted in the imposition of study restrictions on a widespread basis, affecting large numbers of people who were previously on temporary admission (and were not restricted from studying) and who suddenly found themselves prohibited from studying as a condition of their immigration bail. During the passage of the Immigration Bill in parliament, the government had made clear the power to impose restrictions on study was to be confined to the 'most exceptional circumstances', where the restriction is necessarily conducive to the statutory purpose, for example, in cases relating to national security, to ensure the individual maintains contact with the defendant, and reduce the risks of non-compliance.[290] In practice, however, the study restriction has been imposed on a far wider scale.

1.194 The *Immigration bail* policy originally suggested that any person who is 'appeal rights exhausted'[291] would be subject to a study restriction, even though there is no such restriction in primary legislation. This was successfully challenged in two judicial reviews, as the result of which the secretary of state has accepted that there should be no general rule that those who are 'appeal rights exhausted' have bail conditions imposed upon them, and that each case is to be considered on its own facts.[292] Those who are 'appeal rights exhausted' may face other practical obstacles to accessing education, for example, due to admissions criteria at the specific education institution or due to inability to qualify for scholarships.

1.195 In respect of electronic monitoring, the *Immigration bail* policy[293] recognises that it may be impractical to impose electronic monitoring

289 V13.0.

290 Hansard HL Debs col 1653, 1 February 2016, per Lord Keen of Elie (Advocate-General).

291 Ie has exhausted all their appeal rights in the UK.

292 *R (Hameed) v SSHD* JR/2814/2019 and *R (Moutsouka) v SSHD* JR/5174/2019; and see *Immigration bail*, v13.0, p14.

293 V13.0, pp34–35.

on everyone falling within Schedule 10 para 2(2) and (3) because 'there will be fewer devices available' and thus 'a need to regulate the use of devices'. The policy therefore identifies a hierarchy of priority groups such foreign national offenders at highest risk of harm to the public should be considered the highest priority for people imposed an electronic monitoring condition.

1.196 IA 2016 Sch 10 paras 2 and 4 do not specify the type of technology to be used for electronic monitoring. Historically the Home Office had used radio frequency technology for the purposes of electronic monitoring. Radio frequency tagging relies on two elements: a home monitoring unit, usually based in the person's residence, connected to the network; and a tag attached to the individual (usually fitted on the person's ankle). Tagging in this way is typically used to enforce curfew conditions, such as that an individual remain at home between 2pm to 4pm and 10pm to midnight. The tag communicates with the base station over radio to detect if the tag is within range of the monitoring unit, and normally only at specified times of the curfew. The information collected is therefore limited to times while the tag is within range of the monitoring unit. In or around December 2020/January 2021, the Home Office made a decision to shift electronic monitoring from using radio frequency technology to global positioning system (GPS) technology. The shift to the use of GPS technology has been subject to criticisms by privacy rights groups because real-time location data can disclose intimate details about a person's day-to-day life beyond what is required for immigration bail purposes. There are also concerns about the impact of doing so on vulnerable people. The use of GPS technology in a blanket way for electronic monitoring is subject to challenge in several cases.[294] At the time of writing, there has been no published judgment on the issue.

1.197 A significant consequence of the introduction of the immigration bail regime under IA 2016 Sch 10 was the repeal of the provision of bail accommodation under IA 1999 s4(1). A detailed discussion of the implications of this is set out at paras 6.201–6.207.

294 *R (KZR) v SSHD* JR-2022-LON-000977 and *R (NA) v SSHD* JR-2022-LON-00711, *R (Roberts) v SSHD* CO/1858/2022.

Immigration detention

Powers

1.198 The Home Secretary, and immigration officers acting on behalf of the Home Secretary, have wide powers to detain those subject to immigration control[295] and those subject to deportation.[296] The powers may be exercised in the following circumstances:

- on arrival in the UK pending determination of whether a person should be granted leave to enter;[297]
- on arrival to the UK where a person has prior leave to enter but on examination has had their leave suspended, pending a decision on whether to cancel leave;[298]
- pending removal from the UK where a person has been refused leave to enter or is an illegal entrant or is reasonably suspected of being such a person;[299]
- pending removal where a person has breached a condition of their leave, remained in the UK beyond their leave, sought leave to remain by deception or has had their ILR revoked;[300]
- family members of persons who are to be removed in the circumstances described in the preceding four bullet points may also be detained;[301]
- where crew members of a ship, aircraft or train have remained beyond the leave granted to enable them to join their ship, aircraft or train or absconded;[302]
- on arrival to the UK where a person seeks leave to enter and has made an asylum or human rights claim, pending a decision on whether to grant or refuse leave to enter or remove following refusal of leave to enter;[303]

295 Broadly speaking, this means all those who require leave to enter or remain, even if they already have it.

296 For a detailed analysis of the Home Office's approach to foreign national offenders subject to deportation including the exercise of detention powers, see L Dubinsky, H Arnott and A Mackenzie *Foreign national prisoners: law and practice*, Legal Action Group, 2012.

297 IA 1971 Sch 2 para 16(1).

298 IA 1971 Sch 2 para 16(1A).

299 IA 1971 Sch 2 paras 8, 9, 16(2).

300 IAA 1999 s10(2)–(7).

301 IA 1971 Sch 2 paras 10A, 16(2); IAA 1999 s10(2)–(7).

302 IA 1971 Sch 2 paras 12–14, 16(2).

303 NIAA 2002 s62(2), (3)(a).

- where a person is liable to deportation following a recommendation by a criminal court pending the making of a deportation order;[304]
- where a person is served with a decision to deport them, pending the making of a deportation order;[305]
- where a deportation order is signed against a person, pending their removal from the UK.[306]

1.199 Where the power exists to detain an individual, immigration officers must have regard to all relevant Home Office policies when deciding whether or not to exercise that power.[307] The guidance aims to implement ECHR Article 5 and the domestic case-law as to how to the power to detain should be exercised. The broad principles reflected in the guidance are as follows:

- there is a presumption in favour of release;
- detention must only be used as a last resort;
- detention must be used for the specific purpose for which it is authorised (for example, to effect removal);
- all reasonable alternative to detention must be considered;
- once detention has been authorised it must be kept under regular review;
- each case must be considered on its own individual merits, with regard to the need to safeguard and promote the welfare of any children involved.

Time limits

1.200 There is no statutory time limit to the length of detention, although a person can only be detained for a period that is 'reasonable in all the circumstances'.[308] Concerns about the absence of a statutory time limit to immigration detention in the UK have consistently been raised over many years by international institutions such as the United Nations High Commissioner for Refugees (UNHCR), independent inspectors appointed by the government such as the

304 IA 1971 Sch 3 para 2(1).
305 IA 1971 Sch 3 para 2(2).
306 IA 1971 Sch 3 para 3.
307 *Detention: general instructions*, v2.0, 14 January 2022, www.gov.uk/government/publications/offender-management. The previous guidance, referred to in existing jurisprudence is set out in chapter 55, *Enforcement instructions and guidance*.
308 *R (I) v SSHD* [2002] EWCA Civ 888 at para 46.

inspectorate of prisons, Home Office commissioned independent reviewers such as Stephen Shaw, and by non-governmental organisations working with immigration detainees. In February 2019, further to an inquiry into the state of immigration detention, the Joint Committee on Human Rights called for a statutory time limit to be introduced as one of its key recommendations.[309] This has thus far been rejected by the government.

Vulnerable groups

1.201 There are specific limits on the secretary of state's power to detain in respect of certain groups of persons considered to be vulnerable: 1) unaccompanied children; 2) families; 3) pregnant women; and 4) adults at risk.

Unaccompanied children

1.202 The IA 2014 amended the detention power under IA 1971 Sch 2 para 16 by prescribing the limited circumstances in which an unaccompanied child can be detained. Under IA 1971 Sch 2 para 18B, an unaccompanied child can only be detained in a short-term holding facility for a maximum period of 24 hours and only if certain conditions are satisfied:

1) The first condition is that: there are either removal directions in force that require the child to be removed from the short-term holding facility within the relevant 24-hour period; or a decision is being made which is likely to result in removal directions of this sort.
2) The second condition is that the immigration officer authorising detention 'reasonably believes' that the child will be removed within the relevant 24-hour period pursuant to the removal directions.

1.203 There is an additional Home Office policy, dealing with children who are subject to disputes as to their age, which must be applied when the secretary of state is seeking to detain a child.[310] The Home Office will accept an individual as under 18 (including those who have

309 Joint Committee on Human Rights, *Immigration detention*, HC 1484 and HL Paper 278, 7 February 2019.

310 See *Assessing age*, v5.0, 14 January 2022, www.gov.uk/government/publications/assessing-age-instruction; *Detention service order 14/2012* on managing age dispute cases in the detention estate.

previously presented themselves as an adult) unless one or more of the following categories apply:[311]

- There is credible and clear documentary evidence that they are 18 or over.
- A *Merton*-compliant[312] age assessment by a local authority is available stating that they are 18 years of age or over.
- Their physical appearance/demeanour very strongly suggests that they are significantly over 18 years of age and no other credible evidence exists to the contrary.
- The individual:
  - prior to detention, gave a date of birth that would make them an adult and/or stated they were an adult; and
  - only claimed to be a child after a decision had been taken on their asylum claim; and
  - only claimed to be a child after they had been detained; and
  - has not provided credible and clear documentary evidence proving their claimed age; and
  - does not have a *Merton*-compliant age assessment stating they are a child; and
  - does not have an unchallenged court finding indicating that they are a child; and
  - their physical appearance/demeanour very strongly suggests that they are 18 years of age or over.

1.204 The effect of the legislative amendment introduces what is in effect a prohibition on the detention of an unaccompanied child such that the question of age is not a matter of 'reasonable belief' on the part of the secretary of state.[313] If the child can demonstrate that he or she was a child at the time of the detention, the decision to detain and maintain their detention will be unlawful. This overturns the Supreme Court's judgment in *R (AA (Sudan)) v SSHD*[314] which was decided prior to the amendment.

311 Note that this does not apply to individuals previously sentenced by the criminal courts as an adult.

312 Ie an assessment of the child's age which complies with the criteria for a lawful assessment, as set out in *R (B) v Merton LBC* [2003] EWHC 1689 (Admin). For the detailed criteria, see paras 11.30–11.79.

313 *R (AA (Sudan)) v SSHD* [2017] EWCA Civ 138, [2017] 1 WLR 2894.

314 [2013] UKSC 49, [2013] 1 WLR 2224.

Families

1.205 The detention of families is subject to detailed policy requirements[315] and is underpinned by the duty under BCIA 2009 s55 (the detail of which has already been set out above at paras 1.24–1.31.) A child must not be separated from their parent (in a single-parent family) if the consequence of that decision is that the child is taken into care.[316] Any such decision must treat the child's best interests as a primary consideration. The decision-maker must fully document how they have considered all factors.[317]

1.206 There are three stages to the separation process:

1) **Stage one: identifying family life.**[318] This requires case owners to consider 'all of the available information'.[319] If a genuine and subsisting family life exists, then the decision-making must move on to the second sage.
2) **Stage two: whether separation is lawful, necessary and proportionate.**[320] The impact of separation **must** be considered, including on the child's emotional and identity development. Any separation should be for 'as short a time as possible' and must consider the purpose and duration of detention.[321] Even where a child has lived with an alternative caregiver for a short time, they may have significant ties with their primary caregiver and thus be impacted by separation. Where a local authority is involved in the care of any child, the case owner must obtain information from them about the family's circumstances relevant when considering family separation. In particular, the case owner '**must request** OCC [Office of the Children's Champion] for advice for the removal or separation' where it is intended to be permanent or the case involves a child in care.[322] Where the conclusion is that separating the family would not be necessary and proportionate,

315 *Family separations*, v4.0, 11 December 2017; *Criminality: Article 8 ECHR cases*, v8.0, 13 May 2019, www.gov.uk/government/publications/criminality-guidance-in-article-8-echr-cases.

316 *Family separations*, v4.0, p5.

317 *Family separations*, v4.0, p5.

318 *Family separations*, v4.0, pp8–12.

319 *Family separations*, v4.0, p10.

320 *Family separations*, v4.0, pp13–20.

321 *Family separations*, v4.0, p15.

322 *Family separations*, v4.0, p18 (emphasis added).

the case owner 'must not continue pursue a family separation'.[323] Otherwise the case owner should proceed to the final stage.

3) **Stage three: responsibilities, review points and authorities.**[324] Reviews are required at least when case owners are conducting a detention review or where they have become aware of significant changes to the family's circumstances. The review must be recorded.

1.207 The stages of the decision-making process must be recorded on the Family Separations Form ICD 5025.[325] Significant changes in the family circumstances must prompt a review of the initial decision to detain.[326]

1.208 Notwithstanding the comprehensive guidance in operation to prevent unlawful separation of families by immigration detention, the secretary of state's exercise of detention powers in this context has been subject to judicial criticisms and criticisms by reputable organisations.[327]

1.209 Frequently, in separated families cases, the local authority will be involved, whether because the child is already in its care or is taken into care as a direct result of the parent's detention. The duties owed to children who are looked after by the local authority in the circumstances include the duty to promote contact between the child and the parent, a duty that the secretary of state should also facilitate pursuant to BCIA 2009 s55. Where there are positive parenting capacity assessments, they may serve as important evidence of the parent–child relationship as well as well the impact of separation on the child. Separation of families can engage ECHR Article 8 and result in damages being awarded for just satisfaction. In one such case, *AJU and AJS v SSHD*,[328] the secretary of state admitted that it was unlawful to keep separate a three-year-old child from her father for three months in circumstances where the family court had found

323 *Family separations*, v4.0, p21.

324 *Family separations*, v4.0, pp21–25.

325 *Family separations*, v4.0, pp9, 14, 19, 23–25.

326 *Family separations*, v4.0, pp19, 21–22.

327 *R (MXL) v SSHD* [2010] EWHC 2397 (Admin); *R (NXT) v SSHD* [2011] EWHC 969 (Admin); *AJS and AJU v SSHD* (CO/88/2018); Bail for Immigration Detainees, 'Fractured childhoods: the separation of families by immigration detention', April 2013; Amnesty International UK, 'A matter of routine: the use of immigration detention in the UK', 15 December 2017, www.amnesty.org.uk/resources/matter-routine-use-immigration-detention-uk-0.

328 CO/88/2018, reported on the Bhatt Murphy Solicitors' website, https://bhattmurphy.co.uk/.

the father to be a suitable carer notwithstanding his criminal conviction and that the child should be returned to his care. An award of £10,000 was made to the child for an admitted breach of ECHR Article 8.

Pregnant women

1.210 Under IA 2016 s60, there are now specific limitations on the detention of pregnant women. Section 60(2) provides that a woman may not be detained unless the secretary of state is satisfied that the woman will be shortly removed from the UK or there are 'exceptional circumstances' which justify detention. Even in such circumstances, a pregnant woman may not detained for more than 72 hours from the time at which detention beings, with the time limit extendable only by authority of a minister and only to a maximum of seven days in total. This is the only provision in which any time limit is imposed on the length of detention.

Adults at risk

1.211 For nearly 20 years, the secretary of state adopted a policy of not detaining certain vulnerable individuals, including those with serious mental illness and those with independent evidence of torture, save in very exceptional circumstances. This operated as a high threshold and a very strong presumption against detention for vulnerable groups. It did not, however, operate effectively and did not fulfil the policy objective. In February 2015, the government commissioned Stephen Shaw to carry out an independent inquiry into the detention of vulnerable people. His report, *Review into the welfare in detention of vulnerable persons*, was published in January 2016.[329] An overall conclusion of the Shaw Review was that:

> . . . there is too much detention; detention is not a particularly effective means of ensuring that those with no right to remain do in fact leave the UK; and many practices and processes associated with detention are in urgent need of reform.[330]

1.212 The government, in a Written Statement dated 14 January 2016, accepted 'the broad thrust of [Mr. Shaw's] recommendations', in particular the recommendation 'to adopt a wider definition of those at risk . . . and

329 Available at: www.gov.uk/government/publications/review-into-the-welfare-in-detention-of-vulnerable-persons.

330 Shaw Review, para 11.1.

to recognise the dynamic nature of vulnerabilities'.[331] In a statement published in March 2016, the government consequently announced the introduction of a new 'adults at risk' concept into decision-making on immigration detention with a 'clear presumption' that people who are at risk should not be detained. The purpose is directed at achieving fewer vulnerable people being detained, and where detention is necessary, for the period to be shorter than at present.

1.213 This came in the form of IA 2016 s59, which came into force on 12 July 2016. It did not define an 'adult at risk' or prescribe how the secretary of state would deal with them. Instead, it imposed a duty on the secretary of state to issue guidance 'specifying matters to be taken into account' when determining:

a) whether a person ('P') would be particularly vulnerable to harm if P were to be detained or to remain in detention; and
b) if P is identified as being particularly vulnerable to harm in those circumstances, whether P should be detained or remain in detention.

1.214 The statutory guidance, *Adults at risk in detention*, states the objective of the framework:[332]

- to 'lead to a reduction in the number of vulnerable people detained and a reduction in the duration of detention before removal';
- to introduce 'a more holistic approach to the consideration of individual circumstances, ensuring that genuine cases of vulnerability are consistently identified, in order to ensure that vulnerable people are not detained inappropriately';
- to apply a 'clear presumption' that 'detention will not be appropriate of a person is considered to be "at risk" ' unless 'immigration control considerations outweigh the risk factors'.

1.215 An adult is defined in the guidance as 'at risk' if they 'declare that they are suffering from a condition, or have experienced a traumatic event (such as trafficking, torture or sexual violence), that would be likely to render them particularly vulnerable to harm if they are placed in detention or remain in detention'.[333] A person does not

331 See Government's Response (Immigration Minister James Brokenshire MP) to the Shaw Review- Written statement, Hansard HCWS 470; statements have also been made to parliament by ministers to the same effect.

332 *Immigration Act 2016: guidance on adults at risk in immigration detention*, May 2021, paras 1–3, www.gov.uk/government/publications/adults-at-risk-in-immigration-detention.

333 *Immigration Act 2016: guidance on adults at risk in immigration detention*, para 7.

need to self-identify as vulnerable in these terms – it is sufficient if an immigration officer or member of detention centre staff believes that a person is a risk, for example, on the basis of medical evidence indicating vulnerability. Indicators of risk include serious physical disability; serious health conditions or diseases; mental health conditions; being a victim of torture, or a potential victim of torture or slavery; being over 70 years old; being pregnant; or being transgender.

1.216 There is a hierarchical structure to the weight to be placed on the evidence of risk, ranked from level 1–3:

1) Level 1 relates to all self-declared indicators of risk.
2) Level 2 evidence is determined by 'professional evidence (for example, from a social worker, medical practitioner or NGO [non-governmental organisation]), or official documentary evidence, which indicates that the individual is an adult at risk'.[334] It should be afforded 'greater weight'.[335]
3) Level 3 (the highest) evidence is 'professional evidence . . . stating that the individual is at risk and that a period of detention would be likely to cause harm – for example, increase the severity of the symptoms or condition' and should be 'afforded significant weight'.[336]

1.217 According to the statutory guidance, adults at risk may only be detained if 'immigration factors' (including whether or not a person has previously absconded, whether they pose a risk of absconding or harm to the public) outweigh the risk of harm to the individual as the result of detention.[337]

1.218 The guidance on adults at risk sounds, on the face of it, to be comprehensive and consistent with the legislative intention. However, the ranking of evidence of risk by levels has been criticised for diluting the intention of protecting vulnerable detainees. This is because the levels of risk go to the weight that can be put on the evidence and the strength of immigration factors which are necessary to displace the presumption against detention. For example, those who have independent evidence of torture in the form of a rule 35(3) report provided under the Detention Centre Rules 2001[338] would have, under the old policy, not been detained other than in 'very

334 *Immigration Act 2016: guidance on adults at risk in immigration detention*, para 9.

335 *Immigration Act 2016: guidance on adults at risk in immigration detention*, para 9.

336 *Immigration Act 2016: guidance on adults at risk in immigration detention*, para 9.

337 *Immigration Act 2016: guidance on adults at risk in immigration detention*, paras 13–17.

338 SI No 238.

exceptional circumstances'. There is no reason why this would not be the case under the adults at risk framework, particularly as the new framework is supposed to strengthen existing protections. However, under the statutory guidance, rule 35(3) reports are treated only as 'level 2' evidence of risk; in practice this has meant that the strength of the presumption against detention has been said by the secretary of state to be outweighed by immigration factors, including past non-compliance, the existence of a criminal offence or the prospects of removal. The balancing exercise is no longer, in practice, subject to a very exceptional circumstances threshold and has been criticised as amounting to a dilution of the safeguards.

Remedies

1.219 Remedies include:

- appeals;
- administrative review;
- judicial review.

Appeals

Overview

1.220 Rights of appeal are set out in NIAA 2002 s82. As mentioned above, the IA 2014 removed all rights of appeal save for in respect of the refusal of a protection or human rights claim or revocation of a person's protection status.[339] The appeal is to the FTT (IAC), a division of the FTT system deciding immigration and asylum appeals.

1.221 The available grounds are identified at NIAA 2002 s84, and are that removal of the appellant would breach the UK's obligations under the Refugee Convention or in respect of persons eligible for humanitarian protection (ie 'asylum/humanitarian protection grounds') or be unlawful under HRA 1998 s6 (ie 'human rights grounds'). In practice, in an asylum appeal, this will involve arguing that the person meets the definition of a refugee (ie has a well-founded fear of persecution for a convention reason); and in a human rights appeal, that removal will breach one of their rights under the ECHR.

339 For a discussion of revocation, see chapter 3.

1.222 The majority of deportation decisions concern ECHR Article 8 and therefore, where that is raised, give rise to a right of appeal on human rights grounds. Deportation appeals raising human rights grounds are subject to specific statutory provisions contained in NIAA 2002 Part 5A[340] (mirrored in the Immigration Rules at paras 398–399A), which attempt to codify the circumstances whereby deportation will or will not be disproportionate in terms of ECHR Article 8. For cases involving sentences of four years or less, it is necessary to demonstrate that one of the statutory 'exceptions' applies, whereby Article 8 rights will outweigh the presumption that deportation is conducive to the public good:

- The first exception applies if the person has been resident in the UK for most of their life, is socially and culturally integrated, and there would be 'very significant obstacles' to their reintegration in the country of origin.[341]
- The second exception applies where the effect of deportation on a partner or qualifying child[342] would be 'unduly harsh'.[343]
- Where the sentence is one of four years or more, or neither exception applies, the appellant will need to show 'very compelling circumstances' over and above those addressed in the exceptions.[344]

Timing of an appeal

1.223 Where an in-country right of appeal is conferred, a notice of appeal must be received by the FTT no later than 14 calendar days after the date on which notice of the decision appealed against is sent.[345]

1.224 It is important to note that not all refusals of a human rights or protection claim generate an in-country right of appeal to the FTT. The IA 2014 created a new 'deport first, appeal later' power for the secretary of state to 'certify' a human rights claim under NIAA 2002 s94B. Where a person is liable to deportation and has made a human rights claim, the claim may be certified under section 94B if the secretary of state considers that removal pending the outcome of the

340 NIAA 2002 ss117A–117D.
341 NIAA 2002 s117C(4).
342 Ie a British child or a child who has been resident in the UK for seven years or more; NIAA 2002 s117D.
343 See also *KO (Nigeria) v SSHD* [2018] UKSC 53, [2018] 1 WLR 5273; *HA (Iraq) v SSHD* [2020] EWCA Civ 1176, [2020] HLR 21.
344 NIAA 2002 s117C(6).
345 Tribunal Procedure (First-tier Tribunal) (Immigration and Asylum Chamber) Rules 2014 r19(1).

appeal would not be incompatible with an ECHR right. The grounds on which a claim may be certified include that the person subject to potential deportation would not, before the appeals process is exhausted, face a real risk of 'serious irreversible harm'. If the claim is certified under section 94B, an appeal against its refusal may only be brought out of country.[346]

1.225 In *R (Kiarie and Byndloss) v SSHD*,[347] the Supreme Court held that out of country appeals may be unlawful where appellants cannot effectively conduct an appeal out of country, including where they may face practical difficulties in securing legal representation or preparing and giving effective evidence. If such an appeal will not be effective, the public interest in removal pending the appeal will be outweighed by these considerations and certification decision will be unlawful. The effect of *Kiarie and Byndloss* is therefore that out of country appeals are not inherently unlawful, but may be depending on the individual facts of the case. The Upper Tribunal has recently given guidance as to when an out of country appeal will or will not be unlawful.[348] Relevant considerations including the possibility of giving evidence, the effectiveness of legal representation, the possibility of securing expert evidence, and the importance of hearing live evidence. Where a person has been deported on the basis of an unlawful certification, the courts may in some circumstances order the person's return to the UK in order that the appeal can be conducted in-country.[349]

1.226 A human rights or protection claim may also be certified as 'clearly unfounded' under NIAA 2002 s94, in which case any appeal against the refusal of such a claim can only be brought out of country.[350] If a person comes from a country of origin listed in section 94(3), the secretary of state must certify the claim unless satisfied that it is not clearly unfounded. A claim is not 'clearly unfounded' if on at least one legitimate view of the facts and law it may succeed

346 NIAA 2002 s92(3)(a).

347 [2017] UKSC 42, [2017] 1 WLR 2380.

348 *Re AJ (s94B: Kiarie and Byndloss questions: Nigeria)* [2018] UKUT 115 (IAC).

349 *R (Nixon and another) v SSHD* [2018] EWCA Civ 3; see also *R (QR (Pakistan)) v SSHD* [2018] EWCA Civ 1413.

350 NIAA 2002 s92(2)(a) and (3)(a).

before a tribunal.[351] It is possible to challenge a decision to certify a claim, under section 94 or section 94B, by way of judicial review.

Determination of appeals

1.227 Appeals in the FTT are determined by FTT judges who will typically specialise in immigration and asylum appeals within the IAC. The procedural rules governing statutory appeals to the immigration tribunal are available online. For appeals to the FTT, the relevant rules are the Tribunal Procedure (First-tier Tribunal) (Immigration and Asylum Chamber) Rules 2014.[352]

1.228 The rules of evidence in the FTT are flexible, enabling, for example, both oral and documentary evidence to be relied on, including hearsay evidence. The 2014 Procedure Rules expressly provide that the tribunal may receive evidence which would not be admissible in a civil trial and evidence not available to the decision-maker who made the decision under appeal.[353] The duty of candour applicable to judicial review, whereby both parties are required to disclose all evidence unfavourable to their case, does not apply in the FTT, though of course there remains an ongoing professional duty on representatives not to mislead the court.

1.229 Appeals involving vulnerable or sensitive appellants or witnesses, or child appellants, including the victims of trafficking and other abuse, are increasingly common in the FTT. In such appeals, the tribunal is duty-bound to take account of relevant practice directions and guidance as to the correct procedure to be adopted, in particular the Joint Presidential Guidance Note No 2 of 2010: *Child, vulnerable adult and sensitive appellant guidance*; and the practice direction on Child, vulnerable adult and sensitive witnesses.[354]

1.230 Detailed guidance on the correct application of these principles, particularly in the case of child appellants, was set out by the Court of Appeal in *AM (Afghanistan) v SSHD*.[355] In *AM* the court recognised

351 *R (Mahamed) v SSHD* [2008] EWHC 1312 (Admin) at para 37 per Cranston J (citing *R (Yogathas) v SSHD* [2002] UKHL 36, [2003] 1 AC 920 at para 34 per Lord Hope); and *R (L) v SSHD* [2003] EWCA Civ 25, [2003] 1 WLR 1230 at para 58.

352 Available at: www.gov.uk/government/publications/immigration-and-asylum-chamber-tribunal-procedure-rules.

353 Tribunal Procedure (First-tier Tribunal) (Immigration and Asylum Chamber) Rules 2014 r14(2); see *R v Immigration Appeal Tribunal ex p Lulu Miah* [1987] Imm AR 143, QBD re the admissibility of hearsay evidence.

354 Tribunals Judiciary, issued 30 October 2008.

355 [2017] EWCA Civ 1123, [2018] 4 WLR 78.

the core principle that 'a child is foremost a child before he or she is a refugee'[356] and emphasised the critical importance of taking into account the practice direction and presidential guidance note, holding that failure to do so will in general amount to an error of law.[357] The court further confirmed that tribunals have the power to appoint a litigation friend where a child litigant lacks capacity, albeit that the tribunal procedure rules contain no express provision for this.[358]

1.231 While the Home Office is typically represented in a FTT appeal by a presenting officer,[359] specialist counsel is sometimes instructed by the Home Office for more complex cases.

1.232 Where an appeal is dismissed, there is a right of onward appeal to the Upper Tribunal (UT) (IAC) 'on a point of law'.[360] The procedure rules governing the UT are the Tribunal Procedure (Upper Tribunal) Rules 2008.[361] Permission to appeal to the UT must first be made to the FTT, to be lodged within 14 calendar days of the day on which the decision dismissing the appeal is sent.[362] If permission to appeal is refused by the FTT, the application can be renewed to the UT within 14 days of the date on which the FTT decision refusing permission is sent.[363] Where the UT finds an error of law in the FTT's original appeal determination it can set it aside, and either remake it in the UT or remit it to the FTT for a re-hearing.[364] There is an onward right of appeal to the Court of Appeal on any point of law, if the appeal meets the 'second appeals' criteria, ie it raises 'some important point of principle or practice' or 'there is some other compelling

356 At para 35 per Sir Ernest Ryder.

357 At para 30.

358 Upholding the judgment of Picken J in *R (C) v First-tier Tribunal* [2016] EWHC 707 (Admin).

359 A civil servant, not required to be qualified as a solicitor or barrister, though some presenting officers are legally qualified. See *Re Awuah and others (wasted costs orders: HOPOs: tribunal powers)* [2017] UKFTT 555 (IAC) for a discussion of the status of presenting officers.

360 Tribunals, Courts and Enforcement Act (TCEA) 2007 s11. The right of appeal is not in fact limited to the losing party, so that, for example, it is possible to appeal against the dismissal of an appeal on asylum grounds, even if it has been allowed on human rights grounds.

361 SI No 2698. Available at: www.gov.uk/government/publications/upper-tribunal-procedure-rules.

362 The date on which the decision is sent, is usually made clear on the face of the decision itself (Tribunal Procedure (First-tier Tribunal) (Immigration and Asylum Chamber) Rules 2014 r33(2)).

363 Tribunal Procedure (Upper Tribunal) Rules 2008 r21(3)(aa)(i).

364 TCEA 2007 s12(1)–(2).

reason for the relevant appellate court to hear the appeal'.[365] An application for permission to appeal must first be made to the UT itself, and if unsuccessful can be renewed directly to the Court of Appeal or Court of Session.[366]

Administrative review

1.233 For certain decisions against which there is no right of appeal to the FTT,[367] it is possible to request an 'administrative review', a process whereby a Home Office caseworker or immigration officer will review a decision taken by one of their colleagues to ascertain if it is 'wrong because of a case working error'.[368]

1.234 An application for administrative review must be made within 14 days of receiving the decision if the applicant is in the UK, seven days if the person is also detained, or 28 days if the applicant is overseas.[369]

1.235 Administrative review may result in the decision being withdrawn or maintained, for the same or additional reasons to the original decision.[370] Within the time period during which an administrative review may be sought, or while it is pending, leave to enter or remain is extended by virtue of IA 1971 s3C.[371]

Judicial review

1.236 Where there is no right of appeal and administrative review has been unsuccessful or the applicant wishes to challenge the decision on grounds other than a 'case-working error', the remedy of last resort is judicial review. Unlike statutory appeals and administrative review, IA 1971 s3C does not extend leave to remain while judicial review is pursued. This leaves individuals exposed to exclusionary provisions on accommodation, support and benefits.

365 TCEA 2007 s13(6).
366 TCEA 2007 s13(4)–(5).
367 Including refusals of applications for leave to remain under tiers 1, 2, 4 and 5 of the points-based system; see Immigration Rules Appendix AR paras AR3.2, AR5.2.
368 Defined as including an incorrect decision to refuse an application for leave or to cancel leave, or where the Immigration Rules or applicable policy guidance was applied incorrectly: Appendix AR paras AR2.11–2.12.
369 Immigration Rules para 34(R).
370 Immigration Rules Appendix AR para AR2.2.
371 IA 1971 s3C(2)(d).

CHAPTER 2

EEA free movement law and the EU Settlement Scheme

Anthony Vaughan and Emma Fitzsimons

continued

continued

Key points

- Prior to the UK's exit from the European Union (EU), European Economic Area (EEA) nationals exercising free movement rights in the UK did not require leave to remain.[1]
- This all changed when the UK left the EU on 31 December 2020. Following an implementation period, between 24 January 2020 and 31 December 2020,[2] and a grace period,[3] between 1 January 2021 and 30 June 2021, EEA nationals and their family members now require leave to remain in precisely the same way as non-EEA nationals do.[4]
- Such leave may be obtained under the UK's EU Settlement Scheme[5] and take the form of settled[6] or pre-settled status.[7] The former is indefinite leave to remain. The latter is limited.
- Otherwise, leave will need to be obtained under the same Immigration Rules (HC 395) applicable to non-EEA nationals.
- Different rules apply to 'frontier workers'[8] and Irish citizens.[9]
- Notwithstanding the UK's exit from the EU, some elements of EU law have been retained.[10]
- In addition, rights of residence under EU law remain relevant for the purposes of establishing eligibility for welfare benefits[11] and housing,[12] for EEA nationals with pre-settled status.[13]

Introduction

2.1 Chapter 1 of this book explains the regime of domestic immigration law in force in the UK, which is derived from Part I – and principally

1 See para 2.7.
2 See paras 2.8–2.13.
3 See paras 2.14–2.20.
4 See paras 2.21–2.24.
5 See paras 2.138–2.176.
6 See paras 2.153–2.165.
7 See paras 2.166–2.168.
8 See paras 2.177–2.181.
9 See paras 2.182–2.184.
10 See paras 2.25–2.29.
11 See paras 4.66–4.83.
12 See paras 7.6–7.27 and 7.64–7.74.
13 The rights are set out at paras 2.41–2.137.

section 3 – of the Immigration Act (IA) 1971. Prior to the UK's exit from the EU, which occurred at 11pm on 31 January 2020, EEA and Swiss nationals, and their families, were not subject to domestic UK immigration law. See para 2.7. The regime applicable to them was based on directly effective EU free movement law derived from the EU Treaties[14] and the 'Citizens' Rights Directive'.[15] These instruments are described at paras 2.30–2.40. The content of the 'free movement' rights to which these instruments gave rise are addressed at paras 2.41–2.137.

2.2 This all changed following the UK's departure from the EU. Following an 'implementation period' (addressed at paras 2.8–2.13) from between 24 January 2020 and 31 December 2020 during which free movement rights continued to apply, and a further 'grace period' (addressed at paras 2.14–2.20) between 1 January 2021 and 30 June 201 to allow EEA nationals and their family members who were resident in the UK before 11pm on 31 December 2020 to apply to the UK's EU Settlement Scheme (EUSS) to acquire, or convert, their residency based on EU law into one based on domestic law, free movement rights have now ended and EEA nationals and their family members require leave to remain under IA 1971 s3. The content and operation of the EUSS is discussed at paras 2.138–2.176.

2.3 EEA nationals who have not, or cannot, obtain leave under the EUSS must obtain leave under the more general provisions of the Immigration Rules applicable to the nationals of other countries which are the subject of chapter 1.[16] The exceptions to this are 'frontier workers' and Irish citizens. Different rules apply to these two specific categories of EEA national which are discussed at paras 2.177–2.181 and 2.182–2.184 respectively.

2.4 The purpose of this chapter is to give an overview of the free movement law that applied prior to the UK's departure from the EU[17] as well as providing an introduction to the EUSS.[18] The reasons for covering the latter topic – the EUSS – are perhaps obvious: advisors using this book may wish to know whether the applicant

14 Principally the Treaty on the Functioning of the European Union (TFEU).

15 Directive 2004/38/EC of the European Parliament and of the Council of 29 April 2004 on the right of citizens of the Union and their family members to move and reside freely within the territory of the Member States.

16 See further the summary at paras 2.23–2.24 below.

17 See paras 2.41–2.137.

18 See paras 2.138–2.176.

they are assisting has, or can obtain[19] or extend, leave under the EUSS, in order to establish whether they are entitled to any of the support outlined in the other chapters of this book.

2.5 The reasons for covering the former topic – free movement rights – are perhaps less obvious. The need to do so relates firstly to the fact that the residence rights of EU nationals and their family members in the UK, under the EUSS, will continue be closely related to free movement law, and/or to the relevant transitional provisions, until about the end of 2025. It is therefore important to understand the application of free movement rights under the pre-2021 law for the purposes of calculating historic rights and any present entitlements which flow from them. This is not least because those granted 'pre-settled status'[20] on the basis of their entry to the UK before 11pm on 31 December 2020 will be eligible to apply for 'settled status',[21] all things being equal, before the end of 2025, if necessary on the basis of their residence under the EUSS. Secondly, free movement rights are relevant for the purposes of establishing whether an EEA national is eligible for welfare benefits (chapter 4) or social housing or homelessness assistance (chapter 7). In these contexts free movement rights are, for certain purposes, treated as still applying and an EEA national may need to demonstrate that they are exercising those rights in order to be eligible for assistance.[22]

2.6 This chapter will discuss: 1) the background to the current situation; 2) the sources and key concepts of free movement laws; 3) rights of residence of EEA nationals under the Immigration (European Economic Area) Regulations ('EEA Regs') 2016;[23] 4) the EU Settlement Scheme; 5) frontier workers; 6) Irish citizens; and 7) termination of rights to reside and enforcement powers.

19 As a general rule, applications to the EUSS needed to be made by 30 June 2021. However, the time limits may be extended in certain limited circumstances. See paras 2.146–2.151.

20 See paras 2.166–2.168.

21 See paras 2.153–2.167.

22 See paras 4.66–4.83, 7.6–7.27 and 7.64–7.74.

23 SI No 1052.

Background

The rights of EEA nationals before Brexit

2.7 Prior to the UK's exit from the EU, free movement law was given effect in UK law by European Communities Act (ECA) 1972 s2, and Immigration Act 1988 s7. The latter absolved EU nationals from the requirement to obtain leave to remain under IA 1971 s3 when exercising free movement rights in the UK.[24] It followed, for example, that EEA nationals were not 'persons subject to immigration control' under Immigration and Asylum Act (IAA) 1999 s115(9), which sets out certain categories of persons who are generally excluded from welfare benefits. UK domestic legislation could not cut down the scope of free movement rights in EU law, which were directly effective by virtue of ECA 1972 s2. The content of these free movement rights is set out at paras 2.41–2.137.

The rights of EEA nationals following Brexit

Rights of EEA nationals during the implementation period, between 24 January 2020 and 31 December 2020

2.8 On 24 January 2020 the UK and the EU signed a treaty governing the terms of the UK's exit from the EU, known as the 'Withdrawal Agreement',[25] under Article 50(2) of the Treaty on the European Union. Article 126 of the Withdrawal Agreement provides for an 'implementation period' commencing on the date of the agreement and ending on 31 December 2020 at 11pm. Article 127(1) states that,

24 For an illustration of this principle in practice, see *Re MS (British citizenship: EEA appeals: Belgium)* [2019] UKUT 356 (IAC), in which the Upper Tribunal held that, where an EU national has no basis to reside in the UK under EU law, they require leave to enter or remain under the IA 1971. If the EU citizen does not have such leave, they will be in the UK unlawfully for the purposes of the statutory provisions regulating leave to remain on the basis of European Convention on Human Rights (ECHR) Article 8, notably Nationality, Immigration and Asylum Act (NIAA) 2002 ss117B(4) and 117C(4)(a). However, depending on the facts, the person may nonetheless be able to argue that they should be treated as if they were here lawfully (see *Rhuppiah v SSHD* [2018] UKSC 58). In *MS*, the tribunal was prepared to treat a former EU citizen child as being lawfully present in the UK where he had been brought here by his parents, who then did nothing to regularise his status.

25 Agreement on the withdrawal of the United Kingdom of Great Britain and Northern Ireland from the European Union and the European Atomic Energy Community (Treaty Series No 3 (2020), CP 219, Vol 1).

unless otherwise provided, EU law 'shall be applicable to and in the United Kingdom' during the implementation period.

2.9 The extension of EU law generally during the implementation period was accompanied by an extension of the specific free movement provisions in the TFEU and subordinate legislation, which are set out in Part Two of the Withdrawal Agreement, entitled 'Citizens' Rights' (from Article 13). Thus, EU citizens arriving in the UK during the implementation period continued to benefit from directly effective free movement rights. Article 127(3) of the Withdrawal Agreement confirms that the EU law applicable in the UK within the implementation period shall produce 'the same legal effects as those which it produces within the Union and its Member States'. Article 127 was reflected in domestic law by European Union (Withdrawal) Act (EUWA) 2018 s7A.

2.10 As well as securing residence rights, the Withdrawal Agreement also sought to protect social security entitlements and the mutual recognition of professional qualifications of those individuals to whom the Agreement applies.

2.11 Article 86 of the Withdrawal Agreement confirms that the jurisdiction of the Court of Justice of the European Union (CJEU) continued with respect to the UK until the end of the implementation period. After that, the European Commission retains the right to bring proceedings against the UK for breach of EU law occurring before the end of the implementation period, within four years of its expiry, under Article 87(1). To assist it, an Independent Monitoring Authority has been established with powers equivalent to the European Commission to conduct inquiries into alleged breaches of Part Two of the Withdrawal Agreement (on Citizens' Rights) and to bring legal proceedings with a view to obtaining adequate remedies.[26]

2.12 Similar agreements were also concluded between the UK and the EEA, which includes the EU states plus Iceland, Liechtenstein and Norway (the EEA EFTA Separation Agreement); and between the

26 Article 159 of the Withdrawal Agreement, and EUWAA 2020 s15 and Sch 2 (in part). It will not be a complaints body to grant remedies in individual cases, but will look at complaints received in the context of its inquiries about wider issues. At the time of writing the Independent Monitoring Authority had been granted permission to seek judicial review of the 'Home Office's position that citizens who fail to apply for Settled Status before the expiry of their Pre-Settled Status automatically lose their rights'. See https://ima-citizensrights.org.uk/news_events/independent-monitoring-authority-receives-permission-for-judicial-review-hearing-against-home-office/.

UK and Switzerland (the Swiss Citizens' Rights Agreement). Both agreements have been in force from exit day (31 January 2020).[27]

2.13 The UK's implementation of the Withdrawal Agreement in domestic law was by means of the European Union (Withdrawal Agreement) Act (EUWAA) 2020, which was given Royal Assent on 23 January 2020. Section 1 of the 2020 Act retains the application of the ECA 1972 (see para 2.7) during the implementation period. The end of the implementation period was 11pm on 31 December 2020 and is known as 'IP completion day'.[28]

Rights of EEA nationals in the UK during the 'grace period' between 1 January 2021 and 30 June 2021

2.14 On IP completion day, the EU free movement law which remained in force during the implementation period was repealed. Other elements of EU law were retained and these are described below at paras 2.25–2.29. The repeals, notably, included IA 1988 s7 and the EEA Regs 2016, together with the other provisions giving effect to EU free movement law. These repeals were effected by Immigration and Social Security Co-ordination (EU Withdrawal) Act 2020 s1, read with Schedule 1 to that Act which lists the repealed provisions. The effect of these changes was to render EEA nationals subject to immigration control under IA 1971 s1(2) and therefore requiring leave to remain from 11pm on 31 December 2020.

2.15 However, for those EEA nationals and their family members who were already resident in the UK in accordance with EU law prior to IP completion day, Title II of Part Two of the Withdrawal Agreement established rights of residence that are based on the previous free movement categories, notably as a worker, self-employed person, self-sufficient person and their family members etc. Beneficiaries of rights under the Withdrawal Agreement are required to apply for and be granted such rights before they can be enjoyed (unlike rights under EU free movement law, which generally arose upon the fulfilment of certain legal criteria). Article 18 of the Withdrawal Agreement is the basis for the UK's Settled Status Scheme, which is set out below.

2.16 Article 18(2) of the Withdrawal Agreement gave temporary protection to EU citizens in the UK on IP completion day by creating directly effective rights of residence applicable until the application

27 EUWAA 2020 s6; and European Union (Withdrawal Agreement) Act 2020 (Commencement No 1) Regulations 2020 SI No 75 reg 4.

28 EUWA 2018 s39.

deadline. This provision prevents EU citizens with rights under the Withdrawal Agreement from being treated as unlawfully present in the UK before they have made an application under the EUSS.

2.17 In domestic law this temporary protection was effected by the Citizens' Rights (Application Deadline and Temporary Protection) (EU Exit) Regulations 2020,[29] which came into force immediately after IP completion day. Regulation 2 specifies the application deadline as 'the end of 30 June 2021' for the submission of an application for residence status under the EUSS. Regulation 3 provides that, between IP completion day and the application deadline – the 'grace period', regs 5–10 of the EEA Regs 2016 continue to have effect, subject to certain modifications. This saving in reg 3 is applied to those with outstanding applications after the application deadline, by reg 4 (ie in-time applications which have not finally been determined by the application deadline, made by EEA nationals who were lawfully resident in the UK or held permanent residence before IP completion day). An application is not finally determined for so long as any appeal against the adverse initial decision remains pending.

2.18 For completeness, it is noted that, to the extent that Article 18 of the Withdrawal Agreement provides for rights that are broader than the savings provisions set out in the Citizens' Rights (Application Deadline and Temporary Protection) (EU Exit) Regulations 2020, EEA citizens are entitled to rely on the direct effect of the Agreement.[30] It should also be noted that EUWA 2018 s7A[31] confirms that all rights and remedies arising under the Withdrawal Agreement have direct effect in UK domestic law.

2.19 Two main categories of beneficiary under EU free movement law do not benefit from rights under the Withdrawal Agreement: British citizens and the family members to whom the cases of *Zambrano*[32] and *Surinder Singh*[33] apply; and posted workers.[34] These groups are nonetheless eligible for leave to remain under the EUSS, which is described below.

29 SI No 1209. Made under EUWAA 2020 s7.

30 Or the equivalent provisions of the EEA EFTA Separation Agreement (Article 17) and the Swiss Citizens' Rights Agreement (Article 16).

31 Inserted by EUWAA 2020 s5, with effect from 11pm on 31 January 2020.

32 *Ruiz Zambrano v Office National de l'Emploi (ONEm)* Case C-34/09 [2012] QB 265, CJEU ('*Zambrano*').

33 *R v Immigration Appeal Tribunal and Surinder Singh ex p SSHD* Case C-370/90 [1992] 3 CMLR 358, ECJ ('*Surinder Singh*').

34 Whose right to reside derived from TFEU Article 56.

2.20 To the extent that individuals enjoy rights under the Withdrawal Agreement but not under the UK's EUSS, Articles 12 and 23 of the Withdrawal Agreement respectively prohibit discrimination on the grounds of nationality; and secure the right to equal treatment of EU nationals residing in the UK as compared with British citizens. Section 14 of the EUWAA 2020 empowers the minister (or other appropriate authority) to make regulations for the purpose of implementing *inter alia* Articles 12 and 23.[35] Like IA 1988 s7, EUWAA 2020 s14 applies both to those falling within the Agreement, and those who do not but would be eligible for settled or pre-settled status.

Rights of EEA nationals after 30 June 2021

2.21 As explained above, since the end of the implementation period[36] and the subsequent grace period,[37] free movement rights have ended and EEA nationals and their family members have required leave to remain under IA 1971 s3. If they have not been able to obtain such leave under the EUSS,[38] then they must seek to do so under the more general provisions of the Immigration Rules applicable to the nationals of other countries which are the subject of chapter 1: one of the supposed benefits of Brexit was said to be 'taking back control' of the UK's borders. The government's strategy to do so lies in its 'skills based' immigration system, under which 'points' are awarded for meeting a specific set of requirements; and which prioritises highly skilled workers and aims to reduce overall levels of migration to the UK. The strategy was first set out in a white paper,[39] and was implemented in January 2021 principally by way of amendments to the Immigration Rules.[40]

2.22 A full account of the new regime is beyond the scope of this chapter, but it is in reality a re-formulation of the existing points-based system which already applied to economic migrants via Tiers 1

35 The only regulations relating to support which, at the time of writing, have been made under EUWAA 2020 s14 are the Education (Student Fees and Support) (Amendment) (No 2) Regulations (Northern Ireland) 2021 SI No 85, which amend the Education (Student Support) (No 2) Regulations (Northern Ireland) 2009 SI No 373.

36 See paras 2.8–2.13.

37 See paras 2.13–2.19.

38 See paras 2.14–2.20.

39 *The UK's future skills-based immigration system*, Home Office, 19 December 2018.

40 Principally the *Statements of Changes to the Immigration Rules*, HC 813, 22 October 2020; and CP 361, 31 December 2020.

and 2 of the previous Points Based System, and to students via Tier 4, prior to January 2021.

2.23 The major changes of present relevance are that the Immigration Rules governing working, living and studying in the UK now apply to EU, EEA and Swiss citizens as they do to citizens from the rest of the world (save for Appendix EU relating to the EU Settled Status Scheme, addressed at paras 2.138–2.176 below). A flavour of the new additions to the Immigration Rules is as follows:

- **For skilled workers**, as set out in 'Appendix Skilled Worker':
  a) 'general salary threshold' of £25,600 applies (subject to exceptions for new entrants to the UK labour market), although the threshold:
     i) could be as low as £20,480 if other criteria are met, such as that the role is on the shortage occupation list or the applicant has a relevant PhD. The minimum salary figures cannot be pro-rated; and
     ii) could be higher than £25,600 in some higher paid occupations.
  b) the job must be above the minimum skill level, at A-level or equivalent qualification ('RQF3 level'), although these qualifications do not actually need to be held.
- **Highly skilled workers** are allowed to enter the UK without a job offer where they have been endorsed by a relevant and competent body, with a small number of highly skilled workers or self-employed people not requiring such endorsement.
- **Students** continue to require leave as under the existing Points Based System (Tier 4) albeit subject to some modifications: see 'Appendix Student'. A **Graduate route** is planned to allow two years of post-study work at any skill level. When thereafter switching into the skilled worker route, a reduced salary threshold will apply for three years.
- **Visitors**: EU, EEA and Swiss citizens do not require a visa to enter the UK when visiting the UK for up to six months: see 'Appendix V: Visitor'. Those seeking to enter the UK for other reasons, such as work or study, will need to apply for entry clearance in advance under the Immigration Rules.

2.24 There will be no new route for low-skilled workers, although a temporary seasonal worker visa is provided for workers in the 'edible horticulture sector': see Appendix T5: Temporary Seasonal Worker. This visa is valid for up to six months in any 12-month period. The youth mobility scheme which grants two-year visas to 18- to 25-year-olds from a limited list of non-EU countries,[41] under Appendix T5, is retained. Appendix T5 contains visa routes for a range of specific jobs which previously fell under Tier 5 of the PBS, for example, ministers of religion, sportspeople and those working in the arts.

Retained EU law

2.25 Although free movement law has been repealed, a large body of EU law remains applicable in the UK. This is referred to as 'retained EU law'. Retained EU law is a 'snapshot' of EU law taken at 11pm on IP completion day, 31 December 2020. The EUWA 2018, as amended by the EUWAA 2020, provides the mechanism by which much of, but not all, EU law was frozen in time and 'converted' or 'preserved' as retained EU law.

2.26 The EUWA 2018 sets out principles for identifying retained EU law. There is no authoritative list of retained EU law although certain EU instruments are specifically excluded from being retained, most notably the Charter of Fundamental Rights.[42]

2.27 Section 2 'preserves' primary and secondary domestic legislation that is 'derived' from EU law as retained EU law. Section 3 'converts' 'directly effective' EU legislation into domestic legislation. Section 4 'converts' into domestic law directly effective treaty rights and provisions of directives that satisfy the conditions for 'direct effect' (ie they could be directly relied upon by individuals to enforce their rights) if they had not been adequately or correctly incorporated into domestic legislation before IP completion day. If these rights had been implemented into domestic law pre-IP completion day, there would be no need for them to be converted by section 4.

2.28 Retained case-law and general principles of EU law also form part of retained EU law. However, the primary purpose of their retention is to aid interpretation of EU law retained by virtue of sections 2, 3 and 4.

2.29 Significant changes to retained EU law are proposed in the Retained EU Law (Revocation and Reform) Bill 2022. The bill

41 Australia, Canada, Japan, Monaco, New Zealand, Hong Kong, Republic of Korea, Taiwan, and British overseas citizens, British overseas territories citizens, and British national (overseas) citizens.

42 See *R (AAA (Syria)) v SSHD* [2022] EWHC 3230 (Admin) at paras 116–118 (currently under appeal) for a discussion of whether Council Directive 2005/85/EC on minimum standards on procedures in Member States for granting and withdrawing refugee status, falls within the body of retained EU law.

proposes to downgrade the status of retained direct EU legislation and to provide ministers with greater powers to amend and remove retained EU law.

Free movement law: sources and key concepts

The basis of free movement law

2.30 The EU is comprised of, now, 27 member states: Austria, Belgium, Bulgaria, Croatia, Cyprus, the Czech Republic, Denmark, Estonia, Finland, France, Germany, Greece, Hungary, Ireland, Italy, Latvia, Lithuania, Luxembourg, Malta, the Netherlands, Poland, Portugal, Romania, Slovakia, Slovenia, Spain and Sweden.

2.31 The EEA comprises the EU countries and also Iceland, Liechtenstein and Norway. It allows them to be part of the EU's single market.

2.32 Switzerland is neither an EU nor EEA member but is part of the single market, meaning that its citizens enjoy the same free movement rights as EEA nationals in host member states.

2.33 Free movement of workers is a fundamental principle of EU law. Its primary basis in EU law is TFEU Article 45 and has been developed by the case-law of the CJEU. Together with the free movement of goods, capital and services, these four pillars comprise the single market.

2.34 TFEU Article 45 provides:

1. Freedom of movement for workers shall be secured within the Union.
2. Such freedom of movement shall entail the abolition of any discrimination based on nationality between workers of the Member States as regards employment, remuneration and other conditions of work and employment.
3. It shall entail the right, subject to limitations justified on grounds of public policy, public security or public health:
   a. to accept offers of employment actually made;
   b. to move freely within the territory of Member States for this purpose;
   c. to stay in a Member State for the purpose of employment in accordance with the provisions governing the employment of nationals of that State laid down by law, regulation or administrative action;
   d. to remain in the territory of a Member State after having been employed in that State, subject to conditions which shall be embodied in regulations to be drawn up by the Commission.

4. The provisions of this Article shall not apply to employment in the public service.

Citizenship of the EU and derivative rights

2.35 The concept of EU citizenship was introduced by the Treaty of Maastricht in 1992. The creation of EU citizenship has significantly influenced the development of free movement law. It marked the shift away from an economic community towards a social and political Union. The right to Union citizenship is found in TFEU Article 20.

2.36 TFEU Article 20(1) provides:

> Citizenship of the Union is hereby established. Every person holding the nationality of a Member State shall be a citizen of the Union. Citizenship of the Union shall be additional to and not replace national citizenship.

2.37 Article 21(1) then goes on:

> Every citizen of the Union shall have the right to move and reside freely within the territory of the Member States, subject to the limitations and conditions laid down in the Treaties and by the measures adopted to give them effect.

2.38 On the basis of EU citizenship, certain categories of third-country nationals can rely on the EU citizenship of their family member to derive certain rights of movement and residence within the EU. These are covered below within paras 2.83–2.113 and 2.114–2.137.

Directive 2004/38/EC[43] and the Immigration (European Economic Area) Regulations 2016

2.39 The key secondary EU instrument on free movement of persons is Directive 2004/38/EC ('Citizens' Rights Directive'). It allows EU citizens and their family members to move and live freely within the member states. The Citizens' Rights Directive was transposed into UK domestic law via the EEA Regs 2016. Those regulations came into force on 1 February 2017, replacing the earlier regulations of

43 Directive 2004/38/EC of the European Parliament and of the Council of 29 April 2004 on the right of citizens of the Union and their family members to move and reside freely within the territory of the Member States amending Regulation (EEC) No 1612/68 and repealing Directives 64/221/EEC, 68/360/EEC, 72/194/EEC, 73/148/EEC, 75/34/EEC, 75/35/EEC, 90/364/EEC, 90/365/EEC and 93/96/EEC.

the same name.[44] The 2016 EEA Regs were revoked at 11pm on 31 December 2020.

2.40 The main rights under the Citizens' Rights Directive are set out below:

- ***Right of entry:*** An EEA national does not need permission to enter or remain, and must be admitted into the members state, provided they can show a valid national passport or identification document.
- ***Initial right to reside for three months:*** Article 6(1) provides that EU citizens have the right to reside in another member state for a period of up to three months without any conditions or formalities other than the requirement to hold a valid identity card or passport. This initial right of residence also extends to the family members who are accompanying or joining the EU citizen (Article 6(2)). Article 6 has to be read in conjunction with Article 14(1), which provides that EU citizens and their family members shall have the right of initial residence as long as they do not become an unreasonable burden on the social assistance system of the host member state. Article 6(3) provides that an expulsion measure shall not be the *automatic* consequence of recourse to the social assistance system of the host member state. The application of this right in EU and domestic law is discussed further at paras 2.41–2.44.
- ***Extended right of residence:*** To stay beyond the initial three-month period, Article 7 of the Directive provides that an EU national needs to be 'exercising a treaty right', which means being a worker, self-employed person, self-sufficient person or student. The application of this right in EU and domestic law is discussed further at paras 2.45–2.71.
- ***Permanent residence:*** Article 16 creates a right to permanent residence for EU citizens and their family members who have resided legally for a continuous period of five years[45] in the host member state. The right to permanent residence is intended to 'promote social cohesion', which is a fundamental aim of the EU, by providing a legal permanent basis for EU citizens who have chosen to

44 SI 2006 No 1003.

45 Note that the Supreme Court has ruled in *Vomero v SSHD* [2019] UKSC 35, [2020] Imm AR 97 that the right to permanent residence can only be acquired *after* the Citizens' Rights Directive entered into force in April 2006. Time before then will not be counted towards the five years required for permanent residence.

settle in another member state.[46] The application of this right in EU and domestic law is discussed further at 2.72–2.82.

Rights of residence of EEA nationals under the Immigration (European Economic Area) Regulations 2016

Initial three-month right of residence

2.41 The initial right of residence was given effect in domestic law by EEA Regs 2016 reg 13.

2.42 The right of initial residence extended to:

- an EEA national with a valid national ID card or EEA passport;[47]
- a person who was not an EEA national but was a family member who has retained a right of residence, provided they had a valid passport;[48]
- the family member of an EEA national residing in the UK under reg 13(1), provided they had a valid passport.[49]

2.43 The three-month period ran from the date of admission to the UK.[50]

2.44 Regulation 13(3) reflected Article 14(1) of the Citizens' Rights Directive in providing that a person, whether an EEA national or family member, who was 'an unreasonable burden on the social assistance system' of the UK did not have the initial right to reside.

The extended right of residence

2.45 Under EEA Regs 2016 reg 14, there was an extended right of residence for more than three months, which applied to a 'qualified person' and their family members[51] for as long as they remained qualified persons. This meant that in order for an EEA national to enjoy the right to reside beyond three months, they were required to be exercising free movement rights.

46 Recital 17 of the Citizens' Rights Directive.
47 EEA Regs 2016 reg 13(1).
48 EEA Regs 2016 reg 13(2).
49 EEA Regs 2016 reg 13(2).
50 EEA Regs 2016 reg 13(1).
51 For family members, see paras 2.114–2.137.

2.46 Regulation 6(1) provided that an EEA national who satisfied the definition of jobseeker, worker, self-employed person, self-sufficient person or student, was to be treated as a 'qualified person' for the purposes of the EEA Regs 2016. These definitions are developed below at paras 2.49–2.71.

2.47 Family members of EEA nationals also enjoyed an extended right to reside if:

- they were the family member of a qualified person residing in the UK for as long as they remained family members;[52]
- they were the family member of an EEA national with a right of permanent residence under reg 15 for as long as they remained family members;[53]
- they had retained the right of residence.[54]

2.48 The rights of family members, and the relevant definitions, are discussed in greater detail at paras 2.114–2.137.

Qualified persons under the Immigration (European Economic Area) Regulations 2016

Workers

2.49 EEA Regs 2016 reg 4(1)(a) provided that a 'worker' meant a worker within the meaning of TFEU Article 45. However, the term 'worker' is not actually defined in the Treaties, nor in the Citizens' Rights Directive. Instead, the CJEU has developed guidance in the case-law as to what economic activity will constitute employed work:

- a person must actually have been employed in the host state;[55]
- work must be 'genuine and effective' as opposed to purely 'marginal and ancillary';[56]
- the person must perform services of some economic value, for and under the direction of another person: if not, the situation is likely to constitute self-employment instead;[57]

52 EEA Regs 2016 reg 14(2).
53 EEA Regs 2016 reg 14(2).
54 EEA Regs 2016 reg 14(3).
55 *Collins v SSWP* Case C138/02 [2005] QB 145, ECJ.
56 *Kempf v Staatssecretaris van Justitie* Case C-139/85 [1986] ECR 1741, ECJ.
57 *Lawrie-Blum v Land Baden-Wurttemberg* Case 66/85 [1986] ECR 2121, ECJ.

- it includes fixed-term contracts and part-time work;[58] 12 hours of employment a week has been found to fall within the definition;[59]
- assessing whether employment of less than 10–12 hours per week is 'genuine and effective' depends on all the circumstance such as entitlement to paid leave, sick pay, duration of employment, and whether a collective agreement applies to the employment;[60]
- work must be a genuine economic activity as opposed to a voluntary or leisure pursuit.[61]

2.50 A woman who gives up work, or seeking work, because of the physical constraints of the late stages of pregnancy and the aftermath of childbirth, retains the status of 'worker' under EU law.[62] The Upper Tribunal has found that, provided a woman returns to work within 52 weeks of childbirth, she will retain worker status.[63]

2.51 A person who was otherwise temporarily off work could retain worker status in the circumstances specified in reg 6(2), which were broadly:

- being temporarily unable to work as the result of an illness of accident;[64]
- being in 'duly recorded involuntary unemployment' following *at least* one year's employment, and satisfied 'conditions A and B' of the jobseeker criteria (see below). In these circumstances, 'worker' status was retained for *a continuous period of* six months;[65]
- being in 'duly recorded involuntary unemployment' following *less than* one year's employment, and satisfied 'conditions A and B' of the jobseeker criteria (see below). In these circumstances, 'worker' status was retained for *a maximum of* six months;[66]

58 *Ninni-Orasche v Bundesminister fur Wissenschaft, Verkehr und Kunst* Case C-413/01 [2003] ECR I-13187, ECJ.

59 *Kempf* Case C-139/85.

60 *Genc v Land Berlin* Case C-14/09 [2010] 2 CMLR 44, CJEU.

61 *Steymann v Staatssecretaris van Justitie* Case C196/87 [1988] ECR 6159, ECJ.

62 *St Prix v SSWP* Case C-507/12 [2014] PTSR 1448, CJEU. This principle also applies to the retention of self-employed status: see *Revenue and Customs Commissioners v Dakneviciute* Case C-544/18 [2020] PTSR 790, CJEU.

63 *SSWP v SFF and others* [2015] UKUT 502 (AAC); see also *Weldemichael v SSHD* [2015] UKUT 540 (IAC).

64 EEA Regs 2016 reg 6(2)(a).

65 EEA Regs 2016 reg 6(2)(b), read with reg 6(1) and (5)–(6).

66 EEA Regs 2016 reg 6(2)(c), read with reg 6(3) and (5)–(6).

- being involuntarily unemployed and had embarked on vocational training;[67] or
- had voluntarily ceased working and had embarked on vocational training that was related to the person's previous employment.[68]

Jobseekers

2.52 Jobseekers also come under the scope of TFEU Article 45 and are recognised in the preamble to the Citizens' Rights Directive.[69] In *Antonissen*[70] the CJEU held that a person should be permitted a period of at least six months to find work and would be a 'worker' during this time, but that even at the end of that six-month period would remain a worker if they provide 'evidence that he is continuing to seek employment and that he has genuine chances of being engaged'.

2.53 However, the EEA Regs 2016 imposed their own criteria as to what amounted to a jobseeker. 'Jobseekers' were defined in the EEA Regs 2016 as an EEA national 'who satisfies conditions A, B and, where relevant, C',[71] which broadly comprised the following requirements:

- **Condition A** was that the person must have:
  - entered the UK in order to seek employment;[72] *or*
  - been present in the UK seeking employment, immediately after enjoying a right to reside as a worker, self-employed person, self-sufficient person or student.[73]
- **Condition B** was that the person provided evidence that they were seeking employment and had a genuine chance of being employed.[74]
- **Condition C** was that the person has had a period of absence from the UK. Condition C applied where: a) the person had previously retained worker/self-employed status for at least six months on the basis that they were involuntarily unemployed but were seeking employment or self-employment; or b) the person was previously a jobseeker for at least 91 days in total; and c) the

67 EEA Regs 2016 reg 6(2)(d).
68 EEA Regs 2016 reg 6(2)(e).
69 Citizens' Rights Directive Recitals 9 and 16.
70 *R v Immigration Appeal Tribunal ex p Antonissen* Case C-292/89 [1991] ECR I-745, ECJ.
71 EEA Regs 2016 reg 6(1).
72 EEA Regs 2016 reg 6(5)(a).
73 EEA Regs 2016 reg 6(5)(b).
74 EEA Regs 2016 reg 6(6).

person had not been continuously absent from the UK for at least 12 months since enjoying the right of residence.[75] In these circumstances, the person could not retain the status of a worker/ self-employed person (having previously worked for a year), or jobseeker, for longer than 'the relevant period'[76] which was:[77]

i) six months (as a worker/self-employed person); the lawfulness of this restriction was supported by a number of cases: *Dano*,[78] *Alimanovic*,[79] and *Mirga*;[80] *or*

ii) in the case of a jobseeker, 91 days minus the total number of days spent as jobseeker, excluding any days pre-dating an absence of a continuous period of 12 months.

2.54 The EEA Regs 2016 provided that an EEA national may not be a jobseeker for longer than 'the relevant period' unless they could provide 'compelling evidence' that they were continuing to seek employment and had a genuine chance of being engaged.[81] For jobseekers, the 'relevant period' was 91 days minus the total of any days during which the person concerned previously enjoyed a right to reside as a jobseeker, unless that previous period was prior to a continuous absence from the UK of more than 12 months.[82]

2.55 An issue that frequently arose in practice was ascertaining whether a person retained jobseeker status beyond the 91 days specified in the EEA Regs 2016. The meaning of 'compelling evidence' was considered by the Administrative Appeals Chamber of the Upper Tribunal in *SSWP v MB*[83] and *KS v SSWP*.[84]

2.56 In *KS*, Upper Tribunal Judge Sir Crispin Agnew QC held at para 12 that the requirement for 'compelling evidence' did not mean that a higher standard of proof was required that the normal civil standard. In *MB*, the Upper Tribunal considered whether the 'compelling evidence' test of genuinely searching for and finding work was compatible with EU law. In doing so, the tribunal considered the meaning of the 'genuine chances' test (at para 42):

75 EEA Regs 2016 reg 6(8)–(10).
76 EEA Regs 2016 reg 6(7).
77 Under EEA Regs 2016 reg 6(1).
78 *Dano v Jobcenter Leipzig* Case C-333/13 [2015] 1 WLR 2519, CJEU.
79 *Jobcenter Berlin Neukolln v Alimanovic* Case C-67/14 [2016] QB 308, CJEU.
80 *Mirga v SSWP* [2016] UKSC 1.
81 EEA Regs 2016 reg 6(7).
82 EEA Regs 2016 reg 6(8)(b).
83 [2016] UKUT 372 AAC.
84 [2016] UKUT 269 (AAC).

> It seems to me that what is contemplated are chances that, as well as being founded on something objective, offer real prospects of success in obtaining work. Such a view is, moreover, consistent with both the French version ('des chances ve?ritables d'e?tre engage?') and with the German ('dass er mit begru?ndeter Aussicht auf Erfolg Arbeit sucht'). It is a significantly higher level than the "not hopeless" suggested by the skeleton arguments for the claimants.

2.57 Further, as the tribunal held (at para 45), a 'genuine chance of being engaged' is 'not something that can only be satisfied if one can point to a particular job (though of course the offer of a specific job will be very powerful evidence)'.

2.58 As to the meaning of 'compelling evidence', the tribunal held (at para 57):

> What in my view the amendment cannot do and does not do is anything more than that. In particular, it cannot raise the bar for what constitutes a genuine chance (or chances) of being engaged higher than it falls to be set in accordance with Antonissen, which I have sought to interpret in this decision. The risk that it may do so arises particularly acutely in the context of proving a chance: the evidence which is likely to be considered more or less compelling is not that going to the existence of the primary facts, but the constellation of primary facts from which a chance may be inferred. Insistence on 'compelling' evidence may, if care is not taken, all too easily result in raising the bar above the level I have found to be required, namely chances that are founded on something objective and offer real prospects of success in obtaining genuine and effective work within a reasonable period.

2.59 The Home Office now accepts that 'compelling evidence' no longer represents a higher threshold than the requirement to prove that a person is actively seeking work and has a genuine chance of finding work.[85]

2.60 Relatedly, it should be noted that, in *KH v Bury MBC*,[86] the Upper Tribunal ruled that the 'genuine chance of being engaged' test was not applicable to the retention of worker status under Citizens' Rights Directive Article 7(3)(b).

85 *European Economic area nationals: qualified persons*, v8.0, Home Office, 22 October 2020, under the headings 'Jobseekers' and 'Compelling evidence'.

86 [2020] UKUT 50 (AAC).

The self-employed

2.61 EU law has traditionally treated self-employment as the right of 'establishment' under TFEU Article 49, whereas employed work has fallen under the free movement of workers and TFEU Article 45.

2.62 TFEU Article 49 guarantees the right to freedom of establishment, which means the right to take up and pursue activities as a self-employed person, and to set up companies or firms etc.

2.63 EEA Regs 2016 reg 4(1)(b) defined a 'self-employed person' as a person who is established in the UK in order to pursue activity as a self-employed person in accordance with TFEU Article 49.

2.64 In *Jany*[87] the CJEU considered that, for economic activity to fall under the definition of self-employment, it must be:

- an economic activity;
- outside of any relationship of subordination concerning the choice of that activity, working conditions and conditions of remuneration;
- under that person's own responsibility; and
- in return for remuneration paid directly to that person.

2.65 As with workers, the economic activity has to be 'genuine and effective', as opposed to 'purely marginal and ancillary'.[88]

Self-sufficient persons and students

2.66 EEA Regs 2016 reg 4(1)(c) reflected Article 7(1)(b) of the Citizens' Rights Directive, and define a 'self-sufficient person' as one who had:

- sufficient resources not to become a burden on the social assistance system of the UK during the person's period of residence; and
- comprehensive sickness insurance cover in the UK.

2.67 Under EEA Regs 2016 reg 4(1)(d) a student was defined as a person who:

- was enrolled, for the principal purpose of following a course of study (including vocational training), at a public or private establishment which was:
  - financed from public funds; or
  - otherwise recognised by the secretary of state as an establishment which had been accredited for the purpose of providing

87 *Jany v Staatssecretaris van Justitie* Case C-268/99 [2001] ECR I-8615, ECJ.

88 *Deliege v Ligue Francophone de Judo et Disciplines Associees ASBL* Joined Cases C51/96 and C191/97 [2000] ECR I-2549, ECJ.

such courses or training within the law or administrative practice of the part of the UK in which the establishment was located;

- had comprehensive sickness insurance cover in the UK; and
- had assured the secretary of state, by means of a declaration, or by such equivalent means as the person may choose, that the person had sufficient resources not to become a burden on the social assistance system of the UK during the person's intended period of residence.

This definition also corresponds to Article 7(1)(c) of the Citizens' Rights Directive.

2.68 Practitioners will note that, for both self-sufficient persons and students, there was a requirement to have comprehensive sickness insurance in order to qualify for the right to reside under EU law. Although EEA nationals have been allowed to use the NHS, this will not meet the definition of comprehensive insurance cover.[89]

2.69 The self-employed and students also needed to show that they had sufficient resources so that they (and their family members, if they also sought to exercise that right) would not become a burden on the UK's social assistance system. Regulation 4(4) provided:

> In paragraph (1)(c) and (d) and paragraph (3), the resources of the student or self-sufficient person and, where applicable, any of their relevant family members, are to be regarded as sufficient if–
> (a) they exceed the maximum level of resources which a British citizen (including the resources of the British citizen's family members) may possess if the British citizen is to become eligible for social assistance under the United Kingdom benefit system; or
> (b) paragraph (a) does not apply but, taking into account the personal circumstances of the person concerned and, where applicable, all their relevant family members, it appears to the decision maker that the resources of the person or persons concerned should be regarded as sufficient.

2.70 The rationale for the requirement of self-sufficiency was to ensure that economically inactive Union citizens did not use the host member state's welfare system to fund their means of subsistence.[90]

89 *Ahmad v SSHD* [2014] EWCA Civ 988, [2014] 3 CMLR 45.
90 *Mirga v SSWP* [2016] UKSC 1, [2016] 1 WLR 481.

2.71 Sources of income that may be counted towards self-sufficiency could include income derived in part from a spouse in a third-country national.[91]

The permanent right of residence

Permanent residence after five years

2.72 The right to permanent residence was automatically acquired after five years' residence in the UK as a 'qualified person' under the EEA Regs 2016. In practice, this required proof that the EEA citizen has exercised treaty rights in the UK over the five-year period, by engaging in one or more of the following economic activities:

- work;
- job seeking;
- self-employment;
- self-sufficiency;
- studying.

2.73 Regulation 15 recognised three circumstances where a person acquired a right of permanent residence following five years residence in the UK:

- an EEA national who has resided in the UK in accordance with the regulations for a period of five years acquires permanent residence;[92]
- a family member[93] of an EEA national who is not an EEA national but who has resided in the UK with the EEA national in accordance with these regulations for a continuous period of five years;[94]
- a person who has resided in the UK in accordance with the regulations for a continuous period of five years *and* was, at the end of the period, a family member who has retained the right of residence under reg 10.[95]

2.74 Extended family members[96] were only entitled to a permanent residence card after a period of five years from the issue of a residence card (even if they could prove that they had resided legally with an

91 *Kuldip Singh v Minister for Justice and Equality* Case C-218/14 [2016] QB 208, CJEU.

92 EEA Regs 2016 reg 15(1)(a).

93 See paras 2.115–2.116.

94 EEA Regs 2016 reg 15(1)(b).

95 EEA Regs 2016 reg 15(1)(f). See paras 2.123–2.127.

96 See paras 2.117–2127.

EU citizen in the host member state continuously for five years as an extended family member).[97]

2.75 Continuous periods of residence which were completed before the transposition of the Citizens' Rights Directive (ie 30 April 2006) in accordance with earlier EU instruments must also be taken into account for the purpose of counting the five-year period for permanent residence.[98]

2.76 Residence in the UK as a result of a derivative right to reside did not constitute residence for the purpose of reg 15.[99]

Permanent residence before five years

2.77 The right to permanent residence could be acquired where a person had spent less than five years in the UK if they were:

- a worker or self-employed person who 'ha[d] ceased activity' in accordance with reg 5;[100]
- the family member[101] of a worker or self-employed person who had 'ceased activity' provided that:
  - they were the family member at the point the worker or self-employed person ceased activity; *and*
  - at that point, the family member enjoyed a right to reside on the basis of being a family member of that worker or self-employed person;[102]
- a person who was the family member of a worker or self-employed person where:
  - the worker or self-employed person had died;
  - the family member resided with the worker or self-employed person immediately before the death; *and*
  - the worker or self-employed person had resided continuously in the UK for at least two years immediately before dying or the death was the result of an accident at work or an occupational disease.[103]

97 *SSHD v Aibangbee* [2019] EWCA Civ 339, [2019] 1 WLR 4747 at para 33.

98 *SSWP v Lassal (Child Action Poverty Group intervening)* Case C-162/09 [2011] 1 CMLR 31, CJEU.

99 EEA Regs 2016 reg 15(3).

100 EEA Regs 2016 reg 15(1)(c).

101 See paras 2.115–2.127.

102 EEA Regs 2016 reg 15(1)(d).

103 EEA Regs 2016 reg 15(1)(e).

When will a worker or self-employed person 'cease activity'?

2.78 A worker or self-employed person 'ceased activity', if they came within one of the three conditions set out at EEA Regs 2016 reg 5.

2.79 Under reg 5(2), if they lived in the UK for three years before they stopped working as a worker or self-employed person at the age at which they are entitled to a state pension, or in the case of worker, to take early retirement. They must have lived in the UK continuously for at least three years prior to retirement, worked as a worker or self-employed person in the UK for at least 12 continuous[104] months prior to retirement, and reached state retirement age or, if a worker, taken early retirement.

2.80 Under reg 5(3), if they stopped working as a worker or self-employed person as a result of permanent incapacity to work; and either had been living in the UK continuously for more than two years prior to termination; or the incapacity was the result of an accident at work or an occupational disease that entitles them to a pension payable in full or in part by an institution in the UK.

2.81 Under reg 5(4), if they are active as a worker or self-employed person in another EEA country but keep their home in the UK and returns to it at least once a week; and previously they had been continuously resident and continuously active as a worker or self-employed person in the UK for at least three years.

2.82 The applicable Home Office guidance interpreting these provisions is *European Economic Area nationals: qualified persons.*[105]

Derivative rights of residence

Overview of derivative rights

2.83 Derivative rights of residence are rights that are derived from sources of EU law, other than the Citizens' Rights Directive, notably EU citizenship in TFEU Articles 20 and 21, the non-discrimination principle, proportionality and the EU Charter of Fundamental Rights. Family members of EU citizens may have had a derivative right to reside in the UK where the EU citizen had a right to reside without being a 'qualified person' under the EEA Regs 2016.

2.84 EEA Regs 2016 reg 16 sought to make provision for the derivative rights that have been recognised by the CJEU. The Home Office's

104 *AT v Pensionsversicherungsanstalt* Case C-32/19 [2020] 1 WLR 2370, CJEU.

105 *European Economic area nationals: qualified persons*, v8.0, Home Office, 22 October 2020: see under heading 'Worker or self-employed person who has ceased activity'.

published guidance explains its approach to decision-making under that regulation, which sets out the Home Office's policy for deciding applications, step by step.[106] This may assist practitioners in seeking to establish that derivative rights were enjoyed prior to the end of the implementation period. In any case involving a child, the Home Office should discharge their duties in accordance with Borders, Immigration and Citizenship Act 2009 s55 and the requirements of ECHR Article 8 as explained in the *ZH (Tanzania)* case.[107]

2.85 Under the EEA Regs 2016, a person could potentially qualify for a derivative right of residence provided that they are not an 'exempt person'. An 'exempt person' was defined in reg 16(7)(c) as a person:

- who has a right to reside in the UK as a result of any other provision of the EEA Regs 2016, for example, a person who is already exercising free movement rights as an EEA national;
- who has a right of abode in the UK by virtue of IA 1971 s2, for example, the person is a British citizen;
- to whom IA 1971 s8, or any order made under subsection (2) of that provision, applies;
- who has indefinite leave to enter or remain in the UK.

2.86 There are broadly three types of derivative residence rights which have been developed by the CJEU in case-law:

- '***Zambrano* carer**': A *Zambrano* carer had the right to reside if they are a non-EEA national primary carer of a British citizen who is residing in the UK, where that carer's removal from the UK would require the British citizen to leave the territory of the EEA.[108] This right is discussed below at paras 2.90–2.100.
- '***Chen* carer**': A *Chen* carer had the right to reside if they are the primary carer of an EEA national child who is exercising free movement rights in the UK as a self-sufficient person, where requiring that carer to leave the UK indefinitely would prevent the EEA national child from continuing to exercise those free movement rights in the UK.[109] This right is discussed below at paras 2.101–2.109.

106 *Free Movement Rights: derivative rights of residence*, v5.0, Home Office, 2 May 2019.

107 *ZH (Tanzania) v SSHD* [2011] UKSC 4.

108 See EEA Regs 2016 reg 16(5); and *Ruiz Zambrano* C-34/09.

109 See EEA Regs 2016 reg 16(2); and *Chen and Zhu v SSHD* Case C-200/02 [2005] QB 325, ECJ ('*Chen*').

- ***Ibrahim/Teixeira* cases:** *Ibrahim/Teixeira* cases involve either the child of an EEA national worker/former worker where that child was in education in the UK, *or* the primary carer of a child of an EEA national worker/former worker where that child was in education in the UK; and where requiring the primary carer to leave the UK would prevent the child from continuing their education in the UK.[110] This right is discussed below at paras 2.110–2.113.

2.87 The type of derivative right a person enjoys affected their eligibility to access certain welfare benefits and housing, as discussed in chapter 4. Prior to 1 January 2021, rights under the Citizens' Rights Directive were more favourable than those arising from derivative rights.

2.88 Under the EEA Regs 2016, persons with derivative rights did not qualify for permanent residence after five years in the UK. This was because residence in the UK as a result of a derivative right to reside does not constitute 'residence' for the purposes of reg 15.[111]

2.89 In contrast to the position under the EEA Regs 2016, the EUSS was, however, open to individuals who enjoyed a derivative right of residence under EEA Regs 2016 reg 16.[112] Such persons could apply for settled and pre-settled status. Following a written Ministerial Statement to Parliament on 7 March 2019,[113] Appendix EU of the Immigration Rules was amended so as specifically to provide that persons with a derivative right to reside or a person with a *Zambrano* right was eligible to apply for settled status. This took effect from 1 May 2019. The Home Office also published detailed guidance to their caseworkers for EUSS applications. There was separate guidance for *Zambrano* cases;[114] and the *Chen* and *Ibrahim/Teixeira* cases

110 See EEA Regs 2016 reg 16(2), read with *Ibrahim v Harrow LBC* Case C-310/08 [2010] PTSR 1913, [2010] 2 CMLR 51, CJEU and *Teixeira v Lambeth LBC* Case C-480/08 [2010] PTSR 1913, [2010] 2 CMLR 50, CJEU.

111 EEA Regs 2016 reg 15(2). See paras 2.72–2.82 on permanent residence.

112 The EUSS is discussed in more detail at paras 2.138–2.176.

113 Written Statement of Caroline Nokes, Minister of State for Immigration, on the EU Settlement Scheme, 7 March 2019 (Statement UIN HCWS1387).

114 *EU Settlement Scheme: person with a Zambrano right to reside,* Home Office. Wherever Home Office guidance documents relating to the EUSS are cited in this chapter, only their title is given, and any applicable sub-heading, since these documents are frequently updated and it is likely that any given version will quickly become out of date. The guidance documents are easily accessible by an internet search of 'Home Office' and the guidance document title.

are dealt with together in a separate document.[115] For the purposes of an application under the EUSS, those applying as holders of derivative residence right did need to show that they, or the relevant EEA child, holds or has held comprehensive sickness insurance.[116]

'*Zambrano* carer'

2.90 The category of '*Zambrano* carer' is derived from the CJEU decision of *Ruiz Zambrano*,[117] which concerned the status of third country national carers of EU citizen children, who had not left their country of residence.

2.91 Mr Zambrano was a Colombian national, who arrived in Belgium in 1999 with a valid visa. His wife, also Colombian, joined him shortly thereafter. They claimed asylum and were refused. Eventually over a lengthy ten-year period of various unsuccessful applications, he challenged the decision to remove him in the Belgian courts. In the meantime, he had two Belgian citizen children and obtained full-time employment, although this was unlawful.

2.92 The CJEU ruled that the right to EU citizenship, protected by TFEU Article 20, precludes a member state from refusing a right of residence to a third country national on whom his minor EU children are dependent, in the member state of residence and nationality of those children; and from refusing to grant a work permit to that third country national, in so far as such decisions deprive those children of 'the genuine enjoyment of the substance of the rights attaching to the status of European Union citizen'.

2.93 The *Zambrano* principle has been supplemented by *Chavez-Vilchez*,[118] a case in which the CJEU held that it is not simply enough to find another parent who can care for the child; there must first be an assessment of the best interests of the child. Although the applicant parent should provide evidence of this, the CJEU recognised that

115 *EU Settlement Scheme: derivative right to reside (Chen and Ibrahim/Teixeira cases)*, Home Office.

116 See the definitions of 'person with a right to reside', 'person with a Zambrano right to reside' and 'person who had a derivative or Zambrano right to reside' at Annex 1 of Appendix EU of the Immigration Rules, which does not require such a person to meet the requirement of comprehensive sickness insurance cover, as is required under the EEA Regs 2016.

117 *Ruiz Zambrano v Office National de l'Emploi (ONEm)* C-34/09 [2011] 2 CMLR 46, [2011] All ER (EC) 491, CJEU.

118 *Chavez-Vilchez and others v Raad van Bestuur van de Sociale Verzekeringsbank* Case C-133/15 [2018] QB 103, CJEU.

that member states are also under a duty to make inquires regarding the circumstances of the child and family in question.

2.94 The scope of the *Zambrano* principle has been considered further by the Supreme Court in *Patel*,[119] which involved two appeals. The first (*Patel*) concerned a non-EU national adult, with no right to remain, who cared for his elderly British parent. The other case (*Shah*) concerned a non-EU national parent, who was the primary carer to his British citizen son, while his British citizen wife worked to support the family.

2.95 The Supreme Court reaffirmed that TFEU Article 20 provides for a right of citizenship, but this does not confer rights on a third country national. However, an EU *citizen's* rights need to be effective; and a third country national may enjoy a derivative right to reside if their removal could deprive an EU citizen of genuine enjoyment of their citizenship rights, as a result of being compelled to leave Union territory by the third country national's departure.[120] This limits the entitlement of a third country national to reside in the EU. There must be a relationship of dependency between the two.

2.96 The court underlined that a distinction is to be drawn between an EU citizen who is an adult and one who is a child. A third country national can have a relationship with an adult EU citizen sufficient to justify a derivative right of residence only in exceptional circumstances.[121] *Chavez-Vilchez* does not relax the need to establish that the adult EU citizen will be *compelled* to leave the EU; it is confined to cases involving children.[122]

2.97 On the facts, Mr Patel's case failed because it was established that his father would not accompany him to India. By contrast, Mr Shah's appeal succeeded: the overarching question was whether the child would be compelled to leave with his father, who was his primary carer. In answering that question, the court was required to have regard to the child's best interests. The compulsion test is a practical one and is to be applied to the actual facts. If a child *will* leave the EU, then it was held that this is sufficient compulsion for the purposes of the *Zambrano* principle.

119 *Patel v SSHD; SSHD v Shah* [2019] UKSC 59, [2020] 1 WLR 228.

120 The importance of effectiveness of EU citizenship was emphasised by the CJEU in *KA v Belgium* Case C-82/16 [2018] 3 CMLR 28, CJEU at paras 47–50, which was discussed in detailed by the Supreme Court in *Patel*.

121 *Patel* at para 17, quoting *KA* at para 65.

122 *Patel* at para 27.

2.98 It is not a precondition to the existence of the *Zambrano*-derived right that the beneficiary of that right lacks any lawful leave to remain.[123]

2.99 Under EEA Regs 2016 reg 16(5), a person who met the following criteria qualified as a *Zambrano* carer:

- they are the primary carer of a British citizen;
- that the British citizen is residing in the UK; and
- that the British citizen would be unable to reside in the UK or in another EEA state if their carer left the UK for an indefinite period.

2.100 *Zambrano* carers could not access to public funds and could not apply to have to access to public funds.

'Chen carer'

2.101 *Chen*[124] concerned an Irish citizen child, born in Belfast to Chinese parents, who had been living in Wales. At that time, Irish nationality law afforded birth right citizenship to any person born on the island of Ireland. The child's mother then sought to apply for residence in the UK based on the child's Irish nationality, and permanently to live in Cardiff. This was rejected by the Home Office. In the course of the appeal, a preliminary reference was made to the CJEU.

2.102 The CJEU held that a self-sufficient EEA national child has the right to be accompanied by their primary carer, where they would be unable to remain in the host member state if the primary carer were

123 Note that Appendix EU Annex 1 defines the term 'person with a *Zambrano* right to reside' as excluding a person from being granted EUSS leave on the *Zambrano* basis if they held limited leave to remain at the relevant time (which was not EUSS leave). This provision, and the corresponding parts of the guidance described in fn 116 above, were declared to be unlawful in *R (Akinsanya) v SSHD* [2021] EWHC 1535 (Admin). The SSHD's appeal was unsuccessful. Following the Court of Appeal's judgment, the Home Office reconsidered the EUSS requirements for applicants relying on being a *Zambrano* primary carer and published their guidance dated 13 June 2022. The SSHD decided that she no longer wishes that definition in Appendix EU to reflect the scope of the EEA Regs 2016 (which have now been revoked) but wishes it to reflect the scope of those who, by the end of the transition period, had an EU law right to reside in the UK as a *Zambrano* primary carer, in line with the originally stated policy intention. She therefore intends to maintain the requirement in sub-paragraph (b) of the definition that the applicant did not, by the end of the transition period and during the relevant period relied upon, have leave to enter or remain in the UK (unless this was under the EUSS). This means applications will be considered under the existing Immigration Rules for the EUSS in Appendix EU.

124 *Chen and Zhu v SSHD* Case C-200/02 [2005] QB 325, ECJ.

required to leave. The EEA national child had the right to reside anywhere in the EU, and to deny her parents residency when she was dependent on them would deprive her rights of any real effect.

2.103 The *Chen* category was reflected in the criteria set down in EEA Regs 2016 reg 16(2):

- the person is the primary carer of an EEA national; and
- the EEA national:
  - is under the age of 18;
  - resides in the UK as a self-sufficient person; and
  - would be unable to remain in the UK if the person left the UK for an indefinite period.

2.104 Self-sufficiency was defined in reg 4(1)(c) as a person who has:

- sufficient resources not to become a burden on the social assistance of the UK during the person's period of residence; and
- comprehensive sickness insurance cover in the UK.

2.105 A *Chen* carer was not permitted to have recourse to public funds.

2.106 An issue which was encountered in practice was establishing self-sufficiency. The Court of Appeal in Northern Ireland made a referral to the CJEU for a preliminary reference on the meaning of 'self-sufficiency' in the case of *Bajratari*.[125] An Albanian couple living in Northern Ireland with two Irish citizen children sought to rely on the *Chen* principle. The father's earnings which were used to justify self-sufficiency were obtained via illegal working. The questions referred were:

- Can income from employment that is unlawful under national law establish, in whole or in part, the availability of sufficient resources under Article 7(1)(b) of the Citizens' Rights Directive?
- If 'yes', can Article 7(1)(b) be satisfied where the employment is deemed precarious solely by reason of its unlawful character?

2.107 The reference was made as the facts of *Chen* suggested that the earnings from illegal working could count towards self-sufficiency, whereas UK domestic law provides that incomes from unlawful working cannot be used to establish self-sufficiency.[126] This is in further conflict with Irish domestic law,[127] which is material as the children in question have Irish citizenship.

125 *Bajratari v SSHD* Case C-93/18 [2020] 1 WLR 2327, CJEU.
126 *W (China) and X (China) v SSHD* [2006] EWCA Civ 1494, [2007] 1 WLR 1514.
127 *OA v Minister for Justice, Equality and Defence* [2014] IEHC 384.

2.108 In its ruling in *Bajratari*[128] the CJEU clarified that an EU citizen child will meet the requirement of 'sufficient resources' for the purposes of Article 7(1)(b) of the Directive even if those resources come from income gained through 'unlawful' employment. This is an important decision because, for many EU citizen children, the only way they can show that they are self-sufficient will be through their parents' incomes. Even where resources are derived from income obtained from a third country national parent without a residence card and work permit, these will be sufficient for the purposes of EU law. Home Office guidance for *Chen* carers applying under the EUSS has been updated to reflect this.[129]

2.109 Relevantly, in *Subdelegación del Gobierno en Ciudad Real v RH*[130] (see at para 49) the CJEU held that where a relationship of dependency exists between an EU citizen and a third country national who is a member of their family, TFEU Article 20 precludes a member state from denying a derived right of residence solely because the EU citizen has insufficient resource.

Ibrahim/Teixeira cases

2.110 In the linked cases of *Ibrahim* and *Teixeria*[131] the CJEU ruled that Article 10 of Regulation (EU) No 492/2011 provides a right of residence for:

- children who are in education in a host member state where the EEA worker is working, or has worked; and
- primary carers of a child of an EEA worker/former worker where that child is in education in the UK, and where the requiring the primary carer to leave the UK would prevent the child from continuing their education in the UK.

2.111 In domestic law, reg 16(3) provided for a derivative right of residence to the child of an EEA national where the child lived in the UK at the

128 *Bajratari v SSHD* Case C-93/18 [2020] 1 WLR 2327, CJEU.

129 *EU Settlement Scheme: derivative right to reside (Chen and Ibrahim/Teixeira cases)*, Home Office: see under heading 'Stage 2: self sufficiency': 'You must, therefore, consider whether the EEA citizen child was self-sufficient before the primary carer started employment in a "*Chen*" capacity. The primary carer may engage in "unlawful employment", ie employment without permission, provided that employment is not engaging in a criminal activity.'

130 Case C-836/18 [2020] 4 WLR 59, CJEU.

131 *Ibrahim v Harrow LBC* Case C-310/08 [2010] PTSR 1913, [2010] 2 CMLR 51, CJEU and *Teixeira v Lambeth LBC* Case C-480/08 [2010] PTSR 1913, [2010] 2 CMLR 50, CJEU.

time when the EEA national parent was a worker and is in education in the UK. Regulation 16(4) provided for a derivative right of residence to the primary carer of the child who meets the definition of reg 16(3).

2.112 'Education' does not include nursery education but does not exclude education received before compulsory school age where that education is equivalent to the education received at or after compulsory school age.[132] Therefore, a child attending reception class is not considered nursery education.

2.113 A 'primary carer' was defined as:

- a direct relative or legal guardian of the child;
- who either has primary responsibility for the child's care; or
- shares equally the responsibility of their care with one of person.[133]

Unlike *Zambrano* and *Chen* cases, persons with *Ibrahim/Teixeria* rights did have recourse to public funds.

Family members and other family members

Family members

2.114 The definition of 'family member' (sometimes referred to as 'direct family members') under EEA Regs 2016 reg 7, which reflected Article 2(2) of the Citizens' Rights Directive, comprised the EEA national's:

- spouse or civil partner;[134]
- direct descendants or the direct descendants of their spouse/civil partner who were under 21 or were dependants of the person or their spouse/civil partner;[135]
- dependent direct relatives in their ascending line, or that of their spouse/civil partner.[136]

132 EEA Regs 2016 reg 16(7), which gave effect to the decision of *Re Shabani (EEA: jobseekers: nursery education)* [2013] UKUT 315 (IAC).

133 EEA Regs 2016 reg 16(8).

134 EEA Regs 2016 reg 7(1)(a).

135 EEA Regs 2016 reg 7(1)(b). This does not include step-children of an EEA national: *Latayan v SSHD* [2020] EWCA Civ 191, [2020] Imm AR 841.

136 EEA Regs 2016 reg 7(1)(c).

Family members of workers, self-employed and self-sufficient persons

2.115 Workers[137] and self-employed persons[138] had a complete and unlimited right to have their family travel with them.[139]

Family members of students and the self-sufficient

2.116 For students and the self-sufficient,[140] the definition of 'family member' was more restrictive. It included only the spouse/civil partner, or dependent child.[141] In addition, students were required to have comprehensive sickness cover in the UK for themselves and any accompanying family members.

'Other family members'

Definition of 'other family members'

2.117 Other family members may also have been eligible to apply for a right to reside, provided they met the definition in Article 3(2) of the Citizens' Rights Directive,[142] which was transposed by EEA Regs 2016 reg 8. Under reg 8, 'other family members' were referred to as 'extended family members' (EFMs). Advisors should be aware of the Home Office guidance on extended family members, which set out its application and interpretation of the EEA Regs 2016.[143]

2.118 Regulation 8 defined an extended family member as a person who is not a 'family member' under reg 7 and who satisfied one of the following conditions:

- *Dependent relative:* Is a relative of the EEA national and is residing in a country other than the UK; and i) is dependent upon the EEA national or is a member of the EEA national's household, and either ii) is accompanying the EEA national to the UK or wants to

137 See paras 2.49–2.51.
138 See paras 2.61–2.65.
139 See para 2.47.
140 See paras 2.66–2.71.
141 EEA Regs 2016 reg 7(2).
142 On 11 August 2022, a Presidential Panel of the Upper Tribunal held in *Batool and others (other family members: EU exit)* [2022] UKUT 219 (IAC) and *Celik (EU exit, marriage, human rights)* [2022] UKUT 220 (IAC) that the appellants could not avail themselves of protections under the Withdrawal Agreement. In *Batool* the Upper Tribunal also dismissed arguments relying on the EU Charter of Fundamental Rights and ECHR Article 8.
143 *Free Movement Rights: extended family members of EEA nationals*, v7.0, Home Office, 27 March 2019.

join the EEA national in the UK; or has joined the EEA national in the UK and continues to be dependent upon the EEA national, or a member of the EEA national's household.[144] In *Chowdhury*[145] the Upper Tribunal ruled that 'continues to be dependent' in reg 8(2)(c) required the applicant to establish that there had not been any break in their dependency.

- *Health grounds:* Is a relative of an EEA national and, on serious health grounds, strictly requires the personal care of the EEA national.[146]
- *Meeting the Immigration Rules for ILR as a dependent relative:* Is a relative of the EEA national and would meet the requirements in the Immigration Rules (other than those relating to entry clearance) for indefinite leave to enter or remain in the UK as a dependent relative of the EEA national.[147]
- *'Durable' partner:* Is the partner (other than a civil partner) of the EEA national, and is able to prove to the Home Office that they are in a 'durable relationship'.[148] Although the *Extended family member* guidance[149] specifies that the applicant and the durable (unmarried) partner of an EEA national must have been living together in a relationship similar to marriage for at least two years, this is not under EU law a fixed rule and depends on the circumstances. The guidance accepts, for example, that a couple who have a child together but have been in a relationship for less than two years may qualify.
- Practitioners should also be aware that, under the old 2006 Regulations, it was possible for the spouse or civil partner of an EEA national to sponsor dependent relatives of theirs as an 'extended family member'.[150] However, from 1 February 2017, the free movement rights of extended family members only applied to the relatives of the EEA national, and not to the relatives of the EEA national's spouse/civil partner.

144 EEA Regs 2016 reg 8(2).

145 *Chowdhury (extended family members: dependency)* [2020] UKUT 188 (IAC) at paras 23–30.

146 EEA Regs 2016 reg 8(3).

147 EEA Regs 2016 reg 8(4).

148 EEA Regs 2016 reg 8(5).

149 *Free Movement Rights: extended family members of EEA nationals*, v7.0, see under heading 'Durable partners: regulation 8(5)', p22.

150 See now repealed reg 8(2) and (3) of the EEA Regs 2006, which enabled an EEA national's spouse/civil partner to sponsor dependent relatives and 'health grounds' cases.

The discretionary nature of residence permits for EFMs and the requirement to make an application

2.119 It should be noted that EFMs enjoyed no automatic right to a residence permit. Even where the EEA national's relative met the definition of an EFM, the secretary of state nevertheless had a discretion whether to grant a residence permit having regard to all the circumstances and following an 'extensive examination of the personal circumstances of the applicant'. See EEA Regs 2016 regs 12(4)–(5) and 17(5)–(6) and Article 3(2) of the Citizens' Rights Directive. As such, an application first had to be made to enable the secretary of state to exercise that discretion before the residence right arose.[151]

Appeal rights for EFMs

2.120 Appeal rights against EEA decisions in general are addressed at the end of this chapter; however, appeal rights for EFMs require particular mention at this stage. Whether an EFM enjoyed a right of appeal to the First-tier Tribunal against an EEA decision – such as the refusal to issue a residence card – was heavily litigated. In *Sala (EFMs: right of appeal)*[152] the Upper Tribunal held that under the 2006 EEA Regs, the decision to refuse an EFM a residence card did not attract a right of appeal because it was not an 'EEA decision', being a matter of discretion, and not entitlement.[153] As a consequence, the Home Office reflected this in the 2016 EEA Regs, meaning that EFMs had no right of appeal as a result of reg 39.

2.121 A reference was made to the CJEU in the case of *Banger*[154] to consider to what extent EFMs were entitled to an effective remedy, and whether such a remedy would be a review or a full merits appeal. The CJEU decision found that judicial review cannot be an adequate remedy, because it does not allow for the full factual assessment of circumstances that happens in an appeal.

2.122 On 29 March 2019 the EEA Regs 2016 were amended so as to remove the exclusion of EFMs from the definition of an appealable 'EEA decision' in reg 2,[155] with the ostensible effect that EFMs would

151 *SSHD v Macastena* [2018] EWCA Civ 1558, [2019] Imm AR 28.

152 [2016] UKUT 411 (IAC).

153 This was subsequently overturned by *Khan v SSHD* [2017] EWCA Civ 1755, [2018] Imm AR 440, meaning EFMs *did* enjoy a right of appeal under the 2006 EEA Regs. This was confirmed by the Supreme Court in *SM (Algeria) v Entry Clearance Officer, UK Visa Section* [2018] UKSC 9, [2018] 1 WLR 1035.

154 *SSHD v Banger* Case C-89/17 [2019] 1 WLR 845, CJEU.

155 Immigration (European Economic Area Nationals) (EU Exit) Regulations 2019 SI No 468 Part 3 reg 3(2).

enjoy a right of appeal against EEA decisions under reg 36. However, the amending legislation failed to address the requirement under reg 36(4) that, in order to exercise a right of appeal, the EFM (other than a durable partner) must produce a valid passport and either an EEA family permit, a qualifying EEA residence card, proof that the criteria for reg 7 is met (direct family member), or proof that the criteria for reg 10 is met (retained right of residence). In practice, then, the amended text of reg 36(4) only afforded a right of appeal to those EFMs who were family members, or those who already possessed valid residence documentation. This was contrary to the ruling of the CJEU in *Banger*. The Home Office accepted this oversight[156] and, as of 15 August 2019, reg 36(4) was amended so as to afford the right of appeal to EFMs in possession of a passport and upon proof that they are an EFM.[157] The Upper Tribunal has indicated[158] that it is open to EFMs who were denied a right of appeal in the intervening periods either to ask the Home Office to make a new decision which attracts a right of appeal, or lodge a notice of appeal to the tribunal, invoking the doctrine of direct effect and seek an extension of time in the light of the *Banger* litigation.

Consequences for family members where the EEA national dies, departs from the UK or the marriage is terminated

2.123 A family member could retain their right to reside under EEA Regs 2016 reg 10 in certain circumstances after the death, divorce or departure of the qualified person.

2.124 If the EEA national sponsor died, their non-EEA family members could retain a right of residence provided they met the criteria contained in reg 10(2), namely that:

- they were the family member of an EEA national who was either a qualified person or had a right of permanent residence when they died;[159]
- they were living in the UK in line with the regulations for at least one year immediately before the EEA national's death;[160]

156 Letter from the Home Office to President of the IAC, Mr Justice Lane, dated 19 June 2019. Available at: www.judiciary.uk/wp-content/uploads/2019/09/letter-from-HO.doc.pdf.

157 Immigration (European Economic Area) (Amendment) Regulations 2019 SI No 1155 reg 2(9)(a)(iii).

158 *Banger (EEA: EFM: right of appeal)* [2019] UKUT 194 (IAC).

159 EEA Regs 2016 reg 10(2)(a).

160 EEA Regs 2016 reg 10(2)(b).

- they would be a worker, self-employed person or self-sufficient person if they were an EEA national, or they are the family member of a person who meets this requirement.[161]

2.125 The direct descendants – either EEA or non-EEA – of an EEA national could retain a right of residence in certain circumstances, as set down in reg 10(3). This applied where:

- the person is the direct descendant of either:
  - a qualified person or an EEA national with permanent residence who has died;
  - a person who ceased to be a qualified person on ceasing to reside in the UK;
  - the spouse or civil partner of the qualified person or EEA national with permanent residence immediately before their death; or
  - the spouse or civil partner of a person who ceased to be a qualified person on ceasing to reside in the UK; and
- the descendant was attending an educational course in the UK immediately before the qualified person or the EEA national with permanent residence died, or ceased to be a qualified person, and continues to attend such a course.

'Parent' here means the parent with the actual custody of a child who satisfies the latter criteria.[162]

2.126 Regulation 10(5) governed the situation where the marriage or civil partnership had broken down. After divorce/termination a former family member retained the right of residence if:

- at the commencement of divorce proceedings, the EEA national resided in the UK as a qualified person or held permanent right of residence (proof from the ex-partner, or, ideally, from HM Revenue and Customs (HMRC) relating to their employment was usually necessary[163]);[164] and
- the marriage/civil partnership had lasted at least three years, of which one year was spent in the UK; or
- the former spouse/civil partner had rights to custody of a child of a qualified person, or a court ordered access in the UK, or the

161 EEA Regs 2016 reg 10(2)(c) read together with reg 10(6).

162 EEA Regs 2016 reg 10(4).

163 See *Amos v SSHD* [2011] EWCA Civ 552, [2011] Imm AR 600. at para 40.

164 *Baigazieva v SSHD* [2018] EWCA Civ 1088; and *SSHD v NA* Case C-115/15 [2017] QB 109, CJEU.

family member needed to stay in the UK due to difficult circumstances such as domestic violence.

2.127 However, the person needed to show that they were presently a worker, self-employed person, self-sufficient person or are the family member of one.[165]

Family members of British citizens

2.128 Under EU law, a British citizen who moved to another member state and exercised Treaty rights had the right to return to the UK with their third country national family members. The rationale for this principle is to ensure that individuals are not deterred from exercising their right to free movement. This was established by the case of *Surinder Singh*.[166]

2.129 In *O and B v Netherlands*,[167] the CJEU elaborated on the *Surinder Singh* principle. In *O*, a Dutch national living in Spain for two months with her Nigerian husband sought to rely on EU law as a basis for her husband's right of residence. The case of *B* concerned a Dutch national living with a Moroccan spouse at weekends in Belgium. The Dutch Court asked the CJEU to clarify whether EU law, in particular TFEU Article 21 and the Citizens' Rights Directive, grants third-country nationals a right of residence in member states of which the citizens in question are nationals.

2.130 The key principles derived from the judgment are:

- TFEU Article 21 and the Citizens' Rights Directive do not provide an autonomous right of residence for third-country nationals. Any rights conferred to third-country nationals are derived from the exercise of free movement by the EU citizen.
- Applying TFEU Article 21, a refusal to allow a derived right of residence for a third-country national family member may interfere with an EU citizen's free movement rights because it will deter them from moving and residing in another member state, if they cannot sponsor their family on return.
- In order for the right to free movement to be effective, TFEU Article 21 allows for a derived right of residence for third country national family members, where:

165 EEA Regs 2016 reg 10(6).

166 *R v Immigration Appeal Tribunal and Surinder Singh ex p SSHD* Case C-370/90 [1992] 3 CMLR 358, ECJ.

167 *O v Minister voor Immigratie, Integratie en Asiel; Minister voor Immigratie, Integratie en Asiel v B* Case C-456/12 [2014] QB 1163, CJEU.

- the EU citizen has exercised their right of free movement by residing in another member state, in accordance with the Citizens' Rights Directive;
- this must be for a minimum period of three months;
- they must genuinely reside in another member state;
- during their residence, a family life has been created and strengthened in that member state.

- Short periods, such as weekend visits and holidays, do not count as residence for these purposes.
- The right is not be exercised 'abusively'.

2.131 The case of *Banger*[168] confirmed that durable partners also benefit from derivative rights under TFEU Article 21 in the *Surinder Singh* situation described above. However, Article 21 does not create a *right* of residence for durable partners; rather, it creates a duty to 'facilitate the provision of a residence authorisation' based on 'an extensive examination of the applicant's personal circumstances' akin to the rights provided to other family members in Article 3(2) of the Citizens' Rights Directive.

2.132 The UK's interpretation of the *Surinder Singh* line of cases was set out at EEA Regs 2016 reg 9. In addition, the Home Office published guidance on the topic, *Free Movement Rights: Family members of British citizens.*[169] In the light of *Banger* and a subsequent case of *Christy,*[170] EEA Regs 2016 reg 9 was amended on 28 March 2019[171] to reflect the correct scope of the derived rights underpinning it.

2.133 Regulation 9(2) treated the returning British citizen as if they were an EEA national, where they met the following conditions:

- the British citizen is residing in an EEA state as a worker, self-employed person, self-sufficient person or student,[172] *or* so resided there immediately before returning to the UK *or* has acquired permanent residence (where such residence would have given rise to permanent residence under reg 15 had it taken place in the UK: reg 9(6));

168 *SSHD v Banger* Case C-89/17 [2019] 1 WLR 845, CJEU.

169 *Free Movement Rights: Family members of British citizens*, v5, Home Office, 9 March 2020.

170 *Christy v SSHD* [2018] EWCA Civ 2378, [2019] 1 WLR 2017.

171 Immigration (European Economic Area Nationals) (EU Exit) Regulations 2019 Part 3 reg 3(4), (5).

172 See EEA Regs 2016 reg 9(7) as to exceptions to the 2016 Regs for these purposes.

- the British citizen and their family member/extended family member resided together in the EEA state;
- the couple's residence in the EEA state was 'genuine';
- the partner of the British citizen was a family member or extended family member of the British citizen during all or part of their joint residence in that EEA state; and
- 'genuine family life' was created or strengthened during their joint residence in the EEA state.

EFMs must also have been lawfully resident in the EEA state from which they seek to come.[173]

2.134 Regulation 9(3) set out the factors relevant to assessing whether the residence of the British citizen and their family member/EFM in the EEA state was 'genuine':

- the length of their joint residence in the EEA state;
- the nature and quality of their accommodation in the EEA state, and whether it is or was British citizen's principal residence;
- the degree of their integration in the EEA state;
- whether the family member/extended family member's first lawful residence in the EU with the British citizen was in the EEA state.

2.135 EEA Regs 2016 reg 9(3)(a) still included 'whether the centre of the [British citizen's] life transferred to the EEA State' as one of the relevant factors in determining 'genuineness' of residence, at the time the regulations were revoked. However, this was notwithstanding that the Upper Tribunal had confirmed in *ZA (reg 9. EEA Regs: abuse of rights: Afghanistan)*[174] that the requirement to have transferred the centre of one's life to the host member state is not a requirement of EU law, nor is it endorsed by the CJEU. The Home Office has accepted that this is the effect of the *ZA* case because it has removed all references to the 'centre of life' criterion in its guidance.[175]

2.136 Whether an exercise of Treaty rights is genuine, or family life was established/strengthened in the EEA state, requires a qualitative, fact-specific assessment, which will need to bear in mind the following:

- any work or self-employment must have been 'genuine and effective' and not marginal or ancillary;

173 EEA Regs 2016 reg 9(1A)(b).

174 *Re ZA (reg 9. EEA Regs: abuse of rights: Afghanistan)* [2019] UKUT 281 (IAC).

175 *Free Movement Rights: extended family members of EEA nationals*, v7.0, under 'Changes from last version of this guidance' (p4).

- the assessment of whether a stay in the host state was genuine does not involve an assessment of the intentions of the parties over and above a consideration of whether what they intended to do was to exercise Treaty rights;
- there is no requirement for the EU national or his family to have integrated into the host member state; nor for the sole place of residence to be in the host state; and there is no requirement to have severed ties with the home member state, although that these factors may, to a limited degree, be relevant to the qualitative assessment of whether the exercise of Treaty rights was genuine.

2.137 Regulation 9 did not apply where the 'purpose of the residence in the EEA state was as a means for circumventing any immigration laws applying to non-EEA nationals' (reg 9(4)(a); application of this ground was recently upheld in *Kaur*[176]). However, in *ZA*, the Upper Tribunal confirmed that, if it is alleged that the stay in the host member state was such that reg 9(4) applies, the burden is on the secretary of state to show that there was an abuse of rights.

The EU Settlement Scheme

Overview

2.138 The EUSS gives effect to the UK's obligations under the Withdrawal Agreement to safeguard the rights of EEA citizens resident in the UK by 11pm on 31 December 2020. The Withdrawal Agreement is discussed at paras 2.8–2.20. The Scheme is set out in Appendix EU of the Immigration Rules[177] and at all times has operated as a freestanding immigration status with a route to settlement which was not affected (and did not affect) the holding of EU free movement rights, while those rights existed in UK law – ie during the implementation period[178] and, indirectly, in the grace period.[179] After 30 June 2021 it is no longer possible to apply for it (subject to what is said at paras 2.146–2.151 below). Settled status exists independently of the

176 *Kaur v SSHD* [2020] EWCA Civ 98.

177 Accessible at: www.gov.uk/guidance/immigration-rules.

178 That is, between 11pm on 31 January 2020 and 11pm on 31 December 2020. See paras 2.8–2.13.

179 That is, after 11pm on 31 December 2020 and 30 June 20201. See paras 2.14–2.20.

proposed new 'skills based' immigration rules discussed at para 2.23 which potentially apply to everyone arriving in the UK after 11pm on 31 December 2020.

2.139 The EUSS was opened fully on 30 March 2019 for applications made from within the UK (for limited/indefinite leave to remain); and on 9 April 2019 for applications made from outside the UK (for limited/indefinite leave to enter). The deadline for applying was 30 June 2021, based on a date of arrival in the UK of no later than 11pm on 31 December 2020 (but see paras 2.146–2.151 below). No fee applied.[180]

The core elements of the EU Settlement Scheme

2.140 The domestic legal basis for the EUSS is Appendix EU of the Immigration Rules, made by the secretary of state under IA 1971 s3. Appendix EU is detailed; and is supplemented by yet more detailed guidance documents, which should be studied carefully by anybody applying under the scheme.[181] At the time of writing they are:

- *EU Settlement Scheme: EU, other EEA and Swiss citizens and their family members* ('the main guidance') which covers the general requirements applicable to these categories of applicant;
- *EU Settlement Scheme: Suitability Requirements* which addresses the circumstances in which 'character' and 'conduct' issues may arise in any application under the scheme;
- three separate guidance documents concerning the eligibility requirements for three distinct subsets of applicants exercising derivative rights of residence, ie:
  - *EU Settlement Scheme: derivative Right to reside (Chen and Ibrahim/Teixera cases)*;
  - *EU Settlement Scheme: Family Member of a qualifying British citizen* (based on *Surinder Singh* situations, as discussed at paras 2.128–2.137 above); and
  - *EU Settlement Scheme: Person with a Zambrano right to reside*;
- a final guidance document concerns applications that involve a change of gender or name and gender, *Interim guidance: Gender identity and sex markers on documents.*

180 Persons who applied under the pre-30 March 2019 pilot scheme and paid fees are entitled to a refund: Immigration and Nationality (Fees) (Refund, Waiver and Amendment) (EU Exit) Regulations 2019 SI No 475.

181 The current versions of the guidance documents can be accessed at: www.gov.uk/government/publications/eu-settlement-scheme-caseworker-guidance.

2.141 The Scheme has two types of status, which are granted under Appendix EU of the Immigration Rules:

- **'Settled status'** (a type of indefinite leave to enter or remain).[182] This is analogous to, but is broader than, the right to permanent residence under the EEA Regs 2016. Settled status is discussed at paras 2.153–2.165.
- **'Pre-settled status'** (five years' limited leave to enter or remain). This is granted to those who were present in the UK at the time of application but do not yet qualify for settled status, commonly because they have not accrued the necessary period of continuous residence in the UK to qualify for settled status (usually five years).[183] A person granted pre-settled status will be eligible for settled status once they have accrued five years' residence in the UK. Not all of this five-year period need be in the same eligibility category on which the initial grant of pre-settled status was based, provided the different basis for eligibility under para EU14 is satisfied.[184] Pre-settled status is discussed at paras 2.166–2.168.

2.142 An applicant cannot choose which status they apply for; they simply apply to the EUSS, and the Home Office will grant them settled status or pre-settled status as applicable.

2.143 Applicants who apply to the EUSS from within the UK will be granted limited or indefinite leave to enter. Applicants who make an application from outside the UK will be granted limited or indefinite leave to enter.

2.144 There are three core criteria under the EUSS:

1) **Identity and validity:** Verifying identity and nationality through passports, national identity cards or biometric residence cards; and use of the required online application process.[185]
2) **Eligibility:** The key eligibility categories for settled status are set out at paras 2.153–2.160 (for settled status) and 2.166–2.168 (for pre-settled status) must be met as at the date of application. The common elements are that the applicant is:
   – resident in the UK;

182 Appendix EU para EU2, read with para EU11 (relating to a 'relevant EEA citizen or their family member, or as a person with a derivative right to reside or a person with a *Zambrano* right to reside') and EU12 (relating to family members of a qualifying British citizen, ie *Surinder Singh* type cases).

183 Appendix EU para EU3, read with paras EU11 and EU12.

184 Appendix EU paras EU2, EU4 and EU14.

185 Appendix EU para EU9.

- the applicant or the relevant EEA citizen has the necessary status;
- if appropriate the necessary family relationship or connection has been established at the date of application;
- a continuous qualifying period of residence has been accrued (settled status only); and
- the application is made by the 'required date' (in most cases 30 June 2021) unless the person has a reasonable excuse, or other limited exceptions apply.

The eligibility criteria encompass the requirements for permanent residence[186] under the EEA Regs 2016/Citizens' Rights Directive, but are considerably broader in that residence on the basis of derived rights and as a *Zambrano* carer[187] does count for the purposes of calculating the necessary continuous residence needed for settled status.

3) **Suitability:** Appendix EU paras EU15 and EU16 set out the basis on which applications may be refused on suitability grounds. This will be assessed on a case-by-case basis and will include consideration of relevant criminal convictions and whether the applicant has been open and honest in the application process. The significance of any potential conduct issue must be considered by the prospective applicant against the detailed rules and guidance[188] before an application is made. The suitability grounds are addressed further below at paras 2.161–2.164.

2.145 Notwithstanding the use of EU law terminology within the rules and guidance, it is the definitions provided in Appendix EU that should primarily be relied upon in applying to the EUSS.

The application deadline and late applications

2.146 The general rule is that applications under the EUSS must have been made before 1 July 2021, which for most people is the 'required date' (see Annex 1 to Appendix EU – Definitions).

2.147 In certain limited circumstances, the 'required date' may be later than 30 June 2021 and are set out in Annex 1 to Appendix EU under the definition of that term.

2.148 Late applications made after the 'required date' can be accepted where there are 'reasonable grounds' for the person's failure to meet

186 See paras 2.72–2.82.

187 See paras 2.90–2.100.

188 See in particular the *EU Settlement Scheme: suitability requirements* guidance.

the application deadline. This exception applies indefinitely. The *EU Settlement Scheme* main guidance directs Home Office caseworkers to adopt a 'flexible and pragmatic approach' to this criterion,[189] and sets out the following principles to guide its application:

- In general, the more time which has elapsed since the deadline applicable to the person under the scheme, the harder it will be for them to establish that, at the date of application, there are reasonable grounds for their failure to meet the deadline.
- 'For the time being', caseworkers are directed to 'give applicants the benefit of any doubt' in determining whether there are reasonable grounds for the late application, 'unless this would not be reasonable'. However the guidance leaves 'any change in approach' an open question for the future.
- An applicant who has provided insufficient information to establish reasonable grounds for its late submission must be contacted by the Home Office caseworker to request more information and given a reasonable opportunity to respond.
- Where the caseworker is not satisfied that reasonable grounds for the late application exist, the application falls for refusal under para EU6 of Appendix EU (non-eligibility).

2.149 The policy gives the following as non-exhaustive examples of reasonable grounds for failing to meet the deadline, which should be evidenced:

- the applicant was a child at the time of the deadline, and their parent, guardian or local authority did not make an application on their behalf, even 'years earlier';
- the applicant lacks the physical or mental capacity to apply to the Scheme, or has care and support needs relevant to their inability to apply in time;
- persons with serious medical conditions or significant medical treatment needs arising from illness or accident, or pregnancy etc;
- being a victim of modern slavery;
- being in an abusive or controlled relationship or situation;
- 'other compelling practical or compassionate reasons';
- not being aware that they had to apply under the scheme, for example, because they held a biometric residence permit evidencing

189 See the *EU Settlement Scheme* main guidance under the heading 'Reasonable grounds for failing to meet the deadline'.

their status under the EEA Regs 2016 which expired after the application deadline.

2.150 Reasonable grounds to make a late application to the Scheme are deemed to exist where:

- the person holds existing leave to remain under the Immigration Rules or outside the Rules (discretionary leave), which expires after 30 June 2021; and
- where the person ceased to be exempt from immigration control on or after 1 July 2021 in which case the deadline is 90 days from the day on which this occurred. Even if that 90-day deadline is not met, the application may still be considered if there are reasonable grounds for failing to meet it.

2.151 In the event that a person without leave is encountered by Immigration Enforcement officers from 1 July 2021, and it appears that the person may be eligible for leave to remain under the settled status scheme, the guidance indicates that the individual should be served with a notice affording them 28 days to make a valid application Scheme. Whether the person had a reasonable excuse for not applying before the applicable deadline will be considered at the time the substantive application is considered.[190]

Evidential flexibility and requesting further evidence from applicants

2.152 Under Annex 3 to Appendix EU the SSHD has the power to request the applicant to provide further evidence or information on certain relevant matters, including that they meet the eligibility requirements, and as to their relationship with another person. The SSHD also has the power to interview the applicant and/or the other person concerned. If the applicant fails within a reasonable specified timeframe to comply with requests for further information, or twice fails to comply with an invitation to attend an interview, the SSHD may draw adverse factual inferences on the relevant issues (although cannot draw adverse inferences on the sole basis that there was such non-compliance).

190 See the *EU Settlement Scheme* main guidance under the heading 'Reasonable grounds for failing to meet the deadline' and 'Encountered by Immigration Enforcement'.

Settled status

Eligibility criteria

2.153 In summary, the eligibility criteria for settled status for EEA citizens and their family members are that any of the following criteria – which correspond to the numbered subcategories listed in para EU11 – are satisfied:[191]

1) **Applicant has a documented right of permanent residence.**[192] An EEA citizen/their family member/a family member who has retained the right of residence, and already has a 'documented right of permanent residence' (under the EEA Regs 2016); and where no 'supervening event' has occurred (broadly, no absence of more than five years since permanent residence acquired and no deportation, removal decisions or exclusion order etc).
2) **Applicant has existing indefinite leave to enter or remain.** An EEA citizen/their family member/a family member who has retained the right of residence, and there is 'valid evidence of their indefinite leave to enter or remain', which is set out under condition 2 of para EU11, where that status is current, and has not lapsed through two years of consecutive absence from the UK.
3) **Applicant has accrued a continuous qualifying period of five years.** An EEA citizen/their family member/a family member who has retained the right of residence/person with a derived right of residence and/or person with a *Zambrano* right to reside,[193] and has completed a 'continuous qualifying period' of five years[194] in any combination of these categories, and since then no supervening event has occurred. The meaning of 'continuous qualifying residence' is discussed at paras 2.156–2.157.

191 As set out in detail in Appendix EU para EU11, read with the definitions in Annex 1 of Appendix EU and the *EU Settlement Scheme* main guidance.

192 For the permanent right of residence see paras 2.72–2.82.

193 Note that the definition of a 'person with a *Zambrano* right to reside' in Appendix EU Annex 1, wrongly includes, at (b), the criterion that the person was 'without leave to enter or remain in the UK, unless this was granted under this Appendix': *R (Akinsanya) v SSHD* [2021] EWHC 1535 (Admin), [2021] Imm AR 1311. The High Court declared that criterion to be unlawful in that case, as were the *EU Settlement Scheme* main guidance and *Person with a Zambrano right to reside* guidance on that point. See further paras 2.90–2.100 on *Zambrano* carers.

194 As to which see Appendix EU para EU13 and the definition of this term in Annex 1 of Appendix EU.

4) **Applicant is an economically active EEA citizen who has ceased activity.** An EEA citizen who is a person who has ceased activity, and since they did so, no 'supervening event' has occurred. The content of para EU11 condition 4 reflects EEA Regs 2016 reg 5, as discussed at paras 2.78–2.82.
5) **Applicant is a family member**[195] of a person in 4). The family member of an EEA citizen who had ceased activity, where the EEA citizen has been or is being granted ILE/ILR under Appendix EU, or would be granted it if they validly applied for it, the applicant was a family member at the point that the EEA citizen ceased activity and the applicant had accrued the continuous qualifying period of residence before that point, and no supervening event has since occurred. The EEA citizen may also be a 'relevant naturalised British citizen'.[196] The particularly convoluted wording of condition 5 should be read against the *EU Settlement Scheme* main guidance.[197]
6) **The applicant's relevant EEA family member has died.** The applicant is the family member of an EEA citizen who i) has died; ii) was resident in the UK as a worker or self-employed person at the time of their death; and iii) was resident in the UK and Islands for a continuous qualifying period of at least two years before death, or the death was as a result of an accident at work or an occupational disease; and the applicant was resident in the UK with the EEA citizen immediately before the death; and since when no supervening event has occurred.
7) **The applicant is a child under the age of 21.** A child under 21 of an EEA citizen, or of their spouse or civil partner and:
   - the marriage/partnership was entered into before the end of the implementation period (11pm on 31 December 2020), or the non-EEA partner was a durable partner before and on that date and is now a spouse/civil partner; and
   - the EEA citizen/their spouse or civil partner:
     - has been or is being granted ILE/ILR under Appendix EU; or
     - in the case of a person who is an Irish citizen has not made a valid application under Appendix EU but would be granted that leave if they made such an application; or

195 See paras 2.114–2.127.

196 As explained in para EU11(5) and as defined in Annex 1 to Appendix EU.

197 Under the headings 'Eligibility: family members of a relevant EEA citizen'/'The relevant EEA citizen has ceased activity'.

– is a relevant naturalised British citizen (under subparas (b), (c) and (d) of the definition in Annex 1 to Appendix EU).

2.154 Under categories 3 to 7 above, it is of particular importance that the basis for the residence in the claimed capacities is fully evidenced, with close reference to Appendix EU, the applicable guidance documents and the free movement principles set out at paras 2.41–2.113. Those granted pre-settled status should be advised to keep paperwork evidencing the basis for that status over the five-year period. They are otherwise likely to face real practical issues in evidencing continuous residence at the end of the five-year period, particularly where the basis for the pre-settled status changes in that time. It would be advisable, where the status changes, to apply again to obtain confirmation of this, prior to the applicable application deadline.

2.155 Categories 1–3 refer to a 'family member who has retained the right of residence', which is discussed above at paras 2.115–2.137. Appendix EU was amended on 14 May 2020 to expand the scope of this criterion so that victims of domestic violence or abuse could apply for status through the EUSS.[198] The 'domestic violence exception' under the EUSS had been restricted to a former spouse or civil partner whose marriage or civil partnership has been legally terminated and who was a victim of domestic violence or abuse while the marriage/civil partnership was subsisting. However, from 24 August 2020 any family member within the scope of the EUSS (a spouse, a civil partner, durable partner, child, dependent parent or dependent relative) whose family relationship with a relevant EEA citizen or with a qualifying British citizen broke down permanently due to domestic violence or abuse has a continued right of residence.

Continuous qualifying residence

2.156 Annex 1 to Appendix EU explains that a 'continuous qualifying period' of residence is not broken unless the applicant has been absent from the UK for more than six months in total, within any given 12-month period, throughout the residence relied upon by the applicant. There are, however, exceptions where:

- There is evidence to show that an absence of more than six months but less than 12 months where 'this is for an important reason' such as pregnancy, child birth, serious illness, vocational

198 See: www.gov.uk/government/publications/statement-of-changes-to-the-immigration-rules-cp-232-14-may-2020.

training or an overseas posting. Specified evidence must, however, be supplied.[199]

- The person served or is serving a sentence of imprisonment of any length in the UK. This has the effect of breaking the continuous residence 'which starts from scratch' upon release,[200] both of the person who served the sentence *and* of any family member. However it should be noted that, once the continuous qualifying period of residence has been accrued, a subsequent sentence of imprisonment cannot affect that fact, as it is not a 'supervening event' under the scheme. Therefore, where a right of permanent residence is accrued under EEA Regs 2016 reg 15, a subsequent sentence of imprisonment is no bar to reliance on that right under the scheme.
- A decision or order to exclude, remove or deport the person from the UK (unless set aside).

2.157 Once a person has completed a continuous qualifying period of residence in the UK of five years, they may rely on this in applying for settled status under condition 3 of para EU11 in the absence of a 'supervening event' following the completion of that five-year period.

Eligibility for settled status for '*Surinder Singh*' family members of British citizens

2.158 Appendix EU para EU12, makes separate provision for settled status to be granted to family members of 'qualifying British citizens', which covers those who derived residence rights on the basis of the *Surinder Singh* case, as described at paras 2.128–2.137 above, and reflected in EEA Regs 2016 reg 9.

2.159 Paragraph EU12 sets out four eligibility criteria. The first three criteria reflect conditions (1)–(3) of EU11 in respect of EEA nationals and their family members, summarised at para 2.153 above.

2.160 The fourth criterion relates to a child under 21 of the spouse of civil partner of the qualifying British citizen where:

- the marriage civil partnership pre-dates 'the date and time of withdrawal' (ie 11pm on 31 January 2020); or
- the person who is now their spouse or civil partner was the durable partner of the qualifying British citizen before and at 11pm on 31 January 2020; and

199 See *EU Settlement Scheme* main guidance under 'Qualifying residence Continuous qualifying period'.

200 See *EU Settlement Scheme* main guidance under 'Qualifying residence Continuous qualifying period'.

- the applicant is in the UK lawfully under EEA Regs 2016 reg 9(1)–(6); and the spouse or civil partner has been or is being granted ILR/ILE under Appendix EU.

Suitability requirements

2.161 Mandatory grounds for refusal include that the applicant is at the date of decision subject to a deportation or exclusion order or decision (see Appendix EU para EU15).

2.162 Discretionary grounds for refusal (see Appendix EU para EU16) can be invoked where, at the date of the decision, the SSHD is satisfied that it would be proportionate to refuse the application where:

- False or misleading information has been submitted (including submitted to any person to obtain a document used in support of the application), *whether or not to the applicant's knowledge*; and where this is material to the decision whether to grant the application.
- The applicant is subject to a removal decision under the EEA Regs 2016 on grounds of non-exercise or misuse of rights under the Citizens' Rights Directive.
- The applicant has previously been refused admission to the UK on public policy grounds, or had settled status or pre-settled status which was cancelled.
- Refusal of the application is justified either:
  - on grounds of public policy, security or health in respect of conduct committed before 11pm on 31 December 2020 in accordance with EEA Regs 2016 reg 27 (including for those to which they do not apply, in which case reg 27 should be read as if it applied to a person otherwise qualifying for settled or pre-settled status); or
  - on the ground that the decision is conducive to the public good, in respect of conduct committed after 11pm on 31 December 2020.
- The applicant is or would be excluded from protection under the Refugee Convention or from humanitarian protection (ie they are a 'relevant excluded person'):
  - based on conduct committed before 11pm on 31 December 2020 and the public policy grounds apply in accordance with EEA Regs 2016 reg 27 (and where they do not apply, as if that regulation referred to a person eligible for settled or pre-settled status); or
  - based on conduct committed after 11pm on 31 December 2020.

2.163 Applicants are required to disclose past offending in their application and this is checked by Home Office caseworkers for consistency against the Police National Computer (PNC) and other databases. A failure to disclose convictions may cause the applicant to fall foul of the first discretionary ground of refusal; although the guidance accepts that genuine errors will not be penalised. As well as 'checking' the honesty of the applicant, this stage serves as a screening point for deportation or exclusion, since any applicant who served a sentence of imprisonment pursuant to a criminal conviction will, according to the *Suitability guidance*, be referred to Immigration Enforcement. The guidance sets out detailed instructions for the correct approach to those already or previously subject to a deportation action.

2.164 In the case of pending prosecution which could lead to a refusal on suitability grounds, the caseworker must consider whether it is reasonable and proportionate to pause consideration of the application until the outcome of the application is known. Where applications have been paused in this way, it is understood that the Home Office will only accept an update to the PNC as proof of resolution of the criminal proceedings, which has led to substantial delays in re-activating the application.

Lapsing of settled status

2.165 In general, settled status lapses if the holder stays outside the UK for a continuous period of five years (or four years in the case of Swiss nationals or their family members).[201] The exceptions to this include members of HM Forces and Crown servants.[202]

Pre-settled status

Eligibility criteria

2.166 The criteria for pre-settled status (limited leave to remain), which are set out in Appendix EU para EU14, are broadly that the person would

201 Immigration (Leave to Enter and Remain) Order 2000 SI No 1161 art 13(4)(za), inserted by Immigration (European Economic Area Nationals) (EU Exit) Order 2019 SI No 686 art 8, which refers to the status as 'unlimited leave', presumably to distinguish it from ILR granted under the non-Appendix EU rules.

202 See Immigration (Leave to Enter and Remain) Order 2000 arts 13(4)(za), 13A–13C (inserted by Immigration (European Economic Area Nationals) (EU Exit) Order 2019 art 8).

have qualified for ILR/ILE had they completed a continuous qualifying period of five years.

2.167 It should be noted that the Home Office practice appears to be that, where applicants are granted pre-settled status, no refusal letter setting out the reasons for not granting settled status is provided. Reasons should always be sought alongside any applications for administrative review or appeals.

2.168 Following the grant of pre-settled status for five years, an application for settled status must be made before the expiry of that leave. Any application which is made out of time, ie after that leave expires, will have to establish a 'reasonable excuse'. The policy approach to late applications is set out above at paras 2.146–2.151. However, it should be noted that the policy hints at the possibility of the more generous approach of giving applicants 'the benefit of the doubt' being changed in the future.

Documentation of rights under the EU Settlement Scheme – 'digital only' status

2.169 An EU, EEA or Swiss citizen granted status under the EUSS must now use a digital document to 'view and prove' their immigration status and are not issued with a physical document such as a biometric residence card. Non-EU, EEA or Swiss citizen family members can use the view and prove service if they have a UKVI account.[203]

2.170 The view and prove service involves visiting a website on which an individual can apply for a 'share code' to provide to a third party that needs to verify their immigration status, such as a prospective landlord or employer. For individuals having difficulty accessing the internet, there is a telephone line that they can call.

2.171 The Home Office's Policy Equality Statement (PES) for the EUSS[204] describes the view and prove system as 'quicker, more secure and cost effective to enable those granted status under the EUSS to access and share evidence of their immigration status using an online service'. The PES also notes that digital only status 'may put at a particular disadvantage certain protected groups', including adults over 75 years old, the Roma community, women and people with certain disabilities. The EU citizens' rights group, the3million,

203 Home Office guide on using the 'view and prove' system: *Your immigration status: an introduction for EU, EEA and Swiss citizens (accessible version) on GOV.UK* (www.gov.uk).

204 Policy equality statement: *EU Settlement Scheme (accessible version) on GOV.UK* (www.gov.uk).

brought a claim for judicial review challenging the discriminatory impact of the digital only status scheme ahead of it becoming mandatory at the end of the implementation period.[205] However, the claim was dismissed as being premature as the Home Office stated that it had not finalised the scheme, having recently introduced the telephone helpline. The Work Rights Centre research shows that there continue to be significant issues with the view and prove scheme, with 42 per cent of individuals contacting them stating that they struggled to issue a share code.[206]

Challenging adverse decisions under the EU Settlement Scheme

2.172 For applications decided after exit day, ie after 31 January 2020, there is a right of appeal against refusal of that application to the First-tier Tribunal. This is dealt with at paras 2.119–2.229

2.173 Administrative review is also available in most cases, whether the application was made or decided before 31 January 2020. Most decisions to refuse settled status is challengeable in the first instance by way of administrative review, which is governed by Appendix AR (EU) of the Immigration Rules, which sets out decisions that are eligible for administrative review and the formal application requirements, as well as the scope of that review. It is noteworthy that the procedure provides a merits review, and so fresh evidence that was not before the original decision-maker is admissible. The Home Office has also published guidance on administrative review which should be carefully considered alongside the Rules before applying under Appendix AR (EU).[207]

2.174 Where an application is refused on suitability grounds under para EU16 of Appendix EU, or is rejected as invalid, there is no right to an administrative review. It is noted that the appeal rights provided under the Immigration (Citizens' Rights Appeals) (EU Exit) Regulations 2020[208] also exclude decisions as to the validity of an application, although decisions on suitability are not excluded.

205 *R (The3million Ltd) v SSHD* [2021] EWHC 1159 (Admin).

206 Work Rights Centre 'EUSS digital-only status remains an issue for 2 in 5 EU citizens', 5 May 2022, https://www.workrightscentre.org/news/euss-digital-only-status-remains-an-issue-for-2-in-5-eu-citizens.

207 *Administrative review: EU Settlement Scheme*, Home Office.

208 SI No 61.

2.175 Applications for administrative review must be made no more than 28 days after the applicant receives notice of the eligible decision.[209] Decisions to refuse settled status, and any refusal to refuse administrative review in respect of that decision, are challengeable by way of judicial review within three months of the original refusal of settled status. However, given that settled status decisions now give rise to a merits appeal in most cases, there is unlikely to be any reason to have recourse to judicial review save for decisions relating to invalidity of an application. An appeal can be lodged following any adverse administrative review determination, as explained below.

2.176 A Freedom of Information Act response has shown that some 89.5 per cent of initial decisions under the EUSS scheme were overturned on administrative review.[210]

Frontier workers

2.177 'Frontier workers' are EEA nationals who – immediately before 31 December 2020 and continuously thereafter – are not primarily resident in the UK, who are workers or self-employed persons in the UK, or have retained worker or self-employed person status.[211] Their right of entry and residence is protected by Article 10 of the Withdrawal Agreement.

2.178 Under the Citizens' Rights (Frontier Workers) (EU Exit) Regulations 2020,[212] frontier workers can obtain a frontier worker permit, which is valid for two years (in the case of a person who has retained frontier worker status) or five years in any other case. The permit is renewable. Those holding such permits are, in general, exempt from immigration control.[213]

2.179 The criterion of 'not primarily resident' in the UK at the 'relevant date' is satisfied if the person has been present in the UK for less than 180 days in the 12-month period immediately before the day on which

209 Appendix AR (EU) para 34R (IA).

210 FOI Reference 55254, letter from UKVI to Alice Walsh dated 16 October 2019 and annexes.

211 Citizens' Rights (Frontier Workers) (EU Exit) Regulations 2020 reg 3(1) and (2). For worker see paras 2.177–2.181; for self-employed person see paras 2.61–2.65; and for worker or self-employed person who has retained their status see paras 2.78–2.82.

212 SI No 1213.

213 Citizens' Rights (Frontier Workers) (EU Exit) Regulations 2020 reg 5.

the relevant date falls; or they have returned to their country of residence at least – i) once in the six-month period immediately before the day on which the relevant date falls; or ii) twice in the 12-month period immediately before the day on which the relevant date falls, unless there are exceptional reasons for not having done so.[214]

2.180 Frontier workers may retain the status of worker or self-employed person after having ceased work.[215] Regulation 4 sets out the criteria, which echo those applicable to retention of worker/self-employed status in the event of temporary inability to work due to illness or accident, involuntary unemployment, or engaging in vocational training.

2.181 Numerous powers exist to refuse, revoke, remove and deport those holding frontier worker permits: see Part 4 of the Citizens' Rights (Frontier Workers) (EU Exit) Regulations 2020. Distinct rights of appeal are provided to the First-tier Tribunal against these decisions.[216]

Irish citizens

2.182 Irish citizens enjoy a right of residence in the UK based on the 'Common Travel Area' arrangements, which are not reliant on the UK's membership of the EU. Therefore, Irish citizens do not need to apply under the EUSS, but can do so if they wish. The eligible family members of an Irish citizen living in the UK will be able to obtain status under the settled status scheme without the Irish citizen doing so.[217]

2.183 Immigration and Social Security Co-ordination (EU Withdrawal) Act 2020 s2(2) inserts a new section 3ZA into the IA 1971 to provide that an Irish citizen does not require leave to enter or remain unless made subject to a deportation order, or a direction that exclusion is conducive to the public good, or is an excluded person. Since 2007 the UK government's policy has been that Irish citizens would only be deported where a court has recommended deportation when sentencing, or where there are exceptional circumstances in the public interest to order deportation.[218]

214 Citizens' Rights (Frontier Workers) (EU Exit) Regulations 2020 reg 3(3).

215 Citizens' Rights (Frontier Workers) (EU Exit) Regulations 2020 reg 4.

216 See paras 2.219–2.229.

217 *EU Settlement Scheme: EU, other EEA and Swiss citizens and their family members*, Home Office, under the heading 'Who can apply' and 'Irish citizen'.

218 Written Ministerial Statement by the Immigration Minister, Liam Byrne, 19 February 2007.

2.184 Under the Good Friday Agreement, an international treaty, all people of Northern Ireland have the right to remain on the territory whether they identify themselves as Irish, British or both; and the right to be accepted as such. These principles may be in tension with deportation action taken in respect of an Irish citizen who identifies as Irish, in order to defeat deportation to the Republic of Ireland. The Good Friday Agreement precludes exclusion and deportation of Irish citizens from Northern Ireland.

Termination of rights to reside and enforcement powers

2.185 The powers to terminate a right of entry or residence and/or to bring enforcement action against a person depends on whether they hold entry clearance, leave to enter or leave to remain granted under the EUSS, or would be so entitled were they to apply under the Scheme. If they do not benefit from entry and residence rights under the EUSS, then the rules governing termination of leave to remain set out in chapter 1 apply.

2.186 If the person does benefit from entry and residence rights under the Scheme, then the applicable rules depend on the type of enforcement action the Home Office is proposing to take in respect of them, and the timing and/or type of conduct giving rise to the enforcement action. This section will address:

- termination of leave to enter or remain under Appendix EU Annex 3;[219]
- administrative removal;[220]
- deportation arising from criminal and other conduct.[221]

Termination of leave to enter or remain under Appendix EU

2.187 Separate powers apply depending on whether:

- the individual is outside the UK or has just arrived at the port of entry; in either case the power is called 'cancellation';[222] or

219 See paras 2.187–2.193.
220 See para 2.194.
221 See paras 2.195–2.204.
222 See paras 2.188–2.189.

- the individual is in the UK, holds limited leave, and there are issues about the honesty of the person, or their ceasing to meet the applicable requirements, in which case, the power is called 'curtailment';[223] or
- the Home Office wishes to remove indefinite leave to enter or remain, in which case the power is called 'revocation'.[224]

Cancellation of leave because of conduct committed after 11pm on 31 December 2020

2.188 A person who holds limited or indefinite leave granted under Appendix EU 'must' have their leave cancelled on or before their arrival in the UK where the Home Office considers that the person's presence in the UK is not conducive to the public good because of conduct committed after the 'specified date' which is 11pm on 31 December 2020 (see Appendix EU Annex 1).[225]

Cancellation of leave because of conduct committed before 11pm on 31 December 2020

2.189 The limited or indefinite leave of a person, which was granted under Appendix EU, 'may' be cancelled on or before their arrival in the UK where the secretary of state or an immigration officer is 'satisfied that it is proportionate to cancel that leave' where:

- the cancellation is justified on grounds of public policy, public security or public health within the meaning of EEA Regs 2016 reg 27 (which is based on Chapter VI of the Citizens' Rights Directive discussed at paras 2.197–2.204 below);[226]
- false or misleading information, representations or documents were submitted (whether to the Home Office or to any person to obtain any supporting document) which is material to the decision in the application, and whether or not to the applicant's knowledge;[227]
- they cease to meet the requirements of Appendix EU.[228]

223 See paras 2.190–2.192.
224 See para 2.193.
225 Appendix EU Annex 3 para A3.1.
226 Appendix EU Annex 3 para A3.2(a).
227 Appendix EU Annex 3 para A3.2(b).
228 Appendix EU Annex 3 para A3.3.

Curtailment of limited leave

2.190 Limited leave to enter or remain held by a person who is in the UK 'may' be curtailed if it is proportionate to curtail that leave where:

- false and misleading information has been submitted in relation to the application which is material to the decision, whether to the applicant's knowledge (as under Annex A para A3.2(b) above);[229]
- the person ceases to meet the requirements of Appendix EU;[230] and
- curtailment is justified on the grounds that 'it is more likely than not that, after the specified date, the person has entered, attempted to enter or assisted another person to enter or to attempt to enter, a marriage, civil partnership or durable partnership of convenience'.[231]

2.191 Whether a marriage is one of convenience has been the subject of much litigation under the misuse of rights provisions under the EEA Regs 2016. The term was defined at EEA Regs 2016 reg 2 in the following terms:

> . . . 'marriage of convenience' includes a marriage entered into for the purpose of using these Regulations, or any other right conferred by the EU Treaties, as a means to circumvent–
> (a) immigration rules applying to non-EEA nationals (such as any applicable requirement under the 1971 Act to have leave to enter or remain in the United Kingdom); or
> (b) any other criteria that the party to the marriage of convenience would otherwise have to meet in order to enjoy a right to reside under these Regulations or the EU Treaties.

2.192 The burden of proof to establish that a marriage is one of convenience rests on the Home Secretary.[232] Surprisingly, a couple may enter

229 Appendix EU Annex 3 para A3.4(a).

230 Appendix EU Annex 3 para A3.4(c). in *Chenchooliah v Minister for Justice and Equality* Case C-94/18 [2020] 1 WLR 1801, CJEU the Grand Chamber of the CJEU ruled that the procedural protections in Articles 15, 30 and 31 of the Citizens' Rights Directive applied 'by analogy' to expulsion decisions taken on the basis that a third country national was no longer a beneficiary of a right of residence under the Directive (and not on the grounds of public policy, security or health). A full right of appeal is afforded in the case of a curtailment of leave: see paras 2.219–2.229 below.

231 Appendix EU Annex 3 para A3.4(b).

232 *Sadovska and another v SSHD* [2017] UKSC 54, [2017] Imm AR 1473. See also guidance of the European Commission issued in respect of the Citizens' Rights Directive (COM) 2009 313) 2 July 2009 which sets out criteria governing whether marriages are of convenience.

into a marriage of convenience, even if they are in a genuine and subsisting relationship. In *Molina*,[233] the Upper Tribunal distinguished between 'sham marriages' under the IAA 1999, and a marriage of convenience under the regulations. Whilst a sham marriage requires there be no genuine relationship between the parties, a marriage of convenience is one where the intention of the parties is to gain an immigration advantage. From 1 January 2021, EEA citizens (except Irish citizens and those with status under the EUSS, or a pending application to the scheme) are liable to be subject to the Home Office's 'sham marriage referral and investigations scheme'.[234] There is no automatic right to disclosure of Home Office records of interview with a suspected party to a marriage of convenience.[235]

Revocation of indefinite leave

2.193 Indefinite leave to enter or remain granted under Appendix EU 'may' be revoked where the secretary of state is satisfied that it is proportionate to revoke that leave where:

- the person is liable to deportation, but cannot be deported for legal reasons;[236] or
- the indefinite leave to enter or remain was obtained by deception.[237]

Administrative removal

2.194 Under IAA 1999 s10, persons who require leave to remain in the UK but do not have it are liable to enforced removal under that provision. This in principle applies to EU, EEA and Swiss nationals present in the UK without leave from 1 July 2021. However, as noted at paras 2.146–2.151 above, the general deadline of 30 June 2021 for submitting a late application to the EUSS is subject to various exceptions. As

233 *R (Molina) v SSHD* [2017] EWHC 1730 (Admin); see also *R (Seferi) v SSHD* [2018] EWHC 287 (Admin).

234 Immigration and Social Security Co-ordination (EU Withdrawal) Act 2020 (Consequential, Saving, Transitional and Transitory Provisions) (EU Exit) Regulations 2020 SI No 1309; see also Home Office, *Marriage Investigations* guidance, 31 December 2020, pp6–7.

235 *Miah (interviewer's comments: disclosure: fairness)* [2014] UKUT 515 (IAC); *Re Nimo (appeals: duty of disclosure: Ghana)* [2020] UKUT 88 (IAC).

236 Appendix EU Annex 3 para A3.5(a).

237 Appendix EU Annex 3 para A3.5(b). The provisions of para A3.5 are consistent with NIAA 2002 s76.

noted above, the policy framework presently expressly accepts that, where it appears to immigration enforcement officers that a person encountered by them from 1 July 2021 may benefit from rights under Appendix EU, the person should be given 28 days to make a late application under the EUSS. No removal can take place while any such application, or onward appeal, remains outstanding.[238]

Deportation

2.195 The test for the deportation of EEA and Swiss nationals and their family members, based on criminal and other conduct, depends on whether the conduct giving rise to deportation action occurred before or after 11pm on 31 December 2020. In the former case, the applicable rules are the EEA deportation provisions notably contained in EEA Regs 2016 reg 27, which is derived from Chapter VI of the Citizens' Rights Directive.[239] In the latter case, the domestic deportation provisions apply,[240] which are much stricter.

Deportation because of conduct occurring after 11pm on 31 December 2020

2.196 Where the secretary of state deems the deportation of an EEA and Swiss nationals and/or their family members to be 'conducive to the public good', such persons are 'liable to deportation' under IA 1971 s3(5). A decision under section 3(5) can only be made on the basis of conduct occurring *after* 11pm on 31 December 2020, so far as EEA/ Swiss nationals and their family members are concerned. Any conduct engaged in before that point in time must be addressed under IA 1971 s3(5A) which applies the protections in the Citizens' Rights Directive to such decisions, in accordance with Article 20 of the Withdrawal Agreement[241] (see next section). Similarly, court recommended deportation is precluded in respect of a 'relevant person's' conduct occurring before the expiry of the implementation period (new section 3(6A) of the IA 1971).

2.197 In addition, where an EEA national or their family members have been convicted of an offence and sentenced to a period of imprisonment of at least 12 months, they are subject to the automatic

238 Withdrawal Agreement Article 18(3).
239 Withdrawal Agreement Article 20(1).
240 Withdrawal Agreement Article 20(2).
241 And its equivalents in Article 19 of the EEA EFTA Separation Agreement; and Article 17 or 20(3) of the Swiss Citizens' Rights Agreement.

deportation regime under UK Borders Act 2007 s32, to which the exceptions in section 33 of that Act apply (see, relevantly, Exception 7 at section 33(6B)–(6D)).

Deportation because of conduct occurring before 11pm on 31 December 2020

2.198 By IA 1971 s3(5A) and Article 20 of the Withdrawal Agreement, conduct occurring before 11pm on 31 December 2020 must be dealt with in accordance with the EEA deportation test, which provides significant protection to EEA nationals and their families against expulsion from the host member state, as compared with the UK's domestic deportation regime. Articles 27 and 28 of the Citizens' Rights Directive are the key provisions from which the following general principles can be derived:

- Member states can only rely on limited grounds to expel an EEA national, namely public policy, public security or public health (Article 27(1)).
- An expulsion decision cannot be taken to pursue economic ends (Article 27(2)).
- An expulsion decision taken on public policy or public security shall comply with the principle of proportionality (Article 27(2)).
- Previous criminal convictions alone are not grounds for an expulsion decision (Article 27(2)).
- Decisions must be taken on the individual's current circumstances and personal conduct (Article 27(2)).
- Relevant considerations are length of residence, age, health, family and economic situation, social and cultural integration (Article 28(1)).
- The same principles apply in cases involving the proposed expulsion of a person holding derived rights of residence. That is by virtue of TFEU Articles 20/21 directly, rather than via Articles 27 and 28.[242]
- The level of protection from expulsion increases with the length of residence in the host member state so that:
  - a person with permanent residence cannot be expelled unless there are *serious grounds* of public policy or public security (Article 28(2));

242 *Robinson (Jamaica) v SSHD* [2020] UKSC 53, [2021] Imm AR 607.

- an EU citizen with ten years' residence cannot be expelled unless there are *imperative grounds* of public security (Article 28(3)(a));
- an EU citizen under the age of 18 cannot be expelled unless there are *imperative grounds* of public security except if expulsion is necessary for the best interests of the child as provided for under the UNCRC (Article 28(3)(b)).

2.199 The Home Office has published detailed guidance relating to decisions taken on grounds of public policy, public security or public health.[243]

2.200 If a person is subject to an expulsion decision, it is important first to ascertain what level of protection they enjoy. This can be a painstaking task, of compiling ten or five years' worth of records, showing the exercise of treaty rights. This is a further reason why it may be (or have been) advisable for EEA nationals and their family members to apply for documentation confirming their right to reside.

2.201 To qualify for enhanced protection from expulsion – ie requiring 'imperative grounds of public safety' after ten years – the CJEU has clarified in *Vomero*[244] that this means the EU national must first acquire permanent residence: ten years' residence in the host member state is not sufficient. The period of ten years is assessed from the date on which the initial expulsion decision is adopted; time spent in prison does not count towards accrual of the ten years.[245] However, a term of imprisonment will not automatically break a ten-year residence period that was accrued before the imprisonment. What the court must look at is the extent to which integrative links have been broken in consequence of the imprisonment.

2.202 Detention in a young offenders institution (YOI) for the purposes of a detention and training order may give rise to a break continuity of residence for the purposes of determining whether a person has enhanced protection from deportation.[246] However, the overall assessment of integration, including taking account of the best interests of the child,[247] still needs to be conducted.

2.203 Articles 27 and 28 of the Citizens' Rights Directive were transposed into domestic law by EEA Regs 2016 reg 27, which broadly

243 *Public policy, public security or public health decisions*, Home Office.

244 *B v Land Baden-Wurttemberg; SSHD v Vomero* Joined Cases C-316/16 and C?424/16 [2019] QB 126, CJEU.

245 *Hafeez v SSHD* [2020] EWCA Civ 406, [2020] Imm AR 1020.

246 *SSHD v Viscu* [2019] EWCA Civ 1052, [2019] Imm AR 1298.

247 *Viscu* at para 51.

reflected the text of those provisions, save for one important difference. Regulation 27(8) directed that a court or tribunal in considering whether the requirements of the regulation are met must (in particular) have regard to the considerations set out in Schedule 1. These were public policy principles to which parliament required the tribunal to have regard. In this respect, they mirrored the provisions in NIAA 2002 s117B (see chapter 1).

2.204 The guidance notes that, whether the criminality or conduct occurred both before and after 11pm on 31 December 2020, the caseworker is given two options:

- either consider the totality of the conduct under the public policy, public security or public health test; or
- consider *only* the conduct that occurred after 31 December 2020 on the ground that it is conducive to the public good and exclude reliance on the conduct that occurred prior to that date.[248]

Appeals

2.205 Distinct appeals regimes apply to refusal decisions made under Appendix EU of the Immigration Rules, and – now of transitional and historic interest only – EEA decisions made under the EEA Regs 2016. Those appellate regimes are described below.

Challenging a negative decision under the Immigration (European Economic Area) Regulations 2016

2.206 Such decisions would only be made in response to an application for a residence permit under the EEA Regs 2016, which will have pre-dated the UK's exit from the EU. There is a right of appeal against an 'EEA decision' under EEA Regs 2016 Part 6, to the First-tier Tribunal (Immigration and Asylum Chamber).[249] In a case which raises national security issues or the relationship with another country, the right of appeal is to the Special Immigration Appeals Commission.[250]

2.207 An 'EEA decision' is defined under reg 2 as a decision under the regulations that concerns:

- a person's entitlement to be admitted to the UK;

248 *Public policy, public security or public health decisions* guidance, Home Office: see under heading 'Conduct committed after 31 December 2020'.

249 EEA Regs 2016 reg 36.

250 EEA Regs 2016 reg 38.

- a person's entitlement to be issued with or have renewed, or not to have revoked, an EEA family permit, a registration certificate, residence card, derivative residence card, document certifying permanent residence or permanent residence card (but does not include a decision that an application for the above documentation is invalid);
- a person's removal from the UK; or
- the cancellation, under reg 25, of a person's right to reside in the UK; but
- does not include a decision to reject an application under reg 26(4) (misuse of a right to reside: material change of circumstances), or any decisions under reg 33 (human rights considerations and interim orders to suspend removal) or reg 41 (temporary admission to submit case in person). Regulation 2 was amended on 28 March 2019 so as to remove an exclusion on the right of appeal against decisions concerning extended family members.[251]

2.208 The only ground of appeal that may be raised in an appeal against an EEA decision is that the decision breaches the person's rights under EU law.[252] A person cannot rely on ECHR Article 8 as a distinct ground of appeal against a refusal of an EEA decision unless a section 120 'one stop' notice has been served and responded to;[253] or unless the Home Office has refused a 'human rights claim'. Human rights claims are discussed in detail in chapter 3.

2.209 Where an appeal has been or could be made against an EEA decision, the Home Secretary has the power to issue a certificate under reg 33 on the basis that removal before the person's appeal has been determined would not be in breach of the ECHR. Removal pursuant to a reg 33 certificate is open to judicial review, in the Upper Tribunal, which may suspend removal in the circumstances set out in reg 33(4). Where removal cannot be so suspended, the person can be removed before the appeal under EEA Regs 2016 Part 6 has been heard. The person will then have to bring their appeal from outside the UK, subject to being granted permission to re-enter for their appeal hearing under reg 41, addressed below.

251 Immigration (European Economic Area Nationals) (EU Exit) Regulations 2019 Part 3 reg 3(2).

252 *Amirteymour v SSHD* [2017] EWCA Civ 353; *Munday (EEA decision: ground of appeal)* [2019] UKUT 91 (IAC).

253 Meaning that the Home Office has served a notice under NIAA 2002 s120, and the recipient has in return served on the Home Office a statement of additional grounds indicating their reliance on ECHR Article 8.

2.210 The Home Office has published guidance on what decision-makers are required to consider when certifying an appeal.[254] The test for certification is that it would not give risk to a breach of Human Rights Act 1998 s6. The Home Office often rely on the need for 'serious, irreversible harm' (reg 33(3)); but this is illustrative, rather than exhaustive. Under the Home Office policy, if a person has the right to permanent residence and has not been sentenced to a period of four years' imprisonment, their case will not usually be certified. Certification must comply with the principle of proportionality and be based solely on the personal conduct of the individual, in accordance with Article 27 the Citizens' Rights Directive: see the *Hafeez* case.[255]

2.211 Two further cases which are important for practitioners when preparing representations as to why certification is not appropriate are *Kiarie and Byndloss*[256] and *OO (Nigeria)*.[257]

2.212 In *Kiarie*, the Supreme Court held that NIAA 2002 s94B (which allows for out of country appeals and is therefore analogous with reg 33) was not unlawful. However, the court did find that the out of country appeal regime did not provide an effective remedy, in particular where the person concerned cannot give oral evidence. The difference under the EEA regime is that re-entry is possible under reg 41 (discussed below). The case is nonetheless helpful in showing the limits of out of country appeals on the right to an effective remedy under the procedural requirements of ECHR Article 8, for example, the ability to give instructions to an advisor; the limits to technology such as Skype or video calling to give oral evidence etc.

2.213 In *OO (Nigeria)*, the Court of Appeal gave guidance on the interaction between the power to certify an appeal out of country (albeit under NIAA 2002 s94) and the ECHR Article 8 rights of foreign criminals and their children, and the impact of BCIA 2009 s55. On the facts of *OO*, the court concluded it would be a disproportionate interference with the ECHR Article 8 rights of a foreign criminal convicted of acquiring criminal property and sentenced to 2½ years' imprisonment, pending his appeal against deportation. The best interests of his son prevailed over the strong public interest in removal, given the mitigation as regards the offence, the offender's

254 *Regulations 33 and 41 of the Immigration (European Economic Area) Regulations 2016*, Home Office.

255 *Hafeez v SSHD* [2020] EWCA Civ 406, [2020] Imm AR 1020.

256 *R (Kiarie and Byndloss) v SSHD* [2017] UKSC 42, [2017] Imm AR 1299.

257 *R (OO (Nigeria)) v SSHD* [2017] EWCA Civ 338.

conduct in relation to it and conduct since it was committed. The certificate was quashed accordingly.

2.214 Importantly the court held that (at para 62):

> A case based on the best interests of an affected child . . . would be much more powerful if it were supported by evidence showing some specific reason why the child would suffer during a period of interim removal. By itself evidence that the child would suffer from separation from the parent risks being too general, and too commonplace, to prevail over the public interest in removal.

2.215 Practitioners therefore will need to consider what particular evidence is necessary to put before the decision-maker *prior to* the certification decision. Asserting that it is not generally in a child's best interests to be separated for an interim period will not suffice.

2.216 As noted above, one of the key differences under the EEA Regs 2016 as compared with the regime under the NIAA 2002 is that a person can apply under reg 41 for re-entry to be present at his appeal. Regulation 41(3) provides that 'the Secretary of State must grant such a request' unless the person's appearance 'may cause serious troubles to public policy or public security'. In *Gabor*,[258] the Upper Tribunal made clear that 'proportionality is not the test, and the cost of facilitating the applicant's appearance is not a relevant consideration'.

2.217 Under reg 37, some appeals are always out of country. A person may not appeal while in the UK against a decision:

- to refuse to admit that person to the UK;
- to revoke that person's admission;
- to make an exclusion order against that person;
- to refuse to revoke a deportation or exclusion decision;
- to refuse to issue an EEA family permit;
- to revoke, refuse to issue or renew a document where the person was outside the UK at the time of the decision;
- to remove a person who entered the UK in breach of a deportation order where they were not entitled to be admitted.

2.218 An appeal against an EEA decision must be filed with the First-tier Tribunal (Immigration and Asylum Chamber) within 14 days of the decision being sent to them, where the appellant is in the UK; within 28 days of their departure from the UK where they are precluded from appealing from within the UK by provisions of the NIAA 2002; or in any other case, not later than 28 days after they receive the

258 *R (Gabor) v SSHD (reg 29AA: interpretation)* [2017] UKUT 287 (IAC).

notice of decision.[259] Note that different rules apply to appeals against settled status decisions, as set out below.

Challenging a negative decision in relation to settled or pre-settled status

2.219 When first piloted, the government had indicated that a refusal under the EUSS would not attract a right of appeal, but instead would be challengeable via administrative review in the first instance, and ultimately by judicial review. However, Article 21 of the Withdrawal Agreement contains a commitment that EU citizens and their family members *do* have the right to an appeal against a decision restricting their residence rights under Part Two of the Agreement.

2.220 Accordingly, the Immigration (Citizens' Rights Appeals) (EU Exit) Regulations 2020 came into force on 31 January 2020,[260] which create a right of appeal to the First-tier Tribunal for those who are refused settled or pre-settled status. The Regulations indicate that only applications submitted *on or after* exit day will attract a right of appeal.[261]

2.221 Appealable decisions are as follows:

- Where a person makes a valid application,[262] on or after exit day, for leave to enter or remain under 'residence scheme immigration rules'[263] they will have a right of appeal against a decision:[264]
  - to vary their existing leave to enter or remain granted under the residence scheme immigration rules so they do not have any leave, or to cancel such leave;
  - not to grant any leave in response to the application; or

259 Tribunal Procedure (First-tier Tribunal) (Immigration and Asylum Chamber) Rules 2014 SI No 2604 (as amended) r19.

260 Made under EUWAA 2020 s11. The Regulations were amended by the Immigration (Citizens' Rights etc) (EU Exit) Regulations 2020 SI No 1372; and the Citizens' Rights (Frontier Workers) (EU Exit) Regulations 2020.

261 Immigration (Citizens' Rights Appeals) (EU Exit) Regulations 2020 reg 3(2) provides that 'relevant application' means an application for leave to enter or remain in the UK made under residence scheme immigration rules on or after exit day.

262 The corollary of this is that there is no appeal right against a decision to treat the application as invalid.

263 Defined in EUWAA 2020 s17(1) (broadly, as Appendix EU to the Immigration Rules and any other rules having effect in connection with the UK's withdrawal from the EU).

264 Immigration (Citizens' Rights Appeals) (EU Exit) Regulations 2020 reg 3.

  - not to grant indefinite leave to enter or remain, where limited leave is granted, or the applicant had limited leave when they made the application.
- There is also a right of appeal against a decision to revoke indefinite leave to enter or remain under NIAA 2002 s76(1) or (2), which was granted under residence scheme immigration rules.[265]
- A person may also appeal against decisions made in respect of applications under 'relevant entry clearance immigration rules',[266] namely:[267]
  - a refusal of the application, or a decision to cancel or revoke scheme entry clearance;
  - where the applicant holds scheme entry clearance, to refuse leave to enter;[268]
  - to cancel or vary leave to enter which was previously held having arrived in the UK with scheme entry clearance.
- A decision made on or after 31 January 2020, to make a deportation order under IA 1971 s5(1) in respect of a person is appealable where the person has EUSS leave, or is in the UK having arrived with EUSS entry clearance.[269] This appeal right does not apply where the removal decision is taken under EEA Regs 2016 reg 23(6)(b) (removal on grounds of public policy, public security or public health).
- Various decisions taken under the Citizens' Rights (Frontier Workers) (EU Exit) Regulations 2020.[270]
- Various decisions taken in relation to persons with a healthcare right of entry granted under Appendix S2 Healthcare visitor of the Immigration Rules.[271]

2.222 Appeals will be to the First-tier Tribunal (Immigration and Asylum Chamber), save for cases that are certified by the secretary of state on grounds relating to national security or international relations, in

265 Immigration (Citizens' Rights Appeals) (EU Exit) Regulations 2020 reg 4.

266 Defined in EUWAA 2020 s17(2) as any immigration rules which are identified as having effect in connection with the granting of entry clearance for the purposes of acquiring leave to remain in the UK by virtue of residence scheme immigration rules.

267 Immigration (Citizens' Rights Appeals) (EU Exit) Regulations 2020 reg 5.

268 Under Immigration (Leave to Enter and Remain) Order 2000 art 7(1).

269 Immigration (Citizens' Rights Appeals) (EU Exit) Regulations 2020 reg 6.

270 Immigration (Citizens' Rights Appeals) (EU Exit) Regulations 2020 regs 6A–6E.

271 Immigration (Citizens' Rights Appeals) (EU Exit) Regulations 2020 regs 6G–6J.

which case it will be Special Immigration and Asylum Commission (SIAC).[272]

2.223 There are two grounds of appeal against any such decision:[273]

- either that the decision breaches any rights which the appellant has by virtue of the Withdrawal Agreement; or
- that the decision was not in accordance with the relevant immigration rule or legislation under which it was made.

In addition, where an NIAA 2002 s120 notice has been served,[274] the person may by their responding section 120 statement raise additional grounds of appeal that are specified in NIAA 2002 s84, which include human rights grounds. The tribunal may consider post-decision evidence up to the date of hearing: reg 9(4)–(5), although procedural restrictions on the raising of 'new matters' apply, as under the principal appeals regime under NIAA 2002 s85.

2.224 Appeals may be brought from either within or outside the UK; and there is no requirement for continued presence within the UK for the duration of the appeal as with the principal appeals regime under the NIAA 2002.[275] Leaving the UK does not mean that the appeal is abandoned.[276]

2.225 Where an appealable decision is made and a decision has also been made (whether before or after the appealable decision) to make a deportation order under IA 1971 s5(1), the secretary of state may certify that the person's removal before the appeal has been determined would not be in breach of the Human Rights Act 1998, under reg 16(3). In relation to the lawfulness of such certifications, see the discussion relating to *Kiarie and Byndloss* discussed at paras 2.211–2.115 above. Only judicial review of the certificate is available.

2.226 Where such a certification is made, the person has a right to return to the UK in order to attend their appeal hearing in person, unless their return may cause serious troubles to public policy or public security. Where a person is permitted to return to the UK to attend their appeal hearing, they will be admitted on immigration

272 Immigration (Citizens' Rights Appeals) (EU Exit) Regulations 2020 reg 7 and Sch 1.

273 Immigration (Citizens' Rights Appeals) (EU Exit) Regulations 2020 reg 8.

274 See para 2.208.

275 Immigration (Citizens' Rights Appeals) (EU Exit) Regulations 2020 reg 14.

276 Immigration (Citizens' Rights Appeals) (EU Exit) Regulations 2020 reg 13(5).

bail for the duration of their time in the UK.[277] This reflects the position for deportation appeals under the EEA Regs 2016.

2.227 There are alternative provisions governing the place from which appeals may be brought in national security cases, and a limited right of review of 'out of country appeal' certifications which are not outlined here.[278]

2.228 The First-tier Tribunal (Immigration and Asylum Chamber) Rules 2014 set out, in rule 19(3A)–(3E), dedicated time limits for the bringing of appeals under the 2020 Regulations against what are called 'citizens' rights immigration decisions'. The time limits are as follows:

- if the person is in the UK, within 14 days after the decision notice is sent to the appellant;
- if the person is outside the UK, not later than 28 days after the person receives the notice of decision.

2.229 However, where the person has applied administrative review of the decision under Appendix AR (EU) of the Immigration Rules, and had not appealed to the FTT before doing so, the time limits for filing the notice of appeal with the FTT are:

- if the person is in the UK, within 14 days after the SSHD's decision on the administrative review is sent to the appellant;
- if the person is outside the UK, not later than 28 days after the person receives the SSHD's decision on the application for administrative review.

277 Immigration (Citizens' Rights Appeals) (EU Exit) Regulations 2020 reg 12 and Sch 3 para 1.

278 Immigration (Citizens' Rights Appeals) (EU Exit) Regulations 2020 reg 15.

CHAPTER 3

Asylum and international protection law

Shu Shin Luh
with Irena Sabic KC and Louise Hooper

continued

Key points

- The UN Geneva Convention of 1951 Relating to the Status of Refugees, as amended by the Protocol to the Convention 1967, provides the foundation for the way in which the UK treats those who enter with a view to seeking protection from persecution.[1]
- However, the UK's legal framework on conferring international protection to those seeking asylum from persecution has been influenced by European Union (EU) law, elements of which remain relevant, notwithstanding the UK's departure from the EU.[2]
- The domestic basis for claiming asylum in the UK is found in the Immigration Rules. What it means to claim asylum and the circumstances in which asylum will be granted, or leave granted on human rights grounds, are discussed at paras 3.31–3.66.
- The procedure for making such claims, and the decision-making process, are discussed at paras 3.67–3.102.
- Claims may be declared 'inadmissible' where the secretary of state takes the view that the applicant has a connection with a safe third country.[3]
- Positive decisions on asylum or related claims should result in a grant of leave.[4] Adverse decisions may be challengeable by means of statutory appeal or judicial review.[5]

Introduction

3.1 The United Nations (UN) Universal Declaration of Human Rights (UDHR)[6] at Article 14 refers to a right to 'seek and to enjoy in other countries asylum from persecution' – but does not define the grounds of persecution. It is in the specialist international and regional conventions that the 'refugee' is given legal meaning. It is this legal meaning that governs the way in which the UK treats those who enter with a view to seeking protection from persecution.

1 See paras 3.4–3.14.
2 See paras 3.15–3.30.
3 See paras 3.131–3.142.
4 See paras 3.103–3.117.
5 See paras 3.118–3.130.
6 Available at: www.un.org/en/about-us/universal-declaration-of-human-rights.

3.2 The main legal reference point is the UN Geneva Convention of 1951 Relating to the Status of Refugees, as amended by the Protocol to the Convention 1967 (collectively known as 'the Refugee Convention').[7] However, the UK's legal framework on conferring international protection to those seeking asylum from persecution is also influenced by EU law. Although the UK has exited the EU, it remains relevant to consider the extent to which retained EU law concerning the legal framework on asylum and international protection affects the rights and entitlements of individuals seeking protection in the UK.

3.3 This chapter provides an outline of the legal framework applicable to all of these people who may seek asylum or other forms of international protection to the extent that it is relevant to individuals' ability to access support. It will cover: 1) the international law on refugees; 2) the domestic law on asylum and international protection; 3) the procedure for making protection claim; and 4) the exclusion, revocation and cessation of protection status.

International law on refugees

The Refugee Convention

3.4 The key international instrument is the Refugee Convention. In broad terms, the Refugee Convention provides a definition of a 'refugee', creates exclusions from the definition and sets out circumstances when a person may cease to be a refugee,[8] and defines the duties owed to and by refugees vis-à-vis their host states.

3.5 A 'refugee' is defined under the Refugee Convention as applying to any person who:

> . . . owing to well-founded fear of being persecuted for reasons of race, religion, nationality, membership of a particular social group or political opinion, is outside the country of his nationality and is unable or, owing to such fear, is unwilling to avail himself of the protection of that country; or who, not having a nationality and being outside the country of his former habitual residence as a result of such events, is unable or, owing to such fear, is unwilling to return to it.[9]

7 Available at: www.unhcr.org/uk/1951-refugee-convention.html.

8 Refugee Convention Article 1.

9 Refugee Convention Article 1A(2).

3.6 The definition has itself changed over time. Originally Article 1A(2) began with the words: 'As a result of events occurring before 1 January 1951' and Article 1B had a geographical limitation to Europe. Most state parties to the 1951 Refugee Convention have, by ratifying the Protocol Relating to the Status of Refugees of 1967 without reservation, agreed to remove the temporal and geographical limitations to the refugee definition.

3.7 There are certain people excluded from the protection under the Refugee Convention. These are listed in Articles 1C–1F. In particular, under Article 1F, the convention will not apply to any person with respect to whom there are 'serious reasons' for considering that they have committed a crime against peace, a war crime, or a crime against humanity, a serious non-political crime outside the country of refuge prior to their admission to that country as a refugee, or have been guilty of acts contrary to the purposes and principles of the UN.

3.8 The principal duty owed to refugees is that under Article 33(1) of *non-refoulement*, defined as the expulsion or return of refugees in any manner whatsoever to the frontiers of territories where their lives or freedom would be threatened on account of their race, religion, nationality, membership of a particular social group or political opinion. However, Article 33(2) excludes the benefit of this provision from being claimed by a refugee whom there are reasonable grounds for regarding as a danger to the security of the country in which he or she is or who, having been convicted by a final judgment of a particularly serious crime, constitutes a danger to the community of that country. The principle of *non-refoulement* effectively requires a state to determine an asylum claim made by someone within its territory (including the border or transit zone at an airport).

3.9 Protection against refoulement is not, however, the only duty owed by signatory states to the Refugee Convention. As a party to the Refugee Convention, the UK must afford all the convention rights to anyone who is a refugee within the meaning of Article 1A to avoid a breach of the UK's international obligations. Article 3 requires states to apply the provisions of the convention to refugees without discrimination as to race, religion or country of origin.

3.10 The Refugee Convention acknowledges that some asylum-seekers may enter a country illegally. Article 31 outlines a state's obligations when it comes to the treatment of those seeking refugee by entering a state in a way that would usually be unlawful. The provision states that:

> 1. The Contracting States shall not impose penalties, on account of their illegal entry or presence, on refugees who, coming directly from a territory where their life or freedom was threatened in the sense of article 1, enter or are present in their territory without authorization, provided they present themselves without delay to the authorities and show good cause for their illegal entry or presence.
> 2. The Contracting States shall not apply to the movements of such refugees restrictions other than those which are necessary and such restrictions shall only be applied until their status in the country is regularized or they obtain admission into another country. The Contracting States shall allow such refugees a reasonable period and all the necessary facilities to obtain admission into another country.

3.11 Article 31(1) extends to the territory under a state's control. Although expressed in terms of the 'refugee', this provision would be devoid of all effect unless it is also extended to asylum-seekers, or in the words of the Divisional Court in *Adimi*,[10] to 'presumptive refugees', those who claim asylum in good faith. In respect of the argument that asylum-seekers and refugees should claim in the first safe country, the Divisional Court held that:

> Some element of choice is indeed open to refugees as to where they may properly claim asylum. I conclude that any merely short term stopover en route to such intended sanctuary cannot forfeit the protection of [Article 31], and that the main touchstones by which exclusion from protection should be judged are the length of stay in the intermediate country, the reasons for delaying there (even a substantial delay in an unsafe third country would be reasonable were the time spent trying to acquire the means of travelling on), and whether or not the refugee sought or found there protection de jure or de facto from the persecution they were fleeing.[11]

3.12 *Adimi* reflects the fact that there is no requirement under international law for refugees to claim asylum in the first safe country they reach. Article 31 exists in recognition that there are no safe and legal routes to travel to the UK (or other countries) for the vast majority of refugees.

3.13 Refugees who come to the UK in circumstances as outlined in Article 31(1) have a statutory defence against certain immigration offences related to document fraud and illegal entry under Immigration and Asylum Act (IAA) 1999 s31.

3.14 Where someone is recognised as a refugee and granted asylum, signatory states are under a duty to secure equal treatment with own

10 *R v Uxbridge Magistrates' Court ex p Adimi* [1999] EWHC Admin 765.

11 At para 18.

nationals, or sometimes with other lawfully resident third country nationals, in respect of religion, personal status, property, freedom of association, gainful occupation, welfare, administrative measures and the issue of special travel documents to be used in place of the refugee's national passport.[12]

EU asylum framework

3.15 The three key directives comprising the EU's asylum policy framework as applicable in the UK are:

- EU Reception Directive;[13]
- EU Qualification Directive;[14]
- EU Procedures Directive.[15]

3.16 During the implementation period following the UK's departure from the EU,[16] the UK is bound to ensure that the results of the directives are achieved, although it is for the UK to choose the form and method of the implementation.[17]

3.17 Additionally, European Union (Withdrawal) Act (EUWA) 2018 s4 provides for the retention and continued effect in domestic law of some EU law after Britain's exit from the EU on 31 December 2020. EUWA 2018 s4(2)(b) retains all 'rights, powers, liabilities, obligations, restrictions, remedies or procedures' which arise under an EU directive and are 'of a kind recognised by the European Court or any court or tribunal in the United Kingdom in a case decided before

12 Refugee Convention Articles 4–30.

13 The full title is Council Directive 2003/9/EC of 27 January 2003 laying down minimum standards for the reception of asylum seekers, https://eur-lex.europa.eu/legal-content/EN/ALL/?uri=celex%3A32003L0009.

14 The full title is Council Directive 2004/83/EC of 29 April 2004 on minimum standards for the qualification and status of third country nationals or stateless persons as refugees or as persons who otherwise need international protection and the content of the protection granted, https://eur-lex.europa.eu/legal-content/en/TXT/?uri=CELEX%3A32004L0083.

15 The full title is Council Directive 2005/85/EC of 1 December 2005 on minimum standards on procedures in Member States for granting and withdrawing refugee status, https://eur-lex.europa.eu/legal-content/EN/ALL/?uri=CELEX%3A32005L0085.

16 See Agreement on the withdrawal of the United Kingdom of Great Britain and Northern Ireland from the European Union and the European Atomic Energy Community (Treaty Series No 3 (2020), CP 219, Volume 1) ('Withdrawal Agreement') Article 127; EUWA 2018 s1A; and paras 2.8–2.13.

17 Treaty of the Functioning of the European Union (TFEU) Article 288.

completion day (whether or not as an essential part of the decision in the case)'.

3.18 The Qualification, Procedures and Reception Directives were retained by EUWA 2018 s4, at least until 30 December 2020.[18] Section 4 of the EUWA 2018 provided for retention where the rights, obligations and procedures set out in the directives are clearly 'of a kind' recognised on numerous occasions by both UK courts and the CJEU (to give just a few examples: *R (MN) v SSHD*,[19] *AS (Egypt) v Advocate General for Scotland*[20] and *SSHD and G v R and H*[21]). This is important in that, as retained EU law, the directives impact on the interpretation of the Refugee Convention, and the relevant parts of the Immigration Rules[22] must be read in line with the directives: *TG (interaction of directives and rules)*.[23]

3.19 The question of whether these directives are now retained EU law has been called into question by the Divisional Court in *R (AAA (Syria)) v SSHD*.[24] It was argued by one of the claimants in that case that the Immigration Rules permitting for the inadmissibility of asylum claims (discussed further at paras 3.131–3.142 below), on which the scheme to relocate asylum-seekers to Rwanda is based, were contrary to requirements under Articles 25 and 27 of the Procedures Directive and therefore unlawful. The details of the directive are discussed below at para 3.24. For this purpose, and in brief, Article 25 identifies the circumstances in which an asylum claim may be treated as inadmissible. Article 25(2)(c) provides that a member state may consider an application for asylum as inadmissible if a country which is not a member state is considered a safe third country for the applicant pursuant to Article 27. Article 27 defines the 'safe third country concept'. It was argued by the claimant that the criteria set down in Article 27 were not met by the Immigration Rules which address inadmissibility of an asylum claim. The claimant relied on EUWA 2018 s4 to state that the Procedures Directive remains 'retained EU law' and therefore the compatibility or otherwise of domestic immigration rules on inadmissibility of asylum claims falls to be considered against the legal framework set down by

18 *G v G* [2021] UKSC 9 at para 84.
19 [2020] EWCA Civ 1746, [2021] 1 WLR 1956.
20 [2020] CSOH 94.
21 [2020] EWCA Civ 1001, [2021] Imm AR 1.
22 HC 395. Available at: www.gov.uk/guidance/immigration-rules.
23 [2016] UKUT 374 (IAC) at para 3. See further paras 2.25–2.29 on the interpretation and application of retained EU law.
24 [2020] EWHC 3230 (Admin).

the Procedures Directive. The secretary of state argued that by reason of section 1 of and Schedule 1 to the Immigration and Social Security Co-ordination (EU Withdrawal) Act (ISSCEWA) 2020, the Procedures Directive ceased to be retained EU law. The Divisional Court accepted the secretary of state's argument and held that the Procedures Directive ceased to be retained EU law with effect from 31 December 2020 by reason of para 6 of Schedule 1. Paragraph 6(1) provides that any:

> EU-derived rights, powers, liabilities, obligations, restrictions, remedies and procedures cease to be recognised and available in domestic law so far as (a) they are inconsistent with, or are otherwise capable of affecting the interpretation, application or operation of, any provision made by or under the Immigration Acts (including, and as amended by, this Act), or (b) they are otherwise capable of affecting the exercise of functions in connection with immigration.

This applies to such rights, powers, liabilities, obligations, restrictions, remedies and procedures that had been retained under EUWA 2018 s4. This issue is subject to an appeal to the Supreme Court in *AAA*.

Reception Directive

3.20 The rights under the Qualification Directive work in tandem with the Reception Directive, which lays down minimum standards for the reception of asylum-seekers to ensure that they are able to enjoy a dignified standard of living and comparable living conditions in the member state while awaiting a decision on their asylum claims. The EU adopted a recast Reception Directive on 26 June 2013[25] but the UK opted out of the recast Directive, and therefore only the Reception Directive is retained EU law and applicable to the UK.

3.21 The UK has sought to comply with the obligations under the Reception Directive by means of the Asylum Seekers (Reception Conditions) Regulations 2005[26] and amendments made to the Immigration Rules, in particular the right of asylum-seekers to seek employment. To the extent that the Reception Directive has been transposed into domestic law, mainly in the form of regulations, it is not affected by the ISSCEWA 2020. Pursuant to the provision of Article 11 of the Reception Directive, asylum claimants who are not

25 Directive 2013/33/EU of the European Parliament and of the Council of 26 June 2013 laying down standards for the reception of applicants for international protection (recast) ('Reception Conditions Directive').

26 SI No 7.

European Economic Area (EEA) nationals may apply to work if their application is outstanding for over a year, but they are currently restricted to employment which is on the Home Office list of shortage occupations.[27] Asylum support is also available to asylum-seekers while they await a decision on their asylum claim. For a discussion of asylum support in the UK, see chapter 5.

Qualification Directive

3.22 The definition of a refugee is contained in the Qualification Directive at Article 2, and is similarly defined as Article 1A of the Refugee Convention, although not an exact mirror image of the convention definition. The EU definition applies only to non-EU nationals, as follows:

> 'refugee' means a third country national who, owing to a well-founded fear of being persecuted for reasons of race, religion, nationality, political opinion or membership of a particular social group, is outside the country of nationality and is unable or, owing to such fear, is unwilling to avail himself or herself of the protection of that country, or a stateless person, who, being outside of the country of former habitual residence for the same reasons as mentioned above, is unable or, owing to such fear, unwilling to return to it . . .

There are similar provisions of exclusion under Article 12 of the directive to Article 1F of the Refugee Convention.

3.23 The Qualification Directive also recognises that there will be those deserving protection under other international instruments who may fall outside it. People may be fleeing torture and inhuman or degrading treatment even though such treatment may not be on the grounds of race, religion, nationality, membership of a social group or political opinion. Expulsion may be contrary to other international human rights obligations. The distinction is recognised under the Qualification Directive by the grant of a subsidiary status under Article 15 to those who cannot be expected to return to their country of origin for reasons not qualifying them for refugee status.

3.24 The Qualification Directive sets out the residence rights which should be granted to recognised refugees and to other persons needing subsidiary protection throughout the EU. The UK has complied with the obligations under the Qualification Directive through domestic regulations: the Refugee or Person in Need of

27 The shortage occupation list is contained in the Immigration Rules at Appendix Shortage occupation list.

International Protection (Qualification) Regulations 2006[28] and amendments to the Immigration Rules. The EU has since adopted a recast Qualification Directive (Directive 2011/95/EU) but the UK has opted out and remains bound by the 2004 Directive.

Procedures Directive

3.25 The Procedures Directive provides for specific procedural safeguards that are to be afforded to asylum applicants.

3.26 Article 7 confers the right to remain in the member state pending a decision on the asylum application. Article 8(1) prohibits member states from rejecting or excluding asylum applications from examination on the sole ground that they have not been made as soon as possible. Article 12 requires that an applicant be given the opportunity of a personal interview prior to any decision on the claim. Article 23 requires member states to process applications in accordance with the principles and guarantees of Chapter II of the directive, and to 'ensure that such a procedure is concluded as soon as possible, without prejudice to an adequate and complete examination', and to inform asylum-seekers of the delay if a decision cannot be taken within six months.

3.27 Article 25 permits member states to consider a person's asylum claim inadmissible if a non-member state third country is considered a 'safe third country' for the applicant pursuant to Article 27. Article 27(2) sets out the limited circumstances in which the 'safe third country concept' may be applied. Article 27(2)(a) requires there to be a connection between the person claiming asylum and the safe third country 'on the basis of which it would be *reasonable* for that person to go to that country' (emphasis added). Recital (23) confirms this as it requires an applicant with a connection to a safe third country to reasonably be expected to seek protection 'in that' third country, not in another third country to which the person has no such connection. Furthermore, recital (24) provides that such an approach is only permissible in relation to third countries 'with respect to which the Council has satisfied itself that the high standards for the safety of the third country concerned'. Article 27(2)(b) requires rules laid down in national legislation governing 'the methodology by which the competent authorities satisfy themselves that the safe third country concept may be applied to a particular country or to a particular applicant'.

28 SI No 2525.

3.28 The Procedures Directive acknowledges that an asylum applicant who was not successful in their initial asylum application may seek to make a further application on the basis of a change in country condition or evidence which was not previously submitted. The Procedures Directive therefore laid down minimum standards that member states must meet for dealing with subsequent applications for asylum and international protection under Article 32. It is permitted under Article 32(3) for member states to first carry out a preliminary examination as to whether by the subsequent application, an applicant has presented new elements or findings not previously considered. If not, the Procedures Directive permits the member state to deal summarily with the subsequent application for asylum; otherwise, member states are required to carry out assessment of the merits.

3.29 The UK has transposed the Procedures Directive by amending the Immigration Rules and the Asylum (Procedures) Regulations 2007.[29] The EU adopted a recast Procedures Directive (2013/32/EU) but the UK opted out of the recast directive.

3.30 Under Article 32, the Procedures Directive recognises that applicants may make subsequent applications for asylum even if their first application was unsuccessful. A procedure for examining such subsequent asylum applications is laid down in Article 32. The Immigration Rules under para 353 broadly reflect the procedural requirements under Article 32 although there is one important difference in respect of such an asylum applicant's eligibility for support pending examination of the subsequent application. While the subsequent asylum application is pending, the Procedures Directive recognises that the applicant is an 'asylum applicant' within the meaning of Article 2(c). There is no requirement under the directive for the application to have undergone the preliminary screening provided under Article 32(3). This differs from the UK's approach. The Home Office treats subsequent applications for asylum as 'further submissions' and not a fresh asylum claim until and unless the Home Office accepts that it meets the 'fresh claim' threshold under para 353.[30] The consequences are significant as in the UK, those with further submissions pending examination as to whether they meet the para 353 threshold are not considered to be eligible for support as an asylum-seeker (as opposed to a failed

29 SI No 3187.

30 For a discussion of 'fresh claims', see paras 3.42–3.43.

asylum-seeker) under IAA 1999 s95.[31] They are instead eligible for support under IAA 1999 s4(2) if they are destitute.[32] There are also specific implications for care leavers in this position and their eligibility for support under the Children Act 1989.[33]

Domestic law on asylum and international protection

Claims for asylum

Overview

3.31 In the UK, the Refugee Convention is transposed into domestic law by providing that it would be unlawful for the secretary of state to make Immigration Rules which are inconsistent with the convention.[34]

3.32 The Immigration Rules are made by the secretary of state for the Home Department (SSHD) under IA 1971 s3(2). They are defined as 'detailed statements by a minister of the Crown as to how the Crown proposes to exercise its executive power to control immigration'.[35] They have a unique legal status – they are not law but a statement of the secretary of state's administrative practice.[36] However, the Immigration Rules have acquired status of 'quasi-law'[37] and the immigration tribunal is required to apply them, although not at the expense of considering wider human rights implications.[38]

3.33 The Immigration Rules provide that refugee status in the UK will be granted if the secretary of state is satisfied of the following:[39]

1) an applicant is in the UK or has arrived at a port of entry in the UK;
2) they are a refugee, as defined in Refugee or Person in Need of International Protection (Qualification) Regulations 2006 reg 2;

31 See paras 5.22–5.28.
32 See paras 6.25–6.36.
33 See paras 6.144–6.153 and 9.235.
34 Asylum and Immigration Appeals Act (AIAA) 1993 s2; Immigration Rules para 334.
35 *Odelola v SSHD* [2009] UKHL 25, [2009] 1 WLR 1230 at para 6 per Lord Hoffmann.
36 Per Lord Reed in *Hesham Ali v SSHD* [2016] UKSC 60, [2016] 1 WLR 4799.
37 Per Sedley LJ in *SSHD v Pankina* [2010] EWCA Civ 719, [2011] QB 376.
38 For a discussion of the status of the Immigration Rules, see paras 1.12–1.14.
39 Immigration Rules para 334.

3) there are no reasonable grounds for regarding them as a danger to the security of the UK;
4) having been convicted by a final judgment of a particularly serious crime, they do not constitute a danger to the community of the UK; and
5) refusing their application would result in them being required to go (whether immediately or after the time limited by any existing leave to enter or remain) in breach of the Refugee Convention, to a country in which their life or freedom would be threatened on account of their race, religion, nationality, political opinion or membership of a particular social group.

Definition of 'asylum-seeker': immigration and support context

3.34 Who is an 'asylum-seeker' is differently defined under the Immigration Rules and in the support context.[40] Immigration Rules para 327 defines an asylum-seeker as an applicant for asylum or other form of international protection. This definition applies to both adults and children. By contrast, for support purposes, whether asylum support or another form of support (such as under the Care Act 2014 or the Children Act 1989), the term asylum-seeker only applies to adults (those 'not under 18') who have 'made a claim for asylum which has been recorded by the Secretary of State but which has not been determined'.[41] In the asylum support context, a claim for asylum includes a claim under the Refugee Convention or a claim under European Convention on Human Rights (ECHR) Article 3 (prohibition of inhuman or degrading treatment or punishment).[42] See further paras 5.17–5.49 and following for a discussion of the meaning of an asylum-seeker for support purposes.

3.35 An asylum claim is a claim that it would be contrary to the UK's obligations under the Refugee Convention for the person who made the claim to be removed from or required to leave the UK.[43]

3.36 The immigration implications of the provisions under the Nationality and Borders Act (NBA) 2022 concerning inadmissibility of asylum claims, by which a person who has claimed asylum may

40 See further the discussion concerning asylum-seekers in chapter 5.

41 IAA 1999 s94(1). See also Nationality, Immigration and Asylum Act (NIAA) 2002 s18(1) and (3) and Sch 3 para 17. Note that asylum-seeker does not include a failed asylum-seeker who had made further submissions which had to be have been accepted by the secretary of state as a fresh claim.

42 IAA 1999 s94(1); NIAA 2002 s18(1) and (3) and Sch 3 para 17.

43 AIAA 1993 s1.

cease to be an asylum-seeker, and the differential treatment of refugees dependant on their mode of entry will be addressed in paras 3.105–3.115 below. The effect on eligibility for asylum support is discussed at paras 5.39–5.44.

Humanitarian protection claim

3.37 Humanitarian protection is the means by which the UK gives effect to the obligation in the Qualification Directive on the UK to provide 'subsidiary protection' to third country nationals and stateless people who do not qualify for refugee status but who face a real risk of suffering serious harm, who are not excluded from protection and who lack the protection of their home country.[44] The Immigration Act (IA) 2014 (amending the NIAA 2002 and in force since October 2014) introduced the concept of 'protection claims', defined as claims under the Refugee Convention or claims for humanitarian protection.[45]

3.38 The Immigration Rules provide a definition for such a claim under para 327EA, namely a request by a person for international protection due to a claim that if they are removed from or required to leave the UK, they would face a real risk of suffering serious harm in their country of origin and they are unable, or owing to such risk, unwilling to avail themself of the protection of that country.

3.39 'Serious harm' is defined under Immigration Rules para 339CA as the death penalty or execution; unlawful killing; torture or inhuman or degrading treatment or punishment in the country of return; or serious or individualised threat to a civilian life because of indiscriminate violence in situations of international or internal armed conflict.

3.40 The grounds on which humanitarian protection can be granted are broader than those under the Refugee Convention, so it may be possible for an applicant who fails to establish they qualify for refugee status to succeed in qualifying for humanitarian protection.

3.41 The UK considers protection and other claims for leave to enter or remain in a hierarchy – the starting point is whether a person qualifies for refugee status and if not, whether they qualify for humanitarian protection and if not, whether they qualify for discretionary leave. Thus someone who makes a humanitarian protection claim will be deemed to be an asylum applicant and to have made an

44 Qualification Directive 2004 Articles 2(e) and 18.

45 NIAA 2002 s82.

application for asylum for the purposes of the Immigration Rules. If the application for refugee status is refused, then the secretary of state will go on to consider the claim as a claim for humanitarian protection.[46]

Fresh claims on asylum and human rights grounds

3.42 Immigration Rules Part 12 para 353 provides for the making of a fresh asylum or human rights claim. Its formulation has not changed much since it was first introduced in October 2004:

> 353. When a human rights or protection claim has been refused or withdrawn or treated as withdrawn under paragraph 333C of these Rules and any appeal relating to that claim is no longer pending, the decision maker will consider any further submissions and, if rejected, will then determine whether they amount to a fresh claim. The submissions will amount to a fresh claim if they are significantly different from the material that has previously been considered. The submissions will only be significantly different if the content:
> (i) had not already been considered; and
> (ii) taken together with the previously considered material, created a realistic prospect of success, notwithstanding its rejection.

3.43 The test imposed by Immigration Rules para 353 is 'somewhat modest' as confirmed by the Court of Appeal in *WM (Democratic Republic of Congo) v SSHD*.[47] The question is whether there is a realistic prospect that an immigration tribunal, equipped with the previous evidence and any new evidence could conclude that a further appeal against the refusal of a protection or human rights claim should be allowed.[48] What this means is a 'more than a fanciful prospect' but not more than that.[49] The tribunal does not have to achieve certainty, but only 'to think' that there is a real risk of the applicant being persecuted on return. Since asylum is in issue the consideration of all the decision-makers, the secretary of state and the tribunal must be informed by the anxious scrutiny of the material that is axiomatic in decisions that if made incorrectly may lead to the applicant's exposure to persecution. A refusal to accept the application as a fresh claim is subject to judicial review.

46 Immigration Rules para 327EC.
47 [2006] EWCA Civ 1495, [2007] Imm AR 337.
48 [2006] EWCA Civ 1495 at para 7 per Buxton LJ.
49 *R (AK (Sri Lanka)) v SSHD* [2009] EWCA Civ 447, [2010] 1 WLR 855.

Human rights claims

Introduction

3.44 A person may make a claim that their removal from the UK would constitute a breach of any rights protected by the ECHR. Most commonly, and in addition to situations which fall within the ambit described above, these are likely to be those otherwise excluded from protection who face a real risk of torture, inhuman or degrading treatment (which can include medical grounds) or punishment (Article 3), a risk of trafficking or slavery (Article 4) or an interference with the right to respect for private and family life (Article 8). People involved in litigation, including as victims of crime or damages claims against the Home Office, may have a claim to remain on Article 6 grounds.[50]

Claims under ECHR Article 3

Overview

3.45 The right not to be tortured or subjected to inhuman or degrading treatment contrary to ECHR Article 3 is an unqualified right and can never be balanced or give way to competing considerations.[51] The landmark case of *Soering v UK*[52] established that extradition to a country where there is a real risk of treatment contrary to Article 3 engages the UK's responsibility under Article 3. The *Soering* principle has since been applied to the removal of rejected asylum-seekers,[53] deportation on national security grounds[54] and, indeed, must be taken to apply to any forced expulsion.[55]

3.46 The absolute nature of Article 3 means that there is no room for balancing the risk of ill-treatment against the reasons for expulsion in determining whether a state's responsibility under Article 3 is

50 *R v SSHD ex p Quaquah (application for judicial review)* [2000] 9 WLUK 7, QBD.

51 *Chahal v UK* App No 22414/93 (1997) 23 EHRR 413, ECtHR at paras 79–80. See also *Ahmed v Austria* App No 25964/94 (1997) 24 EHRR 278, ECtHR at para 41.

52 *Soering v UK* App No A/161 (1989) 11 EHRR 439, ECtHR.

53 See, for example, *Hilal v UK* App No 45276/99 (2001) 33 EHRR 2, [2001] INLR 595, ECtHR (rejection of claim of Tanzanian asylum-seeker and decision to remove him breached Article 3).

54 See *Chahal v UK* above.

55 *Pretty v UK* App No 23 46/02 (2002) 35 EHRR 1, ECtHR at para 52: the ECtHR held that the act of expulsion is 'treatment' within the scope of the negative duty to under Article 3; thus, expulsion which exposes a person to a real risk of ill-treatment abroad is a violation of Article 3.

engaged.[56] In *Vilvarajah v UK*[57] the European Court of Human Rights (ECtHR) held that the expelling state's responsibility was engaged where 'substantial grounds have been shown for believing' that the person concerned faces a real risk of being subjected to torture or inhuman or degrading treatment or punishment in the country to which he is returned.

3.47 In the expulsion context, Article 3 may apply where the risk is posed by state actors as well as non-state actors. In the non-state actor context, Article 3 arises where the risk from non-state actors is real and the authorities of the receiving state are unable to obviate it by providing appropriate protection. Practitioners will likely come across this in two common contexts: cases where it is said expulsion on medical grounds is likely to engage Article 3 or where it is said that the risk of suicide posed by the individual is likely to engage Article 3.

ECHR Article 3 medical cases

3.48 The ECtHR has held that, in the light of the fundamental importance of ECHR Article 3, it may be engaged by expulsion when the source of the harm in the destination country is not human agency at all, but the exacerbation of a naturally occurring severe illness, whether physical or mental, because of inadequate medical provision or the lack of carers in the receiving state. However, the threshold for establishing an Article 3 breach had been set very high following the House of Lords' judgment in *N v SSHD*:

> . . . whether the applicant's illness has reached such a critical stage (ie he is dying) that it would be inhuman treatment to deprive him of the care which he is currently receiving and send him home to an early death unless there is care available there to enable him to meet that fate with dignity.[58]

On this high threshold, few cases succeeded on ECHR Article 3 medical grounds. To give an example, the Upper Tribunal and the Court of Appeal in *GS (India)*[59] dismissed the appeal of a kidney dialysis patient in his thirties who was fit and well when he first arrived lawfully in the UK but would die within a fortnight of removal

56 *Chahal v UK* at para 81 affirmed in *Ahmed v Austria* and subsequently in *Saadi v Italy* App No 37201/06 (2008) 49 EHRR 30, ECtHR.

57 App No 13163/87 (1992) 14 EHRR 248, ECtHR.

58 [2005] UKHL 31, [2005] 2 AC 296 at para 69.

59 *Re GS and EO (Article 3: health cases: India)* [2012] UKUT 397 (IAC); *GS (India) and others v SSHD* [2015] EWCA Civ 40.

because he would receive no medical treatment in his country of origin. It is relevant to note that Lady Hale and Lord Brown both expressed discomfort and unease but this high threshold was reaffirmed by the ECtHR in *N v UK*.[60]

3.49 In December 2016 the European Court's Grand Chamber reconsidered its position on the principles applicable to Article 3 medical cases in *Paposhvili v Belgium*,[61] holding that expulsion on medical grounds is likely to come within the protection of Article 3 in situations involving the removal of a seriously ill person in which:

> . . . substantial grounds have been shown for believing that he or she, although not at imminent risk of dying, would face a real risk, on account of the absence of appropriate treatment in the receiving country or the lack of access to such treatment, of being exposed to a serious, rapid and irreversible decline in his or her state of health resulting in intense suffering or to a significant reduction in life expectancy.[62]

Although the ECtHR continued to describe this as 'high threshold', it has been seen as a loosening of the previous threshold.

3.50 In the UK, the courts considered *Paposhvili* on several occasions with different judges expressing a range of views as to the extent to which it altered the approach to be taken to consideration of ECHR Article 3 involving the removal of a seriously ill person. The Court of Appeal had taken the view that although the *Paposhvili* test was more relaxed than the test in *N*, the difference was a very modest one,[63] holding that the European Court's reference to 'significant reduction in life expectancy' required a serious, rapid and irreversible decline in a person's state of health and therefore required imminence of death. The Court of Appeal's approach was overruled by the Supreme Court, which handed down judgment in *AM (Zimbabwe) v SSHD*[64] in April 2020.

3.51 The background to the case is relevant to consider the significance of the legal development, particularly as it affects many of the vulnerable migrants who require support. The appellant in *AM (Zimbabwe)* arrived in the UK as a child, and was granted indefinite leave to remain. He later committed a number of crimes, including possession of a firearm, for which he was sentenced to seven years in

60 App No 26565/05 (2008) 47 EHRR 39, ECtHR.

61 App No 41738/10 [2017] Imm AR 867, ECtHR.

62 *Paposhvili v Belgium* at para 183.

63 See *AM (Zimbabwe) v SSHD* [2018] EWCA Civ 64 per Sales LJ.

64 [2020] UKSC 17.

prison. He contracted HIV and received treatment in the UK. He suffered serious side effects to conventional antiretroviral therapy and was instead offered a drug called Eviplera. Evidence suggested that this was not available in Zimbabwe, meaning that if he was deported from the UK he would not receive effective treatment, leading to his untimely death.

3.52 The Supreme Court in *AM (Zimbabwe)* found that it was too extreme and unduly narrow to construe the words of the European Court – 'significant reduction in life expectancy'[65] – as requiring imminence of death. The Supreme Court accepted that the test set by the European Court required *either* 'a serious, rapid and irreversible decline in his or her state of health resulting in intense suffering' or 'a significant reduction in life expectancy', not both.[66] However, the Supreme Court did not give much guidance on what the new 'intense suffering or significant reduction in life expectancy' test means in practice. Rather, the Supreme Court observed that 'significant' reduction in life expectancy might mean different things to a 74-year-old and to a 24-year-old.[67]

3.53 The Supreme Court went on to point out that *Paposhvili* is not only about the threshold test in ECHR Article 3 medical treatment cases, but it also establishes procedural requirements. The initial burden of proof is on the applicant to show by evidence that substantial grounds exist for believing that, if removed, they would be expected to a real risk of subjection to treatment contrary to ECHR Article 3.[68] When the applicant does so, the burden shifts to the Home Secretary to dispel 'any doubts raised' by the evidence, subject the alleged risk to close scrutiny and address reports of reputable organisations about treatment in the receiving state.[69] The Home Secretary must also 'verify on a case-by-case basis' whether the care generally available in the receiving state was in practice sufficient to prevent the applicant's exposure to treatment contrary to Article 3.[70] The Home Secretary must also consider the accessibility of the treatment to the particular applicant, including by reference to its cost if any, to the existence of a family network and to its geographical location.[71]

65 *Paposhvili* at para 182 quoted in *AM (Zimbabwe)* at para 22.
66 *AM (Zimbawe)* in the Supreme Court at paras 29–30.
67 *AM (Zimbawe)* in the Supreme Court at para 31.
68 *Paposhvili* at para 186 and *AM (Zimbabwe)* at para 32.
69 *Paposhvili* at para 187 and *AM (Zimbabwe)* at para 23(b).
70 *Paposhvili* at para 189 and *AM (Zimbabwe)* at para 23(c).
71 *Paposhvili* at para 190 and *AM (Zimbabwe)* at para 33.

If serious doubts continue to surround the impact of removal, the Home Secretary had to obtain an individual assurance from the receiving state that appropriate treatment would be available and accessible to the applicant.[72]

3.54 The procedural safeguards are notably only triggered if the applicant submits sufficient evidence in the first place. It logically follows that applicants would be well advised to seek high-quality medical evidence on their prognosis in the UK and what will happen to their body, their quality of life and their lifespan in the event of withdrawal of medical treatment or provision of different or less precise medical treatment. By way of illustration, it should be noted that AM's appeal was later dismissed on remittal by the Supreme Court to the Upper Tribunal (Immigration and Asylum Chamber).[73] That appeal did not turn on a legal dispute but rather on the tribunal's assessment of his evidence. There were findings concerning his credibility, and the inconsistencies between his accounts. Although his character and past criminal conduct were not material factors in assessing his Article 3 claim, they did influence the tribunal's assessment of his evidence. The tribunal found concerning the lack of precise evidence from the treating consultant and two experts (one instructed by the applicant and one by the Home Office) regarding the Zimbabwean healthcare system and the cost of anti-retroviral treatment, monitoring and testing in Zimbabwe, and the risk involving in switching drugs. The Upper Tribunal concluded that there was an effective anti-retroviral treatment available in the public sector and there was also adequate affordable testing and monitoring. AM's appeal determination highlights the importance of clear expert evidence from clinicians who have recent experience of providing relevant treatment and services in the receiving country, and are able to address the treatment options and costs in both public and private sectors. While character and conduct are not directly relevant in ECHR Article 3 cases, the Upper Tribunal's decision shows that credibility is still likely to influence the assessment of an applicant's claim about their resilience and ability to cope following return. Similarly, evidence as to family or community support will likely play a significant role in the tribunal's assessment of the accessibility and availability of treatment.

3.55 The *Paposhvili* test has been applied not only in ECHR Article 3 medical treatment cases but also to 'material deprivation' or 'living

72 *Paposhvili* at para 191 and *AM (Zimbabwe)* at para 33.

73 *AM (Art 3; health cases) Zimbabwe* [2022] UKUT 131 (IAC).

conditions' claims. *Ainte (material deprivation: Art 3: AM (Zimbabwe))*[74] was an appeal against deportation to Somalia. The appellant argued that his removal to Moghadishu would result in him facing 'a real risk of living in conditions of such extreme material deprivation, and so lacking in security' that they would constitute inhuman and degrading treatment under Article 3. The Upper Tribunal held that where the material deprivation is not intentionally caused, the applicable threshold for this type of Article 3 case is the *AM (Zimbabwe)* threshold. The question will be whether conditions of living are such that there is a real risk that the individual concerned will be exposed to intense suffering or a significant reduction in life expectancy.[75] Similar evidential requirements will need to be satisfied.

ECHR Article 3 suicide risk cases

3.56 In a suicide risk case, the Court of Appeal has held in *J v SSHD*[76] that consideration of ECHR Article 3 should be taken in three stages:

1) when the person is informed that a final decision has been made to remove them to their country of origin;
2) when the person is physically removed by airplane; and
3) after the person has arrived in the country of origin.

3.57 The test to be applied at the different stages is different. In 'foreign cases', namely those where the breach arises in respect of the receiving state's conduct, the question is whether the fear of ill-treatment is objectively well-founded. The *Paposhvili* test, discussed above at paras 3.49–3.50, is relevant to this. This objective threshold only applies to 'foreign cases', not 'domestic cases' raising ECHR Article 3. In 'domestic cases' – that is, those engaging the UK's Article 3 obligations – the Court of Appeal in *Y (Sri Lanka) v SSHD*[77] held that if the person's genuine fear of ill-treatment is such that it creates a risk of suicide when the return is enforced by the state seeking to remove the person (ie the UK), then that might give rise to a breach of Article 3. The Court of Appeal approved the test set out in *J v SSHD*[78] (which applies both to domestic and foreign cases). That test is summarised as follows:

74 [2021] UKUT 203 (IAC).

75 See headnote to *Ainte (material deprivation: Art 3: AM (Zimbabwe))* [2021] UKHT 203 (IAC).

76 [2005] EWCA Civ 629, [2005] Imm AR 409 at para 17.

77 [2009] EWCA Civ 362, [2009] HLR 22.

78 [2005] EWCA Civ 629 at paras 26–32.

1) What is the severity of treatment which it is said that an applicant will suffer if removed?
2) Is there a causal link between the act or threatened act of removal or expulsion and the inhuman treatment relied on as violating the applicant's Article 3 rights?
3) Is the alleged inhuman treatment a direct or indirect responsibility of the public authorities of the receiving state?
4) Is the applicant's fear of ill-treatment in the receiving state upon which the risk of suicide is said to be based is objectively well-founded? If not, that will tend to weigh against there being a real risk that the removal will be in breach of Article 3.
5) Does the removing and/or receiving state have effective mechanisms to reduce the risk of suicide? If so, that will also weigh heavily against the applicant's claim that removal will violate their Article 3 rights.

Claims under ECHR Article 8

3.58 Claims based on ECHR Article 8 (right to respect for private and family life) have been, to a large extent and controversially, codified in the Immigration Rules since 2014. The government also introduced a statutory definition of 'the public interest'.[79] The rules now make provision for leave to remain 'on the ground of private life' (paras 276ADE–276DH), for entry and stay based on family life (Appendix FM) and ECHR Article 8 claims arising in the context of deportation (paras 398–399B). The SSHD and the First-tier Tribunal (Immigration and Asylum Chamber) (FTT (IAC)) are required to assess any applications according to the Immigration Rules first. If an applicant does not satisfy the requirement under the rules, it is still necessary to make an assessment of ECHR Article 8 applying the criteria established by case-law.[80] The Immigration Rules concerning family and private life are discussed in more detail at para 1.92.

Claims under ECHR Article 4

3.59 ECHR Article 4 prohibits slavery, servitude and forced labour. It is an absolute right from which no derogation is possible because it enshrines one of the fundamental values of democratic society. The ECtHR has held that the prohibition under Article 4 includes prohibition against human trafficking given 'its very nature and aim of

79 NIAA 2002 ss117A–117D.

80 *SSHD v Izuazu* [2013] UKUT 45 (IAC) at para 41.

exploitation, is based on the exercise of powers attaching to the right of ownership'[81] and the ECHR being a living instrument to be interpreted in the light of developments over time. Like Articles 2, 3 and 8, Article 4 contains positive obligations, which in this context require the state to put in place an appropriate legislative and administrative framework to penalise and prosecute effectively any act aimed at maintaining a person in a situation of slavery, servitude or forced or compulsory labour.[82]

3.60 It is important to be aware of the positive obligation to take operational measures to protect victims or potential victims of treatment in breach of ECHR Article 4. The positive obligation will be triggered if demonstrated that the state authorities were aware or ought to have been aware of circumstances giving rise to a credible suspicion that an individual has been or was at real and immediate risk of being subjected to treatment in breach of Article 4. In *R (TDT) v SSHD*,[83] the Court of Appeal held that the 'credible suspicion' represents a 'relatively low threshold' and concluded that there was a breach of Article 4 in the decision to release a child victim of trafficking out of immigration detention without putting in place any measures to protect him against being re-trafficked. The domestic legal and policy framework for the identification and support of victims and potential victims of trafficking under the National Referral Mechanism (NRM) is discussed in more detail in chapter 11.

3.61 In *MS (Pakistan) v SSHD*[84] the Supreme Court was concerned with the extent to which immigration tribunals are bound to accept decisions of the NRM as to whether a person is or is not a victim of trafficking; and the circumstances in which a decision to remove a person from the UK will be contrary to ECHR Article 4. The appeal arose because the Court of Appeal[85] decided that a judge hearing an asylum or protection appeal (including Article 4) cannot go behind the fact findings made by the 'competent authority' in the conclusive grounds decision made within the NRM process (discussed at paras 11.177–11.178). The Court of Appeal's decision was based on an argument made by the Home Secretary that the immigration tribunal could only go behind NRM decisions and re-determine relevant

81 *Rantsev v Cyprus and Russia* App No 25965/04 (2010) 51 EHRR 1, ECtHR at para 281; and see also *EK (Tanzania) v SSHD* [2013] UKUT 313 (IAC).

82 *Siliadin v France* App No 73316/01 (2006) 43 EHRR 16, ECtHR; and *CN v UK* App No 4239/08 (2013) 56 EHRR 24, ECtHR.

83 [2018] EWCA Civ 1395, (2018) 21 CCLR 525.

84 [2020] UKSC 9, [2020] 1 WLR 1373.

85 [2018] EWCA Civ 594, [2018] 4 WLR 63.

factual issues if the NRM decision was perverse, irrational or a decision not open to the NRM to make. This meant that the only remedy that a victim or potential victim had to challenge an adverse NRM decision was by way of judicial review.

3.62 On appeal to the Supreme Court, the Home Secretary conceded that immigration tribunals were not bound by the decision reached under the NRM.[86] This was described by the Supreme Court to be a proper concession having regard to the statutory jurisdiction of immigration tribunals to carry out a merits review of Home Office decision-making, and prior authority, in particular *Huang v SSHD*[87] which made it 'crystal clear' that tribunals had to decide for themselves factual issues relevant to the immigration decisions falling within their jurisdiction. That is not to say that a decision under the NRM can be totally ignored. It should rather be given 'proper consideration and weight', which will depend on the nature of the decision and its relevance to the issues before the tribunal.

3.63 On the second issue concerning when decisions to remove will be contrary to ECHR Article 4, the Supreme Court held that where the tribunal decides that a person was a victim of trafficking (such as in MS's case), it is necessary for the tribunal to decide for itself whether the person's removal from the UK would amount to a breach of any of the positive obligations under Article 4. In MS's case, the Supreme Court held that the adverse NRM decision on his trafficking status was defective. As such, he was denied the protective measures under Article 4, read in line with the UK's treaty obligations under the Council of Europe Convention on Action against the Trafficking in Human Beings (ECAT). Although, on the facts, MS had been removed from the risk of further exploitation, the Supreme Court noted that it was clear that there had not yet been an effective investigation into his situation as a victim of the crime of trafficking as required by Article 4. The Supreme Court agreed with the Upper Tribunal that it was inconceivable that an effective police investigation could be conducted without the full assistance and co-operation of MS, which realistically would not be feasible if her were removed to Pakistan.[88]

3.64 Further to the coming into force of NBA 2022 s65, it remains to be seen how a human rights claim under ECHR Article 4 will be treated and whether the outcome would be materially different if

86 *MS (Pakistan)*, Supreme Court at para 11.

87 [2007] UKHL 11, [2007] 2 AC 167.

88 *MS (Pakistan)*, Supreme Court at paras 34–35.

considered under Article 4 as opposed to NBA 2022 s65. As was stated by the Supreme Court in *MS (Pakistan)*, there is no direct read across of rights and obligations under the ECAT to ECHR Article 4. Prior to 30 January 2023, the domestic case-law confirmed the secretary of state's intention to implement ECAT Article 14 to its fullest extent. However, since 30 January 2023, the secretary of state has expressly stated in her section 65 policy that she no longer intends to implement Article 14(1)(a) beyond what parliament has prescribed under NBA 2022 s65. It is difficult to see how a human rights claim under ECHR Article 4 could bring in the full ambit of Article 14(1)(a) through a different route. Whether NBA 2022 s65 is compatible with ECHR Article 4 is likely to be a matter that will be heavily litigated in the months and years to come.

3.65 At the writing of this chapter, the Illegal Migration Act 2023 has received royal assent, in which further restrictions are introduced to the identification of victims of trafficking and modern slavery and the protection to which they are entitled if identified. This is not discussed in any detail in this chapter because the provisions that have not come into force remain unknown at this time.

Grant of leave on human rights grounds

3.66 A person who succeeds in showing that their return will breach ECHR Article 3 (prohibition of torture, inhuman and degrading treatment) or Article 8 (right to respect for family and private life) may be granted discretionary leave (DL). DL may also be granted for exceptional cases under consideration of Immigration Rules para 353B or for victims of trafficking. Home Office guidance on *Discretionary leave* is a useful document setting out the criteria on which such a grant will be made and in what circumstances.[89]

Procedure for making protection claim

3.67 This section will cover the procedure for making protection claim:

- registering a claim, interviews and reasons for refusal;
- child asylum applicants;
- negative decisions on asylum: reasons for refusal;

89 *Discretionary leave*, v9.0, 16 December 2021, www.gov.uk/government/publications/granting-discretionary-leave.

- positive decisions on asylum/humanitarian protection and human rights claims: grant of status;
- statutory appeals against refusals of protection and human rights claims;
- inadmissibility and the Rwanda asylum plan.

Registering a claim, interviews and reasons for refusal

3.68 The determination of refugee status is entrusted to the secretary of state. There are detailed Immigration Rules,[90] policies and guidance[91] governing the processing and consideration of claims.

3.69 A partner or child of a principal applicant for asylum can be included as a dependent on their application (subject to the consent of each adult applicant) or they may make an application in their own right, to be considered independently and as soon as possible.[92]

3.70 The ordinary procedure is as follows:

1) claim made at a designated place and in accordance with timing rules;
2) screening interview and routing;
3) substantive asylum interview.

3.71 From 23 February 2023, the Home Office introduced a streamlined asylum processing policy,[93] the stated object of which is to provide a more expedited process by which asylum claims made by people from certain countries with 'high-grant rate of protection status' could be determined. This is discussed below at paras 3.90–3.94.

Claim must be made at a designated place

3.72 A person can claim asylum within the UK, but must normally do so in person at a place designated by the secretary of state. NBA 2022 s14(2) defines what a 'designated place' means, namely:

(a) a place identified in a notice published by the Secretary of State as an asylum intake unit;

90 Immigration Rules paras 339HA–339NE, 357A–358B.

91 There is a suite of asylum policies which can be found on the www.gov.uk website. Policy changes over time and the same policy may be amended. It is advisable to check the government website for the latest list of relevant asylum policy and the version applicable to the individual affected by the policies.

92 Immigration Rules para 349.

93 *Streamlined Asylum Processing*, v1.0, 23 February 2023, https://www.gov.uk/government/publications/streamlined-asylum-processing/streamlined-asylum-processing-accessible.

(b) a removal centre (within the meaning of section 147 of the Immigration and Asylum Act 1999);
(c) a port (within the meaning of section 33 of the Immigration Act 1971);
(d) a place where there is a person present who, for the purposes of the immigration rules, is authorised to accept an asylum claim on behalf of the Secretary of State;
(e) a place to which the claimant has been directed by the Secretary of State or an immigration officer to make the claim;
(f) such other place, or a place of such other description, as the Secretary of State may by regulations designate.

3.73 NBA 2022 s14(7) excludes the possibility of registering a claim whilst a person is in the UK territorial sea. However, for the purposes of section 14(2)(d), it does not include reference to the territorial sea of the UK. When someone is intercepted in UK territorial sea and they ask an official for asylum, they are to be informed that they will be able to do so once they are brought ashore. Once ashore, arrangements will be made so the person can claim asylum.[94]

3.74 Immigration Rules para 327AB provides that an application for asylum will only be recorded as valid if it is made in a designated place as defined in NBA 2022 s14 unless subsequently or otherwise accepted by the Home Secretary. Additionally, it has to be made in person, by a person who is not a British citizen, be particularised (if it is a claim made by an applicant who is 18 or over), and not fall to be considered as a fresh claim under Immigration Rules para 353. Immigration Rules para 327AC now provides that a claim which does not meet these requirements will not be a valid asylum application.

3.75 The same procedural requirements for making an asylum claim apply to claims for humanitarian protection.[95]

3.76 The Home Office's policy expectation is that if a person arrives in the UK with the intention to claim asylum and protection, they should do so at the port of entry on arrival. However, a person may not claim asylum at the port on entry on arrival for a variety of reasons. This could be because they believe that they have become a refugee *sur place*, so that they qualify for refugee status because of a change of situation in their country of origin or personal circumstances since their departure. They may also have otherwise entered the country illegally or overstayed a visa and have protection reasons

94 *Asylum screening and routing*, v7.0, 28 June 2022, www.gov.uk/government/publications/asylum-screening-and-routing.

95 Immigration Rules para 327EB.

for remaining in the UK. These claims should be made at the Asylum Intake Unit located in Croydon.[96]

3.77 In certain situations, related to health, disability or the fact the person wanting to claim asylum is a minor, they may request for screening to be undertaken locally in England and Wales. The request will need to be supported by evidence of a person's inability to travel to the Asylum Intake Unit. The *Asylum screening and routing* policy outlines the Home Office's general approach.

3.78 NBA 2022 s14 does not specifically address the position of foreign national offenders serving a prison sentence. The *Asylum screening and routing* policy provides[97] that an individual detained in a prison can claim asylum through the Prison Operations and Prosecutions (POP). A POP team will be located in a 'hub' prison and will work from there in covering that and other prisons allocated to the relevant 'hub' POP team. A prisoner can make a request for asylum during immigration surgeries held in prison or their request for asylum can be passed to the local POP hub team.

3.79 Further applications for asylum, discussed above at paras 3.42–3.43, have to be made by appointment and in person at the Liverpool or Glasgow Further Submissions Unit.[98] The specified locations may change over time and should be checked against the most current policy.

Delay and promptitude of claim

3.80 NBA 2022 s37(2)(a) provides that for those arriving in the UK, the requirement to claim asylum without delay will only be satisfied for those claiming asylum 'as soon as reasonably practicable after their arrival'. For those already in the UK, when they became a refugee, if they have leave to remain, they must claim asylum before their presence becomes unlawful. If their presence has become unlawful, they must claim asylum as soon as they become aware of their need for protection.

Screening interview and routing

3.81 The first stage in the application process is to have a screening interview, the purpose of which is to identify the 'bio-data' (identity,

96 *Asylum screening and routing*, v7.0.

97 *Asylum screening and routing*, v7.0, p32.

98 See further, *Further submissions*, v10.0, 28 June 2022, p14; and *Submit new evidence to support your asylum claim*, www.gov.uk/submit-new-evidence-asylum-claim.

nationality etc), travel history and documentation, health, family background, and basis of claim (in summary only), and to carry out a security screening. The Home Office's *Asylum screening and routing* policy sets out further details.[99]

3.82 The screening pro forma includes a section which poses a question to the interviewee as to whether they experienced exploitation in their country of origin on en route to the UK. The notes to the screening pro forma and the *Asylum screening and routing*[100] direct interviewing officers to obtain brief details from the asylum applicant where their answer to the pro forma question indicates that they may have experienced exploitation or believe they were going to be exploited. The interviewing officer is directed to consider whether an NRM referral is required based on the information provided by the asylum applicant. A discussion of the NRM is at paras 11.62–11.197.

3.83 The screening pro forma also includes a question to provide the asylum applicant an opportunity to provide reasons for why they should not be detained pending consideration of their asylum claim. This question was added in 2014 further to the judgment in *R (Detention Action) v SSHD*,[101] a case that challenged the 'detained fast track', an accelerated process for processing and deciding asylum claim in a truncated seven-day timescale. The court had considered it a necessary addition to the screening pro forma so that there was at least an opportunity to elicit information from the asylum applicant of reasons that may affect their suitability to be detained. Although the detained fast track was suspended in 2015 in response to further litigation, the Home Office introduced a different detained asylum process, the Detained Asylum Casework in July 2015. In September 2016, the *Adults at risk* statutory framework under IA 2016 s59 and associated statutory guidance (discussed at para 1.211) also came into force. It remains relevant for the Home Office to elicit and consider information about an asylum applicant's vulnerabilities and to consider whether those vulnerabilities mean that they would be unsuitable for detention. The detention question has therefore remained in the screening pro forma.

3.84 After screening, there are different procedures to be followed. First, a person may be detained and processed under the detained

99 V7.0.
100 V7.0, pp69–70.
101 [2014] EWHC 2245 (Admin).

asylum process[102] (also known as Detained Asylum Casework – DAC). Second, the person may also be processed through the non-detained route, in which case they are dealt with via the National Asylum Allocations Unit (NAAU) under the non-detained procedure.[103]

3.85 A third routing procedure was introduced in April 2022 further to the government's announcement of its plan to send people who arrive in the UK illegally to seek asylum to the Republic of Rwanda as part of a memorandum of understanding (MOU) agreed between the UK and Rwanda.[104] Under the Rwanda asylum plan – officially the 'UK and Rwanda Migration and Economic Development Partnership' – the UK's legal responsibilities for certain asylum-seekers would end once they have been relocated to Rwanda. The process by which this could happen is outlined briefly at paras 3.131–3.142 below. At the writing of this chapter the process is under challenge.[105]

3.86 Save where an applicant is detained, there is a requirement to provide a document confirming that an asylum claim has been recorded within three working days.[106] This will be in the form of an 'application registration card' (ARC) which is issued to acknowledge that the individual is an asylum claimant or dependant of an asylum claimant. It is not an identity card.[107] It is, however, used for access to support, to prove entitlement to work (where it exists) and to facilitate reporting. Those who are not detained are subject to 'immigration bail' under IA 2016 Sch 10.[108]

102 *Detained Asylum Casework (DAC) asylum process*, v5, 18 March 2019.

103 *Asylum screening and routing*, v7.0.

104 The MOU is available at: www.gov.uk/government/publications/memorandum-of-understanding-mou-between-the-uk-and-rwanda/memorandum-of-understanding-between-the-government-of-the-united-kingdom-of-great-britain-and-northern-ireland-and-the-government-of-the-republic-of-r.

105 The Divisional Court handed down judgment on 19 December 2022 (*R (AAA (Syria)) v SSHD* [2022] EWHC 3230 (Admin)) but granted the claimants permission to appeal to the Court of Appeal on various grounds of appeal. At the writing of this chapter in February 2023, the Court of Appeal hearing is pending.

106 Immigration Rules paras 359 and 359A. See also *Asylum screening and routing*, v7.0.

107 Immigration Rules para 359B.

108 See chapter 1 at paras 1.188–1.197 for a discussion on immigration bail.

Substantive asylum interview

3.87 Next in the process is a personal interview[109] with a representative of the secretary of state in order to put forward the applicant's case for claiming asylum. This substantive interview is an important part of the process and, where possible, applicants are well advised to have a legal representative present.[110] Interviewers are provided with detailed guidance on the manner and procedure to be followed. The applicant should be prepared to have any inconsistencies in their account put to them so they can have an opportunity to deal with it.

3.88 The Home Office's *Asylum interviews*[111] contains detailed instructions on the conduct and procedure of the substantive interviews and how they apply for particular applicants, for example, children,[112] victims of torture or victims of sexual violence.

3.89 There are circumstances in which it would not be appropriate to interview an applicant, most commonly because they are a vulnerable applicant and the Home Office has sufficient material on which to make a positive decision, or if it is not reasonably practicable for an interview to be conducted, for example where the applicant is not fit or able to attend a personal interview.[113]

Streamlined asylum process

3.90 On 23 February 2023, the Home Office published a new streamlined asylum processing policy, which sets out the circumstances in which it may be appropriate to decide asylum claims without a substantive asylum interview or with a significantly shortened interview. The streamlined asylum processing is said, at this time, to apply to 'legacy claims', that is claims for asylum made prior to 28 June 2022. The significance of the date is that from 28 June 2022 onwards, provisions within the NBA 2022 came into force establishing a new framework for asylum decision-making, including the differentiated asylum system, which allows the UK to treat two groups of refugees differently on the basis of whether they 'came directly' to the UK,

109 Immigration Rules para 339NA.

110 Although note that there is no entitlement to a legal representative: *R v SSHD ex p Lawson* [1994] Imm AR 58, QBD.

111 *Asylum interviews*, v9.0, 28 June 2022, www.gov.uk/government/publications/conducting-the-asylum-interview-process.

112 See *Children's asylum claims*, v4.0, 31 December 2020, www.gov.uk/government/publications/processing-an-asylum-application-from-a-child-instruction.

113 Immigration Rules para 339NA.

made an asylum claim, 'without delay' and, where applicable, showed 'good cause' for their illegal entry or presence. This is discussed further at paras 3.105–3.115 below.

3.91 The streamlined asylum processing model policy states that its intention is to apply this process to the processing of '*manifestly well-founded cases in the legacy caseload*'. It would apply to claimants from Afghanistan, Eritrea, Libya, Syria and Yemen where sufficient evidence is available to confirm their nationality and there are no other factors that would mean a personal interview was required, such as considerations related to whether they should be excluded from the Refugee Convention owing to their involvement in activities of concern, such as war crimes. These nationalities are selected on the basis of the high grant rate of protection status for people of these nationalities in the year ending September 2022. The policy does not preclude the possibility that claimants from other nationalities may be subject to this policy.

3.92 The streamlined process involves the following steps:

1) A screening interview to gather basic information details of the claimant to confirm their identity and a brief overview of why they have come to the UK and claimed asylum.
2) Where the claimant has not had a personal interview, and on the available information, it is deemed possible to decide the claim without such an interview, an asylum questionnaire will be issued, the purpose is to elicit more details on the person's reasons for claiming asylum, what they fear would happen if they were returned to their country of origin, any physical and mental health issues, any experience of exploitation (for identifying potential trafficking or modern slavery), any grounds for suspecting that the person may have been involved in activities of concern that would cause them to be excluded from the Refugee Convention, any family members dependant on the claim, and any further evidence the claimant wishes to provide in support of their claim.
3) The questionnaire must be returned within 20 working days. An extension could be sought so long as it is reasonable and proportionate, although the policy does not explain what would satisfy this criterion. The policy states that if an extension if granted, it would normally be granted for a maximum of 20 working days. The failure to return a questionnaire could result in the person's asylum claim being treated as withdrawn under para 333C of the Immigration Rules.

4) If it is not possible to grant protection status on the basis of the information available pre-personal interview (screening interview and asylum questionnaire) and the required information cannot be sourced via another method, such as writing to the claimant, the caseworker should normally proceed to arranging an interview with the claimant, unless there are other reasons to omit the interview.

3.93 Interviews carried out further to a completed asylum questionnaire do not need to be a full substantive interview, according to the policy. They could be 'targeted interviews' carried out to ascertain a claimant's nationality, lasting 30 to 60 minutes; or 'shorter interviews', where the further information required is limited. Either interview may not be appropriate if more substantial information is required regarding the claim before it can be decided.

3.94 Concerns have been raised by the Immigration Law Practitioners' Association and more than one hundred refugee and migrants' rights organisations, law firms and individuals[114] about the fairness of this process, especially when a vast number of asylum-seekers are unable to secure legal advice and representation. It is not clear from the policy whether there is an assumption that legal advice and assistance is required or not for the purposes of completing the questionnaire. It was the view of the signatories that legal advice and assistance is essential to the fairness of the asylum decision-making process. This is of added importance under the streamlined process given the potentially grave consequences of non-compliance, namely that a person's claim for asylum can be deemed to be withdrawn. The questionnaire is also only provided in English with no translated versions available. The questions set out in the questionnaire are legally complex. At the writing of this chapter, it is not clear whether and to what extent the Home Secretary carried out any public sector equality considerations under section 149 of the Equality Act 2010 prior to implementing this process. In particular, it is not known what considerations have been paid to the potential disadvantage suffered by people with a history of mental illness and mental incapacity and other disability in engaging. Similarly, no consideration appears to have been paid to the potential impaired ability of people who have experienced sexual violence and other traumatic experiences or

114 Joint open letter to Home Secretary dated 1 March 2023. A copy of this was sent to the Office of the Immigration Services Commission and the Legal Aid Agency. https://ilpa.org.uk/joint-open-letter-to-home-secretary-re-remedying-the-asylum-questionnaire-1-march-2023/.

people who have no or little literacy in engaging in this streamlined process without legal advice and assistance. The lawfulness or otherwise of this streamlined process remains to be seen.

Child asylum applicants

3.95 There are special provisions dealing with protection claims for children, both accompanied and unaccompanied. A 'child' is a person under 18 who, in the absence of documentary evidence appears to be under 18.[115]

3.96 In cases where age is disputed, the Home Office's policy is set out in the *Assessing age* policy.[116] In summary, the Home Office's practice is to give the applicant the benefit of the doubt. The Home Office may do otherwise in certain circumstances, such as where there is clear documentary evidence to establish the person is over 18 and the person's physical appearance and/or general demeanour very strongly suggests that they are significantly over 18 and there is no other persuasive evidence to establish claimed age. The details are set out in the *Assessing age* policy. The essential point is that even in cases where the Home Office doubts the person is a child and their age as claimed, their asylum claims should be dealt with in accordance with procedures for considering claims by children until satisfactory evidence establishes that the person is an adult. See further paras 11.130–11.137 concerning the Home Office's policy approach to age disputes.

3.97 In England and Wales, where the asylum applicant is an unaccompanied child, the Home Office must pass the child's details to the Refugee Council's panel of advisers within 24 hours of the claim for asylum being lodged.[117] Age dispute cases must always be referred to the panel unless the applicant is considered to be significantly over 18 and is being treated as an adult in line with the Home Office's *Assessing age* policy. Both Scotland and Northern Ireland have guardianship schemes for children who arrive in the UK unaccompanied and separated from their families who are seeking asylum or who have been trafficked. The process for referral is therefore different and beyond the scope of this book.

115 Immigration Rules para 394.

116 *Assessing age*, v5.0, 14 January 2022, available at: www.gov.uk/government/publications/assessing-age-instruction.

117 *Children's asylum claims*, v4.0.

3.98 In making decisions in respect of child applicants, the Home Secretary must comply with Borders, Citizenship and Immigration Act (BCIA) 2009 s55 and associated statutory guidance issued under that provision.[118] The Immigration Rules and the Home Office policies[119] are useful in clarifying the approach that should be adopted in assessing claims from children. The following points are important to note:

- more weight may need to be given to objective indicators of risk than to the child's state of mind or other subjective indicators of credibility;[120]
- applications from children receive priority at all stages;[121]
- children's claims will be decided by caseworkers trained to deal with asylum claims from children;[122]
- usually children over the age of 12 will be interviewed about their claim, unless it is inappropriate to do so, or if they are unfit;[123]
- particular care is needed when assessing evidence from children, taking into account 'child specific factors' such as age, level of maturity and a more liberal application of the benefit of doubt.[124]

3.99 The Home Office has an obligation to endeavour to trace the family members of an unaccompanied asylum-seeking child (UASC) as soon as possible after the asylum claim is made.[125] The obligation to trace is part of the assessment whether the child qualifies for asylum. The Upper Tribunal has held that being a child is capable of constituting a 'particular social group' under the Refugee Convention.[126]

3.100 In cases where there are no adequate reception facilities on return, the Immigration Rules provide for leave to remain to be

118 See chapter 1 paras 1.24–1.31 for discussion on BCIA 2009 s55.

119 At the time of writing the applicable policy is *Children's asylum claims*, v4.0.

120 At p51.

121 Immigration Rules para 350.

122 Immigration Rules paras 352 and 352ZB.

123 Immigration Rules para 352; and *Children's asylum claims*, v4.0, p39.

124 This is set out in the United Nations High Commissioner for Refugees (UNHCR) Handbook on procedures and criteria for determining refugee status under the 1951 Convention and the 1967 Protocol relating to the Status of Refugees at para 219; and *Children's asylum claims*, v4.0, pp51–53. See also *Re KS (benefit of the doubt)* [2014] UKUT 552 (IAC).

125 Reception Directive Article 19, implemented by the Asylum Seekers (Reception Conditions) Regulations 2005 reg 6. See also *DS (Afghanistan) v SSHD* [2011] EWCA Civ 305, [2011] 3 WLUK 691; *HK (Afghanistan) (by their litigation friend) v SSHD* [2012] EWCA Civ 315; and *KA (Afghanistan) v SSHD* [2012] EWCA Civ 1014.

126 *LQ (age: immutable characteristic) Afghanistan* [2008] UKAIT 5.

granted to an unaccompanied asylum-seeking child under the age of 17.5 if they do not qualify for grant of asylum or humanitarian protection and provided that they do not otherwise qualify for exclusion or revocation of status.[127] Leave is granted for 30 months or until age of 17.5, whichever is the shorter period.

3.101 The Court of Appeal has given guidance on the approach of the courts and tribunals to asylum claims as made by children in *AM (Afghanistan) v SSHD*,[128] endorsing the Practice Direction and Joint Presidential Guidance Note: *Child vulnerable adult and sensitive witnesses.*[129] The court confirmed that a 'child is foremost a child before he or she is a refugee'[130] and in each case the tribunal should carefully consider whether oral evidence is necessary at all, especially if there is objective and medical evidence available to help in assessment of past events and future risk. In cases of clear discrepancies in oral evidence, the tribunal should consider the extent to which the age, vulnerability or sensitivity of the witness is an element of the discrepancy.

Negative decisions on asylum: reasons for refusal

3.102 The Immigration Rules require[131] the Home Secretary to give 'reasons in fact and law' for refusal of asylum in a decision letter. The decision letter will form the basis of an appeal to the FTT (IAC).

Positive decisions on asylum/humanitarian protection and human rights claims: grant of status

Grant of leave as a refugee

3.103 If the Home Secretary concludes that a person is entitled to refugee status on a claim or asylum made prior to 28 June 2022, the person will be issued with a five-year residence permit 'as soon as possible'.[132] Shorter periods may be granted if compelling reasons of national

127 Immigration Rules para 352ZE.

128 [2017] EWCA Civ 1123, [2017] CP Rep 41.

129 *Practice Direction (UT: First-tier and Upper Tribunals: child, vulnerable adult and sensitive witnesses)* [2009] 1 WLR 332; and Joint Presidential Guidance Note No 2 of 2010: *Child, vulnerable adult and sensitive appellant guidance.*

130 *AM (Afghanistan)* at para 35.

131 Immigration Rules para 336.

132 Immigration Rules para 339Q(i). The position post 28 June 2022 is discussed at paras 3.110–115.

security or public order otherwise require or there are reasonable grounds to believe that the applicant is a danger to the security of the UK or having been convicted by a final judgment of a particularly serious crime, the applicant constitutes a danger to the community of the UK or the person's character, conduct or associations otherwise require. Longer periods of leave, including indefinite leave to remain, may also be appropriate if necessary to meet the needs of vulnerable applicants such as children, unaccompanied children, disabled people, pregnant women, single parents with children under 18 or torture victims. The discretion to allow for longer period of leave for this vulnerable cohort reflects the UK obligation under the Qualification Directive.[133]

3.104 At the end of the five-year period of leave, the refugee will be eligible to apply for indefinite leave to remain on the settlement protection route (Immigration Rules Appendix Settlement Protection), subject to any review and applicable policies. If a person is granted indefinite leave to remain, they will be considered 'settled' in the UK. It is always highly advisable to make an in-time application for indefinite or further leave. An out of time application will lead to a review of whether a cessation clause is applicable. The consequence of grant of refugee status is that the person becomes entitled to mainstream benefits.[134]

Differential treatment of refugees under the Nationality and Borders Act 2022

3.105 This long-standing approach to the grant of refugee status changed on 28 June 2022, when NBA 2022 s12 came into force. That provision under the NBA 2022 introduced a discretion to treat refugees differently depending on whether they arrived or are present in the UK unlawfully and/or claimed asylum without delay. Under section 12, the duration of leave that a person is granted will depend on whether they are considered to be a Group 1 or Group 2 refugee:

1) Group 1 refugees are those who a) have come to the UK directly from a country or territory where their life or freedom was threatened; and b) have presented themselves to the authorities

133 Qualification Directive Article 20(2). This used to also be confirmed in the Home Office policy, *Refugee and humanitarian protection leave in asylum claims lodged before 28 June 2022*, v1.0, 28 June 2022, p10. See discussion in paras 3.37–3.41.

134 See chapters 4 and 7.

without delay.[135] For those who have entered or are present in the UK unlawfully, if they can show 'good cause' for their unlawful entry or presence, they may also be treated as a Group 1 refugee.[136]

2) Group 2 refugees are those who do not fit the description of Group 1 refugees.

3.106 As for the meaning of 'coming directly', NBA 2022 s37 states that a refugee has not come directly 'if . . . they stopped in another country outside the United Kingdom, unless they can show that they could not reasonably be expected to have sought protection under the Refugee Convention in that country'. This section seems intended to reverse the Divisional Court's judgment in *Adimi*,[137] discussed above at paras 3.11–3.12.

3.107 NBA 2022 s12(5) gives examples of how the Home Secretary may exercise their discretion to treat Group 1 and Group 2 refugees differently by:

a) the length of any period of limited leave to enter or remain;
b) the requirements that the refugee must meet in order to be given indefinite leave to remain;
c) whether a 'no recourse to public funds' condition is attached to their limited leave, the legal implications, relevance and significance of which are discussed at paras 1.166–1.172; and
d) whether their family members qualify for family reunion.

NBA 2022 s12(6) gives examples of the Home Secretary's discretion to treat the Group 2 refugee's family members differently, which are:

- whether to give them leave to enter or remain;
- the length of their limited leave to enter or remain;
- the requirements for indefinite leave to remain; and
- whether to impose an NRPF condition.

3.108 Under NBA 2022 s12(7), the Home Secretary is not, however, allowed to treat family members differently if they 'are refugees themselves'.

3.109 The apparent intention of differentiation between the two groups of refugees is to deprive Group 2 refugees of the protection of the non-penalisation provision in Article 31(1) of the Refugee Convention, discussed at paras 3.11–3.13 above.

3.110 On 28 June 2022, the Immigration Rules were amended pursuant to NBA 2022 s12(8) to provide for differential treatment of Group 1

135 NBA 2022 s12(2).
136 NBA 2022 s12(3).
137 *R v Uxbridge Magistrates Court ex p Adimi* [1999] EWHC Admin 765.

and Group 2 refugees who claim asylum on or after that date. On the issue of duration of leave as a recognised refugee, the new para 339QA of the Immigration Rules provides that:

a) where the asylum applicant is a Group 1 refugee, they will be granted refugee permission to stay for a minimum period of five years; and
b) where the asylum applicant is a Group 2 refugee, they will be granted temporary refugee permission (TRP) to stay for a minimum of 30 months, unless exceptional circumstances apply.

3.111 Immigration Rules paras 352A, 352AB, 352D and 352DB provide for differentiation with respect to refugee family reunion for pre-flight partners, children under 18 or adult children who remain dependent on their family, with Group 2 refugees having to also demonstrate that there are 'insurmountable obstacles' to the couple or the child and parent 'living together anywhere other than in the UK, and a refusal of their application would breach the UK's obligations under Article 8 of the ECHR'.[138] For a discussion of 'insurmountable obstacles' and the Home Office's approach to Article 8 claims, see paras 1.105–1.106.

3.112 Only Group 1 refugees are entitled to apply for indefinite leave to remain after five years under Immigration Rules Appendix Settlement Protection para 3.1. Group 2 refugees are given temporary refugee protection and they and their dependants are ineligible for the settlement protection route. It will take them much longer to qualify for indefinite leave to remain, after ten years under the general long residence provisions in Immigration Rules Part 7 – see Immigration Rules para 276B.

3.113 The Home Office has published a policy dealing with Group 1 and Group 2 refugees. The *Permission to stay on a protection route for asylum claims lodged on or after 28 June 2022*[139] states that the decision-maker may use the screening and substantive interviews and any other information, such as Border Force case notes or a 'preliminary information questionnaire', to decide whether a refugee is a Group 1 or 2 refugee. The refugee will be given 'an opportunity to rebut' the finding they are a Group 2 refugee and after that a final decision will

138 Immigration Rules para 352AB.
139 V1.0, 28 June 2022, www.gov.uk/government/publications/permission-to-stay-on-a-protection-route-caseworker-guidance.

be made.[140] Matters that may be relevant include personal circumstances, age, situational factors and past trafficking experience. There is no right of appeal or administrative review against the decision of group categorisation. The standard of proof is 'balance of probabilities'. There will be a 'safe return review' at each renewal for a Group 2 refugee. If a safe return review concludes that protection is no longer needed, the person's refugee status or humanitarian protection will be revoked and they will not qualify for further leave on a protection route.

3.114 Group 2 refugees – that is, those with TRP – will not have NRPF imposed, but the conditions attached to TRP may change at a later point. The Immigration Rules as currently drafted do not provide for NRPF. Longer leave will only be granted in the 'most exceptional of circumstances' which is said to mean a situation that is distinguished to a high degree from other cases. Specific evidence must be provided and where there are medical/mental health issues evidence must specifically address why the longer period is necessary.

3.115 Child dependents of Group 2 refugees will normally be granted leave in line with the main applicant (if they do not have protection needs in their own right). The differential treatment provisions will also apply to unaccompanied children so that they may be treated as Group 2 refugees on the basis of how they arrived into the UK. The decision-maker must consider a child's best interests and there may be 'exceptional reasons' to grant children a longer prior of permission to stay (under the *Discretionary leave* policy) but that in the vast majority of cases temporary protection is said, under the policy, to be sufficient. It is said to be 'very unlikely' that best interests considerations will override the wider policy intention of immigration control and discouraging people coming to the UK illegally. At the writing of this chapter, the government has announced that it will not carry on with this policy at present.

Grant of leave under humanitarian protection

3.116 If a person is granted humanitarian protection, the Immigration Rules[141] say that normally, a five-year residence permit will be issued. As with the grant of refugee status, the residence permit leads to immediate and unrestricted access to the labour market and recourse

140 See further *Assessing credibility and refugee status in asylum claims lodged on or after 28 June 2022*, v11.0, 28 June 2022, www.gov.uk/government/publications/considering-asylum-claims-and-assessing-credibility-instruction.

141 Immigration Rules para 339C.

to public funds. There is a five-year route to settlement (indefinite leave to remain) and there is no requirement to demonstrate a knowledge of language and life in the UK when applying for settlement.

3.117 If a human rights claim is successful, a grant of discretionary leave will follow. The duration 'must be determined by considering the individual facts of the case but leave should not normally be granted for more than 30 months at a time'.[142] From 9 July 2012, a person granted DL will become eligible for settlement (indefinite leave to remain) after completing a continuous period of ten years in the UK.[143] That is a significantly longer period of leave than is needed for settlement following a grant of refugee status or humanitarian protection.

Statutory appeals against refusals of protection and human rights claims

Overview

3.118 The IA 2014 significantly amended the legal framework of appeals contained in NIAA 2002 s82. From 20 October 2014, a right of appeal to the FTT lies against refusal of a protection claim,[144] refusal of a human rights claim and revocation of protection status. Previously, there was no right of appeal against the refusal of asylum. Instead, a right of appeal was given against an 'immigration decision', such as a decision that a person is liable to be removed from the UK owing to a refusal of their asylum or protection claim. This was a curious and rather artificial feature of the system and one that the 2014 changes sought to fix by introducing a right of appeal against the protection, human rights or revocation claims.

3.119 NIAA 2002 s77 prohibits the removal of a person from the UK while their asylum claim is 'pending'. A claim is pending until an individual is given notice of the secretary of state's (substantive) decision on it (s77(2)(b)). NIAA 2002 s78 similarly prohibits removal until the final determination of a person's appeal against the refusal of their asylum claim. This is on the basis that to remove them pending the final determination of their asylum claim would breach the UK's obligations under the Refugee Convention, namely the principle of *non-refoulement* under Article 33. This is subject to important caveats set out below concerning the regime for the

142 *Discretionary leave*, v9.0.

143 Immigration Rules para 276B.

144 See paras 3.31–3.41 above for definition of protection claim.

inadmissibility of certain asylum claims and the Rwanda scheme at paras 3.131–3.142.

3.120 There is no entitlement to appeal where an applicant repeats an earlier application for asylum based on the same evidence. To have a further right of appeal, the secretary of state must determine that any further claim is a fresh claim for asylum in order to trigger a further right of appeal.[145]

Certification of an asylum claim and impact on right of appeal

3.121 An appeal to the FTT will be available against refusal of asylum unless they are to be removed to a 'safe third country' in accordance with Asylum and Immigration (Treatment of Claimants, etc) Act (AITCA) 2004 Sch 3 or the claim is certified as 'clearly unfounded'.

3.122 The legislative policy underlying the certification of protection and/or human rights claims is to prevent in-country appeals for claims which are considered hopeless. A further aim was to reduce the costs of financially supporting those whose claims are refused by the Home Office, rather than continue to support during an in-country appeal.[146]

3.123 AITCA 2004 Sch 3 Parts 2–4 (paras 2–16) apply to lists of countries specified by order of the secretary of state and subject to an affirmative resolution by parliament: those include EU and EEA countries and selected other countries. AITCA 2004 Sch 3 Part 5 (paras 17–19), however, permits the secretary of state to certify an individual state as a 'safe third country' for the return of a given *individual* applicant. AITCA 2004 Sch 3 para 17 ('Countries certified as safe for individuals') enables the removal of a person who has made an asylum claim if the secretary of state certifies that it is proposed to remove the person to a specified state, of which the person is not a national or citizen, and the Home Secretary is of the opinion that the specified state is a place where the person's life and liberty will not be threatened by reason of their race, religion, nationality, membership of a particular social group or political opinion, and from which the

145 Immigration Rules para 353 provides for the making of a fresh claim for asylum. An argument based on the 2014 changes to the appeal regime that any protection claim has to be accepted by the SSHD as fresh claim and that an appeal automatically lies to the FTT (IAC) under the 2014 regime failed in *R (Robinson) v SSHD* [2019] UKSC 11, [2020] AC 942.

146 See, for example, the rationale in of the certification system in Home Office, *Certification of protection and human rights claims under section 94 of the Nationality, Immigration and Asylum Act 2002 (clearly unfounded claims)*, v4.0, 12 February 2019.

person will not be sent to another state otherwise than in accordance with the Refugee Convention.

3.124 Unlike AITCA 2004 Sch 3 Parts 2–4, certification under Sch 3 para 17 is not and cannot be based on a 'deeming provision' that the country concerned is safe in general; it requires a careful and individualised consideration of the safety of removal to that state for the particular claimant concerned, focused on the statutory consideration under para 17(c). The effect of certification under para 17 is to disapply NIAA 2002 s77 so that the asylum-seeker/refugee can be removed prior to a decision on their asylum claim: Sch 3 para 18. AITCA 2004 Sch 3 para 19(a) precludes an asylum appeal from being brought within the UK where the claim has been certified under para 17.

3.125 Further, if a person comes from a safe country of origin, their claim has to be certified as clearly unfounded unless the Home Secretary is satisfied that it is not clearly unfounded.[147] NIAA 2002 s94(4) contains a list of countries which are generally considered to be free of serious risk of persecution and ECHR breaches for people entitled to reside there.

3.126 The 'safe third country' concept concerns an individual's connection to a country which is not necessarily one that they came from but it is reasonable and feasible to transfer them there without substantively considering their protection claim in the UK. However, as discussed above at paras 3.24–3.30, the Procedures Directive defines a 'safe third country' in a more specific way, related to a country that the person has a connection with, such as by passing through the country on their way to the UK and to which they could reasonably be expected to seek protection. There is currently a question mark on whether the Procedures Directive is retained EU law, see para 3.30 above. The concept of the 'safe third country' and its parameters have become more important in the context of the government's Rwanda asylum plan, discussed at paras 3.131–3.142 below.

3.127 If a claim for protection has been certified as 'clearly unfounded' by the Home Office, there is no suspensive in-country right of appeal. The only challenge to a clearly unfounded certificate is by way of judicial review.

3.128 The test for 'clearly unfounded' is set out in *R (Yogathas and Thangarasa)*[148] and *R (VL) v SSHD*[149] – it is a claim which is so clearly without substance that it is bound to fail.

147 NIAA 2002 s94(3).
148 [2002] UKHL 36, [2003] 1 AC 920.
149 [2003] EWCA Civ 25.

3.129 In relation to deportees, the IA 2014 inserted section 94B into the NIAA 2002, creating a controversial system of 'deport first, appeal later'. The IA 2016 amended section 94B and extended it to any human rights claim against removal, not just a claim made by a person liable to deportation. The consequence of these provisions was to prevent a person appealing a decision to remove or deport which they claimed would breach their human rights prior to actually being removed or deported.

3.130 In the landmark decision of *R (Kiarie and Byndloss) v SSHD*,[150] the Supreme Court held that the approach to certifying human rights claims under NIAA 2002 s94B was unlawful because it breached the procedural requirements of ECHR Article 8. The court considered the practical difficulties for an appellant who appealed from outside the UK, including the costs of obtaining expert evidence and arranging for video link in what is often a difficult appeal. Since *Kiarie and Byndloss*, the Court of Appeal has applied a similar analysis to other out of country appeals where ECHR Article 8 is engaged. In *Ahsan v SSHD*,[151] the Court of Appeal held that an out of country appeal was not an effective alternative remedy to a decision to remove an applicant who was said to have cheated in their English language test and their proposed or actual removal constituted a breach of the procedural obligations in ECHR Article 8.

Inadmissibility and the Rwanda asylum plan

3.131 NBA 2022 s29 and Sch 4 amend NIAA 2002 s77 to make it easier to remove someone with a pending asylum claim to a 'safe third country'. It makes it possible to remove someone to that country whilst their asylum claim is pending. The changes came into force on 28 June 2022.

3.132 Ahead of these changes, on 14 April 2022, the Home Secretary announced an agreement with Rwanda, which created a mechanism for the relocation to Rwanda of asylum-seekers whose claims are inadmissible for consideration inadmissible in the UK. On relocation, the asylum-seeker's claim will be processed by the Rwandan authorities, with a view to deciding whether to grant the person refugee status or, if refused, to remove them from Rwanda to their country of origin. Under the MOU, published on 14 April 2022, the UK is responsible for initial screening of asylum-seekers prior to

150 [2017] UKSC 42, [2017] 1 WLR 2380.
151 [2017] EWCA Civ 2009.

seeking Rwanda's approval for a given individual's transfer. In addition to the MOU, there are two undated Notes Verbales which confirm the two countries' understanding of the details of the MOU governing asylum processing arrangements and reception and accommodation arrangements in Rwanda. These Notes Verbales have not been published. They are said to contain assurances given by Rwanda of compliance with, and observation of, obligations under the Refugee Convention and of provision of adequate reception for asylum-seekers transferred there.

3.133 On 9 May 2022, the Home Office published an amended *Inadmissibility guidance: safe third country cases*[152] to deal with the circumstances in which claims made in the UK could be determined to be inadmissible so that the person's asylum claim could be transferred to Rwanda for substantive consideration. The introduction to the policy stated that:

> In this first stage of applying the policy, removals of individuals from the UK in accordance with the MEDP are intended to deter people from making dangerous journeys to the UK to claim asylum, which are facilitated by criminal smugglers, when they have already travelled through safe third countries. In particular, but not exclusively, this is aimed at deterring arrivals by small boats.

3.134 The Home Office also published an equality impact assessment (EIA) of the UK–Rwanda asylum plan.[153] The EIA noted that the Home Office research into conditions into Rwanda had raised equalities concerns, but that this would be militated by 'a case-by-case risk assessment when determining suitability for relocation and individual vulnerabilities will be taken into consideration and assessed against our knowledge of the conditions in Rwanda'.[154] The need for an individualised assessment to minimise or prevent unlawful discrimination is emphasised throughout the EIA. However, it was said not to be possible to disclose the criteria for relocation under the scheme, as to do so could incentivise smuggling gangs to target the most vulnerable people. In relation to the protected characteristic of disability, the EIA states that 'mental and physical disabilities will be taken into account in any relocation decision, and will depend on

152 V6.0. It has since been updated to v7.0 on 28 June 2022, www.gov.uk/government/publications/inadmissibility-third-country-cases.

153 EIA available at: www.gov.uk/government/publications/migration-and-economic-development-partnership-with-rwanda.

154 EIA, p2.

both the severity of the disability and the facilities in Rwanda'.[155] However, neither the *Inadmissibility guidance* nor any other published policy set out a process by which mental and physical disabilities would be screened prior to deciding whether to include the person into a process for consideration for inadmissibility of their asylum claim and relocation of them to Rwanda.

3.135 The Home Office also published four 'country policy and information notes' (CPINs), said to be based on interviews with Rwandan officials and the UNHCR, assessing Rwandan asylum processing arrangements and human rights compliance. These CPINs have been relied on by the Home Office to seek to show that Rwanda is a safe third country to which asylum-seekers can be appropriately relocated. However, a more careful consideration of these CPINs shows that the contrary is apparent.

3.136 The UNHCR[156] expressed strong opposition to the UK–Rwanda asylum plan because the arrangements shift asylum responsibilities, evade international obligations, and are contrary to the letter and spirit of the Refugee Convention. The UNHCR urged both countries to rethink the plan and warned that externalisation arrangements only magnified the risk to refugees. On 10 June 2022, the UNHCR published a legal analysis[157] that highlighted significant deficiencies in the process and cast doubt on the reliability of information to the contrary in the CPIN. Five UN Special Rapporteurs with remit on matters concerning human trafficking, modern slavery and migrants also published a communication to the UK government on 1 July 2022 that set out concerns about the arrangements and the risks to victims and potential victims of removal to Rwanda.[158] A commentary published by Asylos, a global network of researchers of country conditions for asylum-seekers, on 13 July 2022, further

155 EIA, p11.

156 'UN refugee agency opposes UK plan to export asylum', 14 April 2022, www.unhcr.org/uk/news/press/2022/4/62585e814/un-refugee-agency-opposes-uk-plan-export-asylum.html.

157 'UNHCR analysis of the legality and appropriateness of the transfer of asylum-seekers under the UK–Rwanda arrangement', 8 June 2022, para 15.

158 Mandates of the Special Rapporteur on trafficking in persons, especially women and children; the Special Rapporteur on the human rights of migrants; the Special Rapporteur on contemporary forms of slavery, including its causes and consequences; the Special Rapporteur on the promotion and protection of human rights and fundamental freedoms while countering terrorism and the Special Rapporteur on violence against women, its causes and consequences, Ref: OL GBR 9/2022, Geneva 1.7.2022 ('UNSR legal analysis').

identified significant gaps and omissions in the description of problems with Rwanda as a safe country for asylum-seekers.

3.137 The *Inadmissibility guidance* is the only published policy that sets out how decisions are made to allocate a person to the process for deciding whether a person's claim is inadmissible and whether they should be relocated to Rwanda. However, the guidance contains little information about the criteria for allocating to and suitability for removal to Rwanda, or how it is to be assessed. It acknowledges that:[159]

1) unaccompanied asylum-seeking children, including those whose ages are disputed but are subject to age assessments, are not suitable for the inadmissibility process;
2) EU nationals, for whom there is a separate inadmissibility process under the Immigration Rules, will not be allocated.

3.138 For those not expressly excluded from the inadmissibility process, the consideration of allocation into and decision-making within that process appears to be as follows:

1) **Screening:** Following registration of an asylum claim, the individual will be subject to a screening interview. This has to date frequently taken place whilst the person is detained under immigration powers. The screening pro forma contains a warning that the asylum claim may be treated as inadmissible 'if you came to the UK after travelling through a safe third country or have connections to a safe third country', and that if inadmissible, it would not be substantively considered in the UK and the individual may be removed to a safe third country. The warning does not mention Rwanda as such a possible country. Nor are the screening pro forma questions directed at eliciting information about why it may not be safe and appropriate to seek a given person's potential removal to Rwanda or another country that he or she had passed through on their way to the UK.
2) **Allocation to inadmissibility process:**[160] The National Asylum Allocation Unit (NAAU) carries out an initial assessment to consider whether to refer the person's case to the Third Country Unit (TCU) to be allocated to the inadmissibility process. That assessment is heavily reliant on information gathered from the screening interview. The timing of the referral shows that in practice the assessment is made *prior* to the completion of any investigations

159 *Inadmissibility guidance*, p11.

160 *Inadmissibility: safe third country cases*, v7.0, 28 June 2022, pp14–19.

into an individual's personal circumstances, including any trafficking investigation. Although the guidance focuses, for suitability for allocation, on those people who could be described as having made a 'dangerous' journey to the UK (for example, by small boat or clandestinely in lorries), that fact should only mean the person '*may* be eligible for removal to Rwanda'. It remains a *discretion*, to be exercised on a case-by-case basis, on whether a given person should be allocated to the process.

3) **Notice of intent:** The TCU will serve a 'notice of intent' (NOI) on the individual where it considers that the case 'appears to' satisfy Immigration Rules paras 345A and 345B. If an individual is being considered for removal to Rwanda, this will be specified in the NOI (*Inadmissibility guidance*, p14). When served with a NOI, the individual has seven calendar days (for detained cases) or 14 calendar days (for non-detained cases) to make representations as to a) why their asylum claim should not be considered inadmissible or b) why they should not be required to leave the UK or be removed to Rwanda (or any other country). To date, as at the time of writing (September 2022), the NOI served on individuals is in English. Other than identifying the country with which they are said to have a connection, nothing in the pro forma NOI sets out the *Inadmissibility guidance* or contains information tailored to the individual claimant. They do not set out the reasons for the decision to allocate the person to the process or the evidence on which it is based. The NOI is served with an 'Information Pack' entitled 'I'm being considered for relocation to Rwanda – what does this mean for me?'. This, again, is only in English.
4) **Decision on inadmissibility and removal:** TCU has to 'fully review the evidence available' including, responses to the NOI and information from additional checks, such as fingerprint checks or inquiries with the third country. The decision-maker also needs to consider whether Rwanda is safe for the individual.

3.139 If representations have been made which raise a real risk of serious harm in Rwanda (or of a risk of refoulement, ie that an individual may be sent from Rwanda to a country where they face such a risk), these will be considered both as part of the inadmissibility decision by the TCU and as an Article 3 human rights claim by a different team.

3.140 If a decision is taken to treat the claim as inadmissible and refuse any human rights claim, those decisions will be taken and served together. The human rights claim is not subject to an inadmissibility threshold and is to be considered substantively. However, where a person's asylum claim has been determined to be inadmissible, the *Inadmissibility guidance* states that any refused human rights claim should also be certified under NIAA 2002 s94 such that the person has no in-country right of appeal in respect of that claim, although in principle the merits of the human rights claim should be considered in its own right. In practice, the decisions will also be served together with a notice of removal, which provides five working days' notice of removal directions.

3.141 The first planned flight to Rwanda was scheduled for 14 June 2022. However, owing to a series of legal challenges, the flight did not depart because all individuals originally planned for the flight had either had their removal directions to Rwanda cancelled by the Home Office on receipt of representations or the issuing of judicial review proceedings, or had been suspended by the Upper Tribunal, the ECtHR or the Court of Appeal.

3.142 The Divisional Court handed down judgment in the challenge to the legality of the Rwanda asylum plan on 19 December 2022.[161] The court found that the Rwanda asylum plan was lawful and rejected the claimants' arguments on all grounds concerning the lawfulness of the plan. The court concluded that it is lawful for the government to make arrangements for relocating asylum-seekers to Rwanda and for their asylum claims to be determined in Rwanda rather than in the UK. The court held that, on the evidence before it, the government has made arrangements with the government of Rwanda which are intended to ensure that the asylum claims of people relocated to Rwanda are properly determined in Rwanda. In those circumstances, the relocation of asylum-seekers to Rwanda was consistent with the Refugee Convention and with the statutory and other legal obligations on the government including the obligations imposed by the Human Rights Act 1998. However, the Divisional Court went on to find that the secretary of state must consider properly the circumstances of each individual claimant. The secretary of state must decide if there is anything about each person's particular circumstances which means that his or her asylum claim should be determined in the UK or whether there are other reasons why he or she should not be relocated to Rwanda. In eight claims, the court found that the secretary of state had not properly considered their individual circumstances. The decisions in those cases that their asylum claim would not be admitted for examination in the UK and their

161 *R (AAA (Syria)) v SSHD* [2022] EWHC 3230 (Admin).

human rights claim certified without a right of appeal in the UK would be set aside and referred back to the secretary of state for a fresh decision. The claimants have appealed the Divisional Court's judgment. At the writing of this appeal, the appeal is due to be heard in late April 2023.

Exclusion, revocation and cessation of protection status

3.143 A person may be excluded from the grant of refugee status or that status may be subject to cancellation, cessation or revocation. These scenarios are outlined below. The broad principle behind these provisions is to deny the benefits of refugee protection to those who do not deserve it because of their conduct or criminality or in order to protect the public.

Exclusion and cessation

3.144 An applicant may be excluded from the grant of refugee status under Article 1F of the Refugee Convention if they have committed war crimes, crimes against humanity, terrorist acts or other serious criminal offences. The Home Office's policy on *Exclusion under Article 1F of the Refugee Convention*[162] advises that any cases which potentially engage Article 1F must be referred to Special Cases Unit (SCU) or where criminality in in the UK, the Criminal Casework Directorate. The exclusion provisions are reflected in the EU Directives and the Immigration Rules.[163]

3.145 Refugee Convention Article 33(2) has a different purpose to Article 1F. It relates to crimes and conduct in the country of refuge. A person's status as a refugee may be revoked and they may be removed: 'where there are reasonable grounds for regarding them as a danger to the security of the country in which he is, or who, having been convicted by a final judgment of a particularly serious crime, constitutes a danger to the community of that country'.[164] NIAA 2002 s71 is the UK's interpretation of Article 33(2) in domestic law. Even if a person comes under Article 33(2), they cannot be removed to a

162 V7.0, 28 June 2022.

163 Immigration Rules para 334(iii) and (iv); and Qualification Directive Article 14(5).

164 Refugee Convention Article 33(2).

country where there is an ECHR barrier to removal (usually ECHR Article 3 breach).

3.146 A person may be excluded from the grant of humanitarian protection on grounds that are identical to those for exclusion from refugee status. Exclusion will apply if there are serious reasons for considering that the person has participated in crimes against peace, war crimes, crimes against humanity or any other serious crimes, or if there are serious reasons for considering that they constitute a danger to the security of the UK.[165]

3.147 The Home Office may review the grant of asylum at any point during the period of five years or when an application for indefinite leave is made or on the expiry of the five-year period. A review may result in revocation or failure to renew if the Home Office is satisfied that the conditions leading to grant of refugee status have ceased (cessation). Immigration Rules para 339A(i)–(vi) deal with cessation and broadly reflect the cessation provisions in Refugee Convention Article 1C(1)–(6). These provisions are concerned with the refugee's voluntary actions such as receiving protection from the country from which asylum was claimed or the acquisition of new nationality which means that refugee protection is no longer needed.

Revocation

3.148 A review of refugee status and possible revocation of asylum may be triggered if a person:

- falls within the scope of Refugee Convention Article 33(2);
- is on the sex offenders register;
- is the subject of an extradition request;
- where the secretary of state considers that their presence is not conducive to the public good.[166]

3.149 If refugee status is being actively reviewed, there are strict procedural requirements set out in the Immigration Rules and based on the Procedures Directive including the opportunity to respond to an allegation of deception, the right to an interview in complex cases and the opportunity to make representations as to why refugee status should be retained.

165 Immigration Rules para 339D.

166 *Revocation of protection status*, v1.0, 28 June 2022, www.gov.uk/government/publications/canceling-ceasing-and-revoking-refugee-status-process.

3.150 If refugee status is revoked, that does not in itself make the person removable. However, as a matter of practice, their leave to remain is likely to be curtailed if asylum is revoked. IAA 1999 s10 (as amended by the IA 2014) provides a single power of removal for those who require but do not have leave to enter or remain. A separate removal decision is not necessary. Those who are in breach of the conditions of their leave, or who obtained leave by deception, may be removed under this power but any extant leave must be brought to an end first (curtailed). All persons removed under this power must still be given notice of removal.[167]

3.151 A right of appeal under NIAA 2002 s82 lies against any decision to revoke a protection claim (ie refugee or humanitarian protection).

167 *Revocation of refugee status*, v1.0, p11.

CHAPTER 4

Welfare benefits for migrants

Tom Royston

continued

Key points[1]

- People in the UK unlawfully (ie people who require leave to remain but do not have it) are ineligible for benefits.[2]
- Most non-European Economic Area (EEA) nationals with limited leave to remain are ineligible for benefits because their leave will have been granted subject to the condition that they do not have recourse to public funds (people with refugee status or humanitarian protection are an important exception to that).[3]
- Non-EEA nationals with indefinite leave to remain are generally eligible for benefits.
- EEA nationals with settled status (a form of indefinite leave to remain) are eligible for benefits.[4]
- EEA nationals with pre-settled status (a form of limited leave to remain) are eligible for benefits if they can show that they are exercising a European Union (EU) law right of residence by being here, which normally requires a history of economic activity in the UK.[5]
- People coming (or returning) to the UK, including UK nationals, often have to wait for several months (sometimes longer) to be able to receive benefits.[6]
- The main ways in which the state can restrict a migrant's access to benefits are:
  - making a migrant's leave to remain conditional on 'not having recourse to public funds' (NRPF).[7]
  - deeming them a 'person subject to immigration control' (PSIC).[8]
  - treating them as not satisfying a residence requirement.[9]

1 This is a general overview, which is subject to many exceptions.
2 See paras 4.32–4.33 and 4.66.
3 See paras 4.35–4.41 and 4.52.
4 See paras 4.76–4.78.
5 See paras 4.79–4.83.
6 See paras 4.138–4.145.
7 See paras 4.35–4.41.
8 See paras 4.32–4.34.
9 See paras 4.42–4.108.

Introduction

> This is about saying: our welfare system is like a national club. It's made up of the contribution of hardworking British taxpayers. Millions of people doing the right thing, paying into the system, generation after generation. It cannot be right that migrants can turn up and claim full rights to this club straightaway.
>
> *David Cameron, 28 November 2014*[10]

4.1 Since the early 2000s, political concerns about migration have been channelled into legislation making migrants' access to cash social security benefits ('benefits'), increasingly restricted, and increasingly complex.

4.2 The purpose of this chapter is to introduce these immigration-based restrictions, to help in the task of assessing whether or not a particular person is excluded from accessing social security benefits as a result of their immigration status.

4.3 No attempt is made here to detail the substantive entitlement conditions for social security benefits. The *Welfare benefits and tax credits handbook*, published by Child Poverty Action Group (CPAG), is a useful introduction to the social security system (and it is nearly 1,800 pages long).

4.4 This book describes the law in England and Wales. Regarding the other parts of the UK, Northern Ireland has a legislatively separate social security system, and a separate adjudication system, although in practice both operate on virtually identical lines to that in England and Wales.

4.5 Scotland's social security system used to be identical to that in England and Wales, but is beginning to diverge under devolution arrangements.

Overview of chapter

4.6 This chapter adopts the following structure:

- About benefits – what kinds of benefits are there?
- Subjection to immigration control:
  - What does it mean to be a person subject to immigration control?
  - Exceptions
- Recourse to public funds
  - what is 'no recourse to public funds'?

10 Prime Minister, Speech made at JCB Staffordshire (www.gov.uk/government/speeches/jcb-staffordshire-prime-ministers-speech).

- Residence requirements:
  - What is habitual residence?
  - What is ordinary residence?
  - What is a right to reside?
  - What residence rights might EEA nationals have?
  - What are presence requirements?
  - What are the special rules for employment related benefits?
- Practicalities:
  - Who needs a national insurance number?
  - How is benefit entitlement affected by a person's partner being a migrant?
  - What is benefit coordination?
- Challenging decisions and non-decisions:
  - How can adverse decisions be challenged?
  - How can delay in processing migrants' benefit claims be dealt with?
  - What can be done if correctly excluded from benefits?

About benefits

What kinds of benefits are there?

4.7 To understand how migrants' access to benefits can be affected by their immigration status, it may help to start by observing that benefits in this country can be roughly categorised into four types, described below:

1) income supplement or replacement benefits;
2) miscellaneous special purpose benefits;
3) employment-related benefits;
4) contributory benefits.

4.8 Income supplement or replacement benefits now have heavy entitlement restrictions for migrants.

4.9 Miscellaneous special purpose benefits have a mixture of different rules, but in general are also quite heavily restricted.

4.10 Employment-related benefits and contributory benefits generally lack formal restrictions related to immigration status, but because they generally depend on having worked in the UK, may in practice be inaccessible to migrants, particularly new migrants.

Means-tested income supplement or replacement benefits

What are they?

4.11 In this category are:

- universal credit (UC) (the main subsistence benefit for all working-age claimants);[11]
- pension credit (PC) and housing benefit (HB) (the main subsistence benefits for pension-age claimants);[12]
- council tax reduction (for anyone on a low income with a liability to pay council tax).[13]

4.12 UC is administered by the Department for Work and Pensions (DWP) and is normally claimed online. PC is also administered by the DWP and is normally claimed by phone. HB and council tax reduction are administered by local authorities, so claim arrangements will vary.

Who gets them and what do they include?

4.13 Means-tested income supplement or replacement benefits are paid where a single adult or an adult couple have no income, or a low income.

4.14 They provide for the members of a household's subsistence costs and housing costs, including those of children. They can include extra amounts where a member of the household is disabled. UC can also include amounts to subsidise the costs of childcare.

Means testing

4.15 The benefits are 'means-tested' in the sense that the more other income a household has (for example, from employment), the less

11 Welfare Reform Act 2012 Part 1; Universal Credit Regulations 2013 SI No 376.

12 State Pension Credit Act 2002; State Pension Credit Regulations 2002 SI No 1792; Social Security Contributions and Benefits Act 1992 s130; Housing Benefit (Persons who have attained the qualifying age for state pension credit) Regulations 2006 SI No 214.

13 Local Government Finance Act 1992 s13A. Council tax reduction, the precise conditions of which are prescribed by a claimant's local authority, is an atypical benefit, because it operates as a reduction in tax liability rather than a cash benefit. But in its rules, purpose, and exclusions for migrants, it closely resembles a means tested benefit.

benefit it receives. Possession of capital (for example, savings) also affects entitlement, and can bar it completely.

4.16 For UC, some earned income can be completely disregarded (if the claimant is a parent or disabled and therefore has a 'work allowance'); other earned income reduces UC by 55p for every £1 of income.[14] Unearned income is either disregarded altogether (for example, some other benefits like personal independence payment or bereavement support payment), or reduces UC pound for pound.[15]

4.17 For PC, some income is disregarded altogether,[16] and other income reduces benefit pound for pound.[17]

4.18 For HB, some income is disregarded altogether, some income reduces benefit pound for pound, and some reduces entitlement by 65p for every £1 of income.[18]

4.19 Council tax reduction schemes vary because they are generally locally designed, but most roughly copy the approach of UC and/or PC, as do the default schemes which take effect if a local authority chooses not to design its own.[19]

Legacy benefits

4.20 For working-age claimants and their families, UC is in the process of replacing a number of older benefits ('legacy benefits'): income support (IS); income-based jobseeker's allowance (JSA); income-related employment and support allowance (ESA); HB for working-age people; child tax credit (CTC); and working tax credit (WTC).

4.21 New claims can in general no longer be made for legacy benefits, so they are not discussed in this chapter, but advisers should be aware that for some years to come, claimants may still be receiving them. The CPAG handbook contains information about their rules.

Miscellaneous special purpose benefits

4.22 This miscellaneous category includes benefits covering a wide variety of purposes. The main examples are:

14 Universal Credit Regulations 2013 reg 22.
15 Universal Credit Regulations 2013 regs 22(1)(a) and 66.
16 State Pension Credit Regulations 2002 Part III.
17 State Pension Credit Act 2002 s2(2).
18 Housing Benefit (Persons who have attained the qualifying age for state pension credit) Regulations 2006 reg 51.
19 Council Tax Reduction Schemes (Default Scheme) (England) Regulations 2012 SI No 2886; Council Tax Reduction Schemes (Default Scheme) (Wales) Regulations 2013 SI No 3035.

- discretionary housing payments (DHPs) (to top-up a shortfall in rent);[20]
- free school meals;[21]
- child benefit (CB);[22]
- Healthy Start food vouchers;[23]
- social fund maternity grants;[24]
- social fund cold weather payments;[25]
- social fund funeral payments;[26]
- social fund winter fuel payments;[27]
- disability living allowance (DLA) (disability benefit for children);[28]
- personal independence payment (PIP) (working age disability benefit);[29]
- attendance allowance (disability benefit for retirees);[30]
- carer's allowance (for people caring for a disabled person).[31]

4.23 Unless otherwise stated in the footnotes, all the benefits mentioned above are administered by the DWP. Information about how to claim them can be found on the gov.uk website.

4.24 Entitlement to some of these benefits is means tested (in a wide variety of ways); entitlement to some others is restricted to those in receipt of another income supplement or replacement benefit.

20 Child Support, Pensions and Social Security Act 2000 s69; Discretionary Financial Assistance Regulations 2001 SI No 1167 (administered by local authorities).
21 Education Act 1996 s512ZB (administered by local authorities).
22 Social Security Contributions and Benefits Act 1992 ss141–147; Child Benefit (General) Regulations 2006 SI No 223 (administered by HM Revenue and Customs (HMRC)).
23 Healthy Start Scheme and Welfare Food (Amendment) Regulations 2005 SI No 3262 (administered by the Department of Health).
24 Social Fund Maternity and Funeral Expenses (General) Regulations 2005 SI No 3061 Part II.
25 Social Fund Cold Weather Payments (General) Regulations 1988 SI No 1724.
26 Social Fund Maternity and Funeral Expenses (General) Regulations 2005 Part III.
27 Social Fund Winter Fuel Payment Regulations 2000 SI No 729.
28 Social Security Contributions and Benefits Act 1992 ss71–76; Social Security (Disability Living Allowance) Regulations 1991 SI No 2890.
29 Welfare Reform Act 2012 Part 4; Social Security (Personal Independence Payment) Regulations 2013 SI No 377.
30 Social Security Act 1975 s35; Social Security (Attendance Allowance) Regulations 1991 SI No 2740.
31 Social Security Contributions and Benefits Act 1992 s70; Social Security (Invalid Care Allowance) Regulations 1976 SI No 409.

4.25 The non-means tested benefits in the list above are winter fuel payment, DLA, PIP and attendance allowance.

4.26 Child benefit is not technically means tested, but an equivalent income tax charge for those on high incomes in receipt of child benefit makes it, in practice, means tested where the claimant or their partner has an income above £50,000 per year.[32]

Employment-related benefits

4.27 These are paid to people who have been working. Most are payable to people who are not working at present (because of a new child or because of illness or accident), although industrial injuries disablement benefits are payable to people in work. They are not means tested, and do not depend on national insurance contributions:

- statutory maternity/paternity/adoption/shared parental pay;[33]
- statutory sick pay (SSP);[34]
- maternity allowance;[35]
- industrial injuries disablement benefits (IIDBs).[36]

4.28 All those benefits are administered by the DWP. The 'statutory pay' benefits are generally claimed and paid through employers; information about how to claim maternity allowance and IIDBs can be found on the gov.uk website.

Contributory benefits

4.29 These benefits are paid where a person (or in the case of bereavement support payment, their spouse or civil partner) has paid or been credited with national insurance contributions. They are not in general means tested. They include:

32 Income Tax (Earnings and Pensions) Act 2003 s681B.

33 Social Security Contributions and Benefits Act 1992 Parts XII–12ZC; Maternity Allowance and Statutory Maternity Pay Regulations 1994 SI No 1230; Statutory Paternity Pay and Statutory Adoption Pay (General) Regulations 2002 SI No 2822; Statutory Shared Parental Pay (General) Regulations 2014 SI No 3051.

34 Social Security Contributions and Benefits Act 1992 Part XI; Statutory Sick Pay (General) Regulations 1982 SI No 894.

35 Social Security Contributions and Benefits Act 1992 ss35–35B; Maternity Allowance and Statutory Maternity Pay Regulations 1994.

36 Social Security Contributions and Benefits Act 1992 Part V.

- state retirement pension;[37]
- contribution-based JSA;[38]
- contribution-based ESA;[39]
- bereavement support payment.[40]

4.30 Those benefits are all administered by the DWP. Information about how to claim can be found on the gov.uk website.

4.31 The rates of retirement pension, JSA and ESA are for the most part calculated only by reference to an individual's contributions (and in the case of ESA, their degree of incapacity). Bereavement support payment is an exception in that it has regard to the needs of children rather than just the individual claimant: it is paid at more than double the rate if the bereaved claimant is a parent.

Subjection to immigration control

What does it mean to be a person subject to immigration control?

4.32 The main restriction on migrants' welfare benefit rights is Immigration and Asylum Act (IAA) 1999 s115(1). It excludes 'persons subject to immigration control' (PSIC) from entitlement to the following benefits:[41]

- the principal income replacement/supplement benefits (UC, PC, HB);[42]
- PIP;
- DLA;

37 Pensions Act 2014 Part 1; Social Security Contributions and Benefits Act 1992 ss43–55. Technically the new 2014 Act pension is simply called 'state pension' but the similar benefit known as 'retirement pension' still exists under the 1992 Act for anyone who reached pensionable age before 6 April 2016.

38 Jobseekers Act 1995; Jobseeker's Allowance Regulations 2013 SI No 378.

39 Welfare Reform Act 2007; Employment and Support Allowance Regulations 2013 SI No 379.

40 Pensions Act 2014 Part 5; Bereavement Support Payment Regulations 2017 SI No 410.

41 Also the legacy benefits IS, CTC, WTC, JSA and ESA. For more information about those benefits consult the third edition of this text (2009).

42 Council tax reduction is not expressly excluded by IAA 1999 s115, but PSIC are required to be excluded from local authority schemes, so the effect is the same: Council Tax Reduction Schemes (Prescribed Requirements) (England) Regulations 2012 SI No 2885 reg 13; Council Tax Reduction Schemes and Prescribed Requirements (Wales) Regulations 2013 SI No 3029 (W 301) reg 29.

- attendance allowance;
- carer's allowance;
- CB;
- a social fund payment;
- a health in pregnancy grant.

4.33 A person subject to immigration control is defined in IAA 1999 s115(9) as:

a person who–
(a) requires leave to enter or remain in the United Kingdom[43] but does not have it;
(b) has leave to enter or remain in the United Kingdom which is subject to a condition that he does not have recourse to public funds;
(c) has leave to enter or remain in the United Kingdom given as a result of a maintenance undertaking; or
(d) has leave to enter or remain in the United Kingdom only as a result of paragraph 17 of Schedule 4.[44]

Exceptions

4.34 Social Security (Immigration and Asylum) Consequential Amendments Regulations 2000[45] Schedule, made under IAA 1999 s115(3), creates exceptions (all quite rare) to the general IAA 1999 s115(1) rule. Those exceptions, who are not excluded from benefits despite being PSIC, are:

a) In the case of UC, HB and a social fund payment:
   – a person given leave pursuant to a maintenance and accommodation undertaking, who has been resident in the UK for a period of at least five years (beginning on the date of entry or

43 See chapter 1.

44 IAA 1999 Sch 4 para 17 was repealed in 2003, but IAA 1999 s115(9)(d) has not been amended to reflect that change. IAA 1999 Sch 4 para 17 made provision for continuation of leave to remain while an immigration appeal was pending. In *EE v City of Cardiff (HB)* [2018] UKUT 418 (AAC) (11 December 2018) the Upper Tribunal decided (at para 31), 'the reference in section 115(9)(d) of the 1999 Act to paragraph 17 of Schedule 4 to that Act *must be construed as a reference to that provision as reenacted in section 3C(1) and (2)(b) and (c) of the Immigration Act [1971]*' (emphasis added). However, query whether *EE* is correctly decided on that point: IA 1971 s3C is not identically worded to IAA 1999 Sch 4 para 17 and it is questionable whether it really can be treated as a 're-enactment'. If *EE* is wrong, a person with IA 1971 s3C leave continues to be eligible for benefit if they had been eligible before their non-section 3C leave expired.

45 SI No 636.

the date on which the undertaking was given in respect of him or her, whichever date is the later);
- a person given leave pursuant to a maintenance and accommodation undertaking, who has not been resident in the UK for the five-year period specified above, but whose sponsor(s) has died;
- a person who is a national of a state which has ratified the European Convention on Social and Medical Assistance (ECSMA) or a state which has ratified the Council of Europe Social Charter (CESC) and who is lawfully present in the UK.

b) In the case of attendance allowance, carer's allowance, DLA, PIP, a social fund payment, a health in pregnancy grant and CB:
- a family member of an EEA national;
- a person, or the family member of a person, lawfully working in Great Britain who is a national of a state with which the EU has concluded an agreement under Treaty on the Functioning of the European Union (TFEU) Article 217 providing, in the field of social security, for the equal treatment of workers who are nationals of the signatory state and their families;
- a person given leave pursuant to a maintenance and accommodation undertaking.

Recourse to public funds

What is 'no recourse to public funds'?

4.35 It is a standard condition of a migrant's leave to remain in the UK that they do not have recourse to public funds.[46] A person subject to that condition who applies for benefit may put their immigration status at risk.

4.36 Public funds are defined in Immigration Rules HC 395 para 6(2):

'Public funds' means–

(a) housing under Part VI or VII of the Housing Act 1996 and under Part II of the Housing Act 1985 . . .; and

(b) attendance allowance, severe disablement allowance, carer's allowance and disability living allowance under Part III of the Social Security Contribution and Benefits Act 1992; income support, council tax benefit and housing benefit under Part VII of that Act; a social fund payment under Part VIII of that Act; child benefit under Part IX of that Act; income based jobseeker's allowance

46 See further paras 1.166–1.172.

under the Jobseekers Act 1995, income related allowance under Part 1 of the Welfare Reform Act 2007 (employment and support allowance) state pension credit under the State Pension Credit Act 2002; or child tax credit and working tax credit under Part 1 of the Tax Credits Act 2002; and

. . .

(d) Universal Credit under Part 1 of the Welfare Reform Act 2012 or Personal Independence Payment under Part 4 of that Act; and

. . .

(f) a council tax reduction under a council tax reduction scheme made under section 13A of the Local Government Finance Act 1992 in relation to England or Wales . . .; and

. . .

(i) a discretionary payment made by a local authority under section 1 of the Localism Act 2011.[47]

4.37 The fact that a migrant, as a condition of their leave in the UK, is prohibited from having access to public funds, does not as a matter of fact always prevent the migrant from receiving them.

4.38 In most cases, a person who has NRPF will *not* be entitled to receive those public funds, whether as a claimant on their own or as part of a household, largely because having NRPF will make the person a PSIC and therefore disentitled to benefit. However, it is important to be aware that this is not always the case.

4.39 In some situations, the immigration status of non-claimant household members is not taken into account when calculating the amount of benefit to which a household is entitled. Therefore the presence in a household of a NRPF adult or child can, if a benefit is claimed, lead to that household receiving more benefit than it otherwise would have, causing the NRPF person to breach the terms of his or her leave to remain.[48] Examples can include where, an eligible person claiming HB and a NRPF person are members of a couple and are joint tenants, or where UC or child benefit is claimed in respect of a NRPF child.

4.40 A person in this position must seek specialist immigration law advice.

4.41 Additionally, a few people whom IAA 1999 s115(1) exempts from being excluded from benefit are, nevertheless PSIC.[49] For the most part, the consequences of this are kept tidy by 'recourse to public

47 References omitted to public funds prescribed under legislation applying only to Scotland or Northern Ireland.

48 Immigration Rules para 6A.

49 See paras 4.32–4.34.

funds' excluding receipt of benefits by an exempt person,[50] but council tax reduction has not been included in the IAA 1999 s115 list, and the wording of Immigration Rules para 6(2) is arguably unclear: a person in this position who can otherwise claim benefits should seek specialist immigration law advice before claiming council tax reduction.

Residence requirements

Introduction and overview

4.42 Although the main cause of a migrant's ineligibility for benefit is being 'subject to immigration control',[51] it was historically the case that most people in that category had either entered the UK unlawfully or had leave subject to a NRPF condition, and few in either group would ever contemplate trying to obtain benefit. Thus legal disputes in that area were comparatively rare.

4.43 Residence requirements, in contrast, are frequently problematic for migrants who are either lawfully in the country and not subject to immigration control, but are unknowingly excluded from benefit; or people who are unknowingly unlawfully in the country. The size of both of these groups (the first of which can include UK nationals) has been considerably expanded by the UK's departure from the EU.

4.44 Paragraphs 4.48–4.108 deal with the different, overlapping ways in which a person can, through residence requirements, be required to demonstrate links with the UK to claim benefits. The various tests which have been invented over the years, and which are often applied to a claimant in combination, give different weight to the three key factors of *where a person is*, *where a person intends to be for the future*, and *what a person is doing*.

4.45 The requirements collectively form a confusing nest of legal tests: typically, a person must be 'in Great Britain' to be entitled to a particular benefit,[52] but cannot be 'in Great Britain' unless they are 'habitually resident',[53] and cannot be 'habitually resident' unless they have a 'right to reside' – and finally, not all residence rights reside qualify as a 'right to reside'.[54]

50 Immigration Rules para 6(2).
51 See paras 4.32–4.34.
52 See paras 4.84–4.106.
53 See paras 4.48–4.63.
54 See paras 4.66–4.83.

4.46 To see how this fits together in practice, see, for example, the UC residence requirements. The primary legislation simply requires that a UC claimant is 'in Great Britain',[55] but here is *part* of how the Universal Credit Regulations 2013 require one to interpret that short statutory provision:[56]

9. Persons treated as not being in Great Britain

(1) For the purposes of determining whether a person meets the basic condition to be in Great Britain, except where a person falls within paragraph (4), a person is to be treated as not being in Great Britain if the person is not habitually resident in the United Kingdom, the Channel Islands, the Isle of Man or the Republic of Ireland.

(2) A person must not be treated as habitually resident in the United Kingdom, the Channel Islands, the Isle of Man or the Republic of Ireland unless the person has a right to reside in one of those places.

(3) For the purposes of paragraph (2), a right to reside does not include a right which exists by virtue of, or in accordance with–

(a) regulation 13 of the EEA Regulations;[57]

(aa) regulation 14 of the EEA Regulations, but only in cases where the right exists under that regulation because the person is–

(i) a qualified person for the purposes of regulation 6(1) of those Regulations as a jobseeker; or

(ii) a family member (within the meaning of regulation 7 of those Regulations) of such a jobseeker;

(b) regulation 16 of the EEA Regulations, but only in cases where the right exists under that regulation because the person satisfies the criteria in regulation 16(5) of those Regulations;

(c) a person having been granted limited leave to enter, or remain in, the United Kingdom under the Immigration Act 1971 by virtue of–

(i) Appendix EU to the immigration rules made under section 3(2) of that Act;

(ii) being a person with a Zambrano[58] right to reside as defined in Annex 1 of Appendix EU to the immigration rules made under section 3(2) of that Act;

55 Welfare Reform Act 2012 s4(1)(c).

56 The main text reads '. . . part of how . . .', because as well as reg 9 repeatedly creating situations where a person sitting opposite your desk is not 'in Great Britain', reg 11 accommodates various absences from this country by the device of pretending that certain persons who are abroad are nevertheless 'in Great Britain'. See paras 4.84–4.106.

57 Immigration (European Economic Area) Regulations 2016 SI No 1052.

58 *Ruiz Zambrano v Office National de l'Emploi (ONEm)* C-34/09 [2012] QB 265, CJEU.

(iii) having arrived in the United Kingdom with an entry clearance that was granted under Appendix EU (Family Permit) to the immigration rules made under section 3(2) of that Act.

(3A) Paragraph (3)(c)(i) does not apply to a person who–
(a) has a right to reside granted by virtue of being a family member of a relevant person of Northern Ireland; and
(b) would have a right to reside under the EEA Regulations if the relevant person of Northern Ireland were an EEA national, provided that the right to reside does not fall within paragraph (3)(a) or (b);

(4) A person falls within this paragraph if the person is–
(za) a person granted leave in accordance with the immigration rules made under section 3(2) of the Immigration Act 1971, where such leave is granted by virtue of–
(i) the Afghan Relocations and Assistance Policy; or
(ii) the previous scheme for locally-employed staff in Afghanistan (sometimes referred to as the ex-gratia scheme);
(zb) a person in Great Britain not coming within sub-paragraph (za) or (e) who left Afghanistan in connection with the collapse of the Afghan government that took place on 15th August 2021;
(zc) a person in Great Britain who was residing in Ukraine immediately before 1st January 2022, left Ukraine in connection with the Russian invasion which took place on 24th February 2022 and–
(i) has been granted leave in accordance with immigration rules made under section 3(2) of the Immigration Act 1971;
(ii) has a right of abode in the United Kingdom within the meaning given in section 2 of that Act; or
(iii) does not require leave to enter or remain in the United Kingdom in accordance with section 3ZA of that Act;
(a) a qualified person for the purposes of regulation 6 of the EEA Regulations as a worker or a self-employed person;
(b) a family member of a person referred to in sub-paragraph (a);
(c) a person who has a right to reside permanently in the United Kingdom by virtue of regulation 15(1)(c), (d) or (e) of the EEA Regulations;
(ca) a family member of a relevant person of Northern Ireland, with a right to reside which falls within paragraph (3)(c)(i), provided that the relevant person of Northern Ireland falls within paragraph (4)(a), or would do so but for the fact that they are not an EEA national;
(cb) a frontier worker within the meaning of regulation 3 of the Citizens' Rights (Frontier Workers) (EU Exit) Regulations 2020;[59]

59 SI No 1213.

(cc) a family member of a person referred to in sub-paragraph (cb), who has been granted limited leave to enter, or remain in, the United Kingdom by virtue of Appendix EU to the immigration rules made under section 3(2) of the Immigration Act 1971;

(d) a refugee within the definition in Article 1 of the Convention relating to the Status of Refugees done at Geneva on 28th July 1951, as extended by Article 1(2) of the Protocol relating to the Status of Refugees done at New York on 31st January 1967;

(e) a person who has been granted, or who is deemed to have been granted, leave outside the rules made under section 3(2) of the Immigration Act 1971.

(f) a person who has humanitarian protection granted under those rules; or

(g) a person who is not a person subject to immigration control within the meaning of section 115(9) of the Immigration and Asylum Act 1999 and who is in the United Kingdom as a result of their deportation, expulsion or other removal by compulsion of law from another country to the United Kingdom.

(5) In this regulation–

'EEA national' has the meaning given in regulation 2(1) of the EEA Regulations;

'family member' has the meaning given in regulation 7(1)(a), (b) or (c) of the EEA Regulations, except that regulation 7(4) of the EEA Regulations does not apply for the purposes of paragraphs (3A) and (4)(ca);

'relevant person of Northern Ireland' has the meaning given in Annex 1 of Appendix EU to the immigration rules made under section 3(2) of the Immigration Act 1971.

4.47 This section of the chapter deals first with the older two residence tests – 'habitual residence'[60] and 'ordinary residence'[61] – then the newer and normally most significant 'right to reside'[62] test. Next the section addresses the special situation of EU nationals post-Brexit,[63] the presence requirement and its exceptions for temporary absence[64] and finally, the scope for special rules applying to employment-related benefits.[65]

60 See paras 4.48–4.63.
61 See paras 4.64–4.65.
62 See paras 4.66–4.60.
63 See paras 4.70–4.83.
64 See paras 4.84–4.106.
65 See para 4.108.

What is habitual residence?

Introduction

4.48 'You are not entitled to benefit because you are not habitually resident' has for several decades been, and probably is still, the most common reason given in government decision letters for refusing migrants' benefit claims, though these days it appears in decision letters for largely historical reasons and the real problem will often be a lack of a relevant right to reside.[66]

Definition

4.49 The 'habitual residence' requirement is not defined in legislation. Case-law establishes that it requires a person to demonstrate:

- a 'settled intention' to reside in the UK,[67] which could, for example, be evidenced by:
  - the claimant's own evidence about their plans;
  - registration of children in education;
  - registration with a doctor;
  - employment;
  - a place to live in the medium or long term;
- that a person has been continually resident in the UK for 'an appreciable period',[68] unless:
  - they are returning to the UK following a temporary absence; or
  - *possibly*, they have come to the UK having worked in the EU.

4.50 That case-law definition (described below as 'actual' habitual residence) was in the mid-2000s added to by legislation which deems a person not to be habitually resident unless they have a 'right to reside'.

When does a claimant have to demonstrate habitual residence?

4.51 Being habitually resident in the common travel area (the UK, Ireland, the Channel Islands and the Isle of Man) is a condition of entitlement to:

66 See paras 4.66–4.83.

67 *Nessa v Chief Adjudication* Officer [1999] 1 WLR 1937, HL at pp1943C–1943D.

68 *Nessa* at pp1942G–1942H.

- all the current income replacement/supplement benefits (UC,[69] PC,[70] HB,[71] council tax reduction[72]);
- DLA;[73]
- PIP;[74]
- attendance allowance;[75]
- carer's allowance.[76]

4.52 The following people are exempt from the habitual residence test[77] – though note that after 30 June 2021, a person can rely on the EEA-related exemptions only if they have also obtained leave to remain under the EU Settlement Scheme (EUSS):[78]

- an EEA national exercising free movement rights as a worker or a self-employed person or retaining that status;
- an EEA national with a right to reside permanently as a retired or permanently incapacitated ex worker or self-employed person;
- a family member of an EEA national in either of the two situations described above;
- a refugee, person with humanitarian protection or person with exceptional leave to enter or remain;
- a person who is not a PSIC and who is in the UK as a result of their deportation, expulsion or other removal by compulsion of law from another country to the UK;
- a person granted leave under the *Afghan Relocations and Assistance* policy[79] or the previous scheme for locally employed staff in Afghanistan;[80]

69 Universal Credit Regulations 2013 reg 9.

70 State Pension Credit Regulations 2002 reg 2.

71 Housing Benefit (Persons who have attained the qualifying age for state pension credit) Regulations 2006 reg 10.

72 Council Tax Reduction Schemes (Prescribed Requirements) (England) Regulations 2012 reg 12; Council Tax Reduction Schemes and Prescribed Requirements (Wales) Regulations 2013 reg 28.

73 Social Security (Disability Living Allowance) Regulations 1991 reg 2.

74 Social Security (Personal Independence Payment) Regulations 2013 reg 16.

75 Social Security (Attendance Allowance) Regulations 1991 reg 2.

76 Social Security (Invalid Care Allowance) Regulations 1976 reg 9.

77 For example, Universal Credit Regulations 2013 reg 9(4).

78 Immigration and Social Security Co-ordination (EU Withdrawal) Act 2020 (Consequential, Saving, Transitional and Transitory Provisions) (EU Exit) Regulations 2020 SI No 1309 Sch 4.

79 Ministry of Defence, January 2021, last updated May 2023.

80 See para 7.46 for a discussion of the analogous rule in the housing context.

- other persons in Great Britain who left Afghanistan in connection with the collapse of the Afghan government that took place on 15 August 2021;[81]
- a person in Great Britain who was residing in Ukraine immediately before 1 January 2022, who left Ukraine in connection with the Russian invasion which took place on 24 February 2022 and either has a right of abode in the UK, has been granted leave under the Immigration Rules or does not require such leave;[82]
- a family member of a 'relevant person of Northern Ireland';[83]
- a frontier worker;[84]
- a family member of a frontier worker granted leave to enter or remain in the UK under Immigration Rules Appendix EU.[85]

4.53 A person is not exempt by virtue of being a UK national.

Habitual residence and EU law

4.54 As indicated above, EU law still plays a part in habitual residence law because a person exercising EU law rights can still rely on them provided they also have leave to remain under the EUSS.

4.55 In *Collins v SSWP*,[86] considering the habitual residence test, the European Court of Justice (ECJ) emphasised the importance of giving a restrictive definition to what establishing actual habitual residence requires:

> [72] . . . while a residence requirement is, in principle, appropriate for the purpose of ensuring such a connection, if it is to be proportionate it cannot go beyond what is necessary in order to attain that objective. More specifically, its application by the national authorities must rest on clear criteria known in advance and provision must be made for the possibility of a means of redress of a judicial nature. In any event, if compliance with the requirement demands a period of residence, the period must not exceed what is necessary in order for the national authorities to be able to satisfy themselves that the person concerned is genuinely seeking work in the employment market of the host Member State.

81 See para 7.47 for a discussion of the analogous rule in the housing context.
82 See paras 7.56–7.60 for a discussion of the analogous rule in the housing context.
83 See paras 7.52–7.55 for a discussion of the analogous rule in the housing context.
84 See paras 2.177–2.181.
85 See paras 2.114–2.127.
86 Case C-138/02 [2005] QB 145, ECJ.

4.56 In *Swaddling v Adjudication Officer*,[87] the ECJ held that a UK national who had exercised free movement rights by working (and being habitually resident) in another member state and had then settled back in the UK could not lawfully be subjected to a requirement of being resident in the UK for an 'appreciable period' when claiming a special non-contributory benefit (SNCB) covered by Regulation (EEC) No 1408/71.[88]

4.57 In CIS/15484/96 a Social Security Commissioner held that *Swaddling* extended to an EEA non-UK national who had previously lived in the UK.

4.58 In *Nessa v Chief Adjudication Officer* the House of Lords held that the *Swaddling* principle would not apply to a person who had not previously lived in the UK.[89] However, that was not an EU law case and doubt may remain about whether the EU law answer would be the same.

4.59 There is also doubt as to whether *Swaddling* applies to a person claiming a benefit other than a SNCB. That latter question has been made more significant by the UK government taking the view that UC, now the main working age income replacement benefit, is not a SNCB (in contrast with its position on JSA and ESA).[90]

Habitual residence and domestic law

4.60 While *Nessa* demonstrates the requirement to show residence for an 'appreciable period' in addition to other factors (save where EU law requires otherwise or a person is resuming a past period of habitual residence, for example, following a holiday abroad), it also emphasises that an 'appreciable period' is a flexible concept, and where other factors point strongly in favour of habitual residence being established, it may be met in a short time, perhaps a month or so (*Nessa* at p1943).

Limited importance of 'actual' habitual residence

4.61 Unless a migrant is only visiting for a short time, or is maintaining a residence outside the UK as well as here, the effect on benefit

87 Case C-90/97 [1999] 2 CMLR 679, ECJ.

88 Regulation (EEC) No 1408/71 of the Council of 14 June 1971 on the application of social security schemes to employed persons and their families moving within the Community.

89 [1999] 1 WLR 1937, HL at p1943.

90 Regulation (EC) No 883/2004 of the European Parliament and of the Council on the coordination of social security systems Annex X.

entitlement of 'actual' habitual residence in the sense discussed above is likely to be modest, because after a while a claimant will have completed an appreciable period of residence and will be able to demonstrate the other indices of habituality. It would be a very unusual case where this took more than three months.

4.62 A claimant found not to be habitually resident can in general challenge a decision by way of application for revision, and on appeal, but can also repeatedly re-apply, emphasising what has changed since the last application (including the mere passage of time).

4.63 Much more important than 'actual' habitual residence, therefore, is the situation where a person cannot *ever* be held habitually resident for benefit purposes unless he or she can demonstrate a suitable right to reside in the UK.[91]

What is ordinary residence?

4.64 It is a condition of entitlement to the following benefits that a claimant be 'ordinarily resident' in Great Britain:[92]

- CB (and the child must be too);[93]
- social fund funeral payment;[94]
- winter fuel payment;[95]
- bereavement support payment;[96]
- category D retirement pension.[97]

4.65 The meaning of ordinary residence is not defined in legislation. Case-law suggests that it depends on a person living in the UK 'for settled purposes', it can begin immediately upon arrival, it does not require a fixed address, it need not be interrupted by temporary

91 See paras 4.66–4.60.
92 Technically, for child benefit and funeral payments, the UK.
93 Social Security Contributions and Benefits Act 1992 s146; Child Benefit (General) Regulations 2006 reg 23(1).
94 NB the ordinary residence requirement actually attaches to the deceased. The claimant is subject to a 'living in' England and Wales requirement: Social Fund Maternity and Funeral Expenses (General) Regulations 2005 reg 7(5) and (9A).
95 Social Fund Winter Fuel Payment Regulations 2000 reg 2. Note the exception for some people who have moved to EEA countries but retain a link to the UK: regs 2(1)(a)(ii) and 4.
96 Pensions Act 2014 s30(1)(c).
97 Social Security (Widow's Benefit and Retirement Pensions) Regulations 1979 SI No 642 reg 10.

absence, and it is possible to be ordinarily resident in more than one country simultaneously.[98]

What is a right to reside?

4.66 Having a right to reside in the UK is a condition of entitlement to income replacement/supplement benefits (UC,[99] PC,[100] HB,[101] council tax reduction[102]) and also CB.[103]

4.67 The way the 'right to reside' test is implemented is (save for child benefit) by deeming a person with no right to reside not to be habitually resident in the UK. This explains why benefit refusals may, counterintuitively, state that a person who has been living for years in the UK is 'not habitually resident'.

4.68 In most cases it is easy to recognise whether or not a person has a right of residence:

- a UK or Irish citizen has a right of residence in the UK;
- a Commonwealth citizen has a right of residence in the UK if they have the right of abode here;
- a person with leave to enter or remain in the UK under the IA 1971 (which includes EEA nationals given leave under the EUSS) has a right of residence in the UK.

4.69 Note, however:

- a person with limited leave to remain will frequently be a PSIC and excluded from entitlement to benefits on that basis, and/or have leave on condition that they do not have recourse to public funds);
- an EEA national (or their family member) with limited leave to remain granted under Immigration Rules Appendix EU will not

98 See *R v Barnet LBC ex p Shah* [1982] UKHL 14, [1983] 2 AC 309, discussed and updated in *GC v HMRC (TC) (residence and presence conditions: ordinary residence)* [2014] UKUT 251 (AAC) (30 May 2014).

99 Universal Credit Regulations 2013 reg 9.

100 State Pension Credit Regulations 2002 reg 2.

101 Housing Benefit (Persons who have attained the qualifying age for state pension credit) Regulations 2006 reg 10.

102 Council Tax Reduction Schemes (Prescribed Requirements) (England) Regulations 2012 reg 12.

103 Child Benefit (General) Regulations 2006 reg 23. CB is unusual because in contrast to the other 'right to reside' benefits, where a lack of right of residence leads to deemed non-habitual residence, CB has an 'ordinary residence' test instead of a 'habitual residence' test, and a lack of right of residence leads directly to deemed non-presence in the UK.

on the basis of that alone have a right of residence qualifying them for benefit, though see para 4.80 on whether that purported limitation is lawful, and see paras 4.81-4.83 on the possibility that they can establish entitlement by showing they are, in addition to having pre-settled status, exercising a right of residence under the Immigration (European Economic Area) Regulations ('EEA Regs') 2016.[104]

What rights might EEA nationals have?

4.70 If, after 30 June 2021, an EEA national does not have pre-settled or settled status, and does not have some other right of residence under the IA 1971, it is likely that they are in the UK unlawfully; they would accordingly be excluded from most benefit entitlement by IAA 1999 s115(9) (requiring leave to enter or remain in the UK but not having it). This is the case even if they entered the UK lawfully and exercised EU law rights of residence throughout their time here. Any such person should seek urgent specialist immigration advice.

4.71 An EEA national with settled status (or a non-Appendix EU grant of leave) will be in the same position as a non-EEA national.

4.72 The most complex situation, from a social security perspective, is that of EEA nationals with pre-settled status. However, before exploring that, it is necessary to recap the Appendix EU scheme.

The Appendix EU scheme

4.73 The UK government published rules, in Appendix EU to the Immigration Rules, under which EEA nationals who had come to the UK before the end of 2020 could apply for leave to remain.

4.74 Chapter 2 of this book sets out the rules of that scheme in detail.[105] The key points from a social security perspective are:

- The scheme was available to EEA nationals and family members who began residence in the UK before 11 pm on 31 December 2020, and operated until 30 June 2021.
- On application, a person with five years' residence in the UK, or a permanent EU law right of residence, would be granted indefinite leave to remain, referred to as 'settled status'. To benefit from the five-year rule, a person would not need to prove exercise of EU

104 SI No 1052.
105 See paras 2.138–2.176.

law rights at any point in that period, but would simply need to prove residence.

- A person who failed to demonstrate five years' residence would be granted limited leave to remain, for a period of five years, referred to as 'pre-settled status'. A person would not need to prove exercise of EU law rights at any point at all to obtain that status (save in the sense that they would have exercised an EU law right by coming to the UK in the first place).

4.75 Late applications are discussed at paras 2.146–2.151.

Settled status[106]

4.76 A grant of settled status under Appendix EU gives a person a right to reside which entitles them to claim benefit.

4.77 It is unclear whether the government plans any future change to that principle. The Statement of Intent on the Appendix EU scheme, published in June 2018, stated that the right of EEA nationals to receive benefits will be 'determined according to the same rules as now'. Implementing that proposal would have implied excluding settled status from being an automatically qualifying right of residence for benefit purposes, because its recipients will not necessarily have exercised EU law rights for five years (the rule when the UK was a member of the EU).

4.78 However, at present, settled status granted under Appendix EU is *not* an excluded right of residence, and it is not subject to a NRPF condition (indeed such a condition could not be added without an amendment to the Immigration Act 1971 itself[107]). So *for most EEA nationals who have been in the UK for at least five years, a grant of settled status is the most straightforward way to obtain access to benefits, since it does not require the claimant to demonstrate past or present exercise of EU law residence rights.*

Pre-settled status

4.79 The UK government decided that pre-settled status should be excluded from being a qualifying right of residence for the purposes of benefit entitlement. Therefore it made regulations requiring a person with pre-settled status who wishes to claim benefit to

106 See paras 2.153–2.165.
107 Immigration Act 1971 s3.

demonstrate some alternative right of residence, based on the EU law that used to apply.[108]

4.80 The regulations giving effect to that exclusion were held unlawful by the Court of Appeal in *Fratila v SSWP*,[109] as inconsistent with the ratio of *Trojani v Centre Public d'Aide Sociale de Bruxelles (CPAS)*,[110] and thereby constituting direct discrimination on the grounds of nationality contrary to TFEU Article 18.[111] However, the CJEU in *CG v Department for Communities in Northern Ireland*[112] subsequently reached a different conclusion, holding that TFEU Article 18 does not apply in this scenario, and Directive 2004/38/EC ('Citizens' Rights Directive')[113] applies instead. The Grand Chamber held that the protection against discrimination set out in Article 24 of the Directive was not available to CG as she had no right of residence under the Directive, because she lacked sufficient resources to keep herself from becoming an unreasonable burden on the social assistance system of the UK.[114] Article 24, the court concluded, did not preclude the UK from excluding from eligibility for welfare benefits 'economically inactive Union citizens who do not have sufficient resources and to whom that State has granted a temporary right of residence, where those benefits are guaranteed to nationals of the Member State concerned who are in the same situation'.[115] However, it said consideration will still need to be given in an individual case to whether the denial of support would give result in breach of the person's fundamental rights under the Charter of Fundamental Rights of the European Union.[116] Following the decision of the CJEU

108 Social Security (Income-related Benefits) (Updating and Amendment) (EU Exit) Regulations 2019 SI No 872; and Council Tax Reduction Schemes (Prescribed Requirements) (England) (Amendment) Regulations 2020 SI No 23.

109 [2020] EWCA Civ 1741, [2020] WLR(D) 694.

110 Case C-456/02 [2004] 3 CMLR 38, ECJ.

111 Agreement on the withdrawal of the United Kingdom of Great Britain and Northern Ireland from the European Union and the European Atomic Energy Community (Treaty Series No 3 (2020), CP 219, Vol 1) (Withdrawal Agreement) Article 12 contains an equivalent provision applicable following the departure of the UK from the EU.

112 Case C-709/20 [2021] 1 WLR 5919, CJEU.

113 Directive 2004/38/EC of the European Parliament and of the Council of 29 April 2004 on the right of citizens of the Union and their family members to move and reside freely within the territory of the Member States.

114 *CG v Department for Communities in Northern Ireland* C-709/20 at paras 72–81.

115 *CG v Department for Communities in Northern Ireland* C-709/20 at para 93.

116 *CG v Department for Communities in Northern Ireland* C-709/20 at paras 88–91 and 93.

in *CG*, the Supreme Court allowed the Secretary of State for Work and Pensions' appeal in the cases of *Fratila*,[117] and declined to consider the Charter issues raised by *CG*. The Upper Tribunal has since confirmed that destitute EU nationals with pre-settled status may rely on the Charter to obtain access to UC, where they and their children would otherwise be exposed to an 'actual and current risk' that they could not live in the UK in 'dignified conditions'.[118]

4.81 Meanwhile, a person with pre-settled status, whose circumstances are not sufficiently dire so as to engage the protection of the Charter, is in a rather odd position. They are by virtue of their pre-settled status in the UK lawfully, regardless of what they are doing, and EU law has in general ceased to apply in the UK, but in order to have a right to reside entitling them to benefit, they must additionally show that they are exercising one of the traditional rights of residence derived from EU law which used to be available to EEA nationals in the UK. The EEA Regs 2016 are preserved to that extent.[119] So a person with pre-settled status wanting to claim benefit must additionally show that he or she is a worker, a person who has retained worker status due to unemployment or illness etc. A detailed discussion of the different rights of residence which existed under those regulations can be found at paras 2.41–2.137.

4.82 There may also be scope for arguments that a person with pre-settled status can assert entitlement to benefit by virtue of rights given to them under the Withdrawal Agreement (such arguments are likely to require specialist advice, and probably litigation).

4.83 Note finally that not all of the old EEA rights of residence which entitle a person to reside in the UK are sufficient to make a person eligible for benefit. An EEA national (or their family member) with pre-settled status, who additionally has a right to reside under the EEA Regs 2016, will not be entitled to benefit if the only additional right is as a:

- person with an initial three-month right of residence;
- jobseeker;
- self-sufficient person;
- '*Zambrano*' carer.[120]

117 [2021] UKSC 53, [2022] PTSR 448.
118 *SSWP v AT* [2022] UKUT 330 (AAC). This decision is under appeal.
119 Immigration and Social Security Co-ordination (EU Withdrawal) Act 2020 (Consequential, Saving, Transitional and Transitory Provisions) (EU Exit) Regulations 2020 Sch 4.
120 *Ruiz Zambrano v Office National de l'Emploi (ONEm)* C-34/09 [2012] QB 265, CJEU. See paras 2.90–2.100.

What are presence requirements?

Presence of claimant normally required

4.84 A claimant must be *in* Great Britain (or sometimes 'the UK') to claim a lot of the benefits administered in Great Britain:

- UC;[121]
- PC and HB;[122]
- council tax reduction;[123]
- CB;[124]
- DLA (disability benefit for children);[125]
- PIP (working age disability benefit);[126]
- attendance allowance (disability benefit for retirees);[127]
- carer's allowance (for people caring for a disabled person).[128]

Healthy Start vouchers, maternity grants, funeral payments, cold weather payments and discretionary housing payments in practice have a presence test too because they include a requirement to qualify for a means tested benefit with a presence test.[129]

Temporary absences

4.85 In some circumstances, temporary absence can be treated as presence.

121 UC: Universal Credit Regulations 2013 reg 9.

122 PC: State Pension Credit Regulations 2002 reg 2. Housing benefit: Housing Benefit (Persons who have attained the qualifying age for state pension credit) Regulations 2006 reg 10.

123 Council Tax Reduction Schemes (Prescribed Requirements) (England) Regulations 2012 reg 12.

124 Social Security Contributions and Benefits Act 1992 s146.

125 Social Security (Disability Living Allowance) Regulations 1991 reg 2(1)(a)(ii).

126 Social Security (Personal Independence Payment) Regulations 2013 reg 16(a).

127 Social Security (Attendance Allowance) Regulations 1991 reg 2(1)(a)(ii).

128 Social Security (Invalid Care Allowance) Regulations 1976 reg 9(1)(b).

129 Healthy Start Scheme and Welfare Food (Amendment) Regulations 2005 reg 3(b) (Healthy Start vouchers); Social Fund Maternity and Funeral Expenses (General) Regulations 2005 reg 5(2) (maternity grants), reg 7(4) (funeral payments); Social Fund Cold Weather Payments (General) Regulations 1988 reg 1A(2) (cold weather payments); Discretionary Financial Assistance Regulations 2001 reg 2(1) (discretionary housing payments).

Temporary absence – UC

4.86 If a claimant was entitled to UC immediately before they left Great Britain, and is temporarily absent, they can continue to be entitled for:[130]

- one month where the absence is not expected to exceed and does not exceed one month;
- two months where the absence is in connection with the death of a close relative and it would not be reasonable to return within one month;
- six months where the absence is not expected to exceed and does not exceed six months and it is:
  - for the medical treatment of the claimant, their partner or their child;
  - due to being a mariner or continental shelf worker.

Temporary absence – PC

4.87 If a claimant was entitled to PC immediately before they left Great Britain and is temporarily absent, they can continue to be entitled for up to:[131]

- four weeks where the absence is not expected to be longer;
- eight weeks where the absence is in connection with the death of a close relative and it would not be reasonable to return within four weeks;
- 26 weeks for the medical treatment of the claimant, their partner or their child.

Temporary absence – HB

4.88 A claimant can receive HB while temporarily absent for up to:[132]

- four weeks, provided the absence is not expected to be longer;
- eight weeks where the absence is in connection with the death of a close relative and it would not be reasonable to return within four weeks;
- 26 weeks where the absence is not expected to exceed and does not exceed 26 weeks and it is due to being:
  - a member of the armed forces posted overseas;
  - a mariner or continental shelf worker.

130 Universal Credit Regulations 2013 reg 11.
131 State Pension Credit Regulations 2002 reg 3.
132 Housing Benefit (Persons who have attained the qualifying age for state pension credit) Regulations 2006 reg 7.

Temporary absence – CB

4.89 A claimant can receive child benefit for a child during the claimant's absence of:[133]

- eight weeks for any reason;
- 12 weeks where the absence relates to obtaining treatment for the illness or disability of a relative, or to the death of a relative.

Temporary absence – disability benefits

4.90 A claimant can receive DLA, PIP or attendance allowance during an absence of:[134]

- 13 weeks for any reason;
- 26 weeks where being treated for an illness or physical or mental disability which commenced before the absence;
- indefinite duration in certain cases relating to the armed forces, mariners, airmen, continental shelf workers and their families etc.

4.91 A claimant can receive carer's allowance during an absence of:[135]

- four weeks for any reason;
- longer, where the absence is temporary and the person is caring for a person who continues to receive the relevant disability benefit for their care needs;
- indefinite duration in certain cases relating to the armed forces, mariners, airmen, continental shelf workers and their families etc.

Presence of partner

4.92 There are rules about the presence of a partner in a household which apply whether the partner is abroad or simply absent from the household.

4.93 For UC, PC and HB, if a claimant separates from their partner with the intention that the separation will be permanent, they must immediately claim as a single person rather than as a member of a couple.[136]

4.94 If a claimant separates temporarily from their partner, they must claim as a single person rather than as a member of a couple if:

133 Child Benefit (General) Regulations 2006 reg 24.
134 Social Security (Disability Living Allowance) Regulations 1991 reg 2; Social Security (Personal Independence Payment) Regulations 2013 regs 17–19.
135 Social Security (Invalid Care Allowance) Regulations 1976 reg 9.
136 Welfare Reform Act 2012 s1.

- for UC, the couple are separated (or expect to be separated) for more than six months;[137]
- for PC and HB, the couple are likely to be separated for more than 52 weeks (subject to certain exceptions).[138]

Presence of children

Temporary absence – UC

4.95 A claimant can receive UC in respect of a child for whom they are responsible. A person cannot be responsible for a child if the child is absent from Great Britain for periods longer than those allowed for a claimant absent from Great Britain (see above).[139]

Temporary absence – CB

4.96 A claimant can receive child benefit for a child during a temporary absence by the child of:[140]

- 12 weeks for any reason;
- any period where the child is absent receiving full-time education in an EEA state or Switzerland; or being engaged in a recognised educational exchange or visit;
- any period where being treated for an illness or physical or mental disability which commenced before the absence.

Disability benefit past presence requirement

4.97 A 'past presence test' applies to:[141]

- DLA;
- PIP;
- attendance allowance;
- carer's allowance.

4.98 Subject to exceptions described below, it requires that a claimant has been present in Great Britain for periods amounting to at least 104 out of the last 156 weeks.

137 Universal Credit Regulations 2013 reg 3.

138 State Pension Credit Regulations 2002 reg 5; Housing Benefit (Persons who have attained the qualifying age for state pension credit) Regulations 2006 reg 21.

139 Universal Credit Regulations 2013 reg 4(7)(b).

140 Child Benefit (General) Regulations 2006 reg 21.

141 Social Security (Disability Living Allowance) Regulations 1991 reg 2; Social Security (Personal Independence Payment) Regulations 2013 reg 16; Social Security (Attendance Allowance) Regulations 1991 reg 2; Social Security (Invalid Care Allowance) Regulations 1976 reg 9.

Full exemption

4.99 The past presence test does not apply to a person with refugee leave or humanitarian protection (or their dependants).

4.100 It does not apply to attendance allowance, DLA or PIP where the claimant is terminally ill.

4.101 It does not apply to people who fall within the personal scope of Regulation (EC) No 883/2004 and have a 'genuine and sufficient' link to the UK. In assessing the existence of such a link, 'evidence of the motives, intentions and expectations of the applicant are not to be ignored if they are relevant to proof of the link and are convincing'.[142]

Part exemption

4.102 A child under six months old claiming DLA has to have been present for at least 13 weeks in their life.[143]

4.103 A child between six months and three years old claiming DLA has to have been present for at least 26 weeks in their life.[144]

Returning UK national children

4.104 In late 2020 the Upper Tribunal found, in an appeal brought by UK national children who had been abroad outside the EU, that the extension of the requirement to have been present in Great Britain from 26 weeks out of 52 to 104 weeks out of 156 was a breach of their rights under Article 14 of the European Convention on Human Rights. It disapplied the legislation requiring that longer period: *TS and EK v SSWP (DLA)*.[145]

4.105 The secretary of state has not appealed, and should therefore apply *TS and EK* in other similar cases. She will at some stage have to expressly amend the legislation to remove the parts identified to be unlawful by the Upper Tribunal.

Child benefit past presence requirement

4.106 A CB claimant must generally have been living in the UK for the last three months.

142 *Kavanagh and another v SSWP* [2019] EWCA Civ 272 at para 69.
143 Social Security (Disability Living Allowance) Regulations 1991 reg 2(6).
144 Social Security (Disability Living Allowance) Regulations 1991 reg 2(7).
145 [2020] UKUT 284 (AAC).

4.107 There are exemptions for various groups, the most significant of which are:[146]

- EEA nationals with a right to reside (or retained right to reside) as a worker or self-employed person;
- non EEA nationals who would be a worker or self-employed person if they were an EEA national;
- refugees and people with humanitarian protection;
- people with leave outside the Immigration Rules but access to public funds;
- people with leave granted pending an application for indefinite leave to remain as a victim of domestic violence;
- people returning to the UK after absence of less than 52 weeks, where on leaving the UK the person had been ordinarily resident for at least the last three months.

What are the special rules about migrants and employment-related benefits?

4.108 At the time of writing, migrants were not excluded from access to employment-related benefits. However, Welfare Reform Act 2012 s63 will, if and when brought into force, require a claimant to demonstrate that they had an entitlement to work in the employment they rely upon in order to receive:

- maternity allowance;
- statutory maternity/paternity/adoption/shared parental pay;
- statutory sick pay.

Practicalities

Who needs a national insurance number?

4.109 It is a general condition of entitlement to most benefits that a claimant, and any other person in respect of whom she is claiming benefit, must either have a national insurance number (NINO) or apply for one,[147] including in the application information or evidence enabling such a number to be so allocated. There are exceptions to this rule for:

146 Child Benefit (General) Regulations 2006 reg 23(6).

147 Social Security Administration Act 1992 s1(1A).

- a child claiming DLA;[148]
- payments of elements in respect of children in UC and HB;[149]
- payments in respect of a member of a couple who is a PSIC in income supplement or replacement benefits;[150]
- benefits which do not require a claim.

4.110 NINOs are usually allocated to individuals in the UK shortly before they turn 16.

4.111 A migrant who has not previously worked or claimed benefit in the UK may well not have a NINO (although NINOs are sometimes now issued with a biometric residence permit, in which case it will be on the reverse of the card).

4.112 Where a person does not have a NINO, a claim for benefit should be treated automatically as an application for a NINO, but it is not the only mechanism for obtaining one. A person with the right to work or study in the UK is entitled to be allocated one on application. Given the frequency of delays in processing NINO applications, it can be a good idea to apply for a NINO at the earliest possible opportunity.[151]

4.113 In the UC system, payments of benefit are not made until a NINO has been allocated to a claimant. The legality of this practice was challenged unsuccessfully in *R (Bui) v SSWP*,[152] reliant on earlier case-law which had emphasised that the relevant entitlement condition for a person without a NINO is merely that the person has *applied* for a NINO with sufficient evidence or information to allow a NINO to be allocated; and that it is not necessary for the application actually to have been processed for benefit to be awarded.[153] An attempt is being made to appeal in *Bui*. Meanwhile, affected claimants

148 Social Security (Disability Living Allowance) Regulations 1991 reg 1A.

149 Universal Credit, Personal Independence Payment, Jobseeker's Allowance and Employment and Support Allowance (Claims and Payments) Regulations 2013 2013 SI No 380 reg 5; Housing Benefit (Persons who have attained the qualifying age for state pension credit) Regulations 2006 reg 4.

150 State Pension Credit Regulations 2002 reg 1A; Universal Credit Regulations 2013 reg 3(3); Housing Benefit (Persons who have attained the qualifying age for state pension credit) Regulations 2006 reg 4.

151 See paras 5.278–5.281 for a discussion of the delays faced by recently recognised refugees in obtaining a NINO and a biometric residence permit and making the transition from asylum support to mainstream support.

152 [2022] UKUT 189 (AAC).

153 Social Security Commissioner's Decision CH/4085/2007, 8 October 2008.

may need to challenge any delay in allocating NINOs by way of judicial review.[154]

How is benefit entitlement affected by a person's partner being a migrant?

4.114 Many benefits are claimed by individuals, in respect of their individual circumstances, in which case the immigration status of any partner does not matter.

4.115 Means tested income supplement or replacement benefits are a significant exception: where a person is a member of a couple, a UC,[155] state pension credit[156] or HB[157] claim must ordinarily be made as a couple claim, and both must satisfy the entitlement conditions.

4.116 Where one member of a couple is excluded from entitlement because a PSIC, and one is not, a claim for UC or PC can (and must) be made as a single person.[158] UC takes the excluded person's income and capital into account; PC does not.

What is benefit coordination?

Overview

4.117 Benefit coordination rules exist to minimise situations where two different states are responsible for paying benefits to an individual, and also to reduce (but not eradicate) situations where a person loses benefit entitlement as a result of migrating from one country to another.

4.118 The rules apply to contributory benefits, as well as to various special purpose benefits and employment-related benefits. They do not generally apply to income supplement or replacement benefits.

4.119 EEA nationals are the most likely to be affected by coordination rules, but coordination issues can arise with nationals of other states with which the UK has made benefit coordination agreements.

154 See paras 4.134–4.137 and 4.142.

155 Welfare Reform Act 2012 s1(2)(a).

156 State Pension Credit Act 2002 s2(5).

157 Social Security Contributions and Benefits Act 1992 s136(1).

158 Universal Credit Regulations 2013 reg 3(3)(b); State Pension Credit Regulations 2002 reg 5(1)(h).

Detailed rules outside scope of this book

4.120 The rules relating to exportation, aggregation and competence are very complex. Note, for example, that Part 6 of the CPAG *Benefits for migrants handbook* provides 50 pages of introduction. Further, the UK's exit from the EU may lead to significant change in benefit coordination rules.

Exportation

4.121 Where a person was receiving a benefit abroad, they may be entitled to continue receiving it, via the UK authorities, when in the UK. Likewise they may be entitled to continue receiving a UK benefit when abroad.

4.122 An example of this principle is a person who moves to the UK seeking work and is able to receive another state's unemployment benefit, albeit paid via the UK authorities.

Aggregation

4.123 Where a UK benefit has a condition that a person has a history of residence or national insurance contributions in the UK, they may be able to rely on residence or national insurance contributions accumulated in another country to satisfy the conditions. Likewise UK residence or national insurance contributions may sometimes be relied on to claim foreign benefits.

4.124 An example is a person who works for a few years in one EEA state, moves here, and works for a few more years, who then retires and is able to receive a retirement pension from the UK based on the contributions in both countries.

Competence

4.125 Where another EEA state is responsible ('competent') for paying a particular kind of benefit to a claimant, that may mean the claimant is not entitled to receive that kind of benefit from the UK authorities.

4.126 An example of this is a person who cannot receive a disability benefit because they are already receiving disability benefits from another EEA state.

4.127 If EEA states disagree about which is the competent state, there is a dispute resolution process and a mechanism for the making of interim payments.

Challenging decisions and non-decisions

How can adverse decisions be challenged?

Appeals

Overview

4.128 There exists a statutory right of appeal to the First-tier Tribunal (FTT) (Social Entitlement Chamber (SEC)) against most decisions made in relation to social security benefits.[159] Thus a claimant who is dissatisfied with the decision of the government can, without a court fee or a risk of paying the government's costs, appeal to an independent judge, who will look at the decision afresh and come to their own decision.

Two-stage process

4.129 Before exercising a right of appeal to the FTT (SEC) against a decision, it is normally necessary to apply to the decision-maker for the decision to be revised.[160] This is known informally as an application for mandatory reconsideration (MR). That request can be made in writing or orally.

4.130 If, following MR, a claimant still wishes to challenge a decision, they can appeal to the tribunal. Tribunal appeals can be made online (for some benefits) or by post. Appeal forms are all available online.

Inquisitorial process

4.131 An important feature of the FTT is that it operates an inquisitorial process. It can ask questions to uncover information which a claimant may not have known to be relevant (or may have been unable to present in writing), and it can uncover relevant documentation, in particular by making directions to the DWP.[161]

159 Social Security Act 1998 s12; Child Support, Pensions and Social Security Act 2000 Sch 7 para 6. An exception is council tax reduction, which has its own procedure: see the Valuation Tribunal for England (Council Tax and Rating Appeals) (Procedure) Regulations 2009 SI No 2269.

160 Universal Credit, Personal Independence Payment, Jobseeker's Allowance and Employment and Support Allowance (Decisions and Appeals) Regulations 2013 SI No 381 reg 7. The only major exception to the requirement to seek reconsideration before appeal is HB, where an appeal can be made immediately upon receipt of a decision.

161 *Kerr v Department for Social Development* [2004] UKHL 23, [2004] 1 WLR 1372 at para 62.

4.132 An important instance of this power relates to directing the DWP to locate and produce documentary evidence about the circumstances of someone related to the claimant.[162] Migrants' eligibility for benefits will often depend on their relationship with another person. For example, a spouse of an EU national working in the UK will have a right to reside in the UK arising out of that marital relationship. If the parties are estranged, it may be impossible for the claimant to obtain evidence themself about their estranged partner's work. An attempt to have the DWP obtain relevant documents pre-appeal (for example, the partner's national insurance records or their own benefit claim history) will often be declined with vague references to 'data protection'. Even if that were a valid reason for the DWP's inaction pre-appeal, a tribunal certainly can direct the DWP to provide information about a third party, notwithstanding the absence of that third party's consent: *PM v SSWP (IS)*.[163] So where necessary a tribunal should be asked to make such directions to assist a claimant with their appeal.

Time limits

4.133 A MR application must normally be made within one month of a decision,[164] then an application to appeal within a month of the MR decision.[165] Late applications are possible (in particular, a MR application can generally be made to the DWP at any point up to 13 months after the initial decision,[166] and even if the DWP rejects the reasons for lateness, its response will trigger a right of appeal to the FTT[167]) but the complex law relating to the precise conditions of this lies outside the scope of this book.

162 A good example of a FTT being criticised by the higher courts, in an immigration law context, for failure properly to exercise this jurisdiction is *AS v SSWP (UC)* [2018] UKUT 260 (AAC).

163 [2014] UKUT 474 (AAC) at para 4.

164 For example, Universal Credit, Personal Independence Payment, Jobseeker's Allowance and Employment and Support Allowance (Decisions and Appeals) Regulations 2013 reg 5.

165 Tribunal Procedure (First-tier Tribunal) (Social Entitlement Chamber) Rules 2008 SI No 2685 r22.

166 Universal Credit, Personal Independence Payment, Jobseeker's Allowance and Employment and Support Allowance (Decisions and Appeals) Regulations 2013 reg 6.

167 *R (CJ) and SG v SSWP (ESA)* [2017] UKUT 324 (AAC).

Judicial review

4.134 If there is a right of appeal against a decision, it will not normally be necessary or appropriate to resort to judicial review, because the statutory tribunal appeals process will provide a suitable alternative remedy.

4.135 Two exceptions to this, discussed below, are: (i) where no decision has been made, and (ii) where there is extreme urgency of a kind which the tribunal's powers of expedition cannot accommodate.

How can delay in processing migrants' benefit claims be dealt with?

4.136 Migrants are particularly likely to experience delays in benefits processing and decision-making.[168]

4.137 They are also particularly likely to experience delay where claims are refused on the ground that they are not eligible for benefit, and they have to apply for mandatory reconsideration, or appeal.

Where no entitlement decision has yet been made

Claim interim payment

4.138 A payment on account of benefit (also known as an 'interim payment' or a 'short-term benefit advance') can be made on application, even where no entitlement decision has been made, if:[169]

- 'it appears to the secretary of state likely' that the claimant will be entitled to the benefit once a decision is made; and
- the secretary of state is satisfied that the claimant is in financial need.

4.139 The benefits in respect of which interim payments may be made are:

- the principal income supplement or replacement benefits (UC and PC); for pensioners' HB see below;
- the principal contributory benefits (JSA, ESA, retirement pension – NB not bereavement support payment);
- carer's allowance;
- industrial injuries benefits.

168 See paras 5.278–5.281 for a discussion of the particular problems faced by recently recognised refugees in making the transition from asylum-support to mainstream support.

169 Social Security (Payments on Account of Benefit) Regulations 2013 SI No 383 reg 5.

4.140 Similar but not identical powers to make interim payments exist in respect of CB and guardian's allowance,[170] and HB.[171]

4.141 There is no right of appeal against a refusal to make an interim payment, so if a claim is refused, it can be challenged only by an application for judicial review.

Argue delay unlawful

4.142 There is no right of appeal against a failure to decide a benefit claim within a reasonable time, so it must be challenged by making an application for judicial review.[172] It may in particular be worth arguing that the secretary of state's decision-making apparatus is, if it causes foreign nationals to wait longer than UK nationals for benefit decisions, indirectly discriminatory, and that the treatment is not justified in your particular case.

Seek local authority support

4.143 The public authority of last resort is the local authority. They may have relevant powers or duties:

- in respect of children in the household (see chapter 8);
- in respect of people who need care and support (see chapter 9).

4.144 The local authority may also operate a local welfare provision scheme, providing emergency support in kind or in cash. The website advice-local.uk contains a database of all such schemes.

Where a claim has been refused

Challenge local authority if it rubber-stamps DWP decision

4.145 Where a person claims local authority support which has an immigration eligibility requirement, the local authority may rely on an adverse eligibility decision by the Secretary of State for Work and Pensions to refuse assistance automatically. Rather than simply let matters take their course on appeal, that approach should be challenged and the local authority asked to revisit its decision: the local authority's duty is to make its own decision, and although it is entitled

170 Child Benefit and Guardian's Allowance (Administration) Regulations 2003 SI No 492 reg 22.

171 Housing benefit works slightly differently, and under a different legislative power: if a claim is not decided within 14 days and certain qualifying conditions are met, payments on account of benefit in respect of a housing association or private sector tenancy must be paid: Housing Benefit (Persons who have attained the qualifying age for state pension credit) Regulations 2006 reg 74.

172 *R (C and W) v SSWP and another* [2015] EWHC 1607 (Admin).

to take the DWP's view into account, if new evidence or representations are put before it, it must make its own decision.[173]

Try to expedite process

4.146 As discussed at paras 4.128–4.133, FTT appeals are free, and relatively user-friendly, but they can be slow.

4.147 If an application is made for mandatory reconsideration and the Secretary of State for Work and Pensions is slow in considering it, the failure to make a decision is amenable to judicial review, just as is a failure to make an initial decision on a claim.[174]

4.148 Once the secretary of state has rejected an application for mandatory reconsideration, and a claimant has in response lodged a notice of appeal, the timescale for further consideration of the application lies in the hands of the FTT. Normally an appeal will take months: the appeal notice will be sent to the decision-maker, the decision-maker will have 28 days to respond,[175] the appellant will have a further month to put in submissions and evidence,[176] then an appeal hearing will be listed on a date typically some months in the future. However, the FTT has a broad power to modify those normal time limits,[177] and an obligation to ensure it uses its rules to deal with cases fairly and justly. There is no reason in principle why, in a sufficiently urgent case, it could not be asked to dispose of an appeal in days rather than months.[178] Migrants' appeals are particularly likely to be urgent, because a decision that they are ineligible for benefits will often affect all sources of household income (and quite possibly other social assistance too).

4.149 Alternatively, if the FTT refuses to assist by expediting a hearing, or the urgency is even greater than can realistically be accommodated by varying its rules, a claimant may in principle be entitled to apply for judicial review of the secretary of state's decision, arguing that there is no suitable alternative remedy, and potentially seeking interim relief, including payment of benefit. However, this is likely to

173 See, for example, Social Security Commissioner's Decision R(H) 9/04, 5 June 2004 at para 40.

174 See paras 4.134–4.142.

175 Tribunal Procedure (First-Tier Tribunal) (Social Entitlement Chamber) Rules 2008 r24(1)(c).

176 Tribunal Procedure (First-Tier Tribunal) (Social Entitlement Chamber) Rules 2008 r24(7).

177 Tribunal Procedure (First-Tier Tribunal) (Social Entitlement Chamber) Rules 2008 r5(3)(a).

178 A refusal to exercise this power could be challenged by judicial review.

be a realistic option only in exceptional cases, given the potential for seeking to expedite FTT proceedings, and the possibility of obtaining emergency support from a local authority.[179]

What can be done if correctly excluded from benefits?

Local support

4.150 The public authority of last resort is the local authority. Even when a person is excluded from access to public funds, it may have relevant powers or duties:

- in respect of children in the household (see chapter 8);
- in respect of people who need care and support (see chapter 9).

4.151 Local charitable support may also be available. A citizens' advice bureau, or local authority social services department, is likely to know what local resources exist.

4.152 Be aware that a local authority is required to notify the Home Secretary if a person requesting support is, or may be, excluded from receiving care and support on the basis that they are: suspected or known to be unlawfully present in the UK, a refused asylum-seeker who has not complied with removal directions, or a refused asylum-seeker with dependent children who has been certified by the secretary of state as having failed to take steps to leave the UK voluntarily.[180]

Challenging a NRPF condition

4.153 If a person is not lawfully in the UK, their lack of access to public funds will be an inevitable incident of that lack of lawful immigration status (though steps can obviously be taken to attempt to regularise that status).

4.154 However, where a person is granted leave to remain in the UK *subject to a NRPF condition,*[181] that condition represents an exercise of discretion by the Home Secretary.

179 *R (Sanneh) v SSWP and another* [2013] EWHC 793 (Admin) at para 96.
180 Nationality, Immigration and Asylum Act 2002 Sch 3 para 14.
181 See further paras 1.166–1.172.

4.155 The Home Office policy on NRPF condition waiver is now very detailed and should be consulted carefully where a challenge to a NRPF condition is contemplated.[182] In summary, the policy provides:

Criteria for the non-imposition or lifting of the NRPF condition
The NRPF condition must not be imposed, and if imposed must be lifted if the applicant is assessed and found

- to be destitute
- to be at risk of imminent destitution
- there are reasons relating to the welfare of a child which outweigh the considerations for imposing the condition
- that they are faced with exceptional financial circumstances[183]

4.156 An NRPF condition can in some circumstances be avoided by making submissions in advance of the grant of leave, or if imposed, challenged, either on the basis that it was wrong from the start or that the claimant's circumstances have changed such that it is no longer appropriate. Applications to have an NRPF condition lifted can be made online free of charge and should be supported by evidence.[184]

4.157 NRPF conditions which adversely affect the welfare of children may be particularly vulnerable to challenge because of the Home Secretary's duty under Borders, Citizenship and Immigration Act 2009 s55 to 'have regard to the need to safeguard and promote the welfare of children who are in the United Kingdom': as the guidance acknowledges, 'destitution' is usually the relevant test for adults but the lower test of 'very low income' may be sufficient in child cases.[185] Needs arising from an applicant's disability may also provide a basis

182 *Family Policy: Family life (as a partner or parent), private life and exceptional circumstance*, v18.0, Home Office, 11 August 2022, pp76–85, www.gov.uk/government/publications/family-life-as-a-partner-or-parent-private-life-and-exceptional-circumstance. Home Office policy on imposition and removal of NRPF conditions have been found, or accepted to be, unlawful, on a number of occasions in recent years. See *R (W (a child)) v SSHD* [2020] EWHC 1299 (Admin), [2020] 1 WLR 4420; *ST (a child) v SSHD* [2021] EWHC 1085 (Admin); *R (AB) v SSHD* [2022] EWHC 1524 (Admin); and https://dpglaw.co.uk/home-offices-no-recourse-to-public-funds-nrpf-policy-found-unlawful-for-the-fifth-time-in-five-years/. At the time of writing, the current policy is due to be updated in light of the most recent concession that the guidance and rules fail to comply with the Equality Act 2010.

183 *Family Policy: Family life (as a partner or parent) and exceptional circumstances*, v18.0, p77.

184 At: www.gov.uk/government/publications/application-for-change-of-conditions-of-leave-to-allow-access-to-public-funds-if-your-circumstances-change.

185 *Family Policy: Family life (as a partner or parent) and exceptional circumstances*, v18.0, p84.

for challenging an NRPF condition, irrespective of whether the applicant is facing destitution.[186]

4.158 'Destitution' in this context has the same meaning as it does in the asylum support context.[187] Consistently with this, the guidance observes that 'there are no fixed monetary values attached to the destitution test in this context'. However, it recognises that households who are receiving local authority support under Children Act 1989 s17[188] owing to their financial circumstances, and those who had previously been in receipt of support under IAA 1999 s4(2)[189] or s95(1)[190] may, in the absence of a change of circumstances, generally be regarded as destitute.[191]

186 See https://dpglaw.co.uk/wp-content/uploads/2023/03/4030643-Final-sealed-order.pdf.

187 See paras 5.57–5.90.

188 See paras 9.12–9.69.

189 See paras 6.9–6.200.

190 See paras 5.9–5.277.

191 *Family Policy: Family life (as a partner or parent) and exceptional circumstances*, v18.0, p83.

CHAPTER 5

Asylum support

Connor Johnston

continued

Key points

- Asylum support under Immigration and Asylum Act (IAA) 1999 s95(1) is available to asylum-seekers and the dependants of asylum-seekers who appear to the Secretary of State for the Home Department to be destitute or likely to become destitute within 14 days.[1]
- In this context, an asylum-seeker is a person who has made a claim that it would be contrary to the UK's obligations under the Refugee Convention or under European Convention on Human Rights (ECHR) Article 3 (prohibition on inhuman or degrading treatment or punishment), for them to be removed from, or required to leave, the UK.[2]
- Asylum support under IAA 1999 s95(1) may also be available to certain failed asylum-seeking households with children.[3]
- Where a family with children appear to be eligible for support under IAA s95(1), local authority social services departments may not provide them with support of the kind available under section 95(1).[4]
- However, responsibility for 'infirm destitute' asylum-seeking adults (ie those eligible for care and support under the Care Act 2014[5]) will lie with social services. Unaccompanied asylum-seeking children (UASCs) will also be the responsibility of social services; and, generally, so will care leavers who are asylum-seekers, but not necessarily if their immigration status changes.[6] Asylum support will *not* usually be provided to these groups.
- There are certain exclusions from asylum support which apply to those who (among other things) lodge their asylum claim late or fail to co-operate with inquiries into their application for asylum support.[7]
- Temporary support under IAA 1999 s98(1) may be available to an applicant while their application for asylum support under IAA 1999 s95(1) is considered.[8]

1 See paras 5.9–5.90. For those who are already receiving support, the prescribed period is 56 days.
2 See paras 5.17–5.44.
3 See paras 5.45–5.49.
4 See paras 5.103–5.111.
5 See paras 5.94–5.103 and 8.7–8.195.
6 See paras 5.112–5.117.
7 See paras 5.118–5.140.
8 See paras 5.282–5.301.

- Asylum support can consist of accommodation or financial subsistence payments, or both.[9]
- Applicants seeking accommodation will normally be dispersed across the UK. Accommodation is generally offered on a no-choice basis, though exceptions apply to certain vulnerable applicants.[10]
- Accommodation is currently provided, or secured, by Clearsprings, Mears Group or Serco.[11]
- Subsistence payments are generally made at a fixed rate prescribed under regulations. The sum currently in payment is £45 per week. Lower payments are made in cases where applicants are in full-board accommodation, as elements of their essential living needs are met by the full board provision. Applicants and their dependants may be eligible for additional payments, or to recover certain expenses, in some cases.[12]
- Applications for asylum support under IAA 1999 s95(1) are made using the ASF1 form. Currently, the organisation Migrant Help is contracted by the Home Office to assist with the application process[13] (although there is no bar on others assisting) and applications should be submitted to the Home Office through Migrant Help.
- Support may come to an end either where the applicant ceases to be destitute or ceases to be an asylum-seeker, or where there has been a breach of conditions on the part of the applicant or a member of their household. Applicants will generally have a grace-period before they are required to leave their accommodation. The length of this grace-period will vary from case to case, but it is invariably short.[14]
- Applicants who are unhappy with the service with which they have been provided may seek to complain to the Home Office and, if that complaint is not dealt with satisfactorily, onward to the Parliamentary and Health Service Ombudsman (PHSO). The timescales involved in this process mean that it will not be suitable for urgent matters.[15] Judicial review may also be available.

9 See paras 5.141–5.220.
10 See paras 5.169–5.184.
11 See para 5.145.
12 See paras 5.185–5.214.
13 See paras 5.221–5.229.
14 See paras 5.251–5.277.
15 See paras 5.372–5.374.

- An entitlement to a statutory appeal to the First-tier Tribunal (FTT) (Asylum Support) will arise where the secretary of state has decided that an applicant does not qualify for support under IAA 1999 s95(1). An appeal right will also arise where the secretary of state has decided to discontinue the applicant's support before it would otherwise have come to an end.[16]
- Save for this, an applicant wishing to challenge an unlawful act on the part of the secretary of state will need to seek judicial review.[17]
- Certain limits are placed on the circumstances in which an applicant who has had their support refused or discontinued may seek to make a further application.[18]

Introduction

Chapter overview

5.1 This chapter will consider the provision of accommodation and financial support to asylum-seekers and their dependants in England and Wales by the Home Office, under IAA 1999 Part VI. The provision of accommodation to failed asylum-seekers by the Home Office is dealt with in chapter 6.[19] Those seeking a historical account of the development of the current regime should refer to the Introduction.

5.2 The chapter begins with a brief summary of the key features of the asylum support regime,[20] followed by an overview of amendments to the system contained in the Nationality, Immigration and Asylum Act (NIAA) 2002, Immigration Act (IA) 2016 and the Illegal Migration Act (IMA) 2023 which are not yet in force.[21] The chapter will then consider who is eligible for asylum support under IAA 1999 s95(1),[22]

16 See paras 5.310–5.327.

17 See paras 5.317–5.318.

18 See para 5.371.

19 The term 'asylum support' is sometimes used to refer both to the support which is available to asylum-seekers and to the support which is available to failed asylum-seekers. In this chapter we use it to refer solely to the support which is available to asylum-seekers.

20 See above.

21 See paras 5.7–5.8.

22 See paras 5.9–5.140.

what support they will receive,[23] how they go about getting it[24] and how it comes to an end.[25] This section forms the substantial part of the chapter.

5.3 A similar exercise will then be carried out in relation to the temporary support under IAA 1999 s98(1) which may be available to an applicant while their application for asylum support is considered.[26] The final section will consider the various appeal rights, remedies and avenues of challenge which may be available to a person who is unhappy with the outcome of their application, or the services with which they have been provided.[27]

5.4 Throughout this chapter, the person who is seeking or receiving support will be referred to as 'the applicant'.

5.5 Some of the cases and materials mentioned in this chapter refer to the National Asylum Support Service or NASS. This is the body which was originally set up to administer the asylum support scheme introduced by the IAA 1999. It ceased to exist in April 2006, although the term 'NASS accommodation' is still frequently used both in Home Office policy and by those who work in the sector. Asylum support is now administered by the UK Visas and Immigration (UKVI) department of the Home Office.

5.6 Decisions of the FTT (Asylum Support) are referred to throughout this chapter.[28] These decisions are not binding, although certain decisions will be marked by the tribunal as 'Landmark Decisions' which tend to be guideline cases and hold persuasive value when considering related points on appeal.[29] Decisions can be accessed as follows:

- Decisions which feature the initials of the applicant (for example, *MG v SSHD* AS/17/05/36760, 12 May 2017, FTT (Asylum Support)) can be found on the FTT (Asylum Support) database.[30]
- Most other decisions (in the form AS/17/05/36760, 12 May 2017, FTT (Asylum Support)) can be found on the website of the

23 See paras 5.141–5.220.
24 See paras 5.221–5.246.
25 See paras 5.247–5.277.
26 See paras 5.282–5.301.
27 See paras 5.310–5.374.
28 See paras 5.343–5.344.
29 See *R (SSHD) v First-Tier Tribunal (Social Entitlement Chamber)* [2021] EWHC 1690 (Admin), [2022] 1 WLR 22 at para 44 per Chamberlain J.
30 See: www.gov.uk/asylum-support-tribunal-decisions.

Asylum Support Appeals Project (ASAP).[31] Anonymised decisions can also be requested directly from the FTT (Asylum Support).

Changes within the Nationality, Immigration and Asylum Act 2002, Immigration Act 2016 and Illegal Migration Act 2023

5.7 NIAA 2002 Part 2 contains a statutory framework for the establishment of 'accommodation centres' to accommodate destitute asylum-seekers. Applicants may be accommodated in such centres either under IAA 1999 s95(1)[32] or under NIAA 2002 s17(1). There are various procedural safeguards contained within NIAA 2002 Part 2 governing the introduction and use of accommodation centres including a prior consultation requirement, where the centre is to be established in Scotland, Northern Ireland or Wales,[33] and a six-month limit on the time which an individual may be continuously accommodated in a centre.[34] The operative provisions of NIAA 2002 Part 2 have not yet been brought into force; however, the Secretary of State for the Home Department has stated that 'new asylum reception centres to provide basic accommodation and process claims' are to be introduced,[35] facilitated by new provisions in Nationality and Borders Act (NBA) 2022 s13, which raise the possibility that they could be brought into effect in the not too distant future.[36] Building on the provisions contained in the NBA 2022, the IMA 2023 contains provisions that will render persons whose claims are declared inadmissible[37] pursuant to the Act (which is intended to be directed at those arriving in the UK on small boats) ineligible for support under IAA 1999 s95(1) and brings them within the scope of IAA 1999 s4(2)[38] instead.[39]

31 See: www.asaproject.org/.
32 NIAA 2002 s22.
33 NIAA 2002 ss40–42.
34 NIAA 2002 s25(1).
35 *New plan for immigration policy statement*, HM Government, March 2021, pp19–20.
36 See paras 5.152–5.153. As discussed in that section, facilities such as Napier Barracks, which are accommodation centres in all but name, are already being used to provide accommodation for asylum-seekers.
37 See paras 3.131–3.142 and 5.39–5.44 for the current legal framework governing declarations of inadmissibility, which the IMA 2023 builds on.
38 See paras 6.9–6.200.
39 IMA 2023 s9.

5.8 There are a number of significant changes to the asylum support regime under IAA 1999 Part VI which are either contained in the IA 2016, or which the IA 2016 paves the way for. At the time of writing, these changes have not come into force. It is not known when (or if) they will come into effect. In outline, the changes are as follows:

- The definition of an 'asylum-seeker'[40] will be extended to include those who have been refused protection and have either lodged further submissions relating to their claim which have not been determined, or have been granted permission to apply for judicial review in relation to the rejection of their further submissions.[41] This means that applicants falling within these categories may be eligible for asylum support under IAA 1999 s95(1). Currently, such applicants would generally need to seek support under IAA 1999 s4(2),[42] as it is only applicants whose further submissions have been accepted by the secretary of state as constituting a fresh claim who will fall within the definition of asylum-seeker, for asylum support purposes.[43]
- Support for failed asylum-seekers under IAA 1999 s4(2)[44] will be abolished and replaced with a more limited form of support under IAA 1999 s95A.[45]
- The extended definition of asylum-seeker under IAA 1999 s94(5) encompassing certain failed asylum-seeking households with children[46] will be abolished.[47] This means that this category of person will no longer be eligible for asylum support under IAA 1999 s95(1).
- The 'grace period'[48] during which this category of person is able to remain in accommodation provided under IAA 1999 s95(1) following the rejection of their asylum claim will be increased from 21 days to 90 days.[49]

40 See paras 5.17–5.49.

41 IA 2016 Sch 11 Part 1 para 3. See further *Reforming support for migrants without immigration status*, Home Office, January 2016, para 19.

42 See paras 6.15–6.38.

43 See paras 5.23–5.28.

44 See paras 6.9–6.200.

45 IA 2016 Sch 11 Part 1 paras 1 and 9. See further *Reforming support for migrants without immigration status*, paras 31–37.

46 See paras 5.45–5.49.

47 IA 2016 Sch 11 Part 1 para 7(5). See further *Reforming support for migrants without immigration status*, para 31.

48 See paras 5.29–5.44 and paras 5.252–5.255.

49 *Reforming support for migrants without immigration status*, paras 23–26.

- This category will either be able to seek support from the Home Office under IAA 1999 s95A[50] or from their local authority under NIAA 2002 Sch 3 para 10A, subject to meeting the eligibility criteria under those provisions.[51]

Support under Immigration and Asylum Act 1999 s95(1)

The eligibility criteria

5.9 Under IAA 1999 s95(1) the secretary of state may provide, or arrange for the provision of support (which may take the form of accommodation and subsistence or subsistence only)[52] for:[53]

- asylum-seekers or dependants of asylum-seekers;
- who appear to the secretary of state to be destitute or likely to become destitute within a 'prescribed period'.

5.10 The prescribed period is 14 days for new applicants.[54] For those who are already receiving support, the prescribed period is 56 days.[55]

5.11 These eligibility criteria contain a number of legal definitions which are discussed in detail below.[56] Where the secretary of state decides that an applicant does not meet these qualifying criteria, they have a statutory right of appeal to the FTT (Asylum Support).[57] It should be noted that the eligibility criteria are subject to a number of statutory exclusions discussed at paras 5.118–5.140. A person subject to one of these exclusions will not be able to access support even if he or she meets the other eligibility criteria.

5.12 Support under IAA 1999 s95(1) is legally distinct, although similar in many practical respects, from the temporary support which is provided under IAA 1999 s98(1) pending a decision by the

50 IA 2016 Sch 11 Part 1 para 9. See further *Reforming support for migrants without immigration status*, paras 31–37.

51 IA 2016 Sch 12 para 10. See further *Reforming support for migrants without immigration status*, paras 51–63.

52 See paras 5.141–5.200.

53 IAA 1999 s95(1).

54 Asylum Support Regulations ('AS Regs') 2000 SI No 704 reg 7(a).

55 See para 5.60.

56 For 'asylum-seeker' see paras 5.17–5.49. For 'dependant' see paras 5.50–5.56. For 'destitute' see paras 5.57–5.90.

57 See paras 5.314–5.327.

secretary of state as to whether a person is eligible for asylum support.[58]

5.13 In contrast to many mainstream welfare benefits provided under the social security legislation,[59] IAA 1999 s95(1) is unusual in that it is expressed to be a power, rather than a duty, to provide support where the relevant conditions are satisfied. In *R (Sathanantham) v SSHD*[60] Edis J described IAA 1999 s95 as forming one of a 'collection of powers to provide support in an immigration context'.[61] Similarly, in *R (Husain) v Asylum Support Adjudicator*[62] Stanley Burnton J observed that:

> Unusually, if not uniquely, Part VI is clearly drafted so as to authorise, but not to oblige, the Secretary of State to provide, or to arrange for the provision of, support for destitute asylum-seekers . . . The effect of the use of the word 'may' in section 95, instead of the usual 'shall', is obvious. Nowhere in Part VI is there a reference to any obligation imposed on the Secretary of State to provide support.[63]

5.14 The purpose of this drafting, he inferred, was an attempt on the part of the government to 'take asylum-seekers' benefit outside the scope of [ECHR] Article 6' (right to a fair trial).[64] There was however, he noted, 'a degree of unreality in regarding support for asylum-seekers as in any real sense discretionary'[65] as a failure to provide support where the relevant conditions were satisfied might amount to discrimination,[66] a failure to meet a substantive legitimate expectation[67] or a breach of ECHR Article 3.[68] This latter point was put beyond doubt by the House of Lords in the case of *R (Limbuela) v SSHD*,[69] where it was confirmed that the state would be under a duty

58 See paras 5.282–5.301.

59 Social Security Contributions and Benefits Act 1992.

60 [2016] EWHC 1781 (Admin), [2016] 4 WLR 128.

61 *Sathanantham* at para 66.

62 [2001] EWHC Admin 852.

63 *Husain* at para 36. See also para 39.

64 *Husain* at para 38. In contrast, the judge held, that once the secretary of state had made a decision to grant support, there was a duty to continue providing that support, and it could not be suspended or withdrawn unless any of the criteria in AS Regs 2000 reg 20(1) were satisfied. This, he concluded, amounted to a civil right for the purposes of ECHR Article 6. See paras 42–57.

65 *Husain* at para 39.

66 *Husain* at para 39.

67 *Husain* at para 41.

68 *Husain* at paras 51–53.

69 [2005] UKHL 66, [2006] 1 AC 396.

to provide asylum support in circumstances where it was necessary to avoid an applicant facing destitution sufficient to breach Article 3.[70]

5.15 However, any debate as to the nature of the power under IAA 1999 s95 has been rendered academic by the Asylum Seekers (Reception Conditions) Regulations 2005.[71] These regulations implement, in part, Council Directive 2003/9/EC[72] ('Reception Directive') laying down minimum standards for the reception of asylum-seekers.[73] Asylum Seekers (Reception Conditions) Regulations 2005 reg 5(1) provides that:

> If an asylum seeker or his family member applies for support under section 95[(1)] of the 1999 Act and the Secretary of State thinks that the asylum seeker or his family member is eligible for support under that section he must offer the provision of support to the asylum seeker or his family member.

5.16 To similar effect the Explanatory Memorandum[74] to these regulations records that the regulation means that the secretary of state 'must' offer support to a person who he or she thinks is eligible for it, altering the 'existing provisions which provide that he may provide support to destitute asylum seekers and their dependants'. This effectively converts IAA 1999 s95(1) into a duty, in circumstances where the eligibility criteria are satisfied.[75] Those criteria are discussed in detail below. The Court of Appeal has described the duty as being 'absolute and immediate'.[76]

70 *R (Limbuela) v SSHD* [2005] UKHL 66, [2006] 1 AC 396 at paras 6–9 per Lord Bingham, discussed at paras 5.127–5.128 and para 5.264.

71 SI No 7.

72 Council Directive 2003/9/EC of 27 January 2003 laying down minimum standards for the reception of asylum seekers.

73 The Asylum Seekers (Reception Conditions) Regulations 2005 implement, in part, the Reception Directive. See *R (Refugee Action) v SSHD* [2014] EWHC 1033 (Admin) at para 22 per Popplewell J. See *R (NB and others) v SSHD* [2021] EWHC 1489 (Admin) at paras 145–158 for the continued effect of the Reception Directive following the departure of the UK from the EU.

74 Explanatory Memorandum to the Asylum Seekers (Reception Conditions) Regulations 2005 para 4.5.

75 *R (Refugee Action) v SSHD* [2014] EWHC 1033 (Admin) at para 13 per Popplewell J; *R (JM) v SSHD* [2021] EWHC 2514 (Admin) at para 15 per Farbey J; *Asylum support: policy bulletins instruction*, v9.0, UKVI, May 2021, para 25.1 (www.gov.uk/government/publications/asylum-support-instructions-policy-bulletins).

76 *R (A) v National Asylum Support Service* [2003] EWCA Civ 1473, [2004] 1 WLR 752 at para 59 per Waller LJ. See further paras 5.154 and 5.245.

Asylum-seeker

5.17 The term 'asylum-seeker' has a special definition under IAA 1999 Part VI. It means:

> . . . a person who is not under 18 and has made a claim for asylum which has been recorded by the Secretary of State but which has not been determined.[77]

5.18 It will be noted that the term 'asylum-seeker', in this context, applies only to those aged 18 or over. Unaccompanied asylum-seeking children (UASCs) will normally access support from local authority children's services under the Children Act (ChA) 1989[78] instead. The terms 'claim for asylum', 'which has been recorded' and 'which has not been determined' are all legal terms of art with specific meanings in the asylum support context. These will be explored in turn.

'Claim for asylum'

5.19 A 'claim for asylum' means a claim that it would be contrary to the UK's obligations under the UN Convention relating to the Status of Refugees 1951 ('Refugee Convention')[79] or under ECHR Article 3,[80] for the applicant to be removed from, or required to leave, the UK.[81]

5.20 There are two particular points to note about this definition. First, the definition differs from that set out in Immigration Rules[82] para 327 (and in the Reception Directive) which refers to an asylum applicant, for the purposes of immigration and asylum law, as a person who has made a request to be recognised as a refugee under the Refugee Convention or for 'international protection'. Second, although it expressly includes those seeking leave to remain to avoid a breach of ECHR Article 3, it does not also encompass those seeking leave to remain pursuant to Article 8.[83]

5.21 The word 'claim' is not defined in the IAA 1999. However, used in the context of the phrase 'person who . . . has made a claim for asylum' it connotes the positive assertion of a right.[84] Thus, in

77 IAA 1999 s94(1).

78 See chapter 8 on support under the ChA 1989 generally; and paras 11.4–11.115 for issues affecting UASCs specifically.

79 See paras 3.31–3.43 for a discussion of claims under the Refugee Convention.

80 See paras 3.44–3.57 for a discussion of ECHR Article 3 claims.

81 IAA 1999 s94(1).

82 HC 395. Available at: www.gov.uk/guidance/immigration-rules.

83 See paras 1.92–1.117 for a discussion of ECHR Article 8 claims.

84 *R (EAT) v Newham LBC* [2013] EWHC 344 (Admin) at para 78 per John Powell QC sitting as a deputy High Court judge.

R (EAT) v Newham LBC[85] John Powell QC sitting as a deputy High Court judge held that, judged objectively, the claimant's mother could not be regarded as having made a claim for asylum, in circumstance where she had not expressly or impliedly invited the secretary of state to consider her application for leave to remain under ECHR Article 3. The fact that her application for leave to remain, which she had made under ECHR Article 8, had been considered by the secretary of state as encompassing a claim under Article 3 did not affect that result.

'Which has been recorded'

5.22 Generally, where an applicant makes an initial claim for asylum, that claim will be recorded at the point at which it is made. This may be 'at port', for those who make their claim on arrival in the UK at an airport or seaport, for example, or for those who make their claim 'in-country', at the Asylum Intake Unit at Lunar House in Croydon or from detention.[86]

5.23 Different considerations apply in instances where an applicant, who has previously had a claim for asylum rejected or withdrawn, makes 'further submissions' in support of a 'fresh claim' for asylum.[87] In such cases, the Home Office's policy is to not treat such further submissions as having been 'recorded' until the secretary of state has made a determination that the applicant's further submissions satisfy the requirements of Immigration Rules para 353 and do, in fact, constitute a fresh claim. Under Immigration Rules para 353, further submissions will amount to a fresh claim only if they are 'significantly different from the material that has previously been considered'.[88] The submissions will only be regarded as 'significantly different' if the content has not already been considered and, taken together with the previously considered material, creates a realistic prospect of success.

5.24 The difference in approach to eligibility for asylum support as between applicants who are making their first claim for asylum and applicants who are seeking to make further submissions having

85 [2013] EWHC 344 (Admin).

86 See further paras 3.67–3.151 for a detailed discussion of the asylum process. Note that additional, temporary, regional Asylum Intake Units were set up in response to the COVID-19 pandemic in Glasgow, Belfast, Liverpool, Leeds, Solihull and Cardiff.

87 See paras 3.42–3.43 for a discussion of fresh claims.

88 Immigration Rules para 353. See further *Asylum and human rights policy instruction: further submissions*, Home Office, June 2022.

previously had a claim rejected was explained by Collins J in *R (Nigatu) v SSHD*:[89]

> 21. There is a real difference between the situation when an initial claim for asylum is made and that when attempts are made to prevent removal following rejection and the exhaustion of all the appeal processes of that claim. The Secretary of State is indeed entitled to consider whether the representations made can properly be said to amount to a fresh claim so as to make the individual an asylum seeker. He will record that, and the evidence before me is that he does record that, when that preliminary decision is made and that the individual in question is notified when that happens. A record is made of that decision at that time.
>
> 22. I am bound to say that Parliament must have meant something by requiring that the claim be recorded. One would have thought that if all that was meant was that it was received, that would have been said. Normally speaking, that will perhaps make no great difference because no system of sensible administration could work unless every application and every claim were recorded by someone when it was made. The question really turns on whether what was put before the Secretary of State can be said to have amounted to a claim for asylum. For the reasons that I have given, in my judgment, it does require the Secretary of State to decide the initial question as to whether it should be regarded as a claim for asylum before any right to support within section 95 can arise.

5.25 The decision in *Nigatu,* it should be noted, does not deal with a number of relevant principles of EU law. In particular, the judge did not consider the effect of the Reception Directive[90] because the case pre-dated the transposition deadline of the Reception Directive in the UK.[91] In addition, the decision pre-dated the implementation of Council Directive 2005/85/EC on minimum standards on procedures in member states for granting and withdrawing refugee status ('Procedures Directive'). Since *Nigatu* was decided, there have been a number of reported decisions (including three decisions of the Supreme Court) dealing with the question of whether a person who has made further submissions which have not yet been recognised as a fresh claim, should be regarded as having made a claim for asylum either as a matter of domestic law or EU law under the Reception

89 [2004] EWHC 1806 (Admin). See further *R (AW) v Croydon LBC* [2005] EWHC 2950 (Admin), (2006) 9 CCLR 252 at paras 63–64 per Lloyd Jones J.

90 See *R (NB and others) v SSHD* [2021] EWHC 1489 (Admin) at paras 145–158 for the continued effect of the Reception Directive following the departure of the UK from the EU.

91 The transposition deadline was 6 February 2005. See: https://eur-lex.europa.eu/legal-content/EN/NIM/?uri=celex:32003L0009.

and Procedures Directives. These outcomes in these cases, which are discussed in detail at paras 6.25–6.36, have not been altogether consistent. For present purposes, suffice to say that these legal developments leave a question mark over whether the reasoning in *Nigatu* would now be upheld by the Court of Appeal or the Supreme Court. However, for now at least, this reasoning continues to be applied by the secretary of state and by the FTT (Asylum Support) in determining applications and appeals relating to eligibility for asylum support.

5.26 The practical effect of this approach is that an applicant who lodges further submissions will only be treated as an asylum-seeker for support purposes once the secretary of state has recognised the further submissions as a fresh claim. At that juncture, their claim will be regarded as having been recorded. Prior to this stage the applicant is likely to be regarded as a failed asylum-seeker[92] and may be entitled to support under IAA 1999 s4(2).[93] The approach of the FTT (Asylum Support) in considering eligibility for support, has been to place the burden of proof on the applicant to establish that they have made a claim for asylum that has been recorded.[94] In contrast, the burden of establishing that an application for asylum, once made, is no longer under consideration lies on the secretary of state.[95]

5.27 Particular difficulties can sometimes arise in circumstances where an applicant has succeeded in an application for judicial review of a refusal by the secretary of state to accept their further submissions as a fresh claim.[96] The fact that an applicant has succeeded in their judicial review means that the parties have agreed or the High Court has decided that the secretary of state made an error of law in deciding the further submissions did not amount to a fresh claim, which will generally lead to that decision being quashed. However, that does not necessarily denote an acceptance on the part of the secretary of state or a finding on the part of the court that the submissions do amount to a fresh claim, or that such a decision will inevitably result when the matter is reconsidered by the secretary of state.

92 An example of an exception to this would be where the applicant's initial asylum claim was treated as withdrawn, perhaps because they absconded, and was never properly determined. In this instance an applicant who has lodged further submissions is likely to be entitled to support under IA 2016 Sch 10. See paras 6.201–6.272.

93 See paras 6.9–6.200.

94 *AAA v SSHD* AS/04/06/82286, 7 July 2004, FTT (Asylum Support) at para 18; *AA v SSHD* AS/08/06/1779, 25 June 2008, FTT (Asylum Support) at para 15.

95 *AA v SSHD* AS/08/06/1779, 25 June 2008, FTT (Asylum Support) at para 16.

96 See paras 3.42–3.43.

Whether that is the case will depend on exactly what has been agreed or decided and why – meaning that in such cases, whether or not the applicant's claim can be regarded as having been recorded will generally depend on the precise terms of the judgment or court order, or the consent order compromising the claim. The claim should certainly be regarded as having been recorded when the judgement order expressly says that the further submissions constitute a fresh claim. Disputes tend to arise where the court order is less clear. In such cases careful consideration will need to be given to the wording and the practical and legal consequences of the order to ascertain its true effect. For example, in AS/15/03/32865[97] the recital to the consent order compromising the applicant's judicial review claim stated as follows:

> Upon the Claimant having 10 weeks from the date of this order to serve further evidence in support of his claim under para 353 HC395 and the Defendant agreeing to make a new decision on the Claimant's claim within 3 months (excluding exceptional circumstances) of the receipt of the Claimant's further evidence and if the Defendant's new decision refuses the Claimant's asylum claim, the Defendant agrees to give the Claimant an in-country right of appeal . . .

5.28 In that case, the Home Office refused the applicant's application for asylum support under IAA 1999 s95(1), asserting that the applicant remained a failed-asylum-seeker. The FTT (Asylum Support) held that this was incorrect. Although the order did not expressly stipulate that the applicant's fresh claim for asylum had been recorded as such, this conclusion followed from the fact that, under the terms of the order, any further negative decision on the applicant's case carried with it an in-country right of appeal. And a right of appeal could only lie if the secretary of state had accepted that the applicant's further submissions amounted to a fresh claim. A decision that further submissions do not amount to a fresh claim does not give rise to a right of appeal. At the other end of the spectrum, a court order which simply quashes the secretary of state's decision that further submissions do not amount to a fresh claim is unlikely to result in the applicant's claim being recorded. An applicant in such circumstances is likely to remain a failed asylum-seeker.

'Which has not been determined'

5.29 For support purposes, the point at which a claim for asylum (in the extended sense discussed above at paras 5.5.19–5.21) is treated as

97 AS/15/03/32865, 10 April 2015, FTT (Asylum Support).

having been 'determined' depends on whether the claim is accepted, rejected or declared inadmissible (pursuant to new provisions introduced under the NBA 2022) and, if it is rejected, whether the applicant has an in-country right of appeal and duly exercises that right of appeal within the statutory time limit.[98] Different rules apply in respect of asylum-seekers with dependent children under the age of 18 in their household. The situation in which the claim is accepted or rejected is discussed at paras 5.30–5.38. The situation where the claim is declared inadmissible is discussed at paras 5.39–5.44. The rules that apply where the household contains dependent children are discussed at paras 5.45–5.49.

5.30 Dealing first with cases where the claim is accepted or rejected,[99] in summary:

- If the asylum claim is accepted, it is treated as having been determined at the end of the 28-day period beginning on the day on which the secretary of state notifies the applicant in writing of their decision.[100]
- If the asylum claim is rejected but, at the same time, the secretary of state decides to grant the applicant limited leave to enter or remain in the UK instead, the asylum claim is treated as having been determined at the end of the 28-day period beginning on the day on which the secretary of state notifies the applicant in writing of his decision.[101]
- If the asylum claim is rejected and the applicant is successful in appealing against that decision, then the asylum claim is treated as having been determined at the end of the 28-day period beginning on the day on which the appeal is allowed.[102]
- If the asylum claim is rejected and the applicant does not appeal against that decision then the asylum claim is treated as having been determined at the end of the 21-day period beginning on the day on which the applicant is notified in writing of that decision.[103]

98 IAA 1999 s94(3)–(4B).

99 An applicant whose claim is rejected may be eligible for support under IAA 1999 s4(2). See chapter 6.

100 IAA 1999 s94(3)(a) and (8); AS Regs 2000 reg 2(2) and (2A)(a); *Ceasing section 95 support instruction*, v1.0, Home Office, June 2022, p9.

101 IAA 1999 s94(3)(a) and (8); AS Regs 2000 reg 2(2) and (2A)(b); *Ceasing section 95 support instruction*, v1.0, p9.

102 IAA 1999 s94(3)(b); AS Regs 2000 reg 2(2) and (2A)(c). Save where the appeal has been lodged out of time. See para 5.34.

103 IAA 1999 s94(3)(a) and (8); AS Regs 2000 reg 2(2); *Ceasing section 95 support instruction*, v1.0, p8.

- If the asylum claim is rejected and the applicant is unsuccessful in appealing against that decision, then the asylum claim is treated as having been determined at the end of the 21-day period beginning on the day on which the appeal is finally disposed of.[104] This is often described as the date on which the applicant becomes 'appeal rights exhausted' or 'ARE'.

5.31 The category referred to in the final bullet point at para 5.30 above requires some understanding of the appeal rights available to an applicant whose asylum claim is refused,[105] and when such an appeal can be regarded as having been disposed of. An appeal is disposed of when 'it is no longer pending for the purposes of the Immigration Acts or the Special Immigration Appeals Commission Act 1997'.[106] The Immigration Acts in this context are listed in UK Borders Act 2007 s61(2) and include, among others, the NIAA 2002.[107] Under the NIAA 2002 a person may appeal to the FTT (Immigration and Asylum) where the secretary of state has decided to refuse their 'protection claim' or human rights claim.[108] Tribunals, Courts and Enforcement Act 2007 ss11 and 13 provide such a person with onward rights of appeal to the Upper Tribunal and then the Court of Appeal, respectively. A 'protection claim', in this context, is a claim that removal of the person from the UK would result in a breach of the UK's obligations under the Refugee Convention, or obligations owed to those eligible for a grant of humanitarian protection.[109] This is a different definition to 'asylum claim' for the purposes of asylum support, which is discussed above at paras 5.19–5.21, but under NIAA 2002 s82, an appeal right is also provided for in respect of a 'human rights' claim, which would include a claim under ECHR Article 3. Thus, in practical terms this right of appeal is available to all of those who have made an 'asylum claim', within the meaning of IAA 1999 s94(1), including Article 3 claims, which has been refused. No appeal lies against a refusal to accept that further submissions amount to a fresh claim.[110] The remedy there is judicial review.

104 IAA 1999 s94(3)(a) and (4); AS Regs 2000 reg 2(2); *Ceasing section 95 support instruction*, v1.0, p8. See further paras 3.118–3.130 for a discussion of asylum appeal rights and time-limits.
105 See paras 3.118–3.130 for a fuller discussion of appeal rights in asylum cases.
106 IAA 1999 s94(4).
107 UK Borders Act 2007 s61(2)(f).
108 NIAA 2002 s82(1).
109 NIAA 2002 s82(2).
110 *R (Robinson) v SSHD* [2019] UKSC 11.

5.32 Under NIAA 2002 s104 an appeal is 'pending' until the latest of the following dates:[111]

- the final date for seeking permission to appeal to the Upper Tribunal or Court of Appeal;
- the date on which permission to appeal is refused by the Upper Tribunal or Court of Appeal;
- the date on which any substantive appeal is refused;
- the date on which the appeal is withdrawn or abandoned;
- the date on which any rehearing, following a successful appeal, has taken place.

5.33 A person who is inside the UK has 14 days in which to lodge an appeal at the FTT (Immigration and Asylum Chamber (IAC)).[112] The same time limit applies to any subsequent application to the FTT (IAC) for permission to appeal to the Upper Tribunal.[113] Where permission to appeal is refused by the FTT (IAC) the person has a further 14 days in which to seek permission to appeal directly from the Upper Tribunal.[114] No appeal lies against a refusal to grant permission to appeal by the Upper Tribunal: judicial review is the only remedy.[115] Where permission is granted to appeal to the Upper Tribunal but the appeal itself is unsuccessful, permission to appeal to the Court of Appeal can be sought from the Upper Tribunal within 12 working days (in general) or seven working days (if the person is detained).[116] Time limits of ten and five working days, respectively, are substituted where the decision is sent out electronically.[117] If the Upper Tribunal refuses permission to appeal, then permission may be sought directly from the Court of Appeal[118] within 28 days.[119]

5.34 Where an appeal is lodged out of time, it will not be regarded as pending, notwithstanding the fact that the court has a discretion to

111 NIAA 2002 s104(1)–(2).

112 Tribunal Procedure (First-tier Tribunal) (Immigration and Asylum Chamber) Rules 2014 SI No 2604 r19.

113 Tribunal Procedure (First-tier Tribunal) (Immigration and Asylum Chamber) Rules 2014 r33.

114 Tribunal Procedure (Upper Tribunal) Rules 2008 SI No 2698 r21(3). Save in fast-track cases where only four working days are allowed. See para 3.83 for fast-track cases.

115 See *R (Cart) v Upper Tribunal* [2011] UKSC 28, [2012] 1 AC 663.

116 Tribunal Procedure (Upper Tribunal) Rules 2008 r44(3A)–(3B).

117 Tribunal Procedure (Upper Tribunal) Rules 2008 r44(3C).

118 Tribunals, Courts and Enforcement Act 2007 s13(5).

119 Civil Procedure Rules 1998 SI No 3132 Practice Direction 16 para 3.3.

entertain such an appeal,[120] unless and until the court decides to grant an extension of time to appeal. At that point, the appeal becomes a pending appeal.[121]

5.35 These rules on appeals are complex and advisers wishing to establish whether their client's asylum claim has been determined in these circumstances will need to check carefully against the wording of the relevant regulations to establish whether the applicable time limit(s) for appealing have elapsed. In a typical case, where the applicant has not sought permission to appeal against the refusal of their asylum claim, that claim will be treated as determined at the end of the 35-day period beginning on the day the decision letter is sent out. Similarly, where permission to appeal is refused by the FTT (IAC) and then the Upper Tribunal in turn – another fairly common scenario – the claim will be treated as determined at the end of the 21-day period following the refusal of permission by the Upper Tribunal.

5.36 The use of the word 'notified' in IAA 1999 s94(3) and AS Regs 2000 reg 2(2A), which implies that the applicant has acquired knowledge of the asylum decision, suggests that the applicant must actually have received the decision in order for their asylum claim to be regarded as having been determined. In that vein, in the FTT (Asylum Support) landmark decision in *Arama v SSHD*[122] Principal Judge Storey, applying the principle set down by the House of Lords in *R (Anufrijeva) v SSHD*[123] that 'a constitutional state must accord to individuals the right to know of a decision before their rights can be adversely affected',[124] held that the mere placing of the decision refusing the applicant's asylum claim on the applicant's file, by the secretary of state, was not sufficient. In those circumstances case, she held, the applicant continued to be an asylum-seeker for support purposes and remained entitled to asylum support. However, IAA 1999 s94(9) provides a statutory exception to this rule, to the effect that notices which are sent by the secretary of state by first class post addressed to either the applicant's representative or last known

120 *R (Erdogan) v SSHD* [2004] EWCA Civ 1087, [2004] INLR 503.
121 *R (Akinola) v Upper Tribunal* [2021] EWCA Civ 1308 at para 48.
122 AS/04/09/8617, 5 October 2004, FTT (Asylum Support).
123 [2003] UKHL 36, [2004] 1 AC 604.
124 *Anufrijeva* at para 28 per Lord Steyn.

address, will be treated as having been received on the second day after posting.[125]

5.37 It will be noted that IAA 1999 s94(3) and AS Regs 2000 reg 2(2) and (2A) deal only with the situation where the secretary of state has made a decision on the applicant's asylum claim. However, what if no substantive decision has been made? This may happen, for example, because the asylum claim has been withdrawn. The withdrawal of asylum claims forms the subject of Immigration Rules para 333C, which provides that consideration of an asylum claim by the secretary of state may be discontinued if the application for asylum has been withdrawn either explicitly or implicitly. An application will be treated as explicitly withdrawn where the applicant signs a form to that effect. An application will be treated as implicitly withdrawn if the applicant:

- leaves the UK without authorisation at any time prior to the conclusion of their asylum claim;
- fails to complete an asylum questionnaire as requested by the secretary of state; or
- fails to attend their asylum interview (unless the applicant demonstrates within a reasonable time that that failure was due to circumstances beyond their control).[126]

5.38 Most typically one or more of these criteria will be engaged, and the asylum application will be treated as implicitly withdrawn, in circumstances where the applicant has absconded prior to any decision being reached on the merits of their asylum claim.[127] The approach

125 IAA 1999 s94(9). This statutory exception, which applies only in the asylum support context, is considerably narrower than the normal rules that apply in relation to immigration decisions under Immigration (Notices) Regulations 2003 SI No 658 reg 7(2) which permits service to be effected by leaving the decision on file, in certain circumstances.

126 Immigration Rules para 333C.

127 For further reading on this subject see *Support for absconders and others who have withdrawn their asylum claims*, ASAP, 30 May 2019. Note that para 4.3 of that document considers the position of applicants who lodged asylum claims prior to 7 April 2008 or 27 February 2015. Such cases are relatively esoteric and are not dealt with here.

of both the secretary of state[128] and the FTT (Asylum Support)[129] has generally been that where an applicant's asylum claim has been withdrawn under Immigration Rules para 333C, the applicant can no longer be regarded as an asylum-seeker, unless and until further submissions are lodged which are accepted as a fresh claim,[130] and is therefore ineligible for support under IAA 1999 s95(1).[131] However, arguably, the applicant cannot be regarded as a failed asylum-seeker either, since the asylum claim has never been 'rejected', meaning that support under IAA 1999 s4(2) would not be available.[132] In these circumstances, the applicant may be eligible for support under IA 2016 Sch 10. This is discussed in detail at paras 6.201–6.274. However, practitioners advising clients in these circumstances should be aware that the Home Office has in place a policy setting out a particular procedure which should be followed before an asylum claim can be treated as implicitly withdrawn.[133] Where there has been a failure to follow this procedure, or where an applicant has not been notified of the withdrawal of their claim, it may be that the asylum claim cannot be regarded as having been properly withdrawn and that the applicant remains an asylum-seeker for support purposes.[134]

128 *Asylum policy instruction withdrawing asylum claims*, Home Office, May 2020, p18; *Ceasing section 95 support instruction*, v1.0, p7.

129 For example, AS/13/05/29889, 4 June 2013, FTT (Asylum Support); AS/13/07/30183, 29 July 2013, FTT (Asylum Support); AS/15/01/32416, 26 January 2015, FTT (Asylum Support); and *XC v SSHD* AS/18/06/38201, 22 June 2018, FTT (Asylum Support). The jurisdiction of the Asylum Support Adjudicator (since replaced by the FTT (Asylum Support)) to consider the issue of whether or not an applicant is an asylum-seeker in the context of a statutory appeal, was confirmed in *R (Malaj) v Chief Asylum Support Adjudicator* [2006] EWHC 3059 (Admin), (2006) Times, December 22. See further paras 5.314–5.327 on appeals.

130 See paras 5.23–5.28 and Immigration Rules para 353, which expressly encompasses the lodging of further submissions following a withdrawn claim.

131 Cases in which the applicant has a child under the age of 18 provide an exception to this rule. Under IAA 1999 s94(5) the applicant should continue to be characterised as an asylum-seeker, notwithstanding the withdrawal of their asylum claim, so long as the child is under the age of 18 and the applicant and the child remain in the UK. See paras 5.45–5.49.

132 IAA 1999 s4(2)(b). The point is described as arguable as there has been a divergence in approach to this issue at the FTT (Asylum Support). See paras 6.19–6.24.

133 *Asylum policy instruction withdrawing asylum claims*, pp14–17.

134 AS/14/09/31873, 19 September 2014, FTT (Asylum Support); AS/18/07/3437, 9 August 2018, FTT (Asylum Support); AS/21/03/42880, 7 April 2021, FTT (Asylum Support); AS/22/01/43710, 17 March 2022, FTT (Asylum Support).

5.39 The discussion at paras 5.30–5.38 has focused on the situation where the asylum-claim is 'determined' as a result of having been accepted or rejected. However, as noted, at para 5.29, a claim is also treated as determined where it has been declared inadmissible under NIAA 2002 ss80A–80B.[135] These provisions were introduced by NBA 2022 ss15–17 and came into force on 28 June 2022.[136]

5.40 In outline, NIAA 2002 s80A[137] requires the secretary of state to declare an asylum claim made by a person who is a member of an EU member state inadmissible, save where there are 'exceptional circumstances'. This declaration of inadmissibility precludes her from considering the claim.[138] The term 'exceptional circumstances' is defined, non-exhaustively, in NIAA 2002 s80A(5) and includes the situation where there would be a breach of the applicant's rights under the ECHR.

5.41 Under NIAA 2002 s80B[139] the secretary of state also has a discretion to declare inadmissible (and hence refrain from considering) an asylum claim made by a person who has a 'connection to a safe third State'.[140] A 'safe third State' is one where the applicant's life or liberty will not be threatened on any of the grounds protected by the Refugee Convention, where they will not be sent on to another state in contravention of the Refugee Convention or ECHR Article 3, and where they may apply to be recognised as a refugee.[141] An applicant will have a 'connection' with such a state where the criteria in NIAA 2022 s80C are satisfied.[142] In very broad terms, the criteria in NIAA 2022 s80C will be satisfied where the applicant has, or reasonably could have, made their claim in the safe third state. Notwithstanding the making of a declaration of inadmissibility under NIAA 2002 s80B(1), the secretary of state may consider an applicant's claim for asylum in any event if they decide either that it is unlikely to be possible to remove the applicant to a safe third state within a

135 IAA 1999 s94(4A). See further paras 3.131–3.142 on declarations of inadmissibility.

136 The IMA 2023 paves the way for declarations of inadmissibility to be used more widely.

137 See further paras 3.131–3.142.

138 NIAA 2002 s80A(1)–(4).

139 See further paras 3.131–3.142.

140 The fact that an applicant's claim is declared inadmissible because they have a connection with a safe third state does not mean that they have to be removed to *that* state: NIAA 2002 s80B(6). They could, for example, be removed to Rwanda under the Migration and Economic Development Partnership.

141 NIAA 2002 s80B(4).

142 NIAA 2002 s80B(5).

reasonable period, or that there are exceptional circumstances, or in any other circumstances set out in the Immigration Rules.[143]

5.42 NIAA 2002 s80B has thus far been applied to the UK's Migration and Economic Development Partnership with Rwanda, referred to at paras 3.131–3.142 as the 'Rwanda asylum plan'.[144] Under this scheme, the secretary of state can make a decision to declare an applicant's asylum claim inadmissible, and seek the applicant's removal to Rwanda, for their asylum claim to be examined there.[145] In order to make that decision, the secretary of state would first issue a Notice of Intent to declare the applicant's claim for asylum inadmissible. The applicant would have an opportunity to respond to that Notice of Intent before a decision on inadmissibility is made. Until the applicant has been notified of the declaration of inadmissibility, the applicant remains an asylum-seeker for the purposes of asylum support. Thus the service of a Notice of Intent would not, on its own, render the claim inadmissible.

5.43 Where a declaration of inadmissibility is made under NIAA 2002 s80A or s80B, the applicant's asylum claim will, for asylum support purpose, be treated as having been determined at the end of the 21-day period beginning with the day on which the secretary of state notifies the applicant of that decision.[146] If the applicant is in receipt of IAA 1999 s95(1) support at this point, they will be notified that this support may end[147] and that they may be able to apply for support under IAA 1999 s4(2).[148] However, if the secretary of state subsequently decides to consider the applicant's claim in any event, pursuant to NIAA 2002 s80B(7), because, for example, it becomes apparent that it will not be possible to remove them to the safe third state within a reasonable period, then the applicant will be considered to be an asylum-seeker for support purposes once more.[149] If the applicant had been receiving IAA 1999 s4(2) support during this

143 NIAA 2002 s80B(7).

144 See further paras 3.131–3.142. The legality of this scheme was upheld by the High Court in *R (AAA (Syria)) v SSHD* [2022] EWHC 3230 (Admin). That decision is under appeal.

145 *Inadmissibility: safe third country cases*, v7.0, Home Office, June 2022, pp7 and 17.

146 IAA 1999 s94(3), (4A) and (4C); AS Regs 2000 reg 2(2). The deeming provision in IAA 1999 s94(3) is necessary as the declaration of inadmissibility does not constitute a refusal of the claim: NIAA 2002 ss80A(3) and 80B(3).

147 See further paras 5.247–5.256.

148 *Ceasing section 95 support instruction*, v1.0, p10. See chapter 6 for support under IAA 1999 s4(2).

149 IAA 1999 s94(4B); *Ceasing section 95 support instruction*, v1.0, p10.

time, they will automatically be transitioned back to IAA 1999 s95(1) support.[150]

5.44 It is important to note that the phrase 'asylum claim' as used in NIAA 2002 ss80A–80B has a different meaning to the phrase 'claim for asylum' (and 'asylum-seeker') used in IAA 1999 Part VI. As discussed at paras 5.19–5.21, the latter includes a claim under the Refugee Convention and/or a claim under ECHR Article 3,[151] whereas the former has a narrower meaning and refers only to claims under the Refugee Convention.[152] Thus, under NIAA 2002 ss80A–80B, the secretary of state's declaration of inadmissibility only applies to a claim made under the Refugee Convention and not a human rights claim raising ECHR Article 3.[153] An applicant who makes a claim under both the Refugee Convention and ECHR Article 3 will be regarded as an asylum-seeker for asylum support purposes. However, whether the applicant will remain an asylum-seeker for asylum support purposes, depends on how the secretary of state deals with their claim under the Refugee Convention and ECHR Article 3. If the claim under the Refugee Convention is declared inadmissible but the human rights claim remains undetermined, then for asylum support purposes, the applicant's 'claim for asylum' within the meaning of IAA 1999 s94(1) remains pending. They remain an 'asylum-seeker' for support purposes. Similarly, if the human rights claim is refused but not certified as clearly unfounded so as to attract an in-country right of appeal, then, if that appeal right is exercised, the applicant remains an 'asylum-seeker' for support purposes. However, and in practice, it is the secretary of state's stated policy to deal with the human rights claim in line with the decision on inadmissibility such that if the claim under the Refugee Convention is declared inadmissible, the human rights claim is most likely to be refused and certified as clearly unfounded without an in-country right of appeal. This means that the applicant will cease to be an asylum-seeker for support purposes.

150 *Ceasing section 95 support instruction*, v1.0, p10.

151 IAA 1999 s94(1).

152 NIAA 2002 ss80A(6), 80B(8)(a) and 113(1).

153 An ECHR Article 3 claim cannot be declared inadmissible, save where it is based on the same facts as a claim for asylum that has been declared inadmissible. Accordingly any such claim has to be considered substantively. Such a claim may however be certified under Asylum and Immigration (Treatment of Claimants, etc) Act 2004 Sch 3. See Immigration Rules para 327F and *Inadmissibility: safe third country cases*, v7.0, pp11 and 20. See further paras 3.121–3.130.

Households including children

5.45 Different rules apply to certain households containing children. IAA 1999 s94(5) contains a special deeming provision which treats certain failed asylum-seekers (that is those with claims which have been determined against them and who have exhausted available appeal rights), who have a dependant child as continuing to be asylum-seekers for support purposes until the child reaches their majority. Specifically, IAA 1999 s94(5) provides that:

> If an asylum-seeker's household includes a child who is under 18 and a dependant of his, he is to be treated (for the purposes of this Part) as continuing to be an asylum-seeker while–
> (a) the child is under 18; and
> (b) he and the child remain in the United Kingdom.

5.46 The FTT (Asylum Support) had in the past interpreted this provision as applying only to households who were in receipt of asylum support at the time their asylum claim was rejected, the view being that:

> Section 94(5) is not intended to enable person who have exhausted their appeal rights from qualifying for support under Section 95 unless they are already in receipt of such support. Otherwise the use of the word 'continuing' in subsection 5 would have no relevance.[154]

5.47 This analysis was relied on by Judge Sally Verity Smith in *YY v SSHD*[155] who added that IAA 1999 s94(5) 'prevents support from being withdrawn from such persons and ensures continuity of support'.[156]

5.48 Arguably, the approach described above in *YY v SSHD* is wrong and in more recent decisions, such as AS/18/12/39001,[157] the FTT (Asylum Support) has taken a different approach which, in the authors' view, reflects the correct interpretation of the statute and current Home Office policy.[158] The word 'continuing' in IAA 1999 s94(5) is expressed to refer to the applicant's status as an asylum-seeker and not to their entitlement to support. The more natural way to read IAA 1999 s94(5) is that an asylum-seeker with a dependant child under the age of 18 in their household at the time their asylum

154 See the landmark decisions of *EH v SSHD* AS/02/02/1872, 26 February 2002, FTT (Asylum Support) at para 11; and *RB v SSHD* AS/02/02/1877, 26 February 2002, FTT (Asylum Support) at para 10.

155 AS/07/02/14740, 22 February 2007, FTT (Asylum Support).

156 *YY v SSHD* AS/07/02/14740, 22 February 2007, FTT (Asylum Support) at para 10. See further *GA v SSHD* AS/12/10/29002, 26 October 2012, FTT (Asylum Support) at paras 11–14.

157 15 January 2019, FTT (Asylum Support), June 2019 *Legal Action* 30.

158 *Ceasing section 95 support instruction*, v1.0, pp9–10.

claim is rejected, shall continue to be treated as an asylum-seeker until the child reaches the age of 18, providing they remain in the UK.[159] Such a person remains eligible for asylum support during that time, provided that the other eligibility criteria are met. But there is no requirement that the applicant should have previously received asylum support prior to the rejection of their asylum claim or have been in receipt of asylum support at the time their claim was finally determined.

5.49 This reflects the approach of the High Court in *R (VC) v Newcastle City Council*.[160] In that case VC made an asylum claim in December 2002 and thereafter began to receive asylum support. Her asylum claim was rejected in January 2003 and her asylum support was terminated later that year. The following year, in August 2004, VC gave birth to a son. Later that month she lodged further submissions which, in January 2005, were accepted as amounting to a fresh claim, but refused. In subsequent judicial review proceedings, the parties to the claim accepted that this second asylum claim brought VC within the ambit of IAA 1999 s94(5) and meant that she fell to be treated as an asylum-seeker, notwithstanding the fact she had not been in receipt of asylum support at the time her appeal rights were exhausted and that there was no question of ensuring 'continuity of support'[161] for the household since VC had not received asylum support since before the birth of her son. The Divisional Court endorsed the agreement reached by the parties on this issue.[162]

Dependant

5.50 The word 'dependant' in the asylum support context does not necessarily denote an actual relationship of dependency, whether financial, emotional, practical or otherwise. Rather, a dependant is someone who satisfies the special statutory definition contained in

159 This reading of IAA 1999 s94(5) was described as 'probably right' by Warby J in *R (FA) v Redbridge LBC* [2018] EWHC 2189 (Admin), [2018] 4 WLUK 538 at paras 29–30, albeit he did not decide the issue and did not regard it as 'plain or obvious'.

160 [2011] EWHC 2673 (Admin), [2012] 2 All ER 227.

161 The phrase used in *YY v SSHD* AS/07/02/14740, 22 February 2007, FTT (Asylum Support) at para 10.

162 See *R (VC) v Newcastle City Council* [2011] EWHC 2673 (Admin), [2012] 2 All ER 227 at paras 4 and 55–56 per Munby LJ and the description of IAA 1999 s94(5) given at para 41 which would seem to accord with the description of the law put forward here. See also *R (Chen) v SSHD* [2012] EWHC 2531 (Admin) at para 9 per Beatson J. Neither judge added the gloss to IAA 1999 s94(5) given in the FTT (Asylum Support) decisions referred to above.

IAA 1999 s94(1) and AS Regs 2000 reg 2.[163] Specifically, a dependant, in relation to an asylum-seeker, a person who is receiving asylum support or an applicant for asylum support, means a person in the UK who:[164]

- is their spouse or civil partner;[165]
- is a child of theirs, or of their spouse or civil partner, who is dependent on them[166] and who is, or was at the relevant time, under 18;[167]
- is a member of their, or their spouse or civil partner's, close family and is, or was at the relevant time, under 18;[168]
- had been living as part of their household either since birth or for at least six out of the 12 months before the relevant time and is, or was at the relevant time, under 18;[169]
- is in need of care and attention from them, or from a member of their household, by reason of a disability and would fall within

163 See *R v Camden LBC ex p Diirshe* [2000] 2 WLUK 875, QBD (in the context of the Asylum Support (Interim Provisions) Regulations 1999 SI No 3056) applied by the Principal Judge in the landmark decision in *GM v SSHD* AS 04/05/8109, 3 June 2004, FTT (Asylum Support).

164 IAA 1999 s94(1); AS Regs 2000 reg 2(1), (4) and (7).

165 IAA 1999 s94(1)(a); AS Regs 2000 reg 2(4)(a). For a marriage that took place abroad to be valid under UK law it must have been recognised as a valid ceremony satisfying the legal requirements of the country in which it took place. Marriages in the UK must have met the requirements of the Marriage Act 1949. The Home Office guidance observes that 'it may not always be reasonable to expect a couple who have fled persecution to be able to provide a marriage certificate unless the marriage has taken place since they arrived in the UK'. See *Dependants on an asylum support application*, Home Office, January 2015, para 2.2 (www.gov.uk/government/publications/dependants-on-an-asylum-support-application-instruction).

166 In AS/15/07/33507, 30 July 2015, FTT (Asylum Support) it was held that a child may be properly regarded as dependent on both parents and still qualify as a dependant of the parent who is applying for asylum support.

167 IAA 1999 s94(1)(b); AS Regs 2000 reg 2(4)(b). This provision means that a person does not cease to be a dependant on turning 18. *Dependants on an asylum support application*, section 6 provides that: 'Children who have been accepted as a dependant on an asylum support application should not be expected to apply for support in their own right on turning 18 unless the main applicant is a failed asylum-seeker and has no other child dependants. Their support will continue until such time as the main applicant becomes ineligible for support.' See further See *DAG v SSHD* AS/12/02/28098, 27 April 2012, FTT (Asylum Support).

168 AS Regs 2000 reg 2(4)(c). See fn 179.

169 AS Regs 2000 reg 2(4)(d). See fn 179.

one of the previous two categories but for the fact that they are not, and were not at the relevant time, under 18;[170]

- had been living with them as a member of a cohabiting couple for at least two of the three years before the relevant time;[171]
- is living as part of their household and was, immediately before 6 December 1999, receiving assistance from a local authority under ChA 1989 s17;[172]
- is living as part of their household and was, immediately before 3 April 2000, receiving assistance from a local authority under Children (Scotland) Act 1995 s22 or Children (Northern Ireland) Order 1995[173] art 18;[174]
- has made a claim for leave to enter or remain in the UK, or for variation of any such leave, which is being considered on the basis that they are dependant on the asylum-seeker.[175]

5.51 AS Regs 2000 regs 2(4) and (5) go on to provide that if a supported person, or an applicant for support, is a dependant of an asylum-seeker then, conversely, the asylum-seeker will also be regarded as their dependant (providing they are in the UK). However, a person who would otherwise meet the definition of dependant of a supported person or applicant for support is not classed as a dependant unless they are also a dependant of the asylum-seeker or the asylum-seeker.

5.52 The purpose of these provisions is to deal with the situation where the application for support is made by a dependant of the asylum-seeker, for example, their spouse.[176] The structure of the legislation is such that it is necessary, in these circumstances, to treat the asylum-seeker as a dependant of the applicant, so that they can be included

170 AS Regs 2000 reg 2(4)(e). See AS/18/03/37905, 16 March 2018, FTT (Asylum Support) for an example of a case where the 'care and attention' criterion was found to be satisfied.

171 AS Regs 2000 reg 2(4)(f). In *R (Chen) v SSHD* [2012] EWHC 2531 (Admin) the High Court rejected an argument that this provision, which treats cohabitants less favourably than married couples and short-term cohabitants less favourably than long-term cohabitants, resulted in unjustified discrimination contrary to ECHR Articles 8 and 14.

172 AS Regs 2000 reg 2(4)(g). See paras 9.12–9.69 for support under ChA 1989 s17.

173 SI No 755 (NI 2).

174 AS Regs 2000 reg 2(4)(h).

175 AS Regs 2000 reg 2(4)(i).

176 The legislation permits applications for asylum support to be made either by an asylum-seeker or their dependant: IAA 1999 s95(1); AS Regs 2000 reg 3(1). See paras 5.221–5.224.

in the application,[177] the assessment of destitution[178] and the provision of support.[179] Treating the asylum-seeker as a dependant of their dependant – even if this does not reflect the reality of the situation – is a necessary fiction in order to ensure that they can access support even though they are not the applicant. Further, the provisions ensure that in such cases the only other dependants who may be included in the application are those who are also dependants of the asylum-seeker. Take, for example, the case where the application is made by the spouse of the asylum-seeker. A person under the age of 18 who has been living as part of the spouse's household for at least six out of the 12 months, but who is not a child or close family member, would only be classed as their dependant if they had also been part of the asylum-seeker's household during that period.[180] In simple terms, whether the application is made by the asylum-seeker or by their dependant, the only other people who may be included in the application are the dependants of the asylum-seeker.

5.53 The various categories of dependant set out above include a number of terms which are defined expressly within the AS Regs 2000. In particular:

- the 'relevant time' means the time at which the application for asylum support was made or,[181] where the person in question has later joined a supported person in the UK, the time when they joined the supported person;[182]
- 'cohabiting couple' means two people who, though not married to, or civil partners of, each other, are living together as if they were a married couple or civil partners.[183]

5.54 The terms 'close family', 'household, 'disability' and 'care and attention', however, are not defined in the IAA 1999 or the AS Regs 2000 and presumably should assume their ordinary English meaning. To the extent that definitions and interpretations from other statutory schemes may assist in understanding these terms, it may be of use to note that:

177 AS Regs 2000 reg 3(2).
178 IAA 1999 s95(3)–(4); AS Regs 2000 reg 5.
179 IAA 1999 s96(1)(b)–(c).
180 AS Regs 2000 reg 2(4)(d) and (5).
181 See AS 20/01/41402, 3 February 2020, FTT (Asylum Support) for a discussion of the 'relevant time', in a case where there had been multiple applications for support.
182 AS Regs 2000 reg 2(6).
183 AS Regs 2000 reg 2(1).

- The word 'family', in the context of the Rent Act 1977, has been 'applied flexibly, and does not cover only legally binding relationships'. Rather, it implies a relationship which bears the 'hall marks . . . of mutual inter-dependence, of the sharing of lives, of caring and love, of commitment and support'.[184] By way of illustration, in *Sheffield City Council v Wall's personal representatives*[185] the Court of Appeal held that a long-term foster child would, in the absence of any express statutory provision to the contrary, 'undoubtedly' be regarded as a member of his foster-mother's family.
- 'Household', in the context of legislation governing houses in multiple occupation (HMOs) has been held to be 'a question of fact and degree'. Factors relevant to the assessment of whether a group of people together form a household will include the size of the group, whether the composition of the group fluctuates or is 'durable and intimate' in character, and whether the arrangement is temporary.[186] This approach was followed by the Principal Judge in the landmark decision in *GM v SSHD*,[187] where she held that an applicant, her sister and her nephew, together formed a household by virtue of the small size of the group, their close relationship which was both intimate and durable, their shared domestic arrangements, and the permanent nature of their situation (notwithstanding the temporary nature of the applicant's immigration status).
- In the context of the Equality Act 2010, a 'disability' is a physical or mental impairment with a substantial and long-term adverse effect on a person's ability to carry out normal day-to-day activities.[188]
- 'Care and attention' under National Assistance Act (NAA) 1948 s21 meant 'looking after', ie 'doing something for the person being cared for which he cannot or should not be expected to do for himself'.[189]

184 *Fitzpatrick v Sterling Housing Association Ltd* [1999] UKHL 42, [2001] 1 AC 27 at paras 22–23 per Lord Slynn.

185 [2010] EWCA Civ 922, [2010] HLR 47 at paras 20–26 per Ward LJ.

186 See *Simmons v Pizzey* [1979] AC 37, HL at pp59E–60D per Lord Hailsham.

187 AS 04/05/8109, 3 June 2004, FTT (Asylum Support).

188 Equality Act 2010 s6 and Sch 1.

189 *R (M) v Slough BC* [2008] UKHL 52, [2008] 1 WLR 1808 at para 33 per Baroness Hale. Note that this provision has now been superseded by support under the Care Act 2014. See paras 8.7–8.178.

5.55 However, a note of caution should be sounded before importing definitions from other statutes since the interpretation of a given phrase will always depend on the context in which it is used and the legislative objective.

5.56 A person's immigration status does not have any bearing on whether or not they are a dependant for the purposes of IAA 1999 s94(1) and AS Regs 2000 reg 2. For example, in the FTT (Asylum Support) landmark decision in *GM v SSHD*[190] the applicant's nephew was found to be a dependant for asylum support purposes notwithstanding the fact he was a British citizen. This is reflected in Home Office policy which provides that 'the definition of dependant for support purposes does not exclude British citizens or persons with valid leave to remain in the UK'.[191] However, where a dependant, by virtue of their immigration status, has access to other public funds this may impact on the separate question of whether the applicant is destitute.

Destitution

5.57 For asylum support purposes, an applicant is destitute if they:[192]

- do not have adequate accommodation or any means of obtaining it (whether or not their other essential living needs are met); or
- have adequate accommodation or the means of obtaining it, but cannot meet their other essential living needs.

5.58 If the applicant has dependants,[193] then the destitution test will be satisfied if the applicant, taken together with his or her dependents, are without adequate accommodation or unable to meet their essential living needs.[194]

5.59 What it means to be without 'adequate accommodation'[195] and unable to meet 'essential living needs'[196] are considered in more detail below.

5.60 In assessing destitution, the secretary of state must ignore any asylum support or support under IAA 1999 s98[197] which the applicant

190 AS 04/05/8109, 3 June 2004, FTT (Asylum Support).
191 *Dependants on an asylum support application*, Home Office, para 3.1.
192 IAA 1999 s95(3).
193 See paras 5.50–5.56.
194 IAA 1999 s95(4). See further AS Regs 2000 reg 5.
195 See paras 5.72–5.82.
196 See paras 5.83–5.90.
197 See paras 5.282–5.3010.

and any of their dependants are being provided with or might be provided within the next 14-day period.[198] In *Assessing destitution*, the Home Office notes that income which is 'clearly provided for reasons unrelated to covering the costs of their accommodation or meeting their essential living needs', such as 'small cash sums' paid by local authorities to help applicants meet disability or care related needs or occasional charitable payments to 'fund travel to attend classes or to buy course materials', should be disregarded.[199] As should financial support from the Salvation Army or its subcontractors to potential or confirmed victims of modern slavery, as that cash allowance 'takes into account, where appropriate, that the person's essential living needs are being met under sections 95, 98 or 4 of the 1999 Act and is provided for other purposes'.[200]

5.61 However, the secretary of state must take into account:[201]

- any other income which the applicant, or any dependants, has or might reasonably be expected to have within that period;[202]
- any other support which is available to the applicant or any dependants, or might reasonably be expected to be so available within that period;[203]
- any assets (whether held in the UK or elsewhere) which are available to the applicant or any dependants, or might reasonably be expected to be so available within that period.

5.62 It is important to note that these various forms of income, support and assets can only be taken into account where they are actually available, or where they might 'reasonably be expected' to be available. This requires the secretary of state to have reasonable grounds

198 IAA 1999 s95(1) and Sch 8 paras 1–2; AS Regs 2000 reg 6(3); AS Regs 2000 reg 7(a). For those who are already in receipt of support the period is 56 days: AS Regs 2000 reg 7(a).

199 *Assessing destitution*, v4.0, Home Office, November 2021, p12 example 2 (www.gov.uk/government/publications/assessing-destitution-instruction).

200 *Assessing destitution*, v4.0, p12 example 3. See further *R (K) v SSHD* [2018] EWHC 2951 (Admin), [2019] 4 WLR 92. See paras 11.198–11.212.

201 AS Regs 2000 reg 6(4).

202 This includes income which a dependant might receive by way of mainstream welfare benefits such as income support or jobseeker's allowance. See *R (SSHD (National Asylum Support Service)) v The Asylum Support Adjudicators and (1) Berkadle (2) Perera* [2001] EWHC Admin 881 at para 76(11)–(12) per Gibbs J.

203 This includes support available from social services: *R (Westminster City Council) v National Asylum Support Service* [2002] UKHL 38, [2002] 1 WLR 2956; *R (SG) v Haringey LBC* [2015] EWHC 2579 (Admin), (2015) 18 CCLR 444 at para 12. See paras 5.94–5.102.

to expect the resources to be available.[204] Or, to put it another way, there must be an evidential basis for the expectation. Value judgments or presumptions as to whether or not it would be reasonable for a family member (for example) to assist the applicant, have little if any part to play in this assessment.[205] It is the expectation which must be reasonable under AS Regs 2000 reg 6(4) rather than the conduct of the applicant or third party. Public law requires public bodies to act reasonably. No such legal obligation is placed on the individual.

5.63 The assets which must be taken into account by the secretary of state in this assessment are:[206]

- cash;[207]
- savings;[208]
- investments;[209]
- land;[210]
- cars or other vehicles;[211] and
- goods held for the purpose of a trade or other business.[212]

5.64 This list is exhaustive. The secretary of state must ignore any assets which are not included within the list.[213] On a literal reading of the list, this means that jewellery, for example, may not be taken into account unless it can properly be regarded as having been acquired or kept as form of 'saving' or 'investment'. A previous version of the ASF1 application form for asylum support asked applicants to declare any 'valuable' jewellery, among other items. While the secretary of state might legitimately inquire into the existence of such

204 See, by analogy, *British Home Stores Ltd v Burchell* [1980] ICR 303, EAT in which it was held that one of the core ingredients for a reasonable belief on the part of an employer, that an employee was guilty of misconduct was that there should be a reasonable basis for holding that belief.

205 See, by analogy, *Hotak v Southwark LBC* [2015] UKSC 30, [2016] AC 811 at para 70 per Lord Neuberger, on third-party support in the homelessness context.

206 AS Regs 2000 reg 6(5).

207 AS Regs 2000 reg 6(5)(a). Account should be taken of any commissioning charges incurred in converting the currency into pound sterling. *Assessing destitution*, v4.0, p11.

208 AS Regs 2000 reg 6(5)(b). Bank statements covering the previous six-months will normally be required. *Assessing destitution*, v4.0, p11.

209 AS Regs 2000 reg 6(5)(c).

210 AS Regs 2000 reg 6(5)(d).

211 AS Regs 2000 reg 6(5)(e).

212 AS Regs 2000 reg 6(5)(f).

213 AS Regs 2000 reg 6(6).

jewellery on the footing that the sale of the jewellery is a matter of which he or she would need to be notified,[214] the natural reading of AS Regs 2000 reg 6 is that it should not be factored into the assessment of destitution.

5.65 In the landmark decision, *ZN v SSHD*,[215] Principal Judge Storey held, relying on the definition of 'land' contained in the Law of Property Act 1925 which extends to the buildings thereon,[216] that an applicant's home constituted land for asylum support purposes and might therefore be regarded as an asset which should be taken into account under AS Regs 2000 reg 6(5). Similarly, personal possessions that can 'easily be converted to cash', she held, might reasonably be treated as cash, savings or investments.

5.66 As to the first of these propositions, the judge's reliance on the definition of land contained in the Law of Property Act 1925 is misplaced. The word 'land' is defined differently across a number of different statutes, sometimes so as to encompass the buildings that are upon the land and sometimes not.[217] In addition, the definition within Law of Property Act 1925 s205(1) is expressed, by the opening words of that provision, to apply only for the purposes of that Act, and save where the context dictates otherwise. It does not purport to be a general definition and other statutes have tended to stipulate expressly where the same definition is intended to apply.[218]

5.67 However, the judge's conclusion may be justified by application of the definition of land contained in the Interpretation Act 1978 which 'includes buildings and other structures'.[219] The critical question in cases involving applicants with assets in the form of land abroad is likely to be whether those assets are 'available' or might reasonably be expected to become available within 14 days.[220] The practical problems inherent in selling property within such a short space of time might mean that it does not satisfy these requirements. For example,

214 AS Regs 2000 reg 15(2)(b).

215 AS/17/09/37288, 27 April 2018, FTT (Asylum Support) at para 24.

216 ' "Land" includes land of any tenure, and mines and minerals, whether or not held apart from the surface, buildings or parts of buildings (whether the division is horizontal, vertical or made in any other way) and other corporeal hereditaments . . .': Law of Property Act 1925 s205(1)(ix).

217 See, for example, Legal Aid, Sentencing and Punishment of Offenders Act 2012 Sch 4 Part 2 para 6; Civil Aviation Act 2012 s72; and Finance Act 2013 s174.

218 See, for example, Trusts of Land and Appointment of Trustees Act 1996 s23.

219 Interpretation Act 1978 s5 and Sch 1 para 1.

220 For those who are already in receipt of support the period is 56 days: AS Regs 2000 reg 7(a).

putting a property on the market, finding a buyer, carrying out surveys, allowing the prospective buyer to obtain credit or a mortgage and carry out a survey, conveyancing etc, are the kind of task which may be required (with the necessary allowances made for different processes for buying and selling property in other countries) and which can take some considerable time. Likewise, the fact that family members are living in the property, might mean that selling the property is not an available option. However, where the property is not occupied, the secretary of state might perhaps lawfully impose conditions upon the provision of asylum support to the applicant, requiring the applicant to take reasonable steps to sell the property.[221]

5.68 The second of the Principal Judge's propositions in *ZN v SSHD*, however, is arguably wrong. First, it conflicts with the two-stage approach implicit in AS Regs 2000 reg 6(5) and (6), which invites consideration, of: (i) whether an item is an asset; and, if so, (ii) whether that asset is available or can reasonably be expected to become available within 14 days.[222] The Principal Judge's approach involves a different approach of considering the single composite question of whether an item can easily become an asset within 14 days. That approach does not reflect the statutory rubric. Second, this approach involves interpreting the word 'cash' as meaning 'cash, or items that are not cash but might be converted cash within a reasonable period'. This interpretation requires words to be read into the regulations, a practice that is permissible only in rare circumstances.[223] Third, it conflicts with AS Regs 2000 reg 6(6), which provides that assets not mentioned in the list in reg 6(5) 'must' be ignored.[224] Bearing in mind that a great many personal possessions might potentially be sold, and thereby converted into cash, the judge's approach has the effect of expanding the list of assets in AS Regs 2000 reg 6(5) to one of indefinite length and uncertain scope. That arguably conflicts with the parliamentary intention underpinning a precisely defined list. Had parliament intended such a result, it seems

221 See IAA 1999 s95(9), AS/16/05/35309, 18 May 2016, FTT (Asylum Support) and paras 5.215–5.219. See further *Assessing destitution*, v4.0, p12 example 1.

222 For those who are already in receipt of support the period is 56 days: AS Regs 2000 reg 7(a).

223 See *Jones v Wrotham Park Settled Estates* [1980] AC 74, HL at pp105E–106A per Lord Diplock for the criteria which must be satisfied where for a court to be justified in reading words into legislation which are not expressly included. The criteria would not appear to be satisfied in this instance.

224 See further *Assessing destitution*, v4.0, p11.

more likely that AS Regs 2000 reg 6 would have been drafted so as to leave the question of what constitutes an asset to be taken into account in assessing destitution entirely within the discretion of the secretary of state.

5.69 Giving practical guidance on the assessment of destitution, the Principal Judge in *ZN v SSHD* went on to observe that in cases where the applicant has obtained entry clearance abroad prior to coming to the UK, and the FTT (Asylum Support) is asked to make findings about the applicant's financial situation in their own country, it would be helpful for the tribunal to have access to legible copies of the documents which underpinned the entry clearance application, and details of any checks that were carried out to establish their authenticity.[225] This issue tends to arise where applicants have falsely exaggerated their assets in order to obtain entry clearance so that they are able to come to the UK to lodge their asylum claim. The information in their entry clearance application is frequently relied on by the Home Office as the basis for finding that the applicant is not destitute. The Principal Judge's view was that 'in the absence of robust checks overseas, and given the view taken by the [Home Office] that applicants often exercise deception in order to secure entry, it is unlikely that asylum support judged will feel able to make findings on these matters'. More limited guidance is provided in the Home Office's *Assessing destitution* policy, which states that where the applicant claims that the figures given for income and assets on the visa application were inaccurate or fabricated, the decision-maker 'will need to decide if that claim is credible, taking account of all the available evidence and applying the normal balance of probabilities test'.[226] If the claim is not considered credible, the income and assets declared to the visa officer should be taken into account 'in the normal way'.

5.70 A previous version of the *Assessing destitution* guidance referred to the 'intentional deprivation of capital', in the context of assessing destitution, suggesting that where an applicant has deliberately divested themself of income or assets in order to qualify for asylum support, then they might properly be refused support.[227] Although this guidance was withdrawn in February 2017, the phrase 'intentional deprivation of capital' is still sometimes used in refusal letters.

225 *ZN v SSHD* AS/17/09/37288, 27 April 2018, FTT (Asylum Support) at para 32.

226 *Assessing destitution*, v4.0, Home Office, November 2021, p15.

227 *Assessing destitution*, v2.0, Home Office, July 2014, para 2.4.

It is important to note that this phrase is one borrowed from social security law[228] and does not have any legal foundation in IAA 1999 Part VI. To the extent that Home Office decision-making suggests that whether an applicant has intentionally deprived themself of capital is determinative of the question of whether the applicant is destitute, it is wrong. To the same end, whether the applicant has behaved foolishly or recklessly in spending their income or assets money is not the issue.[229] The question posed by AS Regs 2000 reg 6(4) is whether or not the applicant has income, support or assets which are either available or might reasonably be expected to become available within 14 days.[230] Accordingly, in a case where an applicant has divested themself of income or assets which might have been used to avoid destitution, the question is not whether the 'deprivation of capital' was 'intentional'. Rather, the question is whether the applicant can reasonably be expected to recover the income or assets within 14 days.[231] This is reflected in the latest *Assessing destitution* policy which requires decision-makers to consider first whether the applicant's claim to have depleted their funds is credible and, if so, to refuse support only 'if the assets or income can be recovered'.[232]

Overlap between assessment of destitution and applicant's substantive asylum claim

5.71 Issues may sometimes arise in the course of the determination of an applicant's asylum support appeal which overlap with their substantive asylum claim. In *ZN v SSHD*[233] the Principal Judge expressed the view that 'it is *never* the role of [the FTT (Asylum Support)] to evaluate a first instance asylum claim and thus, nothing that is decided in an asylum support appeal should impact on the appellant's asylum claim/appeal'. However, she went on to observe that judges in asylum support appeals would still need to determine the issues arising in the appeal, irrespective of whether they overlapped

228 See, for example, Housing Benefit Regulations 2006 SI No 213 reg 49.

229 See, for example, *IS v SSHD* AS/17/01/36364, 25 January 2017, FTT (Asylum Support) at para 13: 'whether the appellant has spent his money most unwisely (which I find he has) or prudently and frugally makes little difference to my accepting the respondent's finding that the appellant's family's destitution'.

230 AS Regs 2000 reg 6(3)–(4); AS Regs 2000 reg 7(a). For those who are already in receipt of support the period is 56 days: AS Regs 2000 reg 7(a).

231 For those who are already in receipt of support the period is 56 days: AS Regs 2000 reg 7(a).

232 *Assessing destitution*, v4.0, p15.

233 AS/17/09/37288, 27 April 2018, FTT (Asylum Support) at para 29.

with matters arising in the applicant's asylum claim or appeal. Findings of credibility on those issues, she explained, would not be binding on any immigration or asylum judge or any other judge of the FTT (Asylum Support).[234]

'Does not have adequate accommodation or any means of obtaining it'[235]

5.72 What constitutes 'adequate' accommodation is not defined in IAA 1999 Part VI, but the Court of Appeal has explained that the word 'adequate' takes its meaning from the statutory purpose of asylum support, which is to provide accommodation to asylum-seekers to prevent their destitution.[236] In addition, the Reception Directive refers to the need for accommodation to be adequate to ensure a 'dignified standard of living'.[237] However, this does not mean that there is one single standard of adequacy which must be applied across the board. Whether accommodation is adequate 'must be tested by reference to the needs of persons to whom the duty is owed', which will involve consideration of the applicant's personal circumstances such as the age of any children and whether anyone within the household has a disability.[238] Taking this type of approach, the FTT (Asylum Support) has held that accommodation occupied by an applicant, which consisted of a single-room which he occupied with his disabled wife, and where his presence in the accommodation was merely 'tolerated' by the accommodation provider and could be 'terminated at any time', was not adequate.[239]

5.73 In determining whether a person's accommodation is adequate, IAA 1999 s95 and the AS Regs 2000 prescribe certain matters which the secretary of state must, and must not, take into account. In particular, the secretary of state must have regard to whether:[240]

234 *ZN v SSHD* at paras 30–31. See further paras 5.343–5.344.

235 See paras 5.154–5.168 for a discussion adequacy in the context of the secretary of state's duty to provide adequate accommodation.

236 *R (A) v National Asylum Support Service* [2003] EWCA Civ 1473, [2004] 1 WLR 752 at paras 52–53 per Waller LJ.

237 Reception Directive Articles 13–14 and recital 7. See *R (NB and others) v SSHD* [2021] EWHC 1489 (Admin) at paras [145]–[158] for the continued effect of the Reception Directive as a piece of retained EU law following the departure of the UK from the EU. See paras 2.25–2.29 for retained EU law more generally.

238 *R (A) v National Asylum Support Service* [2003] EWCA Civ 1473, [2004] 1 WLR 752 at para 53 per Waller LJ.

239 *JN v SSHD* AS/08/02/17248, 13 March 2008, FTT (Asylum Support).

240 IAA 1999 s95(5)(a); AS Regs 2000 reg 8(1).

- it would be reasonable for the applicant to continue to occupy the accommodation;[241]
- the accommodation is affordable;[242]
- the accommodation is provided under IAA 1999 s98, or otherwise on an emergency basis, while the claim for asylum support is being determined;[243]
- the applicant can secure entry to the accommodation;[244]
- the accommodation consists of a moveable structure, vehicle or vessel designed or adapted for human habitation, whether there is a place where the applicant is entitled or permitted both to place it and reside in it;[245]
- the accommodation is available for occupation by the applicant together with any dependants;[246]
- it is probable that the applicant's continued occupation of the accommodation will lead to domestic violence against the applicant or their dependants.[247] Domestic violence in this context means 'violence from a person who is or has been a close family member, or threats of violence from such a person which are likely to be carried out'.[248] The courts have generally taken an expansive approach to the meaning of 'violence' and 'domestic violence' holding that the term 'includes physical violence, threatening or intimidating behaviour and any other form of abuse which, directly or indirectly, may give rise to the risk of harm'.[249]

5.74 In determining whether it would be reasonable for the applicant to continue to occupy accommodation, the secretary of state may have

241 AS Regs 2000 reg 8(3)(a). The secretary of state does not have to have regard to this factor where 'the person indicates to the Secretary of State that he wishes to remain in the accommodation'. See AS Regs 2000 reg 8(2).

242 AS Regs 2000 reg 8(3)(b). The secretary of state does not have to have regard to this factor where 'the person indicates to the Secretary of State that he wishes to remain in the accommodation'. See AS Regs 2000 reg 8(2).

243 AS Regs 2000 reg 8(3)(c).

244 AS Regs 2000 reg 8(3)(d).

245 AS Regs 2000 reg 8(3)(e).

246 AS Regs 2000 reg 8(3)(f).

247 AS Regs 2000 reg 8(3)(g). Surprisingly, the secretary of state does not have to have regard to this factor where 'the person indicates to the Secretary of State that he wishes to remain in the accommodation'. See AS Regs 2000 reg 8(2).

248 AS Regs 2000 reg 8(6)(a).

249 *Yemshaw v Hounslow LBC* [2011] UKSC 3, [2011] 1 WLR 433 at para 28 per Baroness Hale; *Hussain v Waltham Forest LBC* [2015] EWCA Civ 14, [2015] HLR 16. See further *Domestic abuse: responding to reports of domestic abuse from asylum seekers*, v2.0, Home Office, July 2019, p8.

regard to the general circumstances prevailing in relation to housing in the district of the local housing authority[250] where the accommodation is. The phrase 'reasonable to continue to occupy' is one that is well known in the context of mainstream homelessness law,[251] having been first used in the Housing (Homeless Persons) Act 1977 and in each subsequence iteration of the homelessness legislation.[252] Having chosen to incorporate a phrase with over 20 years of judicial learning attached to it into the scheme of IAA 1999 Part VI, it might reasonably be assumed that parliament intended a similar interpretation to be adopted and reference to the extensive case-law in the homelessness jurisdiction might usefully be made where necessary.[253] For example, in the landmark decision of *MAS v SSHD*[254] the secretary of state argued that an applicant held in immigration detention should not be regarded as destitute. The Principal Judge disagreed, holding that the applicant could not be regarded as adequately accommodated, in such circumstances, and that it would not be 'reasonable to continue to occupy a prison cell' where there was an alternative available.[255] Accordingly, he was to be regarded as destitute and would be eligible for accommodation if released on bail. In doing she followed the decision in *R (B) v Southwark LBC*[256] where Owen J held, in the context of the homelessness legislation, that a cell in a young offender's institution did not amount to 'accommodation' and, in addition, could not be regarded as 'reasonable to continue to occupy'.

250 This has the meaning given by Housing Act 1996 s217(3). See AS Regs 2000 reg 8(6)(b).

251 The same can be said of much of AS Regs 2000 reg 8, the drafting of which is based heavily on Housing Act 1996 ss175–177.

252 It was originally used in the context of determining whether an applicant had become homeless intentionally. See the Housing (Homeless Persons) Act 1977. However, the use of the term was later extended so as to become an integral part of the definition of homelessness itself. See Housing Act 1985 s58, as amended by Housing and Planning Act 1986 s14 (reversing the effect of the decision of the House of Lords in *R v Hillingdon LBC ex p Puhlhofer* [1986] AC 484, HL), replaced by Housing Act 1996 s175.

253 See, for example, Arden, Vanhegan and Bates *Homelessness and allocations*, Legal Action Group, 11th edn, 2018; and Luba, Davies, Johnston and Buchanan *Housing allocation and homelessness*, Lexis, 5th edn, 2018.

254 AS/05/05/9315, 7 June 2005, FTT (Asylum Support).

255 This approach was followed in AS/18/06/38186, 12 July 2018, FTT (Asylum Support).

256 [2003] EWHC 1678 (Admin), [2004] HLR 3. See further *Stewart v Lambeth LBC* [2002] EWCA Civ 753, [2002] HLR 40 at para 21 per Longmore LJ.

5.75 The central issue in *MAS*, as to whether an applicant in immigration detention should be regarded as destitute, has assumed a greater importance in recent times, even though it is a case dealing with the provision of support for failed asylum-seekers under IAA 1999 s4(1)(c) rather than section 95 with which this chapter is concerned. Prior to 15 January 2018, an applicant in immigration detention would have been able to access support under IAA 1999 s4(1)(c) provided that he or she would be destitute if released on bail, or would become destitute with 14 days.[257] However, on 15 January 2018, IAA 1999 s4(1) was repealed and replaced with a new form of support under IA 2016 Sch 10 para 9(2).[258] Support under Schedule 10, which is discussed in more detail in chapter 6, is intended to operate as a last resort rather than a like for like replacement of IAA 1999 s4(1)(c). Thus detainees requiring accommodation on release are directed by the Home Office policy to seek support under IAA 1999 s95(1) if they are asylum-seekers or under section 4(2) if they are failed asylum-seekers in the first instance.[259]

5.76 Under this approach, the Home Office has, in some (though not all) cases, continued to adopt the position taken in the *MAS* case that detention is adequate accommodation and that support should therefore been refused, and that the applicant can make a further application if and when he or she is released from detention.[260] The approach of the FTT (Asylum Support) in such cases has been to ask whether or not there is any real prospect of the applicant being granted bail within the next 14 days.[261] If there is, then detention cannot be regarded as adequate accommodation because there is an alternative available, meaning the applicant is destitute. Alternatively, if there is no prospect of release within this timescale then the applicant is not destitute. In considering this question, the FTT (Asylum Support)

257 *Asylum support, section 4 policy and process*, para 5.7.3 (archived on 5 January 2018). See paras 6.201–6.203.

258 See paras 6.201–6.273.

259 See paras 6.9–6.200 for a discussion of the eligibility criteria for IAA 1999 s4(2).

260 See, for example, AS/19/01/39139, 11 February 2019, FTT (Asylum Support). It should be noted, however, that Home Office practice has not been consistent and there have been instances where the polar opposite position has been taken. See, for example, AS/19/08/40290, 9 September 2019, FTT (Asylum Support) at para 19: '[the presenting officer] confirms that UKVI accepts that detention does not offer adequate accommodation.'

261 See, for example, *SM v SSHD* AS/18/12/38967, 8 January 2019, FTT (Asylum Support); and AS/19/02/39185, 15 February 2019, FTT (Asylum Support).

has tended to focus on whether or not the FTT (IAC) has made a grant of bail, or bail in principle subject to accommodation being made available.

5.77 On the one hand, this approach provides a practical solution to the problems faced by detainees seeking asylum support. In order to obtain accommodation they should first seek a grant of bail in principle from the FTT (IAC) and then make their application for asylum support. On the other hand, this approach is, arguably, wrong in law for several reasons. First, it is based on a mischaracterisation of the decision of the High Court in *R (B) v Southwark LBC*, which was not simply that it was not reasonable for the applicant to continue to occupy his cell, but that the cell could not properly be described as accommodation at all.[262] The FTT (Asylum Support) in considering the destitution of detainees solely with reference to the question of whether there is a real prospect of release within 14 days seems to have conflated the issue of whether an cell or room in immigration detention is reasonable to continue to occupy (which informs the assessment of whether or not it can be regarded as 'adequate' accommodation), with the prior issue of whether the cell or room can properly be described as 'accommodation' at all. Arguably, following *R (B) v Southwark LBC*, it cannot and a detainee should be regarded as destitute irrespective of their prospects of release. Second, this approach does not factor in the question of whether accommodation can be considered to be adequate where the person's detention (and therefore their requirement to 'reside' in the said cell) is unlawful. Where there no lawful justification for compelling a person to remain in the cell, that should arguably the starting point for considering whether the accommodation is adequate.[263]

5.78 The words 'continue to occupy' refer to occupation over time and will necessitate consideration of how long the applicant is expected to stay in the accommodation.[264] This means that accommodation

262 [2003] EWHC 1678 (Admin), [2004] HLR 3 at para 29 per Owen J.

263 Accommodation which is occupied unlawfully is not normally regarded as being reasonable to continue to occupy. See *Chishimba v Kensington and Chelsea RLBC* [2013] EWCA Civ 786, [2014] PTSR 49; and AS Regs 2000 reg 8(3)(a).

264 *Godson v Enfield LBC* [2019] EWCA Civ 486, [2020] HLR 1 at para 49 per Lewison LJ; *Safi v Sandwell BC* [2018] EWCA Civ 2876, [2019] HLR 16 at para 30 per David Richards LJ.

may not to be reasonable to continue to occupy, even though the occupiers could get by in it for a little while longer.[265]

5.79 In determining whether an applicant's accommodation is affordable, the secretary of state must have regard to:

- any income, or any of the assets referred to in para 5.63 whether held in the UK or elsewhere, available to the applicant or any dependants (aside from asylum support or support under IAA 1999 s98) or which might reasonably be expected to be available;[266]
- the cost of the accommodation;[267]
- the applicant's reasonable living expenses.[268]

5.80 In determining whether an applicant's accommodation is adequate, the secretary of state must not have regard to:[269]

- the fact that the applicant concerned has no enforceable right to occupy the accommodation;[270]
- the fact that the applicant shares the accommodation, or any part of the accommodation, with one or more other persons;
- the fact that the accommodation is temporary;
- the location of the accommodation.

5.81 In determining whether the applicant has the means of obtaining adequate accommodation, as a general rule, the cost of obtaining accommodation should be established by obtaining an average price for bed and breakfast in the local area.[271] However, the secretary of state is not restricted to simply considering whether the applicant has enough money to pay for accommodation. The word 'means' is amply broad enough to encompass practical considerations such as whether the applicant can actually access that money (for example, because their bank accounts are frozen or cannot be accessed from abroad) or whether, if the applicant can access it, he or she is in a position to spend it. For example, in *MYA v SSHD*[272] the FTT

265 *R (Ali and others) v Birmingham City Council; Moran v Manchester City Council* [2009] UKHL 36, [2009] 1 WLR 1506 at paras 36–39 per Baroness Hale.
266 AS Regs 2000 reg 8(5)(a).
267 AS Regs 2000 reg 8(5)(b).
268 AS Regs 2000 reg 8(5)(c).
269 IAA 1999 s95(5)(b) and (6).
270 Such as a tenancy or an occupation order granted under the Family Law Act 1996.
271 *Assessing destitution*, v4.0, p13.
272 AS/19/02/39259, 5 March 2019, FTT (Asylum Support).

(Asylum Support) found an applicant to be destitute, notwithstanding the fact that he had access to funds, on the basis that the restrictions on the right to rent imposed on certain migrants by the Immigration Act 2014[273] would make it 'disproportionately difficult for the appellant to successfully enter into a rental contract'.[274]

5.82 See further AS/17/12/37628,[275] in which the applicant's appeal against a refusal of support was granted in circumstances where he had access to funds and had been granted permission to rent under the right to rent scheme, but his ability to find a landlord who would rent to him was stymied by the failure of the Home Office to provide him with an asylum registration card to prove his identification and status. Home Office policy provides that permission to rent should normally be granted to asylum-seekers,[276] that the applicant's records should be updated swiftly to reflect this and that landlord's may contact the Home Office landlord's checking service to establish that they can rent to the applicant.[277] However, as the decisions of the FTT (Asylum Support) demonstrate, these aspirations do not necessarily reflect reality and an applicant who might notionally be eligible for permission to rent is entitled to adduce evidence to establish either that permission has not in fact been granted or that permission has been granted but finding a landlord willing to provide accommodation has nevertheless provided impracticable.

'Cannot meet his other essential living needs'

5.83 IAA 1999 s95 and AS Regs 2000 reg 9 provide a list of factors and items that may not be taken into account in the assessment of the essential living needs of an applicant taken together with any dependants. In determining whether an applicant's essential living needs are met the secretary of state must not have regard to any 'personal preferences' which the applicant might express as to clothing, albeit 'individual circumstances' as regards clothing should be considered.[278]

273 See paras 7.389–7.438.

274 *MYA v SSHD* AS/19/02/39259, 5 March 2019, FTT (Asylum Support) at paras 38–44. Note, however, that, since the decision in *MYA*, the Court of Appeal has upheld the legality of the right to rent scheme. See *R (Joint Council for the Welfare of Immigrants) v SSHD* [2020] EWCA Civ 542.

275 AS/17/12/37628, 4 January 2018, FTT (Asylum Support).

276 And to failed-asylum-seekers who are eligible for support under IAA 1999 s4(2). See paras 6.9–6.200.

277 *Assessing destitution*, v4.0, p14.

278 IAA 1999 s95(7)(b); AS Regs 2000 reg 9(1)–(2).

In addition, none of the following items may be regarded as essential living needs:[279]

- the cost of faxes;[280]
- computers and the cost of computer facilities;[281]
- the cost of photocopying;[282]
- travel expenses, save for the expense of the initial journey to the place where the applicant is to reside;[283]
- toys and other recreational items;[284]
- entertainment expenses.[285]

5.84 Any items not included in this list may or may not be regarded as essential living needs.[286] This means that the question of whether an item not on this list is regarded as an essential living need will, in the first instance, require a value judgment on the part of the secretary of state, but one that should be made objectively with reference to the minimum standards set out in the Reception Directive[287] which requires 'full respect for human dignity, so as to ensure a dignified standard of living' and for the special needs of vulnerable people to be met, among other things.[288] Adopting this approach in *R (Refugee Action) v SSHD*[289] Popplewell J held that the following are be regarded as essential living needs:

279 IAA 1999 s95(8); AS Regs 2000 reg 9(3).

280 AS Regs 2000 reg 9(4)(a).

281 AS Regs 2000 reg 9(4)(b).

282 AS Regs 2000 reg 9(4)(c).

283 AS Regs 2000 reg 9(4)(d) and (5). See *IAO v SSHD* AS/19/05/39577, 21 May 2019, FTT (Asylum Support). Note, however, that those being released from immigration detention or prison should generally be provided with travel warrants. See *Detention services order 01/2018: release of detainees from immigration detention*, Home Office, February 2018, para 21; PSI 72/2011 para 2.29.

284 AS Regs 2000 reg 9(4)(e).

285 AS Regs 2000 reg 9(4)(f).

286 AS Regs 2000 reg 9(6).

287 See *R (NB and others) v SSHD* [2021] EWHC 1489 (Admin) at paras 145–158 for the continued effect of the Reception Directive following the departure of the UK from the EU.

288 *R (Refugee Action) v SSHD* [2014] EWHC 1033 (Admin), [2014] 4 WLUK 360 paras 83–91 per Popplewell J. See further *R (SG and others) v SSHD* [2016] EWHC 2639 (Admin), [2016] 10 WLUK 497 at paras 35–36 and 138–139 per Flaux J. The Court of Appeal refused permission to appeal against this decision in *R (JK (Burundi)) v SSHD* [2017] EWCA Civ 433, [2017] 1 WLR 4567.

289 [2014] EWHC 1033 (Admin), [2014] 4 WLUK 360. See paras 92–119.

- essential household goods such as washing powder, cleaning materials and disinfectant;
- nappies, formula milk and other special requirements of new mothers, babies and very young children;
- non-prescription medication;[290]
- the opportunity to maintain interpersonal relationships and a minimum level of participation in social, cultural and religious life.

5.85 Previous Home Office guidance on assessing destitution[291] provided a set of benchmark figures which (used in conjunction with average bed and breakfast rates for the local area) were intended to provide a 'guide to the level of funds which the Home Office expect would meet a person's accommodation costs and essential living needs'. The rationale behind these benchmark figures was to indicate that an applicant 'with funds available to him in excess of the relevant threshold in the tables is unlikely to be destitute'. The guidance stressed that the benchmark figures should be used as 'a guideline only' and 'that each case should be examined on its own merits'. One example given in the guidance was of an applicant who was without any winter clothes and who might therefore need to deplete his funds faster than would otherwise be the case. To enable such factors to be taken into account in the assessment of essential living needs, the benchmark figures were to be used 'a starting point only'.[292]

5.86 However, the benchmark figures are no longer included in the current November 2021 version of the *Assessing destitution* policy, which is much more limited, and simply states that 'as a general rule, the cost to a person of meeting essential their essential living needs should be assessed' with the current asylum support rates[293] which reflect 'the amount of weekly cash that the average asylum-seeker needs to cover most of their essential living needs'.[294]

5.87 The approach described in the current *Assessing destitution* policy – which refers to the comparison with asylum-support rates as being the 'general rule' appropriate for the 'average' asylum-seeker –

290 See further AS/18/09/38647, 4 October 2018, FTT (Asylum Support), December 2018 *Legal Action* 27.

291 *Assessing destitution*, v2.0, Home Office, July 2014, withdrawn in February 2017.

292 *Assessing destitution*, v2.0, Home Office; July 2014, withdrawn in February 2017.

293 See paras 5.185–5.200.

294 *Assessing destitution*, v4.0, p13.

necessarily implies that the assessment of essential living needs should be carried out on a case-by-case basis with regard to the personal circumstances of the applicant taken together with any dependants, in order to establish whether the general rule should be disapplied. This reflects the approach endorsed by the courts.[295] For example, in *R (A) v National Asylum Support Service*[296] Waller LJ disapproved an earlier decision of Collins J[297] in which he had taken the view that the assessment had to be based upon the needs of an able bodied adult or child, without regard to any special peculiarities or disabilities which the applicant or their dependants might have. Similarly, in *R (SSHD (National Asylum Support Service)) v Asylum Support Adjudicators and (1) Berkadle (2) Perera*,[298] it was held that while benchmark figures may assist in the assessment of whether or not an applicant is in a position to meet their essential living needs, the assessment is not a purely mathematical one.[299]

5.88 That case concerned two 'mixed households', ie households where the applicants were asylum-seekers but their dependants were not. In both cases the applicants had joined their wives who were already in the UK. The applicants' wives, who lived with their dependant children, were already in receipt of mainstream welfare benefits: income support and jobseeker's allowance respectively. In both cases, the applicants were refused asylum support as the levels of income support and jobseeker's allowance which the wives were receiving were in excess of the benchmark figures for weekly expenditure used by NASS meaning, NASS concluded, that the applicants, taken together with their dependants, could not be regarded as destitute. These refusals were overturned by Asylum Support Adjudicators in both cases, who held that:

> Parliament would [not] have intended an asylum seeker to be ineligible for support . . . simply because his partner has, under benefits legislation, been provided with a minimum amount necessary to provide for

295 See further Reception Directive Article 17; and Asylum Seekers (Reception Conditions) Regulations 2005 reg 4, for further statutory authority on the requirement to consider needs on a case-by-case basis.

296 [2003] EWCA Civ 1473, [2004] 1 WLR 752 at paras 2–5 and 21 per Waller LJ. See further *R (Refugee Action) v SSHD* [2014] EWHC 1033 (Admin), [2014] 4 WLUK 360 at paras 67–76 per Popplewell J.

297 *R (Ouji) v SSHD* [2002] EWHC 1839 (Admin), (2002) 5 CCLR 533.

298 [2001] EWHC Admin 881.

299 [2001] EWHC Admin 881 at para 76 per Gibbs J.

the essential living needs of herself and their children, but which takes no account of the needs of the subsequently arriving spouse.[300]

And that:

> Parliament cannot have intended that the standard of living enjoyed by a woman and her children should be reduced below the very basic level permitted by her applicable amount simply because she has permitted her asylum seeker husband to live with her.[301]

5.89 The secretary of state sought judicial review of these decisions. Allowing the application, Gibbs J held that any mainstream welfare benefits which were paid to the dependant of the applicant could properly be taken into account in the assessment of whether the applicant was in a position to meet their essential living needs. However, the fact that a dependant was in receipt of welfare benefits and that such benefits would generally be higher than the NASS benchmark figures did not automatically mean that the applicant should not be regarded as destitute. An individualised assessment of the applicant's essential needs was still required. If the income received by the dependant by way of welfare benefits was not available to the applicant, perhaps because of relationship breakdown, then that would be an in instance where the welfare benefits award could not be regarded as sufficient to meet the applicant's essential living needs. Alternatively, 'on the particular facts of a case there might simply not be enough left to contribute to the applicant's own essential needs from the family's Social Security budget, once their own more extensive and permanent needs have been met from it'. As such, in cases where a dependant was in receipt of welfare benefits, it would always be necessary 'to consider how far, in reality, in each particular case, those benefits were or might reasonably be expected to be actually available, if at all, to meet the applicant's own essential needs'. Cases where the welfare benefits award would be sufficient to meet the essential living needs of the applicant, taken together with his dependants, were likely to be 'rare'.[302]

5.90 In cases, such as those involving mixed households, where the applicant, taken together with any dependants have some form of income, support or assets available to them, but not sufficient to meet their essential living needs, then asylum support should still be provided. However, the secretary of state will take the income,

300 [2001] EWHC Admin 881 at para 7.
301 [2001] EWHC Admin 881 at para 13.
302 See [2001] EWHC Admin 881 at paras 75–83.

support or assets into account in determining what level or kind of support to provide[303] and may require the applicant pay contributions toward the cost of their support.[304] The level or kind of support provided will vary from case to case according to the composition and circumstances of the household. Some guidance may be found in the *Asylum support: policy bulletins instruction*[305] which provides that households in which the spouse or partner of the asylum-seeker is in receipt of jobseeker's allowance (JSA) or income support (IS) and is liable for rental and utility costs, will generally be provided with asylum support sufficient to 'top-up' their joint income to 95 per cent of the income-based JSA or IS couple rate.[306] If the spouse or partner has only utility costs to meet, then asylum support will be provided at a level which will top-up their joint income to 85 per cent of the income-based JSA or IS couple rate.

Change of circumstances

5.91 Under AS Regs 2000 reg 15(1), applicants must notify the secretary of state of any 'relevant' change of circumstances. A relevant change of circumstances occurs where an applicant or their dependant:[307]

- is joined in the UK by a dependant (or a further dependant);
- receives or gains access to any money, or other asset mentioned in AS Regs 2000 reg 6(5),[308] that has not previously been declared to the secretary of state;
- becomes employed;
- becomes unemployed;
- changes their name;
- gets married or forms a civil partnership;
- starts living with a person as if married to, or in a civil partnership with, that person;
- gets divorced or obtains a dissolution order in respect of the civil partnership;
- separates from a spouse or civil partner, or from a person with whom they have been living as if married to, or in a civil partnership with;

303 AS Regs 2000 reg 12. See paras 5.185–5.195. *Assessing destitution*, v4.0, p13.

304 AS Regs 2000 reg 16. See para 5.201.

305 V9.0, para 7.2.

306 See AS/20/01/41413, 3 February 2020, FTT (Asylum Support).

307 AS Regs 2000 reg 15(2).

308 See para 5.63.

- becomes pregnant;
- has a child;
- leaves school;
- starts to share their accommodation with another person;
- moves to a different address, or otherwise leaves their accommodation;
- goes into hospital;
- goes to prison or is otherwise held in custody;
- leaves the UK; or
- dies.

5.92 In broad terms, the list covers the various changes in circumstances which might potentially impact on the applicant's ongoing eligibility for support, or on the level or nature of support which they require.[309] A failure to report a change of circumstances may constitute a criminal offence[310] and result in the discontinuation of the applicant's support.[311]

Relationship with community care services

Overview

5.93 There are a number of situations in which an applicant (or their dependant) who appears to be eligible for asylum support may also appear to be in need of, or eligible for, community care services from their local authority under the ChA 1989[312] or Care Act 2014.[313] In such cases, the question will arise as to who should be responsible for meeting their needs. Should it be the Home Office, the local authority, or some combination of the two? The answer to this question will vary according to the applicant's personal circumstances. In some circumstances the answer is provided expressly within IAA 1999 Part VI. In other circumstances, it has been left to the courts to determine the answer to the question. Below we consider the common scenarios in which the question is likely to arise and the answers that have, thus far, been provided by the legislation and the courts.

309 See paras 5.92–5.90 and 5.141–5.219.
310 IAA 1999 s105(1)(c)–(d). See paras 5.230–5.231.
311 See paras 5.257–5.266.
312 See paras 9.12–9.194 for support under the ChA 1989.
313 See paras 8.7–8.178 for support under the Care Act 2014.

The infirm destitute[314]

5.94 Until the Care Act 2014[315] came into force, residential accommodation for adults who, by reason of age infirmity or other circumstances, were in need of care and attention which was not otherwise available, was provided by social services under NAA 1948 s21. In *R v Hammersmith and Fulham LBC ex p M*[316] the Court of Appeal held that the destitute asylum-seekers who were in need of care and attention by reason of 'the problems under which they are labouring' such as 'the lack of food and accommodation . . . their inability to speak the language, their ignorance of this country and the fact they have been subject to the stress of coming to this country in circumstances which at least involve their contending to be refugees' should be supported under this provision.[317]

5.95 One of the key objectives of IAA 1999 Part VI was to deal with the consequences of this decision by transferring the responsibility of supporting destitute asylum-seekers from local authorities to the Home Office.[318] One of the ways in which this objective was to be achieved was by IAA 1999 s116, which amended NAA 1948 s21 by inserting a new subsection (1A) prohibiting social services from providing accommodation to any person falling within the ambit of IAA 1999 s115 whose need for care and attention arose 'solely' from the fact they were destitute. This was sometimes referred to as the 'destitution plus' test. In *R v Wandsworth LBC ex p O*,[319] the Court of Appeal interpreted this provision to mean that a person subject to immigration control, within the meaning of IAA 1999 s115, would be eligible for accommodation under this provision provided that their need for care and attention was to any material extent made more acute by some circumstance other than the mere lack of

314 The phrase 'infirm destitute' was used by Lord Hoffmann in *R (Westminster City Council) v National Asylum Support Service* [2002] UKHL 38, [2002] 1 WLR 2956 and is adopted here as it is still used in the courts. However, a more accurate description under the current statutory regime contained in the Care Act 2014 would be 'destitute adults with care and support needs'. See further paras 8.7–8.178 for a detailed discussion of the care and support available to adults under the Care Act 2014.

315 See paras 8.7–8.178 for support under the Care Act 2014.

316 (1998) 30 HLR 10, CA.

317 *R v Hammersmith and Fulham LBC ex p M* (1998) 30 HLR 10, CA at p20 per Lord Woolf MR. See the Introduction.

318 See the Introduction for a fuller discussion of the background to IAA 1999 Part VI.

319 [2000] 1 WLR 2539, CA at 2553G–2558A per Hale LJ.

accommodation and money. This meant that the infirm and destitute claimant in that case, who was an overstayer with chronic and relapsing psychiatric problems, fell to be accommodated by social services.

5.96 This did not, however, resolve the issue of where responsibility lay for the accommodation of infirm destitute asylum-seekers. That issue was decided by the House of Lords in *R (Westminster City Council) v National Asylum Support Service.*[320] The court held that the new regime for supporting asylum-seekers under IAA 1999 Part VI endowed the secretary of state with residual powers to accommodate asylum-seekers, available only where no other support was available. The effect of NAA1948 s21(1A) had only been to exclude the 'able-bodied destitute' from local authority support. The 'infirm destitute' remained the responsibility of social services.[321]

5.97 A variation on the scenario in *R (Westminster City Council) v National Asylum Support Service*[322] was considered by the Court of Appeal in *R (O) v Haringey LBC.*[323] That case concerned an infirm destitute asylum-seeker together with her two young children, aged three and five. The court decided, although the provision of accommodation for the mother remained the responsibility of social services under NAA 1948 s21, the family as a whole were to be regarded as destitute and thereby fell within the scheme of IAA 1999 Part VI as that accommodation was not available for the whole household. The consequence of this was that the secretary of state was under a duty to 'arrang[e] for the provision of, adequate accommodation for the child as part of the eligible person's household'.[324] However, the secretary of state was still entitled to have regard to the availability of the accommodation under NAA 1948 s21 in deciding how to accommodate the household.[325] In practice this meant that the whole family were to be accommodated by social services, but with the secretary of state making a financial contribution to social services 'to represent the children's share'.[326]

320 [2002] UKHL 38, [2002] 1 WLR 2956.

321 See further *Asylum seekers with care needs*, v2, Home Office, August 2018.

322 [2002] UKHL 38, [2002] 1 WLR 2956.

323 [2004] EWCA Civ 535, [2004] 2 FLR 476.

324 IAA 1999 s122(3). See paras 5.103–5.106.

325 See AS Regs 2000 reg 12.

326 *R (O) v Haringey LBC* [2004] EWCA Civ 535, [2004] 2 FLR 476 at para 61 per Carnwath LJ.

5.98 In *R (Refugee Action) v SSHD*,[327] Popplewell J described the effect of this decision in the following terms:

> The upshot is that the Secretary of State has the residual responsibility for the essential living needs of the disabled and destitute plus, for whom the accommodation responsibility falls on local authorities under s. 21(1), if and insofar as such needs fall outside the scope of the accommodation related services . . ..

5.99 The final case of significance in this context is *R (SL) v Westminster City Council*.[328] In that case, the Supreme Court had to decide whether a failed asylum-seeker with depression and post-traumatic stress disorder (PTSD) who required support comprising of weekly meetings with his social worker at which he was offered advice and encouragement, and general monitoring of his mental condition and progress (among other things) was entitled to support under NAA 1948 s21(1). The Supreme Court held that he was not. The court did not question the dividing line established in the *R (Westminster City Council) v National Asylum Support Service* case, between local authority and Home Office support. It was accepted by the parties that if SL was not entitled to the former then he was entitled to the latter.[329] However, the court took the view that the Court of Appeal in *R v Wandsworth LBC ex p O* had gone wrong, in so far as it 'endorsed the proposition that if an applicant's need for care and attention is to any extent made more acute by circumstances other than the lack of accommodation and funds, he "qualifies for assistance [under section 21(1)(a)]" '.[330] An applicant who met this threshold would satisfy the destitution plus test, and would not be excluded from support by NAA 1948 s21(1A). However, that did not automatically mean that they qualified for support under NAA 1948 s21(1). To qualify for support, the applicant would need to go further and establish a need for care and attention which was 'accommodation related'. This means that it has to be care and attention of a sort which is normally provided in the home or will be effectively useless if the claimant has no home.[331] The result of this decision was to create an 'undistributed middle' consisting of 'people who do have a need for care and attention which is made more acute by circumstances other than the

327 [2014] EWHC 1033 (Admin), [2014] 4 WLUK 360 at para 54.
328 [2013] UKSC 27, [2013] 1 WLR 1445.
329 *R (SL) v Westminster City Council* [2013] UKSC 27, [2013] 1 WLR 1445 at para 4 per Lord Carnwath.
330 *R (SL) v Westminster City Council* at para 47 per Lord Carnwath.
331 *R (SL) v Westminster City Council* at para 48 per Lord Carnwath.

lack of accommodation and funds but who nevertheless do not qualify for accommodation under section 21'.[332]

5.100 Following the decision in *SL* the position, in summary, was as follows. Infirm destitute asylum-seekers (ie asylum-seekers in need of care and support) were generally the responsibility of social services. However, if they did not meet the destitution plus threshold (as explained in *R v Wandsworth LBC ex p O*) or they do not meet the eligibility criteria for accommodation under NAA 1948 s21, then they would be the responsibility of the Home Office.

5.101 The relevant provisions of the NAA 1948 have since been superseded by the Care Act 2014 which contains an analogous exclusion to that found in NAA 1948 s21(1A).[333] However, the nature of the duty to provide care and support under the Care Act 2014 is not identical to the duty to provide accommodation under NAA 1948 s21. In particular, under the Care Act 2014, there is no longer a duty to provide residential care where a person is in need of care and attention. Rather, there is a duty to 'meet the adult's needs for care and support which meet the eligibility criteria'.[334] How that duty is fulfilled is a matter of judgment for the local authority. For example, the duty may be fulfilled by the provision of accommodation among other things.[335] Alternatively it may be fulfilled by the local authority 'arranging for a person other than it to provide a service'.[336] As a consequence the question of whether an infirm destitute applicant asylum-seeker should be accommodated by the local authority under the Care Act 2014 instead of the secretary of state under IAA 1999 s95(1) is less clear-cut than it was previously when the NAA 1948 was in force. On the one hand, the discretion under Care Act 2014 s8 is broad enough such that it may conceivably leave open the possibility that the local authority might arrange for the Home Office to provide accommodation under IAA 1999 s95(1) as part of a package of support to meet identified care and support needs. On the other hand, a series of cases dealing with a variety of statutory provisions across the community care context have consistently stressed that support under the IAA 1999 is 'residual' in nature, meaning that is available

332 *R (SL) v Westminster City Council* at para 47 per Lord Carnwath.
333 Care Act 2014 s21(1).
334 Care Act 2014 s18(1).
335 Care Act 2014 s8(1)(a).
336 Care Act 2014 s8(2)(a).

only where other forms of local authority support are not available,[337] and which raises the question of whether the amendments to the Care Act 2014 were intended to (or were capable of) changing this fundamental characteristic of the IAA 1999 support regime. It may be that the High Court will need to grapple with these competing arguments at some point.[338]

5.102 Home Office policy in relation to this cohort is that any asylum-seeker who presents with urgent needs that may require either residential care, specific accommodation or day-to-day assistance with personal care, should be referred to the local authority in which they are physically present for a needs assessment.[339] Those with urgent care needs will not generally be admitted to initial accommodation as the expectation is that the local authority has the primary power under Care Act 2014 s19(3) to accommodate them while the needs assessment takes place.[340] Clearly, however, if the local authority does not agree to accommodate, then the secretary of state will need to act compatibly with its obligations to provide accommodation to avoid a breach of the applicant's rights under the ECHR.[341]

Households with dependant children

5.103 Households containing dependant children are subject to two special rules in relation to the provision of asylum support. These rules are contained in IAA 1999 s122.

5.104 The first of the two rules is designed – in broad terms – to ensure that households containing children are provided with support, as a household, under IAA 1999 s95(1). Specifically, the rule applies to:[342]

337 *R (Westminster City Council) v National Asylum Support Service* [2002] UKHL 38, [2002] 1 WLR 2956 at paras 38 and 41; *R (SO) v Barking and Dagenham LBC* [2010] EWCA Civ 1101, [2011] 1 WLR 1283 at para 40; *R (VC) v Newcastle City Council* [2011] EWHC 2673 (Admin), [2012] PTSR 546 at para 86.

338 The issue arose in the case of *R (SG) v Haringey LBC* [2015] EWHC 2579 (Admin), (2015) 18 CCLR 444 in relation to asylum support under IAA 1999 s95(1) but was resolved following a concession by the local authority that the availability of support under the IAA 1999 should be ignored in deciding whether or not to provide accommodation under the Care Act 2014 and so the court was not required to adjudicate on the matter. See para 12.

339 *Asylum seekers with care needs*, v2, pp6–7.

340 See chapter 8 on the Care Act 2014.

341 See paras 6.90–6.135 and 9.203–9.217.

342 IAA 1999 s122(1)–(2).

- an applicant for asylum support;
- who appears to the secretary of state to be a person for whom support may be provided; and
- whose household includes a dependant child under the age of 18.

5.105 If it appears to the secretary of state that adequate accommodation is not being provided for the child, then they must offer and, if the offer is accepted, provide or arrange the provision of adequate accommodation for the child as part of the applicant's household.[343] Similarly, if it appears to the secretary of state that any of the child's essential living needs are not being met, they must offer and, if the offer is accepted, provide or arrange the provision of essential living needs for the child as part of the applicant's household.[344]

5.106 This rule was of particular significance when IAA 1999 Part VI came into force as it converts the powers to provide asylum support under IAA 1999 s95(1) and temporary support under IAA 1999 s98(1) into duties, in relation to households with children.[345] The importance of this has diminished somewhat following the coming into force of the Asylum Seekers (Reception Conditions) Regulations 2005 reg 5(1) which requires the secretary of state to provide support in all cases where he or she 'thinks that the asylum seeker or his family member is eligible for support'.[346] The significance of this rule now lies primarily in the fact that, where this rule is engaged, NIAA 2002 s55(1) – which prohibits the secretary of state from providing asylum support to applicants who do not claim asylum as soon as reasonably practicable following entry[347] – does not apply.[348]

5.107 The second of the two rules provides a counterpoint to the first and is designed to ensure that these same households are excluded from accessing certain types of support from social services. This has been described as 'part of a legislative structure to place responsibility for children, with their household, on [the Home Office]'.[349] The rule has the effect that no local authority may provide 'assistance'

343 IAA 1999 s122(3).

344 IAA 1999 s122(4).

345 See *R (A) v National Asylum Support Service* [2003] EWCA Civ 1473, [2004] 1 WLR 752 at paras 85–87 per Brooke LJ.

346 See paras 5.15–5.16.

347 See paras 5.132–5.136.

348 NIAA 2002 s55(5)(b).

349 See *R (O) v Haringey LBC* [2004] EWCA Civ 535, [2004] 2 FLR 476 at paras 26 and 58 per Carnwath LJ.

under ChA 1989 s17[350] in respect of a dependant under the age of 18 or any member of their family at any time when:[351]

- the secretary of state is accommodating the household pursuant to IAA 1999 s122(3) or meeting the child's essential living needs pursuant to IAA 1999 s122(4); or
- there are reasonable grounds for believing that the person is eligible for asylum support and that the secretary of state would be required to provide such support, pursuant to IAA 1999 s122(3) or (4), if the person had applied for it.

5.108 Where a person meets these criteria, then they may not be provided with 'assistance' under ChA 1989 s17, even if there are disabled children in the household,[352] but only to the extent that the 'assistance' concerns the 'provision of accommodation or of any essential living needs'.[353] IAA 1999 s122 does not operate as a complete bar to the provision of support under ChA 1989 s17. It only operates as a bar to the provision of accommodation or essential living needs, that is the support provided under IAA 1999 s95. Where a child has needs over and above the provision of accommodation or essential living needs, it is open to social services to meet those additional needs under ChA 1989 s17 notwithstanding the fact that the household may be eligible or in receipt of asylum support. Whether a local authority does so must be based on an assessment of the child's needs pursuant to the assessment framework under the ChA 1989, discussed at paras 9.30–9.48.

5.109 Although the two rules set out above might appear straightforward at first glance, their application can sometimes prove difficult in practice, particularly in instances where there is some ambiguity as to whether or not the household is eligible for asylum support. The case of *R (FA) v Redbridge LBC*[354] provides an illustration of the complexities that may arise. FA was a failed asylum-seeker with a seven-year-old daughter. She had had asylum claims rejected on two occasions. The second had been rejected after the birth of her daughter. The pair became homeless and presented to Redbridge LBC seeking support under ChA 1989 s17. This was refused in the first instance. Redbridge took the view that FA fell within the extended

350 See paras 9.12–9.169 for support under ChA 1989 s17.

351 IAA 1999 s122(5)–(7).

352 See *R (A) v National Asylum Support Service* [2003] EWCA Civ 1473, (2003) 6 CCLR 538 at paras 65–68 per Waller LJ.

353 IAA 1999 s122(6).

354 [2018] EWHC 2189 (Admin), [2018] 4 WLUK 538.

definition of asylum-seeker contained in IAA s94(5)[355] and was therefore eligible for IAA 1999 s95(1) support, meaning she was excluded from accessing support under the ChA 1989 by IAA 1999 s122(5). FA duly applied to the secretary of state for support under both IAA 1999 s95(1) and, for good measure, support under IAA 1999 s4(2)[356] in the alternative. The secretary of state refused the application for support under IAA 1999 s4(2) and (at first) failed to reach a decision on FA's eligibility for support under IA 1999 s95(1). FA then appealed to the FTT (Asylum Support) against the refusal of IAA 1999 s4(2) support. Her appeal was dismissed, with the judge refusing to accept that she was destitute. In the course of the appeal the judge was invited to consider whether FA might be eligible for IAA 1999 s95(1) support in the alternative. He did not decide the issue but gave an indication that she was probably not eligible. A person whose asylum claim had been refused, he suggested, and who had never previously been in receipt of asylum support, could not avail herself of the extended definition of asylum-seeker contained in IAA 1999 s94(5). In light of this refusal, FA sought judicial review of Redbridge's refusal to provide accommodation under ChA 1989 s17. Warby J granted an interim injunction requiring Redbridge to accommodate FA and her daughter under ChA1989 s17 pending the determination of permission, on the basis that, relying on the FTT (Asylum Support) judge's indication that FA was ineligible for IAA 1999 s95(1) support, it was *arguable* that FA was not subject to the IAA 1999 s122(5) exclusion.[357] The Home Office later accepted that FA was eligible for support under IAA 1999 s95(1) putting it beyond doubt that the IAA 1999 s122(5) exclusion did, in fact, apply. As a result, permission to proceed with the judicial review was refused.[358]

5.110 It is the authors' view that the indication given by the judge of the FTT (Asylum Support) in FA's case was wrong, and that an asylum-seeker with a dependant child under the age of 18 in their household at the time their asylum claim is rejected, should continue to be treated as an asylum-seeker for support purposes – and therefore eligible for support under IAA 1999 s95(1) – until the child reaches

355 See paras 5.45–5.49.

356 Support for failed asylum-seekers. See paras 6.9–6.200.

357 See further *R (Ezeh) v Barking and Dagenham LBC* [2013] EWHC 4486 (Admin) where it was acknowledged that: 'It is at the very least arguable that s122(5) cannot operate so as to relieve a Local Authority of its duties under s17 if in fact an application has been made to the Secretary of State under s95 and has been refused.'

358 *R (FA) v Redbridge LBC* February 2018 *Legal Action* 24, FTT (Asylum Support).

the age of 18.[359] However, the important point for present purposes is that if there is any ambiguity over an applicant's eligibility for IAA 1999 s95 support, then deciding whether or not the IAA 1999 s122(5) exclusion applies, and deciding whether or not support should be sought from social services or the Home Office, can be very difficult. In cases like that of FA, the important practical point for advisers will be to obtain a clear chronology from the applicant to ascertain when their children were born in relation to any decisions made on their asylum claim. This will assist in establishing whether the applicant falls within the extended definition of asylum-seeker. However, where there remains ambiguity over the applicant's status it may be prudent to request support from both social services and the Home Office, while encouraging the two bodies to co-operate with each other to resolve the ambiguity.

5.111 Whether or not the IAA 1999 s122(5) exclusion applies is to be judged objectively. The subjectively held opinion of the local authority in question is not determinative of this issue. In *R (EAT) v Newham LBC*[360] the claimant's mother had applied to the secretary of state for indefinite leave to remain pursuant to ECHR Article 8, but not Article 3, and had sought accommodation for the claimant and herself from Newham LBC under ChA 1989 s17 in the meantime. Her application for leave to remain was refused by the secretary of state in a decision which recorded, among other things, that her application had been 'considered under the provisions of Article 3 Medical of the ECHR' and that reached the conclusion that removal from the UK would not result in a breach of Article 3.[361] The claim that she had advanced under Article 8 was also rejected. An appeal was lodged against this decision asserting that the household's removal from the UK would result in a breach of Article 8. However, as per the original application, no suggestion was made that removal would result in a breach of Article 3. Throughout this decision-making process, for reasons that evolved as the process went on, Newham had maintained a refusal to support the household. On the claimant's application for judicial review of Newham's refusal to provide support, the issue arose as to whether or not the IAA 1999 s122(5) exclusion applied. Newham contended that it did, taking the position that the claimant's mother had made a claim which had been recorded and considered by the Home Office as encompassing

359 See paras 5.46–5.49 for a detailed discussion of this issue.
360 [2013] EWHC 344 (Admin).
361 [2013] EWHC 344 (Admin) at para 20.

a claim under Article 3 and which was still pending. As such she was to be regarded as an asylum-seeker and was eligible for asylum support under IAA 1999 s95(1) and ineligible for support under ChA 1989 s17. John Powell QC sitting as a deputy High Court judge allowed the claimant's application. The second limb of the IAA 1999 s122(5) exclusion applies where there are 'reasonable grounds' for believing that the applicant is eligible for asylum-support and that the secretary of state would be required to provide it if the applicant had applied for it. The relevant belief is that of the local authority. However, it must be a belief based on 'reasonable grounds', which is an objective criterion, albeit one that 'admits of a margin of error'.[362] On the facts of this case, no claim for asylum had ever been made and there were no reasonable grounds for believing that there had been such a claim. The word 'claim', in this context, connoted the assertion of a right. The claimant's mother had never asserted any right under Article 3, impliedly or expressly, and the fact that the Home Office had proceeded on the basis that she had did not change that. Accordingly, the IAA 1999 s122(5) exclusion did not apply.

Unaccompanied asylum-seeking children

5.112 To be regarded as an asylum-seeker for asylum support purposes it is necessary for the applicant to be over the age of 18.[363] This means that an unaccompanied asylum-seeking child (UASC) is not, in the asylum support context, regarded as an asylum-seeker and is ineligible for asylum support. Such applicants are the responsibility of their local authority under ChA 1989 Part III.[364]

Care leavers

5.113 Certain young people who are over the age of 18, and who were looked after, accommodated or fostered by their local authority for a period in excess of 13 weeks while they were children, acquire 'leaving care rights': a package of rights and entitlements under ChA 1989 Part III, for which their local authority is responsible, which can continue until they are 25 years old and which may include the provision of accommodation.[365] The case of *R (SO) v Barking and*

362 [2013] EWHC 344 (Admin) at para 75 per John Powell QC sitting as a deputy High Court judge.

363 IAA 1999 s94(1). See paras 5.17–5.18.

364 See paras 9.70–9.117 and 11.4–11.126.

365 See paras 9.118–9.194.

Dagenham LBC[366] is the leading authority on the relationship between leaving care rights and support under the IAA 1999.

5.114 The claimant, SO, was an Eritrean national. He arrived in the UK as a child and claimed asylum. From his arrival in the UK until he reached the age of 18 he was accommodated by Barking and Dagenham LBC under ChA 1989 s20[367] with the consequence that he became entitled to leaving care rights. This meant that SO was entitled, among other things, to 'assistance to the extent his welfare requires it' under ChA 1989 s23C(4)(c).

5.115 Following his 18th birthday, the secretary of state refused SO's asylum claim. Further submissions were also rejected, with the secretary of state taking the view that they did not amount to a fresh claim.[368] Barking and Dagenham sought to terminate SO's accommodation and support, asserting that, since he was a failed asylum-seeker, the responsibility for accommodating SO lay with the secretary of state under IAA 1999 s4(2).[369]

5.116 SO sought judicial review of Barking and Dagenham's decision. The judge at first instance dismissed the claim holding that 'other assistance', for the purposes of ChA 1989 s23C(4)(c), did not encompass the provision of accommodation. The Court of Appeal overturned this decision. Accommodation could be provided under ChA 1989 s23C(4)(c). And where an applicant was, notionally, entitled to such support it could not be refused on the basis that the applicant would be entitled to support under IAA 1999 s4(2) or s95(1). Following the reasoning of the House of Lords in *R (Westminster City Council) v National Asylum Support Service*[370] and the Court of Appeal in *R (A) v National Asylum Support Service*[371] it could be seen that:

> . . . the powers under s95 (and s4) of the Immigration and Asylum Act 1999 are residual, and cannot be exercised if the asylum seeker (or failed asylum seeker) is entitled to accommodation under some other provision, a local authority is not entitled, when considering whether a former relevant child's welfare requires that he be accommodated by it, to take into account the possibility of support from NASS.[372]

366 [2010] EWCA Civ 1101, [2011] 1 WLR 1283.
367 See paras 9.70–9.117.
368 See paras 3.42–3.43.
369 See paras 6.9–6.200.
370 [2002] UKHL 38, [2002] 1 WLR 2956.
371 [2003] EWCA Civ 1473, [2004] 1 WLR 752.
372 *R (SO) v Barking and Dagenham LBC* [2010] EWCA Civ 1101, [2011] 1 WLR 1283 at para 40 per Tomlinson LJ.

5.117 Although the case turned specifically on the application of ChA 1989 s23C(4)(c), this same logic would presumably extend to the other powers and duties under that part of the ChA 1989 relating to care leavers.

Statutory exclusions

5.118 The eligibility criteria for asylum support under IAA 1999 s95(1) are subject to a number of statutory exclusions. A person subject to one or more of these exclusions will not be able to access asylum support even if they meet the other eligibility criteria.[373] The same exclusions also apply to the provision of temporary support under IAA 1999 s98(1).[374]

The Immigration and Asylum Act 1999 s95(2) and Asylum Support Regulations 2000 reg 4 exclusion

5.119 By virtue of IAA 1999 s95(2), an applicant who would otherwise be eligible for support under IAA 1999 s95(1) is excluded in 'prescribed circumstances'. Those prescribed circumstances are set out in AS Regs 2000 reg 4. An applicant may not be provided with asylum support if:[375]

- They are a person to whom interim support applies.[376] This exclusion is of historic interest only. It applied to asylum-seekers who fell to be supported by local authorities during the 'interim period', which ended on 3 April 2006, following the coming into effect of the new asylum support regime under IAA 1999 Part VI.[377]
- They are a person to whom social security benefits apply.[378] This is a niche category.[379] The majority of persons subject to immigration control, within the meaning of IAA 1999 s115(9), are excluded from accessing mainstream welfare benefits such as

373 Discussed at paras 5.9–5.90.

374 See paras 5.282–5.301.

375 AS Regs 2000 reg 4(4).

376 AS Regs 2000 reg 4(4)(a).

377 See Asylum Support (Interim Provisions) Regulations 1999.

378 AS Regs 2000 reg 4(4)(b). See *R (AT (Guinea)) v SSHD* [2019] EWHC 2709 (Admin) at paras 46–49 for a discussion relating to the operation of this exclusion.

379 See further para 4.34.

IS, JSA or universal credit (UC).[380] However, there are certain exceptions to this rule contained in Social Security (Immigration and Asylum) Consequential Amendments Regulations 2000[381] reg 2. They include, for example cases where a person has been given leave to enter or remain in the UK on the basis of an undertaking given by a sponsor, where the sponsor has died, and cases where the person is a national of a state which has ratified the European Convention on Social and Medical Assistance (ECSMA) or the Council of Europe Social Charter (CESC), and is lawfully present in the UK.[382] Such persons are eligible for certain mainstream welfare benefits and, as a consequence, are prescribed as ineligible for asylum support.

- They have not made a claim for leave to enter or remain in the UK, or for variation of any such leave, which is being considered on the basis that they are an asylum-seeker or dependent on an asylum-seeker.[383]

5.120 These exclusions will apply if the applicant:

- is applying for support by themself;[384] or
- forms part of a group who are seeking asylum support and all members of the group fall within the terms of one of the exclusions.[385]

5.121 This means that if the applicant forms part of a group who are seeking asylum support and there is at least one person within the group who does not fall within the terms of one of these exclusions, then the applicant will remain eligible for support.

380 IAA 1999 s115(1), (3) and (9).

381 SI No 636.

382 Social Security (Immigration and Asylum) Consequential Amendments Regulations 2000 reg 2 and Sch 1 paras 2 and 4.

383 AS Regs 2000 reg 4(4)(c).

384 AS Regs 2000 reg 4(2).

385 AS Regs 2000 reg 4(3).

The Nationality, Immigration and Asylum Act 2002 s54 and Sch 3 exclusions[386]

5.122 The effect of NIAA 2002 s54 and Sch 3[387] is to exclude certain categories of migrant from certain forms of state support. However, as explained below, the exclusions have little practical effect as – in practice – a person who is eligible for asylum support by virtue of being destitute will generally fall within one of the exceptions to the exclusions.

5.123 The particular types of support to which the exclusion applies are contained in NIAA 2002 Sch 3 para 1 and include support under any provision of the IAA 1999.[388]

5.124 In the present context, the exclusions apply to:

- a person, together with any dependants, who is not an EEA national but who has been granted refugee status by an EEA state other than the UK;[389]
- certain failed asylum-seekers with dependant children in their household, together with any dependants, who fall within the extended definition of asylum-seeker contained in NIAA 2002 s18(2),[390] and whom the secretary of state has certified as having failed, without reasonable excuse, to take reasonable steps to leave the UK voluntarily, or to place themselves in a position in which they are able to leave the UK.[391]

5.125 However, the exclusions are subject to exceptions. In particular, the exclusions do not prevent the provision of support to:

- a British citizen;[392]

386 See further paras 9.195–9.217.

387 As amended by Immigration and Social Security Co-ordination (EU Withdrawal) Act 2020 (Consequential, Saving, Transitional and Transitory Provisions) (EU Exit) Regulations 2020 SI No 1309 reg 13(4) and subject to the transitional modifications specified in Citizens' Rights (Application Deadline and Temporary Protection) (EU Exit) Regulations 2020 SI No 1209 reg 12(1)(k) during the grace period. See further paras 2.14–2.19.

388 IAA 1999 Sch 3 para 1(1)(l).

389 NIAA Sch 3 para 4 as amended by Immigration, Nationality and Asylum (EU Exit) Regulations 2019 SI No 745 reg 12.

390 Which provides that a person shall continue to be treated as an asylum-seeker while their household includes a dependent child who is under 18, and they do not have leave to enter or remain in the UK. This is similar, though not identical, to the extended definition of asylum-seeker contained in IAA 1999 s94(5). See paras 5.45–5.49.

391 NIAA 2002 Sch 3 para 7A.

392 NIAA 2002 Sch 3 para 2(1)(a).

- a child;[393] or
- any person, to the extent necessary to avoid a breach of their rights under the ECHR.[394]

5.126 The first two exceptions are self-explanatory. For obvious reasons they are more likely to be applicable to a dependant of an asylum-seeker, rather than the asylum-seeker themself.

5.127 The third exception will most typically be invoked in asylum support cases in instances where the applicant, but for the provision of support, will face street homelessness thereby occasioning the risk of a breach of their rights under the ECHR.[395] In relation to ECHR Article 3, in *R (Limbuela) v SSHD*,[396] Lord Bingham explained that:

> A general public duty to house the homeless or provide for the destitute cannot be spelled out of article 3. But I have no doubt that the threshold may be crossed if a late applicant with no means and no alternative sources of support, unable to support himself, is, by the deliberate action of the state, denied shelter, food or the most basic necessities of life.[397]

5.128 The Article 3 threshold, he went on to observe, would be likely to be crossed 'if there were persuasive evidence that a late applicant[398] was obliged to sleep in the street, save perhaps for a short and foreseeably finite period, or was seriously hungry, or unable to satisfy the most basic requirements of hygiene'.[399] The ECHR Article 3 threshold is

393 NIAA 2002 Sch 3 para 2(1)(b).

394 NIAA 2002 Sch 3 para 3.

395 The provision of support to avoid a breach of the ECHR is discussed further at paras 6.90–6.135 and 9.203–9.217.

396 [2005] UKHL 66, [2006] 1 AC 396. See further the Introduction for the facts of, and background to, this decision.

397 *R (Limbuela) v SSHD* [2005] UKHL 66, [2006] 1 AC 396 at para 7 per Lord Bingham.

398 A 'late applicant' is a reference to a person who did not claim asylum as soon as reasonably practicable. This relates to the NIAA 2002 s55 exclusion discussed below at paras 5.132–5.136.

399 *R (Limbuela) v SSHD* [2005] UKHL 66, [2006] 1 AC 396 at para 9 per Lord Bingham, paras 56–63 per Lord Hope and para 78 per Baroness Hale. See para 5.264 on the overlap between the ECHR Article 3 threshold and the destitution test. For recent examples of cases where the Article 3 threshold was met see further *R (Humnyntskyi) v SSHD* [2020] EWHC 1912 (Admin), [2021] 1 WLR 320; *NH and others v France* App No 28820/13 [2020] ECHR 202; *R (W (a child)) v SSHD* [2020] EWHC 1299 (Admin), [2020] 1 WLR 4420; *Re Mahmud's application for judicial review* [2021] NIQB 6 and [2021] NIQB 37; and *R (CVN) v Croydon LBC* [2023] EWHC 464 (Admin). And for examples of cases where the threshold was not met, see *R (AR) v Hammersmsmith and Fulham LBC* [2018] EWHC 3453 (Admin), (2019) 22 CCLR 56; *R (Aburas) v Southwark LBC* [2019] EWHC 2754 (Admin), (2019) 22 CLR 537; *R (NB and others) v SSHD* [2021] EWHC 1489 (Admin); and *AO v Home Office* [2021] EWHC 1043 (QB).

not exactly the same as the destitution test under IAA 1999 s95(1).[400] However, as discussed at para 5.264, there is a very significant degree of overlap meaning that the a person who is eligible for asylum support will generally, by virtue of their destitution, fall within the Article 3 exception meaning that the NIAA 2022 Sch 3 exclusion will not apply. As such, the exclusion, in practice, has little effect in the asylum support context.

5.129 Similarly, ECHR Article 8 does not give rise to a general duty to house the homeless,[401] but is capable of giving rise to a positive obligation to provide accommodation either in circumstances where the Article 3 threshold is also met or where the welfare of children is at stake and the provision of welfare support is necessary to enable family life to continue.[402]

5.130 *R (Bernard) v Enfield LBC*[403] and *R (de Almeida) v Kensington and Chelsea RLBC*[404] provide examples of cases in which a failure to provide accommodation has been found to give rise to a breach of ECHR Article 8.[405] In the former case, it was a failure to provide suitable accommodation, as opposed to a complete failure to accommodate, which occasioned the breach. The claimant in that case was severely disabled and 'suitable accommodation was necessary not merely to facilitate the normal incidents of family life, but to secure [her] physical and psychological integrity'.[406] In the latter case, the High Court

400 See paras 5.57–5.90.

401 *Wandsworth LBC v Michalak* [2002] EWCA Civ 271, [2003] 1 WLR 617 at para 18 per Brooke LJ.

402 *R (Anufrijeva) v Southwark LBC* [2003] EWCA Civ 1406, [2004] 2 WLR 603 at para 43 per Lord Woolf MR.

403 [2002] EWHC 2282 (Admin), [2003] HLR 27.

404 [2012] EWHC 1082 (Admin), (2012) 15 CCLR 318.

405 For examples of cases where the courts have found no breach of ECHR Article 8, see: *R (McDonagh) v Enfield LBC* [2018] EWHC 1287 (Admin), [2018] HLR 43 (failure to provide suitable accommodation for over two years to a family with a severely disabled young child, in breach of Housing Act 1996 s188(1), not a breach of ECHR Article 8); *R (Idolo) v Bromley LBC* [2020] EWHC 860 (Admin), [2021] HLR 17 (delay in rehousing a disabled resident under Housing Act 1996 Part VI did not constitute a breach in circumstances where there was no lack of respect, maladministration or culpability on the part of the local authority); *R (NB) v SSHD* [2021] EWHC 1489 (Admin) (unlawful and dangerous conditions in which asylum-seekers were housed at the Napier barracks did not constitute a breach); and *R (SSHD) v First-Tier Tribunal (Social Entitlement Chamber)* [2021] EWHC 1690 (Admin) (no blanket requirement under Article 8 to provide support to failed asylum-seekers to protect public health during the COVID-19 pandemic).

406 *R (Bernard) v Enfield LBC* [2002] EWHC 2282 (Admin), [2003] HLR 27 at para 33 per Sullivan J.

found that the local authority's refusal to provide accommodation under NAA 1948 s21(1) to a terminally ill Portuguese national with advanced and untreatable HIV/AIDS, hepatitis C and cancer, was incompatible with his rights under ECHR Articles 3 and 8.

5.131 *R (MG (Iran)) v SSHD*[407] was another ECHR Article 8 case, involving a slightly different factual matrix. In that case, the Home Office's refusal to provide either accommodation or travel expenses in order to facilitate contact between a father and his son, who lived 130 miles away, constituted a disproportionate interference with his right to respect for family life under ECHR Article 8.

The Nationality, Immigration and Asylum Act 2002 s55 exclusion

5.132 Perhaps the most infamous exclusion to which the eligibility criteria for asylum support are subject is contained in NIAA 2002 s55[408] which prohibits the Home Office from providing asylum support to an applicant in circumstances where 'the secretary of state is not satisfied that the claim was made as soon as reasonably practicable after the person's arrival in the United Kingdom'.[409] As with the NIAA 2002 Sch 3 exclusions,[410] this does not preclude the provision of support in circumstances where it is necessary to avoid a breach of the individual's rights under the ECHR.[411] In addition, NIAA s2002 s55 does not preclude the provision of support to a household containing a dependant child.[412]

5.133 The background to this rule and the hardship which it engendered, culminating in the case of *R (Limbuela) v SSHD*,[413] are discussed in the Introduction. The circumstances in which support will be necessary to avoid a breach of the ECHR are discussed at paras 5.127–5.131.

5.134 In *R (Q) v SSHD*[414] the Court of Appeal held that the phrase 'as soon as reasonably practicable' required the secretary of state to consider:

> On the premise that the purpose of coming to this country was to claim asylum and having regard both to the practical opportunity for

407 [2015] EWHC 3142 (Admin). See para 5.184.
408 See the Introduction for a discussion of the background to this exclusion.
409 NIAA 2002 s55(1)–(2).
410 See paras 5.122–5.131.
411 NIAA 2002 s55(5)(a).
412 NIAA 2002 s55(5). See further paras 5.103–5.111 on households containing dependant children.
413 UKHL 66, [2006] 1 AC 396.
414 [2003] EWCA Civ 364, [2004] QB 36.

claiming asylum and to the asylum seeker's personal circumstances, could the asylum seeker reasonably have been expected to claim asylum earlier than he or she did?[415]

5.135 The burden lies on applicants to establish that they claimed as soon as reasonably practicable, though it is important for the secretary of state 'to probe the facts of each case in order to ensure that he has a reasonably full picture'.[416] In assessing whether they have done so the secretary of state will need to take account of their state of mind and anything they may have been told by agents (or the like) who facilitated their entry to the UK.[417]

5.136 Home Office policy[418] on NIAA 2002 s55 is that 'each case must be considered on its own merits, taking into account the information provided by the applicant and his particular circumstances, including his state of mind and the effect of any instructions given by third parties'.[419] However, 'bearing this in mind, if a person can demonstrate that he claimed asylum within three days of arrival in the UK, it should usually be accepted that he did so as soon as reasonably practicable if the person has given a credible account'.[420] The Home Office policy contains specific guidance on dealing with vulnerable applicants.[421] Of note, the policy provides that households containing pregnant women should normally receive a positive NIAA 2002 s55 decision.[422] In addition, NIAA 2002 s55 should not be applied to households including dependant children.[423]

The Nationality, Immigration and Asylum Act 2002 s57 exclusion

5.137 The last of the exclusions from asylum support which is considered in this chapter is, strictly speaking, not an exclusion in the true sense

415 *R (Q) v SSHD* [2003] EWCA Civ 364, [2004] QB 36 at para 37 per Lord Phillips MR giving the judgment of the court.

416 *R (Q) v SSHD* at para 89.

417 *R (Q) v SSHD* at paras 40, 43 and 89.

418 Which has been drafted so as to take into account the decisions in both *R (Q) v SSHD* and *R (Limbuela) v SSHD*.

419 *Nationality, Immigration and Asylum Act 2002 (section 55 guidance)*, Home Office, June 2015, p7 (www.gov.uk/government/publications/nationality-immigration-and-asylum-act-2002-process).

420 *Nationality, Immigration and Asylum Act 2002 (section 55 guidance)*, p7.

421 *Nationality, Immigration and Asylum Act 2002 (section 55 guidance)*, paras 3.4 and 3.10.

422 *Nationality, Immigration and Asylum Act 2002 (section 55 guidance)*, para 3.10.1.

423 *Asylum support: policy bulletins instruction*, v9.0, Q14.

of the word. Rather, it is a legal provision which the secretary of state may rely on to justify refusing to consider the application at all. This means that even applicants who are entitled to support may be unable to access it as a consequence. However, from the applicant's point of view, this is an exclusion in all but name and so it is convenient to deal with it in this section of the chapter.

5.138 The exclusion in question was introduced into IAA 1999 Sch 8 para 12 by NIAA 2002 s57,[424] and decisions relating to this exclusion are commonly referred to as 'section 57 decisions'. Under IAA 1999 Sch 8 para 12 the secretary of state is entitled to make regulations with respect to procedural requirements including 'the circumstances in which an application may not be entertained'. In particular, the regulations may provide for an application not to be entertained where the secretary of state is not satisfied that the information provided is complete or accurate or that the applicant is co-operating with further inquiries which the secretary of state has sought to make into their application for asylum support.[425]

5.139 This is then put into effect by AS Regs 2000 reg 3(4) which provides, in similar terms to the primary legislation, that the application may not be entertained by the secretary of state where they are not satisfied that:[426]

- the information provided by the applicant is complete or accurate; or
- the applicant is co-operating with further inquiries which he has made about any matter connected with the application.

5.140 In practice, this provision is sometimes erroneously relied on by the secretary of state to justify a finding that an applicant is not destitute. For example, the decision may suggest that the applicant has failed to provide evidence in response to further inquiries made by the secretary of state designed to establish whether or not the applicant is destitute, and that NIAA 2002 s57 is being relied on as a basis to refuse to entertain the application. Such decisions should be scrutinised carefully by advisers. If there has been a genuine failure to co-operate on the part of the applicant, particularly where it has put the secretary of state in a position where he or she cannot make a decision (whether positive or negative), then reliance on NIAA 2002 s57 may be justified. However, if, in reality, a decision has been made and the decision

424 See *Asylum support: policy bulletins instruction*, v9.0, chapter 10.
425 IAA 1999 Sch 8 para 12(c)–(d).
426 See further paras 5.221–5.224.

is that the applicant has failed to provide sufficient evidence does establish that they are destitute, then that cannot properly be described as an NIAA 2002 s57 decision. In such cases, the secretary of state has entertained the application and, having done so, has reached an adverse decision. The distinction is an importance one as a right of appeal may lie against the latter, but not the former.[427] However, in the former situation the applicant may simply seek to gather the required information and make a fresh application.[428]

The provision of support

Overview

5.141 Support under IAA 1999 s95(1) may be provided in the following ways:[429]

- by providing accommodation that appears to the secretary of state to be adequate for the needs of the applicant together with any dependants;[430]
- by providing what appear to the secretary of state to be essential living needs of the applicant together with any dependants;[431]
- by enabling the applicant (if they are the asylum-seeker) to meet certain expenses incurred in connection with the asylum claim;[432]
- by enabling the applicant and any dependants to attend bail proceedings in connection with the detention of the applicant or the dependants under any provision of the Immigration Acts;[433]
- by providing, in cases that appear to the secretary of state to be exceptional, such other support as he considers necessary to enable the applicant and any dependants to be supported.[434]

5.142 It is the first two forms of support – accommodation and subsistence – which are sought by the majority of applicants for asylum support. Although they can be, and often are, provided together, they do not

427 See further the discussion of this issue at paras 5.317–5.318; and 'Briefing note on when it is possible to appeal a decision under section 57 of the Nationality and Immigration Act 2002', ASAP, September 2016.

428 See paras 5.239 on repeat applications.

429 IAA 1999 s96(1).

430 IAA 1999 s96(1)(a).

431 IAA 1999 s96(1)(b).

432 IAA 1999 s96(1)(c).

433 IAA 1999 s96(1)(d) and (e).

434 IAA 1999 s96(2).

have to be under IAA 1999 s95(1).[435] Applicants may apply for one or other or both,[436] and will be asked to indicate which of these options they are seeking within their application form.[437] Beyond this, applicants are provided with little choice as to the way in which they are supported. In determining how to provide support under IAA 1999 s95(1) the secretary of state may disregard any preference which the applicant, or any dependants, may express as to the way in which the support is to be given.[438] Legal challenges as to the type, level or location of support provided to an applicant need to be brought by way of judicial review. There is no right of appeal in relation to such matters.[439]

5.143 When deciding whether to provide support to an applicant or dependant who is a 'vulnerable person', the secretary of state is required to take into account the special needs of that person. 'Vulnerable' in this context encompasses:[440]

- a child under the age of 18;
- a disabled person;
- an elderly person;
- a pregnant woman;
- a lone parent with a child under the age of 18; or
- a person who has been subjected to torture, rape, or other serious forms of psychological, physical or sexual violence;
- who has had an 'individual evaluation of his situation that confirms he has special needs'.

5.144 The various forms of support will now be considered in turn.[441]

435 This differs materially to support for failed asylum-seekers under IAA 1999 s4(2), in which accommodation and support are provided hand in hand. See para 6.154.

436 See: www.gov.uk/asylum-support/what-youll-get.

437 See paras 5.221–5.246 on the application process.

438 IAA 1999 s97(7).

439 See paras 5.314–5.320.

440 Asylum Seekers (Reception Conditions) Regulations 2005 reg 4 implementing Reception Directive Article 17.

441 For accommodation see paras 5.145–5.184. For subsistence see paras 5.185–5.206. For expenses in connection with asylum claims and bail proceedings see paras 5.207–5.209. For additional payments in exceptional cases see paras 5.210–5.214.

Accommodation

5.145 From 2012 to 2019, accommodation for asylum-seekers was provided by means of six regional 'Commercial and Operational Managers Procuring Asylum Support Services' (COMPASS) contracts. These six contracts were held by three separate companies:[442] Clearsprings, G4S and Serco. In September 2019, the COMPASS contracts were replaced by Asylum Accommodation and Support Services Contracts (AASSC), which are intended to remain in place until 2029.[443] The contracts have been awarded to Clearsprings Ready Homes, Mears Group and Serco as follows:[444]

- Midlands and East of England – Serco;
- North East, Yorkshire and Humberside – Mears Group;
- North West – Serco;
- Northern Ireland – Mears Group;
- Scotland – Mears Group;
- South – Clearsprings Ready Homes;
- Wales – Clearsprings Ready Homes.

5.146 These companies will either secure accommodation themselves or will rely on subcontractors which may, in turn, rely on private landlords.[445] The precise arrangements vary from region to region. The fact that the Home Office has chosen to discharge its statutory functions by means of private contractual arrangements with these companies does not alter the fact that it is the Home Office that is legally responsible for the proper discharge of those functions.[446]

442 *An inspection of the Home Office's management of asylum accommodation provision February – June 2018*, Independent Chief Inspector of Borders and Immigration, November 2018, paras 5.12–5.13.

443 See: www.gov.uk/government/news/new-asylum-accommodation-contracts-awarded.

444 See: www.gov.uk/government/news/new-asylum-accommodation-contracts-awarded. The contracts do not appear to be available online but the Statement of Requirements set out in Schedule 2 to the contracts can be accessed at http://data.parliament.uk/DepositedPapers/Files/DEP2018-1112/AASC_-_Schedule_2_-_Statement_of_Requirements.pdf.

445 *COMPASS contracts for the provision of accommodation for asylum seekers*, HC 880, National Audit Office, January 2014.

446 See, for example, *Ali (Iraq) v Serco Ltd* [2019] CSIH 54 at paras 52–57 per Lady Dorian; *R (AQS) v SSHD* [2020] EWHC 843 (Admin) at para 22 per Robin Knowles J; *Re Mahmud's application for judicial review* [2021] NIQB 6 at para 134 per Friedman J; and *R (AXG) v SSHD* [2022] EWHC 56 (Admin) at para 15 per Steyn J.

5.147 Accommodation is provided on a 'no-choice' basis.[447] IAA 1999 s97(2) expressly provides that in exercising his or her power to provide accommodation, the secretary of state must not have regard to any preference to the locality in which the accommodation is provided. This is supplemented by AS Regs 2000 reg 13 which requires the secretary of state to disregard any personal preferences the applicant might have about the nature of accommodation to be provided or the standard of fixtures and fittings. These provisions do not, however, obviate the need for the secretary of state to consider the applicant's 'individual circumstances, as they relate to his accommodation needs'.[448]

5.148 Where accommodation is provided for an applicant and their family, the secretary of state is required to 'have regard to family unity and ensure, in so far as it is reasonably practicable to do so, that family members are accommodated together', save where they do not agree to being accommodated together.[449]

5.149 Accommodation is provided, in the first instance, in 'initial accommodation'[450] following which applicants are dispersed around the country to longer-term placements, referred to by the Home Office as 'dispersal accommodation'.[451] As of 30 June 2022, there were in excess of 33,364 people in initial accommodation, with 72,564 in dispersal accommodation.[452] The Home Office aims to move applicants on from initial accommodation within 35 days, although, in practice, many stay much longer than this,[453] the delay to dispersal having become worse during and as a result of the COVID-19 pandemic.

447 See *Allocation of accommodation policy*, v8.0, Home Office, December 2022, p5; and *Al-Ameri v Kensington and Chelsea RLBC* [2004] UKHL 4, [2004] 2 AC 159 at paras 16–17 per Lord Bingham.

448 AS Regs 2000 reg 13(2). See further paras 5.169–5.184 on dispersal.

449 Asylum Seekers (Reception Conditions) Regulations 2005 reg 3, implementing Reception Directive Article 8.

450 Initial accommodation is generally, but not always, provided pursuant to IAA 1999 s98(1) (see paras 5.282–5.301), as a temporary expedient while the secretary of state determines whether the applicant is eligible for IAA 1999 s95(1) support. However, in certain circumstances those in receipt of IAA 1999 s95(1) support may still be placed in initial accommodation. See *Asylum support: policy bulletins instruction*, v9.0, para 1.1.3. See further *R (JM) v SSHD* [2021] EWHC 2514 (Admin), [2022] PTSR 260 at para 40 per Farbey J.

451 See paras 5.169–5.184.

452 See *Immigration statistics asylum and resettlement – asylum seekers in receipt of support*, Home Office, August 2022.

453 *Asylum accommodation and support*, HC 375, National Audit Office, July 2020, para 3.15 and figure 8.

5.150 Historically, initial accommodation has typically been 'hostel-style, full-board accommodation' and dispersal accommodation has typically been a furnished flat or shared house (with utility bills and council tax paid).[454] However, this changed markedly during the COVID-19 pandemic in two ways. First, military camps/barracks at Penally and Napier were pressed into use as accommodation[455] as well as numerous hotels, to house the increased numbers who required accommodation during the pandemic as a result of factors such as the temporary cessation of evictions and obstacles to people returning to their countries of origin. Such provision was generally referred to by the Home Office as 'contingency accommodation'.[456]

5.151 The use of hotels has persisted even as the pandemic has receded. The Refugee Council reported that as of 31 December 2021 26,380 applicants remained in hotel accommodation, 3,254 of whom had been in such accommodation in excess of six months.[457] Serious concerns have been expressed about the use of such accommodation, particularly for families with children.[458] The use of hotels for this purpose has also given rise to planning disputes with local authorities concerned about the change of use from hostel to hotel, seeking interim injunctions.[459] The Home Office intention is that the use of hotel accommodation will end, though no date has been given for when this will happen.[460]

5.152 In contrast, the use of large centres for accommodating asylum-seekers, such as the Ministry of Defence facilities at Napier and

454 *An inspection of the Home Office's management of asylum accommodation provision February – June 2018*, Independent Chief Inspector of Borders and Immigration, November 2018, paras 5.3 and 5.7; *Asylum accommodation*, HC 637, House of Commons Home Affairs Committee, January 2017, para 49 (https://publications.parliament.uk/pa/cm201617/cmselect/cmhaff/637/637.pdf).

455 See further para 5.159.

456 See, for example, *An inspection of contingency asylum accommodation May 2021 – November 2021*, Independent Chief Inspector of Borders and Immigration, May 2022. In practice, there has been little functional difference between initial and contingency accommodation in terms of what applicants actually get.

457 *Lives on hold: Experiences of people living in hotel asylum accommodation*, Refugee Council, July 2022, pp6–7.

458 See para 5.159.

459 See, for example, *Ipswich BC v Fairview Hotels (Ipswich) Ltd* [2022] EWHC 2868 (KB) and *Great Yarmouth BC v Al-Abdin* [2022] EWHC 3476 (KB).

460 *New plan for immigration policy statement*, p19.

Penally,[461] is set to increase.[462] NIAA 2002 Part 2 contains a statutory framework for the establishment of 'accommodation centres' to accommodate destitute asylum-seekers. Applicants may be accommodated in such centres either under IAA 1999 s95(1)[463] or under NIAA 2002 s17(1). There are various procedural safeguards contained within NIAA 2002 Part 2 governing the introduction and use of accommodation centres including a prior consultation requirement[464] and a time limit on the time which an individual may be continuously accommodated in a centre.[465] This framework has recently been amended and supplemented by NBA 2022 s13 which provides among other things for different types of accommodation to be provided to applicants depending on the stage of their asylum claim and their previous compliance with conditions.[466] The relevant provisions of the NIAA 2002 are not yet in force. Their amendment by the NBA 2022, coupled with the government's stated intention to increase the use of accommodation centres suggests that the relevant provisions will be brought into force in due course.[467]

5.153 It should be noted that when the Home Office started to use Napier and Penally in Autumn 2020 to house asylum-seekers, it did not use the legal framework under the NIAA 2002 relating to accommodation centres. The provision of accommodation at Napier and Penally was instead done through executive policy. This meant that many of the safeguards provided for under the NIAA 2002 were not available to those accommodated at these two facilities. However,

461 The use of the Penally camp has ended. The use of Napier Barracks has continued. Although the making of the Town and Country Planning (Napier Barracks) Special Development Order 2021 SI No 962, which granted planning permission to use the site for asylum support accommodation for a further five years, was held to have been unlawful as contrary to Equality Act 2010 s149 in *R (Hough) v SSHD* [2022] EWHC 1635 (Admin).

462 *New plan for immigration policy statement*, pp19–20.

463 NIAA 2002 s22.

464 NIAA 2002 ss40–42.

465 NIAA 2002 s25(1).

466 NBA 2022 s13(1) inserting a new subsection (3A) into IAA 1999 s97.

467 The parliamentary debates over the relevant clause (Public Bill Committee (Eighth Sitting) Nationality and Borders Bill Deb 21 October 2021, c272) and the tender for the provision of accommodation centres (www.find-tender.service.gov.uk/Notice/019531-2021#procedure-heading) both imply that this will be the case.

they were accommodation centres in all but name.[468] The Home Office appears therefore to be of the view that accommodation centres may be operated solely under the framework of the IAA 1999. The lawfulness of such an approach remains to be tested; it will depend on the nature and functions of the accommodation facility among other things, and whether or not the use of the facility outside of the statutory framework of the NIAA 2002 and NBA 2022 is, in effect, subverting the statutory scheme.

Adequacy of accommodation

5.154 IAA 1999 s96(1)(a) regulates the standards of accommodation that may be provided under section 95(1), by requiring that such accommodation should 'appear . . . to the Secretary of State to be adequate for the needs of the supported person and his dependants'. The meaning of the word 'adequate', which is also part of the statutory test for destitution, is discussed at para 5.72. The Court of Appeal in *R (A) v National Asylum Support Service*[469] described the duty to provide adequate accommodation as being 'absolute and immediate', while acknowledging that what is adequate in the short term may not be adequate in the long term.[470] More recent decisions of the High Court have characterised the duty as a 'reasonable endeavours' or 'best efforts'[471] duty, or a duty to provide adequate accommodation within a 'reasonable period of time'.[472] But it is questionable whether these decisions are consistent with the Court of Appeal's statement of principle in the *R (A) v National Asylum Support Service* case. The better view may be that the duty is immediate and unqualified but that the High Court in judicial review proceedings will be unlikely to

468 The government's official position was that Napier was not categorised as an accommodation centre. See Letter from Tom Pursglove MP, Parliamentary Under Secretary of State, to the Chairs of the Nationality and Borders Bill Committee House of Commons, 26 October 2021.

469 [2003] EWCA Civ 1473, [2004] 1 WLR 752 at para 59 per Waller LJ. See also *R (AXG) v SSHD* [2022] EWHC 56 (Admin) at para 71 per Steyn J.

470 See further para 5.245 on that nature of the duty and delay in its performance.

471 See *R (Chkharchkhalia) v SSHD* [2019] EWHC 2232 (Admin) at para 37 but contrast *R (AMA) v SSHD* [2021] EWHC 2646 (Admin) at para 10.

472 See *R (JM) v SSHD* [2021] EWHC 2514 (Admin), [2022] PTSR 260 at para 98; *R (AMA) v SSHD* [2021] EWHC 2646 (Admin) at para 10; *R (ALW) v SSHD* [2022] EWHC 557 (Admin).

grant a mandatory order to compel compliance with the duty where the secretary of state is doing all that she reasonably can to comply.[473]

5.155 The statutory test contained in IAA 1999 s96(1)(a) contains a subjective element, providing that accommodation must 'appear . . . to the Secretary of State to be adequate', suggesting that the secretary of state has a degree of judgment to exercise in deciding what is or is not adequate. However, the statutory requirement of adequacy must be interpreted in light of the requirements of Reception Directive Article 13(2) which requires 'a standard of living adequate for the health of applicants and capable of ensuring their subsistence' to be provided. Construing IAA 1999 s96(1)(a) in light of Article 13(2), in effect, converts the requirement of adequacy into an objective standard and a decision to provide accommodation that falls short of the standard contained in Article 13(2) will not be lawful or rational.[474]

5.156 Historically it has been clear that, at a systemic level, the duty to provide adequate accommodation has not always been met. In January 2014 the National Audit Office (NAO) noted severe defects in a significant number of properties across the country.[475] Reporting three years later in January 2017, the Home Affairs Select Committee put flesh on the bones of the NAO's statistics, remarking that:

> The poor standard of asylum accommodation was the most significant issue identified in the evidence we received, which focused largely on contracts administered by G4S and Serco. It is clear that in too many cases Providers are placing people in accommodation that is substandard, poorly maintained and, at times, unsafe. Some of this accommodation is a disgrace and it is shameful that some very vulnerable people have been placed in such conditions.[476]

5.157 Particular concerns were expressed in relation to the 'presence of vermin in some accommodation' and the lack of adequate provision for 'particularly vulnerable asylum seekers, such as expectant mothers, those living with mental health needs and victims of trafficking, rape and torture' who were, at times, having to share

473 See *R (Elkundi) v Birmingham City Council* [2022] EWCA Civ 601 and *R (Parul) v SSHD* [2022] EWHC 2143 (Admin) discussing and applying *Elkundi* when considering the grant of relief in the asylum support context.

474 See *R (NB and others) v SSHD* [2021] EWHC 1489 (Admin) at paras 116 and 145–158 per Linden J, explaining how it is that these requirements of the Reception Directive remain applicable following the departure of the UK from the EU.

475 *COMPASS contracts for the provision of accommodation for asylum seekers*, HC 880, p29.

476 *Asylum accommodation*, HC 637, para 68.

rooms or being placed in large houses in multiple occupation (HMOs).[477]

5.158 These concerns were echoed by David Bolt, the Independent Chief Inspector of Borders and Immigration, in November 2018 following his inspection of the Home Office's management of asylum accommodation provision. Two-thirds of the submissions he received as part of his inspection 'focused on poor property standards, with frequent references to defects, damp, dirt and vermin' and almost half 'referred to the unsuitability of the accommodation provided for particular groups of asylum seekers, including survivors of torture, victims of domestic violence, pregnant women and new mothers, and LGBTQI+ asylum seekers'.[478] In a follow-up report in December 2018, the Home Affairs Select Committee described the Independent Chief Inspector's report as forming part of a body of 'overwhelming evidence' indicating that standards of accommodation remained 'unacceptably poor'. The Committee urged the Home Office to 'show a greater urgency about the degrading conditions in which very vulnerable people are being housed under its contracts, including torture survivors, individuals suffering PTSD, pregnant women and mothers with small children'.[479]

5.159 It was hoped that the implementation of the new AASSCs[480] would address this.[481] However, recent reports suggest that this is not the case.[482] Indeed the increased reliance on hotel accommodation during the COVID-19 pandemic, which can be particularly problematic for those with disabilities or family commitments, has generated

477 *Asylum accommodation*, HC 637, paras 61 and 97.

478 *An inspection of the Home Office's management of asylum accommodation provision February – June 2018*, Independent Chief Inspector of Borders and Immigration, November 2018, para 3.8. See further paras 3.9, 7.3, 7.12–7.13, 8.75 and 10.25.

479 *Asylum accommodation: replacing COMPASS*, HC 1758, House of Commons Home Affairs Committee, December 2018, recommendation 15, paras 57–58.

480 See para 5.145.

481 See *Asylum accommodation and support*, HC 375, figure 4 for the expected improvements under the new contracts.

482 *WAKE UP CALL: How government contracts fail people seeking asylum*, Asylum Matters and Refugee Action, July 2020, pp10–11 (available at: www.refugee-action.org.uk/wake-up-call/); 'Asylum seekers in PM's constituency claim accommodation "not fit to live in" ' *Guardian*, 22 December 2021.

new problems.[483] The use of largescale centres for accommodating asylum-seekers[484] has proved equally problematic and in *R (NB and others) v SSHD*,[485] Linden J held that the accommodation provided to asylum-seekers at the Napier Barracks in Kent, which at that time posed a risk of fire as well as a risk of contracting COVID-19, to those placed there, was inadequate.[486]

5.160 The AASSCs (like the predecessor COMPASS contracts) contain specific provision designed to ensure that the secretary of state's duty to provide adequate accommodation is discharged. These place a contractual obligation on the providers with whom the Home Office contracts[487] to provide accommodation that is 'safe, habitable, fit for purpose and correctly equipped', and contain detailed requirements to that end.[488] In *R (NB and others) v SSHD*, Linden J, in *obiter* remarks, expressed the view that the fact that accommodation did not meet the standards set out in the AASSC would not necessarily mean that it is inadequate.[489] Nevertheless, many of those requirements (which address matters of safety and fitness of habitation, among other things) will certainly be relevant to the overall assessment of adequacy, and did inform the judge's decision, particularly the serious concerns about fire safety at the barracks.

5.161 Also relevant to the assessment of adequacy (or potentially giving rise to a freestanding legal challenge) are the policies maintained by the secretary of state which deal with the type of accommodation that should be provided to particular applicants. In particular, the *Healthcare needs and pregnancy dispersal policy*, v3.0 provides that as a general rule:[490]

483 *Lives on hold: Experiences of people living in hotel asylum accommodation*, Refugee Council, July 2022, pp6–7; *An inspection of contingency asylum accommodation May 2021 – November 2021*, Independent Chief Inspector of Borders and Immigration, May 2022. See further *R (MQ) v SSHD* [2023] EWHC 205 (Admin).

484 See para 5.152.

485 [2021] EWHC 1489 (Admin).

486 See *A re-inspection of Napier Barracks March 2022: March 2022*, Independent Chief Inspector of Borders and Immigration, June 2022 for a more recent appraisal of conditions at Napier following improvements subsequent to the judgment in *NB*.

487 See para 5.145.

488 See para 2.2.1 of the Statement of Requirements contained in Schedule 2 to the AASSC discussed at para 5.145.

489 [2021] EWHC 1489 (Admin) at paras 173 and 179.

490 *Healthcare needs and pregnancy dispersal policy*, v3.0, Home Office, January 2016, para 4.9.

- accommodation provided to pregnant women must be suitable not just for them (factoring in any mobility issues), but also for the mother and baby, post birth;
- those with mobility problems (but who are not wheelchair users) should generally be accommodated on the ground floor or in level access accommodation with a lift;
- wheelchair users will require accommodation that allows them access to all the key areas of the accommodation, ie kitchen, bathroom and sleeping area;
- it will not be appropriate for those with active infectious diseases to share rooms; and
- those with HIV should be provided with their own room.

5.162 The policy as a whole is essential reading for advisers working with pregnant women, new mothers and others with healthcare needs. However, it should be borne in mind that for applicants who have a need for care and attention which does not arise solely from their destitution, it may be the case that social services rather than the Home Office should in fact assume responsibility for their accommodation.[491]

5.163 Specific guidance on how to deal with the accommodation needs of victims of domestic abuse is provided in *Domestic abuse: responding to reports of domestic abuse from asylum seekers*, v2.0. 'Domestic abuse' is defined for this purpose as 'any incident or pattern of incidents of controlling, coercive or threatening behaviour, violence or abuse between those aged 16 or over who are or have been intimate partners or family members regardless of gender or sexuality'. 'Abuse' can encompass but is not limited to psychological, physical, sexual, financial and emotional abuse. 'Controlling behaviour' is a range of acts designed to make a person subordinate and or dependent by isolating them from sources of support, exploiting their resources and capacities for personal gain, depriving them of the means needed for independence, resistance and escape and regulating everyday behaviour. 'Coercive behaviour' is an act or pattern of acts of assault, threats, humiliation and intimidation or other abuse that is used to harm, punish, or frighten their victim.

5.164 Where a report of domestic abuse is received from an applicant accommodated under the IAA 1999, the presumption is that the applicant should be believed, corroborating evidence is not required and the applicant and their children must immediately be offered

491 See paras 5.94–5.102.

safe alternative accommodation and (if that offer is accepted) transferred without delay.[492] The alternative accommodation 'must be suitable for the individuals concerned, including children' and, for example:

> . . . may need to be within close proximity of specialist support services which might include independent domestic violence advocates (IDVAs), LGBTQI+ organisations that support people who have experienced domestic abuse, specialist organisations that support men, specialist BME women's organisations, counsellors and other specialist health services, including rape crisis centres, specialist advisors and services for women within refugee agencies.[493]

5.165 The policy provides the possibility that the victim may wish to remain in their current accommodation, and in these cases, the policy directs that consideration must be given to relocating the perpetrator. The possibility of doing so may be important for many victims and their dependant children where their support networks are in the area of their current accommodation and relocation as a result of abuse may disrupt those networks at a time when they critically depend on them. Further discussion on the policy approach concerning asylum support for victims of domestic abuse is set out in paras 11.249–11.261.

5.166 Until May 2021, there was no comparable policy on responding to other forms of abuse, threats and anti-social behaviour in the asylum support context, even though individuals and families may often be placed in shared dispersal accommodation with strangers and conflict may arise. The Home Office does have powers to discontinue or suspend support if it 'has reasonable grounds to suspect' that a supported person has 'failed without reasonable excuse' to comply with a condition of their support under AS Regs 2000 reg 20.[494] This includes where they have 'reasonable grounds to believe' that the supported person or a dependant 'has committed an act of *seriously violent behaviour* whether or not that act occurs in accommodation provided by way of asylum support or at the authorised address or elsewhere'. However, the *Breach of conditions* policy as operated prior to May 2021 provided no specific guidance on what the Home Office and accommodation providers are to do to address the immediate and potential safeguarding problems that victims

492 See Home Office policy, *Domestic reports abuse: of domestic responding abuse asylum seekers*, v2.0, 21 January 2022, p10.

493 *Domestic abuse: responding to reports of domestic abuse from asylum seekers*, v2.0, p10.

494 See paras 5.257–5.265.

of violence and abuse (in a non-domestic abuse context) face. In *R (XN) v SSHD*[495] the claimant and her child faced anti-social behaviour and threats of violence in shared asylum support accommodation from another resident. Despite repeated complaints raised and requests for safeguarding investigations, no steps were taken to relocate the perpetrator or to offer the claimant safe alternative accommodation. The claimant challenged the *Breach of conditions* policy as framed at that time for being deficient in failing to make comparable provision for the relocation of the perpetrator as is set out in the policy concerning domestic abuse victims 'in a case in which perpetrator and victim are not part of the same immediate residence, but part of broader communal shared accommodation'. The Home Office subsequently settled the case[496] with an agreement to review and amend the policy to deal with such cases. Further to a short consultation with stakeholders, this led to an amended *Conditions of support* policy.[497] The policy now highlights[498] the requirement on accommodation providers to refer serious or persistent incidents of anti-social behaviour to the Home Office for investigation. The potential outcomes now include the possibility of relocation of the perpetrator as an alternative to relocating the victim and any dependants; the presumption is that the perpetrator is moved if the allegations are established, unless it is in the victim's interest to be relocated.

5.167 Applicants who feel that their accommodation is inadequate may, in the first instance, seek to raise this either via Migrant Help[499] or with the Home Office or accommodation provider directly. If this does not provide adequate redress, judicial review may be available. Recent examples of judicial review claims challenging the adequacy of accommodation include *R (O) v SSHD*,[500] *R (Chkharchkhalia)*

495 [2020] EWHC 2117 (Admin).

496 See: https://dpglaw.co.uk/wp-content/uploads/2020/12/3039784-Consent-Order-03-12-20.pdf.

497 *Conditions of support*, v1.0, Home Office, May 2021. This replaced the previous *Breach of Conditions* policy. This has since been replaced with *Conditions of support*, v2.0, Home Office, March 2023.

498 *Conditions of Support*, v2.0, p18.

499 *A Home Office guide to living in asylum accommodation*, UKVI, July 2019, p13 or p16 (www.gov.uk/government/publications/living-in-asylum-accommodation).

500 [2019] EWHC 2734 (Admin). Successful judicial review of failure to provide adequate accommodation to household with autistic child who required self-contained accommodation to stay safe.

v SSHD,[501] *R (AMA) v SSHD*,[502] *R (ALW) v SSHD*,[503] *R (K) v SSHD*[504] and *R (MQ) v SSHD*.[505]

5.168 The accommodation standards set out in Landlord and Tenant Act 1985 ss9A and 11, which give rise to a private law cause of action against the landlord of a property, do not generally apply to asylum support accommodation as those standards apply only to tenancies and asylum-seekers generally occupy their accommodation under contractual licenses rather than tenancies.[506] However, applicants in inadequate accommodation may be able to seek assistance from the environmental health department of the local authority tasked with enforcing the housing standards imposed under the Environmental Protection Act 1990 and the Housing Act 2004,[507] which safeguard occupiers (among others) against statutory nuisances and hazardous accommodation respectively.[508]

Dispersal

5.169 The dispersal of applicants for asylum-support to accommodation located around the UK is one of the key concepts underpinning the statutory regime for asylum support introduced by IAA 1999 Part VI.

501 [2019] EWHC 2232 (Admin). Failure to provide accommodation closer to place where applicant receiving therapy not unlawful owing to lack of affordable properties.

502 [2021] EWHC 2646 (Admin). Not unlawful to accommodate applicant and son in cramped, shared room some distance from the school and hospital the household required.

503 [2022] EWHC 557 (Admin). Inadequacy conceded by secretary of state in case where there was a two-year delay in providing appropriate accommodation for household containing severely disabled child who needed space for wheelchair.

504 [2020] EWHC 3639 (Admin). Mandatory interim injunction granted in case where family of five sleeping in single room of hotel, with three-week-old baby sleeping on the floor.

505 [2023] EWHC 205 (Admin). Not unlawful to accommodate applicant and family in single room in hotel where concerns had been raised about quality of food and extent of living space.

506 Whether a particular applicant occupies their accommodation under a licence or tenancy will depend on the precise terms of their occupation agreement. See *Street v Mountford* [1985] AC 809, HL for the relevant principles.

507 Note, however, that the draft Houses in Multiple Occupation (Asylum-Seeker Accommodation) (England) Regulations 2023 exclude certain asylum support accommodation, where occupation commenced between the coming into force of these Regulations and 30 June 2024, from the definition of a 'house in multiple occupation' within the meaning of Housing Act 2004 s254, limiting the degree of local authority regulation.

508 See J Luba, C O'Donnell and G Peaker *Housing conditions: tenant's rights*, Legal Action Group, 6th edn, 2019.

The idea is that accommodation is provided, in the first instance, in initial accommodation[509] following which applicants are dispersed around the country to longer-term placements. The Home Office aims to disperse applicants within 35 days but takes much longer than this in some cases.[510] Dispersal generally takes place in date order though applicants are free to make representations as to why their case should be dealt with more quickly.[511] The policy underpinning dispersal was described in the following terms by the Home Affairs Select Committee:

> The policy of dispersal was first introduced under the Immigration and Asylum Act 1999 when the then Labour Government sought to alleviate the pressure on local authorities in London and the south-east of England where most asylum seekers were making their claims for asylum. Beyond the aim of relocating asylum seekers away from the southeast of England, the two main factors driving the distribution of asylum accommodation are availability and cost.[512]

5.170 It used to be the case that providers could only place applicants in areas where the local authority had agreed to take asylum-seekers, and only up to a 'cluster limit' of one asylum-seeker per 200 residents.[513] However, the majority of local authority areas refused to participate,[514] meaning that that the burden fell on the minority that had, which led to a perception among some local authorities that 'the propensity to place families in low value housing in the north of England was placing enormous strain on schools in already deprived areas'.[515] This policy changed in May 2022 and asylum-seekers can now be dispersed to the areas of all local authorities in England, Scotland and Wales irrespective of whether they have volunteered for that purpose.[516]

5.171 The statutory basis for dispersal in found in IAA 1999 s97(1)(b) which provides that the secretary of state, when exercising their

509 See paras 5.149–5.150 and 5.286 for initial accommodation.
510 *Asylum accommodation and support*, HC 375, para 3.15 and figure 8.
511 *R (MQ) v SSHD* [2023] EWHC 205 (Admin).
512 *Asylum accommodation*, HC 637, para 31.
513 *An inspection of the Home Office's management of asylum accommodation provision February – June 2018*, Independent Chief Inspector of Borders and Immigration, November 2018, para 5.6.
514 As of March 2020, 180 out of 382 local authorities had agreed to house asylum-seekers in their area. See *Asylum accommodation and support*, HC 375, para 4.7 and figure 14.
515 *Asylum accommodation*, HC 637, para 38.
516 *R (Wolverhampton City Council and others) v SSHD* [2022] EWHC 1721 (Admin).

power to provide accommodation under IAA 1999 s95(1), must have regard to 'the desirability, in general, of providing accommodation in areas in which there is a ready supply of accommodation'. This is then supplemented by AS Regs 2000 reg 19, which allows the secretary of state to refuse or discontinue support to an applicant who fails to comply with a condition that they should reside in the accommodation to which they have been dispersed to.

5.172 These statutory provisions provide the legal basis for the Home Office policy on dispersal which provides that:

> The overriding principle when allocating accommodation is that it is offered on a 'no choice basis' and as a general rule is provided outside London and the South East and only in areas of the UK where the Home Office has a ready supply.
>
> Caseworkers must, however, consider requests to be allocated accommodation in London, the South East, or another specific location and consider whether there are exceptional circumstances that make it appropriate to agree to the request.
>
> All requests should be considered on a case by case basis, balancing the overarching principle that accommodation is offered on a 'no choice basis' against the strength of the exceptional circumstances that might make it appropriate to agree to the request to provide accommodation in a particular location.
>
> . . .
>
> Requests for accommodation in a particular location should normally be made in writing and be supported, where appropriate, with other documentary evidence, for example from medical practitioners.[517]

5.173 The allocation of accommodation is a function falling within Borders, Citizenship and Immigration Act (BCIA) 2009 s55(2), meaning that decisions on dispersal must be made with due regard to safeguard and promote the welfare of any children involved, who are in the UK.[518] In practice this necessitates 'the child's interests being made a primary, although not the only consideration'.[519]

5.174 At the time of writing, there are two main Home Office policies dealing with dispersal.[520] The first, which provides generalised guidance, is the *Allocation of accommodation policy*, v8.0. The second, which provides more specific guidance tailored to certain vulnerable applicants, is the *Healthcare needs and pregnancy dispersal policy*, v3.0.

517 *Allocation of accommodation policy*, v8.0, pp5-6.

518 BCIA 2009 s55(1). See paras 5.302–5.309.

519 *Allocation of accommodation policy*, v8.0, p7.

520 The High Court in *R (MQ) v SSHD* [2023] EWHC 205 (Admin) rejected a claim that there was a further unpublished policy relating to the order in which applicants are dispersed.

These policies are essential reading for those advising applicants on dispersal.

5.175 The *Allocation of accommodation policy*, v8.0, deals with a number of 'typical request scenarios', setting out some of the commonly received requests from applicants to be accommodated in a particular location, and how the Home Office typically will deal with them:[521]

- Requests for accommodation in a particular area because the applicant or a dependant is receiving medical treatment there will generally be refused, save where there are exceptional circumstances, on the basis that treatment for most medical conditions is available in all parts of the UK and the transfer of patients within the NHS is a normal everyday occurrence. However, requests made in order to avoid unreasonable disruption of medical treatment or related assistance 'should be considered carefully, balancing the degree of disruption that may be caused by a move to another area against the overriding principle of allocating accommodation on a "no choice basis" and outside London and the South East'.
- A similar approach is taken in instances where an applicant has requested accommodation in a particular area because they or a dependant have a disability and need to be, or stay, within that area in order to avoid unreasonable disruption of any treatment or assistance they are receiving to cope with the disability. In such cases decision-makers will need to have 'particular regard' to any local authority support that the applicant or dependant is receiving.
- Requests for accommodation in a particular area in order to maintain family ties should be considered on a case-by-case basis with regard to ECHR Article 8. However, in cases where an applicant needs to maintain contact with a child, the making of additional payments to cover travel expenses[522] in order to allow them to travel to see the child may be considered more appropriate.
- Requests for accommodation in a particular area because children are attending school there will normally be refused, as arrangements can be made for the children to transfer schools. However, an exception may be made if the child has started their final school or college year leading up to their GCSE, Scottish Highers, AS or A-level exams (or equivalents), so long as they have been enrolled in the school for a significant part of the last school year. In those cases, accommodation may temporarily be

521 *Allocation of accommodation policy*, v8.0, pp8–10.
522 See paras 5.210–5.214.

arranged in the area requested. Exceptions may also be made in respect of households including a child with special educational needs (SEN) who has gained entry to an appropriate school. In those cases, accommodation should normally be provided near to the school, save where it is clear that accommodation could be arranged near to an alternative location in which there is an appropriate school that the child could be transferred to.

- Requests for accommodation in a particular area made because the applicant or a dependant is a member of a particular ethnic or religious group and there is a community in the area will normally be refused. However, requests made for accommodation located within reasonable travelling distance of a particular place of worship used by a religious group (for example, a church, mosque or temple) should be agreed wherever possible.
- Requests for accommodation in a particular area because the applicant's legal advisers are nearby will normally be refused.

5.176 Special provision is made for those who are receiving (or who are to receive) treatment from either Freedom from Torture or the Helen Bamber Foundation.[523] In these cases, applicants should generally be accommodated near to the centre where their treatment is taking place. This means accommodation within Zones 1–6 for those in London, and within one hour of the centre elsewhere. Where the applicant commences treatment after accommodation has been provided, then their accommodation needs should be re-assessed and consideration should be given to relocating them to suitable accommodation near to the treatment centre. If the applicant's accommodation is more than three miles from the centre, then reasonable travel expenses should normally be met.

5.177 Specific rules also apply in relation to the use of Napier barracks and 'other communal dormitory forms of accommodation where there is room sharing between unrelated individuals'.[524]

5.178 The policy provides that women and children should not be accommodated there. Nor should those who have been referred into the National Referral Mechanism for the identification of victims of trafficking, persons assessed to be vulnerable, persons with serious mobility problems or physical disabilities and persons with complex mental health problems, among others.

523 *Allocation of accommodation policy*, v8.0, pp11–14.

524 *Allocation of accommodation policy*, v8.0, pp15–17. See paras 5.150–5.152 above on Napier barracks more generally.

5.179 The *Healthcare needs and pregnancy dispersal policy*, v3.0, is a detailed policy dedicated to the accommodation of the most vulnerable categories of applicant. The policy is not prescriptive. Whether, when, how and to where a person is dispersed will vary from case to case. However, the thrust of the policy is to try to ensure that applicants are able to maintain access to appropriate healthcare and treatment. For those receiving general medical treatment, factors relevant to dispersal decisions will include:[525]

- the nature of the treatment being provided;
- whether it can be readily transferred elsewhere in the UK;
- whether the effectiveness of the course of treatment would be affected if interrupted; and
- the effect on any support network.

5.180 Specific provision is made within the *Healthcare needs and pregnancy dispersal policy*, v3.0, for pregnant women, those with HIV, active tuberculosis and severe mental health problems among other things.[526] In particular:

- **Pregnancy**[527] – Cases are to be considered 'sympathetically' on the merits as 'no single solution is likely to be in the interests of all pregnant women'.[528] Those currently accessing care should be accommodated close to a maternity unit as well as existing sources of family and social support. Those with high-risk pregnancies (for example, applicants with HIV, pre-eclampsia or chronic diseases) should be accommodated in areas where they can access the current treating facility. Dispersal at the late stages of pregnancy should only take place at the applicant's or her medical adviser's request. Where there has been a miscarriage, the applicant should not be dispersed until all related procedures and recovery are complete. For still-births, this means that the parent(s) should not be moved until they have been given time for any funeral to take place.
- **HIV**[529] – The Home Office is required to take account of the fact that long-term relationships between doctor and patient are a crucial aspect of successful management which may be disrupted

525 *Healthcare needs and pregnancy dispersal policy*, v3.0, para 4.10.

526 *Healthcare needs and pregnancy dispersal policy*, v3.0, chapter 7. Note, however, that such applicants may be eligible for care and support under the Care Act 2014. See paras 5.94–5.102 and 8.7–8.178.

527 *Healthcare needs and pregnancy dispersal policy*, v3.0, pp38–42.

528 *Healthcare needs and pregnancy dispersal policy*, v3.0, para 7.4.

529 *Healthcare needs and pregnancy dispersal policy*, v3.0, pp31–32.

by dispersal. Also, treatment for associated conditions may be protracted and require input from a variety of specialists, which may not be widely available.

- **Tuberculosis**[530] – Applicants should not be dispersed while their condition is contagious, and thereafter only where the treating clinician advises that onward dispersal can take place.
- **Mental health**[531] – Where the applicant is receiving psychological or psychiatric services, the dispersal process 'must not adversely affect the mental health of an individual and the care he receives'.[532] If the applicant is not receiving psychological or psychiatric services, the decision-makers should not assume this means they are not experiencing mental health problems and should be aware that some applicants 'may be used to a more holistic approach to mental health issues, which may rely more heavily on the support of family and other networks rather than counselling and medication'.[533]

5.181 Vulnerable applicants seeking to avoid dispersal as a result of health problems will invariably need to obtain medical evidence setting out the nature and effect of their conditions, addressing the four bullet points set out at para 5.179 and attesting to the likely impact of dispersal on the applicant. A short letter from the applicant's GP, or an email update from a medical professional working with the applicant (such as a treating consultant), may provide a helpful starting-point which might justify requesting the secretary of state to defer dispersing the applicant until further, more comprehensive evidence can be obtained. Ideally, such evidence will be in the form of detailed report setting out reasoned conclusions in relation to these matters. In obtaining such evidence the qualifications of the medical professional and the extent of their personal knowledge of the applicant should be borne in mind. For example, evidence provided by more senior medical professionals, with specialist qualifications, who have treated the applicant personally over a period of time will often carry the most weight. However, realistically, commissioning an expert report will not be a viable option for many applicants, even those who are ably assisted by third-sector advisers. In such cases written representations focused on the criteria set out above, rooted in a detailed description of the applicant's health conditions as they affect

530 *Healthcare needs and pregnancy dispersal policy*, v3.0, pp34–35.
531 *Healthcare needs and pregnancy dispersal policy*, v3.0, pp35–36.
532 *Healthcare needs and pregnancy dispersal policy*, v3.0, para 7.3.
533 *Healthcare needs and pregnancy dispersal policy*, v3.0, para 7.3.

them on a day-to-day basis, may suffice. Where appropriate, such representations could invite the secretary of state to make further inquiries to obtain any necessary expert evidence.

5.182 The Home Office is likely to seek its own medical advice, usually from NowMedical, to assist in the evaluation of any such evidence submitted by the applicant. Such advice is usually provided following a paper review of the applicant's case and without any face-to-face assessment, often by a practitioner with limited, if any, specialist qualifications. The limitations of such advice, which may need to be drawn to the attention of the Home Office and (if appropriate) the High Court, are discussed at paras 6.81–6.82. In summary, whilst the advice provided by such medical advisers may be of some assistance, the limited extent and character of the medical expertise needed to be borne in mind by decision-makers. The function of the medical adviser in these circumstances is usually to help decision-makers understand the medical issues and to evaluate for themselves the expert evidence placed before them. The medical adviser's advice cannot itself ordinarily constitute expert evidence of the applicant's condition. And decision-makers must give adequate reasons if they are to adopt such medical advice over first-hand expert evidence provided on behalf of an applicant.

5.183 The consequences of a failure to travel to dispersal accommodation are discussed in detail at paras 5.270–5.277. In practical terms, a refusal may lead to the withdrawal of the applicant's support and the cautious option (where practicable) may be for an applicant to accept the offer and then subsequently seek to challenge the dispersal decision.

5.184 There is currently no right of appeal against a dispersal decision. Under IAA 1999 s103(7) the secretary of state may, by regulations, provide for a right of appeal against decisions as to where support is provided. However, that power has never been exercised. This means that a challenge to a dispersal decision would need to be brought by way of judicial review.[534] Examples of judicial review challenges in this context include:

- *R (M) v SSHD*:[535] Decision to disperse father and young son with complex behavioural and educational needs unlawful in circumstances where secretary of state had failed to consider the significant detriment to the son caused by the disruption of the move.

534 See para 5.317.
535 [2002] EWHC 1924 (Admin).

- *R (Blackwood) v SSHD*:[536] Decision to accommodate vulnerable asylum-seeker outside of London, where she had lived for over half her life and where her support network was located, was irrational. In addition, there was a strong case that dispersal would result in a breach of the applicant's rights under ECHR Article 8.
- *R (Muwangusi) v SSHD*:[537] Dispersal of applicant with 'full blown AIDS' and severe depression to Leeds not irrational in circumstances where adequate medical treatment available there. Where dispersal affects an applicant's support networks it is capable of resulting in an ECHR Article 8 breach. However, the interference was proportionate on facts of this particular case.
- *R (Wanjugu) v SSHD*:[538] Maintaining decision to disperse applicant to Swansea not appropriate in the light of subsequent evidence that adequate medical treatment for her PTSD unavailable in the area.
- *R (Gezer) v SSHD*:[539] No breach of ECHR Article 3 where family had suffered 'extremely distressing levels of racist abuse and harassment' following dispersal to Glasgow.
- *R (MG (Iran)) v SSHD*:[540] Dispersal of applicant to accommodation 130 miles from his young son, coupled with a refusal to pay travel expenses, contrary to ECHR Article 8 and BCIA 2009 s55[541] as it impeded the applicant's relationship with his son to the extent that the son's welfare was not being properly safeguarded or promoted. Contact between son and father by telephone or Skype was not an adequate solution.
- *IO v SSHD*:[542] Decision to disperse individual with poor mental health and diagnosis of PTSD away from Bristol, where his long-term support network was located and where he was receiving medical treatment from primary and mental health services, unlawful. The secretary of state had erred in failing to consider the multiple factors set out in the *Healthcare needs and pregnancy dispersal policy*, v3.0, and considering instead solely whether it was 'medically essential' for the claimant to live in Bristol: a question which has no foundation in the policy.

536 [2003] EWHC 97 (Admin), [2003] HLR 44.
537 [2003] EWHC 813 (Admin).
538 [2003] EWHC 3116 (Admin).
539 [2004] EWCA Civ 1730, [2005] HRLR 7.
540 [2015] EWHC 3142 (Admin).
541 See paras 5.302–5.309.
542 [2020] EWHC 3420 (Admin).

Subsistence

5.185 The word 'subsistence' refers here to support under IAA 1999 s95(1) made 'by providing what appear to the secretary of state to be essential living needs of the supported person his dependants (if any)'.[543]

5.186 The prescribed rate of asylum support subsistence payments is set out in AS Regs 2000 reg 10.[544] This is reviewed from time to time. The rate in payment as at March 2023 is £45 per person per week, though reg 10 has not yet been amended to reflect this.[545] This money is paid by means of an allowance which is loaded onto a special debit card (an ASPEN card) each week.[546] Applicants may use their ASPEN card to make payments and to withdraw cash from ATMs. The card cannot be used to make contactless, telephone or internet payments. Any money left over at the end of the week will carry over to the next.[547] Albeit, the Home Office have been known to monitor spending and query the destitution of those who do not spend their full allowance each week.

5.187 Historically, in real terms, asylum support rates have been more generous than they currently are.[548] When the scheme was first introduced in 2000, the rates were set at 70 per cent of income support (IS) rates for adults,[549] and 100 per cent of the IS rates in respect of child dependants. Different rates were adopted in respect of single adults between the ages of 18 and 24 and those aged 25 and over, reflecting a distinction drawn under the IS regime. The rationale for setting the adult rates at a level lower than IS (which is itself intended to meet only subsistence needs) was that asylum-seekers were provided with furnished accommodation and did not have to pay utility bills, coupled with the fact that asylum support was intended to be 'a measure of last resort provided on a short-term basis'. Until 2008 (save in the case of 16- and 17-year-olds) rates were increased annually in line with increases to IS. Then, in 2008, the link with IS was broken and a unitary rate for all single adults was introduced,

543 IAA 1999 s96(1)(b).

544 The power to set the rates in this manner is found in IAA 1999 Sch 8 paras 1 and 3.

545 https://www.gov.uk/asylum-support/what-youll-get.

546 See: www.gov.uk/asylum-support/what-youll-get.

547 *A Home Office guide to living in asylum accommodation*, p27.

548 See *R (Refugee Action) v SSHD* [2014] EWHC 1033 (Admin), [2014] 4 WLUK 360 at para 17 per Popplewell J.

549 IAA 1999 s97(5) specifically allows for rates to be limited to a proportion of certain mainstream welfare benefits.

taking effect from the following year. The rates (with certain exceptions) were then increased in line with the Consumer Price Index (CPI) until the 2011/12 financial year, and were then frozen throughout the financial years 2012/13 and 2013/14. By the end of that period, the rate of asylum support paid to a single adult over the age of 25 had reduced from 70 per cent of IS to 51 per cent.

5.188 In *R (Refugee Action) v SSHD*[550] the High Court allowed a judicial review challenge to the decision to keep the rates of support for the financial year 2013/14 frozen at £36.62, the level which had applied since 2011. Popplewell J found that there were a number of essential living needs which had been overlooked by the secretary of state in reaching this decision.

5.189 Following this case, the secretary of state reconsidered the setting of the rates relying on a new methodology and, in August 2014, reached the decision that the levels of support payable to single adults should nevertheless remain the same. Those rates were then increased very slightly in April 2015 to £36.95, while in July 2015 the rates payable in respect of child dependants was cut significantly from £52.96 to £36.95, bringing them in line with that payable in respect of adults. The High Court dismissed a challenge to the setting of these rates in *R (SG and others) v SSHD*[551] and permission to bring an appeal, focusing on a failure to have due regard to the need to safeguard and promote children's welfare in the setting of the rates, was refused by the Court of Appeal.[552]

5.190 In February 2018, the rates were increased by 80p per week to £37.75[553] further to a review of the cash allowance conducted in 2017, and published in January 2018.[554] This rate was then frozen until June 2020 when, following a provisional review of the cash allowance, it was increased to £39.60.[555] The completion of that review

550 [2014] EWHC 1033 (Admin), [2014] 4 WLUK 360.

551 [2016] EWHC 2639 (Admin), [2016] 10 WLUK 497.

552 *R (JK (Burundi)) v SSHD* [2017] EWCA Civ 433, [2017] 1 WLR 4567.

553 Asylum Support (Amendment) Regulations 2018 SI No 30 reg 2(2).

554 See: https://assets.publishing.service.gov.uk/government/uploads/system/uploads/attachment_data/file/673545/Report_on_review_of_cash_allowance_paid_to_asylum_seekers_-_2017_-_final.pdf.

555 Letter from Chris Philp MP, Parliamentary Under-Secretary of State, to all Chief Executives dated 8 June 2020. This change was implemented in practice without any amendment to AS Regs 2000 reg 10.

led to a decision that the rate should be increased to £39.63[556] and AS Regs 2000 reg 10 was amended to reflect this.[557] The rate was subsequently increased to £40.85,[558] to take account of inflation, and then £45, pursuant to a mandatory order granted by the High Court after the secretary of state failed to act on advice provided to her, recommending that rates be further increased in line with rapidly escalating inflation to ensure essential living needs were met.[559] The reviews contain useful information describing the categories of needs which the secretary of state considers to constitute essential living needs under IAA 1999 s95(1), and the cash value that the secretary of state has allocated to each category. The categories are: food/drink, toiletries, healthcare, household cleaning items, clothing/footwear, travel and communications. Healthcare needs, for example, include 'essential generic non-prescription medication' for headaches (paracetamol and ibuprofen tablets), indigestion and colds (cough linctus, hot drink sachets, nasal inhalers and decongestant/cold and flu capsules). For further details of the cash value breakdown for each category of essential living needs, see the table set out in the judgment of *R (AXG) v SSHD*[560] which should now be read in light of the discussion in *R (CB) v SSHD* as to the need to update these figures for inflation.[561]

5.191 The rate prescribed in AS Regs 2000 reg 10 is the rate which will be paid in the majority, though not all, cases:[562] AS Regs 2000 reg 10(2) provides that 'as a general rule' the prescribed rate is the amount that may be expected to be paid in respect of essential living needs. For example, those in full-board accommodation, whose essential living needs should be met in part by the provision of food at the accommodation, should receive a reduced sum, the reduction

556 Letter from Chris Philp MP, Parliamentary Under-Secretary of State, to all Chief Executives dated 27 October 2020. See further *R (JM) v SSHD* [2021] EWHC 2514 (Admin), [2022] PTSR 260 at paras 48–54 per Farbey J and *R (AXG) v SSHD* [2022] EWHC 56 (Admin) at paras 17–26 per Steyn J for an overview of changes, and the review process underpinning them, between 2017and 2020.

557 Asylum Support (Amendment) Regulations 2021 SI No 99 reg 2

558 Asylum Support (Amendment) Regulations 2022 SI No 78 reg 2.

559 *R (CB) v SSHD* [2022] EWHC 3329 (Admin). The judgment contains a useful overview of the earlier case-law and reviews and the context of the increase to £45.

560 [2022] EWHC 56 (Admin) at para 20.

561 [2022] EWHC 3329 (Admin).

562 See paras 11.208–11.212 for subsistence payments to asylum-seekers who are also potential victims of modern slavery.

calculated by reference to the categories of essential living needs which are actually provided as part of the full catering component of the accommodation.[563] Applying this principle, in October 2020, the Home Office indicated that applicants in full board accommodation would start to receive a weekly payment of £8 to meet the 'costs for buying items to meet needs related to clothes, non-prescription medicines and travel'.[564] The Home Office also announced that it would provide payments to applicants who had been in receipt of support at the relevant time, backdated to March 2020 (in relation to clothing) and July 2020 (in relation to travel). This was provided on an apparent acceptance that those categories of essential living needs (identified in previous reviews of cash allowance) were not met within the full board accommodation.

5.192 The provision of £8 per week represented an improvement on the previous situation whereby those in full board accommodation had generally not received any cash payment at all. The difficulty this caused asylum-seekers supported in such accommodation came into stark relief during the pandemic when charity support, often the safety net for destitute asylum-seekers, stopped being readily available.

5.193 The failure of full board accommodation arrangements to meet all of the accepted categories of essential living needs was challenged in the case of *R (JM) v SSHD*.[565] There, the claimant, had been provided with full board accommodation from 1 May 2020 to 1 February 2021. The claimant received some financial support in addition to the full board provision, but this did not meet all of his essential living needs. In particular, the claimant challenged the failure on the part of the secretary of state to make any provision for communication needs, both in respect of the weekly payment and the backdated payments, and the failure to make backdated payments for travel costs to cover the period prior to July 2020. Farbey J held that the failure to make provision for communication needs was unlawful. But the limitation on backdated payments for travel costs was not. In light of the restrictions on travel in effect prior to July 2020 as a result of the COVID-19 pandemic, it was not irrational for the secretary of state to conclude that travel was not an essential need during that period.

563 AS Regs 2000 reg 10(5).

564 Letter from Chris Philp MP, Parliamentary Under-Secretary of State, to all Chief Executives dated 27 October 2020.

565 [2021] EWHC 2514 (Admin), [2022] PTSR 260.

5.194 In a separate challenge in *R (AXG) v SSHD*[566] the claimant mounted a further challenge to the failure of the secretary of state to make adequate provision for essential living needs to asylum-seekers in full board accommodation. She and her young daughter had been provided with full board accommodation from 1 November 2019 to 28 June 2021, encompassing a period preceding the COVID-19 pandemic and the lockdown restrictions which took effect on 27 March 2020. She argued that the £8 per week that started to be provided to asylum-seekers in full-board accommodation from October 2020 did not accurately reflect her essential living needs which were unmet by the full board provision. In addition to the unlawful failure to meet communications needs that the High Court had already identified in *JM*, the claimant, AXG, also identified the failure to meet healthcare needs, in particular non-prescription medication. She further challenged the secretary of state for the ongoing failure to make any provision for communications, travel, clothing/footwear, non-prescription medication and (to a limited extent) laundry from November 2019 to October 2020, that is prior to the long-stop date for the backdated payments scheme announced by the Home Office, contending that backdated payments should extend to prior to the COVID-19 pandemic.[567] The claimant argued that the secretary of state did not have a discretion as to what essential living needs are met for asylum-seekers in full board accommodation. The duty under IAA 1999 s95 is to meet all needs that the secretary of state has deemed to be essential. Steyn J accepted that the list of essential living needs is that identified in the periodic review of cash allowance for asylum support. The onus is on the secretary of state to determine what essential living needs are not met by the full board provision and to ensure those needs are met by way of provision either in kind or in cash. The failure to do so, Steyn J accepted, would be a breach of IAA 1999 s95. In respect of the claimant's arguments, Steyn J accepted that as a matter of fact and law, the secretary of state had acted unlawfully in failing to provide for essential living needs in relation to communications, travel, clothing/footwear and non-prescription medication during the period claimed by the claimant, including the period prior to the COVID-19 pandemic. Nevertheless, the judge held that the secretary of state had a discretion as to how to remedy that illegality and the decision to impose a long-stop of March

566 [2022] EWHC 56 (Admin).

567 Save for travel, as the legality of the long-stop for that need was dealt with in *JM*.

2020 in relation to the backdated payments was not unlawful. However, the judge did find that the failure to make any backdated payments at all in relation to non-prescription medication from the beginning of the COVID-19 pandemic restrictions, that is from 27 March 2020, was unlawful. The secretary of state had decided not to make any such payment on the premise that healthcare needs were being met in the full board accommodation. There was no evidence that could rationally form a basis for that premise. At the time of writing, this situation has not yet been remedied.

5.195 A further example of a situation in which the secretary of state might depart from the 'general rule' is where the applicant forms part of a mixed household, in which their spouse or partner is in receipt of mainstream welfare benefits such as income support or jobseeker's allowance. This situation is discussed at paras 5.88–5.90 above.

5.196 Additional payments toward the essential living needs of pregnant women and young children are paid at the following rates:[568]

- pregnant woman – £3;
- child aged under one – £5;
- child aged at least one and under three – £3.

5.197 These additional payments are made pursuant to AS Regs 2000 reg 10A. They were introduced in 2003,[569] following a case in which the refusal by the secretary of state to make exceptional payments pursuant to IAA 1999 s96(2)[570] in respect of a mother with HIV who was contemplating breast-feeding her child owing to not having enough money to buy formula milk, was held to be unlawful.[571] The payments are 'intended to allow supported asylum seekers to purchase healthy foods'.[572] They have remained fixed at the same level since their introduction.

5.198 A one-off maternity payment of £300 may also be provided to those supported under IAA 1999 s95(1) or s98(1),[573] to help with the

568 AS Regs 2000 reg 10A.

569 By Asylum Support (Amendment) Regulations 2003 SI No 241 reg 2.

570 See paras 5.210–5.214.

571 *R (T) v Secretary of State for Health* [2002] EWHC 1887 (Admin), [2002] 7 WLUK 747.

572 *Asylum support: policy bulletins instruction,* v9.0, para 24.5.

573 See paras 5.282–5.301 for support under IAA 1999 s98(1).

costs arising from the birth of a new baby.[574] To be eligible for a maternity payment:[575]

- an application must have been lodged in writing and signed by the father or mother of the child;[576]
- the birth must be expected in eight weeks (or less) or the child less than six weeks old;
- the application must have been received by the Home Office within this time window;
- the mother (or expectant mother) must be receiving asylum support;
- the original full birth certificate must have been submitted, or original formal medical evidence of the estimated date of delivery (EDD).

5.199 Maternity payments may also be made where the child was born outside of the UK to a person who is eligible for asylum support and the child is less than three months old, or simply where the child is born to a person in receipt of asylum support and 'the case is an exceptional one'. No guidance is given as to what constitutes an exceptional case, leaving it open to any applicant whose circumstances fall outside of the normal run of cases, to argue that their case is exceptional.

5.200 Provision for maternity payments is made within the *Asylum support: policy bulletins instruction*, v9.0, rather than in the AS Regs 2000. It is to be presumed that the statutory basis for the making of such payments is IAA 1999 ss95(1) and 96(1)(b), and that they are to be regarded as payments to meet essential living needs. It seems unlikely that they could be intended to be exceptional payments, pursuant to IAA 1999 s96(2),[577] since the normal needs of pregnant women and children are not, by definition, exceptional.[578]

Contributions

5.201 In cases where an applicant for asylum support has (or might reasonably be expected to have) some form of income, support or assets

574 See *Asylum support: policy bulletins instruction*, v9.0, paras 24.2–24.4.

575 *Asylum support: policy bulletins instruction*, v9.0, para 24.3.

576 See para 5.235 for how to make an application.

577 See paras 5.210–5.214.

578 *R (Refugee Action) v SSHD* [2014] EWHC 1033 (Admin), [2014] 4 WLUK 360 at paras 36–38 per Popplewell J.

available,[579] but not sufficient to keep them and any dependants from destitution, the secretary of state may this into account in determining what level or kind of support to provide.[580] Alternatively, the secretary of state may decide to pay the applicant asylum support at the standard rate but then require the applicant to make contributions toward the cost of that support.[581] Theoretically, the provision of asylum support to the applicant in such cases may be made conditional upon the prompt payment of these contributions,[582] meaning that if the applicant fails to pay promptly their support may be terminated.[583] However, in practice there is no system for collecting contributions and so the secretary of state delays or reduces the first payment (or payments) of asylum support instead.[584]

Recovery of overpayments

5.202 Under the IAA 1999 and the AS Regs 2000 the secretary of state is entitled to recover payments of asylum support that have been made to an applicant in a variety of circumstances, and by several different methods. We will refer to this as the recovery of 'overpayments' as this is the commonly used term and that which has been adopted in the Home Office policy. However, it will be seen that, in certain circumstances, the use of the term is not strictly accurate.

5.203 The particular circumstances in which the secretary of state is entitled to recover an overpayment of asylum support are as follows:

- An overpayment is recoverable where an applicant for asylum support has, at the time of their application, assets (in the UK or otherwise) which are not capable of being realised but those assets subsequently become available.[585] Although this cannot truly be described as an overpayment (as the applicant was entitled to the support they were provided with at the time it was provided) the

579 See para 5.63 for the types of income, support and assets that may be taken into account.

580 AS Regs 2000 reg 12. See paras 5.88–5.90 on mixed households for an illustration of this.

581 IAA 1999 Sch 8 paras 1 and 10; AS Regs 2000 reg 16(1)–(3).

582 AS Regs 2000 reg 16(4).

583 See paras 5.215–5.219 on the imposition of conditions and paras 5.257–5.277 on the termination of support.

584 'Factsheet 15: Suspending, delaying or reducing s95 payments and back payments of support', Asylum Support Appeals Project, September 2018.

585 IAA 1999 Sch 8 para 11; AS Regs 2000 reg 17. The realisation of the assets would have needed to have been reported to the secretary of state under AS Regs 2000 reg 15(1) and (2)(b).

secretary of state may recover some or all of the asylum support which has been paid to the applicant, 'as if it were a debt'[586] or by way of deductions from any subsequent payments of asylum support. The maximum amount which the secretary of state may recover is whichever is the less of the monetary value of all the asylum support that has been provided to the applicant and the monetary value of the assets concerned.[587]

- An overpayment made in respect of an applicant and any dependants at a time when, it later transpires, they were not actually destitute, may be recovered from the applicant.[588] The maximum amount recoverable is the total value of the support paid during the period when the person in question was not destitute. The overpayment can be recovered as if it were a debt,[589] where the applicant fails to repay it within a reasonable period. What constitutes a reasonable period in this context, is not defined.[590]
- An overpayment made as a result of a misrepresentation or non-disclosure on the part of the applicant is recoverable.[591] To recover overpayments falling within this category, the secretary of state should make an application to the county court for an order requiring the applicant to repay the amount which has been overpaid as a result of the misrepresentation or non-disclosure.[592]
- An overpayment of asylum support made during any period in which the applicant was the subject of an undertaking given by a sponsor pursuant to the Immigration Rules to maintain and accommodate them, may be recovered from the sponsor following proceedings in the magistrates' court.[593] The magistrates'

586 The phrase 'as if were a debt' is used in both the IAA 1999 and the AS Regs 2000 but is not defined. The ordinary meaning of the words would suggest that the secretary of state would be entitled to institute civil proceedings to obtain a judgment in respect of the overpayment, which could then be enforced in accordance with the procedures contained within the Civil Procedure Rules (CPR).

587 AS Regs 2000 reg 17(3).

588 European Communities Act 1972 s2(2); Reception Directive Article 16(1)(b); AS Regs 2000 reg 17A.

589 See fn 609.

590 There is likely to be some overlap between this category and the second category. In such cases, the method of recovery relevant to that category might also be used.

591 IAA 1999 s112.

592 There is likely to be some overlap between this category and the second category. In such cases the method of recovery relevant to that category might also be used.

593 IAA 1999 s113.

court may order the sponsor to repay a sum which is deemed to be 'appropriate' having regard to all the circumstances including the sponsor's income. The sum should not exceed the amount of asylum support which the applicant has received. The order of the magistrates' court will be enforceable as if it were a maintenance order within the meaning of the Magistrates' Courts Act 1980.

- Overpayments made as a result of an error on the part of the Home Office may also be recovered from the applicant.[594] The overpayment may be recovered either as if it were a debt[595] or by way of deductions from future payments of asylum support, but only where it is considered appropriate to do so taking into account the household's circumstances.[596]

5.204 In cases where the secretary of state is entitled to recover the overpayment by means of deductions from future payments of asylum support, the Home Office policy provides that the normal rate of recovery for adults is a 15 per cent weekly deduction. However, applicants should first be given the chance to make representations.[597] The policy might be read as suggesting that overpayments may be recovered by way of deductions in respect of all of the categories of overpayment set out above.[598] However, that is unlikely to be the case. Given the comprehensive nature of the statutory code governing the recovery of overpayments, it is unlikely that the secretary of state has the power to recover overpayments save where the IAA 1999 or AS Regs 2000 expressly allow them to do so.[599]

Backdating

5.205 Applicants may be entitled to receive a back-payment of support where payments have been missed owing to an error on the part of the Home Office or circumstances beyond the applicant's control.[600] Where it is clear that the applicant was at fault, then requests for back-payments will generally be refused. However, the overriding principle in dealing with requests for back-payments 'is one of

594 IAA 1999 s114; AS Regs 2000 reg 18.

595 See fn 609.

596 *Conditions of support*, v2.0, p25 (www.gov.uk/government/publications/withdrawal-of-asylum-support-where-a-breach-of-conditions-has-occurred-instruction).

597 *Conditions of support*, v2.0, p25.

598 *Conditions of support*, v2.0, p25.

599 See *R (Child Poverty Action Group) v SSWP* [2010] UKSC 54, [2011] 2 AC 15.

600 *Conditions of support*, v2.0, p25.

fairness, both in terms of operating the system and in terms of transparency in applying the system requirements'.[601]

5.206 Where an applicant is successful in an appeal against a refusal of support[602] the FTT (Asylum Support) may substitute the correct decision, with effect from the date of the original decision appealed against, with the effect that the award should be backdated to the time of the refusal.[603]

Expenses

5.207 As well as support in the form of accommodation and subsistence payments, the secretary of state may provide support under IAA 1999 s95(1):

- to enable the applicant (if they are the asylum-seeker) to meet what appear to the secretary of state to be expenses (other than legal expenses or other expenses of a prescribed description) incurred in connection with their claim for asylum;[604]
- to enable the asylum-seeker and any dependants to attend bail proceedings in connection with their detention under any provision of the Immigration Acts;[605]
- to enable the asylum-seeker and any dependants to attend bail proceedings in connection with the detention of a dependant of theirs under any provision of the Immigration Acts.[606]

5.208 Surprisingly, given the importance of these matters, at the time of writing there is no publicly available guidance or policy setting out when such support will be provided or how applicants might go about obtaining it.[607] However, the Explanatory Notes to the IAA 1999 provide that the first of these three categories of support would encompass 'the costs of preparing and copying certain documents,

601 *Conditions of support*, v2.0, p25.

602 See paras 5.310–5.274 on appeals and remedies.

603 *R (SSHD (National Asylum Support Service)) v Asylum Support Adjudicators and (1) Berkadle (2) Perera* [2001] EWHC Admin 881 at paras 92–93 per Gibbs J. See further *Asylum support: policy bulletins instruction*, v9.0, para 15.6.

604 IAA 1999 s96(1)(c).

605 IAA 1999 s96(1)(d).

606 IAA 1999 s96(1)(e). The Immigration Acts in this context are listed in UK Borders Act 2007 s61(2).

607 Transport is generally provided for an applicant to attend their own bail hearing from detention so the lack of guidance in relation to such travel expenses is unlikely to cause problems in practice. More generally, the procedure for making applications for asylum-support is set out at paras 5.221–5.246.

and travelling to interviews with the [Home Office] associated with the asylum seeker's claim for asylum'.[608]

5.209 Applicants are also entitled to 'reasonable travelling expenses' in connection with attendance at the FTT (Asylum Support) for the purposes of a statutory appeal against an adverse asylum support decision.[609] Tickets will generally be sent to applicants in advance of the hearing date and section 2 of the Notice of Appeal asks applicants to provide an address to which travel documents can be sent.

Additional payments in exceptional cases

5.210 IAA 1999 s96(2) provides that:

> If the Secretary of State considers that the circumstances of a particular case are exceptional, he may provide support under section 95 in such other ways as he considers necessary to enable the supported person and his dependants (if any) to be supported.

Support provided under this provision is generally referred to as 'additional support'.

5.211 In *R (Refugee Action) v SSHD*[610] Popplewell J explained that IAA 1999 s96(2) is not a general power to provide support in exceptional circumstances. Rather, it is a power to meet an applicant's essential living needs, either by payments in cash or in kind,[611] in exceptional cases where the applicant's needs fall outside the scope of that which would generally be covered by means of the weekly subsistence payments of £45.[612] It is important to note the focus of IAA 1999 s96(2) is materially different to section 96(1) and concerns needs that are additional to the generality of essential living needs identified in the review of the cash allowance discussed above at paras 5.188–5.194. Thus, just as an applicant cannot seek additional support under IAA 1999 s96(2) for needs which are already accounted for in asylum support subsistence payments, the secretary of state cannot refuse to meet 'essential living needs' of the kind intended to be met

608 IAA 1999 Explanatory Notes para 300. See further para 5.220 for ways in which travel expenses may be met outside of IAA 1999 Part VI.

609 IAA 1999 s103(9). See further paras 5.330–5.371 for appeals.

610 [2014] EWHC 1033 (Admin), [2014] 4 WLUK 360 at paras 36–38. See further *R (JM) v SSHD* [2021] EWHC 2514 (Admin), [2022] PTSR 260 at para 147 per Farbey J.

611 Home Office policy suggests needs may also be met by changes to accommodation arrangements or by changes to 'other arrangements'. See *Applications for additional support*, Home Office, March 2017, p4.

612 See paras 5.185–5.200.

by these subsistence payments by asking the applicant to make a request for section 96(2) support.

5.212 The circumstances in which such payments may be made, and the application process for obtaining such support, is contained in the Home Office policy *Applications for additional support*. The policy suggests that, in the opinion of the Home Office, the weekly subsistence payments should generally be sufficient to cover the following needs:[613]

- food;
- clothing;
- toiletries;
- non-prescription medication;
- household cleaning items;
- communications;
- travel;
- the ability to access social, cultural and religious life.

5.213 Other essential living needs such as warmth, fuel, towels and bedding are intended to be met by the provision of furnished accommodation with utilities bills paid and household goods and linens provided. As such, in order to be granted additional support an applicant will generally need to show either that:[614]

- they have a need that is essential and different from the needs of asylum-seekers in general; or
- they have an essential need which is common to all asylum-seekers but which is more costly to meet owing to their particular circumstances.

5.214 Examples of circumstances in which IAA 1999 s96(2) support are given include a person who needs to make a large amount of additional journeys (perhaps in order to maintain family ties),[615] a person who needs extra help with shopping following an operation and a person who needs to replace belongings after a fire. Needs that can

613 *Applications for additional support*, p4.

614 *Applications for additional support*, p5. The policy does, however, stress that while this is the general rule, applications will need to be considered on a case-by-case basis.

615 See *Allocation of accommodation policy*, v8.0, p7 on the payment of travel expenses to maintain family ties. See further *R (MG (Iran)) v SSHD* [2015] EWHC 3142 (Admin) where the dispersal of an applicant to a location 150 miles from his son coupled with a failure to pay travel expenses constituted a breach of ECHR Article 8.

be met elsewhere, for example, by the provision of support by a local authority, will not generally be met.

Conditions

5.215 The provision of support under IAA 1999 s95(1) may be made subject to conditions.[616] For example, a condition that the applicant should reside at the accommodation provided to them will invariably be imposed. The conditions must be set out in writing and a copy provided to the applicant.[617] This document is known as the 'asylum support agreement'.[618]

5.216 Conditions of support which limit the ability of applicants freely to enter or leave their accommodation (for example, curfews) will require careful scrutiny as they may constitute false imprisonment or a breach of ECHR Article 5 (right to liberty and security).[619]

5.217 Breach of certain conditions (for example, conditions relating to residence,[620] reporting[621] and conduct[622]) may be taken into account by the secretary of state in deciding whether to provide, suspend or discontinue the provision of support,[623] or in deciding what kind and level of support to provide.[624] Conditions may be attached to the provision of any of the various types of support which may be provided under IAA 1999 s95(1).[625]

5.218 If the secretary of state has reason to believe that:[626]

- an applicant or any dependants are not residing at the accommodation which has been provided for them;
- an applicant or any dependants are using the accommodation for some other purpose; or
- someone other than the applicant together with any dependants is residing in the accommodation,

616 IAA 1999 s95(9).

617 IAA 1999 s95(10)–(11).

618 *Discontinuing asylum support after failure to report with an ARC*, Home Office, October 2016, p5 (www.gov.uk/government/publications/discontinuing-asylum-support-after-failure-to-report-with-arc-instruction).

619 *R (NB and others) v SSHD* [2021] EWHC 1489 (Admin) at paras 279–331 per Linden J applying *R (Jalloh) v SSHD* [2020] UKSC 4, [2021] AC 262.

620 AS Regs 2000 regs 19(1)–(2) and 20(1)(d), (k) and (6)(c).

621 AS Regs 2000 reg 20(1)(i) and (6)(d).

622 AS Regs 2000 reg 20(1)(a)–(c).

623 See further paras 5.247–5.277 on how support may be brought to an end.

624 AS Regs 2000 regs 19–20.

625 See paras 5.141–5.201 for the various ways in which support may be provided.

626 IAA 1999 s125.

they may apply to the magistrates' court for a warrant to enter the accommodation. The warrant should be granted where the justice of the peace is satisfied that there is reason to believe that one or more of these criteria are met. The warrant may only be executed at reasonable times and with reasonable force.

5.219 The secretary of state has analogous powers to attach conditions to the provision of temporary support under IAA 1999 s98(1)[627] and to obtain a warrant to enter premises.[628]

Other miscellaneous forms of support

5.220 The additional forms of support set out below may also be available to asylum-seekers. Although they are not all provided under IAA 1999 Part VI, they are dealt with here for completeness to set out the spectrum of entitlements which asylum-seekers may potentially access:

1) Asylum-seekers living outside of the three-mile radius of their reporting location and receiving asylum support may be eligible to receive assistance with travel expenses for reporting.[629] The statutory basis for this was previously NIAA 2002 s69 which has now been superseded by IA 2016 Sch 10 para 35.[630]
2) Those in receipt of asylum support are entitled to access primary and secondary NHS services without charge. Those with an HC2 certificate may also access: free NHS prescriptions; free NHS dental treatment; free NHS wigs and fabric supports; free NHS eye tests; vouchers towards the cost of glasses; and refunds of necessary travel costs to and from hospital for NHS treatment under the care of a consultant.[631]
3) Assistance with funeral costs may be available in certain limited circumstances.[632]
4) The secretary of state may provide services by way of education (including English language lessons) and sporting or other developmental activities, to recipients of asylum support for the

627 See paras 5.282–5.301.
628 IAA 1999 s125(1).
629 *Reporting and offender management*, Home Office, January 2018, pp31–33.
630 Note, however, the provisions are not identical and their scope may not be the same.
631 See *Asylum support: policy bulletins instruction*, v9.0, Q13; www.gov.uk/asylum-support/what-youll-get; and chapter 10 on healthcare.
632 *Asylum support: policy bulletins instruction*, v9.0, chapter 18.

purpose of maintaining good order. At the time of writing, no such services have been made available.[633]

5) School-age children of those in receipt of asylum support may be eligible for free school meals.[634]
6) Two-year-old children of those in receipt of asylum support may be eligible for free nursery places.[635]
7) Those in receipt of asylum support who are also receiving civil legal aid in respect of their asylum claim are, in certain circumstances, entitled to the costs of their travel for the purposes of giving instructions to their legal adviser.[636] This only applies where the applicant is destitute and where, at the point the matter was started, no more local provider was available to take on the case. The disbursement 'will be the cost of the return fare on the cheapest available mode of public transport'.

The application process

Making an application

Overview

5.221 The procedure for making an application for asylum-support has its legal basis in IAA 1999 Sch 8 para 12 and AS Regs 2000 reg 3. Either an asylum-seeker or a dependant of an asylum-seeker may make an application for support.[637] The application may be for the applicant alone or for the applicant together with any dependants.[638] The application must be made by completing, in full and in English, the

633 IAA 1999 Sch 8 para 4; AS Regs 2000 reg 14.

634 Education Act 1996 s512ZB; *Free school meals guidance for local authorities, maintained schools, academies and free schools*, Department for Education, April 2018.

635 Childcare Act 2006 s7; Local Authority (Duty to Secure Early Years Provision Free of Charge) Regulations 2014 SI No 2147. This provision is to be extended to the children of parents in receipt of support under IAA 1999 s4(2). See *Extending eligibility for the free early education entitlement for two year olds*, Department for Education, August 2019.

636 *2018 Standard civil contract specification category specific rules: immigration and asylum*, Legal Aid Agency (LAA), paras 8.48–8.50 (available from: www.gov.uk/government/publications/standard-civil-contract-2018).

637 IAA 1999 s95(1); AS Regs 2000 reg 3(1). See AS/15/03/32761, 19 March 2014, FTT (Asylum Support).

638 See *Change of address*, Home Office, January 2015.

application form issued by the secretary of state for that purpose.[639] The form currently in use is the ASF1.[640] The ASF1 form needs to be sent to the asylum support casework team, and can either be completed online and emailed or printed out and posted.[641]

5.222 The secretary of state may not entertain an application if:[642]

- the ASF1 form has not been used;
- the ASF1 form has not been completed in full;
- the ASF1 form has not been completed in English;
- the secretary of state is not satisfied that the information provided is complete or accurate;
- the secretary of state is not satisfied that the applicant is co-operating with any further inquiries which the secretary of state has made about any matter connected with the application.[643]

5.223 Where the secretary of state elects to make further inquiries a 'Request for further information' will be sent to the applicant.[644] The applicant is required to respond to this request within five working days of receipt.[645] If the applicant fails, without reasonable excuse, to respond within that time-frame, then the secretary of state is entitled to conclude that they are not co-operating with inquiries.[646] An applicant has no right of appeal against a refusal by the secretary of state to entertain their application.[647] In addition, a refusal to entertain an application in these circumstances has the consequence that any support provided to the applicant under IAA 1999 s98(1) will

639 AS Regs 2000 reg 3(3). This requirement does not apply if the applicant is already receiving support and is seeking to add a dependant to their application: AS Regs 2000 reg 3(6). See para 5.232.

640 See: www.gov.uk/government/publications/application-for-asylum-support-form-asf1.

641 See: www.gov.uk/asylum-support/how-to-claim.

642 AS Regs 2000 reg 3(4). This rule was introduced pursuant to NIAA 2002 s57. See paras 5.137–5.140; and *Asylum support: policy bulletins instruction*, v9.0, chapter 10. The rule does not apply if the applicant is already receiving support and is seeking to add a dependant to their application: AS Regs 2000 reg 3(6). See para 5.232.

643 Such inquiries are made pursuant to AS Regs 2000 reg 3(5).

644 At the time of writing, the making of such requests has decreased significantly.

645 AS Regs 2000 reg 3(5A). 'Working days' in this context means any day other than a Saturday, a Sunday, Christmas Day, Good Friday or 'a day which is a bank holiday under section 1 of the Banking and Financial Dealings Act 1971 in the locality in which the applicant is living': AS Regs 2000 reg 3(7).

646 AS Regs 2000 reg 3(5B).

647 See para 5.317.

come to an end.[648] This means it is very important for applicants to respond to requests for further information within the prescribed timescale or, where they fail to so, provide the secretary of state with good reason for that failure without delay.

5.224 The secretary of state has statutory powers under IAA 1999 ss126–127 to obtain information from the postal service and from property owners which may be used (among other circumstances) to check the accuracy of information provided by applicants in connection with their applications.

The role of Migrant Help

5.225 Although the decision as to whether an applicant is eligible for support is made by the Home Office, at the present time applications are sent via the charity Migrant Help. The Home Office has contracted with Migrant Help to provide advice to asylum-seekers accessing asylum support[649] and its assistance in making the application can be obtained by calling the asylum support customer contact centre. It also serves as a 'post box' for corresponding with the Home Office. Migrant Help will generally be the first point of contact for applicants seeking any of various forms of support outlined in this chapter. However, it is the Home Office which retains ultimate responsibility for decision-making and, in legal terms, the actions of Migrant Help are attributable to the secretary of state.[650]

5.226 In January 2019 the Home Office announced that Migrant Help had been awarded a new contract for 'the Advice, Issue Reporting and Eligibility Assistance services (AIRE), which will be a single integrated and national service for asylum seekers'.[651] The purpose of the service is to 'provide advice and guidance to service users on the asylum process, their rights and signposting different services'. This contract commenced in September 2019. As well as providing advice in relation to asylum support (including payment issues), the topics Migrant Help is contracted to assist with include: how to claim

648 AS Regs 2000 reg 3(5C). See para 5.300.

649 *An inspection of the Home Office's management of asylum accommodation provision February – June 2018*, Independent Chief Inspector of Borders and Immigration, November 2018, para 2.1.

650 *Ali (Iraq) v Serco Ltd* [2019] CSIH 54 at paras 52–57 per Lady Dorian; *R (AQS) v SSHD* [2020] EWHC 843 (Admin) at para 22 per Robin Knowles J; *Re Mahmud's application for judicial review* [2021] NIQB 6 at para 134 per Friedman J.

651 See further: www.gov.uk/government/news/new-asylum-accommodation-contracts-awarded.

asylum; finding legal representation; the asylum process; accessing healthcare; and any other asylum issues.[652]

5.227 Organisations advocating on behalf of asylum-seekers who are seeking advice in relation to an applicant's entitlement to support should also consider contacting the Asylum Support Appeals Projects (ASAP) telephone advice line.[653]

Evidence

5.228 The ASF1 form is designed to illicit the information necessary to establish that the applicant and any dependants are eligible for asylum-support.[654] Unsurprisingly, much of the form is given over to the questions designed to establish whether the applicant is destitute,[655] inquiring into the applicant's accommodation situation and assets. Since the burden of proof lies on the applicant to establish that they are eligible for asylum support, it is vitally important to provide sufficient evidence and explanatory material to prove that they are destitute. For, example:

- If an applicant has been asked to leave the accommodation which they have been occupying it will be important to provide some evidence that this is that case. A letter from the person or organisation which has provided the accommodation will often suffice. The letter will need to make clear when the applicant is required to leave, since an applicant who has adequate accommodation available for a period in excess of 14 days will not be regarded as destitute if their other essential living needs are being met. A clear explanation from the accommodation provider as to why the applicant has to leave may also assist, to avoid any suggestion on the part of the Home Office that the accommodation provider and the applicant have colluded to try to make it appear that the applicant is eligible for support. Where an individual who has been accommodating the applicant is not willing to provide a letter then the applicant should provide an explanation for why this is.
- Where an applicant is applying for asylum support in circumstances where they have been without support for a prolonged period, an explanation and evidence to show how they have managed without support to date and what has changed, is likely

652 *A Home Office guide to living in asylum accommodation*, p14.

653 See: www.asaproject.org/contact/adviceline.

654 See paras 5.9–5.90.

655 See paras 5.57–5.90.

to be essential. The *Assessing destitution* policy suggests that, in such cases, 'it will usually be a reasonable assumption that they have had access to alternative forms of accommodation or other forms of assistance during the period' and that '[a]n explanation of why this accommodation and assistance is no longer available will therefore usually be required'.[656]

- Any contradictions within any documents or evidence provided by the applicant, or that emerge from checks carried out by the Home Office (such as Experian searches), will need to be explained as inconsistencies are likely to be taken by the Home Office as an indicator that the applicant is not being truthful. This issue tends to arise in circumstances where applicants have falsely exaggerated their assets in order to obtain entry clearance so that they are able to come to the UK to lodge their asylum claim. The information in their entry clearance application may then be relied on by the Home Office as the basis for finding that the applicant is not destitute.[657] In such cases, it is important for applicants to explain the reasons for the inconsistency and provide evidence to establish that their assets are at the level presently claimed, and not the level asserted at the time they sought entry clearance.
- Where an applicant has assets abroad (for example, a family home or a car) which cannot be realised within 14 days,[658] an explanation of why this is, is likely to be needed. The difficulties in selling a property from abroad within 14 days are perhaps obvious, but it is less clear why a car could not be sold within this time period and this begs an explanation. Evidence of any particular difficulties involved in carrying out a specific transaction is likely be of assistance. For example, if a lawyer is needed, if the applicant needs the consent of co-owners, if a witness is needed to a signature, if the transfer of funds requires access to a UK bank account or if the applicant needs to be present in person for the transaction to take place.
- Where an applicant has one or more bank accounts, bank statements will generally need to be obtained going back at least six months in order to establish the availability of any funds.[659] Where bank statements cannot be obtained, evidence of why that is and what steps have been taken to obtain them (including any steps

656 *Assessing destitution*, v4.0, p9.
657 See paras 5.69–5.71.
658 AS Regs 2000 reg 6(4). See paras 5.57–5.70.
659 *Assessing destitution*, v4.0, p11.

that have been taken to try to register for online banking, for example) is likely to be essential. Applicants may also need to provide evidence of any closed bank accounts, particularly where the account was closed recently, and bank statements to show what happened to any funds that had been in those accounts.

5.229 There are no prescribed forms of evidence which the secretary of state can or cannot accept. However, in general, documentary evidence (such as bank statements) which have, where necessary and practicable, been translated by means of a certified translation,[660] and the provenance of which can be readily verified, will usually carry more weight than less formal evidence (such as emails or text messages from friends in the applicant's country of origin), evidence of questionable provenance or evidence in the applicant's mother tongue. However, the realities of the situation need to be born in mind. Evidence falling in the latter category is better than nothing, and particularly for those who have fled their home country at very short notice and who do not have anyone left whom they can contact, or any means of contacting them, when the amount of formal documentary evidence which they can access is likely to be minimal. In those circumstances, an explanation of why it is that the evidence cannot be obtained should be provided instead.

False or dishonest statements and delay or obstruction

5.230 At the beginning of the ASF1 form applicants are warned that a 'Failure to disclose all necessary information or to provide false information regarding yourself or any dependant may lead to information being passed to the police or other agencies for investigation'. At the end of the form applicants are then invited to sign to acknowledge that they may be prosecuted if they give false information. These warnings refer (without saying so expressly) to IAA 1999 ss105–107 which create a series of criminal offences, with which those who have made false or dishonest statements in order to obtain benefits or payments under IAA 1999 Part VI, and those who, without reasonable excuse, withhold information or delay or obstruct the exercise by the Home Office of its functions under IAA 1999

660 Note, however, *ZN v SSHD* AS/17/09/37288, 27 April 2018, FTT (Asylum Support) where the Principal Judge accepted at para 35 that it may not be reasonable to expect applicants to produce certified translations and that the Home Office may be better placed to do so. The Home Office, in general, does not insist on certified translations and in some cases has been known to pay for documents to be translated where they are critical to an applicant's case.

Part VI, may be charged. IAA 1999 ss109A–109B endow the secretary of state with certain powers of entry, search, seizure and arrest in connection with the commission of these offences. These are supplemented by more general powers under IAA 1999 ss125–127 permitting the secretary of state to enter premises and obtain information in respect of the applicant's circumstances.[661]

5.231 The existence of such punitive powers means that it is imperative that advisers assisting applicants in filling out their applications go through the form with the applicant extremely carefully to check that the information that has been recorded is accurate.

Adding dependants

5.232 Generally, applicants who wish support to be provided to them together with their dependants[662] will have made that clear within the appropriate section of the ASF1 form. However, where that has not been done – for example, because the dependant arrived in the UK after the asylum-seeker was granted support – a request to this effect can be made in writing, supplemented by evidence to establish that the person is a dependant for asylum support purposes. It is not necessary for a new ASF1 form to be completed.[663]

Requests from non-dependants to be accommodated together

5.233 Circumstances may arise where two or more applicants for support wish to be accommodated together, but there is no relationship of dependancy between them for asylum support purposes.[664] Most commonly this will arise where a household containing a young adult – for example, a son or daughter aged 18 or over – enter the UK together and seek asylum. Under IAA 1999 Part VI and the AS Regs 2000, the secretary of state is not obliged to accommodate non-dependants together in such circumstances. However, under Human Rights Act 1998 s6 and ECHR Article 8, any interference by the secretary of state with the household's family life must be necessary and proportionate, which may, in practice, require the secretary of state to secure accommodation for them together or, at the very least, in such a way as to ensure that family life can continue. This is reflected in Home Office policy which provides that:

661 See paras 5.215–5.219 and 5.221–5.224.
662 See paras 5.50–5.56 and 5.141–5.143.
663 *Dependants on an asylum support application*, para 3.
664 See paras 5.50–5.56.

> When considering requests for separate support applications to be 'linked together' in this way, caseworkers should take into account the wishes of all parties, the availability of suitable accommodation, [and] Article 8 ECHR considerations (right to respect for private and family life) . . .[665]

Additional payments and expenses

Additional payments toward the essential living needs of pregnant women and young children[666]

5.234 Applicants who are seeking the additional payments which are payable as a result of the presence of a pregnant woman or young child in the household can make this known by providing the relevant information within the ASF1 form. Alternatively, where a person to whom support is already being provided becomes eligible for such payments then a written request for these payments should be made, signed by the applicant and supported by 'original, credible written confirmation of pregnancy such as form MAT B1,[667] a letter from a community midwife or a letter from a GP' or, as the case may be, the child's original birth certificate.[668]

Maternity payment[669]

5.235 Applicants who are seeking the £300 maternity payment[670] will need to submit a form MAT B1, an original birth certificate or other 'original formal evidence' in order to apply for the payment.[671] The grant can either be requested at the time the initial application for asylum support is made or, if the applicant becomes pregnant after support has been provided, by contacting the support team who dealt with the initial application.[672]

Expenses[673]

5.236 At the time of writing there is no publicly available guidance or policy setting out how applicants should go about seeking financial

665 *Dependants on an asylum support application*, para 5.

666 See paras 5.196–5.197.

667 A maternity certificate, verifying the pregnancy and giving the expected due date (EDD).

668 *Asylum support: policy bulletins instruction*, v9.0, para 24.6.

669 See paras 5.198–5.200.

670 See para 5.198.

671 *Asylum support: policy bulletins instruction*, v9.0, para 24.2.

672 See: www.gov.uk/asylum-support/what-youll-get.

673 See paras 5.207–5.209.

assistance either to meet expenses (other than legal expenses) in connection with their claim for asylum, or to attend bail proceedings. Applicants seeking such assistance might sensibly contact Migrant Help in the first instance.

Additional payments in exceptional cases[674]

5.237 Applicants who are seeking the additional support which is available in exceptional cases where an applicant's essential living needs are not being met by the provision of accommodation and subsistence payments alone,[675] will need to complete a form ASF2[676] setting out:[677]

- the details of their need;
- their particular circumstances;
- the further support required;
- its cost;
- its likely duration.

Where possible, documentary evidence should be provided to support the application.

Backdating[678]

5.238 Applicants seeking back payments of support should direct their request to the casework team dealing with their application, together with evidence that the payment was missed owing to an error on the part of the Home Office, or that the applicant had a valid reason for failing to collect the payment. Home Office policy requires applications for back payments to be considered within five working days.[679]

Repeat applications

5.239 If an applicant has been refused asylum support and their appeal to the FTT (Asylum Support)[680] has been dismissed, then the secretary of state may not entertain any further application for support unless

674 See paras 5.210–5.214.
675 See paras 5.185–5.200.
676 See: www.gov.uk/government/publications/application-for-additional-asylum-support-form-asf2.
677 *Applications for additional support*, pp5–6.
678 See paras 5.205–5.206.
679 See *Asylum support: policy bulletins instruction*, v9.0, paras 15.1–15.7 and Q48–Q49.
680 See paras 5.310–5.371.

they are satisfied that there has been a 'material change in the circumstances'.[681] Save for this there is nothing within IAA 1999 Part VI or the AS Regs 2000 to prevent an applicant who has been refused asylum support from making a fresh application for support. Indeed, some applicants make multiple applications. However, unless there has been a material change in the applicant's circumstances since the previous refusal then it is very likely that the secretary of state will reach the same decision for precisely the same reasons.

5.240 Different considerations apply where an applicant has had their support suspended or discontinued.[682] In this situation, the way in which the secretary of state will approach the application will depend on the reason why support was suspended or discontinued. The cases fall into two categories.

5.241 The first category encompasses those cases where support has been suspended or discontinued because either the applicant has abandoned their accommodation[683] or has failed to comply with a reporting requirement.[684] In either of these situations, if the applicant is traced or voluntarily reports to the police, the secretary of state or an immigration officer, then 'a duly motivated decision based on the reasons for the disappearance shall be taken as to the reinstatement of some or all of the supported person's or his dependant's or both of their asylum support'.[685]

5.242 The second category encompasses those cases where support has been suspended or discontinued for any other reason. In such cases, the secretary of state is not to entertain the application unless:[686]

- there has been a material change in circumstances since the suspension or discontinuation;
- there are exceptional circumstances which justify the application being entertained.

5.243 In this context, a material change of circumstances is one which, if the applicant were a supported person, would have had to have been notified to the secretary of state under AS Regs 2000 reg 15.[687]

681 IAA 1999 s103(6).
682 See paras 5.257–5.265 on the suspension and discontinuation of support.
683 AS Regs 2000 reg 20(1)(d).
684 AS Regs 2000 reg 20(1)(i).
685 AS Regs 2000 reg 20(5).
686 AS Regs 2000 reg 21(1); *Conditions of support*, v2.0, p17.
687 See paras 5.91–5.92.

Delay

5.244 Regrettably, delay in the administration of the asylum support system is commonplace. Delay is, in some respects, less problematic in relation to applications for support under IAA 1999 s95(1), owing to the availability of interim support under IAA 1999 s98(1),[688] than it is in respect of applications for support under IAA 1999 s4(2).[689] However, this is not to say that it is not a serious problem. For example, it can be problematic in cases where the Home Office does not accept that the applicant is entitled to support under IAA 1999 s98(1) or there is a delay in providing that support also. Alternatively, there may be delay in providing accommodation that is adequate for the needs of the applicant and his or her household.[690]

5.245 Whether an applicant can challenge the delay in their case, and the precise legal basis of that challenge, turns on the nature of the duty under IAA 1999 s95(1), read with Asylum Seekers (Reception Conditions) Regulations 2005 reg 5(1) and, in cases where the delay is in the provision of adequate accommodation, IAA 1999 s96(1). Perhaps surprisingly, the nature of this duty is not (or at least as not been treated by the High Court as) entirely settled. The Court of Appeal in *R (A) v National Asylum Support Service*[691] described the duty to accommodate as being 'absolute and immediate', and described the duty to provide adequate accommodation in similar terms. Similarly, Steyn J in *R (AXG) v SSHD*[692] remarked that: 'The s95 duty applies from the moment a determination is made that it is owed.' This would tend to suggest that, from the point at which the duty is accepted, any failure to provide (adequate) accommodation is unlawful and challengeable by way of judicial review. That would mirror the approach set out by the Court of Appeal in relation to the mainstream homelessness legislation, which operates in a very similar context.[693] However, several recent decisions of the High Court have characterised the duty as a 'reason-

688 See paras 5.282–5.301.

689 See paras 6.9–6.200.

690 See paras 5.154–5.168 for adequacy of accommodation provided under IAA 1999 s95(1).

691 [2003] EWCA Civ 1473, [2004] 1 WLR 752 at para 59 per Waller LJ.

692 [2022] EWHC 56 (Admin) at para 71.

693 *R (Elkundi) v Birmingham City Council* [2022] EWCA Civ 601, where the Court of Appeal characterised the analogous duty to provide 'suitable' accommodation to homeless persons under Housing Act 1996 Part VII as 'immediate, unqualified and non-deferrable'.

able endeavours' or 'best efforts'[694] duty, or a duty to provide adequate accommodation within a 'reasonable period of time'.[695] Such characterisations reflect the general principle of public law that statutory functions must be discharged within a reasonable period.[696] However, they would seem to conflict with the Court of Appeal's statement of principle in the *R (A) v National Asylum Support Service* case, and to have been formed without any close consideration of the language or purpose of the statutory provisions in question.[697] The better view may be that the duty is immediate and unqualified but that the High Court in judicial review proceedings will be unlikely to grant a mandatory order to compel compliance with the duty where the secretary of state is doing all that they reasonably can to comply.[698] Whether or not the secretary of state is doing all that they reasonably can is generally something that can be identified in pre-action correspondence, by requesting details of what steps have been taken and when to identify alternative accommodation. In addition, what is reasonable, is context specific: greater efforts will be expected in more urgent and serious cases, such as those where the applicant is facing homelessness or a risk of harm.

5.246 In any event, in an asylum support case, the fact that the applicant is facing destitution should generally constitute a compelling factor militating in favour of a swift process. In addition, in some cases,[699] a failure to act expeditiously may also result in a breach of Human Rights Act 1998 s6 as the failure to provide accommodation and/or subsistence to meet essential living needs may well result in a breach

694 See *R (Chkharchkhalia) v SSHD* [2019] EWHC 2232 (Admin) at para 37 but contrast *R (AMA) v SSHD* [2021] EWHC 2646 (Admin) at para 10.

695 See *R (JM) v SSHD* [2021] EWHC 2514 (Admin), [2022] PTSR 260 at para 98; *R (AMA) v SSHD* [2021] EWHC 2646 (Admin) at para 10; *R (ALW) v SSHD* [2022] EWHC 557 (Admin).

696 See, for example, *R (Sathanantham) v SSHD* [2016] EWHC 1781 (Admin), [2016] 4 WLR 128 at para 87 per Edis J (in the context of delays in the provision of support under IAA 1999 s4(1)); *R (Humnyntskyi) v SSHD* [2020] EWHC 1912 (Admin), [2021] 1 WLR 320 at paras 166–167 per Johnson J (in the context of delays in the provision of support under IA 2016 Sch 10 para 9(2)); and *R (DMA) v SSHD* [2020] EWHC 3416 (Admin) at para 178 per Robin Knowles J (in the context of delays in the provision of support under IAA 1999 s4(2)).

697 Contrast with the approach of the Court of Appeal in *R (Elkundi) v Birmingham City Council* [2022] EWCA Civ 601, which treated the matter as a question of statutory construction.

698 See *R (Elkundi) v Birmingham City Council* [2022] EWCA Civ 601 and *R (Parul) v SSHD* [2022] EWHC 2143 (Admin) discussing and applying *Elkundi* when considering the grant of relief in the asylum support context.

699 Typically those where the applicant has not been accommodated in initial accommodation under IAA 1999 s98(1). See paras 5.282–5.301.

of ECHR Article 3.[700] In the related context of support for destitute failed asylum-seekers under IAA 1999 s4(2),[701] Home Office policy used to provide that in cases where a refused asylum-seeker had submitted further submissions in support of a fresh claim for asylum[702] and sought support IAA 1999 s4(2) while those submissions were considered, their application for support would not generally be considered substantively until up to 15 working days had elapsed. In *MK v SSHD*[703] Foskett J held this policy was unlawful in that it gave rise to 'a significant risk that the Article 3 rights of a significant number of applicants for section 4 support will be breached'.[704] More recently, in *R (DMA) v SSHD*,[705] the High Court was called upon once again to consider systemic delays in the provision of support under IA 1999 s4(2). Robin Knowles J held that the delays in the cases before him[706] were unlawful and that the secretary of state was in breach of their duties under IAA 1999 s4(2) and Human Rights Act 1998 s6 in failing to properly monitor the delays in the provision of accommodation.[707]

Ending the provision of support

5.247 There are two situations in which an applicant's entitlement to asylum support may come to an end.[708] The first is where the applicant is no longer eligible for support.[709] Typically this will be because their asylum claim has been determined, meaning that they are no longer an asylum-seeker; alternatively, it may be that there has been a change in circumstances meaning that the applicant is no longer destitute. The second is where there has been some default on the part of the applicant, or their dependants, which gives the secretary of state a discretion either to suspend or to discontinue the provision of support. These two categories will be discussed in turn at paras

700 See *R (Limbuela) v SSHD* [2005] UKHL 66, [2006] 1 AC 396 discussed at paras 5.127–5.131.
701 See paras 6.9–6.200.
702 See paras 3.42–3.43.
703 [2012] EWHC 1896 (Admin).
704 [2012] EWHC 1896 (Admin) at para 184 per Foskett J.
705 [2020] EWHC 3416 (Admin).
706 Consisting of 45 days, 60 days, 105 days and 151 days, respectively.
707 See further *R (Humnyntskyi) v SSHD* [2020] EWHC 1912 (Admin), [2021] 1 WLR 320.
708 See *Asylum support: policy bulletins instruction*, v9.0, Q28.
709 See paras 5.9–5.90 for the eligibility criteria.

5.251–5.256 and 5.257–5.277, respectively. Where an applicant's support is discontinued before it otherwise would have been, the applicant has a right of appeal to the FTT (Asylum Support).[710]

5.248 The procedure by which the applicant's support will come to an end will vary according to which of these two categories the applicant falls within. However, there is one element of the procedure which is common to both situations and which may conveniently be dealt with at the outset. That is the means by which the applicant's right to occupy any accommodation which they have been provided with is brought to an end.

5.249 In accordance with the common law,[711] a notice to quit must be served on an applicant in order to bring their right to occupy the accommodation provided under IAA 1999 Part VI to an end. Although the requirement to serve a notice to quit arises from the common law, the form and content of the notice are prescribed by IAA 1999 Sch 8 para 9 and AS Regs 2000 reg 22. If, as a result of the provision of asylum support, an applicant has a tenancy or licence to occupy accommodation and he or she is given a notice in writing specifying a period:

- of not less than seven days, in cases where support is being terminated either as a result of some default on the part of the applicant or their dependants, of the applicant ceasing to be destitute or of the applicant being moved to other accommodation;[712]
- that is either seven days or that ends on the date on which the applicant's asylum claim is treated as determined[713] (whichever is greater), in cases where support is being terminated as a result of a final decision having been reached on the applicant's asylum claim,[714]

then their tenancy or licence is treated as ending with the period specified in that notice.[715]

710 See paras 5.310–5.371.

711 The statutory regimes for security of tenure contained in the Housing Acts 1985 and 1988 do not apply to accommodation provided under the IAA 1999. See Housing Act 1985 ss79–80 and Sch 1 para 4A; and Housing Act 1988 s1 and Sch 1 para 12A.

712 AS Regs 2000 reg 22(3)(a).

713 See paras 5.29–5.35 for how to calculate this date.

714 AS Regs 2000 reg 22(3)(b).

715 AS Regs 2000 reg 22(1). Exceptionally, notice of less than seven days may be given where the circumstances of the case justify it. See AS Regs 2000 reg 22(4). The use of this power may be appropriate in circumstances where it was necessary to move an occupant at short notice, for example, because of a fire at the property or because he or she was being subject to domestic violence. See *Asylum support: policy bulletins instruction*, UKVI, December 2015, Q59.

5.250 These statutory requirements displace the normal common law rules on the termination of licences and tenancies.[716] A written notice from the applicant's accommodation provider meeting these requirements will be sufficient to bring the applicant's occupation rights to an end. Save for these requirements the notice does not need to be in any particular form – a simple letter will suffice – and nor does it need to contain any particular information. The formalities of Protection from Eviction Act 1977 s5, which provides that a notice to quit will only be valid where (among other things) it contains certain prescribed information about the occupant's rights,[717] do not apply in relation to accommodation provided under IAA 1999 Part VI.[718] Similarly, Protection from Eviction Act 1977 s3 does not apply meaning that the accommodation provider or the Home Office is not required to institute court proceedings before requiring the applicant to leave the accommodation.[719]

Applicant no longer eligible for support

5.251 If an applicant ceases to be:

- an asylum-seeker;[720] or
- destitute,[721]

then their entitlement to support will end, since the requirements of IAA 1999 s95(1) are no longer satisfied.

716 At common law, to be valid, a notice to quit would need to expire either at the end of the rental period of the tenancy or on the first day of any period. See *Crate v Miller* [1947] KB 946, CA. In respect of a bare (ie non-contractual) licence with no rental period, only 'reasonable' notice is required. See *Minister of Health v Bellotti* [1944] KB 298, CA. These requirements do not apply. However, any contractual requirement within the applicant's occupation agreement stipulating a longer notice period would take precedence over these minimal statutory requirements, on the footing that accommodation providers are free to provide more generous rights than those guaranteed under the statute.

717 See Notices to Quit etc (Prescribed Information) Regulations 1988 SI No 2201.

718 Protection from Eviction Act 1977 s3A(7A).

719 See *Ali (Iraq) v Serco Ltd* [2019] CSIH 54 for an unsuccessful attempt, on the part of a failed asylum-seeker, to argue that a court order was required under the analogous legislation in Scotland. It is understood that the reclaimer intends to appeal in that case.

720 See paras 5.17–5.49.

721 See paras 5.57–5.90.

Applicant ceases to be an asylum-seeker

5.252 An applicant will (save for the exception discussed at para 5.253 below) cease to be an asylum-seeker for asylum support purposes at the point at which their claim is 'determined'. This question of when a claim is regarded as having been determined is discussed in detail at paras 5.29–5.44. In broad terms, the asylum claim will be treated as having been determined either 28 days after the applicant is notified of a positive decision or is successful in their appeal, or 21 days after they have been notified of a negative decision or declaration of inadmissibility, or have exhausted any appeal rights. For present purposes, the important point is that there is a 'grace period' built into the statutory scheme meaning that an applicant does not cease to be an asylum-seeker for asylum support purposes the moment a decision is reached on their claim. They will continue to be eligible for support for at least a further 21 or 28 days,[722] and longer if an appeal is lodged. According to Home Office policy, this 'gives applicants the opportunity to make arrangements for additional accommodation and support or to make arrangements for their departure from the UK'.[723]

5.253 The exception to the general rule arises where the applicant's household includes a dependant child aged under 18. In these circumstances, if the applicant's asylum claim is rejected, they will continue to be treated as an asylum-seeker for asylum support purposes so long as the child is under 18 and they remain in the UK.[724] Such applicants remain eligible for support.[725]

5.254 Home Office policy is to notify applicants that their support may come to an end in 21 or 28 days at the point at which they are advised of the decision on their asylum claim.[726] However, where the decision is negative, 'a review should be set for the 11th day after the decision to refuse leave was received by the applicant to establish whether an appeal has been submitted'.[727] The Home Office will also need to notify the accommodation provider so that the appropriate notice to quit can be served.[728]

722 An additional two-days may be added to these periods where the decision is posted. See IAA 1999 s94(9); and para 5.36.

723 *Ceasing section 95 support instruction*, v1.0, p13.

724 IAA 1999 s94(5)–(6). See paras 5.45–5.49.

725 *Ceasing section 95 support instruction*, v1.0, p13.

726 *Ceasing section 95 support instruction*, v1.0, p6.

727 *Ceasing section 95 support instruction*, v1.0, p7.

728 *Ceasing section 95 support instruction*, v1.0, p9. See paras 5.249–5.250.

5.255 An applicant will also cease to be an asylum-seeker for asylum support purposes if their asylum claim is withdrawn.[729] They will cease to be eligible for support at this juncture. There is no grace period of 21 or 28 days though, if the applicant has been accommodated, a notice to quit[730] will still need to be served by the accommodation provider.[731]

Applicant ceases to be destitute

5.256 Applicants are required to notify the secretary of state of changes in their employment status and financial circumstances under AS Regs 2000 reg 15(1)–(2).[732] Where the change is such that the applicant is no longer destitute then they will no longer be entitled to support under IAA 1999 s95(1). Home Office policy is that any such change must be verified prior to support being terminated or suspended. If a Home Office caseworker receives information which leads them to believe that an applicant's change in circumstances warrants further investigation, then the applicant's case should be referred to a compliance officer. Support should not be terminated or suspended until the investigation has concluded.[733] If the applicant has been accommodated, a notice to quit will need to be served by the accommodation provider.[734]

Default on the part of the applicant or their dependants

5.257 The secretary of state may suspend or discontinue the provision of asylum support under IAA 1999 s95(1) if:[735]

- the secretary of state has reasonable grounds to believe that the applicant or their dependant has committed a serious breach of the rules of their accommodation;[736]
- the secretary of state has reasonable grounds to believe that the applicant or their dependant has committed an act of seriously violent behaviour, whether in their accommodation or elsewhere;[737]

729 See paras 5.37–5.38.
730 See paras 5.249–5.250.
731 *Ceasing section 95 support instruction,* v1.0, p7.
732 See paras 5.91–5.92.
733 *Ceasing section 95 support instruction,* v1.0, p8.
734 AS Regs 2000 reg 22(1) and (2)(c). See paras 5.249–5.250.
735 AS Regs 2000 reg 20.
736 AS Regs 2000 reg 20(1)(a).
737 AS Regs 2000 reg 20(1)(b). See further paras 11.249–11.261.

- the applicant or their dependant has committed an offence under IAA 1999 Part VI, which includes (but is not limited to) a failure to report a relevant change of circumstances;[738]
- the secretary of state has reasonable grounds to believe that the applicant or their dependant has abandoned their accommodation, without first informing the secretary of state;[739]
- the applicant has failed to respond to a request for further information by the secretary of state, relating to their eligibility for asylum support, within a reasonable period (of not less than five working days);[740]
- the applicant has failed, without reasonable excuse, to attend an interview relating to their asylum support claim;[741]
- the applicant has failed to respond to a request for further information by the secretary of state, relating to their asylum claim, within a reasonable period (of not less than ten working days);[742]
- the secretary of state has reasonable grounds to believe that the applicant or their dependant has unduly benefited from the provision of asylum support as a result of having concealed financial resources;[743]
- the applicant or their dependant has not complied with a reporting requirement;[744]
- the secretary of state has reasonable grounds to believe that the applicant or their dependant has made a second claim for asylum prior to their first claim being determined;[745]
- the applicant or their dependant have failed to comply with a residence condition.[746]

738 AS Regs 2000 reg 20(1)(c); IAA 1999 s105(1)(c)–(d); AS Regs 2000 reg 15; *Asylum support: policy bulletins instruction*, UKVI, December 2015, Q43. For changes in circumstances see paras 5.91–5.92. For offences under IAA 1999 Part VI see paras 5.230–5.231.

739 AS Regs 2000 reg 20(1)(d).

740 AS Regs 2000 reg 20(1)(e).

741 AS Regs 2000 reg 20(1)(f). The applicant must have been given no less than five working days' notice of the interview: AS Regs 2000 reg 20(2).

742 AS Regs 2000 reg 20(1)(g).

743 AS Regs 2000 reg 20(1)(h).

744 IAA 1999 s95(9A); AS Regs 2000 reg 20(1)(i).

745 AS Regs 2000 reg 20(1)(j).

746 AS Regs 2000 regs 20(1)(k), 20(6)(c) and 19(2).

5.258 The distinction between the discontinuance and suspension of support is that the former refers to a permanent state of affairs[747] whereas the latter is temporary. Home Office policy is that a suspension will only be appropriate for a maximum of 30 days.[748] A decision to discontinue support carries with it a right of appeal[749] whereas a decision to suspend does not and would (if appropriate) need to be challenged by way of judicial review.

5.259 The circumstances in which support provided to a destitute asylum-seeker by a local authority (prior to the coming into force of IAA 1999 Part VI) could be discontinued were considered by the Court of Appeal in the case of *R v Kensington and Chelsea RLBC ex p Kujtim*.[750] The court held that where an applicant:

> . . . either unreasonably refuses to accept the accommodation provided or if, following its provision, by his conduct he manifests a persistent and unequivocal refusal to observe the reasonable requirements of the local authority in relation to the occupation of such accommodation, then the local authority is entitled to treat its duty as discharged and to refuse to provide further accommodation.[751]

5.260 However, such a decision should be made:

> . . . only after being satisfied of [the applicant's] persistent and unequivocal refusal to comply with the local authority's requirements, coupled with a careful consideration of his current needs and circumstances. Either or both may involve consideration of any relevant medical condition or infirmity known to the local authority. Before concluding that there has been such refusal, it will plainly be desirable for a local authority to write a letter of final warning of the kind written by the respondents to the applicant in this case.[752]

5.261 This approach – of requiring 'persistent and unequivocal' conduct in order to justify a discontinuance of support – has been applied by the FTT (Asylum Support) in a number of cases.[753] The FTT (Asylum Support) has also, in several cases, proceeded on the basis that

747 In this chapter we use the words 'discontinuance' and 'termination' of support interchangeably.

748 *Ceasing section 95 support instruction*, v1.0, p12.

749 See paras 5.321–5.327.

750 [1999] 4 All ER 161, (2000) 32 HLR 579, CA.

751 *Kujtim* at p593 per Potter LJ.

752 *Kujtim* at p594 per Potter LJ.

753 See the landmark decision of *DK v SSHD* AS/02/04/2665, 1 May 2002, FTT (Asylum Support) at para 35; *JKV v SSHD* AS/12/03/28234, 12 April 2012, FTT (Asylum Support) at para 22; *XZC v SSHD* AS/11/08/27297, 25 August 2011, FTT (Asylum Support) at para 22.

although the civil standard of proof applies in establishing a breach of conditions, given the importance of what is at stake for the applicant, a high degree of probability will be required.[754]

5.262 Particular care will need to be taken prior to taking any decision to suspend or discontinue the support that is being provided to a household with children.[755] In particular, the Home Office will need to take into account the impact of any decision on the family before proceeding.[756] Before taking any action to discontinue support, the Home Office 'should liaise with the local authority, notifying them that the Home Office plans to discontinue support from the family'.[757]

5.263 Account must also be taken of the special needs of any person who is vulnerable within the meaning of Reception Directive Article 17.[758] This encompasses:[759]

- a child under the age of 18;
- a disabled person;
- an elderly person;
- a pregnant woman;
- a lone parent with a child under the age of 18; or
- a person who has been subjected to torture, rape, or other serious forms of psychological, physical or sexual violence,

who has had an 'individual evaluation of his situation that confirms he has special needs'. Any decision to discontinue support must be taken 'individually, objectively and impartially . . . based on the particular situation of the person concerned' and reasons must be given to explain the decision.[760] Decisions should also be proportionate and a complete withdrawal of all support may result in a breach of the

754 See *JKV v SSHD* AS/12/03/28234, 12 April 2012, FTT (Asylum Support) at para 16; and *XZC v SSHD* AS/11/08/27297, 25 August 2011, FTT (Asylum Support) at para 14, relying on the analogous approach advocated by Lord Scarman in *R v SSHD ex p Khawaja* [1984] AC 74, HL.

755 In such a case the duty under BCIA 2009 s55 will be engaged. See paras 5.302–5.309.

756 *Conditions of support*, v2.0, p13.

757 *Conditions of support*, v2.0, p14. See paras 9.12–9.69 for the local authority's duties.

758 See AS Regs 2000 reg 20(3), *Conditions of support*, v2.0, pp6–8 and 13; and *Discontinuing asylum support after failure to report with an ARC*, pp10–11. See further *R (NB and others) v SSHD* [2021] EWHC 1489 (Admin) at paras 145–158 for the continued effect of the Reception Directive following the departure of the UK from the EU.

759 Reception Directive Article 17 implemented by Asylum Seekers (Reception Conditions) Regulations 2005 reg 4.

760 AS Regs 2000 reg 20(3).

Reception Directive, particularly where there are children involved.[761] The decision letter will need to explain why the discontinuation of support is consistent with the Home Office's obligations under BCIA 2009 s55.[762]

5.264 Support should not be discontinued where it would result in a breach of the applicant's rights under ECHR Article 3 or Article 8.[763] This is not the same test as the statutory destitution[764] test under IAA 1999 s95(1). However, there is a significant degree of overlap between the destitution test under IAA 1999 s95(1) and the ECHR Article 3 threshold. In *R (Limbuela) v SSHD* Lord Bingham explained that the threshold would be likely to be crossed 'if there were persuasive evidence that a late applicant was obliged to sleep in the street, save perhaps for a short and foreseeably finite period, or was seriously hungry, or unable to satisfy the most basic requirements of hygiene'.[765] Whereas the destitution test will be satisfied where the applicant does not have adequate accommodation or any means of obtaining it (whether or not their other essential living needs are met) or has adequate accommodation or the means of obtaining it, but cannot meet their other essential living needs.[766] Plainly these two tests are not identical[767] and there will be some divergence in the outcome of the application of these two tests around the margins. For example, an applicant might have adequate accommodation available to them and have some charitable support toward clothing and meals. However, they might be lacking the resources to obtain washing powder, cleaning materials and disinfectant and other such 'essential

761 *Haqbin v Federaal Agentschap voor de opvang van asielzoekers* Case C-233/18 [2020] 1 WLR 2633, CJEU. See *R (NB and others) v SSHD* [2021] EWHC 1489 (Admin) at paras 145–158 for the continued effect of the Reception Directive following the departure of the UK from the EU.

762 *Conditions of support*, v2.0, p14. See paras 5.302–5.309.

763 Human Rights Act 1998 s6. See paras 5.127–5.131. It is these Articles which are most likely to be relevant. However, see the landmark decision of *DK v SSHD* AS/02/04/2665, 1 May 2002, FTT (Asylum Support) for an unusual example of a case where an applicant unsuccessfully sought to rely on ECHR Article 9 to resist the discontinuance of support. Article 4 may also be of relevance in cases involving victims of human trafficking. See paras 11.156–11.161.

764 See paras 5.57–5.90.

765 [2005] UKHL 66, [2006] 1 AC 396 at para 9 per Lord Bingham; paras 56–63 per Lord Hope; and para 78 per Baroness Hale. See further the Introduction.

766 IAA 1999 s95(3).

767 See *R (Limbuela) v SSHD* [2005] UKHL 66, [2006] 1 AC 396 at paras 57–58 and 62 per Lord Hope.

living needs'.[768] Such an applicant would be regarded as destitute as their essential living needs were not being met but would be unlikely to meet the ECHR Article 3 threshold. In addition, the Article 3 threshold will be crossed where there is an 'imminent prospect' of breach.[769] Whereas support under IAA 1999 s95 is available to those asylum-seekers who appear to be destitute or *likely to become destitute within 14 days*.[770] Meaning that an adequately accommodated applicant who was facing homelessness in the next ten days might be eligible for support under IAA 1999 s95(1) without crossing the Article 3 threshold. However, an applicant facing imminent street homelessness will satisfy both the Article 3 threshold and the destitution test. The practical consequence of this is that there will be a significant core of applicants who would, by virtue of their having been eligible for asylum support in the first place, face an Article 3 breach were their support to be discontinued.[771] In such cases, the only lawful way in which the secretary of state could exercise their discretion would be to maintain the provision of asylum support.

5.265 Guidance on some of the circumstances in which support may be suspended or discontinued can be found spread across various Home Office policies. These are discussed below at paras 5.266–5.277. The circumstances in which an applicant whose support has been discontinued may seek to re-apply for support are discussed at paras 5.239–5.243.

Guidance on changes of circumstances

5.266 Very limited guidance on the discontinuation of asylum support following a failure to report a relevant change of circumstances[772] is contained in the *Conditions of support* policy,[773] which simply provides that the 'level and type of support provided may need to be reassessed following a change in circumstances'.

768 See paras 5.83–5.90.

769 See *R (Limbuela) v SSHD* [2005] UKHL 66, [2006] 1 AC 396 at para 8 per Lord Bingham and para 62 per Lord Hope.

770 IAA 1999 s95(1); AS Regs 2000 reg 7. The period is 56 days where the applicant is already in receipt of support.

771 The obvious exceptions to this would be where discontinuance is proposed on the basis that the applicant is no longer destitute and/or has concealed financial resources. See para 5.256 and AS Regs 2000 reg 20(1)(h).

772 AS Regs 2000 reg 20(1)(c); IAA 1999 s105(1)(c)–(d); AS Regs 2000 reg 15; *Asylum support: policy bulletins instruction*, UKVI, December 2015, Q24. See paras 5.91–5.92 for the obligation to report a relevant change of circumstances.

773 Home Office, May 2021, pp10–12.

Guidance on discontinuation where the applicant is absent from accommodation

5.267 Absence from accommodation[774] is dealt with in the *Asylum support: policy bulletins instruction*[775] which provides that the applicant should not be absent without caseworker permission for 'more than seven consecutive days and nights, or for more than a total of 14 calendar days and nights in a six-month period'.[776] However, before discontinuing support in these circumstances, the Home Office caseworker dealing with the case should write to the applicant:[777]

- stating that there is evidence to suggest that they are in breach of their residence condition;
- giving particulars of any specific absences with dates (where available);
- inviting the applicant to explain their absence;
- explaining that support may be discontinued and the accommodation withdrawn if the applicant does not either continue to reside there or provide a reasonable explanation for their absence;
- informing them of their right to appeal against any decision to discontinue support;
- reminding them that they are under a duty to comply with the conditions attached to their support.

5.268 Caseworkers are then required to consider any explanation offered by the applicant for their absence prior to making a decision on whether to discontinue support. Examples of circumstances in which it might be deemed unreasonable to discontinue support are where the applicant has absented themself owing to harassment or other unacceptable behaviour, or where the applicant has been temporarily staying with friends or family (who do not have the capacity to support them in the long term) owing to ill-health.

Guidance on discontinuation where the applicant fails to report

5.269 Guidance on the discontinuation of support where an applicant has failed to report[778] is contained in *Discontinuing asylum support after failure to report with an ARC*. The policy provides that attempts should be made to contact the applicant to ascertain whether they

774 Which might fall within either AS Regs 2000 reg 20(1)(d) or (k).

775 UKVI, May 2021. See further *Conditions of support*, v2.0, pp14–15.

776 *Asylum support: policy bulletins instruction*, v9.0, Q39.

777 *Asylum support: policy bulletins instruction*, v9.0, Q39.

778 IAA 1999 s95(9A); AS Regs 2000 reg 20(1)(i).

had a reasonable excuse for failing to report. Examples of situations in which an applicant may have a reasonable excuse for failing to report include where they 'may not have been able to report due to circumstances beyond their control, perhaps because of illness, family emergency, family death, an asylum interview, transport strike, or adverse weather conditions'.[779]

Guidance on discontinuation where the applicant fails to travel to dispersal accommodation

5.270 Guidance on how to deal with cases in which an applicant has failed to travel to dispersal accommodation made available under IAA 1999 s95(1) can be found in chapter 19 of the *Asylum support: policy bulletins instruction.*[780] We deal with this guidance here, under the heading of discontinuation, because in practical terms – as will be become apparent – this is what happens. An applicant who fails to travel to dispersal accommodation will find that their support comes to an end. However, strictly speaking, whether or not this amounts to a discontinuation, within the meaning of AS Regs 2000 reg 20, is open to debate.

5.271 Current Home Office policy does not treat a failure to travel as a circumstance which would permit support to be discontinued, stating that 'a failure to travel will not result in a decision to discontinue or suspend support'.[781] Rather, it is treated as a circumstance in which the Home Office has made accommodation available to the applicant in performance of its duty, but the applicant has chosen not to avail themself of it.[782] The practical consequence of which is that, unless the applicant had a reasonable excuse for failing to travel or is willing to adhere to new travel arrangements, a decision will be made to withdraw the offered accommodation. Examples of reasonable justifications for a failure to travel include medical issues or circumstances in which there was a misunderstanding over the travel arrangements.[783] The applicant will also be required to leave any Home Office accommodation which they currently occupy, though the offer of dispersal accommodation will remain open to them

779 *Discontinuing asylum support after failure to report with an ARC*, pp7–8.

780 V9.0, UKVI, May 2021.

781 *Asylum support: policy bulletins instruction*, v9.0, para 19.1.

782 Some support for this approach may be found in the context of homelessness law in the case of *R (Brooks) v Islington LBC* [2015] EWHC 2657 (Admin), [2016] PTSR 389.

783 *Asylum support: policy bulletins instruction*, v9.0, para 19.1.1.

should they change their position.[784] The policy provides that single applicants and childless couples will have to leave their current accommodation on the third working day after the decision is served on them; and households including children will have to leave on the sixth working day after the decision is served.[785] If the applicant does change their position and agree to take up the dispersal accommodation then, if the same address is no longer available, alternative accommodation should be sought in the same area. However, where the applicant maintains their position not to take up the dispersal accommodation, then they will be left without support.

5.272 The approach set out in this policy seeks to characterise the withdrawal of support in these circumstances as something other than a discontinuance, within the meaning of AS Regs 2000 reg 20. The policy instead refers to 'clos[ing] off the existing accommodation and support arrangements',[786] and telling applicants that they are 'required to leave their current accommodation and that they will not be able to continue to access subsistence (cash) support'[787] and that they 'no longer have permission to remain in their current accommodation'.[788] The distinction between closing off an applicant's support because they failed to travel to dispersal accommodation and discontinuing an applicant's support because they failed to comply with a condition that they should reside at their dispersal accommodation[789] is – from the applicant's point of view – a purely semantic one. However, the legal ramifications of this distinction are significant. By characterising the withdrawal of support as something other than a discontinuance, the applicant faces the loss of their support without any right of appeal.[790] In addition, this approach allows support to be withdrawn at shorter notice than would be the case if this situation were treated as a discontinuance. As noted, for single applicants or childless couples, support will be withdrawn upon two days' notice.[791] Whereas seven days' notice would normally need to

784 *Asylum support: policy bulletins instruction*, v9.0, Q58 and para 19.1.1.
785 *Asylum support: policy bulletins instruction*, v9.0, Q58 and paras 19.1.1–19.2.
786 *Asylum support: policy bulletins instruction*, v9.0, para 19.1.
787 *Asylum support: policy bulletins instruction*, v9.0, Q58.
788 *Asylum support: policy bulletins instruction*, v9.0, para 19.1.1.
789 AS Regs 2000 reg 20(1)(k).
790 *Asylum support: policy bulletins instruction*, v9.0, para 19.1.
791 *Asylum support: policy bulletins instruction*, v9.0, para 19.1.1.

be given if support were being discontinued as the result of a failure to comply with a residence condition.[792]

5.273 It is questionable whether the approach set out in the current Home Office policy is entirely correct. The issue of whether or not the withdrawal of support following a failure to travel to dispersal accommodation constituted a discontinuation decision carrying with it a right of appeal, was the subject of the Court of Appeal decision in *Dogan v SSHD*.[793] The applicant in that case was a destitute asylum-seeker. He applied to the Home Office for asylum support and, together with his wife, was provided with temporary support under IAA 1999 s98(1)[794] in accommodation in Luton, while his application was considered. In due course the Home Office accepted that the applicant was eligible for asylum support and offered him dispersal accommodation in Liverpool. The documentation which accompanied the offer of accommodation in Liverpool stated that 'support will only be available to you in a dispersal area', that 'should you fail to travel, you will not receive any further support at your current address' and 'there should be no expectation that an alternative will be offered'. Failure to travel, the applicant was informed, was a breach of the conditions of his agreement with the Home Office which provided that 'when you receive notice about the accommodation we have offered you, you must move to the accommodation in line with the travel instructions we give you'. A travel date to Liverpool was fixed for around two weeks later, during which time the applicant remained in the accommodation in Luton which was now provided pursuant to IAA 1999 s95(1). In the event, the applicant did not travel to Liverpool and his support in Luton was withdrawn.

5.274 The applicant appealed to the asylum support adjudicator.[795] In the course of the proceedings, the secretary of state sought to argue that the adjudicator lacked the jurisdiction to decide the appeal. An appeal right under IAA 1999 s103(2)[796] only arises where 'the Secretary of State decides to stop providing support for a person under section 95 before that support would otherwise have come to an end'. The decision in Mr Dogan's case, the secretary of state

792 AS Regs 2000 regs 20(1)(k) and 22(1), (2)(a) and (3)(a). See further paras 5.249–5.250 on notices to quit.

793 [2003] EWCA Civ 1673, [2004] HLR 25.

794 See paras 5.282–5.301.

795 The predecessor of the FTT (Asylum Support).

796 See paras 5.310–5.371 for appeal rights.

argued, did not fall within the ambit of that provision. The Chief Asylum Support Adjudicator rejected this argument, reasoning that:

> The words 'stop providing support' must be given their ordinary everyday meaning. This must therefore include suspension or discontinuation of support. The fact that in this and other similar cases the Secretary of State argues that he has not decided to discontinue support but merely to suspend it until the open offer of accommodation if taken up in a dispersal area, does not entitle the Secretary of State to deprive the appellant of his right of appeal . . .[797]

5.275 She went on to allow the applicant's appeal on the footing that he had not been given adequate notice of the proposed dispersal. In *R (SSHD) v Chief Asylum Support Adjudicator*[798] Silber J allowed the secretary of state's application for judicial review of this decision, holding that:

> 32. . . . a decision to stop support to an asylum seeker only gives rise to an appeal under section 103(2) if before the decision under challenge to stop payment is made, the claimant already possessed an existing right to section 95 support which then had been prematurely terminated by the decision under challenge in the appeal proceedings. The claimant could only have possessed that right to pre-existing section 95 support if he or she had already and previously been granted to him or her. In other words, the right of appeal under section 103(2) of the 1999 Act for a stoppage appeal only arises if the asylum seeker can show that two separate decisions had been made, namely a first one to grant it and then a second later one, being the one being challenged, to terminate it prematurely.
>
> 33. So an asylum seeker cannot pursue a stoppage appeal if the Secretary of State only makes one decision granting either support for a limited period of time or support subject to a condition, such as that it will only be provided if the claimant moves to a particular area; in that event, there is no decision to stop providing support in the words of section 103(2) before that support would otherwise come to an end . . .

The Court of Appeal upheld this decision. The adjudicator had no jurisdiction to hear an appeal in these circumstances.

5.276 The important point about the courts' analyses for present purposes is that neither the judgment of the High Court or the Court of Appeal provides authority for the secretary of state's proposition – which is reflected in the current policy – that the withdrawal of support where an applicant fails to travel does not constitute a discontinuance, because support remains available but the applicant has

797 [2003] EWCA Civ 1673, [2004] HLR 25 at para 16.
798 [2002] EWHC 2218 (Admin).

chosen not to avail themself of it. That proposition was rejected by the Chief Asylum Support Adjudicator in the passage quoted above and did not form part of the arguments advanced by the secretary of state in the litigation or in the reasoning of the High Court or the Court of Appeal. Applying Silber J's guidance, it is an oversimplification to say that withdrawing support upon a failure to travel is not a discontinuation giving rise to a right of appeal. Rather, whether or not such a decision amounts to a discontinuation will depend on the circumstances of the case. If the secretary of state makes a single decision to grant support that is conditional upon an applicant travelling to dispersal accommodation and support is then stopped after they fail to do so, that will not constitute a discontinuation decision. If, on the other hand, a decision is taken to provide support to an applicant in dispersal accommodation and a second decision is subsequently taken to prematurely terminate that support because, for example, the applicant is failing to comply with a condition of residence then, arguably at least, that will constitute a discontinuation decision under AS Regs 2000 reg 20(1)(k),[799] will give rise to a right of appeal under IAA 1999 s103(2) and will necessitate the service of a notice to quit complying with AS Regs 2000 reg 22(3)(a).[800]

5.277 However, whatever the correct legal analysis, the underlying fact is that a refusal to travel to dispersal accommodation is likely to lead to the applicant's support being stopped. As such, where an applicant is concerned about the adequacy of location of dispersal accommodation consideration should be given to accepting the offer, traveling to the accommodation and then subsequently seek to challenge the dispersal decision.

Making the transition to mainstream support

5.278 In theory, once an applicant has been granted asylum as well as having the right to work, they should, if necessary, be entitled to access a wide range of mainstream welfare benefits, such as UC, and accommodation under Housing Act 1996 Parts VI and VII.[801] Ideally, applicants should be able to make the transition seamlessly from asylum support to employment or mainstream support without any break in entitlement. However, in practice there are frequently problems and delays in making this transition, and the consequences

799 Read with AS Regs 2000 regs 20(6)(c) and 19(2).

800 See paras 5.249–5.250.

801 See chapters 4 and 7.

may be dire. In a report written in 2014, *The move on period: an ordeal for new refugees*,[802] the British Red Cross observed that:

> Accessing both the labour market and mainstream benefits is particularly difficult when individuals recently granted status do not have specific documents, such as the Biometric Residence Permit (BRP) and a National Insurance number (NINo) – as recently demonstrated in a Refugee Council report (Doyle, 2014). Many people become destitute because of such difficulties.[803]
>
> Destitution during the move-on period can have dramatic consequences. A baby boy, known as 'EG', starved to death as his ill mother fell unconscious for several days. The family had become destitute as she struggled to obtain benefits and support once her asylum application was approved (Westminster Safeguarding Children Board, 2012).
>
> In 2013, the Home Affairs Select Committee (2013: 38) described the situation of destitute refugees as 'especially concerning'. They recommended that: 'asylum support should not be discontinued until the Department for Work and Pensions has confirmed that the recipient is receiving mainstream benefits'.

5.279 In a follow up report in 2018, *Still an ordeal: the move-on period for new refugees*,[804] the British Red Cross observed that not only did these problems persist but that they had actually been exacerbated by certain policy changes, such as the continued roll-out of UC:

> Under the Universal Credit system, the risk of destitution is particularly acute for refugees due to the design of key aspects of the application process. In particular, the incompatibility of the 28-day move-on period (after which asylum support is terminated) with the minimum five-week (35-day) waiting period for the first Universal Credit payment leaves refugees facing almost inevitable destitution. All of the refugees in our sample who had applied for Universal Credit experienced difficulties and/or delays with their applications, none of them received their Universal Credit payment promptly at the end of the five-week period, and all were also left destitute at the end of the 28-day move-on period, for periods ranging from six days to 72 days (ten weeks).[805]

5.280 Guidance published by the DWP suggests that such problems might be avoided or mitigated by the applicant seeking an advance payment

802 Carnet, Blanchard and Apollonio, British Red Cross, 2014.

803 At pp14–15.

804 *Policy, Research and Advocacy*, British Red Cross, 2018, https://naccom.org.uk/faq-items/still-an-ordeal-the-move-on-period-for-new-refugees-british-red-cross-december-2018/.

805 *Still an ordeal: the move-on period for new refugees*, pp2–3.

of UC.[806] However, there are several problems with this. First, it puts the applicant in debt to the DWP at the outset of their claim. This debt will be recovered by monthly instalments deducted from subsequent monthly payments of UC. The result being that the applicant receives less than the 'standard allowance' during those months and may be left struggling to pay for essentials. Second, in any event, obtaining an advance is easier said than done. In particular, to obtain UC applicants require a bank account, something that newly recognised refugees are unlikely to have and may struggle to obtain until they have a letter from the DWP which they can use as proof of address. However, that proof of address is unlikely to be provided until the UC application has been processed and the first payment made, thereby leaving applicants, in the words of the British Red Cross, in a 'chicken and egg' situation.[807] In addition, delays and mistakes in the issue of BRPs may cause further difficulties.[808]

5.281 In the meantime, applicants experiencing difficulties in making the transition to mainstream benefits might consider one or more of the following options:

- Asking the secretary of state to continue to support them while the problems are resolved. Although the secretary of state cannot be compelled to provide support under IAA 1999 s95(1) after the applicant's statutory entitlement to support has ended, arguably at least, they have a discretion to continue to accommodate the applicant on a non-statutory basis thereafter. Any such discretion would need to be exercised in a manner compatible with the applicant's human rights and, in particular, to avoid a breach of ECHR Article 3[809] occasioned by state induced destitution.
- Consider the possibility of an application for judicial review against, as appropriate, either the secretary of state or the DWP challenging the delay in providing the applicant with a BRP[810] (for example) or in processing their universal credit application. Challenges based on unreasonable delay in discharging statutory functions are discussed at para 5.245.

806 *Claiming universal credit and other benefits if you are a refugee*, DWP, 1 October 2019.

807 *Still an ordeal: the move-on period for new refugees*, pp25–26.

808 *Still an ordeal: the move-on period for new refugees*, p27.

809 See paras 5.127–5.131.

810 In *Husson v SSHD* [2020] EWCA Civ 329 the Court of Appeal accepted that an individual who had experienced a two-year delay in obtaining his permit had established an arguable case that the secretary of state owed a tortious duty of care to issue the permit promptly, giving rise to a claim in damages for breach.

- Consider whether the obstacle that is seemingly standing in the way of making the transition to mainstream support, really is a genuine obstacle or not. For example, a local housing authority may be reluctant to provide homelessness assistance to a recently recognised refugee who is lacking a BRP to establish their immigration status. However, possession of a BRP is not a necessary requirement in order to establish eligibility for homelessness assistance under Housing Act 1996 Part VII[811] and a local housing authority imposing eligibility requirements over and above those set down by the legislative scheme is likely to be acting unlawfully.
- Consider requesting support from the local authority under the Localism Act 2011.[812]

Temporary support under Immigration and Asylum Act 1999 s98(1)

The eligibility criteria

5.282 Deciding whether or not an applicant is eligible for asylum support under IAA 1999 s95(1)[813] may not be straightforward. For example, assessing whether an applicant is destitute may be an involved process necessitating consideration of extensive documentary evidence and the making of further inquiries of the applicant. In order to avoid the prospect of applicants being left without accommodation or unable to meet their essential living needs, during this time IAA 1999 s98(1) permits the secretary of state to provide, or arrange for the provision of, 'temporary support' for:[814]

- asylum-seekers or dependants of asylum-seekers;
- who it appears to the secretary of state may be destitute.

5.283 The terms 'asylum-seeker', 'dependant' and 'destitute' have the same meaning as they do in the context of asylum support under IAA 1999 s95(1).[815] In addition, support under IAA 1999 s98(1) may be made

811 Housing Act 1996 s185; Allocation of Housing and Homelessness (Eligibility) (England) Regulations 2006 SI No 1294 reg 5(1)(a). See paras 7.6–7.90.

812 See paras 8.138–8.156.

813 See paras 5.9–5.90.

814 IAA 1999 s95(1).

815 IAA 1999 ss94(1) and 98(3). For asylum-seeker see paras 5.17–5.49. For dependants see paras 5.50–5.56. For destitute see paras 5.57–5.900.

subject to the same conditions as support under IAA 1999 s95(1) and the eligibility criteria are subject to the same exclusions.[816]

5.284 Temporary support under IAA 1999 s98(1) may be provided until the secretary of state is able to determine whether support may be provided under IAA 1999 s95(1).[817] The principal distinctions between IAA 1999 ss98(1) and 95(1) are that:

- Support under IAA 1999 s98(1) is directed at those who it appears *may* be destitute, as opposed to those who appear to be destitute. The use of the word 'may' implies that this is a low threshold to meet.
- Support under IAA 1999 s98(1) is only available to those who may be destitute now, as opposed to those who are likely to become destitute within 14 days.

5.285 When deciding whether to provide support under IAA 1999 s98(1) to an applicant or dependant who is a 'vulnerable person', the secretary of state is required to take into account the special needs of that person.[818] 'Vulnerable' in this context encompasses:

- a child under the age of 18;
- a disabled person;
- an elderly person;
- a pregnant woman;
- a lone parent with a child under the age of 18; or
- a person who has been subjected to torture, rape, or other serious forms of psychological, physical or sexual violence,

who has had an 'individual evaluation of his situation that confirms he has special needs'.

5.286 Support under IAA 1999 s98(1) is sometimes referred to by the terms 'emergency support' or 'initial accommodation'. While there is nothing inherently wrong with these terms, they do not reflect the term used in the statute which is 'temporary support'. In addition, the use of the phrase initial accommodation is apt to confuse, since initial accommodation can also be made available to applicants under

816 IAA 1999 s98(3); AS Regs 2000 reg 4(8)–(9); NIAA 2002 Sch 3 para 1; IAA 1999 s55(2); AS Regs 2000 reg 3(5C). See paras 5.215–5.219 for conditions that may be attached to support; and paras 5.118–5.140 for exclusions.

817 IAA 1999 s98(2).

818 Asylum Seekers (Reception Conditions) Regulations 2005 reg 4 implementing Reception Directive Article 17. See *R (NB and others) v SSHD* [2021] EWHC 1489 (Admin) at paras 145–158 for the continued effect of the Reception Directive following the departure of the UK from the EU.

IAA 1999 s95(1) prior to dispersal.[819] In this chapter, for the sake of clarity, we will generally use the term 'IAA 1999 s98(1) support' to refer to temporary accommodation provided under that section pending a decision on eligibility for support under IAA 1999 s95(1). Where the term 'initial accommodation' is used, this should be understood as a reference to accommodation provided prior to dispersal.

5.287 There is no right of appeal against a refusal to provide temporary support under IAA 1999 s98(1). A legal challenge to a refusal or failure to provide support would need to be brought by way of judicial review.[820]

The provision of support

5.288 Home Office policy describes support under IAA 1999 s98(1) as 'temporary full board or self catering accommodation . . . intended for short term use' available to those 'awaiting a decision from the Secretary of State on whether he may provide asylum support'.[821] In some cases, however, applicants will be placed in self-catering accommodation and provided with cash support in order to buy food.[822]

5.289 The Home Office aims, in most cases, to move applicants on from initial accommodation provided under IAA 1999 s98(1) within 19 days, during which time their application for asylum support under IAA 1999 s95(1) will have been assessed and longer-term dispersal accommodation found for their occupation.[823] The Home Office has access to initial accommodation in the following locations:[824]

- Liverpool;
- Birmingham;
- Derby;
- Glasgow;
- Belfast;
- Wakefield;

819 See paras 5.169–5.184 and *Asylum support: policy bulletins instruction*, v9.0, para 1.1.3.

820 See para 5.320.

821 *Asylum support: policy bulletins instruction*, v9.0, Q1 and para 1.1.

822 *Factsheet 17: Section 98 support*, ASAP, November 2018.

823 *An inspection of the Home Office's management of asylum accommodation provision February – June 2018*, David Bolt (Independent Chief Inspector of Borders and Immigration), November 2018, para 5.4.

824 *Healthcare needs and pregnancy dispersal policy*, v3.0, p9.

- Cardiff;
- London.

The application process

5.290 The process for obtaining support under IAA 1999 s98(1) is not especially clear from either Home Office policy[825] or the information published by the Home Office on the internet.[826] The lack of a clear published policy setting out the application process may be the cause of disadvantage to some applicants, since the lack of transparency has the potential to result in confusion over their legal rights. However, on the other hand, the lack of a fixed procedure also allows for a degree of flexibility.

5.291 In practice, applicants may request support under IAA 1999 s98(1) at their initial appointment to claim asylum at the Asylum Screening Unit (ASU).[827] Those who are homeless do not need to make an appointment with the ASU in order to lodge their asylum claim, and may simply attend the ASU between Monday–Friday, 07.30–16.00 to lodge their claim, at which point support under IAA 1999 s98(1) may be requested. Applicants will need to provide sufficient evidence to establish that they may be destitute.[828]

5.292 Home Office policy also provides that, in certain exceptional circumstances, applicants may be provided with support under IAA 1999 s98(1) and permitted admission to initial accommodation outside of 'normal office hours'[829] prior to their asylum claim being recorded. This only applies to applicants who are regarded as 'particularly vulnerable'. Namely:[830]

- families with a dependent child or children aged under 18 years;
- visibly pregnant women, or women able to prove that they are pregnant;
- asylum-seekers who are disabled but are not considered to have clear and urgent care needs;
- asylum-seekers whose individual needs appear to require special consideration.

825 *Asylum support: policy bulletins instruction*, v9.0, paras 1.1–1.1.1.

826 See: www.gov.uk/asylum-support/how-to-claim.

827 *Factsheet 17: Section 98 support*, ASAP, November 2018.

828 See paras 5.9–5.90.

829 Defined as 17.30–09.00 on weekdays, and weekends and public holidays.

830 *Asylum support: policy bulletins instruction*, v9.0, para 1.1.1.

The applicant must attend the ASU on the next working day to have their asylum claim recorded.

5.293 For applicants who elect to seek support under IA 1999 s98(1) after they have lodged their claim for asylum, an Initial Accommodation Referral Form needs to be completed and emailed to the 'IA Validation Team' at the Home Office.[831] Applicants may seek assistance with this process from Migrant Help,[832] which might be done at the point of making their application under IAA 1999 s95(1). The Home Office should respond to a request for accommodation 'before the end of the working day on which the application is received'.[833]

Ending the provision of support

Decision made on eligibility for asylum support

5.294 The secretary of state may only provide temporary support to an applicant under IAA 1999 s98(1) until he or she is able to determine whether asylum support may be provided under IAA 1999 s95(1).[834] As a consequence, most typically, temporary support under IAA 1999 s98(1) will come to an end because the secretary of state has decided that the applicant is either eligible or ineligible for asylum support.

5.295 If the secretary of state decides that the applicant is eligible, then the applicant should transition seamlessly from temporary support to asylum support. Often the applicant will remain in the initial accommodation for a short time following this decision until dispersal accommodation[835] is allocated and travel arrangements are made.

5.296 Alternatively, if the secretary of state decides that the applicant is not eligible for asylum support – either because the applicant is not an asylum-seeker,[836] is not destitute[837] or is subject to one of the statutory exclusions from asylum support[838] – then the temporary

831 *Factsheet 17: Section 98 support*, ASAP, November 2018. The form is available at: https://ellis.custhelp.com/app/answers/detail/a_id/220.

832 See paras 5.225–5.229.

833 *Asylum support: policy bulletins instruction*, v9.0, para 1.1.1.

834 IAA 1999 s98(1).

835 See paras 5.169–5.184.

836 See paras 5.17–5.49.

837 See paras 5.57–5.90.

838 See paras 5.118–5.140.

support will be brought to an end. Home Office policy provides that, in these circumstances 'initial accommodation to those supported under Section 98 must end as soon as is reasonable; ordinarily the next working day'.[839] This is a shorter period then would generally be the case where asylum support comes to an end.[840] AS Regs 2000 reg 22, which deals with the minimum period which must be provided in a notice to quit accommodation, does not apply to accommodation provided under IAA 1999 s98(1).[841]

5.297 However, the policy, by use of the phrase 'as soon as is *reasonable*', provides a degree of flexibility to the Home Office in determining the time at which support should end. This reflects the public law requirement that public bodies should act reasonably in terminating the provision of accommodation[842] and complements the common law principle (applicable to the licensor of the accommodation) that 'where the relevant period has not been specified by the licence itself, a licensee is entitled, following revocation of the licence, to whatever in all the circumstances is a reasonable time to remove himself and his possessions'.[843] Accordingly, where an applicant's personal circumstances are out of the ordinary and require a longer period than normal to vacate the accommodation, this should be made known to the Home Office and to the accommodation provider as soon as practicable. In practice, the Home Office will usually allow pregnant women and households with children to remain in their accommodation until any appeal against the refusal of support is determined.

Decision made on asylum claim

5.298 Home Office policy specifically caters for the possibility that a decision is made on the applicant's asylum claim while they are being provided with temporary support under IAA 1999 s98(1).[844] The policy reflects that fact that there is a 'grace period' built into the statutory scheme meaning that an applicant does not cease to be an asylum-seeker for asylum support purposes the moment a decision

839 *Asylum support: policy bulletins instruction*, v9.0, para 1.1.2.

840 See paras 5.247–5.250.

841 See AS Regs 2000 reg 21(a) which refers specifically to a tenancy or licence granted 'as a result of asylum support' which, under reg 2(1), means 'support provided under section 95 of the Act'.

842 See *R v Newham LBC ex p Ojuri (No 5)* (1999) 31 HLR 631, QBD; *R v Secretary of State for the Environment ex p Shelter* [1997] COD 49, QBD.

843 See *Gibson v Douglas* [2016] EWCA Civ 1266, [2017] HLR 11 at paras 20–21 per Munby P; and *Minister of Health v Bellotti* [1944] 1 KB 298, CA.

844 *Asylum support: policy bulletins instruction*, v9.0, para 1.1.2.

is reached on their claim.[845] The general rule is that the applicant will continue to be regarded as an asylum-seeker for 28 days after they are notified of a positive decision or is successful in their appeal, or 21 days after they have been notified of a negative decision or have exhausted their appeal rights. In these circumstances, the applicant will continue to be eligible for temporary support under IAA 1999 s98(1) either until the end of the grace period, until a decision is reached as to the whether the applicant is destitute[846] or until a decision is reached that the applicant is subject to one of the statutory exclusions from asylum support,[847] whichever comes first.

5.299 The exception to this general rule is where the applicant's household includes a dependant child aged under 18. In these circumstances, if the applicant's asylum claim is rejected, they will continue to be treated as an asylum-seeker for asylum support purposes so long as the child is under 18 and they remain in the UK.[848] Such applicants will remain eligible for temporary support under IAA 1999 s98(1) either until a decision is reached as to destitution or whether one of the statutory exclusions applies.

Applicant fails to co-operate with inquiries

5.300 Where the secretary of state decides that an applicant has failed, without reasonable excuse, to co-operate with inquiries, then temporary support provided under IAA 1999 s98(1) must come to an end.[849] This is sometimes referred to as a 'section 57 decision' (referring to NIAA 2002 s57).

Default on the part of the applicant or their dependants

5.301 By virtue of AS Regs 2000 reg 20A, the powers within regs 19–20 apply to temporary support under IAA 1999 s98(1) as they do to asylum support under IAA 1999 s95(1). The effect of this is that the secretary of state is entitled to refuse or discontinue support following certain acts or omissions on the part of the applicant or their dependant, such as abandonment of the accommodation or actions of seriously violent behaviour. These circumstances are described in detail at paras 5.257–5.277.

845 See paras 5.252–5.255.
846 See paras 5.57–5.90.
847 See paras 5.118–5.140.
848 IAA 1999 s94(5)–(6). See paras 5.45–5.49.
849 AS Regs 2000 reg 3(5C). See paras 5.221–5.224 and 5.137–5.140.

Borders, Citizenship and Immigration Act 2009 s55[850]

5.302 By virtue of BCIA 2009 s55, the secretary of state is required to make arrangements for ensuring that:[851]

- the secretary of state's functions in relation to immigration,[852] asylum or nationality (among other things) are discharged having regard to the need to safeguard and promote the welfare of children[853] who are in the UK; and
- any services provided by another person pursuant to arrangements made by the secretary of state relating to the discharge of those functions, are provided having regard to that need.

5.303 The immigration and asylum functions to which BCIA 2009 s55(1) applies, encompass the secretary of state's functions in relation to asylum support under IAA 1999.[854] The fact that the duty extends to the provision of services by another person means that services provided by contractors (such as the provision of accommodation by Serco, Mears Group or Clear Springs Ready Homes or their subcontractors)[855] must also be provided, having due regard to the welfare of any children.[856]

5.304 In *ZH (Tanzania) v SSHD*[857] Baroness Hale described BCIA 2009 s55(1) as reflecting the 'spirit, if not the precise language'[858] of United Nations Convention on the Rights of the Child 1989 (UNCRC) Article 3(1), which provides that:

850 See further paras 1.24–1.31.
851 BCIA 2009 s55(1) and (2)(a).
852 See *R (HZ) v SSHD* [2023] EWHC 660 (Admin) for a discussion of 'function[s] in relation to immigration, asylum or nationality'. In that case it was held that the provision of accommodation in bridging hotels to recently arrived Afghans was not a function relating to immigration, as the Afghan nationals in question had been granted leave to remain, and accommodating them did not involve 'entry to, abode in and removal from the United Kingdom'. As such, BCIA 2009 s55(1) did not apply.
853 'Children' in this context means persons under the age of 18: BCIA 2009 s55(6).
854 See, for example, *Asylum support: policy bulletins instruction*, v9.0, p3.
855 See para 5.145.
856 See *Every child matters: change for children*, Home Office, November 2009, para 2.37. The secretary of state is required to have regard to this guidance by virtue of BCIA 2009 s55(3).
857 [2011] UKSC 4, [2011] 2 AC 166.
858 *ZH (Tanzania) v SSHD* [2011] UKSC 4, [2011] 2 AC 166 at para 23.

> In all actions concerning children, whether undertaken by public or private social welfare institutions, courts of law, administrative authorities or legislative bodies, the best interests of the child shall be a primary consideration.

5.305 Consistently with this, guidance on the application of the BCIA 2009 s55(1) duty which features in the majority, if not all, of the various Home Office policies on asylum support explains that the duty requires decision-makers to demonstrate that the child's interests have been treated as 'a primary, although not the only consideration'.[859] In addition, children should be treated fairly and to the same standard as a British child, and the Home Office must be alert to identify those children who might be at risk from harm.[860]

5.306 In relation to the analogous duty under Children Act (ChA) 2004 s11(2), which applies to various public bodies other than the Home Office,[861] the courts have taken the view that the obligation to have regard to the need to safeguard and promote the welfare of the child when discharging functions applies not only to the formulation of general policies and practices, but also to their application in an individual case. However, ChA 2004 s11(2) and BCIA 2009 s55(1) do not redefine or create new functions. Rather, the effect of these provisions is to ensure that existing functions are carried out in a way which takes account of the need to safeguard and promote the welfare of children.[862]

5.307 In practical terms, the duty will require the Home Office to identify the principal needs of any children, both individually and collectively, and to have regard to the need to safeguard and promote them when making the decision. These interests should then be treated as a primary consideration. This does not mean that they are a 'trump card', but that there should be no other consideration that 'is inherently more significant than the best interests of the child' and that '[t]

859 *Asylum support: policy bulletins instruction*, v9.0, p3.

860 See, for example, *Asylum support: policy bulletins instruction*, v9.0, p3.

861 The duties in ChA 2004 s11(2) and BCIA 2009 s55(1) are not materially different. See *Every child matters*, p4 para 4. The fact that the newer duty applies to the Home Office only whereas the older duty applies to other public bodies arises from the fact that the UK had in place a general reservation to the UNCRC concerning immigration matters which was not lifted until 2008: *ZH (Tanzania) v SSHD* [2011] UKSC 4, [2011] 2 AC 166 at para 23 per Baroness Hale.

862 *Nzolameso v Westminster City Council* [2015] UKSC 22, [2015] PTSR 549 at paras 22–24 per Baroness Hale; and *R (Castle) v Commissioner of Police of the Metropolis* [2011] EWHC 2317 (Admin), [2012] 1 All ER 953 at para 51 per Pitchford LJ. See further *Every child matters*, para 1.3.

he question to be addressed, if the best interests point to one conclusion, is whether the force of other considerations outweigh it'.[863] Any decision letter will need to provide sufficient information to demonstrate that this has been done.[864] Merely paying 'lip-service' to the performance of the duty will not suffice.[865] For example, in *Re JO and others (section 55 duty: Nigeria)*,[866] a decision which referred to only one of three children, without identifying the children by name or initials or otherwise, and did not engage with the evidence relating to the children, was described as showing only 'cursory' consideration to the children's interests in breach of BCIA 2009 s55(1). By extension, a standard paragraph referring to the duty is unlikely to be sufficient.

5.308 The approach of the FTT (Asylum Support) in reviewing the Home Office's discharge of the duty under BCIA 2009 s55(1) has not been entirely consistent. For example, in AS/17/05/36776[867] one judge took the view that the BCIA 2009 s55(1) duty had no bearing on a decision as to whether the applicant was entitled to support under IAA 1999 s95(1), where the issue on the appeal was whether the applicant was destitute.[868] If the applicant was not destitute then he could be expected to accommodate, support and care for his family, including his disabled son. Whereas if he was destitute then he was entitled to support. 'Neither outcome', the judge explained, 'is dependant on section 55'.[869] Whereas in AS/17/02/36490[870] another judge remitted an IAA 1999 s95(1) destitution decision for reconsideration by the Home Office in circumstances where, he held, the BCIA 2009 s55(1) duty had not been discharged, without reaching any conclusion as to whether the applicant was destitute.

5.309 In the absence of a settled approach at the FTT (Asylum Support), the observation of Baroness Hale in *Nzolameso v Westminster City Council*, in the context of ChA 2004 s11(2), that '[s]ome statutory questions do leave room for the consideration of the child's welfare'

863 *R (Project for the Registration of Children of British Citizens) v SSHD* [2021] EWCA Civ 193, [2021] 1 WLR 3049 at para 70 per David Richards LJ.

864 See *Nzolameso v Westminster City Council* [2015] UKSC 22, [2015] PTSR 549 at paras 27 and 37 and (more generally) the standard guidance on the application of BCIA 2009 s55(1), placing the burden on the Home Office to demonstrate the discharge of the duty.

865 *R (MG (Iran)) v SSHD* [2015] EWHC 3142 (Admin) at para 20 per Michael Kent QC sitting as a deputy High Court judge.

866 [2014] UKUT 517 (IAC).

867 18 May 2017, FTT (Asylum Support).

868 See paras 5.57–5.90.

869 AS/17/05/36776, 18 May 2017, FTT (Asylum Support) at para 13.

870 28 February 2017, FTT (Asylum Support).

whereas others do not, is instructive. In making this point, she drew a distinction between findings of fact and binary questions the answer to which cannot differ by taking into account welfare considerations, to which ChA 2004 s11(2) would not be relevant, and the exercise of a discretion or the making of an evaluative judgment, to which the duty would be relevant.[871] The same reasoning would apply to BCIA 2009 s55(1). Accordingly, BCIA 2009 s55(1) is unlikely, for example, to be relevant to decisions on the credibility of the applicant, or whether the applicant is an asylum-seeker,[872] the assets which the applicant has available, or whether the applicant has provided sufficient evidence to establish they are destitute.[873] On the other hand, BCIA 2009 s55(1) may have a role to play in determining the essential living needs of the applicant and their dependants,[874] in a case where the household contains a child with particular needs, or in determining where a household with children should be accommodated[875] or whether or not the household requires a longer than usual notice period before their accommodation is terminated.[876]

Appeals and remedies

Overview

5.310 It will be apparent from the foregoing sections of this chapter that there are numerous decisions which the secretary of state might make in the course of determining an application for asylum support under IAA 1999 s95(1). For example:

- At the outset, the secretary of state may need to decide whether to provide temporary support under IAA 1999 s98(1),[877] while the application for asylum support is considered.
- Then consideration will need to be given to whether the applicant meets the eligibility criteria for asylum support.[878] In making this assessment, consideration may need to be given to whether one

871 *Nzolameso v Westminster City Council* [2015] UKSC 22, [2015] PTSR 549 at paras 25–26.
872 See paras 5.17–5.49.
873 See paras 5.57–5.70.
874 See paras 5.83–5.90.
875 See paras 5.169–5.184.
876 See paras 5.247–5.250.
877 See paras 5.282–5.301.
878 See paras 5.9–5.90.

of the statutory exclusions applies,[879] such as the exclusion contained in NIAA 2002 s55 which prohibits the Home Office from providing asylum support to an applicant in circumstances where 'the Secretary of State is not satisfied that the claim was made as soon as reasonably practicable after the person's arrival in the United Kingdom'.[880]

- If the decision is reached that the applicant is eligible for support, then further decisions may need to be made in relation to the level of subsistence which should be provided to the applicant[881] and where in the country they should be accommodated.[882]
- In all cases, ultimately, a decision to terminate support will be made.[883]

An applicant who is aggrieved by the outcome of any one of these decisions might wish to challenge the decision. The question then arises: how should they go about doing so?

5.311 The same question might arise in the context of a variety of other issues which might not be the subject of a formal decision. For example, an applicant whose accommodation is in a poor state of repair might wish to take action to remedy this. How should they do so?

5.312 In broad terms, there are three routes by which an applicant who is aggrieved by a decision made on their application, or who is unhappy with the services with which they have been provided, may seek to obtain a remedy:

1) by way of a statutory appeal under IAA 1999 s103;[884]
2) by means of a complaint[885] (whether to the accommodation provider, the Home Office or the Parliamentary and Health Service Ombudsman (PHSO));
3) by judicial review.

5.313 Which of these remedies is appropriate will depend on the particular decision or situation that forms the subject of the challenge. In overview:

- Statutory appeal:

879 See paras 5.118–5.140.
880 NIAA 2002 s55(1)(b); see also s55(1)–(2). See paras 5.132–5.136.
881 See paras 5.185–5.200.
882 See paras 5.169–5.184.
883 See paras 5.247–5.277.
884 See paras 5.310–5.370.
885 See paras 5.372–5.374.

- An entitlement to a statutory appeal will arise where the secretary of state has decided that the applicant does not qualify for support under IAA 1999 s95(1).[886]
- An entitlement to a statutory appeal will also arise where the secretary of state has decided to discontinue the applicant's support before it would otherwise have come to an end.[887]

- Complaint: An applicant who is unhappy with the service which they have received may seek to complain to the Home Office (usually via Migrant Help) and, if that complaint is not dealt with satisfactorily, onward to the PHSO. The timescales involved in this process mean that it will not be suitable for urgent matters.[888]
- Judicial review: An applicant who does not have a statutory right of appeal who wishes to challenge an unlawful act on the part of the secretary of state may seek judicial review. Examples of situations in which judicial review may be appropriate are to challenge: a refusal to provide temporary support under IAA 1999 s98(1); delay in the provision of support; a decision that the applicant is subject to the exclusions from support contained in NIAA 2002 s55 or s57; or a dispersal decision.[889]

The right to appeal

Appeals against a refusal to provide support

5.314 Under IAA 1999 s103(1) a person has a right of appeal to the FTT (Asylum Support) if:

- they have made an application for asylum support under IAA 1999 s95(1); and
- the secretary of state decides that they do not qualify support under that provision.

5.315 This is sometimes referred to as a 'non-qualification' appeal.[890] This right of appeal will arise from any decision that an applicant does not meet the eligibility criteria for support under IAA 1999 s95(1) which are discussed at paras 5.9–5.90. To that end, in *R (Malaj) v Chief*

886 See paras 5.9–5.90.
887 See paras 5.256–5.277.
888 See paras 5.372–5.374.
889 See paras 5.317–5.320.
890 See *Dogan v SSHD* [2003] EWCA Civ 1673, [2004] HLR 25 at para 4 per Laws LJ.

Asylum Support Adjudicator[891] HHJ Gilbart QC (sitting as a deputy High Court judge) observed that IAA 1999 s103(1) 'gives a right of appeal where the issue of qualification for support is in issue, whatever that reason may be'.[892] Specifically, an applicant will have a right of appeal against any decision that they are not:

- destitute;[893]
- likely to become destitute within 14 days;
- an asylum-seeker;[894] or
- the dependant of an asylum-seeker.[895]

5.316 Appealable decisions falling within the third category (ie that the applicant is not an asylum-seeker) include decisions that:

- the applicant has not made a claim for asylum;[896]
- the applicant's claim for asylum has not been recorded;[897]
- the applicant's claim for asylum has been determined;[898]
- the applicant does not fall within the extended definition of asylum-seeker, encompassing certain failed asylum-seeking households including children.[899]

5.317 The right of appeal under IAA 1999 s103(1) will only arise where the secretary of state has decided 'that the applicant does not qualify for support'. Accordingly, no right of appeal will lie against:

- a refusal to entertain an application because the applicant has not used the correct application form;[900]
- a refusal to entertain an application because the information provided by the applicant is not complete or accurate;[901]

891 [2006] EWHC 3059 (Admin), (2006) Times, December 22.

892 *R (Malaj) v Chief Asylum Support Adjudicator* [2006] EWHC 3059 (Admin), (2006) Times, December 22 at para 25. The court in that case held that a decision that an applicant was not an asylum-seeker gave rise to a right of appeal. See further *Dogan v SSHD* [2003] EWCA Civ 1673, [2004] HLR 25 at para 6 per Laws LJ.

893 See paras 5.57–5.90.

894 See paras 5.17–5.49.

895 See paras 5.50–5.56.

896 See paras 5.19–5.21.

897 See paras 5.22–5.28.

898 See paras 5.29–5.44.

899 See paras 5.45–5.49.

900 AS Regs 2000 reg 3(4)(a). See paras 5.221–5.224.

901 NIAA 2002 s57; IAA 1999 Sch 8 para 12(c); AS Regs 2000 reg 3(4)(b). See paras 5.137–5.140; and *Asylum support: policy bulletins instruction*, v9.0, Q36.

- a refusal to entertain an application because the applicant is not co-operating with inquiries;[902]
- a refusal to entertain a repeat application because there has been no material change in circumstances since the previous application or appeal was rejected;[903]
- a decision that there is no power to provide support because the applicant falls within NIAA 2002 Sch 3;[904]
- a decision that there is no power to provide support because the applicant did not lodge their claim for asylum as soon as reasonably practicable after their arrival in the UK;[905]
- decisions as to the adequacy or location of accommodation provided to an applicant;[906]
- decisions as to the level of financial subsistence provided to an applicant;[907]
- decisions as to the conditions which are attached to the provision of support;[908]
- any delay in the provision of support.[909]

5.318 No right of appeal lies in these cases because none of these decisions touch on whether or not the applicant meets the qualifying criteria under IAA 1999 s95(1). An applicant seeking to challenge any one of these decisions will *generally* need to seek judicial review. However, in practice, there have been two exceptions to this, both of which have arisen in the context of refusals by the secretary of state to entertain an application:

- The first is that the FTT (Asylum Support) has been willing to consider an appeal against a refusal to entertain an application for

902 NIAA 2002 s57; IAA 1999 Sch 8 para 12(c); AS Regs 2000 reg 3(4)(b). See paras 5.137–5.140; and *Asylum support: policy bulletins instruction*, v9.0, Q36.

903 IAA 1999 s103(6); AS Regs 2000 reg 21(1). See para 5.239.

904 See paras 5.122–5.131.

905 NIAA 2002 s55(1)–(2). See paras 5.132–5.136; and *CS v SSHD* AS/12/12/29244, 21 December 2012, FTT (Asylum Support).

906 See paras 5.154–5.168 and paras 5.169–5.184. Under IAA 1999 s103(7) the secretary of state may, by regulations, provide for a right of appeal against decisions as to where support is provided. That power, which would allow for a right of appeal to be provided in relation to dispersal decisions, has never been exercised.

907 See paras 5.185–5.200.

908 See paras 5.215–5.219.

909 See paras 5.244–5.246.

asylum support, in circumstances in which the secretary of state had no power to refuse to entertain the application.[910]

- The second is where the refusal to entertain the application has been improperly characterised as such. This tends to arise in cases where the secretary of state seeks to invoke the NIAA 2002 s57 exclusion, asserting that an application has not been entertained and that support has been refused as the applicant has failed to provide complete or accurate information or has failed to co-operate with inquiries.[911] In such cases, advisers will wish to carefully scrutinise the decision to decide whether the NIAA 2002 s57 exclusion has been properly invoked. If no consideration has been given to the merits of the application, then it may accurately be described as a situation in which the application has not been entertained. However, if, in fact, the application has been considered substantively and a decision has been reached that the applicant does not meet the qualifying criteria for asylum support because they have not supplied sufficient evidence in response to a request for further information, then the decision cannot truly be characterised as an NIAA 2002 s57 decision, and dressing it up as such by citing a lack of co-operation on the part of the applicant will not oust their right to appeal under IAA 1999 s103(1). This is a matter of substance and not form. The issue is not whether the decision letter describes itself as an NIAA 2002 s57 decision or uses the words 'refused to entertain', or the like. The real issue is whether, as a matter of substance, the secretary of state has made a decision that a person does not qualify for support. If so, then a right of appeal will lie to the FTT (Asylum Support).[912]

5.319 Whether or not a right of appeal arises against a refusal to provide support made on the basis that the applicant is a person to whom AS

910 See the landmark decision in *JT v SSHD* AS/04/05/8025, 14 May 2004, FTT (Asylum Support).

911 See paras 5.137–5.140.

912 See, for example, AS/16/11/36087, 18 November 2016, FTT (Asylum Support); and AS/17/03/36540, 14 March 2017, FTT (Asylum Support). The fact that the FTT (Asylum Support) has been willing to look to the substance of the underlying decision may be taken as an application of the principle that it is for the tribunal to satisfy itself that it has jurisdiction. See the landmark decision in *MC v SSHD* AS/01/10/0986, 24 October 2001, FTT (Asylum Support); and (more generally) *Anisminic v Foreign Compensation Commission* [1969] 2 AC 147, HL.

Regs 2000 reg 4 applies[913] is perhaps open to debate. Although, given the exclusion in AS Regs 2000 reg 4 is not frequently applied, it may be that this debate is of academic interest only. On the one hand, the language of AS Regs 2000 reg 4(1) suggests that this is a circumstance in which there is no power to provide support even if the applicant meets the qualifying criteria under IAA 1999 s95(1). That would militate against a right of appeal. On the other hand, the language of IAA 1999 s95(2) suggests that this is a circumstance in which the applicant is excluded from qualification under IAA 1999 s95(1). That would suggest that there could be a non-qualification appeal.

5.320 There is no right of appeal under IAA 1999 s103(1) against a refusal to provide temporary support under IAA 1999 s98(1). An applicant wishing to challenge such a decision would need to seek judicial review.

Appeals against the discontinuation of support

5.321 Under IAA 1999 s103(2), a person will also a have a right of appeal to the FTT (Asylum Support) if:

- they are receiving asylum support under IAA 1999 s95; and
- the secretary of state decides to stop providing that support before it would otherwise have come to an end.

5.322 This is sometimes referred to as a 'stoppage' appeal.[914] The language of IAA 1999 s103(2) is broader than that of section 103(1) in that it confers a right of appeal on any person who has been provided with asylum support under IAA 1999 s95(1), and not solely the person who made the application for support. Accordingly, a dependant of the principal applicant may appeal against the discontinuation of support under IAA 1999 s103(2).[915]

5.323 There is no right of appeal under IAA 1999 s103(2) against a decision to discontinue temporary support under IAA 1999 s98(1). An applicant wishing to challenge such a decision would need to seek judicial review.

913 IAA 1999 s95(2); AS Regs 2000 reg 4(1). See para 5.119. This is the exclusion which applies to applicants eligible for interim support or social security benefits, as well as those who have not made an application for leave that is being considered on the basis that they are an asylum-seeker or dependent on an asylum-seeker.

914 See *Dogan v SSHD* [2003] EWCA Civ 1673, [2004] HLR 25 at para 4 per Laws LJ.

915 See the landmark decision of *CDO v SSHD* AS/04/09/8678, 8 October 2004, FTT (Asylum Support).

5.324 The Explanatory Notes to the IAA 1999 state that IAA 1999 s103(2) is intended to provide a right of appeal against 'the termination of support before the applicant's asylum application has been determined (for example, when he is required to leave accommodation because of misbehaviour)'.[916] However, that description does not reflect the language of IAA 1999 s103(2), and in *Dogan v SSHD*[917] the Court of Appeal rejected this interpretation with Laws LJ describing it as 'fundamentally erroneous':

> 18. ... There is nothing in Section 103(2) to suggest that the words 'would otherwise have come to an end' refer only to the statutory termination of support fixed by reference to the definition of 'asylum seeker'. The Secretary of State is perfectly at liberty to provide the support subject to conditions, so that where there is a breach of condition the person's support will end automatically, or may end pursuant to a further discretionary decision. I do not think these possibilities are in the least constrained by Schedule 8(7) and (8) which I have read. In either event, it cannot be said that support has been stopped before it would 'otherwise have come to an end'. The imposition of the condition contemplates that support will or at least may be stopped by the original intention of the Secretary of State if the condition is not fulfilled.
>
> 19. The possibility that the stoppage for breach of condition may not be automatic but may depend on the Secretary of State's discretion cannot help the appellant's argument, as, in fairness, Mr Cox was inclined to concede this morning. The support was always liable to come to an end if the condition was violated.

5.325 In that case, the Home Office had terminated the applicant's asylum support after he refused to travel to the dispersal accommodation that had been arranged for him. The court held that there was no right of appeal against that decision.[918]

5.326 The circumstances in which an applicant's asylum support may be discontinued are discussed in detail at paras 5.247–5.277. In outline, support will come to an end where:

- the applicant ceases to be an asylum-seeker;[919]
- the applicant ceases to be destitute;[920]

916 IAA 1999 Explanatory Notes para 317.

917 [2003] EWCA Civ 1673, [2004] HLR 25.

918 See paras 5.273–5.276 for a detailed discussion of the decision in *Dogan v SSHD* [2003] EWCA Civ 1673, [2004] HLR 25, and when a right of appeal might lie against a discontinuance of support in circumstances in which an applicant has failed to travel.

919 See paras 5.252–5.255.

920 See para 5.256.

- there has been some default on the part of the applicant or their dependants (for example, a serious breach of the rules of their accommodation).[921]

5.327 The consequence of the decision in *Dogan v SSHD*[922] is that a right of appeal will arise in circumstances where the secretary of state has discontinued the applicant's support, and there is a dispute as to whether the relevant criterion is satisfied. For example, where the secretary of state asserts that the applicant is no longer destitute or an asylum-seeker, but the applicant does not accept that this is the case; or where there is a dispute as to whether the applicant breached the conditions of their support.[923]

The appeal process

5.328 The statutory right of appeal under IAA 1999 s103 lies to the to the FTT (Asylum Support). The FTT (Asylum Support) is currently located at Import Building (formerly Anchorage House), 2 Clove Crescent, London E14 2BE.

5.329 The FTT was established under Tribunal, Courts and Enforcement Act 2007 s3 and comprises of a number of different 'chambers'.[924] The FTT (Asylum Support) forms a part of the Social Entitlement Chamber.[925] Its functions extend to 'cases regarding support for asylum seekers [and] failed asylum seekers' but do not encompass functions relating to immigration and asylum matters which fall within the remit of the Immigration and Asylum Chamber.[926] An appeal from a decision of the Social Entitlement Chamber would generally lie to the Administrative Appeals Chamber of the Upper Tribunal.[927] However, by virtue of IAA 1999 s103(5), decisions of the FTT (Asylum Support) are final, meaning that there is no right of appeal in an asylum support cases. The right of appeal to the FTT (Asylum Support) replaced the earlier right of appeal to an Asylum

921 AS Regs 2000 reg 20(1)(a). See paras 5.257–5.277 for the full list and for a detailed discussion of when support may be terminated in these circumstances.

922 [2003] EWCA Civ 1673, [2004] HLR 25.

923 See paras 5.257–5.277.

924 Tribunals, Courts and Enforcement Act 2007 s7.

925 First-tier Tribunal and Upper Tribunal (Chambers) Order 2010 SI No 2655 arts 2(d) and 6(a).

926 First-tier Tribunal and Upper Tribunal (Chambers) Order 2010 art 6.

927 First-tier Tribunal and Upper Tribunal (Chambers) Order 2010 art 10.

Support Adjudicator from November 2008.[928] The process of the FTT (Asylum Support) is governed by the Tribunal Procedure (First-tier Tribunal) (Social Entitlement Chamber) Rules ('Tribunal Procedure Rules') 2008.[929]

Timetable

5.330 A rudimentary timetable for the appeal process is contained in the Tribunal Procedure Rules 2008, which will then be supplemented by directions issued by the FTT (Asylum Support)[930] which may vary from case to case. The timetable is generally very short, reflecting the urgency arising from the fact that the applicant may be destitute during the appeal process. A typical timetable for the consideration of an appeal is set out in the table below. Where an action must be carried out by a particular day, it must be completed before midnight on that day.[931] If the deadline to complete an action falls on a non-working day, then the action is completed in time providing it is done on the next working day.[932]

928 See IAA 1999 ss102–103 as originally enacted; Tribunals, Courts and Enforcement Act 2007 s30 and Part 4 and Sch 4; Transfer of Tribunal Functions Order 2008 SI No 2833 art 3, Sch 1 table 1 and Sch 3 para 181.

929 SI No 2685. Available at: www.gov.uk/government/publications/social-entitlement-chamber-tribunal-procedure-rules.

930 See paras 5.355–5.357.

931 Tribunal Procedure Rules 2008 r12(1).

932 Tribunal Procedure Rules 2008 r12(2).

Table 5.1

Action	Deadline
Notice of appeal[933] must be received by the FTT (Asylum Support.	Within three days after the date on which the applicant received written notice of the decision being challenged.[934]
The FTT (Asylum Support) must send a copy of the notice of appeal and any accompanying documents to the Home Office.	The day that the FTT (Asylum Support) receives the notice of appeal, or (if that is not reasonably practicable) as soon as reasonably practicable on the following day.[935]
Home Office response to the appeal must be received by the FTT (Asylum Support).	Within three days after the date on which the FTT (Asylum Support) received the notice of appeal.[936]
Notice of the time and place of the hearing must be given to the parties.	At least one day and not more than five days before the hearing.[937]
Hearing of appeal.	Generally within seven to nine days of notice of appeal being lodged.
Decision notice issued to applicant by FTT (Asylum Support).	The day of the hearing.[938]
Written statement of reasons for the decision must be sent to the applicant by the FTT (Asylum Support).	Within three days after the hearing.[939]

5.331 Any document which is to be provided to the FTT (Asylum Support) should be:[940]

- sent by pre-paid post;
- delivered by hand;
- sent by fax; or
- sent or delivered by such other method as the tribunal may permit or direct, such as email.[941]

933 See paras 5.332–5.334
934 Tribunal Procedure Rules 2008 r22(1)(a).
935 Tribunal Procedure Rules 2008 r22(7)(a).
936 Tribunal Procedure Rules 2008 r24(1)(a).
937 Tribunal Procedure Rules 2008 r29(1) and (2)(a).
938 Tribunal Procedure Rules 2008 r33(3).
939 Tribunal Procedure Rules 2008 r34(1)(a).
940 Tribunal Procedure Rules 2008 r13.
941 See the 'Notice of Appeal' form EO9 for example which permits filing by email.

The notice of appeal

5.332 The Tribunal Procedure Rules 2008 provide that a notice of appeal must be completed in English or Welsh and must be signed by the applicant.[942] In addition, the notice must state:[943]

- the name and address of the applicant;
- the name and address of the applicant's representative (if any);
- an address where documents may be sent or delivered;
- the grounds of appeal on which the applicant relies;
- whether the applicant will require an interpreter at any hearing, and if so for which language or dialect;
- whether the applicant intends to attend or be represented at any hearing.

5.333 All of these matters are dealt with within the form E09 notice of appeal currently used by the FTT (Asylum Support).[944]

5.334 Together with the notice of appeal, the applicant must provide a copy of the decision under challenge and any documents in support of their case which have not been supplied to the Home Office.[945] If the decision is not provided then the appeal will be marked as invalid by the FTT (Asylum Support) and will not go ahead.

Extension of time

5.335 The Tribunal Procedure Rules 2008 provide that a notice of appeal must be received by the FTT (Asylum Support) within three days of the date on which the appellant received written notice of the decision being challenged.[946] However, the FTT (Asylum Support) has a discretion to extend this time limit.[947] In exercising this discretion, the FTT (Asylum Support) must seek to give effect to the 'overriding objective'[948] of dealing with cases fairly and justly, which includes (among other things) the need to avoid delay, so far as that is compatible with proper consideration of the issues.[949] An applicant seeking to appeal out of time should complete section six, part three of the notice of

942 Tribunal Procedure Rules 2008 r22(3).

943 Tribunal Procedure Rules 2008 r22(3) and (5).

944 See: www.gov.uk/government/publications/form-t200-notice-of-appeal-form-eo9.

945 Tribunal Procedure Rules 2008 r22(4) and (6).

946 Tribunal Procedure Rules 2008 r22(2)(a).

947 Tribunal Procedure Rules 2008 r5(3)(a).

948 See para 5.353.

949 Tribunal Procedure Rules 2008 r2(1), (2) and (3)(a).

appeal, explaining why the appeal is late and giving reasons (supported by evidence if necessary) why the FTT (Asylum Support) should consider the appeal out of time. In practice, the FTT (Asylum Support) routinely accepts out of time appeals, which is perhaps a reflection of the importance of the matters at stake and the difficulties destitute applicants may have in meeting such a tight deadline.

The hearing

5.336 The FTT (Asylum Support) must hold an oral appeal hearing in all cases save where:[950]

- each party has consented (or has not objected) to the matter being decided without a hearing; and
- the FTT (Asylum Support) considers that it is able to decide the matter without a hearing.

5.337 Section four of the notice of appeal[951] allows applicants to specify whether they wish to have an oral hearing or whether they want the appeal to be determined on the papers. Although the FTT (Asylum Support) may overrule this preference and decide to list the appeal for an oral hearing in any event if it is deemed appropriate.

5.338 An oral hearing may be conducted via video-link.[952] The practice of the FTT (Asylum Support) is that video-link hearings are only likely to be conducted where there are exceptional circumstances making it difficult for the applicant to attend the FTT (Asylum Support) in London. Applicants wishing to have their hearing conducted via video-link should make this known on their notice of appeal.[953]

5.339 Hearings are conducted in public save where the FTT (Asylum Support) directs otherwise.[954] Applicants are entitled to attend their hearing[955] and would generally be well-advised to do so, in order to have the chance to explain their case and respond to any concerns that the FTT (Asylum Support) may have. An interpreter will be provided by HM Courts and Tribunals Service (HMCTS), where one has been requested in the notice of appeal. Where the applicant fails

950 Tribunal Procedure Rules 2008 r27(1).

951 See paras 5.332–5.334.

952 Tribunal Procedure Rules 2008 r1(3).

953 See paras 5.332–5.334.

954 Tribunal Procedure Rules 2008 r30(1) and (3).

955 Tribunal Procedure Rules 2008 r28. The FTT (Asylum Support) does, however, have a discretion to exclude a disruptive applicant from a hearing: Tribunal Procedure Rules 2008 r30(5).

to attend the hearing, the FTT (Asylum Support) may proceed in their absence, provided it is satisfied that reasonable steps have been taken to notify the applicant of the party and that it is in the interests of justice to proceed.[956]

5.340 The rules on evidence in the FTT (Asylum Support) are considerably more relaxed than those that apply in the generality of civil proceedings.[957] In particular, the FTT (Asylum Support) may admit evidence whether or not the evidence would be admissible in a civil trial in the UK, or was available to Home Office at the time the decision was made.[958] In practice, the FTT (Asylum Support) is generally willing to consider documentary evidence from any source, or witness evidence from any person, providing it is relevant to the matters in issue in the appeal. The FTT (Asylum Support) is generally also willing to consider fresh evidence (whether oral or documentary) provided at the hearing itself. However, if the evidence is of significant probative value in relation to the matters raised in the appeal and the secretary of state has not previously had the chance to consider it, then the FTT (Asylum Support) may choose to exercise its power to remit the case[959] to allow the secretary of state the opportunity to do so.

5.341 Applicants in asylum support appeals will frequently be vulnerable. The President of the Upper Tribunal (Immigration and Asylum Chamber) and the Acting President of the FTT (Immigration and Asylum Chamber) have issued joint guidance on dealing with children and vulnerable adults.[960] This guidance should be followed by the FTT (Asylum Support).[961] Failure to follow the guidance is likely to amount to a material error of law.[962]

5.342 Issues may sometimes arise in the course of the determination of an applicant's asylum support appeal which overlap with their

956 Tribunal Procedure Rules 2008 r31.

957 See Civil Procedure Rules Parts 32–33 for the evidential rules in civil proceedings. These do not apply at the FTT (Asylum Support).

958 Tribunal Procedure Rules 2008 r15(2).

959 See paras 5.360–5.365.

960 Joint Presidential Guidance Note No 2 of 2010: *Child, vulnerable adult and sensitive appellant guidance*.

961 *ZN v SSHD* AS/17/09/37288, 27 April 2018, FTT (Asylum Support) at para 36. See further AS/18/05/38061, 15 May 2018, FTT (Asylum Support).

962 *AM (Afghanistan) v SSHD* [2017] EWCA Civ 1123, [2018] 4 WLR 78 at paras 30–38 per Ryder LJ.

substantive asylum claim. In the landmark decision in *ZN v SSHD*[963] the Principal Judge expressed the view that 'it is *never* the role of [the FTT (Asylum Support)] to evaluate a first instance asylum claim and thus, nothing that is decided in an asylum support appeal should impact on the appellant's asylum claim/appeal'. This is entirely in keeping with the jurisdiction of the FTT (Asylum Support) as described above.[964] However, she went on to observe that judges in asylum support appeals would still need to determine the issues arising in the appeal, irrespective of whether they overlapped with matters arising in the applicant's asylum claim or appeal. Findings of credibility on those issues, she explained, would not be binding on any immigration or asylum judge or any other judge of the FTT (Asylum Support).[965] In reaching this decision, she referred with approval to two earlier decisions of the FTT (Asylum Support) in which another judge had stressed the need for caution in assessing evidence which overlaps with the applicant's asylum claim.[966] In the second of the two cases, *MG v SSHD*, the judge had suggested that where an issue in the asylum support claim overlapped with an issue in the applicant's asylum claim, the FTT (Asylum Support) should not seek to evaluate the substance of the facts relied upon and should only refuse support where the evidence relied on 'relating to both the asylum claim and the issue of destitution is to be characterised as clearly abusive or manifestly unfounded'.[967] It is not altogether easy to reconcile the approach taken by the Principal Judge in *ZN* and that taken by the judge in *MG*. The former would seem to suggest that findings of fact should be made on the overlapping issues, presumably on the balance of probabilities, to the extent necessary to determine the asylum support appeal. The latter would seem to suggest that the applicant's evidence on overlapping issues should be accepted save where manifestly hopeless or abusive. The two approaches are not the same and may yield different results. However, what is plain from the approach in both cases is that caution should be exercised by judges when evaluating overlapping issues.

963 AS/17/09/37288, 27 April 2018, FTT (Asylum Support) at para 29 (emphasis in original) (available at: www.gov.uk/asylum-support-tribunal-decisions/zn-v-secretary-of-state-for-the-home-department-as-17-09-37288).

964 See para 5.239.

965 See *ZN v SSHD* AS/17/09/37288, 27 April 2018, FTT (Asylum Support) at paras 29, 30–31.

966 *RG v SSHD* AS/16/09/35812, 23 September 2016, FTT (Asylum Support); and *MG v SSHD* AS/17/05/36760, 12 May 2017, FTT (Asylum Support).

967 *MG v SSHD* AS/17/05/36760, 12 May 2017, FTT (Asylum Support).

Directions

5.355 The FTT (Asylum Support) may give directions either or on its own initiative or on the application of one of the parties.[986] Applications for directions, supported by reasons, can be made either by means of a written application to the FTT (Asylum Support) or orally during the course of a hearing.[987] Typically, the directions that the FTT (Asylum Support) will give in the lead up to an appeal will relate to the preparation by the Home Office of the appeal bundle[988] and the lodging (by either party) of evidence or submissions on issues arising in the case by 12.00 on the day before the hearing.[989]

5.356 Directions can often seem daunting to applicants, as they will often provide a long list of instructions requiring the applicant to produce specific pieces of evidence which they may not previously have been asked for. However, directions generally provide a helpful indication of the evidence that the FTT (Asylum Support) thinks it may need to see in order to establish that the applicant is eligible for support.

5.357 The free telephone advice service operated by ASAP, which can be accessed by those advocating on behalf of asylum-seekers, may be of assistance to applicants who need advice to assist them to understand or comply with directions.[990]

Strike out

5.358 Under Tribunal Procedure Rules 2008 r8(2), the FTT (Asylum Support) is required to strike out an appeal in circumstances where it lacks the jurisdiction to hear the case. In other circumstances the FTT (Asylum Support) has a discretion either to strike out all or part of an appeal, or to bar the Home Office from taking part in the proceedings, if:[991]

- either party has failed to comply with a direction which stated that failure to comply could lead to the striking out of all or part of the proceedings (known as 'an unless order');
- either party has failed to co-operate with the FTT (Asylum Support) to such an extent that the FTT (Asylum Support) cannot deal with the proceedings fairly and justly; or

986 Tribunal Procedure Rules r6(1).
987 Tribunal Procedure Rules r6(2)–(3).
988 Tribunal Procedure Rules r5(3)(i).
989 Tribunal Procedure Rules r15(1)(a)–(b).
990 See: www.asaproject.org/contact/adviceline.
991 Tribunal Procedure Rules 2008 r8(3) and (7).

- the FTT (Asylum Support) considers there is no reasonable prospect of the party's case, or part of it, succeeding.

5.359 Before striking out an applicant's case, or barring the Home Office from participating, the party should be given the opportunity to make representations.[992] An applicant whose appeal has been struck out because they have failed to comply with an unless order may seek to have it reinstated.[993]

Powers on appeal

5.360 On an appeal under IAA 1999 s103, the FTT (Asylum Support) may:[994]

- remit the matter for reconsideration by the secretary of state;
- substitute its own decision for the decision appealed against; or
- dismiss the appeal.

5.361 These powers are broad. The task of the FTT (Asylum Support) is not restricted to reviewing the legality or procedural propriety of the Home Office's decision-making. Rather, the purpose of the appeal is for the FTT (Asylum Support) to decide for itself, having considered all of the evidence, whether the applicant is a person who qualifies for support or whether the applicant's support should continue. In deciding whether to exercise the power to substitute its own decision for the decision appealed against, 'the Tribunal can, of course, take into account the policy which the SSHD says that he or she is going to apply'.[995]

5.362 The power to remit, may be likened to the power of the High Court, on an application for judicial review, to quash an administrative decision. In practical terms this means that the situation in which the applicant was in prior to the decision will pertain. That is, an applicant who is accommodated will continue to be accommodated until a new decision is made. Conversely, an applicant who is without support will continue to be without support. In the latter scenario, an applicant without accommodation following a successful IAA 1999 s95(1) qualification appeal might wish to seek temporary support under IAA 1999 s98(1).[996]

5.363 Where the FTT (Asylum Support) exercises its power under IAA 1999 s103(3)(b) to substitute a decision that the applicant qualifies

992 Tribunal Procedure Rules 2008 r8(4).
993 Tribunal Procedure Rules 2008 r8(5).
994 IAA 1999 s103(3).
995 *R (Razai) v SSHD* [2010] EWHC 3151 (Admin) at para 59 per Nicol J.
996 See paras 5.282–5.301.

for asylum support under IAA 1999 s95(1), then the secretary of state should provide accommodation forthwith.[997] In practice, there are frequently delays in doing so.[998]

5.364 The situation will sometimes arise where an applicant for asylum support under IAA 1999 s95(1) is actually eligible for support under IAA 1999 s4(2)[999] or vice versa. How should the FTT (Asylum Support) proceed when faced with an appeal from an applicant who has been refused one type of support, where it appears that they may actually be eligible for the other type of support? One option is to remit the decision in order for the secretary of state to consider whether the applicant is eligible for the other type of support.[1000] The other course may be for the FTT (Asylum Support) to consider for itself whether the applicant is eligible for the other type of support and, if so, substitute a decision to that effect for the decision appealed against. Although the Home Office has been known to resist this approach, the FTT (Asylum Support) has been willing to adopt this approach in a number of cases.[1001]

5.365 This latter approach would seem to be more in keeping with the powers conferred on the FTT (Asylum Support) by IAA 1999 s103. The FTT (Asylum Support) has the jurisdiction, under IAA 1999 s103(1)–(2), to consider appeals against decisions to refuse or discontinue asylum support under IAA 1999 s95(1). It also has the jurisdiction, under IAA 1999 s103(2A), to consider appeals against decisions to refuse or discontinue support under IAA 1999 s4. The powers conferred by IAA 1999 s103(2) to dismiss an appeal, remit a decision for consideration or substitute its own decision are common to both of these jurisdictions. More specifically, there is only one single power available to the FTT (Asylum Support) under IAA 1999 s103(3)(b) to substitute its own decision for that appealed against, which may be exercised in either IAA 1999 s4 or s95(1) or appeals. By necessary implication, the power must be broad enough to allow the FTT (Asylum Support) to grant either form of support. Also, there is nothing within the language of IAA 1999 s103(3)(b) to

997 See *Asylum support: policy bulletins instruction*, v9.0, para 6.4.

998 See paras 5.244–5.246.

999 See para 6.9–6.200.

1000 This was the course adopted in *CS v SSHD* AS/12/12/29244, 21 December 2012, FTT (Asylum Support).

1001 See, for example, AS/15/04/33047, 11 May 2015, FTT (Asylum Support); AS/15/02/32615, 26 February 2015, FTT (Asylum Support); AS/13/07/30183, 29 July 2013, FTT (Asylum Support); and the decision of the Principal Judge in AS/21/03/42880, 7 April 2021, FTT (Asylum Support).

suggest there is a limitation on the circumstances in which that power may be exercised. This would suggest that if the court is satisfied that an applicant in an IAA 1999 s95(2) case is eligible for section 4 support (or vice versa), then it has the power to make a decision to that effect. Any other interpretation of the legislation would seem to conflict with the object of IAA 1999 s103 which is designed to ensure that destitute migrants are able to access the support which they qualify for. To the extent there is any ambiguity over the ambit of IAA 1999 s103(3)(b), the imperatives placed on the FTT (Asylum Support) under Human Rights Act 1998 ss3[1002] and 6[1003] would seem to militate in favour of a broad interpretation of the power, in order to avoid a situation where a destitute applicant who qualified for support faces the risk of an ECHR Article 3 breach.[1004]

Costs

5.366 The FTT (Asylum Support) has no power to make any order in respect of costs.[1005]

Correcting or setting-aside a decision

5.367 The FTT (Asylum Support) has very limited powers to amend or set aside a decision once made. The power to amend a decision is limited to a power to correct any 'clerical mistake or other accidental slip or omission' in a decision. All parties should be notified of any such correction.[1006] An applicant seeking to have an accidental slip corrected should make an application to that effect.[1007] The power may be exercised at any time.

5.368 The power to set aside and re-make a decision (or part of a decision) which disposes of an appeal is found in Tribunal Procedure Rules 2008 r37. The power will only arise where:[1008]

- a document relating to the proceedings was not sent to, or was not received at an appropriate time by, a party or a party's representative;
- a document relating to the proceedings was not sent to the FTT (Asylum Support) at an appropriate time;

1002 To interpret legislation compatible with the ECHR.
1003 To act compatibly with the ECHR.
1004 See paras 5.127–5.131.
1005 Tribunal Procedure Rules 2008 r10.
1006 Tribunal Procedure Rules 2008 r36.
1007 Tribunal Procedure Rules 2008 r41.
1008 Tribunal Procedure Rules 2008 r37(1)–(2).

- a party, or a party's representative, was not present at a hearing; or
- there was some other procedural irregularity in the proceedings.

5.369 Providing one or more of these criteria is satisfied the FTT (Asylum Support) may set aside the decision but only where it considers that it would be in the interests of justice to do so.[1009] A party seeking to have the FTT (Asylum Support) exercise this power must act quickly, ensuring that a written application is received by the FTT (Asylum Support) no later than one month after the date on which the decision was sent to the party.[1010]

Challenging a decision of the FTT (Asylum Support)

5.370 No right of appeal lies against a decision of the FTT (Asylum Support) following the determination of an appeal.[1011] An applicant who wishes to challenge such a decision on the basis that it contains an error of law, can only do so by way of judicial review observing the time-limits and procedure set out in the Civil Procedures Rules and the Judicial Review Pre-action Protocol.

New applications

5.371 The circumstances in which an applicant who has had their appeal against an adverse IAA 1999 s95(1) decision dismissed may seek to make a further application for support are discussed at paras 5.239–5.243.

Complaints

5.372 An applicant who is unhappy with the standard of service they have received in connection with an application for asylum support may seek to complain to the Home Office using its internal complaints process.[1012] Complaints should be made within three months, unless there are 'exceptional circumstances'. The Home Office aims to deal with complaints within 20 working days or, for complaints raising issues of serious professional misconduct, 12 weeks. However, different timescales apply to complaints where financial redress is

1009 Tribunal Procedure Rules 2008 r37(1).
1010 Tribunal Procedure Rules 2008 r37(3).
1011 IAA 1999 s103(5).
1012 See: www.gov.uk/government/organisations/uk-visas-and-immigration/about/complaints-procedure.

sought.[1013] Plainly, the timescales involved means that the complaints process will not be an effective remedy where urgent relief is needed. Those who have received a final response to their complaint and are unhappy with the outcome may request that their case be considered by the Independent Examiner of Complaints.[1014]

5.373 Complaints about accommodation may also, in the first instance, be made to the accommodation provider directly[1015] or via Migrant Help.[1016] Under their contracts with the Home Office,[1017] providers are required to seek to resolve any complaints within five working days. However, more urgent problems will need dealt with more quickly. For example, complaints in relation to gas leaks and floods should be dealt with within four hours, and lack of heating, hot water or electricity in 24 hours.[1018]

5.374 An applicant who has exhausted these internal complaints mechanisms, who remains unsatisfied with the way in which their grievance has been dealt with, may seek to complain to the PHSO.[1019] An applicant seeking to complain to the PHSO will need to seek a referral from the local member of parliament (MP).[1020]

1013 See: www.gov.uk/government/publications/ex-gratia-guidance.

1014 See: https://www.gov.uk/guidance/make-a-complaint-to-the-independent-examiner-of-complaints#complaints-the-oiec-can-look-at.

1015 *An inspection of the Home Office's management of asylum accommodation provision February – June 2018*, Independent Chief Inspector of Borders and Immigration, November 2018, paras 9.21–9.22.

1016 *A Home Office guide to living in asylum accommodation*, p13 or p16.

1017 See para 5.145.

1018 *A Home Office guide to living in asylum accommodation*, p24.

1019 See: www.ombudsman.org.uk.

1020 The complaint form can be found at: www.ombudsman.org.uk/making-complaint/complain-us-getting-started/complaint-forms. Details of how to find the applicant's MP can be found at: www.parliament.uk/mps-lords-and-offices/mps/.

CHAPTER 6

Support for failed asylum-seekers and those on immigration bail

Shu Shin Luh and Connor Johnston

continued

Key points

- Support under Immigration and Asylum Act (IAA) 1999 s4(2) is available to failed asylum-seekers,[1] together with any dependants,[2] who are destitute and who face certain statutorily prescribed legal or practical obstacles to return[3] to their country of origin.
- Support under IAA 1999 s4(2) consists of accommodation together with financial subsistence payments[4] which, in contrast to IAA 1999 s95(1), cannot be provided separately.
- Accommodation is generally offered on a no-choice basis and applicants are dispersed around the UK away from the South East.[5] Exceptions may be made for certain vulnerable applicants.
- Responsibility for infirm destitute failed asylum-seekers (ie those in need of care and support and eligible for support under the Care Act 2014[6]) will normally lie with social services.[7] The position of care leavers will depend on their immigration status and whether they have outstanding appeals or further submissions in support of a fresh claim.[8] Support under IAA 1999 s4(2) is usually only available to this group where support from children's services is not available. The same applies to households with children.[9]
- Accommodation is currently provided, or secured, by Clearsprings Ready Homes, G4S or Mears Group through contractual arrangements made with the Home Office.
- Subsistence payments are made at the rate of £45 per week.[10] Applicants may be eligible for additional payments, or payments to cover certain expenses, in some cases.[11]

1 See paras 6.15–6.38.
2 See para 6.39.
3 See paras 6.46–6.135.
4 See paras 6.154–6.173.
5 See para 6.159.
6 See paras 8.7–8.178.
7 See paras 6.139–6.140.
8 See paras 6.144–6.153.
9 See paras 6.141–6.143.
10 See paras 6.160–6.162.
11 See paras 6.163–6.173.

- Applications for support under IAA 1999 s4(2) are made using the ASF1 form, with the charity Migrant Help also contracted to assist with the application process as they are for section 95 applications discussed in chapter 5.[12]
- Similar principles of cessation of support apply to IAA 1999 s4(2) as they do to section 95 cases so that support may come to an end either where the applicant ceases to be destitute, is no longer classed as a failed asylum-seeker or is in a position to return to their country of origin, or where there has been some default on the part of the applicant or a member of their household.[13]
- Applicants who are unhappy with the service provided to them may complain to the Home Office and, if that complaint is not dealt with satisfactorily, onward to the Parliamentary and Health Service Ombudsman (PHSO). The timescales involved in this process mean that it will not be suitable for urgent matters.[14]
- An entitlement to a statutory appeal to the First-tier Tribunal (Asylum Support) ('FTT (Asylum Support)') will arise where the Secretary of State for the Home Department (SSHD) has decided that the applicant does not qualify for support under IAA 1999 s4(2) or where support has been discontinued.[15]
- Support under Immigration Act (IA) 2016 Sch 10 para 9(2) is available, in exceptional circumstances, to persons who do not have leave to remain in the UK but are not eligible for support under IAA 1999 s95 or s4(2). On the literal wording of the accommodation power, a person needs to be subject to a residence condition of immigration bail to receive accommodation, although in practice this is not strictly a prerequisite.[16] This support will typically be required by those seeking release from immigration detention but may also apply to those who are not asylum-seekers or failed asylum-seekers, but who are destitute and face a legal or practical obstacle to leaving the UK.[17]

12 See paras 6.178–6.187.
13 See paras 6.188–6.194.
14 See para 6.198.
15 See paras 6.195–6.197.
16 See paras 6.213–6.220.
17 See paras 6.227–6.250.

- There is no statutory right of appeal against a refusal of support under IA 2016 Sch 10 para 9(2). The remedy is judicial review[18] or a complaint, although as with complaints related to section 4 provision, that procedure will not be suitable for urgent matters.

Introduction

Overview of chapter

6.1 The provision of accommodation and financial support, by the Home Office, to asylum-seekers in England and Wales formed the subject of chapter 5. This chapter addresses the position of those who are not, or are no longer, asylum-seekers. Specifically, this chapter will deal with the provision of accommodation and support under IAA 1999 s4(2) to failed asylum-seekers and their dependants, and under the residual powers set out in IA 2016 Sch 10 para 9(2).

6.2 The IA 2016 brought into force changes to the structure of support for migrants who do not meet the eligibility criteria for support as asylum-seekers or failed asylum-seekers under IAA 1999 ss4(2) and 95 provisions, by repealing[19] existing residual powers to provide accommodation under IAA 1999 s4(1) and introducing a new and more limited power to provide accommodation and support under IA 2016 Sch 10 para 9(2). This new accommodation power forms part of the immigration bail regime under the IA 2016, which was introduced on 15 January 2018, and which requires anyone who is subject to immigration control and who does not yet have leave to enter or remain in the UK to be subject to bail.[20]

6.3 Transitional arrangements were made under IA 2016 Sch 11 para 46 for those individuals who were in receipt of support under IAA 1999 s4(1) prior to 15 January 2018 or had applications for section 4(1) accommodation which had not yet been determined. At the time of writing, the vast majority of recipients of section 4(1) support will have moved on from the transitional arrangements.

18 See paras 6.272.

19 See IA 2016 Sch 11 para 1. The repeal was brought into force by the Immigration Act 2016 (Commencement No 7 and Transitional Provisions) Regulations 2017 SI No 1241.

20 See paras 6.201–6.207 for a discussion of the effect of the changes further to the repeal of IAA 1999 s4(1). The two regimes are not identical.

6.4 The changes brought about by the IA 2016 Sch 10 regime are substantial and have wider implications for how persons subject to immigration control who require but do not yet have leave to remain are monitored in the UK. From a support perspective, the new regime has not altered the eligibility criteria for support under IAA 1999 s4(2) discussed below, but has meant that certain categories of persons previously eligible for support under IAA 1999 s4(1) must endeavour either to bring themselves within the eligibility criteria for support under IAA 1999 s95 or s4(2), or, if they are ineligible for either, to seek accommodation and support under Schedule 10 instead. This principally affects persons released from immigration detention and those whose asylum claims were withdrawn prior to determination. The implications of these changes are discussed in more detail at paras 6.201–6.250 below.

6.5 The chapter is structured as follows:

- The chapter begins with a summary of the key features of the support regimes for failed asylum-seekers and for those who can only seek support under IA 2016 Sch 10.[21]
- The chapter will consider the legal framework and policy governing IAA 1999 s4(2), including eligibility;[22] nature and level of support;[23] process for accessing support;[24] how it comes to an end;[25] and the various appeal rights, remedies and avenues of challenge which may be available if applicants are unhappy with the outcome of their application or the services with which they have been provided.[26]
- Similar detailed consideration will be given to the framework for support under IA 2016 Sch 10 para 9 for those who are unable to qualify for support under the IAA 1999, with particular consideration of the emerging issues under that regime.[27]
- The amendments contained in the IA 2016 and Illegal Migration Act (IMA) 2023 that have not yet been brought into force are discussed at paras 5.7–5.8.

6.6 Throughout this chapter, the person who is seeking or receiving support will be referred to as 'the applicant'. As explained in chapter

21 See above.
22 See paras 6.9–6.137.
23 See paras 6.154–6.173.
24 See paras 6.178–6.187.
25 See paras 6.188–6.194.
26 See paras 6.195–6.200.
27 See paras 6.201–6.272.

5, some case-law and material may refer to the National Asylum Support Service or NASS, the body originally set up to administer the asylum support scheme introduced by the IAA 1999. This ceased to exist in April 2006, although the term 'NASS support' is still frequently used. UK Visas and Immigration (UKVI) now administers the asylum support regime. Decisions of the FTT (Asylum Support) will be referred to throughout this chapter as illustrative of legal issues arising under the IAA 1999 s4(2) regime but, as with decisions related to IAA 1999 s95 appeals, these determinations are not binding, although those designated by the tribunal to be landmark decisions will be treated as persuasive by other tribunal judges and the Home Office.[28]

Borders, Citizenship and Immigration Act 2009 s55

6.7 The duty placed on the secretary of state by Borders, Citizenship and Immigration Act (BCIA) 2009 s55(1), to exercise functions in relation to immigration and asylum (among other things), with regard to the need to safeguard and promote the welfare of children who are in the UK, applies to the provision of accommodation and support under the IAA 1999 and IA 2016. This duty is discussed at paras 5.302–5.309.

Overview of support arrangements under the Immigration and Asylum Act 1999 and Immigration Act 2016

6.8 The statutory regimes by which destitute asylum-seekers and failed asylum-seekers and other destitute migrants who require support but do not qualify for the IAA 1999 provisions (or for mainstream support) are complex, made more so by the changes introduced by IA 2016 Sch 10. Table 6.1 gives a basic overview[29] of what support is generally available to whom, how they may get it and what they can do if support is refused, together with cross-references to the relevant section of this chapter and chapter 5.

28 See paras 5.343–5.344.

29 The table is not intended to be exhaustive and does not cover every situation. Reference should be made to the more detailed commentary in this chapter and chapter 5 for the full eligibility criteria.

Table 6.1

Status	Potential form of support	Application process	Right of appeal?
Asylum-seekers[30]	IAA 1999 s95(1)	ASF1 form (submitted via Migrant Help)	Yes
Refused asylum-seekers[31]	IAA 1999 s4(2)	ASF1 form (submitted via Migrant Help)	Yes
Applicants who have lodged further submissions[32]	IAA 1999 s95(1) once further submissions accepted as fresh claim under Immigration Rules para 353	ASF1 form (submitted via Migrant Help)	Yes
	IAA 1999 s4(2) until further submissions accepted as fresh claim, if previous asylum claim was rejected	ASF1 form (submitted via Migrant Help)	Yes
	IA 2016 Sch 10 para 9(2) until further submissions accepted as fresh claim, if previous asylum claim was withdrawn explicitly or implicitly	Form Bail 409	No
Detainees (not including foreign national offender (FNO) 'harm cases')[33]	IAA 1999 s95(1) for asylum-seekers	ASF1 form (submitted via Migrant Help)	Yes
	IAA 1999 s4(2) for failed asylum-seekers	ASF1 form (submitted via Migrant Help)	Yes
	IA 2016 Sch 10 para 9(2) otherwise	Form Bail 409	No

30 See paras 5.9–5.281.
31 See paras 6.9–6.200.
32 See paras 5.23–5.28, 6. 25–6.36, 6.113–6.114 and 6.239.
33 See paras 5.74–5.77, 6.157–6.158 and 6.244–6.250.

Applicants released on bail by Special Immigration Appeals Commission[34]	IA 2016 Sch 10 para 9(2)	Form Bail 401 or B1	No
FNOs granted immigration bail who have been classified as 'harm cases'[35]	IA 2016 Sch 10 para 9(2) if not eligible for IAA 1999 s4(2) or s95	Form Bail 401 or B1	No
Applicants who have withdrawn asylum claim (including absconders)[36]	IA 2016 Sch 10 para 9(2)	Form Bail 409	No
Former unaccompanied asylum-seeking child (UASC) care leavers whose immigration claims were determined prior to 18[37]	Children Act (ChA) 1989 if continue to be eligible, which will depend on care history and outcome of claim	Referral to local authority (if not already supported by it)	No
	IA 2016 Sch 10 para 9(2) otherwise	Form Bail 409	No
Former UASC care leavers whose claims were determined post-18[38]	ChA 1989 if continue to be eligible, which will depend on care history and outcome of claim	Referral to local authority (if not already supported by it)	No
	IAA 1999 s4(2) otherwise	ASF1 form (submitted via Migrant Help)	Yes

34 See para 6.231.

35 See paras 6.232–6.235.

36 See paras 6.20–6.24 and 6.236–6.243.

37 See paras 6.147–6.151 and paras 9.118–9.194. Note that the situation may be more complex in cases where further submissions have been made.

38 See paras 6.152–6.153 and 9.118–9.194. Note that the situation may be more complex in cases where further submissions have been made.

Care leavers who have not sought asylum	ChA 1989 if continue to be eligible, which will depend on care history and immigration status post-18.	Referral to local authority (if not already supported by it)	No
	IA 2016 Sch 10 para 9(2) otherwise.	Form Bail 409	No
Applicants who have never claimed asylum but face obstacles to leaving UK (eg extant European Convention on Human Rights (ECHR) Article 8 (right to respect for private and family life) application)[39]	IA 2016 Sch 10 para 9(2)	Form Bail 409	No

Support under Immigration and Asylum Act 1999 s4(2)

> . . . what is unique about asylum support under section 4 of the [IAA 1999] is that once charity is exhausted it is the only (lawful) gateway to some of the bare necessities of existence.[40]

The eligibility criteria

Overview

6.9 Under IAA 1999 s4(2) the secretary of state may provide, or arrange for the provision of, facilities for the accommodation of a person who:

- was (but is no longer) an asylum-seeker; and
- has had their asylum claim rejected; or
- has had their claim declared inadmissible.

6.10 The meaning of these terms will be discussed below at paras 6.15–6.18, 6.19–6.24 and 6.37–6.38, respectively. The application of these

39 See paras 6.236–6.243.

40 *Re Mahmud's application for judicial review* [2021] NIQB 37 at para 41 per Friedman J.

legal tests in cases where an applicant has lodged further submissions in support of a fresh claim for asylum will be discussed at paras 6.25–6.36.

6.11 There is a corresponding power, contained in IAA 1999 s4(3), to provide, or arrange for the provision of, facilities for the accommodation of a dependant of a person who is entitled to support under IAA 1999 s4(2). However, in contrast to support under IAA 1999 s95(1), dependants are not themselves entitled to make an application for support. The meaning of 'dependant' will be discussed at para 6.39.

6.12 Although these two powers under IAA 1999 s4(2) and (3) are framed very broadly, they are supplemented by regulation-making powers, by which the secretary of state may specify criteria which are to be used in determining whether or not to provide or arrange, or continue to provide or arrange, accommodation under IAA 1999 s4,[41] as well as specifying the services and facilities which an eligible applicant may be provided.[42] These powers have been exercised in the form of the Immigration and Asylum (Provision of Accommodation to Failed Asylum-Seekers) Regulations ('IA (PAFAS) Regs') 2005[43] and the Immigration and Asylum (Provision of Services or Facilities) Regulations ('IA (PSF) Regs') 2007.[44] The former contains the eligibility criteria for IAA 1999 s4(2) support. The latter set out the nature and level of support with which an applicant will be provided. The regulations operate alongside various policy and guidance documents issued by the secretary of state.

6.13 The nature and level of support with which an applicant will be provided is dealt with later in this chapter.[45] As for eligibility, an applicant qualifies for support under IAA 1999 s4(2) or (3)[46] if:

a) they appear to the secretary of state to be destitute;[47] and additionally
b) they satisfy one or more of the following criteria, prescribed under the IA (PAFAS) Regs 2005:[48]

41 IAA 1999 s4(5)–(6).
42 IAA 1999 s4(10)–(11).
43 SI No 930.
44 SI No 3627.
45 See paras 6.154–6.173.
46 That is, a person who was (but is no longer) an asylum-seeker (see paras 6.15–6.18) who has had their asylum claim rejected (see paras 6.19–6.24) together with their dependant(s) (see para 6.39).
47 IA (PAFAS) Regs 2005 reg 3(1)(a). See paras 6.40–6.45.
48 IA (PAFAS) Regs 2005 reg 3(1)(b). See paras 6.46–6.47.

i) *Applicant taking all reasonable steps to return*: They are taking all reasonable steps to leave the UK or place themself in a position in which they are able to leave the UK, which may include complying with attempts to obtain a travel document to facilitate their departure.[49]

ii) *Applicant faces obstacle to travel*: They are unable to leave the UK by reason of a physical impediment to travel or for some other medical reason.[50]

iii) *Applicant has no safe route of return*: They are unable to leave the UK because in the opinion of the secretary of state there is currently no viable route of return available.[51]

iv) *Applicant pursuing judicial review challenge to an asylum decision*: They have made an application for judicial review of a decision in relation to their asylum claim and have been granted permission to proceed by the court.[52]

v) *Applicant needs support to avoid a human rights breach*: The provision of support is necessary for the purpose of avoiding a breach of a person's ECHR rights, within the meaning of the Human Rights Act 1998.[53]

6.14 What it means to be destitute, and the scope of these five gateways to support, are discussed in detail below. It should be noted that unlike IAA 1999 s95(1), it is not enough to appear to be destitute, or to be likely to become destitute within a prescribed period of time.[54] Failed asylum-seekers must additionally establish that they meet one or more of the five gateways to eligibility for support. This additional requirement is referable to the fact that the failed asylum-seeker, by their very immigration status, has had their claim for asylum rejected and appeal rights exhausted, and has no permission to remain in the UK. The requirement to meet at least one of the five gateways is to advance the policy objective that a failed asylum-seeker should only be supported by the Home Office in circumstances where they cannot reasonably be expected, as a matter of law or practicality, to return to their country of origin to seek support.

49 IA (PAFAS) Regs 2005 reg 3(2)(a). See paras 6.48–6.58.
50 IA (PAFAS) Regs 2005 reg 3(2)(b). See paras 6.59–6.83.
51 IA (PAFAS) Regs 2005 reg 3(2)(c). See paras 6.84–6.85.
52 IA (PAFAS) Regs 2005 reg 3(2)(d). See paras 6.86–6.89.
53 IA (PAFAS) Regs 2005 reg 3(2)(e). See paras 6.90–6.135.
54 See para 5.60.

Was, but is no longer, an asylum-seeker

Definition

6.15 The term 'asylum-seeker', has the same meaning in the context of support under IAA 1999 s4(2) as it does in the context of asylum support under IAA 1999 s95(1).[55] The definition of this term is discussed in detail at paras 5.17–5.49. In outline, an asylum-seeker is a person:[56]

- who is not under 18;
- who has made a claim for asylum;[57]
- which has been recorded by the secretary of state;[58]
- which has not been determined.[59]

Therefore, an applicant who once met these requirements but, for whatever reason, has ceased to do so, will be regarded as a person who was, but is no longer, an asylum-seeker.

Children

6.16 The term 'asylum-seeker', in this context, applies only to those aged 18 or over.[60] This means that an unaccompanied seeking child (UASC) whose claim is determined before they turn 18 cannot be regarded as a person who was, but is no longer, an asylum-seeker. This means they will not satisfy the first criterion for becoming eligible for support under IAA 1999 s4(2). Instead, and as children who are not excluded from support under Nationality, Immigration and Asylum Act (NIAA) 2002 Sch 3, they are almost inevitably going to qualify for support from their local authority under the ChA 1989.[61] What happens to the children when they turn 18 is a different matter, discussed at paras 6.144–6.153 below.

55 IAA 1999 s4(4).
56 IAA 1999 s94(1).
57 See paras 5.19–5.21.
58 See paras 5.22–5.28.
59 See paras 5.29–5.44. As a result of amendments to the IAA 1999 introduced by the Nationality and Borders Act (NBA) 2022, a claim is treated as having been determined if it is declared inadmissible. The IMA 2023 paves the way for more asylum claims to be dealt with in this way. See paras 5.39–5.44.
60 UASCs normally access support under the ChA 1989 instead. See chapter 9 on support under the ChA 1989 generally, and paras 11.4–11.126 for support for UASCs specifically.
61 See paras 9.70–9.117.

Households including children

6.17 Special rules apply to certain households that include children. As explained at paras 5.45–5.49, an applicant with dependant children, whose asylum-claim is rejected before the child reaches the age of 18, may benefit from the extended definition of asylum-seeker contained in IAA 1999 s94(5). If an applicant falls within this extended definition they will not be, for the purposes of support, regarded as a person who was, but is no longer, an asylum-seeker. They will therefore be ineligible for support under IAA 1999 s4(2), and instead, continue to be eligible for asylum support under IAA 1999 s95(1) along with their dependant children until the youngest child in the household reaches the age of 18. However, once that child reaches the age of 18, the applicant will cease to be regarded as an asylum-seeker, unless there has been a material change in their immigration status, and will have to seek support under IAA 1999 s4(2) as a failed asylum-seeker subject to meeting the eligibility criteria. If they do not meet the criteria under section 4(2), they may need to consider whether they qualify for support under IA 2016 Sch 10 para 9(2).

6.18 If an applicant's asylum claim was finally determined[62] prior to them having dependant children, they will not be beneficiaries of the deeming provision under IAA 1999 s94(5) and the household's eligibility for support will fall to be considered under IAA 1999 s4(2) if local authority support is not available. See further paras 6.141–6.143 below.

Has had their claim for asylum rejected

6.19 At the time of writing, there has been some divergence in the approach of the FTT (Asylum Support) as to what it means for an asylum claim to have been 'rejected'. It is uncontroversial that a claim will be regarded as having been rejected in circumstances where the secretary of state has adjudicated on the merits of the claim and made a decision that the applicant does not meet the criteria for the grant of refugee status, and the applicant has exhausted any available in-country right of appeal. This scenario encompasses the majority of cases in which support under IAA 1999 s4(2) is sought.

6.20 However, the position is less clear where the secretary of state has made a decision that consideration of the claim will cease, and that the merits of the claim will not be adjudicated upon, owing to procedural failings on the part of the applicant. Does this also constitute a

62 See paras 5.29–5.44.

rejection? This question will affect any applicant whose asylum claim is no longer under consideration by the Home Office because it has been treated as having been withdrawn, for example, because they absconded before the claim was determined.[63] The answer to this question is a matter of statutory construction. However, little direct assistance can be found in the statute itself: the word 'rejected' is not defined in the IAA 1999 or in the IA (PAFAS) Regs 2005. Recourse to the dictionary definition of the word does little to resolve the ambiguity. The *Chambers Dictionary* includes 'to discard' or 'to refuse to accept' as possible meanings of the word 'reject'; concepts which are potentially broad enough to encompass either or both of the scenarios above.

6.21 The secretary of state's view is that a claim will only have been rejected where a decision has been taken on its merits, and that a claim that is treated as being implicitly withdrawn prior to this has not been 'rejected':

> If an asylum claim is withdrawn under [Immigration Rules] paragraph 333C, as no formal decision has been made on the claim, the claimant will not be a failed asylum seeker and as a result will not be eligible for section 4(2) support.[64]

6.22 This view has been endorsed by the FTT (Asylum Support) in a number of cases.[65] If this interpretative approach to 'rejected' is correct, then the applicant will have to look to the possibility of qualifying for support under IA 2016 Sch 10 instead.[66]

6.23 The alternative view, which has found some currency at the FTT (Asylum Support), is that a 'rejection', when used in the context of the Immigration Rules,[67] does not necessarily require a formal decision on the merits of the claim. For example, in AS/19/11/40826,[68] Judge Lewis noted that Immigration Rules para 336 uses the word 'refusal' in the context of a decision that an applicant does not meet

63 See paras 5.37–5.38. See further *Support for absconders and others who have withdrawn their asylum claims*, Asylum Support Appeals Project (ASAP), December 2019, for further discussion of this issue.

64 *Asylum policy instruction: withdrawing asylum claims*, v6.0, Home Office, May 2020, p18 (www.gov.uk/government/publications/withdrawing-asylum-applications).

65 For example, AS/13/05/29889, 4 June 2013, FTT (Asylum Support); AS/13/07/30183, 29 July 2013, FTT (Asylum Support); AS/15/01/32416, 26 January 2015, FTT (Asylum Support); *XC v SSHD* AS/18/06/38201, 22 June 2018, FTT (Asylum Support); AS/22/01/43710, 17 March 2022, FTT (Asylum Support).

66 See paras 6.201–6.272.

67 HC 395.

68 AS/19/11/40826, 19 November 2019, FTT (Asylum Support).

the criteria for the grant of refugee status. Whereas the word 'reject' is used in para 339M to encompass the situation where the secretary of state has made a decision that the applicant will not be granted asylum owing to procedural failings on their part, for example, failing to report to a designated place to be fingerprinted or failure to complete an asylum questionnaire. Relying on this distinction, Judge Lewis reasoned that:

> The element of non-compliance, and for example in particular the failure to provide substantiation of a claim, and/or the failure to make full disclosure of material facts, suggest that a rejection of the claim does not involve substantive consideration of the claim. This is comparable to a failure to attend an interview resulting in an implied withdrawal decision that has the effect of avoiding substantive consideration.[69]

On this approach, the applicant in this situation would be treated as a failed asylum-seeker who, depending on whether they also meet one of the five gateways, to be discussed below, may be eligible for support under IAA 1999 s4(2). This approach was followed by the judge in AS/19/11/40868[70] but was not followed by the judges in *HMA v SSHD*,[71] AS/21/03/42880[72] and AS/22/01/43710.[73]

6.24 This divergence in the approach of the FTT (Asylum Support) means that, at present, the most that can be said is that it is arguable that an applicant whose claim has been treated as implicitly withdrawn as a result of absconding, has had their claim rejected. However, in future it may be that this is an issue on which guidance from the High Court may be needed. In considering this issue the court may need to address the consequences of the amendments to the IAA 1999 made by the NBA 2022, discussed further at paras 3.131–3.142 (in the context of the asylum process), 5.39–5.44 (in the context of IAA 1999 s95(1)) and at paras 6.37–6.38 below, which have the consequence of bringing applicants whose claims for asylum have been declared inadmissible within the scope of IAA 1999 s4(2).[74] A declaration of inadmissibility does not involve any substantive consideration of the merits of the claim. The express inclusion of a cohort of former asylum-seekers who have not had their claims

69 At para 19.
70 AS/19/11/40868, 25 November 2019, FTT (Asylum Support).
71 AS/20/08/42323, 9 September 2020, FTT (Asylum Support).
72 AS/21/03/42880, 7 April 2021, FTT (Asylum Support).
73 AS/22/01/43710, 17 March 2022, FTT (Asylum Support).
74 IAA 1999 s4(2)(b) as amended by NBA 2022 s17(2).

considered on the merits within the scope of IAA 1999 s4(2) might be taken to support the argument that the broad construction of section 4(2) described at para 6.23 should be favoured. On the other hand, the fact that a declaration of inadmissibility is not defined as a rejection but is a separate eligibility criterion,[75] and that parliament saw the need to amend the legislation to bring this cohort within the scope of section 4(2), indicating a belief that the 'rejected' criterion was not broad enough to encompass this particular cohort, might be taken to suggest that the narrow construction described at paras 6.21–6.22 is the right one.

Cases in which the applicant has lodged further submissions

6.25 An applicant who was but is no longer an asylum-seeker[76] who has had their asylum claim rejected[77] may seek to make further submissions in support of a new asylum claim. Provision for doing so is made under Immigration Rules para 353 and supplemented by the Home Office's *Further submissions* policy.[78] Historically, further submissions could only be lodged at the Further Submissions Unit (FSU) in Liverpool. The position is now more complex. The process by which further submissions are lodged depend on the legal basis of the submissions and the applicant's circumstances, for example, whether they are subject to removal action or is unable to travel.[79]

6.26 What is the status of an applicant who lodges further submissions? Are they to be described as an asylum-seeker because they are, on any view, seeking asylum, even though their first claim had failed?[80] If the question is answered by reference solely to the EU law position, then it would have to be answered in the affirmative. Council Directive 2005/85/EC on minimum standards on procedures in Member States for granting and withdrawing refugee status

75 Under IAA 1999 s4(2)(b) an applicant may be eligible for asylum support if they have had their asylum claim rejected *or* declared inadmissible. They are distinct criteria.

76 See paras 6.15–6.18.

77 See paras 6.19–6.24. Note that the further submissions process does not apply to asylum inadmissibility decisions. See paras 6.37–6.38 below.

78 *Further submissions*, v10.0, Home Office, June 2022. See further paras 3.42–3.43.

79 *Further submissions*, v10.0, pp13–21.

80 Immigration Rules para 327 defines an asylum-seeker as a person who has made a request to be recognised as a refugee or for international protection. However, this applies to the applicant's first asylum claim only. Fresh claims are dealt with under Immigration Rules para 353.

('Procedures Directive') Article 2(c)[81] defines an asylum applicant as someone who has made a 'request' for international protection. It does not distinguish between an initial or subsequent request, although the directive does provide for member states to make different arrangements for examining subsequent claims. The same definition is used in Council Directive 2003/09/EC laying down minimum standards for the reception of asylum seekers ('Reception Directive') Article 2(c).

6.27 The position in domestic law is, however, different. The High Court in *R (Nigatu) v SSHD*[82] took the view that the lodging of further submissions would not, by itself, be sufficient for the applicant to meet the domestic definition of an asylum-seeker for support purposes.[83] The judge's conclusion was based on the premise that it was not sufficient for the applicant to have sought to claim for asylum; the claim needed to have been 'recorded'. Although what is necessary for a claim to be 'recorded' is not set out in the IAA 1999, the judge held that this necessarily required the secretary of state to make a determination that the applicant's further submissions satisfied the requirements of Immigration Rules para 353[84] and constituted a fresh claim, ie that the further submissions were 'significantly different from the material that has previously been considered' and created a realistic prospect of success before an appeal tribunal when considered together with the previously considered material. It was only then that the claim would be recorded and the applicant would become an asylum-seeker once more and could seek asylum support under IAA 1999 s95(1).[85] Unless and until that time, the applicant would continue to be classed as a failed asylum-seeker for support purposes and would need to seek support under IAA 1999 s4(2).[86]

6.28 Surprisingly, the correctness of the decision in *R (Nigatu) v SSHD* has never directly been called into question in the context of

81 But see *R (AAA (Syria)) v SSHD* [2022] EWHC 3230 (Admin) at paras 116–118 (currently under appeal) for a discussion of whether the Procedures Directive falls within the body of retained EU law. See paras 2.25–2.39 for retained EU law.

82 [2004] EWHC 1806 (Admin) at paras 21–22 per Collins J. See further *R (AW) v Croydon LBC* [2005] EWHC 2950 (Admin) at paras 63–64 per Lloyd Jones J.

83 IAA 1999 ss4(4) and 94(1). See paras 5.17–5.49.

84 Immigration Rules para 353 governs the acceptance of fresh claims. See further paras 3.42–3.43; and *Further submissions*, v10.0.

85 See paras 5.9–5.90.

86 Different considerations apply when the applicant has lodged further submissions because their initial asylum claim was withdrawn (for example, because they absconded). See paras 6.20 and 6.239.

eligibility for support under the IAA 1999, even though it was a case that needed to be read with caution as it pre-dated the transposition of the Reception Directive and Procedures Directive[87] in the domestic law in the UK. Although the Reception Directive had been adopted by EU member states by the time *Nigatu* was heard by the High Court, no argument was raised by reference to the Reception Directive. This seems to be a significant omission particularly as the interpretation adopted by the judge was one that was, on its face, incongruent with the EU law definition of an asylum applicant for the purposes of providing reception conditions pending the determination of the asylum claim. The *Nigatu* decision was not revisited in the support context for nearly 15 years until 2018. In the meantime, the question as to the precise status of those who have further submissions outstanding, and the rights and entitlements that flow from that status, was the subject of vigorous debate at the highest levels of the courts in various related contexts, resulting in a series of decisions at the Supreme Court level, but which has not produced a clear answer.[88]

6.29 The first is the decision of the Supreme Court in the case of *R (BA (Nigeria)) v SSHD*,[89] which arose in the context of two deportees who had previously failed in their asylum claims but had, in the course of challenging an immigration decision to deport them, sought to rely on further submissions to argue that their removal would be in breach of the Refugee Convention.[90] They contended that those further submissions made on asylum grounds gave them an in-country right of appeal. The Home Secretary argued that an asylum claim for the purposes of the statutory appeal provisions under the NIAA 2002 only related to first asylum claims or those further submissions which had been recorded as fresh claims. The Supreme Court rejected that argument, finding that for the purposes of a right of appeal against an 'immigration decision' under the version of NIAA 2002 s92(4)(a) in force at that time, an 'asylum claim' included any second or subsequent claim that the applicant

87 But see *R (AAA (Syria)) v SSHD* [2022] EWHC 3230 (Admin) at paras 116–118 (currently under appeal) for a discussion of whether the Procedures Directive falls within the body of retained EU law. See paras 2.25–2.39 for retained EU law.

88 The comments of Lord Neuberger in *R (ZA (Nigeria)) v SSHD* [2010] EWCA Civ 926, [2011] QB 722 at para 51 illustrate the potential for debate as to the effect of these cases.

89 [2009] UKSC 7, [2010] 1 AC 444.

90 UN Convention relating to the Status of Refugees 1951.

might make, irrespective of whether it had been accepted as constituting a fresh claim for asylum under Immigration Rules para 353, and thus, in those two appeals, gave rise to exercisable in-country rights of appeal. EU law arguments were not advanced before the Supreme Court.

6.30 *R (ZO (Somalia)) v SSHD*,[91] another Supreme Court judgment, concerned the meaning of the term 'asylum-seeker' for the purposes of a right to make a request under Immigration Rules para 360 for permission from the Home Secretary to work pending the determination of a claim for asylum. The appellant had failed in his first claim but made further submissions in support of a fresh claim under Immigration Rules para 353. He contended that as a matter of EU law, and particularly the definition of an asylum applicant under Reception Directive Article 2(c), he was an asylum applicant. He was entitled, under Reception Directive Article 11(2), to make a request for permission to work pending the determination of his asylum application even though this was not a first application. The Supreme Court held in that case that a person who had lodged further submissions which had yet to be considered by the secretary of state was to be regarded as an asylum-seeker for the purposes of entitlement to seek permission to work under Immigration Rules para 360. The Supreme Court arrived at this conclusion by construing the immigration rule consistently with Reception Directive Article 11(2) and with the definition of an asylum applicant contained in the Directive.

6.31 More recently, the Supreme Court had occasion to consider the *BA (Nigeria)* decision in the context of further submissions made on human rights (rather than asylum) grounds in *R (Robinson) v SSHD*.[92] It confined *BA (Nigeria)* to cases where there was already an appealable decision (in that case an immigration decision to seek the appellant's deportation). It was not authority for disapplying Immigration Rules para 353 in the context of determining whether there was a right of appeal against further submissions raised on human rights grounds. Moreover, *BA (Nigeria)* was decided under a different statutory appeal regime, in which the appeal is made against an appealable immigration decision, which was prescribed under NIAA 2002 s82 prior to amendments made to it by the Immigration Act (IA) 2014. Further to the amendments made under the IA 2014, appeals were no longer brought under NIAA 2002 s82 against specified immigration decisions but rather against a refusal of a

91 [2010] UKSC 36, [2010] 1 WLR 1948.

92 [2019] UKSC 11, [2019] 2 WLR 897.

protection or human rights claim. The Supreme Court held that the phrase 'human rights claim'[93] under NIAA 2002 s82(1)(b) did not encompass any and all human rights claims; rather it was confined to the applicant's original claim and any subsequent claim which had been accepted as amounting to a fresh claim under Immigration Rules para 353.

6.32 These three cases were not decided in the context of statutory support for asylum-seekers and failed asylum-seekers, although *ZO (Somalia)* comes the closest, it being decided under the same rubric of the Reception Directive. But all three touch so very closely on the question which lay at the heart of *Nigatu* – whether, under domestic or EU law, a person who has lodged further submissions which have yet to be considered should be regarded as an asylum-seeker or a failed-asylum-seeker – that their impact has to be considered.

6.33 In *R (Mustafa) v Kent CC*[94] the High Court was called upon to do exactly that.[95] The applicant in that case was a care leaver who had failed in his first asylum claim but had made further submissions in support of a fresh claim which had yet to be considered by the secretary of state. He sought support from his local authority under ChA 1989 s23C as a former 'relevant child', having previously been 'looked after' by the local authority for the requisite period of time.[96] Whether he was entitled to support under that provision turned on whether he was a person to whom the exclusions from support contained in NIAA 2002 Sch 3 applied.[97] This, in turn, was a question of whether he fell within the definition of 'asylum-seeker' contained in NIAA 2002 s18(3) and Sch 3 para 17. Importantly, for the purposes of this chapter, that definition is identical to that which applies in the context of support under IAA 1999 ss4(2) and 95(1).[98] The applicant argued that the relevant provisions of the NIAA 2002 should be interpreted in line with the definition of an asylum applicant under the Reception

93 The rules governing fresh claims in Immigration Rules para 353 encompass claims brought on both asylum and other human rights grounds. Although the facts of *Robinson* involved a claim under ECHR Article 8 (right to respect for private and family life), the *ratio* of the case also extends to asylum claims.

94 [2018] EWHC 2025 (Admin), (2019) 22 CCLR 138.

95 The decision in *Mustafa* pre-dates the decision of the Supreme Court in *Robinson*. However, the Supreme Court upheld the decision of the Court of Appeal in that case.

96 See paras 9.118–9.194.

97 See paras 9.195–9.217.

98 See IAA 1999 ss4(4) and 94(1).

Directive and Procedures Directive,[99] which lay down minimum standards for the procedure for processing subsequent asylum application, and that, consistently with the decision in *ZO (Somalia)*, he should be regarded as an asylum-seeker. The local authority conceded that as a matter of EU law the applicant was an asylum-seeker, but contended that the margin of appreciation permitted the UK, as a member state, to adopt a different definition of an asylum-seeker so that different support arrangements could be made for asylum-seekers and failed asylum-seekers with further submissions awaiting consideration by the secretary of state. The High Court accepted the local authority's argument, and, relying on *Nigatu*, concluded that the applicable meaning of the phrase 'asylum-seeker' was derived from domestic law and referred to a person pursuing either an initial claim for asylum or a subsequent claim that the secretary of state had accepted as amounting to a fresh claim in line with Immigration Rules para 353. It further held that it was unnecessary to adopt the same definition as that used in the Reception Directive, providing the UK's obligations under the Directive were 'fulfilled in the result'.[100] The result required by the Reception Directive was the provision of a minimum standard of reception conditions for those seeking asylum.[101] That result, where necessary, could be achieved by means of the provision of support under IAA 1999 s4(2).[102]

6.34 The practical consequence of this series of cases is that, at least at the level of the FTT (Asylum Support), the decision in *Nigatu* remains good law and that an applicant who has lodged further submissions should continue to be regarded as a failed asylum-seeker[103] unless and

99 See *R (AAA (Syria)) v SSHD* [2022] EWHC 3230 (Admin) at paras 116–118 (currently under appeal) for a discussion of whether the Procedures Directive is retained EU law. See paras 2.25–2.39 for retained EU law.

100 *R (Mustafa) v Kent CC* [2018] EWHC 2025 (Admin), (2019) 22 CCLR 138 at para 41 per Upper Tribunal Judge Markus QC sitting as a High Court judge.

101 Reception Directive Articles 13–14.

102 The applicant in *Mustafa* pursued an appeal against this decision but subsequently withdrew it in the light of material changes in his factual circumstances.

103 Cases in which the applicant's initial asylum claim was never 'rejected' as a result of having been withdrawn provide an exception to this rule. See paras 5.37–5.38 and 6.20–6.24. In such circumstances the applicant may be entitled to support under IA 2016 Sch 10. See paras 6.201–6.272.

until their further submissions have been determined.[104] However, the complexity of the issues is such that *Mustafa* may not be the last word on the subject and this may be an issue which the higher courts have to return to in due course. Alternatively, parliament could bring into force IA 2016 Sch 11 para 3, which provides for an extended definition of an asylum-seeker for support purposes, which encompasses those with further submissions outstanding which had not yet been determined under Immigration Rules para 353. If that provision were brought into force, then the question of who is an asylum-seeker as a matter of domestic law may finally be settled.

6.35 The position on eligibility for support may decisively change once the Home Office has determined the applicant's further submissions in line with Immigration Rules para 353; there are three possible outcomes:[105]

- The applicant is granted refugee status, humanitarian protection or discretionary leave to remain. Thereafter the 'asylum-seeker' question falls away. The grant of refugee status or humanitarian protection affords a person entitlement to mainstream welfare benefits, meaning that they will have a different source of state support to avoid destitution once they are in receipt of the benefits[106] and thus no longer require support under the IAA 1999. Those who have been granted discretionary leave to remain may also access mainstream welfare benefits if they have recourse to public funds.
- The secretary of state accepts that the further submissions amount to a fresh claim but rejects the claim. This would normally give rise to an in-country right of appeal.[107] The applicant would in those circumstances be regarded as an asylum-seeker, meaning they should be eligible for asylum support under IAA 1999 s95(1),[108] until the point at which they exhaust their appeal

104 Note, however, that this will change if IA 2016 Sch 11 para 3 is brought into force. This will amend the definition of an asylum- seeker set out in IAA 1999 s94(1) to include those who have further submissions outstanding. Such applicants would then be entitled to seek asylum support under IAA 1999 s95(1).

105 *Asylum support, section 4(2): policy and process*, v3.0 (the '*Section 4(2) policy*'), Home Office, June 2022, p14 (www.gov.uk/government/publications/asylum-support-section-42-policy).

106 See paras 6.40–6.45.

107 See paras 3.118–3.130.

108 See chapter 5.

rights.[109] If the outcome at the end of the appeal process is negative, they will revert to the status of a failed asylum-seeker thereafter. Eligibility for section 4(2) support will depend on whether they meet the destitution criterion and one of the five additional qualifying conditions under the IA (PAFAS) Regs 2005, the detail of which is discussed at paras 6.46–6.135 below.

- The secretary of state decides that the further submissions do not amount to a fresh claim. There is no right of appeal against such a decision. The applicant remains a failed asylum-seeker.

6.36 The further submissions process does not apply to asylum inadmissibility decisions.[110] As explained in paras 3.131–3.142 and 5.39–5.44, individuals subject to the inadmissibility process will be served by the Home Office a Notice of Intent to declare their asylum claim inadmissible and to relocate them to another country which the Home Office considers a 'safe third country' and with which the UK has an agreement concerning the relocation of asylum-seekers. Individuals served this Notice have an opportunity to make representations as to why an inadmissibility decision should not be made. The Home Office's policy directs that those representations must be 'carefully considered' but do not need to meet the test set out in Immigration Rules para 353.[111] Such consideration may lead to 'them no longer being declared inadmissible',[112] meaning the applicant will become an asylum-seeker once more for support purposes.[113] Alternatively, if the representations are unsuccessful then the application a will fall within the scope of IAA 1999 s4(2).[114]

Has had their claim for asylum declared inadmissible

6.37 Declarations of inadmissibility are discussed in more detail at paras 3.131–3.142 in the context of the asylum process generally, and specifically in relation to asylum support, at 5.39–5.44. In outline, the secretary of state must declare an asylum claim to be inadmissible where an applicant is a national of an EU member state and may do so where the applicant has a connection with a safe third state.[115] The

109 See paras 5.29–5.44.
110 See further paras 5.39–5.44 and 6.37–6.38 for declarations of inadmissibility.
111 See *Inadmissibility: safe third country cases*, v7.0, Home Office, June 2022, p29 and *Further submissions*, v10.0, pp40–41.
112 The *Section 4(2) policy*, p14.
113 IAA 1999 s94(4B).
114 See paras 6.19 and 6.19–6.24.
115 NIAA 2002 ss80A–80C.

consequence of such a declaration is that substantive consideration of the applicant's asylum claim ceases and they may be removed either to the third country in question or, potentially, to another third country identified by the secretary of state. At the writing of this chapter, the secretary of state has identified Rwanda as a safe third country.[116]

6.38 In safe third state cases, the secretary of state may resume consideration of the applicant's claim, notwithstanding the earlier declaration of inadmissibility, if, for example, it becomes apparent that it will not be possible to remove them to the safe third state within a reasonable period.[117] If that happens, the applicant will become an asylum-seeker once more for support purposes,[118] and so will no longer be eligible for support under IAA 1999 s4(2).[119] If the applicant had been receiving IAA 1999 s4(2) support prior to the resumption of consideration of the claim, they will automatically be transitioned back to IAA 1999 s95(1) support.[120] If they were not previously in receipt of support, a new application can be made.

Dependant

6.39 The word 'dependant' has the same meaning in the context of support under IAA 1999 s4(2) as it does in the context of asylum support under IAA 1999 s95(1).[121] However, in contrast to support under IAA 1999 s95(1), dependants are not themselves entitled to make an application for support. The definition of this term is discussed in detail at paras 5.50–5.56. There is no requirement for the dependant to have been treated as a dependant on the person's asylum claim.[122]

116 See *R (AAA (Syria)) v SSHD* [2022] EWHC 3230 (Admin) at paras 116–118 (currently under appeal) on the legality of the Rwanda scheme.

117 NIAA 2002 s80B(7).

118 IAA 1999 94(4B); *Ceasing section 95 support instruction*, v1.0, Home Office, June 2022, p10.

119 Because the requirement that they were, but are no longer, an asylum-seeker (see para 6.15) will not be met.

120 *Ceasing section 95 support instruction*, v1.0, p10.

121 IAA 1999 s4(4).

122 The *Section 4(2) policy*, p7.

Destitution[123]

Overview

6.40 As explained at paras 6.9–6.14, an applicant who was (but is no longer) an asylum-seeker[124] who has had their asylum claim rejected,[125] together with their dependant(s),[126] will be eligible for support under IAA 1999 s4(2) if they appear to the secretary of state to be destitute[127] and to fall within one or more of the various gateways to support.[128]

6.41 The word 'destitute' for IAA 1999 s4(2) purposes means the same as it does under IAA 1999 s95(3).[129] This means that an applicant for section 4(2) support is destitute if they:[130]

- do not have adequate accommodation or any means of obtaining it (whether or not their other essential living needs are met); or
- have adequate accommodation or the means of obtaining it, but cannot meet their other essential living needs.

This test for establishing whether an applicant is destitute is discussed in detail at paras 5.57–5.90 in the context of asylum support under IA 1999 s95(1).

6.42 There is one notable difference in the statutory language of the destitution criterion as between IAA 1999 s4(2) and s95(1). When determining whether an applicant is eligible for asylum support under IAA 1999 s95(1), the statute requires the secretary of state to adopt a forward-looking approach, and ask whether the applicant 'is' or 'is likely to become' destitute within 14 days.[131] By contrast, an applicant only qualifies for section 4(2) support if they appear to be

123 Destitution very frequently arises as an issue between the Home Office and applicants for asylum support and a plethora of useful decisions of the FTT (Asylum Support) may be found through the ASAP website: www.asaproject.org/.

124 See paras 6.15–6.18.

125 See paras 6.19–6.24.

126 See para 6.39.

127 IA (PAFAS) Regs 2005 reg 3(1)(a).

128 IA (PAFAS) Regs 2005 reg 3(1)(b). See paras 6.46–6.135.

129 IA (PAFAS) Regs 2005 reg 2. This means that in assessing destitution for the purposes of IAA 1999 s4(2) the relevant provisions of the Asylum Support Regulations ('AS Regs') 2000 SI No 704 should also be applied. See *R (AW) v Croydon LBC* [2007] EWCA Civ 266, [2007] 1 WLR 3168.

130 IAA 1999 s95(3).

131 The 14-day test applies to new applicants. See AS Regs 2000 reg 7(a). For those who are already receiving support, the equivalent period is 56 days.

destitute now[132] and not whether they *are likely to become* destitute within 14 days. However, as a matter of policy, the Home Office has elected to apply a 14-day test to section 4(2) support applicants (or the 56-day test for those already in receipt of support) in any event.[133] This ensures a degree of parity between asylum-seekers and failed asylum-seekers in establishing eligibility for support and ensures that neither cohort has to wait until their situation has reached crisis point before support can be provided.

Destitution issues specific to Immigration and Asylum Act 1999 s4(2) applicants

6.43 As with applications for asylum support under IAA 1999 s95(1), it is for the person seeking section 4(2) support to provide evidence to support their claim to be destitute. The standard of proof is the balance of probabilities. For those who had previously been provided with IAA 1999 s95(1) asylum support but are no longer eligible, for example, because their asylum claim has been finally determined, the *Section 4(2) policy* requires the Home Office to take account of:[134]

- the lapse of time since any support was provided under IAA 1999 s95(1);
- the evidence available to support the application for IAA 1999 s4(2) support;
- whether the person has, or has had, access to accommodation or financial support and if so the evidence about the continued availability of this support.

6.44 For applicants who were not previously supported under IAA 1999 s95(1), or whose support was discontinued some time ago, the *Section 4(2) policy* considers it 'usually reasonable' to assume that they have been able to access alternative sources of support prior to making their section 4(2) applications and that they can continue to do so unless a good explanation is provided as to why such support is no longer available.[135] It is therefore vital in these circumstances for applicants to be in a position to provide a clear explanation of how they had been supported previously and provide evidence to demonstrate that this support is no longer available or sufficient. Due to the transient nature of the living and support arrangements, it can be

132 IA (PAFAS) Regs 2005 reg 3(1)(a).

133 The *Section 4(2) policy*, p9.

134 The *Section 4(2) policy*, p9.

135 The *Section 4(2) policy*, pp9–10. See further *Assessing destitution*, Home Office, November 2019, p10.

challenging for a section 4(2) applicant fully to evidence their recent history of accommodation and support. Many will have lived at a series of temporary or insecure addresses for months or even years after the refusal of their asylum claim. They may have lived with other migrants on the floors of hostels, sharing food and attempting to keep their whereabouts in the UK an unknown. They may have relied on soup kitchens, mosques, churches, casual acquaintances or voluntary organisations for food, toiletries and clothing. Such organisations will rarely provide receipts or keep records of whom they have supported and when. In some cases, in desperation, failed asylum-seekers may have worked illegally to make ends meet. Even if the available evidence is limited, the applicant still needs to do their best to provide a clear explanation as to how they have supported themself in the past.

6.45 Difficulties in evidencing a complete history of accommodation and support should not necessarily render applicants ineligible for section 4(2) support. The relevant question is not whether the applicant was able, in the past, to access support and accommodation without recourse to assistance from the secretary of state. Rather, the decision-maker must ask whether the applicant is *currently* destitute. Generally speaking, if the applicant has given a cogent account of their recent accommodation and support history, and where the evidence indicates that support is no longer available, the decision-maker should be satisfied that the applicant is destitute.

The five gateways to support

Overview

6.46 In addition to satisfying the secretary of state that they appear to be destitute, the IAA 1999 s4(2) applicant must qualify under one or more of the following gateways to support, as set out in IA (PAFAS) Regs 2005 reg 3(2), namely that:[136]

1) the applicant is taking all reasonable steps to return;[137]
2) the applicant faces obstacle to travel;[138]
3) the applicant has no safe route of return;[139]

136 IA (PAFAS) Regs 2005 reg 3(1)(b) and (2).
137 IA (PAFAS) Regs 2005 reg 3(2)(a). See paras 6.48–6.58.
138 IA (PAFAS) Regs 2005 reg 3(2)(b). See paras 6.59–6.83.
139 IA (PAFAS) Regs 2005 reg 3(2)(c). See paras 6.84–6.85.

4) the applicant has been granted permission to bring a judicial review challenge to an asylum decision;[140]
5) the applicant needs support to avoid a human rights breach.[141]

6.47 The five gateways are directed at the overarching question of whether it would be unreasonable to expect an applicant to leave the UK, reflecting an underlying 'policy that failed asylum-seekers should leave the country if possible'.[142] They do not have to be met cumulatively. However, where an applicant does (or believes that they) satisfy more than one condition, this should be made clear within their application for support.[143] This is because the Home Office may, for example, disagree with an applicant's contention that they meet one of the gateways while accepting that they meet another. So long as they meet one of the gateways, it does not matter that their application has been rejected under another.

Taking all reasonable steps to leave the UK – Immigration and Asylum (Provision of Accommodation to Failed Asylum-Seekers) Regulations 2005 reg 3(2)(a)

6.48 Applicants must show that they are taking 'all reasonable steps' to leave the UK or to place themselves in a position in which they are able to leave the UK. The use of the word 'all' means that there is an expectation on applicants to be proactive. It is not enough for an applicant to have taken some steps when there are other possible steps that could reasonably be taken. If the Home Office is able to point to a single reasonable step which has not been taken, that can be a ground for refusing to provide support under IAA 1999 s4(2). In addition, the use of the present tense ('*taking*' all reasonable steps)[144] indicates that the applicant's obligation is a continuing one, and that they will only remain eligible for support so long as they continue to take steps to leave. To that end, the *Section 4(2) policy* provides that eligibility under reg 3(2)(a) should be 'reviewed regularly and should usually be discontinued after 3 months unless the person provides satisfactory evidence to show why they have not left the UK'.[145]

140 IA (PAFAS) Regs 2005 reg 3(2)(d). See paras 6.86–6.89.
141 IA (PAFAS) Regs 2005 reg 3(2)(e). See paras 6.90–6.135.
142 *R (SSHD) v First-Tier Tribunal (Social Entitlement Chamber)* [2021] EWHC 1690 (Admin) at para 133 per Chamberlain J.
143 See paras 6.178–6.179.
144 As opposed to an applicant who 'has taken' all reasonable steps.
145 The *Section 4(2) policy*, p10.

6.49 On the other hand, the requirement is only that the applicant should be taking all 'reasonable' steps. Thus an applicant should not be penalised for failing to take a step which it would be unreasonable to expect them to take. Or, to put it another way, the Home Office cannot demand the impossible. Nor can the Home Office insist on the taking of steps that are futile.[146] Neither the IAA 1999 nor the IA (PAFAS) Regs 2005 define what constitutes a 'reasonable step'. According to reg 3(2)(a), reasonable steps 'may include complying with attempts to obtain a travel document'. However, this is intended as an example only and is not exhaustive. It also does not require the attempts to be successful; that can often be entirely out of the hands of the applicant. The *Section 4(2) policy* sets out a more expansive list of factors to be taken into account in determining whether an applicant is taking all reasonable steps. In particular, consideration should be given to whether the applicant:[147]

- has applied for Assisted Voluntary Return (AVR);
- has applied to their national embassy for any necessary travel document needed to facilitate their departure from the UK;
- has fully complied with the Home Office's processes to obtain a travel document on their behalf, including by supplying accurate information to support an application for an Emergency Travel Document;
- is being prosecuted under Asylum and Immigration (Treatment of Applicants, etc) Act 2004 s35 because they have failed to comply with directions issued by the secretary of state to take specified action to assist with the re-documentation process.

6.50 The FTT (Asylum Support) has by and large faithfully followed this list as benchmarking the sorts of reasonable steps that an applicant is expected to be able to show that they have taken. In the landmark case of *SK v SSHD*,[148] Chamber President Aitken and Principal Judge Storey approved, in substance, the reasonable steps cited above, while also acknowledging the possible challenges that some individuals may face depending their country of nationality.[149] The judges went on to give the following additional examples of steps that might be regarded as reasonable:

146 See AS/16/06/35415, 10 June 2016, FTT (Asylum Support).
147 The *Section 4(2) policy*, p10.
148 *SK v SSHD* AS/17/01/36372, 23 February 2018, FTT (Asylum Support).
149 At paras 49–50.

- establishing, where available, independent voluntary routes of return;
- collecting evidence independently to support the applicant's claimed nationality (where challenged or not established) or seeking assistance to do so from charities working on the ground in the country of nationality;
- approaching an embassy to obtain travel documents, either in the UK or, where there is no embassy in the UK, the embassy nearest to the UK;
- keeping relevant appointments whether arranged independently or by the Home Office;
- requesting financial assistance, if required, to cover the cost of return; and
- assisting the Home Office's efforts to effect a voluntary return.

6.51 Evidence of the taking of such reasonable steps can include:

- copies of letters, faxes and emails that the applicant has sent to their embassy;
- a schedule of telephone calls that they have made to their embassy, the Home Office and advice agencies in relation to re-documentation and assisted return;
- notes of any such telephone conversations;
- notes from any visits to their embassy or the Home Office; and/or
- copies of travel documents or tickets.

6.52 The FTT (Asylum Support) has consistently identified applying for voluntary return as an example of a reasonable step under IA (PAFAS) Regs 2005 reg 3(2)(a). The Assisted Voluntary Return (AVR) scheme used to involve registering with a scheme called *Choices* which was operated by the charity Refugee Action. However, this arrangement came to an end in 2015 and applications for voluntary return are now to be submitted to the Voluntary Returns Services operated by the Home Office. At the time of writing, those eligible for voluntary return[150] can apply for up to £2,000 of financial support which is for the purposes of helping the returnee find somewhere to live, and secure employment or start a business.

6.53 Not everyone is eligible to apply for voluntary return. Those excluded from the scheme include individuals who:

- are being investigated by the police or detained by the Home Office;

150 The eligibility criteria are scan be accessed at: www.gov.uk/return-home-voluntarily.

- have been given a prison sentence that is 12 months or longer;
- have been convicted of an immigration offence and made subject to a deportation order.

6.54 Persons who are ineligible for voluntary return cannot reasonably be expected to pursue this option in order to establish eligibility for support under IA (PAFAS) Regs 2005 reg 3(2)(a), although there may be other options which are available to them and which they can be expected to pursue.[151]

6.55 For certain nationalities, the re-documentation process can be complex and time-consuming. For example, nationals of certain countries such as Eritrea may find their embassy is not willing to issue them with a travel document because they cannot prove they are Eritrean.[152] Other challenges may involve tensions in diplomatic relations and matters which are well outside the control of the applicant. For an example of this, see *R (Sino) v SSHD*[153] which at paras 119–141 detailed the complex procedures for obtaining emergency travel documents for undocumented Algerians and which lasted several years in Mr Sino's case. Whether, in such circumstances, an applicant has taken all reasonable steps will need to be assessed by reference to available evidence such as the Home Office's policy on returns to that country and what is known about the documentation process.

6.56 In some cases, applicants may be reluctant to take a particular step because they are concerned that, in doing so, they may expose themselves to danger. Whether that taking of such a step is regarded as reasonable will depend on the circumstances of the case. In *R (Rasul) v Asylum Support Adjudicator*[154] the High Court declined to 'express any view, however tentative' on whether it would be reasonable to expect the applicant to seek to return to Iraq voluntarily in circumstances where, it was said, the journey by road through Northern Iraq which this would entail, was unsafe. However, the FTT (Asylum Support) has subsequently taken the view that such concerns are not relevant to the determination of eligibility under IA (PAFAS) Regs 2005 reg 3(2)(a). Rather, an applicant who is concerned about the danger to which they would be exposed in their country of

151 *UA v SSHD* AS/12/11/2199, 15 February 2013, FTT (Asylum Support).

152 See *UA v SSHD* AS/12/11/2199, 15 February 2013, FTT (Asylum Support) for an example of this.

153 [2011] EWHC 2249 (Admin).

154 [2006] EWHC 435 (Admin).

origin, by seeking to return voluntarily, must seek to raise this in the context of a fresh claim for asylum.[155]

6.57 In discontinuing support[156] on the basis that there is a reasonable step which the applicant has failed to take, it is incumbent on the secretary of state to identify what that step is. This does not mean that every possible step which could be taken needs to be set out within the decision letter. What is reasonable will vary from case to case.[157]

6.58 On appeal,[158] the FTT (Asylum Support) is not concerned with whether or not the applicant thinks they have taken all reasonable steps or whether the secretary of state's opinion that they have not is reasonably held. Rather, the question for the FTT (Asylum Support) is whether, judged objectively, all reasonable steps have been taken.[159] However, the factors which are personal to the applicant may be relevant to this assessment, for example, where the applicant has mental health difficulties which impede their understanding of, or ability to pursue, a particular step.[160] To put it another way, what is reasonable to expect from one applicant may not be reasonable to expect from another.

Unable to leave the UK – Immigration and Asylum (Provision of Accommodation to Failed Asylum-Seekers) Regulations 2005 reg 3(2)(b)

Overview

6.59 To qualify through the IA (PAFAS) Regs 2005 reg 3(2)(b) gateway, applicants must show that they are 'unable to leave the United Kingdom by reason of a physical impediment to travel or for some other medical reason'. The question is not whether it is undesirable or unreasonable for an applicant to leave the UK; it is not enough to for an applicant to be receiving medical treatment that does not prevent travel or that might not be available following the applicant's departure from the UK.[161] What must be demonstrated is that the applicant has a physical or medical condition which means that they

155 *SHH v SSHD* ASA/06/06/13556, 26 June 2006, Asylum Support Adjudicator at para 28; *AEA v SSHD* AST/0707/15572, 20 July 2007, FTT (Asylum Support) at paras 16–26.

156 See paras 6.188–6.194 on ending the provision of support.

157 See *SK v SSHD* AS/17/01/36372, 23 February 2018, FTT (Asylum Support) at para 50.

158 See paras 6.195–6.197 on appeals.

159 *AEA v SSHD* AST/0707/15572, 20 July 2007, FTT (Asylum Support) at para 19.

160 AS/13/10/30532/SB, 24 October 2013, FTT (Asylum-Support).

161 The *Section 4(2) policy*, p11.

are 'unable' to travel 'on any given day'.[162] In *R (SSHD) v Chief Asylum Support Adjudicator, Osman and others*[163] Holman J observed that reg 3(2)(b) requires a two-step approach:

a) first, it is necessary to consider whether the applicant is unable to leave the UK;
b) second, if so, it is then necessary to determine whether that inability to leave is by reason of a physical impediment to travel or some other medical reason.[164]

6.60 The judge went on to explain that 'unable' was a simple word in ordinary daily usage and that it would be unwise and unnecessary to seek to paraphrase it to assist in the application of the statutory test. However, with that caveat, he observed that the word was synonymous with 'not able', as opposed to a word with more positive force, such as 'impossible', which would put the test too high. On the other hand, there was no justification for implying a test of reasonableness into the assessment of whether a person was unable to travel.[165]

Pregnancy and maternity[166]

6.61 In the context of maternity, a relevant factor is whether an airline would be unable to carry the applicant on a long-haul flight either because she is in the latter stages of pregnancy or because she has recently given birth. The Home Office accepts that women falling into these categories may be unable to leave the UK as the result of a physical impediment to travel.

6.62 In respect of pregnant women, the *Section 4(2) policy* states that:

> Unless there are complications with the pregnancy, supported by medical evidence that the person's health and or that of the unborn child may be at risk, support must not normally be granted until around 6 weeks before the EDD [expected delivery date].[167]

6.63 The NHS assesses the average length of pregnancy in the UK to be around 40 weeks, meaning that eligibility for support will generally

162 *R (SSHD) v Chief Asylum Support Adjudicator, Osman and others* [2006] EWHC 1248 (Admin) at para 60 per Holman J.

163 [2006] EWHC 1248 (Admin).

164 [2006] EWHC 1248 (Admin) at para 21 per Holman J. This is commonly referred to as the '*Osman* test'.

165 [2006] EWHC 1248 (Admin) at paras 22–30 per Holman J.

166 See further, *Factsheet 8: Section 4 support for pregnant refused asylum seekers*, ASAP, October 2018.

167 The *Section 4(2) policy*, p11.

arise around the 34th week of pregnancy. Eligibility for support will then be reviewed six weeks after the EDD or (if known to the Home Office) the birth. In practice, this review does not always take place and the Home Office will often continue to provide support well beyond this point.

6.64 The *Section 4(2) policy* mirrors the Civil Aviation Authority's (CAA) *Guidelines for health professionals on fitness to fly*, which state that airlines will generally not accept pregnant women after the 36th week of pregnancy. However, the CAA guidelines, like the *Section 4(2) policy*, do not seek to draw bright lines as to when a pregnant woman is fit to fly and when she is not. Indeed, the guidelines refer to the 36-week benchmark being applicable to single, uncomplicated pregnancies. In respect of women with multiple pregnancies, the CAA considers that they should not travel from 32 weeks onwards, and should be required to provide medical certification as to their fitness to fly from 28 weeks onwards. The primary concern of the CAA guidelines is the health and well-being of the mother and baby and the need for airlines to consider the risks of pre-term birth and emergency complications while in flight or when forced to divert in flight to an alternative location. It is clear when the CAA guidelines are read as a whole, that they are not meant to operate as an immutable threshold as to when a pregnant woman is or is not fit to fly. Fitness to fly assessments should depend on the particular pregnant woman's personal and medical circumstances. For example, in *NS v SSHD*,[168] the FTT (Asylum Support) allowed the applicant's appeal in circumstances where his wife was 27 weeks pregnant but her pregnancy was complicated by 'severe mental illness which includes auditory and visual hallucinations'. Similarly, survivors of female genital mutilation may face complications which do not typically arise in more routine pregnancies.

6.65 In respect of women who have just given birth, the Home Office accepts that where the dependant child is less than six weeks old, the mother and child will normally be unable to travel from the UK for the purposes of IAA (PAFAS) Regs 2005 reg 3(2)(b).[169] Establishing this will require the production of the child's birth certificate or a letter from a medical professional confirming the date of the birth of the child. As with pregnant women, eligibility for support will be reviewed six weeks after birth. However again, as with pregnant women, the six-week benchmark does not operate as a bright line rule, and eligibility

168 AS/11/12/27841, 3 January 2012, FTT (Asylum Support).
169 The *Section 4(2) policy*, p11.

must still be considered in the context of the individual case. Ultimately the question is not whether the applicant is six or seven weeks post-birth, for example, but whether she is unable to travel.

Psychological and mental health conditions

6.66 Eligibility for support through the IA (PAFAS) Regs 2005 reg 3(2)(b) gateway is not restricted to those with physical impediments to travel. An applicant may also qualify if they are unable to travel by reason of another 'medical reason'. Neither the IA (PAFAS) Regs 2005 nor the *Section 4(2) policy* seek to define what is meant by a 'medical reason'. The phrase is amply broad enough to encompass psychological or mental health conditions, and the fact that it is used in contrast to an impediment of a physical nature suggests that this was the legislative intention.

6.67 Examples of cases in which such conditions have given rise to entitlement under reg 3(2)(b) include:

- AS/16/10/35949:[170] An Iranian applicant was diagnosed with depression and post-traumatic stress disorder (PTSD) which presented in the form of significant low mood, helplessness and hopelessness. His psychotherapist expressed a clinical view that this would deteriorate substantially should the applicant be instructed to organise travel back to Iran. This had already been exhibited in group therapy sessions during which the applicant exhibited significant anxiety and distress at the thought of return to Iran. The applicant's GP supported this clinical view. In allowing the appeal on reg 3(2)(b) grounds, the FTT (Asylum Support) accepted evidence that the nature and extent of the applicant's mental health conditions were such 'that he would not be able to make it even if he wanted to'.
- AS/17/01/36347/LP:[171] The applicant suffered from depression and PTSD, and the medical evidence indicated that his anxiety and panic was worse in enclosed spaces and that he might present as a threat to himself or others if put in a vehicle to be deported.
- AS/15/03/32762:[172] Psychiatric evidence submitted on behalf of the applicant indicated that there was a high likelihood that she would attempt to take her own life were she required to leave the UK. The judge found that, on the particular facts of that case, the applicant 'unequivocally satisfies the *Osman* test'.

170 AS/16/10/35949, 24 October 2016, FTT (Asylum Support).
171 See also AS/17/01/36347/LP, 24 January 2017, FTT (Asylum Support).
172 AS/15/03/32762, 20 March 2015, FTT (Asylum Support).

6.68 However, the FTT (Asylum Support) has emphasised in a number of cases that the existence of a suicide risk is not in and of itself sufficient for an applicant to qualify for support. Thus, in the landmark decision in *MAA v SSHD*,[173] the medical evidence adduced in support of the establishment of PTSD and a contention of associated suicide risks creating a medical impediment to removal under reg 3(2)(b) did not succeed because the trauma upon which the medical expert diagnosed the appellant as having PTSD had been held to be fabricated. Perceived risks of suicide or situational depression worsened by negative decisions on support did not by themselves meet the threshold under reg 3(2)(b). In these circumstances, the apparent medical impediments could be avoided by co-operating with the Home Office removal process and the secretary of state arranging 'suitable escort(s) who will if required, medicate or restrain the appellant to ensure that they do not self-harm whilst in transit'.[174] In *YT v SSHD*,[175] another appeal turning on an argument about suicide risk failed in circumstances where the evidence pointed to a subjective fear but was insufficient to establish an objective foundation for a real risk of suicide in breach of ECHR Article 3. In that case, the judge contemplated that the outcome might be different if the applicant pursued a fresh claim, relying on the medical evidence on suicide risks and immigration and asylum case-law[176] establishing that such risk may found a meritorious ECHR Article 3 claim.[177]

6.69 These suicide risk cases illustrate the importance of applicants seeking to establish eligibility in these circumstances providing evidence to show precisely how the risk that they face is linked to their ability to travel, and why it is that the provision of an escort would not alleviate that risk. Where the risk is subjective and could be eliminated or substantially reduced so that it is not an impediment by co-operating with the Home Office removal process, there may be no impediment that satisfies the reg 3(2)(b) gateway. That said, the burden of proof in this context is not entirely one way. Where the Home Office suggests that the applicant can return to

173 AS/15/05/33112, 12 February 2016, FTT (Asylum Support).

174 *MAA v SSHD* AS/15/05/33112, 12 February 2016, FTT (Asylum Support) at para 59. Note that this case concerned eligibility for support under IA (PAFAS) Regs 2005 reg 3(2)(e). See paras 6.90–6.135.

175 AS/18/01/37699, 29 January 2018, FTT (Asylum Support). As with *MAA v SSHD*, this case also concerned reg 3(2)(e).

176 See *J v SSHD* [2005] EWCA Civ 629; and *Y (Sri Lanka) v SSHD* [2009] EWCA Civ 362.

177 See paras 3.56–3.57 for a discussion of the relevant threshold.

their home country with the assistance of a medical escort, questions still need to be asked as to whether this has actually been arranged and will take place and as to how the presence of an escort will mitigate the risk.[178] The same also arises in respect of any proposal by the Home Office to use physical restraint or sedation during the flight to prevent self-harm or disruption to other passengers.

6.70 Much turns on the nature and quality of the medical evidence, the severity of the psychological or mental health condition, and the risk of suicide posed by removal. If it can be shown that removal would cause 'intense physical or mental suffering'[179] to a threshold of a real risk of an ECHR Article 3 breach, then the applicant might properly be regarded as unable to leave the UK and therefore eligible for support under reg 3(2)(b).[180] Alternatively, as was hinted by the judge in *YT*, in such cases the applicant may be eligible for support under reg 3(2)(e),[181] which requires the provision of support to avoid a breach of human rights, while the applicant makes further submissions in support of a fresh claim for asylum or humanitarian protection or until practical arrangements are put in place for the applicant's safe return to their country of origin.[182]

Relevance of third-party support

6.71 The cases referred to at para 6.68 above raise an important issue as to the relevance of third-party support (Home Office escorts in those cases) to the question of whether or not the applicant is unable to leave the UK. It is implicit in the decisions referred to above that in assessing whether or not an applicant is able to travel, it is permissible to take into account the support which may be provided to them by a third-party (in this instance, in-flight escorts provided by the Home Office) in order to make that possible.

178 See paras 6.71–6.77.

179 See *Pretty v UK* App No 2346/02 (2002) 35 EHRR 1, ECtHR. See further *Y (Sri Lanka) v SSHD* [2009] EWCA Civ 362, in which the Court of Appeal held that a fear of ill-treatment upon return that creates a risk of suicide when the return is enforced by the state might give rise to a breach of ECHR Article 3. In *YT v SSHD* AS/18/01/37699, 29 January 2018, FTT (Asylum Support), the tribunal accepted in principle, at para 51, that this might be of relevance in the support context.

180 On the basis that Human Rights Act 1998 s3 requires IS (PAFAS) Regs 2005 reg 3(2)(b) to be read compatibly with the ECHR.

181 See paras 6.90–6.135.

182 See AS/15/11/34454, 16 November 2015, FTT (Asylum Support) in which the applicant's appeal was rejected under IA (PAFAS) Regs 2005 reg 3(2)(b) but allowed under reg 3(2)(e), until removal was effected.

6.72 However, a different approach prevailed in AS/17/09/37284.[183] That case concerned a mentally incapacitated applicant with severe learning disability and epilepsy. He was found by medical professionals (including the Home Office's own doctor) not to be fit to fly by himself owing to his complex mental health needs and his dependency on his parents in all aspects of his daily activities. However, the Home Office still found that he was ineligible for support, influenced by its medical advisor's view that 'the appellant could probably travel if accompanied by his parents' back to their home country of Pakistan. Judge Penrose of the FTT (Asylum Support) substituted this for a decision finding that the applicant was eligible, reasoning that:

> This is of no relevance to the question of whether the appellant can travel independently, which is the question posed in the regulation. His parents may or may not accompany the appellant on travel, (they have yet to make up their minds it would appear) but satisfaction of the Regulation in respect of this appellant should not be contingent on the actions of any third party.[184]

6.73 Superficially, this case differs from the suicide risk cases referred to at para 6.68 above because the support available relied on is from family members as opposed to state support from the Home Office. However, as a matter of principle there does not seem to be any statutory basis for drawing a distinction between different types of third-party support in considering eligibility under IA (PAFAS) Regs 2005 reg 3(2)(b). It is either something which the IA (PAFAS) Regs 2005 allow to be taken into account or it is not. So, which of these two approaches is correct?

6.74 In AS/19/05/39578,[185] Judge Lewis preferred the approach taken in the suicide risk cases of considering the availability of third-party support, describing it as representing the 'long-standing orthodoxy in section 4 medical cases',[186] and took the view that AS/17/09/37284[187] was wrong in so far as it decided otherwise. Although there is no binding authority on the issue, it seems probable that the reasoning of Judge Lewis is correct. Although IA (PAFAS) Regs 2005 reg 3(2)(b) does not expressly require or mandate consideration of third-party support, it does not exclude such support from being taken into consideration. To disregard or ignore the availability and possibility of

183 AS/17/09/37284, 5 October 2017, FTT (Asylum Support).
184 AS/17/09/37284, 5 October 2017, FTT (Asylum Support) at para 17.
185 AS/19/05/39578, 28 June 2019, FTT (Asylum Support).
186 AS/19/05/39578, 28 June 2019, FTT (Asylum Support) at para 74.
187 AS/17/09/37284, 5 October 2017, FTT (Asylum Support).

third-party support as relevant mitigation against any impediment to leaving the UK would, as Judge Lewis observed,[188] mean reading the phrase 'unable to leave the United Kingdom' as 'unable to leave the United Kingdom *independently*' [emphasis in original]. That added, in his view, an unwarranted gloss to the plain words of the regulations.

6.75 Further support for Judge Lewis' analysis, together with an important caveat, may be found in the reasoning of the Supreme Court in a slightly different statutory context. The case of *Hotak v Southwark LBC*[189] related to the correct approach to be taken in assessing whether or not a homeless applicant should be regarded as 'vulnerable' for the purposes of Housing Act 1996 s189(1)(c) and, as a result, whether or not a duty to accommodate them had arisen. In deciding this, the Supreme Court had to consider whether or not it was permissible for a local housing authority to take into account the support which might be available to the applicant from a third party, in assessing the risk of harm which they would face when homeless. The support in that case was provided to the applicant by his brother. The local housing authority accepted that without this support the applicant would be vulnerable, but argued that the availability of that support could not be overlooked. The Supreme Court agreed,[190] finding that third-party support could be taken into account. The court's reasoning was that the question of whether the applicant was vulnerable needed to assessed 'with reference to his situation if and when homeless'. It was not a clinical assessment. Rather it was a contextual and practical assessment. The court held that 'the fact that it is a contextual and practical question points strongly in favour of the conclusion that, when deciding if he is "vulnerable" ' and that this 'must take into account such services and support that would be available to the applicant if he were homeless'.[191] It would seem 'contrary to common sense' if one were to disregard 'any aspect of the actual or anticipated factual situation when assessing vulnerability'.[192] If an applicant had a health condition which could satisfactorily be treated by medication, which they could obtain and administer

188 AS/19/05/39578, 28 June 2019, FTT (Asylum Support) at para 78.

189 [2015] UKSC 30, [2016] AC 811.

190 With Baroness Hale dissenting. In her opinion the source of the third-party support matters. Statutory support could be taken into account. But other less steady forms of support, such as charitable support and support from friends and families, should not. See paras 94–96.

191 *Hotak v Southwark LBC* [2015] UKSC 30, [2016] AC 811 at para 62 per Lord Neuberger.

192 *Hotak* at para 63 per Lord Neuberger.

for themself, then it would be unrealistic to disregard that medication in assessing whether the applicant was vulnerable. Once that point was acknowledged, then it was hard to justify ignoring other forms of assistance or support.[193]

6.76 Many of these points would apply with equal force to the assessment of whether an applicant is unable to leave the UK for the purposes of reg 3(2)(b). This is not a purely medical question but rather one which is practical and contextual, to be judged with reference to the applicant's situation when leaving the UK.[194] If an applicant has a health condition which does not impact on their ability to travel because it can be appropriately managed by medication when travelling, then it would be unrealistic to disregard the availability and effect of that medication when considering whether the applicant can leave the UK. That same logic would apply to third-party support.

6.77 Be that as it may, in the absence of binding authority from the higher courts, the point would seem to be open to debate. However, even assuming that the analysis at paras 6.74–6.76 is correct, it should not be taken as carte blanche for the Home Office to refuse support in any case where third-party support might be available. Rather, the Supreme Court's warning that third-party support should only be relied 'with considerable circumspection'[195] would need to be kept in mind. Specifically, third-party support should only be taken into account where it will be available on a 'consistent and predictable' basis and where it is sufficient to alleviate any risk posed to (or by) the applicant.[196] Putting this in the context of IA (PAFAS) Regs 2005 reg 3(2)(b), an applicant may still be eligible for support notwithstanding the notional eligibility of third-party support, if there is a question mark over if, when or how that support will be made available. The facts of AS/17/09/37284,[197] in which it was unclear whether the applicant's parents would accompany him to Pakistan, provide an

193 *Hotak* at para 64 per Lord Neuberger.

194 An obvious example of the practical nature of the question may be found in the pregnancy cases discussed at paras 6.61–6.65, where the focus is not solely on the medical consequences of travel for the mother to be, but whether or not an airline would be willing to accept her on a long-haul flight.

195 *Hotak* at para 61 per Lord Neuberger.

196 *Hotak* at paras 66 and 70 per Lord Neuberger.

197 AS/17/09/37284, 5 October 2017, FTT (Asylum Support).

illustration of this.[198] Cases where there is no evidence as to when the Home Office intends to provide the applicant with an escort, but simply an assertion that an escort *could* be provided, might provide another.[199] Further, an applicant will still be eligible for support notwithstanding the availability of an escort from the Home Office, where such arrangements would not be sufficient to enable them to fly safely. An illustration of this is provided by AS/16/11/36081/CA,[200] in which the applicant's appeal was allowed in circumstances where '[t]he respondent has not set out in any detail how they intend to overcome the appellant's immense physical health and functional problems in the confines of a plane'.

Medical evidence

6.78 Demonstrating inability to travel will almost always require written evidence from a medical practitioner who is able to explain the exact nature of the physical impediment or medical reason that prevents the person from leaving the UK, to explain why this is the case and to indicate how long this state of affairs will persist. The Home Office asks for this information to be provided on the 'Section 4(2) Medical Declaration' form, although it is also possible to provide the information by way of medical letters and reports, providing that the salient points are dealt with. The Home Office provides medical practitioners with a fee for completing the medical declaration form.[201]

6.79 The Home Office also has a specific form for medical declarations in respect of pregnant women. The 'MATB1' form is to be completed by a doctor or a midwife up to 20 weeks prior to the EDD. The Home

198 *Hotak* supports the judge's reasoning in that case, that Home Office decision-making should not be based on assumptions about what a reasonable parent (or other third-party) would do in such circumstances. See para 70 per Lord Neuberger: 'whether a particular applicant will in fact receive support and if so what support, must be a case-specific question, to which the answer must be based on evidence (which can of course include appropriate inferences)'.

199 See *MN v SSHD* AS/15/05/33235, 12 June 2015, FTT (Asylum Support) in which the applicant's case was remitted for reconsideration under IA (PAFAS) Regs 2005 reg 3(2)(b), among other things, with a direction that the Home Office should consider seven practical questions such as who would be responsible for providing an escort and when. In such cases it may also be that the applicant is entitled to support under IA (PAFAS) Regs 2005 reg 3(2)(e) until the practical arrangements are put in place to remove them. See AS/15/11/34454, 16 November 2015, FTT (Asylum Support) in which the applicant's appeal was rejected under IA (PAFAS) Regs 2005 reg 3(2)(b) but allowed under reg 3(2)(e), until removal was effected.

200 AS/16/11/36081/CA, 21 November 2016, FTT (Asylum Support).

201 The *Section 4(2) policy*, p11.

Office usually sets a date six weeks after the EDD or the birth of the child to review the situation.

6.80 The credentials of the medical professionals providing evidence of the applicant's medical condition will be critical to the proper determination of whether an applicant meets the criterion for accommodation under IA (PAFAS) Regs 2005 reg 3(2)(b). Questions such as the specialism of the medical professional, whether they have seen the applicant and how well they know the applicant are all highly relevant and go to the value of and the weight to be put on the medical opinion.[202]

6.81 The Home Office routinely instructs medical advisers to comment on the medical evidence submitted by applications in order to provide decision-makers with a view on whether the applicant's condition poses an impediment that means they are unable to leave the UK. The medical view obtained is almost always based on a paper review and not on a clinical judgment informed by an assessment of the applicant. In the context of homelessness applications under Housing Act 1996 Part VII, where the use of such advisers has been a long-standing feature of local authority decision-making, the courts have cautioned against overreliance on such medical advice. In *Shala v Birmingham City Council*[203] the Court of Appeal held that whilst the advice provided by such medical advisers may be of some assistance, the limited extent and character of the medical expertise needed to be borne in mind by decision-makers. The function of the medical adviser in these circumstances is usually to help decision-makers understand the medical issues and to evaluate for themself the expert evidence placed before them. The medical adviser's advice 'cannot itself ordinarily constitute expert evidence of the applicant's condition'.[204] The Court of Appeal in *Guiste v Lambeth LBC*[205] reaffirmed the principles set down in *Shala*, emphasising that decision-makers must give adequate reasons addressing the matters outlined at para 6.80 if they are to adopt such medical advice over first-hand expert evidence provided on behalf of an applicant:

202 *Shala v Birmingham City Council* [2007] EWCA Civ 624, [2008] HLR 8: a case decided under the Housing Act 1996 but applied routinely by the FTT (Asylum Support), for example, in the landmark decision in *MAA v SSHD* AS/15/05/33112, 12 February 2016, FTT (Asylum Support) at paras 48–50. See further *Guiste v Lambeth LBC* [2019] EWCA Civ 1758 at paras 64–65.

203 [2007] EWCA Civ 624, [2008] HLR 8.

204 *Shala v Birmingham City Council* [2007] EWCA Civ 624, [2008] HLR 8 at para 22. See fn 216 above.

205 [2019] EWCA Civ 1758.

> If Ms Ubiam was intending to base her conclusion on the views of the two psychiatrists instructed by NowMedical, she needed to explain why their views should prevail over that of Dr Freedman, when they were less highly qualified that she is, and (more importantly) they had never met or interviewed Mr Guiste. Equally, I find it hard to see how Ms Ubiam could rationally have given more weight to the report of the consultation at St George's Hospital in September 2017 than to the more recent and much fuller report of Dr Freedman, which (unlike the earlier report) also focused on the critical question of the effect that homelessness would have on Mr Guiste's mental health.[206]

6.82 In AS/16/11/36081/CA,[207] the FTT (Asylum Support) was asked to find that a Kuwaiti applicant who was wheelchair-bound and had significant renal difficulties was unable to leave the UK because of a physical impediment. The applicant produced several medical declarations and a report from her treating consultant, a professor of renal medicine, as to why she was unable to fly. Her treating consultant explained at some length how the immunosuppressive medication she had to take made her vulnerable to infection and how an environment of proximity to so many people within the cabin of a plane would be a particular risk. However, the Home Office's medical adviser, on a paper review of the documents, expressed the view that while the applicant faced difficulties in flight, these were not insurmountable and that the evidence did not support a conclusion that the applicant was unable to travel. The Home Office relied on the medical adviser's opinion instead of the opinion of the applicant's treating consultant. On an appeal, the tribunal preferred the evidence of the applicant's treating consultant on the basis of that the consultant had first-hand detailed knowledge of the applicant's condition and was able, in his evidence, to specifically address the applicant's ability to travel.

6.83 What is clear from the above is that clearly reasoned medical evidence to show a link between the health need and the inability to travel, whether for a physical or psychological reason, is paramount. The FTT (Asylum Support) will invariably issue directions in IA (PAFAS) Regs 2005 reg 3(2)(b) cases to elicit such information. However, the short timescale in which the appeal process takes place[208] may mean that obtaining this information in the time between the giving of directions and the hearing of the appeal may be impracticable. For that reason, it is vital that detailed medical evidence, addressing the *Osman* test and explaining how and why it is

206 *Guiste v Lambeth LBC* [2019] EWCA Civ 1758 at para 64; see also para 65.

207 AS/16/11/36081/CA, 21 November 2016, FTT (Asylum Support).

208 See paras 6.195–6.197 on appeals.

that the applicant is unable to leave the UK, should be sought at the earliest opportunity. Of course, if such evidence can be obtained at the point the application for support is made,[209] it also increases the chance of the application being granted meaning that the case never needs to progress to an appeal.

No viable route of return – Immigration and Asylum (Provision of Accommodation to Failed Asylum-Seekers) Regulations 2005 reg 3(2)(c)[210]

6.84 Support may be provided where the applicant is unable to leave the UK because, in the opinion of the secretary of state, there is currently no viable route of return available.

6.85 In *R (Rasul) v Asylum Support Adjudicator and others*,[211] Wilkie J held that the opinion of the Home Secretary, for the purposes of reg 3(2)(c), is a policy decision which is taken in respect of a whole country and is not a decision related to a particular individual or the journey to be undertaken. On appeal, the role of the FTT (Asylum Support) is limited to considering whether the secretary of state's opinion is truly held. That is, it is not open to the FTT (Asylum Support) to adjudicate on the substantive merits of the opinion.[212] At the time of writing, there are no countries to which the secretary of state considers that there is no viable route of return.

Permission granted in judicial review – Immigration and Asylum (Provision of Accommodation to Failed Asylum-Seekers) Regulations 2005 reg 3(2)(d)[213]

6.86 An applicant will be eligible for support under IA (PAFAS) Regs 2005 reg 3(2)(d) where they have made an application for judicial review in England or Wales in relation to their asylum claim and have been granted permission to proceed pursuant to Civil Procedure Rules (CPR) Part 54.[214] This gateway applies only to judicial review challenges relating to the applicant's asylum claim. It does not apply to judicial review of other types of immigration decision.[215] Judicial

209 See paras 6.178–6.187 on applications.

210 IA (PAFAS) Regs 2005 reg 3(2)(c).

211 [2006] EWHC 435 (Admin).

212 *R (Rasul) v Asylum Support Adjudicator and others* [2006] EWHC 435 (Admin).

213 IA (PAFAS) Regs 2005 reg 3(2)(d).

214 Analogous provisions also apply to those who made their judicial review claim in Scotland or Northern Ireland. See IA (PAFAS) Regs 2005 reg 3(2)(d).

215 In such cases, the applicant may, however, qualify for support under IA (PAFAS) Regs 2005 reg 3(2)(e). See paras 6.90–6.135.

review claims of asylum decisions may, for example, relate to: the Home Office's refusal to accept further submissions as a fresh claim under Immigration Rules para 353;[216] the certification of the applicant's asylum or human rights claim;[217] or a declaration that the applicant's asylum claim is inadmissible.[218]

6.87 Since November 2013, claims for judicial review brought in England and Wales have predominantly been the responsibility of the Upper Tribunal (Immigration and Asylum Chamber). This includes circumstances where the challenge to the immigration decision is brought together with a challenge to removal directions.[219] A claim can still be brought in the Administrative Court division of the High Court if the judicial review also involves a challenge to a person's detention under immigration powers or where there is a wider argument about the lawfulness of a policy or rule and its operation. In Scotland, the responsible court for determining judicial reviews of immigration decisions is the Court of Session. In Northern Ireland it is the High Court in Belfast.

6.88 The existence of a judicial review claim and the grant of permission for the claim to proceed may be evidenced by the sealed claim form and the production of the court order granting permission. The requirement of permission being granted is a mandatory qualifying condition under this gateway; anything short of this will not suffice. An applicant who has filed a judicial review application with the court but is awaiting a decision on whether permission will be granted will not qualify under reg 3(2)(d), but is likely qualify on human rights grounds under reg 3(2)(e).[220] The same would apply to an applicant who has issued their claim and been granted interim relief without any decision being taken on permission. Judicial review claims which have been dismissed by the first instance court following a substantive hearing but which have been granted permission to appeal would arguably qualify under this condition but not if the application for permission to appeal yet to be determined.

216 See paras 3.42–3.43 and 6.25–6.36.

217 NIAA 2002 s94(1). See paras 3.121–3.130.

218 The *Section 4(2) policy*, p12. See paras 5.39–5.44 and 6.37–6.38 for declarations of inadmissibility.

219 Consolidated Direction given in respect of the Mandatory Transfer of Judicial Review applications to the Upper Tribunal under the Senior Courts Act 1981 s31A(2), made by the Lord Chief Justice in accordance with Constitutional Reform Act 2005 Sch 2 and Tribunals, Courts and Enforcement Act 2007 s18.

220 See paras 6.90–6.135.

6.89 The availability of support under reg 3(2)(e) for applicants who have issued judicial review proceedings but have not yet been granted permission means that, in practice, applications for support under reg 3(2)(d) are rare, since the majority of applicants will already have applied for and been granted support before their application for judicial review reaches the permission stage.

Support to avoid a breach of human rights – Immigration and Asylum (Provision of Accommodation to Failed Asylum-Seekers) Regulations 2005 reg 3(2)(e)[221]

6.90 To qualify for support though the IA (PAFAS) Regs 2005 reg 3(2)(e) gateway, an applicant must establish that the provision of accommodation is necessary for the purpose of avoiding a breach of a person's 'Convention rights' within the meaning of the Human Rights Act 1998. This encompasses ECHR Articles 2–12 and 14, Articles 1–3 of the First Protocol, and Article 1 of the Thirteenth Protocol, as read with Articles 16–18.[222] In contrast to the other gateways to support, reg 3(2)(e) does not focus solely on the applicant – its ambit is wider than that. The question is whether the applicant needs accommodation in order to avoid a breach of 'a person's' rights under the ECHR. This might, for example, mean that an applicant should be provided with accommodation in order to avoid a breach of a dependant's ECHR rights[223] or even the rights of the public at large.[224]

6.91 Despite the apparently broad scope of reg 3(2)(e), there is relatively little by way of direct authority from the higher courts in this particular statutory context as to what sort of case will qualify through this gateway. In *R (NS (Somalia)) v First-tier Tribunal (Social Entitlement Chamber)*[225] the High Court was invited to give guidance as to how the gateway operated. The applicant in that case had made further submissions in support of a fresh claim for asylum. The secretary of state rejected these submissions concluding that they did not amount

221 IA (PAFAS) Regs 2005 reg 3(2)(e). This is the same test as under NIAA 2002 Sch 3 para 3, which allows a person who would normally be excluded from state support (including support under the IAA 1999) on the basis of their immigration status to access that support to avoid a breach of their human rights. See paras 6.136–6.137.

222 Human Rights Act 1998 s1(1).

223 See, however, paras 6.141–6.143 on the relationship with community care support, for cases where a failed asylum-seeker and a dependant child require accommodation.

224 *R (SSHD) v First-tier Tribunal (Social Entitlement Chamber)* [2021] EWHC 1690 (Admin) at paras 129–130 per Chamberlain J.

225 [2009] EWHC 3819 (Admin).

to a fresh claim. The applicant sought judicial review of this decision. In the meantime, the secretary of state terminated the applicant's accommodation provided under IAA 1999 s4(2). On appeal to the FTT (Asylum Support), the tribunal upheld the secretary of state's decision to terminate support and held that an applicant who was seeking judicial review of an asylum decision would only be eligible for support where they could bring themself within the reg 3(2)(d) gateway. In this case, the applicant had issued her claim for judicial review, but permission had not been granted. Therefore she did not qualify under reg 3(2)(d) and nor could she qualify under reg 3(2)(e):

> . . . if I were to accept that position, then regulation [3(2)(d)] would have no legal effect. It was clearly Parliament's intention to make a distinction following the rejection of further representations presumably by there being some kind of check on the application by virtue of it having to satisfy the High Court that it requires permission in order to proceed.[226]

6.92 The applicant sought judicial review of this decision. Stadlen J allowed the application (which was not ultimately contested by the secretary of state), accepting that the FTT (Asylum Support) had erred by imposing a requirement that, in such a case, permission to proceed with the judicial review of the asylum decision was necessary in order to qualify for support through the reg 3(2)(e) gateway. However, the judge declined to give more general guidance on the true interpretation of the ambit of the reg 3(2)(e) gateway, emphasising simply that there were 'a variety of factual circumstances' in which it may apply and each case should be considered on its own merits.[227]

6.93 Similarly, in *R (SSHD) v First-tier Tribunal (Social Entitlement Chamber)*, Chamberlain J remarked that it would 'not be wise, to attempt to define here the precise boundaries of the category of destitute failed asylum-seekers whose ECHR rights require the provision of accommodation under reg 3(2)(e)' and that the most that could be said for present purposes was that 'a multifactorial assessment would be required in each individual case'.[228]

6.94 However, some general guidance on the circumstances in which support may be necessary to avoid a breach of the ECHR may be drawn from other statutory contexts. The applicant in *R (Kimani) v*

226 [2009] EWHC 3819 (Admin) at para 9.

227 [2009] EWHC 3819 (Admin) at paras 10–14.

228 *R (SSHD) v First-tier Tribunal (Social Entitlement Chamber)* [2021] EWHC 1690 (Admin) at para 137 per Chamberlain J.

Lambeth LBC[229] sought asylum support from her local authority under the Asylum Support (Interim Provisions) Regulations 1999.[230] The local authority refused to provide her with support, on the footing that it was precluded from doing so by virtue of the exclusions from local authority support contained in NIAA 2002 Sch 3[231] paras 1 and 5 as she was the spouse of a European Economic Area (EEA) national. NIAA 2002 Sch 3 para 3 provides that these exclusions do not prevent the exercise of a power or the performance of a duty to the extent necessary to avoid a breach of a person's rights under the ECHR. However, the local authority concluded, on the facts of the applicant's case, the refusal of support would not result in any such breach. This decision was upheld by the High Court and the Court of Appeal. Lord Phillips MR observed that:

> A State owes no duty under the Convention to provide support to foreign nationals who are permitted to enter their territory but who are in a position freely to return home. Most people who fall into this category are given leave to enter on condition that they do not have recourse to public funds.[232]

6.95 The effect of the decision in *Kimani* was considered by the Court of Appeal in *R (Clue) v Birmingham City Council*.[233] Dyson LJ explained that:

> 39. Secondly, the court seems to have been of the view that the essential question was whether it was reasonable to expect a claimant to look for sustenance or support to his home country. Thus, at [24], Lord Phillips said that the objective of Schedule 3 to the 2002 Act is to discourage classes of persons who can *reasonably* be expected to look to other countries for their livelihood. At [26], he said that it was not *reasonable* to expect an asylum-seeker with an outstanding claim for asylum to look to his or her home country for sustenance or support. At [40], he said that Strasbourg jurisprudence would not require this country to permit a claimant, seeking to enter the UK for family

229 [2003] EWCA Civ 1150, [2004] 1 WLR 272. The application of the *Kimani* approach in the asylum support context was endorsed by Chamberlain J in *R (SSHD) v First-tier Tribunal (Social Entitlement Chamber)* [2021] EWHC 1690 (Admin) at para 136.

230 SI No 3056. These regulations provided a system of support for asylum-seekers, to be provided by local authorities, during the interim period which ended on which ended on 3 April 2006, following the coming into effect of the new asylum support regime under IAA 1999 Part VI. See chapter 5.

231 See paras 5.122–5.131 and 9.195–9.217.

232 *R (Kimani) v Lambeth LBC* [2003] EWCA Civ 1150, [2004] 1 WLR 272 at para 49.

233 [2010] EWCA Civ 460, [2011] 1 WLR 99.

reasons, to be permitted to enter or to remain here on public support pending the resolution of his claim. Implicit in this is the proposition that it is reasonable to expect such a claimant to return to his country of origin *because the claim can be pursued from that country*. Indeed, that was the position at the time of the decision in *Kimani*. It was, therefore, reasonable to require the claimant to return pending the determination of the appeal. The same point appears from [49] where the court said that no infringement of article 8 would result from requiring the claimant to return *pending the determination of the appeal*.

40. Thirdly, the penultimate sentence of [49] should not be misunderstood. The court said that a state owes no duty under the Convention to provide support to foreign nationals who are permitted to enter their territory 'but who are in a position *freely* to return home' (emphasis added). What is meant by 'freely'? Asylum seekers who have outstanding applications for asylum clearly cannot be required to return home although, in one sense, they are 'free' to do so. Similarly, as I have said, it is implicit in the reasoning of the court that a person who it is not reasonable to require to return home is not 'free' to return home in the sense in which the court was using the word 'free'.[234]

6.96 The claimant in *Clue* was a Jamaican national whose visitor visa has expired and who remained in the UK in breach of immigration laws. Following the breakdown of her relationship with her British partner, she applied for indefinite leave to remain on human rights grounds and sought support for herself and her four children under ChA 1989 s17(1).[235] The local authority refused to provide support, on the basis that the claimant was excluded from support by virtue of NIAA 2002 Sch 3 para 7,[236] and that any breach of her ECHR rights could be avoided by her returning to Jamaica, which the local authority was willing to fund. The High Court allowed the claimant's application for judicial review and that decision was upheld by the Court of Appeal. Applying the reasoning in *Kimani*, Dyson LJ proceeded to give guidance as to the approach which should be taken in deciding whether or not to provide support in such cases. Elements of this guidance relate to the statutory exclusions from local authority support under NIAA 2002 Sch 3, which are not relevant here, and to the specific considerations that may arise where the person seeking support has made an application for leave to remain that implicitly or explicitly raises ECHR issues.[237] However, elements of the guidance

234 Emphasis in original.
235 See paras 9.12–9.69.
236 See paras 9.195–9.217.
237 This latter guidance may sometimes be relevant to an applicant's eligibility for support under IAA 1999 s4(2). See para 6.115.

are of more general application to any context – including support under IAA 1999 s4(2) – where it is necessary to determine whether the state is required provide support in order to avoid a breach of a person's rights under the ECHR. In outline, Dyson LJ advocated a two-staged approach:[238]

1) It is necessary to decide whether and, if so, the extent to which it is necessary to exercise a power or perform a duty for the purpose of avoiding a breach of a person's rights under the ECHR. If the withholding of assistance would not cause a person to suffer from destitution amounting to a breach of their rights under the ECHR (typically Article 3), the investigation ends there.
2) However, if there are no other sources of assistance which would save the person from destitution amounting to a breach of a right under the ECHR, it is necessary consider whether there is a practical or legal impediment to the person returning to their country of origin. If, and only if, such an impediment exists, then support will need to be provided.

6.97 The Principal Judge of the FTT (Asylum Support), in the landmark case of *AM v SSHD*,[239] accepted that 'many of the principles laid down by Dyson LJ have equal relevance for asylum support judges'[240] and this two-staged approach has been incorporated into the *Section 4(2) policy*.[241]

6.98 In the context of eligibility for support under IAA 1999 s4(2), stage one of this test is fairly straightforward.[242] In *R (Limbuela) v SSHD*,[243] Lord Bingham explained that:

> A general public duty to house the homeless or provide for the destitute cannot be spelled out of article 3. But I have no doubt that the threshold may be crossed if a late applicant with no means and no

238 *R (Clue) v Birmingham City Council* [2010] EWCA Civ 460, [2011] 1 WLR 99 at paras 53–75.

239 AS/14/11/32141, 10 August 2015, FTT (Asylum Support).

240 *AM v SSHD* AS/14/11/32141, 10 August 2015, FTT (Asylum Support) at para 27. See further *SK v SSHD* AS/17/01/36372, 23 February 2018, FTT (Asylum Support) at paras 41–42; and *R (SSHD) v First-Tier Tribunal (Social Entitlement Chamber)* [2021] EWHC 1690 (Admin) at para 136 where Chamberlain J endorsed the application of the *R (Kimani) v Lambeth LBC* [2003] EWCA Civ 1150, [2004] 1 WLR 272 approach in the asylum support context.

241 The *Section 4(2) policy*, pp12–13.

242 The *Section 4(2) policy*, p12.

243 [2005] UKHL 66, [2006] 1 AC 396. See further the Introduction for the facts of, and background to, this decision.

alternative sources of support, unable to support himself, is, by the deliberate action of the state, denied shelter, food or the most basic necessities of life.[244]

6.99 The ECHR Article 3 threshold, he went on to observe, would be likely to be crossed 'if there were persuasive evidence that a late applicant was obliged to sleep in the street, save perhaps for a short and foreseeably finite period, or was seriously hungry, or unable to satisfy the most basic requirements of hygiene'.[245] Although the Article 3 threshold is not identical to the statutory destitution test contained in the IAA 1999, there is a significant degree of overlap between the two standards.[246] A failed asylum-seeker who is seeking support under IAA 1999 s4(2) because they are facing imminent homelessness, or they are without food or funds, is likely to satisfy both the statutory destitution test for the purposes of IA (PAFAS) Regs 2005 reg 3(1)[247] and to meet the Article 3 threshold for the purposes of reg 3(2)(e).

6.100 However, by itself, this will not be sufficient to establish eligibility for support. In order to establish eligibility for support by means of IA (PAFAS) Regs 2005 reg 3(2)(b), an applicant who has satisfied the first stage of Dyson LJ's two-stage test, must then move on to the second stage, and establish that they face a legal or practical impediment to return which means that they cannot reasonably be expected to return to their country of origin[248] to alleviate their destitution and avoid the prospective Article 3 breach.[249]

6.101 There are a number of situations featuring in or analogous to the case-law or guidance in which a destitute applicant may, or may arguably, face a practical or legal impediment to return such as to give rise to an entitlement to IAA 1999 s4(2) support through the IA (PAFAS) Regs 2005 reg 3(2)(e) gateway. These include cases:

- in which further submissions have, or are to be, made;[250]

244 *R (Limbuela) v SSHD* [2005] UKHL 66, [2006] 1 AC 396 at para 7 per Lord Bingham.

245 *Limbuela* at para 9 per Lord Bingham, paras 56–63 per Lord Hope and para 78 per Baroness Hale. See further, the *Section 4(2) policy*, p12.

246 See paras 6.40–6.45 for the destitution test and para 5.264 for a discussion of the overlap between the two tests.

247 See paras 6.40–6.45.

248 Characterised by Dyson LJ as 'the essential question' in such cases. See para 6.95.

249 The *Section 4(2) policy*, p13.

250 See paras 6.103–6.114.

- where the applicant has an extant application for leave to remain under ECHR Article 8 or other grounds;[251]
- where the applicant has been referred to the National Referral Mechanism (NRM), the formal identification process for victims of trafficking, for a decision as to whether they are victims of trafficking;[252]
- where the applicant is preparing to seek, or has applied for, judicial review of an asylum decision, but permission has not yet been granted;[253]
- where the applicant is seeking to pursue an out of time appeal against the refusal of their asylum claim;[254]
- where an applicant is pursuing an appeal against the rejection of an ECHR Article 3 claim having had his or her claim under the Refugee Convention declared inadmissible;[255]
- where the applicant has made an application to the European Court of Human Rights (ECtHR);[256]
- where the applicant needs to remain in the UK temporarily because of court proceedings.[257]

6.102 These categories will be explored in turn below. While these are the main cohorts of applicants to whom reg 3(2)(e) may apply, it is important to note that this list is by no means exhaustive and that the *Section 4(2) policy* reminds decision-makers that situations in which there is said to be an obstacle to return must be considered on a case-by-case basis.[258] As *NS v First-tier Tribunal* did not prescribe any limitations on entitlement to support to avoid a breach of the ECHR, whether an individual applicant can satisfy that it would be unreasonable for them to take steps to leave the UK in the context reg 3(2)(e) will turn very much on the factual circumstances of their case.[259]

251 See para 6.115. An applicant pursuing an application for leave to remain on ECHR Article 3 grounds would be classed as an asylum-seeker (see paras 5.19–5.21) and so would be eligible for asylum support under IAA 1999 s95(1) rather than support under IAA 1999 s4(2).

252 See paras 6.116–6.123.

253 See paras 6.124–6.127.

254 See para 6.128.

255 See para 6.129.

256 See paras 6.130–6.132.

257 See paras 6.133–6.135.

258 The *Section 4(2) policy*, p13.

259 See further *R (SSHD) v First-tier Tribunal (Social Entitlement Chamber)* [2021] EWHC 1690 (Admin) at para 137 per Chamberlain J.

Further submissions

6.103 The most common 'impediment to return', which may give rise to an entitlement to IAA 1999 s4(2) support through the IA (PAFAS) Regs 2005 reg 3(2)(e) gateway arises in cases where the applicant has made further submissions[260] in support of a fresh claim for asylum under Immigration Rules para 353.[261] Where further submissions have been made[262] and acknowledged as having been received by the Home Office, the secretary of state is barred from removing the applicant from the UK pending consideration of the further submissions by operation of Immigration Rules para 353A. The legal impediment to return arises as a matter of law immediately.

6.104 Home Office policy provides that an applicant who has lodged further submissions, which have yet to be considered, who does not have access to accommodation and the means to live (or will shortly be in this position) may require support in order to avoid a breach of their rights under the ECHR.[263] Although the policy is couched in discretionary terms, support is provided in the majority of such cases, consistently with Immigration Rules para 353A, which provides that an applicant is not to be removed before the secretary of state has considered the further submissions under Immigration Rules para 353 or otherwise. However, support will be refused where the further submissions are found to be 'clearly abusive, manifestly unfounded or repetitious'.[264]

6.105 The *Section 4(2) policy*, in this respect, mirrors the guidance given by the Principal Judge in the landmark case of *AM v SSHD*,[265] in which she stipulated that judges of the FTT (Asylum Support) should accept that applicants who have made further submissions are eligible for support save where those submissions are 'obviously hopeless or abusive'.[266] In reaching her decision in that case, the Principal Judge applied the reasoning of the Court of Appeal in *R (Clue) v Birmingham*

260 See paras 3.42–3.43.

261 A 'claim for asylum' in this context is a claim that it would be contrary to the UK's obligations under the Refugee Convention or under ECHR Article 3, for the applicant to be removed from, or required to leave, the UK. See IAA 1999 ss4(4) and 94(1). See further paras 5.19–5.21 and 6.15.

262 Not including submissions addressing declarations of inadmissibility which are discussed at para 6.114.

263 The *Section 4(2) policy*, p13.

264 The *Section 4(2) policy*, p13.

265 AS/14/11/32141, 10 August 2015, FTT (Asylum Support).

266 See further *R (AW) v Croydon LBC* [2005] EWHC 2950 (Admin) at para 69 per Lloyd Jones J.

City Council.[267] *Clue* involved a household with an extant application for leave to remain on human rights grounds who were seeking local authority support under ChA 1989 s17(1).[268] One of the main issues in the case was whether or not, in deciding whether such support was necessary to avoid of the household's rights under the ECHR, the local authority should adjudicate on the substantive merits of their immigration application. The Court of Appeal held that it should not and that support should be provided in such cases save where immigration application was 'obviously hopeless or abusive'. The example was given of an application 'which is not an application for leave to remain at all' or which is 'merely a repetition of an application which has already been rejected'.[269]

6.106 The *Section 4(2) policy* only deals with the situation where the applicant has lodged their further submissions. It does not deal with cases in which an applicant intends to make further submissions at some point in the future, but has not done so yet. In *AM v SSHD*[270] the Principal Judge expressed the view that a 'mere assertion' that further submissions are in the process of being lodged, would not be sufficient to establish eligibility and, in practice, the Home Office routinely refuses applications for IAA 1999 s4(2) support unless the further submissions have actually been lodged. However, it is important to bear in mind that the test for eligibility in this context is not whether or not further submissions have been lodged yet, but whether or not support is necessary to avoid a breach of the ECHR. That is to be judged with reference to whether or not the applicant faces a legal or practical impediment to return which means that it is unreasonable to expect them to return to their country of origin to avoid destitution.[271] Whether this is the so will turn on the facts of the individual case. There is no bright-line rule.

6.107 In practice the FTT (Asylum Support) has tended to approach cases where further submissions are to be made in future as existing on a spectrum. At one end of the spectrum are those cases where the applicant has made a 'mere assertion' that they intend to lodge further submissions, but they have no appointment at the FSU (or equivalent) to do so, are not receiving legal assistance, have not

267 [2010] EWCA Civ 460, [2011] 1 WLR 99. See paras 6.95–6.96.

268 See paras 9.12–9.69.

269 *R (Clue) v Birmingham City Council* [2010] EWCA Civ 460, [2011] 1 WLR 99 at para 66 per Dyson LJ.

270 AS/14/11/32141, 10 August 2015, FTT (Asylum Support).

271 See paras 6.94–6.100.

prepared the further submissions, and are unable to give a clear indication of what the basis of their further submissions will be and how they differ from that which has been considered previously. Applications and appeals of this nature will invariably be refused. A history of unmeritorious applications and a failure to produce corroborative evidence are further factors which are likely to weigh against applicants in such cases.[272]

6.108 At the other end of the spectrum lies the applicant who has an appointment to lodge further submissions that have already been prepared, possibly with the assistance of legal representation, that are supported by evidence and are materially different from what had previously been considered by the Home Office. Unless there is some credible reason to believe that the applicant will not attend the appointment at the FSU to tender the submissions, or the lodging of the further submissions has been delayed by some act or omission on the part of the applicant, then their position ought not to be treated any differently from the applicant who has already lodged their further submissions. In both cases the applicant has a prospective fresh claim, which is neither hopeless nor abusive, which they are going to pursue. If it is not reasonable to expect the latter applicant to return to their country of origin to avoid destitution then it may not be reasonable to expect it of the former. In these cases, appeals against refusals to grant support are more likely to be granted and, reflecting these principles, counsel for the secretary of state in *R (SSHD) v First-tier Tribunal (Social Entitlement Chamber)* accepted that those who 'were about to lodge' their further submissions, should qualify under reg 3(2)(e).[273]

6.109 For example, in AS/18/01/37672,[274] the applicant, an Iranian failed asylum-seeker, was able to secure an appointment to attend the FSU but the appointment was some ten weeks later. She was refused IAA 1999 s4(2) support by the Home Office. On appeal, she provided an explanation as to the steps that she had taken and was taking to prepare her further submissions. She explained that her further submissions could not yet be finalised due to the instructed psychiatrist cancelling and rescheduling an appointment for preparing a medical report. She did, however, produce evidence from her solicitors to confirm the basis of her further submissions, which, on those

272 *SK v SSHD* AS/17/01/36372, 23 February 2018, FTT (Asylum Support) at para 58.

273 [2021] EWHC 1690 (Admin) at para 135 per Chamberlain J.

274 AS/18/01/37672, 17 January 2018, FTT (Asylum Support).

facts, related to her conversion to Christianity. She was able to provide copies of some relevant documents from her church to support this basis for a further asylum claim. This basis of claim had not previously been raised in her initial failed asylum claim. Nor had she previously adduced psychiatric evidence to support her initial failed asylum claim. The FTT (Asylum Support) accepted that the delay in making further submissions was beyond the applicant's control and held that, in circumstances where she was now 'poised' to submit her further submissions, she could not be expected to return to Iran to alleviate her destitution and was entitled to support.

6.110 In AS/18/05/38069,[275] Judge Lewis gave the following guidance in relation to cases in which further submissions were yet to be lodged, drawing together the principles outlined at paras 6.107–6.109 in conjunction with a number of practical suggestions as to how such cases might sensibly be approached by applicants, advisers and decision-makers:

- The 'mere assertion' that further submissions are in the process of being lodged will not be sufficient to satisfy that eligibility under reg 3(2)(e) is established.
- To take matters beyond 'mere assertion', it will be necessary to demonstrate that genuine concrete steps are being taken in pursuit of lodging further submissions. The mere making of an FSU appointment is insufficient because it does not take matters meaningfully beyond the assertion that submissions are in the process of being lodged. Nonetheless, as a bare minimum an applicant might reasonably be expected to have at least secured an appointment at the FSU.
- In a similar way to a case where representations have been lodged at the FSU, the applicant also needs to demonstrate that proposed representations 'are not obviously hopeless or abusive'. If it were otherwise, an applicant who has not yet lodged further submissions might be in a better position than an applicant who has.
- To demonstrate that the proposed representations are not obviously hopeless or abusive, an applicant will need to articulate the nature of the further submissions, and demonstrate how they are different from what has previously been considered. This latter element would require the production of the earlier decisions by the secretary of state and/or the FTT (Immigration and Asylum Chamber (IAC)) to assist in undertaking this comparative analysis.

275 AS/18/05/38069, 17 May 2018, FTT (Asylum Support).

- If further submissions have already been drafted, it would make sense to submit them in draft. However, a failure to produce a draft will not be fatal if the basis of such proposed representations is adequately articulated.
- If the basis of the further submissions is not provided, then the application or appeal is likely to be refused, as it will not be possible to establish that they are not hopeless or abusive.
- Cases in which multiple sets of further submissions have been rejected previously are more likely to be characterised as hopeless or repetitive.
- The secretary of state or FTT (Asylum Support) will need to be satisfied that it is more likely than not that the applicant will present the proposed further submissions at the FSU.
- Applicants can reasonably be expected to demonstrate that any new evidence is both real and pertinent. Generalised assertions about new evidence being sought are unlikely to be sufficient to establish that any further submissions are more than speculative or that they are different to that which has been considered previously.
- If further submissions rely upon new evidence, the applicant should be in a position to indicate what such evidence is and what stage any evidence gathering has reached.

6.111 Although this guidance is not binding on the FTT (Asylum Support), many of these points seem to reflect well-established principles, and given the considerable delays that many applicants experience in obtaining appointments at the FSU to lodge their further submissions, such guidance is to be welcomed. Potential difficulties arise in the requirement that the applicant provides a draft of the further submissions, which the Home Office will see in advance of its submission to the FSU. This may be addressed by the applicant providing a summary of the basis of the further submissions and identifying the matters that distinguish them from previous material so that it is possible to determine that the further submissions are not clearly hopeless or abusive, adopting a broad-brush approach and bearing in mind that the role of the Home Office in this context and that of the FTT (Asylum Support) is not to determine the merits or otherwise of the further submissions.

6.112 One situation which is not covered by the guidance set out above is where the applicant is not yet ready to book an appointment with the FSU because they are seeking to obtain a medico-legal report (MLR) in support of their case, which may take many months. Home

Office policy in relation to medical evidence in asylum claims recognises that it may take five months or more to obtain, and decisions on an applicant's initial asylum claim will generally be put on hold during this time.[276] Similar timescales may be required for independent experts not from the Medical Foundations. If applicants can demonstrate that a medical report is being prepared, for example, by a confirmation letter from the Medical Foundations or the relevant instructed expert, then applicants may still be able to establish eligibility through the reg 3(2)(e) gateway because they have demonstrated proactive steps being taken to progress the prospective further submissions.[277]

6.113 Fortunately, given the potential delays involved in lodging and assessing further submissions, the Home Office does not require decision-makers to wait until the determination of the further submissions before deciding the application for IAA 1999 s4(2) support. Decisions on support should generally be made within five working days and should be made within two working days in cases involving (for example): people who are street homeless; families with children; disabled people; elderly people; pregnant women; persons who have been subjected to torture, rape or other serious forms of psychological, physical or sexual violence; and potential victims of trafficking.[278]

6.114 As noted at para 6.103, the discussion above centres on further submissions falling within the scope of Immigration Rules para 353 and does not encompass the situation in which further submissions are made in relation to a declaration of inadmissibility,[279] which are not subject to that rule (or to the rule in para 353A).[280] Nevertheless, by analogy, a similar approach should be adopted in the context of eligibility under reg 3(2)(e). Such submissions, which may in due course lead to the applicant 'no longer being declared inadmissible'[281] and becoming an asylum-seeker once more for support purposes,[282] should constitute a practical/legal impediment to removal giving rise

276 *Medical evidence in asylum claims*, v1.0, Home Office, 5 August 2021 (www.gov.uk/government/publications/medical-evidence-in-asylum-claims).

277 See, for example, AS/19/10/40661, 28 October 2019, FTT (Asylum Support).

278 The *Section 4(2) Policy*, pp13–14. See further paras 6.185–6.186 on delay.

279 See further paras 5.39–5.44 and 6.37–6.38 for declarations of inadmissibility.

280 See *Inadmissibility: safe third country cases*, v7.0, p29 and *Further submissions*, v10.0, pp40–41.

281 The *Section 4(2) policy*, p14.

282 IAA 1999 s94(4B).

to reg 3(2)(e) eligibility providing that the submissions are not hopeless or abusive.

Immigration applications raising ECHR Article 8 and other grounds

6.115 Cases in which the applicant has sought to make further submissions in support of a fresh claim for asylum[283] are the most common instances in which the applicant may establish an impediment to return to their country of origin for the purposes of IA (PAFAS) Regs 2005 reg 3(2)(e). However, certain applicants who have a different type of immigration application outstanding may also face a practical or legal impediment to return. In particular, in the landmark case of *AM v SSHD*,[284] the Principal Judge of the FTT (Asylum Support) accepted that an applicant with an extant application for leave to remain on ECHR Article 8 grounds[285] could potentially qualify for support by means of IA (PAFAS) Regs 2005 reg 3(2)(e). The Principal Judge in that case applied the reasoning of the Court of Appeal in *R (Clue) v Birmingham City Council*.[286] The rationale in these cases would seem to apply equally to cases in which another ground of the ECHR was relied on as a basis for the applicant's immigration application. Likewise, support may need to be provided where the applicant is pursuing an application that they are stateless.[287]

Victims of trafficking

6.116 Victims, and potential victims, of human trafficking may face an impediment to return for the purposes of IA (PAFAS) Regs 2005 reg 3(2)(e) while the Home Office investigates their case. Article 10 of the Council of Europe Convention on Action against Trafficking (ECAT)

283 See paras 6.25–6.36. A 'claim for asylum' means a claim that it would be contrary to the UK's obligations under the Refugee Convention or under ECHR Article 3, for the applicant to be removed from, or required to leave, the UK. See IAA 1999 ss4(4) and s94(1).

284 AS/14/11/32141, 10 August 2015, FTT (Asylum Support).

285 Such an applicant may be eligible for leave under Appendix FM of the Immigration Rules or for leave outside of the rules. Applicants might qualify for such leave by, for example, long-residence or the fact they have a spouse or child with British citizenship or settled status. See paras 1.92–1.117.

286 [2010] EWCA Civ 460, [2011] 1 WLR 99. See paras 6.95–6.100. See further AS/17/11/37467, 20 November 2017, FTT (Asylum Support).

287 *SK v SSHD* AS/17/01/36372, 23 February 2018, FTT (Asylum Support) at para 18 (acknowledging a previous stage in the applicant's support history where a statelessness application had provided a basis for support) and AS/15/05/33059, 11 May 2015, FTT (Asylum Support).

directs signatory states, of which the UK is one, not to remove victims of trafficking from their territories pending the completion of the victim identification process. This obligation was implemented by the UK through the NRM and the *Modern Slavery Act statutory guidance for England and Wales (under s49 of the Modern Slavery Act 2015) and Non-Statutory Guidance for Scotland and Northern Ireland* ('*Modern Slavery Act statutory guidance*').[288] The process is described in further detail at paras 11.162–11.197. In brief, the NRM process is triggered in an individual case by a referral of the potential victim by a designated 'First Responder'. There are then two stages to the decision-making:

1) an initial decision that there are reasonable grounds for believing the individual is a potential victim of modern slavery (a reasonable grounds decision);
2) followed by a decision as to whether, on the balance of probabilities, there are sufficient grounds to conclude that the individual is a victim of human trafficking or slavery, servitude and forced or compulsory labour (a conclusive grounds decision).

6.117 The operation of the NRM and the arrangements for victim support are dealt with in more detail in chapter 11. What follows is an overview for the purposes of addressing the question of eligibility under reg 3(2)(e) for failed asylum-seekers who are (or may be) victims of trafficking. These cases fall into five categories, explained below:

a) applicants who have been referred to the NRM in respect of whom no decision has yet been made;
b) applicants who have received a positive reasonable grounds decision;
c) applicants who have received a negative reasonable grounds decision;
d) applicants who have received a negative conclusive grounds decision;
e) applicants who have received a positive conclusive grounds decision.

6.118 The first category encompasses applicants who have been referred to the NRM in respect of whom no decision has yet been made. They will not normally be entitled to access specialist support arranged by the Home Office under the Modern Slavery Victim Care Contract ('the MSVC contract') save in exceptional circumstances. However,

288 V3.1, Home Office, January 2023.

as the NRM identification process remains ongoing, the potential victim cannot be removed or be expected to leave the UK and thus, as a matter of fact and law, faces an impediment to removal, and therefore is likely to satisfy the gateway for IAA 1999 s4(2) support under IA (PAFAS) Regs 2005 reg 3(2)(e). The bar on removal arises from the UK's obligations under Articles 10 and 13 of the ECAT.

6.119 The second category encompasses applicants who have received a positive reasonable grounds decision. The bar on removing such victims remains as the NRM identification process still has not yet concluded. There will remain a legal impediment to the victim leaving the UK. Such victims are eligible for accommodation and support through the NRM.[289] As a result they will not normally be eligible for support under IAA 1999 s4(2) because they are unlikely to be accepted as being destitute given their eligibility to access adequate accommodation and support. In principle, there should be no need to provide section 4(2) support to such victims to avoid a breach of their rights under the ECHR for the purposes of IA (PAFAS) Regs 2005 reg 3(2)(e).

6.120 Problems do, however, arise in several ways. First, the Home Office will frequently seek to divert potential victims of trafficking entitled to NRM support to accommodation under IAA 1999 s4(2), supplemented by outreach support provided under the MSVC contract. The *Modern Slavery Act statutory guidance* certainly indicates a preference for victims, where eligible, being housed in IAA 1999 accommodation rather than NRM safe houses.[290] Thus, even though NRM support is mandatory in nature, as opposed to support under IAA 1999 s4(2) which is framed as a discretionary provision, the Home Office may in practice treat victims eligible for NRM support as being eligible for IAA 1999 s4(2) support. Second, as there are a finite number of bed spaces under the MSVC contract, the Home Office may not always be able to offer a bed space for a victim notwithstanding their eligibility for NRM support. This problem arose in AS/18/01/37708.[291] It was not in dispute in that case that the applicant might potentially fall within IA (PAFAS) Regs 2005 reg 3(2)(e) as a result of having 'something outstanding' with the Home Office, as she was awaiting a conclusive grounds decision. However, the case was remitted for the Home Office to consider whether alternative accommodation might be available to

289 *Modern Slavery Act statutory guidance*, para 8.20.
290 *Modern Slavery Act statutory guidance*, para 15.14.
291 AS/18/01/37708, 6 February 2018, FTT (Asylum Support).

her under the NRM. If accommodation is not available under the NRM in such a case this should give rise to eligibility under IA (PAFAS) Regs 2005 reg 3(2)(e), not only to alleviate the applicant's destitution, thereby avoiding a breach of their human rights, but also to discharge the state's obligation to provide victims of trafficking with accommodation and support for their recovery pending the completion of the NRM identification process.

6.121 The third category encompasses applicants who have received a negative reasonable grounds decision. They will cease to be eligible for NRM support because they have been found not to be a victim. In addition, the impediment to their removal that had previously existed by virtue of their status as a potential victim of trafficking, will fall away, meaning that they are unlikely to be eligible for support under IAA 1999 s4(2) by means of IA (PAFAS) Regs 2005 reg 3(2)(e) unless there is some other reason why they cannot reasonably be expected to return to their country of origin to alleviate their destitution. This may arise because they have separately made further submissions in support of a fresh claim for asylum or they are seeking judicial review of the negative reasonable grounds decision.[292]

6.122 The fourth category encompasses applicants who have received a negative conclusive grounds decision. They will no longer be eligible for NRM support under the MSVC contract, save for a short grace period[293] and, as with those who have received a negative reasonable grounds decision, would be unlikely to satisfy the requirements of IA (PAFAS) Regs 2005 reg 3(2)(e) on this basis alone. Similar to those with negative reasonable grounds decisions, if there are other outstanding immigration matters, such as further submissions, or a judicial review challenge of the negative conclusive grounds decision, this may separately result in in them being eligible.

6.123 The fifth category encompasses applicants who have received a positive conclusive grounds decision. This situation is not as straightforward as might have been hoped. The positive decision, in and of itself, confers no grant of leave to remain, although the recognised victim of trafficking is automatically entitled to be considered for a residence permit, which, if granted, would give the victim recourse to public funds. However, the Home Office's practice is

292 See paras 6.103–6.114 and 6.124–6.127.

293 The current grace period is nine working days although there is a discretion to extend this by a formal request. See *Modern Slavery Act statutory guidance*, paras 7.13 and 8.27. See also paras 11.198–11.129 for more details on the support arrangements for victims of trafficking.

generally to defer consideration of a victim's eligibility for a residence permit until any outstanding asylum claim, including further submissions, has been determined. The problems with such an approach are discussed at paras 11.186–11.192. In the meantime, recognised victims will inevitably face an impediment to leaving the UK which will undoubtedly mean that they meet the IA (PAFAS) Regs 2005 reg 3(2)(e) gateway subject to any preceding question about whether the victim is destitute. The question of destitution is what makes the legal position complex. The Home Office accepts that recognised victims with a positive conclusive grounds decision are in principle entitled to access support for their needs associated with trafficking under the NRM, if a needs assessment determines that they have continuing recovery needs.[294] This approach is consistent with the UK's international obligations under the EU Directive on preventing and combating trafficking in human beings and protecting its victims[295] and the ECAT.[296] However, the Home Office will consider whether the victim has access to other forms of support, including section 4(2) support, and will only allow them to remain in MSVC contract accommodation where 'necessary to meet a recovery need arising from their modern slavery experiences which cannot be adequately addressed through other accommodation options'.[297] It is therefore still possible that a recognised victim will meet the gateway criteria for support under IAA 1999 s4(2), relying on reg 3(2)(e) if they are failed asylum-seekers (or IAA 1999 s95(1) if they are asylum-seekers).

Pre-permission judicial review claims

6.124 As was established in *NS v First-tier Tribunal*,[298] applicants who are seeking judicial review of an immigration decision, but have not yet been granted permission to proceed, may potentially face an impediment to return for the purposes of IA (PAFAS) Regs 2005 reg 3(2)(e). A number of specific instances in which the lodging of a judicial

294 See *Recovery needs assessment (RNA)*, v7.0, Home Office, March 2023 (https://assets.publishing.service.gov.uk/government/uploads/system/uploads/attachment_data/file/1138946/MARCH_2023_-_Recovery_Needs_Assessment_v7.pdf) pp18–19.

295 Directive 2011/36/EU of the European Parliament and of the Council of 5 April 2011 on preventing and combating trafficking in human beings and protecting its victims.

296 See *R (G and others) v SSHD* [2016] EWHC 942 (Admin), [2016] 1 WLR 4031.

297 *Recovery needs assessment (RNA)*, v7.0, p19.

298 *R (NS (Somalia)) v First Tier Tribunal (Social Entitlement Chamber)* [2009] EWHC 3819 (Admin). See paras 6.91–6.92.

review claim will operate as an impediment to an applicant's removal from the UK may be found in the Home Office policy on *Judicial reviews and injunctions*.[299] The policy provides that the threat of judicial review by itself does not require removal action to be deferred. However:

- Removal will 'normally' be deferred where an application for judicial review has been lodged with the relevant court in England and Wales, Scotland or Northern Ireland in accordance with the relevant procedural rules. However, it is not automatic where there has been less than six months since a previous judicial review claim or statutory appeal, or the person is within a removal window, or the person is being removed by special arrangements (including a charter flight).[300]
- Removal will be deferred if the claim has been issued and there has been non-compliance with the relevant procedural rules if either the court decides that there is a valid reason for the non-compliance and gives directions accordingly, permission to proceed with the judicial review has been granted, or the court has not yet reached a decision on this matter by the time of the removal.[301]
- Removal may be deferred where the claim has not yet been filed, owing to the Administrative Court or Upper Tribunal office being closed, but an out of hours application has been made and the Home Office has been provided with a copy of the detailed grounds.[302]
- Removal must be deferred where an injunction to that effect has been granted by the court.[303]
- Removal must be deferred where the judicial review is the applicant's first challenge to a decision to certify an immigration decision, the result of which being there is either no appeal or any appeal right is out of country only.[304]

6.125 These examples are not an exhaustive statement of the circumstances in which an applicant will face a practical or legal impediment which means that it is not reasonable for them to return to their country of origin, but these are specified instances where Home Office explicitly

299 *Judicial reviews and injunctions*, v22.0, Home Office, 10 August 2022.
300 *Judicial reviews and injunctions*, v22.0, p19.
301 *Judicial reviews and injunctions*, v22.0, p19.
302 *Judicial reviews and injunctions*, v22.0, p19.
303 *Judicial reviews and injunctions*, v22.0, p28.
304 *Judicial reviews and injunctions*, v22.0, p31.

recognises that removal will not be appropriate. The FTT (Asylum Support) has identified additional instances, such as where an applicant has not yet lodged an application for judicial review, but will do so in future, which may also fall within the ambit of reg 3(2)(e). As with those cases where the applicant has not yet lodged further submissions in support of a fresh claim but intends to do so in future,[305] these cases sit on a spectrum. Where the claim for judicial review is merely speculative, support is likely to be refused. Whereas in cases where preparations to make the judicial review claim are well advanced and there is clarity as the nature and timing of the claim and the further steps that are to be taken in order to issue the claim, support is more likely to be granted.

6.126 For example, in *CC v SSHD*,[306] support was granted to an applicant who had sent a pre-action letter to the Home Office in contemplation of a judicial review challenge to the refusal to recognise her further submissions as a fresh claim and, following receipt of the Home Office response to that letter, had applied for legal aid with a view to issuing the judicial review. Judge Lewis remarked that 'the guiding principle is the reasonableness of the expectation that a person be expected to quit the UK rather than await the outcome of some pending matter'.[307] Pre-action correspondence, he noted, is part of the judicial review process and some 'element of hiatus' prior to the issuing of the claim was inevitable.[308] In circumstances where, he found, on the balance of probabilities the applicant intended to pursue the judicial review claim and where the substance of that claim was neither hopeless nor abusive,[309] nor an attempt to frustrate the removal process, it was appropriate to grant support.

6.127 In contrast, *BM v SSHD*[310] and *HM v SSHD*[311] provide examples of cases in which the applicant had not taken sufficient concrete steps to progress the intended judicial review claim to qualify for support by means of reg 3(2)(e). The former was a case in which the pre-action protocol had been concluded but the applicant had not heard from her solicitor for two months and was not aware of any further steps having been taken to initiate judicial review proceed-

305 See para 6.107.
306 AS/12/07/28659, 25 July 2012, FTT (Asylum Support).
307 AS/12/07/28659 at para 14. See paras 6.94–6.100.
308 AS/12/07/2865 at para 15.
309 See further para 6.105.
310 AS/14/02/31105, 17 March 2014, FTT (Asylum Support).
311 AS/15/07/33510, 20 July 2015, FTT (Asylum Support).

ings. Given the lack of progress, it was not unreasonable to expect her to make arrangements to return to her country of origin. The latter was a case in which the applicant had been refused permission to pursue his judicial review claim on the papers. His evidence was that he believed his solicitors were to seek to renew the application for permission at an oral hearing. However his solicitor had not confirmed whether legal aid had been granted or when he would next be in touch and by the time the matter came before the FTT (Asylum Support) the deadline for making the renewed application had passed. Judge Carter took the view that the applicant's plans to renew the judicial review claim were 'not sufficiently evidenced or tangible to represent a legal or practical obstacle to prevent him from taking steps to leave the United Kingdom'.[312]

Out of time appeals

6.128 The *Section 4(2) policy* recognises that applicants who have submitted a late appeal against the rejection of their asylum claim will face a legal impediment to return, for the purposes of IA (PAFAS) Regs 2005 reg 3(2)(e), while the FTT (Immigration and Asylum) considers whether to allow their appeal to proceed out of time.[313] The same logic would presumably apply to late applications to the Upper Tribunal.

Extant ECHR Article 3 appeal where declaration of inadmissibility made

6.129 The *Section 4(2) policy* provides that where an applicant's claim under ECHR Article 3 has been rejected (but not certified) and they have had the Refugee Convention element of their claim declared inadmissible, they will be eligible under IA (PAFAS) Regs 2005 reg 3(2)(e) so long as they have an outstanding appeal against the ECHR Article 3 decision.[314] Declarations of inadmissibility are discussed further at paras 5.39–5.44 and 6.37–6.38.

Applications to the European Court of Human Rights

6.130 An application to the ECtHR may constitute an impediment to an applicant returning to their country of origin for the purposes of IA (PAFAS) Regs 2005 reg 3(2)(e). In order to qualify for IAA 1999

312 *HM v SSHD* AS/15/07/33510, 20 July 2015, FTT (Asylum Support) at para 28.
313 The *Section 4(2) policy*, p13.
314 The *Section 4(2) policy*, p13.

s4(2) support in these circumstances, the applicant will need to show that they have:[315]

- exhausted all domestic remedies;
- lodged an application to the ECtHR that is individuated, fully reasoned, supported by all relevant documentation and has substance as opposed to being merely fanciful or speculative; and
- raised the possibility of an imminent risk of serious and irreparable damage in the event of a return to their country of origin, which may or may not include a request for interim measures (such as a suspension on removal) under Rules of Court r39.

6.131 Guidance on the requirement to exhaust all domestic remedies was laid down by the ECtHR in *Sufi and Elmi v UK*:[316]

- the burden of proof is on the responding state to demonstrate that an effective remedy is available in theory and in practice at the relevant time;
- the remedy must be one which is accessible and capable of providing redress in respect of the applicant's complaints; and
- the remedy must offer reasonable prospects of success.

6.132 Doubts on the part of the applicant as to the prospects of success of national remedies do not absolve them from the obligation to exhaust those remedies. However, it was accepted in *Sufi and Elmi* that there might be instances where an applicant can show that they have been advised by counsel that an appeal offers no prospects of success, or by providing relevant domestic case-law or other suitable evidence, that an available remedy, which has not been used, was bound to fail.[317] The burden of proof to evidence such an assertion is on the applicant.

Ongoing court proceedings

6.133 Applicants involved in ongoing court proceedings may potentially face an impediment to return to their country of origin for the purposes of IA (PAFAS) Regs 2005 reg 3(2)(e) where they engage an applicant's rights under the ECHR.

315 See the landmark decisions in: *ZH v SSHD* AS/11/04/26681, 23 May 2011, FTT (Asylum Support); *MMA v SSHD* AS/11/06/26857, 24 August 2011, FTT (Asylum Support); and *SH v SSHD* AS/11/12/27820, 27 March 2013, FTT (Asylum Support).

316 *Sufi and Elmi v UK* App Nos 8319/07 and 11449/07 (2012) 54 EHRR 9, ECtHR.

317 At paras 203–205.

6.134 Decisions relating to the entry, stay and deportation of immigrants do not involve the determination of civil rights, and therefore fall outside the scope of ECHR Article 6(1) (right to a fair trial).[318] However, it is possible for ECHR Article 6 to be engaged in circumstances where an individual has an ongoing private law claim for damages arising out of their immigration detention, as was the case in *R v Chief Immigration Officer ex p Quaquah*.[319] There, the claimant challenged his removal to Ghana in circumstances where he had brought proceedings for malicious prosecution against the Home Office and its contractor. He contended that removal would significantly impair his ability to pursue his claims against the same legal entity which was now seeking to remove him. The prospects of success in his civil proceedings would be diminished if he could not have ready access to the solicitor whom he had instructed in those proceedings. There were numerous stages of the civil proceedings at which a party needed to be in communication with his advisers for the purposes of providing adequate instructions and being able to respond to requests from other parties. If he was removed, he would suffer great disadvantages in the preparatory stages of the litigation. The court agreed with the claimant and held that under both the CPR and ECHR Article 6 the principle of 'equality of arms' was firmly established. There was a need to recognise that he was not to be placed at a disadvantage when compared with the Home Office in the conduct of proceedings. The Home Office had a discretion to permit him to remain pending the civil proceedings and had erred in the exercise of that discretion. The question was not whether the claimant needed to be in the UK but a lower threshold of whether there was a reasonable requirement that in order to conduct his litigation with reasonable efficiency, he should not be removed. The Home Office had failed adequately to consider the impact of the claimant's removal on the work his solicitors needed to be able to perform before his case was ready for trial. The Home Office also failed to consider the difficulties put in the claimant's way, hindering his ability to prepare for trial.

6.135 In a case such as *Quaquah*, it is at least arguable that an applicant might need support under IAA 1999 s4(2) in order to remain in the UK and pursue their claim, and thereby avoid a breach of their rights under ECHR Article 6. Analogous considerations might also apply to proceedings relating to contact between a parent and child in

318 *Maaouia v France* App No 39652/98 (2001) 33 EHRR 42, ECtHR.

319 [2000] HRLR 325, QBD.

which ECHR Article 8 is engaged (right to respect for private and family life).[320] However, the bare existence of legal proceedings is unlikely to establish eligibility. For example, in *MS v SSHD*[321] the FTT (Asylum Support) found that the applicant, who had issued a personal injury claim, did not require support in order to avoid a breach of his rights under ECHR Article 6 in circumstances where no explanation had been given as to why his witness statement had not been prepared already or why it could not be prepared remotely, if he were to return to his country of origin.

Statutory exclusions from support

6.136 As discussed at paras 5.122–5.131, the effect of NIAA 2002 s54 and Sch 3 is to exclude certain categories of migrant from certain forms of state support. This includes support under IAA 1999 s4(2).[322] The effect will be no different to those affected who are likely recipients of support under IAA 1999 s95(1). A detailed discussion of the exclusions under Schedule 3 may be found at paras 9.195–9.217. Those caught by the NIAA 2002 Sch 3 exclusions are ineligible for support save where they fall within certain categories of exception. As with cases concerning access to local authority children's services and adult social care or IAA 1999 s95(1) support, the most relevant exception in the IAA 1999 s4(2) context is that set out under NIAA 2002 Sch 3 para 3,[323] which requires support to be provided to the extent that it is necessary to avoid a breach of the applicant's rights under the ECHR. This exception is worded in the same language as the gateway under IA (PAFAS) Regs 2005 reg 3(2)(e). As such, in practical terms, the Schedule 3 scheme has no bearing on eligibility for IAA 1999 s4(2) support and is not applied by the Home Office in considering eligibility for support. The gate-keeping mechanism under NIAA 2002 Sch 3 para 3 is already built into the IA (PAFAS) Regs 2005 such that if a person demonstrates that they are destitute[324] and that they face some legal or practical barrier to returning

320 See *MS (Ivory Coast) v SSHD* [2007] EWCA Civ 133.

321 AST/07/04/15053, 24 April 2007, FTT (Asylum Support).

322 NIAA 2002 Sch 3 para 1(1)(l).

323 As amended by Immigration and Social Security Co-ordination (EU Withdrawal) Act 2020 (Consequential, Saving, Transitional and Transitory Provisions) (EU Exit) Regulations 2020 SI No 1309 reg 13(4) and subject to the transitional modifications specified in Citizens' Rights (Application Deadline and Temporary Protection) (EU Exit) Regulations 2020 SI No 1209 reg 12(1)(k) during the grace period. See further paras 2.14–2.19.

324 IA (PAFAS) Regs 2005 reg 3(1)(a). See paras 6.40–6.45.

to their country of origin,[325] they will qualify for support under IAA 1999 s4(2) *and* satisfy the NIAA 2002 Sch 3 para 3 exception.

6.137 The NIAA 2002 s55 exclusion[326] also applies to the provision of support under section 4(2).[327] In practice this exclusion is rarely, if ever, invoked in respect of failed asylum-seekers.

Relationship with community care services

6.138 As with IAA 1999 s95, there will be particular cases where questions arise as to whether an applicant's needs are to be met under section 4(2) or through community services from their local authority's social services department under the ChA 1989[328] or Care Act 2014.[329] The principles, for the most part, are similar to those governing the relationship between asylum support under IAA 1999 s95(1) and local authority community care support,[330] although there are some differences, given IAA 1999 s4(2) is a form of support of last resort for those who have not succeeded in their asylum and international protection claims but for legal or practical reasons are unable to leave the UK. Cross-references are made to the more detailed commentary on this subject in chapter 5 where appropriate.

The infirm destitute[331]

6.139 As explained at paras 5.94–5.102, under the previous regime before the Care Act 2014 came into force, there was a duty under National Assistance Act (NAA) 1948 s21 to provide residential accommodation for adults who, by reason of age, infirmity or other circumstances, were in need of care and attention which was not otherwise available. Persons subject to immigration control within the meaning of IAA 1999 s115, were excluded from this duty by operation of NAA 1948 s21(1A), if their need for care and attention had arisen solely because of they were destitute.[332] This was often described as the

325 IA (PAFAS) Regs 2005 reg 3(1)(b) and (2). See paras 6.46–6.47.

326 Applying to applicants who did not claim asylum as soon as reasonably practicable after arrival in the UK. See paras 5.132–5.136.

327 NIAA 2002 s55(2)(a); the *Section 4(2) policy*, p8.

328 See paras 9.12–9.69 for support under the ChA 1989.

329 See paras 8.7–8.178 for support under the Care Act 2014.

330 The exception is where support is required by households with children. See paras 6.141–6.143.

331 See paras 5.94–5.102.

332 NAA 1948 s21(1A) was inserted by IAA 1999 s116.

'destitution plus' test, and created a division between those who were described by the courts as the 'able-bodied destitute' and the 'infirm destitute'. The Court of Appeal in *R (AW) v Croydon LBC*[333] confirmed that infirm destitute failed asylum-seekers were the responsibility of their local authority and not the Home Office and fell to be supported under NAA 1948 s21, rather than IAA 1999 s4(2).[334]

6.140 The relevant provisions of the NAA 1948 have been repealed and replaced with the Care Act 2014 which contains an analogous exclusion to that found in NAA 1948 s21(1A).[335] However, as discussed at para 5.101, the nature of the duty to provide care and support under the Care Act 2014 has also been reframed meaning that the question of whether an infirm destitute applicant should be accommodated by the local authority under the Care Act 2014 instead of the secretary of state under IAA 1999 s4(2) is less clear-cut than it was previously when the NAA 1948 was in force. It may be that guidance on this issue is needed from the High Court at some point.

Households with dependant children

6.141 As explained at paras 6.17–6.18, responsibility for failed asylum-seeking households with dependent children will depend on when the children were born. Where the household contains a child who was born before the final determination of the applicant's asylum claim (that is before all appeal rights were exhausted), then the applicant is likely to fall within the extended definition of an 'asylum-seeker' contained in IAA 1999 s94(5)[336] and will be eligible for support under IAA 1999 s95(1) rather than s4(2), meaning that they will be ineligible for destitution-based support (that is accommodation and essential living needs) from children's services under ChA 1989 s17 by virtue of IAA 1999 s122.[337] Where the children were born after determination of the applicant's asylum claim and the applicant does not fall within the extended definition of an asylum-seeker, the question arises as to whether the Home Office should support the destitute household under IAA 1999 s4(2) or whether the local authority children's services should provide support under ChA 1989 s17. This was the vexed question under consideration in

333 [2007] EWCA Civ 266, [2007] 1 WLR 3168.

334 See further *R (SL) v Westminster City Council* [2013] UKSC 27, [2013] 1 WLR 1445 at para 4.

335 Care Act 2014 s21(1).

336 See paras 5.45–5.49 and 6.17–6.18.

337 See paras 5.103–5.111.

R (VC) v Newcastle City Council.[338] There, the parent was a failed asylum-seeker whose appeal rights had been exhausted prior to her children being born.[339] When she presented to the local authority in need of support to meet her and her children's accommodation and essential living needs, the local authority assessed her children as being 'in need' within the meaning of ChA 1989 s17(10), but turned her away on the basis that she should apply for support under IAA 1999 s4(2). The relationship between ChA 1989 s17 and IAA 1999 s4(2) thus fell to be determined in the case.

6.142 In finding against the local authority on its refusal to provide support under ChA 1989 s17, Munby LJ observed that 'the mere fact that support is or may be available under section 4 does not of itself exonerate a local authority from what would otherwise be its powers and duties under section 17'.[340] He went on to explain that a local authority will not be able to justify the refusal to provide support under ChA 1989 s17 unless it can be shown:

- that the secretary of state is able and willing (or if not willing, can be compelled) to provide IAA 1999 s4(2) support; and
- that support under IAA 1999 s4(2) will suffice to meet the child's assessed needs.

6.143 That does not mean that support under ChA 1989 s17 will always trump support under IAA 1999 s4(2). It will depend on the needs of the children as assessed. However, given the Spartan nature of support under IAA 1999 s4(2), Munby LJ went on to suggest that, in practical terms 'a local authority faced with a child who is assessed as being "in need" is . . . very unlikely in the general run of such cases to be able to justify non-intervention by reliance upon section 4'.[341]

338 [2011] EWHC 2673 (Admin), [2012] PTSR 546.

339 Following this, and subsequent to the birth of her eldest child, VC made further submissions based on ECHR Article 3 (prohibition of inhuman or degrading treatment) which the secretary of state accepted as amounting to a fresh claim but refused. VC's appeal against that decision was dismissed. As a result of these events, VC actually fell within the extended definition of 'asylum-seeker' contained in IAA 1999 s94(5) and was excluded from support under ChA 1989 s17. However, this was not known to the parties at the time the application for judicial review was brought. These facts only came to light during the hearing. As a result, the court proceeded to decide the issue of principle on the basis that VC was a failed asylum-seeker who was notionally eligible for support under IAA 1999 s4(2) or ChA 1989 s17. See paras 4, 10 and 55–56.

340 *R (VC) v Newcastle City Council* [2011] EWHC 2673 (Admin), [2012] PTSR 546 at para 86.

341 *R (VC) v Newcastle City Council* at para 92; see also paras 91–94.

Former unaccompanied asylum-seeking children and care leavers

Overview

6.144 As explained above at para 6.16 and in the previous chapter at paras 5.19–5.21, for the purposes of the support regime under the IAA 1999, the applicant has to be over the age of 18 to be regarded as an asylum-seeker.[342] UASCs, thus, cannot qualify for asylum support under IAA 1999 s95(1) in their own right by virtue of their being under 18, and will be the responsibility of the local authority children's services department under ChA 1989 Part III, almost certainly under ChA 1989 s20[343] until their 18th birthday.

6.145 The questions of what form of support the applicant will be entitled to post-18 if their asylum claim is rejected, and from whom, are not always straightforward. The answers to these questions will depend on a number of variables:

- the applicant's age at the time the asylum claim is determined (ie the point at which the applicant exhausts their appeal rights[344]);
- whether the applicant has acquired 'leaving care rights': a package of rights and entitlements under ChA 1989 Part III, available to a young person (a care leaver) from their local authority if they were looked after, accommodated or fostered for a period in excess of 13 weeks starting on or after their 14th birthday and ending on or after their 16th birthday. These rights continue until the age of 21, and longer in some cases, and may include the provision of accommodation;[345]
- the status of any further submissions made in support of a fresh claim for asylum.[346]

6.146 The various different scenarios will now be discussed in turn.

UASC is under 18 at the time their most recent asylum claim was determined

6.147 If a UASC's asylum claim is rejected, the Home Office's general policy is to grant 'UASC leave' under Immigration Rules para

342 IAA 1999 ss4(4) and 94(1).

343 See paras 9.70–9.117.

344 IAA 1999 s94(1) and (3); AS Regs 2000 reg 2(2) and (2A). See paras 5.29–5.44.

345 See paras 9.118–9.194.

346 See further paras 6.25–6.36.

352ZC, until the child is 17½ years old.[347] During this time, the applicant should continue to be accommodated by their local authority, generally under ChA 1989 s20. If the applicant is still under 18 at the time they exhaust their appeal rights against the adverse asylum-decision, then they are neither an asylum-seeker nor a failed-asylum-seeker for support purposes.[348]

6.148 The first question to ascertain at this point in order to determine what support may be available is whether or not the applicant has acquired leaving care rights. If the applicant has leaving care rights, then, if they are entitled to support at all, it is likely to be from children's services under ChA 1989 s23C.[349] However, whether the applicant is eligible for this support and, if so, the level of support which they will be provided with, will depend on their particular circumstances.

6.149 An applicant who is not an asylum-seeker[350] who is in the UK in breach of immigration laws within the meaning of British Nationality Act 1981 s50A will be excluded from support under ChA 1989 s23C by virtue of NIAA 2002 Sch 3 para 7, save to the extent necessary to avoid a breach of their human rights.[351] In practical terms, this means that, in order to access support under ChA 1989 s23C, an applicant who is a care leaver will need to demonstrate that they face a practical or legal impediment to return to their country of origin and that they will be facing destitution if support is not provided.[352] The support that is provided to an applicant who meets these criteria will be limited to that which is necessary to avoid the human rights breach that they would otherwise face. Theoretically, the secretary of state would have the power to provide support to an applicant in these circumstances under IA 2016 Sch 10 para 9(2).[353] However, as a matter of policy, the secretary of state has adopted the position that this power will not be exercised in circumstances where

347 *Children's asylum claims*, v4.0, Home Office 31 December 2020, pp64–65 (www.gov.uk/government/publications/processing-an-asylum-application-from-a-child-instruction).

348 IAA 1999 s94(1) (see paras 5.17–5.18); IAA 1999 s4(2)(a) and (4) (see para 6.16).

349 See paras 9.118–9.194 for support under ChA 1989 s23C, generally.

350 The term 'asylum-seeker', as used in NIAA 2002 Sch 3, has the same meaning as in IAA 1999 s94(1). See NIAA 2002 Sch 3 para 17(1).

351 See paras 6.136–6.137 and paras 9.195–9.217.

352 See paras 9.195–9.217. *R (CVN) v Croydon LBC* [2023] EWHC 464 (Admin) discussed at paras 9.212 and 9.217, provides a recent example of such a case, where support was required.

353 See paras 6.201–6.272.

alternative forms of support, such as support under the ChA 1989, are available.[354]

6.150 It is very often the case that care leavers who are former UASCs will seek to make further submissions in support of a fresh claim for asylum. The effect of these further submissions on the applicant's status and their entitlement to support will generally be as follows:

a) The lodging of the further submissions will not be sufficient for the applicant to be regarded as an asylum-seeker for support purposes[355] – meaning that while the further submissions are outstanding, the applicant will continue to be classed as a person who, for support purposes, is neither an asylum-seeker nor a failed asylum-seeker and will be subject to the NIAA 2002 Sch 3 exclusions. However, the existence of the further submissions will mean that there is a legal impediment to the applicant's removal[356] and, assuming they face destitution, support will need to be provided under ChA 1989 s23C to avoid a breach of their human rights.
b) If the applicant is granted asylum, then they will no longer be caught by NIAA 2002 Sch 3 and will be entitled to mainstream support[357] as well as support under ChA 1989 s23C to the extent that their welfare requires it.
c) If the Home Office accepts that the further submissions meet the threshold for being treated as a fresh claim for asylum[358] but rejects the claim with a right of appeal, then the applicant will be an asylum-seeker for support purposes until the point at which their appeal rights are exhausted.[359] During this time, the applicant will not be caught by NIAA 2002 Sch 3 and will be entitled to support under ChA 1989 s23C to the extent that their welfare requires it.

Destitute asylum-seekers in other circumstances generally fall to be supported by the Home Office under IAA 1999 s95(1). However, the Court of Appeal has held, in relation to care leavers, that 'the powers under s95 (and s4) of the Immigration and Asylum Act 1999 are residual, and cannot be exercised if the

354 See *Immigration bail policy*, v15.0, p88 (https://assets.publishing.service.gov.uk/government/uploads/system/uploads/attachment_data/file/1014714/immigration_bail.pdf); and para 6.238.

355 *R (Mustafa) v Kent CC* [2018] EWHC 2025 (Admin), (2019) 22 CCLR 138. See paras 6.25–6.36.

356 Immigration Rules para 353A. See further para 6.103.

357 See chapters 4 and 7.

358 See para 6.27.

359 IAA 1999 s94(1) and (3). See paras 5.29–5.44.

asylum seeker (or failed asylum seeker) is entitled to accommodation under some other provision' with the consequence that 'a local authority is not entitled, when considering whether a former relevant child's welfare requires that they be accommodated by it, to take into account the possibility of support from NASS'.[360] In these circumstances, support under ChA 1989 s23C takes precedence over support under IAA 1999 s95(1).

d) Once the applicant in the circumstances described at (c) above has exhausted their appeal rights, they will become a failed asylum-seeker for support purposes and will be caught by NIAA 2002 Sch 3 once more. Support under ChA 1989 s23C will be available to the extent necessary to avoid a breach of their human rights if they are facing destitution and there is some other practical or legal impediment to removal – because, as noted above, support under ChA 1989 s23C will generally take precedence over support under IAA 1999 s4(2).[361] However, this hierarchy only pertains where the applicant can establish that support is needed to avoid a human rights breach and thereby escape the strictures of NIAA 2002 Sch 3. In *R (Mustafa) v Kent CC*[362] the applicant was a care leaver and failed asylum-seeker who had further submissions outstanding. His local authority had concluded that he was caught by NIAA 2002 Sch 3 and that support was not necessary to avoid a breach of his human rights. That conclusion was challenged initially upon his application for judicial review but, by the time of the substantive hearing, this ground of challenge had fallen away following a revised assessment by the local authority.[363] In these circumstances, the court held, to the extent the applicant was entitled to support at all, it would need to be provided by the Home Office under IAA 1999 s4(2) rather than by the local authority.

e) If the Home Office rejects the further submissions, finding that they do not meet the threshold for being treated as a fresh claim for asylum, the applicant will continue to be neither an asylum-seeker nor a failed asylum-seeker, and will be back where they started.[364] That is, support under ChA 1989 s23C will be available to the extent necessary to avoid a breach of the applicant's human

360 *R (SO) v Barking and Dagenham LBC* [2010] EWCA Civ 1101, [2011] 1 WLR 1283 at para 40 per Tomlinson LJ. See further paras 5.113–5.117.

361 *R (SO) v Barking and Dagenham LBC* at para 40 per Tomlinson LJ.

362 [2018] EWHC 2025 (Admin), (2019) 22 CCLR 138. See para 6.33.

363 See *Mustafa v Kent CC* [2018] EWHC 2025 (Admin), (2019) 22 CCLR 138 at paras 4–5.

364 See para 6.147.

rights, if they are facing destitution and there is some other practical or legal impediment to removal.

6.151 If the applicant does not have leaving care rights, then the position will generally be as follows:

a) As a person who is neither an asylum-seeker nor a failed asylum-seeker, support under IAA 1999 s4(2) or 95(1) is not available, but they may be able to access support under IA 2016 Sch 10 para 9(2) if they are destitute and face impediments to leaving the UK.[365] The lodging of further submissions is one way in which that impediment will arise.
b) If, following the making of further submissions, the applicant is granted refugee status then they will be entitled to mainstream support.[366]
c) If the Home Office accepts that the further submissions meet the threshold for being treated as a fresh claim for asylum but rejects the claim with a right of appeal, then the applicant will be an asylum-seeker for support purposes until the point at which their appeal rights are exhausted. During this time the applicant will be eligible for asylum support under IAA 1999 s95(1) if they are facing destitution.[367]
d) Once the applicant has exhausted their appeal rights, they will become a failed-asylum-seeker for support purposes and will be eligible for support under IAA 1999 s4(2) if they are destitute and satisfy one of the IA (PAFAS) Regs reg 3(2) gateways.[368]
e) Alternatively, if the Home Office rejects the further submissions on the basis that those submissions do not constitute a fresh claim under Immigration Rules para 353, the applicant will continue to be neither an asylum-seeker or a failed asylum-seeker, and will be back where they started meaning that they may be able to seek support under IA 2016 Sch 10 para 9(2).

UASC is over 18 at the time their most recent asylum claim was determined

6.152 If the applicant is over 18 at the time they become appeal rights exhausted, then they will be a failed asylum-seeker for support

365 See paras 6.201–6.272.
366 See chapters 4 and 7.
367 See paras 5.9–5.90.
368 See paras 6.46–6.135.

purposes. If the applicant has leaving care rights, then the position will generally be as follows:

a) The applicant will be caught by the NIAA 2002 Sch 3 exclusions, where if they are destitute and face a practical or legal impediment to the applicant returning to their country of origin, support will need to be provided under ChA 1989 s23C to the extent necessary to avoid a breach of their human rights for similar reasons as discussed above if they have further submissions pending.[369] If and once those submissions are accepted to meet the threshold for being treated as a fresh claim for asylum, they will be considered asylum-seekers while they go through any appeal process. Those with refugee status will have access to mainstream support; otherwise, they will be entitled to support under ChA 1989 s23C to the extent their welfare requires it.[370]
b) An appeal rights exhausted care leaver, as a failed asylum-seeker, will be caught by NIAA 2002 Sch 3 again. Support under ChA 1989 s23C will be depend on whether it is necessary to avoid a breach of the applicant's human rights if they face destitution and there is some other practical or legal impediment to removal. The same applies if the Home Office rejects the further submissions, finding that they do not meet the threshold for being treated as a fresh claim for asylum.

6.153 If the applicant does not have leaving care rights, then the position is as follows:

a) The applicant will be eligible for support under IAA 1999 s4(2) if they met the qualifying conditions. If their claim is resolved positively by way of a grant of refugee status or another form of leave to remain, they will be entitled to mainstream support.
b) A rejection of the further submissions but the grant of a right of appeal will make the applicant an asylum-seeker for support purposes until the point at which their appeal rights are exhausted, and, subject to satisfying the destitution threshold, mean they are eligible for asylum support under IAA 1999 s95(1).

An appeal rights exhausted applicant will be a failed asylum-seeker eligible for support under IAA 1999 s4(2) if they meet the qualifying conditions. The same applies if the Home Office rejects the further submissions, finding that they do not meet the threshold for being treated as a fresh claim for asylum.

369 See para 6.150 bullet point (d).
370 See para 6.145 bullet point (c).

The provision of support

Overview

6.154 The power under IAA 1999 s4(2) allows the secretary of state to 'provide, or arrange for the provision of, facilities for the accommodation'.[371] Notably, in contrast with IAA 1999 s95(1), section 4(2) refers only to 'accommodation' and not to 'support'. However, as was noted in the case of *R (AW (Kenya)) v SSHD*[372] 'the words "facilities for the accommodation of a person" obviously go wider than the accommodation itself'[373] as the power to provide accommodation under IAA 1999 s4(2) is supplemented by section 4(10)–(11) which allows the secretary of state to make regulations 'permitting a person who is provided with accommodation under this section to be supplied also with services or facilities of a specified kind' and, 'in particular, permit a person to be supplied with a voucher which may be exchanged for goods or services'.[374] Such support principally takes the form of weekly subsistence payments.[375] Because these subsistence payments are ancillary to the provision of accommodation, an applicant for support under IAA 1999 s4(2) cannot, for example, seek subsistence only support while living with a partner who is receipt of mainstream benefits.[376] This may be contrasted with asylum support under IAA 1999 s95(1) which may be provided in the form of either accommodation or subsistence or both.[377]

6.155 The regulation-making power under IAA 1999 s4(10) has been exercised in the form of the Immigration and Asylum (Provision of Services and Facilities) Regulations ('IA (PSF) Regs') 2007. The IA (PSF) Regs 2007 allow for the provision of:

371 For accommodation see paras 6.156–6.159.

372 [2006] EWHC 3147 (Admin).

373 At para 28 per Sir Michael Harrison sitting as a deputy High Court judge. However, the court held, the power did not extend to the provision of clothing as this was not 'linked to the accommodation'.

374 Under the regulations applicants may not be provided with money: IAA 1999 s4(11)(b).

375 For subsistence payments see paras 6.160–6.173. The current rate £45 per week.

376 *R (MK (Iran)) v SSHD* [2011] EWCA Civ 671, [2012] 1 WLR 765. However, the secretary of state may be requested to assume legal/financial responsibility for accommodation in which an applicant already resides with a family member or carer, and thereby discharge her responsibilities in that way: see *R (Hussain) v SSHD* [2021] 11 WLUK 450, QBD District Registry (Leeds).

377 See paras 5.141–5.144.

- assistance with travel;[378]
- assistance with telephone calls and letters;[379]
- vouchers for pregnant women, new mothers and children;[380]
- support to meet exceptional needs.[381]

Each of these various forms of support will be explored in turn below.

Accommodation

6.156 Accommodation is not provided directly by the Home Office. Instead, like arrangements made for support under IAA 1999 s95(1), the provision of accommodation is arranged by contract from three companies – Serco, Mears Group and Clearsprings Ready Homes – by means of regional contracts. These contractual arrangements are discussed at para 5.145.

Adequacy

6.157 Serious and sustained concerns have been expressed over a number of years in relation to the quality of accommodation that is provided pursuant to the IAA 1999.[382] In contrast to accommodation provided to asylum-seekers pursuant to IAA 1999 s95(1), there is no statutory requirement that accommodation provided to failed asylum-seekers under IAA 1999 s4(2) is 'adequate'.[383] However, it is arguable that as section 4(2) accommodation is provided to those who are destitute and unable to obtain adequate accommodation other than by the provision of statutory support that, read together with IA (PAFAS) Regs 2005 reg 3(1), there is an implicit, if not explicit, requirement for facilities provided to the applicant to be adequate.[384] This stat-

378 See paras 6.163–6.167.
379 See paras 6.168–6.170.
380 See para 6.171.
381 See paras 6.172–6.173.
382 See paras 5.156–5.159.
383 See IAA 1999 s96(1) and paras 5.154–5.155. This is a legal rather than a practical distinction: there is often no difference between accommodation provided under IAA 1999 s4(2) and s95(1) and some hostels and houses in multiple occupation (HMOs) will house applicants on both types of support.
384 Note, however, the opinion of Court of Appeal in *R (MK (Iran)) v SSHD* [2011] EWCA Civ 671, [2012] 1 WLR 765 was that unlike IAA 1999 s95(1), the power under IAA 1999 s4(2) is not a power to alleviate destitution. See at para 15 per Sullivan LJ and para 27 per Gross LJ, approving the *dicta* of Sir Michael Harrison in *R (AW (Kenya)) v SSHD* [2006] EWHC 3147 (Admin). See further *R (DMA) v SSHD* [2020] EWHC 3416 (Admin) at para 205 per Robin Knowles J.

utory objective would be defeated by the provision of accommodation which is inadequate.

6.158 Applicants who find themselves housed in substandard conditions may seek to raise this with the Home Office or with their accommodation provider. Where this does not result in any improvement, applicants may consider seeking the help of the local authority environmental health department; make a complaint; or alternatively challenge the adequacy of accommodation by way of judicial review, depending on the nature of the inadequacy and the applicant's personal situation.[385]

Dispersal

6.159 Dispersal of applicants for IAA 1999 s4(2) support to accommodation located outside of London and the South East is also a central feature of the support regime as it is with section 95(1) recipients. This is not stipulated in statute, unlike IAA 1999 s97(1),[386] but it is set out in the *Section 4(2) policy* which provides that accommodation if offered 'on a no-choice basis' and will 'usually be outside London and the south-east of England'.[387] However, as is the case in IAA 1999 s95(1) cases, accommodation may be provided in a particular location 'if there are particular reasons to do so, for example medical reasons'.[388] Guidance on the allocation of accommodation specific to the needs of certain vulnerable applicants may be found in the *Healthcare needs and pregnancy dispersal policy*[389] discussed at paras 5.169–5.184.

Subsistence

6.160 Subsistence payments are generally made at a standard rate of £45 per week, in line with IAA 1999 s95(1) rates,[390] which is intended to cover 'food, clothing and toiletries'.[391] However, those in full-board accommodation, whose needs should be partially met by the provision of food at the accommodation, receive a weekly payment of

385 See paras 5.167–5.168.

386 See paras 5.169–5.184 for the statutory framework governing the dispersal of asylum-seekers.

387 The *Section 4(2) policy*, p6.

388 The *Section 4(2) policy*, p6.

389 V3.0, Home Office, January 2016 (www.gov.uk/government/publications/healthcare-needs-and-pregnancy-dispersal-instruction).

390 See paras 5.185–5.200.

391 See: www.gov.uk/asylum-support/what-youll-get; and the *Section 4(2) policy*, p6. Compare fn 388 above.

only £8.[392] In contrast with IAA 1999 s95(1), there is no specified power in statute to set the level of financial support to be provided to failed asylum-seekers.[393] The weekly financial support rate is, instead, set by an exercise of the secretary of state's general power under IAA 1999 s4(2). Until relatively recently, the rates have been slightly lower than the IAA 1999 s95(1) rates, but they were brought in line during the COVID-19 pandemic.

6.161 To access their support, applicants are provided with an ASPEN payment card, to which these payments are loaded, which can be used at shops that accept Visa. However, unlike the ASPEN card which is provided to asylum-seekers in receipt of IAA 199 s95(1) support, the section 4(2) card cannot be used to withdraw cash from ATMs.[394]

6.162 In addition to this weekly payment, additional payments and facilities, set out at paras 6.163–6.173, may also be made available to certain applicants. Applicants who are seeking to obtain any or all of these payments may apply by means of a single application form, supported by the appropriate evidence.[395]

Travel

6.163 The secretary of state may supply, or arrange for the supply of, facilities for travel for a 'qualifying journey' for an applicant who is in receipt of support under IAA 1999 s4(2), in order for them to:[396]

- receive healthcare treatment, where the applicant has provided evidence that the qualifying journey is necessary; or
- register a birth.

In such cases, where necessary, arrangements can also be made for the applicant's dependants to travel too.[397]

392 Letter from Chris Philp MP, Parliamentary Under-Secretary of State, to all Chief Executives dated 27 October 2020. See further para 5.190.

393 See para 5.186. The power to set the asylum support rates for the purposes of IAA 1999 s95 is contained in IAA 1999 Sch 8 paras 1 and 3 and the rates are prescribed by AS Regs 2000 regs 10 and 10A. The IAA 1999 and IA (PAFAS) Regs 2005 do not contain any equivalent provisions in respect of the rates of support under IAA 1999 s4(2). See *Mensah v Salford City Council* [2014] EWHC 3537 (Admin), [2015] PTSR 157 at para 40 per Lewis J.

394 See para 5.186 and *A Home Office guide to living in asylum accommodation*, UKVI, July 2019, p27 (www.gov.uk/government/publications/living-in-asylum-accommodation).

395 See: www.gov.uk/government/publications/application-for-section-4-extra-services-or-facilities. See further paras 6.178–6.183 on the application process.

396 IA (PSF) Regs 2007 reg 3(1).

397 IA (PSF) Regs 2007 reg 3(2).

6.164 A qualifying journey is one that is either:[398]

- three miles or more;
- less than three miles, in cases where the applicant has a 'specified need'.

6.165 An applicant will have a specified need if they:[399]

- are unable, or virtually unable, to walk a distance of up to three miles by reason of a physical impediment or for some other reason;
- have a dependant child who is aged under five;
- have a dependant child who is unable, or virtually unable, to walk a distance of up to three miles by reason of a physical impediment or for some other reason.

6.166 If the applicant is seeking assistance to fund travel costs for healthcare treatment they should, where possible, submit written evidence from their healthcare provider to demonstrate that they need to travel to receive the treatment. This evidence should, where possible, be submitted on headed paper with the details of the healthcare provider. Alternatively, an appointment card will suffice. In cases where the need to travel is clear and obvious (for example, where a trip to Accident and Emergency is necessary), then a verbal statement may be sufficient.[400]

6.167 Those seeking assistance to fund the cost of registering a birth will need to provide evidence that the birth has taken place such as the midwife's notes, the baby's national health number or, more simply, evidence that there is a baby in the household.[401] In England and Wales births need to be registered within 42 days.

Telephone calls and letters

6.168 The secretary of state may supply, or arrange for the supply of, facilities to a supported person aged 18 or over, to make telephone calls:[402]

- regarding medical treatment or care;
- to a qualified person;
- to a court or tribunal;
- to a voluntary sector partner;
- to a citizens' advice bureau;

398 IA (PSF) Regs 2007 reg 2.
399 IA (PSF) Regs 2007 reg 2.
400 The *Section 4(2) policy*, p19.
401 The *Section 4(2) policy*, p19.
402 IA (PSF) Regs 2007 reg 5(1).

- to a local authority;
- to an immigration officer;
- to the secretary of state.

6.169 The secretary of state may also supply, or arrange for the supply of, stationery and postage for correspondence with these same people and organisations.[403]

6.170 The support which is made available to assist in making telephone calls consists of a single £5 payment which will be uploaded to the applicant's ASPEN card. Only one such payment will generally be made in any six-month period.[404] Support toward stationery costs consists of a payment of £2.50, which will also be made available on the applicant's ASPEN card.

Vouchers and additional payments for pregnant women, new mothers and children

6.171 The IA (PSF) Regs 2007 provide for the following support to be provided in respect of pregnant women, new mothers and children, in addition to the £45 weekly payment:

- Vouchers redeemable for goods to the value of £250, payable to expectant mothers during the ante-natal period in respect of each expected child.[405] Applications will not be accepted where the mother had previously been supported under IAA 1999 s95(1) and had already received the equivalent maternity payment which is made available to asylum-seekers.[406] Applications should normally include either an MATB1 form showing the expected delivery date (EDD) of the child, or a letter from a community midwife or GP, or the child's full birth certificate, unless this information has already been provided.[407]
- £3 per week to pregnant women throughout the duration of the pregnancy.[408] This will be credited to the applicant's ASPEN card.[409] The applicant must provide an original MATB1 form

403 IA (PSF) Regs 2007 reg 5(2).
404 The *Section 4(2) policy*, p21.
405 IA (PSF) Regs 2007 reg 6(1). Applications can also be made following the birth of the child under reg 6(2).
406 IA (PSF) Regs 2007 reg 6(3). See paras 5.198–5.200 for maternity payments.
407 The *Section 4(2) policy*, p22.
408 IA (PSF) Regs 2007 reg 7(1).
409 The *Section 4(2) policy*, p22.

showing the expected delivery date of the child, with the application.[410]

- £5 per week in respect of children aged under one.[411] This will be credited to the applicant's ASPEN card.[412]
- £3 per week in respect of children aged between one and three.[413] This will be credited to the applicant's ASPEN card.[414]
- £5 per week in respect of children under the age of 16, for clothing costs.[415] This will be credited to the applicant's ASPEN card.[416]

Additional support to meet exceptional needs

6.172 Additional support may also be provided if the secretary of state is satisfied that an applicant has an exceptional need for:[417]

- facilities for travel;
- facilities to make telephone calls;
- stationery and postage;
- essential living needs.

6.173 This support may be provided even if the applicant would not have qualified for similar support under IA (PSF) Regs 2007 reg 3, 5 or 6.[418] The term 'essential living needs' is used in the context of assessing eligibility for support under IAA 1999 s95(1). The same interpretation is to be adopted in this context.[419] A discussion of what is, or is not, an essential living need may be found at paras 5.83–5.84 and 5.211. Whether a particular need is sufficiently exceptional to qualify for additional support under IA (PSF) Regs 2007 reg 9(1) is to be decided on a case-by-case basis.[420]

410 The *Section 4(2) policy*, p22.
411 IA (PSF) Regs 2007 reg 7(2).
412 The *Section 4(2) policy*, p22.
413 IA (PSF) Regs 2007 reg 7(3).
414 The *Section 4(2) policy*, p22.
415 IA (PSF) Regs 2007 reg 8.
416 The *Section 4(2) policy*, p22.
417 IA (PSF) Regs 2007 reg 9(1).
418 IA (PSF) Regs 2007 reg 9(1). See paras 6.163–6.167 for support under reg 3, paras 6.168–6.170 for support under reg 5 and para 6.171 for support under reg 6.
419 IA (PSF) Regs 2007 reg 9(2).
420 The *Section 4(2) policy*, p23.

Conditions

6.174 The provision of support under IAA 1999 s4(2) may be subject to conditions requiring the applicant or any dependant to:[421]

- comply with specified standards of behaviour;
- comply with a reporting requirement;
- comply with a requirement to reside at an authorised address;
- comply with a requirement to limit any absences from that address to no more than seven consecutive days and nights or no more than a total of 14 days and nights in any six-month period, unless the secretary of state grants permission to be away for longer than this;
- comply with specified steps to facilitate their departure from the UK. Such conditions might include a requirement that the applicant applies for a passport from their national embassy or attends a Home Office re-documentation interview and provides accurate information to support an application for an Emergency Travel Document.[422]

6.175 Any such conditions must be set out in writing,[423] and will generally be provided with the decision letter granting the applicant support. Breach of any such conditions may lead to support being discontinued.[424]

Review of eligibility for support

6.176 Support under IAA 1999 s4(2) is not intended to be a long-term provision because it is support directed toward those facing a temporary impediment to return to their country of origin.[425] However, in practice, people can stay on section 4(2) support for long periods of time, mainly because those with an impediment to leaving the UK would more often than not be regularising their status by seeking leave to remain, and the immigration decision-making process can be lengthy. However, and because the support is in principle not intended to be long-term, the *Section 4(2) policy* directs a review of an applicant's continued eligibility for support no later than three months after the date on which support was granted, and at intervals

421 IA (PAFAS) Regs 2005 reg 6.
422 The *Section 4(2) policy*, p15.
423 IA (PAFAS) Regs 2005 reg 6(1)(b).
424 See paras 6.188–6.194; and the *Section 4(2) policy*, p15.
425 IA (PAFAS) Regs 2005 reg 3(2). See paras 6.46–6.135.

of no more than three months thereafter.[426] Earlier review dates will be scheduled where:[427]

- The applicant is supported on the basis that they are taking all reasonable steps to leave the UK.[428] As part of the review, the Home Office will check whether the applicant is co-operating with efforts to arrange travel documents or departure, and whether they have approached their embassy for the purposes of obtaining a passport and the like.
- The applicant is supported because she is in the later stages of her pregnancy or has just given birth, and so is unable to travel.[429] A review is normally set for six weeks from the expected delivery date (EDD) or (if known) the actual birth date.

6.177 If the review concludes that the applicant is no longer eligible for IA 1999 s4(2) support, then support will be discontinued.[430]

The application process

Making an application

6.178 In contrast to the procedure for making an application for asylum support under IAA 1999 s95(1), the application process for failed asylum-seekers does not have a statutory basis.[431] However, in practice, the application process is very similar.[432] Applications for IA 1999 s4(2) support are made using form ASF1,[433] which is sent to the Home Office via Migrant Help,[434] which is able to assist with the application process.

6.179 An applicant for asylum support under IAA 1999 s95(1) who does not co-operate with further inquiries made of them in connection with their application may find that the secretary of state refuses

426 The *Section 4(2) policy*, p15.
427 The *Section 4(2) policy*, p15.
428 IA (PAFAS) Regs 2005 reg 3(2)(a). See paras 6.48–6.58.
429 IA (PAFAS) Regs 2005 reg 3(2)(b). See paras 6.59–6.83.
430 See paras 6.188–6.194.
431 See paras 5.221–5.243. The statutory basis for the application process for asylum support under IAA 1999 s95(1) is contained in IAA 1999 Sch 8 para 12 and AS Regs 2000 reg 3. There are no equivalent provisions contained in IAA 1999 or the IA (PAFAS) Regs 2005 in respect of support under IAA 1999 s4(2).
432 See paras 5.221–5.243 for a more detailed discussion of the process.
433 See paras 5.221–5.224.
434 See paras 5.225–5.227.

to entertain the application.[435] There is no equivalent statutory sanction in respect of section 4(2) applications. Instead, the *Section 4(2) policy* provides that an applicant who fails to provide evidence in response to a further inquiry relating to their application should be refused support 'on the basis that the person has not established that they are eligible to receive support'.[436] This distinction is important. A refusal to accept that an applicant is eligible for support, unlike a refusal to entertain their application, carries with it a right of appeal.[437]

Evidence in support of the application

6.180 Applications should be supported by supported by evidence that the applicant is destitute[438] and meets one or more of the gateway criteria contained in IA (PAFAS) Regs 2005 reg 3(2).[439] A general discussion of evidence which might usefully be submitted alongside the ASF1 form to establish that the applicant is destitute, together with suggestions on how to overcome common evidential problems can be found at paras 5.228–5.229. In addition, Table 6.2 contains suggestions of evidence which might assist in establishing that one of the IA (PAFAS) Regs 2005 reg 3(2) gateways applies.[440] This list is not exhaustive and the evidential requirements for any particular application will vary from case to case.

435 AS Regs 2000 reg 3(4). This rule was introduced pursuant to NIAA 2002 s57. See paras 5.137–5.140.

436 The *Section 4(2) policy*, p10.

437 See paras 6.195–6.197.

438 See paras 6.40–6.45.

439 See paras 6.46–6.135.

440 See *Factsheet 6: Evidence for s4 support*, ASAP, October 2018. These suggestions would also apply to evidence in support of an appeal.

Table 6.2

Gateway	Suggested evidence
Applicant taking all reasonable steps to leave the UK[441]	• Copies of letters and faxes sent to/from embassy, Home Office, advice agencies and voluntary returns service • Contemporaneous notes of any relevant telephone conversations with such organisations • Inventory of telephone calls • Evidence of any visits to any of the above, eg travel tickets
Applicant unable to leave the UK by reason of physical impediment to travel or some other medical reason[442]	• IAA 1999 s4(2) Medical Declaration Form[443] • Up-to-date evidence, on headed paper, from a relevant medical practitioner explaining that the applicant is unable to leave the UK, why this is and how long the situation is likely to pertain for. Particularly in the case of applicants with mental health issues it can assist if the medical practitioner can explain how long they have known the applicant and the duration/frequency of any assessments
Applicant granted permission to seek judicial review of asylum decision[444]	• Sealed claim form • Court order granting permission
Applicant needs support to avoid breach of ECHR[445]	• Further submissions cases:[446] – Copy/outline of further submissions – Evidence in support of further submissions – Evidence of appointment with FSU – Evidence that further submissions have been submitted – Previous immigration decisions

441 IA (PAFAS) Regs 2005 reg 3(2)(a). See paras 6.48–6.58.
442 IA (PAFAS) Regs 2005 reg 3(2)(b). See paras 6.59–6.83.
443 See: www.gov.uk/government/publications/section-42-medical-declaration.
444 IA (PAFAS) Regs 2005 reg 3(2)(d). See paras 6.86–6.89.
445 IA (PAFAS) Regs 2005 reg 3(2)(e). See paras 6.90–6.135.
446 See paras 6.103–6.114.

	– Written account from immigration solicitor explaining the progress that has been made in submitting further submissions, any outstanding further steps and the timeline in which those steps will be taken – Applications for leave under ECHR Article 8 and statelessness application:[447] – Copy of application – Evidence that application has been submitted • Pre-permission judicial review proceedings:[448] – Pre-action correspondence and any response – Copy of issued claim form and/or grounds for judicial review – Written account from immigration solicitor explaining the progress that has been made in lodging judicial review claim (eg whether legal aid application has been made), any outstanding further steps and the timeline in which those steps will be taken • Out of time immigration appeals:[449] – Copy of Appeal Notice – Evidence that Appeal Notice has been submitted – Any correspondence/directions and decisions from the Tribunal • Applications to the ECtHR:[450] – Copy of the application – Proof of submission to the ECtHR – Any further correspondence with the ECtHR and directions – Any rule 39 requests and outcome – Evidence of exhaustion of domestic remedies • Ongoing court proceedings:[451]

447 See para 6.155.
448 See paras 6.124–6.127.
449 See para 6.128.
450 See paras 6.130–6.132.
451 See paras 6.133–6.135.

	– Pleadings – Directions – Hearing notices – Outline of the remaining steps in the litigation and evidence or explanation of why the applicant needs to remain in the UK to undertake those steps and why the fairness of the proceedings will be compromised if those steps cannot be taken • All cases: – Any medical evidence relating to difficulties that the applicant might have in taking any of the steps or gathering any of the evidence referred to above, or difficulties which they would face in leaving the UK (falling short of establishing eligibility by means of IA (PAFAS) Regs 2005 reg 3(2)(b))

Dependants

6.181 Generally, applicants who wish support to be provided to them together with their dependants[452] will have made that clear within the appropriate section of the ASF1 form. However, where that has not been done a request to this effect can be made in writing, supplemented by evidence to establish that the person is a dependant for asylum-support purposes. It is not necessary for a new ASF1 form to be completed.[453]

6.182 Circumstances may arise where two or more applicants for support wish to be accommodated together, but there is no relationship of dependancy between them for support purposes. Most commonly this will arise where a household contains a young adult. The secretary of state is not obliged to accommodate non-dependants together in such circumstances. However, under Human Rights Act 1998 s6 and ECHR Article 8 (right to respect for private and family life), any interference by the secretary of state with the household's family life must be necessary and proportionate, which may, in practice, require the secretary of state to secure accommodation for them

452 See para 6.39.

453 *Dependants on an asylum support application*, Home Office, January 2015, para 3 (www.gov.uk/government/publications/dependants-on-an-asylum-support-application-instruction).

together or, at the very least, in such a way as to ensure that family life can continue.[454]

Additional support

6.183 Applicants who are seeking additional support in the form of:

- assistance with travel;[455]
- assistance with telephone calls and letters;[456]
- vouchers for pregnant women, new mothers and children;[457]
- support to meet exceptional needs;[458]

may apply by means of a single application form, supported by the appropriate evidence.[459] Applications for additional support from pregnant women or new mothers should be supported by evidence of the expected delivery date or birth of the child, unless this has been provided already, such as an MATB1 form (showing the expected delivery date of the child), a letter from a community midwife or GP, or the child's full birth certificate.[460]

Repeat applications

6.184 If an application for IAA 1999 s4(2) support is refused or discontinued and the applicant has not appealed that decision, or any appeal has been dismissed, any further application for support 'should not be entertained unless the application is made on a different basis or there has been a material change of circumstances'.[461]

Delay

6.185 Delay in the processing of applications for support under IAA 1999 s4(2) is commonplace. This can be particularly problematic as the statute does not provide for a power to grant interim support while a decision is made as to the applicant's eligibility. This contrasts with the position for applicants for IAA 1999 s95(1) support who may be

454 *Dependants on an asylum support application*, para 5.
455 See paras 6.163–6.167.
456 See paras 6.168–6.170.
457 See para 6.171.
458 See paras 6.172–6.173.
459 See: www.gov.uk/government/publications/application-for-section-4-extra-services-or-facilities.
460 The *Section 4(2) policy*, p22.
461 The *Section 4(2) policy*, p17; IAA 1999 s103(6).

provided with temporary support under IAA 1999 s98(1)[462] while their application is considered.

6.186 The *Section 4(2) policy* does provide for an urgent process for decision-making. Although decisions on applications should generally be made within five working days, 'careful consideration should be given to any additional factors that call for the case to be given higher priority and the decision made more quickly'.[463] Where the application relates to any of the following individuals or groups, reasonable efforts should be made to determine the application within two working days:[464]

- people who are street homeless;
- families with minors;
- disabled people;
- elderly people;
- pregnant women;
- persons who have been subjected to torture, rape, or other serious forms of psychological, physical or sexual violence;
- potential victims of trafficking.

6.187 More generally, there is a general principle of public law that statutory functions must be discharged within a reasonable period and in cases where the secretary of state has failed to provide accommodation under IAA 1999 s4(2) within a reasonable timescale an applicant may seek judicial review.[465] Equally, judicial review may be available where the applicant is facing an imminent breach of his or her rights under the ECHR.[466] In *R (DMA) v SSHD*,[467] the High Court was called upon to consider the systemic delays in the provi-

462 See paras 5.282–5.301.

463 The *Section 4(2) policy*, p14. This guidance features in the 'further submissions' section of the policy. However, given the purpose of the guidance is to ensure expeditious decision-making in urgent cases to avoid a breach of the ECHR it is presumably intended to be of general application.

464 The *Section 4(2) policy*, p14.

465 See, for example, *R (Sathanantham) v SSHD* [2016] EWHC 1781 (Admin), [2016] 4 WLR 128 at para 87 per Edis J (in the context of delays in the provision of support under IAA 1999 s4(1)); *R (Humnyntskyi) v SSHD* [2020] EWHC 1912 (Admin), [2021] 1 WLR 320 at paras 166–167 per Johnson J (in the context of delays in the provision of support under IA 2016 Sch 10 para 9(2)); and *R (DMA) v SSHD* [2020] EWHC 3416 (Admin) at para 178 per Robin Knowles J (in the context of delays in the provision of support under IAA 1999 s4(2)).

466 See paras 6.90–6.135 for when support may be needed to avoid an ECHR breach.

467 [2020] EWHC 3416 (Admin).

sion of support under IA 1999 s4(2). Robin Knowles J held that the delays in the cases before him[468] were unlawful and that the secretary of state was in breach of her duties under IAA 1999 s4(2) and Human Rights Act 1998 s6 in failing to properly monitor the delays in the provision of accommodation.[469] Other recent examples of challenges to delay in individual cases include *AO v Home Office*,[470] *R (Babbage) v SSHD*[471] and *R (Parul) v SSHD*.[472] Delay, including the principles relevant to the grant of relief in judicial review proceedings, is discussed further at paras 5.244–5.246.

Ending the provision of support

6.188 There are two situations in which an applicant's entitlement to support under IAA 1999 s4(2) may come to an end.

6.189 The first is where the applicant is no longer eligible for support. This can happen where the person is no longer destitute,[473] or no longer satisfies one of the gateway criteria contained in IA (PAFAS) Regs 2005 reg 3(2)[474] or because they are no longer classed as a person 'who was, but is no longer, an asylum-seeker'.

6.190 The second is where the applicant has breached the conditions[475] on which their support was granted. In these cases, the secretary of state has a discretion either to suspend or to discontinue the provision of support. Support should only be terminated where the applicant has been given an opportunity to explain why they did not comply with the conditions and has failed to provide a reasonable explanation.[476] A reasonable explanation might, for example, be that the applicant was suffering from a serious illness that meant they were not able to take the required action. Such an explanation would need

468 Consisting of 45 days, 60 days, 105 days and 151 days respectively.

469 See further *R (Humnyntskyi) v SSHD* [2020] EWHC 1912 (Admin), [2021] 1 WLR 320.

470 [2021] EWHC 1043 (QB) (failure to properly deal with application for accommodation, and source accommodation, for around 11 months unreasonable).

471 [2021] EWHC 2995 (Admin) (one month constituted reasonable period to find accommodation and delay thereafter unlawful).

472 [2022] EWHC 2143 (Admin) (ongoing delay of 146 days to provide adequate accommodation to disabled applicant unlawful).

473 See paras 6.40–6.45.

474 See paras 6.46–6.135.

475 See paras 6.174–6.175.

476 The *Section 4(2) policy*, p15.

to be supported by medical evidence. The principles outlined at paras 5.259–5.264 are relevant in this context.

6.191 In contrast to the procedure for ending the provision of support made available to an asylum-seeker under IAA 1999 s95(1),[477] the procedure for doing so under section 4(2) does not have a statutory basis.[478] The *Section 4(2) policy* provides that:

> Where it is decided to refuse support or to stop providing it, a letter setting out the reasons must be sent to the person, copied to their representative if they have one. Where the decision is to stop providing support the person should be informed that the decision will take effect 14 working days from the date of the letter. The accommodation provider should also be given separate notice of the decision, with instructions that any eviction notice served on the person should ordinarily give them no less than 7 days to vacate the accommodation.[479]

6.192 In the majority of cases, compliance with the *Section 4(2) policy* is likely to be all that is required in order to terminate an applicant's accommodation. However, there may be exceptional circumstances in which this is not the case, in which it may assist to consider the two sets of legal principles which are engaged when an occupier has to leave their accommodation.

6.193 The first are the common law[480] rules governing the termination of licences.[481] In respect of a bare (ie non-contractual) licence with no rental period, the landlord[482] must provide 'reasonable' notice.[483] What is reasonable will vary from case to case and it is possible – for

477 See paras 5.247–5.277.

478 The statutory basis for terminating asylum support under IAA 1999 s95(1) is contained in AS Regs 2000 regs 19–22. There are no equivalent provisions contained in the IA (PAFAS) Regs 2005 in respect of support under IAA 1999 s4(2). However, the legal basis for continuing the provision of support for a short period after an applicant has ceased to meet the statutory eligibility criteria may be found in the Royal Prerogative. See, by analogy, *R (SSHD) v First-tier Tribunal (Social Entitlement Chamber)* [2021] EWHC 1690 (Admin) at para 58 per Chamberlain J.

479 The *Section 4(2) policy*, p16.

480 The statutory regimes for security of tenure contained in the Housing Acts 1985 and 1988 do not apply to accommodation provided under the IAA 1999. See Housing Act 1985 ss79–80 and Sch 1 para 4A; and Housing Act 1988 s1 and Sch 1 para 12A.

481 Accommodation under IAA 1999 s4(2) is typically provided under a licence rather than a tenancy.

482 The landlord will almost certainly be the accommodation provider rather than the Home Office, though this will turn on the relevant contractual arrangements between the two.

483 *Minister of Health v Bellotti* [1944] KB 298, CA.

example, in the case of disabled occupants who might need longer in order to vacate the accommodation and remove their possessions – that a period in excess of 14 days might be needed.[484] Contractual licences will be governed first and foremost by any clause within the contract specifying a notice period. In the absence of any such clause, the common law rules would apply. A written notice from the applicant's accommodation provider meeting these requirements will be sufficient to bring their occupation rights to an end. The notice does not need to be in any particular form – a simple letter will suffice. The formalities of Protection from Eviction Act (PEA) 1977 s5, which provides that a notice to quit will only be valid where (among other things) it contains certain prescribed information about the occupant's rights,[485] do not apply in relation to accommodation provided under IAA 1999 s4(2).[486] Similarly, PEA 1977 s3 does not apply meaning that neither the accommodation provider (nor the Home Office) is required to institute court proceedings before requiring the applicant to leave the accommodation.[487]

6.194 The second are the public law principles which require public bodies to act reasonably in requiring an occupier to give up their accommodation.[488] Particularly in cases involving families, these rules might, in an appropriate case, require the Home Office to allow the applicant a longer period than that which is set out in the *Section 4(2) policy*, before vacating the accommodation.

Appeals and remedies

6.195 There are three routes by which an applicant who is aggrieved by a decision made on their section 4(2) application, or who is unhappy with the services with which they have been provided, may seek to obtain a remedy:

1) by way of a statutory appeal under IAA 1999 s103;

484 See *Gibson v Douglas* [2016] EWCA Civ 1266, [2017] HLR 11 at paras 20–21 per Sir James Munby for a general discussion of how reasonable notice may vary from case to case.

485 See Notices to Quit etc (Prescribed Information) Regulations 1988 SI No 2201.

486 PEA 1977 s3A(7A).

487 See *Ali (Iraq) v Serco Ltd* [2019] CSIH 54 for an unsuccessful attempt to argue that a court order was required under the analogous legislation in Scotland. It is understood that the reclaimer intends to appeal in that case.

488 See *R v Newham LBC ex p Ojuri (No 5)* (1999) 31 HLR 631, QBD; *R v Secretary of State for the Environment ex p Shelter and the Refugee Council* [1997] COD 49, QBD.

2) by means of a complaint (whether to the accommodation provider, the Home Office or the Parliamentary and Health Service Ombudsman (PHSO));
3) by judicial review.

Appeal

6.196 A right to appeal will arise where the secretary of state:[489]

- refuses to provide support for a person under IAA 1999 s4;[490] or
- decides to discontinue the applicant's support.

6.197 The right of appeal is to the FTT (Asylum Support). The appeal process is described in detail at paras 5.310–5.371.

Complaint

6.198 An applicant who is unhappy with the service which they have received may seek to complain to the Home Office and, if that complaint is not dealt with satisfactorily, onward to the PHSO.[491] The timescales involved in this process mean that it will not be suitable for urgent matters.

Judicial review

6.199 An applicant who does not have a statutory right of appeal, for whom the complaints process does not provide a suitable remedy, who wishes to challenge an unlawful act on the part of the secretary of state, may seek judicial review. Examples of situations in which judicial review may be appropriate are to challenge:

- delay in the provision of support;[492]
- a decision that the applicant is subject to the exclusions from support contained in NIAA 2002 s55 or Sch 3;[493]
- the location or adequacy of accommodation;[494]
- a refusal to accept a repeat application;[495]

489 IAA 1999 s103(2A).

490 The appeal right encompasses all forms of support under IAA 1999 s4, and so encompasses a refusal to provide any of the additional payments described at paras 6.163–6.173 which are granted pursuant to regulations enacted under the power contained in IAA 1999 s4(10).

491 See paras 5.372–5.374.

492 See paras 6.185–6.187.

493 See paras 6.136–6.137.

494 See paras 6.157–6.159.

495 See para 6.184.

- the reasonableness, in public law terms, of the notice period which the applicant has been given to vacate their accommodation;[496]
- decisions as to the reasonableness of any conditions attached to the provision of support.[497]

6.200 Damages may be recoverable in a claim for a breach of human rights arising from unlawful failure to make any or adequate IAA 1999 s4(2) provision. For example in *R (DMA) v SSHD*, the claimants succeeded in recovering £1,000 for delays in the provision of support to them.[498] In *Re Mahmud's application for judicial review*,[499] where the applicant was street homeless for nearly six months on account of the Home Office's failure to provide him with accommodation and support under IAA 1999 s4(2), the court found a breach of ECHR Article 3 and made an award of £1,750, observing that the awards in *DMA* appeared to be too low for the length of time spent of street homeless.

Support under Immigration Act 2016 Sch 10 para 9(2)

Overview

6.201 As was foreshadowed in the introduction to this chapter, support under IAA 1999 s4 underwent significant reform under the IA 2016. Prior to 15 January 2018, the IAA 1999 included a provision under section 4(1) which allowed the secretary of state to provide accommodation to persons:

- temporarily admitted to the UK under Immigration Act (IA) 1971 Sch 2 para 21;
- released from detention under that paragraph; or
- released on bail from detention under any provision of the Immigration Acts.

6.202 The exercise of the IAA 1999 s4(1) power was not dependent on the person's status as either an asylum-seeker or a failed asylum-seeker. In addition, the statutory eligibility requirements applicable to IAA 1999 s4(2) – the destitution test and the five conditions under the

496 See paras 6.188–6.194.
497 See paras 6.174–6.175.
498 [2020] EWHC 3416 (Admin) at paras 336–341.
499 [2021] NIQB 37.

IA (PAFA) Regs 2005 – did not form part of the statutory criteria for IAA 1999 s4(1) eligibility, although the destitution test was applied as a matter of policy.[500]

6.203 The availability of accommodation under IAA 1999 s4(1) bridged the gap to ensure that certain categories of persons who, irrespective of whether they had an outstanding asylum claim or had made one previously,[501] were provided with accommodation and essential living needs if they were destitute. The largest group of individuals in receipt of IAA 1999 s4(1) support were those who were released from immigration detention on temporary release or by a grant of immigration bail. This group were provided with accommodation under section 4(1)(c). A smaller number of people were also supported under IAA 1999 s4(1)(a) and (b) because they were destitute, could not access other avenues of support and were in need of support to avoid a breach of their human rights, on the basis that 'the person cannot reasonably be expected to leave the United Kingdom'.[502] Examples of groups falling within subsections (a) and (b) of section 4(1) were:

- people who had never made a previous asylum application but who have outstanding applications for leave to remain that were not asylum claims – for example, applications made under Appendix FM of the Immigration Rules, under ECHR Article 8 or based on statelessness;
- those taking steps to leave the UK who had never claimed asylum;
- individuals who were too ill to travel who had never claimed asylum;
- those who had withdrawn their asylum claims but were seeking to re-instate them;
- those who stopped engaging with the Home Office, whose asylum claims were treated as being implicitly withdrawn; and
- former UASCs whose asylum claims had been determined before they reached the age of 18 and who did not qualify for local authority support.

500 *Asylum support: section 4 policy and process*, v7, Home Office, March 2016, paras 1.1.2, 1.1.3 and 5.4 (withdrawn in January 2018).

501 For example, in respect of support under IAA 1999 s4(1)(c) for those released on bail, the policy expressly provided that an applicant 'could be an asylum seeker, a failed asylum-seeker, or a person who has never had an asylum application but is otherwise in detention'. See *Asylum support: section 4 policy and process*, v7, para 5.1 (withdrawn in January 2018).

502 *Asylum support: section 4 policy and process*, v7, para 1.1.3 (withdrawn in January 2018).

6.204 The changes brought into force by the IA 2016 represented a significant change to the approach taken to governing the conditions on which individuals who require but do not yet have leave to remain are permitted to be in the UK temporarily. Understanding these changes is important to understanding the impact of the modifications to the support regime that had previously existed under IAA 1999 s4(1). Previously, a person could be admitted to the UK temporarily under IA 1971 Sch 2 para 21 without being subject to immigration bail. The category of persons subject to immigration bail was largely limited to those on bail granted by the Special Immigration and Asylum Commission (SIAC), deportees granted immigration bail under IA 1971 Sch 3 para 2, and others granted immigration bail on release from immigration detention. Not all deportees or persons liable to be removed from the UK were required to be subject to immigration bail in order to be released from immigration detention; they could instead be granted temporary admission or temporary release. This changed on 15 January 2018 when, by the IA 2016, the regime of temporary admission and temporary release under IA 1971 Sch 2 paras 21 and 22 was repealed[503] and the 'various pre-existing alternatives to detention' were replaced with 'a single power to grant immigration bail', whereby all persons who require leave to enter or remain but do not have it are subject to immigration bail, overseen by the SSHD and the FTT (IAC).[504]

6.205 Alongside the repeal of the temporary admission and temporary release regime was also the repeal of the power to provide support under IAA 1999 s4(1).[505] This did not affect the qualifying criteria for support under IAA 1999 s4(2), but left a gap in the availability of accommodation and subsistence support for those who had previously qualified for it under IAA 1999 s4(1). Although there is a power to provide facilities for accommodating those who are on immigration bail under IA 2016 Sch 10 para 9(2), that power is not intended to, and does not, in practice, operate as a mirror image replacement of IAA 1999 s4(1).[506]

6.206 The introduction of the new regime has not been without its difficulties. For some considerable time after the new regime was brought

503 The necessary repeals were effected by IA 2016 Sch 10 Part 2.

504 *Immigration bail policy*, v15.0, p8. See paras 6.213–6.220.

505 By IA 2016 Sch 11 para 1 and to the extent specified in Immigration Act 2016 (Commencement No 7 and Transitional Provisions) Regulations 2017 reg 2(d)(i). See paras 6.268–6.271 for the transitional provisions governing the move from the IAA 1999 s4(1) to the IA 2016 Sch 10 regime.

506 The two statutory provisions are very different, although their underlying purpose is similar. See paras 6.244–6.250.

into effect, there was no application process by which applicants could apply for support under IA 2016 Sch 10 para 9(2).[507] Although an application process has now been put in place, it is far from perfect. Much of the practical detail as to what support is available and where is not prescribed by statute or policy and is left to the discretion of the secretary of state, a situation which is not ideal for migrants seeking to establish what support they are entitled to. In addition, the Home Office policy does not deal comprehensively or adequately with all situations in which an applicant might require support.[508] Added to that are potentially wider concerns as to the compatibility of the immigration bail regime with ECHR Article 5 (right to liberty and security).[509] There are also no statutory rights of appeal against refusal to support under Schedule 10 para 9(2), which raises questions as to whether the scheme infringes constitutional principles related to access to justice, particularly when it concerns a regime where people are subject to immigration bail irrespective of their immigration history and conduct and are subject to criminal and civil sanctions including immigration detention and prosecution for a breach of condition.

6.207 The rest of this chapter is given over to a discussion of who is entitled to support under IA 2016 Sch 10 para 9(2), how they can go about obtaining that support, what they can do if they are wrongly refused support and, generally, how they might seek to navigate the difficulties described above along the way.

The eligibility criteria

Overview

6.208 Under IA 2016 Sch 10 para 9(2), the secretary of state may provide, or arrange for the provision of, facilities for the accommodation of a person who:

- is on immigration bail;[510]
- is subject to a bail condition requiring them to reside at a specified address;[511]
- would not otherwise be able to support themself at that address.[512]

507 See paras 6.255–6.258.
508 See paras 6.244–6.250.
509 See para 6.216.
510 IA 2016 Sch 10 para 9(1)(a). See paras 6.213–6.220.
511 IA 2016 Sch 10 para 9(1)(a). See paras 6.220–6.226.
512 IA 2016 Sch 10 para 9(1)(b). See para 6.227.

6.209 This power may only be exercised to the extent that the secretary of state thinks that there are 'exceptional circumstances' to justify its use.[513] Each of these four statutory conditions will be explored below. The power is to be exercised to provide accommodation at the address specified in the bail condition.[514]

6.210 It is important to note that the power under IA 2016 Sch 10 para 9(2) may only be exercised in respect of the person who satisfies these conditions. It does not, on the face of it, extend to the provision of accommodation for such a person together with their dependants. Adult dependants may, if they are vulnerable, be able to seek accommodation from social services under the Care Act 2014.[515] Otherwise they will need to establish that they are eligible under IA 2016 Sch 10 para 9(2) in their own right. Child dependants would need to be supported by social services under the ChA 1989.[516] The relationship between support under IA 2016 Sch 10 para 9(2) and these community care services is discussed further at para 6.251.

6.211 The wording of IA 2016 Sch 10 para 9 is unusual. The power to provide accommodation may only be exercised to allow an individual to reside at the address specified in their bail conditions. On the face of it, the power will not arise until the individual has been made subject to such a bail condition.[517] However, such a bail condition cannot be imposed until the address of the accommodation has been provided, which can only be done once the power to provide accommodation has been exercised. This means that the power to provide accommodation can only arise in circumstances where the power to provide accommodation has already arisen. Moreover, there should be no requirement, in principle, to impose a condition of residence on everyone who requires it by reason of their destitution. The power to impose bail conditions under IA 2016 Sch 10 para 2 only requires such conditions to be imposed if necessary to meet the bail objectives of ensuring a person keeps in contact with the Home Office and

513 IA 2016 Sch 10 para 9(3). See paras 6.228–6.250.

514 IA 2016 Sch 10 para 9(2).

515 See paras 8.7–8.178.

516 See paras 9.12–9.177. In such a case it might be expected that the applicant would seek to be accommodated by social services with their dependant rather than seeking Home Office support.

517 See *R (AT (Guinea)) v SSHD* [2019] EWHC 2709 (Admin) at paras 50–51 per Nigel Poole QC sitting as a deputy High Court judge.

protect the public from potential risks of harm. Thus, as drafted, the accommodation power under Schedule 10 para 9 can appear circular and, applied literally, can result in absurdity.

6.212 However, the Home Office has indicated that it intends to take a pragmatic approach to the exercise of the power under IA 2016 Sch 10 para 9(2) and that para 9(1)(a) should be read as referring to 'either an address that is already specified or one that is to be specified'.[518] That is, the bail condition need not refer to a specific address in order for secretary of state to provide accommodation. This pragmatic approach, if applied consistently, should ensure that the objective of IA 2016 Sch 10 para 9, to provide accommodation in exceptional circumstances to persons on immigration bail, is not frustrated and that the power to accommodate can be exercised in a way that ensures compliance with the ECHR.[519]

Condition 1: Applicant is on immigration bail[520]

6.213 The first eligibility requirement in order for an applicant to access support under IA 2016 Sch 10 para 9(2) is that they are on immigration bail.[521] By virtue of the changes made under IA 2016 Sch 10 para 20 repealing the regime of temporary admission and temporary release, all those previously subject to these alternatives to detention at the time IA 2016 Sch 10 came into force on 15 January 2018 were, from that point forward, treated as though they had been granted immigration bail under the new regime.[522]

6.214 The detail of the administration of the immigration bail regime is set out in the Home Office's *Immigration bail policy*.[523] However, the fundamentals of the statutory regime are as follows. Under IA 2016 Sch 10 para 1, the secretary of state may grant immigration bail to any person who is detained, or liable to be detained, under any of the following provisions:[524]

518 *R (Humnyntskyi) v SSHD* [2020] EWHC 1912 (Admin), [2021] 1 WLR 320 at para 19 per Johnson J.

519 If the legislation were not construed in this way there could be a risk of a breach of ECHR Article 3 (see paras 6.90–6.135) if a destitute applicant was unable to access accommodation under this provision. Such a construction may therefore be justified (and required) under Human Rights Act 1998 s3.

520 See further paras 1.188–1.197.

521 IA 2016 Sch 10 para 9(1)(a).

522 IA 2016 Sch 10 para 13; Immigration Act 2016 (Commencement No 7 and Transitional Provisions) Regulations 2017 reg 1.

523 *Immigration bail policy*, v15.0, Home Office, January 2023.

524 IA 2016 Sch 10 para 1(1) and (2).

- IA 1971 Sch 2 para 16(1), (1A) or (2) (detention of persons liable to examination or removal);
- IA 1971 Sch 3 para 2(1), (2) or (3) (detention pending deportation);
- NIAA 2002 s62 (detention of persons liable to examination or removal); or
- UK Borders Act 2007 s36(1) (detention pending deportation).

6.215 These statutory provisions are labyrinthine. However, in practical terms they encompass any person who requires leave to enter or remain in the UK but does not have it. The FTT (IAC) has analogous powers to grant bail to any person detained under one of these provisions, upon that person's application to the tribunal.[525]

6.216 The statutory language used under IA 2016 Sch 10 para 1 authorises the secretary of state to exercise the power to impose immigration bail on any person who is 'liable to be detained', irrespective of whether it would be lawful to detain them.[526]

6.217 When considering whether to grant bail, the Home Secretary and the FTT (IAC) must have regard to the following statutorily prescribed considerations:[527]

- the likelihood of the person failing to comply with a bail condition;
- whether the person has been convicted of an offence (anywhere and at any time);
- the likelihood of a person committing an offence while on immigration bail;
- the likelihood of the person's presence in the UK, while on immigration bail, causing a danger to public health or being a threat to the maintenance of public order;
- whether the person's detention is necessary in that person's interests or for the protection of any other person, and
- such other matters as the secretary of state or the FTT (IAC) think relevant.

525 IA 2016 Sch 10 para 1(3). Save that the FTT (IAC) has no power to grant immigration bail without the consent of the Home Secretary if there are removal directions in place requiring the person to be removed within 14 days of the date of the bail decision: IA 2016 Sch 10 para 3(4).

526 IA 2016 Sch 10 para 1(2) and (5); *R (Kaitey) v SSHD* [2021] EWCA Civ 1875, [2022] 3 WLR 121 (where this was interpretation was affirmed and held to be compatible with ECHR Article 5).

527 IA 2016 Sch 10 para 3(1)(a) and (2).

6.218 Regard will also need to be had to whether the grant of bail is necessary to protect the applicant's rights under the ECHR, for example, by allowing them to access accommodation and thereby avoid a breach of their rights under Article 3.[528]

6.219 Once a person has been granted immigration bail, they will remain on bail until they:[529]

- are granted leave to enter or remain in the UK;
- are detained;
- are removed from, or otherwise leave, the UK; or
- in a case where the person could not be lawfully detained, are no longer under consideration for deportation.

6.220 Any decision to grant or refuse to grant immigration bail must be notified in writing to the person.[530] That notice must state when the grant of immigration bail commences, and the bail conditions the person would be subjected to.[531] The commencement of a grant of immigration bail may be conditional on arrangements being put in place to ensure that the person is able to comply with the bail conditions.[532] This may be of significance in a case where support under IA 2016 Sch 10 para 9(2) is sought, as it allows for bail to commence at the point where accommodation is made available to the person.[533]

Condition 2: Applicant subject to residence condition

6.221 The second eligibility requirement in order for an applicant to access support under IA 2016 Sch 10 para 9(2) is that they are subject to a bail condition requiring them to reside at a specified address.[534] As discussed at para 6.211, there is a circular logic to this requirement and to ensure the effective operation of the statutory regime, the Home Office has indicated that this requirement should be interpreted as a condition requiring the applicant to reside either at a specified address or an address that is to be specified.

6.222 The power to impose bail conditions is contained in IA 2016 Sch 10 para 2 and may be exercised by either the secretary of state or the

528 Human Rights Act 1998 s6. See *R (Ganpot) v SSHD* [2023] EWHC 197 (Admin) where the point was accepted as 'strongly arguable'.
529 IA 2016 Sch 10 para 8.
530 IA 2016 Sch 10 para 3(5)–(6).
531 IA 2016 Sch 10 para 3(7).
532 IA 2016 Sch 10 para 3(8).
533 See paras 6.221–6.226 for a discussion of the residence condition requirement, necessary to establish eligibility for support under IA 2016 Sch 10 para 9.
534 IA 2016 Sch 10 para 9(1)(a).

FTT (IAC) upon the grant of bail. The list of conditions which may be imposed, including a residence condition,[535] are contained in IA 2016 Sch 10 para 2(1). When considering what bail conditions are appropriate, the Home Secretary and the FTT (IAC) must have regard to statutory bail considerations set out in Sch 10 para 3.[536] At least one bail condition must be imposed in all cases,[537] but conversely, there is no requirement to impose more than one condition. The applicant must be notified in writing of their conditions,[538] which in practice is on a Bail 401 form.

6.223 Applicants for support under Schedule 10 para 9(2) who are already subject to immigration bail but require a residence condition to be imposed in order to become eligible for support, may apply to have their bail conditions varied.[539]

6.224 The requirement for a residence condition in order to establish eligibility for support does not sit at all easily with the principle that bail conditions amount to a restriction on liberty and that the minimum conditions necessary should be imposed to avoid a disproportionate interference with this right.[540] If such a condition is needed to avoid an applicant sleeping on the streets, then it might perhaps be viewed as the lesser of two evils. However, this is not a satisfactory way in which to approach the imposition of measures to restrict a person's liberty in circumstances where the residence condition may not be necessary to meet the objectives of bail, to ensure that the bailee remains in contact with the Home Office, and refrains from offending or causing harm to the public.

6.225 The date on which bail commences may be conditional on arrangements, such as the provision of accommodation under IA 2016 Sch 10 para 9(2), being put in place to ensure that the applicant can comply with their bail conditions.[541] Notably, however, Schedule 10 para 3(8), which sets out the power to postpone commencement of the grant of bail, does not confer a comparable power on the secret-

535 IA 2016 Sch 10 para 2(1)(c).

536 IA 2016 Sch 10 para 3(1)(a) and (2).

537 IA 2016 Sch 10 para 2(1).

538 IA 2016 Sch 10 para 3(5)–(7).

539 IA 2016 Sch 10 para 6. See the *Immigration Bail policy*, v15.0, pp81–83

540 *Guidance on Immigration Bail for Judges of the First-tier Tribunal (Immigration and Asylum Chamber)*, Tribunals Judiciary, 15 January 2018, para 12. See further the *Immigration Bail policy*, v15.0, p18 where it is said that a residence condition will only usually be imposed where 'necessary to enable a high level of contact or mitigate against a serious risk of non-compliance'.

541 IA 2016 Sch 10 para 3(8).

ary of state or the FTT (IAC) to impose an expiry date for the bail grant if a condition imposed is not satisfied. Once bail is granted, whether unconditionally or conditionally, changes to the person's circumstances can be dealt with under other provisions under IA 2016 Sch 10, such as para 6 which sets out powers to vary or remove the conditions of bail having regard to the same statutory matters under Sch 10 para 3(2) which inform the grant of bail. Routinely, however, the FTT (IAC) grants conditional bail for a prescribed period, frequently 14 or 21 days, after which the grant of bail 'expires'. There is no statutory basis for this practice, which seems to have developed by way of guidance issued by the Tribunals Judiciary.[542] Conditional bail – or 'Bail in Principle' – is most prolifically used where there is an identified need for bail accommodation but the secretary of state has either not considered the applicant's eligibility under IA 2016 Sch 10 para 9, or has yet to identify an actual bail address for release.[543]

6.226 Imposing a specific time period for the conditional bail grant may well be a pragmatic way by which some pressure is exerted on the secretary of state to act promptly to identify suitable arrangements under Schedule 10 para 9, in circumstances where similar problems with delays in accommodation arrangements plague Schedule 10 para 9 cases as they do cases under IAA 1999 ss4(2) and 95. However, problems arise where no accommodation is identified before the expiry of the period of the conditional bail grant. The FTT (IAC) has entertained requests for an extension of the conditional bail grant period by applicants, although there is no statutory basis for the power to extend bail grants because there is no statutory basis to impose a time limit in the first place. The existence of a power to extend conditional bail grant periods is also not set out in the tribunal guidance. Nor is it informed to applicants. Where the conditional bail grant period expires, the only remedy for the applicant is a fresh bail application, which may be met again by another conditional bail grant if accommodation under Schedule 10 para 9 is still not made available by the secretary of state. It is not uncommon for immigration detainees to be subject to several conditional bail grants before accommodation is identified under Schedule 10 para 9, and often only after judicial review proceedings are issued.[544]

542 Presidential Guidance Note No 1 of 2018: *Guidance on Immigration Bail for Judges of the First-tier Tribunal (Immigration and Asylum Chamber)*, para 58.

543 As noted in *R (Humnyntskyi) v SSHD* [2020] EWHC 1912 (Admin), [2021] 1 WLR 320 at para 19 per Johnson J.

544 See, for example, *R (SML) v SSHD* [2020] EWHC 3267 (Admin).

Condition 3: Applicant not otherwise able to support themself

6.227 The third eligibility requirement to qualify for accommodation IA 2016 Sch 10 para 9(2) is that the applicant would not otherwise be able to support themself at the address specified in their bail conditions.[545] There is no definition or explanation of this requirement in either the IA 2016 or the *Immigration bail policy*. The ordinary meaning of the words – 'unable to support himself or herself at the address' – suggest that this requirement is broader than a simple requirement that the applicant is unable to meet their contractual liability to pay the rent or occupation charge. The legislative focus on the applicant's ability to support themself, suggests that this requirement will also be fulfilled where an applicant is unable to meet their essential living needs such as food, clothing, warmth etc, while living at the accommodation. These are, after all, basic needs which any person must meet in order to support themself from day to day. Applicants who are seeking support under IA 2016 Sch 10 para 9(2) in order to avoid destitution in breach of ECHR Article 3 will certainly meet this threshold.[546]

Condition 4: Exceptional circumstances

Overview

6.228 The fourth eligibility requirement is that 'the Secretary of State thinks that there are exceptional circumstances' to justify the provision of support.[547] This element of the statutory test is not defined in the IA 2016. Rather, the question of what constitutes exceptional circumstances has been left for the secretary of state to determine.

6.229 In the *Immigration bail policy*, the secretary of state has indicated that the following cases are normally to be regarded as exceptional:[548]

- SIAC cases;[549]
- harm cases;[550]
- ECHR Article 3 cases.[551]

545 IA 2016 Sch 10 para 9(1)(b).
546 See paras 6.236–6.243.
547 IA 2016 Sch 10 para 9(3).
548 *Immigration bail policy*, v15.0, pp86–90.
549 See para 6.231.
550 See paras 6.232–6.23.
551 See paras 6.236–6.243.

6.230 These three classes of case will each be considered in turn, although it should be noted that these classes should not be regarded as exhaustive of the categories of exceptionality. There is no legislative fetter on the circumstances which the secretary of state might regard as exceptional for the purposes of IAA 2016 Sch 10 para 9. Further, while the secretary of state is entitled to adopt a policy as to how they intend to exercise their judgment in this regard, they must always be willing to consider applications from those who fall outside of the terms of the policy but who contend that their case is, nevertheless, exceptional.[552]

SIAC cases

6.231 These are national security cases involving applicants who have been granted bail by the SIAC. Strict bail conditions will invariably be imposed in such cases, including a residence condition, in order to control the risk which the applicant has been adjudged to pose. It is unsurprising that such cases are regarded by the secretary of state as exceptional and qualifying for accommodation under IAA 2016 Sch 10 para 9.[553] The *Immigration bail policy* suggests that accommodation should be provided to asylum-seekers and failed asylum-seekers who are SIAC cases, even if they would otherwise be eligible for asylum support under IAA 1999 s4(2) or s95(1).[554]

Harm cases

6.232 'Harm cases' are defined under the *Immigration bail policy* as those involving:[555]

- applicants (including foreign national offenders (FNOs)) who are granted bail and are currently assessed by His Majesty's Prison and Probation Service as being at a high or very high risk of causing serious harm to the public;
- FNOs at high risk of harmful reoffending against an individual, who have been assessed using the Offender Group Reconviction Scale with a minimum score of 70 per cent.

6.233 Serious harm in this context means 'an event, which is life-threatening and/or traumatic, from which recovery, whether physical or psycho-

552 *British Oxygen Co Ltd v Board of Trade* [1971] AC 610, HL at p625 per Lord Reid; *R (Humnyntskyi) v SSHD* [2020] EWHC 1912 (Admin), [2021] 1 WLR 320.

553 *Immigration bail policy*, v15.0, p86.

554 *Immigration bail policy*, v15.0, pp86 and 92.

555 *Immigration bail policy*, v15.0, pp86–87.

logical, can be expected to be difficult or impossible'.[556] The risk of such harm being caused will be classified as high or very high if the potential event either could happen at any time, or is more likely than not to happen imminently, and the impact would be serious.

6.234 These cases are regarded as exceptional for the purposes of IA 2016 Sch 10 para 9 either if the applicant has nowhere suitable to live in accordance with their licence conditions or multi-agency public protection (MAPPA) arrangements, or where the secretary of state considers it to be in the interest of public protection. The position of other immigration detainees who are not adjudged to pose high or very high risk of harm is discussed at paras 6.244–6.250 below.

6.235 The *Immigration bail policy* suggests that accommodation should be provided to asylum-seekers and failed asylum-seekers who meet the criteria above, even if they would otherwise be eligible for support under IAA 1999 s4(2) or s95(1).[557]

ECHR cases

6.236 An applicant's case will be regarded as exceptional for the purposes of IA 2016 Sch 10 para 9 if:[558]

- they do not have adequate accommodation or the means of obtaining it; and
- the provision of accommodation is necessary to avoid a breach of their rights under the ECHR.

6.237 Quite properly, the *Immigration bail policy* recognises that any breach of the ECHR should be regarded as exceptional. However, the policy suggests that, in practical terms, it is ECHR Article 3 which will most typically be in issue.[559] The circumstances in which support will be necessary to avoid a breach of ECHR Article 3 are discussed at paras 5.127–5.128 and 6.98–6.100. This threshold will generally be met where:

- there is evidence that the applicant would otherwise be street homeless, seriously hungry, or unable to satisfy the most basic requirements of hygiene;[560] and

556 *Immigration bail policy*, v15.0, p87.

557 *Immigration bail policy*, v15.0, p92.

558 *Immigration bail policy*, v15.0, pp87–90.

559 This may, however, be in conjunction with another Article, such as ECHR Article 8. See para 6.115. See further paras 6.116–6.135 for other Articles of the ECHR that may be engaged.

560 *R (Limbuela) v SSHD* [2005] UKHL 66, [2006] 1 AC 396 at para 9 per Lord Bingham, paras 56–63 per Lord Hope and para 78 per Baroness Hale. See further, the *Immigration bail policy*, v15.0, p88.

- the applicant faces a practical or legal impediment to return to their country of origin, meaning that it would not be reasonable to expect the applicant to look to their home country for sustenance or support.[561]

6.238 In order to meet the first limb of this test, the applicant will need to establish that they cannot access alternative forms of support. In particular, asylum-seekers, failed asylum-seekers, applicants with dependent children and applicants with care and support needs are unlikely to be eligible for IA 2016 Sch 10 para 9(2) support as they should be entitled to other forms of state support.[562] Examples of applicants who might be ineligible for other forms of state support and might therefore require support under IA 2016 Sch 10 para 9(2)[563] include those whose initial asylum claim was withdrawn[564] and former UASCs whose asylum claims were determined before they reached the age of 18 and who do not qualify for local authority support under the ChA 1989.[565] These two cohorts are not classed as asylum-seekers or failed asylum-seekers and may need support under IA 2016 Sch 10 para 9(2) to avoid the destitution arising from the legal limbo in which they find themselves.

6.239 As to the second limb of the test, the *Immigration bail policy* gives the following examples of cases in which it will not be reasonable to expect an applicant to seek support in their country of origin owing to the existence of a practical or legal impediment to return:[566]

- cases in which the applicant's initial asylum claim was withdrawn, where they are seeking to make further submissions in support of a fresh claim for asylum;

561 *R (Clue) v Birmingham City Council* [2010] EWCA Civ 460, [2011] 1 WLR 99 at paras 39–40 and 53–75 per Dyson LJ. See further, the *Immigration bail policy*, v15.0, p89.

562 *Immigration bail policy*, v15.0, p88. Asylum-seekers should be eligible for support under IAA 1999 s95(1) (see paras 5.9–5.90); failed asylum-seekers should be eligible for support under IAA 1999 s4(2); applicants with children should be eligible for support under ChA 1989 s17(1) (see paras 9.12–9.69); adults in need of care and attention should be eligible for support under Care Act 2014 s18(1) (see paras 8.7–8.178).

563 *Immigration bail policy*, v15.0, p90.

564 Often this will be because the applicant absconded before the secretary of state determined the initial asylum claim. See paras 5.37–5.38 and 6.20–6.24.

565 See paras 6.147–6.151. Note, however, that many former UASCs are eligible for support as care leavers under the ChA 1989. See paras 9.118–9.194. If that is the case, then the applicant would be unlikely to qualify for support under IA 2016 Sch 10 para 9(2).

566 *Immigration bail policy*, v15.0, p90.

- cases in which the applicant is taking reasonable steps to leave the UK;
- cases in which the applicant is unable to leave the UK because of a physical impediment, or other medical reason;
- cases in which the applicant was refused asylum and exhausted their appeal rights before they reached the age of 18.

6.240 The Bail 409 application form,[567] by which applicants may apply for support under IA 2016 Sch 10 para 9(2),[568] contains the following additional examples of impediments to return:[569]

- cases in which, in the opinion of the secretary of state, there is currently no viable route of return available;
- cases in which the applicant has an extant appeal or has been granted permission to proceed with a judicial review of an immigration decision.

6.241 These categories of case in which applicants face a recognised form of impediment to return will be familiar to advisors who are accustomed to working with failed asylum-seekers who are applying for support under IAA 1999 s4(2) as they mirror closely the various gateways to support under IA (PAFAS) Regs 2005 reg 3(2).[570] This reflects the fact that the underlying rationale for the provision of support is the same whether it is sought under IA 2016 Sch 10 para 9(2) or IAA 1999 s4(2): that the state will need to provide support to destitute migrants who cannot reasonably return to their country of origin to alleviate their destitution, in order to avoid a breach of the ECHR.

6.242 With that rationale in mind, there are several further categories of case which are not referred to expressly within the *Immigration bail policy* in which an applicant, who is not an asylum-seeker or a failed asylum-seeker, may require support under IA 2016 Sch 10 para 9(2) in order to avoid a breach of the ECHR. These include:

- cases in which the applicant has an extant application for leave to remain under ECHR Article 8 or where the applicant is stateless;[571]

567 See: www.gov.uk/government/publications/application-for-immigration-bail-accommodation-exceptional-circumstances-article-3-echr-bail-409-form.

568 See paras 6.255–6.268 for the application process.

569 See: www.gov.uk/government/publications/application-for-immigration-bail-accommodation-exceptional-circumstances-article-3-echr-bail-409-form.

570 See paras 6.46–6.135 for a detailed discussion of the scope of those gateways.

571 See para 6.115 and *R (Ganpot) v SSHD* [2023] EWHC 197 (Admin).

- cases in which the applicant is seeking judicial review of an immigration decision but has not yet been granted permission;[572]
- cases in which the applicant has an extant application to the ECtHR including a request for interim measures (such as a suspension on removal) under Rules of Court r39.[573]

6.243 These three categories are relatively well established as giving rise to a legal or practical impediment to an applicant returning to their country of origin. Destitute applicants falling within one of these categories should consider making an application for support under IA 2016 Sch 10 para 9(2) and should not be deterred by the fact that their circumstances are not referred to expressly within the *Immigration bail policy*. First, because the categories of 'exceptional' case for the purposes of IA 2016 Sch 10 para 9 are not closed and the secretary of state, as a matter of public law, must always be open to considering whether any given case is exceptional.[574] Second, because a case where an applicant, but for the provision of support, is facing a breach of the ECHR must be deemed to be exceptional in order to ensure that the power under IA 2016 Sch 10 para 9(2) is exercised compatibly with the ECHR.[575]

Other immigration detention cases

6.244 The sections on the *Immigration bail policy* relating to SIAC and harm cases provide a means by which certain detainees may qualify for support under IA 2016 Sch 10 para 9(2) by virtue of their exceptional circumstances. However, the policy appears to suggest it only applies to those detainees who are adjudged by the secretary of state to pose a high or very high risk of harm to the public. This applies mostly to foreign national offenders. Many of those in immigration detention, even those with criminal convictions, cannot be characterised as posing such a level of risk, yet they may be in equal need of accommodation in order to secure their release from detention. The FTT (IAC) in particular may be reluctant to release a

572 See paras 6.124–6.127.

573 See paras 6.130–6.132.

574 *British Oxygen Co Ltd v Boardr of Trade* [1971] AC 610, HL at p625 per Lord Reid; *R (Humnyntskyi) v SSHD* [2020] EWHC 1912 (Admin), [2021] 1 WLR 320.

575 See Human Rights Act 1998 ss3 and 6. The issue could be characterised as one of statutory construction (s3), in relation to the meaning of the word 'exceptional', or the appropriate way for the secretary of state to exercise their discretion (s6). Either way, the result is the same.

detainee on bail unless satisfied that they have accommodation to be released to.

6.245 Prior to the introduction of IA 2016 Sch 10, the position was relatively straightforward. Any detainee released on bail, or seeking to be released on bail, could apply for accommodation under IAA 1999 s4(1)(c).[576] Home Office policy was that accommodation should be provided to any applicant provided that they would be destitute if released on bail, or would become destitute within 14 days.[577] The precise immigration status of the detainee was not particularly important. Applicants could qualify whether they were asylum-seekers, failed asylum-seekers or neither.[578] Similarly, the section 4(1)(c) provision applied whether the detainee was an FNO with criminal convictions.

6.246 The repeal of IAA 1999 s4(1)(c)[579] and its replacement by IA 2016 Sch 10 para 9, as supplemented by the *Immigration bail policy*, has complicated matters. The *Immigration bail policy* provides that support under IA 2016 Sch 10 para 9(2) will not generally be granted to asylum-seekers or failed asylum-seekers. These cohorts will, instead, need to seek support under IAA 1999 s95(1) or s4(2) respectively. Exception is made for SIAC and high harm FNOs but not explicitly for detainees posing low, medium or no risk. If a detainee in the latter group is an asylum-seeker or failed asylum-seeker, they will have to pursue support under IAA 1999 s95(1) or s4(2) in the first instance. In doing so, they may well encounter the problems in establishing destitution that are described at paras 5.74–5.77: namely, a perception on the part of the Home Office that an applicant in immigration detention is adequately accommodated and therefore not destitute.

6.247 Diverting detainees to the IAA 1999 regime also does not address the residual category of detainees who are neither asylum-seekers nor failed asylum-seekers. Their only option, if they do not have the means to access accommodation by themselves and they face a legal impediment to being removed from the UK, is to seek support under IA 2016 Sch 10 para 9(2) in order to secure their release. This category

576 *Asylum support: section 4 policy and process*, v7, para 5.4 (withdrawn in January 2018).

577 *Asylum support: section 4 policy and process*, v7, para 5.7.3 (withdrawn in January 2018).

578 See *Asylum support: section 4 policy and process*, v7 (withdrawn in January 2018).

579 By IA 2016 Sch 11 para 1 and to the extent specified in Immigration Act 2016 (Commencement No 7 and Transitional Provisions) Regulations 2017 reg 2(d)(i).

does not fit neatly within any of the classes of exceptional case set out in the *Immigration bail policy*.[580]

6.248 The failure to deal with this cohort within the *Immigration bail policy* potentially raises a number of legal issues. There is now a clear line of authority establishing that the secretary of state is under a public law obligation to make reasonable efforts to provide accommodation where the person would otherwise remain in detention[581] and that '[d]etention is not a proper substitute for [bail] accommodation once detention cannot otherwise be justified'.[582] In *R (Diop) v SSHD*[583] the claimant's embassy had refused to issue him with an emergency travel document, thereby limiting his prospects of removal. The High Court concluded that he had been unlawfully detained for a period of around four weeks in circumstances where the sole reason that he remained in detention for that period of time was the failure to provide bail accommodation under IAA 1999 s4(1)(c). The same rationale would apply equally to a failure to provide support under IA 2016 Sch 10 para 9(2). Such a failure may raise ECHR Article 5 issues of the type canvassed in *Diop*,[584] as well as the public law issues on which the claim was decided. As such, cases in which an applicant who faces an impediment to removal requires accommodation under IA 2016 Sch 10 para 9(2) in order to secure their release from detention arguably constitute an important example of the exceptional type of case in which the power to provide accommodation should be exercised. If that is correct, then the failure to set out within the *Immigration bail policy* the circumstances in which the power will be exercised in relation to this cohort is concerning. As the Supreme Court observed in *R (Lumba) v SSHD*,[585] 'the rule of law calls for a transparent statement by the executive of the circumstances in which the broad statutory criteria will be exercised'.

580 See paras 6.228–6.243. In particular, they do not fit within the rubric of the typical ECHR Article 3 case described at paras 6.236–6.243, since the applicant would need to be released before the Article 3 risk could arise.

581 *R (Razai) v SSHD* [2010] EWHC 3151 (Admin) at para 26 per Nicol J, *R (Sathanantham) v SSHD* [2016] EWHC 1781 (Admin, [2016] 4 WLR 128 at para 69 per Edis J and *R (Humnyntskyi) v SSHD* [2020] EWHC 1912 (Admin), [2021] 1 WLR 320 at paras 166–167 per Johnson J.

582 *R (MS) v SSHD* [2017] EWHC 2797 (Admin) at para 79 per Martin Griffiths QC, sitting as a deputy High Court judge.

583 [2018] EWHC 1934 (Admin).

584 See *R (Diop) v SSHD* [2018] EWHC 1934 (Admin) at paras 10–20.

585 [2011] UKSC 12, [2012] 1 AC 245 at para 34 per Lord Dyson.

6.249 This problem with the way the secretary of state operated the category-based exceptional circumstances as they applied to foreign national offenders who have not been deemed to be high harm came to the fore in the case of *R (Humnyntskyi) v SSHD*.[586] Although the *Immigration bail policy* provided for the accommodation power to be exercised where it is required to avoid a breach of the ECHR, in practice the secretary of state did not apply that aspect of the policy to foreign national offenders who were not high harm cases, thereby making it excessively difficult for these foreign national offender detainees to secure bail accommodation for their release from immigration detention. This policy approach was successfully challenged by way of judicial review.[587] Each of the three claimants had been refused bail accommodation under IA 2016 Sch 10 para 9(2). They argued that the refusals were unlawful, and that the system for providing Schedule 10 accommodation was unlawful both by reason of inherent unfairness and because the secretary of state had fettered her discretion as to the circumstances in which she would provide accommodation. The court held that the *Immigration bail policy* was intended to recognise ECHR Article 3 cases as a discrete category that applied to all foreign national offenders.[588] However, in practice, that was not how the secretary of state treated the applications. The decision-making process, mandated by unpublished guidance, resulted in IA 2016 Sch 10 accommodation not being considered for an FNO who did not pose a high risk, because a bail residence condition was not necessary in such a case. The policy did not require FNOs to be informed of a caseworker's decision that they were not eligible for Schedule 10 para 9(2) accommodation. In those circumstances, the policy did not satisfy the minimum criteria necessary to secure fairness.

6.250 The court also held that producing an exhaustive list of circumstances capable of being exceptional so as to merit the grant of IA 2016 Sch10 para 9(2) accommodation and to refuse to contemplate any others would be unlawful. The wording of the *Immigration bail policy* gave the impression that only three specified categories of case could amount to exceptional circumstances. This created the unintended risk that caseworkers would regard the categories as closed. It was unlikely that that was the intention behind the unpublished guidance, but the evidence presented by the claimants was that this was how the policy had been operated. In this way, the secretary of

586 [2020] EWHC 1912 (Admin), [2021] 1 WLR 320.

587 *R (Humnyntskyi) v SSHD* [2020] EWHC 1912, [2021] 1 WLR 320 (Admin).

588 See at paras 279–286.

state had unintentionally but unlawfully fettered her discretion as to what might amount to exceptional circumstances such as to merit a grant of IA 2016 Sch 10 para 9(2) accommodation.[589] The order made by the court did not direct the secretary of state to make changes to the *Immigration bail policy* but the policy should now be read in the light of the findings of systemic unfairness made by the court in the judgment.

Relationship with community care services and support under the Immigration and Asylum Act 1999

6.251 The *Immigration bail policy* provides[590] that support under IA 2016 Sch 10 para 9(2) will not be provided in circumstances where the applicant is eligible for other forms of state support such as community care services under the ChA 1989[591] or Care Act 2014[592] or support under IAA 1999 s4(2)[593] or s95(1).[594] In this respect, in relation to community care services, the policy follows the position that has been consistently adopted by the courts which is that Home Office support, in these circumstances, is a residual form of support of last resort and that the notional availability of such support cannot be used by a local authority to justify refusing community care services,[595] save where the applicant's eligibility for Home Office support means that they are subject to an express statutory exclusion from those services.[596]

589 See *R (Humnyntskyi) v SSHD* [2020] EWHC 1912 (Admin) at paras 287, 290–291, 293, 295–297.

590 *Immigration bail policy*, v15.0, p88.

591 See paras 9.12–9.69.

592 See paras 8.7–8.178.

593 See paras 6.9–6.200.

594 See paras 5.9–5.90.

595 *R (Westminster City Council) v National Asylum Support Service* [2002] UKHL 38, [2002] 1 WLR 2956 (support for vulnerable adults under NAA 1948 s21 takes precedence over support under IAA 1999 s95(1)); *R (AW) v Croydon LBC* [2007] EWCA Civ 266, [2007] 1 WLR 3168 (support for vulnerable adults under NAA 1948 s21 takes precedence over support under IAA 1999 s4(2)); *R (SO) v Barking and Dagenham LBC* [2010] EWCA Civ 1101, [2011] 1 WLR 1283 (support for care leavers under ChA 1989 takes precedence over support under IAA 1999 ss4(2) and 95(1)); *R (VC) v Newcastle City Council* [2011] EWHC 2673 (Admin), [2012] PTSR 546 (support for households with dependant children under ChA 1989 s17(1) takes precedence over support under IAA 1999 s4(2)).

596 Of the type found in ChA 1989 s122 or Care Act 2014 s21.

The provision of support

6.252 Under IA 2016 Sch 10 para 9(2) the secretary of state has the power to 'provide, or arrange for the provision of, facilities for the accommodation'. This is the same statutory formulation as appears in IAA 1999 s4(2).[597] This permits the secretary of state to provide accommodation together with subsistence payments, but not subsistence payments only. The *Immigration bail policy* says little about the nature of the support that will be provided, referring only the provision of accommodation and other 'assistance' to meet the applicant's 'daily living needs'. There is no publicly available data on the number of grants of support under IA 2016 Sch 10 para 9(2). The numbers were reportedly low in the first five months of the regime in 2018, according to a Freedom of Information Act request made by Bail for Immigration Detainees (BID), and were almost exclusively granted to detained and SIAC cases.[598]

6.253 The Home Office seems to be providing financial support at the rates equivalent to the asylum support rates under IAA 1999 s95(1),[599] paid by means of an ASPEN card which the applicant can use to pay for goods in shops or withdraw cash, alongside hostel style accommodation.

Travel expenses

6.254 Under IA 2016 Sch 10 para 9(4) the secretary of state may pay travel expenses to an applicant who is on immigration bail for the purposes of allowing them to comply with bail conditions, to the extent that the secretary of state thinks that there are exceptional circumstances to justify the payment of those expenses.[600] The *Immigration bail policy* provides the example of an applicant who is subject to a reporting condition that requires travel which they are unable to afford, where

597 See para 6.154.

598 In the first five months of the new regime, 24 applications for support were granted. This information comes from a Home Office response to a Freedom of Information request made by BID, reported on BID's twitter feed on 25 June 2018 at https://twitter.com/BIDdetention/status/1011548806305939461?ref_src=twsrc%5Etfw%7Ctwcamp%5Etweetembed%7Ctwterm%5E1011548806305939461&ref_url=https%3A%2F%2Frighttoremain.org.uk%2Fpost-detention-accommodation-briefing-from-bid%2F.

599 See paras 5.185–5.200.

600 IA 2016 Sch 10 para 9(5).

the secretary of state is unwilling to vary that condition to move it to a location closer to where the applicant is living.[601]

The application process

6.255 When IA 2016 Sch 10 first came into force on 15 January 2018, the Home Office did not put in place any application process by which applicants could seek support under IA 2016 Sch 10 para 9(2). The original version of the *Immigration bail policy* was silent on how someone may be able to ask the Home Office to exercise the power, and there was no publicly available application form. This position was only rectified following a legal challenge to the lack of policy and process in the case of *MSM v SSHD*,[602] and on 5 April 2019 an amended version of the *Immigration bail policy*[603] was published alongside a Bail 409 application form. This form is intended to be used by those who are in immigration detention and are seeking accommodation so that they can be released on bail and by those in the community on immigration bail who are seeking to have their bail conditions varied so that they can access accommodation.[604] The former category will need to complete the Bail 409 form in addition to the appropriate bail application form. The completed Bail 409 form can only be submitted, it would appear, by post, to PO Box 471, Dover CT16 9FN, whereas IAA 1999 s95 or s4(2) applications can be sent by email to Migrant Help, the secretary of state's contractor for operating the asylum support regime.

6.256 The *Immigration bail policy* stipulates that the Bail 409 application form is not to be used by FNOs or in SIAC cases. Instead they should 'set out their needs in the bail application form', which is form B1 (where bail is sought from the FTT (IAC)) or BAIL 401 (where bail is sought from the secretary of state),[605] and 'these will be assessed as part of the bail consideration process'.[606] Neither form is well suited to this purpose. The court in *Humnyntskyi* made comments to the

601 *Immigration bail policy*, v15.0, p93.

602 CO/4687/2018.

603 V4.0, Home Office, 5 April 2019.

604 *Immigration bail policy*, v15.0, p92: www.gov.uk/government/publications/. application-for-immigration-bail-accommodation-exceptional-circumstances-article-3-echr-bail-409-form.

605 See: www.gov.uk/bail-immigration-detainees/apply-for-bail.

606 *Immigration bail policy*, v15.0, p92.

same effect,[607] noting that these forms are designed to apply for bail and not for accommodation. The court also expressed concerns[608] over evidence adduced in the judicial review proceedings which indicated that individuals requiring IA 2016 Sch 10 para 9(2) accommodation were not informed of its existence or how they might be eligible for it, or how they might apply for it. In detained cases, this has had the consequence of individuals remaining longer in detention. In community cases, this has led to street homeless.

6.257 When the *Immigration bail policy* was first issued, it also did not contain any timescales for decision-making on the application for bail accommodation. This was amended in February 2020 further to a successful judicial review claim challenging the failure to provide for timescales and in particular for prioritising consideration of applications from vulnerable applicants.[609] The current *Immigration bail policy*, now provides that decision on Bail 409 applications from non-detained cases should generally be made within five working days but that 'careful consideration' should be given to 'any additional factors that call for the case to be given higher priority and make the decision more quickly'.[610] In particular, if any of the following circumstances apply, applications should be decided within two working days:[611]

- people who are street homeless;
- families with children under the age of 18;
- people with disabilities (physical and/or mental);
- elderly people;
- pregnant women;
- people who have been subjected to torture, rape, or other serious forms of psychological, physical or sexual violence;
- potential victims of trafficking.

607 *R (Humnyntskyi) v SSHD* [2020] EWHC 1921 (Admin) at para 37 per Johnson J.

608 See *Humnyntskyi* at para 60 per Johnson J.

609 The consent order compromising the claim can be found at: https://dpglaw.co.uk/wp-content/uploads/2020/04/2750648-Signed-Consent-Order-31-03-2020-redacted.pdf. As well are referring to the amendments to the policy, the order recorded a concession on the part of the SSHD that 'if there is a delay in providing non-foreign national offenders with accommodation under Paragraph 9 of Schedule 10 to the Immigration Act 2016, once an application has been approved, she/he may enter initial accommodation in the interim period'.

610 *Immigration bail policy*, v15.0, p92.

611 *Immigration bail policy*, v15.0, p92. See further, paras 6.185–6.187 on delay.

6.258 Concern has been expressed in the voluntary sector as to whether advice and assistance in connection with applications for support under IA 2016 Sch 10 para 9(2) are regulated by the Office of the Immigration Services Commissioner (OISC). The concern arises from the fact that advice and representation in connection with applications for bail under the Immigration Acts are 'immigration services' for the purposes of IAA 1999 s82(1), which has the consequence that any person providing such services is required either to be registered with, and accredited by, the OISC or to be authorised by a designated professional body[612] to practise as a member of the profession whose members the body regulates.[613] The answer, unsatisfactorily, is not entirely clear. The questions within the application form for support under IA 2016 Sch 10 para 9(2) are not directed toward the grant of variation of immigration bail. In the main, they are directed toward other matters relevant to the provision of support such as destitution and the obstacles faced by the applicant in leaving the UK. An adviser could fill out, or assist an applicant to fill out, this form without ever providing any advice or making any representations on the subject of bail.[614] However, on the other hand, the form expressly describes itself as being 'designed for persons who are applying for Immigration Bail with a residence condition' and applicants must be on immigration bail which is subject to a residence condition in order to qualify for support.[615] This means that, in practice, the subject of immigration bail may be unavoidable and the form itself might reasonably be viewed as an application for bail or for a variation of bail conditions. In these circumstances it would seem prudent for advisers assisting with such applications to seek to clarify the position with the OISC.

Ending the provision of support

Overview

6.259 Both IA 2016 Sch 10 and the *Immigration bail policy* are silent as to how and when support provided under IA 2016 Sch 10 para 9(2) may be brought to an end. Certainly support may be terminated if

612 Such as the Solicitors Regulation Authority (SRA).

613 IAA 1999 s84(1).

614 Save for checking the box to acknowledge that the applicant will be destitute if granted bail.

615 See paras 6.213–6.226.

the applicant ceases to meet the eligibility criteria.[616] Arguably, it is also implicit within the statutory scheme that support may be withdrawn if the applicant evinces a rejection of that support by means of a persistent and unequivocal refusal to observe any reasonable conditions which have been attached to the provision of their support by the secretary of state.[617] Before deciding to terminate support in these circumstances, the secretary of state would need to consider any relevant medical conditions or infirmities which the applicant might have and provide the applicant with a letter of final warning, to give them the opportunity to change their behaviour or provide representations in response.[618]

6.260 As to the procedure by which support can be brought to an end, there are two sets of legal principles to consider:

1) the private law rules governing the termination of licences;
2) the public law rules which require public bodies to act reasonably in requiring an occupier to give up their accommodation.

Private law rules

6.261 The first set of legal principles to consider are the private law rules governing the termination of licences.[619] These rules apply to the accommodation provider, as opposed to the Home Office. The position here is a little complicated and depends principally on whether or not the PEA 1977 applies to accommodation provided under IA 2016 Sch 10 para 9(2). This, it will be seen, is open to debate.

6.262 The private law principles begin with the common law, which requires that an occupier must be given notice to quit their accommodation before they can be required to leave. This requirement is overlaid by PEA 1977 s5(1A) which provides that a notice to quit premises which are occupied as a 'dwelling' under a licence will not be valid unless:

616 See paras 6.208–6.250.

617 *R v Kensington and Chelsea RLBC ex p Kujtim* [1999] 4 All ER 161, (2000) 32 HLR 579, CA at p593 per Potter LJ.

618 *Kujtim* at p594 per Potter LJ.

619 Accommodation secured by the Home Office is typically provided under a licence rather that a tenancy. Where, exceptionally, the accommodation is provided under a tenancy it is likely that the tenancy would be assured shorthold attracting statutory protection under the Housing Act 1988. Unlike support under IAA 1999 ss4(2) and 95(1), support under IA 2016 Sch 10 para 9(2) is not excluded from security of tenure under Housing Act 1988 s1 and Sch 1 para 12A: see para 5.249 fn 711.

- it is in writing and contains such information as may be prescribed, and
- it is given not less than four-weeks before the date on which it is to take effect.

The prescribed information is set out in Notices to Quit etc (Prescribed Information) Regulations 1988.

6.263 Once the notice to quit has expired, the landlord will need to institute proceedings in the county court in accordance with CPR Part 55 in order to recover possession.[620] For the landlord to seek to recover possession without recourse to the courts is both a civil wrong,[621] for which damages may be recoverable,[622] and a criminal offence.[623]

6.264 On the face of it, these significant procedural protections would seem to apply to accommodation provided under IA 2016 Sch 10 para 9(2). The various forms of accommodation to which the safeguards within the PEA 1977 do not apply are set out in PEA 1977 s3A. The other principal forms of Home Office accommodation, support under IA 1999 ss4 and 95, have been explicitly excluded from protection.[624] Accommodation under IA 2016 Sch 10 para 9(2) has not been excluded. From this, it might reasonably be inferred that parliament intended that occupiers under IA 2016 Sch 10 para 9(2) should have the full protection of the PEA 1977.

6.265 The counter-argument to this might be that accommodation provided under IA 2016 Sch 10 para 9(2) is of a sufficiently short-term and transient nature that, like interim homelessness accommodation provided under Housing Act 1996 Part VII, it is not usually occupied as a 'dwelling' and therefore does not attract statutory protection.[625] And if the PEA 1977 does not apply, then an occupier of accommodation under IA 2016 Sch 10 para 9(2) would benefit only from the more limited private law protection described at para 6.193. In outline, the occupier would need to be provided with reasonable notice, which need not be very long. And the notice need not be in any particular form. A letter would suffice.

6.266 On balance, it seems likely that the PEA 1977 does apply. Parliament made two amendments to PEA 1977 s3A under the IA

620 PEA 1977 s3(1) and (2B).

621 PEA 1977 s3.

622 See Arden, Brown and Madge-Wyld *Quiet enjoyment: protection from rogue landlords*, Legal Action Group, 8th edn, 2017.

623 PEA 1977 s1.

624 PEA 1977 s3A(7A).

625 *R (N) v Lewisham LBC* [2014] UKSC 62, [2015] AC 1259.

2016[626] and therefore plainly had in mind, when enacting the IA 2016, the types of accommodation which should and should not attract statutory protection. In those circumstances, it seems more likely than not that if parliament had intended accommodation under IA 2016 Sch 10 para 9(2) to fall outside of the protection of the Act, it would have said so expressly.

Public law rules

6.267 In addition to these private law rules, the second set of legal principles which are relevant are the public law rules which require public bodies to act reasonably in requiring an occupier to give up their accommodation.[627] These rules apply to the Home Office and, like the private law rules, will require some notice to be given to the occupier before they can be required to leave. However, in practice, a relatively short notice period is likely to satisfy these requirements. More notice will generally be required in cases where children are accommodated.

Transitional cases

6.268 IAA 1999 s4(1) was repealed on 15 January 2018[628] and replaced with the new regime under IA 2016 Sch 10 para 9 described above at paras 6.201–6.267. However, there remain, at the time of writing, some applicants who have not yet transitioned to the new regime and continue to be accommodated under IAA 1999 s4(1). Such applicants will continue to receive support under IAA 1999 s4(1) until the Home Office discontinues it.[629] However, once they come off section 4(1) support, they will not be able to request it again and will need to consider other options under IA 2016 Sch 10 para 9(2),[630] IAA 1999 s4(2)[631] or IAA 1999 s95(1),[632] depending on their personal circumstances.

626 See IA 2016 s33E(5) and Sch 11 para 2(b)(i) (not yet in force).
627 See *R v Newham LBC ex p Ojuri (No 5)* (1999) 31 HLR 631, QBD; *R v Secretary of State for the Environment ex p Shelter and the Refugee Council* [1997] COD 49, QBD.
628 By IA 2016 Sch 11 para 1 and to the extent specified in Immigration Act 2016 (Commencement No 7 and Transitional Provisions) Regulations 2017 reg 2(d)(i).
629 IA 2016 Sch 11 para 46(1)–(2).
630 See paras 6.201–6.271.
631 See paras 6.9–6.173.
632 See paras 5.9–5.220.

6.269 The Home Office's policy *Support provided under section 4(1) of the Immigration and Asylum Act 1999: handling transitional cases*[633] explains that the entitlement of any applicant who remains on IAA 1999 s4(1) support should be reviewed at least every three months.[634] Where possible, the applicant should be transferred onto IA 2016 Sch 10 para 9(2), or IAA 1999 s4(2) or s95(1) support and they should be notified of this change. There should be no change to their support arrangements, with the exception of those who are transferred to asylum support under IAA 1999 s95(1) in respect of whom steps should be taken to enable them to use their ASPEN cards to make cash withdrawals.[635]

6.270 Home Office policy provides that applicants should only remain on IAA 1999 s4(1) support following a review if discontinuing support would amount to a breach of the ECHR. In cases where the applicant was eligible for support under IAA 1999 s4(1)(a) or (b) by virtue of having been granted temporary admission to the UK, this does not constitute a significant change from the old regime. The majority of applicants who were on support under that category would have been assisted for ECHR reasons. If nothing has changed in their circumstances since they were granted support, then they should remain entitled. In cases where the applicant was eligible for support under IAA 1999 s4(1)(c) by virtue of having been released on immigration bail this amounts to a more significant change.[636] In order to remain eligible for support, they will need to demonstrate that there is some kind of practical or legal obstacle that stops them from leaving the UK to alleviate their destitution.[637]

6.271 Applicants have a right of appeal against a decision to discontinue support under IAA 1999 s4(1)[638] and there have been a number of successful appeals against discontinuation decisions based on the fairness of the procedure adopted by the Home Office in bringing the

633 V1.0, Home Office, 16 February 2018 (www.gov.uk/government/publications/asylum-support-section-41-handling-transitional-cases).

634 *Support provided under section 4(1) of the Immigration and Asylum Act 1999: handling transitional cases*, v1.0, Home Office, 16 February 2018, p6.

635 See para 5.186.

636 Contrast with the position as described in *Asylum support, section 4 policy and process*, Home Office, April 2016, chapter 5 (archived on 5 January 2018).

637 See by analogy paras 6.90–6.102.

638 IAA 1999 s103; *Support provided under section 4(1) of the Immigration and Asylum Act 1999: handling transitional cases*, v1.0, p8. See paras 6.195–6.197. This right of appeal will be abolished in respect of discontinuation decisions made after 15 January 2018 if and when IA 2016 Sch 11 para 2 is brought into effect. See IA 2016 Sch 11 para 46(2).

applicant's support to an end.[639] The FTT (Asylum Support) in these cases has taken the view that the Home Office is required, as a matter of public law, to administer the transitional cases policy fairly, and that unfairness may arise if support is discontinued without the applicant first being given the opportunity and the information necessary to make representations as to why their support should continue, or why they should be granted a different form of support.

Remedies

6.272 There is no statutory right of appeal against a refusal to provide support under IA 2016 Sch 10 para 9(2). The remedy is judicial review. In appropriate cases, applicants may also rely on the complaints mechanisms described at paras 5.372–5.374.

639 See, for example, AS/19/07/39953, 16 July 2019, FTT (Asylum Support), AS/19/04/39465, 17 April 2019, FTT (Asylum Support); AS/19/03/39332, 18 March 2019, FTT (Asylum Support).

CHAPTER 7

Housing for migrants

Tessa Buchanan

continued

Key points

- Applicants who are homeless or threatened with homelessness may apply to a local housing authority for immediate accommodation or assistance in obtaining accommodation under Housing Act (HA) 1996 Part VII (in England) or Housing (Wales) Act (H(W)A) 2014 Part 2 (in Wales). Applicants who are seeking an allocation of social housing on a long-term basis may apply to a local housing authority under HA 1996 Part VI.
- Persons subject to immigration control will be ineligible for either homelessness assistance or an allocation of social housing unless they are within a class prescribed as eligible by regulations. Other 'persons from abroad' will be ineligible for such assistance if:
  - they are not habitually resident, unless they fall within a class prescribed as exempt from the habitual residence test; or
  - they fall within a class prescribed as ineligible by regulations.
- Local housing authorities are subject to a range of duties owed to those who are homeless or threatened with homelessness under HA 1996 Part VII (in England) or H(W)A 2014 Part 2 (in Wales). Some of these duties require the provision of accommodation and others do not. What duty, if any, will be owed to an eligible applicant for homelessness assistance will depend on whether they are homeless or threatened with homelessness; whether they have a priority need; and whether they became homeless intentionally.
- Local housing authorities are required by HA 1996 Part VI to have schemes for allocating social housing which must meet certain statutory requirements, including giving reasonable preference to specific classes of people. Local housing authorities in England may disqualify certain classes of people from their allocation schemes.
- There is a serious shortage of social housing and many people are obliged (or choose) to rent in the private rented sector. The right to rent scheme, introduced in 2014, makes it unlawful for private landlords, and some social landlords, to rent to certain people who are disqualified due to their immigration status. This scheme has been upheld as lawful by the Court of Appeal.

Introduction

Overview

7.1 This chapter is concerned with access to what may be described as 'mainstream' accommodation in the social housing and private rented sectors, namely the provision of urgent assistance by a local housing authority to a person facing immediate or imminent homelessness; or an allocation of long-term accommodation in the social housing sector; or a licence or tenancy in the private rented sector. It is usually only when a person is unable to obtain accommodation by one of these routes that they are obliged to seek housing through a different avenue, such as from the Home Office (see chapters 5 and 6) or social services (see chapters 8 and 9).

Structure of this chapter

7.2 This chapter is structured as follows:

- The chapter deals firstly with the eligibility rules which restrict access for migrants both to short-term emergency homelessness assistance from local housing authorities, and longer-term allocations of accommodation from social housing providers. In England, there are two types of registered providers of social housing: public registered providers (local housing authorities) and private registered providers (most commonly housing associations). In Wales, there are local housing authority landlords and registered social landlords.
- The chapter then looks at the framework which governs access to such housing (or assistance with housing) for eligible applicants.
- Finally, the chapter discusses the right to rent provisions and their impact on migrants seeking accommodation in the private rented sector.

Housing Act 1996 and Housing (Wales) Act 2014

7.3 The HA 1996 contains the framework for long-term allocations of social housing (in England and Wales) as well as the provision of short-term emergency homelessness assistance (in England only). Homelessness law in Wales is contained in H(W)A 2014 Part 2.

7.4 HA 1996 Part VI sets out the provisions with which local housing authorities must comply when allocating housing accommodation.[1]

1 HA 1996 s159(1).

An allocation of social housing takes place when a local housing authority selects or nominates a person to be a long-term (secure, introductory, or assured) tenant of a social housing provider.[2] HA 1996 Part VI applies to both England and Wales, albeit with some differences as explained in the rest of this chapter.

7.5 HA 1996 Part VII governs the provision of homelessness assistance by local housing authorities. It contains the powers and duties which local housing authorities have towards those who are homeless or threatened with homelessness. Unlike HA 1996 Part VI, however, it applies only in England. The equivalent legislation in Wales is set out in H(W)A 2014 Part 2.

Eligibility for homelessness assistance and housing allocations

Introduction

7.6 The most significant barrier preventing migrants from accessing either homelessness assistance or an allocation of social housing is the eligibility requirement.[3] This is a criterion based on immigration or residence status. (In Wales, 'eligibility' can also refer to misconduct-related provisions whereby an applicant may be excluded from a local housing allocation scheme due to past unacceptable behaviour.[4] This is discussed at para 7.359.)

7.7 Applicants who are ineligible are excluded from virtually all forms of *homelessness assistance* in both England and Wales. In England, this is the result of HA 1996 s185(1), which provides that an ineligible person is not 'eligible for assistance under this Part'. 'Assistance' is defined at HA 1996 s183(2) to mean 'the benefit of any function under the following provisions of this Part relating to accommodation or assistance in obtaining accommodation'. This means that ineligible applicants in England will not be entitled to the benefit of any of the powers or duties from HA 1996 s184 onwards.[5] In Wales,

2 HA 1996 s159(2): see paras 7.354–7.56 for a more detailed discussion of the definition of an allocation.

3 At the time of writing, the Retained EU Law (Revocation and Reform) Bill was awaiting its second reading in the House of Lords. This bill may, if enacted, impact upon the rules governing eligibility.

4 HA 1996 s160A.

5 This does not absolve local housing authorities of the obligation under HA 1996 s184 to make inquiries into whether an applicant is eligible and, if they decide the applicant is not, to issue a decision to that effect.

ineligible applicants are excluded from help under H(W)A 2014 ss66, 68, 74 and 75.[6] Although apparently defined more narrowly than the exclusion under HA 1996 Part VII, the result is in practical terms the same.[7] However, in both England and Wales an ineligible applicant can still benefit from the local housing authority's general duty to provide an information and advisory service on homelessness and can obtain free advice and information about homelessness and the prevention of homelessness.[8] The eligibility criterion applies to all applicants seeking homelessness assistance under HA 1996 Part VII (in England) or H(W)A 2014 Part 2 (in Wales).

7.8 In both England and Wales, applicants who are ineligible may not be made an *allocation* of social housing.[9] The eligibility criterion applies to most applicants seeking an allocation of long-term social housing under HA 1996 Part VI (England and Wales). There are, however, some important exceptions where it does not apply. In England, the eligibility rules do not affect an applicant who is already a secure, introductory or assured tenant of social housing, where:

1) the allocation involves a transfer;
2) the transfer is at the applicant's own request; and
3) the applicant is entitled to a reasonable preference within the local housing authority's allocation scheme under HA 1996 s166A(3): see para 7.366.[10]

7.9 In Wales, the eligibility rules do not apply to an applicant who is already a contract-holder in relation to housing accommodation allocated to them by a local housing authority in Wales.[11]

7.10 It is the eligibility of the *applicant* which will determine whether or not they can access homelessness assistance or an allocation of social housing. This is straightforward in respect of homelessness applications, as such applications can only be made by

6 H(W)A 2014 Sch 2 para 1(1). See paras 7.275–7.293 for a description of the duties contained in these sections.

7 Technically, ineligible applicants in Wales can still benefit from the discretionary power to provide interim accommodation pending review under H(W)A 2014 s69(11). However, it seems unlikely that this discretion would often be exercised in favour of an applicant who is ineligible.

8 HA 1996 s179(1) (England) and H(W)A 2014 s60(1) (Wales).

9 HA 1996 ss160ZA(1) (England) and 160A(1) (Wales).

10 HA 1996 ss159(4A) and (4B) and 160ZA(5).

11 HA 1996 s160A(6).

an individual.[12] Applications for an allocation of social housing can, however, be made jointly by two or more persons.[13] In the case of a joint application, if any one of the applicants is ineligible, no allocation can be made.[14] If, therefore, a particular person within a family is ineligible, then the application for homelessness assistance or for an allocation of social housing should be made by another member of the household, if they are able to do so. This does not mean, however, that the immigration position of other members of the household is irrelevant. The status of another member of the household can affect what obligations are subsequently owed pursuant to the application for homelessness assistance or for an allocation of social housing. This is discussed below at paras 7.75–7.85.

7.11 The rules on eligibility are, in summary, as follows:

1) **persons who are subject to immigration control** will be ineligible for assistance unless they are within a class prescribed as eligible by regulations;
2) **other 'persons from abroad'** will be ineligible for assistance only if:
   a) they are not habitually resident, unless they fall within a class prescribed as exempt from the habitual residence test (in which case they will be eligible); or
   b) they fall within a class prescribed as ineligible by regulations.

Each of these two rules is examined further below.

7.12 Local housing authorities have no discretion to disapply the eligibility provisions. An applicant *must* be found to be ineligible if the relevant criteria are met, and if they are ineligible, they *cannot* be made an allocation of social housing[15] or, with limited exceptions,[16] be supported under the homelessness provisions.[17]

7.13 This section will discuss the two rules on eligibility: the eligibility of members of the household; and challenging a decision that an applicant is not eligible.

12 HA 1996 Part VII and H(W)A 2014 Part 2 both refer to 'a person' making the application: HA 1996 s183(1) and H(W)A 2014 s62(1). See also *Hynds v Midlothian DC* (1986) SLT 54, (1985) November SCOLAG 163, CS (OH) at p295 per Lord Ross.

13 This possibility is expressly recognised at HA 1996 ss160ZA(1)(a) (England) and 160A(1)(c) (Wales).

14 HA 1996 ss160ZA(1) (England) and 160A(1) (Wales).

15 HA 1996 ss160ZA(1) (England) and 160A(1) (Wales).

16 See paras 7.119 and 7.339–7.345.

17 HA 1996 s185(1) (England) and H(W)A 2014 Sch 2 para 1(1) (Wales).

Persons subject to immigration control

7.14 Persons who are subject to immigration control will be ineligible for homelessness assistance or for an allocation of social housing unless they fall within a class of persons prescribed as eligible.[18]

Who is subject to immigration control?

7.15 The term 'persons subject to immigration control' has a special meaning in the context of homelessness and allocations. Although the same phrase is used in respect of welfare benefits, its definition in that field is different.[19] In the housing context, 'persons subject to immigration control' has the meaning given by the Asylum and Immigration Act (AIA) 1996.[20] Under the AIA 1996, a person is subject to immigration control if they require leave to enter or remain in the United Kingdom (UK) under the Immigration Act (IA) 1971, whether or not such leave has been given.[21]

7.16 The following persons do not require leave to enter or remain in the UK:

1) British citizens;[22]
2) Irish citizens;[23]
3) Commonwealth citizens with the right of abode in the UK;[24]
4) people who are exempt from immigration control under the Immigration Acts (this includes certain diplomats and military personnel);[25] and
5) certain European Economic Area (EEA) nationals.[26]

7.17 These people are not subject to immigration control and will therefore be eligible for homelessness assistance or an allocation of social housing, unless they fall within the second excluded category of

18 For allocations: HA 1996 ss160ZA(2) (England) and 160A(3) (Wales). For homelessness: HA 1996 s185(2) (England) and H(W)A 2014 Sch 2 para 1(2) (Wales).

19 See paras 4.32–4.33.

20 In respect of allocations, this is the result of HA 1996 ss160ZA(2) (England) and 160A(3) (Wales). In respect of homelessness, this is the result of HA 1996 s185(2) (England) and H(W)A 2014 Sch 2 para 1(2) (Wales).

21 AIA 1996 s13(2).

22 IA 1971 s3(1).

23 IA 1971 s3ZA(1).

24 IA 1971 ss2 and 3(1).

25 IA 1971 s8.

26 See paras 7.18–7.27.

'persons from abroad' who are ineligible: see paras 7.64–7.74. Everyone else is a person subject to immigration control and will be ineligible for assistance, unless they fall within a class of persons which has been statutorily prescribed as eligible even though subject to immigration control. This means that a person who was born in the UK and has never left it could be a person subject to immigration control, as was confirmed by the Court of Appeal in the case of *Ehiabor v Kensington and Chelsea RLBC*.[27] This is discussed further at paras 7.64–7.70 below.

Which EEA nationals are not subject to immigration control?

7.18 'EEA nationals' as used in this chapter refers to:

1) members of the European Union (EU), namely: Austria, Belgium, Bulgaria, Croatia, Cyprus, Czech Republic, Denmark, Estonia, Finland, France, Germany, Greece, Hungary, Ireland, Italy, Latvia, Lithuania, Luxembourg, Malta, Netherlands, Poland, Portugal, Romania, Slovakia, Slovenia, Spain, and Sweden;
2) those members of the EEA who are not in the EU, namely: Iceland, Liechtenstein, and Norway; and
3) Swiss nationals.[28]

7.19 Before 1 January 2021, an EEA national with a right to reside[29] in the UK under the Immigration (European Economic Area) Regulations ('EEA Regs') 2016,[30] or arising directly from EU law, did not require leave to enter or remain in the UK under the IA 1971 by virtue of Immigration Act (IA) 1988 s7(1). Such a person was therefore not subject to immigration control. IA 1988 s7 and the EEA Regs 2016 were then repealed as of 11pm on 31 December 2020. The default or starting position now is therefore that an EEA national is subject to immigration control. However, the repeal of these enactments was subject to a number of different transitional, saving and transitory provisions,[31] the effect of which is that certain EEA nationals will not be subject to immigration control or will be treated as not subject to

27 [2008] EWCA Civ 1074, [2008] 5 WLUK 191. See also *Barnet LBC v Ismail* [2006] EWCA Civ 383, [2006] 1 WLR 2771.

28 Although Switzerland is not in the EEA, Swiss nationals have had the same rights as EEA nationals to freedom of movement and social security within the EEA since 1 June 2002.

29 See paras 2.41–2.137 for a discussion of rights to reside.

30 SI No 1052.

31 Unfortunately, there is no single document containing all the changes made to the EEA Regs 2016 and ascertaining which set of modifications apply in any particular case, and what those modifications are, is not an easy task. This is a confusing and unsatisfactory position.

immigration control in the housing context. Such EEA nationals will therefore be eligible for homelessness assistance and an allocation of social housing unless they fall within one of the classes of person prescribed as ineligible.

7.20 There are three classes[32] of EEA nationals who are not subject to immigration control or are treated as not being subject to immigration control in the housing context.[33]

7.21 **The first class**[34] comprises EEA nationals and their family members who have limited leave to enter or remain in the UK where that leave was granted under Appendix EU of the Immigration Rules.[35] Such leave is referred to by the Home Office,[36] and commonly known, as 'pre-settled status'.[37] People in this class – referred to as 'member[s] of the post-transition period group'[38] – are to be treated

32 There was, for a brief time, a fourth class by virtue of Citizens' Rights (Application Deadline and Temporary Protection) (EU Exit) Regulations 2020 SI No 1209 regs 3 and 12(1)(g). This comprised EEA nationals who were 'lawfully resident in the UK by virtue of free movement law immediately before the end of the transition period, and who do not yet have status': Citizens' Rights (Application Deadline and Temporary Protection) (EU Exit) Regulations 2020 Explanatory Memorandum para 2.2. This class only applied during the 'grace period', namely the time between 11pm on 31 December 2020 (the end of the implementation period) and 30 June 2021 (the deadline for submission of an application for residence status pursuant to the Withdrawal Agreement) and is therefore of mainly historic interest.

33 Guidance is available in the statutory codes: *Homelessness code of guidance*, Ministry of Housing, Communities and Local Government (MHCLG), February 2018, paras 7.9–7.10; *Allocation of accommodation: guidance for local housing authorities in England*, Department for Levelling Up, Housing and Communities (DLUHC), June 2012, paras 3.9–3.10; and *Addendum to guidance affecting certain persons subject to immigration control*, Welsh Government, February 2023, paras 9–12.

34 Immigration and Social Security Co-ordination (EU Withdrawal) Act 2020 (Consequential, Saving, Transitional and Transitory Provisions) (EU Exit) Regulations 2020 SI No 1309 reg 83 and Sch 4 paras 5–6.

35 Or under 'any other immigration rules which are identified in the Immigration Rules as having effect in connection with the withdrawal' of the UK from the EU: European Union (Withdrawal Agreement) Act 2020 s17(1)(b) and Immigration and Social Security Co-ordination (EU Withdrawal) Act 2020 (Consequential, Saving, Transitional and Transitory Provisions) (EU Exit) Regulations 2020 reg 83 and Sch 4 paras 1, 5 and 6.

36 See, for example: *EU Settlement Scheme: EU, other EEA and Swiss citizens and their family members*, Home Office, July 2021.

37 See paras 2.166–2.168 for a detailed explanation of pre-settled status. See paras 7.72–7.74 for the eligibility of EEA nationals with pre-settled status.

38 Immigration and Social Security Co-ordination (EU Withdrawal) Act 2020 (Consequential, Saving, Transitional and Transitory Provisions) (EU Exit) Regulations 2020 Sch 4 para 1.

as not being subject to immigration control for the purposes of determining eligibility for homelessness assistance or an allocation of social housing.[39]

7.22 **The second class**[40] is made up of EEA nationals who:

1) have made a valid application for leave to enter or remain in the UK under Appendix EU of the Immigration Rules[41] which was submitted on or before 30 June 2021[42] and which has not been determined or withdrawn;[43]
2) were lawfully resident in the UK, or had a right of permanent residence in the UK, by virtue of the EEA Regs 2016 immediately before 11pm on 31 December 2021;[44] and
3) are currently exercising a right of residence under the EEA Regs 2016.[45]

7.23 A person will only remain in this class for 'the relevant period'. This began at the end of 30 June 2021[46] and will end:

1) when they are granted leave to enter or remain in the UK;
2) if leave is refused and the person does not appeal, on the first day on which they are no longer entitled to appeal; or

39 Immigration and Social Security Co-ordination (EU Withdrawal) Act 2020 (Consequential, Saving, Transitional and Transitory Provisions) (EU Exit) Regulations 2020 Sch 4 para 5.

40 Citizens' Rights (Application Deadline and Temporary Protection) (EU Exit) Regulations 2020 regs 4(2), (5) and 12(1)(g).

41 Or under 'any other immigration rules which are identified in the immigration rules as having effect in connection with the withdrawal' of the UK from the EU: European Union (Withdrawal Agreement) Act 2020 s17(1)(b) and Citizens' Rights (Application Deadline and Temporary Protection) (EU Exit) Regulations 2020 reg 4(6)(a).

42 30 June 2021 was the deadline for submission of an application for residence status pursuant to the Withdrawal Agreement: Citizens' Rights (Application Deadline and Temporary Protection) (EU Exit) Regulations 2020 reg 2.

43 Citizens' Rights (Application Deadline and Temporary Protection) (EU Exit) Regulations 2020 reg 4(2)(a) and (6)(a).

44 Citizens' Rights (Application Deadline and Temporary Protection) (EU Exit) Regulations 2020 reg 4(2)(b). In determining this, the EEA Regs 2016 as they were in effect immediately before 11pm on 31 December 2020 should be applied.

45 Citizens' Rights (Application Deadline and Temporary Protection) (EU Exit) Regulations 2020 regs 4(5) and 12(1)(g). In determining this, the EEA Regs 2016 as modified by Citizens' Rights (Application Deadline and Temporary Protection) (EU Exit) Regulations 2020 regs 5–10 should be applied.

46 Citizens' Rights (Application Deadline and Temporary Protection) (EU Exit) Regulations 2020 regs 1, 2 and 3(5).

3) if leave is refused and the person does appeal, on the day on which that appeal is finally determined, withdrawn, abandoned, or lapses.[47]

7.24 An applicant will have been lawfully resident immediately before 11pm on 31 December 2021, or will be currently exercising a right of residence, where they were or are exercising one of the four rights of residence contained in the EEA Regs 2016. As referred to above at para 7.19, although these regulations have now been repealed, that repeal is subject to several different saving and transitional provisions, with the confusing result that a different version of the EEA Regs 2016 will apply depending on whether the decision-maker is looking at:

- the situation as of 31 December 2020 – in which case the EEA Regs 2016 as they were in effect immediately before 11pm on 31 December 2020 should be applied; or
- the applicant's current position – in which case the EEA Regs 2016 as modified by Citizens' Rights (Application Deadline and Temporary Protection) (EU Exit) Regulations 2020 regs 5–10 should be applied.

7.25 A detailed discussion of EU Treaty rights, including the consequences of Brexit, is contained in chapter 2. In summary, in order to fall within this second class an applicant must have been exercising one of the following four rights immediately before 11pm on 31 December 2020[48] and must be exercising one of them when they apply for homelessness assistance or an allocation:[49]

1) The initial right of residence for three months.[50]
2) The extended right of residence for a person who is a jobseeker, a worker, self-employed, self-sufficient or a student.[51]

47 Citizens' Rights (Application Deadline and Temporary Protection) (EU Exit) Regulations 2020 reg 4(6)(b).

48 Citizens' Rights (Application Deadline and Temporary Protection) (EU Exit) Regulations 2020 reg 4(2)(b).

49 Citizens' Rights (Application Deadline and Temporary Protection) (EU Exit) Regulations 2020 regs 4(5) and 12(1)(g).

50 EEA Regs 2016 reg 13, as in force immediately prior to 11pm on 31 December 2020 and continuing in effect and modified by Citizens' Rights (Application Deadline and Temporary Protection) (EU Exit) Regulations 2020 reg 6. See paras 2.41–2.44.

51 EEA Regs 2016 reg 14 as in force immediately prior to 11pm on 31 December 2020 and continuing in effect and modified by Citizens' Rights (Application Deadline and Temporary Protection) (EU Exit) Regulations 2020 reg 6. The definition for 'jobseeker' is found in reg 6 of the EEA Regs 2016 and the definitions for 'worker', 'self-employed', 'self-sufficient', and 'student' are found in reg 4 of the EEA Regs 2016: Citizens' Rights (Application Deadline and Temporary Protection) (EU Exit) Regulations 2020 reg 5. See paras 2.45–2.71.

3) The permanent right of residence[52] which can be acquired by:
   a) an EEA national who has resided in the UK in accordance with the regulations or lawfully for a continuous period of five years;
   b) a non-EEA national who is a family member[53] of an EEA national and who has resided with that person in the UK in accordance with the regulations for a continuous period of five years;
   c) a worker or self-employed person who has ceased activity;
   d) a person who is the family member of a worker or self-employed person who has ceased activity, provided that they were a family member at the point that the activity ceased and, at that point, they had a right to reside on the basis of being that family member;
   e) a person who is the family member of a worker or self-employed person, where that person has died but had resided continuously in the UK for at least two years immediately prior to death, or that person died due to an accident at work or an occupational disease, and the family member resided with them immediately prior to the death;
   f) a person who has resided in the UK in accordance with the regulations or lawfully for a continuous period of five years and who at the end of that period was a family member retaining the right of residence.
4) The derivative rights of residence,[54] which are based on declarations by the Court of Justice of the European Union (CJEU). The derivative rights of residence are the rights of residence held by:
   a) a primary carer of an EEA national child where the child is self-sufficient and would have to leave the UK if the primary carer left;

52 EEA Regs 2016 reg 15 as in force immediately prior to 11pm on 31 December 2020 and continuing in effect and modified by Citizens' Rights (Application Deadline and Temporary Protection) (EU Exit) Regulations 2020 reg 6. See paras 2.72–2.82.

53 'Family member' is defined at EEA Regs 2016 reg 7 as in force immediately prior to 11pm on 31 December 2020 and continuing in effect and modified by Citizens' Rights (Application Deadline and Temporary Protection) (EU Exit) Regulations 2020 reg 5. See paras 2.114–2.137.

54 EEA Regs 2016 reg 16 as in force immediately prior to 11pm on 31 December 2020 and continuing in effect and modified by Citizens' Rights (Application Deadline and Temporary Protection) (EU Exit) Regulations 2020 reg 6. See paras 2.83–2.113.

b) a person whose parent is an EEA national, where they have both resided in the UK at the same time during which period the parent was a worker, and the person is in education in the UK;
c) a primary carer of b), where b) would be unable to continue their education in the UK if the primary carer left the UK;
d) a primary carer of a British citizen residing in the UK who would be unable to reside in the UK or another EEA state if the primary carer left the UK;
e) a child whose primary carer has a derivative right to reside under a), c), or d) which they would be prevented from exercising if the child left the UK.

7.26 **The third class**[55] of EEA nationals who are not subject to immigration control or are treated as not being subject to immigration control in the housing context comprises EEA nationals who are exercising their rights as 'frontier workers'. A 'frontier worker' is defined[56] as a person who:

1) was an EEA national immediately before 11pm on 31 December 2020 and has remained an EEA national since that date;
2) was not 'primarily resident' in the UK immediately before 11pm on 31 December 2020 and has not been primarily resident in the UK since that date;[57] and
3) was either a 'worker', a 'self-employed person', or a person with retained 'worker' or 'self-employed' status in the UK[58] immediately before 11pm on 31 December 2020 and has been a 'worker', a 'self-employed person', or a person with retained 'worker' or 'self-employed' status in the UK continuously since that date.[59]

55 Citizens' Rights (Frontier Workers) (EU Exit) Regulations 2020 SI No 1213 reg 5(1).
56 Citizens' Rights (Frontier Workers) (EU Exit) Regulations 2020 reg 3.
57 The circumstances in which a person is to be treated as not being primarily resident are set out at Citizens' Rights (Frontier Workers) (EU Exit) Regulations 2020 reg 3(3).
58 The circumstances in which a person who is no longer a worker in the UK or a self-employed person in the UK will continue to be treated as such are set out in Citizens' Rights (Frontier Workers) (EU Exit) Regulations 2020 reg 4.
59 A person may change between these statuses without losing 'frontier worker' rights: Citizens' Rights (Frontier Workers) (EU Exit) Regulations 2020 reg 3(2). The EEA Regs 2016 do not apply directly to determining whether a person is a frontier worker, but the definitions of 'worker', 'self-employed person', and 'retained' worker or self-employed status contained in those regulations will assist in determining whether or not the criteria for frontier worker status have been met.

7.27 If an EEA national falls within one of these three classes, they will not be subject to immigration control and will be eligible unless they are not habitually resident (and are not exempt from the habitual residence test)[60] or they fall within a class of persons who are prescribed as ineligible.[61] If an EEA national does not fall within one of these three classes, they will be subject to immigration control and will be ineligible unless they fall within one of the classes prescribed as eligible.[62]

Subject to immigration control but still eligible

7.28 There are certain classes of people who are prescribed as eligible for homelessness assistance or an allocation of social housing even though they are subject to immigration control. In respect of England, there are 14 classes. These are found in the Allocation of Housing and Homelessness (Eligibility) (England) Regulations ('Eligibility (England) Regs') 2006.[63] Regulation 3 of those Regulations sets out the classes in respect of allocations and reg 5 does so in respect of homelessness.[64] In respect of Wales, there are 13 classes. These are contained in the Allocation of Housing and Homelessness (Eligibility) (Wales) Regulations ('Eligibility (Wales) Regs') 2014.[65] Again, reg 3 relates to allocations and reg 5 deals with homelessness.[66]

7.29 The classes are denoted by letters of the alphabet. For the first four classes (discussed at paras 7.30–7.36 below), each class has the same letter for both England and Wales and for both homelessness and allocations. Unfortunately, however, the effect of successive amendments to the two sets of regulations is that matters become more complicated after Class D, with the same class being referred to by a different letter of the alphabet depending on whether it applies to homelessness or allocations, or England or Wales, and sometimes both.

60 See paras 7.65–7.70.

61 See paras 7.71–7.74.

62 See paras 7.30–7.63.

63 SI No 1294.

64 Guidance is also available in the statutory codes: *Homelessness code of guidance*, para 7.14; and *Allocation of accommodation: guidance for local housing authorities in England*, para 3.14.

65 SI No 2603 (W 257).

66 Guidance is available in the *Code of guidance to local authorities on the allocation of accommodation and homelessness*, Welsh Government, March 2016, para 2.14 and *Addendum to guidance affecting certain persons subject to immigration control*, paras 1–8 and 19–32.

Classes that apply to both England and Wales

Class A

7.30 The first class which applies to both England and Wales is Class A.[67] This is comprised of people who are recorded by the secretary of state as refugees and who have leave to enter or remain in the UK. As refugees are entitled to family reunion under the Immigration Rules,[68] their family members will not be subject to conditions of no recourse to public funds (NRPF).

Class B

7.31 Class B[69] consists of people who have exceptional leave to remain in the UK which is granted without a condition of NRPF. 'Exceptional leave to remain' historically referred to the leave granted to asylum-seekers whose claim for full refugee status had failed but who had been allowed to remain in the UK due to compelling humanitarian or compassionate factors. However, exceptional leave to remain was replaced in April 2003 by humanitarian protection (which is granted under the Immigration Rules and which is covered by Class D below) and discretionary leave to remain (granted outside the Immigration Rules). There have been a number of developments since 2003 and discretionary leave to remain[70] is now only one of a number of species of leave which may be granted outside the rules. Other examples include leave outside the rules on the basis of compelling compassionate circumstances[71] as well as leave for survivors of the Grenfell Tower fire.[72] In summary, anyone who has been granted leave to enter or remain outside the Immigration Rules has been treated

67 Eligibility (England) Regs 2006 regs 3(a) (allocations) and 5(1)(a) (homelessness); Eligibility (Wales) Regs 2014 regs 3(a) (allocations) and 5(1)(a) (homelessness).

68 Immigration Rules HC 395 paras 352A–352F.

69 Eligibility (England) Regs 2006 regs 3(b) (allocations) and 5(1)(b) (homelessness); Eligibility (Wales) Regs 2014 regs 3(b) (allocations) and 5(1)(b) (homelessness).

70 Guidance on discretionary leave to remain is available at: https://assets.publishing.service.gov.uk/government/uploads/system/uploads/attachment_data/file/658372/discretionary-leave-v7.0ext.pdf.

71 Guidance on this form of leave is available at https://assets.publishing.service.gov.uk/government/uploads/system/uploads/attachment_data/file/684049/lotr-compelling-compassionate-grounds-v1.0ext.pdf.

72 See the guidance at: https://assets.publishing.service.gov.uk/government/uploads/system/uploads/attachment_data/file/697989/grenfell-tower-immigration-cases-v6.0.pdf.

'exceptionally' and may therefore be said to have been granted 'exceptional leave to remain'.[73]

7.32 A further example of those who would qualify under Class B are persons who have been granted an initial period of leave to remain under the Destitution Domestic Violence (DDV) Concession.[74] Leave may be granted under the DDV Concession to a person who is destitute and who entered the UK as the spouse of a British citizen or a person who is settled in the UK, where that relationship has broken down due to domestic violence. Under current Home Office policy, the successful applicant is given three months' limited leave to remain with recourse to public funds and services whilst their application for indefinite leave to remain as a settled person in their own right is determined.

7.33 There will be other potential classes of persons who may fall within Class B but the immigration rules and policies are complex and oft-changing so consideration of whether any particular person is eligible for housing assistance by virtue of falling within Class B may require specialist immigration advice.

Class C

7.34 Class C[75] comprises people who are habitually resident[76] in the Common Travel Area (the UK, Channel Islands, Isle of Man, and Republic of Ireland) and whose leave to remain is not subject to any limitation or condition. This does not include people who have been resident in the UK for less than five years[77] and whose leave was given upon a written undertaking from a sponsor(s) that they would be responsible for the applicant's maintenance and accommodation, unless the sponsor has died (or, if more than one, all sponsors have died).

73 This was certainly the position of the government in power in 2003, as set out in a letter dated 25 March 2003 from the Homelessness Directorate (Office of the Deputy Prime Minister) to Chief Executives and Housing Directors of English local housing authorities.

74 For a discussion of the DDV Concession, see chapter 1.

75 Eligibility (England) Regs 2006 regs 3(c) (allocations) and 5(1)(c) (homelessness); Eligibility (Wales) Regs 2014 regs 3(c) (allocations) and 5(1)(c) (homelessness).

76 See paras 7.65–7.70 for the habitual residence test.

77 Beginning with the date of entry or the date on which the sponsor's undertaking was given, which is the later.

7.35 Settled status is a form of unlimited leave to remain.[78] EEA nationals who are habitually resident in the Common Travel Area and who have settled status will be eligible by virtue of this class.

Class D

7.36 Class D[79] consists of people who have humanitarian protection granted under the Immigration Rules.

Class F/G

7.37 The next class is referred to (for both England and Wales) as Class F in respect of allocations and Class G in respect of homelessness.[80] It comprises people who have limited leave to enter or remain in the UK on European Convention on Human Rights (ECHR) Article 8 grounds which was granted under Immigration Rules para 276BE(1), para 276DG or Appendix FM. People who are subject to an NRPF condition are excluded. People who were granted leave on ECHR Article 8 grounds prior to the introduction of Immigration Rules para 276BE(1), para 276DG or Appendix FM would be eligible under Class B.[81]

Class G/H

7.38 Class G for allocations and Class H for homelessness[82] consists of people who:

- are habitually resident in the Common Travel Area;[83]
- have been transferred to the UK under Immigration Act (IA) 2016 s67 (commonly known as the 'Dubs amendment'); and
- have been granted limited leave to remain under Immigration Rules para 352ZH.

7.39 The 'Dubs amendment', named after the peer who introduced it, aimed to assist children affected by the refugee crisis. It requires the

78 See paras 2.153–2.165 for a discussion of settled status.

79 Eligibility (England) Regs 2006 regs 3(d) (allocations) and 5(1)(d) (homelessness); Eligibility (Wales) Regs 2014 regs 3(d) (allocations) and 5(1)(d) (homelessness).

80 Eligibility (England) Regs 2006 regs 3(f) (allocations) and 5(1)(g) (homelessness); Eligibility (Wales) Regs 2014 regs 3(f) (allocations) and 5(1)(g) (homelessness).

81 This was confirmed in a letter from the Department of Communities and Local Government to Chief Executives and Chief Housing Officers of Local Authorities in England dated October 2016.

82 Eligibility (England) Regs 2006 regs 3(g) (allocations) and 5(1)(h) (homelessness); Eligibility (Wales) Regs 2014 regs 3(g) (allocations) and 5(1)(h) (homelessness).

83 See paras 7.65–7.70 for habitual residence and para 7.34 for the Common Travel Area.

secretary of state to 'make arrangements to relocate to the UK and support a specified number of unaccompanied refugee children from other countries in Europe'.

7.40 Immigration Rules para 352ZH provides for leave to remain to be granted to children transferred under this provision. This class enables such people to access housing allocations and homelessness assistance.

Class H/I

7.41 Class H for allocations and Class I for homelessness[84] consists of people who are habitually resident in the Common Travel Area[85] and who have 'Calais leave to remain' under Immigration Rules para 352J. 'Calais leave' was introduced following the clearing of the migrant camp at Calais in 2016, during which 769 unaccompanied asylum-seeking children were transferred to the UK from France. Two hundred and twenty of these children were relocated under the Dubs amendment (see paras 7.38–7.39) and the remaining 549 were brought to the UK to be reunited with family members. A large number of those reunited with family members – 115 children – did not qualify for leave under the existing immigration provisions and therefore a new form of leave – 'Calais leave' – was introduced by Immigration Rules para 352J to ensure that they had a legal basis to remain in the UK. The inclusion of this class of persons enables them to access housing allocations and homelessness assistance.

Class J/K and I/J

7.42 The next class[86] – in England, Class J for allocations and Class K for homelessness; and in Wales, Class I for allocations and Class J for homelessness – comprises persons who are habitually resident in the Common Travel Area[87] and who have limited to leave to remain as a stateless person under Immigration Rules para 405. Stateless persons are those who are not considered a national by any other state. Article 21 of the 1954 UN Convention Relating to the Status of Stateless

84 Eligibility (England) Regs 2006 regs 3(h) (allocations) and 5(1)(i) (homelessness); Eligibility (Wales) Regs 2014 reg 3(h) (allocations) and 5(1)(i) (homelessness).

85 See paras 7.65–7.70 for habitual residence and para 7.34 for the Common Travel Area.

86 Eligibility (England) Regs 2006 regs 3(j) (allocations) and 5(1)(k) (homelessness); Eligibility (Wales) Regs 2014 regs 3(i) (allocations) and 5(1)(j) (homelessness).

87 See paras 7.65–7.70 for habitual residence and para 7.34 for the Common Travel Area.

Persons, which has been ratified by the UK, requires that such persons are accorded treatment in respect of housing which is 'as favourable as possible and, in any event, not less favourable than that accorded to aliens generally in the same circumstances'. This class gives effect to that obligation.

Class K/L and J/K

7.43 The next class[88] – in England, Class K for allocations and Class L for homelessness; and in Wales, Class J for allocations and Class K for homelessness – consists of people who have limited leave to enter or remain in the UK by virtue of Immigration Rules Appendix Hong Kong British National (Overseas). In order to qualify for this class, that leave must not be subject to a condition requiring them to maintain and accommodate themselves and their dependants with NRPF and the person must be habitually resident in the Common Travel Area.[89]

7.44 This class arises from the introduction of a new form of leave for people from Hong Kong with British National (Overseas) status following what the government described as 'the imposition by the Chinese government of a national security law on Hong Kong that restricts the rights and freedoms of the people of Hong Kong, in breach of the Sino-British Joint Declaration'.[90] The class is intended to ensure that beneficiaries of this form of leave can access homelessness assistance and allocations of social housing.

Class L/M and K/L

7.45 The next class[91] – in England, Class L for allocations and Class M for homelessness; and in Wales, Class K for allocations and Class L for homelessness – came into force on 16 September 2021 in England[92] and 15 October 2021 in Wales.[93] It consists of two categories.

88 Eligibility (England) Regs 2006 regs 3(k) (allocations) and 5(1)(l) (homelessness); Eligibility (Wales) Regs 2014 regs 3(j) (allocations) and 5(1)(k) (homelessness).

89 See paras 7.65–7.70 for habitual residence and para 7.34 for the Common Travel Area.

90 Letter from Lucy Rodger and Frances Walker, MHCLG, to all Local Authorities, 8 June 2021.

91 Eligibility (England) Regs 2006 regs 3(l) (allocations) and 5(1)(m) (homelessness); Eligibility (Wales) Regs 2014 regs 3(k) (allocations) and 5(1)(l) (homelessness).

92 Allocation of Housing and Homelessness (Eligibility) (England) and Persons subject to Immigration Control (Housing Authority Accommodation and Homelessness) (Amendment) Regulations 2021 SI No 1045 regs 1 and 2.

93 Allocation of Housing and Homelessness (Eligibility) (Wales) (Amendment) (No 2) Regulations 2021 SI No 1147 (W 282) regs 1, 3 and 5.

7.46 **The first category** comprises people who have leave to enter or remain in the UK which was granted in accordance with the Immigration Rules by virtue of the *Afghan relocations and assistance policy* or the previous scheme for locally employed staff in Afghanistan (the *Afghanistan locally employed staff ex-gratia scheme*). The *Afghan relocations and assistance policy* was launched in April 2021. It provides relocation or other assistance to 'those who served alongside our armed forces in Afghanistan and provided important support to Her Majesty's Government defence and security mission there'.[94] The previous scheme for locally employed staff in Afghanistan was established on 4 June 2013 for the purpose of making 'ex gratia offers to eligible locally employed staff (LES) who have been or will be made redundant as a direct consequence of the UK's military drawdown from Afghanistan'.[95] It was subsequently expanded to include those who were made redundant or who resigned on or after 1 May 2006 with 12 months' or more continuous service 'outside the wire on the frontline mostly in Helmand'.[96] The ex-gratia scheme remained open until 30 November 2022, after which the locally employed staff have to apply through the *Afghanistan relocations and assistance policy*.[97]

7.47 **The second category** consists of people who have leave to enter or remain in the UK which does not fall within the first category but who left Afghanistan in connection with the collapse of the Afghan government on 15 August 2021. A person will be excluded from this class if they are subject to an NRPF condition. A person will also be excluded if they have been resident in the UK for less than five years[98] and their leave was given upon a written undertaking from a sponsor(s) that they would be responsible for the applicant's maintenance and accommodation, unless the sponsor has died (or, if more than one, all sponsors have died). This category encompasses

94 *Afghanistan resettlement and immigration policy statement*, Home Office, 13 September 2021, para 15. More details on eligibility for this scheme are contained in the guidance *Afghan relocations and assistance policy: further information on eligibility criteria, offer details and how to apply*, Ministry of Defence, January 2021, subsequently updated.

95 *Afghanistan locally employed staff ex-gratia scheme: further information on eligibility criteria and offer details*, Foreign, Commonwealth & Development Office and Ministry of Defence, October 2013, subsequently updated.

96 *Afghanistan locally employed staff ex-gratia scheme: further information on eligibility criteria and offer details.*

97 *Afghanistan locally employed staff ex-gratia scheme: further information on eligibility criteria and offer details.*

98 Beginning with the date of entry or the date on which the sponsor's undertaking was given, which is the later.

those who fled Afghanistan after the Taliban takeover in 2021 and who have leave to remain but who do not come within one of the two schemes discussed in the previous paragraph. It will include those granted leave pursuant to the Afghan Citizens Resettlement Scheme (provided that their leave is not subject to an NRPF condition or a sponsorship undertaking). This was opened on 6 January 2022 and prioritises 'those who have assisted the UK efforts in Afghanistan and stood up for values such as democracy, women's rights, freedom of speech, and rule of law' as well as 'vulnerable people, including women and girls at risk, and member of minority groups at risk (including ethnic and religious minorities and LGBT+)'.[99]

Class O/P and M/N

7.48 The final class[100] which applies to both England and Wales – in England, Class O for allocations and P for homelessness; and in Wales, Class M for allocations and Class N for homelessness – came into force on 30 January 2023.[101] This class consists of people who have limited leave[102] to remain granted in accordance with Immigration Rules Appendix Temporary Permission to Stay for Victims of Human Trafficking or Slavery.[103] A person is eligible for leave under this Appendix if they are in the UK and have received a positive conclusive grounds decision that they are a victim of trafficking or slavery[104] and the grant of permission to stay is necessary for the purpose of:

1) assisting the person in their recovery from any physical or psychological harm arising from the relevant exploitation; or

99 *Afghan citizens resettlement scheme*, Home Office, 18 August 2021.

100 Eligibility (England) Regs 2006 regs 3(o) (allocations) and 5(1)(p) (homelessness); Eligibility (Wales) Regs 2014 regs 3(m) (allocations) and 5(1)(n) (homelessness).

101 Allocation of Housing and Homelessness (Eligibility) (England) and Persons Subject to Immigration Control (Housing Authority Accommodation and Homelessness) (Amendment) (No 4) Regulations 2022 SI No 1371 reg 2(2) and (3) (England) and Allocation of Housing and Homelessness (Eligibility) (Wales) (Amendment) Regulations 2023 SI No 76 (W 14) regs 3(c) and 4(c) (Wales).

102 Eligibility (Wales) Regs 2014 regs 3(m) (allocations) and 5(1)(n) (homelessness) refer to 'temporary leave' rather than 'limited leave'. Appendix Temporary Permission to Stay for Victims of Human Trafficking or Slavery itself refers to 'temporary permission to stay'. Nothing appears to turn on these slight differences in terminology.

103 Guidance on this type of leave has been published in *Temporary permission to stay considerations for victims of human trafficking or slavery*, Home Office, February 2023.

104 As defined by Nationality and Borders Act 2022 s69(1): see paras 11.131–11.145 and 11.177–11.178.

2) enabling the person to seek compensation in respect of the relevant exploitation; or
3) enabling the person to co-operate with a public authority in connection with an investigation or criminal proceedings in respect of the relevant exploitation.

7.49 Permission to stay will not be necessary for the purpose of assisting the person in their recovery from any physical or psychological harm if the applicant's need for assistance is capable of being met in their own country or a country to which they may be removed. Permission to stay will not be necessary for the purpose of enabling the person to seek compensation if the applicant is capable of seeking compensation from outside the UK and it would be reasonable for them to do so in the circumstances. Permission will be granted for a period not exceeding 30 months (or 12 months where it is being granted on the basis that it is necessary for the purpose of enabling the person to seek compensation).

7.50 Prior to the introduction of Immigration Rules Appendix Temporary Permission to Stay for Victims of Human Trafficking or Slavery, leave for victims of trafficking or modern slavery was granted as a form of discretionary leave outside the Immigration Rules. Recipients of such leave were eligible for an allocation of housing or homelessness assistance under Class B.[105] This regime has now been replaced by Appendix Temporary Permission to Stay for Victims of Human Trafficking or Slavery, but the creation of this new class ensures victims of trafficking and slavery can still access social housing and homelessness assistance.

Classes that apply only to England

7.51 There are two further classes which apply only to England.

Class I/J

7.52 Class I for allocations and Class J for homelessness[106] applies to a person who:

1) has been given pre-settled status (namely limited leave to enter or remain by virtue of Immigration Rules Appendix EU);
2) is a family member of a 'relevant person of Northern Ireland' in accordance with the Immigration Rules; and

105 See paras 7.31–7.33.

106 Eligibility (England) Regs 2006 regs 3(i) (allocations) and 5(1)(j) (homelessness).

3) would have been considered eligible under the Eligibility (England) Regs 2006 reg 4(2)(d) (in respect of an allocation) or reg 6(2)(d) (in respect of homelessness) if the relevant person of Northern Ireland were a person specified in reg 4(2)(a)–(c) (in respect of an allocation) or reg 6(2)(a)–(c) (in respect of homelessness).

7.53 The first criterion applicable to this class, pre-settled status, is discussed at paras 2.166–2.168.

7.54 As to the second criterion, a 'relevant person of Northern Ireland' is defined as a person who:

1) is a British or Irish citizen (or both);
2) was born in Northern Ireland; and
3) at the time of their birth had at least one parent who was a British or Irish citizen (or both) or was otherwise entitled to reside in Northern Ireland without restriction.[107]

7.55 The third criterion requires more discussion. Regulations 4(1)(a) and 6(1)(a) of the Eligibility (England) Regs 2006 provide that a person who is not subject to immigration control is nevertheless to be treated as ineligible if they are not habitually resident in the Common Travel Area.[108] Regulations 4(2)(d) and 6(2)(d) of the Eligibility (England) Regs 2006 provide an exception to this test for family members of workers and self-employed persons, who are not to be deemed ineligible even if they are not habitually resident.[109] The difficulty with this criterion is that Eligibility (England) Regs 2006 regs 4 and 6 only apply to persons who are not subject to immigration control, but Class I/J itself applies only to persons who *are* subject to immigration control. In the light of this it is unclear what the remit of class will be. It appears that the aim of the provision may have been to ensure that family members of relevant persons of Northern Ireland are able to access homelessness assistance and allocations of social housing on the same basis as the family member of an Irish national in order to protect the right, enshrined in the Good Friday Agreement, for persons of British and Irish nationality to 'identify themselves

107 Eligibility (England) Regs 2006 reg 2(1).

108 See paras 7.65–7.70 for habitual residence and para 7.34 for the Common Travel Area.

109 The exception also applies to the family member of a person who is to be treated as a worker pursuant to the Accession of Croatia (Immigration and Worker Authorisation) Regulations 2013 SI No 1460, but as the accession period following Croatia's joining of the EU ended on 30 June 2018, this exception is unlikely to be of any practical application.

and be accepted as Irish or British, or both, as they may so choose'.[110] It is, however, unclear whether that has been achieved by the drafting.

Class M/N

7.56 Class M for allocations and Class N for homelessness[111] came into force on 22 March 2022.[112] This class applies to a person who is in the UK and who:

1) was residing in Ukraine immediately before 1 January 2022;
2) left Ukraine in connection with the Russian invasion on 24 February 2022;
3) has been granted leave in accordance with immigration rules made under IA1971 s3(2); and
4) is not subject to an NRPF condition.

7.57 Following the Russian invasion of Ukraine on 24 February 2022, the UK government established two schemes to support Ukrainians seeking to flee to the UK. The Ukraine Family Scheme enables Ukrainians who left Ukraine in connection with the invasion and who have family members settled in the UK to join them. The Homes for Ukraine Scheme allows Ukrainians, with or without family ties to the UK, to come to the UK under the sponsorship of an individual, charity, community group or business.[113] Leave granted under the Ukraine Family Scheme or the Homes for Ukraine Scheme includes access to public funds.[114] This class gives effect to these schemes and enables those who have fled the war in Ukraine to apply for an allocation of social housing or homelessness assistance in the UK.

Class N/O

7.58 Class N for allocations and Class O for homelessness[115] make eligible for assistance a person in the UK who has limited leave to remain granted in accordance with Appendix Ukraine Scheme of the

110 Belfast Agreement, Constitutional Issues, Article 1(vi).

111 Eligibility (England) Regs 2006 regs 3(m) (allocations) and 5(1)(n) (homelessness).

112 Allocation of Housing and Homelessness (Eligibility) (England) and Persons subject to Immigration Control (Housing Authority Accommodation and Homelessness) (Amendment) Regulations 2022 SI No 339 regs 1(1) and 2.

113 Allocation of Housing and Homelessness (Eligibility) (England) and Persons subject to Immigration Control (Housing Authority Accommodation and Homelessness) (Amendment) Regulations 2022 Explanatory Memorandum para 7.1.

114 Immigration Rules Appendix Ukraine Scheme paras UKR 10.2 and UKR 20.2.

115 Eligibility (England) Regs 2006 regs 3(n) (allocations) and 5(1)(o) (homelessness).

Immigration Rules pursuant to an application made by that person from within the UK. A person who is subject to an NRPF condition is excluded.

7.59 The Appendix Ukraine Scheme of the Immigration Rules creates three routes to leave for people affected by the war in Ukraine. The first two – the Ukraine Family Scheme and the Homes for Ukraine Sponsorship Scheme – are discussed above at para 7.57. These routes assist persons who were living in Ukraine immediately before the invasion. Such persons will already be eligible for homelessness assistance or an allocation of social housing by virtue of Class M/N.[116]

7.60 The third route – the Ukraine Extension Scheme – is aimed at Ukrainians who had been living in the UK but who cannot return because of the war. These persons would not have fallen within Class M/N because they were not residing in Ukraine immediately before 1 January 2022 and did not leave Ukraine in connection with the Russian invasion. Class N/O was therefore created in order to encompass this group.[117] The creation of Class N/O would, however, appear to make Class M/N[118] redundant, as it is likely that anyone who fell within Class M/N will now be eligible by virtue of Class N/O. It is probably for this reason that the Eligibility (Wales) Regs 2014, which contain a very similar category to Class N/O, do not contain an equivalent to Class M/N.[119]

Classes that apply only to Wales

7.61 There are two classes which apply only to Wales.

Class E/F

7.62 The first[120] class is Class E for allocations and Class F for homelessness. This class consists of people who have been granted limited leave to enter the UK as a relevant Afghan citizen under Immigration Rules para 276BA1 and who are habitually resident in the Common Travel Area.[121] The leave granted under para 276BA1 originally

116 See paras 7.56–7.57.

117 Allocation of Housing and Homelessness (Eligibility) (England) and Persons subject to Immigration Control (Housing Authority Accommodation and Homelessness) (Amendment) (No 2) Regulations 2022 SI No 601 Explanatory Memorandum paras 7.4 and 7.6.

118 See paras 7.56–7.57.

119 See paras 7.56–7.57.

120 Eligibility (Wales) Regs 2014 regs 3(e) (allocations) and 5(1)(f) (homelessness).

121 See paras 7.65–7.70 for habitual residence and para 7.34 for the Common Travel Area.

applied only to local staff in Afghanistan who 'worked in particularly dangerous and challenging roles in Helmand'.[122] It has since been amended and now covers those who fall within the *Afghan relocations and assistance policy* and the *Afghanistan locally employed staff ex-gratia scheme.*[123] Such persons will now be eligible for an allocation of social housing and homelessness assistance by virtue of the class discussed at paras 7.45–7.47 above (in England, Class L for allocations and Class M for homelessness; and in Wales, Class K for allocations and Class L for homelessness). This means that this class is now likely to be redundant, and it has in fact been repealed in England with effect from 16 September 2021.[124]

Class L/M

7.63 The second class[125] which applies only to Wales is Class L for allocations and Class M for homelessness. This class is very similar to Class N/O in respect of England.[126] It applies to a person who has been granted leave to enter or remain in the UK by virtue of the Appendix Ukraine Scheme of the Immigration Rules. As discussed above at paras 7.57–7.60. Appendix Ukraine Scheme creates three pathways to leave for those displaced by the Russian invasion of Ukraine: the Ukraine Family Scheme, the Homes for Ukraine Sponsorship Scheme and the Ukraine Extension Scheme. This class makes persons granted leave under any of those routes eligible for an allocation of social housing or homelessness assistance. There are two key differences between this class and its equivalent in the Eligibility (England) Regs 2006.[127] The first is that persons who are subject to an NRPF condition are excluded from assistance under this class in England,[128] but not in Wales. The second is that in order to be eligible under this class in England, a person must have applied for limited leave to remain under Immigration Rules Appendix Ukraine Scheme from within the UK.[129] No such requirement applies in Wales.

122 Secretary of State for Defence, Written Ministerial Statement, 4 June 2013.

123 See para 7.46.

124 Allocation of Housing and Homelessness (Eligibility) (England) and Persons subject to Immigration Control (Housing Authority Accommodation and Homelessness) (Amendment) Regulations 2021 reg 2(2)(a).

125 Eligibility (Wales) Regs 2014 regs 3(l) and 5(1)(m).

126 See paras 7.58–7.60.

127 Class N/O, discussed above at paras 7.58–7.60.

128 Eligibility (England) Regs 2006 regs 3(n) (allocations) and 5(1)(o) (homelessness).

129 Eligibility (England) Regs 2006 regs 3(n) (allocations) and 5(1)(o) (homelessness).

'Other persons from abroad'

7.64 Even if a person is not subject to immigration control, they may still be ineligible for an allocation of social housing or homelessness assistance if they are to be treated as a person from abroad who is ineligible.[130] An applicant may be a 'person from abroad' even if they are born and brought up in – and indeed have never left – the UK.[131] This category, of persons who are not subject to immigration control but who are ineligible, is comprised of two classes:

1) those who are not habitually resident in the Common Travel Area; and
2) those who are members of a prescribed excluded class.

These two categories are considered in turn.

Habitual residence

7.65 The first class is made up of people who are not habitually resident in the Common Travel Area.[132] They will be ineligible for assistance unless they are exempt from the habitual residence test. If they are exempt from the habitual residence test, then they will be eligible regardless of whether they are habitually resident, unless they are ineligible for another reason.[133]

7.66 Habitual residence is not determined by a person's immigration status. It is made up of:

1) a settled purpose of establishing residence; and
2) an appreciable period of such residence.[134]

7.67 Whether or not a person is habitually resident is a question of fact. If a person has been continuously resident in the Common Travel Area for two years prior to their application, statutory guidance advises that they should generally be considered habitually resident without

130 For allocations: HA 1996 ss160ZA(4) (England) and 160A(5) (Wales). For homelessness: HA 1996 s185(3) (England) and H(W)A 2014 Sch 2 para 1(4) (Wales).

131 See *Ehiabor v Kensington and Chelsea RLBC* [2008] EWCA Civ 1074, [2008] 5 WLUK 191; and *Barnet LBC v Ismail* [2006] EWCA Civ 383, [2006] 1 WLR 2771.

132 See para 7.34 for Common Travel Area.

133 Eligibility (England) Regs 2006 regs 4(1)(a) and (2) (allocations) and 6(1)(a) and (2) (homelessness); Eligibility (Wales) Regs 2014 regs 4(1)(a) and (2) (allocations) and 6(1)(a) and (2) (homelessness).

134 *R (Paul-Coker) v Southwark LBC* [2006] EWHC 497 (Admin) at para 20.

further inquiry.[135] This does not mean that a person cannot be habitually resident if they have been resident for a shorter period of time. The 'two-year' benchmark simply creates a presumption. There is, in law, no minimum length of residence that must be met.[136] The decision-maker should take into account all the circumstances, including the applicant's ties with the UK; their nationality; whether they are seeking to bring family members to the UK; and whether they have brought property to the UK. A detailed discussion of the 'habitual residence' test which is applicable equally in the housing assistance and welfare benefits context is found at paras 4.48–4.63.

7.68 The following people are exempt from the habitual residence test and will be eligible even if not habitually resident (unless excluded for a different reason):[137]

1) an EEA national who is a worker: see paras 2.49–2.51;[138]
2) an EEA national who is self-employed: see paras 2.61–2.65;[139]

135 *Allocation of Accommodation: guidance for local housing authorities in England*, para 3.21 and *Homelessness code of guidance*, para 7.22 (England); *Code of guidance to local authorities on the allocation of accommodation and homelessness*, para 2.22 (Wales).

136 *R (Paul-Coker) v Southwark LBC* [2006] EWHC 497 (Admin) at para 21.

137 Eligibility (England) Regs 2006 regs 4(2) (allocations) and 6(2) (homelessness); Eligibility (Wales) Regs 2014 regs 4(2) (allocations) and 6(2) (homelessness). Guidance on the position of EEA nationals is available in the statutory codes: *Homelessness code of guidance*, paras 7.18–7.20; *Allocation of accommodation: guidance for local housing authorities in England*, paras 3.17–3.19; and *Addendum to guidance affecting certain persons subject to immigration control*, paras 15–18.

138 Pursuant to Eligibility (England) Regs 2006 reg 2(2)(a) and Eligibility (Wales) Regs 2014 reg 2(2)(a), 'worker' has the same meaning as for the purposes of the definition of a 'qualified person' in EEA Regs 2016 reg 6. However, this regulation must be applied as continued in effect and modified by Immigration and Social Security Co-ordination (EU Withdrawal) Act 2020 (Consequential, Saving, Transitional and Transitory Provisions) (EU Exit) Regulations 2020 reg 71 (England) and reg 76 (Wales) and Sch 4 (for members of the post-transition period group) and the Citizens' Rights (Application Deadline and Temporary Protection) (EU Exit) Regulations 2020 regs 4 and 11 (for EEA nationals with an in-time application for leave).

139 Pursuant to Eligibility (England) Regs 2006 reg 2(2)(a) and Eligibility (Wales) Regs 2014 reg 2(2)(a), 'self-employed person' has the same meaning as for the purposes of the definition of a 'qualified person' in EEA Regs 2016 reg 6. However, this regulation must be applied as continued in effect and modified by the Immigration and Social Security Co-ordination (EU Withdrawal) Act 2020 (Consequential, Saving, Transitional and Transitory Provisions) (EU Exit) Regulations 2020 regs 71 (England) and 76 (Wales) and Sch 4 (for members of the post-transition period group) and the Citizens' Rights (Application Deadline and Temporary Protection) (EU Exit) Regulations 2020 regs 4 and 11 (for EEA nationals with an in-time application for leave).

3) until 30 June 2018, a person who is to be treated as a worker pursuant to the right of residence given to a Croatian national with worker authorisation;[140]
4) a family member of 1), 2) or 3): see paras 2.114–2.116.[141] This does not include 'extended' family members: see paras 2.117–2.118;[142]
5) a person with a permanent right to reside in the UK because:
   a) they are an EEA national who is a worker or self-employed person who has ceased activity: see paras 2.78–2.82;
   b) they are the family member of 5)a), provided that they were a family member at the point that the activity ceased and, at that point, they had a right to reside on the basis of being that family member: see para 2.77; or
   c) they are the family member of an EEA national worker or self-employed person, where that person has died but had resided continuously in the UK for at least two years immediately prior to death or had died due to an accident at work or an occupational disease, and the family member resided with them immediately prior to the death: see para 2.77;[143]

140 The right of residence is contained in Accession of Croatia (Immigration and Worker Authorisation) Regulations 2013 reg 5. This category is unlikely to be of any practical relevance.

141 Pursuant to Eligibility (England) Regs 2006 reg 2(2)(b) and Eligibility (Wales) Regs 2014 reg 2(2)(b), 'family member' is to be construed in accordance with EEA Regs 2016 reg 7. However, this regulation must be applied as continued in effect and modified by Immigration and Social Security Co-ordination (EU Withdrawal) Act 2020 (Consequential, Saving, Transitional and Transitory Provisions) (EU Exit) Regulations 2020 reg 71 (England) and reg 76 (Wales) and Sch 4 (for members of the post-transition period group) and Citizens' Rights (Application Deadline and Temporary Protection) (EU Exit) Regulations 2020 regs 4 and 11 (for EEA nationals with an in-time application for leave).

142 Eligibility (England) Regs 2006 reg 2(3) and Eligibility (Wales) Reg 2014 reg 2(3).

143 These rights are contained in EEA Regs 2016 reg 15(1)(c), (d), and (e) as continued in effect and modified by Immigration and Social Security Co-ordination (EU Withdrawal) Act 2020 (Consequential, Saving, Transitional and Transitory Provisions) (EU Exit) Regulations 2020 reg 71 (England) and reg 76 (Wales) and Sch 4 (for members of the post-transition period group) and Citizens' Rights (Application Deadline and Temporary Protection) (EU Exit) Regulations 2020 regs 4 and 11 (for EEA nationals with an in-time application for leave). 'Worker', 'self-employed person' and 'family member' are to be given the same meaning as in, or construed in accordance with, EEA Regs 2016 regs 6 and 7. These regulations must be applied as continued in effect and modified by Immigration and Social Security Co-ordination (EU Withdrawal) Act 2020 (Consequential, Saving, Transitional and Transitory Provisions) (EU Exit) Regulations 2020 reg 71 (England) and reg 76 (Wales) and Sch 4 (for members of the post-transition period group) and Citizens' Rights (Application Deadline and Temporary Protection) (EU Exit) Regulations 2020 regs 4 and 11 (for EEA nationals with an in-time application for leave).

6) a person who has been deported to the UK;
7) a frontier worker;[144]
8) a person who has pre-settled status[145] and who is the family member (see paras 2.114–2.116) of a frontier worker.[146] This does not include 'extended' family members: see paras 2.117–2.118;[147]
9) a person who left Afghanistan in connection with the collapse of the Afghan government on 15 August 2021; and
10) a person who was residing in Ukraine immediately before 1 January 2022 and who left Ukraine in connection with the Russian invasion on 24 February 2022.

7.69 It will be noted that the majority of these exemptions apply to EEA nationals or their family members. These exceptions will only be relevant to those EEA nationals, and family members of EEA nationals, who are not subject to immigration control.[148] Following the UK's departure from the EU, many EEA nationals and their family members will be subject to immigration control and neither the habitual residence test nor the exceptions to it will apply to them: they will only be eligible if they fall within one of the classes of people who are eligible despite being subject to immigration control.[149] The three categories of EEA nationals (and their family members) who are not subject to immigration control, and to whom these exemptions may therefore be relevant, are discussed at paras 7.18–7.27.

144 'Frontier worker' is defined in Citizens' Rights (Frontier Workers) (EU Exit) Regulations 2020 reg 3: Eligibility (England) Regs 2006 reg 2(2)(ab) and Eligibility (Wales) Regs 2014 reg 2(2)(ab).

145 See paras 2.166–2.168 for a discussion of 'pre-settled status'.

146 Pursuant to Eligibility (England) Regs 2006 reg 2(2)(b) and Eligibility (Wales) Regs 2014 reg 2(2)(b), 'family member' is to be construed in accordance with EEA Regs 2016 reg 7. This regulation must be applied as continued in effect and modified by Immigration and Social Security Co-ordination (EU Withdrawal) Act 2020 (Consequential, Saving, Transitional and Transitory Provisions) (EU Exit) Regulations 2020 reg 71 (England) and reg 76 (Wales) and Sch 4 (for members of the post-transition period group) and Citizens' Rights (Application Deadline and Temporary Protection) (EU Exit) Regulations 2020 regs 4 and 11 (for EEA nationals with an in-time application for leave). 'Frontier worker' is defined in Citizens' Rights (Frontier Workers) (EU Exit) Regulations 2020 reg 3: Eligibility (England) Regs 2006 reg 2(2)(ab) and Eligibility (Wales) Regs 2014 reg 2(2)(ab).

147 Eligibility (England) Regs 2006 reg 2(3) and Eligibility (Wales) Reg 2014 reg 2(3).

148 Eligibility (England) Regs 2006 regs 4 (allocations) and 6 (homelessness) and Eligibility (Wales) Regs 2014 regs 4 (allocations) and 6 (homelessness) only apply to persons who are not subject to immigration control.

149 See paras 7.30–7.63.

7.70 The last two categories were added in the wake of the Taliban takeover of Afghanistan in August 2021 and the Russian invasion of Ukraine in February 2022, respectively. Most people fleeing those events will be subject to immigration control. These categories will not assist them, but they should be eligible by virtue of amendments made to Eligibility (England) Regs 2006 regs 3 and 5 and Eligibility (Wales) Regs 2014 regs 3 and 5.[150] However, some people who have left Afghanistan or Ukraine in the wake of those events will not be subject to immigration control because, for example, they are British citizens. These new categories of persons exempt from the habitual residence test ensure that such people are not excluded from an allocation of social housing or homelessness assistance on the grounds that they are not habitually resident in the Common Travel Area. They will be eligible even if not habitually resident.

Member of an excluded class

7.71 The second class of persons who are not subject to immigration control but who are to be treated as ineligible for an allocation of social housing or homelessness assistance consists of EEA nationals whose only right to reside in either the UK or the rest of the Common Travel Area is one of certain specified rights ('an excluded right'). Again, this will only affect EEA nationals who are not subject to immigration control by virtue of falling within one of the three classes described above at paras 7.18–7.27.

7.72 An EEA national who is not subject to immigration control but whose only right to reside in the UK is derived from one of the following will not be eligible:[151]

1) their status as a jobseeker, or the family member of a jobseeker: see paras 2.52–2.60;[152]

150 See paras 7.56–7.60 and 7.63.

151 Eligibility (England) Regs 2006 regs 4(1)(b) (allocations) and 6(1)(b) (homelessness); Eligibility (Wales) Regs 2014 regs 4(1)(b) (allocations) and 6(1)(b) (homelessness).

152 Pursuant to Eligibility (England) Regs 2006 reg 2(2)(a) and (b) and Eligibility (Wales) Regs 2014 reg 2(2)(a) and (b), 'jobseeker' has the same meaning as in, and 'family member' is to be construed in accordance with, EEA Regs 2016 regs 6 and 7. However, these regulations must be applied as continued in effect and modified by Immigration and Social Security Co-ordination (EU Withdrawal) Act 2020 (Consequential, Saving, Transitional and Transitory Provisions) (EU Exit) Regulations 2020 regs 71 (England) and 76 (Wales) and Sch 4 (for members of the post-transition period group) and Citizens' Rights (Application Deadline and Temporary Protection) (EU Exit) Regulations 2020 regs 4 and 11 (for EEA nationals with an in-time application for leave).

2) the exercise of the initial three-month right to reside: see paras 2.41–2.44;[153] or
3) the exercise of a derivative *Zambrano* right to reside as the primary carer of a British citizen: see paras 2.90–2.100.[154]

7.73 An EEA national who is not subject to immigration control but whose only right to reside in the Channel Islands, Isle of Man or Republic of Ireland is derived from one of the following will also not be eligible:

1) their status as a jobseeker, or the family member of a jobseeker: see paras 2.52–2.60;[155]
2) the exercise of the initial three-month right to reside: see paras 2.41–2.44;[156] or
3) the exercise of a derivative right to reside as the primary carer of a British citizen: see paras 2.90–2.100.[157]

7.74 For the purposes of determining whether an EEA national's *only* right to reside is one of these excluded rights, a right to reside by virtue of having been granted limited leave to enter or remain under

153 This right is contained in EEA Regs 2016 reg 13 as continued in effect and modified by Immigration and Social Security Co-ordination (EU Withdrawal) Act 2020 (Consequential, Saving, Transitional and Transitory Provisions) (EU Exit) Regulations 2020 regs 71 (England) and 76 (Wales) and Sch 4 (for members of the post-transition period group) and Citizens' Rights (Application Deadline and Temporary Protection) (EU Exit) Regulations 2020 regs 4 and 11 (for EEA nationals with an in-time application for leave).

154 This right was recognised by the CJEU in the case of *Zambrano v Office national de l'emploi (ONEm)* Case C-34/09 [2012] QB 265, CJEU.

155 Pursuant to Eligibility (England) Regs 2006 reg 2(2)(a) and (b) and Eligibility (Wales) Regs 2014 reg 2(2)(a) and (b), 'jobseeker' has the same meaning as in, and 'family member' is to be construed in accordance with, EEA Regs 2016 regs 6 and 7. However, these regulations must be applied as continued in effect and modified by Immigration and Social Security Co-ordination (EU Withdrawal) Act 2020 (Consequential, Saving, Transitional and Transitory Provisions) (EU Exit) Regulations 2020 regs 71 (England) and 76 (Wales) and Sch 4 (for members of the post-transition period group) and Citizens' Rights (Application Deadline and Temporary Protection) (EU Exit) Regulations 2020 regs 4 and 11 (for EEA nationals with an in-time application for leave).

156 This right is contained in EEA Regs 2016 reg 13 as continued in effect and modified by Immigration and Social Security Co-ordination (EU Withdrawal) Act 2020 (Consequential, Saving, Transitional and Transitory Provisions) (EU Exit) Regulations 2020 regs 71 (England) and 76 (Wales) and Sch 4 (for members of the post-transition period group) and Citizens' Rights (Application Deadline and Temporary Protection) (EU Exit) Regulations 2020 regs 4 and 11 (for EEA nationals with an in-time application for leave).

157 This right was recognised by the CJEU in the case of *Zambrano v Office national de l'emploi (ONEm)* Case C-34/09 [2012] QB 265, CJEU.

Appendix EU of the Immigration Rules[158] (pre-settled status) is to be disregarded.[159] In short, an EEA national who would have been ineligible without pre-settled status, because their only right to reside was an excluded right, will still be ineligible: having pre-settled status will not assist them. An applicant with pre-settled status must therefore still have some other qualifying right to reside in order to be eligible for housing assistance. A challenge to a similar provision in the field of welfare benefits, which argued that the measure constituted discrimination on the ground of nationality contrary to Article 18 of the Treaty on the Functioning of the European Union (TFEU), failed in the Supreme Court.[160] The Supreme Court followed *CG v Department for Communities in Northern Ireland*,[161] in which the Grand Chamber of the CJEU had held that TFEU Article 18 was of no application. The court refused to allow the claimant to raise an argument based on the Charter of Fundamental Rights of the European Union. The matter has since been considered by the Upper Tribunal.[162]

Eligibility of members of the household

7.75 As explained at the beginning of this chapter, it is the status of the *applicant*, not members of their household, which determines whether or not the applicant is eligible for homelessness assistance or an allocation of social housing. However, the status of a member of the household can be relevant to what duty is owed and how it is performed.

Homelessness assistance

7.76 In respect of homelessness assistance under HA 1996 Part VII, the status of a member of the household and their eligibility is potentially relevant in three ways.

158 Or leave to enter by virtue of an entry clearance granted under Appendix EU: Family Permit of the Immigration Rules: Eligibility (England) Regs 2006 regs 4(1A) (allocations) and 6(1A) (homelessness); Eligibility (Wales) Regs 2014 regs 4(1A) (allocations) and 6(1A) (homelessness).

159 Eligibility (England) Regs 2006 regs 4(1A) (allocations) and 6(1A) (homelessness); Eligibility (Wales) Regs 2014 regs 4(1A) (allocations) and 6(1A) (homelessness). See paras 2.166–2.168 for pre-settled status.

160 *Fratila v SSWP* [2021] UKSC 53, [2022] 3 All ER 1045.

161 Case C-709/20 [2021] 1 WLR 5919, CJEU.

162 See further para 4.80.

7.77 **First**, the eligibility of a household member can affect *what* duty is owed.[163] In the case of certain applicants, a member of the household who is ineligible in their own right for housing assistance (applying the tests set out above) must be disregarded when the local housing authority is considering whether the applicant is homeless[164] or threatened with homelessness[165] and whether the applicant has a priority need.[166] In other words, the local housing authority will proceed as though the ineligible member does not exist when deciding whether the applicant is homeless, threatened with homelessness, or has a priority need.

7.78 This only applies to an applicant who:

1) is subject to immigration control;[167] and
2) is eligible as a result of falling within one of the classes prescribed as eligible by regulations;[168] but
3) was not, immediately before 1pm on 31 December 2020, an EEA national who fell within a class of persons who are subject to immigration control but who are prescribed as eligible within by regulations.[169]

7.79 The effect of this can be to alter what duty, if any, is owed to the applicant. If, for example, an applicant only has a priority need because their household contains a particular person who is vulnerable,[170] but that vulnerable person is ineligible for housing assistance, then the main housing duty will not apply. (The 'main housing duty' is, in summary, the duty owed to applicants who are homeless, are eligible for assistance, did not become homeless intentionally, have a priority need, and in respect of whom the relief duty[171] has ended. It requires the local housing authority to secure that accommodation is available for occupation by the applicant.[172] A detailed discussion of the main housing duty is at paras 7.263–7.269 and 7.284–7.293 below.)

163 HA 1996 s185(4) (England) and H(W)A 2014 Sch 2 para 1(5) (Wales).
164 See paras 7.121–7.133.
165 See paras 7.134–7.135.
166 See paras 7.136–7.151.
167 See paras 7.152–7.157.
168 See paras 7.30–7.63.
169 HA 1996 s185(5) (England) and H(W)A 2014 Sch 2 para 1(6) (Wales).
170 'Vulnerability' in the context of housing assistance is discussed at para 7.138 below.
171 See paras 7.187–7.193 and 7.221–7.335.
172 HA 1996 s193(1) and (2); and H(W)A 2014 s75(1).

7.80 **Second**, for certain other applicants, an ineligible member of the household can alter the *nature* of the duty owed. This applies in a 'restricted' case.[173] An applicant's case will be 'restricted' where the following criteria are met:

1) the applicant is eligible for assistance;[174]
2) in the applicant's household, there is a person (known as a 'restricted person'):[175]
   a) who is not eligible for assistance under HA 1996 Part VII (in England) or H(W)A 2014 Part 2 (in Wales);[176] and
   b) who is subject to immigration control;[177] and
   c) who does not have leave to enter or remain in the UK; or
   d) whose leave to enter or remain is subject to an NRPF condition;
3) the applicant is owed the main housing duty[178] under HA 1996 s193; and
4) the applicant is only owed the main housing duty because of the presence of the restricted person.

7.81 In such 'restricted' cases, the local housing authority *must* bring the main housing duty to an end by making a private rented sector offer so far as is reasonably practicable.[179] A private rented sector offer is, in England, an offer:

1) of an assured shorthold tenancy;
2) made by a private landlord to the applicant;
3) in relation to accommodation which is or may become available for the applicant to occupy;
4) made with the approval of the local housing authority;
5) made pursuant to arrangements made by the local housing authority with the landlord with a view to bringing the main housing duty to an end; and

173 HA 1996 s193(3B) (England); and H(W)A 2014 s76(5) (Wales). An applicant will know whether or not they are a restricted case because the local housing authority must notify them of this when informing them of the decision on their application: HA 1996 s184(3A) (England); and H(W)A 2014 s63(2) (Wales).

174 For eligibility see paras 7.6–7.74.

175 HA 1996 s184(7) (England); and H(W)A 2014 s63(5) (Wales).

176 For eligibility see paras 7.6–7.74.

177 See paras 7.15–7.17.

178 See paras 7.263–7.269.

179 HA 1996 s193(7AD) (England); and H(W)A 2014 s76(5) (Wales).

6) of a tenancy which is for a fixed term of at least 12 months.[180]

In Wales, a private rented sector offer is an offer:

1) of a tenancy which is an occupation contract in relation to accommodation in Wales or an assured shorthold tenancy in relation to any accommodation in England;
2) made by a private landlord to the applicant;
3) in relation to accommodation which is available for the occupant's occupation;
4) made with the approval of the local housing authority;
5) made pursuant to arrangements made by the local housing authority with a view to bringing the main housing duty[181] to an end; and
6) of a tenancy which is for a fixed term of at least six months.[182]

7.82 This creates a potential difference between restricted cases and other cases as to the way in which the main housing duty[183] will be brought to an end. For example, in non-restricted cases the local housing authority may bring the duty to an end by – amongst other methods – making an offer of long-term accommodation under HA 1996 Part VI.[184] However, as in reality private rented sector offers are increasingly common even in non-restricted cases, this is a distinction of decreasing significance.

7.83 **Third**, restricted cases are dealt with differently in another way which applies only in England. This relates to the special provisions at HA 1996 s195A. HA 1996 s195A(1) provides that an applicant who re-applies for homelessness assistance within two years of accepting a private rented sector offer[185] will be owed the main housing duty[186] regardless of whether or not they have a priority need[187] provided they are homeless,[188] eligible[189] and did not become homeless intentionally.[190] Pursuant to HA 1996 s195A(5), this special provision does

180 HA 1996 s 193(7AC).
181 See paras 7.284–7.293.
182 H(W)A 2014 s76(4).
183 See paras 7.263–7.269.
184 There are several other circumstances in which the main housing duty under HA 1996 s193(2) can be brought to an end: see para 7.265.
185 See para 7.265.
186 See paras 7.263–7.269.
187 See paras 7.136–7.151.
188 See paras 7.121–7.133.
189 See paras 7.6–7.74.
190 See paras 7.152–7.157.

not apply if the local housing authority would not have been satisfied that an applicant is homeless, eligible and did not become homeless intentionally had it not had regard to a restricted person. In such cases, an applicant re-applying within two years of accepting a private rented sector offer will still need to have a priority need in order to be entitled to the main housing duty.

Housing allocations

7.84 In relation to allocations, the eligibility of a household member for housing assistance is potentially relevant in two ways.

7.85 **The first** relates to the question of what property would be suitable for an applicant who has successfully applied for an allocation of social housing. In considering what sort of property would be appropriate for an applicant, the local housing authority must take into account the number, and needs, of members of their household.[191] It is for the local housing authority to set its own rules, which should be contained in its allocation scheme, as to how the make-up of a household will be determined.[192] The local housing authority, applying its rules, may decide that a particular person does not form part of the applicant's household and therefore that that person can be ignored when considering what size or type of property is suitable for the applicant. In deciding whether or not a particular person is part of the applicant's household, the immigration status of a person may be taken into account.

7.86 In *R (Ariemuguvbe) v Islington LBC*,[193] it was held that the local housing authority had been entitled to take into consideration the fact that the applicant's five adult children were subject to NRPF conditions when determining whether the applicant should be allocated a large property which would accommodate them all. However, this does not mean that a family member of uncertain immigration status can be automatically discounted. In *R (Kimvono) v Tower*

191 In *R (Bibi) v Camden LBC* [2004] EWHC 2527 (Admin), [2005] HLR 18, the local housing authority had erred by failing to consider whether the applicant's children formed part of her family, and therefore her household, for the purposes of its allocation scheme.

192 In Complaint against Kettering BC, Local Government Ombudsman Report 16 012 028, November 2017 *Legal Action* 41, 3 August 2017, the Local Government and Social Care Ombudsman found fault with a local housing authority's scheme which was unclear as to in what circumstances adult children would be assessed as being part of an applicant's household.

193 [2009] EWCA Civ 1308, [2010] HLR 14.

Hamlets LBC,[194] the local housing authority was wrong to disregard the claimant's 13-year-old daughter simply because she did not have indefinite leave to remain (her application had not yet been determined) when assessing the household's needs.

7.87 **Secondly**, the eligibility of a member of the household may affect what priority[195] an applicant is given within the local housing authority's allocation scheme. A local housing authority's allocation scheme must be framed so as to give reasonable preference[196] to certain categories of applicant.[197] This includes:

1) people who are statutorily homeless;[198]
2) in England, people who are owed a duty under HA 1996 s190(2),[199] s193(2)[200] or s195(2);[201] and
3) in Wales, people who are owed a duty under H(W)A 2014 s66,[202] s73[203] or s75.[204]

7.88 However, the presence of a restricted person[205] may lead to the removal of reasonable preference. If an applicant would be entitled to a reasonable preference under any of the categories set out in the preceding paragraph, but would not have been so entitled without

194 (2001) 33 HLR 78, QBD.

195 See para 7.366.

196 See para 7.366.

197 HA 1996 s166A(3) (England); and H(W)A 2014 s167(2) (Wales).

198 This means people who are homeless within the meaning of HA 1996 Part VII (England) or H(W)A 2014 Part 2 (Wales): see paras 7.121–7.133.

199 The short-term accommodation duty owed to an applicant who is homeless, is eligible for assistance and has a priority need, but who became homeless intentionally: HA 1996 s190(1). See paras 7.260–7.262.

200 The main housing duty owed to a person who is homeless, is eligible for assistance, has a priority need, did not become homeless intentionally and in respect of whom the relief duty has ended: HA 1996 s193(1). See paras 7.263–7.269.

201 The prevention duty owed to a person who is threatened with homelessness and is eligible for assistance: HA 1996 s195(1). See paras 7.181–7.186.

202 The prevention duty owed to an applicant who is threatened with homelessness and eligible for assistance: H(W)A 2014 s66(1). See paras 7.211–7.220.

203 The relief duty owed to an applicant who is homeless and eligible for assistance: H(W)A 2014 s73(1). See paras 7.221–7.227.

204 The main housing duty owed to a person who is homeless, is eligible for assistance, has a priority need and did not become homeless intentionally: H(W)A 2014 s75(2). See paras 7.284–7.293.

205 As defined at HA 1996 s184(7): see para 7.80.

the local housing authority taking into account a restricted person, then the reasonable preference will be removed.[206]

Challenging a decision that an applicant is ineligible

Homelessness[207]

7.89 An applicant who wishes to challenge a decision made by a local housing authority as to their eligibility for assistance may request that the local housing authority review that decision.[208] The review must be requested within 21 days of the date on which the applicant is notified of the decision, or such longer period as the authority may in writing allow.[209] The review is a *de novo* consideration of all the circumstances of the case. The decision on review must be made within eight weeks of the day on which the request for review was made or such longer period as the applicant and reviewer agree in writing.[210]

7.90 If an applicant is dissatisfied with the decision made on the review, they may appeal the review decision on a point of law to the county court.[211] Alternatively, if the applicant has requested a review but no decision has been made within eight weeks (or by any agreed extended deadline) then they may appeal the original decision to the county court.[212] However, unlike with the review procedure, this right of challenge is limited to points of law.

7.91 In *R (Sambotin) v Brent LBC*,[213] the claimant successfully challenged the local housing authority's attempt to revoke its decision that he was eligible. The claimant applied to Waltham Forest LBC which decided that he was ineligible. He then applied to Brent LBC and provided it with a copy of Waltham Forest's decision, but Brent concluded that he was eligible and referred him to Waltham Forest under HA 1996 s198.[214] When Waltham Forest disputed his eligibility, Brent purported to reach a new decision that he was not, in fact,

206 HA 1996 s166A(4) (England); and H(W)A 2014 s167(2ZA) (Wales).

207 See paras 7.326–7.335 for a discussion of reviews and appeals in respect of homelessness decisions more generally.

208 HA 1996 s202(1)(a) (England); and H(W)A 2014 s85(1)(a) (Wales).

209 HA 1996 s202(3) (England); and H(W)A 2014 s85(5) (Wales).

210 Homelessness (Review Procedure etc) Regulations 2018 SI No 223 reg 9(1) (England); and Homelessness (Review Procedure) (Wales) Regulations 2015 SI No 1266 (W 76) reg 6(1) and (2) (Wales).

211 HA 1996 s204(1)(a) (England); and H(W)A 2014 s88(1)(a) (Wales).

212 HA 1996 s204(1)(b) (England); and H(W)A 2014 s88(1)(b) (Wales).

213 [2018] EWCA Civ 1826, [2019] HLR 5.

214 See paras 7.308–7.317.

eligible. The Court of Appeal rejected Brent's argument that the first decision had not been final and could be revoked. After the first decision had been reached, Brent was *functus officio* and not entitled to reach a new decision absent fraud or a fundamental mistake of fact.

Allocations[215]

7.92 An applicant who has been found to be ineligible for an allocation of social housing accommodation must be notified of that decision and of the grounds for it.[216] The local housing authority's scheme must provide applicants with a right to request a review of such a decision.[217] If it does not, the applicant's remedy would be to apply for a judicial review of the scheme and to seek a mandatory order requiring the local housing authority to amend its scheme to introduce such a right.

7.93 There is no statutory right of appeal against an adverse decision on review. An applicant who is dissatisfied with such a decision would have to apply for judicial review. Such a challenge would be limited to points of law.

Housing for eligible applicants

7.94 Applicants who are eligible for housing assistance may be entitled to urgent homelessness assistance under HA 1996 Part VII (in England) or H(W)A 2014 Part 2 (in Wales), or to a longer-term allocation of social housing under HA 1996 Part VI (England and Wales).

Homelessness assistance

Legal framework

7.95 The statutory provisions relating to homelessness are contained in HA 1996 Part VII (in respect of England) and H(W)A 2014 Part 2 (in respect of Wales) and in regulations made under those Acts. There are also statutory codes of guidance for both jurisdictions. The

215 See paras 7.326–7.335 for a discussion of reviews and appeals in respect of allocations decisions more generally.
216 HA 1996 ss160ZA(9) (England) and 160A(9) (Wales).
217 HA 1996 ss166A(9)(c) (England) and 167(4A)(d) (Wales). The procedure to be followed on such a review, including the timescale by which it must be concluded, is for the local housing authority to determine and should be set out in the allocation scheme.

Homelessness code of guidance[218] applies to local housing authorities in England. The relevant guidance for local housing authorities in Wales is the *Code of guidance to local authorities on the allocation of accommodation and homelessness* together with the supplementary guidance *Additional provisions under section 75(3)*,[219] *Code of guidance: addendum*,[220] and *Addendum to guidance affecting certain people subject to immigration control*.[221]

England

7.96 HA 1996 Part VII was substantially amended by the Homelessness Reduction Act 2017. The amendments apply to all applications for homelessness assistance made to local housing authorities in England on or after 3 April 2018.[222] The aim of the amendments was to ensure that local housing authorities engaged in 'more robust' work to prevent homelessness, at an earlier stage, and irrespective of whether or not the applicant had a priority need[223] for accommodation.[224] As a result of the amendments made by the Homelessness Reduction Act 2017, HA 1996 Part VII now contains a number of different, sometimes overlapping, duties. What follows is a brief summary of how these duties fit together. Subsequent sections contain a more detailed discussion of when the duties will arise and what they entail.

7.97 When a person applies to a local housing authority in England for homelessness assistance, the first question for the authority will be whether or not it has reason to believe that they may be homeless,[225] eligible[226] and have a priority need.[227] If it does, the interim accommodation duty under HA 1996 s188(1) will be owed.[228]

218 MHCLG, February 2018 (subsequently updated).
219 Welsh Government, December 2019.
220 Welsh Government, October 2022.
221 Welsh Government, February 2023.
222 Homelessness Reduction Act (Commencement and Transitional and Savings Provisions) Regulations 2018 SI No 167 reg 3.
223 See paras 7.136–7.131.
224 Gousey *No one turned away: changing the law to prevent and tackle homelessness*, Crisis, 2016.
225 See paras 7.121–7.133.
226 See paras 7.6–7.93.
227 See paras 7.136–7.151.
228 See paras 7.253–7.259.

7.98 The next question will be whether the applicant is eligible for assistance.[229] If not, no further duty will be owed.[230] If the applicant *is* eligible, then the local housing authority will have to determine whether the applicant is either homeless[231] or threatened with homelessness.[232] If the applicant is eligible and either homeless or threatened with homelessness, then the authority will be subject to the duty imposed by HA 1996 s189A to make an assessment of the applicant's case and prepare a personalised housing plan.[233] If the applicant is eligible and threatened with homelessness (but not actually homeless), the local housing authority will also owe the prevention of homelessness duty under HA 1996 s195(2).[234] If the applicant is eligible and homeless (rather than just threatened with homelessness), the relief of homelessness duty imposed by HA 1996 s189B(2) will arise.[235]

7.99 No further duty is owed at the end of the prevention duty if the applicant's homelessness is successfully prevented; or the applicant becomes ineligible; or the applicant remains threatened with homelessness but has not actually become homeless. If, however, by the end of the prevention duty the applicant has become homeless, the relief duty will arise.[236]

7.100 What duty, if any, is owed at the end of the relief duty will depend on the applicant's circumstances at that time. If the applicant is no longer homeless, or has become ineligible, no duty will arise. If the applicant remains homeless and eligible, but has no priority need, then no further duty will be owed (unless the applicant is re-applying for homelessness assistance within two years of accepting a private rented sector offer and did not become homeless intentionally, in which case the special provisions at HA 1996 s195A(1) will apply).[237] If the applicant is homeless and eligible and has a priority need but became homeless intentionally, then the local housing authority will be required to secure that accommodation is available for a reason-

229 See paras 7.6–7.70.

230 Save for certain miscellaneous non-accommodation duties which may arise, such as referring the applicant to social services and/or taking steps to protect their belongings: see paras 7.195–7.200.

231 See paras 7.121–7.133.

232 See paras 7.134–7.135.

233 See paras 7.169–7.180.

234 See paras 7.181–7.186.

235 See paras 7.187–7.193.

236 See paras 7.187–7.193.

237 See para 7.254.

able period and to provide advice and assistance pursuant to HA 1996 s190(2).[238] It is only if the applicant is homeless and eligible, has a priority need and did not become homeless intentionally that the main housing duty under HA 1996 s193(2) will be owed.[239] Even in these circumstances, the main housing duty will *not* be owed if:

1) the applicant refused a final accommodation offer[240] or a final Part 6 offer[241] during the course of the relief duty.[242] If so, the main housing duty does not apply and no further duty is owed; or
2) the applicant has been given a notice during the course of the relief duty[243] by the local housing authority stating that it considers they deliberately and unreasonably failed to take a step required by their personalised housing plan.[244] In this instance, the main housing duty does not apply but the local housing authority will be required to secure accommodation under HA 1996 s193C(4).[245]

Wales

7.101 The amendments made by the Homelessness Reduction Act 2017 to HA 1996 Part VII were based upon the provisions of H(W)A 2014 Part 2. H(W)A 2014 Part 2 contains a similar emphasis on preventing homelessness and on assisting all eligible applicants but its framework is considerably simpler.

7.102 On receipt of an application for homelessness assistance, one of the first questions for a local housing authority in Wales to consider will be whether a duty to provide interim accommodation is owed.[246] This can arise in two situations. The first[247] is where the authority has reason to believe that an applicant may be homeless,[248] eligible[249] and have a priority need.[250] The second[251] is where:

238 See paras 7.260–7.262.
239 See paras 7.263–7.269. Save for the special circumstances under HA 1996 s195A(1): see para 7.254.
240 See para 7.273.
241 See para 7.273.
242 See paras 7.187–7.193.
243 See paras 7.187–7.193.
244 See paras 7.169–7.180.
245 See paras 7.270–7.274.
246 See paras 7.275–7.283.
247 H(W)A 2014 s68(2).
248 See paras 7.121–7.133.
249 See paras 7.6–7.93.
250 See paras 7.136–7.151.
251 H(W)A 2014 s68(3).

1) the local housing authority has reason to believe that an applicant has a priority need; or
2) the local housing authority is satisfied that the applicant has a priority need; or
3) the applicant's case has been referred to the local housing authority from a local housing authority in England under HA 1996 s198(1);[252] and
4) the applicant is owed the relief duty.[253]

In addition to this, if it appears to the local housing authority that the applicant may be homeless or threatened with homelessness then the assessment duty under H(W)A 2014 s62(1) will arise.[254] As part of this, the authority must consider whether or not the applicant is eligible for assistance.[255]

7.103 If the applicant is not eligible, no further duties will arise.[256] If the applicant *is* eligible for assistance, then the local housing authority will have to determine whether they are homeless or threatened with homelessness.[257] If the applicant is eligible and threatened with homelessness, the authority will be subject to the prevention of homelessness duty under H(W)A 2014 s66(1).[258] If the applicant is eligible and homeless, the relief duty under H(W)A 2014 s73(1) will apply.[259]

7.104 If the applicant remains homeless at the end of the relief duty then the main housing duty under H(W)A 2014 s75(1)[260] will arise if:

1) the relief duty[261] came to an end because 56 days had elapsed *or* because the local housing authority was satisfied (before the end of the 56-day period) that reasonable steps had been taken to help to secure that suitable accommodation was available for occupation by the applicant;[262]

252 See paras 7.221–7.228.
253 Under H(W)A 2014 s73(1): see paras 7.221–7.227.
254 See paras 7.294–7.325.
255 H(W)A 2014 s62(4): see paras 7.6–7.93.
256 Save for certain non-accommodation duties which may be relevant, such as referring the applicant to social services and/or taking steps to protect their belongings: see paras 7.228–7.235.
257 See paras 7.120–7.135.
258 See paras 7.211–7.220.
259 See paras 7.221–7.227.
260 See paras 7.284–7.293.
261 Under H(W)A 2014 s73(1): see paras 7.221–7.227.
262 H(W)A 2015 s75(1).

2) the local housing authority is satisfied that the applicant does not have suitable accommodation which is available for their occupation either at all or for at least six months;[263]
3) the local housing authority is satisfied that the applicant is eligible;[264]
4) the local housing authority is satisfied that the applicant has a priority need for accommodation;[265] and
5) if the local housing authority is having regard to the intentional homelessness test:[266]
   a) it is not satisfied that the applicant became homeless intentionally;[267] or
   b) it is satisfied that the applicant became homeless intentionally, but the applicant falls within one of the groups of people to whom the main housing duty is owed despite the applicant being homeless intentionally[268] by virtue of H(W)A 2014 s75(3) and the local housing authority had not within the last five years secured an offer of accommodation to the applicant on the basis that they fell within H(W)A 2014 s75(3).[269]

Applying as homeless

Making a homelessness application

7.105 A person seeking homelessness assistance can apply to their local housing authority for help. There is no requirement that the application be made in any particular form.[270] In England, provided that the local housing authority has 'reason to believe' that the person 'may be homeless or threatened with homelessness',[271] then the local housing authority will come under a duty to make inquiries into

263 H(W)A 2014 s75(2)(a).
264 H(W)A 2014 s75(2)(b). See paras 7.6–7.93.
265 H(W)A 2014 s75(2)(c). See paras 7.136–7.151.
266 See para 7.152.
267 H(W)A 2014 s75(2)(d): see paras 7.152–7.157.
268 These groups are specified at H(W)A 2014 s75(3)(e) and are discussed at para 7.155.
269 H(W)A 2014 s75(3): see para 7.156.
270 *Homelessness code of guidance*, para 18.5 (England); *Code of guidance to local authorities on the allocation of accommodation and homelessness*, paras 10.7–10.8 (Wales); *R v Chiltern DC ex p Roberts* (1991) 23 HLR 387, QBD at p392 per Pill J; *R (Edwards) v Birmingham City Council* [2016] EWHC 173 (Admin), [2016] HLR 11 at para 37 per Hickinbottom J.
271 See para 7.117.

their case.[272] A very similar test applies in Wales: if it 'appears' to the local housing authority that the person 'may be homeless or threatened with homelessness', then the local housing authority will come under a duty to 'carry out an assessment' of their case.[273]

7.106 The duty to make inquiries (owed by local housing authorities in England) and the duty to assess (owed by local housing authorities in Wales) are similar but not exactly coterminous. The duty (in England) to make inquiries is aimed solely at determining what duty, if any, is owed to the applicant. The duty (in Wales) to assess an applicant's case will address this issue, but is more wide-ranging. The local housing authority in Wales must (if the applicant is eligible)[274] and may (if it has not yet determined whether the applicant is eligible) consider the circumstances that have caused the applicant to become homeless or threatened with homelessness as well as the housing and support needs of the applicant and their household.[275] There is a similar duty of assessment on local housing authorities in England,[276] but this is separate to the duty to make inquiries.

7.107 In England, a person who is homeless or threatened with homelessness may also come to the attention of the local housing authority via the public authority referral duty. This duty is contained in HA 1996 s213B. It applies where a 'specified' public authority 'considers' that a person in England in relation to whom the body 'exercises functions' is, or may be, homeless or threatened with homelessness.[277] The public authorities which are subject to this duty are contained in the Homelessness (Review Procedure etc) Regulations 2018 at reg 10 and Sch 1. They include:

- a governor of a prison, young offender institution, or secure training centre;
- a youth offending team (YOT);
- a provider of probation services;
- a social services authority;
- an NHS Trust or NHS Foundation Trust, but only in connection with emergency services, urgent treatment centres and in-patient treatment; and
- a designated officer at a Jobcentre Plus.

272 HA 1996 s184(1).
273 H(W)A 2014 s62(1).
274 See paras 7.6–7.93.
275 H(W)A 2014 s62(5) and (7).
276 Under HA 1996 s189A.
277 HA 1996 s213B(1).

7.108 If the specified public authority considers that a person in relation to whom it exercises functions may be homeless or threatened with homelessness, then it must ask that person to agree to the authority notifying a local housing authority of this concern.[278] The person should also be asked to agree to the local housing authority being notified of how they may be contacted.[279] If the person does agree, and identifies to which local housing authority they would like to be referred, then the public authority must then make the notification.[280]

7.109 The English *Homelessness code of guidance*[281] states that a referral under HA 1996 s213B does not constitute an application for the purposes of HA 1996 Part VII. This is questionable: if the notification gives the local housing authority reason to believe that the person may be homeless or threatened with homelessness, then there would seem to be no reason why the duty to make inquiries under HA 1996 s184(1) should not arise. In any event, the guidance is clear that local housing authorities 'should always respond to any referral received'.[282]

7.110 Some people seeking homelessness assistance may experience what is known as 'gatekeeping' from the local housing authority to which they seek to apply. This is an unlawful practice whereby local housing authorities, often overstretched, seek to deter the person from making an application or refuse to accept an application. Migrants may be particularly vulnerable to gatekeeping if, for example, their immigration situation is complex or they are unfamiliar with the intricacies of the system. Migrant applicants may face assertions that the 'right' paperwork has not been produced. Some migrant applicants may, for example, have been granted leave pursuant to which they are eligible for homelessness assistance, but have not yet been issued with a biometric residence permit, and the local housing authority may say that this is needed before an application can be progressed.

7.111 It is important to note that an applicant seeking homelessness assistance is not required to prove their case: the burden is on the local housing authority to make inquiries.[283] Moreover, a local

278 HA 1996 s213B(2)(a).

279 HA 1996 s213B(2)(b).

280 HA 1996 s213B(3).

281 *Homelessness code of guidance*, para 4.20.

282 *Homelessness code of guidance*, para 4.20.

283 *R v Woodspring DC ex p Walters* (1984) 16 HLR 73, QBD at p77 per Taylor J. See also *Code of guidance to local authorities on the allocation of accommodation and homelessness*, para 10.22.

housing authority cannot refuse to accept or progress an application until the applicant produces a particular document.[284] A local housing authority which failed to take an application from such an applicant or refused to accept that they were eligible because of the absence of this particular type of proof is likely to be acting unlawfully. Where there is uncertainty regarding an applicant's immigration status, the local housing authority should make inquiries of the Home Office, as advised at para 7.13 of the English *Homelessness code of guidance*, rather than send the applicant away to obtain further proof.

7.112 However, a local housing authority in England or Wales *may* lawfully refuse to accept an application where the applicant has made a previous application to the local housing authority and there has been no change in the applicant's circumstances since that application was disposed of. In England, this limit on repeated applications comes from case-law. The Court of Appeal has confirmed that if the application does not reveal any new facts which 'are said to render that application different from the earlier application', or if any new facts disclosed are 'fanciful or trivial', then the local housing authority may refuse to entertain the application.[285] There is, however, no requirement for there to be a material change of circumstances.[286] Where there is a change (or alleged change) of circumstances, it is not necessary that the alleged change ' "might" or "could" lead to a different conclusion' in order for a new application to be accepted.[287] Furthermore, the local housing authority is not entitled to investigate the accuracy of the new facts relied upon before accepting the application.[288]

7.113 In Wales, the restriction has been enshrined in statute. Pursuant to H(W)A 2014 s62(1) and (2), the local housing authority is not required to carry out an assessment of an applicant's case if:

284 See Complaint against Hounslow LBC, 17 018 631, 3 October 2018, February 2019 *Legal Action* 44; and Complaint against Tower Hamlets LBC, Local Government Ombudsman Report 19 000 068, April 2020 *Legal Action* 45, 11 November 2019.

285 *Begum v Tower Hamlets LBC* [2005] EWCA Civ 340, [2005] 1 WLR 2103 at paras 59–60 per Neuberger LJ. See also *R (Bukartyk) v Welwyn Hatfield BC* [2019] EWHC 3480 (Admin), [2020] HLR 19.

286 *Begum v Tower Hamlets LBC* [2005] EWCA Civ 340, [2005] 1 WLR 2103 at para 50.

287 *Minott v Cambridge City Council* [2022] EWCA Civ 159, [2022] HLR 27 at para 68 per Lewison LJ.

288 *Begum v Tower Hamlets LBC* [2005] EWCA Civ 340, [2005] 1 WLR 2103 at para 61. See also *Minott v Cambridge City Council* [2022] EWCA Civ 159, [2022] HLR 27 at para 76.

> . . . the person has been assessed by a local housing authority under this section on a previous occasion and the authority is satisfied that–
> (a) the person's circumstances have not changed materially since that assessment was carried out, and
> (b) there is no new information that materially affects that assessment.

7.114 Applications cannot be made by dependant children.[289] Nor can they be made by persons without mental capacity:[290] in such cases the application would have to be made by another member of the household, if possible, or by a deputy appointed by the Court of Protection under the Mental Capacity Act 2005.

Determining homelessness applications

7.115 The obligation to make inquiries into (or, in Wales, to assess) the applicant's case is aimed at establishing what duties, if any, the local housing authority owes to the applicant under HA 1996 Part VI or H(W)A 2014 Part 2.[291]

7.116 The local housing authority may owe a number of different duties to the same applicant. Furthermore, these duties may arise at different points and last for different durations. Some may overlap and others may only arise consequent upon other duties ending.[292] Each of the duties is discussed in more detail below, but first this chapter considers the various issues which must be determined in order to establish what duties, if any, are owed.

Reason to believe an applicant may be homeless, eligible for assistance and have a priority need

7.117 The first question for the local housing authority is whether there is 'reason to believe' that the applicant may be homeless,[293] eligible for assistance[294] and have a priority need.[295] If these criteria are met, the local housing authority will be under a duty to provide interim accommodation whilst it undertakes further inquiries into the applicant's

289 *R v Oldham MBC ex p Garlick* [1993] AC 509, [1993] 2 WLR 609, HL.
290 *WB v W District Council* [2018] EWCA Civ 928, [2018] 3 WLR 2035.
291 See para 7.106 for the difference between the duty to make inquiries (as owed by local housing authorities in England) and the duty to assess (as owed by local housing authorities in Wales).
292 See paras 7.96–7.104 for an explanation of how the duties fit together.
293 See paras 7.121–7.133.
294 See paras 7.96–7.104.
295 See paras 7.136–7.151.

case.[296] It has been confirmed repeatedly that this is a low threshold to meet.[297]

Eligible

7.118 The local housing authority will then need to determine whether or not the applicant is eligible for assistance.[298] A discussion of the eligibility criteria is set out above at paras 7.6–7.93.

7.119 If the local housing authority concludes that the applicant is not eligible for assistance, then it need not inquire further into the applicant's case. This does not mean, however, that the local housing authority may immediately wash its hands of the applicant. If the local housing authority was providing interim accommodation, this must be brought to an end lawfully.[299] In addition, the local housing authority may still owe a duty to protect the applicant's property or to seek the applicant's consent for them to be referred to the local children's services authority.[300]

Homeless or threatened with homelessness

7.120 If the applicant is found to be eligible,[301] then the local housing authority must then determine whether or not the applicant is homeless[302] or threatened with homelessness.[303] The local housing authority in Wales will also at this point become subject to a duty to assess:

a) the circumstances that have caused the applicant to be homeless or threatened with homelessness;

296 HA 1996 s188(1) (England) and H(W)A 2014 s68(1) and (2) (Wales). See further at paras 7.253–7.259 and 7.275–7.283. In Wales, the local housing authority will also owe an interim accommodation duty to applicants to whom the relief duty under H(W)A 2014 s73(1) applies, where the local housing authority has reason to believe the applicant has a priority need, or the local housing authority is satisfied that the applicant has a priority need; or the applicant has been referred from a local housing authority in England under HA 1996 s198(1).

297 *R (Kelly and Mehari) v Birmingham City Council* [2009] EWHC 3240 (Admin) at para 7 per Hickinbottom J; *R (M) v Hammersmith and Fulham LBC* [2008] UKHL 14, [2008] 1 WLR 535 at para 36 per Baroness Hale; *Homelessness code of guidance*, para 15.5; *Code of guidance to local authorities on the allocation of accommodation and homelessness*, paras 11.3–11.4 (Wales).

298 HA 1996 s184(1)(a) (England); and H(W)A 2014 s62(4) (Wales).

299 See para 7.256.

300 HA 1996 s211 (England); and H(W)A 2014 s93 (Wales). See paras 7.194–7.200 and 7.228–7.235.

301 See paras 7.6–7.93.

302 See paras 7.121–7.133.

303 See paras 7.134–7.135.

b) the housing needs of the applicant and any person with whom the applicant lives or might reasonably be expected to live; [and]
c) the support needed for the applicant and any person with whom the applicant lives or might reasonably be expected to live to retain accommodation which is or may become available.[304]

Homeless

7.121 'Homelessness' is defined at HA 1996 ss175–177 and at H(W)A 2014 ss55–57. A person is homeless if they have no accommodation available for their occupation, in the UK or elsewhere,[305] which they:

1) are entitled to occupy by virtue of an interest in it or an order of court;
2) have a licence to occupy; or
3) are entitled to occupy by virtue of an enactment or rule of law.[306]

7.122 Accommodation will not be 'available' for a person's occupation unless it is available for occupation by the person together with:

1) any other person who normally resides with them as a member of their family; or
2) any other person who might reasonably be expected to reside with them.[307]

7.123 A person is also homeless if they have accommodation but:

1) they cannot secure entry to it; or
2) it consists of a moveable structure, vehicle or vessel which is designed or adapted for human habitation, and there is no place where they are entitled or permitted both to place it and to reside in it.[308]

7.124 In England, a special provision applies in respect of applicants who accepted a private rented sector offer[309] made pursuant to a previous homelessness application and then re-applied as homeless (to the same or a different local housing authority) within two years of the date on which they accepted that offer. If the applicant has received a notice from their landlord under Housing Act (HA) 1988 s21 stating that possession of their home is required, then they will be deemed to be homeless on the day on which that notice expires.[310]

304 H(W)A 2014 s62(5) and (7).
305 The availability of accommodation abroad may be of particular relevance to migrants: see para 7.154.
306 HA 1996 s175(1) (England); and H(W)A 2014 s55(1) (Wales).
307 HA 1996 s176 (England); and H(W)A 2014 s56(1) (Wales).
308 HA 1996 s175(2) (England); and H(W)A 2014 s55(2) (Wales).
309 See para 7.254.
310 HA 1996 s195A(2).

7.125 A person shall not be treated as having accommodation unless it is accommodation which it would be reasonable for them to *continue to occupy*.[311] Thus, for example, it was not reasonable for a woman who had fled to a refuge to escape domestic violence to continue to occupy that refuge, with the result that she was homeless.[312] This criterion applies whether or not the applicant is in actual occupation of the accommodation. It is necessarily forward-looking: the local housing authority must consider not just whether the accommodation is reasonable for the applicant to continue to occupy at the present moment but also whether it will be reasonable for the applicant to continue to occupy on the basis that 'the accommodation is to be available "indefinitely" '[313] or, if the applicant is likely to obtain suitable alternative accommodation, until that accommodation will be provided.[314] In *Safi v Sandwell MBC*[315] the Court of Appeal held that the local housing authority should have asked itself two questions: first, was it reasonable, 'looking to the foreseeable future as well as the present', for the applicant to continue to occupy her property; and second, if not, 'how long in the short term was it reasonable for them to continue to occupy the flat and, in the light of that period, would they be able to obtain suitable accommodation in that period through the operation of the housing list'.[316]

7.126 In determining whether it would be reasonable for a person to continue to occupy accommodation, regard may be had to the general circumstances prevailing in respect of housing in the district of the local housing authority to which the applicant has applied.[317] The local housing authority must also have regard to the affordability of the accommodation.[318]

311 HA 1996 s175(3) (England); and H(W)A 2014 s55(3) (Wales).

312 *R (Aweys) v Birmingham City Council* [2009] UKHL 36, [2009] 1 WLR 1506. See also the statutory guidance *Improving access to social housing for victims of domestic abuse*, MHCLG, November 2018, para 31.

313 *Samuels v Birmingham City Council* [2019] UKSC 28, [2019] 4 All ER 773 at para 35 per Lord Carnwath.

314 *Safi v Sandwell MBC* [2018] EWCA Civ 2876, [2019] HLR 16; *Godson v Enfield BC* [2019] EWCA Civ 486, [2020] HLR 1.

315 [2018] EWCA Civ 2876, [2019] HLR 16. See also *Waltham Forest LBC v Maloba* [2007] EWCA Civ 1271, [2008] HLR 26 at para 57 per Toulson LJ.

316 *Safi v Sandwell MBC* [2018] EWCA Civ 2876, [2019] HLR 16 at para 30 per David Richards LJ.

317 HA 1996 s177(2) (England); and H(W)A 2014 s57(3)(a) (Wales).

318 Homelessness (Suitability of Accommodation) Order 1996 SI No 3204 art 2 (England); and H(W)A 2014 s57(3)(b) (Wales). See *Samuels v Birmingham City Council* [2019] UKSC 28 for the correct approach to determining affordability.

7.127 It is prescribed in statute that it will not be reasonable for a person to continue to occupy accommodation if it is probable that this will lead to violence or domestic abuse (in England) or abuse (in Wales) against them or a member of their household.[319] 'Domestic abuse' consists of physical or sexual abuse, violent or threatening behaviour, controlling or coercive behaviour, economic abuse, or psychological, emotional or other abuse between two people who are 'personally connected'.[320] 'Violence' means violence from another person or threats of violence[321] from another person which are likely to be carried out.[322] 'Abuse' (the term used in H(W)A 2014 s57) means physical violence, threatening or intimidating behaviour and any other form of abuse which, directly or indirectly, may give rise to the risk of harm.[323] This behaviour will constitute domestic abuse where the victim is associated with the abuser.[324]

7.128 One argument which migrants in particular sometimes face when applying as homeless is the suggestion that they are not homeless because they have property available to them elsewhere – often outside of the UK. In order to reach such a conclusion, the local housing authority will have to have satisfied itself that:

1) the accommodation is available to the applicant;
2) it is also available for their family members or any other person who might reasonably be expected to reside with them;
3) the applicant has a right to occupy that accommodation;
4) the applicant can secure entry to it; and
5) it is reasonable for the applicant to occupy that accommodation (taking into account features such as its nature, size, condition, location and affordability).[325]

319 HA 1996 s177(1) (England); and H(W)A 2014 s57(1) and (2) (Wales). 'Member of the household' has the same meaning as in HA 1996 s176 (England); and H(W)A 2015 s56(1) (Wales).
320 HA 1996 s177(1A) and Domestic Abuse Act 2021 s1. 'Personally connected' is defined in Domestic Abuse Act 2021 s2.
321 This could include a single threat, pursuant to Interpretation Act 1978 s6(c) which states that 'unless the contrary intention appears . . . words in the singular includes the plural' and vice versa.
322 HA 1996 s177(1A).
323 H(W)A 2014 s58(1).
324 H(W)A 2014 s58(1). The circumstances in which people are associated with one another are set out in H(W)A 2014 s58(2)–(4).
325 If the local housing authority is not satisfied of these matters then the definition at HA 1996 ss175–177 and H(W)A 2014 ss55–57 will not be met.

7.129 The decision-maker must make specific findings on each question. In one case, the Court of Appeal quashed a decision which found that the applicant had had accommodation available for his occupation under either a licence or a tenancy, without determining which:

> 41. With respect to the learned Judge that does not satisfy in my view the requirements of s175 of the HA 1996. The section can only be satisfied if the appellant either has an interest at the time for consideration (namely the review) which confers on him an entitlement to occupy (subs.(a)) or he has an express or implied licence to occupy (subs.(b)).
>
> 42. . . . It is difficult to see how the section can be satisfied unless one knows the nature of the interests and then satisfies oneself that the relevant interest confers on the appellant a right to occupy the property.[326]

7.130 In another case, a finding that the appellant was not homeless because a different local authority owed a duty to accommodate him was quashed. As the local authority had not identified any specific property in which he could live, it could not be said that there was accommodation available for his occupation:

> . . . the language of s175(1) is simply not apt to refer to unspecified accommodation which may in the future become available, if the applicant were to apply to another authority.[327]

7.131 Where a migrant applicant has accommodation available to them abroad, then the question of whether or not it would be reasonable for them to continue to occupy it is likely to be key. A local housing authority considering such a property must take into account not just its size and physical qualities, but also whether it would be reasonable to expect the applicant to move to it.[328] In *Waltham Forest LBC v Maloba*,[329] the applicant had been born and brought up in Uganda but had lived much of his adult life in the UK and was a British citizen. He met his wife on a visit to Uganda. They married and lived there in the applicant's family home for two years before returning to the UK. His application for homelessness assistance was refused on the basis that they could live in the family home in Uganda. The applicant appealed this decision successfully to the county court. The Court of Appeal dismissed the local housing authority's appeal against the circuit judge's decision. The court rejected the local housing authority's argument that the property's location in Uganda

326 *Fletcher v Brent LBC* [2006] EWCA Civ 960, [2007] HLR 12 per Peter Smith J.

327 *Johnston v City of Westminster* [2015] EWCA Civ 554, [2015] HLR 35 at para 27 per Gloster LJ.

328 *Waltham Forest LBC v Maloba* [2007] EWCA Civ 1281, [2008] HLR 26.

329 [2007] EWCA Civ 1271, [2008] HLR 26.

was irrelevant, finding that the council had adopted an unduly narrow approach to the question of reasonableness:

> Consider, for example, the case of a woman who was born in England and has lived all her life here. Her family originated in India, where she continues to have relatives. She marries or forms a relationship and has children. Her husband or partner subsequently dies or leaves her, and she finds herself homeless with dependent children. Her grandparents have always said that they would be happy for her and her children to live with them in India. She has never wished to do so and does not wish to do so now. Nor would anyone reasonably expect her to do so. It would mean uprooting the family from the country in which all the members were born, had lived their lives and had their cultural roots. It would also involve disruption of the children's education. It may be said that those would be unusual facts, but the question whether it would be reasonable to expect a person to occupy particular accommodation is necessarily a fact specific question. As a matter of statutory construction, I see no warrant for imposing the restrictions contended for by the council as to what may be relevant to that question.[330]

7.132 Moreover, any finding that the applicant could go or return to a different country is very likely to engage the ECHR Article 8 rights of the applicant and their household. In *Kumaning v Haringey LBC*,[331] a decision that an applicant was not homeless because he owned a house in Ghana was quashed. The judge found that it was unrealistic for the local housing authority to suggest that it was not an inevitable implication of its decision that the applicant and his family would have to move to Ghana, and consequently the council had an obligation to carry out a proportionality analysis of the impact of its decision on the father and son's Article 8 rights.

7.133 Any decision that a migrant applicant can reside in a property located abroad should therefore be carefully scrutinised. Advisers will want to make full representations as to the implications of requiring the applicant to move to a different country, which may involve considering the circumstances in which the applicant came to the UK in the first place. For example, an applicant who has been granted refugee status or leave to remain in the UK on human rights grounds is likely to have compelling reasons for not being able to return to a property located in their country of origin.

330 *Waltham Forest LBC v Maloba* [2007] EWCA Civ 1281, [2008] HLR 26 at para 61 per Toulson LJ.

331 April 2012 *Legal Action* 47, County Court (Central London).

Threatened with homelessness

7.134 A person is 'threatened with homelessness' if it is likely that they will become homeless within 56 days.[332] In England, specific provision is made for a person who has been served with a notice under HA 1988 s21. This is a notice served by a landlord to an assured shorthold tenant, informing them that possession of the rented property is required. The notice can be given without the need for any fault on the part of the tenant or any particular reason for requiring possession on the part of the landlord. The recipient of such a notice will be threatened with homelessness if:

1) a valid notice has been given to them under HA 1988 s21;
2) the notice is in respect of the only accommodation which they have that is available for their occupation; and
3) the notice will expire within 56 days.[333]

7.135 If an applicant to a local housing authority is eligible for assistance and threatened with homelessness or homeless, then certain short-term duties arise:

1) in England, the local housing authority will become subject to a duty to assess the applicant's case and prepare a personalised housing plan;[334]
2) in England and Wales, if an applicant is eligible and threatened with homelessness, the local housing authority will owe the prevention duty;[335]
3) in England and Wales, if an applicant is eligible and homeless, the local housing authority will owe the relief duty.[336]

332 HA 1996 s175(4) (England); and H(W)A 2014 s55(4) (Wales).

333 HA 1996 s175(5). See para 7.254 for the special provision which applies in respect of HA 1988 s21 notices to applicants who accepted a private rented sector offer made pursuant to a previous homelessness application and then re-applied as homeless (to the same or a different local housing authority) within two years of the date on which they accepted that offer.

334 HA 1996 s189A. As discussed above at paras 7.103 and 7.105–7.106, a local housing authority in Wales owes a similar assessment duty (although not a duty to prepare a personalised housing plan) but this is not distinct from the duty to make inquiries and determine what duty is owed (as it is in England) and it arises before the local housing authority has determined whether or not the applicant is homeless or threatened with homelessness.

335 HA 1996 s195(1) (England); and H(W)A 2014 s66(1) (Wales). See paras 7.181–7.186 and 7.211–7.220.

336 HA 1996 s189B(2) (England); and H(W)A 2014 s73(1) (Wales). See paras 7.187–7.193 and 7.221–7.227.

Priority need

7.136 In order to determine what longer-term duty may be owed, the local housing must go on to consider whether or not the applicant has a 'priority need' for accommodation. If an applicant does not have a priority need for accommodation, then no further duty arises.[337] The exception to this is if an applicant to a local housing authority in England falls within the special provisions of HA 1996 s195A. This applies where the applicant is re-applying for homelessness assistance within two years of accepting a private rented sector offer[338] made pursuant to a previous application. If the local housing authority is satisfied that the applicant is homeless[339] and eligible for assistance,[340] and is not satisfied that the applicant became homeless intentionally,[341] then the main housing duty[342] will apply regardless of whether the applicant has a priority need.[343]

7.137 The categories of person who will have a priority need are prescribed at HA 1996 s189(1) and the Homelessness (Priority Need for Accommodation) Order 2002[344] ('Priority Need Order') (in respect of England); and in H(W)A 2014 s70 (in respect of Wales). There is a significant degree of overlap between the two sets of categories in England and Wales, but they are not identical.

7.138 In England, the following categories of person will have a priority need:

1) a pregnant woman or a person with whom she resides or might reasonably be expected to reside;[345]
2) a person with whom dependent children reside or might reasonably be expected to reside;[346]
3) a person who is vulnerable as a result of old age, mental illness or handicap or physical disability or other special reason, or with whom such a person resides or might reasonably be expected to

337 Save perhaps for a duty to protect the applicant's belongings: see paras 7.197–7.200 and 7.233–7.235. See paras 7.96–7.104 for a description of how the duties fit together.

338 'Private rented sector offer' is defined at HA 1996 s193(7AC).

339 See paras 7.121–7.133.

340 See paras 7.6–7.93.

341 See paras 7.152–7.157.

342 Under HA 1996 s193(2): see paras 7.263–7.269.

343 See paras 7.77–7.79 for a discussion of how this provision applies differently in restricted cases.

344 SI No 2051.

345 HA 1996 s189(1)(a).

346 HA 1996 s189(1)(b).

reside.[347] The Supreme Court has confirmed that 'vulnerable' means ' "significantly more vulnerable than ordinary vulnerable" as a result of being rendered homeless' when compared with the ordinary person if made homeless;[348]

4) a person who is homeless (or threatened with homelessness) as a result of an emergency such as a flood, fire, or other disaster;[349]
5) a person who is homeless as a result of that person being a victim of domestic abuse;[350]
6) a 16- or 17-year-old who is not a relevant or looked after child[351] under the Children Act (ChA) 1989;[352]
7) a person who is under 21 and who was looked after, accommodated, or fostered[353] between the ages of 16 and 18;[354]
8) a person who is vulnerable as a result of an institutional background (having been looked after, accommodated or fostered;[355] having been in the naval, military or air forces; or having been in prison[356]);[357] and
9) a person who is vulnerable as a result of ceasing to occupy accommodation by reason of violence (excluding domestic abuse) from another person or threats of violence from another person which are likely to be carried out.[358]

347 HA 1996 s189(1)(c).

348 *Hotak v Southwark LBC* [2015] UKSC 30, [2016] AC 811 at paras 53 and 57 per Lord Neuberger. See *Panayiotou v Waltham Forest LBC* [2017] EWCA Civ 1624, [2018] QB 1232 for the meaning of 'significantly' more vulnerable.

349 HA 1996 s189(1)(d).

350 HA 1996 s189(1)(e). 'Domestic abuse' has the meaning given by Domestic Abuse Act 2021 s1: see para 7.127. See *Homelessness code of guidance*, chapter 21.

351 See paras 7.144, 9.85–9.89 and 9.136–9.140 for the meaning of 'relevant child' and 'looked after child'.

352 Priority Need Order 2002 arts 2 and 3. A child who is a category 2 young person within the meaning of Social Services and Well-being (Wales) Act (SSWB(W)A) 2014 s104(2) or who is owed a duty under SSWB(W)A 2014 s76 is also excluded. See paras 9.258-9.261.

353 Priority Need Order 2002 art 1(3) defines 'looked after, accommodated or fostered' as having the meaning given by ChA 1989 s24(2), which is set out at para 7.144. See further paras 9.85–9.89.

354 Priority Need Order 2002 arts 2 and 4.

355 See fn 353.

356 Defined as having served a custodial sentence within the meaning of Powers of Criminal Courts (Sentencing) Act (PCC(S)A) 2000 s76 or Sentencing Act 2020 s222; having been committed for contempt of court or any other kindred offence; or having been remanded in custody within the meaning of PCC(S)A 2000 s88(1)(b), (c) or (d).

357 Priority Need Order 2002 arts 2 and 5.

358 Priority Need Order 2002 arts 2 and 6.

7.139 The categories which apply to Wales are as follows:

1) a pregnant woman or a person with whom she resides or might reasonably be expected to reside;[359]
2) a person with whom a dependent child resides or might reasonably be expected to reside;[360]
3) a person who is vulnerable as a result of some special reason (such as old age, physical or mental illness or physical or mental disability), or with whom such a person resides or might reasonably be expected to reside.[361] A person will be 'vulnerable' if they would be less able to fend for themself as a result of the special reason if the person were to become street homeless than would an ordinary homeless person who becomes street homeless and this would lead to the person suffering more harm than would be suffered by the ordinary homeless person;[362]
4) a person who is homeless or threatened with homelessness as a result of an emergency such as flood, fire or other disaster, or with whom such a person resides or might reasonably be expected to reside;[363]
5) a person who is homeless as a result of being subject to domestic abuse, or with whom such a person (other than the abuser) resides or might reasonably be expected to reside;[364]
6) a person who is aged 16 or 17 (at the time of their homelessness application) or with whom such a person resides or might reasonably be expected to reside;[365]
7) a person who is aged 18, 19, or 20 (at the time of their homelessness application) who is at particular risk of sexual or financial exploitation, or with whom such a person (other than the exploiter or potential exploiter) resides or might reasonably be expected to reside;[366]
8) a person who is aged 18, 19, or 20 (at the time of their homelessness application) who was looked after, accommodated or

359 H(W)A 2014 s70(1)(a).
360 H(W)A 2014 s70(1)(b).
361 H(W)A 2014 s70(1)(c).
362 H(W)A 2014 s71(1). See also *Code of guidance to local authorities on the allocation of accommodation and homelessness*, paras 16.71–16.78.
363 H(W)A 2014 s70(1)(d).
364 H(W)A 2014 s70(1)(e).
365 H(W)A 2014 s70(1)(f).
366 H(W)A 2014 s70(1)(g).

fostered at any time while under the age of 18 or with whom such a person resides or might reasonably be expected to reside;[367]

9) a person who has served in the regular armed forces of the Crown who has been homeless since leaving those forces or with whom such a person resides or might reasonably be expected to reside;[368]
10) a person who has a local connection with the area of the local housing authority and who is vulnerable as a result of having been to prison[369] or with whom such a person resides or might reasonably be expected to reside;[370]
11) as of 24 October 2022, a person who is street homeless or with whom such a person resides or might reasonably be expected to reside.[371] A person will be street homeless if they have no accommodation available for their occupation in the UK or elsewhere which they are entitled to occupy by virtue of an interest in it or by virtue of an order of a court; which they have a licence to occupy; or which they occupy as a residence by virtue of any enactment or rule of law giving them the right to remain in occupation or restricting the right of another person to recover possession.[372]

7.140 The category of being vulnerable for another 'special reason' may be of peculiar relevance to migrants, who are likely to face particular challenges which are different from other applicants. In *R v Kensington and Chelsea RLBC ex p Kihara*,[373] the Court of Appeal held that 'being vulnerable' was not limited to 'physical or mental weakness' but instead entailed 'an examination of all the personal circumstances of an applicant'.[374] The court found that, while financial impecuniosity on its own was not a special reason, the situation of

367 H(W)A 2014 s70(1)(h). See paras 9.258–9.261.

368 H(W)A 2014 s70(1)(i).

369 Defined as having served a custodial sentence within the meaning of PCC(S)A 2000 s76 or Sentencing Act 2020 s222; having been remanded in or committed to custody by a court order; or having been remanded to youth detention accommodation under Legal Aid, Sentencing and Punishment of Offenders Act 2012 s91(4).

370 H(W)A 2014 s70(1)(j).

371 H(W)A 2014 s70(1)(k), as introduced by Homelessness (Priority Need and Intentionality) (Wales) Regulations 2022 SI No 1069 (W 225) reg 2. Guidance on this category is provided at paras 1–38 of *Code of guidance: addendum*.

372 H(W)A 2014 s71(2).

373 (1997) 29 HLR 147, CA.

374 At p159 per Neill LJ.

asylum-seekers who had no income or capital, who were prohibited from working and therefore had no means of earning money, who had no family or friends in the UK, and who did not understand English did amount to this. This case pre-dates significant changes to the rules on eligibility, it being decided at a time when asylum-seekers who were awaiting a determination of their immigration status were able to access mainstream housing assistance.[375] It must also be read in light of the Supreme Court's decision in *Hotak v Southwark LBC*[376] which clarified the meaning of vulnerability in the context of priority need.[377] Nevertheless, *ex p Kihara* remains authority for the proposition that a constellation of factors, including but not limited to destitution, are capable of constituting a special reason by virtue of which an applicant may have a priority need.

7.141 The Welsh *Code of guidance to local authorities on the allocation of accommodation and homelessness* reminds local housing authorities of the need to take into account the difficulties experienced by former asylum-seekers, who:

> ... may well have experienced persecution or trauma in their country of origin or severe hardship in their efforts to reach the UK and may be vulnerable as a result. They are likely to have poor English language skills, have little knowledge or understanding of the cultural, social and economic customs and less likely to have any social networks on which they can call on for support.[378]

7.142 Victims of trafficking or modern slavery are not automatically considered to be in priority need and will therefore need to fit within one of the prescribed categories of persons described above. Given what is known about the experiences of many victims of trafficking and the acknowledged forms of exploitation, however, it is highly likely that an applicant who has experienced trafficking or modern slavery will have a special reason giving rise to vulnerability, if indeed they are not vulnerable on the grounds of physical or mental illness.[379] The English *Homelessness code of guidance* states:

> A person who has been a victim of trafficking or modern slavery may have a priority need for accommodation if they are assessed as being vulnerable according to section 189(1)(c) of the 1996 Act. In assessing whether they are vulnerable a housing authority should take into

375 See the Introduction.

376 [2015] UKSC 30, [2016] AC 811.

377 See para 7.138.

378 *Code of guidance to local authorities on the allocation of accommodation and homelessness*, para 16.32. See also paras 12.143–12.144.

379 See paras 11.127–11.224 (trafficking section of special cases chapter).

account advice from specialist agencies providing services to the applicant, such as their assigned support provider under the NRM. Many victims of modern slavery suffer from poor mental health and often lack support structures in the area they are residing. If a victim of modern slavery is threatened with homelessness or is homeless this significantly increases their risk to being re-trafficked or exposed to further exploitation.[380]

7.143 Other priority need categories which may be particularly pertinent for migrants are those relating to care leavers.[381] In England, there are two such categories. The first comprises a person, other than a relevant student, who is under the age of 21 and who was looked after, accommodated or fostered by a local authority at any time after reaching the age of 16 but before reaching the age of 18 (and who has now ceased so to be).[382] The second comprises a person who has reached the age of 21, who is not a relevant student, and who is vulnerable as a result of having been looked after, accommodated or fostered.[383]

7.144 Priority Need Order 2002 art 1(3) defines 'looked after, accommodated or fostered' as having the meaning given by ChA 1989 s24(2), which is:

(a) looked after[384] by a local authority (without subsequently being looked after by a local authority in Wales);
(b) accommodated by or on behalf of a voluntary organisation;
(c) accommodated in a private children's home;
(d) accommodated for a consecutive period of at least three months–
   (i) by any Local Health Board, Special Health Authority or by a local authority in the exercise of education functions, or
   (ii) in any care home or independent hospital or in any accommodation provided pursuant to arrangements made by the Secretary of State, the National Health Service Commissioning Board or a clinical commissioning group under the National Health Service Act 2006 or by a National Health Service trust or an NHS foundation trust, or by a local authority in Wales in the exercise of education functions; or
(e) privately fostered.

380 *Homelessness code of guidance*, para 25.22.

381 Priority Need Order 2002 arts 4 and 5; and H(W)A 2014 s70(1)(h): see paras 7.138 and 7.139. Although the term 'care leaver' is commonly used, in fact an applicant need not necessarily have been in care in order to fall within these categories: they may qualify if they were privately fostered.

382 Priority Need Order 2002 art 4.

383 Priority Need Order 2002 art 5(1).

384 See paras 9.85–9.89.

7.145 A child has been looked after if they were in the care of a local authority or provided with accommodation by the local authority in the exercise of any of its social services functions (apart from ChA 1989 s17, s23B or s24B) for more than 24 hours.[385]

7.146 'Relevant students' are excluded. Such persons are owed separate accommodation duties by children's services: see para 9.160. A 'relevant student' is a person:

1) who is under the age of 25;
2) who qualifies for advice and assistance by virtue of ChA 1989 s24(1A)[386] or (2)(a),[387] or would have done were they under 21;
3) who is in full-time further or higher education; and
4) whose term-time accommodation is not available during a vacation.[388]

7.147 These provisions mean that most recent care leavers aged between 18 and 20 will have a priority need for accommodation whether or not they are vulnerable. Care leavers aged 21 or over will have a priority need only if they are vulnerable as a result of having been looked after, accommodated or fostered (at any age). When determining whether a care leaver is vulnerable for this reason, relevant factors will include:

a) the length of time that the applicant was looked after, accommodated or fostered;
b) the reasons why they were looked after, accommodated or fostered;
c) the length of time since the applicant left care, and whether they have been able to obtain and maintain accommodation during any of that period;
d) whether the applicant has any existing support networks, particularly including family, friends or a mentor.[389]

385 ChA 1989 s22(1)–(2). For a more detailed discussion of the looked after child and leaving care regimes, see paras 9.71–9.185.

386 ChA 1989 s24(1A) states that it 'applies to a person– (a) who has reached the age of sixteen but not the age of twenty-one; (b) with respect to whom a special guardianship order is in force (or, if he has reached the age of eighteen, was in force when he reached that age); and (c) who was, immediately before the making of that order, looked after by a local authority'.

387 ChA 1989 s24(2)(a) refers to being 'looked after by a local authority (without subsequently being looked after by a local authority in Wales)'.

388 Priority Need Order art 1(3).

389 *Homelessness code of guidance*, para 22.22.

7.148 The relevant category in Wales refers to a person who has reached the age of 18 (at the time of their application for homelessness assistance) but not the age of 21, and who was looked after, accommodated or fostered at any time whilst under the age of 18. The category extends to a person residing with someone who meets this criteria (or who might reasonably be expected to reside with such a person).[390] 'Looked after, accommodated or fostered' is defined as meaning:

(a) looked after[391] by a local authority (within the meaning of section 74 of the Social Services and Well-Being (Wales) Act 2014 or section 22 of the Children Act 1989),
(b) accommodated by or on behalf of a voluntary organisation,
(c) accommodated in a private children's home,
(d) accommodated for a continuous period of at least three months–
   (i) by any Local Health Board or Special Health Authority,
   (ii) by or on behalf of a clinical commissioning group or the National Health Service Commissioning Board,
   (iii) by or on behalf of a county or county borough council in Wales in the exercise of education functions,
   (iv) by or on behalf of a local authority in England in the exercise of education functions,
   (v) in any care home or independent hospital, or
   (vi) in any accommodation provided by or on behalf of an NHS Trust or by or on behalf of an NHS Foundation Trust, or
(e) privately fostered (within the meaning of section 66 of the Children Act 1989).[392]

7.149 Pursuant to SSWB(W)A 2014 s74, a child is 'looked after' by a local authority if they are in its care or if they are provided with accommodation for a continuous period of more than 24 hours by the local authority in the exercise of any of its social services functions other than functions under SSWB(W)A 2014 s15, s109, s114 or s115.[393]

7.150 This category means that, in respect of Wales, all care leavers aged between 18 and 20, together with members of their household, will have a priority need. Although there is no special provision for care leavers over the age of 21 who are vulnerable as a result of their experiences in care, such applicants may well fall within the general category of vulnerability.[394]

390 H(W)A 2014 s70(1)(h).
391 See paras 9.258–9.261.
392 H(W)A 2014 s70(2).
393 See paras 9.258–9.261.
394 H(W)A 2014 s70(1)(c): see para 7.139.

7.151 Many of these applicants will be owed other duties of support by Children's Services under ChA 1989 ss23C–24D (in England) or the SSWB(W)A 2014 (in Wales): see paras 9.160–9.185 and 9.262.

Becoming homeless intentionally

7.152 If the applicant does have a priority need[395] for accommodation, then the last matter which the local housing authority will have to decide is whether or not the applicant became homeless intentionally. For local housing authorities in England, this test will apply to every applicant who has met the preceding criteria. For local housing authorities in Wales, however, the intentional homelessness test only applies where the authority has made an express decision to have regard to it.[396]

7.153 A person is intentionally homeless if they deliberately do, or fail to do, anything in consequence of which they cease to occupy accommodation.[397] The accommodation must have been available to the person and it must have been reasonable for them to continue to occupy it.[398] An act or omission is not deliberate if it was done in good faith by a person who was unaware of a relevant fact.[399] The deliberate act or omission, and the resulting loss of accommodation, must be an operative cause of the person's current homelessness.[400] The causal chain can be broken by supervening events including if the applicant obtains settled accommodation.[401]

7.154 A migrant who gives up accommodation abroad to come to the UK may find that in doing so they have made themself intentionally homeless. A situation which has been considered a number of times by the courts is that of applicants who arrived in the UK believing that they would have accommodation available to them, or employ-

395 See paras 7.136–7.151.

396 H(W)A 2014 s78. A local housing authority in Wales may only apply the intentional homelessness test to an applicant who falls within a category specified in the Homelessness (Intentionality) (Specified Categories) (Wales) Regulations 2015 SI No 1265, but as the categories specified therein mirror exactly the categories of persons who may have a priority need, this in practice includes all applicants to whom the test would be relevant. Having decided that it will apply the intentional homelessness test to all or some of those categories, the local housing authority must then publish a notice of that decision: H(W)A 2014 s78(2). It is understood that most local housing authorities in Wales have 'opted in' to this test to some extent.

397 HA 1996 s191(1) (England); and H(W)A 2014 s77(2) (Wales).

398 HA 1996 s191(1) (England); and H(W)A 2014 s77(2) (Wales). See paras 7.125–7.127.

399 HA 1996 s191(2) (England); and H(W)A 2014 s77(3) (Wales).

400 *Haile v Waltham Forest LBC* [2015] UKSC 34, [2015] AC 1471.

401 *Haile v Waltham Forest LBC* [2015] UKSC 34, [2015] AC 1471.

ment which would enable them to obtain accommodation, but who discovered on arrival that this was not in fact the case.[402] Such applicants have sought to argue that their deliberate act of leaving their accommodation abroad did not make them intentionally homeless because they were acting in ignorance of a relevant fact, namely the lack of accommodation and/or employment available to them in the UK. In considering such case, the Court of Appeal has distinguished between relevant facts (ignorance of which may mean that the applicant was not intentionally homeless) and 'matters of hope' (which will not).[403] An applicant whose chances of obtaining employment rested upon 'little more than a wing and a prayer' had not acted in ignorance of a relevant fact.[404]

7.155 An applicant who is homeless,[405] eligible[406] and in priority need,[407] but who became homeless intentionally, will *not* be owed the main housing duty[408] – subject to one important exception which applies only in Wales. By virtue of H(W)A 2014 s75(3),[409] certain categories of applicant in Wales will be owed the main housing duty under section 75(1) even if they became homeless intentionally. The relevant categories of applicant are as follows:

1) a pregnant woman or a person with whom she resides or might reasonably be expected to reside;
2) a person with whom a dependent child resides or might reasonably be expected to reside;
3) a person under the age of 21 or a person with whom a person under the age of 21 resides or might reasonably be expected to reside; and
4) a person who is aged 21 to 24 years who had been looked after, accommodated or fostered when a child, or a person with whom such a person resides or might reasonably be expected to reside.[410]

402 For a recent example, see *Ciftci v Haringey LBC* [2021] EWCA Civ 1772, [2022] HLR 9.

403 *R v Ealing LBC ex p Sukhija* (1994) 26 HLR 726, CA at p730.

404 *Aw-Aden v Birmingham City Council* [2005] EWCA Civ 1834, July 2006 *Legal Action* 29.

405 See paras 7.121–7.133.

406 See paras 7.6–7.93.

407 See paras 7.136–7.151.

408 Under HA 1996 s193(2) (England); and H(W)A 2014 s75(1) (Wales). See paras 7.263–7.269 and 7.284–7.293.

409 This was brought into force on 2 December 2019 by the Housing (Wales) Act 2014 (Commencement Order No 10) Order 2019 SI No 1479 (W 263).

410 H(W)A 2014 s75(3)(e).

7.156 Such an applicant will be owed the main housing duty, regardless of whether they became homeless intentionally,[411] provided that:

1) the relief duty[412] owed to the applicant has come to an end because the period of 56 days has ended *or* because the local housing authority is satisfied (before the end of the 56-day period) that reasonable steps have been taken to help to secure that suitable accommodation is available for occupation by the applicant;[413]
2) the local housing authority is satisfied that the applicant is homeless;[414]
3) the local housing authority is satisfied that the applicant is eligible;[415]
4) the local housing authority is satisfied that the applicant has a priority need;[416] and
5) the applicant had not previously been offered accommodation under the main housing duty pursuant to H(W)A 2014 s75(3) within the preceding five years.[417]

7.157 Advice on the operation of this provision is contained in supplementary guidance published by the Welsh Government in December 2019, entitled *Additional provisions under section 75(3)*.

Challenging decisions on homelessness applications

7.158 If a local housing authority refuses to accept a homelessness application, the applicant's remedy would be to apply for judicial review and seek a mandatory order requiring the authority to accept and make inquiries into their application.

411 H(W)A 2014 s75(1) and (3).

412 Under H(W)A 2014 s73(1). See paras 7.221–7.227.

413 H(W)A 2015 s75(1). This means that if, for example, the relief duty ended under H(W)A 2014 s74(5) because the applicant, having been informed of the consequences of refusal or acceptance, refused an offer of suitable accommodation which was likely to be available for at least six months, the main housing duty will not be owed.

414 H(W)A 2014 s75(3)(b).

415 H(W)A 2014 s75(3)(c).

416 H(W)A 2014 s75(3)(d).

417 H(W)A 2014 s75(3)(f). This appears to be the intended result of H(W)A 2014 s75(3)(f) although the drafting is somewhat unclear. H(W)A 2014 s75(3)(f)(i) refers to the period of '5 years before the day on which the applicant was notified under section 63 that a duty was owed to him or her under this section', which is difficult to understand given that the effect of H(W)A 2014 s 75(3)(f) is presumably that an applicant who falls foul of that subsection is not owed a duty under H(W)A 2014 s75 at all.

7.159 If a local housing authority in England, having accepted an application, considers that it does not have reason to believe that the applicant may be homeless,[418] eligible[419] and have a priority need[420] such that the interim accommodation duty[421] does not arise, then the applicant's remedy would again lie in an application for judicial review. The position is different in Wales. If a Welsh local housing authority considers that the interim accommodation duty[422] does not apply, or that it has come to an end, then the applicant in question has a statutory right to request a review of this decision and subsequently to appeal to the county court on a point of law.[423]

7.160 There are statutory rights of review and appeal in both England and Wales in respect of decisions that the applicant is not eligible, not homeless or threatened with homelessness, not in priority need, or became homeless intentionally.[424]

7.161 In England, these arise by virtue of HA 1996 s202(1)(b), which gives the applicant the right to request a review of any decision of a local housing authority as to what duty (if any) is owed[425] to them under:

1) HA 1996 s189B: the relief duty, owed to an applicant who is homeless and eligible.[426]
2) HA 1996 s190: the short-term accommodation duty, owed to an applicant who is homeless and eligible and has a priority need but who became homeless intentionally.[427]
3) HA 1996 s193: the main housing duty, owed to an applicant who is homeless and eligible for assistance, has a priority need, and did not become homeless intentionally.[428]

418 See paras 7.121–7.133.
419 See paras 7.6–7.93.
420 See paras 7.136–7.151.
421 HA 1996 s188(1): see paras 7.253–7.259.
422 H(W)A 2014 s68(1) and (2): see paras 7.275–7.283.
423 H(W)A 2014 ss85(1)(b) and (c) and 88(1).
424 See paras 7.326–7.350 for a discussion of the nature of the review and appeal process.
425 This includes a decision that a duty is no longer owed: *Warsame v Hounslow LBC* (2000) 32 HLR 335, CA.
426 See paras 7.187–7.193.
427 See paras 7.260–7.262.
428 See paras 7.263–7.269.

4) HA 1996 s193A: this section provides that if an applicant who is owed the relief duty[429] refuses a final offer of accommodation,[430] the relief duty will end and the main housing duty[431] will not apply.
5) HA 1996 s193C: this provides that if an applicant who is owed the relief or prevention duty[432] deliberately and unreasonably refuses to co-operate, the relief or prevention duty (whichever is applicable) will end and the main housing duty (if the applicant would be owed this) will not apply. A different accommodation duty will be owed instead.[433]
6) HA 1996 s195: the prevention duty, owed to an applicant who is threatened with homelessness and eligible.[434]

7.162 The decision that an applicant is not homeless or threatened with homelessness, does not have a priority need or became homeless intentionally will result in a decision that one or more of these duties does or does not apply, and thus the right to request a review will arise. HA 1996 s204(1) gives the applicant the right subsequently to appeal on a point of law to the county court against a decision made on review (or, if no decision has been made within the applicable timeframe, the original decision).

7.163 In Wales, the means of challenging a decision that the applicant is not eligible,[435] not homeless[436] or threatened with homelessness,[437] not in priority need,[438] or that they became homeless intentionally[439] arises by virtue of H(W)A 2014 s85(1)(b) and (c). These provisions give the applicant the right to request a review of a decision by a local housing authority that a duty is not owed (or has ended) under:

429 Under HA 1996 s189B(2). See paras 7.187–7.193.

430 This means either a 'final accommodation offer', defined at HA 1996 s193A(4), or a 'final Part 6 offer', defined at HA 1996 s193C(5). The applicant must first have been informed of the consequences of refusal and of the right to request a review of the suitability of the accommodation: HA 1996 s193A(1)(b).

431 See paras 7.263–7.269.

432 See paras 7.181–7.186 and 7.187–7.193.

433 See paras 7.270–7.274.

434 See paras 7.181–7.186.

435 See paras 7.6–7.93.

436 See paras 7.121–7.133.

437 See paras 7.134–7.135.

438 See paras 7.136–7.151.

439 See paras 7.152–7.157.

1) H(W)A 2014 s66: the prevention duty, owed to an applicant who is eligible and threatened with homelessness.[440]
2) H(W)A 2014 s68: the interim accommodation duty, owed to an applicant who the authority has reason to believe may be homeless, eligible for help and have a priority need for accommodation.[441] It is also owed to an applicant to whom the relief duty[442] applies and who the local housing authority has reason to believe, or is satisfied, has a priority need or who has been referred from a local housing authority in England under HA 1996 s198(1).[443]
3) H(W)A s73: the relief duty, owed to an applicant who is eligible and homeless.[444]
4) H(W)A s75: the main housing duty to secure accommodation for applicants in priority need once the relief duty has ended.[445]

7.164 As with the case of applicants to local housing authorities in England, a decision that an applicant to a local housing authority in Wales is not homeless or threatened with homelessness, does not have a priority need or did become homeless intentionally will result in a decision that one or more of these duties does or does not apply, and thus the right to request a review will arise.[446]

Non-accommodation duties

7.165 The aim of virtually all applicants seeking homelessness assistance is to secure an offer of accommodation from the local housing authority. However, not all eligible applicants achieve this outcome.[447] For

440 See paras 7.211–7.220.

441 See paras 7.275–7.283.

442 Under H(W)A 2014 s73(1). See paras 7.221–7.227.

443 HA 1996 s198(1) applies to applicants who would be owed the main housing duty under HA 1996 s193 but in whose case the conditions for referral to another local housing authority are met. See paras 7.294–7.317.

444 See paras 7.221–7.227.

445 The HW(A) 2014 s75(1) duty will not apply to applicants who have secured their own accommodation under the relief or prevention duty, who have refused offers of suitable accommodation made under the relief duty, or (in certain circumstances) who became homeless intentionally: H(W)A 2014 s73(2) and (3). See paras 7.221–7.227.

446 See paras 7.326–7.350 for a discussion of reviews and appeals in respect of homelessness decisions.

447 In January to March 2022 in England, 11,060 out of 15,800 applicants were found to be owed the main housing duty: *Table MD1 – Number of households by decision on duty owed at end of relief duty, England, January to March 2022*, DLUHC, July 2022.

many years, applicants who were not owed the main housing duty[448] were offered little help under the homelessness legislation. Applicants who had a priority need[449] but who had become homeless intentionally[450] were (and still are) entitled to accommodation for such period as the local housing authority considered would give them a reasonable opportunity of securing their own accommodation.[451] However, all that the local housing authority was required to do in respect of other applicants, who did not have a priority need, was to provide advice and assistance in any attempts they may make to secure their own accommodation.[452] Despite, or perhaps because of, the limited nature of this duty, it was often neglected.[453]

7.166 Concerns about the lack of assistance available beyond the main housing duty led to legislative changes aimed at requiring more robust prevention work and greater provision for applicants who did not have a priority need. These took place firstly in Wales, with the H(W)A 2014 (which came into force on 27 April 2015) and then in England, via amendments to the HA 1996 (which came into force on 3 April 2018).

7.167 Both regimes introduced three substantive new duties owed to applicants regardless of whether or not they have a priority need or became homeless intentionally. These are:

1) the duty to assess an applicant's case and (in England) to prepare a personalised housing plan;[454]
2) the prevention duty;[455]
3) the relief duty.[456]

448 See paras 7.263–7.269 and 7.284–7.293.

449 See paras 7.136–7.151.

450 See paras 7.152–7.157.

451 Provided that they were also homeless and eligible: HA 1996 s190(2)(a) (England) and H(W)A 2014 s69(5) (Wales). See paras 7.260–7.262 and 7.280. By virtue of H(W)A 2014 s75(3), some applicants in Wales are now entitled to the main housing duty despite having become homeless intentionally: see paras 7.285–7.286.

452 By virtue of HA 1996 ss190(3) and 192(2), which are no longer in force. These provisions ceased to apply to Wales when the H(W)A 2014 Part 2 came into force by virtue of H(W)A 2014 Sch 3 para 4. They were repealed in respect of England by Homelessness Reduction Act 2017 s5(5)(c) and (6) respectively.

453 See, for example, *More than a Roof: A report into Tackling Homelessness*, Department for Transport, Local Government and the Regions, March 2002; and *No one's priority: the treatment of single homeless people by local authority homelessness services*, Crisis, 2009.

454 See paras 7.204–7.210 and 7.169–7.180.

455 See paras 7.181–7.186 and 7.204–7.210.

456 See paras 7.187–7.193 and 7.221–7.227.

7.168 These duties are owed in addition to existing non-accommodation duties, which are considered at the end of this section.

England

Assessment and planning duty

7.169 If a local housing authority in England is satisfied that an applicant is homeless[457] or threatened with homelessness[458] and eligible for assistance,[459] the authority must 'make an assessment of the applicant's case'.[460] This must include an assessment of:

1) the circumstances that caused the applicant to become homeless or threatened with homelessness;
2) the applicant's housing needs, including what accommodation would be suitable for them; and
3) what support would be necessary for the applicant to be able to have and retain suitable accommodation.[461]

The authority must notify the applicant in writing of the outcome of the assessment.[462]

7.170 After completing the assessment, the authority must try to agree with the applicant what steps it and the applicant are to take for the purposes of securing that the applicant has and can retain suitable accommodation.[463] If these steps are agreed, they should be recorded in writing.[464] If they cannot be agreed, the authority should record this in writing together with any steps it considers it would be reasonable for the applicant to take for the purposes of securing that they have and can retain suitable accommodation as well as the steps it will take for the same purposes.[465] This written record of the steps to be taken – whether agreed or not – must be given to the applicant.[466] This will then constitute the applicant's personalised housing plan.[467]

457 See paras 7.121–7.133.

458 See paras 7.134–7.135.

459 See paras 7.6–7.93.

460 HA 1996 s189A(1). Guidance on the assessment process is found in *Homelessness code of guidance*, chapter 11.

461 HA 1996 s189A(2).

462 HA 1996 s189A(3).

463 HA 1996 s189A(4).

464 HA 1996 s189A(5).

465 HA 1996 s189A(6).

466 HA 1996 s189A(8).

467 Guidance on the contents of the personalised housing plan is found in *Homelessness code of guidance*, chapter 11.

7.171 The steps which the applicant has agreed or is required to take are important. If the applicant fails to take any of these steps, the local housing authority could decide that they have deliberately and unreasonably refused to co-operate.[468]

7.172 Determining that an applicant has deliberately and unreasonably refused to co-operate involves a two-stage process. First, the local housing authority must serve the applicant with a 'relevant warning'. This is a written notice which:

1) is given to the applicant by the local housing authority after the applicant has deliberately and unreasonably refused to take any step which they agreed to take or which was recorded by the local housing authority as being reasonable for the applicant to take for the purposes of securing that they have and can retain suitable accommodation;
2) warns the applicant that, if they deliberately and unreasonably refuse to take any such step after receiving the notice, the authority intends to give notice that they have deliberately and unreasonably refused to co-operate; and
3) explains the consequences of such a notice being given.[469]

7.173 The applicant must then be given a 'reasonable period' in which to take the step in question.[470] If the applicant still does not comply, then the local housing authority may give them notice that they have deliberately and unreasonably refused to co-operate.[471] The decision to give such a notice must be made by 'an officer of that local authority' and then authorised by a person who works for the authority, who was not involved in the decision to give the notice, and who is at least as senior as the officer who made that decision.[472]

7.174 An applicant may request a review of the decision to give notice of a deliberate and unreasonable refusal to co-operate.[473] The review

468 Under HA 1996 s189A(7), the local housing authority may also record in the personalised housing plan 'any advice for the applicant that the authority consider appropriate (including any steps the authority consider it would be a good idea for the applicant to take but which the applicant should not be required to take)'. A refusal by the applicant to comply with these advisory (but not compulsory) steps cannot amount to a deliberate and unreasonable refusal to co-operate: HA 1996 s193B(2).

469 HA 1996 s193B(5).

470 HA 1996 s193B(4)(b).

471 HA 1996 s193B(2).

472 Homelessness (Review Procedure etc) Regulations 2018 reg 3.

473 HA 1996 s202(1)(bb). See paras 7.326–7.350 for a discussion of reviews and appeals.

must be requested within 21 days of the date on which the applicant received the notice.[474] The applicant may then appeal to the court against the review decision (or against the original decision if no decision is made on the review) on a point of law.[475]

7.175 A decision that an applicant has deliberately and unreasonably refused to co-operate should not be made lightly. The English *Homelessness code of guidance* advises that, before even a warning is given, the authority should review its assessment of the applicant's case and the appropriateness of the steps therein and explain the consequences of not co-operating.[476] Before giving the final notice, it should be satisfied of the following:

1) the steps recorded in the applicant's personalised housing plan are reasonable in the context of the applicant's particular circumstances and needs;
2) the applicant understands what is required of them in order to fulfil the reasonable steps, and is therefore in a position to make a deliberate refusal;
3) the applicant is not refusing to co-operate as a result of a mental illness or other health need, for which they are not being provided with support, or because of a difficulty in communicating;
4) the applicant's refusal to co-operate with any step was deliberate and unreasonable in the context of their particular circumstances and needs.

7.176 The consequences of an applicant being given notice of a decision that they have deliberately and unreasonably refused to co-operate are that the prevention[477] or relief[478] duty (whichever is owed) will come to an end.[479] No further duty will be owed unless the local housing authority is satisfied that the applicant is (still) eligible for assistance and is homeless and has a priority need. If the local housing authority is satisfied of those matters, and also satisfied that the applicant did not become homeless intentionally, then the accommodation duty at HA 1996 s193C(4) will apply.[480] If, however, the local housing authority is satisfied that the applicant *did* become

474 HA 1996 s202(3).
475 HA 1969 s204(1).
476 *Homelessness code of guidance*, para 14.50.
477 See paras 7.181–7.186.
478 See paras 7.187–7.193.
479 HA 1996 s193C(2).
480 See paras 7.270–7.274.

homeless intentionally then the short-term accommodation duty at HA 1996 s190(2) will apply instead.[481]

7.177 The steps set out in the personalised housing plan for the applicant to take are therefore of significance. As to the steps the local housing authority is to take, the *Homelessness code of guidance* gives examples of measures the authority may wish to consider:[482]

1) attempting mediation/conciliation where an applicant is threatened with parent/family exclusion;
2) assessing whether applicants with rent arrears might be entitled to Discretionary Housing Payments (DHPs);
3) providing support to applicants, whether financial or otherwise, to access private rented accommodation;
4) assisting people at risk of violence and abuse wishing to stay safely in their home through provision of 'sanctuary' or other measures;
5) helping to secure or securing an immediate safe place to stay for people who are sleeping rough or at high risk of sleeping rough.

The assessment and the personalised housing plan must be kept under review and updated as necessary.[483]

7.178 An assessment does not have to 'deal with and set out every need that an applicant might possibly have' but it should contain 'the key needs' which would provide the ' "nuts and bolts" for any offer of accommodation'.[484] The assessment of the applicant's case, and the steps that were then to be taken to secure accommodation for the applicant, do not necessarily have to be contained within a single document:[485] determining whether the duty to provide a lawful assessment and personalised housing plan has been discharged requires an assessment of 'the totality of the written housing file as it might be viewed by a "reasonable and sensible housing officer" '.[486] The documentation should distinguish between an applicant's needs and their wishes so that it is 'obvious to the "reasonable and sensible

481 See paras 7.260–7.262.

482 *Homelessness code of guidance*, para 11.23.

483 HA 1996 s189A(9)–(11).

484 *XY v Haringey LBC* [2019] EWHC 2276 (Admin) at para 51 per Clive Sheldon QC sitting as a deputy judge of the High Court.

485 *XY v Haringey LBC* at para 54 per Clive Sheldon QC sitting as a deputy judge of the High Court.

486 *R (ZK) v Havering LBC* [2022] EWHC 1854 (Admin) at para 39 per Susie Alegre sitting as a deputy judge of the High Court.

housing officer" what exactly is needed for the . . . [applicant] . . . to find and retain suitable accommodation'.[487]

7.179 There is no right to request a review of the assessment. There is, however, a right to request a review of the local housing authority's decision regarding what steps it will take to help the applicant secure and retain accommodation.[488] The review process is subject to stricter deadlines than apply to other decisions: representations must be submitted by the applicant within two weeks and the decision itself made within three.[489] An applicant dissatisfied with the decision on review (or who has requested but not received a decision on review) may appeal to the county court on a point of law.[490]

7.180 It appears that there is no right to request a review – and therefore no right to an appeal – of the local housing authority's decision regarding what steps *the applicant* is to take to secure and retain accommodation.[491] This is surprising given the possible consequences for the applicant of failing to take those steps.[492] The remedy for an applicant who wished to challenge such a decision would be to apply for a judicial review on the basis of an error of law.

Prevention of homelessness duty

7.181 If a local housing authority in England is satisfied that an applicant is eligible for assistance[493] and threatened with homelessness,[494] then the prevention duty under HA 1996 s195(2) will apply.[495] The duty requires the local housing authority to 'take reasonable steps to help

487 *R (ZK) v Havering LBC* at para 45 per Susie Alegre sitting as a deputy judge of the High Court.

488 HA 2006 s202(1)(ba)(i) and (bc)(i). See paras 7.326–7.350 for a discussion of reviews and appeals.

489 Homelessness (Review Procedure etc) Regulations 2018 regs 5(3)(b) and 9(1)(a).

490 HA 1996 s204(1).

491 HA 1996 s202(1)(ba)(i) and (bc)(i) refer to a decision of a local housing authority as to the steps 'they' – implying the authority – are to take. The *Homelessness code of guidance* supports this interpretation, stating that applicants 'have a right under section 202 to request a review of the steps the housing authority is to take': para 11.36.

492 See paras 7.171–7.176.

493 See paras 7.6–7.93.

494 See paras 7.134–7.135.

495 Guidance on the prevention duty is found in *Homelessness code of guidance*, chapter 12.

the applicant to secure that accommodation does not cease to be available for the applicant's occupation'.[496]

7.182 In deciding what steps it will take, the local housing authority must have regard to its assessment of the applicant's case under HA 1996 s189A.[497] These steps should in any event have already been set out in the applicant's personalised housing plan.[498] The applicant has a right to request a review of, and thereafter to appeal, the steps which the local housing authority is to take.[499] The local housing authority has a power to provide accommodation under the prevention duty[500] but is not required to do so.

7.183 The *Homelessness code of guidance* suggests that:

> The first option to be explored with the applicant should be enabling them to remain in their current home, where suitable. Where this is not possible, the focus should be on helping to secure alternative accommodation that the applicant can move into in a planned way.[501]

7.184 The local housing authority can bring the prevention duty to an end by notifying the applicant that:

1) the local housing authority is satisfied that the applicant has suitable accommodation available for their occupation and a reasonable prospect of having suitable accommodation available for at least six months;[502]
2) the local housing authority is satisfied that it has complied with the prevention duty and 56 days have passed since the day on which the duty arose.[503] However, the duty cannot be ended on this ground if the applicant was served with a valid notice under HA 1988 s21 in respect of the only accommodation which is available

496 HA 1996 s195(2).
497 HA 1996 s195(3). See paras 7.169–7.180.
498 HA 1996 s189A(4)–(6). See also *Homelessness code of guidance,* para 12.7. See paras 7.169–7.180.
499 HA 1996 ss202(1)(bc)(i) and 204(1). See paras 7.326–7.350 for a discussion of reviews and appeals.
500 HA 1996 s205(3).
501 *Homelessness code of guidance,* para 12.4.
502 HA 1996 s195(8)(a). The *Homelessness code of guidance,* suggests at para 14.11 that 'a move into accommodation in a lodging or sponsorship arrangement whereby the household shares accommodation in a private home with a "host" household, such as the sponsorship arrangements in place under the Homes for Ukraine scheme' may amount to suitable accommodation for the purposes of this subsection.
503 HA 1996 s195(8)(b).

to the applicant and that notice has expired or is due to expire within 56 days;[504]

3) the local housing authority is satisfied that the applicant has become homeless.[505] Provided that the applicant remains eligible,[506] the local housing duty will now owe the relief duty under HA 1996 s189B(2)[507] and may also owe the interim accommodation duty under HA 1996 s188(1);[508]
4) the local housing authority is satisfied that the applicant has refused an offer of suitable accommodation and on the date of refusal there was a reasonable prospect that suitable accommodation would be available for at least six months;[509]
5) the local housing authority is satisfied that the applicant has become homeless intentionally[510] from any accommodation that was made available under the prevention duty;[511]
6) the local housing authority is satisfied that the applicant is no longer eligible[512] for assistance;[513]
7) the local housing authority is satisfied that the applicant has withdrawn their homelessness application;[514] or
8) the local housing authority considers that the applicant has deliberately and unreasonably refused to co-operate following a warning.[515]

7.185 In all of these circumstances, the applicant must be given a formal notice bringing the duty to an end. In the first seven situations, the applicant must be given a written notice specifying on what basis the duty is being brought to an end and informing the applicant of their

504 HA 1996 s195(6).
505 HA 1996 s195(8)(c). See paras 7.121–7.133 for a discussion of the meaning of 'homelessness'.
506 See paras 7.6–7.93.
507 See paras 7.187–7.193.
508 See paras 7.253–7.259.
509 HA 1996 s195(8)(d).
510 See paras 7.152–7.157.
511 HA 1996 s195(8)(e). Case-law has established that an applicant in interim accommodation remains homeless and therefore cannot become homeless intentionally from that accommodation: *Alam v Tower Hamlets LBC* [2009] EWHC 44 (Admin). In order for the applicant to be able to become homeless intentionally from the accommodation provided under the prevention duty, the accommodation will probably have to be reasonably permanent, in which case the prevention duty is likely to have already ended under a different provision.
512 See paras 7.6–7.93.
513 HA 1996 s195(8)(f).
514 HA 1996 s195(8)(g).
515 HA 1996 ss193B(2), 193C(2) and 195(10). See paras 7.171–7.176.

right to request a review within 21 days.[516] The notice brings the duty to an end.[517] In the last circumstance, the applicant must be given a written notice setting out the reasons for the notice, its effect and the applicant's right to request a review within 21 days.[518] Again, the notice brings the duty to an end.[519]

7.186 An applicant may request a review of the decision to give notice that the prevention duty has come to an end where the local housing authority states that it is satisfied of one of the matters set out at para 7.184 1)–7) above.[520] An applicant may also request a review of the decision to notify them that they have deliberately and unreasonably refused to co-operate.[521] An applicant may also request a review of the suitability of any accommodation[522] offered in discharge of the prevention duty.[523] The applicant may appeal any decision on review (or the original decision in the absence of a review decision) to the county court on a point of law.[524]

Relief of homelessness duty

7.187 If the local housing authority is satisfied that an applicant is homeless[525] and eligible for assistance,[526] then the relief duty under HA 1996 s189B(2) will arise. The local housing authority must 'take reasonable steps to help the applicant to secure that suitable accommodation becomes available for the applicant's occupation' for at least six months.

7.188 The relief duty will not, however, arise if the local housing authority refers the applicant to another local housing authority in England.[527] This exception does not apply in respect of the prevention duty,[528] the performance of which cannot be referred.

516 HA 1996 s195(7). See paras 7.326–7.350 for a discussion of reviews and appeals.
517 HA 1996 s195(5).
518 HA 1996 s193B(3).
519 HA 1996 ss193B(1) and 193C(1) and (2).
520 HA 1996 s202(1)(bc)(ii).
521 HA 1996 s202(1)(bb). This is the situation described at para 7.184 8).
522 See paras 7.239–7.252.
523 HA 1996 s202(1)(f).
524 HA 1996 s204(1). See para 7.326–7.350 for a discussion of reviews and appeals in respect of homelessness decisions.
525 See paras 7.121–7.133.
526 See paras 7.6–7.93.
527 HA 1996 s189B(2). An applicant's case may be referred to another local housing authority in England under HA 1996 s198(A1) where certain conditions are met: see paras 7.294–7.317.
528 See paras 7.181–7.186.

7.189 In deciding what steps to take, the authority must have regard to its assessment of the applicant's case under HA 1996 s189A.[529] These steps should in any event have already been set out in the applicant's personalised housing plan.[530] The applicant has a right to request a review of, and thereafter to appeal, the steps which the local housing authority is to take.[531] The local housing authority has a power to provide accommodation under the relief duty[532] but is not required to do so.

7.190 The relief duty can come to an end in ten different circumstances:

1) if the local housing authority is satisfied that the applicant has a priority need[533] and is not satisfied that the applicant became homeless intentionally,[534] then the duty will end 56 days after it arose;[535]
2) the local housing authority is satisfied that the applicant has suitable accommodation available for their occupation and a reasonable prospect of having suitable accommodation available for at least six months;[536]
3) the local housing authority is satisfied that it has complied with the relief duty and 56 days have passed since the day on which the relief duty arose;[537]
4) the local housing authority is satisfied that the applicant has refused an offer of suitable accommodation and on the date of refusal there was a reasonable prospect that suitable accommodation would be available for at least six months;[538]

529 HA 1996 s189B(3). See paras 7.169–7.180.

530 HA 1996 s189A(4)–(6). See also *Homelessness code of guidance*, para 13.5. See paras 7.169–7.180.

531 HA 1996 ss202(1)(ba)(i) and 204(1). See paras 7.326–7.350 for a discussion of reviews and appeals.

532 HA1996 s205(3).

533 See paras 7.136–7.151.

534 See paras 7.152–7.157.

535 HA 1996 s189B(4).

536 HA 1996 s189B(7)(a). The *Homelessness code of guidance*, suggests at para 14.11 that 'a move into accommodation in a lodging or sponsorship arrangement whereby the household shares accommodation in a private home with a "host" household, such as the sponsorship arrangements in place under the Homes for Ukraine scheme' may amount to suitable accommodation for the purposes of this subsection.

537 HA 1996 s189B(7)(b).

538 HA 1996 s189B(7)(c).

5) the local housing authority is satisfied that the applicant has become homeless intentionally from any accommodation that was made available under the relief duty;[539]
6) the local housing authority is satisfied that the applicant is no longer eligible for assistance;[540]
7) the local housing authority is satisfied that the applicant has withdrawn their application for homelessness assistance;[541]
8) the applicant has refused a final accommodation offer,[542] having been informed of the consequences of refusal and of their right to request a review of the suitability of the accommodation offered.[543] Such an offer cannot be made if the applicant is under contractual or other obligations in respect of their existing accommodation which they are unable to bring to an end before being required to take up the offer;[544]
9) the applicant has refused a final Part 6 offer,[545] having been informed of the consequences of refusal and of their right to request a review of the suitability of the accommodation offered.[546] Such an offer cannot be made if the applicant is under contractual or other obligations in respect of their existing accommodation which they are unable to bring to an end before being required to take up the offer;[547] or
10) the local housing authority has notified the applicant that it considers they have deliberately and unreasonably refused to co-operate following a warning.[548]

539 HA 1996 s189B(7)(d). Case-law has established that an applicant in interim accommodation remains homeless and therefore cannot become homeless intentionally from that accommodation: *Alam v Tower Hamlets LBC* [2009] EWHC 44 (Admin). In order for the applicant to be able to become homeless intentionally from accommodation provided under the relief duty, the accommodation will probably have to be reasonably permanent, in which case the relief duty is likely to have already ended under a different provision. See paras 7.152–7.157 for the meaning of becoming homeless intentionally.

540 HA 1996 s189B(7)(e). See paras 7.6–7.93 for the meaning of 'eligible for assistance'.

541 HA 1996 s189B(7)(f).

542 This is defined at HA 1996 s193A(4).

543 HA 1996 ss189B(9)(a) and 193A(2). See paras 7.239–7.252 for a discussion of suitability.

544 HA 1996 s193A(7).

545 This is defined at HA 1996 s193A(5).

546 HA 1996 ss189B(9)(a) and 193A(2). See paras 7.239–7.252 for a discussion of suitability.

547 HA 1996 s193A(7).

548 HA 1996 ss189B(9)(b), 193B(2) and 193C(2). See paras 7.171–7.176.

7.191 In the first situation, there is no requirement to give written notice. The duty will end automatically. In the second to seventh circumstances, the applicant must be given a written notice specifying on what basis the duty is being brought to an end and informing the applicant of their right to request a review within 21 days.[549] The notice brings the duty to an end.[550] In the eighth and ninth scenarios, there is no requirement to give notice specifically bringing the duty to an end, but the applicant must be informed of the consequences of refusal of the offer, which will include the fact that the relief duty will end.[551] There is a specific requirement that the final Part 6 offer must be in writing.[552] There is no such statutory requirement in respect of a final accommodation offer, but it is likely that it will also be made in writing. The duty ends when the offer is refused.[553] In the tenth situation, the applicant must be given a written notice setting out the reasons for the notice, its effect, and the applicant's right to request a review within 21 days.[554] Again, the notice brings the duty to an end.[555]

7.192 An applicant may request a review of:

1) the decision that the relief duty has come to an end because the applicant has a priority need, did not become homeless intentionally, and 56 days have passed;[556]
2) the decision to give notice to the applicant that the relief duty has come to an end because the local housing authority is satisfied of one of the matters set out at para 7.190 2)–7) above;[557]
3) the decision to notify the applicant that they have deliberately and unreasonably refused to co-operate;[558] and
4) the suitability of any accommodation offered to bring the relief duty to an end or as a final Part 6 or final accommodation offer.[559]

549 HA 1996 s189B(6). See paras 7.326–7.350 for a discussion of reviews and appeals.
550 HA 1996 s189B(5).
551 HA 1996 s193A(1)(b).
552 HA 1996 s193A(5).
553 HA 1996 s193A(2).
554 HA 1996 s193B(3).
555 HA 1996 ss193B(1) and 193C(1) and (2).
556 HA 1996 s202(1)(b).
557 HA 1996 s202(1)(ba)(ii).
558 HA 1996 s202(1)(bb).
559 HA 1996 s202(1)(f) and (h). See paras 7.239–7.252 for a discussion of suitability.

7.193 The applicant may appeal any decision on review (or the original decision in the absence of a review decision) to the county court on a point of law.[560]

Other non-accommodation duties

7.194 In addition to the above duties of assessment,[561] planning,[562] prevention[563] and relief,[564] the local housing authority in England may be subject to a number of other non-accommodation duties in respect of a homelessness applicant.

7.195 **First**, where the applicant's household contains a child,[565] and the local housing authority has reason to believe that the applicant may be ineligible for assistance or may have become homeless intentionally,[566] then the authority must invite the applicant to agree that 'the essential facts' of their case be referred to social services.[567] If the applicant does so consent, the local housing authority must then make the social services authority aware of those facts and of any subsequent decision reached by the local housing authority in the applicant's case.[568]

7.196 A social services authority which has been made aware that an applicant has been found to be ineligible or to have become homeless intentionally may request the local housing authority to provide it with advice and assistance in the exercise of its functions under ChA 1989 Part III.[569] The local housing authority which has received such a request must provide 'such advice and assistance as is reasonable in the circumstances'.[570]

7.197 **Second**, the local housing authority may be subject to a duty to protect an applicant's belongings.[571] This duty will apply where:

560 HA 1996 s204(1). See paras 7.326–7.350 for a discussion of reviews and appeals in respect of homelessness decisions.

561 See paras 7.169–7.180.

562 See paras 7.169–7.180.

563 See paras 7.181–7.186.

564 See paras 7.187–7.193.

565 Defined as a person under 18: HA 1996 s213A(1).

566 HA 1996 s213A(1). See paras 7.6–7.93 for eligibility and 7.152–7.157 for intentional homelessness.

567 HA 1996 s213A(2)(a).

568 HA 1996 s213A(2)(b).

569 See paras 9.7–9.69 for a discussion of the functions which the social services authority may have a duty or power to exercise following such a referral.

570 HA 1996 s213A(5).

571 See *Homelessness code of guidance*, chapter 20.

1) the local housing authority has reason to believe that there is a danger of loss of, or damage to, the applicant's personal property due to the applicant's inability to protect or deal with it;[572]
2) the local housing authority has reason to believe that no other suitable arrangements have been or are being made;[573] and
3) the local housing authority is or has been subject to:[574]
   a) the interim duty to accommodate;[575]
   b) the relief duty;[576]
   c) the prevention duty;[577]
   d) the short-term accommodation duty owed in certain cases of intentional homelessness;[578]
   e) the main housing duty;[579] or
   f) any of the accommodation duties owed where an applicant is owed the main housing duty but is being considered for referral to another local housing authority.[580]

7.198 The duty requires the local housing authority to take reasonable steps to prevent the loss of property or to prevent or mitigate damage to the property.[581] The local housing authority may decline to take action except upon such conditions as it considers appropriate, which may include conditions as to the levying of charges or disposal of the property in specified circumstances.[582] If no duty arises, the local housing authority has a power to take any steps it considers reasonable for the same purpose.[583]

7.199 The duty will end:

1) once the local housing authority considers that there is no longer any reason to believe that there is a danger of loss of or damage to the applicant's property due to their inability to protect or deal with it;[584] or

572 HA 1996 s211(1)(a).
573 HA 1996 s211(1)(b).
574 HA 1996 s211(2).
575 Under HA 1996 s188: see paras 7.253–7.259.
576 Under HA 1996 s189B(2): see paras 7.187–7.193.
577 Under HA 1996 s195(2): see paras 7.181–7.186.
578 Under HA 1996 s190(2): see paras 7.260–7.262.
579 Under HA 1996 s193(2): see paras 7.263–7.269.
580 Under HA 1996 s200: see paras 7.320–7.322.
581 HA 1996 s211(2).
582 HA 1996 s211(4).
583 HA 1996 s211(3).
584 HA 1996 212(3).

2) if the authority has, at the applicant's request, moved the property to a location specified by them.[585]

7.200 If the local housing authority decides it is not subject to this duty, then there is no right to request a review. An applicant seeking to challenge such a decision would have to apply for judicial review on the basis that the local housing authority had erred in law or bring a claim in the county court for breach of duty.[586]

7.201 **Finally**, where a local housing authority is satisfied that an applicant is homeless,[587] eligible for assistance,[588] has a priority need[589] and became homeless intentionally,[590] then it must provide them (or secure that they are provided with) advice and assistance in any attempts they may make to secure that accommodation becomes available for their occupation.[591]

7.202 In deciding what advice and assistance to provide, the local housing authority must:

1) take into account its assessment of the applicant's case under HA 1996 s189A;[592] and
2) provide information about 'the likely availability' in its district of 'types of accommodation appropriate to the applicant's housing needs'.[593]

7.203 This duty arises once the relief duty[594] has ended and exists in tandem with the duty to provide accommodation for such period as it considers will give the applicant a reasonable opportunity of securing their own accommodation.[595]

Wales

Assessment duty

7.204 If a person has applied for homelessness assistance to a local housing authority in Wales, and it appears to the authority that they may be

585 HA 1996 s212(2).
586 See, for example, *Deadman v Southwark LBC* (2001) 33 HLR 75, CA.
587 See paras 7.121–7.133.
588 See paras 7.6–7.93.
589 See paras 7.136–7.151.
590 See paras 7.152–7.157.
591 HA 1996 s190(2)(b).
592 HA 1996 s190(4).
593 HA 1996 s190(5).
594 Under HA 1996 s189B(2). See paras 7.187–7.193.
595 Under HA 1996 s190(2)(a). See paras 7.260–7.262.

homeless[596] or threatened with homelessness,[597] then the authority must 'carry out an assessment' of their case.[598] The only exception to this is if the applicant had been previously assessed by a local housing authority in Wales and the authority in receipt of the new application is satisfied that:

a) the person's circumstances have not changed materially since that assessment was carried out, and
b) there is no new information that materially affects that assessment.[599]

7.205 The assessment must include a determination of whether or not the applicant is eligible for help.[600] If the applicant is eligible, the assessment must also include an assessment of:

1) the circumstances that caused the applicant to become homeless or threatened with homelessness;[601]
2) the housing needs of the applicant and their household;[602]
3) the support needed for the applicant and their household to be able to retain any accommodation which is or may become available;[603]
4) whether or not the local housing authority has any duty under H(W)A 2014 Part 2;[604]
5) what outcome the applicant seeks from their application;[605] and
6) whether 'the exercise of any function' under H(W)A 2014 Part 2 could 'contribute to the achievement of that outcome'.[606]

7.206 The local housing authority may proceed to consider these matters before having determined whether or not the applicant is eligible.[607]

596 See paras 7.121–7.133.
597 See paras 7.134–7.135.
598 H(W)A 2014 s62(1). Guidance on the duty to assess is contained in *Code of guidance to local authorities on the allocation of accommodation and homelessness*, chapter 10, and in *Code of guidance: addendum*, paras 42–48.
599 H(W)A 2014 s62(2).
600 H(W)A 2014 s62(4). See paras 7.6–7.93 for eligibility.
601 H(W)A 2014 s62(5)(a).
602 H(W)A 2014 s62(5)(b).
603 H(W)A 2014 s62(5)(c).
604 H(W)A 2014 s62(5)(d).
605 H(W)A 2014 s62(6)(a).
606 H(W)A 2014 s62(6)(b).
607 H(W)A 2014 s62(7).

7.207 The local housing authority should aim to complete the assessment process, and notify the applicant of the outcome, 'as soon as possible' and in most cases within ten days.[608]

7.208 The local housing authority must keep its assessment under review for as long as it owes a duty to the applicant under H(W)A 2014 Part 2.[609] It is, however, specifically required to review its assessment in two circumstances:[610]

1) The first situation is where an applicant has been notified that the prevention duty[611] is owed, and it appears to the local housing authority that this duty has or is likely to come to an end because the applicant is homeless.
2) The second situation is where an applicant has been notified that the relief duty[612] is owed and it appears to the local housing authority that this duty has or is likely to come to an end in circumstances where the main housing duty[613] may be owed.

7.209 The local housing authority must notify the applicant of the outcome of the assessment (or any review of its assessment).[614] If any issue has been decided against the applicant's interests, then the notification must include reasons.[615] The notification must be in writing and must inform the applicant of the right to request a review of the decision within 21 days.[616]

7.210 There is not, as in England, a requirement to prepare a personalised housing plan,[617] but the Welsh *Code of guidance to local authorities on the allocation of accommodation and homelessness* suggests that it would be 'best practice' to prepare such a document.[618]

608 *Code of guidance to local authorities on the allocation of accommodation and homelessness*, para 10.5.
609 H(W)A 2014 s62(8).
610 H(W)A 2014 s62(9).
611 Under H(W)A 2014 s66. See paras 7.211–7.220.
612 Under H(W)A 2014 s73. See paras 7.221–7.227.
613 Under H(W)A 2014 s75. See paras 7.284–7.293.
614 H(W)A 2014 s63(1).
615 H(W)A 2014 s63(1).
616 H(W)A 2014 s63(4). See paras 7.326–7.335 for a discussion of reviews of homelessness decisions.
617 See paras 7.169–7.180.
618 *Code of guidance to local authorities on the allocation of accommodation and homelessness*, para 12.17.

Prevention of homelessness duty

7.211 If a local housing authority in Wales is satisfied that an applicant is eligible for assistance[619] and threatened with homelessness,[620] then the prevention duty under H(W)A 2014 s66(1) will apply. The duty requires the local housing authority to 'help to secure that suitable accommodation does not cease to be available for occupation' by the applicant.[621]

7.212 The ambit of 'help to secure' is clarified at H(W)A 2014 s65 which states that the local housing authority:

a) is required to take reasonable steps to help, having regard (among other things) to the need to make the best use of the authority's resources;
b) is not required to secure an offer of accommodation under HA 1996 Part VI (allocation of housing);
c) is not required to otherwise provide accommodation.

7.213 Further guidance is given in H(W)A 2014 s64, which gives examples of the ways in which the local housing authority may secure or help to secure that suitable accommodation is available or does cease to be available. These include:

1) arranging mediation;
2) providing information and advice;
3) making or guaranteeing payments;
4) providing accommodation
5) supporting applicants in managing debts, mortgage arrears or rent arrears;
6) putting in place security measures for applicants at risk of abuse; and
7) providing advocacy or other representation.[622]

7.214 The local housing authority may provide these services itself or arrange for someone else to provide them.[623]

7.215 Chapter 12 of the Welsh *Code of guidance to local authorities on the allocation of accommodation and homelessness* contains numerous examples of steps that may be taken in performance of this duty.[624]

619 See paras 7.6–7.93.
620 See paras 7.134–7.135.
621 HW(A) 2014 s66(1).
622 H(W)A 2014 s64(2).
623 H(W)A 2014 s64(1).
624 *Code of guidance to local authorities on the allocation of accommodation and homelessness*: see particularly para 12.13.

Chapter 12 also contains guidance on assisting 'Groups Most at Risk of Homelessness', which include refugees, former asylum-seekers and people from ethnic minority backgrounds.[625] Paragraphs 12.68–12.69 set out a number of issues which local housing authorities should consider when assisting such applicants:

> 12.68 . . .
>
> 1. A lack of awareness of housing procedures and rights and a lack of confidence to enforce rights, especially for recently settled migrants and refugees. This barrier is often compounded due to the presence of language barriers. There is also a fear of being viewed as 'a trouble maker' by housing staff.
>
> 2. The visibility, accessibility and appropriateness of housing services and support. The barrier in terms of the perceived lack of cultural sensitivity of mainstream housing and related services for BME people. Also identified was a lack of effective signposting between services and the need to address wider support needs that could impact on a person's ability to sustain their tenancy if not addressed.
>
> 3. The appropriateness of accommodation and access to good quality and affordable housing.
>
> 12.69 Other issues to note are:
>
> - Hidden homelessness i.e. BME people not presenting at all to services when they find themselves in housing need. It is important to note that people from the Gypsy or Traveller communities might be deterred from approaching the Local Authority for help due to the fear of being placed in bricks and mortar housing.
> - A lack of awareness of refugee specific experiences in statutory services.
> - A preference for 'own' services (ie services delivered by those within their own community) due to perceptions that specialist organisations are more appropriate and sensitive to their culture.
> - Fear of racial harassment in social and private rented housing and in temporary accommodation.

7.216 Paragraph 12.70 recommends that, to address such issues, local housing authorities should:

1) ensure that advice and information about homelessness and the prevention of homelessness is available in a range of languages;
2) ensure that a good quality interpretation service is available;
3) monitor local BME and migration data;
4) ensure that checks aimed at establishing eligibility are carried out 'in a manner that does not discriminate on the basis of race,

625 *Code of guidance to local authorities on the allocation of accommodation and homelessness*, paras 12.65–12.70 and 12.143–12.148.

colour, nationality, national or ethnic origins and deals with applicants in a sensitive manner';
5) ensure that homelessness services are 'culturally sensitive to the needs of different communities'; and
6) when addressing housing need, consider issues such as proximity to places of worship or community facilities.

7.217 The prevention duty will come to an end where the applicant is notified[626] that the local housing authority is satisfied that:
1) the applicant has become homeless;[627]
2) the applicant is no longer threatened with homelessness and suitable accommodation is likely to be available for the applicant for at least six months;[628]
3) the applicant, having been informed of the consequences of acceptance and refusal, has refused an offer of suitable accommodation where the accommodation was likely to be available for at least six months;[629]
4) the applicant is not, or is no longer, eligible;[630]
5) a mistake of fact led to the applicant being notified that a duty was owed to them;[631]
6) the applicant has withdrawn their application;[632] or
7) the applicant is unreasonably failing to co-operate with the local housing authority in connection with its homelessness functions.[633]

7.218 As indicated, in all these circumstances, the applicant must be notified of the local housing authority's decision that the duty is ended. The notice must be in writing[634] and must inform the applicant:

626 Under H(W)A 2014 s84.

627 H(W)A 2014 s67(2). In this situation, the local housing authority must review its assessment of the applicant's case: H(W)A 2014 s62(9). See paras 7.121–7.133 for homelessness.

628 H(W)A 2014 s67(3). See paras 7.134–7.135 for threatened with homelessness.

629 H(W)A 2014 s67(4). See paras 7.239–7.252 for suitability.

630 H(W)A 2014 s79(2). See paras 7.6–7.93 for eligibility.

631 H(W)A 2014 s79(3).

632 H(W)A 2014 s79(4).

633 H(W)A 2014 s79(5). Guidance on unreasonable failure to co-operate is given at paras 15.86–15.89 of the Welsh Government's *Code of guidance to local authorities on the allocation of accommodation and homelessness*, and at paras 53–54 and 59 of *Code of guidance: addendum*.

634 H(W)A 2014 s84(3).

1) that the local housing authority no longer regards itself as being subject to the duty in question;
2) why it considers the duty to have come to an end; and
3) that the applicant has the right to request a review, which must be done within 21 days of the day on which the applicant is notified of the decision.[635]

7.219 Moreover, in the third situation – refusal of an offer of suitable accommodation – the applicant must also have been notified in writing, prior to their refusal, of the possible consequences of acceptance and refusal.[636]

7.220 An applicant may request a review of the decision that the prevention duty has come to an end.[637] They may also request a review of the suitability of any accommodation[638] offered in, or in connection with, the discharge of the prevention duty, whether or not the accommodation has been accepted.[639] The applicant may then appeal the review decision (or, if no decision is made on the review, the original decision) to the county court on a point of law.[640]

Relief of homelessness duty

7.221 If a local housing authority in Wales is satisfied that an applicant is eligible for assistance[641] and homeless,[642] then the relief duty under H(W)A 2014 s73(1) will apply. The duty requires the local housing authority to 'help to secure that suitable accommodation is available for occupation by an applicant'.[643]

7.222 The relief duty will not, however, arise if the local housing authority refers the applicant to another local housing authority in either England or Wales.[644] This exception does not apply in respect of the prevention duty,[645] the performance of which cannot be referred.

635 H(W)A 2014 s84(1). See paras 7.326–7.350 for a discussion of reviews and appeals.
636 H(W)A 2014 s67(4).
637 H(W)A 2014 s85(1)(c).
638 See paras 7.239–7.252.
639 H(W)A 2014 s85(3).
640 H(W)A 2014 s88(1).
641 See paras 7.6–7.93.
642 See paras 7.121–7.133.
643 H(W)A 2014 s73(1).
644 H(W)A 2014 s73(2). An applicant's case may be referred under H(W)A 2014 s80 to another local housing authority where certain conditions are met: see paras 7.294–7.325.
645 See paras 7.211–7.220.

7.223 The scope of 'help to secure' is clarified at H(W)A 2014 s65 and examples as to how this duty may be discharged are contained at H(W)A 2014 s64 and in the Welsh *Code of guidance to local authorities on the allocation of accommodation and homelessness* in chapters 12 and 13.

7.224 The relief duty will come to an end where the applicant is notified[646] that:

1) 56 days have passed since the day on which the applicant was notified of the outcome of the assessment of their case;[647]
2) the local housing authority is satisfied that reasonable steps have been taken to help to secure that suitable accommodation is available for occupation by the applicant;[648]
3) the local housing authority is satisfied that the applicant has suitable accommodation available for their occupation which is likely to be available for at least six months;[649]
4) the applicant, having been informed of the possible consequences of acceptance and refusal, refuses an offer of suitable accommodation where the accommodation was likely to be available for at least six months;[650]
5) the local housing authority is satisfied that the applicant is not, or is no longer, eligible;[651]
6) the local housing authority is satisfied that a mistake of fact led to the applicant being notified that a duty was owed to them;[652]
7) the local housing authority is satisfied that the applicant has withdrawn their application;[653] or
8) the local housing authority is satisfied that the applicant is unreasonably failing to co-operate with the local housing authority in connection with its homelessness functions.[654]

646 Under H(W)A 2014 s84.
647 H(W)A 2014 s74(2) and (6).
648 H(W)A 2014 s74(3). See paras 7.239–7.252 for suitability.
649 H(W)A 2014 s74(4).
650 H(W)A 2014 s74(5).
651 H(W)A 2014 s79(2). See paras 7.6–7.93 for eligibility.
652 H(W)A 2014 s79(3).
653 H(W)A 2014 s79(4).
654 H(W)A 2014 s79(5). Guidance on unreasonable failure to co-operate is given in the *Code of guidance to local authorities on the allocation of accommodation and homelessness*, paras 15.86–15.89 and in the *Code of guidance: addendum*, paras 53–54 and 59.

7.225 As indicated, in all these circumstances the applicant must be notified of the local housing authority's decision that the duty is ended. The notice must be in writing[655] and must inform the applicant:

1) that the local housing authority no longer regards itself as being subject to the duty in question;
2) why it considers the duty to have come to an end; and
3) what the applicant has the right to request a review, which must be done within 21 days of the day on which the applicant is notified of the decision.[656]

7.226 Moreover, in the fourth situation – refusal of an offer of suitable accommodation – the applicant must also have been notified, prior to their refusal, of the possible consequences of acceptance and refusal.[657]

7.227 An applicant may request a review of the decision that the relief duty has come to an end.[658] Where the duty ended because 56 days had passed,[659] or because the local housing authority was satisfied that reasonable steps had been taken to help to secure that suitable accommodation was available,[660] then an applicant may request a review of whether or not reasonable steps were in fact taken during the period in which the relief duty was owed.[661] They may also request a review of the suitability of any accommodation[662] offered in, or in connection with, the discharge of the relief duty, whether or not the accommodation has been accepted.[663] The applicant may then appeal the review decision (or, if no decision is made on the review, the original decision) to the county court on a point of law.[664]

655 H(W)A 2014 s84(3).

656 H(W)A 2014 s84(1). See paras 7.326–7.350 for a discussion of reviews and appeals.

657 H(W)A 2014 s74(5). This provision does not actually stipulate that such a notice must be given in writing but the Court of Appeal has held that '"notify" requires the giving of a notice which imports a degree of formality sufficient to constitute the document, as it will usually be, a notice': *Ali v Birmingham City Council* [2009] EWCA Civ 1279, [2011] HLR 17 at para 39 per Sir Anthony May.

658 H(W)A 2014 s85(1)(c).

659 H(W)A 2014 s74(2).

660 H(W)A 2014 s74(3).

661 H(W)A 2014 s85(2).

662 See paras 7.239–7.252.

663 H(W)A 2014 s85(3).

664 H(W)A 2014 s88(1).

Other non-accommodation duties

7.228 In addition to the above duties of assessment,[665] prevention[666] and relief,[667] the local housing authority in Wales may be subject to a number of other non-accommodation duties in respect of a homelessness applicant.

7.229 The first arises where the applicant's household contains a child,[668] and the local housing authority has reason to believe that:

1) the applicant may be ineligible for assistance;[669]
2) the applicant may be homeless[670] and a duty under H(W)A 2014 s68,[671] s73[672] or s75[673] is not likely to apply; or
3) the applicant may be threatened with homelessness[674] and the duty under (HW)A 2014 66[675] is not likely to apply.[676]

7.230 Where the duty applies, the local housing authority must invite the applicant to agree that 'the essential facts' of their case be referred to social services.[677] If the applicant does so consent, the local housing authority must then make the social services department aware of those facts and of any subsequent decision reached by the local housing authority in the applicant's case.[678]

7.231 Where the local housing authority has decided that an applicant is ineligible,[679] became homeless intentionally[680] or became threatened with homelessness intentionally, then it must provide the social services department with 'such advice and assistance as the social services department may reasonably request'.[681]

665 See paras 7.204–7.210.
666 See paras 7.211–7.220.
667 See paras 7.221–7.227.
668 Defined as a person under 18: H(W)A 2014 s96(1).
669 See paras 7.6–7.93.
670 See paras 7.121–7.133.
671 The interim accommodation duty. See paras 7.275–7.283.
672 The relief duty. See paras 7.221–7.227.
673 The main housing duty. See paras 7.284–7.293.
674 See paras 7.134–7.135.
675 The prevention duty. See paras 7.211–7.220.
676 H(W)A 2014 s96(1).
677 H(W)A 2014 s96(2). See paras 9.250–9.257 for the duties that may subsequently be owed by social services.
678 H(W)A 2014 s96(2).
679 See paras 7.6–7.93.
680 See paras 7.152–7.157.
681 H(W)A 2014 s96(4).

7.232 Second, the local housing authority may be subject to a duty to protect an applicant's belongings.[682] This duty will apply where:

1) the local housing authority has reason to believe that there is a danger of loss of, or damage to, the applicant's personal property due to the applicant's inability to protect or deal with it;[683]
2) the local housing authority has reason to believe that no other suitable arrangements have been or are being made;[684]
3) the local housing authority is or has been subject to:[685]
   a) the prevention duty,[686] but only where the applicant has a priority need;[687]
   b) the interim accommodation duty;[688]
   c) the main housing duty;[689] or
   d) the accommodation duties owed to an applicant whose case is considered for referral or is referred, to another local housing authority, but only where the applicant has a priority need.[690]

7.233 The duty requires the local housing authority to take reasonable steps to prevent the loss of property or to prevent or mitigate damage to the property.[691] The duty is subject to any conditions that the local housing authority may consider appropriate, which may include conditions as to the levying of charges or disposal of the property in specified circumstances.[692]

7.234 The duty will end:

1) once the local housing authority considers that there is no longer any reason to believe that there is a danger of loss or damage to the applicant's property due to their inability to protect or deal with it;[693] or

682 See *Code of guidance to local authorities on the allocation of accommodation and homelessness*, paras 11.15–11.21.
683 H(W)A 2014 s93(1)(a).
684 H(W)A 2014 s93(1)(b).
685 H(W)A 2014 s93(2).
686 Under H(W)A 2014 s66(1): see paras 7.152–7.157.
687 See paras 7.136–7.151.
688 Under H(W)A 2014 s68(1): see paras 7.253–7.259.
689 Under H(W)A 2014 s75(1): see paras 7.284–7.293.
690 Under H(W)A 2014 s82: see paras 7.323–7.325.
691 H(W)A 2014 s93(1).
692 H(W)A 2014 s93(4).
693 H(W)A 2014 s94(6).

2) if the authority has, at the applicant's request, moved the property to a location specified by them and the applicant is informed that the duty has come to an end.[694]

7.235 If the local housing authority decides it is not subject to this duty, then there is no right to request a review. An applicant seeking to challenge such a decision would have to apply for judicial review on the basis that the local housing authority had erred in law or bring a claim in the county court for breach of duty.[695]

Accommodation duties

7.236 Despite recent attempts to shift the focus of homelessness assistance onto preventing homelessness and helping applicants to secure their own accommodation, for most people who apply as homeless to their local housing authority, being provided with an actual unit of accommodation by that authority remains of the utmost importance.

7.237 In both England and Wales, there are a number of different duties under which the local housing authority must secure that accommodation is available for occupation by the applicant. In England, these are:

1) the interim duty under HA 1996 s188 to accommodate an applicant pending inquiries into their case;
2) the short-term duty under HA 1996 s190 to accommodate applicants who are homeless and eligible and have a priority need but became homeless intentionally;
3) the main housing duty under HA 1996 s193 to accommodate applicants who are homeless, eligible, have a priority need and did not become homeless intentionally; and
4) the duty under HA 1996 s193C to accommodate applicants who would have been owed the main housing duty but who deliberately and unreasonably refused to co-operate with their homelessness application.

In Wales, these are:

1) the duty under H(W)A 2014 s68 to secure interim accommodation; and
2) the main housing duty under H(W)A 2014 s75.

7.238 Some of these necessitate the provision of accommodation on an interim basis only. Others require accommodation to be secured for

694 H(W)A 2014 s94(4).
695 See, for example, *Deadman v Southwark LBC* (2001) 33 HLR 75, CA.

a potentially indefinite period. However, it is now well established that accommodation provided under even the highest form of duty which can be owed, the main housing duty,[696] need not be offered under a permanent or secure tenancy.[697] Moreover, the – deliberate – result of various legislative reforms over the years has been to introduce and then increase the use of offers of accommodation in the private rented sector as a means of bringing homelessness duties to an end.[698]

Standard of accommodation

7.239 Although it is possible for a local housing authority to resolve an applicant's homelessness application by making them an offer of social housing under HA 1996 Part VI,[699] accommodation provided under HA 1996 Part VII (England) or H(W)A 2014 Part 2 (Wales) is intended to be a solution to a short-term crisis rather than a route into longer-term social housing. Nevertheless, certain standards must still be met.

7.240 The first standard is that the accommodation must be available not just for occupation by the applicant, but for occupation by the applicant together with any other person who normally resides with them as a member of their family, or any other person who might reasonably be expected to reside with them.[700]

7.241 The second is that the accommodation must be suitable.[701] It must be suitable not just for the applicant but also for members of their household.[702] When determining whether or not a particular unit of accommodation is suitable for an applicant and their household, there are certain factors which local housing authorities must take into account. These are:

696 Under HA 1996 s193(2) (England); and H(W)A 2014 s75(1) (Wales).

697 This was first confirmed by the then House of Lords in *R v Brent LBC ex p Awua* [1996] AC 55, HL.

698 See the amendments made to the HA 1996 by the Homelessness Act 2002; Housing and Regeneration Act 2008; Localism Act 2011; H(W)A 2014; and Homelessness Reduction Act 2017.

699 Under HA 1996 ss193A(1), 193(6)(c) and (7), and 193C(6)(b) (England) and H(W)A 2014 s76(2)(a) and (3)(c) (Wales).

700 HA 1996 s176 (England); and H(W)A 2014 s56(1) (Wales).

701 HA 1996 s206(1) (England); and H(W)A 2014 ss68(1) and 75(1) (Wales).

702 *Homelessness code of guidance*, para 17.2 (www.gov.uk/guidance/homelessness-code-of-guidance-for-local-authorities) (England); *Code of guidance to local authorities on the allocation of accommodation and homelessness*, para 19.11 (Wales).

1) the provisions of the HA 1985 which relate to slum clearance and overcrowding;[703]
2) the provisions of HA 2004 Parts 1–4 which relate to housing conditions, houses in multiple occupation and the licensing of accommodation;[704]
3) the affordability of the accommodation;[705]
4) the location of the accommodation.[706] Local housing authorities are required to secure that accommodation is available within their district so far as reasonably practicable;[707]
5) the public sector equality duty (PSED) under Equality Act (EqA) 2010 s149;
6) the best interests of any child in the household;[708]
7) the right to education in respect of any school-age child in the household;[709]
8) the guidance given in the relevant code of guidance;[710]
9) the local housing authority's own homelessness strategy;[711] and
10) in Wales only, the provisions of H(W)A 2014 Part 1 which relate to the regulation of private rented housing.[712]

703 HA 1996 s210(1) (England); and H(W)A 2014 s59(1)(a) and (b) (Wales); HA 1985 Parts IX and X.

704 HA 1996 s210(1) (England); and H(W)A 2014 s59(1)(c)–(f) (Wales).

705 Homelessness (Suitability of Accommodation) Order 1996 art 2 (England); and H(W)A 2014 s59(2) (Wales). See *Samuels v Birmingham City Council* [2019] UKSC 28 for the correct approach to determining affordability.

706 For England: Homelessness (Suitability of Accommodation) (England) Order 2012 SI No 2601 art 2. The obligation applies differently in England in respect of some recent migrants: see paras 7.243–7.245. For Wales: *Code of guidance to local authorities on the allocation of accommodation and homelessness*, paras 19.13–19.25 and (in respect of a person who is or may be in priority need) Homelessness (Suitability of Accommodation) (Wales) Order 2015 SI No 1268 (W 87) art 3(d)–(g) (Wales).

707 HA 1996 s208(1) (England); and H(W)A 2014 s91(1) (Wales).

708 Pursuant to the duty under Children Act 2004 s11 (England) and s28 (Wales) to safeguard and promote the welfare of children, as confirmed by the Supreme Court in *ZH (Tanzania) v SSHD* [2011] UKSC 4, [2011] 2 AC 166. See *Nzolameso v Westminster City Council* [2015] UKSC 22 for a discussion of the best interests of children and offers of accommodation.

709 Human Rights Act 1998 Sch 1 Part II art 2. See also *R (E) v Islington LBC* [2017] EWHC 1440 (Admin), [2018] PTSR 349.

710 HA 1996 s182(2); and *Homelessness code of guidance*, chapter 17 (England); and H(W)A 2014 s98(1) and *Code of guidance to local authorities on the allocation of accommodation and homelessness*, chapter 19 (Wales).

711 Homelessness Act 2002 s1(5) (England); and H(W)A 2014 s50(4) (Wales).

712 H(W)A 2014 s59(1)(g).

7.242 Welsh local authorities are also statutorily required to take into account the following factors when determining whether or not accommodation is suitable for a person who is or may be in priority need:

1) the specific health needs of the applicant or members of their household;
2) the proximity and accessibility of family support;
3) any disabilities;
4) the proximity and accessibility of medical facilities and other support services which are currently used by or provided to the applicant or members of their household and which are essential to that person's well-being;
5) the distance of the accommodation from the authority's area (if it is located outside the authority's area);
6) the significance of any disruption caused by the location of the accommodation to the employment, caring responsibilities or education of the person; and
7) the proximity of alleged perpetrators and victims of domestic abuse.[713]

7.243 The requirement to take into account the location of accommodation[714] applies differently in respect of some recent migrants who are applying to local housing authorities in England. Pursuant to Homelessness (Suitability of Accommodation) (England) Order 2012 art 2, when determining whether accommodation is suitable, local housing authorities in England must take into account the location of the accommodation including: the distance of the accommodation from the authority's district (where the accommodation is situated outside of the district); the significance of any disruption which would be caused by the location of the accommodation to the employment, caring responsibilities or education of the applicant or members of their household; the proximity and accessibility of the accommodation to medical facilities and other support which are currently used by or provided to the applicant or members of their household and which are essential to that person's well-being; and the proximity and accessibility of the accommodation to local services, amenities and transport.[715] However, this obligation does not apply to an applicant who makes a homelessness application to a local housing authority (in England) on or after 1 June 2022 and within

713 Homelessness (Suitability of Accommodation) (Wales) Order 2015 art 3.

714 See para 7.241(4).

715 Local housing authorities in Wales are under a similar obligation by virtue of Homelessness (Suitability of Accommodation) (Wales) Order 2015 art 3.

two years of the date on which they arrived in the UK; who is eligible for assistance under HA 1996 Part VII;[716] and who did not have a right to occupy accommodation in the UK for an uninterrupted period of six months or more in the three years prior to the date on which they arrived in the UK.[717] The local housing authority must still take into account the significance of any disruption which would be caused by the location of the accommodation to any caring responsibilities of the applicant or members of their household for 'persons for whom there are family associations'.[718] The *Homelessness code of guidance* states that 'family associations' may extend beyond 'partners, parents, adult children of siblings' and that 'the actual closeness of the family association and level of caring responsibilities may count for more than the degree of blood relation'.[719]

7.244 This exception for recent migrants was brought into force on 1 June 2022 and will expire on 1 June 2023.[720] According to the Explanatory Memorandum produced with the Homelessness (Suitability of Accommodation) (Amendment) (England) Order 2022,[721] its purpose is 'to open up a broader supply of accommodation which local authorities can use to discharge their homelessness duties and reduce the administrative burden on local authorities when making out of area placements, in order to cope with pressures from recent arrivals following on from two international humanitarian crises in quick succession'.[722]

716 See paras 7.6–7.93 for eligibility. This particular criterion is a curious one. It is likely to be largely irrelevant because if an applicant is ineligible then in the vast majority of cases the local housing authority will not owe them a duty, or have a power, to accommodate them. Its only application would appear to be where the local housing authority has a duty under HA 1996 s188(1) to accommodate an applicant pending inquiries into their application because it has reason to believe that they may be eligible (and homeless and in priority need) or where the local housing authority has a power to accommodate an applicant under HA 1996 s188(3) or s204(4) pending the review or appeal of an adverse decision on their case: see paras 7.253–7.259, 7.275–7.283 and 7.336–7.350. Where an applicant is being accommodated under one of these provisions, and has either not yet been accepted as eligible or has been found not to be eligible, then they would appear to fall outside the exception discussed. They will therefore – perhaps surprisingly – be in a better position than an applicant who has been accepted as eligible.

717 Homelessness (Suitability of Accommodation) (England) Order 2012 arts 2 and 2A(1).

718 Homelessness (Suitability of Accommodation) (England) Order 2012 art 2A(2).

719 *Homelessness code of guidance*, para 17.62.

720 Homelessness (Suitability of Accommodation) (Amendment) (England) Order 2022 arts 1(1) and 2.

721 SI No 521.

722 Homelessness (Suitability of Accommodation) (Amendment) (England) Order 2022 Explanatory Memorandum para 7.11.

Those crises are the Taliban takeover in Afghanistan in August 2021 and the Russian invasion of Ukraine in February 2022.[723]

7.245 The effect of the amendment is likely to be fairly limited. The obligation imposed on local housing authorities by HA 1996 s208(1) to secure that accommodation is available within their district so far as reasonably practicable remains in place. Although local housing authorities are no longer required by Homelessness (Suitability of Accommodation) (England) Order 2012 art 2 to take location into account (except in respect of the significance of any disruption caused to caring responsibilities), they are not prohibited from doing so. Indeed, where location is a relevant factor, it may well be a public law error for them not to take it into account. The *Homelessness code of guidance* reminds local housing authorities that they must still comply with their responsibilities under the EqA 2010 and Children Act 2004 s11.[724]

7.246 In addition to these issues, where the accommodation being offered is in the private rented sector, various mandatory standards must, in certain cases, be met. In England, accommodation in the private rented sector will not be suitable unless it complies with the standards set out in the Homelessness (Suitability of Accommodation) (England) Order 2012 art 3(1).[725] This applies to:[726]

1) a private rented sector offer made to bring the main housing duty[727] to an end;[728]
2) a final accommodation offer made to bring the relief duty[729] to an end;[730]
3) a final accommodation offer made to bring the HA 1996 s193C(4) duty[731] to an end;[732] and

723 Homelessness (Suitability of Accommodation) (Amendment) (England) Order 2022 Explanatory Memorandum paras 7.1 and 7.2.

724 *Homelessness code of guidance*, para 17.63.

725 These requirements include that the accommodation is in a reasonable physical condition, reasonable fire safety precautions have been taken, the landlord is a fit and proper person to act as landlord, there is a current gas safety record, and a written tenancy agreement has been provided.

726 Homelessness (Suitability of Accommodation) (England) Order 2012 art 3(2).

727 Under HA 1996 s193(2). See paras 7.263–7.269.

728 HA 1996 s193(7AA).

729 Under HA 1996 s189B(2). See paras 7.187–7.193.

730 HA 1996 s193A(1)(b) and (4).

731 Owed to applicants who would be owed the main housing duty but who have deliberately and unreasonably refused to co-operate. See paras 7.270–7.274.

732 HA 1996 s193C(6) and (7).

4) an offer of accommodation which is made pursuant to the prevention[733] or relief[734] duty to an applicant who has a priority need.

7.247 In Wales, a private rented sector offer which is intended to bring the main housing duty[735] to an end will not be suitable if the local housing authority is of the view that:

1) the accommodation is not in a reasonable physical condition;
2) the accommodation does not comply with all statutory requirements such as (where applicable) requirements relating to fire, gas, electrics, carbon monoxide and other safety, planning, and licences for housing in multiple occupation (HMO); or
3) the landlord is not a fit and proper person within the meaning of H(W)A 2014 s20.[736]

7.248 Special rules also apply in both England and Wales to accommodation provided in a 'bed and breakfast'. The position in England is as follows. Bed and breakfast accommodation is defined as accommodation which is not separate and self-contained; in which the toilet, personal washing facilities and/or cooking facilities are shared by more than one household; which is not owned or managed by a local housing authority, a non-profit registered provider of social housing or a voluntary organisation; and which is not accommodation provided in a private dwelling.[737] Such accommodation is not to be regarded as suitable for an applicant with family commitments unless no other accommodation is available and the applicant does not occupy such accommodation for more than six weeks.[738] An applicant with family commitments means an applicant who is pregnant or an applicant with whom a pregnant woman or dependent children reside or might reasonably be expected to reside.[739] This rule only applies to accommodation provided under HA 1996 ss188(1), 190(2), 193(2) and 200(1), or (unless the accommodation is

733 Under HA 1996 s195(2). See paras 7.181–7.186.
734 Under HA 1996 s189B(2). See paras 7.187–7.193.
735 Under H(W)A 2014 s75(1). See paras 7.284–7.293.
736 Homelessness (Suitability of Accommodation) (Wales) Order 2015 art 8.
737 Homelessness (Suitability of Accommodation) (England) Order 2003 SI No 3326 art 2.
738 Homelessness (Suitability of Accommodation) (England) Order 2003 arts 3 and 4(1) and (2).
739 Homelessness (Suitability of Accommodation) (England) Order 2003 art 2.

that occupied by the applicant at the time of their application) s195(2).[740]

7.249 However, this rule applies differently to an applicant who makes a homelessness application on or after 1 June 2022 and within two years of the date on which they arrive in the UK; who is eligible for assistance under HA 1996 Part VII;[741] and who did not have a right to occupy accommodation in the UK for an uninterrupted period of six months or more in the three years prior to the date on which they arrived in the UK.[742] For such applicants, the maximum six-week period does not apply. Bed and breakfast accommodation will still be automatically unsuitable for recent migrant applicants with family commitments unless no other accommodation is available, which means that if other accommodation *is* available then bed and breakfast accommodation will still be deemed to be unsuitable. If, however, no alternative accommodation is available then such applicants can remain in bed and breakfast accommodation without it being deemed to be unsuitable after six weeks – although it may still be unsuitable due to the applicant's particular circumstances. This exception for recent migrants was brought into force on 1 June 2022 together with the exception, discussed above at para 7.243, which removes location from the list of obligatory factors to be considered when assessing the suitability of accommodation provided to recent migrants.[743] As with that measure, the purpose of the exception is to 'open up a

740 Homelessness (Suitability of Accommodation) (England) Order 2003 art 3. These provisions contain, respectively, the interim accommodation duty, the short-term accommodation duty owed to a person who is homeless and eligible and has a priority need but became homeless intentionally, the main housing duty, the interim accommodation duty owed pending referral of an applicant's case under HA 1996 s198(1), and the prevention duty.

741 See paras 7.6–7.93 for eligibility. This criterion is only relevant where the applicant is being accommodated under the interim accommodation duty at HA 1996 s188(1), as all the other provisions to which the restriction on bed and breakfast accommodation applies are engaged only in respect of applicants who have been found to be eligible. As discussed at para 7.243, it is a curious feature of the drafting that applicants who may not be eligible are thereby placed in a better position than applicants who have been accepted as eligible.

742 Homelessness (Suitability of Accommodation) (England) Order 2003 art 4(3).

743 Homelessness (Suitability of Accommodation) (Amendment) (England) Order 2022 art 1(1).

broader supply of accommodation which local authorities can use to discharge their homelessness duties'.[744] It expires on 1 June 2023.[745]

7.250 There is one more feature of the restriction on the use of bed and breakfast accommodation in England which is of particular interest to migrants. The definition of bed and breakfast accommodation was amended with effect from 1 June 2022 to exclude 'accommodation provided in a private dwelling'.[746] This means that accommodation provided in a private home will not constitute bed and breakfast accommodation, even if it would otherwise have fit the definition for such accommodation, and will not therefore be deemed to be unsuitable for applicants with family commitments. This change was introduced with the provisions discussed at paras 7.243–7.245 and 7.249, and as with those measures the intention was to ease the burden on local housing authorities following the anticipated increase in homelessness applications arising from the recent crises in Afghanistan and Ukraine.[747] However, unlike the other two measures, this amendment is not limited to recent migrants and has no fixed expiry date. It is therefore capable of applying much more widely than the other changes made.

7.251 Special provisions in respect of bed and breakfast accommodation also apply in Wales. In Wales, bed and breakfast accommodation is defined as accommodation which is not separate and self-contained; in which toilet facilities, personal washing facilities and/ or cooking facilities are either not available or are shared by more than one household; which is not accommodation owned or managed by a local housing authority, a registered social landlord, or a voluntary organisation or an establishment registered under the Care Standards Act 2000; and which is commercially provided.[748] Such accommodation is not to be regarded as suitable for a person who is, or may be, in priority need[749] unless:

744 Homelessness (Suitability of Accommodation) (Amendment) (England) Order 2022 Explanatory Memorandum para 7.11.

745 Homelessness (Suitability of Accommodation) (Amendment) (England) Order 2022 art 2.

746 Homelessness (Suitability of Accommodation) (England) Order 2003 art 2, as amended by Homelessness (Suitability of Accommodation) (Amendment) (England) Order 2022 art 3(2).

747 Homelessness (Suitability of Accommodation) (Amendment) (England) Order 2022 Explanatory Memorandum.

748 Homelessness (Suitability of Accommodation) (Wales) Order 2015 art 2.

749 See paras 7.136–7.151.

a) the local housing authority believes that the applicant may be homeless or threatened with homelessness as a result of an emergency such as a fire, flood or other disaster, and no other accommodation is reasonably available to the authority;[750]
b) the authority has offered suitable accommodation to the applicant but the applicant wishes to be accommodated in other accommodation;[751]
c) the applicant does not occupy the accommodation for longer than a prescribed period. The length of that period depends on whether the bed and breakfast is of a 'basic standard' or 'higher standard'. The period may be extended or disapplied if the authority offers suitable alternative accommodation but the applicant chooses to remain in the bed and breakfast.[752]

Similar restrictions apply in Wales to 'shared accommodation'.[753]

7.252 In addition to these mandatory requirements, there is a wide range of other issues which may or may not be relevant to the suitability of the accommodation depending on the circumstances of the particular case. Issues which may be of particular relevance to migrant applicants could include:

- Any particular accommodation needs arising from the applicant's past experiences. In *R v Brent LBC ex p Omar*,[754] the applicant successfully challenged accommodation which consisted of a damp basement flat with high windows and cockroaches. She asserted that it was unsuitable because it reminded her of the prison in Somalia where she had been incarcerated.[755] The English *Homelessness code of guidance* advises local housing authorities to take account of any special considerations in respect of victims of modern slavery that might affect the suitability of the

750 Homelessness (Suitability of Accommodation) (Wales) Order 2015 arts 4 and 6(a).

751 Homelessness (Suitability of Accommodation) (Wales) Order 2015 arts 4 and 6(b).

752 Homelessness (Suitability of Accommodation) (Wales) Order 2015 arts 4 and 7(1). The 'basic standard' is defined at art 1 and the 'higher standard' is defined at art 1 and the Sch to the 2015 Order.

753 Homelessness (Suitability of Accommodation) (Wales) Order 2015 arts 2, 5, 6 and 7.

754 (1991) 23 HLR 446, QBD.

755 See, however, *Poshteh v Kensington and Chelsea RLBC* [2017] UKSC 36, [2017] AC 624, in which an applicant's challenge to the suitability of accommodation which she asserted reminded her of her former prison cell in Iran was unsuccessful.

accommodation.[756] Where there is no other option but hostel accommodation for such applicants, 'the accommodation may need to be gender-specific, or have specific security measures in place'.[757] The code also reminds local housing authorities to consider the particular needs of victims of domestic violence.[758]

- The medical needs of the applicant and any members of their household. This could include a need for specialised treatment from, for example, a psychiatrist or the Helen Bamber Foundation.
- The need to be near a particular religious or ethnic community.
- The need to be near a particular source of support or assistance such as Freedom From Torture or the Helen Bamber Foundation or an immigration solicitor.
- A cultural need for a particular type of accommodation, such a Gypsy or Traveller who has a cultural aversion to bricks-and-mortar accommodation.

England

Interim duty to accommodate

7.253 If a local housing authority has reason to believe that an applicant may be homeless,[759] eligible[760] and have a priority need,[761] then it must secure that accommodation is available for the applicant's occupation pending further inquiries pursuant to HA 1996 s188(1). Having 'reason to believe' that an applicant 'may' meet these criteria is a low threshold.[762]

7.254 If an applicant accepted a private rented sector offer[763] made pursuant to a previous homelessness application and then re-applied as homeless (to the same or a different local housing authority) within two years of the date on which they accepted that offer, then the test is slightly different. Such an applicant is owed the main

756 At para 25.25. See also paras 11.127–11.224 below for further discussion of modern slavery.

757 *Homelessness code of guidance*, para 25.25.

758 *Homelessness code of guidance*, paras 21.41–21.45.

759 See paras 7.121–7.133.

760 See paras 7.6–7.93.

761 See paras 7.136–7.151.

762 *R (Kelly and Mehari) v Birmingham City Council* [2009] EWHC 3240 (Admin), [2009] 11 WLUK 179 at para 7 per Hickinbottom J; *R (M) v Hammersmith and Fulham LBC* [2008] UKHL 14, [2008] 1 WLR 535 at para 36 per Baroness Hale; and *Homelessness code of guidance*, para 15.5.

763 See para 7.265(8).

housing duty[764] if the local housing authority is satisfied that the applicant is homeless,[765] eligible for assistance[766] and did not become homeless intentionally,[767] regardless of whether or not the applicant has a priority need.[768] This means that when it comes to the interim accommodation duty, the local housing authority need only have reason to believe that an applicant may be homeless, may be eligible and may not have become homeless intentionally: there is no need for there be a potential priority need.[769] There is, however, an exception to this: if the applicant would only be owed the main housing duty because of the presence in their household of a restricted person, then the applicant must, like other applicants, have a priority need in order to be entitled to the main housing duty.[770] In these circumstances, the local housing authority would have to have reason to believe that an applicant may have a priority need before the interim accommodation duty was owed.

7.255 The interim accommodation duty is absolute, and must be performed immediately. Any attempt to postpone performance of the duty, or to avoid it by determining the application on the same day as it is made, is likely to be unlawful.[771] A failure by a local housing authority to comply with this duty may be challenged by an application for judicial review.

7.256 The ways in which this duty can be brought to an end are complex:

1) If the local housing authority concludes its inquiries and decides that the applicant does not have a priority need and also that the applicant is not owed the relief duty[772] (ie because they are not eligible or not homeless), then the interim accommodation duty will end when the applicant is notified of that decision.[773]

764 See paras 7.263–7.269.
765 See paras 7.121–7.133.
766 See paras 7.6–7.93.
767 See paras 7.152–7.157.
768 HA 1996 s195A(1). See paras 7.136–7.151.
769 HA 1996 s188(1A). Although note the extra requirement to have reason to believe the applicant may not have become homeless intentionally.
770 HA 1996 s195A(5). See para 7.80.
771 See, for example, *R (Kelly and Mehari) v Birmingham City Council* [2009] EWHC 3240 (Admin), [2009] 11 WLUK 179; and *R (Khazai) v Birmingham City Council* [2010] EWHC 2576 (Admin), December 2010 *Legal Action* 37. See also *R (Edwards) v Birmingham City Council* [2016] EWHC 173 (Admin), [2016] HLR 11.
772 Under HA 1996 s189B(2). See paras 7.187–7.193.
773 HA 1996 s188(1ZA)(a). A decision that the applicant does not have a priority need is not, on its own, sufficient to end the interim accommodation duty: see *R (Mitchell) v Islington LBC* [2020] EWHC 1478 (Admin), [2021] HLR 5.

2) If the local housing authority concludes its inquiries and decides that the applicant does not have a priority need, but accepts that the relief duty[774] is owed, then the interim accommodation duty will end when the applicant is notified that once the relief duty has ended and no duty will be owed under HA 1996 s190 or s193.[775]
3) If the local housing authority concludes its inquiries and decides that the applicant does have a priority need, or if it has not yet determined the issue either way, then the interim accommodation duty will end upon the later of:
   a) the relief duty ending[776] or the local housing authority notifying the applicant that it does not owe them the relief duty (ie because they are not eligible or not homeless);[777] and
   b) the local housing authority notifying the applicant of what duty (if any) will be owed once the relief duty comes to an end.[778]
4) If the applicant is owed the interim accommodation duty in circumstances where the local housing authority has reason to believe that they may be owed the main housing duty regardless of a priority need because they are re-applying within two years of accepting a private rented sector offer,[779] then the interim accommodation duty will end upon the later of:[780]
   a) the relief duty ending[781] or the local housing authority notifying the applicant that it does not owe them the relief duty (ie because they are not eligible or not homeless);[782] or
   b) the local housing authority notifying the applicant of what duty (if any) will be owed once the relief duty comes to an end.[783]

774 Under HA 1996 s189B(2). See paras 7.187–7.193.

775 HA 1996 s188(1ZA)(b). The duties in both HA 1996 s190 and s193 require the applicant to have a priority need, so neither would apply where there is no priority need.

776 The relief duty is at HA 1996 s189B(2). See paras 7.190–7.191 for a discussion as to the circumstances in which the relief duty can come to an end.

777 HA 1996 s188(1ZB)(a).

778 HA 1996 s188(1ZB)(b).

779 Under HA 1996 s195A. See para 7.254.

780 HA 1996 s188(1A).

781 The relief duty is at HA 1996 s189B(2). See paras 7.190–7.191 for a discussion as to the circumstances in which the relief duty can come to an end.

782 HA 1996 s188(1ZB)(a).

783 HA 1996 s188(1ZB)(b).

5) If the applicant has been made a final accommodation offer[784] or a final Part 6 offer[785] and the applicant requests a review of the suitability of the accommodation offered,[786] then the interim accommodation duty will not end until the decision on review has been notified to the applicant.[787]

7.257 In *R (Brooks) v Islington LBC*,[788] Lewis J held that if an applicant refuses suitable accommodation offered under the interim accommodation duty, then the duty will have been performed, and there is no obligation to make a further offer unless circumstances change to render that previous offer unsuitable, in which case further accommodation must be secured.

7.258 Although there is no statutory requirement to notify the applicant that the interim accommodation duty has ended, the applicant will in most circumstances have been notified of the circumstances which have caused the interim accommodation duty to end, namely:

1) the decision that the relief duty is not owed;
2) the decision that the relief duty has come to end;
3) the decision as to what further duty, if any, will be owed once the relief duty comes to an end; or
4) the decision which has been made pursuant to the applicant's request for a review of the suitability of a final accommodation offer or final Part 6 offer.

7.259 There is no right to request a review of the ending of the interim accommodation duty. However, the decisions that the relief duty is not owed, or it has come to an end, or of what further duty, if any, will be owed once the relief duty comes to an end, all carry a right of review.[789] Although there is no requirement that the interim accommodation duty continue pending such a review[790] the local housing authority has the power to continue to secure accommodation in this

784 Defined at HA 1996 s193A(4). See para 7.253.

785 Defined at HA 1996 s193A(5). See para 7.253.

786 Under HA 1996 s202(1)(h). See paras 7.326–7.347 for a discussion of reviews and appeals; and paras 7.239–7.252 for a discussion of suitability.

787 HA 1996 s188(2A). This is because the relief duty under HA 1996 s189B(2) is not taken to have to have come to an end under HA 1996 s193A(2) – refusal of a final accommodation offer or a final Part 6 offer – until the decision on the review is notified to the applicant.

788 [2015] EWHC 2657 (Admin), [2016] PTSR 389.

789 Under HA 1996 s202(1)(a), (b), and (ba)(ii).

790 In contrast to where the review is of the suitability of a final accommodation offer or final Part 6 offer under HA 1996 s202(1)(h).

period.[791] A refusal to exercise this power can only be challenged by judicial review.

Short-term duty to accommodate applicants who are in priority need but intentionally homeless

7.260 If the local housing authority is satisfied that an applicant is eligible for assistance,[792] is homeless,[793] and has a priority need,[794] but is also satisfied that they became homeless intentionally[795] then, once the relief duty[796] has ended, it must secure that accommodation is available for the applicant 'for such period as they consider will give him a reasonable opportunity of securing accommodation for his occupation'.[797]

7.261 This duty only arises once the relief duty has ended. It is owed in conjunction with the duty to provide advice and assistance in any attempt the applicant may make to secure accommodation.[798]

7.262 What period is 'reasonable' will depend on the circumstances of the applicant in question and the situation in the particular local housing authority's area.[799] Any challenge to the length of period allowed by the local housing authority must be brought by judicial review.

Main housing duty

7.263 Subject to the below four exceptions, if the local housing authority is satisfied that an applicant is eligible for assistance,[800] is homeless,[801]

791 Under HA 1996 s188(3). See paras 7.336–7.347.

792 See paras 7.6–7.93.

793 See paras 7.121–7.133.

794 See paras 7.136–7.151.

795 See paras 7.152–7.157.

796 Under HA 1996 s189B(2). See paras 7.187–7.193.

797 HA 1996 s190(1) and (2)(a).

798 Under HA 1996 s190(2)(b). See para 7.201.

799 See *Homelessness code of guidance*, para 15.15 for suggestions as to the factors that should be considered when deciding for what period to provide accommodation. See also *De Falco v Crawley BC* [1980] QB 460, CA, [1980] 2 WLR 664; *R (Nipyo) v Croydon LBC* [2008] EWHC 847 (Admin), [2008] HLR 37; *Newman v Croydon LBC* [2008] EWCA Civ 1591, April 2009 *Legal Action* 22; *Anwar v Manchester City Council* [2009] EWHC 2876 Admin, January 2010 *Legal Action* 36; *R (Conville) v Richmond upon Thames LBC* [2006] EWCA Civ 718, [2006] HLR 45; and *R (Savage) v Hillingdon LBC* [2010] EWHC 88 (Admin), 2010 March *Legal Action* 31 for examples of challenges to what constitutes a reasonable period.

800 See paras 7.6–7.93.

801 See paras 7.121–7.133.

has a priority need[802] and did not become homeless intentionally[803] then, once the relief duty[804] has ended, it will owe the applicant the main housing duty.[805] This requires it to secure that accommodation is available for the applicant.[806]

1) The first exception creates an *additional* category of applicant who is entitled to the main housing duty. If the applicant accepted a private rented sector offer[807] made pursuant to a previous homelessness application and then re-applied as homeless (to the same or a different local housing authority) within two years of the date on which they accepted that offer, then they will be owed the main housing duty regardless of whether or not they have a priority need, provided the other criteria are met.[808] However, if the applicant would only be owed the main housing duty because of the presence in their household of a restricted person,[809] then this exception does not apply and the applicant will need to have a priority need to be owed the main housing duty.[810]

In contrast, three further exceptions all provide that the main housing duty will *not* apply, even though the applicant meets the criteria of homelessness, eligibility, priority need and non-intentional homelessness, in the following circumstances:

2) If the relief duty[811] came to an end because the applicant refused a final accommodation offer[812] or final Part 6 offer,[813] then the main housing duty will not apply.[814]
3) If the relief duty[815] came to an end because the applicant was notified that they had deliberately and unreasonably refused to

802 See paras 7.136–7.151.
803 See paras 7.152–7.157.
804 Under HA 1996 s189B(2). See paras 7.187–7.193.
805 HA 1996 s193(1).
806 HA 1996 s193(2).
807 See para 7.265(8).
808 HA 1996 s195A(1).
809 See para 7.80.
810 HA 1996 s195A(5). See paras 7.80–7.83 for a discussion of restricted cases.
811 Under HA 1996 s189B(2). See paras 7.187–7.193.
812 Defined at HA 1996 s193A(4).
813 Defined at HA 1996 s193A(5).
814 HA 1996 ss193(1A)(a) and 193A(3).
815 Under HA 1996 s189B(2). See paras 7.187–7.193.

co-operate,[816] then the main housing duty will not apply.[817] The applicant will be owed the accommodation duty under HA 1996 s193C(4) instead.[818]

4) If the local housing authority has notified the applicant that it has notified, or it intends to notify, another local housing authority that the conditions for referral of the applicant's case are met, then it will not be subject to the main housing duty.[819] However, it will be required to continue to accommodate the applicant until they are notified of the decision regarding whether or not the referral conditions are met.[820]

7.264 The main housing duty arises as soon as the local housing authority is satisfied that the criteria are met. It is 'an immediate, non-deferrable, unqualified duty to secure that suitable accommodation is available'.[821]

7.265 The main housing duty will end in the following circumstances:

1) The applicant, having been informed of the possible consequences of refusal or acceptance and of the right to request a review of the suitability of the accommodation,[822] refuses suitable accommodation (which is not an offer of accommodation under Part 6 or a private rented sector offer[823]) and the local housing authority notifies the applicant that the duty has ceased.[824]
2) The applicant ceases to be eligible for assistance.[825]
3) The applicant becomes homeless intentionally from the accommodation made available for their occupation pursuant to the main housing duty.[826]
4) The applicant accepts an offer of accommodation under HA 1996 Part VI.[827]

816 HA 1996 s193B(2).
817 HA 1996 ss193(1A)(b) and 193C(4).
818 See paras 7.270–7.274.
819 HA 1996 s200(1). See paras 7.294–7.322 for referrals for homelessness cases.
820 HA 1996 s200(1).
821 *R (Elkundi) v Birmingham City Council* [2022] EWCA Civ 601, [2022] QB 604.
822 See paras 7.239–7.252 for suitability and 7.326–7.347 for reviews.
823 Defined at HA 1996 s193(7AC).
824 HA 1996 s193(5).
825 HA 1996 s193(6)(a). See paras 7.6–7.93 for eligibility.
826 HA 1996 s193(6)(b). See paras 7.152–7.157 for becoming homeless intentionally.
827 HA 1996 s193(6)(c). See paras 7.351–7.388.

5) The applicant accepts an offer of an assured (non-shorthold) tenancy from a private landlord.[828]
6) The applicant voluntarily ceases to occupy as their only or principal home the accommodation made available for their occupation pursuant to the main housing duty.[829]
7) The applicant, having been informed of the possible consequences of refusal or acceptance and of the right to request a review of the suitability of the accommodation,[830] refuses a final offer of accommodation under HA 1996 Part VI.[831] Such an offer must be in writing and state that it is a final offer for the purposes of HA 1996 s193(7).[832] It cannot be made if the applicant is under contractual or other obligations in respect of their existing accommodation which they are unable to bring to an end before being required to take up the offer.[833]
8) The applicant, having been informed in writing of the possible consequences of refusal or acceptance of the right to request a review of the suitability of the accommodation,[834] and of the effect of a further application within two years of acceptance of the offer,[835] accepts or refuses a private rented sector offer.[836] The offer must be of an assured shorthold tenancy for a fixed term of at least 12 months.[837] It cannot be made if the applicant is under contractual or other obligations in respect of their existing accommodation which they are unable to bring to an end before being required to take up the offer.[838]

828 HA 1996 s193(6)(cc).
829 HA 1996 s193(6)(d).
830 See paras 7.239–7.252 for suitability and 7.326–7.347 for reviews.
831 HA 1996 s193(7A).
832 HA 1996 s193(7) and (7A).
833 HA 1996 s193(8).
834 See paras 7.239–7.252 for suitability and 7.326–7.347 for reviews.
835 Under HA 1996 s195A: see para 7.254. Unless the case is a restricted case as defined at HA 1996 s193(3B), in which case only the first two matters must be notified in advance. See paras 7.80–7.83 for further discussion of restricted cases.
836 'Private rented sector offer' is defined at HA 1996 s193(7AC) as an offer of an assured shorthold tenancy made by a private landlord, with the approval of the authority, in pursuance of arrangements made by the authority with a view to bringing the main housing duty to an end, which relates to accommodation which is or may become available for the applicant's occupation and where the tenancy offered is a fixed-term tenancy for a period of at least 12 months.
837 HA 1996 s193(7AA) and (7AC).
838 HA 1996 s193(8).

7.266 Save for the first of these situations, the ending of the duty is automatic: it ends when the circumstance in question arises, not when the applicant is notified that it is ending. However, in practice, some form of letter notifying the applicant that the local housing authority considers the duty to have ended is almost invariably sent, not least because the applicant will have to be told that the accommodation they are occupying is to be withdrawn.

7.267 Where the applicant's case is a restricted case,[839] the local housing authority *must* bring the main housing duty to an end by way of a private rented sector offer 'so far as reasonably practicable'.[840]

7.268 Most decisions relating to the existence or performance of the main housing duty carry statutory rights of review and appeal.[841] These include:

- a decision that the main housing duty is not owed;[842]
- a decision that the main housing duty has ended for one of the reasons set out above at para 7.265;[843]
- a decision that accommodation offered in discharge of the main housing duty is suitable;[844]
- a decision that accommodation offered as a final offer under HA 1996 Part VI is suitable;[845] and
- a decision that accommodation offered pursuant to a private rented sector offer is suitable.[846]

7.269 If, however, the local housing authority accepts that the duty is owed but has simply failed to take any or any adequate steps to comply with it – by, for example, not making any offers of accommodation or by providing accommodation which is acknowledged to be unsuitable – then the applicant's remedy would be to seek a judicial review.[847]

839 As defined at HA 1996 s193(3B): see paras 7.80–7.83.

840 HA 1996 s193(7AD).

841 See paras 7.326–7.347 for reviews and appeals.

842 HA 1996 ss202(1)(b) and 204(1).

843 HA 1996 ss202(1)(b) and 204(1). A decision that a duty has ended has been held to be a decision as 'what duty (if any) is owed': *Warsame v Hounslow LBC* [2000] 1 WLR 696, (2000) 32 HLR 335, CA.

844 HA 1996 ss202(1)(f) and 204(1).

845 HA 1996 ss202(1)(f) and 204(1).

846 HA 1996 ss202(1)(g) and 204(1).

847 See *R (Elkundi) v Birmingham City Council* [2022] EWCA Civ 601, [2022] QB 604.

Duty to accommodate applicants who would be owed the main housing duty but who deliberately and unreasonably refused to co-operate

7.270 A local housing authority may notify an applicant[848] if it considers that they have deliberately and unreasonably refused to take any step which they had agreed to take,[849] or which was recorded by the authority as being reasonable to require the applicant to take, for the purposes of securing or retaining accommodation.[850]

7.271 The effect of this notice is not just to bring the prevention[851] or relief[852] duty to an end[853] but also to disapply the main housing duty.[854] Even if an applicant is homeless,[855] eligible for assistance,[856] has a priority need[857] and did not become homeless intentionally,[858] the main housing duty will not be owed.

7.272 However, applicants who would, but for the notice of a deliberate and unreasonable refusal to co-operate, have been owed the main housing duty are still owed an accommodation duty. This is contained in HA 1996 s193C(4) and requires the local housing authority to 'secure that accommodation is available for occupation by the applicant'.

7.273 This duty will end in the following circumstances:

1) The applicant ceases to be eligible for assistance.[859]
2) The applicant becomes homeless intentionally from accommodation made available for their occupation.[860]
3) The applicant accepts an offer of an assured tenancy from a private landlord.[861]
4) The applicant voluntarily ceases to occupy as their only or principal home the accommodation made available for their occupation.[862]

848 HA 1996 s193B(2).
849 HA 1996 s189A(4). See paras 7.171–7.176.
850 HA 1996 s189A(6).
851 Under HA 1996 s195A(2). See paras 7.181–7.186.
852 Under HA 1996 s189B(2). See paras 7.187–7.193.
853 HA 1996 s193C(2).
854 HA 1996 s193C(4). See paras 7.263–7.269.
855 See paras 7.121–7.133.
856 See paras 7.6–7.93.
857 See paras 7.136–7.151.
858 See paras 7.152–7.157.
859 HA 1969 s193C(5)(a). See paras 7.6–7.93 for eligibility.
860 HA 1996 s193C(5)(b). See paras 7.152–7.157 for becoming homeless intentionally.
861 HA 1996 s193C(5)(c).
862 HA 1996 s193C(5)(d).

5) The applicant, having been informed of the possible consequences of refusal or acceptance, and of their right to request a review of the suitability of the accommodation,[863] refuses or accepts a final accommodation offer.[864] Such an offer cannot be made if the applicant is under contractual or other obligations in respect of their existing accommodation which they are unable to bring to an end before being required to take up the offer.[865]
6) The applicant, having been informed of the possible consequences of refusal or acceptance, and of their right to request a review of the suitability of the accommodation,[866] refuses or accepts a final HA 1996 Part 6 offer.[867] Such an offer cannot be made if the applicant is under contractual or other obligations in respect of their existing accommodation which they are unable to bring to an end before being required to take up the offer.[868]

7.274 An applicant can request a review of (and subsequently appeal):[869]

1) a decision to give notice that the applicant has deliberately and unreasonably refused to co-operate;[870]
2) a decision that the HA 1996 s193C(4) duty is or is not owed;[871]
3) a decision that the HA 1996 s193C(4) duty has ended for one of the reasons set out above at para 7.273;[872]

863 See paras 7.239–7.252 for suitability and 7.326–7.347 for reviews.

864 HA 1996 s193C(6)(a). 'Final accommodation offer' is defined at HA 1996 s193C(7) as an offer of an assured shorthold tenancy made by a private landlord to the applicant in relation to any accommodation which is or may become available for the applicant's occupation, which is made with the approval of the authority and in pursuance of arrangements made by the authority with a view to bringing its duty under HA 1996 s193C(4) to an end, and which is an offer of a tenancy with a minimum fixed term of six months.

865 HA 1996 s193C(10).

866 See paras 7.239–7.252 for suitability and 7.326–7.347 for reviews.

867 HA 1996 s193C(6)(b). 'Final Part 6 offer' is defined at HA 1996 s193C(8) as an offer of accommodation under HA 1996 Part VI which is made in writing and states that it is a final offer for the purposes of HA 1996 s193C(8). See paras 7.351–7.388 for a discussion of allocations under HA 1996 Part VI.

868 HA 1996 s193C(10).

869 See paras 7.326–7.347 for reviews and appeals.

870 HA 1996 ss202(1)(bb) and 204(1).

871 HA 1996 ss202(1)(b) and 204(1).

872 HA 1996 ss202(1)(b) and 204(1). A decision that a duty has ended has been held to be a decision as 'what duty (if any) is owed': *Warsame v Hounslow LBC* [2000] 1 WLR 696, (2000) 32 HLR 335, CA.

4) a decision that accommodation offered in discharge of the HA 1996 s193C(4) duty is suitable;[873]
5) a decision that accommodation offered as a final accommodation offer is suitable;[874] and
6) a decision that accommodation offered as a final HA 1996 Part 6 offer is suitable.[875]

Wales

Interim duties to accommodate

7.275 A local housing authority in Wales will be subject to an interim duty to secure accommodation in two situations.[876]

7.276 The first is where the local housing authority has reason to believe that an applicant may be homeless,[877] eligible[878] and have a priority need.[879] In these circumstances, the local housing authority must secure that suitable accommodation is available for the occupation of the applicant until the duty comes to an end.[880] This duty mirrors the interim duty owed in the same circumstances by local housing authorities in England[881] and, as with that duty, having 'reason to believe' that an applicant 'may' meet these criteria is a low threshold.[882]

7.277 The second situation in which an interim accommodation duty is owed is where:[883]

1) the local housing authority has reason to believe that an applicant has a priority need;[884] or
2) the local housing authority is satisfied that the applicant has a priority need; or

873 HA 1996 ss202(1)(f) and 204(1).
874 HA 1996 ss202(1)(h) and 204(1).
875 HA 1996 ss202(1)(h) and 204(1).
876 H(W)A 2014 s68(1).
877 See paras 7.123–7.133.
878 See paras 7.6–7.93.
879 H(W)A 2014 s68(2). See paras 7.136–7.151 for priority need.
880 H(W)A 2014 s68(1): see para 7.278.
881 See paras 7.253–7.259.
882 *R (Kelly and Mehari) v Birmingham City Council* [2009] EWHC 3240 (Admin), [2009] 11 WLUK 179 at para 7 per Hickinbottom J; *R (M) v Hammersmith and Fulham LBC* [2008] UKHL 14, [2008] 1 WLR 535 at para 36 per Baroness Hale; and *Code of guidance to local authorities on the allocation of accommodation and homelessness*, paras 11.3–11.4.
883 H(W)A 2014 s68(3).
884 See paras 7.136–7.151 for priority need.

3) the applicant's case has been referred to the local housing authority from a local housing authority in England under HA 1969 s198(1);[885] and
4) the applicant is owed the relief duty.[886]

7.278 The interim accommodation duty will end where:

1) the local housing authority has decided that the relief duty[887] is not owed and the applicant is notified of that decision;[888]
2) the applicant, having been notified of the possible consequence of refusal, refuses an offer of interim accommodation which the local housing authority is satisfied is suitable;[889]
3) the local housing authority is satisfied that the applicant has become homeless intentionally[890] from their interim accommodation, provided the accommodation was suitable;[891]
4) the local housing authority is satisfied that the applicant has voluntarily ceased to occupy (as their only or principal home) the interim accommodation, provided the accommodation was suitable;[892]
5) the local housing authority is no longer satisfied that the applicant is eligible;[893]
6) the local housing authority is satisfied that a mistake of fact led to the applicant being notified that they were owed the interim accommodation duty;[894]
7) the local housing authority is satisfied that the applicant has withdrawn their application;[895] or
8) the local housing authority is satisfied that the applicant is unreasonably failing to co-operate with the homelessness application process.[896]

885 HA 1996 s198(1) allows an applicant's case to be referred to another local housing authority at the stage that the main housing duty would be owed: see paras 7.294–7.325.
886 Under H(W)A 2014 s73(1). See paras 7.221–7.227.
887 Under H(W)A 2014 s73(1). See paras 7.221–7.227.
888 H(W)A 2014 s69(2).
889 H(W)A 2014 s69(7). See paras 7.239–7.252 for suitability.
890 See paras 7.152–7.157.
891 H(W)A 2014 s69(8). See paras 7.239–7.252 for suitability.
892 H(W)A 2014 s69(9). See paras 7.239–7.252 for suitability.
893 H(W)A 2014 s79(2). See paras 7.6–7.93 for eligibility.
894 H(W)A 2014 s79(3).
895 H(W)A 2014 s79(4).
896 H(W)A 2014 s79(5).

7.279 There is a further way in which the duty can come to an end which applies only where the duty arose because the *second* set of criteria (see para 7.277) were met:

9) the interim accommodation duty will end where the local housing authority notifies the applicant:
   a) that the relief duty[897] has come to an end; and
   b) of their decision as to whether or not the main housing duty[898] is owed.[899]

7.280 If, however, the local housing authority has decided that the main housing duty is not owed because the applicant became homeless intentionally, or because the applicant has within the last five years been offered accommodation under H(W)A 2015 s75(3),[900] then the interim accommodation duty cannot be brought to an end on this ground until the local housing authority is satisfied that the interim accommodation has been available for a sufficient period to allow the applicant a reasonable opportunity of securing accommodation for their occupation.[901] This 'reasonable period' starts on the day on which the applicant is notified that the main housing duty does not apply[902] and cannot end within 56 days of the date on which the applicant was notified that they were owed the relief duty.[903] This provision is similar to the duty owed by local housing authorities in England to applicants who are homeless and eligible and have a priority need but became homeless intentionally.[904]

7.281 In all of these circumstances, the interim accommodation duty will not end unless and until the applicant is notified in writing:

1) that the local housing authority no longer regards itself as being subject to the relevant duty;
2) why it considers the duty has ended;

897 Under H(W)A 2014 s73(1). See paras 7.221–7.227.
898 Under H(W)A 2014 s75. See paras 7.284–7.293.
899 H(W)A 2014 s69(3).
900 H(W)A 2014 s75(3) provides that the main housing duty will still be owed to an applicant who falls within one of the categories contained at H(W)A 2014 s75(3)(e) even if they became homeless intentionally. However, it appears that this exception is only capable of applying once in a five-year period: H(W)A 2014 s75(3)(f). See para 7.286.
901 H(W)A 2014 s69(4) and (5).
902 H(W)A 2014 s69(5).
903 H(W)A 2014 s69(6). Pursuant to H(W)A 2014 s74(2) and (6), one of the ways in which the relief duty under H(W)A 2014 s73(1) can end is where 56 days have passed.
904 HA 1996 s190(2)(a): see paras 7.270–7.274.

3) that the applicant has the right to request a review; and
4) of the time within which the review must be requested.[905]

7.282 As this demonstrates, an applicant has the right to request a review of the decision that the interim accommodation duty has come to an end.[906] An applicant may also request a review of the suitability of any accommodation offered in (or in connection with) the discharge of the interim accommodation duty, regardless of whether or not the offer has been accepted.[907]

7.283 If the applicant does request a review, the local housing authority has a power, but not a duty, to secure accommodation pending that review.[908] There is also a power to accommodate the applicant pending any appeal of the review decision to the county court,[909] but this is only available where the local housing authority had previously been subject to the interim accommodation duty,[910] the main housing duty[911] or the duty to secure accommodation pending referral of the applicant's case to another local housing authority.[912]

Main housing duty

7.284 The main housing duty arises where the following criteria are met:

1) the relief duty[913] has come to an end because the period of 56 days has ended *or* because the local housing authority is satisfied (before the end of the 56-day period) that reasonable steps have been taken to help to secure that suitable accommodation is available for occupation by the applicant;[914]

905 H(W)A 2014 ss69(1), 79(1) and 84.
906 H(W)A 2014 s85(1)(c). See paras 7.326–7.347 for a discussion of reviews and appeals.
907 H(W)A 2014 s85(3).
908 H(W)A 2014 s69(11).
909 H(W)A 2014 s88(5).
910 Under H(W)A 2014 s68.
911 Under H(W)A 2014 s75.
912 Under H(W)A 2014 s82. See paras 7.320–7.325.
913 Under H(W)A 2014 s73(1). See paras 7.221–7.227.
914 H(W)A 2014 s75(1). This means that if, for example, the relief duty ended under H(W)A 2014 s74(5) because the applicant, having been informed of the consequences of refusal or acceptance, refused an offer of suitable accommodation which was likely to be available for at least six months, the main housing duty will not be owed.

2) the local housing authority is satisfied that the applicant does not have suitable accommodation which is available for their occupation either at all or for at least six months;[915]
3) the local housing authority is satisfied that the applicant is eligible;[916]
4) the local housing authority is satisfied that the applicant has a priority need[917] for accommodation;[918] and
5) if the local housing authority is having regard to the intentional homelessness test,[919] it is not satisfied that the applicant became homeless intentionally.[920]

7.285 By virtue of H(W)A 2014 s75(3),[921] special provisions apply where an applicant is:

1) a pregnant woman or a person with whom she resides or might reasonably be expected to reside;
2) a person with whom a dependent child resides or might reasonably be expected to reside;
3) a person under the age of 21 or a person with whom a person under the age of 21 resides or might reasonably be expected to reside; or
4) a person who is aged 21–24 years who had been looked after, accommodated or fostered when a child, or a person with whom such a person resides or might reasonably be expected to reside.[922]

7.286 Such an applicant will be owed the main housing duty, regardless of whether they became homeless intentionally,[923] provided that:

1) the relief duty[924] owed to the applicant has come to an end because the period of 56 days has ended *or* because the local housing authority is satisfied (before the end of the 56-day period) that

915 H(W)A 2014 s75(2)(a). The six-month period starts on the day on which the applicant is notified that the relief duty does not apply. See paras 7.239–7.252 for suitability.
916 H(W)A 2014 s75(2)(b). See paras 7.6–7.93 for eligibility.
917 See paras 7.136–7.151.
918 H(W)A 2014 s75(2)(c).
919 See para 7.152.
920 H(W)A 2014 s75(2)(d).
921 This was brought into force on 2 December 2019 by the Housing (Wales) Act 2014 (Commencement Order No 10) Order 2019 2019 SI No 1479 (W 263).
922 H(W)A 2014 s75(3)(e).
923 H(W)A 2014 s75(1) and (3). See paras 7.152–7.157 for becoming homeless intentionally.
924 Under H(W)A 2014 s73(1). See paras 7.221–7.227.

reasonable steps have been taken to help to secure that suitable accommodation is available for occupation by the applicant;[925]

2) the local housing authority is satisfied that the applicant does not have suitable accommodation which is available for their occupation either at all or for at least six months;[926]
3) the local housing authority is satisfied that the applicant is eligible;[927]
4) the local housing authority is satisfied that the applicant has a priority need;[928] and
5) the applicant had not previously been offered accommodation under the main housing duty pursuant to H(W)A 2014 s75(3) within the preceding five years.[929]

7.287 Advice on the operation of this provision is contained in supplementary guidance published in December 2019, entitled *Additional provisions under section 75(3)*.

7.288 The main housing duty requires the local housing authority to 'secure that suitable accommodation is available for occupation by the applicant'.[930]

7.289 The main housing duty will come to an end in the following circumstances:

1) the applicant accepts an offer of suitable accommodation made under HA 1996 Part VI;[931]
2) the applicant accepts an offer of suitable accommodation in Wales under a tenancy which is an occupation contract;[932]

925 H(W)A 2015 s75(1). This means that if, for example, the relief duty ended under H(W)A 2014 s74(5) because the applicant, having been informed of the consequences of refusal or acceptance, refused an offer of suitable accommodation which was likely to be available for at least six months, the main housing duty will not be owed.

926 H(W)A 2014 s75(3)(b). The six-month period starts on the day on which the applicant is notified that the relief duty does not apply. See paras 7.239–7.252 for suitability.

927 H(W)A 2014 s75(3(c). See paras 7.6–7.93 for eligibility.

928 H(W)A 2014 s75(3)(d). See paras 7136–7.151 for priority need.

929 H(W)A 2014 s75(3)(f). This appears to be the intended result of H(W)A 2014 s75(3)(f) although the drafting is somewhat unclear. H(W)A 2014 s75(3)(f)(i) refers to the period of '5 years before the day on which the applicant was notified under section 63 that a duty was owed to him or her under this section', which is difficult to understand given that the effect of H(W)A 2014 s75(3)(f) is presumably that an applicant who falls foul of that subsection is not owed a duty under H(W)A 2014 s75 at all.

930 H(W)A 2014 s75(1).

931 H(W)A 2014 s76(2)(a). See paras 7.351–7.388 for allocations under HA 1996 Part VI; and paras 7.239–7.252 for suitability.

932 H(W)A 2014 s76(2)(aa).

3) the applicant accepts an offer of suitable accommodation in England under an assured tenancy (including an assured shorthold tenancy);[933]
4) the applicant, having been notified in writing of the possible consequences of refusal or acceptance, refuses an offer of suitable interim accommodation made under the main housing duty;[934]
5) the applicant, having been notified in writing of the possible consequences of refusal or acceptance, refuses a suitable private rented sector offer;[935]
6) the applicant, having been notified in writing of the possible consequences of refusal or acceptance, refuses a suitable offer of accommodation under HA 1996 Part VI;[936]
7) the local housing authority is satisfied that the applicant has become homeless intentionally from suitable interim accommodation made available for their occupation under the main housing duty;[937]
8) the local housing authority is satisfied that the applicant has voluntarily ceased to occupy (as their only or principal home) suitable interim accommodation made available under the main housing duty;[938]
9) the local housing authority is no longer satisfied that the applicant is eligible;[939]
10) the local housing authority is satisfied that a mistake of fact led to the applicant being notified that they were owed the interim accommodation duty;[940]
11) the local housing authority is satisfied that the applicant has withdrawn their application;[941] or

933 H(W)A 2014 s76(2)(b).
934 H(W)A 2014 s76(3)(a).
935 H(W)A 2014 s76(3)(b). 'Private rented sector offer' is defined at H(W)A 2014 s76(4): see para 7.285(5).
936 H(W)A 2014 s76(3)(c).
937 H(W)A 2014 s76(6). This includes accommodation which was originally provided under the interim accommodation duty and has continued under the main housing duty: H(W)A 2014 s76(6). See paras 7.152–7.157 for becoming homeless intentionally.
938 H(W)A 2014 s76(7). This includes accommodation which was originally provided under the interim accommodation duty and has continued under the main housing duty: H(W)A 2014 s76(7).
939 H(W)A 2014 s79(2). See paras 7.6–7.93 for eligibility.
940 H(W)A 2014 s79(3).
941 H(W)A 2014 s79(4).

12) the local housing authority is satisfied that the applicant is unreasonably failing to co-operate with the homelessness application process.[942]

7.290 Where the applicant is a restricted case,[943] the local housing authority must bring the main housing duty to an end by way of a private rented sector offer 'so far as reasonably practicable'.[944]

7.291 In all of these circumstances, the main housing duty will not end unless and until the applicant is notified in writing:

1) that the local housing authority no longer regards itself as being subject to the relevant duty;
2) why it considers the duty has ended;
3) that the applicant has the right to request a review; and
4) of the time within which the review must be requested.[945]

7.292 As this demonstrates, an applicant has the right to request a review of the decision that the main housing duty has come to an end.[946] An applicant may also request a review of the suitability of any accommodation offered in (or in connection with) the discharge of the main housing duty, regardless of whether or not the offer has been accepted.[947]

7.293 If the applicant does request a review, the local housing authority has a power, but not a duty, to secure accommodation pending that review.[948] There is also a power to accommodate the applicant pending any appeal of the review decision to the county court,[949] but this is only available where the local housing authority had previously been subject to the interim accommodation duty,[950] the main housing duty[951] or the duty to secure accommodation pending referral of the applicant's case to another local housing authority.[952]

942 H(W)A 2014 s79(5).
943 As defined at H(W)A 2014 s76(5): see paras 7.80–7.83.
944 H(W)A 2014 s76(5).
945 H(W)A 2014 ss76(1), 79(1) and 84.
946 H(W)A 2014 s85(1)(c). See paras 7.326–7.350 for reviews and appeals.
947 H(W)A s85(3). See paras 7.239–7.252 for suitability.
948 H(W)A 2014 s69(11).
949 H(W)A 2014 s88(5).
950 Under H(W)A 2014 s68. See paras 7.275–7.283.
951 Under H(W)A 2014 s75.
952 Under H(W)A 2014 s82. See paras 7.323–7.325.

Referral of cases to other local housing authorities

Overview

7.294 A homeless person may apply to any local housing authority for assistance with accommodation. If the authority rejects the application on the grounds that the applicant is not from its area, or does not have a connection with its area, this will constitute unlawful gatekeeping.[953] The authority must accept the application and commence inquiries into it.[954]

7.295 However, this does not mean that any duties which arise will inevitably fall upon that local housing authority. In some circumstances, an applicant's case may be referred by the local housing authority which took the application ('the first authority') to another local housing authority ('the second authority').

7.296 Referring a case is, however, a power, not a duty: the first local housing authority is not required to refer an applicant's case to the second authority even if the conditions for doing so are met (and, indeed, even if the applicant themself wishes to be referred).[955] While a local housing authority may have a general policy as to how it will exercise its power to refer, it must consider in each case whether or not to exercise its discretion, taking into account the applicant's personal circumstances.[956]

7.297 It is also a power which is strictly circumscribed. Local housing authorities can only refer cases at certain stages of the homelessness application process and in certain situations, and while doing so they must comply with any duties that arise.

7.298 With the aim of minimising legal disputes between authorities, the Local Government Association (LGA), the Convention of Scottish Local Authorities (CSLA) and the Welsh Local Government Association (WLGA) have agreed upon a set of guidelines and procedures (the *Referral guidelines*) to assist local housing authorities which are making or receiving referrals.[957] The English *Homelessness code of guidance* reminds local housing authorities that while these

953 See para 7.110.

954 Under HA 1996 s184(1) (England) and H(W)A 2014 s62(1) (Wales).

955 There is no right to request a review of a decision by a local housing authority *not* to refer an applicant's case and any challenge would have to be brought by judicial review: *Hackney LBC v Sareen* [2003] EWCA Civ 351, [2003] HLR 54.

956 *R v East Devon DC ex p Robb* (1997) 30 HLR 922, QBD and *Ozbek v Ipswich BC* [2006] EWCA Civ 534, [2006] HLR 41.

957 *Procedures for referrals of homeless applicants to another local authority; Guidelines for local authorities on procedures for referral*, LGA, CSLA, WLGA (undated).

guidelines are 'now widely used', each case should be considered 'individually on its own particular facts'.[958]

The stages at which a case may be referred

England

7.299 In England, there are two stages at which an applicant's case may be referred to another local housing authority if the conditions for doing so are satisfied.

7.300 *First*, an applicant's case may be referred at the relief duty[959] stage, but only to another local housing authority in England – it cannot be referred at this stage to a local housing authority in Wales.[960] If the first local housing authority would be subject to the relief duty, but considers that the conditions for referral to the second local housing authority are met, it may notify the second authority of this opinion. In order for the relief duty to arise, the first local housing authority must be satisfied that the applicant is homeless[961] and eligible for assistance.[962] There is no requirement that the applicant have a priority need[963] or have not become homeless intentionally.[964]

7.301 If the first local housing authority decides to notify the second local housing at this stage that it considers the conditions for referral to be met, then two duties to notify the applicant arise:

1) If the first local housing authority has notified or intends to notify the second local housing authority of its opinion that the conditions for referral are met, it must at the same time notify the applicant of that decision and the reasons for it.[965] In what appears to be a drafting error in the legislation, the notice must inform the applicant of their right to request a review of the decision and of the time within which such a request must be made, but in fact there is no such right of review: any challenge would have to be brought by judicial review.
2) Once the decision has been made as to whether or not the conditions for referral are in fact met,[966] the first local housing authority

958 At para 10.2.
959 Under HA 1996 s189B(2). See paras 7.187–7.193.
960 HA 1996 s198(A1).
961 See paras 7.121–7.133.
962 See paras 7.6–7.93.
963 See paras 7.136–7.151.
964 See paras 7.152–7.157.
965 HA 1996 s184(4).
966 This decision may be made either by agreement between the two local housing authorities or by a referee.

must notify the applicant of the decision and the reasons for it.[967] The notice must inform the applicant of their right to request a review of the decision (which right does in this case exist)[968] and of the time within which such a request must be made.[969]

7.302 *Second*, an applicant's case may be referred at the main housing duty[970] stage.[971] In order for the main housing duty to arise, the local housing authority must be satisfied that the applicant is homeless, eligible for assistance, has a priority need and did not become homeless intentionally.[972] If the first local housing authority would be subject to the main housing duty, but considers that the conditions for referral to another local housing authority are met, it may notify the second local housing authority of this opinion. Unlike referral at the relief duty stage, referral at this point may be to a local housing authority in England, Wales or Scotland.[973]

7.303 If the first local housing authority decides to notify the second local housing authority at this stage that it considers the conditions for referral to be met, then the duties of notification to the applicant are slightly different from those which apply to referral at the relief duty stage:

1) If the first local housing authority has notified or intends to notify the second local housing authority of its opinion that the conditions for referral are met, then it *may* notify the applicant of this decision and the reasons for it, but – in contrast to the same decision at the relief duty stage – it is not required to do so.[974] If it does decide to give this notification, it cannot do so until the relief duty[975] has come to an end.[976] Although there is a right to request a review of such a decision,[977] perhaps surprisingly, there is no

967 HA 1996 s199A(3).

968 HA 2996 ss198(5) and 202(1)(d).

969 HA 1996 s199A(3).

970 Under HA 1996 s193(2). See paras 7.263–7.269.

971 HA 1996 s198(1).

972 See para 7.254 for the limited exceptions to this.

973 HA 1996 s198(1).

974 HA 1996 s200(1). It is worth noting that the English *Homelessness code of guidance* appears to assume that the first notification is in fact required, or at least will always be given: para 10.47.

975 Under HA 1996 s189B(2). See paras 7.187–7.193.

976 HA 1996 s200(1A).

977 HA 1996 s202(1)(c).

statutory requirement that the notice inform the applicant of this right.[978]

2) However, once the decision has been made as to whether or not the conditions for referral are in fact met,[979] then – as at the relief duty stage – the first local housing authority *must* notify the applicant of the decision and the reasons for it.[980] In this case, the notice must inform the applicant of their right to request a review of the decision[981] and of the time within which such a request must be made.[982]

Wales

7.304 In Wales, there is only one stage at which an applicant's case may be referred and this is at the relief duty[983] stage.[984] Thus if the first local housing authority would be subject to the relief duty, but considers that the conditions for referral to another local housing authority are met, it may notify the second local housing authority of this opinion. However, it may only do so in respect of an applicant who has a priority need[985] and did not become homeless intentionally,[986] which means that the local housing authority will have to have satisfied itself of these matters before the applicant's case is referred.[987]

7.305 Unlike the HA 1996, which deals with referral to local housing authorities in Scotland as well as Wales and England, the H(W)A 2014 only provides for referrals to local housing authorities in Wales or England. It appears therefore that it is not possible for a Welsh local housing authority to refer a case to Scotland.

7.306 Two duties to notify the applicant arise where a case is to be referred to a local housing authority in either England or Wales:

1) First, if the first local housing authority has notified or intends to notify the second local housing authority of its opinion that the conditions for referral are met, it must at the same time notify the applicant of that decision and the reasons for it.[988] The notice

978 HA 1996 s200(1).
979 By agreement between the two local housing authorities or by a referee.
980 HA 1996 s200(2).
981 Under HA 1996 s202(1)(d) and (e).
982 HA 1996 s200(2).
983 Under H(W)A 2014 s73(1). See paras 7.221–7.227.
984 H(W)A 2014 s80(1).
985 See paras 7.136–7.151.
986 See paras 7.152–7.157.
987 H(W)A 2014 s80(2)(b).
988 H(W)A 2014 s63(3).

must inform the applicant of their right to request a review of this decision and of the time within which such a review must be requested.[989]

2) Second, once the decision has been made as to whether or not the conditions for referral are in fact met, the first local housing authority must notify the applicant of the decision and the reasons for it.[990] The notice must inform the applicant of their right to request a review of the decision and of the time within which such a request must be made.[991]

The circumstances in which a case may be referred

7.307 There are three situations in which an applicant's case may be referred to a different local housing authority:

1) The first applies to referrals by local housing authorities in England and Wales to other local housing authorities in England and Wales (and, for referrals coming from England, in Scotland). An applicant's case may be referred where the applicant has a local connection with another local housing authority and does not have a local connection with the authority to which they have applied.[992]
2) The second applies only to referrals by local housing authorities in England to local housing authorities in England. An applicant's case may be referred to a local housing authority from whom they had accepted a private rented sector offer[993] within the last two years.[994]
3) The third applies only to referrals by local housing authorities in England to local housing authorities in England or Wales. An applicant's case may be referred back to a local housing authority where that authority, within the last five years, placed the applicant in the district of the local housing authority to which the applicant has applied.[995]

989 H(W)A 2014 ss63(4) and 84(1).
990 H(W)A 2014 s82(2).
991 H(W)A 2014 s84(1).
992 See paras 7.308–7.317.
993 See para 7.265(8).
994 See para 7.318.
995 See para 7.319.

Local connection referrals

7.308 An applicant's case may be referred by a local housing authority in England or Wales to a second local housing authority in England or Wales[996] where the following conditions are met:[997]

1) neither the applicant nor any person who might reasonably be expected to reside with them has a local connection[998] with the district of the first local housing authority;
2) the applicant or a person who might reasonably be expected to reside with them has a local connection with the district of the second local housing authority;
3) neither the applicant nor any person who might reasonably be expected to reside with them will run the risk of domestic abuse[999] in the area of the second local housing authority; and
4) neither the applicant nor any person who might reasonably be expected to reside with them has suffered (in England) violence[1000] or (in Wales) abuse[1001] (other than domestic abuse) in the district of the second local housing authority – unless it is not probable that the victim's return to the district will lead to further violence or abuse of a similar kind against them.

7.309 The key concept here is local connection. The question is whether or not a local connection exists as at the date of the decision on whether the conditions for referral are met and not, for example, as at the date of the original application.[1002] The ways in which a person can have a local connection are prescribed by statute:[1003] any ties that may exist with another local housing authority which do not fall within the statutory categories of local connection are irrelevant. There are five types of local connection that apply to applicants to local housing authorities in both England and Wales and two types that apply only to applicants in England.

996 Or Scotland, but only where the referral comes from a local housing authority in England.

997 HA 1996 s198(2) and (2A) (England) and H(W)A 2014 s80(3) and (4) (Wales).

998 See paras 7.309–7.317.

999 As defined in Domestic Abuse Act 2021 s1 (England) and H(W)A 2014 s58(1) (Wales).

1000 As defined in HA 1996 s198(3)(b).

1001 As defined in H(W)A 2014 s58(1).

1002 *Mohamed v Hammersmith and Fulham LBC* [2001] UKHL 57, [2002] 1 AC 547.

1003 At HA 1996 s199 (England) and H(W)A 2014 s81 (Wales).

Types of local connection that apply to applicants to local housing authorities in both England and Wales

7.310 The five types of local connection that apply to applicants to local housing authorities in England and Wales are as follows:

1) The first type of local connection which applies to both England and Wales arises where a person has a local connection with the district of a local housing authority because they are, or were in the past, normally resident there and that residence is or was of their own choice.[1004] 'Normal residence' means 'a place where at the relevant time the person in fact resides'.[1005] Temporary accommodation provided by a local housing authority pursuant to its duties under HA 1996 Part VII may constitute normal residence.[1006] The concept of residence of their 'own choice' was discussed by the then House of Lords in *Al-Ameri v Kensington and Chelsea RLBC*.[1007] This case concerned accommodation provided to former asylum-seekers under the Immigration and Asylum Act (IAA) 1999 s95.[1008] This accommodation had been allocated with no regard to the appellants' preferred locality and they were informed that if they refused it, no further offer would be made. The House of Lords held that they did not reside in this accommodation of their own choice:

   > . . . such residence must be of the resident's own choice. So the question to be asked of each respondent is 'Did you reside in Glasgow of your own choice?' To that question there can be, in the case of each respondent, only one possible answer: 'No. I was given no choice about where I resided. I resided in Glasgow because, and only because, that was the only place where I was offered accommodation and the means to meet the most basic of human needs'.[1009]

1004 HA 1996 s199(1)(a) (England) and H(W)A 2014 s81(2)(a) (Wales).

1005 *Mohamed v Hammersmith and Fulham LBC* [2001] UKHL 57, [2002] 1 AC 547 at para 18 per Lord Slynn.

1006 *Mohamed v Hammersmith and Fulham LBC* [2001] UKHL 57, [2002] 1 AC 547 and *Minott v Cambridge City Council* [2022] EWCA Civ 159, [2022] PTSR 786 at para 37 per Macur LJ. In *Minott*, Underhill LJ stated in obiter dicta at para 100 that even residence which 'is in some sense unlawful' may still constitute normal residence.

1007 [2004] UKHL 4, [2004] 2 AC 159.

1008 The position of applicants who have previously been provided with accommodation under IAA 1999 s95 is now dealt with at HA 1996 s199(6) and H(W)A 2014 s81(5): see para 7.312(5).

1009 *Al-Ameri v Kensington and Chelsea RLBC* [2004] UKHL 4, [2004] 2 AC 159 at para 17 per Lord Slynn. See also Lord Hope at paras 41–44.

Statute has also provided that residence is *deemed* not to be of a person's own choice where a person is detained in the district under the authority of an Act of Parliament or enactment.[1010]

2) The second type of local connection which applies to both England and Wales arises where a person has a local connection with the district of a local housing authority because they are employed there.[1011]
3) The third type of local connection which applies to both England and Wales arises where a person has a local connection with the district of a local housing authority because of family associations.[1012] In *Ozbek v Ipswich BC*,[1013] Mr Ozbek, a Turkish asylum-seeker who had been granted indefinite leave to remain, applied to Ipswich Borough Council as homeless. Two of his brothers, three cousins, a first cousin once removed and a relative of his wife lived in the Ipswich area. The *Referral guidelines*[1014] stated that a local connection through family associations normally arose where an applicant had parents, adult children or siblings who had been resident in that district for at least five years. Applying this, Ipswich Borough Council found that no local connection existed with its district. The Court of Appeal upheld this decision, finding that the reviewing officer could not be criticised in the light of the contents of the *Referral guidelines*. They did, however, note that family associations could be based on relationships other than those specifically mentioned in the *Referral guidelines*.[1015]
4) The fourth type of local connection which applies to both England and Wales arises where a person has a local connection with the district of a local housing authority because of special circumstances.[1016] The English *Homelessness code of guidance* suggests that this could include the need to be near special medical or support services which are only available in a particular district.[1017] In *R v Kensington and Chelsea RLBC ex p Bishop*[1018] the applicant's

1010 HA 1996 s199(3)(b) (England); and H(W)A 2014 s81(3) (Wales).
1011 HA 1996 s199(1)(b) (England); and H(W)A 2014 s81(2)(b) (Wales).
1012 HA 1996 s199(1)(c) (England); and H(W)A 2014 s81(2)(c) (Wales).
1013 [2006] EWCA Civ 534, [2006] HLR 41.
1014 See para 7.298.
1015 [2006] EWCA Civ 534, [2006] HLR 41 at para 43.
1016 HA 1996 s199(1)(d) (England); and H(W)A 2014 s81(2)(d) (Wales).
1017 *Homelessness code of guidance*, para 10.11.
1018 11 February 1983, unreported, QBD.

traumatic experiences prior to fleeing as a refugee, together with the existence of an ethnic minority community of same-language speakers in the local housing authority's district and enrolment at a local college, constituted special circumstances.

7.311 In all these situations, the mere presence of one of these statutory factors will not, on its own, suffice: it must give rise to 'a connection in real terms'.[1019]

7.312 This is in contrast to the last local connection category which applies to both England and Wales and which may be of particular importance to migrants:

5) A person has a local connection with the district of a local housing authority if they were, at any time,[1020] provided with accommodation in that district under IAA 1999 s95.[1021] This only applies to the most recent section 95 accommodation provided.[1022]

7.313 This category was introduced in response to the decision of the (then) House of Lords in *Al-Ameri v Kensington and Chelsea RLBC*[1023] in which it was held that an asylum-seeker did not reside in accommodation provided under IAA 1999 s95 of his own choice and therefore did not have a local connection with the area in which he had been accommodated for the purposes of HA 1996 s199(1)(a).[1024] The introduction of this category means that former asylum-seekers *are* now deemed to have a local connection with the district in which they were accommodated under IAA 1999 s95.

7.314 This deeming provision does not, however, apply to accommodation provided under IAA 1999 s4 or s98.[1025] The decision in *Al-Ameri v Kensington and Chelsea RLBC*[1026] is still relevant to accommodation

1019 *R v Eastleigh BC ex p Betts* [1983] 2 AC 613, HL.

1020 The phrase 'at any time' indicates that this local connection will last forever, although it may of course be rendered irrelevant by the subsequent formation of local connections with other areas.

1021 HA 1996 s199(6) (England); and H(W)A 2014 s81(5) (Wales). See chapter 5 for further discussion of the support available under IAA 1999 s95.

1022 HA 1996 s199(7) (England); and H(W)A 2014 s81(6) (Wales).

1023 [2004] UKHL 4, [2004] 2 AC 159.

1024 See para 7.310(1).

1025 The deeming provision also does not apply to accommodation provided under the Asylum Support (Interim Provisions) Regulations 1999 SI No 3056, although it is doubtful that anybody is still supported under these regulations, or to the provision of accommodation in an accommodation centre under Nationality, Immigration and Asylum Act (NIAA) 2002 s22, but this has never been brought into force.

1026 [2004] UKHL 4, [2004] 2 AC 159.

provided under these sections. Such accommodation will not, therefore, give rise to a local connection because the occupant does not reside there of their own choice. It appears that the deeming provision will also not apply to accommodation provided under the power contained at IA 2016 Sch 10 para 9.[1027] As the applicant is unlikely to reside in such accommodation of their own choice, it would appear probable that this too cannot give rise to a local connection.[1028]

7.315 This category does not apply to people provided with accommodation under IAA 1999 s95 in Scotland. Such accommodation is not capable of giving rise to a local connection because residence there is not of a person's own choice.[1029] However, a person who has been accommodated in Scotland under IAA 1999 s95 and who then applies to a local housing authority in England (not Wales) gains little from this exception because by virtue of Asylum and Immigration (Treatment of Claimants, etc) Act 2004 s11(2) and (3), the main housing duty[1030] is disapplied in respect of them.[1031] Even if they are homeless,[1032] eligible for assistance,[1033] have a priority need for accommodation[1034] and became homeless unintentionally,[1035] the main housing duty will not arise and instead the local housing authority has a power to provide accommodation for a period that would give them a reasonable opportunity of obtaining accommodation and to provide advice and assistance with any attempts they may make to obtain their own accommodation.[1036]

Types of local connection that apply only to applicants to local housing authorities in England

7.316 There are two further types of local connection which *only* apply in England:

1027 This gives the secretary of state the power to arrange for a person to be accommodated at a particular address where they are on immigration bail subject to a condition requiring them to reside at that address and that they would be unable to support themself at that address unless the power was exercised.

1028 See paras 6.201–6.272.

1029 Housing (Scotland) Act 1987 s27(2)(iii).

1030 Under HA 1996 s193(2). See paras 7.263–7.269.

1031 Unless the person has a local connection under one of other categories: Asylum and Immigration (Treatment of Claimants, etc) Act 2004 s11(2)(d).

1032 See paras 7.123–7.133.

1033 See paras 7.6–7.93.

1034 See paras 7.136–7.151.

1035 See paras 7.152–7.157.

1036 Asylum and Immigration (Treatment of Claimants, etc) Act 2004 s11(3)(b).

1) The first applies where a person is owed a duty under ChA 1989 s23C. This provision contains the duties owed by local authorities to former relevant children. A 'former relevant child' is defined[1037] as a person who:
   a) is aged between 18 and 21[1038] (or between 18 and 25 where they are engaged in a programme of education or training which is set out in their pathway plan);[1039] and
   b) was looked after by the local authority for a period of at least 13 weeks beginning after their 14th birthday and ending after their 16th birthday.[1040]

   The duties owed by social services authorities to the former relevant children for whom they are responsible include keeping in touch, maintaining a pathway plan, continuing with the appointment of a personal adviser and providing various other forms of assistance.[1041] The duties are owed by the authority which was last responsible for the person or which was looking after them when they turned 18.[1042] A person who is owed any of the duties imposed by ChA 1989 s23C will be deemed to have a local connection with the district of the local authority which is subject to the duty.[1043] This connection will last for as long as the duty is owed.[1044]
2) The second type of local connection arises where:
   a) a person is aged under 21;[1045]
   b) they were normally resident[1046] in the district of a local housing authority by virtue of accommodation provided under ChA 1989 s22A;[1047]

1037 At ChA 1989 s23C(1). See paras 9.160–9.164.
1038 ChA 1989 s23C(1) and (6).
1039 ChA 1989 s23C(7).
1040 ChA 1989 ss23A and 23C(1) and Sch 2 para 19B; and Care Planning, Placement and Care Review (England) Regulations 2010 SI No 959 reg 40.
1041 ChA 1989 s23C(2)–(5A). See paras 9.160–9.174 for a full discussion of the duties owed to former relevant children.
1042 ChA 1989 s23C(1).
1043 HA 196 s199(8). HA 1996 s199(8) states that if the local authority subject to the duty is also the local housing authority, the connection will be with its district. Otherwise, the connection will be with every district of the local housing authority that falls within the area of the local authority subject to the duty.
1044 HA 1996 s199(8).
1045 HA 1996 s199(11).
1046 See para 7.310(1) for normal residence.
1047 ChA 1989 s22A contains the duty imposed on local authorities to provide accommodation for children in their care: see paras 9.85–9.89.

c) they were normally resident there for a continuous period of at least two years; and
d) that two-year period began before they reached the age of 16.

A person who meets these criteria will be deemed to have a local connection with the district of the local housing authority in which they were normally resident.[1048]

7.317 These two categories may be of particular relevance to migrant care leavers who are, perhaps, more likely to have been accommodated in certain areas (such as Kent, where many unaccompanied asylum-seeking children (UASCs) first come to the attention of social services, or Croydon, where many UASCs present to the Home Office). They may also be more likely than other applicants to lack a local connection to other districts.

Referral following prior acceptance of a private rented sector offer

7.318 An applicant's case may be referred by one local housing authority in England (the first local housing authority) to another local housing authority in England (the second local housing authority) where the following conditions are met:[1049]

1) the applicant accepted a private rented sector offer[1050] made by the *second* local housing authority pursuant to a previous homelessness application;
2) within two years of the date of acceptance, the applicant applies to the *first* local housing authority;
3) neither the applicant, nor any person who might reasonably be expected to live with them, will run the risk of domestic abuse[1051] in the district of the second local housing authority; and
4) neither the applicant, nor any person who might reasonably be expected to live with them, has suffered violence[1052] (other than domestic abuse) in the district of the second local housing authority, unless it is not probable that the victim's return to the district will lead to further violence or abuse of a similar kind against them.

Referral following placement in the local housing authority's area

7.319 An applicant's case may be referred by a local housing authority in England (the first local housing authority) to another local housing

1048 HA 1996 s199(10).
1049 HA 1996 s198(2ZA) and (2A).
1050 Under HA 1996 s193(7AA).
1051 As defined in Domestic Abuse Act 2021 s1.
1052 As defined in HA 1996 s198(3)(b).

authority in England or Wales (the second local housing authority) where the following conditions are met:[1053]

1) the applicant was placed in accommodation in the district of the *first* local housing authority by the *second* local housing authority;
2) that placement was made pursuant to the second local housing authority's functions under HA 1996 Part VII or H(W)A 2014 Part 2; and
3) the application to the first local housing authority is made within the period of five years plus the time between the date of the application to the second local housing authority and the date when the applicant was placed in the accommodation.[1054]

Duties owed in referral cases

England

7.320 Where the first authority has informed the applicant that it has notified, or intends to notify, the second authority of its opinion that the conditions for referral are met (either because it is required to do so, as the referral is being made at the relief duty[1055] stage,[1056] or because it has chosen to do so, where the referral is being made at the main housing duty[1057] stage[1058]) then any interim accommodation duty owed by the first authority under HA 1996 s188(1)[1059] ends[1060] and the first authority does not become subject to the relief duty[1061] or main housing duty[1062] (as the case may be).[1063] This does not mean, however, that the first authority may immediately cease accommodating the applicant. If the notification is given at the stage where the relief duty would be owed, then (provided it has reason to believe that the applicant may have a priority need) the first authority must continue to secure that accommodation is available for the applicant's occupation until the applicant is notified of the decision as to

1053 HA 1996 s198(4) and (4A).
1054 Allocation of Housing and Homelessness (Miscellaneous Provisions) (England) Regulations 2006 SI No 2527 reg 3.
1055 Under HA 1996 s189B(2). See paras 7.187–7.193.
1056 See para 7.300.
1057 Under HA 1996 s193(2). See paras 7.263–7.269.
1058 See para 7.302.
1059 See paras 7.253–7.259.
1060 HA 1996 ss199A(1)(a) and 200(1)(a).
1061 Under HA 1996 s189B(2). See paras 7.187–7.193.
1062 Under HA 1996 s193(2). See paras 7.263–7.269.
1063 HA 1996 ss199A(1)(b) and 200(1)(b).

whether or not the conditions for referral are met.[1064] If the notification is given at the stage where the main housing duty would be owed, the first authority must continue to secure that accommodation is available for the applicant's occupation until the applicant is notified of the decision as to whether or not the conditions for referral are met.[1065]

7.321 If it is then decided that the conditions for referral are met, the duties which would otherwise have been owed by the first authority will fall upon the second authority. This means that, if the referral was made at the relief duty stage, the second authority will be subject to the relief duty[1066] and, if it appears that the applicant may have a priority need, the interim accommodation duty.[1067] If the referral was made at the main housing duty stage, the second authority will be subject to this duty (under HA 1996 s193(2) in England and H(W)A 2014 s73 in Wales).[1068]

7.322 If, however, it is decided that the conditions for referral are not met, then the first authority will become subject to the duties which would have been owed had the question of referral not arisen.[1069] The authority cannot change its mind about what duties are owed because the referral was rejected.[1070]

Wales

7.323 Where the first authority has informed the applicant that it has notified or intends to notify the second local housing authority of its opinion that the conditions for referral are met, then the interim accommodation duty[1071] will cease[1072] and the first authority will not be subject to the main housing duty.[1073] However, the first authority must secure that accommodation is available for occupation by the

1064 HA 1996 s199A(2). See paras 7.136–7.151 for priority need.

1065 HA 1996 s200(1).

1066 The second authority can only revisit the decision that this duty would be owed in specific circumstances, as set out in HA 1996 s199A(5)(c).

1067 HA 1996 s199A(5)(a).

1068 HA 1996 s200(4) (England); and H(W)A 2014 s83(2) (Wales).

1069 HA 1996 ss199A(4) and 200(3).

1070 *R (Sambotin) v Brent LBC* [2018] EWCA Civ 1826, [2019] HLR 5.

1071 Under H(W)A 2014 s68: see paras 7.275–7.283. This will have arisen because only applicants who have a priority need may be referred: see para 7.304.

1072 Under H(W)A 2014 s75: see paras 7.284–7.293. H(W)A 2014 s82(1)(a).

1073 H(W)A 2014 s82(1)(b).

applicant until the applicant is notified of the decision as to whether or not the conditions for referral are met.[1074]

7.324 If it is then decided that the conditions for referral are indeed met, the duties which would otherwise have been owed by the first authority will fall upon the second authority. If the second authority is in Wales, it will be subject to the main housing duty under H(W)A 2014 s75.[1075] If the second authority is in England, it will be subject to the main housing duty under HA 1996 s193(2).[1076]

7.325 If, however, it is decided that the conditions for referral are not met, the first authority will be subject to the main housing duty under H(W)A 2014 s75.[1077]

Reviews and appeals

7.326 The HA 1996 and H(W)A 2014 both provide a statutory means of challenging certain decisions made in respect of a homelessness application.[1078] This consists of a right to request that the local housing authority review the decision in question[1079] followed by a right to appeal to the county court on a point of law.[1080]

7.327 In England, the decisions which attract a right of review and subsequent appeal are as follows:

1) any decision as to an applicant's eligibility for assistance;[1081]
2) any decision as to what duty (if any) is owed to an applicant under HA 1996 ss189B–193C and 195;[1082]
3) any decision as to the steps the local housing authority is to take under the relief duty or to give notice bringing the relief duty to an end;[1083]
4) any decision to give notice to the applicant under HA 1996 s193B(2) that they have deliberately and unreasonably refused to co-operate;[1084]

1074 HW(A) 2014 s82(1).
1075 H(W)A 2014 s82(4). See paras 7.284–7.293.
1076 HA 1996 s201A(2). See paras 7.263–7.269.
1077 H(W)A 2014 s82(3).
1078 The decisions to which this applies are set out at HA 1996 s202(1) (England); and H(W)A 2014 s85(1) (Wales).
1079 HA 1996 s202 (England); and H(W)A 2014 s85 (Wales).
1080 HA 1996 s204(1) (England); and H(W)A 2014 s88(1) (Wales).
1081 HA 1996 s202(1)(a).
1082 HA 1996 s202(1)(b).
1083 HA 1996 s202(1)(ba).
1084 HA 1996 s202(1)(bb).

5) any decision as to the steps the local housing authority is to take under the prevention duty or to give notice bringing the prevention duty to an end;[1085]
6) any decision to notify another local housing authority under HA 1996 s198(1) that the conditions for referral of the applicant's case are met;[1086]
7) any decision under HA 1996 s198(5) as to whether the conditions are met for referral of the applicant's case;[1087]
8) any decision under HA 1996 s200(3) or (4) as to the duty owed to an applicant whose case is being referred;[1088]
9) any decision as to the suitability of accommodation offered to an applicant in discharge of the duty under HA 1996 ss189B–193C, 195, 200(3) or (4) or pursuant to HA 1996 s193(7);[1089]
10) any decision as to the suitability of accommodation offered by way of a private rented sector offer;[1090] and
11) any decision as to the suitability of accommodation offered by way of a final accommodation offer or a final Part 6 offer.[1091]

7.328 In Wales, the applicant has a right to request a review (and may subsequently appeal) any of the following:

1) a decision as to the applicant's eligibility;[1092]
2) a decision that a duty is not owed to the applicant under H(W)A 2014 s66, s68, s74 or s75;[1093]
3) a decision that a duty owed under H(W)A 2014 s66, s68, s73 or s75 has come to an end (including where the local housing authority has referred the applicant's case to another authority or decided that the conditions for referral are met);[1094]
4) whether or not reasonable steps were taken during the period in which the relief duty was owed to help to secure that suitable accommodation would be available for the applicant's occupation.

1085 HA 1996 s202(1)(bc).
1086 HA 1996 s202(1)(c).
1087 HA 1996 s202(1)(d).
1088 HA 1996 s202(1)(e).
1089 HA 1996 s202(1)(f).
1090 HA 1996 s202(1)(g).
1091 HA 1996 s202(1)(h).
1092 H(W)A 2014 s85(1)(a).
1093 H(W)A 2014 s85(1)(b).
1094 H(W)A 2014 s85(1)(c).

This right only accrues where the relief duty has come to an end under HW(A) 2014 s74(2) or (3);[1095]

5) the suitability of any accommodation offered to the applicant in discharge of, or in connection with the discharge of, a homelessness duty.[1096]

7.329 Where a decision falls outside this process, the applicant's only recourse is to seek a judicial review or to make a complaint to the local housing authority and/or the ombudsman.[1097]

7.330 The procedure which must be followed on the review is set out:

- for England, at HA 1996 s203 and in the Homelessness (Review Procedure etc) Regulations ('Homelessness (Review Procedure) Regs') 2018;[1098] and
- for Wales, at H(W)A 2014 s86 and in the Homelessness (Review Procedure) (Wales) Regulations ('Homelessness (Review Procedure) (Wales) Regs') 2015.[1099]

7.331 Where the original decision was made by an officer of the local housing authority and the review decision is also to be made by an officer of the authority, the review must be conducted by someone who was not involved in the original decision.[1100] In England, that person must also be an officer who is senior to the officer who made the original decision.[1101] The local housing authority should notify the applicant of the procedure that will be followed on the review and of their right to make representations.[1102] In England, this initial right to make representations is limited to representations in writing,[1103] but in Wales the applicant should be invited to make

1095 H(W)A 2014 s85(2).

1096 H(W)A 2014 s85(3).

1097 In England, a complaint would lie to the Local Government and Social Care Ombudsman (LGSCO). In Wales, the complaint would be to the Public Services Ombudsman for Wales.

1098 SI No 223. These regulations apply to any request for a review made after 3 April 2018 (see reg 11). The Allocation of Housing and Homelessness (Review Procedures) Regulations 1999 SI No 71 apply in respect of any request for a review made before this date.

1099 SI No 1266 (W 86).

1100 Homelessness (Review Procedure) Regs 2018 reg 8(2)(a) (England); and Homelessness (Review Procedure) (Wales) Regs 2015 reg 3 (Wales).

1101 Homelessness (Review Procedure) Regs 2018 reg 8(2)(b).

1102 Homelessness (Review Procedure) Regs 2018 reg 5(3) (England); and Homelessness (Review Procedure) (Wales) Regs 2015 reg 2(2) (Wales).

1103 Homelessness (Review Procedure) Regs 2018 reg 5(3)(a).

representations orally or in writing or both.[1104] Those representations must, of course, be taken into account by the reviewing officer.[1105]

7.332 The review process is not limited to errors of law but is a reconsideration of all the relevant facts and law. The reviewing officer must consider all matters afresh as they exist at the date of the review.[1106] The only exceptions to this are:

1) Where the reviewing officer is considering the applicant's reasons for refusing an offer of accommodation. In those cases, the reviewing officer will look at the facts as at the date of the refusal.[1107]
2) Where the original decision unlawfully deprived the applicant of a benefit to which they were entitled at the date of the original decision. In such cases, the reviewing officer should ensure that the applicant is accorded that benefit even if on the facts as at the date of the review they are no longer so entitled.[1108]
3) Where an applicant to a local housing authority in Wales has or may have a priority need[1109] on the basis that they are aged 16 or 17,[1110] or aged between 18 and 21 and at particular risk of sexual or financial exploitation,[1111] or aged between 18 and 21 and were looked after, accommodated or fostered at any time while under the age of 18[1112] (or are a person with whom any of these people resides or might reasonably be expected to reside). In these cases, the question of priority need will depend on the age that the applicant (or the person residing with the applicant) was at the date on which the application was made to the local housing authority.[1113] This means that the reviewing officer must look, insofar as they are concerned with the issue of age, to the situation as it was when the application was made.

1104 Homelessness (Review Procedure) (Wales) Regs 2015 reg 2(2)(a).

1105 Homelessness (Review Procedure) Regs 2018 reg 7(1) (England); and Homelessness (Review Procedure) (Wales) Regs 2015 reg 5(1) (Wales).

1106 *Temur v Hackney LBC* [2014] EWCA Civ 877, [2014] HLR 39 at paras 33–34 per Jackson LJ.

1107 *Omar v Westminster City Council* [2008] EWCA Civ 421, [2008] HLR 36.

1108 *Robinson v Hammersmith and Fulham LBC* [2006] EWCA Civ 1122, [2007] HLR 7.

1109 See paras 7.136–7.151.

1110 H(W)A 2014 s70(1)(f).

1111 H(W)A 2014 s70(1)(g).

1112 H(W)A 2014 s70(1)(h).

1113 H(W)A 2014 s70(1)(f), (g) and (h).

7.333 A special procedural safeguard applies where the reviewing officer considers that there is a deficiency or irregularity[1114] in the original decision, or in the way in which it was made, but is still minded to make a decision which is against the interests of the applicant. In such cases, the reviewing officer must notify the applicant:

1) that they are so minded, and why; and
2) that the applicant may make further representations orally or in writing or both.[1115]

7.334 An applicant who is dissatisfied with a review decision may appeal to the county court. However, unlike with the review procedure, this right of challenge is limited to points of law. This has been described as encompassing:

> . . . not only matters of legal interpretation but also the full range of issues which would otherwise be the subject of an application to the High Court for judicial review, such as procedural error and questions of vires, to which I add, also of irrationality and (in)adequacy of reasons.[1116]

7.335 A decision of the county court may be appealed to the Court of Appeal. Any such appeal will be a second appeal and must therefore meet the second appeals test at Civil Procedure Rules 1998[1117] (CPR) 52.7(2):

> (2) The Court of Appeal will not give permission unless it considers that–
> (a) the appeal would–
> (i) have a real prospect of success; and
> (ii) raise an important point of principle or practice; or
> (b) there is some other compelling reason for the Court of Appeal to hear it.

Accommodation pending review and appeal

England

7.336 In general, there is no duty on local housing authorities in England to provide accommodation pending review.

1114 'Deficiency or irregularity' is not limited to errors of law (*Hall v Wandsworth LBC* [2004] EWCA Civ 1740, [2005] 2 All ER 192 at para 29). It will exist where an important aspect of the case was either not addressed, or not addressed adequately, by the original decision-maker. This may arise because of a subsequent change in the facts: *NJ v Wandsworth LBC* [2013] EWCA Civ 1373, [2014] PTSR 497 at para 70 per Lewison LJ.

1115 Homelessness (Review Procedure) Regs 2018 reg 7(2) (England); and Homelessness (Review Procedure) (Wales) Regs 2015 reg 5(2) (Wales).

1116 *Tower Hamlets LBC v Begum (Nipa)* [2000] 1 WLR 306, (2000) 32 HLR 445, CA at p452 per Auld LJ.

1117 SI No 3132.

7.337 The exception to this is where:

1) an applicant is owed the relief duty;[1118]
2) the applicant has refused a final accommodation offer[1119] or a final Part 6 offer;[1120] and
3) the applicant has requested a review of the suitability of the offered accommodation.[1121]

7.338 The refusal of the offer would ordinarily bring the relief duty to an end, which is itself one of the triggers for the interim accommodation duty[1122] to end. However, HA 1996 s188(2A) provides that the relief duty is not to be taken as having come to an end until the decision on review has been notified to the applicant. The effect of this is that, for applicants with a priority need,[1123] the interim accommodation duty will continue until the decision on review has been notified to the applicant.

7.339 Otherwise, there is no obligation for accommodation to be provided pending a review. However, a local housing authority has the *power* to do so.[1124] When considering whether or not to provide accommodation, the local housing authority should consider:

- the strength of the applicant's case on review;
- whether any new material, information or argument has become available to the local housing authority since the original decision was made;
- the personal circumstances of the applicant and the consequences for them if accommodation is refused;[1125]
- its duties under the EqA 2010;[1126]
- the best interests of any children involved;[1127] and
- any other relevant considerations.

1118 Under HA 1996 s189B(2). See paras 7.187–7.193.
1119 Defined at HA 1996 s193A(4).
1120 Defined at HA 1996 s193A(5).
1121 Under HA 1996 s202(1)(h). See paras 7.239–7.252 for suitability.
1122 Under HA 1996 s188(1). See paras 7.253–7.259.
1123 See paras 7.136–7.151.
1124 Under HA 1996 s188(3).
1125 The three factors at para 7.339(1)–(3) are known as the *Mohammed* factors after the case from which they derive: *R v Camden LBC ex p Mohammed* (1998) 30 HLR 315, QBD.
1126 Including in particular the PSED at EqA 2010 s149.
1127 Children Act 2004 s11. See *Nzolameso v Westminster City Council* [2015] UKSC 22, [2015] 2 All ER 942 for a discussion of the best interests of children and offers of accommodation.

7.340 Pursuant to NIAA 2002 Sch 3[1128] para 1, this power is not available in respect of:

1) a refugee given refugee status by an EEA state (where that person is not an EEA national or a British citizen) or the dependant of such a person;[1129]
2) a former asylum-seeker who has failed to comply with removal directions or the dependant of such a person;[1130]
3) a person (who is not an asylum-seeker) who is unlawfully present in the UK;[1131] and
4) a failed asylum-seeker with a dependent child or children who has failed to leave the UK voluntarily or the dependant of such a person.[1132]

7.341 If it appears to a local authority that the exclusion in NIAA 2002 Sch 3 para 1 applies or may apply to a person falling within categories (2), (3) or (4) then it must inform the Home Office.[1133]

7.342 However, nothing in NIAA 2002 Sch 3 para 1 prevents the power being exercised in support of:

1) a British citizen;[1134]
2) a child;[1135] or
3) if it would be necessary to provide accommodation to avoid a breach of a person's rights under the ECHR.[1136]

7.343 A refusal to provide accommodation pending review can only be challenged by way of judicial review proceedings.

7.344 There is no duty to accommodate an applicant pending appeal. The exception above in respect of accommodation pending review does not apply.[1137] However, a local housing authority again has a

1128 See further paras 5.122-5.131 and 9.195-9.217 for a detailed discussion on the NIAA 2002 Sch 3 exclusions.

1129 NIAA 2002 s54 and Sch 3 paras 1 and 4.

1130 NIAA 2002 s54 and Sch 3 paras 1 and 6.

1131 NIAA 2002 s54 and Sch 3 paras 1 and 7.

1132 NIAA 2002 s54 and Sch 3 paras 1 and 7A. A further category has been added by IA 2016 Sch 12 para 9 but this has not yet come into force. At the time of writing no date has been set for it to do so.

1133 See *Homelessness code of guidance*, para 7.26.

1134 NIAA 2002 Sch 3 para 2(1)(a).

1135 NIAA 2002 Sch 3 para 2(1)(b).

1136 NIAA 2002 Sch 3 para 3. See paras 5.127–5.131, 6.90–6.135 and 9.203–9.217 for the circumstances in which support may be needed to avoid a breach of the ECHR.

1137 See para 7.337.

power to do so. When considering whether or not to exercise this power, the local housing authority should consider the same factors as when considering whether or not to accommodate pending review.[1138] As with the power to accommodate pending review, this discretion cannot be exercised in respect of:

1) a refugee given refugee status by an EEA state (where that person is not an EEA national or a British citizen) or the dependant of such a person;[1139]
2) a former asylum-seeker who has failed to comply with removal directions or the dependant of such a person;[1140]
3) a person (who is not an asylum-seeker) who is unlawfully present in the UK;[1141] and
4) a failed asylum-seeker with a dependent child or children who has failed to leave the UK voluntarily or the dependant of such a person.[1142]

7.345 Again, however, nothing in NIAA 2002 Sch 3 para 1 prevents the power being exercised in support of:

1) a British citizen;[1143]
2) a child;[1144] or
3) if it would be necessary to provide accommodation to avoid a breach of a person's rights under the ECHR.[1145]

7.346 The power to accommodate pending appeal is subject to another restriction. Local housing authorities only have the power to accommodate an applicant pending appeal where they have been under a

1138 See para 7.339.

1139 NIAA 2002 s54 and Sch 3 paras 1 and 4.

1140 NIAA 2002 s54 and Sch 3 paras 1 and 6.

1141 NIAA 2002 s54 and Sch 3 paras 1 and 7.

1142 NIAA 2002 s54 and Sch 3 paras 1 and 7A. A further category has been added by IA 2016 Sch 12 para 9 but this has not yet come into force. At the time of writing no date has been set for it to do so.

1143 NIAA 2002 Sch 3 para 2(1)(a).

1144 NIAA 2002 Sch 3 para 2(1)(b).

1145 NIAA 2002 Sch 3 para 3. See paras 5.127–5.131, 6.90–6.135 and 9.203–9.217 for the circumstances in which support may be needed to avoid a breach of the ECHR.

duty pursuant to HA 1996 s188,[1146] s190,[1147] s199A[1148] or s200.[1149] The common factor here is that the local housing authority will either have been satisfied, or have had reason to believe, that the applicant has a priority need.[1150]

7.347 A refusal to accommodate pending appeal can be the subject of an appeal to the county court under HA 1996 s204A.[1151]

Wales

7.348 Local housing authorities in Wales have the power to accommodate pending review.[1152] This power is not restricted in respect of certain migrants as it is in England. When considering whether or not to exercise it, local housing authorities should have regard to:

- the strength of the applicant's case on review;
- whether any new material, information or argument has become available to the local housing authority since the original decision was made;
- the personal circumstances of the applicant and the consequences for them if accommodation is refused;[1153]
- its duties under the EqA 2010;[1154]
- the best interests of any children involved;[1155] and
- any other relevant considerations.

7.349 A refusal to accommodate pending review can only be challenged by way of judicial review.[1156]

1146 The interim accommodation duty. See paras 7.253–7.259.

1147 The duty to persons becoming homeless intentionally. See paras 7.270–7.274.

1148 The duties owed to an applicant whose case is considered for referral or referred at the relief stage. See paras 7.320–7.325.

1149 HA 1996 s204(4). HA 1996 s200 contains the duties owed to an applicant whose case is considered for referral or referred at the main housing duty stage. See paras 7.320–7.325.

1150 See paras 7.136–7.151.

1151 See paras 7.326–7.335 for appeals.

1152 H(W)A 2014 s69(11).

1153 The three factors at para 7.348(1)–(3) are known as the *Mohammed* factors after the case from which they derive: *R v Camden LBC ex p Mohammed* (1998) 30 HLR 315, QBD.

1154 Including in particular the PSED at EqA 2010 s149.

1155 Children Act 2004 s28.

1156 The Welsh Government, *Code of guidance to local authorities on the allocation of accommodation and homelessness* states that a refusal to accommodate pending review can be challenged by way of an appeal to the county court under H(W)A 2014 s89 but on the wording of section 89 this does not appear to be correct.

7.350 Local housing authorities in Wales have the power to accommodate an applicant pending appeal but, as in England, it only applies where the authority had been subject to one or more of certain duties. Local housing authorities in Wales may only accommodate pending appeal where they had been under a duty pursuant to H(W)A 2014 s68,[1157] s75[1158] or s82.[1159] As with the power to accommodate pending appeal in England, the common factor is the presence of an actual or potential priority need.[1160] A refusal to accommodate pending appeal can be challenged by way of an appeal to the county court under H(W)A 2014 s89.[1161]

Allocation of social housing

Legal framework

7.351 The law relating to the allocation of social housing is contained in HA 1996 Part VI. This applies, with some variations, to both England and Wales.

7.352 There are also statutory codes of guidance for both jurisdictions. For local housing authorities in England, the relevant codes are:

- *Allocation of accommodation: guidance for local housing authorities in England*;[1162]
- *Providing social housing for local people: statutory guidance on social housing allocations for local authorities in England*;[1163]
- *Right to move: statutory guidance on social housing allocations for local housing authorities in England*;[1164]

1157 The interim accommodation duty. See paras 7.275–7.283.

1158 The main housing duty. See paras 7.284–7.293.

1159 H(W)A 2014 s88(5). H(W)A 2014 s82 contains the duty to secure accommodation pending referral of the applicant's case to another local housing authority. See paras 7.320–7.325.

1160 See paras 7.136–7.151.

1161 See paras 7.326–7.335 for appeals.

1162 Department for Communities and Local Government (DCLG – now the Department for Levelling Up, Housing and Communities (DLUHC)), June 2012 (subsequently updated). It is available at: www.gov.uk/guidance/allocation-of-accommodation-guidance-for-local-authorities.

1163 DCLG, December 2013, www.gov.uk/government/collections/social-housing-allocations-guidance.

1164 DCLG, March 2015, www.gov.uk/government/publications/right-to-move-statutory-guidance-on-social-housing-allocations-for-local-housing-authorities-in-england.

- *Improving access to social housing for victims of domestic abuse*;[1165] and
- *Improving access to social housing for members of the armed forces.*[1166]

7.353 For local housing authorities in Wales, the guidance is contained in the Welsh *Code of guidance to local authorities on the allocation of accommodation and homelessness.*[1167]

What is an allocation?

7.354 The term 'allocation' is defined, for the purposes of HA 1996 Part VI, at HA 1996 s159(2). In England, a local authority allocates housing accommodation when it:

1) selects a person to be a secure or introductory tenant of housing accommodation that it holds;
2) nominates a person to be a secure or introductory tenant of housing accommodation held by another authority; or
3) nominates a person to be an assured tenant of housing accommodation held by a social landlord.

In Wales, a local authority allocates housing accommodation when it:

1) selects a person to be a tenant under a secure contract or an introductory standard contract of housing accommodation held by it; or
2) nominates a person to be a tenant under a secure contract or an introductory standard contract of housing accommodation held by another person.

7.355 This means that not every occasion on which a person becomes a tenant of a local housing authority or a housing association will constitute an allocation. In addition to this, a number of exceptions to the above definition have been created. The consequence is that, in England, no 'allocation' takes place where a person becomes a tenant of social housing as a result of:[1168]

1165 MHCLG, November 2018 (subsequently updated), www.gov.uk/government/publications/improving-access-to-social-housing-for-victims-of-domestic-abuse.

1166 MHCLG, June 2020 (subsequently updated), www.gov.uk/government/publications/improving-access-to-social-housing-for-members-of-the-armed-forces.

1167 Welsh Government, March 2016.

1168 IA 2014 Sch 2 para 2 provides that certain of these situations are to be treated as allocations for the purpose of the 'right to rent' legislation: see paras 7.389–7.434.

- the succession to the tenancy on the death of the tenant;[1169]
- the devolution of a fixed-term secure tenancy on the death of the tenant;[1170]
- the lawful assignment of a secure or introductory tenancy;[1171]
- the vesting or disposal of a secure or introductory tenancy pursuant to a court order made under the provisions of certain family law statutes;[1172]
- an introductory tenancy becoming a secure tenancy;[1173]
- an order relating to a social housing tenancy made under Family Law Act 1996 Sch 7 Part II;[1174]
- the allocation of accommodation to an existing secure, introductory or assured tenant, unless the allocation involves a transfer for which the tenant had applied and the local housing authority is satisfied that the tenant is to be given reasonable preference[1175] within the allocation scheme;[1176]
- the provision of suitable alternative accommodation under Land Compensation Act 1973 s39 by the local housing authority to a tenant or owner-occupier who has been displaced from their accommodation;[1177]
- the grant of a secure tenancy following the acquisition of a defective dwelling-house under HA 1985 ss554–555;[1178]
- the grant of a tenancy to a person currently occupying a property under a family intervention tenancy;[1179] or
- a tenancy granted pursuant to a surrender and re-grant procedure where two social housing tenants, one of whom is a flexible or assured shorthold tenant, are exchanging homes.[1180]

7.356 In Wales, no 'allocation' takes place where a person obtains a tenancy of social housing as a result of:

1169 HA 1996 s160(2)(a) and (3)(b).
1170 HA 1996 s160(2)(b).
1171 HA 1996 s160(2)(c), (2)(d) and (3)(c).
1172 HA 1996 s160(2)(e)(i)–(iv) and (3)(d)(i)–(iv). The family law statutes in question are specified at HA 1996 s160(2)(e) and (3)(d).
1173 HA 1996 s160(3)(a).
1174 By virtue of Family Law Act 1996 Sch 7 para 7(1).
1175 See para 7.366 for reasonable preference.
1176 HA 1996 s159(4A) and (4B).
1177 Allocation of Housing (England) Regulations 2002 SI No 3264 reg 3.
1178 Allocation of Housing (England) Regulations 2002 reg 3.
1179 Allocation of Housing (England) Regulations 2002 reg 3.
1180 HA 1996 s160(2)(da).

- the succession to the secure occupation contract on the death of the tenant. This includes a substitute succession under Renting Homes (Wales) Act 2016 s80;[1181]
- the transfer of a secure contract to a potential successor;[1182]
- the transfer of a secure contract to another secure contract-holder;[1183]
- the vesting or disposal of a secure contract or standard introductory contract pursuant to a court order made under the provisions of certain family law statutes;[1184]
- an introductory standard contract becoming a secure contract;[1185]
- a prohibited conduct standard contract becoming a secure contract;[1186]
- an order relating to a social housing tenancy made under the Family Law Act 1996 Sch 7 Part II;[1187]
- the allocation of housing accommodation to a person who is already a tenant under a secure contract or an introductory standard contract unless the allocation involves a transfer for which the tenant applied;[1188]
- the provision of suitable alternative accommodation under Land Compensation Act 1973 s39 by the local housing authority to a tenant or owner-occupier who has been displaced from their accommodation;[1189] or
- the grant of a secure contract following the acquisition of a defective dwelling-house under HA 1985 ss554–555.[1190]

The law relating to allocations does not apply to such cases.

1181 HA 1996 s160(3A)(a).
1182 HA 1996 s160(3A)(b).
1183 HA 1996 s160(3A)(c).
1184 HA 1996 s160(3A)(d). The family law statutes in question are specified at HA 1996 s160(3A)(d)(i)–(iv).
1185 HA 1996 s160(3A)(e)(i).
1186 HA 1996 s160(3A)(e)(ii). The provision reads '(e) an introductory standard contract becomes – . . . (ii) a prohibited conduct standard contract becomes a secure contract . . .' but this appears to be a drafting error.
1187 By virtue of Family Law Act 1996 Sch 7 para 7(1).
1188 HA 1996 s159(5).
1189 Allocation of Housing (Wales) Regulations 2003 SI No 239 (W 36) reg 3.
1190 Allocation of Housing (Wales) Regulations 2003 reg 3.

Eligibility

7.357 An applicant for social housing must be 'eligible' before they can even join the waiting list to be allocated a property.

7.358 Eligibility is concerned with an applicant's immigration or residence status. These rules are discussed at paras 7.6–7.63.

7.359 In Wales (but not in England), eligibility also has a second meaning. Welsh local housing authorities may decide that an applicant is to be treated as ineligible if they are satisfied that:

1) the applicant, or a member of their household, has been guilty of unacceptable behaviour serious enough to make them unsuitable to be a tenant of the local housing authority; and
2) in the circumstances at the time the application is considered, they are unsuitable to be a tenant of the local housing authority by reason of that behaviour.[1191]

Qualification

7.360 Local housing authorities in England have an additional mechanism for controlling entry onto their registers. HA 1996 s160ZA allows them to decide that certain classes of person will, or will not, qualify for an allocation and to refuse to allocate a property to a person who does not qualify.

7.361 Unlike with eligibility,[1192] where two or more persons have made a joint application for an allocation, only one of them needs to qualify in order to be considered for an allocation.[1193]

7.362 Who will or will not qualify is largely a matter for the individual local housing authority to decide. HA 1996 s160ZA(7) states that 'a local housing authority may decide what classes of persons are, or are not, qualifying persons'. This freedom is, however, subject to a number of limitations:

1) A local housing authority may not allocate accommodation to a person who is ineligible.[1194] This means that a local housing authority cannot circumvent the eligibility requirements by designating such persons as qualifying for an allocation.
2) The secretary of state may prescribe classes of person who are, or are not, to be treated as qualifying. They may also prescribe criteria that may *not* be used to decide what classes of person do

1191 HA 1996 s160A(7).
1192 See paras 7.6–7.93.
1193 HA 1996 s160ZA(6)(b).
1194 HA 1996 s160ZA(7). See paras 7.6–7.93 for eligibility.

not qualify.[1195] Currently, two sets of regulations have been made under this power:

a) *Allocation of Housing (Qualification Criteria for Armed Forces) (England) Regulations 2012*:[1196] These regulations provide that local authorities must not disqualify on the grounds of 'local connection'[1197] certain specified members, veterans, or widows/widowers of veterans, of the armed forces.[1198]
b) *Allocation of Housing (Qualification Criteria for Right to Move) (England) Regulations 2015*:[1199] These state that local authorities must not disqualify on the grounds of 'local connection'[1200] someone transferring from the district of another local authority in England who is a social housing tenant, who is entitled to a reasonable preference[1201] on the grounds that they are occupying insanitary, overcrowded or otherwise unsatisfactory housing, and who needs to move because of work.[1202]

3) The setting of qualification criteria is subject to the obligation to give certain groups of people a reasonable preference under HA 1996 s166A(3).[1203] This means that a local housing authority must not adopt qualifying criteria which disqualify a class of people by reference to the criterion which entitles them to a reasonable preference. Thus, for example, a qualifying class which excluded 'homeless applicants placed in long term suitable temporary accommodation under the main homeless duty' infringed the requirement to give a reasonable preference to persons who are owed the HA 1996 s193(2) main housing duty.[1204] What has been less clear is whether a local housing authority may lawfully adopt qualifying criteria which are of general reference (for example, excluding people without a local connection or who have rent arrears) but which operate so as to exclude persons who are

1195 HA 1996 s160ZA(7).

1196 SI No 1869.

1197 As defined by HA 1996 s199: see paras 7.308–7.317.

1198 Allocation of Housing (Qualification Criteria for Armed Forces) (England) Regulations 2012 reg 3.

1199 SI No 967.

1200 As defined by HA 1996 s199: see paras 7.308–7.317.

1201 See para 7.366.

1202 Allocation of Housing (Qualification Criteria for Right to Move) (England) Regulations 2015 regs 3–5.

1203 *R (Jakimaviciute) v Hammersmith and Fulham LBC* [2014] EWCA Civ 1438, [2015] 3 All ER 490 at para 31. See para 7.366 for reasonable preference.

1204 *R (Jakimaviciute) v Hammersmith and Fulham LBC* [2014] EWCA Civ 1438, [2015] 3 All ER 490.

entitled to a reasonable preference. In *R (HA) v Ealing LBC*,[1205] the judge held that a residency requirement was unlawful because it excluded people who were entitled to a reasonable preference. In *R (Ward and Gullu) v Hillingdon LBC*[1206] Lewison LJ noted (obiter) that:

> All eligible persons included in the 'reasonable preference' groups must be treated as qualifying for inclusion in the allocation policy.

However, in *R (Montero) v Lewisham LBC*,[1207] the court held that a qualification criterion which excluded those without a local connection was not unlawful even though it disqualified persons who fell within a reasonable preference category. The judge held that *R (HA) v Ealing LBC*[1208] had been incorrectly decided. The current position therefore appears to be that qualification criteria can lawfully exclude persons entitled to a reasonable preference, although given the conflicting first instance decisions on the topic it may be that clarification from the Court of Appeal is needed.

4) When setting and applying their qualifying criteria (if any), local housing authorities must not infringe any other legal obligations to which they are subject. In particular, local housing authorities must take into account their obligations under the EqA 2010. This includes complying with the PSED[1209] and ensuring that any criteria are not unlawfully discriminatory.[1210] Local housing authorities must also ensure that any qualifying criteria comply with their duty to treat the best interests of children as a primary consideration.[1211] See para 7.367 for further discussion of these factors.

7.363 It is important that local housing authorities retain a discretion within their schemes to override the qualification criteria in exceptional cases. Statutory guidance encourages authorities 'to make explicit provision for dealing with exceptional cases within their qual-

1205 [2015] EWHC 2375 (Admin), [2016] PTSR 16.

1206 [2019] EWCA Civ 692, [2019] HLR 30 at para 6.

1207 [2021] EWHC 1359 (Admin), [2022] HLR 4.

1208 [2015] EWHC 2375 (Admin), [2016] PTSR 16.

1209 At EqA 2010 s149.

1210 Direct discrimination is defined at EqA 2010 s13 and indirect discrimination at s19. EqA 2010 s29 prohibits discrimination in the provision of public services or in the exercise of a public function.

1211 Children Act 2004 s11 (England); and s28 (Wales).

ification rules'[1212] and a scheme which retains no discretion is likely to be unlawful.[1213]

7.364 Common qualifying and non-qualifying criteria in allocation schemes include local connection;[1214] anti-social behaviour;[1215] housing need; means; and community participation.

Allocation schemes

7.365 Pursuant to HA 1996 Part VI, every local housing authority in England and Wales is required to have an allocation scheme and to allocate accommodation in accordance with that scheme.[1216] Although local housing authorities have a significant degree of freedom in setting their schemes, there are nevertheless certain obligations with which they must comply.

Housing Act 1996 Part VI requirements

7.366 HA 1996 Part VI contains a number of statutory requirements with which each particular scheme must comply:

1) First, each scheme must contain the local housing authority's policy for 'determining priorities' in allocating housing accommodation.[1217]
2) Second, the scheme must contain 'the procedure to be followed' in allocating accommodation. 'Procedure' includes 'all aspects of the allocation process, including the persons or descriptions of persons by whom decisions are taken'.[1218]
3) Third, the scheme must include:

   . . . a statement of the authority's policy on offering people who are to be allocated housing accommodation–
   (a) a choice of housing accommodation; or
   (b) the opportunity to express preferences about the housing accommodation to be allocated to them.[1219]

1212 *Allocation of accommodation: guidance for local housing authorities in England*, para 3.31.
1213 See *Hillingdon LBC v Holley* [2016] EWCA Civ 1052, [2017] HLR 3 at para 27.
1214 See paras 7.308–7.317.
1215 See, for example, *R (YA) v Hammersmith and Fulham LBC* [2016] EWHC 1850 (Admin), [2016] HLR 39.
1216 HA 1996 s166A(1) and (14) (England); and s167(1) and (8) (Wales).
1217 HA 1996 s166A(1) (England); and s167(1) (Wales).
1218 HA 1996 s166A(1) (England); and s167(1) (Wales).
1219 HA 1996 s166A(2) (England); and s167(1A) (Wales).

4) Fourth, the scheme must also 'be framed so as to secure that reasonable preference is given to' five categories of person.[1220] The categories are:
   a) people who are homeless;[1221]
   b) people who are owed a duty under HA 1996 s190(2),[1222] s193(2)[1223] or s195(2)[1224] (in England) or under H(W)A 2014 s66,[1225] s73[1226] or s75[1227] (in Wales);
   c) people occupying insanitary or overcrowded housing or otherwise living in unsatisfactory housing conditions;
   d) people who need to move on medical or welfare grounds (including any grounds relating to a disability); and
   e) people who need to move to a particular locality in the district of the authority, where failure to meet that need would cause hardship.

   The meaning of 'reasonable preference' has been discussed by the courts on a number of occasions. It is clear that there is no requirement that these groups of people be given *absolute* preference within a particular local housing authority's scheme.[1228] Indeed, it is quite possible for a scheme to give reasonable preference to a person within one of the statutory categories and for 'that person never to be allocated Pt 6 housing'.[1229] Nor is there any obligation to give equal preference to the different reasonable preference categories[1230] or for the scheme to give more priority to a person falling within more than one group.[1231] What amounts to reasonable preference is largely a matter for the local housing authority to decide.[1232]

1220 HA 1996 s166A(3) (England); and s167(2) (Wales). See paras 7.87–7.88 for the impact of a 'restricted person' on reasonable preference.
1221 As defined by HA 1996 Part VII (England); or H(W)A 2014 Part 2 (Wales): see paras 7.121–7.133.
1222 The short-term duty owed to people who are in priority need but who became homeless intentionally: see paras 7.260–7.262.
1223 The main housing duty: see paras 7.263–7.269.
1224 The prevention duty: see paras 7.181–7.186.
1225 The prevention duty: see paras 7.211–7.220.
1226 The relief duty: see paras 7.221–7.227.
1227 The main housing duty: see paras 7.284–7.293.
1228 *R (Ahmad) v Newham LBC* [2009] UKHL 14, [2009] HLR 31.
1229 *R (Lin) v Barnet LBC* [2007] EWCA Civ 132, [2007] HLR 30 at para 25.
1230 This is confirmed in the English code of guidance, *Allocation of accommodation: guidance for local housing authorities in England*, para 4.5.
1231 *R (Ahmad) v Newham LBC* [2009] UKHL 14, [2009] HLR 31.
1232 *R (Lin) v Barnet LBC* [2007] EWCA Civ 132, [2007] HLR 30.

In Wales, local housing authorities are not required to give reasonable preference to a person in respect of whom they are satisfied that:

a) they, or a member of their household, have been guilty of unacceptable behaviour serious enough to make them unsuitable to be a tenant of the authority; and
b) in the circumstances, the person deserves not to be given reasonable preference.[1233]

5) Fifth, in England only, the scheme must give additional preference to a person with urgent housing needs who falls within one or more of the reasonable preference categories and who:
   a) is serving in the regular forces and is suffering from a serious injury, illness or disability which is attributable to their service;
   b) formerly served in the regular forces;
   c) has recently ceased, or will cease, to be entitled to reside in accommodation provided by the Ministry of Defence following the death of their spouse or civil partner who has served in the regular forces and whose death is attributable to that service; or
   d) is serving, or has served, in the reserve forces and is suffering from a serious injury, illness or disability which is attributable to their service.[1234]
6) Finally, in both England and Wales, a scheme must provide the applicant with a right to:
   a) request such general information as will enable them to assess how their application is likely to be treated, including whether they are likely to be given a reasonable preference;[1235]
   b) request such general information as will enable them to assess whether suitable accommodation is likely to be made available to them, and if so when;[1236]
   c) request to be informed of any decision about the facts of their case which is likely to be, or has been, taken into account in considering whether to allocate housing accommodation to them;[1237]

1233 HA 1996 s167(2B) and (2C).
1234 HA 1996 s166A(3).
1235 HA 1996 s166A(9)(a)(i) (England); and s167(4A)(a)(i) (Wales).
1236 HA 1996 s166A(9)(a)(ii) (England); and s167(4A)(a)(ii) (Wales).
1237 HA 1996 s166A(9)(b) (England); and s167(4A)(c) (Wales).

d) request a review of certain decisions and to be informed of the decision on review;[1238] and
e) in Wales only, to be notified in writing of any decision that the applicant is to be denied reasonable preference on the basis of anti-social behaviour, and the grounds for it.[1239]

Duties owed by local housing authorities

7.367 In addition to the requirements contained in HA 1996 Part VI, allocation schemes must comply with other duties owed by local housing authorities:

1) Both when drafting their scheme, and when applying it to individual cases, local housing authorities must comply with the PSED imposed by EqA 2010 s149. This requires them to:

   . . . have due regard to the need to–
   (a) eliminate discrimination, harassment, victimisation and any other conduct that is prohibited by or under this Act;
   (b) advance equality of opportunity between persons who share a relevant protected characteristic and persons who do not share it;
   (c) foster good relations between persons who share a relevant protected characteristic and persons who do not share it.[1240]

   A breach of the PSED was found to have occurred in *R (Ward and Gullu) v Hillingdon LBC*, where the authority had failed to consider the impact of its scheme on non-UK nationals even after a judicial review had been brought on that point.[1241] In contrast, there was no breach in *R (C) v Islington LBC* in respect of a local lettings policy which prioritised for a new development applicants currently living on the estate on which the new homes had been built.[1242] In *R (H) v Ealing LBC*, the Court of Appeal had concerns as to the adequacy of the equality impact assessment (EIA) which the local housing authority had undertaken, but decided not to grant relief given that a review was underway.[1243]
2) Local housing authorities must also ensure that, when drawing up and applying their allocation schemes, they do not unlawfully

1238 HA 1996 s166A(9)(c) (England); and s167(4A)(d) (Wales): see paras 7.384–7.386.

1239 HA 1996 s167(4A)(b) (Wales).

1240 EqA 2010 s149(1).

1241 [2019] EWCA Civ 692, [2019] HLR 30.

1242 [2017] EWHC 1288 (Admin), [2017] HLR 32.

1243 [2017] EWCA Civ 1127, [2018] HLR 2.

discriminate under either the EqA 2010 or ECHR Article 14 (prohibition of discrimination).[1244]

EqA 2010 s29 prohibits discrimination by a person providing services to the public or exercising a public function. The allocation of housing accommodation will fall within this section.[1245] Discrimination may be 'direct', ie when a person is treated less favourably because of a protected characteristic;[1246] or 'indirect', ie where an apparently neutral practice or policy puts persons with a protected characteristic at a particular disadvantage.[1247] Indirect discrimination is capable of being justified on the basis that it is a 'proportionate means of achieving a legitimate aim'.[1248]

In order for discrimination to be prohibited by ECHR Article 14, it must impact upon the enjoyment of another ECHR right. The right most commonly relied on in allocation cases is Article 8, which enshrines a person's right to respect for their private and family life, home and correspondence. In a recent case which challenged a London borough's allocations arrangements with a charity that provided housing for members of the Orthodox Jewish Community, the Court of Appeal held that Article 8 was not engaged,[1249] but this was doubted in the Supreme Court[1250] and then disapproved in the European Court of Human Rights.[1251]

1244 See *R (Osman) v Harrow LBC* [2017] EWHC 274 (Admin); *R (XC) v Southwark LBC* [2017] EWHC 736 (Admin), [2017] HLR 24; *R (C) v Islington LBC* [2017] EWHC 1288 (Admin), [2017] HLR 32; *R (H) v Ealing LBC* [2017] EWCA Civ 1127, [2018] HLR 2; *R (Ward and Gullu) v Hillingdon LBC* [2019] EWCA Civ 692, [2019] HLR 30; *R (Z) v Hackney LBC* [2020] UKSC 40, [2020] 1 WLR 4327; and *R (Nur) v Birmingham City Council (No 2)* [2021] EWHC 1138 (Admin).

1245 *R (Ward and Gullu) v Hillingdon LBC* [2019] EWCA Civ 692, [2019] HLR 30 at para 9; *R (Z) v Hackney LBC and another* [2019] EWHC 139 (Admin), [2019] HLR 29 at para 49; and *R (Nur) v Birmingham City Council (No 2)* [2021] EWHC 1138 (Admin) at paras 138–150.

1246 EqA 2010 s13. The protected characteristics are set out at EqA 2010 s4: age; disability; gender reassignment; marriage and civil partnership; pregnancy and maternity; race; religion or belief; sex; sexual orientation (although EqA 2010 Part 3 does not apply to the protected characteristics of age, so far as relating to persons who have not attained the age of 18, or marriage and civil partnership).

1247 EqA 2010 s19.

1248 EqA 2010 s19(2)(d).

1249 *R (Z) v Hackney LBC* [2019] EWCA Civ 1099, [2019] HLR 44.

1250 *R (Z) v Hackney LBC* [2020] UKSC 40, [2020] 1 WLR 4327.

1251 *LF v UK* App No 19839/21 (2022) 75 EHRR SE5, ECtHR.

3) The scheme must also be drawn up and applied in compliance with the local housing authority's duty to have regard to the need to safeguard and promote the welfare of children.[1252] This means treating the best interests of children as a primary consideration[1253] and actively promoting their welfare.[1254]
4) Local housing authorities in Wales must also comply with the socio-economic duty contained at EqA 2010 s1. This duty requires public authorities, 'when making decisions of a strategic nature' about how to exercise their functions, to have 'due regard to the desirability of exercising them in a way that is designed to reduce the inequalities of outcome which result from the socio-economic disadvantage'.[1255] It was brought into force in respect of Wales on 31 March 2021[1256] and applies to county councils and county borough councils.[1257] The Welsh government has produced statutory guidance in respect of this duty entitled *A more equal Wales: The socio-economic duty Equality Act 2010.*[1258] Although breach of the duty does not confer a cause of action at private law,[1259] it can be challenged by way of a claim for judicial review.[1260]

Further suggestions

7.368 Beyond these requirements, each local housing authority 'may decide on what principles the scheme is to be framed'.[1261] HA 1996 Part VI

1252 Children Act 2004 s11 (England); and s28 (Wales). See *R (Woolfe) v Islington LBC* [2016] EWHC 1907 (Admin), [2016] HLR 42; *R (M) v Islington LBC* [2016] EWHC 332 (Admin), [2016] HLR 19; *R (J and L) v Hillingdon LBC* [2017] EWHC 3411 (Admin); *R (H) v Ealing LBC* [2017] EWCA Civ 1127, [2018] HLR 2; *R (KS) v Haringey LBC* [2018] EWHC 587 (Admin), [2018] HLR 41; and *R (Z) v Hackney LBC* [2019] EWCA Civ 1099, [2019] HLR 44.

1253 *ZH (Tanzania) v SSHD* [2011] UKSC 4, [2011] 2 AC 166.

1254 *R (J and L) v Hillingdon LBC* [2017] EWHC 3411 (Admin).

1255 EqA 2010 s1(1).

1256 Equality Act 2010 (Commencement No 15) (Wales) Order 2021 SI No 298 (W 75) art 2(a). The duty has not yet been brought into force in respect of England.

1257 EqA 2010 s1(3A)(b).

1258 Welsh Government, 2021.

1259 EqA 2010 s3.

1260 *A more equal Wales: The socio-economic duty Equality Act 2010*, p7.

1261 HA 1996 s166A(11) (England); and s167(6) (Wales).

does, however, contain some suggestions as to how this discretion may be exercised:[1262]

- A scheme may be framed so as to give additional preference to particular descriptions of people within the reasonable preference groups.[1263]
- A scheme may contain provision for determining priorities within the reasonable preference groups. The factors which may be taken into account include an applicant's financial resources, behaviour and local connection with the authority's district.[1264]
- A scheme may contain provision concerning the allocation of a particular unit of accommodation to a person who makes a specific application for that accommodation, or to persons of a particular description.[1265]

Residency requirements in allocation schemes

7.369 Many local housing authorities include provisions in their schemes which penalise applicants who have not been resident in their area for a particular period of time. Some schemes disqualify such applicants, meaning that they cannot enter the housing register at all. Other schemes do not wholly exclude such applicants but give them reduced priority within the scheme. Given the shortage of social housing,[1266] this can often mean in practice that they will never be given an allocation. Such requirements are, almost by definition, likely to be particularly difficult for migrants to meet.

1262 Further guidance is provided in the codes of guidance: for England, see *Allocation of accommodation: guidance for local housing authorities in England*, chapter 4; *Providing social housing for local people: statutory guidance on social housing allocations for local authorities in England*, paras 11–27; *Right to move: statutory guidance on social housing allocations for local housing authorities in England*, paras 35–47; *Improving access to social housing for victims of domestic abuse*, paras 15–28; and *Improving access to social housing for members of the armed forces*, paras 12–37. For Wales, see *Code of guidance to local authorities on the allocation of accommodation and homelessness*, chapter 3.

1263 HA 1996 s166A(3) (England); and s167(2) (Wales). In England, local housing authorities must give additional preference to the people specified at HA 1996 s166A(3): see para 7.366.

1264 HA 1996 s166A(5) (England); and s167(2A) (Wales).

1265 HA 1996 s166A(6) (England); and s167(2E) (Wales).

1266 In January 2019, a report published by the housing charity Shelter, *Building for our future: a vision for social housing*, concluded that 3.1 million more units of social housing were needed.

7.370 In the code of guidance issued in 2012, the secretary of state referred to qualifying criteria based on residency rules and advised local housing authorities to:

> . . . consider the implications of excluding all members of such groups. For instance, when framing residency criteria, authorities may wish to consider the position of people who are moving into the district to take up work or to escape violence, or homeless applicants or children in care who are placed out of borough.[1267]

7.371 The supplementary code of guidance published in 2013, *Providing social housing for local people: statutory guidance on social housing allocations for local authorities in England*, took a different tone. It 'strongly' encouraged local housing authorities to consider including residency criteria in their schemes. It opined that a reasonable minimum period of residency would be 'at least two years'. It also reminded local housing authorities of their 'ability to take account of any local connection between the applicant and their district when determining relative priorities between households who are on the waiting list'.[1268] More recent statutory guidance, however, has encouraged local housing authorities to make exceptions to residency criteria, including for victims of domestic abuse[1269] and spouses and civil partners of armed forces personnel.[1270]

7.372 Given their propensity to disadvantage large numbers of people, many of whom are likely to be vulnerable, it is perhaps unsurprising that schemes involving residence requirements have been challenged in the courts on a number of occasions.

7.373 In *R (HA) v Ealing LBC*,[1271] the local housing authority's scheme disqualified applicants who had not been resident in the borough for the last five years. The criterion was challenged by an applicant who had recently fled to the borough to escape domestic violence and who could not, therefore, meet the threshold. The court found that the requirement discriminated against female victims of domestic violence and no rational justification for the discrimination had been advanced.

1267 *Allocation of accommodation: guidance for local housing authorities in England*, para 3.28.

1268 *Providing social housing for local people: statutory guidance on social housing allocations for local authorities in England*, paras 13 and 26.

1269 *Improving access to social housing for victims of domestic abuse*, paras 15–20.

1270 *Improving access to social housing for members of the armed forces*, paras 16–18.

1271 [2015] EWHC 2375 (Admin), [2016] PTSR 16.

7.374 A similar rule came before the Court of Appeal in two joined cases: *R (Ward) v Hillingdon LBC* and *R (Gullu) v Hillingdon LBC*.[1272] Hillingdon's scheme as it existed at the start of the litigation had excluded all those who had not been living in its borough for at least ten years. There were some exceptions but they did not extend to all those who fell within the reasonable preference groups. During the course of the litigation, it was amended and by the time it came before the Court of Appeal it operated such that a person who had not been living in Hillingdon for ten years, but who was entitled to a reasonable preference, qualified for the housing register but was placed in Band D. A person who had not lived in Hillingdon for ten years and who did not fall within a reasonable preference group did not qualify at all.

7.375 This residency rule was challenged by two sets of claimants, the first consisting of Irish Travellers and the other a Kurdish refugee. Neither could meet the residency requirement. The Court of Appeal, with Lewison LJ giving the judgment of the court, agreed with the claimants that the rule was indirectly discriminatory, noting (in respect of the latter claimant) that a 'long line of cases has accepted that a residence requirement disadvantages non-UK nationals'.[1273]

7.376 The question was therefore whether the provision could be justified. What was required was for the 'discrimination as regards that particular group' to be justified: 'If a policy amounts to indirect discrimination against group E, I do not consider that it is an answer for the policy maker to say that it has considered groups A, B, C and D'.[1274] Hillingdon's argument that the scheme was saved by the presence of 'safety valves' failed:

> 86. . . . the key principle is that the goal is equality of outcome. If a PCP results in a relative disadvantage as regards one protected group, any measure relied on as a 'safety valve' must overcome that relative disadvantage. Put simply, if the scales are tilted in one direction, adding an equal weight to each side of the scales does not eliminate the tilt . . .
>
> 87. In addition, there is no evidence that the 'safety valves' within the allocation policy have actually operated to eliminate the disadvantage to the two protected groups in issue on these appeals . . .

1272 [2019] EWCA Civ 692, [2019] HLR 30.

1273 *R (Ward) v Hillingdon LBC; R (Gullu) v Hillingdon LBC* [2019] EWCA Civ 692, [2019] HLR 30 at para 60.

1274 *Ward and Gullu* at para 81.

7.377 Lewison LJ concluded that Hillingdon had not justified the discrimination, but held that it was 'still open to them to do so if better evidence were to be provided' and made declarations accordingly.[1275]

7.378 Lewison LJ also considered whether Hillingdon had failed to comply with its PSED under EqA 2010 s149. His Lordship accepted the authority's submission that there was no obligation to 'assess the potential indirect discriminatory effect on every conceivable group that shares a protected characteristic'.[1276] In consequence, although the initial equality impact assessment had not considered non-UK nationals or refugees, this did not constitute a breach of EqA 2010 s149 because it had not been shown that there was any particular reason for it to do so. However, by the time of the next assessment Mr Gullu had brought his application for judicial review and in the light of that, Hillingdon 'ought at least to have *considered* the position of non-UK nationals' – in failing to do so, it had breached EqA 2010 s149.[1277]

7.379 Mr Gullu's argument that his rights under ECHR Articles 8 and 14 had been breached, on the basis that being a refugee was a particular status under Article 14 and the provision of social housing engaged Article 8, was left open.[1278]

Private registered providers of social housing and allocations

7.380 Private registered providers (most commonly, housing associations) have an important role to play in the social housing sector. Indeed, more lettings of social housing are made by private registered providers than by local housing authorities.[1279] There are two main ways in which a person may become a tenant of a private registered provider:

1) The first is via a direct let made by the private registered provider to a person who applies to it for a home. In 2020/21, 37.5 per cent of general needs social rent lettings made by private registered providers in England were made to applicants who had applied directly to that provider.[1280] Private registered providers must have

1275 *Ward and Gullu* [2019] EWCA Civ 692, [2019] HLR 30 at para 111.

1276 *Ward and Gullu* at para 72.

1277 *Ward and Gullu* at para 74. Emphasis in original.

1278 *Ward and Gullu* at paras 108–109.

1279 *Social housing lettings: April 2020 to March 2021*, DLUHC, July 2022.

1280 *Social housing lettings in England, 2020–21: Continuous Recording (CORE) summary tables, Table 3j*, MHCLG, December 2020.

a set of rules governing how they will determine priority as between applicants and what procedure will be followed when allocating housing accommodation.[1281]

2) The second is via a nomination made by a local housing authority of a person who has applied to it under HA 1996 Part VI for an allocation of social housing. HA 1996 s170 requires every private registered provider or registered social landlord to 'co-operate to such extent as is reasonable in the circumstances in offering accommodation to people with priority under the authority's allocation scheme' on receipt of a request from a local housing authority. This duty does not extend to requiring a private registered provider to accept an applicant who does not fall within its own criteria.[1282] In a recent case in the Supreme Court, a local housing authority's nominations agreement with a housing association was challenged on the grounds that the housing association's policy was impermissibly discriminatory and the nominations agreement was consequently unlawful. The claimant's case failed. The housing association's policy was lawful and therefore the local housing authority did not act unlawfully in nominating applicants to the association.[1283]

Decision-making in allocations

Overview

7.381 Local housing authorities must ensure that individual allocations decisions are made in accordance with their allocations scheme.[1284] Authorities must also comply with general public law principles of legality, rationality and procedural propriety. The best interests of any children affected by the decision must be treated as a primary consideration.[1285] In making decisions, local housing authorities must

1281 Housing Act 1985 s106(2).

1282 *R (Z) v Hackney LBC* [2020] UKSC 30, [2020] 1 WLR 4327.

1283 *R (Z) v Hackney LBC*. A subsequent challenge to the European Court of Human Rights was declared to be inadmissible: *LF v United Kingdom* App No 19839/21 (2022) 75 EHRR SE5, ECtHR.

1284 HA 1996 s166A(14) (England); and s167(8) (Wales).

1285 Children Act 2004 s11 (England); and s28 (Wales). See para 7.367. See *ZH (Tanzania) v SSHD* [2011] UKSC 4, [2011] 2 AC 166 for an explanation of this duty. For 'best interests' decisions in an allocations context, see *R (Woolfe) v Islington LBC* [2016] EWHC 1907 (Admin), [2016] HLR 42; *R (J and L) v Hillingdon LBC* [2017] EWHC 3411 (Admin); *R (KS) v Haringey LBC* [2018] EWHC 587 (Admin), [2018] HLR 41; and *R (Z) v Hackney LBC* [2019] EWCA Civ 1099, [2019] HLR 44.

comply with the PSED under EqA 2010 s149 and must avoid unlawful discrimination.[1286]

Notification

7.382 There are three decisions in respect of which the local housing authority is under a direct statutory obligation to notify the applicant of its determination, in writing, with reasons. These are:

1) any decision that the applicant is not eligible for an allocation on the grounds of immigration or residence status;[1287]
2) in England only, any decision that the applicant is not a qualifying person;[1288] and
3) in Wales only, any decision that the applicant is to be treated as not eligible on the grounds of unacceptable behaviour.[1289]

7.383 In addition to these, however, HA 1996 Part VI provides that every local housing authority's scheme must 'be framed so as to secure'[1290] that an applicant has the right to be notified of certain other decisions. A scheme must give applicants the right:

1) to request the authority to inform them of any decision about the facts of their case which is likely to be, or has been, taken into account in considering whether to allocate housing accommodation to them;[1291]
2) to be informed of any decision made on a review of a decision about the facts of their case which has been taken into account in considering whether to allocate accommodation to them;[1292]

1286 See para 7.367. For allocations cases alleging breaches of the EqA 2010, see *R (HA) v Ealing LBC* [2015] EWHC 2375 (Admin), [2016] PTSR 16; *R (YA) v Hammersmith and Fulham LBC* [2016] EWHC 1850 (Admin), [2016] HLR 39; *R (C) v Islington LBC* [2017] EWHC 1288 (Admin), [2017] HLR 32; *R (H) v Ealing LBC* [2017] EWCA Civ 1127, [2018] HLR 2; *R (Osman) v Harrow LBC* [2017] EWHC 274 (Admin); *R (XC) v Southwark LBC* [2017] EWHC 736 (Admin), [2017] HLR 24; and *R (Z) v Hackney LBC* [2020] UKSC 30, [2020] 1 WLR 4327.

1287 HA 1996 s160ZA(9)(a) (England); and s160A(9)(a) (Wales). See paras 7.357–7.359 for eligibility.

1288 HA 1996 s160ZA(9)(b). See paras 7.360–7.364 for qualification criteria.

1289 HA 1996 s160A(9)(b). See para 7.359 for ineligibility on the grounds of unacceptable behaviour.

1290 HA 1996 ss166A(9) (England); and s167(4A) (Wales).

1291 HA 1996 s166A(9)(b) (England); and s167(4A)(c) (Wales).

1292 HA 1996 s166A(9)(c) (England); and s167(4A)(d) (Wales).

3) to be informed of any decision made on a review of a decision that they are ineligible on the grounds of immigration/residence status;[1293]
4) in England only, to be informed of any decision made on a review of a decision that they are not a qualifying person;[1294]
5) in Wales only, to be informed of any decision made on a review of a decision that they are to be treated as ineligible on the grounds of unacceptable behaviour;[1295] and
6) in Wales only, to be notified in writing of any decision that they are not to be given any reasonable preference due to unacceptable behaviour.[1296]

Reviews

7.384 Each local housing authority's allocation scheme must ensure that an applicant has the right to request a review of:

1) any decision about the facts of their case which is likely to be, or has been, taken into account in considering whether to allocate housing accommodation to them;[1297]
2) any decision that a person is ineligible for an allocation of accommodation (including, in Wales, on anti-social behaviour grounds);[1298]
3) in England, any decision that a person does not qualify for an allocation of accommodation;[1299] and
4) in Wales, any decision that they are a person who is to be denied reasonable preference on the grounds of anti-social behaviour.[1300]

7.385 If a scheme made no provision for an applicant to request a review of one or more of these decisions, the aggrieved applicant would firstly have to seek judicial review of this omission, inviting the court to require the authority to remedy the scheme.[1301] Once the scheme was

1293 HA 1996 s166A(9)(c) (England); and s167(4A)(d) (Wales). See paras 7.357–7.359 for eligibility.

1294 HA 1996 s166A(9)(c). See paras 7.360–7.364 for qualification criteria.

1295 HA 1996 s167(4A)(d). See para 7.359 for ineligibility on the grounds of unacceptable behaviour.

1296 HA 1996 s167(4A)(b). See para 7.366 for denying reasonable preference on the grounds of anti-social behaviour.

1297 HA 1996 s166A(9)(c) (England); and s167(4A)(d) (Wales).

1298 HA 1996 s166A(9)(c) (England); and s167(4A)(d) (Wales). See paras 7.357–7.359 for ineligibility and para 7.359 for ineligibility on the grounds of unacceptable behaviour.

1299 HA 1996 s166A(9)(c). See paras 7.360–7.364 for qualification criteria.

1300 HA 1996 s167(4A)(d). See para 7.366 for denying reasonable preference on the grounds of anti-social behaviour.

1301 See paras 7.387–7.388 for a discussion of judicial review.

amended, they could then exercise their right to request a review of the decision in issue.

7.386 There are no statutory provisions or regulations governing how the review should be carried out. However, in both England and Wales codes of guidance provide recommendations on good practice. The English code contains the following 'general principles of good administrative practice':

(i) Applicants should be notified of the timescale within which they must request a review. 21 days from the date the applicant is notified of the decision is well-established as a reasonable timescale. A housing authority should retain the discretion to extend this time limit in exceptional circumstances.

(ii) Applicants should be notified that the request for review should be made in writing, and that it would also be acceptable for the request to be submitted by a representative on their behalf. Applicants should also be advised of the information which should accompany the request.

(iii) Authorities should consider whether to advise that provision can be made for verbal representations, as well as written submissions, to be made.

(iv) The review should be carried out by an officer who is senior to the person who made the original decision. Alternatively, authorities may wish to appoint a panel to consider the review. If so, it should not include any person involved in the original decision.

(v) The review should be considered on the basis of the authority's allocation scheme, any legal requirements and all relevant information. This should include information provided by the applicant on any relevant developments since the original decision was made – for instance, the settlement of arrears or establishment of a repayment plan, or departure of a member of the household responsible for anti-social behaviour.

(vi) Reviews should be completed wherever practicable within a set deadline. Eight weeks is suggested as a reasonable timescale. The applicant should be notified of any extension to this deadline and the reasons for this.

(viii) Applicants must be notified in writing of the outcome of the review. The notification must set out the reasons for the decision. This will assist the applicant and the authority if, for example, the applicant is not satisfied with the outcome and decides to seek a judicial review or to take their case to the Local Government Ombudsman.[1302]

1302 *Allocation of accommodation: guidance for local housing authorities in England*, para 5.19. Similar guidance is contained at *Code of guidance to local authorities on the allocation of accommodation and homelessness*, para 2.55.

Allocations and judicial review

7.387 There is no statutory right of appeal against an adverse decision on review. If the decision contains an error of law, then a dissatisfied applicant may apply for judicial review. If the decision is not challengeable on a point of law, then the applicant would have to seek redress via the local housing authority's complaints process and/or the ombudsman.[1303]

7.388 An application for judicial review may, where appropriate, challenge not just the decision made in the applicant's individual case but also the scheme itself. Thus, for example, it may be asserted that in formulating the scheme the local housing authority failed to comply with its PSED under EqA 2010 s149;[1304] or that the scheme unlawfully discriminates against persons with a particular protected characteristic;[1305] or that the scheme was drafted without the requisite consideration having been given to the best interests of children.[1306]

Right to rent

Legal framework

7.389 The 'right to rent' provisions were brought in by the Immigration Act (IA) 2014 as part of the government's attempts to create a 'hostile environment' for those without a lawful right to remain in the UK.[1307] The IA 2014 received royal assent on 1 May 2014 and a pilot scheme began on 1 December 2014 in five West Midlands council areas. The

1303 In England, a complaint would lie to the Local Government and Social Care Ombudsman. In Wales, the complaint would be to the Public Services Ombudsman for Wales.

1304 See, for example, *R (C) v Islington LBC* [2017] EWHC 1288 (Admin) [2017] HLR 32.

1305 See, for example, *R (HA) v Ealing LBC* [2015] EWHC 2375 (Admin), [2016] PTSR 16.

1306 See, for example, *R (KS) v Haringey LBC* [2018] EWHC 587 (Admin), [2018] HLR 41.

1307 In an interview with the *Telegraph* published on 25 May 2012, then Home Secretary Theresa May stated 'The aim is to create here in Britain a really hostile environment for illegal migration' (James Kirkup and Robert Winnett 'Theresa May interview: "We're going to give illegal migrants a really hostile reception" ' *Telegraph*, 25 May 2012). She repeated this terminology when introducing the Immigration Bill for its second reading, stating 'This is not just about making the UK a more hostile place for illegal migrants; it is also about fairness' (Hansard HC Debs col 264, 22 October 2013).

provisions were then rolled out across all of England with effect from 1 February 2016. They do not currently apply to Wales, Scotland or Northern Ireland.

7.390 The government has produced a number of guidance documents:[1308]

- *Code of practice for landlords: avoiding unlawful discrimination when conducting 'right to rent' checks in the private rented residential sector;*[1309]
- *Coronavirus (COVID-19): landlord right to rent checks;*[1310]
- *Right to rent: landlords' penalties;*[1311]
- *Code of practice on right to rent: civil penalty scheme for landlords and their agents;*[1312]
- *Right to rent checks from 1 July 2021: information for landlords;*[1313]
- *Landlord's guide to right to rent checks;*[1314] and
- *Right to rent checks: a guide to immigration documents for tenants and landlords.*[1315]

Application of the right to rent provisions

Overview

7.391 The right to rent provisions do not apply to tenancies which began before the date on which the scheme commenced (that is, 1 December

1308 Limited guidance is also available at Home Office policy document *Immigration bail*, v4.0, April 2019, pp17, 18 and 56.

1309 Home Office, October 2014 (subsequently updated) (www.gov.uk/government/publications/right-to-rent-landlords-code-of-practice).

1310 Home Office, March 2020 (subsequently updated) (www.gov.uk/guidance/coronavirus-covid-19-landlord-right-to-rent-checks).

1311 Home Office, November 2020 (https://assets.publishing.service.gov.uk/government/uploads/system/uploads/attachment_data/file/934469/right-to-rent-landlords-v7.0-gov-uk.pdf).

1312 Home Office, July 2021 (subsequently updated) (www.gov.uk/government/publications/right-to-rent-landlords-code-of-practice).

1313 HM Government, July 2021 (subsequently updated) (www.gov.uk/government/publications/right-to-rent-checks-from-july-2021-important-information-for-landlords).

1314 Home Office, November 2020 (subsequently updated) (www.gov.uk/government/publications/landlords-guide-to-right-to-rent-checks).

1315 Home Office, April 2022 (subsequently updated) (https://assets.publishing.service.gov.uk/government/uploads/system/uploads/attachment_data/file/1069600/2022.04.12_RTR_User_Guide.pdf). This appears to have replaced the previous guidance, *Right to rent checks: a user guide for tenants and landlords*, published in September 2021.

2014 in the West Midlands[1316] and 1 February 2016 in the rest of England), nor to the renewal of such a tenancy where the agreement is between the same parties, in respect of the same property, without a break.[1317]

7.392 The scheme applies mainly, but not solely, in the private rented sector. It applies to a 'residential tenancy agreement', which is defined as a tenancy, lease, licence, sub-lease or sub-tenancy (or an agreement for any of those things) which:

1) grants a right of occupation of premises for residential use;
2) provides for payment of rent (whether or not a market rent); and
3) is not an excluded agreement.[1318]

Excluded agreements

7.393 The agreements which are *excluded* from the right to rent provisions are set out at IA 2014 Sch 3.

7.394 The first excluded agreement is 'an agreement that grants a right of occupation in social housing'.[1319] This is defined as accommodation provided to a person by virtue of HA 1985 Part II or HA 1996 Parts VI and VII.[1320] It is important to note that certain agreements are to be treated as allocations made by virtue of HA 1996 Part VI for the purposes of the right to rent provisions even though they do not constitute allocations for the purposes of HA 1996 Part VI itself.[1321] This means that certain tenancies and licences which do not fall within the definition of an allocation under HA 1996 Part VI are nevertheless to be treated as such for the purposes of IA 2014 Sch 3 para 1, with the result that they are excluded from the right to rent provisions. These are:

- an allocation of accommodation by a local housing authority in England to a person who is already a secure or introductory tenant or an assured tenant of housing accommodation held by a private registered provider of social housing or a registered social landlord;[1322]
- a succession to the tenancy on the death of the tenant;[1323]

1316 Namely Birmingham, Wolverhampton, Dudley, Sandwell, and Walsall.
1317 IA 2014 s35(1) and (2).
1318 IA 2014 s20(2).
1319 IA 2014 Sch 3 para 1(1).
1320 IA 2014 Sch 3 para 1(2) and (3).
1321 IA 2014 Sch 3 para 2.
1322 IA 2014 Sch 3 para 2(2).
1323 IA 2014 Sch 3 para 2(3); HA 1996 s160(2)(a) and (3)(b).

- the devolution of a fixed-term secure tenancy on the death of the tenant;[1324]
- the lawful assignment of a secure or introductory tenancy;[1325]
- the vesting or disposal of a secure or introductory tenancy pursuant to a court order made under the provisions of certain family law statutes;[1326]
- an introductory tenancy becoming a secure tenancy;[1327]
- the provision of suitable alternative accommodation under Land Compensation Act 1973 s39 by the local housing authority to a tenant or owner-occupier who has been displaced from their accommodation;[1328]
- the grant of a secure tenancy following the acquisition of a defective dwelling-house under HA 1985 ss554–555;[1329]
- in England, the grant of a tenancy to a person currently occupying a property under a family intervention tenancy;[1330] and
- in England, a tenancy granted pursuant to a surrender and re-grant procedure where two social housing tenants, one of whom is a flexible or assured shorthold tenant, are exchanging homes.[1331]

7.395 The remaining categories of excluded agreement, to which the right to rent scheme does *not* apply, are contained at IA 2014 Sch 3 paras 3–13. They are:

- an agreement that grants a right of occupation in a care home;[1332]
- an agreement that grants a right of occupation in a hospital or hospice;[1333]
- accommodation relating to healthcare provision;[1334]

1324 IA 2014 Sch 3 para 2(3); HA 1996 s160(2)(b).
1325 IA 2014 Sch 3 para 2(3); HA 1996 s160(2)(c), (2)(d) and (3)(c).
1326 IA 2014 Sch 3 para 2(3); HA 1996 s160(2)(e)(i)–(iv) and (3)(d)(i)–(iv). The family law statutes in question are specified at HA 1996 s160(2)(e) and (3)(d).
1327 IA 2014 Sch 3 para 2(3); HA 1996 s160(3)(a).
1328 IA 2014 Sch 3 para 2(3); HA 1996 s160(4); Allocation of Housing (England) Regulations 2002 reg 3 (England); and Allocation of Housing (Wales) Regulations 2003 reg 3 (Wales).
1329 IA 2014 Sch 3 para 2(3); HA 1996 s160(4); Allocation of Housing (England) Regulations 2002 reg 3 (England); and Allocation of Housing (Wales) Regulations 2003 reg 3 (Wales).
1330 IA 2014 Sch 3 para 2(3); HA 1996 s160(4); Allocation of Housing (England) Regulations 2002 reg 3.
1331 IA 2014 Sch 3 para 2(3), HA 1996 s160(2)(da).
1332 IA 2014 Sch 3 para 3.
1333 IA 2014 Sch 3 para 4.
1334 IA 2014 Sch 3 para 5.

- an agreement that grants a right of occupation in a non-commercial hostel or refuge;[1335]
- any other agreement under which accommodation is provided to a person as a result of a duty imposed on a local authority, or as a result of a power conferred on a local authority which is exercised to provide accommodation to a person who is homeless or threatened with homelessness;[1336]
- accommodation provided by virtue of IAA 1999 s4, s95 or s98;[1337]
- accommodation provided by virtue of the NIAA 2002 Sch 3 para 10A or 10B (when these provisions come into force);[1338]
- a Mobile Homes Act 1983 agreement;[1339]
- an agreement that grants a right of occupation of tied accommodation;[1340]
- student accommodation;[1341] and
- long leases.[1342]

7.396 The result of the above is that the right to rent provisions *do* apply to most, but not all, accommodation agreements in the private rented sector, and do *not* apply to most, but not all, accommodation agreements in the social housing sector. They do, for example, apply where a private registered provider makes an offer of a social housing tenancy to an individual which is not made pursuant to arrangements made by the local housing authority.[1343]

7.397 Some agreements will be readily identifiable as either falling within, or being excluded from, the right to rent scheme. Accommodation occupied by a migrant under an assured shorthold tenancy granted by a private landlord for a market rent will clearly be included, while accommodation occupied by a migrant under the main housing duty[1344] will not.[1345]

7.398 Other agreements, however, will be less clear cut. By way of example, various schemes provide for individuals or families to 'host'

1335 IA 2014 Sch 3 para 6.
1336 IA 2014 Sch 3 para 7.
1337 IA 2014 Sch 3 para 8. See chapters 5 and 6.
1338 IA 2014 Sch 3 para 8A.
1339 IA 2014 Sch 3 para 9.
1340 IA 2014 Sch 3 para 10.
1341 IA 2014 Sch 3 paras 11–12.
1342 IA 2014 Sch 3 para 13.
1343 See para 7.380.
1344 Under HA 1996 s193(2). See paras 7.263–7.269.
1345 By virtue of IA 2014 Sch 3 para 1.

refugees in their spare rooms.[1346] If the individual owns their own home, and does not charge rent, then the arrangement should not fall within the scheme.[1347] If any rent at all was charged – even a peppercorn rent, or rent in kind through the provision of services – then the right to rent provisions would apply. The provision of services for other purposes, such as in return for food, should not bring the agreement within the scheme.

7.399 If, however, the individual is a rent-paying tenant themself, then the situation may be different. The right to rent scheme extends to occupiers as well as tenants. Even though the tenant may not be demanding rent from the person hosted, if the tenancy agreement grants a right of occupation to that person (whether or not they are named) then the landlord will be liable if they fail to make reasonable inquiries as to the identity of the proposed occupiers.[1348] If the tenancy agreement contains no such right, but the tenant subsequently seeks and is granted permission from the landlord to take in a lodger, then this will amount to a variation of the agreement. Where a landlord consents to a variation which grants a right of occupation to a new occupier, this is to be treated as the entering into of a residential tenancy agreement.[1349] A landlord consenting to the lodger may therefore be liable should the lodger be a disqualified person.[1350]

7.400 Certain types of hostel and refuge accommodation are also excluded from the right to rent provisions. Advisers assisting migrant clients who reside within such places will want to consider carefully the definitions provided at IA 2014 Sch 3 para 6. A 'hostel' is stated to be a building which:

a) is used for:
   i) the provision of residential accommodation (other than in separate and self-contained premises) to persons generally or a class of person; and
   ii) the provision of board or facilities for the preparation of food adequate to the needs of those persons;

1346 See, for example, the Homes for Ukraine scheme launched to assist those fleeing the Russian invasion of Ukraine in February 2022.

1347 The right to rent scheme only applies to agreements which provide for the payment of rent: IA 2014 s20(2)(b).

1348 IA 2014 s22(4)(c) and (6).

1349 Immigration (Residential Accommodation) (Prescribed Cases) Order 2014 SI No 2873 art 3(a).

1350 See paras 7.403–7.410 for the meaning of a disqualified person. The statutory excuses which may be available to such a landlord are set out at para 7.413.

b) and:
  i) is managed by a registered housing association; or
  ii) is not operated on a commercial basis, and the costs of its operation are provided wholly or in part by a government department or agency or a local authority; or
  iii) is managed by a voluntary organisation or charity.[1351]

7.401 A 'refuge' is defined as being a building which is not operated on a commercial basis, and its costs of operation are provided wholly or in part by a government department or agency or a local authority and which is used wholly or mainly for providing accommodation to persons who have been subject to:

a) controlling, coercive or threatening behaviour;
b) physical violence;
c) abuse of any other description (whether physical or mental); or
d) threats of any such violence or abuse.[1352]

7.402 A migrant occupying a room, with shared catering facilities, in a hostel which is run by a charity on a not-for-profit basis would *not* therefore be subject to the right to rent regime.

Disqualified persons

7.403 The right to rent scheme operates so as to preclude landlords from letting properties to persons who are referred to as 'disqualified' persons. A person will be disqualified if:[1353]

1) they are not a 'relevant national'; and
2) they do not have a right to rent in relation to the premises.

7.404 The first question is therefore whether a person is a 'relevant national'. A 'relevant national' means:[1354]

1) a British citizen;[1355]
2) an Irish citizen;[1356]

1351 IA 2014 Sch 3 para 6(2)–(4).
1352 IA 2014 Sch 3 para 6(5).
1353 IA 2014 s21(1).
1354 IA 2014 s21(5) as amended by Immigration and Social Security Co-ordination (EU Withdrawal) Act 2020 (Consequential, Saving, Transitional and Transitory Provisions) (EU Exit) Regulations 2020 reg 20(2).
1355 IA 2014 s21(5)(a).
1356 IA 2014 s21(5)(aa), as inserted by Immigration and Social Security Co-ordination (EU Withdrawal) Act 2020 (Consequential, Saving, Transitional and Transitory Provisions) (EU Exit) Regulations 2020 reg 20(2).

3) a person who is not an Irish citizen and who has leave to enter or remain in the UK which was granted by virtue of Appendix EU to the Immigration Rules;[1357] or
4) an EEA national[1358] who has made a valid application for leave to enter or remain in the UK under Appendix EU to the Immigration Rules[1359] which was submitted on or before 30 June 2021[1360] and which has not been determined or withdrawn,[1361] and who was lawfully resident in the UK, or had a right of permanent residence in the UK, by virtue of the EEA Regs 2016 immediately before 11 pm on 31 December 2021.[1362]

7.405 The result of this is that the following people are relevant nationals, and will therefore not be disqualified persons:

- British citizens;
- Irish citizens;
- EEA nationals with settled status;[1363]

1357 Or under 'any other immigration rules which are identified in the immigration rules as having effect in connection with the withdrawal' of the UK from the EU. Rules, or changes to Appendix EU, which are identified as not having effect in connection with the residence scheme that operates in connection with the withdrawal of the UK from the EU are excluded: European Union (Withdrawal Agreement) Act 2020 s17(1) and IA 2014 s21(5)(ab) as inserted by Immigration and Social Security Co-ordination (EU Withdrawal) Act 2020 (Consequential, Saving, Transitional and Transitory Provisions) (EU Exit) Regulations 2020 reg 20(2).

1358 See para 7.18 for the meaning of EEA national.

1359 Or under 'any other immigration rules which are identified in the immigration rules as having effect in connection with the withdrawal' of the UK from the EU. Rules, or changes to Appendix EU, which are identified as not having effect in connection with the residence scheme that operates in connection with the withdrawal of the UK from the EU are excluded: European Union (Withdrawal Agreement) Act 2020 s17(1)(b) and Citizens' Rights (Application Deadline and Temporary Protection) (EU Exit) Regulations 2020 reg 4(6)(a).

1360 30 June 2021 was the deadline for submission of an application for residence status pursuant to the Withdrawal Agreement: Citizens' Rights (Application Deadline and Temporary Protection) (EU Exit) Regulations 2020 reg 2.

1361 Citizens' Rights (Application Deadline and Temporary Protection) (EU Exit) Regulations 2020 reg 4(2)(a) and (6)(a).

1362 Citizens' Rights (Application Deadline and Temporary Protection) (EU Exit) Regulations 2020 regs 4(2)(b) and 12(1)(n). See the discussion of this group at paras 7.22–7.25.

1363 See paras 2.153–2.165 for settled status.

- EEA nationals with pre-settled status;[1364] and
- EEA nationals with an in-time application for settled or pre-settled status which has not yet been determined (or withdrawn).[1365]

7.406 If the person is not a relevant national, the next question is whether they have a right to rent in relation to the premises. The person will not have a right to rent if:[1366]

1) they require leave to enter or remain in the UK but do not have it; or
2) their leave to enter or remain in the UK is subject to a condition preventing them from occupying the premises, unless the Secretary of State for the Home Department has granted them permission to occupy premises.

7.407 A person will have a limited right to rent if they have been granted leave to enter or remain in the UK for a limited period.[1367] The government's guidance states this will include EEA nationals with pre-settled status.[1368]

7.408 The secretary of state has the power to grant a person permission to rent. This is found at IA 2014 s21(3). Guidance on how this power will be exercised is contained in *Right to rent: landlords' penalties*.[1369] A migrant who seeks permission to rent, or who wishes to know whether or not they already have permission to rent, can make an application to the Home Office. The guidance suggests that the request could be made in correspondence, at a reporting event at a reporting centre, or at a personal appointment concerning an application.[1370] Some applicants are able to check their right to rent status

1364 See paras 2.166–2.168 for pre-settled status.

1365 See *Landlord's guide to right to rent checks*, p57.

1366 IA 2014 s21(2) and (3).

1367 IA 2014 s21(4); and *Landlord's guide to right to rent checks*, p16. As amended by Immigration and Social Security Co-ordination (EU Withdrawal) Act 2020 (Consequential, Saving, Transitional and Transitory Provisions) (EU Exit) Regulations 2020 reg 20(2). IA 2014 s21(4) states that '(4) References in this Chapter to a person with a "*limited right to rent*" are references to– (a) a person who has been granted leave to enter or remain in the United Kingdom for a limited period, or (b) a person who– (i) is not a relevant national' (emphasis added). This appears to be a mistake, because pursuant to IA 2014 s21(1) a person who is not a relevant national will be disqualified if they do not have a right to rent pursuant to IA 2014 s21(1): the status of not being a relevant national does not in itself (according to IA 2014 s21(1)) confer a right to rent.

1368 *Landlord's guide to right to rent checks*, p16.

1369 At pp13–18.

1370 At p17.

online.[1371] The Home Office's policy is that permission will 'normally' be granted to:[1372]

1) individuals with an outstanding protection claim, or an outstanding claim under ECHR Article 3,[1373] or an outstanding appeal against the refusal of such a claim;
2) individuals who have lodged further submissions against the refusal of a protection claim and those submissions have been outstanding for more than five working days;
3) individuals who have an outstanding appeal which cannot be pursued from abroad;
4) individuals who have been given permission to bring a judicial review in circumstances where the judicial review would 'as a matter of policy' be treated as suspensive of removal. If the outcome of the judicial review requires the Home Office to carry out a reconsideration, the permission to rent will normally last until this has been undertaken;
5) individuals who have been granted bail by an immigration tribunal or the courts with a residence or electronic monitoring restriction;[1374]
6) potential victims of modern slavery[1375] – permission would normally be granted from the date of a positive reasonable grounds decision[1376] until two weeks after the conclusive grounds decision;[1377]
7) recognised victims of modern slavery[1378] – permission would normally be granted from the date of a positive reasonable grounds decision[1379] until two weeks after the conclusive grounds decision;[1380]
8) recognised victims of modern slavery[1381] who have an associated outstanding application for discretionary leave to remain;[1382]

1371 See www.gov.uk/prove-right-to-rent.
1372 At pp13–14.
1373 See paras 3.43–3.46.
1374 See paras 1.188–1.197.
1375 See paras 11.131–11.145.
1376 See paras 11.170–11.176.
1377 See paras 11.177–11.178.
1378 See paras 11.131–11.145.
1379 See paras 11.170–11.176.
1380 See paras 11.177–11.178.
1381 See paras 11.131–11.145.
1382 See paras 1.126–1.136 and 11.52–11.53.

9) families with one or more children under the age of 18 who are co-operating with the family returns process; and
10) individuals who are complying with the voluntary departure process – this will include those with 'genuine obstacles' to returning, providing that they are 'taking all reasonable steps to address these'.[1383]

7.409 Even if a person does not meet one or more of the above criteria, the Home Office must still consider whether to make a 'discretionary' grant of permission to rent.[1384] The Home Office's policy requires decision-makers to pay particular regard to three factors:[1385]

1) whether the Home Office will 'better progress' the migrant's case if permission to rent is granted;
2) whether the migrant is a vulnerable person or unable to make their own decisions; and
3) whether permission to rent should be granted to avoid a breach of human rights.

7.410 A decision to grant, or not to grant, permission to rent must be communicated to the applicant in writing.[1386] If permission is refused, the decision-maker must explain why the criteria are not met and why the individual's circumstances are 'not sufficiently compelling to exercise discretion beyond the criteria'.[1387] A migrant who is dissatisfied with a decision not to grant them permission to rent may request an internal review of this decision on the grounds that the criteria were not correctly applied. The decision-maker must then review their decision. If the decision-maker decides to uphold the decision, they must request a peer or manager to consider whether the criteria were properly applied.[1388] If the review decision remains adverse, an applicant's remedy would be to apply for a judicial review. A fresh application may only be made where the individual's circumstances have changed such that permission to rent should now be granted.[1389]

1383 *Right to rent: landlords' penalties,* p14. See paras 6.48–6.58 for a discussion of analogous rules in the asylum support context.
1384 *Right to rent: landlords' penalties,* p14.
1385 *Right to rent: landlords' penalties,* p14. These three factors are elaborated on at pp15–16.
1386 *Right to rent: landlords' penalties,* p18.
1387 *Right to rent: landlords' penalties,* p18.
1388 *Right to rent: landlords' penalties,* p18.
1389 *Right to rent: landlords' penalties,* p18.

Implications of the right to rent scheme for landlords

7.411 Under IA 2014 s22, a landlord 'must not authorise an adult to occupy premises under a residential tenancy agreement if the adult is disqualified as a result of their immigration status'. A landlord will be taken to have authorised a disqualified adult to occupy premises where:

1) a tenancy agreement is entered into that grants a right to occupy to a disqualified tenant or adult named in the agreement;
2) a tenancy agreement is entered into that grants a right to occupy to a disqualified adult who is not named in the agreement, and either reasonable inquiries were not made of the tenant prior to the tenancy beginning as to who would occupy the property, or if reasonable inquiries were made, it was or should have been apparent that the adult in question was likely to occupy the property; or
3) a tenancy agreement is entered into that grants a right to occupy premises to an adult with a 'limited right to rent',[1390] and that adult subsequently becomes disqualified but remains in occupation.

7.412 To comply with the scheme, landlords are required to obtain and verify, and retain, copy or record, identity documents of prospective tenants and occupiers.[1391]

7.413 If a landlord or agent contravenes IA 2014 s22, then they face penalisation. The secretary of state may issue a notice requiring the payment of a penalty of up to £3,000.[1392] There are a number of statutory defences to any penalty notice, which are set out at IA 2014 s24 (for landlords) and s26 (for agents). The recipient of a penalty notice may object to it by giving notice of objection to the secretary of state[1393] and, if unsuccessful, may subsequently appeal to the county court.[1394]

7.414 In addition to a penalty notice, a landlord or agent who falls foul of the right to rent provisions also faces criminal sanctions. The IA 2014 creates four separate criminal offences for breach of the right to rent rules:

1390 See para 7.407.
1391 Immigration (Residential Accommodation) (Prescribed Requirements and Codes of Practice) Order 2014 SI No 2874 arts 3–5.
1392 IA 2014 ss23 and 25.
1393 IA 2014 s29.
1394 IA 2014 s30.

1) A landlord will commit an offence if their property is occupied by a disqualified adult and the landlord knows or has reasonable cause to believe that this is the case.[1395]
2) A landlord will commit an offence if there has been a post-grant contravention of the right to rent provision and the landlord knows or has reasonable cause to believe the contravention has happened.[1396]
3) An agent will commit an offence if they knew or had reasonable cause to believe that the landlord would contravene IA 2014 s22 by entering into the tenancy agreement and they had sufficient opportunity to notify the landlord of that fact before the landlord entered the agreement but did not do so.[1397]
4) An agent will commit an offence if a landlord commits a post-grant contravention and the agent is responsible for the contravention and knows or has reasonable cause to believe that there has been a contravention.[1398]

7.415 A landlord or agent who is guilty of an offence under the right to rent provisions is liable on conviction on indictment to imprisonment for up to five years and/or an unlimited fine or on summary conviction to imprisonment for a term not exceeding the general limit in a magistrates' court or a fine or both.[1399] Conviction could also lead to loss of a letting licence (under HA 2004 Parts 2 and 3) or a banning order (under Housing and Planning Act 2016 s14).

Eviction under the right to rent scheme

7.416 The IA 2014 provides for landlords to be able to evict occupiers from their homes where their occupation contravenes the right to rent rules. The method of eviction available to the landlord depends on whether all, or one or more but not all, of the occupiers are disqualified persons.

7.417 Under IA 2014 s33D, where the secretary of state has given the landlord a notice or notices identifying that the occupier of premises

1395 IA 2014 s33A(1)–(3). There are statutory defences to this offence at IA 2014 s33A(4) and (6).

1396 IA 2014 s33A(10). There are statutory defences to this offence at IA 2014 ss33A(10)(d) and 24(6)(a)–(c).

1397 IA 2014 s33B(2).

1398 IA 2014 s33B(3) and (4). There are statutory defences to this offence at IA 2014 ss33B(4)(b) and 26(6)(a) and (b).

1399 IA 2014 s33C.

is (or, if there is more than one occupier, all the occupiers are) disqualified, then the landlord 'may terminate the residential tenancy agreement by giving notice in writing and in the prescribed form to the tenant', or to all of the tenants under a joint tenancy, 'specifying the date on which the agreement comes to an end'.[1400] This notice 'is to be treated as a notice to quit in a case where a notice to quit would otherwise be required' and is 'enforceable as if it were an order of the High Court'.[1401] The prescribed form of notice is contained in the Immigration (Residential Accommodation) (Termination of Residential Tenancy Agreements) Order 2016.[1402]

7.418 The statutory assertion that a notice served under IA 2014 s33D is 'enforceable as if it were an order of the High Court' is somewhat problematic. The government's view is that, if the tenants do not leave by the date specified in the notice, then the landlord may:[1403]

1) apply to the District Registry of the High Court to ask for High Court enforcement officers to evict the tenants, without the need for a possession order;
2) exclude the tenants from the property 'peacefully . . . for example by changing the locks'; or
3) alternatively, take 'other steps to recover vacant possession'.

7.419 However, if the statute itself does not permit the landlord to use 'self-help' to effect re-entry – by, for example, going in and changing the locks themself – then the assertion in government guidance is irrelevant. It is at least arguable, by analogy with the approach of the Court of Appeal in *Haniff v Robinson*[1404] and with reference to the identical wording of County Courts Act 1984 s42(5) and to CPR 83.13(1),[1405] that IA 2014 s33D(7) requires the use of High Court enforcement orders (HCEOs) and that if parliament had intended otherwise it would have said so expressly. The point is not yet settled.

7.420 In *R (Goloshvili) v SSHD*,[1406] the claimant sought to have a notice issued in respect of her by the secretary of state under IA 2014 s33D quashed. The court refused to entertain the claim on the basis that it was academic because the notice had been withdrawn. In obiter

1400 IA 2014 s33D(3).
1401 IA 2014 s33D(6) and (7).
1402 SI No 1060.
1403 *Landlord's guide to right to rent checks*, p68.
1404 [1993] QB 419, CA.
1405 Which provides only three specified ways in which a High Court order may be enforced.
1406 [2019] EWHC 614 (Admin), [2019] HLR 37.

comments, however, the judge indicated that he would in any event have dismissed the claim. Although the issuing of a notice under IA 2014 s33D did amount to direct discrimination on the basis of race, such discrimination was exempt by virtue of EqA 2010 Sch 3 paras 2 and 17.

7.421 The second method applies where some, but not all, of the occupiers are disqualified persons. In this situation, the landlord may bring proceedings under the HA 1988, which has been amended to include a new ground for seeking possession where the secretary of state has given a written notice identifying that at least one of the tenants or occupiers is a disqualified person and the person named in the notice is in fact disqualified.[1407]

7.422 The nature of the right to rent provisions is that they will impact upon households who are already excluded from accessing accommodation under HA 1996 Part VI or Part VII (as such households are very unlikely to be eligible for homelessness or allocations assistance).[1408] The scheme closes off another avenue of accommodation, namely the private rented sector, for such households. Where the household includes a child, there may be no option but for the family to seek assistance from social services pursuant to ChA 1989 s17.[1409] The inaccessibility of private rented sector accommodation due to the right to rent scheme may be a relevant factor in any assessment of the child's needs completed by social services.[1410]

Discrimination and the right to rent

7.423 Even before it was introduced, the government was warned that the right to rent scheme would result in discrimination. In its response to the government's consultation on the proposed measures, the Joint Council for the Welfare of Immigrants (JCWI) stated:

> JCWI's main concern is that these proposals are very likely to lead to racial profiling and discrimination against BME [Black and Minority Ethnicity] prospective tenants . . . [The proposed immigration status checks] will serve to encourage indirect discrimination and in many cases direct discrimination. It will be far easier for a landlord to let his

1407 HA 1988 Sch 2 Part I Ground 7B. The Rent Act 1977 has also been amended, although Rent Act tenancies are now extremely rare.

1408 See paras 7.6–7.93.

1409 See paras 9.12–9.69.

1410 *R (U (children)) v Milton Keynes Council* [2017] EWHC 3050 (Admin), (2018) 21 CCL Rep 199. See paras 9.55–9.57.

or her property to a British/EU national who will simply have to produce their passport to confirm status.[1411]

7.424 The government acknowledged these warnings in the impact assessment issued on 25 September 2013, in which it noted that:

> Particular concern was raised that the regulations would result in discrimination motivated not because of overt prejudice but because of administrative convenience where some people are more likely than others to have readily available documentation.[1412]

7.425 Nevertheless, the government proceeded to implement the proposals, first in a pilot scheme in the West Midlands and then across the whole of England. To address the risk of unlawful discrimination, statutory guidance was published entitled *Code of practice for landlords: avoiding unlawful discrimination when conducting 'right to rent' checks in the private rented residential sector*.

7.426 As the right to rent scheme unfolded, observers noted with concern that the fears over the discriminatory effects of the provisions were, it seemed, being realised. An evaluation published by the JCWI in September 2015 found that 42 per cent of landlords surveyed said that the rules had made them less likely to consider people without a British passport; 27 per cent were reluctant to engage with applicants with 'foreign accents or names'.[1413] Further research published in February 2017 found that the scheme was causing foreign nationals and BME applicants to experience discrimination and that there was no evidence it was encouraging irregular migrants to leave the UK.[1414]

7.427 In January 2018, the JCWI lodged an application for judicial review of the scheme. The claim challenged the scheme itself, and the proposal to extend it to Wales, Scotland and Northern Ireland, under ECHR Articles 8 and 14 and EqA 2010 s149.

7.428 The JCWI succeeded in the Administrative Court.[1415] Martin Spencer J held that the scheme came within the ambit of Article 8

1411 Quoted in *R (Joint Council for the Welfare of Immigrants) v SSHD* [2019] EWHC 452 (Admin), [2019] HLR 35 at para 9. The position in respect of EU nationals has now changed: see paras 7.18–7.27.

1412 Quoted in *R (Joint Council for the Welfare of Immigrants) v SSHD* [2019] EWHC 452 (Admin), [2019] HLR 35 at para 10.

1413 *'No passport equals no home': an independent evaluation of the 'right to rent' scheme*, JCWI, September 2015, p11.

1414 *Passport please: the impact of the right to rent checks on migrants and ethnic minorities in England*, JCWI, February 2017.

1415 *R (Joint Council for the Welfare of Immigrants) v SSHD* [2019] EWHC 452 (Admin), [2019] HLR 35.

because it interfered with the process of seeking a home[1416] and that it infringed the right to non-discrimination under Article 14:

> In my judgment the evidence, when taken together, strongly showed not only that landlords are discriminating against potential tenants on grounds of nationality and ethnicity but also that they are doing so because of the Scheme.[1417]

7.429 The judge found that the secretary of state had 'not come close' to justifying the scheme[1418] and granted the claimant's request for a declaration that IA 2014 ss20–37 were incompatible with ECHR Article 14 in conjunction with Article 8.[1419] He also declared that any decision to extend the scheme to Wales, Scotland and Northern Ireland would, without further consideration of the efficacy and discriminatory impact of the scheme, be irrational and a breach of EqA 2010 s149.[1420]

7.430 The secretary of state appealed to the Court of Appeal, which unanimously allowed the appeal.[1421] The leading judgment was given by Hickinbottom LJ, with whom Henderson LJ agreed. Hickinbottom LJ concurred with Martin Spencer J that the scheme caused discrimination. Those who had a right to rent but who did not have British passports were the subject of discrimination on the basis of their actual or perceived nationality and the discrimination 'was caused by the scheme in the sense that, but for the Scheme, that level of such discrimination would not have occurred'.[1422] Hickinbottom LJ also accepted for the purposes of the judgment that the facts of the case fell within the ambit of Article 8.[1423] The question remaining was therefore whether the measure was justified.

7.431 There was disagreement between the parties as to whether the question of justification should be considered by reference to the manifestly without reasonable foundation test or the usual balancing exercise. Hickinbottom LJ stated that, had he been required to determine the matter, he would have held that the manifestly without reasonable foundation criterion applied, but that in any event the

1416 [2019] EWHC 452 (Admin), [2019] HLR 35 at para 37.

1417 [2019] EWHC 452 (Admin), [2019] HLR 35 at para 93.

1418 [2019] EWHC 452 (Admin), [2019] HLR 35 at para 123.

1419 [2019] EWHC 452 (Admin), [2019] HLR 35 at paras 127 and 134.

1420 [2019] EWHC 452 (Admin), [2019] HLR 35 at paras 131–134.

1421 *R (Joint Council for the Welfare of Immigrants) v SSHD* [2020] EWCA Civ, [2020] 1 WLR 1151 at 542.

1422 [2020] EWCA Civ, [2020] 1 WLR 1151 at para 66.

1423 [2020] EWCA Civ, [2020] 1 WLR 1151 at para 110.

result should be the same whichever threshold was used. This was because there was no bright line separating measures involving an element of economic or social policy from other cases: the position was simply that 'where there is a substantial degree of economic and/or social policy involved in a measure, the degree of deference to the assessment of the democratically-elected or -accountable body that enacts the measure must be accorded great weight'.[1424] The 'greater the element of economic and/or social policy involved, the greater the margin of judgment and the greater the deference that should be afforded'.[1425] Conversely, where the measure involved adverse discriminatory effects, then the margin of judgment would be reduced.[1426]

7.432 Even applying the usual balancing exercise, however, the measure was justified. The scheme was capable of being operated in a proportionate way, as shown by the fact that the majority of landlords complied with the scheme without committing discrimination. This on its own was a complete answer to the claim.[1427] Even if that were not so, however, the scheme would have been justified. The measure was 'an Act of Parliament implementing a socio-economic policy' and therefore 'very considerable deference' must be given to parliament's assessment of the public interest.[1428] It was clear that parliament had been aware of the risk of discrimination and it was not proper to speculate as to 'what might have been the expectation of Parliament . . . with regard to the management of that risk'.[1429] The scheme appeared to be successful in that there was 'no evidence that irregular immigrants do now obtain' private rented accommodation.[1430] The scheme itself 'does not intend, encourage or directly create discrimination'.[1431] Landlords engaging in discrimination were doing so as private citizens.[1432] The nature and level of the discrimination was relevant and, whilst the discrimination may give rise to

1424 [2020] EWCA Civ, [2020] 1 WLR 1151 at para 140.
1425 [2020] EWCA Civ, [2020] 1 WLR 1151 at para 140.
1426 [2020] EWCA Civ, [2020] 1 WLR 1151 at paras 134–140. On the issue of proportionality see also *R (SC) v SSWP* [2021] UKSC 26, [2022] AC 223.
1427 [2020] EWCA Civ, [2020] 1 WLR 1151 at para 119.
1428 [2020] EWCA Civ, [2020] 1 WLR 1151 at para 143.
1429 [2020] EWCA Civ, [2020] 1 WLR 1151 at para 147.
1430 [2020] EWCA Civ, [2020] 1 WLR 1151 at para 144.
1431 [2020] EWCA Civ, [2020] 1 WLR 1151 at para 148(i).
1432 [2020] EWCA Civ, [2020] 1 WLR 1151 at para 148(ii).

delay for some people in finding accommodation, they did not necessarily become homeless.[1433]

7.433 Davis LJ disagreed with the conclusion that the scheme caused discrimination. He stated that 'so far from encouraging or incentivising discrimination', the scheme actually sought to do the opposite, and in so far as there was discrimination on the part of a minority, that was because they had chosen not to comply with the law.[1434] He also disagreed that the facts of the case came within the ambit of ECHR Article 8, stating that 'a degree of delay and inconvenience in securing a letting' did not suffice to bring the case within that Article.[1435]

7.434 The Supreme Court subsequently refused permission to appeal against this decision.

Conclusion

7.435 A settled home is a prerequisite to achieving stability in other areas of life. This is often particularly true for migrants who may have come to the UK as a result of difficult and traumatic experiences. This chapter is intended to assist advisers who are helping migrant clients meet the fundamental human need for shelter.

1433 [2020] EWCA Civ, [2020] 1 WLR 1151 at para 150.
1434 [2020] EWCA Civ, [2020] 1 WLR 1151 at paras 157–165.
1435 [2020] EWCA Civ, [2020] 1 WLR 1151 at para 175. See, however, *LF v UK* App No 19839/21 (2022) 75 EHRR SE5, ECtHR.

CHAPTER 8

Adult care for migrants

Shu Shin Luh and Connor Johnston

continued

Key points

- The Care Act 2014 is the principal legal framework in England by which local authorities are required to meet the needs of adults for care and support.[1]
- The Care Act 2014 also allows for the provision of support to carers.[2]
- The first step toward the provision of care and/or support is an assessment of the adult's needs, or the needs of their carer.[3]
- Following this, a decision will be made as to whether the assessed needs meet the statutory eligibility criteria.[4]
- If so, a decision will be made as to how to meet those needs and a care and support plan (or, in the case of carers, a support plan) will be prepared.[5]
- If not, the local authority retains a power to meet the adult's needs in any event.[6]
- The local authority has a wide degree of latitude in deciding, in conjunction with the adult carer, how to meet needs.[7]
- In some cases, accommodation may need to be provided as a vehicle effectively to deliver care and support.[8]
- Needs which should be met either by the National Health Service (NHS) or by local housing authorities cannot generally be met under the Care Act 2014.[9]
- However, support under the Care Act 2014 generally takes precedence over Home Office support.[10]
- The Care Act 2014 is subject to a number of immigration-based exclusions from support. However, there are exceptions to these exclusions.[11]

1 See paras 8.89–8.97.
2 See paras 8.98–8.99.
3 See paras 8.33–8.70.
4 See paras 8.71–8.87.
5 See paras 8.107–8.117.
6 See paras 8.89–8.97.
7 See paras 8.118–8.122.
8 See paras 8.123–8.131.
9 See paras 8.132–8.137.
10 See para 8.157.
11 See paras 8.158–8.178.

- Under the Mental Health Act 1983 'after-care' should be made available to certain categories of person who have been detained under that Act.[12]
- For Wales, the counterpart to the Care Act 2014 is the Social Services and Well-Being (Wales) Act 2014. It contains broadly equivalent provisions.[13]

Introduction

8.1 This chapter and the next chapter examine the relationship between immigration status and access to community care services for different cohorts of migrants: adults, families, and lone children and young people.

8.2 The background to how the relationship has evolved is important to note at the outset, particularly as there used to be a time when immigration concerns played no or little part in the decision on eligibility for community care services. However, over time the approach in law and policy changed significantly. Changes to eligibility for mainstream state benefits and community care services are discussed in some detail in the Introduction.

8.3 For the purposes of this and next chapters, the significant changes affecting access to community care services provided by local authority social care departments were brought about by the Immigration and Asylum Act (IAA) 1999 which, by sections 115 and 116, introduced sweeping exclusions which made persons subject to immigration control ineligible for virtually all state welfare benefits and for many local authority community care services. The creation of the asylum support regime under the IAA 1999 (discussed in chapters 5 and 6) provided a self-contained safety-net system for asylum-seekers and certain qualifying failed asylum-seekers through the provision of accommodation and support on a temporary basis pending the determination of their claims and/or departure from the UK. That support, however, was generic in nature rather than needs-based, and directed at providing a minimum standard of support to avoid destitution and street homeless. It was also only made available to those asylum-seekers who satisfied that threshold and qualifying failed asylum-seekers.

12 See paras 8.196–8.202.

13 See paras 8.203–8.219.

8.4 Through Nationality, Immigration and Asylum Act (NIAA) 2002 s54 and Sch 3, further and more significant exclusions were introduced, including a general presumption that certain categories of migrants with no permission to remain in the UK would be excluded from mainstream benefits and community care services unless it could be shown that withdrawal or withholding of support would breach their rights under the European Convention on Human Rights (ECHR) or European Union (EU) Treaties. Yet more changes have subsequently been brought into force affecting access to housing and other aspects of a person's day-to-day life, but do not bear on the adult care provisions that this chapter is concerned with.

8.5 What is apparent from the sustained introduction of restrictions over more than two decades is that there is now a tiered system of support, in which eligibility is heavily focused on the immigration status of the individual.

8.6 In this chapter, the focus will be on social care arrangements for vulnerable adults (including those discharged from psychiatric hospital wards) and for those who care for them. It will give an overview of the general structure governing adult social care assessments, eligibility criteria and support[14] and focus on the exclusions applicable to persons subject to immigration control and the remedies available to individuals against acts, omissions and decisions made by the local authorities from whom they are seeking support.

Care Act 2014

Overview

8.7 Adult community care services mean the care and support provided by local social services authorities (and sometimes NHS authorities) pursuant to their responsibilities towards adults who need extra support to do the everyday things that others may often take for granted – such as getting out of bed, washing and getting dressed, cooking meals, managing their affairs, and participating in the community at large. It might also include:

- emotional support at times of difficulty or stress, or to prevent the risk of a deterioration in mental health, and respite and other

14 For a comprehensive and in-depth examination of adult social care, see L Clements *Community care and the law*, Legal Action Group, 7th edn, 2019.

support to help people who are caring for a family member or friend;
- supported accommodation, subsistence and other financial assistance and facilities to get to and from activities and appointments.

8.8 The typical cohorts of eligible persons include:
- the elderly;
- people with learning disabilities and other cognitive impairments;
- physically disabled people;
- people with mental health problems;
- people who lack mental capacity; and
- drug and alcohol misusers and their carers.

8.9 The legislative framework for arranging adult community care services had become a confusing patchwork of conflicting statutes enacted and amended over a period of 60 years. Until 2014, there was no single, modern statue to which those receive support and those providing support could turn in order to understand whether (and if so what kind of) services can or must be provided. In May 2011, the Law Commission published a report on adult social care[15] which made 76 recommendations for changes to the adult care legal framework, aimed at consolidating and simplifying the way in which needs are identified and met. In 2012, the government responded by publishing the white paper, *Caring for our future: reforming care and support*,[16] which proposed a new structure for adult social care, aimed at promoting well-being and independence and at reducing the risk of people reaching a crisis point.

8.10 In 2014, parliament enacted the Care Act 2014, applicable to local authorities in England, to give effect to the policies in the white paper and recommendations by the Law Commission to modernise the legal framework governing the way in which care and support needs for adults are assessed, eligibility is determined and care and support arrangements are made. In Wales, the Welsh Assembly similarly passed the Social Services and Well-being (Wales) Act (SSWB(W)A) 2014, applicable to local authorities in Wales, with the same aim. Scotland and Northern Ireland have separate legal frameworks for the arrangement of adult social care.

15 Law Commission, *Adult social care*, HC 941, 10 May 2011.
16 Cm 8378, July 2012.

8.11 The purpose of these new Acts was to consolidate existing community care legislation as applied in England and in Wales.[17] Responsibility for arranging adult community care services remains predominantly on local authority adult care departments, although the burden continues to be shared with the relevant NHS body where the support required is for preventing a deterioration in a person's mental state and to avert risks of re-hospitalisation under the Mental Health Act (MHA) 1983.

8.12 The approach to reform taken by England and Wales was, however, materially different. In England, as is indicated by the long title to the Act,[18] the Care Act 2014 is aimed only at adults. It sought to 'make provision to reform the law relating to care and support for adults and the law relating to support for carers'. By contrast, the Welsh SSWB(W)A 2014 is more ambitious, seeking to consolidate not only legislation relating to adult social care but also provisions relating to children, young adults and their families. The Welsh act, as introduced, thus covers a wider terrain than the Care Act 2014, and includes greater safeguarding powers and major reform to the law concerning 'children in need' (and consequent repeal to parts of the Children Act (ChA) 1989 in Wales).

8.13 For the purposes of this chapter, the discussion will be primarily based on the Care Act 2014[19] but will touch briefly on the Welsh Act as it applies to adults.[20] The provision of after-care when a patient leaves hospital following compulsory detention under the MHA 1983

17 In England, by the Care Act 2014 and Children and Families Act 2014 (Consequential Amendments) Order 2015 SI No 914, the following community care duties were repealed in their application to local authorities in England: National Assistance Act 1948 ss21 and 29; Chronically Sick and Disabled Persons Act 1970 s2 (as it applied to disabled adults, but not to disabled children) and National Health Service and Community Care Act 1990 s47, save in respect of its applicability to MHA 1983 s117. In Wales, by the Social Services and Well-being (Wales) Act 2014 (Consequential Amendments) Regulations 2016 SI No 413, the same provisions were repealed in Wales.

18 The long title to the Care Act 2014 is 'an Act to make provision to reform the law relating to care and support for adults and the law relating to support for carers; to make provision about safeguarding adults from abuse or neglect; to make provision about care standards; to establish and make provision about Health Education England; to establish and make provision about the Health Research Authority; to make provision about integrating care and support with health services; and for connected purposes'.

19 See paras 8.7–8.195.

20 See paras 8.203–8.219. The SSWB(W)A 2014 provisions that apply to children are discussed at paras 9.249–9.265.

will also be addressed below.[21] The primary framework for and discussion around the duties and powers of NHS bodies and the arrangements for NHS care are set out in chapter 10.

Terminology

8.14 As part of the reform brought about by the Care Act 2014, the language used to describe those receiving support and those caring for them also changed.

8.15 The Care Act 2014 does not talk of the disabled, elderly or infirm. The term 'disability' is not used. Instead, the phrase used throughout is of an 'adult', which is generally qualified by the person 'needing care', or having 'needs for care and support'. Unlike the ChA 1989,[22] the Care Act 2014 contains no broad definition of what makes an adult 'in need'. However, the Care and Support (Eligibility Criteria) Regulations ('Eligibility Regs') 2015,[23] do, however, provide that an adult is in effect 'in need' and therefore qualify for care and support if their needs meet the eligibility criteria,[24] arise from or are related to 'a physical or mental impairment or illness'.[25] Although what constitutes an impairment or illness is not defined in regulations, the *Care and support statutory guidance*, issued under the Care Act 2014, explains that this includes anyone who has a 'condition as a result of either physical, mental, sensory, learning or cognitive disabilities or illnesses, substance misuse or brain injury'.[26] The statutory guidance also advises that local authorities should base their judgment on the assessment of the adult and a formal diagnosis of the condition

21 See paras 8.196–8.202.

22 ChA 1989 s17(10) defines a child as 'in need' if: '(a) he is unlikely to achieve or maintain, or to have the opportunity of achieving or maintaining, a reasonable standard of health or development without the provision for him of services by a local authority . . .; (b) his health or development is likely to be significantly impaired, or further impaired, without the provision for him of such services; or (c) he is disabled.' By section 17(11), a child is disabled if 'he is blind, deaf or dumb or suffers from mental disorder of any kind or is substantially and permanently handicapped by illness, injury or congenital deformity or such other disability as may be prescribed; and . . . "development" means physical, intellectual, emotional, social or behavioural development; and "health" means physical or mental health'.

23 SI No 313.

24 See paras 8.71–8.87.

25 Eligibility Regs 2015 reg 2.

26 *Care and support statutory guidance*, Department of Health & Social Care, 2 November 2022, para 6.104, www.gov.uk/government/publications/care-act-statutory-guidance/care-and-support-statutory-guidance.

should not be required.[27] By this explanation, it is clear that phrases such as 'adults needing care' are intended to be given a pragmatic, rather than an unduly clinical or formalistic, interpretation.

8.16 'Carer' is used to describe 'an adult who provides or intends to provide care for another adult' but who is not contracted to do so or providing the care as formal 'voluntary work'.[28] The Care Act 2014 includes provision for 'young carers', defined as carers who are under 18.[29]

8.17 Where the Care Act 2014 refers to 'individuals', depending on the context, it can mean either an adult needing care and support or a carer.

8.18 An important innovation of the Care Act 2014 is its move away from the focus on 'services' to a focus on the 'provision of care and support' in the case of adults and 'provision of support' for carers, with a focus on meeting needs rather than fitting people's needs to particular commissioned services. The MHA 1983 has continued to supplement the consolidated adult care and support framework in respect of those mentally ill patients who are discharged from hospital.

Key concepts

8.19 A significant change brought about by the Care Act 2014 was the enshrining of a person-centric approach to assessing needs and determining care arrangements in primary legislation. This was done through the introduction of a cluster of general duties imposed on local authorities to:

- promote individual well-being;
- prevent the development or deterioration of needs for care and support; and
- co-operate with other authorities to achieve this.

Well-being duty

8.20 Care Act 2014 s1 is the first of these general duties and has the most prominent role. It imposes a general duty on the local authority, in the exercise of a function under Part 1 of the Act in the case of an individual, to 'promote that individual's well-being'. This duty is

27 *Care and support statutory guidance*, para 6.104.
28 Care Act 2014 s10(3) and (9)–(10).
29 Care Act 2014 ss63 and 64.

referred to in the statutory guidance to the Care Act 2014 as the 'guiding principle'.[30] The well-being obligation applies whenever a local authority exercises 'a function' under Care Act 2014 Part 1 in 'the case of an individual'.[31] Arguably it must not only inform the way in which care and support for an individual with qualifying needs is arranged, it must also inform broader macro decisions around how the local authority determines the social care budget across its area, particularly given the local authority's duty to take preventative action against people in its area developing a need for care and support,[32] its duty to provide information and advice relating to care and support for adults and support for carers,[33] and its duty to promote the efficient and effective operation of a market in services for meeting care and support needs.[34]

8.21 'Well-being' is not itself defined, but Care Act 2014 s1(2) lists the nine factors relevant to determining an adult's well-being:

a) personal dignity (including treatment of the individual with respect);
b) physical and mental health and emotional well-being;
c) protection from abuse and neglect;
d) control by the individual over day-to-day life;
e) participation in work, education, training or recreation;
f) social and economic well-being;
g) domestic, family and personal relationships;
h) suitability of living accommodation;
i) the individual's contribution to society.

8.22 Additionally, when discharging any obligation under the Act, the local authority 'must have regard to' eight further principles set out under section 1(3) that inform the approach to considering 'well-being' This includes:

a) the assumption that the 'individual' is best placed to judge well-being;
b) the individual's views, wishes and feelings;
c) the importance of preventing or delaying the development of needs for care and support or needs for support and the importance of reducing needs of either kind that already exist;

30 *Care and support statutory guidance*, para 1.2.
31 Care Act 2014 s1(1).
32 Care Act 2014 s2.
33 Care Act 2014 s3.
34 Care Act 2014 s4.

d) the need to take into account all the individual's circumstances (and non-discriminatory in terms of stereotyping etc);
e) the importance of the individual participating (with support if needs be) as fully as possible in decisions about them;
f) the importance of striking a balance between the individual's well-being and that of any friends or relatives involved in their care;
g) the need to protect people from abuse and neglect;
h) the need to ensure that any restrictions are kept to the minimum necessary.

8.23 The statutory guidance explains how the well-being principle fits with the concept in Care Act 2014 Part 1 of 'meeting needs' – which is distinct from a model based on fitting people's needs to particular services: everyone's needs are different and personal to them; care and support can be provided in a number of ways; some aspects of well-being will be more relevant to some people than others.[35] Local authorities are required explicitly to consider the most relevant aspects of well-being to the individual concerned, and assess how their needs impact on them.[36]

8.24 The well-being principle is intended to cover intended to cover the key components of independent living, as expressed in the UN Convention on the Rights of Persons with Disabilities 2006, in particular, Article 19. Supporting people to live as independently as possible, for as long as possible, is a guiding principle of the Care Act 2014.[37]

8.25 In *R (JF) v Merton LBC*[38] the High Court held that there was a statutory duty to have regard to the matters listed in Care Act 2014 s1(2) and (3). It has been held to be maladministration for a local authority to impose 'restrictive interpretations of Care Act outcomes' that fail to take proper account of an adult's well-being.[39]

35 *Care and support statutory guidance*, paras 1.9–1.12.

36 *Care and support statutory guidance*, para 1.12.

37 *Care and support statutory guidance*, para 1.19.

38 [2017] EWHC 1519 (Admin). See further *R (Davey) v Oxfordshire CC* [2017] EWHC 354 (Admin), [2017] PTSR 904 at paras 20–22 (upheld by Court of Appeal in *R (Davey) v Oxfordshire CC* [2017] EWCA 1308, (2017) 20 CCLR 303 at paras 52 and 136).

39 Complaint against Hammersmith and Fulham LBC, Local Government Ombudsman Report 15 011 661, 21 July 2016 at para 25.

Prevention duty

8.26 The second innovation of the Care Act 2014 is the general duty under section 2 to provide a range of preventative services that the local authority considers will contribute toward preventing or delaying the development by adults and carers in its area of needs for care and support or reducing the adult or carer's need for care and support.

8.27 As is made clear in the statutory guidance, services provided under this general duty are to be provided for people regardless of whether they satisfy eligibility criteria and even if they do not have any current support needs. The steps taken can be population-wide measures, or targeted to individuals. Examples of prevention measures that are given in the statutory guidance are the promotion of exercise classes or befriending schemes; fall prevention clinics; adaptations to housing; handyman services; telecare services; and intermediate care (a programme of care provided for a limited period of time to assist a person to maintain or regain the ability to live independently). The statutory guidance, in particular, recognises the significant benefit of preventative services, particularly in the context of supporting young carers, directing local authorities to consider how supporting the adult with needs for care and support can prevent the young carer from undertaking excessive or inappropriate care and support responsibilities.[40]

8.28 The rationale behind the prevention duty is, as explained in the government's white paper, to promote early intervention to avoid adults in need and their carers reaching a crisis point.[41] However, as was noted by the House of Commons Committee of Public Accounts in July 2014[42] at around the time the Care Act 2014 received Royal Assent, local authorities were facing severe problems in relation to levels of social care funding at a time when demand for social care support was rising. The Department of Health (as it was called then) admitted that it was doubtful whether preventative services and lower-level intervention made a difference in staving off crises.[43] The Association of Directors of Adult Social Services and the Local Government Association both expressed doubts about investing in

40 *Care and support statutory guidance*, para 2.50.

41 Government white paper, *Caring for our future: reforming care and support*, Cm 8378, July 2012, chapter 2.

42 House of Commons Committee of Public Accounts, *Adult social care in England*, Sixth report of Session 2014–2015, HC 518, 2 July 2014.

43 House of Commons Committee of Public Accounts, *Adult social care in England*, Sixth report of Session 2014–2015, HC 518, 2 July 2014, p7.

preventative services given the overall reduction in adult care budgets from central government. In July 2018, the Local Government Association launched its own green paper, *The lives we want to lead*, setting out options for how the adult care system could be improved and why this was urgently needed given the scale of the funding crisis around adult social care despite the increasing demand for the support. Subsequent white papers on social care reforms have not put a focus on the development of preventative services. The COVID-19 pandemic in fact led to temporary curtailment of certain social care duties while the government at the central and local level sought to respond to the immediate public health crisis. Social care reforms, such as on capping costs of care, were delayed as a result of the COVID-19 pandemic. Other reforms, such as the introduction of an appeal system for social care disputes, were shelved. At the time of writing (September 2022), there appears little prospect of an injection of public funds into the development of preventative services.

8.29 Without a significant injection of investment into preventative services, it was, and remains, difficult to see how the preventative duty can be given full effect. The reality at present is that to invest in more preventative services without new money would be to require a local authority to disinvest in an existing area, and in many local authority areas, this would mean disinvesting in crisis services.

Integration and co-operation duties

8.30 Care Act 2014 s3 places a duty to promote integration with health provision where it would promote the well-being of adults with needs and their carers, contribute to preventing the development of needs in adults or carers, or improve quality of care for adults and carers. This duty is intended to run in tandem with the obligations under the Health and Social Care Act (HSCA) 2012 to promote the integration of health and social care services. The ambition of the government was to provide joined-up services that meet the needs of those who require health, care and support. In practice, this is complicated by the differences in the practical operational realities of local authorities and health bodies.

8.31 Further duties under Care Act 2014 ss6 and 7 also seek to require public bodies to co-operate to work more closely and effectively with each other. Care Act 2014 s6 creates a general duty to co-operate and section 7 a specific duty when requested by a local authority. Section 7 is new to adult social care, and is based on a similar provision in ChA

1989 s27 which provides a basis for children's services to request assistance from other public bodies. The introduction of Care Act 2014 s7 strengthened what used only to be a duty on adult care services to notify housing and health bodies where such relevant needs were identified in the course of a community care assessment with no attendant obligation on the public body notified to act upon the needs identified. By that section, adult social care is now able to request assistance from a housing authority or health authority, unless it would be incompatible with those public bodies' duties or adversely impact on their exercise of functions.

8.32 Like ChA 1989 s27, Care Act 2014 s7 is drafted as to only apply between different authorities. However, it seems likely that this co-operation duty will be interpreted, consistent with the object of the Care Act 2014 to require a similar degree of co-operation to take place between departments where the need concerns a unitary authority.[44] This is supported by the *Care and support statutory guidance* which stresses the importance of co-operation not just between the local authority and its external partners but also internal co-operation within the local authority.[45] For example, the statutory guidance states that it is important for local authority officers responsible for housing to work in co-operation with adult care and support given that housing and suitability of living accommodation play a significant role in supporting a person to meet their needs and can contribute to delaying that person's deterioration. Similarly, the transition of a young person with care needs from children's social care to adult care and support would require the respective departments in the local authority to co-operate to share information, prepare for transition and ensure the young person's needs are met on reaching the age of 18. Young carers will also require co-operation between adult care and children's services to ensure the young carer's needs are assessed properly under both the Care Act 2014 and the ChA 1989.

44 See *R (M) v Islington LBC* [2016] EWHC 332 (Admin) [2016] HLR 19, in which the High Court noted that it was possible that parliament considered that unitary authorities would ensure that there was the necessary co-operation between their various departments so that there would be no need for a statutory requirement to achieve it. However, government guidance required the same degree of co-operation between departments in a unitary authority meaning that the requirements of ChA 1989 s27 applied indirectly.

45 *Care and support statutory guidance*, para 15.23.

The assessment of need

8.33 The decision-making structure for the Care Act 2014 is fairly straightforward and not dissimilar to the previous regime for determining support provisions. It involves an assessment to determine whether and to what extent the adult or carer has a need for care and/or support, whether it is an eligible need giving rise to a duty on the local authority to provide for and how it will be provided in the circumstances. This three-step process – assessment of needs; determination of eligible needs; and planning for support – is standard across all community care law, whether applied to lone adults, families or lone children. This section of the chapter deals with assessments – eligibility determinations are discussed at paras 8.71–8.87; and care planning is discussed at paras 8.107–8.117.

Assessing an adult's need for care and support

8.34 Care Act 2014 s9 contains the duty to assess adults to determine whether they have a need for care and support. The trigger for an assessment is the 'appearance of need' and arises regardless of the 'level' of those needs, the person's financial resources or their location. The threshold test – where it 'appears' to the local authority that an adult 'may have' a need for care and support – is very low, and the consequent duty to assess is absolute and not dependent on whether resources are available to carry out assessments or on whether the local authority would be likely to provide relevant services.[46]

8.35 The duty to assess is only disapplied where an individual refuses an assessment, unless the person lacks capacity in this respect or is experiencing or at risk of abuse.[47] However, where the individual later requests an assessment or there is a change of circumstances, the assessment duty is once again triggered.[48]

8.36 The assessment must have specific regard to the well-being criteria under Care Act 2014 s1(2) and (3),[49] and focus on the outcomes that the adult wishes to achieve in day-to-day life and whether, and to what extent, the provision of care and support could contribute to the achievement of those outcomes. The assessment is

46 For a similar conclusion related to the previous legislative provision, National Health Service and Community Care Act 1990 s47; see *R v Bristol City Council ex p Penfold* (1997–98) 1 CCLR 315, QBD.

47 Care Act 2014 s11(2).

48 Care Act 2014 s11(4).

49 See paras 8.20–8.25.

one of the key interactions between a local authority and an individual, whether an adult needing care or a carer. It is the tool for gaining a full picture of the individual's needs so that the local authority can identify the appropriate response at the right time to meet the level of the person's needs.

8.37 Reflecting the person-centric approach, described at paras 8.19–8.32, Care Act 2014 s9(5) provides that in carrying out a needs assessment, the local authority 'must involve' the adult, any carer the adult has and any person whom the adult asks the authority to involve or, where the adult lacks capacity to ask the authority to do that, any person who appears to be interested in the adult's welfare.

8.38 Although the Care Act 2014 envisages that the assessment may be carried out over the phone or online, instead of face to face, it is difficult to see how eliciting the adult's needs, the impact they have on the adult's well-being and the impact of caring on the carer can be achieved other than by a face-to-face assessment, unless the adult agrees this is not necessary. The *Care and support statutory guidance* repeatedly reminds local authorities that assessments must be person-centred and must establish 'the total extent of needs'.[50]

8.39 For those individuals whose needs may fluctuate, the local authority must recognise this and seek to establish the ongoing level of need by considering the person's care and support history over a suitable period of time, taking account of both the frequency and the degree of fluctuation. The local authority must, in the circumstances, take into account what fluctuations can be reasonably be expected based on its experience of others with a similar condition and by obtaining information from the individual about this.[51]

8.40 To support the person's involvement, the local authority should establish the individual's communication needs and seek to adapt the assessment process accordingly. In order to assist the adult with needs for care and support, or the carer, to prepare for the assessment, the local authority should provide in advance, and in an accessible format, the list of questions to be covered in the assessment.[52] The purpose of this is to help the individual or carer to think through what their needs are and the outcomes they want to achieve in advance of the discussion with the social worker.

8.41 During the assessment, the local authorities must consider all of the adult's care and support needs, and disregard any support which

50 *Care and support statutory guidance*, para 6.10.

51 *Care and support statutory guidance*, paras 6.58–6.59.

52 *Care and support statutory guidance*, para 6.37.

is being provided by the adult's carer.[53] As such, a needs assessment will not fulfil the requirements of Care Act 2014 s9 'if it does not include all the individual's needs, whether currently being met or not'.[54]

8.42 The Care Act 2014, its associated regulations and statutory guidance also place important obligations on local authorities in relation to the advocacy and safeguarding needs of individuals that are identified during the assessment and care planning processes. These are addressed further below at paras 8.33–8.70 and 8.107–8.117.

8.43 Although there is no set timescale for completing assessments under the Care Act 2014, the statutory guidance directs that an assessment should be carried out over 'an appropriate and reasonable timescale',[55] taking into account the urgency of needs and a consideration of any fluctuation in needs.[56] The local authority should provide to the individual an indicative timescale over which the assessment will be conducted and keep the person informed throughout the assessment process.

8.44 Detailed regulations in the form of the Care and Support (Assessment) Regulations ('Assessment Regs') 2014[57] have been issued concerning the process that must be followed during an assessment. This is further reinforced by a new duty on the local authority to ensure that anyone carrying out an assessment has the relevant skills, knowledge and competence and is appropriately trained.[58]

8.45 In *R (Davey) v Oxfordshire CC*[59] the Court of Appeal held that the assessment duty requires an assessment of the matters set out in Care Act 2014 s9(4), namely, the impact of the adult's need for care and support on their well-being, the outcomes that the adult wishes to achieve in day-to-day life, and whether, and to what extent, the provision of care and support could contribute in achieving these outcomes. Failure to assess by reference to these statutory

53 *Care and support statutory guidance*, para 6.15.

54 *R (Antoniak) v Westminster City Council* [2019] EWHC 3465 (Admin) at para 30.

55 *Care and support statutory guidance*, para 6.29.

56 See further *R (D) v Brent LBC* [2015] EWHC 3224 (Admin) at paras 19 and 27 per David Casement KC sitting as a deputy High Court judge.

57 SI No 2827.

58 Assessment Regs 2014 reg 5. See also *Care and support statutory guidance*, paras 6.86–6.88.

59 [2017] EWCA Civ 1308, [2018] PTSR 281.

considerations and to the well-being principles would constitute a breach of statutory duty.

8.46 In *R (JF) v Merton LBC*[60] the High Court summarised the requirements, stating that an assessment will be unlawful if it:[61]

- fails to assess the impact of the adult's needs for care and support on the well-being factors listed in Care Act 2014 s1(2);
- fails to assess the outcomes that the adult wishes to achieve in day-to-day life, and whether, and if so to what extent, the provision of care and support could contribute to the achievement of those outcomes;
- fails to have regard to the matters specified in Assessment Regs 2014 reg 3(2), namely the adult's wishes and preferences, the outcomes they seek and the severity and overall extent of their needs;
- is neither appropriate nor proportionate.

8.47 In relation to adults in need such as JF, who have learning difficulties, autism and no verbal communications abilities, inevitably the assessment process will mean that the local authority must have regard to the views expressed by their parents or carers. Failure properly to take account of their views would be unlawful.[62]

Assessing a carer's need for support

8.48 The duty to assess a carer is similarly triggered where it 'appears' to the local authority that the carer may have needs for support. There is no need for the carer to provide or intend to provide any particular level of care in order for an assessment to be commenced.

8.49 Carers' assessments must ascertain whether the carer is able and willing to continue to provide the care, the impact on the carer's well-being, the outcomes the carer wishes to achieve in day-to-day life, and whether the carer works or wishes to work or participate in education, training or recreation.[63]

8.50 Although the principal carer assessment duty is only owed to adult carers caring for other adults, the Care Act 2014 contains

60 [2017] EWHC 1519 (Admin). The judgment affirmed (on this point) *R (Davey) Oxfordshire CC* [2017] EWHC 354 (Admin) at para 136.

61 *JF v Merton* at para 47.

62 *JF v Merton* at para 54. See further Care Act 2014 s9(5)(b) and Assessment Regs 2014 reg 4(1)(a).

63 The details relating to carers' assessments lie outside of the scope of this text. For further reading, see L Clements *Community care and the law*, Legal Action Group, 7th edn, 2019.

specific provisions covering carers of disabled children and young carers who are in transition into adulthood. These are complemented by measures in the Children and Families Act 2014, which create significant new duties in relation to parent carers and young carers as well as enhanced obligations on local authorities to 'identify any children who are involved in providing care'.[64]

Independent advocacy

8.51 Care Act 2014 s67 and the regulations[65] place a duty on local authorities to arrange an independent advocate for an adult if the authority considers that:

- the adult would experience 'substantial difficulty' in participating in (among other things) their assessment and/or the preparation of their care and support plan; and
- there is no one appropriate available to support and represent their wishes. This criterion does not apply to certain hospital discharges and NHS continuing care disputes.

8.52 The duty within the Act was a new introduction for local authorities, consistent with the focus of the Care Act 2014 on facilitating the individual who may have care and support needs to participate in the assessment process more effectively. Some people, in specific circumstances and subject to certain decisions, already have access to independent advocacy, for example, an independent mental capacity advocate (IMCA), appointed under the Mental Capacity Act (MCA) 2005 for those who lack mental capacity to make decisions about where they live and about serious treatment options, or an independent mental health advocate (IMHA) if they are a qualifying patient subject to certain restrictions and the MHA 1983.[66]

8.53 The threshold for qualifying for independent advocacy under the Care Act 2014 is lower than both the MCA 2005 and MHA 1983. A

64 *Care and support statutory guidance*, para 6.68. Specific provision is made under ChA 1989 ss17ZA–17ZF, directing the exercise of the ChA 1989 s17 discretion in cases involving child young carers and adults caring for disabled children (parent carers). The details of those provisions lie outside of the scope of this text. For further reading see S Broach, L Clements and S Read *Disabled children: a legal handbook* Legal Action Group, 2nd edn, 2015.

65 Care and Support (Independent Advocacy Support) (No 2) Regulations ('IAS Regs') 2014 SI No 2889 reg 4.

66 An IMHA may be appointed where a person is detained under the MHA 1983 (save under section 4 or 5 or under emergency powers under sections 135 and 136), liable to be detained, subject to a community treatment order or guardianship order or a conditionally discharged restricted patient.

person does not need to lack mental capacity or a clinical diagnosis of mental ill-health in order to qualify for and be entitled to an advocate under Care Act 2014 s67. An advocate must be provided if without support an individual would experience 'substantial difficulty' in any one of these areas:[67]

- understanding relevant information;
- retaining that information;
- using or weighing that information as part of the process of being involved;
- communicating the individual's views, wishes or feelings (whether by talking, using sign language or any other means).

8.54 In considering whether an individual would experience a 'substantial difficulty' within the meaning of Care Act 2014 s67(4), the IAS Regs 2014[68] stipulate that the local authority 'must have regard to' the following factors:

- any health condition the individual has;
- any learning difficulty the individual has;
- any disability the individual has;
- the degree of complexity of the individual's circumstances, whether in relation to the individual's needs for care and support or otherwise;
- where the assessment or planning function is the carrying out of an assessment, whether the individual has previously refused an assessment; and
- whether the individual is experiencing, or at risk of, abuse or neglect.

8.55 The duty to arrange independent advocacy arises in relation to any of the following functions of the Care Act 2014:

- a needs assessment (under section 9);
- a carer's assessment (under section 10);
- the preparation of a care and support plan or support plan (under section 25);
- a review of a care and support plan or support plan (under section 27);
- a child's needs assessment (under section 60);
- a child's carer's assessment (under section 62);
- a young carer's assessment (under section 65).

67 Care Act 2014 s67(4).

68 IAS Regs 2014 reg 3.

8.56 The appointment of an independent advocate should be made 'as early as possible in the assessment process' so that the individual's involvement can be supported throughout all stages of the process. Individuals may require help to understand information provided, assistance in weighing up the information, and support in communicating their wishes and preferences.[69] Not infrequently this role will be fulfilled by a family member or friend[70] but if there is no one appropriate, then the local authority must arrange for an independent advocate.[71]

8.57 The IAS Regs 2014[72] detail the competency requirements for independent advocates, requiring:

- appropriate experience;
- having undertaken appropriate training;
- being competent to represent and support the individual;
- integrity and good character; and
- arrangements to be in place for appropriate supervision.

8.58 The duty does not apply if there is an 'appropriate person' available to facilitate the individual's involvement, but the individual must consent or, in cases of incapacity, the local authority must be satisfied they will act in the individual's best interests.

8.59 In *R (SG, by her litigation friend the Official Solicitor) v Haringey LBC*[73] a core reason given by the court for quashing the Care Act assessment completed by the local authority was its failure to make provision for an independent advocate. The claimant in that case was a woman of Afghan nationality who was a victim of torture, rape, and emotional and physical abuse, and who suffered from severe mental health problems, including complex post-traumatic stress disorder (PTSD), insomnia, depression and anxiety. She was also illiterate and did not speak English. The local authority did not dispute that her conditions meant she was entitled to an independent advocate under Care Act 2014 s67. She was, however, not given one. The court rejected the local authority's submission that the absence of an advocate did not lead to a flawed assessment process and did not prejudice the outcome of the assessment, describing the claimant's case as 'the paradigm case' where an advocate was required given she was

69 *Care and support statutory guidance*, para 6.34.
70 *Care and support statutory guidance*, para 7.19.
71 Care Act 2014 s67(2) and (5).
72 IAS Regs 2014 reg 2.
73 [2015] EWHC 2579 (Admin).

otherwise in no position to participate in the assessment process or influence matters.[74]

8.60 In a Local Government Ombudsman complaint determination,[75] a similar conclusion was reached. There, a family member made a complaint about the support provided to her two siblings who lived with her and who had learning disabilities. During the complaints process, she lost confidence with the council and stopped responding to emails. As a result, the siblings received no support. Given the impasse between the local authority and the family member, the duty under Care Act 2014 s67 arose and obliged the local authority to appoint independent advocates for the two siblings to support them to express their views. The failure to appoint an advocate caused avoidable frustration and delay in the local authority agreeing support plans for the two siblings and in their being able to access support and funding to meet their eligible needs.

Assessing adults in prison and immigration detention

Prison

8.61 There has been much research carried out into the care needs of prisoners and those detained in prison. It has been demonstrated that relative to the general population, prisoners experience poorer physical and mental health,[76] and that around 36 per cent of prisoners have a disability as compared with 19 per cent of the general population.[77] The prison population is also aging rapidly; the number of prisoners aged 60 or over increased by 243 per cent between 2002 and 2020.[78]

8.62 These trends are not new. However, as the Law Commission noted in its consultation on adult social care which preceded the report that led to the Care Act 2014, there were few examples of local authorities providing social care service for older prisoners. The reasons for this, the Law Commission observed, were varied and

74 *R (SG) v Haringey LBC* [2015] EWHC 2579 (Admin) at paras 38–40.

75 Complaint against Walsall MBC, Local Government Ombudsman Report 16 004 955, 8 December 2016.

76 *Adult social care: a consultation paper*, Consultation Paper No 192, Law Commission, 1 April 2010, para 11.39.

77 *Estimating the prevalence of disability amongst prisoners*, Ministry of Justice (MoJ), March 2012.

78 *Ageing prison population*, Fifth report of session 2019–21, House of Commons Justice Committee, 22 July 2020.

included a lack of clarity in the law[79] and the ordinary residence rules.[80] The case of *R (Howard League for Penal Reform) v SSHD (No 2)*[81] marked a turning point in respect of needs assessment of children in custody under the ChA 1989, establishing that the assessment duty did not end when the prison gates closed. The Law Commission's view was that same principle applied to adult prisoners.[82] The Law Commission noted there was nothing to prevent prisoners being an identified class of persons for whom assessments could be undertaken and services could be provided, while recognising that there might be some practical issues concerning direct payments and the practicalities of providing care and support (such as ordinary residence and eligibility).

8.63 The Law Commission recommended that, unless a policy decision were taken to exclude prisoners from support, the legal framework should facilitate the provision of support to this cohort and deal with the practical barriers they face in accessing it.[83]

8.64 This intention is reflected in Care Act 2014 s9 as well as other provisions such as section 76, which contains special rules on ordinary residence applying to prisoners.[84] Section 9 contains no geographical restriction on the carrying out of an assessment, nor does it exclude those who are in particular settings, such as prisons. The duty to assess an adult in a custodial setting arises as soon as the local authority is aware that the adult may have care and support needs. As such, the trigger for the assessment is based on the adult's needs rather than where they are living, or how they are accommodated. However, the duty to provide care and support only arises where the adult is 'ordinarily resident in the authority's area or is present in its area but of no settled residence'.[85] Therefore, it may make practical sense for the referral requesting the assessment to be made to the authority in which the adult is ordinarily resident (or, if the adult has no settled residence, the area in which the prison is physically located) since it is that authority that will be responsible for providing services. The ordinary residence rules are discussed at paras 8.100–8.106. Referrals for an assessment can be made by the person in a

79 *Adult social care: a consultation paper*, para 11.39.

80 *Adult social care*, HC 941, Law Commission, 10 May 2011, para 11.133. See paras 8.100–8.106 on the ordinary residence rules.

81 [2002] EWHC 2497 (Admin), (2003) 6 CCLR 47.

82 *Adult social care: a consultation paper*, paras 11.40–11.41.

83 *Adult social care*, HC 941, Law Commission, 10 May 2011, para 11.134.

84 See para 8.105.

85 Care Act 2014 ss18, 19 and 24.

custodial setting, by managers of custodial settings or by the prison's health providers.

8.65 It is a general principle of community care law that assessments should be forward-looking, and consider not only current needs but imminent changes of needs.[86] In the context of the Care Act 2014, this principle is reinforced by the obligations under the well-being and prevention duties under Care Act 2014 ss1–2[87] which require a local authority in discharging its functions to have regard to the need to prevent or delay the development of needs for care and support take steps to arrange services to that end. In the context of prisoners who are soon to be released from custody, this may require an assessment of need to be carried out prior to release to ensure that plans can be put in place to support them in the community.

8.66 The approach to assessment and determination of need is the same as would be applied to someone in the community. The *Care and support statutory guidance* reminds local authorities that they have to bear in mind that the adult in a custodial sentence will no longer have the benefit of support they may have relied upon in the community.[88] There will be inevitable complexities for carrying out assessments in custodial settings, and the statutory guidance directs consideration to be given to how such assessments can be carried out in an efficient way for all involved (for example, making appointments and consideration of the number and type of staff required to be involved). Reception screening and health assessments are useful sources of information for establishing whether an individual has been receiving care and support before entering custody. Existing processes such as interviews for court purposes conducted by the National Probation Service could be used to obtain information about current social care needs.

8.67 The guidance notes that the threshold for the provision of care and support does not change in custodial settings and that when an individual is in a custodial setting, this should not in any way affect the assessment and recording of eligible needs.[89] While the setting in which the care and support will be provided is likely to be different from community or other settings, and this should be taken into account when considering how to meet the need for care and support as part of the care planning process, the extent and nature of need

86 *R (K) v Manchester City Council* [2006] EWHC 3164 (Admin).

87 See paras 8.20–8.29.

88 *Care and support statutory guidance*, paras 17.17–17.28.

89 *Care and support statutory guidance*, para 17.123.

should be identified before taking into account the environment in which the individual lives. This is particularly important when individuals move between prisons and/or from prison into the community. Where an individual does not meet the eligibility criteria, the local authority must give the individual written information about what can be done to meet or reduce needs and what services are available; and what can be done to prevent or delay the development of needs for care and support in the future. The Care Act 2014 s19 power[90] to provide for non-eligible needs for care and support exist similarly in the custodial setting as in the community.

8.68 Prisoners, especially those serving long sentences, may develop eligible needs over time. Local authorities should consider how best to provide information and advice to both individuals and establishments on what can be done to prevent or delay the development of care and support needs.[91] In doing so, it is important to consider the prison regime and the environment, as well as the individual's capacity to understand the information that is being provided. Individuals in custodial settings, like people in the community, may benefit from low-level preventative support and information and advice that will help them maintain their own health and well-being.

Immigration detention

8.69 The *Care and support statutory guidance* makes no reference to those detained in immigration detention. As explained at para 8.104 below, in line with Home Office policy, in general it may be expected that those in need of care and support under the Care Act 2014 should not ordinarily be detained, since they are likely to be classed as 'adults at risk' whom Home Office policy presumes should not be placed in detention. However, as with prisoners, assessments may nevertheless be needed in advance of release to ensure that prior arrangements can be made for care and support to be provided in the community. The scheme of the Care Act 2014 permits this: as stated above, the duty to assess under Care Act 2014 s9 applies irrespective of how and where the person is accommodated.

8.70 As with prisoners, it may make practical sense for the referral requesting the assessment to be made to the authority in which the adult is ordinarily resident (or, if the adult has no settled residence, the area in which they will be physically present upon release) since it is that authority that will be responsible for providing services

90 See paras 8.89–8.97.

91 *Care and support statutory guidance*, para 17.125.

when they leave detention. Where a person being released from immigration detention does not have accommodation otherwise than that provided by the state, then the relevant local authority to whom a referral requesting an assessment should be made should be the authority where the immigration removal centre is located.

Eligibility for care and/or support

8.71 This section covers eligibility for:

- care and support for adults;
- support for carers.

Eligibility for care and/or support (adults)

Overview

8.72 Where an assessment identifies that an individual has needs for care/support, then the authority must decide if any of the needs are sufficient to meet the eligibility criteria, and if so, consider with the individual how to meet those needs.[92] The Care Act 2014 placed eligibility criteria on a statutory footing under Care Act 2014 s13 with the detail spelt out in the Eligibility Regs 2015, which address the separate criteria for adults in need and for carers.

8.73 The introduction of national eligibility criteria represented a significant legislative change from the pre-Care Act 2014 position. A key concept to be grasped with the Care Act 2014 eligibility process concerns the interlocking nature of the various criteria. If it is determined that the adult does not satisfy the eligibility criteria, then there will be no duty to provide support[93] but a power to provide support will arise instead.[94] Further, they may still be entitled to support because their carer is deemed eligible and, even if this does not trigger a duty to provide support, the 'safeguarding obligations' may require that support is provided. For the safeguarding obligations, see paras 8.179–8.184 below.

8.74 Additionally, even if the assessment concludes that the adult is not eligible for care and support, the local authority must provide written advice on prevention, including what can be done to meet/

92 Care Act 2014 s13.

93 Care Act 2014 s18. See paras 8.88–8.92.

94 Care Act 2014 s19. See paras 8.93–8.94.

reduce existing needs; and to prevent or delay the development of care and support needs.[95]

8.75 To be eligible for care and support, an adult must satisfy three requirements under Eligibility Regs 2015 reg 2(1):

1) the adult's needs arise from or are related to a physical or mental impairment or illness;
2) as a result of the adult's needs the adult is unable to achieve two or more of the outcomes specified in reg 2(2); and
3) as a consequence there is, or is likely to be, a significant impact on the adult's well-being.

8.76 Michael Fordham QC sitting as a deputy High Court judge in the case of *R (Aburas) v Southwark LBC*[96] described such needs compendiously as 'looked-after needs' as they are 'in the nature of being looked-after',[97] referring to how needs for 'care and attention' had been analysed by the courts under the predecessor legislation, the National Assistance Act (NAA) 1948. However, the Court of Appeal in *R (BG) v Suffolk CC*[98] deprecated this formulation holding the phrase 'does not reflect the development in the approach which local authorities are now to adopt as set out in sections 1, 9 and 18 CA 2014 which recognise the autonomy of the individual'[99] and that needs for care and support were broader in scope than this, encompassing wider matters such as needs for financial assistance to pay for recreational activities.[100]

8.77 Eligibility Regs 2015 reg 2(2) lists the 'outcomes' referred to in reg 2(1)(b) as being:

- managing and maintaining nutrition;
- maintaining personal hygiene;
- managing toilet needs;
- being appropriately clothed;
- being able to make use of the adult's home safely;
- maintaining a habitable home environment;
- developing and maintaining family or other personal relationships;
- accessing and engaging in work, training, education or volunteering;

95 Care Act 2014 s13(5).

96 [2019] EWHC 2754 (Admin), (2019) 22 CCLR 537.

97 *R (Aburas) v Southwark LBC* [2019] EWHC 2754 (Admin), (2019) 22 CCLR 537 at para 5.

98 [2022] EWCA Civ 1047.

99 [2022] EWCA Civ 1047 at para 70.

100 See further paras 8.118–8.122.

- making use of necessary facilities or services in the local community including public transport, and recreational facilities or services; and
- carrying out any caring responsibilities the adult has for a child.

8.78 The *Care and support statutory guidance* provides examples[101] of how local authorities should consider each of the above outcomes, while emphasising that the guidance does not constitute an exhaustive list of examples.[102] One of the most notable omissions from the list of 'outcomes' under the Eligibility Regs 2015 is 'keeping safe', which had been included in the pre-Care Act 2014 framework. It is difficult to imagine a more important outcome for an individual who has care and support needs. The omission also does not accord with the existence of the safeguarding duty (see paras 8.179–8.184) owed by the local authority to provide support to protect people from harm. However, it would appear, at least from the explanations in the statutory guidance, that the omission is compensated by outcomes such as being able to make use of the home safely, and making use of necessary facilities or services in the local community including public transport and recreational facilities or services.

8.79 Although the assessment process requires the local authority to involve carers and others who have knowledge about the adult's needs, the eligibility determination must be made based only on the adult's needs and how these impact on their well-being. Local authorities must only take consideration of whether the adult has a carer, or what needs may be met by a carer, after the eligibility determination when a care and support plan is prepared.[103] The determination must be based solely on the adult's needs. If an adult does have a carer, the care they are providing will be taken into account later on, when considering whether and how the needs must be met. Local authorities are not required to meet any eligible needs which are being met by a carer, but those needs should be recognised and recorded as eligible during the assessment process. This is to ensure that should there be a breakdown in the caring relationship, the needs are already identified as eligible, and therefore local authorities must take steps to meet them without further assessment.

101 *Care and support statutory guidance*, para 6.106.

102 For more detailed analysis of the outcomes and what they entail, see L Clements *Community care and the law*, Legal Action Group, 7th edn, 2019.

103 *Care and support statutory guidance*, paras 6.15 and 6.115. See further *R (Antoniak) v Westminster City Council* [2019] EWHC 3465 (Admin) at paras 29–30.

Unable to achieve outcomes

8.80 Eligibility Regs 2015 reg 2(2) defines the specified outcomes. These are set out above at para 8.77. To meet the relevant eligibility criterion, the adult must be 'unable to achieve' two or more outcomes. The statutory guidance elaborates on what is meant by being 'unable to achieve' an outcome under Eligibility Regs 2015 reg 2.[104] It includes any of the following circumstances, where the adult:

- **Is unable to achieve the outcome without assistance:** This would include where an adult would be unable to do so even when assistance is provided. It also includes where the adult may need prompting – for example, some adults may be physically able to wash but need reminding of the importance of personal hygiene.
- **Is able to achieve the outcome without assistance but doing so causes the adult significant pain, distress or anxiety:** For example, an older person with severe arthritis may be able to prepare a meal, but doing so will leave them in severe pain and unable to eat the meal.
- **Is able to achieve the outcome without assistance, but doing so endangers or is likely to endanger the health or safety of the adult, or of others:** For example, if the health or safety of another member of the family, including any child, could be endangered when an adult attempts to complete a task or an activity without relevant support.
- **Is able to achieve the outcome without assistance but takes significantly longer than would normally be expected:** For example, an adult with a physical disability is able to dress themself in the morning, but it takes them a long time to do this, leaves them exhausted and prevents them from achieving other outcomes.

Significant impact on well-being

8.81 Where the adult is unable to achieve more than one of the outcomes, the local authority should move on to the next stage of the eligibility criteria and consider whether 'as a consequence there is, or is likely to be, a significant impact on the adult's well-being'.[105] The local authority should not consider the impact of each outcome that the adult is unable to achieve in isolation, but should consider whether the cumulative effect of being unable to achieve those outcomes has a 'significant impact on wellbeing'.[106]

104 *Care and support statutory guidance*, para 6.105.
105 Eligibility Regs 2015 reg 2(1).
106 *Care and support statutory guidance*, para 6.108.

8.82 What is 'significant' is not defined in the Eligibility Regs 2015. The statutory guidance also avoids a precise definition of what 'significant' means. It describes 'significant' as having an 'everyday meaning'[107] and adds that the authorities will have to 'consider whether the adult's needs and their consequent inability to achieve the relevant outcomes will have an important, consequential effect on their daily lives, their independence and their wellbeing'.[108] The statutory guidance goes on to state that:

> In making this judgment, local authorities should look to understand the adult's needs in the context of what is important to him or her. Needs may affect different people differently, because what is important to the individual's wellbeing may not be the same in all cases. Circumstances which create a significant impact on the wellbeing of one individual may not have the same effect on another.[109]

8.83 Guidance issued by the Social Care Institute for Excellence (SCIE) suggests that additionally a 'significant impact' could be a consequence of:[110]

- **a single effect:** this means that the inability to achieve two or more outcomes affects at least one of the areas of well-being in a significant way;
- **a cumulative effect:** this means that the individual may have needs across several of the eligibility outcomes, perhaps at a relatively low level, but as these needs affect the individual in various areas of their life, the overall impact on the individual is significant;
- **a domino effect:** this means that currently the individual may have needs in relation to few eligibility outcomes, but it can be anticipated that in the near future other outcomes will be affected, causing a significant impact on the individual's well-being.

Eligibility criteria for support (carers)

8.84 The eligibility criteria for carers measure whether as a consequence of providing care, the carer is unable to undertake certain key roles or

107 *Care and support statutory guidance*, para 6.109.
108 Care and support statutory guidance, para 6.109.
109 *Care and support statutory guidance*, para 6.110.
110 SCIE online guidance: *Eligibility determination for the Care Act 2014: What does significant impact mean?* at: www.scie.org.uk/care-act-2014/assessment-and-eligibility/eligibility/what-does-significant-mean#:~:text=Significant%20impact%20could%20be%20a%20consequence%20of%20a%20domino%20effect,impact%20on%20the%20individual's%20wellbeing.

tasks, such as household activities, employment, education, recreation, or whether their health is at significant risk.

8.85 Eligibility Regs 2015 reg 3(1) provides that a carer's needs are eligible if:

- the needs arise as a consequence of providing necessary care for an adult;
- the effect of the carer's needs is that any of the circumstances specified in reg 3(2) apply to the carer;
- as a consequence there is, or is likely to be, a significant impact on the carer's well-being.

8.86 The circumstances specified in Eligibility Regs 2015 reg 3(2) are as follows:

- the carer's physical or mental health is, or is at risk of, deteriorating;
- the carer is unable to achieve any of the following outcomes:
  – carrying out any caring responsibilities the carer has for a child;
  – providing care to other persons for whom the carer provides care;
  – maintaining a habitable home environment in the carer's home (whether or not this is also the home of the adult needing care);
  – managing and maintaining nutrition;
  – developing and maintaining family or other personal relationships;
  – engaging in work, training, education or volunteering;
  – making use of necessary facilities or services in the local community, including recreational facilities or services; and
  – engaging in recreational activities.

8.87 'Unable to achieve' is defined in similar terms under Eligibility Regs 2015 reg 3(3) to that for adults needing support.[111] As with the 'adults in need' criteria, the statutory guidance amplifies on what is encompassed by these impacts and outcomes.[112]

111 See para 8.80.

112 *Care and support statutory guidance,* paras 6.116–6.129. A detailed analysis of these impacts and outcomes for carers is provided in L Clements *Carers and their rights,* Legal Action Group, 6th edn, 2016.

Powers and duties to meet needs

8.88 This section will explain:

- the duty to meet eligible needs and power to meet non-eligible needs (adults);
- the duty to meet eligible needs and power to meet non-eligible needs (carers);
- ordinary residence.

The duty to meet eligible needs and power to meet non-eligible needs (adults)

8.89 Once the assessment concludes that an adult's needs meet the eligibility criteria, there is a duty under Care Act 2014 s18 to ensure their care and support needs are met if:

- they are ordinarily resident in the local authority's area;[113] or
- they are present in the area but of no settled residence;[114] and
- there is no charge for meeting the needs; or
- the adult's resources are below the financial limit; or
- their resources are above the financial limit but they ask the local authority to meet their needs in any event; or
- the adult lacks capacity to arrange for the provision of care and support and there is no-one authorised to do so on their behalf.[115]

8.90 The Care Act 2014 s18(1) duty to meet needs does not apply where needs are being met by a willing carer.[116] However, as the High Court explained in *R (P) v Croydon LBC*, any decision that needs can be met by a carer must be 'reasoned, procedurally fair, and reasonable'.[117] In that case, the court held, the local authority had acted unlawfully by failing to meet the applicant's needs for care and support, in circumstances where it had initially determined that she required 24/7 support but subsequently decided to fund only 35 hours on the footing that the initial decision had not factored in the care provided by the applicant's family, without informing the applicant and her family or giving them reasons.

113 See paras 8.100–8.106.

114 This requires only physical presence. See *Care and support statutory guidance*, para 19.44.

115 Care Act 2014 s18.

116 Care Act 2014 s18(7).

117 [2022] EWHC 2886 (Admin) at para 44.

8.91 For persons subject to immigration control, the duty to meet the adult's eligible needs for care and support will also be subject to any exclusions on account of their immigration status, for which see further below at paras 8.159–8.172 in respect of the application of Care Act 2014 s21 and paras 8.173–8.178 and 9.195–9.207 in respect of the operation of NIAA 2002 Sch 3.

8.92 Care Act 2014 s18 reflects the Law Commission's proposal that there should be one duty based on having care needs that meet the eligibility criteria.[118] The Law Commission had also proposed that pre-Care Act 2014 provision under NAA 1948 s21, which related to a duty to arrange residential care, should be retained in substance as a 'long-stop' for cases that did not meet the eligibility criteria.[119] However, the government declined to follow this recommendation, instead introducing a power under Care Act 2014 s19 to deal with those who do not meet the eligibility criteria. The power also allows the local authority to act in urgent cases and in cases where the adult is ordinarily resident elsewhere.

8.93 Specifically, the Care Act 2014 s19 power applies where:

- the person is ordinarily resident in the area, or is present there but of no settled residence, and the authority is satisfied that the person has no eligible needs;[120] or
- the person's needs do meet the eligibility criteria but the person is ordinarily resident in the area of another authority and the assessing authority has notified the other authority of its intention to meet the needs;[121] or
- the local authority has not yet a) carried out an assessment, or b) made a determination under Care Act 2014 s13(1) as to whether any of the assessed needs meet the eligibility criteria,[122] but the adult's needs for care and support appear to the local authority to be *urgent* (regardless of whether the adult is ordinarily resident in its area).[123] This power is not restricted to a first assessment and is also available pending a re-assessment of needs.[124]

118 *Adult social care,* HC 941, Law Commission, 10 May 2011, paras 6.12 and 6.16.
119 *Adult social care,* HC 941, Law Commission, 10 May 2011, para 6.32.
120 Care Act 2014 s19(1).
121 Care Act 2014 s19(2).
122 See paras 8.71–8.87.
123 Care Act 2014 s19(3).
124 *R (Raja) v Redbridge LBC* [2020] EWHC 1456 (Admin), [2020] PTSR 2129.

8.94 In *R (Aburas) v Southwark LBC*,[125] Michael Fordham QC sitting as a deputy High Court judge held that the power under Care Act 2014 s19 would become a duty in circumstances where a person had needs for care and support which were not eligible needs, and where the provision of support was necessary in order to avoid a breach of the ECHR.[126]

8.95 The nature of support to be provided to someone for whom there is a duty under Care Act 2014 s18 or a power under s19 was considered in *R (BG) v Suffolk CC*.[127] The case arose out of an appeal by the local authority against the decision of the High Court quashing its decisions made under the Care Act 2014 and the Eligibility Regs 2015 to withdraw funding for holidays and recreational activities for the respondents, two brothers who were disabled adults. Both respondent adults had autism, learning disabilities, anxiety and other conditions. They required support with daily living. Their mother was their primary carer, with support from other family members. The local authority had assessed both adults as requiring recreational outings and activities and family holidays and sought to meet this by direct payments, which included a budget for respite. However, in 2019, the local authority decided, further to another assessment, that neither holidays nor recreational activities were 'eligible needs' although the local authority also found that without their mother's support, neither respondent adult could access anything outside the home, and that would have a significant impact on their well-being. As a consequence of the assessment, the local authority informed the mother that it would no longer fund holidays and recreational activities and would end direct payments. It stated that paying holiday costs, as opposed to meeting the cost of support that they needed to achieve a holiday, was not an eligible need, thus there was no duty under Care Act 2014 s18 to provide this.

8.96 The High Court found that there was no statutory basis for the local authority's restrictive interpretation of needs. It determined that the local authority had a duty to provide financial support for recreational activity and holidays under Care Act 2014 s18 and that if the eligibility criteria were not met, it had a discretionary power to do so under section 19.

125 [2019] EWHC 2754 (Admin), (2019) 22 CCLR 537.
126 [2019] EWHC 2754 (Admin), (2019) 22 CCLR 537 at paras 10 and 23.
127 [2022] EWCA Civ 1047, [2022] 4 WLR 107.

8.97 The Court of Appeal upheld the High Court's decision and dismissed the local authority's appeal. It held that Care Act 2014 s1(1) imposed a general duty on the local authority to promote an individual's well-being, including their autonomy, when exercising a function under the Act. The statutory guidance, issued under Care Act 2014 s78, also stated the same. Support for the purposes of the Care Act 2014 therefore needed to be tailored to address the needs and wishes of the particular individual. Consistent with the greater emphasis placed upon the autonomy of the individual linked to well-being and support, the intention of the legislation was to broaden the discretion and flexibility of local authorities in their provision of care and support to adults. Both respondents had needs for care and support that required assistance. The provision of recreational activities and holidays were to assist them to meet eligible needs, namely, to develop and maintain family or other personal relationships, and make use of necessary facilities and services in the local community including public transport and recreational facilities or services. This cannot be achieved by making available the facilities if the mother could not afford to pay for the entry requirements. The financial support previously provided by the local authority was not just to meet the cost of recreational activities and to go on holiday but a means of meeting needs which arose from and were related to their physical and mental disability. These needs could not be met without financial support from the local authority. To find that the mother could meet their eligible needs notwithstanding the absence of funding was to ignore a key element of those needs, namely the ability to fund the means to access and take part in recreational activities.

The duty to meet eligible needs and power to meet non-eligible needs (carers)

8.98 As for carers, Care Act 2014 s20 outlines the duties and powers to meet eligible needs for support. The duty under section 20(1) arises:

- where the adult needing care is ordinarily resident in the local authority's area;[128] or
- is present in its area but of no settled residence;[129] and

128 See paras 8.100–8.106.

129 This requires only physical presence. See *Care and support statutory guidance*, para 19.44.

- where meeting the carer's needs involves the provision of support to the carer, there is either:
  - no charge for meeting them; or
  - if the carer has resources above the financial limit, the carer nevertheless asks the authority to meet the needs; and
- where meeting the carer's needs involves the provision of care and support to the adult needing care, either:
  - there is no charge and the adult has agreed to the provision or support; or
  - if the adult has above the financial limit, the adult asks the authority to meet the needs.

8.99 Care Act 2014 s20(6) contains a comparable power to section 19[130] for meeting a carer's non-eligible needs for support, but where this involves the provision of care and support to the adult in need, this has to be with the adult's agreement that the needs are to be met in that way. Section 20(7) provides the local authority with the power to meet some or all of the carer's needs for support in a way which involves the provision of care and support to the adult needing care, even if the authority would not be required to meet the adult's needs under section 18.

Ordinary residence

8.100 Ordinary residence becomes relevant in determining where responsibilities lie between local authorities for the funding and provision of care and support.[131] The key test which applies in the majority of cases[132] to determine ordinary residence remains that in *R v Barnet LBC ex p Shah*:

> ... unless ... it can be shown that the statutory framework or the legal context in which the words are used requires a different meaning, I unhesitatingly subscribe to the view that 'ordinarily resident' refers to a man's abode in a particular place or country which he has adopted voluntarily and for settled purposes as part of the regular order of his life for the time being, whether of short or long duration.[133]

8.101 The test for ordinary residence, which determines which local authority would be responsible for meeting needs, applies differently

130 See paras 8.89–8.97.
131 Care Act 2014 ss18(1)(a) and 20(1)(a).
132 Save where the adult is detained in prison, on which see para 8.105.
133 [1983] 2 AC 309, HL at p343. See further *Care and support statutory guidance*, paras 19.12–19.15.

in relation to adults with needs for care and support and carers. For adults with care and support needs, the local authority in which the adult is ordinarily resident will be responsible for meeting their eligible needs.[134] For carers, however, the responsible local authority will be the one where the adult for whom they care is ordinarily resident.[135]

8.102 Where a person lacks mental capacity to decide where to live, direct application of the test in *ex p Shah* will not assist since that test requires the voluntary adoption of a place, which an incapacitated person cannot do. A modified approach is necessary, as outlined in the *Care and support statutory guidance*,[136] further to the Supreme Court's decision on this issue in *R (Cornwall Council) v Secretary of State for Health*.[137] What local authorities should do is adopt the *ex p Shah* approach but place no regard to the fact that the adult, by reason of their lack of capacity, cannot be expected to be living there voluntarily. This involves considering all the facts, such as the place of the person's physical presence, their purpose for living there, the person's connection with the area, their duration of residence there, and the person's views, wishes and feelings (insofar as these are ascertainable and relevant) to establish whether the purpose of the residence has a sufficient degree of continuity to be described as settled, whether of long or short duration.

8.103 Physical presence provides a starting point for considering ordinary residence but does not necessarily equate to ordinary residence because a person can be physically present in an area but of no settled residence.[138] In certain situations, ordinary residence could be deemed to be in a different area to that in which a person is physically present.[139] There are other permutations regarding factual circumstances where ordinary residence is not entirely straightforward, set out in the *Care and support statutory guidance*.[140]

134 Care Act 2014 s18(1)(a).

135 Care Act 2014 s20(1)(a).

136 *Care and support statutory guidance*, paras 19.16–19.33.

137 [2015] UKSC 46, [2016] AC 137.

138 *Care and support statutory guidance*, paras 19.33 and 19.44–19.46.

139 *Care and support statutory guidance*, paras 19.44–19.59.

140 *Care and support statutory guidance*, paras 19.37–19.41 (in respect of children transitioning to adulthood) and paras 19.70–19.74 (in respect of temporary absences and persons with more than one home).

8.104 Immigration detention is obviously not 'adopted voluntarily'[141] and so a person detained on arrival in the UK will be unlikely to have a place of 'ordinary residence'.[142] People in detention who have previously lived elsewhere in the UK may do. It will depend on the facts of the individual case. The absence of a place of 'ordinary residence' is not fatal to the duty to meet needs arising under Care Act 2014 s18. This is because by section 18(1)(a), the duty arises in respect of an eligible adult who is present in the local authority's area but of no settled residence. This requires only 'physical presence'.[143] Those in immigration detention who have no other ordinary residence in England would meet this requirement and should be treated the same as those who are ordinarily resident there.[144] However, Home Office policy is clear that 'adults at risk' – a broad category which encompasses persons suffering from conditions that would be likely to render them particularly vulnerable to harm if detained – should not be detained.[145] In consequence, there should not generally be a need to provide support under the Care Act 2014 to persons in immigration detention since such persons are likely to fall within the cohort of person who should not be detained in the first place. However, an assessment of a detainee's need for care and support may nevertheless be necessary in advance of release in order to ensure that arrangements for care and support can be put in place for them in the community, and there is nothing within the Care Act 2014 to preclude such assessments being undertaken.[146]

8.105 Different rules apply to prisoners. Care Act 2014 s76 deems any prisoner to be ordinarily resident in the area in which they are in prison.[147] The same applies to adults residing in approved premises or residing in any other premises pursuant to a bail condition imposed in criminal proceedings.[148] The relative vulnerability of prisoners comparative with the population at large and the aging prison population make the provision of community care services to

141 See, by analogy, *Al-Ameri v Kensington and Chelsea RLBC* [2004] UKHL 4, [2004] 2 WLR 354.

142 *Care and support statutory guidance,* para 19.45.

143 *Care and support statutory guidance,* paras 19.43–19.45.

144 *Care and support statutory guidance,* paras 19.43–19.45.

145 *Adults at risk in immigration detention,* v7.0, Home Office, November 2021.

146 See further paras 8.33–8.70 on assessments.

147 'Prison' is defined in Care Act 2014 s76(11) and includes a young offender institution among other things.

148 Care Act 2014 s76(1)–(3).

prisoners vital, as discussed at paras 8.61–8.68. Care Act 2014 s76 is intended to facilitate this.

8.106 Should there be any dispute about the client's place of ordinary residence, two (or more) local authorities can be approached and they should decide between them which will take responsibility. Care and support must not be withheld while the dispute is resolved. The Care and Support (Disputes Between Local Authorities) Regulations 2014[149] set out the procedures local authorities must follow when inter-authority disputes arise regarding a person's ordinary residence. Care should be provided in the interim either by the authority in which the adult is currently receiving care or otherwise the authority in which they are living. If they are not living in any authority, the duty falls to the authority in which they are present.[150]

Care planning

Care and support plans and support plans

8.107 Where a duty to meet the needs for care and support arises, or where the local authority has decided to exercise a power to meet those needs, Care Act 2014 s24 requires the local authority to produce a care and support plan in respect of an eligible adult, and a support plan in respect of an eligible carer.[151] The plan is to explain how the eligible needs will be met, for example, whether they are going to be met by direct payments, and help the adult with deciding how to have the needs meet.

8.108 In order that the individual can determine whether their assessed needs are fully addressed in the care plan, they must be given a record of their needs[152] and also their final care plan.[153] Even if it is decided that none of an individual's needs are eligible needs, the authority must nevertheless provide them with 'information and advice about what can be done to prevent, delay, or reduce their needs'.[154]

149 SI No 2829.

150 For further reference see Care Act 2014 ss39–41; Care and Support (Ordinary Residence) (Specified Accommodation) Regulations 2014 SI No 2828; Care and Support (Disputes Between Local Authorities) Regulations 2014; and *Care and support statutory guidance*, chapter 19 and Annexes H1–H8.

151 Care Act 2014 s24(1).

152 Care Act 2014 s13(2); and *Care and support statutory guidance*, para 6.98.

153 Care Act 2014 s25(9); and *Care and support statutory guidance*, para 10.87.

154 Care Act 2014 s24(2); and *Care and support statutory guidance*, para 2.52.

8.109 The Care Act 2014 uses the language of 'meeting needs', which is a shift from the previous terminology of 'providing services' that would have been used in relation to the predecessor legislation, the NAA 1948. The concept is meant to have a broader scope than a duty to arrange a particular service; this is further exemplified by the statutory language of section 8, which gives examples of how a local authority may meet identified eligible needs.[155]

8.110 Care Act 2014 s25 details what must be in every care and support plan:[156]

- the needs identified by the assessment;
- whether, and to what extent, the needs meet the eligibility criteria;
- the needs that the authority is going to meet and how it intends to do so;
- for a person needing care, for which of the desired outcomes care and support could be relevant;
- for a carer, the outcomes the carer wishes to achieve, and their wishes around providing care, work, education and recreation where support could be relevant;
- the personal budget;
- information and advice on what can be done to reduce the needs in question, and to prevent or delay the development of needs in the future;
- where needs are being met via a direct payment, the needs to be met via the direct payment and the amount and frequency of the payments.

8.111 Pre-Care Act 2014 case-law concerning care plans remain relevant as the principles and importance of care planning are not materially different. Thus in *R v Islington LBC ex p Rixon*,[157] it was held that the care plan was of central importance as it was 'the means by which the local authority assembles the relevant information and applies it to the statutory ends, and hence affords good evidence to any inquirer of the due discharge of its statutory duties'. In *R (J) v Caerphilly CBC*,[158] it was held that care plans must 'set out the operational objectives with sufficient detail – including detail of the "how, who, what and when" – to enable the care plan itself to be used as a means of checking whether or not those objectives are being met'.[159]

155 See further paras 8.118–8.131 on how to meet needs.

156 See further *Care and support statutory guidance*, para 10.36.

157 [1997] ELR 66, (1997–98) 1 CCLR 119, QBD.

158 [2005] EWHC 586 (Admin), (2005) 8 CCLR 255.

159 At para 46.

Although that case arose in the context of the ChA 1989, the conclusion as to the importance of care planning applies with equal force to the Care Act 2014 context. The Local Government Ombudsman has also found maladministration where the local authority failed to provide sufficient detail in an assessment and care plan.[160]

8.112 In the same way that the individual (whether the adult in need or the carer) should be involved in the assessment process, the individual must also be 'genuinely involved and influential throughout the planning process'.[161] It should be made clear that the plan 'belongs' to the person it is intended for, with the local authority role being 'to ensure the production and sign-off of the plan to ensure that it is appropriate to meet the identified needs'.[162]

8.113 The 'sign off of a plan' should only occur once the authority has 'taken all reasonable steps' to reach agreement with the person for whom the plan is being prepared and any third party involved.[163] This agreement should be recorded and a copy placed within the plan.[164] If the plan is not agreed, then the authority should 'state the reasons for this and the steps which must be taken to ensure that the plan is signed-off'.[165]

Review of care and support plans

8.114 Care Act 2014 s27(1) contains a general duty to keep care and support plans under review. The local authority must undertake a further assessment and revise the plan accordingly, if it believes that circumstances have changed materially.[166] The statutory duty creates an expectation that the care and support plans will be reviewed 'no later than every 12 months' although a light-touch review should be considered every six to eight weeks after the plan and the personal budget have been signed off.[167]

8.115 Reviews can be triggered by a planned date set out in the care and support plan, an unforeseen change in needs or circumstances, or by

160 Complaint against Kent CC, Local Government Ombudsman Report 15 015 067, 26 August 2016.

161 *Care and support statutory guidance*, para 10.2.

162 *Care and support statutory guidance*, para 10.2; see also Care Act 2014 s25(3).

163 *Care and support statutory guidance*, para 10.86

164 *Care and support statutory guidance*, para 10.83.

165 *Care and support statutory guidance*, para 10.86.

166 Care Act 2014 s27(4). For example, the loss of accommodation. See *R (Campbell) v Ealing LBC* [2023] EWHC 10 (Admin) at para 61.

167 *Care and support statutory guidance*, paras 10.42 and 13.32.

the request of the person to whom the plan relates, or an interested party on their behalf.[168]

8.116 Reviews must be person-centred, accessible and proportionate, and must involve the person needing care.[169] They must not be used as a mechanism arbitrarily to reduce the level of a person's personal budget.[170] In one complaint the Local Government Ombudsman found maladministration where reductions in the care package occurred without assessing the carer and explicitly clarifying (and recording) whether the carer is 'able and willing' to provide the additional care.[171] However, in *R (MG) v Brent LBC*,[172] the High Court held that it was not unlawful to implement a reduction in the care package of an individual who suffered from schizophrenia on the basis that the reduction would be gradual and subject to ongoing reviews.

8.117 Reviews should not be 'overly-complex or bureaucratic' and should cover the specified matters, which 'should be communicated to the person before the review process begins'.[173] These should include:

- whether the person's needs or circumstances have changed;
- what parts of the plan are working, not working or need changing;
- whether the outcomes identified in the plan have been achieved or not;
- whether the person has new outcomes they want to meet;
- whether improvements could be made to achieve better outcomes;
- whether the person's personal budget enables them to meet their needs and the outcomes identified in their plan;
- whether the current method of managing it is still the best one for what they want to achieve, or should direct payments be considered;
- whether the personal budget still meets the sufficiency test;
- whether there any changes in the person's informal and community support networks which might impact negatively or positively on the plan;

168 Care Act 2014 s27(1); and *Care and support statutory guidance*, para 13.13.

169 *Care and support statutory guidance*, para 13.2.

170 *Care and support statutory guidance*, para 13.4.

171 Complaint against Bromley LBC, Local Government Ombudsman Report 15 020 384, 7 September 2016.

172 [2018] EWHC 1777 (Admin), [2018] 21 CCLR 504.

173 *Care and support statutory guidance*, para 13.12.

- whether there have been any changes to the person's needs or circumstances which might mean they are at risk of abuse or neglect;
- whether the person, carer or independent advocate is satisfied with the plan.

How to meet needs

Overview

8.118 The Care Act 2014 does not contain any definitive list of what can be provided to an adult or carer with eligible needs. Instead, Care Act 2014 s8(1) contains an illustrative list of what may be provided, namely:

- accommodation in a care home or in premises of some other type;
- care and support at home or in the community;
- counselling and other types of social work;
- goods and facilities;
- information, advice and advocacy.

8.119 The absence of arrangements such as 'adaptations', 'travel' and 'holidays', which were previously specified in the Chronically Sick and Disabled Persons Act 1970, was at first considered problematic by the Select Committee,[174] but the government confirmed, in response, that such services were within the ambit of section 8. To that end, the guidance makes clear that the purpose of moving away from the previous terminology of 'providing services', adopted in relation to the predecessor legislation, was to enable a 'greater variety of approaches' in how needs can be met.[175] Thus if adaptations or travel are required, there is no reason why the section 8 power could not encompass meeting needs in that way.

8.120 This broad approach to the meeting of needs was affirmed by the Court of Appeal in the case of *R (BG) v Suffolk CC*.[176] In that case, the court held that the phrase 'care and support' under the Care Act 2014 was intended to be broader in scope than the phrase 'care and attention' which had been used in the predecessor legislation the NAA 1948. 'Care and attention' had meant 'looked-after needs'.

174 *Draft Care and Support Bill*, HL Paper 143, HC 822, Joint Committee on the Draft Care and Support Bill, 2013, paras 168–170.

175 *Care and support statutory guidance*, paras 10.10–10.11.

176 [2022] EWCA Civ 1047, [2022] 4 WLR 107.

However, that phrase 'does not reflect the development in the approach which local authorities are now to adopt as set out in Care Act 2014 ss1, 9 and 18 which recognise the autonomy of the individual' and 'does not properly reflect the individual nature of the assessment, its recognition of the autonomy of the individual and the tailored and broad nature of the support which can be provided'.[177] In light of this, the court held, in meeting a need for support under Care Act 2014 s18, a local authority was entitled to provide financial assistance to take part in recreational activities including holidays.

8.121 Care Act 2014 s8(2) and *Care and support statutory guidance*, para 10.11 give examples of ways of meeting needs, including:

- the local authority directly providing some type of support – for example, by providing a re-ablement or short-term respite service;
- making a direct payment, which allows the person to purchase their own care and support;
- some combination of the above – for example, the local authority arranging a homecare service whilst also providing a direct payment to meet other needs.

8.122 The statutory guidance elaborates further by directing that in considering how to meet eligible or identified needs, the local authority should take into account the preferences of the individual, and the comparative cost of different options.[178] These factors are recognised in current case-law as relevant factors in the way decisions are made on what services are provided in discharge of a duty to meet an assessed eligible need.[179]

The provision of accommodation

8.123 One of the most litigated areas under the previous legislation, the NAA 1948, was the circumstances in which accommodation was an eligible need qualifying for residential care under NAA 1948 s21. Under that provision, a local authority could make arrangements for providing residential accommodation for persons aged 18 and over who by reason of age, disability or any other circumstances were in need of care and attention which was not otherwise available to them.

177 *R (BG) v Suffolk CC* [2022] EWCA Civ 1047, [2022] 4 WLR 107 at para 70 per Nicola Davies LJ.

178 *Care and support statutory guidance*, paras 10.20 and 10.27.

179 See, for example, *Khana v Southwark LBC* [2001] EWCA Civ 999, (2001) 4 CCLR 267 at para 58, on taking into account preferences and cost factors when deciding on how to meet needs.

Approvals and directions under NAA 1948 s21(1) were made by the secretary of state in LAC (93) 10 which converted the power into a duty by directing local authorities to make arrangements in relation to persons who were ordinarily resident in their area who qualified under that provision.

8.124 The statutory test posed three conditions for the provision of accommodation: 1) whether the person was in need of care and attention; 2) whether the need arose by reason of age, disability or any other circumstances; and 3) whether the care and attention was not available otherwise. The leading cases on these three questions were *R (M) v Slough BC*[180] and *R (SL) v Westminster City Council*.[181]

8.125 In *M v Slough*, the claimant, who was HIV positive, had an assessed need to keep his medication in a fridge and to see his doctor every three months. The House of Lords held that this did not amount to a 'need for care and attention'. While the House of Lords recognised that 'care and attention' was a wider concept than a need for nursing or personal care, it must equally mean 'something more than "accommodation" '.[182] This was because the NAA 1948 was not intended to be a general power to provide housing – that is dealt with by housing legislation, with its own criteria for eligibility. Otherwise, every homeless person who did not qualify for housing under the Housing Act 1996 would be able to turn to social services for accommodation. That could not, the House of Lords held, be parliament's intention. The natural meaning of the words 'care and attention' was 'looking after', that is, doing something for the person being cared for which they cannot or should not be expected to do for themself. This might be household tasks which the person could no longer perform or could only perform with great difficulty. It might be protection from risks which a mentally disabled person could not perceive. It might be personal care, such as feeding, washing or toileting. That list was not exhaustive, but the House of Lords held while providing M with a refrigerator to keep HIV anti-retroviral in would in one sense have been doing something for him which (if he had no money) he could not do for himself, 'care and attention' did not involve 'the mere provision of physical things', even things as important as food and accommodation.[183]

180 [2008] UKHL 52, [2008] 1 WLR 1808.

181 [2013] UKSC 27, [2013] 1 WLR 1445.

182 *R (M) v Slough BC* [2008] UKHL 52, [2008] 1 WLR 1808 at para 33 per Lady Hale.

183 *R (M) v Slough* at para 56 per Lord Neuberger.

8.126 In the subsequent case of *SL v Westminster*, the Supreme Court went on to tighten the test for 'care and attention', giving rise to an entitlement to residential accommodation. There, the claimant, SL, suffered depression and PTSD and required weekly supervision from his care coordinator, a social worker employed by the council. While the supervision was necessary for his mental stability the local authority found that SL did not require residential accommodation as the support provided did not relate to any need for accommodation. In upholding that decision, the Supreme Court held that in the context of a request for accommodation, the provision of 'care and attention' has to be associated with the duty to provide residential care, albeit it does not need to be only care and attention which can only be delivered in residential accommodation of a specialised kind.[184] What is required is 'care and attention of a sort which is normally provided in the home' or which 'will be effectively useless if the claimant has no home'.[185] The Supreme Court found, on the facts of *SL*, the test was not met. While the supervision was necessary for his mental stability, it could not be said to be 'accommodation-related'.[186]

8.127 The decision in *SL v Westminster* fundamentally changed the understanding of the law on residential accommodation operating up and until then. It had previously been thought, even following *M v Slough*, that there was no requirement to establish any nexus between the need for care and attention and the need for a home. If the person needed 'looking after' in some way, and did not have available accommodation, it had been thought that the person would be eligible for and require residential accommodation under NAA 1948 s21. Post *SL v Westminster*, what needed to be demonstrated was not only a need for care and attention, but a need for care and attention that is 'normally provided in the home', and would be effectively useless unless a home was provided.

8.128 The Care Act 2014 repealed NAA 1948 s21 and did not replace it with a like provision. Section 8(1) only refers to accommodation being a possible way to meet a person's eligible needs without imposing any duty to do so, seemingly leaving much of the decision-making to the local authority's judgment. The Law Commission had recommended that NAA 1948 s21 be retained in substance as a 'long stop'

184 *R (SL) v Westminster City Council* [2013] UKSC 27, [2013] 1 WLR 1445 at paras 42–44 per Lord Carnwath.

185 *R (SL) v Westminster* at para 48 per Lord Carnwarth.

186 *R (SL) v Westminster* at para 48 per Lord Carnwarth.

for cases that did not the meet the eligibility criteria for care and support[187] but the government rejected this as creating an anomaly to the overall approach of providing a single coherent framework for assessing, determining the eligibility and arranging for care and support for adults and their carers.[188] When the Care Bill was produced, the government further explained the underlying aim of having one duty:

> One of the key aims of the new statute is to remove anomalies and difference resulting from the type of care setting, and provide a single route through which consistent entitlement to care and support can be established . . . Clauses 18–19 provide this single route, replacing the precedents with a clear duty to meet an adult's needs for care and support.[189]

8.129 A question therefore arose, when the Care Act 2014 came into force, whether 'accommodation' referred to in Care Act 2014 s8 was intended to be available more widely to include ordinary accommodation to meet an identified and eligible need without needing to demonstrate the other criteria required under NAA 1948 s21.

8.130 This was considered in two cases brought soon after Care Act 2014 Part 1 came into force on 1 April 2015: (*R (SG) v Haringey LBC*[190] and *R (GS) v Camden LBC*[191]). The argument was that because Care Act 2014 s8(1) was materially different to NAA 1948 s21, the previous case-law, setting a high threshold for the provision of residential accommodation, should no longer apply. This argument was unsuccessful in the High Court. In *R (SG) v Haringey LBC*[192] the court held that for a local authority potentially to be required to provide accommodation under section 18, as part of the provision of care and support under that section:

- the services must be accommodation related – that is, the care and support must be of a sort which is normally provided in the home or will be 'effectively useless' if the claimant has no home;

187 *Adult social care*, HC 941, Law Commission, 10 May 2011, para 6.32.

188 *Reforming the law for adult care and support: the government's response to the Law Commission*, Cm 8379, July 2012.

189 *The Care Bill explained: including a response to the consultation and pre-legislative scrutiny on the Draft Care and Support Bill*, May 2013, paras 71–72.

190 [2015] EWHC 2579 (Admin).

191 [2016] EWHC 1762 (Admin), [2017] PTSR 140.

192 [2015] EWHC 2579 (Admin) at para 54. Take note, however, that the Court of Appeal ([2017] EWCA Civ 322) declined to determine this point and so the issue remains unresolved.

- the matter will generally be best left of the judgment and good sense of the local authority.

See further *R (GS) v Camden LBC*[193] – in that case, the court held that a need for accommodation by itself does not constitute a need for care and support.[194]

8.131 Michael Fordham QC sitting as a deputy High Court judge in the case of *R (Aburas) v Southwark LBC*[195] endorsed this approach to the provision of accommodation under the Care Act 2014. Summarising the principles above, he explained that 'the need for accommodation is not itself a "looked-after need", but the provision of accommodation may be called for under CA14 so as to secure effective care and support for a "looked-after need" '.[196] In other words, 'accommodation may be assessed to be the necessary and appropriate conduit for the practical and effective delivery of care and support for the relevant "looked-after needs" '.[197] He went on to use the formulation 'accommodation so as to secure the support of a social worker' to encapsulate the relevant legal tests.[198] Although this formulation should not, and was not intended to, supplant the statutory eligibility criteria or the questions of whether the care and support is accommodation related and would be effectively useless without it, it is nevertheless a helpful shorthand which gives a practical description of the kind of case in which accommodation may be needed.

Relationship with other community care and state services

Relationship with the NHS[199]

8.132 A number of amendments were made to the Care Bill to ensure that the boundary between local authority responsibilities and the NHS

193 [2016] EWHC 1762 (Admin), [2017] PTSR 140 at paras 28–29.

194 The decision of the Court of Appeal in *R (BG) v Suffolk CC* [2022] EWCA Civ 1047 discussed at paras 8.95–8.97, emphasising the broad scope of the concept of 'support' encompassing financial assistance to pay for recreational activities, may now cast doubt on the correctness of this point.

195 [2019] EWHC 2754 (Admin), (2019) 22 CCLR 537.

196 *Aburas* at para 6. The Court of Appeal in *BG v Suffolk CC* explained that the use of the phrase 'looked-after needs' is no longer apt under the Care Act 2014, but did not cast doubt on the judge's reasoning more generally. However, see fn 194 above.

197 *Aburas* at para 6.

198 *Aburas* at paras 12 and 21.

199 For healthcare, see chapter 10.

(the so called 'NHS Continuing Care' boundary as defined in the *Coughlan* Court of Appeal judgment[200]) remained unchanged when the Care Act 2014 was introduced. The phrasing of Care Act 2014 s22 seeks to achieve the aim[201] by setting out the limits on what a local authority can provide by way of healthcare and so, in effect, set the boundary between the responsibilities of local authorities for the provision of care and support from those of the NHS for the provision of healthcare. Where the NHS has a clear legal responsibility to provide a particular service, then the local authority may not do so. This general rule is intended to provide clarity, avoid overlap and maintain the existing legal boundary.

8.133 However, there is an exception to this general rule, in that the local authority may provide limited healthcare services if doing so would be merely incidental or ancillary to doing something else to meet needs under Care Act 2004 ss18–20, and the service or facility in question would be of a nature that the local authority could be expected to provide.[202]

8.134 Assessment Regs 2014 reg 7 obliges local authorities, when assessing the needs of an individual, who they believe to be eligible for NHS Continuing Healthcare funding, to refer them to the relevant NHS body. Although the regulations create no concomitant obligations on the NHS to respond to such a referral, such a duty exists by virtue of separate NHS regulations[203] and if any specific problem occurred over such a referral the local authority would be able to use its powers to request specific co-operation under Care Act 2014 s7.[204]

Relationship with housing

8.135 Like Care Act 2014 s22 in respect of NHS bodies, section 23 replicated the pre-existing boundary in law between care and support and relevant housing legislation. Where a local authority is required to

200 *R v North and East Devon health authority ex p Coughlan* [2000] 2 WLR 622, [2000] 3 All ER 850, CA.

201 Explanatory Notes to the Care Act 2014 paras 158–167 in respect of section 22 of the Act.

202 Care Act 2014 s22(1); *Care and support statutory guidance*, paras 15.29–15.36.

203 National Health Service Commissioning Board and Clinical Commissioning Groups (Responsibilities and Standing Rules) Regulations 2012 SI No 2996 regs 21–22.

204 For details on NHS healthcare duties as applied to migrants, see chapter 10. For a comprehensive in-depth analysis of the duties and powers of NHS bodies, see D Lock KC and H Gibbs *NHS law and practice*, Legal Action Group, 2018.

meet accommodation-related needs under the Housing Act 1996, or other housing legislation specified in regulations,[205] then the local authority must meet those needs under that housing legislation. Where housing forms part of the solution to meet a person's needs for care and support, or to prevent needs for care and support from developing, then a local authority may include this in the care and support plan even though the housing element is itself provided under housing legislation.[206] Any care and support needed to supplement housing is covered by the Care Act 2014.

8.136 The purpose of Care Act 2014 s23, as formulated in the legislation, is to clarify the boundary in law between a local authority's care and support function and its housing function. It does not prevent joint working, and it does not prevent local authorities in the care and support role from providing more specific services such as housing adaptations, or from working jointly with housing authorities.[207]

8.137 In *R (Idolo) v Bromley LBC*,[208] the claimant was paralysed from the waist down following kidney failure. He was assessed under the Care Act 2014 while in hospital as being substantially bed-bound and requiring two people to hoist him in and out of bed, as well as assistance to dress, prepare meals, wash and use the toilet. Adaptations were made to his home, a two-bedroom flat on the eighth floor of a block, to try to accommodate his needs, but a needs assessment subsequently undertaken by the authority accepted that he required ground-floor, wheelchair-accessible accommodation. As a result, the claimant was placed in the highest band of priority on the local authority's scheme for allocating social housing under Housing Act 1996 Part VI.[209] A further assessment under the Care Act 2014 confirmed that he needed to move in order to meet his care needs. Nevertheless, there was considerable delay in obtaining suitable alternative accommodation and the claimant brought judicial review proceedings, contending that the authority was unlawfully failing to provide him with accommodation under the Care Act 2014. The claim was dismissed. Care Act 2014 s23, the court held, accorded the Housing Act 1996 priority over the Care Act 2014 in relation to the provision of accommodation and '(re)housing needs, even if identified through the Care Act route, cannot shortcut the detailed

205 At the time of writing, no such regulations have been enacted.
206 *Care and support statutory guidance*, para 15.51.
207 See paras 8.30–8.32.
208 [2020] EWHC 860 (Admin), [2021] HLR 17.
209 See chapter 7 for discussion of the housing allocation legal framework.

system of balanced priorities within Housing Act schemes, but must find their proper place within those schemes'.[210] The decision in *Idolo* was followed in the case of *R (Campbell) v Ealing LBC*.[211] In that case, the High Court held that the local authority had no power or duty to accommodate a disabled applicant while he awaited an allocation of accommodation under Housing Act 1996 Part VI. Accordingly, Ealing's decision to terminate the accommodation it had been paying for over the preceding five years was not unlawful.

Relationship with the Localism Act 2011

8.138 The relationship between the power under Localism Act (LA) 2011 s1 and the Care Act 2014, as well as the more general question of whether accommodation can be provided under LA 2011 s1 to a person ineligible for mainstream support as a result of their immigration status, have proved to be particularly complex. The case-law, which has not been entirely consistent, is summarised at paras 8.140–8.154. The principles emerging from the cases are summarised at para 8.155.

8.139 LA 2011 s1 confers a very broad power on local authorities to 'do anything that individuals generally may do'. LA 2011 s1(5) states that this general power is 'not limited by the existence of any other power of the authority' which may overlap with the general power. However, LA 2011 s2 stipulates that where there exists a pre- or post-commencement limitation (including a prohibition, restriction or other limitation), the general power under LA 2011 s1 may not be exercised. These limitations restrict the local authority from:[212]

- doing anything which it is unable to do by virtue of a pre-commencement limitation; or
- doing anything which it is unable to do by virtue of a post-commencement limitation which is expressed to apply to the general power.

8.140 In *R (J (Ghanaian citizen)) v Enfield LBC*,[213] the High Court considered the predecessor provision under Local Government Act (LGA) 2000 s2 in the context of a homeless single mother, who was HIV positive, and her daughter. The local authority carried out a

210 *R (Idolo) v Bromley LBC* [2020] EWHC 860 (Admin), [2021] HLR 17 at para 47.
211 [2023] EWHC 10 (Admin).
212 The full definition of a 'pre-commencement' and 'post-commencement' limitation is set out in LA 2011 s2(4).
213 [2002] EWHC 432 (Admin).

needs assessment under the predecessor provisions to the Care Act 2014 and concluded that the mother did not have any eligible care needs, that her needs arose solely as a result of destitution and therefore she was not eligible for residential accommodation under NAA 1948 s21.[214] The local authority also considered that the claimant and her daughter were not eligible for accommodation together as a family under the ChA 1989.[215] The claimant challenged the local authority's decision that it did not owe a duty to provide her or her daughter with assistance in obtaining accommodation. She argued that the authority's failure to do so amounted to a breach of ECHR Article 8 and that insofar as the ChA 1989 and the NAA 1948 prevented the local authority from exercising a power to accommodate the mother and daughter together with the consequence of forcing their separation, then the two schemes were incompatible with the state's ECHR obligations.

8.141 The Home Secretary intervened in the case to contend that no declaration of incompatibility was needed and that the local authority had a power under LGA 2000 s2 to provide financial assistance to assist the claimant to secure accommodation for herself and her daughter. Although there was a prohibition on the local authority arranging accommodation for someone who is not eligible, there was no bar to the authority providing financial assistance for the purposes of acquiring accommodation. Therefore, there was no gap in the two legislative schemes preventing them from giving effect to the protection of the claimant's and her daughter's human rights. The Home Secretary accepted that LGA 2000 s3 had the effect of prohibiting the local authority from doing anything that which it was unable to do by virtue of 'any prohibition, restriction or limitation on their powers which is contained in any enactment (whenever passed or made)'. However, it was submitted that this limitation did not extend to the provision of financial assistance so that the claimant could acquire accommodation (as opposed to the direct provision of accommodation). Elias J (as he then was) agreed with the Home

214 For further detail on eligibility for accommodation in the context of destitution see paras 8.159–8.172.

215 It should be noted that at the time when *J v Enfield* was decided, the power to assist under ChA 1989 s17(6) did not expressly include the provision of accommodation. An explicit reference to a power to provide accommodation under section 17(6) was inserted on 7 November 2002 by Adoption and Children Act 2002 s116(1). It is highly likely that *J v Enfield* would be decided differently today in the light of the express amendment to ChA 1989 s17(6) and thus there would have been no need, in the circumstances, to turn to LGA 2000 s2. See further chapter 9 on support for children and families.

Secretary's argument and held that the LGA 2000 power was extremely wide and was capable of extending to the grant of financial assistance for acquiring accommodation.[216]

8.142 In *R (Khan) v Oxfordshire CC*,[217] however, the Court of Appeal came to a different conclusion about the effect of the limitation under LGA 2000 s3. There, the Court of Appeal held, in respect of a destitute woman who had to flee her family home because of serious domestic violence inflicted on her by her husband, that the LGA 2000 s2 power could not be used to circumvent the pre-existing prohibition under NAA 1948 s21(1A) on the provision of residential accommodation where the care need arose solely by reason of destitution. Neither accommodation nor payments toward it could be provided under LGA 2000 s2 to persons for whom they could not be provided under NAA 1948 s21. The Court of Appeal acknowledged that the power under LGA 2000 s2 had a broad purpose, but section 3 of the same Act prohibited the local authority doing 'anything' which it was unable to do by virtue of 'any prohibition' on its powers contained in 'any enactment'.[218] In *Khan*, the 'thing' which was under consideration was the provision of residential accommodation to a person who, but for the prohibition in NAA 1948 s21(1A), would be entitled to accommodation under section 21. It is that 'thing' – residential accommodation – which the local authority is prohibited from providing by NAA 1948 s21(1A), and which it cannot provide under any other statutory power, unless it can do so under LGA 2000 s2. The provision of financial assistance to acquire accommodation as opposed to accommodation itself was a difference without distinction in the Court of Appeal's view. Parliament did not intend, by LGA 2000 s2, to circumvent existing legislative schemes and the specified restrictions or prohibitions therein. Human Rights Act (HRA) 1998 s3 did not require a different interpretation of the prohibition.

8.143 The LA 2011 is, in terms, materially the same as the LGA 2000 save for an important difference in the way the prohibition on the exercise of the power is drafted. Instead of imposing a prohibition on the exercise of the power where there is *any* prohibition, restriction, limitation on *any* power within *any* enactment, LA 2011 s2 makes a distinction between limitations contained in acts that pre-date the LA 2011 and those that post-date it. Whereas pre-commencement limitations operate in the same way as they did under LGA 2000 s3,

216 *J v Enfield* at paras 54–58.
217 [2004] EWCA Civ 309, [2004] HLR 41.
218 *Khan v Oxfordshire CC* at paras 36–44 per Dyson LJ.

so that any prohibition on the exercise of any power within any enactment prevents the LA 2011 s1 power from being exercised, the ambit of the 'post-commencement limitation' is drafted more restrictively. LA 2011 s2(2) provides that a post-commencement limitation is one which is 'expressed to apply' to the general LA 2011 s1 power either specifically or as part of a limitation applicable to all of the local authority's powers under any enactment. The significance of this distinction can be seen from the discussion at paras 8.147–8.150.

8.144 *R (MK) v Barking and Dagenham LBC*[219] was the first reported case to consider the application of the power under LA 2011 s2 in the context of care and support, but specifically in the context of access to support under the ChA 1989. In that case, the claimant was a young adult overstayer who had failed in her asylum claim and was homeless. She wished to be accommodated and supported with her aunt and cousins and presented to the local authority to request this under ChA 1989 s17 or alternatively under LA 2011 s1. The local authority refused to do so because the young adult was not a child and therefore did not qualify for services to meet her needs under the ChA 1989 in her own right. The High Court upheld the local authority's decision and held that where the ChA 1989 s17 power did not expressly provide for a local authority to provide support to someone in her position, the power under the LA 2011 did not permit this either.[220]

8.145 *R (GS) v Camden LBC*[221] was the first case to consider the relationship of the LA 2011 to the Care Act 2014 framework. There, the claimant was a Swiss national who was wheelchair-dependent and had severe mental health problems. She had been homeless in Switzerland before arriving in the UK. She was assessed by psychiatrists who agreed that she did not have the mental capacity to decide whether to return to Switzerland or consent to mental health treatment. The local authority provided her with temporary accommodation but the claimant said it was unsuitable for wheelchair access. The local authority carried out a needs assessment to see whether she was entitled to care and support under the Care Act 2014, and concluded that her sole need was accommodation which did not fall

219 [2013] EWHC 3486 (Admin).

220 This particular finding would appear to confuse the important distinction drawn in *R (Khan) v Oxfordshire CC* [2004] EWCA Civ 309, [2004] HLR 41 at para 30 'between the definition of the scope of a power and the imposition of a prohibition, restriction or limitation on the exercise of a power'. As such it is, arguably, wrong.

221 [2016] EWHC 1762 (Admin), [2017] PTSR 140.

within the Act and thus it had no power to meet. The claimant argued that 'care and support' was broad enough to include a simple need for accommodation and pointed to references to accommodation in Care Act 2014 s8. Alternatively, the claimant argued that the local authority had a power to help her under the LA 2011 s1 and that its refusal to do so amounted to inhuman or degrading treatment in breach of ECHR Article 3.

8.146 The High Court rejected the claimant's contention that she was eligible for accommodation under the Care Act 2014 but allowed her claim on the argument that the local authority was under a duty to exercise the power under the LA 2011 s1. The High Court arrived at this conclusion in the following ways:[222]

1) There was a material difference in the wording used to prescribe the application of a pre-commencement limitation and a post-commencement limitation to the general power under LA 2011 s1. Whereas the pre-commencement limitation set out in LA 2011 s2(2)(a) remained broadly drafted so as to preserve the effect of the case-law under the previous LGA 2000 (such as *Khan v Oxfordshire*), the language of section 2(2)(b) showed that parliament must have intended that any post-commencement limitation on the section 1 general power would be specifically stated. The Care Act 2014 commenced after the LA 2011. Although Care Act 2014 s21 contained an express limitation to the power to provide accommodation under that Act, neither that provision nor any other provision in the Care Act 2014 contained an express limitation on the *general* power under LA 2011 s1. It therefore did not qualify as a 'post-commencement limitation' within the meaning of LA 2011 s2(2)(b).
2) Even though a person's immigration status may preclude a local authority from exercising the LA 2011 s1 power by virtue of NIAA 2002 s54 and Sch 3 para 1, the bar is removed where it is necessary to provide accommodation for the purposes of avoiding a breach of the person's ECHR or EU Treaty rights.[223]
3) On the available evidence the claimant, GS, had demonstrated that she was unable to obtain suitable accommodation within her means with the local authority's assistance and that the effects of destitution and homelessness would be exacerbated by her physical and mental health conditions and would constitute a breach

222 *GS v Camden* at para 61.
223 See paras 8.173–8.178.

of the prohibition against inhuman and degrading treatment contrary to ECHR Article 3.[224]

4) Thus the refusal of the local authority to accommodate the claimant by the exercise of the LA 2011 s1 power was held to be unlawful.

8.147 *GS v Camden* was considered in *R (AR) v Hammersmith and Fulham LBC*[225] and held by the High Court in the latter case to be wrongly decided. The facts and context of that case need to be properly considered to understand the difference in outcome.

8.148 The claimant in *AR v Hammersmith and Fulham* was an EU national jobseeker who suffered serious injuries as a result of two separate assaults which led to him being hospitalised for treatment. On each of the two occasions, when he was discharged from hospital, he became homeless. He had continued difficulties with his memory and was unable to work. He suffered periods of depression and attempted suicide, had been assessed under the MHA 1983 and had been signposted to alcohol services. He sought homelessness assistance from the local authority under the Housing Act 1996, but it found him not eligible for housing because he did not have a right to reside under EU law.[226] The claimant did not challenge the refusal of homelessness assistance. The local authority then considered whether the claimant was alternatively eligible for care and support under the Care Act 2014 but concluded that he was not. He challenged the Care Act 2014 decision and contended that in any event that the LA 2011 s1 power ought to be exercised, applying *GS v Camden*, and that he required accommodation to avoid a breach of his human rights under NIAA 2002 Sch 3 para 3.

8.149 The High Court rejected both heads of challenge. In respect of the Care Act 2014 challenge, the High Court upheld the conclusion of the local authority that the claimant's needs were not such that he was unlikely to achieve two or more outcomes, as required under Eligibility Regs 2015 reg 2(1)(b). The High Court considered that the claimant's need for accommodation and subsistence did not, on their own, amount to a need for care and support. The local authority was

224 *GS v Camden* was decided prior to the coming into force of Immigration Act 2016 Sch 10 and the power under para 9 to provide accommodation to enable a person to meet conditions of immigration bail in 'exceptional circumstances'. GS might now be able to access accommodation under that power. See further paras 6.201–6.272.

225 [2018] EWHC 3453 (Admin).

226 See paras 7.6–7.93.

thus rightly precluded under Care Act 2014 s21 from providing him with accommodation.

8.150 As for the LA 2011 argument, the High Court applied the reasoning of the Court of Appeal in *Khan v Oxfordshire*[227] to find that the Housing Act 1996 contained a pre-commencement limitation which fell within the ambit of LA 2011 s2. That limitation had not been considered in *GS v Camden*, which was wrongly decided.[228]

8.151 Alternatively, the court held, even if accommodation could be made available under either the Care Act 2014 or the LA 2011, the claimant was subject to the immigration-based exclusions from support contained in NIAA 2002 Sch 3.[229] On the facts of his case, the judge found, there would be no breach of EU law or the ECHR if support was not provided and so the exceptions to that exclusion did not apply.[230]

8.152 The High Court did not decide whether it was possible to provide financial assistance for the claimant to acquire accommodation[231] notwithstanding the scope of the LA 2011 s2 limitation, as interpreted by the judge, as that did not form part of the claimant's case.[232] However, as the judge observed, resolution of that question would involve consideration of whether 'such provision is "assistance" within Part 7 of the Housing Act and thereby subject to the prohibition in section 185';[233] a question which had not been considered in any of the previous cases. The *Homelessness code of guidance for local authorities*[234] stipulates that financial support to pay for accommodation can be provided under Housing Act 1996 Part VII,[235] and is hence subject to Housing Act 1996 s185, suggesting that – on the judge's analysis in *AR v Hammersmith and Fulham* – this solution may also be unavailable under the LA 2011.

8.153 The availability of the LA 2011 s1 power fell for consideration once more by the High Court in *R (Aburas) v Southwark LBC*.[236] In

227 See discussion at para 8.142.

228 *AR v Hammersmith and Fulham* at paras 28–29.

229 See paras 8.173–8.178.

230 *AR v Hammersmith and Fulham* at paras 31–42.

231 This was the solution arrived at by the High Court in *J v Enfield* as a means to get around the limitation in LGA 2000 s3.

232 *AR v Hammersmith and Fulham* at para 30.

233 *AR v Hammersmith and Fulham* at para 30.

234 *Homelessness code of guidance for local authorities*, Department for Levelling Up, Housing and Communities (DLUHC), 22 February 2018, updated 1 June 2022, www.gov.uk/guidance/homelessness-code-of-guidance-for-local-authorities

235 *Homelessness code of guidance for local authorities*, para 11.23(c).

236 [2019] EWHC 2754 (Admin), (2019) 22 CCLR 537.

that case, the claimant was a homeless failed asylum-seeker who faced barriers to removal to Kuwait. He had a number of mental health issues. The local authority had concluded that he was not eligible for support under the Care Act 2014. He sought judicial review arguing that he had needs for care and support which required accommodation for their effective delivery, and that the failure to provide this would result in a breach of his rights under the ECHR.[237] The High Court rejected this argument finding that there was an insufficient evidential basis to depart from the social worker's conclusion that he did not have a ' "looked-after need" need for social worker support'[238] and that the claimant's destitution could be avoided by his seeking support from the Home Office.[239] In *obiter* comments, the judge agreed with the analysis in *AR v Hammersmith and Fulham*. He expressed the view that where a person has a need for care and support not satisfying the eligibility criteria, and the provision of support is necessary to avoid a breach of the ECHR, then LA 2011 s1 is not needed as the power under Care Act 2014 s19 can be exercised. If the need is for accommodation only, then LA 2011 s1 was not available for the reasons given in *AR v Hammersmith and Fulham*. This left open the question of what circumstances might the LA 2011 s1 power be available to avoid a breach of the ECHR. The fact that this power is contained within a list of provisions set out in NIAA 2002 Sch 3 which may need to be exercised in order to avoid a breach of the ECHR in relation to a person who would otherwise be excluded from support on the grounds of their immigration status,[240] suggested that such circumstances might exist. However, the judge declined to decide what those circumstances would be, leaving the question to be analysed in an appropriate case, while suggesting that such a case might involve 'neither a need for accommodation, nor a "looked-after need", but something else'.[241]

237 See paras 8.173–8.178 for the circumstances in which support will be necessary to avoid a breach of the ECHR.

238 See paras 8.123–8.131 on the circumstances in which accommodation should be provided under the Care Act 2014. Note that the use of the phrase 'looked-after needs' was deprecated by the Court of Appeal in *R (BG) v Suffolk CC* [2022] EWCA Civ 1047 as representing too narrow a view of the types of needs that can be met under the Care Act 2014. See paras 8.123–8.131.

239 *R (Aburas) v Southwark LBC* [2019] EWHC 2754 (Admin), (2019) 22 CCLR 537 at para 21. See chapter 6 for support for failed asylum-seekers.

240 See paras 8.173–8.178.

241 *R (Aburas) v Southwark LBC* [2019] EWHC 2754 (Admin), (2019) 22 CCLR 537 at para 21.

8.154 The High Court was invited to answer this question in the case of *R (Ncube) v Brighton and Hove City Council*.[242] That case concerned the availability of local authority powers to provide accommodation to homeless persons who did not have access to public funds owing to their immigration status, during the COVID-19 pandemic. The court held that emergency and public health related powers to provide such accommodation existed under Local Government Act 1972 s138 and National Health Service Act 2006 s2B. The claimant in that case had argued in the alternative that the pre-commencement limitation in Housing Act 1996 s185 might operate as a pre-commencement limitation preventing a local authority from providing accommodation as a housing authority, but did not prevent it from providing accommodation in its capacity as a social services authority. Further, in any event, reading LA 2011 ss1–2 down, as required by HRA 1998 s3, support could be provided under LA 2011 s1 where necessary to avoid a breach of the ECHR. The court rejected the former argument, on the grounds that it was inconsistent with the authorities summarised above. As to the latter argument, the issue did not arise on the facts of the case as the claimant was not facing a breach of the ECHR owing to the availability of accommodation under other powers, and so it did not require determination.[243]

8.155 Drawing together the threads of the case-law summarised above, the current position would appear to be as follows. There has been a divergence in the High Court as to whether, in cases where there is no risk of an ECHR breach, accommodation may be provided under the LA 2011 to a person with needs for care and support which do not meet the eligibility criteria under the Care Act 2014 but who is not eligible for accommodation under the HA 1996 as a result of their immigration status. One case (*GS v Camden*) suggests that it can be, as the provision of accommodation to such a person is not prohibited by the Care Act 2014, ie there is no post-commencement limitation. The other cases (*AR v Hammersmith and Fulham; Aburas*; and *Ncube*) suggest that it cannot, as the provision of accommodation to such a person is prohibited by HA 1996 s185, ie there is a relevant pre-commencement limitation. The question of whether financial assistance can be provided, in the alternative, to assist in securing accommodation, remains open (see *AR v Hammersmith and Fulham*). That may be a question of whether such assistance can be made

242 [2021] EWHC 578 (Admin), [2021] 1 WLR 4762.

243 *R (Ncube) v Brighton and Hove City Council* [2021] EWHC 578 (Admin), [2021] 1 WLR 4762 at paras 82–139.

available under HA 1996 Part VII. Similarly, the question of whether support may be provided under the LA 2011 in order to avoid a breach of the ECHR and, if so, what type of support (for example, accommodation) remains open (see *Aburas* and *Ncube*) but there has been a suggestion that such support would be limited and would involve 'neither a need for accommodation, nor a "looked-after need", but something else' (see *Aburas*).

8.156 Accepting the divergence and unresolved issues in the case-law, the practical points to draw from this may be that an applicant who is unable to access accommodation under either the Care Act 2014 or the Housing Act 1996 might reasonably ask their local authority to provide it under LA 2011 s1. However, the prudent course would be for the applicant also to seek accommodation under any other available power, for example, the Home Office powers and duties outlined in chapters 5 and 6, at the same time since the local authority may refuse that request and any challenge to that refusal would likely raise one or more of the difficult issues outlined above, which may require resolution by the Court of Appeal.

Relationship with Home Office support

8.157 The relationship between care and support under the Care Act 2014 and the support that is available to asylum-seekers under IAA s95(1), failed asylum-seekers under IAA 1999 s4(2) and those on immigration bail is discussed at paras 5.94–5.102, 6.139–6.140 and 6.251 respectively. In very broad terms, for those who are eligible, support under the Care Act 2014 will generally be expected to take precedence over Home Office support. The relationship between care and support under the Care Act 2014 and Home Office support is closely allied to the question of when a person will be excluded from care and support under the Care Act 2014 as a result of their immigration status. That question is discussed immediately below at paras 8.158–8.178.

Immigration-based exclusions from care and support under the Care Act 2014

Overview

8.158 All people, whatever their immigration status, have a right to be assessed under the Care Act 2014 (where it appears to the local authority they have care and support needs)[244] in order to have a determination as to whether they are eligible for support under the Act. However, in order to access care and support, a migrant must be assessed as having an eligible need for care and support[245] and:

- not be excluded by Care Act 2014 s21, which prevents a local authority from meeting the needs for care and support of a 'person subject to immigration control' where those needs have arisen solely from destitution or its physical effects (the 'destitute plus' test);
- not fall within the immigration-based exclusions contained in NIAA 2002 s54 and Sch 3 or, alternatively, fall within one of the exceptions to those exclusions, for example, a person who needs support to avoid a breach of the ECHR.

This section considers these immigration-based restrictions in turn.

The 'destitute plus' test

8.159 Under the previous NAA 1948 legislative scheme, local authorities were precluded from providing residential accommodation to a person subject to immigration control[246] where the need for care and attention arose solely because of destitution or the physical effects of destitution.[247] This came to be referred to as the 'destitution plus' or 'destitute plus' test.

8.160 Care Act 2014 s21 performs the same function as NAA 1948 s21(1A) previously did, but instead of applying the 'destitution plus' test only to the provision residential accommodation, it applies it to all forms of care and support needs under Care Act 2014 Part 1. Given the language of both provisions is almost identical, case-law interpreting the meaning and application of the test of 'destitute plus' under the previous legislative framework remains applicable to

244 See paras 8.33–8.70 for the duty to assess.

245 See paras 8.71–8.87.

246 As defined in IAA 1999 s115(9).

247 NAA 1948 s21(1A), as inserted by IAA 1999 s116. See the introduction above and para 5.95 for the background that led to the introduction of this provision. Under IAA 1999 s117, other exclusions applied in respect of certain services for older people (under Health Services and Public Health Act 1968 s45) and certain social care and aftercare services for the mentally ill (under National Health Service 2006 Sch 20). The latter two provisions were repealed in Wales by the SSWB(W)A 2014.

the current Care Act 2014 regime, albeit to all services rather than just residential accommodation.

8.161 In *R v Wandsworth LBC ex p O*[248] the applicants were overstayers with no right to accommodation unless they could bring themselves within NAA 1998 s21. They both had health problems and were destitute. The Court of Appeal rejected an argument that they were excluded from consideration for residential accommodation by virtue of NAA 1948 s21(1A). Simon Brown LJ (with whom Hale and Kay LJJ agreed) summarised what is required to meet the 'destitute plus' test; that is where an applicant's need for care and attention is 'to any material extent *made more acute* by some circumstance other than the mere lack of accommodation and funds',[249] despite being subject to immigration control. Simon Brown LJ gave, by way of example, an immigrant who, as well as being destitute, is old, ill or disabled; that person is likely to be more vulnerable and less able to survive than if he were merely destitute. Simon Brown LJ went on to find that the word 'solely' contained in NAA 1948 s21(1A) was a strong one. It was clear, in his view (and that of Hale and Kay LLJ) that NAA 1948 s21 was the 'last refuge of the destitute'. 'If there are to be immigrant beggars on our streets, then let them at least not be old, ill or disabled.'

8.162 This analysis was endorsed in *R (Westminster City Council) v National Asylum Support Service*.[250] There, the claimant was a destitute asylum-seeker suffering from spinal cancer and living with her 13-year-old daughter. She needed assistance from a carer with her mobility indoors and outdoors, with transfers between her bed, chair, bath and wheelchair, and with personal care in respect of washing, dressing and toileting. She also required accommodation with disabled access and its own bedroom, located as close as possible to the hospital where she was receiving ongoing treatment. The dispute arose when the National Asylum Support Service (NASS) refused responsibility for the cost of her accommodation, and the local authority began judicial review proceedings. There was no dispute in that case that the claimant was in need of 'care and attention'; the only issue was whether it was 'otherwise available'.

8.163 Lord Hoffmann summarised[251] the effect of NAA1948 s21(1A) as only excluding 'able bodied destitute' people from the powers and

248 [2000] 1 WLR 2539, (2000) 3 CCLR 237, CA.

249 Emphasis added.

250 [2002] UKHL 38, [2002] 1 WLR 2956.

251 *R (Westminster City Council) v National Asylum Support Service* [2002] UKHL 38, [2002] 1 WLR 2956 at para 32.

duties to provide residential accommodation. The 'infirm destitute' remained eligible for support from social services. This was because their needs arose because they were infirm as well as destitute. They would need care and accommodation even if they were wealthy. Although they would not require accommodation from the state if they were wealthy, Lord Hoffmann observed that 'that is not where section 21(1A) draws the line'.[252]

8.164 Lord Hoffmann rejected the local authority's argument that the claimant's need for care and attention could be satisfied in private accommodation and did not entail a need for local authority accommodation.[253] Concerns had been raised by the Court of Appeal in the case as to whether the 'destitute plus' test had been cast too widely in *ex p O* to include any person whose disability makes his or her need for care and attention 'to any extent more acute' than that which arises merely from their destitution. It was suggested that this might expose the system to abuse. Whilst Lord Hoffmann accepted that the concerns raised by the Court of Appeal were not without substance, he did not find they arose on the facts of the case before it[254] and therefore did not consider the correctness of the test laid down by *ex p O*.

8.165 In *R (Mani) v Lambeth LBC*[255] an opportunity arose to review the 'destitute plus' test set out in *ex p O*. The claimant, a destitute asylum-seeker, suffered from a disability to one leg which impaired his mobility and led to the need for help in tasks such as bed-making, cleaning and carrying shopping. The local authority disclaimed responsibility on the grounds that his needs were not such as to require the provision of accommodation, contending that unless the person's disability was such that it gave rise to an 'accommodation related need for care and attention' it could not be one entitling him to NAA 1948 s21 accommodation.

8.166 At the time when the *Westminster v National Asylum Support Service* case came before the House of Lords, the *Mani* case had been decided at first instance but had not yet reached the Court of Appeal. The High Court was bound by the Court of Appeal's decision in *ex p O* and disagreed with the local authority's submission. When the matter came before the Court of Appeal, the court took the same approach, rejecting the local authority's formulation of requiring the need for

252 *Westminster v National Asylum Support Service* at para 32.
253 *Westminster v National Asylum Support Service* at para 43.
254 *Westminster v National Asylum Support Service* at para 49.
255 [2003] EWCA Civ 836, [2004] HLR 5.

care and attention to be an 'accommodation related need'.[256] Simon Brown LJ did express some doubts as to whether NAA 1948 s21 was intended to provide for all those subject to immigration control who are homeless for reasons which may or may not be connected with their care and attention needs. He concluded, however, that the existing authorities demanded this conclusion, consistent with the government's white paper *Fairer, faster, firmer: a modern approach to immigration and asylum*,[257] which proposed, by means of the introduction of the IAA 1999, to distinguish between the way that 'able-bodied' and 'infirm destitute' persons subject to immigration control were provided with support. It was, Simon Brown LJ held, for the House of Lords to decide otherwise or for parliament to adjust the balance of responsibilities between the asylum support regime and local authorities.[258]

8.167 The matter did not then reach the highest appellate court again for another decade until the Supreme Court in *R (SL) v Westminster City Council*[259] was asked to adjudicate on whether it was necessary for the care and attention need to be 'accommodation related' to satisfy the duty under NAA 1948 s21.

8.168 In the meantime, the House of Lords was asked in *R (M) v Slough BC*[260] to determine whether a claimant, a person subject to immigration control who was HIV positive, was entitled to residential accommodation by reason of his need for a refrigerator in which to keep HIV anti-retroviral medication that he needed for his treatment. The local authority concluded that the claimant had no 'care and attention' need that required accommodation to be provided. The local authority concluded that should a need arise in the future, it would arise solely from the claimant's destitution; the contingent duty to accommodate under the NAA 1948 would, in the circumstances be excluded by section 21(1A).

8.169 The House of Lords was mainly concerned with the meaning of 'in need of care and attention which is not otherwise available to' the person, rather than with the 'destitute plus' test under NAA 1948 s21(1A). The court concluded that the claimant's need for a refrigerator for his HIV anti-retroviral medication was a medical need which was excluded from the ambit of 'need or care and attention' and was

256 *Mani v Lambeth* at paras 18–20.
257 Cm 4018, 27 July 1998.
258 *Mani v Lambeth* at para 21.
259 [2013] UKSC 27, [2013] 1 WLR 1445.
260 [2008] UKHL 52, [2008] 1 WLR 1808.

met by NHS care. The need for ordinary housing was not itself 'care and attention'. Thus, on the facts, the House of Lords found that the claimant, M, was not eligible for residential accommodation because he had no eligible 'care and attention' needs.

8.170 In *R (Z) v Hillingdon LBC*,[261] the first judgment after the *M v Slough* case, the High Court decided that a blind man, receiving help from two friends in connection with shopping, laundry, cooking and getting around, required a sufficient degree of 'looking after' to be in need of care and attention so was entitled to residential accommodation under NAA 1948 s21.

8.171 The test set down in *ex p O* was in this way preserved for more than a decade until it was re-examined by the Supreme Court in *SL v Westminster*. There, a destitute claimant who required mental health supervision from a care coordinator on a weekly basis was held not to be entitled to support under NAA 1948 s21(1) on the basis of a more restrictive interpretation of the statutory test than that set down in *ex p O*. The Supreme Court held that it was not sufficient for the person to have a need for care and attention made more acute by circumstances other than the lack of accommodation and funds. A person who met that threshold would not fall within the NAA 1948 s21(1A) exclusion. However, the fact they did not fall within that exclusion did not automatically mean that they were eligible for accommodation under NAA 1948 s21(1). To be eligible for accommodation, their need had to be 'accommodation-related'. That is, the sort of care and attention normally provided in the home or that which would be rendered effectively useless if the claimant had no home.[262] Where care and attention could be provided independently of the accommodation, the test in NAA 1948 s21(1) would not be met. This meant, the court accepted, that there would be an 'undistributed middle' who had a need for care and attention made more acute by circumstances other than the lack of accommodation and funds (meaning they satisfied the 'destitute plus' test) but who nevertheless were not entitled to accommodation under NAA 1948 s21(1).

8.172 Because NAA 1948 s21(1A) was directed only to the provision of residential accommodation, the case-law to date has only considered the effect of the 'destitute plus' test on access to accommodation. As stated above, Care Act 2014 s21 extends the test to all care and support

261 [2009] EWHC 1398 (Admin), (2009) 12 CCLR 157.

262 *SL v Westminster* at paras 47–48 per Lord Carnwarth. See paras 8.123–8.131 above for a discussion of this approach in the context of accommodation under the Care Act 2014.

arrangements. However, in practice, it seems unlikely that other forms of care and support would be met by the 'destitute plus' test in the same way as accommodation. For example, a person requiring care and support with personal hygiene and day-to-day living will usually require a level of social care intervention that cannot be attributed solely to destitution (even if destitution exacerbates the situation).

The Nationality, Immigration and Asylum Act 2002 exclusions

8.173 In addition to the 'destitute plus' test, NIAA 2002 Sch 3 para 1(1)(n) prevents a local authority from meeting the care and support needs of certain migrants under the Care Act 2014,[263] save where support is necessary to avoid a breach of their rights under the ECHR.[264]

8.174 The exclusion applies to four prescribed classes of 'ineligible persons' set out in NIAA 2002 Sch 3 paras 4–7A.[265] The ones applicable to adults seeking care and support are as follows:

1) non-EEA nationals with refugee status granted by an EEA country (para 4);
2) failed asylum-seekers who have not co-operated with removal directions (para 6);
3) persons in the UK in breach of the immigration laws (who have not claimed asylum) (para 7);
4) failed asylum-seekers with dependant children whom the Home Secretary has certified to have failed without reasonable excuse to take reasonable steps to leave the UK (para 7A).

These classes of person are also excluded from many forms of support under the ChA 1989 and are discussed in more detail at paras 9.195–9.217.

8.175 In outline, the first class is self-explanatory. The third and fourth classes invite consideration of whether a person seeking support is, or has been, an asylum-seeker. An asylum-seeker in this context is a person aged 18 or over who has made a claim for asylum which has

263 NIAA 2002 Sch 3 para 1(1)(o) excludes the provision of care and support under SSWB(W)A 2014 Part 4.

264 NIAA 2002 Sch 3 para 3. See paras 5.127–5.131, 6.90–6.135 and 9.203–9.217 for a detailed discussion of the circumstances in which support is necessary to avoid a breach of the EHCR or the EU Treaties.

265 The Immigration Act 2016 contains further classes of 'ineligible persons' under Schedule 12 para 9 and Schedule 11 Part 2 para 48(8). These have not come into force at the time of writing.

been recorded but not determined.[266] A claim for asylum means a claim that it would be contrary to the UK's obligations under the Refugee Convention or under ECHR Article 3, for the applicant to be removed from, or required to leave, the UK[267] and a claim will be regarded as determined where the Home Secretary has notified the applicant of their decision and the applicant has exhausted their appeal rights, or had their claim declared inadmissible.[268] This is the same definition as contained in IAA 1999 s94 which applies in the context of asylum support, discussed in more detail at paras 5.17–5.44. The High Court has held that in order for an applicant to be regarded as an asylum-seeker for these purposes, in circumstances where they had not been successful in their initial asylum claim and they had made further submissions on asylum and human rights grounds,[269] the Home Secretary needs to have accepted that those submissions amount to a fresh claim under Immigration Rules para 353. It is only at that point, that the claim can be characterised as having been 'recorded'.[270] Whether this position is compatible with the UK's EU law obligations under the Reception Directive[271] remains to be determined by an appellate court.[272]

8.176 If a local authority intends to refuse support by reference to the ineligible classes of persons under NIAA 2002 Sch 3, it must assess whether that would breach the adult's ECHR rights by reference to Schedule 3 para 3. If so, support must be provided to the extent necessary to avoid that breach. A detailed discussion of the circumstances in which support may be necessary to avoid a breach of the ECHR can be found at paras 5.127–5.131, 6.90–6.135 and 9.203–9.217.

8.177 In practice, the requirement for a human rights assessment has often meant adults subject to immigration control (whether they fall within an ineligible class or not) are subject to probing questions about their immigration status and the substance of any pending

266 NIAA 2002 Sch 3 para 17. This mirrors the definition in the IAA 1999 for asylum support purposes. See further paras 5.17–5.44.

267 NIAA 2002 Sch 3 para 17(1)(b) and s18(3).

268 NIAA 2002 Sch 3 para 17(2)–(2B).

269 See paras 3.42–3.43.

270 *R (Mustafa) v Kent CC* [2018] EWHC 2025 (Admin). See further the more detailed discussion of fresh claims at paras 5.23–5.28, in the context of the identical definition of asylum-seeker contained in IAA 1999 s94(1).

271 Council Directive 2003/9/EC of 27 January 2003 laying down minimum standards for the reception of asylum seekers ('Reception Directive').

272 A discussion of the compatibility of the approach of the High Court in *Mustafa v Kent* with Council the Reception Directive can be found at paras 6.26–6.34.

immigration application, and are required to produce documentation that had been submitted to the Home Office. Local authorities have also required adults subject to assessment in these circumstances to give consent to them to contact the Home Office as part of their assessment. Adverse inferences have been drawn by local authorities where the person subject to assessment is deemed to be refusing to co-operate at all or fully.[273]

8.178 A Freedom of Information Act 2000 (FOIA) request made by Project 17, a charity supporting migrant families accessing ChA 1989 support, revealed that local authorities were entering into memorandums of understanding (MOUs) with the Home Office to embed Home Office immigration officers who would participate in the assessment process by conducting interviews in respect of the immigration status of those subject to immigration control who seek support from the local authority. The same response to the FOIA request stated that as at December 2017, within London itself, at least ten of 32 London authorities subscribed to this practice.[274] There is no publicly available information as to the total number of local authorities across England and Wales which have subscribed to this practice. This practice has been controversial and subject to criticisms from support organisations who have raised concerns about the chilling effect it has on vulnerable adults subject to immigration control seeking support that they may be eligible for. Some local authorities have, under pressure from community groups, decided to terminate the practice, but not all have.[275]

Safeguarding

8.179 Prior to the Care Act 2014 coming into force, the safeguarding of vulnerable adults operated under *No secrets: guidance on developing and implementing multi-agency policies and procedures to protect vulnerable adults from abuse*,[276] which was non-statutory guidance issued under Local Authority Social Services Act 1970 s7. The obligations

273 See paras 9.44–9.48 on credibility.

274 Response to Project 17's FOIA request dated 21 December 2017 with attachments of the blank MOU, www.whatdotheyknow.com/request/448245/response/1088568/attach/html/3/FOI%2046332%20Murtagh.pdf.html.

275 Local authorities in London which have publicly stated that they have ended the practice include Southwark LBC, Haringey LBC and Lewisham LBC.

276 Home Office and Department of Health, 20 March 2000, last updated 22 January 2015, www.gov.uk/government/publications/no-secrets-guidance-on-protecting-vulnerable-adults-in-care.

under the *No secrets* guidance were discharged through the use of existing community care provisions, such as assessment and care planning under the National Health Service and Community Care Act 1990, referrals between agencies and the use of lawful information sharing. Those seeking to discern the scope of the duty and enforce it had to draw together public law principles from the community care legal framework, the MCA 2005 and the HRA 1998, alongside common law principles (such as the concept of a duty of care) and the normal mechanisms of the civil and criminal justice systems which formed the legal underpinning to safeguarding. The application of these provisions to achieve the purpose of safeguarding was patchy and inconsistent. In its adult care report, published in 2011, the Law Commission described the legal framework for adult protection as 'neither systematic nor co-ordinated, reflecting the sporadic development of safeguarding policy over the last 25 years'.[277] The absence of directly enforceable duties to investigate safeguarding concerns or to require action to be taken left significant gaps in protection for the most vulnerable in society. The Law Commission found an urgent need for the statute to establish a duty on local authorities not only to make inquiries into adult protection concerns but to also take appropriate action, including the provision of services, monitoring or the use of existing compulsory powers.[278]

8.180 In response to the Law Commission's recommendations, Care Act 2014 ss42–47 placed safeguarding obligations on a statutory footing. This, together with the inclusion of the need to protect adults from abuse and neglect as an aspect of the well-being principle, may be taken to indicate a renewed commitment to safeguarding vulnerable adults. However, in practice, the Care Act 2014 provides local authorities with very little in terms of substance to enhance their safeguarding powers.

8.181 The primary safeguarding obligation is set out in Care Act 2014 s42, which imposes a duty on local authorities to make inquiries if it has reasonable cause to believe that an adult in its area (whether ordinarily resident or not):

- has needs for care and support; and
- is experiencing abuse or neglect; or
- is at risk of abuse or neglect; and
- as a result of their needs for care and support, is unable to protect themself against the abuse/neglect.

277 *Adult social care*, HC 941, Law Commission, 10 May 2011, para 9.1.
278 *Adult social care*, HC 941, paras 9.4, 9.15–9.17.

8.182 What constitutes 'abuse and neglect' is not defined in the Care Act 2014 other than to state that it includes financial abuse.[279] However, the concept of 'abuse and neglect' is expanded on in the *Care and support statutory guidance*[280] with a word of warning to local authorities not to apply the concept in a restrictive way. It encompasses:

- **physical abuse** – including assault; hitting; slapping; pushing; misuse of medication; restraint; and inappropriate physical sanctions;
- **domestic violence** – including psychological, physical, sexual, financial, emotional abuse; and so-called 'honour'-based violence;
- **sexual abuse** – including rape; indecent exposure; sexual harassment; inappropriate looking or touching; sexual teasing or innuendo; sexual photography; subjection to pornography or witnessing sexual acts; indecent exposure; sexual assault; and sexual acts to which the adult has not consented or was pressured into consenting;
- **psychological abuse** – including emotional abuse; threats of harm or abandonment; deprivation of contact; humiliation; blaming; controlling; intimidation; coercion; harassment; verbal abuse; cyber bullying; isolation; and unreasonable and unjustified withdrawal of services or supportive networks;
- **financial or material abuse** – including theft; fraud; internet scamming; coercion in relation to an adult's financial affairs or arrangements, including in connection with wills, property, inheritance or financial transactions; and the misuse or misappropriation of property, possessions or benefits;
- **modern slavery** – encompassing slavery; human trafficking; forced labour and domestic servitude; and traffickers and slave masters using whatever means they have at their disposal to coerce, deceive and force individuals into a life of abuse, servitude and inhumane treatment;
- **discriminatory abuse** – including harassment; and slurs or similar treatment because of race, gender and gender identity, age, disability, sexual orientation or religion;
- **organisational abuse** – including 'neglect and poor care practice within an institution or specific care setting such as a hospital or care home, for example, or in relation to care provided in one's own home. This may range from one off incidents to on-going

279 Care Act 2014 s42(3).

280 *Care and support statutory guidance*, para 14.17.

ill-treatment. It can be through neglect or poor professional practice as a result of the structure, policies, processes and practices within an organisation';

- **neglect and acts of omission** – including ignoring medical, emotional or physical care needs; failure to provide access to appropriate health, care and support or educational services; the withholding of the necessities of life, such as medication, adequate nutrition and heating.

Additional advice is given on **self-neglect** (which covers a wide range of behaviour such as neglecting to care for one's personal hygiene, health or surroundings, and includes behaviour such as hoarding) stating that self-neglect may not always prompt a section 42 inquiry. A decision on whether a response is required under the safeguarding obligations will depend on the adult's ability to protect themself by controlling their own behaviour. There may come a point when they are no longer able to do this, without external support.

8.183 The absence of an attendant obligation on the local authority to respond to the outcome of the inquiry is troubling. All of the statutory powers relate to process duties to inquire and to undertake reviews. The local authority is not required, under the Care Act 2014 itself, to respond by taking any action. This compares unfavourably to the Welsh Act[281] which provides a power of entry, to enable social services to gain access and to speak with a person suspected of being abused.[282] Not only are such powers absent from the Care Act 2014, the previous NAA 1948 s47 power to remove, is repealed. This is made more problematic by the absence of any recognition of 'keeping safe' as an eligible need (unlike the Welsh Act[283]). Aspects of the *Care and support statutory guidance* touch on safeguarding as a basis upon which a need for care and support may arise, but the advice given in the statutory guidance is far from clear.[284]

8.184 However, a failure to act upon the outcomes of a safeguarding inquiry could amount to a breach of the person's ECHR rights where

281 SSWB(W)A 2014 s127.

282 The Scots Act – Adult Support and Protection (Scotland) Act 2007 – contains an additional power to remove: ss7, 8, 11 and 14.

283 SSWB(W)A 2014 s32(1)(b) addresses this issue directly.

284 See, for example, para 6.56 (under chapter 6 headed 'Assessment and eligibility') stating that safeguarding inquiries may result in the provision of care and support under Care Act 2014 s18 or s19. See also para 10.39 (under chapter 10 'Care and support planning') which states that where an inquiry leads to further specific interventions being put in place to address a safeguarding issue, this may be included in the care and support plan.

the inquiry identified credible suspicions of risks of immediate risk of harm which engage the state's positive duties to protect under ECHR Article 3, 4 or 8. In those circumstances the local authority would be required to act upon the inquiry pursuant to HRA 1998 s6.

Remedies

8.185 Remedies include:

- internal complaints;
- complaints to the ombudsman;
- appeals;
- judicial review.

Internal complaints

8.186 All English local authorities are obliged to have in place procedures[285] for dealing with complaints made to them about the discharge of their social services functions under the Care Act 2014 by:[286]

- a person who receives or has received care and support;
- a person who is affected or likely to be affected by an action, omission or decision of the local authority which is the subject of the complaint;
- a representative on behalf of a person who has died, is a child, is unable to make the complaint themself because of physical or mental[287] incapacity, or where the person has requested the representative act on their behalf.

8.187 The procedure for making and determining complaints is set out in the Local Authority Social Services and NHS Complaints Regulations ('LASS and NHS Complaints Regs') 2009.[288] Each local authority must have a complaints manager, whose role is to assist in the coordination of all aspects of the complaints process. A complaint may be made orally or in writing[289] and should be handled and considered speedily and efficiently by the local authority.[290] Generally,

285 LASS and NHS Complaints Regs 2009 reg 3, made under powers in Health and Social Care (Community Health and Standards) Act 2003 ss113–115.

286 LASS and NHS Complaints Regs 2009 reg 5.

287 Reference to mental capacity is a reference to capacity within the meaning of the MCA 2005.

288 SI No 309.

289 LASS and NHS Regs 2009 reg 13.

290 LASS and NHS Regs 2009 reg 3(2).

complaints should be lodged no longer than one year after the grounds to make the complaint arose.[291] However, local authorities have a discretion to consider a complaint made outside of that timescale if they are satisfied that there are good reasons for not making the complaint within that time limit and notwithstanding the delay, it is still possible to investigate the complaint effectively and fairly.[292] The local authority is not required to deal with complaints relating to matters which are the subject of a pending or ongoing investigation by the Local Government Ombudsman.

8.188 Once the complaint has been received by the local authority, it must acknowledge receipt of the complaint either orally or in writing not later than three working days after the day on which it receives the complaint.[293] At the time of acknowledgment, the local authority must offer to discuss with the complainant, at a time to be agreed, the manner in which the complaint is to be handled, and the period within which the investigation is likely to be completed and the response sent to the complainant.[294] If agreement cannot be reached on the response period, the local authority must determine the response period in any event and notify the complainant in writing of that period. As a general rule, complaints should be investigated in a manner appropriate to resolve them speedily and efficiently.[295] The complainant should be kept informed as to the progress of the investigation as far as reasonably practicable.[296] The regulations provide that the investigation should normally conclude within six months, commencing on the date on which the complaint was received, unless a longer period was agreed between the local authority and the complainant. If the local authority cannot meet this six-month long-stop, it must notify the complainant in writing and explain why, and send the complainant in writing a response as soon as reasonably practicable after the expiry of the six months.[297]

8.189 The response provided by the local authority to a complaint after completing the investigation should include an explanation of how the complaint has been considered, what considerations have been reached, and what remedial action is needed. The local authority

291 LASS and NHS Regs 2009 reg 12(1).
292 LASS and NHS Regs 2009 reg 12(2).
293 LASS and NHS Regs 2009 reg 13.
294 LASS and NHS Regs 2009 reg 13(7).
295 LASS and NHS Regs 2009 reg 14(1).
296 LASS and NHS Regs 2009 reg 14(1)(b).
297 LASS and NHS Regs 2009 reg 14(3)–(4).

should also confirm whether it is satisfied that any action needed in consequence of the complaint has been or is proposed to be taken. Local authorities have powers of redress exercisable in cases of maladministration under LGA 2000 s93 as well as more general powers under LA 2011 s1[298] which might appropriately be exercised in such circumstances.

Complaints to the ombudsman

8.190 An applicant who has exhausted these internal complaints mechanisms, and who remains unsatisfied with the outcome of their complaint, may seek to complain to the Local Government and Social Care Ombudsman.[299] Complaints should generally be made within 12 months from the date on which the grounds for complaint arose.

Appeals

8.191 In its scoping report the Law Commission concluded that its review, which went on to form the basis of the Care Act 2014, should consider the efficacy of legal structures in place for complaining about, and seeking redress for failures in, decision-making and service provisions. This included whether or not to create as specialist tribunal akin to that which considers appeals in respect of special educational needs assessments and plans. However, the government's consultation paper did not include redress system as the Department of Health did not want the Commission to cover this.

8.192 The Care Bill introduced in the House of Lords contained no provisions as to appeals. Lord Dubs at the Committee stage tabled an amendment which would enable adults to bring challenges of local authority decisions to a tribunal. In the House of Commons committee stage, Paul Burstow MP introduced an amendment to introduce a mechanism for dispute resolution and redress. Then, on the last day of the Committee stage, the government added a new clause which is now contained in Care Act 2014 s72, containing a regulation-making power to provide for appeals against specific decisions under Care Act 2014 Part 1.

8.193 Care Act 2014 s72, which has not yet been brought into force, does not contain any specifics as to who can bring an appeal, how or when. Instead it provides regulation-making powers to flesh out

298 See further paras 8.138–8.156 on the LA 2011 s1 power.

299 See: www.lgo.org.uk/make-a-complaint.

what this system might look like in future. The government statement announcing the new process explained that it would:[300]

- be a flexible, local, proportionate system avoiding unnecessary bureaucracy;
- include an element of independence from the local authority;
- seek to avoid duplication with existing arrangements for complaints and redress.

8.194 In February 2015, the Department of Health issued a set of consultation proposals, including a proposed new appeal system,[301] proposing that appeals could be brought on a narrow set of issues only and that the 'independent element' of the appeal process would be provided by 'reviewers', appointed by the local authority, who would not routinely meet the complainant, and who could only make recommendations, with the final decision being made by the local authority. In July 2015 the government announced that the proposed appeals system for care and support would be delayed and would be considered as part of the wider Spending Review.[302] In November 2015, the outcome of the Spending Review was announced, but did not include any reference to the appeals system under the Care Act 2014. In a written parliamentary answer given in March 2016, the government said that it planned to introduce the appeals system in April 2020.[303] But in December 2021, the government indicated that plans to implement the system would be kept under review (ie put on hold) indefinitely.[304] A challenge to the legality of this decision, based on a failure adequately to consult and a denial of effective access to a legal remedy to resolve social care disputes, was rejected by the High Court in *R (HL) v Secretary of State for Health and Social Care.*[305]

300 Minister of State (Norman Lamb) Public Bill Committee (Bill 123) 2013–2014, 4 February 2014, p585.

301 *Care Act 2014: cap on care costs and appeals*, Department of Health, 2015, www.gov.uk/government/consultations/care-act-2014-cap-on-care-costs-and-appeals.

302 Written Statement of 17 July 2015, Parliamentary Under Secretary of State, HLWS 135, Department of Health, Lord Prior of Brampton, 17 July 2015.

303 Parliamentary Question 32039, 24 March 2016.

304 *People at the Heart of Care: adult social care reform*, CP560, Department of Health, December 2021 https://www.gov.uk/government/publications/people-at-the-heart-of-care-adult-social-care-reform-white-paper.

305 [2023] EWHC 866 (Admin) At the writing of this chapter, it is under appeal.

Judicial review

8.195 There will be cases in which the complaints mechanisms described above do not provide an individual with an effective remedy to a local authority's refusal or failure to comply with its duties under the Care Act 2014. Typically, this might be the case where urgent remedial action is needed or where a mandatory order is required to compel the local authority to comply with its legal duties, particularly where the need is for care and support provision, such as accommodation. An applicant in these circumstances is likely to need to seek judicial review. The foregoing sections of this chapter are replete with examples of such cases.

The Mental Health Act 1983

After-care under Mental Health Act 1983 s117

8.196 MHA 1983 s117 imposes a duty on the relevant clinical commissioning group and local authority adult social care department to provide 'after-care' services under MHA 1983 s117 to those who cease to be compulsorily detained in certain circumstances and who leave hospital as a result.[306] This applies to those persons compulsorily detained under MHA 1983 s3, 37, 45A, 47 or 48, but not to those who were detained under section 2, which covers detention for an assessment, or to psychiatric treatment as a voluntary patient. The duty to assess a person's need for after-care support derives from the duty under National Health Service and Community Care Act 1990 s47, so this section survives the general repeal of pre-Care Act 2014 legislation[307] and the eligibility criteria applicable to the Care Act 2014 do not apply to such assessments.

8.197 There is no immigration exclusion applicable to MHA 1983 s117 equivalent to Care Act 2014 s21. Nor are after-care services an excluded service under NIAA 2002 Sch 3 para 1. Thus people will be eligible for after-care support under MHA 1983 s117 irrespective of their immigration status.

8.198 Until the Care Act 2014 came into force, what constituted 'after-care' services was not defined under the MHA 1983. By Care Act 2014 s75, a new subsection (6) was inserted into MHA 1983 s117 to

306 MHA 1983 s117(2).

307 Care Act 2014 and Children and Families Act 2014 (Consequential Amendments) Order 2015.

limit after care-services to services provided for the purpose of a) meeting a need arising from or related to the person's mental disorder; *and* b) reducing the risk of a deterioration of the person's mental condition, and accordingly reducing the risk of the person requiring admission to a hospital for treatment for mental disorder.[308] Such services can include social work, support in helping the person with problems of employment, accommodation or family relationships on discharge, the provision of domiciliary services, and the use of day centre and residential facilities.[309] Regulations have been enacted under MHA 1983 s117A[310] which introduce a limited 'choice of accommodation' for persons subject to section 117.[311] Charges cannot be levied for after-care services provided under MHA 1983 s117.[312]

8.199 The local authority responsible for providing after-care services will be the authority where the person was ordinarily resident prior to being detained.[313] MHA 1983 s117(4) gives the secretary of state power to resolve ordinary residence disputes.[314]

8.200 Many individuals entitled to support under MHA 1983 s117 will also have care and support needs under the Care Act 2014. Since the two Acts take a different approach to ordinary residence,[315] there is the risk the authority responsible for the support needs under the Care Act 2014 may be different to the authority responsible for the provision of care and support under section 117. This problem is addressed by Care Act 2014 s39(4) which provides that an adult who is being provided with accommodation under MHA 1983 s117 is to be treated for the purposes of the Care Act 2014 'as ordinarily resid-

308 MHA 1983 s117(6).

309 *Clunis v Camden and Islington Health Authority* [1998] QB 978, CA.

310 Care and Support and After-care (Choice of Accommodation) Regulations 2014 SI No 2670.

311 *Care and support statutory guidance*, Annex A, paras 44–50.

312 *R (Stennett) v Manchester City Council* [2002] UKHL 34, [2002] 2 AC 1127.

313 MHA 1983 s117(3).

314 See further *Care and support statutory guidance*, paras 19.62–19.68 – but note that this guidance should be read subject to the decision of the Court of Appeal in *R (Worcestershire CC) v Secretary of State for Health and Social Care and Swindon BC* [2021] EWCA Civ 1957, [2022] PTSR 833 and the *DHSC's position on the determination of ordinary residence disputes pending the outcome of the Worcestershire case*, Department of Health and Social Care, 22 September 2022.

315 See paras 8.100–8.106. Under the Care Act 2014, responsibility lies where the person is currently ordinarily resident rather than where they were ordinarily resident in the past.

ent in the area of the local authority in England or the local authority in Wales on which the duty to provide the adult with services under that section is imposed'.

8.201 Although the duty to provide after-care begins when the patient leaves hospital, the planning of after-care needs to start as soon as the patient is admitted to hospital. Clinical commissioning groups (CCGs) and local authorities should take reasonable steps, in consultation with the care programme approach care coordinator and other members of the multidisciplinary team to identify appropriate after-care services for patients in good time for their eventual discharge from hospital or prison.[316]

8.202 Assessment and planning should take place within the framework of the Care Programme Approach and should, like the assessment and planning framework under the Care Act 2014, involve, at least, the patient, nearest relative or family members, carers, relevant clinicians and other medical professionals at the hospital and in the community.[317] Where an independent mental health or mental capacity advocate has been appointed, the advocate should also be involved.

The Social Services and Well-being (Wales) Act 2014

Overview

8.203 Like the Care Act 2014 in England, the SSWB(W)A 2014 in Wales was intended to give effect to the recommendations made by the Law Commission in their *Adult social care* report as to the need to have a consolidated set of provisions governing the determination of needs and provision of care and support in Wales. The Welsh Act took a materially different approach from the Care Act 2014, seeking to consolidate adult care legislation but also care and support provision for children and families.[318] This section provides a brief overview of the powers and duties available to local authorities in Wales in respect

316 The *Mental Health Act 1983 Code of Practice*, Department of Health, April 2015, para 33.10.

317 See complete list of people who should be involved in the after-care planning process at para 34.12 of the *Mental Health Act 1983 Code of Practice*.

318 A summary of the duties and powers under the Welsh Act in respect of children and their families is set out at paras 9.249–9.265.

of adult care,[319] insofar as they are likely to be of relevance to migrant adults in need.

8.204 From a structural point of view, the SSWB(W)A 2014 and the Care Act 2014 are similar. Like the Care Act 2014, the SSWB(W)A 2014 sets out new general duties regarding well-being and prevention which did not feature in previous community care legislation. The list of factors relevant to defining well-being are similar in SSWB(W)A 2014 s2(2) as in the Care Act 2014, save that personal dignity is not referred to within the Welsh legislation. However, the importance of promoting and respecting dignity of the individual remains something that the local authority 'must have regard' to under SSWB(W)A 2014 s6(2) – another of the overarching duties governing the Act.

8.205 Another important feature of the SSWB(W)A 2014 is the imposition of a duty on anyone exercising functions under the Act in relation to an adult in need of care and support to 'have due regard' to the United Nations Principles for Older Persons, adopted by the General Assembly of the United Nationals on 16 December 1991.

Care and support for adults

8.206 Under SSWB(W)A 2014 s35 a local authority must provide care and support[320] to an adult[321] if:

- the adult is either ordinarily resident in the local authority's area or of no settled residence and within the local authority's area;
- the adult has a need for care and support which meets the eligibility criteria; or
- the local authority considers it necessary to meet their needs in order to protect them from abuse or neglect or any other harm, or a risk of abuse, neglect or other harm; and
- there is no charge for the care and support needed to meet those needs; or, if there is a charge, either the local authority is satisfied that the adult lacks mental capacity to make arrangements for the provision of care and support and has no one authorised to do so on their behalf under the MCA 2005, or the adult's financial resources are at or below a set limit, or the adult has nevertheless asked the authority to provide care and support.

319 A local authority in this context means either a county or borough council. See SSWB(W)A 2014 s197(1).

320 Defined by the SSWB(W)A 2014 as care or support or both.

321 'Child' means a person under the age of 18. See SSWB(W)A 2014 s3(3).

8.207 The duty under SSWB(W)A 2014 s35 is the counterpart to the duty under Care Act 2014 s18.[322] In order to determine whether the duty to provide care and support is owed, local authorities are required to carry out an assessment of the adult who it appears may need care and support.[323] The duty to assess applies both to an adult who is ordinarily resident in the authority's area and to any other adult who is within the authority's area. It does not appear to be a materially different test to that under Care Act 2014 s18 relating to adults physically present in the local authority's area. A similarly phrased duty to assess and consider the provision of care and support to adults in custodial settings in Wales as in the Care Act 2014 is set out at SSWB(W)A 2014 s185.

8.208 In carrying out the assessment the local authority must:[324]

- seek to identify the outcomes that the adult wishes to achieve in day-to-day life;
- assess whether, and if so, to what extent, the provision of care and support, preventative services or information, advice or assistance could contribute to the achievement of those outcomes or otherwise meet needs identified in the assessment; and
- assess whether, and if so, to what extent, other matters could contribute to the achievement of those outcomes or otherwise meet those needs.

8.209 'Outcomes' are not defined in the SSWB(W)A 2014 but refer back to the well-being principles as the framework for measuring personal outcomes of the adult needing support. This contrasts to the list of 'specified outcomes' contained in the Care Act 2014 framework.[325]

8.210 Under SSWB(W)A 2014 s36(3) local authorities have a power to provide care and support to an adult pending the completion of the assessment. Requirements as to the training and expertise of the person carrying out the assessment and record keeping are set out in Care and Support (Assessment) (Wales) Regulations ('CS(A)(W) Regs') 2015[326] regs 2 and 5.

8.211 Having carried out the assessment, the local authority will then be in a position to determine whether the adult's needs meet the

322 See paras 8.89–8.97.

323 SSWB(W)A 2014 s19(1) and (2).

324 SSWB(W)A 2014 s19(4). For further details about the assessment process and content, see the CS(A)(W) Regs 2015.

325 Care and Support (Eligibility Criteria) Regulations 2015 SI No 313 reg 2(2) as applied to the Care Act 2014.

326 SI No 1305 (W 111).

eligibility criteria. The eligibility criteria are contained in Care and Support (Eligibility) (Wales) Regulations ('CS(E)(W) Regs') 2015.[327] Needs will meet the eligibility criteria if:[328]

- the need arises from the adult's physical or mental ill-health, age, disability, dependence on alcohol or drugs, or other similar circumstances;
- the need relates to the adult's ability to carry out self-care or domestic routines; their ability to communicate; protection from abuse or neglect; involvement in work, education, learning or in leisure activities; the maintenance or development of family or other significant personal relationships; the development and maintenance of social relationships and involvement in the community; or achieving developmental goals;
- the need is one that the adult is unable to meet alone, with the care and support of others who are willing to help, or with the assistance of services in the community to which the adult has access; and
- the adult is unlikely to achieve one or more the outcomes identified in their assessment[329] unless the local authority provides or arranges care and support to meet the need, or enables the need to be met by making direct payments.

8.212 A person is considered to be unable to meet a need if doing so either:[330]

- causes significant pain, anxiety or distress to that person;
- endangers or is likely to endanger the health or safety of that person or another person;
- takes that person significantly longer than would normally be expected.

8.213 Whereas the eligibility criteria for the Care Act 2014 require that the adult is unlikely to achieve *two* or more outcomes to qualify for care and support, the Welsh eligibility criteria only require one or more to be unachievable without support.

8.214 Having completed the assessment process and carried out the eligibility determination, a local authority has a degree of latitude in deciding how to meet the eligible needs of an adult. In particular,

327 SI No 1578 (W 187).

328 CS(E)(W) Regs 2015 reg 3.

329 CS(E)(W) Regs 2015 reg 1(3).

330 CS(E)(W) Regs 2015 reg 6.

SSWB(W)A 2014 s34 provides the following examples of the way in which the adult's needs may be met by a local authority:

- by arranging for a person other than the local authority to provide something;
- by itself providing something;
- by providing something, or by arranging for something to be provided, to a person other than the person with needs for care and support.

8.215 The list of examples outlined in SSWB(W)A 2014 s34 of provision of care and support is not dissimilar to the list set out in Care Act 2014 s8.

8.216 The duties and powers under the SSWB(W)A 2014 to meet care and support needs are subject to the restrictions on the provision of support contained in NIAA 2002 Sch 3.[331]

Remedies

8.217 A person dissatisfied by the provision of services or discharge of social services functions by a local authority in Wales under the SSWB(W)A 2014 may lodge an internal complaint. The procedure for doing so, and the manner in which the complaint will be dealt with, are set out in SSWB(W)A 2014 Part 10 and the Social Services Complaints Procedure (Wales) Regulations 2014.[332]

8.218 If the person is dissatisfied with the outcome of the complaint, then they may seek to pursue their complaint with the Public Services Ombudsman for Wales.[333]

8.219 In circumstances where the complaints process does not provide an adequate remedy to an error of law on the part of a local authority, an affected person may seek judicial review.

331 NIAA 2002 Sch 3 para 1(1)(o). See paras 8.173–8.178.

332 SI No 1794 (W 187).

333 See: www.ombudsman.wales.

CHAPTER 9

Community care services for migrant children, families and care leavers

Shu Shin Luh and Connor Johnston

continued

Key points

- Local authorities in England have a general duty under Children Act (ChA) 1989 s17(1)[1] to make arrangements to safeguard and promote the welfare of children who are 'in need' and in the local authority's area. That general duty is supplemented by a mix of powers and duties under the other subsections of section 17 and Schedule 2 to the ChA 1989. The support that can be provided pursuant to ChA 1989 s17 may include cash, accommodation or assistance in kind, and may be provided to the child and/or to their family. As well as providing a mechanism to meet the needs of vulnerable children, support under ChA 1989 s17 may provide a safety net for destitute migrant families who are unable to access support elsewhere.
- The power is subject to exclusions which are contained in Nationality, Immigration and Asylum Act (NIAA) 2002 Sch 3,[2] which have the effect that support under ChA 1989 s17 may not be provided to a person who is in the UK in breach of immigration laws, among others, save to the extent necessary to avoid a breach of their rights under the European Convention on Human Rights (ECHR) or the European Union (EU) Treaties. This exclusion does not apply to children.
- Local authorities in England owe a duty to accommodate children in need who are without accommodation under ChA 1989 s20.[3] A child who is accommodated under ChA 1989 s20 for a period of 24 hours or more will be classed as a 'looked after' child.[4] This will give rise to additional rights and entitlements,[5] over and above the provision of accommodation, to ensure that the child's needs are met.
- A child who has been looked after by a local authority for a total period of 13 weeks or more, beginning on or after their 14th birthday and ending on or after their 16th birthday, will be classed as an 'eligible child'.[6] If the child ceases to be looked after before reaching the age of 18, they will become a 'relevant child'.[7] When

1 See paras 9.12–9.69.
2 See paras 9.195–9.217.
3 See paras 9.71–9.117.
4 See para 9.85.
5 See paras 9.85–9.195.
6 See paras 9.127–9.135.
7 See paras 9.136–9.159.

an eligible or relevant child reaches the age of 18, they will then be classed as a former relevant child.[8] These cohorts are owed particular duties under ChA 1989 Part III which may continue until they reach the age of 25 or beyond, reflecting the additional needs that they may have as a result of having been looked after for a significant period of time, and which are intended to assist them in making the transition to adulthood. Children and young people who have previously been looked after, but do not fall within one of these cohorts, are referred to as 'qualifying children'.[9] They too have certain, more limited, rights and entitlements, some of which may continue until they reach the age of 25. These young people will be referred to collectively as 'care leavers'.

- Local authorities have a discretion to assist young people who have missed out on the rights and entitlements enjoyed by care leavers as a result of some unlawful act or omission on the local authority's part.[10]
- The duties owed to care leavers are also subject to the restrictions imposed by NIAA 2002 Sch 3.[11]
- Local authorities exercising functions in respect of looked after children and care leavers are subject to a number of overriding principles, reflecting their status as 'corporate parent' to the child or young person, which the local authority must have regard to when exercising its powers and discharging its duties.[12]
- The relationship between support under ChA 1989 Part III and the Immigration and Asylum Act (IAA) 1999 is a complex one. Where a child, family or care leaver appears to be eligible for support under either statute, the question of whether responsibility lies with the Home Office or with the local authority will depend on the circumstances and immigration status of the person seeking support.[13]
- Local authorities in Wales owe similar duties to children, families and care leavers under the Social Services and Well-being (Wales) Act (SSWB(W)A) 2014 as those that are owed under ChA 1989 Part III by local authorities in England.[14]

8 See paras 9.160–9.174.
9 See paras 9.175–9.179.
10 See paras 9.186–9.194.
11 See paras 9.195–9.217.
12 See paras 9.218–9.225.
13 See paras 9.231–9.235.
14 See paras 9.249–9.265.

Introduction

Overview of chapter

9.1 The subject of this chapter is the community care services available from local authority children's services departments to migrant children who are in the UK with their families, and to those who are here as unaccompanied or separated children and young adults.[15] Specifically, this chapter will cover the duties owed to these groups under:

- ChA 1989 Part III (in England); and
- (more briefly) the SSWB(W)A 2014 (in Wales).

9.2 In respect of unaccompanied asylum-seeking children (UASCs), this chapter will look at the broad structure of support framework for them, as children's services will be the main source of the support which is available to this group. However, this group tends to face particular legal issues which are not experienced by other groups of children and young adults – for example, the potential need for an age assessment and the impact of their changing immigration status over the course of their time in care – which may have ramifications over and above the duties owed to them by children's services. The specific common issues pertaining to this group of children and young adults are subject to separate, more detailed examination in chapter 11. Advisers working with UASCs are likely to wish to refer to the relevant sections in this chapter and well as the specialist sections within chapter 11. Cross-references between the two chapters will be made where appropriate.

9.3 Those seeking a more detailed account of the support which is available to meet the needs of vulnerable or disabled children in general should consult *Children in need: local authority support for children and families*[16] and *Disabled children: a legal handbook*.[17]

9.4 This chapter will not set out in detail the law relating to the provision of education, in particular special educational needs (SEN), but

15 The term 'children's services' is used in this chapter, as opposed to 'social services'. The functions discussed in this chapter are, technically, both children's services and social services functions. See Children Act 2004 s18(2) and Local Authority Social Services Act 1970 s1A and Sch 1. However, the term 'children's services' will be used both for the sake of consistency and because it better reflects the administrative arrangements required of local authorities by the Children Act 2004.

16 I Wise KC et al, Legal Action Group, 2nd edn, 2013.

17 S Broach and L Clements, Legal Action Group, 3rd edn, 2020.

will touch on this subject to the extent that it relates to the provision of community care services for the children and young adults. Broadly speaking, any child of statutory school age, defined under Education Act (EdA) 1996 s8 as ages 5–16 years old in England and Wales, is required to be in full-time education irrespective of their immigration status. It is the responsibility of the child's parent to make sure that they receive appropriate education.[18] Children with SEN, irrespective of immigration status, are entitled to additional support, subject to an assessment of their SEN. For children in England, this is governed by Children and Families Act (CFA) 2014 Part 3; for children in Wales, it is governed by EdA 1996 Part IV. Readers seeking further information on this topic may wish to consult *Special educational needs and disability discrimination in schools: a legal handbook*.[19] Access to education as it pertains to UASCs and some common issues concerning access to student finance for this cohort are addressed at paras 11.116–11.126.

Changes within the Immigration Act 2016 and the Illegal Migration Act 2023

9.5 As with the asylum support regimes under IAA 1999 ss4(2) and 95, the Immigration Act (IA) 2016 also sought to introduce very significant changes which, if brought into force, will affect the division of responsibility for dealing with asylum-seekers, failed asylum-seekers and those in the UK in breach of immigration laws (among others), as between the Home Office and local authorities. The impact will, in particular, affect continued access to local authority support by certain children and their families and by certain care leavers, on the grounds of their immigration status. At the time when the IA 2016 was passed, there was much disquiet about the effect the provisions would have on certain categories of migrants' access support. However, four years on, these provisions have not yet been brought into force. At the time of writing in September 2022, it is not known when (or if) these changes will come into effect. Further, highly significant changes are also contained in the Illegal Migration Act (IMA) 2023 which will transfer responsibility for accommodating and supporting unaccompanied migrant children from local authorities to the Home Office.

18 EdA 1996 s7.

19 S Hannett, A McColgan and E Prochaska, Legal Action Group, 2017.

9.6 In outline, the key changes affecting the groups of children and their families addressed in this chapter are as follows:

- The definition of an 'asylum-seeker' in IAA 1999 s94(1)[20] and NIAA 2002 s18 will be extended to include those who have been refused protection and have either lodged further submissions relating to their claim which have not been determined, or have been granted permission to apply for judicial review in relation to the rejection of their further submissions.[21] This change is relevant in different ways to the division of responsibilities as between local authorities and the Home Office for supporting children with families and care leavers who are seeking to make further submissions in relation to their asylum claim.[22] In respect of households with children, responsibility which currently lies with local authorities will shift to the Home Office. In respect of care leavers, those who have made further submissions which have not yet been recorded as a fresh claim for asylum or determined substantively will fall outside of the scope of the exclusions under NIAA 2002 Sch 3.[23]
- The extended definition of asylum-seeker under IAA 1999 s94(5), encompassing certain failed asylum-seeking households with children,[24] will be abolished.[25] Responsibility for supporting this cohort currently lies with the Home Office.[26] Some of this cohort may be able to obtain support from the Home Office under the new power to support failed asylum-seekers contained in IAA 1999 s95A[27] or from their local authority under the new regime to be enacted under NIAA 2002 Sch 3 para 10A.[28] There will,

20 See paras 5.17–5.49.

21 IA 2016 Sch 11 Part 1 paras 3 and 31. See further *Reforming support for migrants without immigration status: the new system contained in Schedules 8 and 9 to the Immigration Bill*, Home Office, January 2016, para 19 (https://assets.publishing.service.gov.uk/government/uploads/system/uploads/attachment_data/file/494240/Support.pdf).

22 See paras 9.233–9.235.

23 See paras 9.195–9.217.

24 See paras 5.45–5.49.

25 IA 2016 Sch 11 para 7(5). See further *Reforming support for migrants without immigration status*, Home Office, January 2016, para 31.

26 See paras 9.232–9.233.

27 To be inserted by IA 2016 Sch 11 Part 1 para 9. See further *Reforming support for migrants without immigration status*, Home Office, January 2016, paras 31–37.

28 To be inserted by IA 2016 Sch 12 para 10. See further *Reforming support for migrants without immigration status*, Home Office, January 2016, paras 51–63.

however, be those who may well fall between those two provisions and are left without support.

- The new regime under NIAA 2002 Sch 3 para 10A is intended to create an entirely separate legal framework for supporting certain destitute migrant families who require leave to enter or remain in the UK but do not have it, and also *Zambrano* carers.[29] These families will no longer be able to access support from their local authority under ChA 1989 s17,[30] as a result of the new exclusion contained in NIAA Sch 3 para 3A,[31] and instead may be provided with support from their local authority under para 10A if certain statutory conditions are met.[32]
- Former relevant children[33] and qualifying children[34] who have limited leave to remain, who are seeking asylum or who have an outstanding application for leave to enter or remain, will no longer be eligible for grants toward their tuition fees from their local authority under ChA 1989 Part III. This will be achieved by means of a new exclusion in NIAA 2002 Sch 3.[35] This will have a consequential impact on the ability of this cohort to continue to be supported by the local authority after their 21st birthday.
- Fundamental changes will be made to the regime for supporting care leavers who do not have leave to remain in the UK but who face some practical or legal impediment to return to their country of origin. This group currently fall to be supported by their local authorities under ChA 1989 Part III.[36] That support will no longer be available.[37] Depending on their precise immigration status, they may be eligible for support from the Home Office under the new power contained in IAA 1999 s95A,[38] or from their local authority under a new regime enacted under NIAA 2002 Sch 3

29 *Ruiz Zambrano v Office National de l'Emploi (ONEm)* Case C-34/09 [2012] QB 265, CJEU. See paras 2.90–2.100. *Zambrano* carers are to be excluded from support under ChA 1989 Part III by means of a new para 7C to be inserted in NIAA 2002 Sch 3 by IA 2016 Sch 12 para 9.

30 See paras 9.12–9.69.

31 To be inserted by IA 2016 Sch 12 para 6.

32 See further C Johnston 'Housing difficulties for destitute migrant families unresolved', November 2016 *Legal Action* 12.

33 See paras 9.160–9.174.

34 See paras 9.175–9.185.

35 NIAA 2002 Sch 3 para 1A to be inserted by IA 2016 Sch 12 para 3.

36 See paras 9.118–9.194.

37 NIAA 2002 Sch 3 para 3B to be inserted by IA 2016 Sch 12 para 6.

38 To be inserted by IA 2016 Sch 11 Part 1 para 9. See further *Reforming support for migrants without immigration status*, Home Office, January 2016, paras 31–37.

para 10B.[39] The precise effect of the changes to support for care leavers is particularly unclear as in the year after the IA 2016 was given royal assent, parliament introduced Children and Social Work Act (CSWA) 2017 s1[40] which put on a statutory footing the corporate parenting role of local authority children's services toward looked after children and care leavers, and prescribed certain considerations to the approach that the local authority must take to fulfilling their role as a corporate parent.

- Under the IMA 2023 the Home Office will be given the power to accommodate and support unaccompanied migrant children under that Act.[41] Allied to this, the secretary of state will have the power to direct local authorities to cease looking after children, and transfer them to be accommodated (and vice versa).[42] The IMA 2023 itself contains little detail as to how these changes will be implemented and operated and it seems likely that such detail will need to be spelt out in regulations or policy.

England – support available to children, families and care leavers under Children Act 1989 Part III

Introduction

9.7 This section of the chapter will consider the community care services available to migrant children, families and care leavers in England under ChA 1989 Part III from their local authority's children's services department. It is concerned with both the services available to unaccompanied children and young people, and to children who are with their families. This section does not deal with the private law orders that may be made by the courts in family proceedings in respect of the upbringing of children under ChA 1989 Part II, or the machinery for taking children into the care of a local authority under ChA 1989 Part IV.

9.8 The material relating to migrant children is of principal relevance to those who have become separated from their families, perhaps owing to the circumstances in which they left their country of origin, or as a result of bereavement or domestic abuse, whether in the UK

39 To be inserted by IA 2016 Sch 12 para 10.

40 See paras 9.218–9.225.

41 IMA 2023 s16.

42 IMA 2023 s17.

or abroad. The law in this area, for the most part, is not significantly different from that which applies to children with British citizenship or indefinite leave to remain. Where that is not the case, that will be made clear. Further reading on the particular issues faced by UASCs may be found in chapter 11.

9.9 The material relating to migrant children with their families is of principal relevance to households who have either entered or remained in the UK without leave to do so, or those who have leave to enter or remain in the UK which is subject to a condition that they should have no recourse to public funds (NRPF).[43] Both of these cohorts are ineligible for mainstream housing[44] and welfare benefits[45] and support from children's services is likely to be the only safety-net available to them in the UK if they are unable to access support from friends, families or charities. However, there are important restrictions on the availability of support from children's services to those in the UK in breach of immigration laws which are contained in NIAA 2002 Sch 3. These are discussed at paras 9.195–9.217. The support available from the Home Office to migrant families seeking asylum is dealt with in chapter 5.[46] However, at paras 9.231–9.235 of this chapter the dividing lines between Home Office and children's services' responsibilities will be discussed, to assist in resolving the potential confusion that can arise from the interplay between the duties under ChA 1989 Part III and the IAA 1999.

9.10 The circumstances and needs of unaccompanied children are likely to be very different from those of migrant children who are with their families. The latter may simply need a roof over their head but be able to get emotional warmth and support from their parents and relatives. The former will inevitably need far more than that. The powers and duties owed to both children in families and unaccompanied children are contained in ChA 1989 Part III. The means by which they can access services is also the same, by way of an assessment of need under ChA 1989 s17.[47] The nature and extent of the support and the duration of the powers and duties may, however, differ as between the different cohorts of children, depending on whether they have family members or friends who are able to assist

43 'Public funds' as defined in Immigration Rules HC 395 para 6(2) (www.gov.uk/guidance/immigration-rules).

44 See chapter 7.

45 See chapter 4.

46 See paras 5.9–5.281.

47 See paras 9.30–9.43.

them in the UK. Where this chapter deals with a particular procedure, power or duty which relates only to unaccompanied children but not to children with families, or vice versa, that will be made clear.

9.11 In terms of structure, this section of the chapter is set out as follows:

- It begins by considering the general duty on local authorities under ChA 1989 s17(1) to provide services in order to safeguard and promote the welfare of children in the area who are in need. Those services may be provided to the children themselves or to their families, and may include the provision of accommodation. This is of particular relevance to migrant families who are without accommodation.
- The section will then move on to consider the specific duties owed to children in need who are without accommodation under ChA 1989 s20, which are supplemented by additional duties on the local authority to 'look after' the child in question. This is of particular relevance to children who have become separated from their families.
- The section will then discuss the duties owed to care leavers, that is, those who were formerly looked after by a local authority.
- The section will finish by considering the exclusions from support set out in NIAA 2002 Sch 3, then the overarching corporate parenting duties owed to looked after children and care leavers, followed by some general principles relating to the ways in which the provision of support under ChA 1989 Part III may be brought to an end.

Children Act 1989 s17 – support and accommodation for children and families

Overview of the Children Act 1989 s17 duty

9.12 ChA 1989 Part III contains the principal legal framework by which the children's services departments of local authorities in England[48] may provide support for children and families. The gateway to services under ChA 1989 Part III is section 17 which introduces the concept of the 'child in need' and places a general duty on local authorities to provide services to such children, and their families, in order to safeguard and promote their welfare. Specifically, under CA 1989 s17(1) it is the 'general duty' of every local authority:

48 ChA 1989 s16B.

- to safeguard and promote the welfare of children within its area who are in need; and
- so far as is consistent with that duty, to promote the upbringing of such children by their families;
- by providing a range and level of services appropriate to those children's needs. In this context, a 'local authority' is the council of a county or a metropolitan district, a London borough council or the Common Council of the City of London.[49] To facilitate the discharge of this duty, local authorities have a number of different powers and duties which are set out in ChA 1989 Sch 2 Part 1.[50]

9.13 The general duty is owed to all children within the area[51] of the local authority who are in need. The nature of this duty is discussed at paras 9.22–9.29 below.

The child in need

9.14 A 'child' is a person under the age of 18.[52] A child is taken to be 'in need' if:[53]

- they are unlikely to achieve or maintain (or to have the opportunity of achieving or maintaining) a reasonable standard of health or development without the provision of services under ChA 1989 Part III; or
- their health or development is likely to be significantly impaired (or further impaired) unless such services are provided; or
- they are disabled.

9.15 The terms 'health', 'development' and 'disabled' are defined by ChA 1989 s17(11):

- 'Health' means physical or mental health.
- 'Development' means physical, intellectual, emotional, social or behavioural development.

9.16 ChA 1989 s17(11) states that a child is disabled if they are 'blind, deaf or dumb or suffers from mental disorder of any kind or is substantially and permanently handicapped by illness, injury or congenital deformity or such other disability as may be prescribed'. Thirty years after its enactment, the language of this provision now seems

49 ChA 1989 s105(1).
50 See ChA 1989 s17(2).
51 See para 9.33.
52 ChA 1989 s105(1).
53 ChA 1989 s17(10).

particularly dated. The definition, it will be noted, does not precisely match the more modern definition of disability contained in Equality Act (EqA) 2010 s6. In particular, the effect of any 'illness, injury or congenital deformity' has to be permanent, in this context, as opposed to long term. However, in practice, there may not be much difference between the two definitions.

9.17 It will be noted that where a child is disabled, they are deemed to be a child in need. There is no margin for discretion here. In contrast, deciding whether a child is in need as a result of health or developmental factors will necessarily require an evaluative judgment on the part of the local authority. One exception to this principle has emerged from the case-law – which is that a child who is without accommodation may be taken to be a child in need.[54]

Services under section 17: what can be provided and to whom?[55]

9.18 Although the target of the duty under ChA 1989 s17(1) is the child in need, any service provided by a local authority in exercising its functions under ChA 1989 s17 and Sch 2 Part 1 may be provided for the family of a particular child in need or for any member of their family, so long as it is provided with a view to safeguarding or promoting the child's welfare.[56] This is consistent with the general duty under section 17(1) to promote the upbringing of children with their families so far as it is consistent with the welfare duty. Family, in this context, is to be interpreted widely, and encompasses any person with parental responsibility for the child as well as any other person with whom the child has been living.[57] The services provided to a child or their family may include (but are not limited to)[58] accommodation; assistance in kind; and cash payments.

9.19 The child's immigration status is irrelevant to whether duties and powers under the ChA 1989 apply. However, and because services

54 *R v Northavon DC ex p Smith* [1994] 2 AC 402, HL at p406; *R (G) v Barnet LBC* [2003] UKHL 57, [2004] 2 AC 208 at p224; *R (G) v Southwark LBC* [2009] UKHL 26, [2009] 1 WLR 1299 at para 28; *R (S and J) v Haringey LBC* [2016] EWHC 2692 (Admin) at para 37; *R (U and U (children)) v Milton Keynes Council* [2017] EWHC 3050 (Admin) at para 23.

55 See further paras 9.49–9.69 for a discussion of the case-law on the provision of financial support and accommodation under ChA 1989 s17(1).

56 ChA 1989 s17(3). See *R (MK) v Barking and Dagenham LBC* [2013] EWHC 3486 (Admin); and *R (OA) v Bexley LBC* [2020] EWHC 1107 (Admin), [2020] PTSR 1654 on the limits of this provision.

57 ChA 1989 s17(10).

58 ChA 1989 s17(6).

provided under ChA 1989 s17 and Sch 2 Part 1 may be provided to the family and not just the child, the immigration status of the parent is of critical importance to whether services will be provided. There are significant restrictions on access to services pursuant to ChA 1989 s17 contained in NIAA 2002 Sch 3, which are of principal application to migrant families who are in the UK in breach of immigration laws. These are discussed at paras 9.195–9.217.

9.20 Services provided under ChA 1989 s17 and Sch 2 Part 1 may be provided outside of the area of the responsible local authority;[59] a point which may be of particular importance to households with an itinerant lifestyle such as Traveller communities, or to households who have been dispersed around the country and require services in order to facilitate family life. However, where children and their families have existing ties to the local authority's area, consideration will always need to be paid to the impact on the children and their families of requiring them to leave the local authority's area in order to receive services.

9.21 The assistance that is provided pursuant to ChA 1989 s17 may either be unconditional or subject to conditions as to repayment.[60] In the context of community care services provided to vulnerable adults, it has been held that it is open to a local authority to attach other reasonable conditions to the provision of support, such as conditions restricting anti-social behaviour in relation to the occupation of accommodation.[61] It is generally accepted that the same principle applies to support provided under ChA 1989 s17.

The nature of the duty under Children Act 1989 s17

9.22 The language of ChA 1989 s17 is a little unusual, when viewed in the wider context of social welfare legislation, in that it is phrased as a 'general duty' which is directed at meeting the needs of children at large, rather than a specific duty owed to a particular child. The nature of this duty was the subject of the House of Lords decision in *R (G) v Barnet LBC*.[62] That case involved a single mother, G, who was a Dutch national of Somali origin. She had come to the UK from Holland with her young son, having been socially ostracised by her community. She applied to Barnet LBC's housing department for

59 *R (J) v Worcestershire CC* [2014] EWCA Civ 1518, [2015] PTSR 127.
60 ChA 1989 s17(7), subject to the limitations imposed by s17(8)–(9).
61 See *R v Kensington and Chelsea RLBC ex p Kujtim* [1999] 4 All ER 161, CA.
62 [2003] UKHL 57, [2004] 2 AC 208.

mainstream housing assistance[63] but was turned down because she did not satisfy the habitual residence test.[64] Following this, she sought assistance from children's services. Barnet assessed her child's needs as being best served by G returning with him to Holland, where she was entitled to welfare benefits and housing, and decided that the accommodation and subsistence payments which she had been provided with in the meantime would be terminated. Barnet accepted that G was suitable to look after her son and that it was not in his best interests to be removed from her care. Nevertheless, their position was that if G refused to return to Holland, they were not prepared to accommodate them together and instead would provide the child with a foster placement. G sought judicial review of Barnet's decision. Her case, by the time it came before the House of Lords, was that ChA 1989 s17(1) requires a local authority to assess the needs of a child who is in need and to meet their needs once they have been assessed. The House held, unanimously, that there was a duty to assess the needs of children within the area of a local authority who are in need.[65] However, a bare majority of three to two dismissed G's appeal, holding that ChA 1989 s17(1) was a general or 'target' duty as opposed to a specific duty to meet the assessed needs of every child in need within the area.[66] As King LJ went on to observe in the case of *R (J) v Worcestershire CC*:

> . . . the authority thereafter has a broad discretion, in the form of a power rather than a duty, to determine how and to what extent they will make provision for the identified needs, subject always to the public law safeguard provided by challenge by way of judicial review.[67]

Or, to put it another way, services under ChA 1989 s17 'are discretionary and not as of right to those who qualify'.[68]

9.23 However, this does not mean that a local authority has an unfettered discretion as to how it fulfils the target duty under ChA 1989 s17. The decision in *R (G) v Barnet* was a finely balanced one, provoking a strong dissenting judgment from Lord Nicholls (with whom Lord Steyn agreed) and there are a number of important

63 See chapter 7.

64 See paras 7.65–7.70.

65 See paras 9.30–9.38.

66 *R (G) v Barnet LBC* [2003] UKHL 57, [2004] 2 AC 208 at para 91 per Lord Hope, paras 106 and 109 per Lord Millet, and para 135 per Lord Scott.

67 [2014] EWCA Civ 1518, [2015] PTSR 127 at para 18.

68 *R (HC) v SSWP* [2017] UKSC 73, [2017] 3 WLR 1486 at para 43 per Baroness Hale.

safeguards which may be drawn from that case and from subsequent decisions and legal developments, which circumscribe the ambit of the local authority's discretion in this area.[69]

9.24 First, as noted above, there are the usual public law constraints. In particular, the exercise of the discretion to provide, or refuse to provide, services must promote the object and purpose of the statute,[70] which can be seen to be the safeguarding and promoting of the welfare of children in need within the area.

9.25 Second, the discretion operates in the context of the overarching obligation under Children Act (ChA) 2004 s11, which requires every local authority in England to make arrangements for ensuring that:

- their functions are discharged having regard to the need to safeguard and promote the welfare of children; and
- any services provided by another person pursuant to arrangements made by the person or body in the discharge of its functions are provided having regard to that need.

9.26 ChA 2004 s11 reflects the 'spirit, if not the precise language' of UN Convention on the Rights of the Child (UNCRC) Article 3 which requires that in all actions involving children, the best interests of the child shall be a primary consideration.[71] The weight that needs to be accorded to those interests may, depending on the facts of the case, result in the child's welfare taking precedence over strong countervailing considerations of public policy.[72]

69 In addition to these safeguards, which are of general application, specific provision is made under ChA 1989 ss17ZA–17ZF, directing the exercise of the CA 1989 s17 discretion in cases involving children with caring responsibilities (young carers) and adults caring for disabled children (parent carers). Parent carer assessments are described at para 9.36. Save for this, the details of those provisions lie outside of the scope of this text. For further reading, see S Broach and L Clements *Disabled children: a legal handbook*, Legal Action Group, 3rd edn, 2020.

70 *Padfield v Minister of Agriculture, Fisheries and Food* [1968] 1 All ER 694, HL; *R (J) v Worcestershire CC*, [2014] EWCA Civ 1518, [2015] PTSR 127 at para 31 per King LJ; *R (VC) v Newcastle City Council* [2011] EWHC 2673 (Admin), [2012] PTSR 546 at para 25 per Munby LJ; and *R (AM) v Havering LBC* [2015] EWHC 1004 (Admin), [2015] PTSR 1242 at para 33 per Cobb J.

71 *ZH (Tanzania) v SSHD* [2011] UKSC 4, [2011] 2 AC 166 at para 23 per Baroness Hale.

72 For example, in *ZH (Tanzania) v SSHD* where giving due weight to the best interests of the children led the Supreme Court to the conclusion that it would be a breach of ECHR Article 8 to remove their mother from the UK notwithstanding her 'appalling' immigration history.

9.27 The practical effect of ChA 2004 s11 in this context[73] is to require a decision-maker to demonstrate how the local authority has had regard to the need to safeguard and promote the welfare of children both individually and collectively.[74] In addition, the decision-maker will be expected to demonstrate that the impact on the child's welfare is proportionate.[75] Commenting on the nature of the ChA 2004 s11 duty in *R (HC) v SSWP*[76] (coupled, in that case, with the duty under Education Act 2002 s175) Baroness Hale observed that: 'Safeguarding is not enough: their welfare has to be actively promoted.'

9.28 Third, decisions made by local authorities about what services to provide under ChA 1989 s17 must be compatible with ECHR Article 8 (right to respect for one's private and family life, home and correspondence).[77] Whether a given decision results in a disproportionate interference with an individual or family's Article 8 rights will depend on the facts of the case.[78] See *R (MG (Iran)) v SSHD*[79] for an example of a case where a refusal to provide services to a father seeking to maintain contact with his son who lived 130 miles away constituted a disproportionate interference with his right to respect for family life under Article 8.[80] A decision which has been made without regard to the requirements of ChA 2004 s11 will not be 'in accordance with the law' for the purposes of Article 8.[81]

9.29 In assessing whether a refusal to provide services under ChA 1989 meets the exacting requirements described above, a court is

73 See para 9.43 for the practical effect of the duty on the assessment process under ChA 1989 s17; and paras 9.65–9.69 for its effect on decisions as to the location of accommodation.

74 *R (C, T, M, U) v Southwark LBC* [2016] EWCA Civ 707, [2016] HLR 36 at para 15 per Ryder LJ, citing *Nzolameso v Westminster City Council* [2015] UKSC 22, [2015] HLR 22 at paras 24–27 per Baroness Hale.

75 *R (C, T, M, U) v Southwark LBC* [2016] EWCA Civ 707, [2016] HLR 36 at para 17 per Ryder LJ and *R (G) v Barnet* [2003] UKHL 57, [2004] 2 AC 208 at para 135 per Lord Scott.

76 [2017] UKSC 73, [2017] 3 WLR 1486 at para 46.

77 Human Rights Act 1998 s6. The same would apply to the other Articles of the ECHR; but Article 8 is most likely to be relevant in this context.

78 *R (G) v Barnet LBC* [2003] UKHL 57, [2004] 2 AC 208 at para 69 per Lord Hope.

79 [2015] EWHC 3142 (Admin). This was an asylum support case. See chapter 5.

80 See further paras 9.203–9.217 for a more general discussion as to the circumstances in which support may be necessary to avoid a breach of the ECHR.

81 *ZH (Tanzania) v SSHD* [2011] UKSC 4, [2011] 2 AC 166 at para 23 per Baroness Hale.

entitled to subject the decision to 'strict and, it may be, sceptical scrutiny'.[82]

The duty to assess

9.30 In order to decide whether or not it is necessary to provide services under ChA 1989 s17 to a child or their family, the first step is for the local authority to carry out an assessment of the child's needs. Section 17, on the face of it, contains no requirement to carry out an assessment. Also, although ChA 1989 Sch 2 Part 1 para 3 empowers a local authority to assess a child's needs, the provision is couched as a discretion. However, as was held by Lord Hope for the majority in *R (G) v Barnet*, ChA 1989 s17(2) provides that, for the purpose of facilitating the discharge of the general duty under section 17(1), every local authority shall have the specific duties and powers set out in Schedule 2 Part 1. Schedule 2 Part 1 para 1 imposes a duty on local authorities to take reasonable steps to identify the extent to which there are children in need in their area. That 'will involve assessing the needs of each child who is found to be in need in their area as paragraph 3 makes clear'.[83] The effect of this analysis is that the obligation on the local authority to discharge its general duty under ChA 1989 s17, read together with Schedule 2 para 3, places local authorities under a duty to assess the needs of any child within the area who appears to be in need.

9.31 According to Department for Education's (DfE) statutory guidance *Working together to safeguard children*, within one working day of a referral being received, a local authority social worker should make a decision about the type of response that is required and acknowledge receipt to the referrer, and the maximum timeframe for the assessment should be no longer than 45 working days from the point of referral.[84]

9.32 The duty to assess under ChA 1989 s17 is a continuing one. Where there is a change in the circumstances upon which the conclusions of an assessment are based, then it will be necessary to carry out a reassessment. For example, in *R (ES) v Barking and Dagenham*

82 *R (VC) v Newcastle City Council* [2011] EWHC 2673 (Admin), [2012] PTSR 546 at para 26 per Munby LJ.

83 *R (G) v Barnet LBC* [2003] UKHL 57, [2004] 2 AC 208 at para 77 per Lord Hope. See also Lord Nicholls at para 32.

84 *Working together to safeguard children*, p33 para 78 and p34 para 82 (www.gov.uk/government/publications/working-together-to-safeguard-children—2).

LBC[85] the local authority had carried out a ChA 1989 s17 assessment concluding that the children in question were not children in need. Subsequently the family became homeless. No reassessment was carried out. Robin Purchas QC sitting as a deputy High Court judge held that the failure to carry out a reassessment following this change in the family's circumstances was unlawful.[86]

9.33 The geographical scope of the duty to assess is circumscribed by ChA 1989 s17(1). This provision applies to any child who is 'within [the] area' of the local authority in question. Unlike other contexts concerning social welfare law, this does not import a test of legal technicality, such as ordinary residence[87] or habitual residence.[88] 'Within the area' under the ChA 1989 requires only physical presence in the area of the local authority.[89] This may have the consequence that two or more local authorities owe the duty simultaneously. For example, in *R (Stewart) v Wandsworth LBC, Hammersmith and Fulham LBC and Lambeth LBC*[90] the claimant was placed by Hammersmith and Fulham (under the Housing Act (HA) 1996) in the area of Lambeth, and her children attended school in Wandsworth. The High Court held that the duty to assess under ChA 1989 s17 fell on both Lambeth and Wandsworth.[91] Although Hammersmith and Fulham was the authority which had placed the family in Lambeth, it had no continuing responsibility for the family under the ChA 1989.[92] The point is made forcefully (in the context of the provision of services to older children) in the statutory guidance, *Prevention of homelessness and provision of accommodation for 16 and 17 year old young people who may be homeless and/or require accommodation*:

> Where a 16 or 17 year old who was living in one local authority area and moves to another local authority area and seeks assistance from children's services in that local authority, the duty to assess falls on the authority area in which the young person is. The authority cannot refuse to consider the young person's immediate needs and expect

85 [2013] EWHC 691 (Admin).

86 See further *R (CO) v Lewisham LBC* [2017] EWHC 1676 (Admin).

87 See paras 8.100–8.106.

88 See paras 7.65–7.70.

89 *R (Stewart) v Wandsworth LBC, Hammersmith and Fulham LBC and Lambeth LBC* [2001] EWHC Admin 709, [2002] 1 FLR 469 at para 23 per Jack Beatson QC sitting as a deputy High Court judge; *R (AM) v Havering LBC* [2015] EWHC 1004, [2015] PTSR 1242 at para 33(xii) per Cobb J.

90 [2001] EWHC Admin 709, [2002] 1 FLR 469.

91 See also *R (AM) v Havering LBC* [2015] EWHC 1004, [2015] PTSR 1242.

92 Note that the placing local authority in such a case may have continuing responsibilities under HA 1996 Part VII. See chapter 7.

them to return to the authority in the area presumed to be their 'home' district.

...

It is essential that disputes about responsibility for the young person in the medium term should not get in the way of the authority that received the young person's request for assistance responding to the young person's immediate needs. The young person concerned must not be passed between local authorities and services whilst a decision is reached about which authority is responsible for assisting them.[93]

9.34 To prevent the possibility of one local authority having to assume an undue financial burden for assessing and supporting children who have come from another area, ChA 1989 s29 provides a mechanism by which the local authority providing services under ChA 1989 Part III may seek to recoup of costs of doing so from the local authority where the child is 'ordinarily resident'.[94] In *R (G) v Southwark LBC*[95] Baroness Hale (in the related context of accommodation under ChA 1989 s20) described this approach as being 'an important innovation in the forerunner provision in the Children Act 1948':

Local authorities have to look after the children in their area irrespective of where they are habitually resident. They may then pass a child on to the area where he is ordinarily resident under section 20(2) or recoup the cost of providing for him under section 29(7). But there should be no more passing the child from pillar to post while the authorities argue about where he comes from.[96]

In such cases, 'needs should be met first and redistribution of resources should if necessary take place afterwards'.[97] Therefore disputes between local authorities about responsibility for the provision of services and support under the ChA 1989 should not preju-

93 *Prevention of homelessness and provision of accommodation for 16 and 17 year old young people who may be homeless and/or require accommodation: guidance to children's services authorities and local housing authorities about their duties under Part 3 of the Children Act 1989 and Part 7 of the Housing Act 1996 to secure or provide accommodation for homeless 16 and 17 year old young people*, Ministry of Housing, Communities and Local Government (MHCLG) and DfE, April 2018 ('*Prevention of homelessness and provision of accommodation for 16 and 17 year old young people*'), paras 3.51 and 3.53 (www.gov.uk/government/publications/provision-of-accommodation-for-16-and-17-year-olds-who-may-be-homeless-and-or-require-accommodation).

94 For the meaning of 'ordinary residence' see *R v Barnet LBC ex p Shah* [1983] 2 AC 309, HL; and ChA 1989 s105(6).

95 [2009] UKHL 26, [2009] 1 WLR 1299.

96 [2009] UKHL 26, [2009] 1 WLR 1299 at para 28.

97 *R (AM) v Havering LBC* [2015] EWHC 1004, [2015] PTSR 1242 at para 33(xvi) per Cobb J.

dice the child and their family. Services should be provided by one or the other local authority while the local authorities access available dispute resolution processes.

9.35 *Working together to safeguard children* contains extensive guidance, promoting the provision of 'early help' as a means to promote the welfare of children, in order to prevent problems arising further down the line.[98] The idea is that this early help can be provided by local agencies and organisations working in conjunction with local authorities and, where appropriate, education, health and housing services, and the police. Whether a child or family would benefit from early help is to be based on an inter-agency early help assessment. In some cases, the guidance suggests, the provision of early help may have the result that a child in need assessment under ChA 1989 s17 is not needed. However, the guidance is clear that the provision of early help is not intended to supplant the role of children's services or be used as a form of gatekeeping, stipulating that 'if at any time it is considered that the child may be a child in need . . . or that the child has suffered significant harm or is likely to do so, a referral should be made *immediately* to local authority children's social care'.[99] Although the ethos underpinning the idea of early help is clearly benevolent, the statutory basis for its provision is unclear. ChA 1989 s17 is precisely the provision one would expect help of this nature to be provided under, yet if that is the case, the suggestions that a referral to children's services or a child in assessment could be dispensed with must surely be misplaced.

9.36 The assessment duty under ChA 1989 s17 is supplemented by an additional assessment duty in cases involving 'parent carers', defined by ChA 1989 s17ZD(2) as 'a person aged 18 or over who provides or intends to provide care for a disabled child for whom the person has parental responsibility' – ie adults caring for disabled children. In such cases, the local authority must carry out a 'parent carer's assessment' if the following criteria are satisfied:[100]

- the parent carer is within the area of the local authority;
- it appears to the local authority that the parent carer may have needs for support, or the local authority receives a request from the parent carer to assess their need for support;

98 *Working together to safeguard children*, p13.
99 *Working together to safeguard children*, pp15–16, para 10 (emphasis in original).
100 ChA 1989 s17ZD(1)–(5).

- the local authority is satisfied that the disabled child cared for by their family are persons for whom it may provide or arrange for the provision of services under ChA 1989 s17.

The purpose of the assessment is to establish whether the parent carer has needs for support and, if so, what those needs are.

9.37 These assessment duties are not contingent on the child's or household's immigration status. Providing the criteria described above are met, the assessment duty will arise irrespective of whether the child or their family have been granted leave to enter or remain or recourse to public funds.

9.38 In recent years there has been an increased tendency among some local authorities, when assessing the needs of families who are in the UK without leave to enter or remain, to involve the Home Office in the assessment process, either by having officers from the Home Office present during the face-to-face part of the assessment process, or by sharing information with the Home Office or otherwise. The reasons for this are rarely explained clearly to the family. Consent is sometimes not sought from the family. The chilling effect can be stark. Many will feel unwilling to give a complete account of their history and current situation for fear that this information will be used against them in some way, jeopardising their chances of remaining in the UK with their child or children. It is questionable whether such practices are consistent with the statutory purpose of the ChA 1989 s17 discretion or with the obligation under ChA 2004 s11.[101]

The duty to co-operate

9.39 In cases of the type described in paras 9.33–9.314, co-operation between local authorities will be essential[102] to ensure that the child is not passed from 'pillar to post' and that the assessment process is started timeously. In order to facilitate this, and the exercise of the functions under ChA 1989 Part III more generally, ChA 1989 s27 places a duty of mutual co-operation on local authorities.[103] Relying on this provision, a local authority may request the help of another local authority, and the latter authority must comply with that request,

101 See paras 9.24–9.27.

102 *R (Stewart) v Wandsworth LBC, Hammersmith and Fulham LBC and Lambeth LBC* [2001] EWHC Admin 709, [2002] 1 FLR 469 at para 28; *R (M) v Barking and Dagenham LBC and Westminster City Council* [2002] EWHC 2663 (Admin) at paras 17–18; *R (AM) v Havering LBC* [2015] EWHC 1004, [2015] PTSR 1242 at para 33(xiv) per Cobb J.

103 See also ChA 2004 s10.

in so far as it is 'compatible with their own statutory or other duties and obligations and does not unduly prejudice the discharge of any of their functions'.[104] Although ChA 1989 s27 does not impose a duty as between departments within a unitary authority,[105] the statutory guidance *Working together to safeguard children*[106] requires 'the same degree of co-operation between departments'.[107]

The requirements of a lawful assessment

9.40 The assessment process should culminate in a 'single plan of action',[108] and 'should set out what services are to be delivered, and what actions are to be undertaken, by whom and for what purpose'.[109] To that end, in the case of *R (AB and SB) v Nottingham City Council*[110] Richards J held that a document which was largely 'a descriptive document rather than an assessment' in which 'there was no clear identification of needs, or what was to be done about them, by whom and by when' did not meet the requirements of a lawful assessment. Similarly, in *R (MM) v Hounslow LBC*,[111] Sir Brian Keith observed that plans must be 'realistic' and not 'just a vague statement of good intent'. However, in considering whether an assessment meets these requirements, it must be remembered that such documents are drafted by busy social workers, meaning that they should not be subject to 'over-zealous textual analysis'.[112]

9.41 A lawful assessment under ChA 1989 s17 must necessarily examine not only the immediate, current circumstances of the child concerned but must also look to imminent changes in those circumstances. Applying this principle, the High Court in *R (K) v Manchester City Council*[113] granted a mandatory order requiring Manchester to

104 ChA 1989 s27(2).

105 For example, as between children's services and the housing department.

106 *Working together to safeguard children*, p34, para 79.

107 *R (M) v Islington LBC* [2016] EWHC 332 (Admin), [2016] HLR 19 at para 14 per Collins J, see also at paras 12–15; *R (C) v Hackney LBC* [2014] EWHC 3670 (Admin), [2015] PTSR 1011.

108 *Working together to safeguard children*, p22.

109 *Working together to safeguard children*, p32, para 71; see more generally paras 46–75.

110 [2001] EWHC Admin 235, (2001) 4 CCLR 295 at para 43.

111 [2015] EWHC 3731 (Admin) at para 9.

112 *R (MM) v Hounslow LBC* [2015] EWHC 3731 (Admin) at para 10 per Sir Brian Keith; *R (Ireneschild) v Lambeth LBC* [2007] EWCA Civ 234 at para 71 per Hallett LJ.

113 [2006] EWHC 3164 (Admin).

carry out a ChA 1989 s17 assessment in respect of a child in custody considering what his needs would be upon release. This approach is reflected in the *Working together to safeguard children* guidance which provides that 'assessment should be a dynamic process, which analyses and responds to the changing nature and level of need and/or risk faced by the child' and that 'known transition points for the child should be planned for in advance'.[114]

9.42 In addition, the assessment should be 'child-centred'[115] and 'must be informed by the views of the child as well as the family'.[116] This latter point reflects the requirement under ChA 1989 s17(4A) that, in providing services under section 17, due consideration should be given to the wishes and feelings of the child in question. This is a point which can sometimes be overlooked when assessing the needs of destitute migrant families who do not have leave to enter or remain in the UK or who are subject to an NRPF condition. In such cases there is sometimes a tendency to focus on the circumstance of the parent and whether their claim to be destitute is truthful.[117] While this is certainly an important factor in deciding whether or not a child is in need and, if so, what services should be provided, it needs to be remembered that ultimately, the assessment under ChA 1989 s17 is of the child and not the parent. A lawful assessment will always need to reflect this. This can be seen from the *Working together to safeguard children* guidance, which suggests that a good assessment will investigate the following 'domains':[118]

- the child's developmental needs, including whether they are suffering or likely to suffer significant harm;
- the capacity of parents or carers (resident and non-resident) and any other adults living in the household to respond to those needs;
- the impact and influence of wider family and any other adults living in the household as well as community and environmental circumstances.

9.43 The assessment (or other contemporaneous documentation, underpinning the decision-making process) will also need to demonstrate

114 *Working together to safeguard children*, p27, para 51 and p33, para 75.

115 *Working together to safeguard children*, p28, para 58.

116 *Working together to safeguard children*, p22.

117 See paras 9.44–9.48.

118 *Working together to safeguard children*, p29, para 59.

that the local authority has discharged its duty under ChA 2004 s11.[119] This means that the assessment should:[120]

- identify how the local authority has had regard to the need to safeguard and promote the welfare of the children both individually and collectively;
- demonstrate that the impact on the child or children's welfare of any decision about service provision is proportionate, when balanced against other countervailing factors such as the resources of the local authority.

The assessment of credibility in the context of determining need

9.44 Recent years have seen a marked increase in the number of cases coming before the courts in which migrant families have been refused support under ChA 1989 s17, because the local authority does not believe the family's claim to be destitute. Such cases often involve parents who have entered the country illegally or overstayed their visas and who have survived in the UK for some time, sometimes many years, relying on informal means of support from friends, family, or place of worship and the like. The parent or parents give only a vague account supported by limited evidence of how they have supported themselves in the UK. In such circumstances, it is perhaps not surprising that local authorities 'making difficult decisions in financially straitened circumstances, against a background of ever greater competing demands on their ever diminishing financial resources'[121] should exercise a degree of caution before accepting such accounts at face value.

9.45 On the other hand, the realities of the situation need to be born in mind. For example:

- Informal support networks are, by definition, informal: those seeking to avoid destitution may often have to rely on the kindness of individuals who they do not know well, if at all, and may only know them by their first name or think of them as their 'Auntie', or some other such term of respect or endearment.
- Those who provide support may be reluctant to be identified, lest their own precarious immigration status become known to the authorities.

119 See paras 9.25–9.27.

120 See *R (C, T, M, U) v Southwark LBC* [2016] EWCA Civ 707, [2016] HLR 36 at paras 15 and 17 per Ryder LJ.

121 *R (O) v Lambeth LBC* [2016] EWHC 937 (Admin) at para 17 per Helen Mountfield QC sitting as a deputy High Court judge.

- Those seeking support may well be vulnerable and have arrived in the UK as a result of trafficking, or have been subject to abuse and exploitation since their arrival. Such traumatic experiences may be difficult to recall or disclose. Mistrust of authorities may also play a role.
- Documentary evidence may also be hard to come by as a result of the restrictions on maintaining bank accounts contained in Immigration Act (IA) 2014 ss40–40G (a feature of the 'hostile environment'[122]) or where a person has occupied accommodation under an informal arrangement or an unlawful subletting agreement.

Factors such as these may mean that it is difficult for a person to present a full account of the means by which they have supported themself in the UK, supported by documentary evidence.

9.46 To assist in navigating these difficult waters, the courts have provided some guidance on how local authorities should approach the task of assessing a child's needs under ChA 1989 s17(1) in cases where there is some dispute as to whether their parent or parents are genuinely destitute. The starting point is that whether or not a child is in need is a question for the judgment and discretion of the local authority, and a local authority may be entitled to draw adverse inferences where a parent has failed to provide information during the assessment process.[123] However, before doing so, consistently with fundamental public law principles of fairness, the local authority must:

- **Make sufficient inquiries**. That is, the local authority should make those inquires which are either suggested by the applicant or which no reasonable authority could fail to undertake in the circumstances. In reviewing the steps taken in this regard 'it behoves courts to satisfy themselves that there has been sufficiently diligent enquiry' as 'such cases are of huge importance to the lives of the vulnerable children with whose interests they are concerned'.[124]

122 See paras 1.2–1.4.

123 *R (MN) v Hackney LBC* [2013] EWHC 1205 (Admin); *R (N) v Newham LBC* [2013] EWHC 2475 (Admin); *R (A) v Lewisham LBC*, Admin Ct, 5 May 2016 and *R (O) v Lambeth LBC* [2016] EWHC 937 (Admin).

124 *R (O) v Lambeth LBC* [2016] EWHC 937 (Admin) at para 17 per Helen Mountfield QC sitting as a deputy High Court judge.

- *Provide adequate reasons* – 'some basis other than "feel" ' must be articulated.[125]
- *Put any concerns to the applicant* so that they have the chance to make observations or representations before adverse inferences are drawn.[126]

9.47 Those seeking support, for their part, are well advised to 'give as much information as possible to assist the decision-maker in forming a conclusion on whether or not they are destitute'[127] and advisers may assist them by seeking to illicit as full an account as possible and seeking to gather documentary evidence in support.

9.48 Examples of cases where these principles have been applied include *R (O) v Lewisham LBC*[128] and *R (AC (children)) v Lambeth LBC*,[129] in which there was no impropriety in the assessment process. In contrast, a lack of procedural fairness led to the quashing of the decisions in *R (S and J) v Haringey LBC*,[130] *R (OK) v Barking and Dagenham LBC*,[131] *R (CO) v Lewisham LBC*,[132] *R (AA) v Bexley LBC*[133] and *R (AA) v Southwark LBC*.[134]

Financial and other support

9.49 As noted at para 9.18, support provided to a child or their family pursuant to ChA 1989 s17 may include (but is not limited to) cash payments.[135] The 'amount of support, in whatever form it may take, will inevitably vary from case to case and will therefore have to be the

125 *R (O) v Lambeth LBC* at para 17 per Helen Mountfield QC sitting as a deputy High Court judge.
126 *R (O) v Lambeth LBC* at para 20 per Helen Mountfield QC sitting as a deputy High Court judge. See further and more generally *Poshteh v Kensington and Chelsea RLBC* [2015] EWCA Civ 711, [2015] HLR 36 at para 45 per Elias LJ; *R v Hackney LBC ex p Decordova* (1995) 27 HLR 108, QBD at p113 per Laws J; and *R (Z) v Croydon LBC* [2011] EWCA Civ 59, [2011] PTSR 748 at para 21 per Sir Anthony May P, on the requirements of procedural fairness in circumstances where a local authority is minded to find that an applicant has lied.
127 *R (O) v Lambeth LBC* [2016] EWHC 937 (Admin) at para 18 per Helen Mountfield QC sitting as a deputy High Court judge.
128 [2017] EWHC 825 (Admin).
129 [2017] EWHC 1796 (Admin).
130 [2016] EWHC 2692 (Admin).
131 [2017] EWHC 2092 (Admin).
132 [2017] EWHC 1676 (Admin).
133 [2019] EWHC 130 (Admin).
134 [2020] EWHC 2487 (Admin).
135 ChA 1989 s17(6).

subject of individual assessment'.[136] As such, it might have been thought that there was little that could be said by way of general comments about the provision of financial support under ChA 1989 s17. However, in recent years, there has been an increasing tendency on the part of local authorities to adopt policies or practices which seek to circumscribe the levels of support that will be provided to destitute migrant families. On the one hand, the adoption of a policy or practice might be seen as laudable. It is readily understandable why a hard-pressed local authority facing an increase in demand for its services from families who are ineligible for mainstream benefits, might seek to ensure that its limited resources are allocated efficiently and consistently as between applicants. On the other hand, there is an obvious tension between a policy or practice which seeks to limit the financial provision that can be made to a family, with a statutory discretion which is designed to meet the individual needs of a particular child, assessed on a case-by-case basis. As such, it is perhaps no surprise that several such cases have fallen for consideration by the courts.

9.50 In *R (PO) v Newham LBC*,[137] Newham had in place a policy whereby a standard rate of subsistence payments would be paid to migrant families with NRPF. The family on whose behalf the case was brought, consisting of a mother and three young children, were paid £50 per week pursuant to the policy. The rates within the policy had been derived from the rates of child benefit payable to families with children by the Department of Work and Pensions (DWP). John Howell QC sitting as a deputy High Court judge held that the policy was unlawful. It is lawful in principle for a local authority to have in place a policy as to the level of services (for example, the level of financial subsistence payments) that it will provide. However, such a policy must have a rational starting point and must permit exceptions where there are exceptional circumstances. The starting point in Newham's policy was flawed: child benefit is not a benefit which is designed to meet the subsistence needs of children. It is a non-means tested benefit payable to those treated as responsible for a qualifying child or young person. In addition, the manner in which the rates in the policy had been derived from the child benefit figures lacked any rational basis. Further the policy was, on the local authority's evidence, operated in a rigid manner that permitted no exceptions.

136 *R (C, T, M, U) v Southwark LBC* [2016] EWCA Civ 707, [2016] HLR 36 at para 38 per Moore-Bick LJ.

137 [2014] EWHC 2561 (Admin), (2014) 17 CCLR 325.

9.51 The case of *R (C, T, M, U) v Southwark LBC*[138] also involved a challenge to the level of financial support provided to a migrant family. The first claimant, who was the mother to three young children, was a Nigerian overstayer. The family, who were awaiting the resolution of their immigration application, were provided with accommodation and subsistence in exercise of the power under ChA 1989 s17. The level of payments varied over time, but reached a maximum of around £216 per week to meet the needs of a family of four. On the claimants' application for judicial review, Bobbie Cheema QC sitting as a deputy High Court judge found that the level of support provided had not been irrational. The amounts provided were said to be the result of a detailed assessment of the children's needs, the assessments were responsive to changes in circumstances and the defendant retained the ability to make one-off payments where necessary. The decision was affirmed on appeal.[139] The Court of Appeal upheld the High Court's judgment on the facts and circumstances the appellants' case, but set down some important points of principles for policy formulation in the context of subsistence support for migrant families under ChA 1989 s17:[140]

- the legislative purpose of ChA 1989 s17, read in the context of ChA 2004 s11, was different to any other legislative scheme, including that contained in IAA 1999 ss4 and 95;[141]
- support provided under ChA 1989 s17 must always primarily be based on an assessment of all appropriate evidential factors and consideration of the child's welfare;
- support provided to a level sufficient solely to avoid destitution, and no more, is unlikely to be adequate;
- as such, the rates of support provided under ChA 1989 s17 should not be fixed by reference to the IAA 1999, child benefit or other such schemes, and it is likely to be irrational to limit support

138 [2014] EWHC 3983 (Admin).

139 *R (C, T, M, U) v Southwark LBC* [2016] EWCA Civ 707, [2016] HLR 36.

140 [2016] EWCA Civ 707, [2016] HLR 36 at paras 21–23 per Ryder LJ and paras 35–44 per Moore-Bick LJ.

141 The statutory regime for providing support to asylum-seekers and failed asylum-seekers in order to keep them from destitution. See chapters 5 and 6. In light of different legislative purposes of these regimes, doubt was expressed about the correctness of the decision in *R (Mensah) v Salford City Council* [2014] EWHC 3537 (Admin) in which a decision to make payments under ChA 1989 s17 in line with the amounts payable by the Home Secretary to failed asylum-seekers under IAA 1999 s4, was held to be lawful. See at para 29 per Ryder LJ and para 44 per Moore-Bick LJ.

to those levels, though they might permissibly be used as a cross-check.

9.52 In *R (BCD, by his litigation friend EGF) v Birmingham Children's Trust*[142] the High Court considered the legality of policies relating to the levels of subsistence support to persons with NRPF, which did not distinguish between households who were subject to NIAA 2002 Sch 3[143] (and thereby limited to support necessary to avoid a breach of the ECHR) and other NRPF households who were not subject to Schedule 3. The claimant, BCD, was a British child who was looked after by his grandmother, EGF, who was a Jamaican national, in the country lawfully in order to look after BCD following his mother's death, but subject to a NRPF condition. Under the defendant's policy the household had been paid subsistence payments in line with the rates paid to asylum-seekers under IAA 1999 s95.[144] The High Court held that it amounted to *Thlimmenos*[145] discrimination to limit the payments made to the claimants in this way, and that they were entitled to receive support sufficient to meet their welfare needs and not simply to avoid destitution.

9.53 The reported cases referred to above have tended to focus on financial support and, in particular, the minimum acceptable levels of financial support which may be provided to families who do not have recourse to public funds, by way of regular payments. However, it is important to remember that support in kind (non-cash) may also be provided under ChA 1989 s17.[146] In addition, these cases should be regarded as setting a floor for what may be acceptable and not a ceiling. If a child has needs which are not met by means of such subsistence payments – for example, if additional funds are needed to purchase a school uniform or allow the child to participate in school trips, have toys to play with or any other such matter which is integral to their development – then there is nothing to preclude the local authority from meeting those needs. As noted above, if a child is in need, their immigration status should not operate as a bar to the local authority meeting their needs under ChA 1989 s17.[147]

142 [2023] EWHC 137 (Admin), (2023) 26 CCLR 135.

143 See paras 9.195–9.205.

144 See paras 5.185–5.200.

145 *Thlimmenos v Greece* App No 34369/97 (2000) 31 EHRR 15, ECtHR: without an objective and reasonable justification, failing to treat differently persons whose situations are significantly different.

146 ChA 1989 s17(6).

147 See para 9.19.

Accommodation

9.54 One of the ways in which local authorities may perform the duty under ChA 1989 s17(1) is by providing accommodation.[148] This is of particular importance to homeless migrant families, who are ineligible for mainstream homelessness assistance[149] and welfare benefits.[150] Case-law has established that a child who is without accommodation is a child in need.[151] The obvious and rational way in which to meet that need will be through the provision of accommodation for the child, together with the child's family, or the provision of the means to pay for it. Some local authorities have been known to threaten to accommodate migrant children separately from their parents, ostensibly as a means of gate-keeping, by discouraging the family from pursuing their claim for support for fear that their household will be split up. Such practices are unlikely to be consistent with the principles outlined at paras 9.23–9.29.

9.55 The potential for migrant families to need accommodation under ChA 1989 s17 has been rendered more acute by the 'right to rent' regime under IA 2014 ss20–21, restricting the right of certain migrants to access accommodation in the private rented sector.[152] This is one of the key features of the 'hostile environment' policy. One of the consequences of the right to rent regime is that even those who have the financial resources to rent privately may lack the legal right to do so, thereby forcing them to turn to children's services for support. Plainly, this is a factor which local authorities called upon to provide accommodation may need to take into account when carrying out an assessment under ChA 1989 s17.

9.56 For example, in *R (U and U (children)) v Milton Keynes Council*[153] the claimants and their mother were overstayers. The mother had an outstanding application for leave to remain. She sought assistance from children's services. This was refused, as the local authority did not accept that she was destitute and (implicitly) thought she had

148 ChA 1989 s17(6).

149 See chapter 7.

150 See chapter 4.

151 *R v Northavon DC ex p Smith* [1994] 2 AC 402, HL at p406; *R (G) v Barnet LBC* [2003] UKHL 57, [2004] 2 AC 208 at p224; *R (G) v Southwark LBC* [2009] UKHL 26, [2009] 1 WLR 1299 at pp1308D–1308F; *R (S and J) v Haringey LBC* [2016] EWHC 2692 (Admin) at para 37; *R (U and U (children)) v Milton Keynes Council* [2017] EWHC 3050 (Admin) at para 23.

152 See paras 7.389–7.434.

153 [2017] EWHC 3050 (Admin), (2018) 21 CCLR 199.

sufficient resources to rent a room. Upper Tribunal Judge Markus QC sitting as a High Court judge found that the local authority had acted unlawfully by failing to have regard to the possible impact of the right to rent provisions on the mother's ability to access accommodation.[154] A suggestion that the family could circumvent the right to rent provisions by staying in a series of different hotels for short periods of time was dismissed, as the suitability of such an arrangement had never been considered.

9.57 In contrast, in the case of *R (Stewart) v Birmingham City Council*[155] a challenge brought in similar circumstances was rejected by the High Court. The family in that case had an in-country right of appeal against the refusal of their application for leave to remain. Jeremy Baker J observed that under the relevant Home Office policy, permission to rent would normally be granted in such cases and 'in the absence of knowledge of particular difficulties to the contrary', the local authority had been entitled to rely on the possibility of the claimant accessing alternative accommodation using his own resources. The different outcome in these two cases makes it difficult to isolate a clear proposition of law as to the impact of the right to rent on decisions about accommodation under ChA 1989 s17. Perhaps the most that can be said is that the personal circumstances of an individual will impact on the likelihood of them obtaining permission to rent and the lesser the chances of them obtaining permission the greater the likelihood that a failure on the part of a local authority to consider this issue will invalidate a refusal to provide accommodation. However, bearing in mind the complexity of the right to rent provisions and the difficulties which a destitute family are likely to have navigating them, it might be best practice for local authorities to consider the impact of the right to rent in all cases.

9.58 The provision of accommodation under ChA 1989 s17 is unlikely to apply to unaccompanied children who will, in the overwhelming majority of cases, meet the criteria for accommodation under ChA 1989 s20 instead.[156] ChA 1989 s20 being a duty, it takes priority over the discretion to accommodation under section 17.[157] Accommodation under ChA 1989 s20 will give rise to a number of associated

154 See *R (AA) v Bexley LBC* [2019] EWHC 130 (Admin) for another example of this.

155 [2018] EWHC 61 (Admin), [2018] PTSR 1204.

156 See paras 9.71–9.117.

157 *R (G) v Southwark LBC* [2009] UKHL 26, [2009] 1 WLR 1299.

entitlements[158] which are of particular importance to children who do not have anyone with parental responsibility who is willing or able to provide them with care and accommodation. It is for that reason that the courts have emphasised that, save in very rare cases (and only where the criteria for accommodation under ChA 1989 s20 are not met), lone children should be accommodated under that provision and not section 17. Describing a placement as 'section 17 accommodation' will not mean that the section 20 duty has not arisen.[159]

9.59 Where accommodation is provided pursuant to ChA 1989 s17, there is no express requirement that such accommodation should be suitable. However, in *R (Yekini) v Southwark LBC*[160] Michael Fordham QC sitting as a deputy High Court judge observed that the public law obligation on a local authority to act reasonably in exercising its power to provide accommodation 'may to a large extent come to, in effect, a requirement of suitability'.[161] However, it is the authors' view that this probably understates the legal requirements of the ChA 1989. Accommodation that is unsuitable for a child is, by definition, accommodation that is detrimental to the child's welfare and that is not appropriate to their needs. As such, a local authority exercising its power under ChA 1989 s17 by providing unsuitable accommodation would not be acting consistently with the object and purpose of that power or with ChA 2004 s11,[162] irrespective of whether its actions could be impugned as irrational or unreasonable.

9.60 In the absence of a detailed statutory code or guidance governing the suitability of accommodation, as can be found in relation to homelessness accommodation provided under HA 1996 Part VII,[163] it has been left to the courts to regulate the position as best they can. In practice, the substantive requirements placed on local authorities have not been especially onerous and the provision of accommodation which is far from optimal has been held to have been lawful in a number of cases.

158 See paras 9.85–9.95.
159 This issue is discussed in detail at paras 9.104–9.117.
160 [2014] EWHC 2096 (Admin).
161 [2014] EWHC 2096 (Admin) at para 47.
162 See paras 9.24–9.27.
163 See paras 7.239–7.252. For example, under Homelessness (Suitability of Accommodation) (England) Order 2003 SI No 3326 arts 3 and 4 it is unlawful for a local housing authority to place an applicant with family commitments in B&B accommodation save where there is no other accommodation available and, even then, for no longer than six weeks.

9.61 In *R (C, T, M, U) v Southwark LBC*[164] the claimants, a mother with three young children, sought to challenge a seven-month period in bed and breakfast (B&B) type accommodation provided pursuant to ChA 1989 s17(1). Bobbie Cheema QC sitting as deputy High Court judge dismissed the claim. It was recognised that 'the accommodating of this mother with young children in a single room in bed and breakfast accommodation for anything longer than a few weeks or so, was inappropriate and bound to have some adverse effect on them'.[165] However, while 'regrettable', it did not have 'such an adverse impact' that it was unlawful or irrational.[166] The court noted in passing that the *Homelessness: code of guidance for local authorities*,[167] which provides detailed guidance to local housing authorities on, among other things, the suitability of accommodation including overcrowding and the use of B&Bs, was not binding on children's services. This decision was upheld by the Court of Appeal.[168]

9.62 In *R (MM) v Hounslow LBC*[169] a decision that accommodation provided in a maisonette on the upper floor of a block of flats was suitable for a 15-year-old autistic boy with challenging behaviour who sometimes needed to use a wheelchair to go outside, was held to be rational.

9.63 In *R (AE) v Brent LBC*[170] a decision that the claimant and her children should be housed within a one-hour journey of the claimant's parents and the children's school was held not to be unreasonable. This was notwithstanding that the claimant had previously been imprisoned for terrorism offences, instigated by her husband, and that there was a need for her to maintain links with her parents both in order to 'safeguard . . . the emotional social and psychological welfare of the children'[171] and 'to support and reinforce the gains she has made in freeing herself from the psychological influenced that [her husband] had upon her and the catastrophic consequences that followed for herself and her children'.[172]

164 *R (C, T, M, U) v Southwark LBC* [2014] EWHC 3983 (Admin) at paras 49–51.
165 [2014] EWHC 3983 (Admin) at para 51.
166 [2014] EWHC 3983 (Admin) at para 51.
167 Department of Communities and Local Government (DCLG), 2006 – since replaced by the 2018 version of the code (www.gov.uk/guidance/homelessness-code-of-guidance-for-local-authorities). See chapter 7.
168 *R (C, T, M, U) v Southwark LBC* [2016] EWCA Civ 707, [2016] HLR 36.
169 [2015] EWHC 3731 (Admin).
170 *R (AE) v Brent LBC* [2018] EWHC 2574 (Admin).
171 [2018] EWHC 2574 (Admin) at para 19.
172 [2018] EWHC 2574 (Admin) at para 18.

9.64 The reluctance of the court to intervene in substantive challenges to the suitability of accommodation provided under ChA 1989 s17 may perhaps reflect the fact that housing is 'the function of the local housing authority' rather than the 'principal or primary purpose' of ChA 1989 Part III,[173] as well as the high threshold which is faced in any public law case by a claimant who seeks to persuade a court that a public body has acted irrationally. However, this is not to say that the courts will not intervene in an appropriate case – but they are perhaps more likely to do so in cases where there has been a procedural failing on the part of the local authority. For example, where the decision to place a family in a given unit of accommodation, or in a given location, is the product of a flawed assessment process.[174] Alternatively, judicial intervention may be appropriate where there has been a failure to discharge the duty under ChA 2004 s11,[175] or where insufficient respect has been afforded to the rights of the child or the child's family under ECHR Article 8. To see how these legal obligations may be relevant to the provision of accommodation under ChA 1989 s17(1), consideration of cases from other jurisdictions may be instructive.[176]

9.65 In *Nzolameso v Westminster City Council*[177] the Supreme Court held that a decision of Westminster City Council to place a single mother with five children in the area of Milton Keynes, pursuant to its homelessness duties under HA 1996 Part VII,[178] was unlawful. Not only had Westminster failed to discharge the particular statutory duties under HA 1996 Part VII relating to the location of accommodation – but there had also been a failure properly to discharge the ChA 2004 s11 duty. Baroness Hale described the interplay between ChA 2004 s11 and HA 1996 Part VII, and the practical effect of ChA 2004 s11, in the following terms:

> The question of whether the accommodation offered is 'suitable' for the applicant and each member of her household clearly requires the local authority to have regard to the need to safeguard and promote the welfare of any children in her household. Its suitability to meet

173 *R (G) v Barnet LBC* [2003] UKHL 57, [2004] 2 AC 208 at para 92 per Lord Hope.

174 See paras 9.40–9.48.

175 See paras 9.25–9.27.

176 A detailed discussion of the suitability of asylum-support accommodation (including the location of such accommodation) may be found at paras 5.154–5.184. Suitability in the context of the provision of accommodation to homeless persons under HA 1996 Part VII is discussed at paras 7.239–7.252.

177 [2015] UKSC 22, [2015] HLR 22.

178 See para 7.241.

their needs is a key component in its suitability generally. In my view, it is not enough for the decision-maker simply to ask whether any of the children are approaching GCSE or other externally assessed examinations. Disruption to their education and other support networks may be actively harmful to their social and educational development, but the authority also have to have regard to the need to promote, as well as to safeguard, their welfare. The decision maker should identify the principal needs of the children, both individually and collectively, and have regard to the need to safeguard and promote them when making the decision.[179]

9.66 The Court of Appeal in *R (C, T, M, U) v Southwark LBC*[180] accepted that these principles applied equally in the context of ChA 1989 s17(1) and that the considerations identified by Baroness Hale would need to be factored into the assessment process.[181]

9.67 In *R (E) v Islington LBC*,[182] further consideration was given to the practical impact of ChA 2004 s11, in relation to the decision of a local housing authority to accommodate a school age child in a different borough. Ben Emmerson QC sitting as a deputy High Court judge explained that:

> . . . it follows from the terms of section 11(2)(b) that where an authority's housing department is considering whether to transfer a school-age child out of borough, the authority must take all necessary steps to satisfy itself that the receiving authority has satisfactory arrangements in place to safeguard the child's educational welfare. If the principles laid down in *Nzolameso* fall to be applied to this statutory duty, as I find they do, then the sending authority would also need to put itself in a position to demonstrate objectively, and by reference to contemporary reasoning and records, how and why it came to the conclusion (if it did) that the delegation of its housing obligations would not imperil the child's educational welfare. In practice, this is something that the sending authority could only be able to do if they had liaised with the education department of the receiving authority and satisfied themselves that suitable arrangements were or would be in place.[183]

9.68 In *R (MG (Iran)) v SSHD*,[184] the court had to consider the impact of Borders, Citizenship and Immigration Act (BCIA) 2009 s55, which

179 *Nzolameso v Westminster City Council* [2015] UKSC 22, [2015] HLR 22 at para 27.

180 [2016] EWCA Civ 707, [2016] HLR 36 at para 15 per Ryder LJ.

181 See para 9.43.

182 [2017] EWHC 1440 (Admin), [2018] PTSR 349.

183 *R (E) v Islington LBC* [2017] EWHC 1440 (Admin), [2018] PTSR 349 at para 117.

184 [2015] EWHC 3142 (Admin). See paras 5.131 and 5.184.

is the counterpart to ChA 2004 s11 that applies in the context of immigration and asylum, on a decision of the Home Office to accommodate a father 150 miles from his son. The court held that the Home Office's refusal to provide either accommodation or travel expenses in order to facilitate contact between the pair constituted a breach of BCIA 2009 s55 and ECHR Article 8. There had been a failure to have regard to the need to promote the son's welfare meaning that the interference with their Article 8 rights had not been justified.

9.69 These cases do not seek to lay down any bright-line rule as to particular types of accommodation which will or will not be suitable. However, they give an indication of the type of factors which are likely to be relevant to the assessment of suitability. Such factors may include:

- the personal circumstances and characteristics of the household;
- location, in relation to schools[185] with places available, appropriate medical facilities and support networks;
- whether the physical layout of the property meets the disability related needs of the child (for example, a property with a lift or without stairs might be required for a child in a wheelchair);
- the space and arrangement of the property (for example, whether two children over the age of ten of the opposite sex have to share a bedroom);[186]
- the physical condition of the property.

Other education-related support

9.70 In addition to the various forms of support set out above, there are a number of additional forms of education-related support which may be available to nursery and school age children to supplement any support they receive under ChA 1989 s17. Although such support is not provided under ChA 1989 Part III, it is included here for completeness. In particular:

- All children in reception, year one and year two, irrespective of immigration status, have a statutory entitlement to free school

185 *Home to school travel and transport guidance*, DfE, July 2014, last updated December 2016 (www.gov.uk/government/publications/home-to-school-travel-and-transport-guidance) sets out recommended maximum travel times to school. A maximum each way journey of 45 minutes represents best practice for a primary school age child and 75 minutes for a secondary school age child. See para 34.

186 See HA 1985 ss324–326.

meals.[187] Until recently, children older than this whose parents did not have recourse to public funds would not normally have been eligible, as eligibility for this cohort is generally linked to the parents' eligibility for certain mainstream benefits. However, during the COVID-19 pandemic the government extended free school meal eligibility to encompass the children of: *Zambrano* carers;[188] families with NRPF with a right to remain under ECHR Article 8; families receiving support under ChA 1989 s17; and families supported under IAA 1999 s4(2) among others,[189] and has since confirmed that this extension will be permanent.[190]

- The following may be eligible for free nursery places: two-year-old children of: *Zambrano* carers; families with no recourse to public funds with a right to remain under ECHR Article 8; families in receipt of support under IAA 1999 s4(2) or s95(1); and families receiving support under ChA 1989 s17.[191]
- All children with SEN, irrespective of immigration status, are entitled to additional support, subject to an assessment of their SEN. For children in England this is governed by CFA 2014 Part 3. For children in Wales it is governed by EdA 1996 Part IV.[192]

187 EdA 1996 s512ZB; *Free school meals: guidance for local authorities, maintained schools, academies and free schools,* DfE, last updated April 2018 (www.gov.uk/government/publications/free-school-meals-guidance-for-schools-and-local-authorities).

188 See paras 2.90–2.100.

189 *Coronavirus (COVID-19): temporary extension of free school meals eligibility to NRPF groups,* DfE, January 2021, updated June 2021 (www.gov.uk/government/publications/covid-19-free-school-meals-guidance/guidance-for-the-temporary-extension-of-free-school-meals-eligibility-to-nrpf-groups).

190 *Providing free school meals to families with no recourse to public funds (NRPF),* DfE, 9 June 2022 (https://www.gov.uk/government/publications/free-school-meals-guidance-for-schools-and-local-authorities/providing-free-school-meals-to-families-with-no-recourse-to-public-funds-nrpf).

191 Childcare Act 2006 s7; Local Authority (Duty to Secure Early Years Provision Free of Charge) Regulations 2014 SI No 2147; *Extending eligibility for the free early education entitlement for two year olds,* DfE, August 2019 (www.gov.uk/help-with-childcare-costs/free-childcare-2-year-olds); 'Extension to two-year-old free early nursery scheme for NRPF families', December 2020/January 2021 *Legal Action* 12.

192 S Hannett, A McColgan and E Prochaska *Special educational needs and disability discrimination in schools: a legal handbook,* Legal Action Group, 2017.

Children Act 1989 s20 – accommodation for children and the duties owed to looked after children

Overview of the Children Act 1989 s20 duty

9.71 The general duty under ChA 1989 s17(1) to provide services with a view to safeguarding and promoting the welfare of children within their area who are in need, is supplemented by two specific duties[193] under ChA 1989 s20 to accommodate certain children in need who require accommodation. These duties are complemented by two further powers to provide accommodation to a child or young person, with a view to safeguarding and promoting their welfare.[194] These powers are exercisable even if the child or young person has suitable accommodation available to them.

9.72 The duties under ChA 1989 s20 are absolute. Where the criteria (considered in detail below) are satisfied, accommodation *must* be provided and a local authority cannot side-step the duty by claiming to have acted under some other power, such as ChA 1989 s17.[195] The legislative purpose underpinning ChA 1989 s20 is clear: that the state should not countenance the ignominy of homeless children. Read together with ChA 1989 s17(1) and (6),[196] IAA 1999 ss95(1) and 122(1)–(3)[197] and HA 1996 ss188(1), 190(2), 193(2) and 193C(3),[198] it forms an integral part of a larger safety net which, when deployed effectively, should ensure that no child within the jurisdiction is without accommodation. An important element of the support that ChA 1989 s20 provides to this safety net is that it does not depend on the child's immigration status. A child who meets the criteria must be accommodated, irrespective of where they come from or whether or not they have leave to remain in the UK.

9.73 It is under ChA 1989 s20 that unaccompanied migrant children in need of accommodation should be accommodated, and not under the general powers under ChA 1989 s17. Such children will, in the overwhelming majority of cases, have needs over and above the need for a roof over their head.[199] The legal duties to meet those needs are

193 ChA 1989 s20(1) and (3). See paras 9.80–9.82 and 9.83 respectively.
194 ChA 1989 s20(4) and (5). See para 9.84.
195 See paras 9.12–9.69.
196 See paras 9.12–9.69.
197 See paras 5.9–5.206.
198 See paras 7.236–7.293.
199 Even in those rare cases where their needs are limited to a roof over their head, they should still be accommodated under ChA 1989 s20 and not s17.

found in ChA 1989 ss22–22D which require the local authority to step into the shoes of the child's parent by 'looking after' and 'maintaining' them.[200] The duties only arise where the child has been accommodated under ChA 1989 s20 for 24 hours or more, and do not arise where the child has been accommodated under ChA 1989 s17(1). A child who has been looked after by a local authority for a period of 13 weeks or more, beginning after their 14th birthday and ending after their 16th birthday, will then be entitled to a further set of duties as a 'care leaver' designed to replicate the support which might be given by a reasonable parent, to assist the child in making the transition to adulthood.[201] It is because of these additional entitlements that the courts have emphasised that, save in very rare cases, lone children should be accommodated under ChA 1989 s20.[202]

9.74 In contrast, ChA 1989 s20 will generally be of limited assistance to migrant families who are without accommodation. In *R (G) v Barnet LBC*,[203] an attempt to press ChA 1989 s20 into service for precisely this purpose was rejected by the House of Lords. That case involved three households, two of whom were migrant families who were without accommodation but who were ineligible for assistance under the HA 1996.[204] The claimants sought to argue that the defendant local authorities were required to accommodate the children under ChA 1989 s20(1) and that 'in fulfilment of this duty they were required by section 23(6) to provide the mothers with accommodation so that their children could live with them'.[205] The effect of ChA 1989 s23(6),[206] on which the claimants sought to rely in advancing their argument, was to require a local authority looking after a child to make arrangements to enable the child to live with their parents. The House of Lords rejected this line of argument. The children had been accommodated by the local authority with their mothers in B&B accommodation during the proceedings. This meant that the children were not being looked after by the respective local authorities, since that would have required them to be accommodated 'by themselves' under ChA 1989 s20(1), meaning that the ChA 1989

200 See paras 9.85–9.89.

201 See paras 9.118–9.174.

202 See *R (G) v Southwark LBC* [2009] UKHL 26, [2009] 1 WLR 1299.

203 *R (G) v Barnet LBC* [2003] UKHL 57, [2004] 2 AC 208.

204 See chapter 7 for assistance under the HA 1996.

205 *R (G) v Barnet LBC* [2003] UKHL 57, [2004] 2 AC 208 at para 95 per Lord Hope.

206 The duty under ChA 1989 s23(6) has since been superseded by ChA 1989 s22C(2) which has similar effect, albeit the structure and language of the two provisions are not identical.

s23(6) duty had not arisen.[207] Even if the children had been accommodated by themselves under ChA 1989 s20(1), the court reasoned, the duty to make arrangements for a child to live with their parents under ChA 1989 s23(6), did not require a local authority to provide accommodation in order for those arrangements to take effect. Rather, ChA 1989 s23(6) was framed on the assumption that 'the person with whom the child is to be placed . . . already has accommodation which will enable the child to live with that person'.[208] For that reason, migrant families who are without accommodation would generally fall to be accommodated under ChA 1989 s17(1).[209]

9.75 The remainder of this section of the chapter is given over to a detailed discussion of ChA 1989 s20:

- It will begin by considering the limitations on the provision of accommodation under section 20.[210] It is convenient to start with the limitations on providing accommodation before discussing the provision of accommodation itself, since the limitations apply to each of the powers and duties under section 20 and so provide important context to the discussion that follows.
- The section will then go on to consider the two duties to accommodate contained in section 20(1) and (3) respectively.[211]
- This is followed by the discretion which local authorities have to accommodate children and certain young adults, under section 20(4)–(5).[212]
- The section will then address the duties owed to looked after children under ChA 1989 ss22–22C,[213] which go hand-in-hand with the provision of accommodation under section 20.
- Following this, the section deals with the requirements as to where, how and with whom the child should be accommodated.[214]
- The section finishes by considering the phenomenon of 'labelling' disputes.[215] That is, disputes which may arise as to whether a local

207 *R (G) v Barnet LBC* [2003] UKHL 57, [2004] 2 AC 208 at para 101 per Lord Hope.

208 [2003] UKHL 57, [2004] 2 AC 208 at para 103, see also at paras 102–104 per Lord Hope. See further *R (G) v Southwark LBC* [2009] UKHL 26, [2009] 1 WLR 1299 at para 24 per Baroness Hale.

209 See paras 9.12–9.13 and 9.54–9.69.

210 See paras 9.76–9.79.

211 See paras 9.80–9.83.

212 See para 9.84.

213 See paras 9.85–9.95.

214 See paras 9.96–9.105.

215 See paras 9.104–9.117.

authority owed or performed the section 20 duty, or whether it acted under another power or did not act at all.

Limitations on the provision of accommodation under Children Act 1989 s20

9.76 Before providing accommodation under ChA 1989 s20, a local authority shall:[216]

- ascertain the child's wishes and feelings regarding the provision of accommodation; and
- give due consideration (having regard to the child's age and understanding) to those wishes and feelings.

9.77 This duty is not absolute. The local authority is only required to take steps to ascertain and consider the child's wishes and feelings so far as is reasonably practicable and only where it is consistent with the child's welfare to do so. In all but the most urgent cases, the local authority will have identified the child's wishes and feelings in the course of the ChA 1989 s17 assessment.[217]

9.78 Subject to the exceptions in the following paragraph, accommodation may not be provided under ChA 1989 s20 if any person who has parental responsibility for the child and is willing and able either to provide or arrange accommodation for them, objects.[218] Where accommodation has been provided for a child under ChA 1989 s20, any person with parental responsibility can remove them from the accommodation at any time.[219] A person with parental responsibility seeking to exercise this right is not required to give notice, in writing or otherwise.[220]

9.79 The right of a person with parental responsibility to veto the provision of accommodation under ChA 1989 s20 is qualified by s20(9)–(10). These cater for court orders which have determined with whom a child is to live. Thus if there is a child arrangements order under ChA 1989 s8 or an order under the inherent jurisdiction of the High Court, providing for the child to live with a particular person or persons, or if there is a special guardianship order, then that parent cannot object or remove the child if the person or persons with whom

216 ChA 1989 s20(6).

217 See paras 9.40–9.43.

218 ChA 1989 s20(7).

219 ChA 1989 s20(8).

220 *Williams v Hackney LBC* [2018] UKSC 37, [2018] 3 WLR 503 at para 44 per Baroness Hale. See, more generally, at paras 38–52 on the limitations of ChA 1989 s20.

the child is to live, or the special guardian or guardians, agree to the child being accommodated.[221] The right of parental veto also does not apply in cases involving children aged 16 or over who have agreed to being accommodated under ChA 1989 s20.[222]

The duty to accommodate under Children Act 1989 s20(1)

9.80 There are four duties and powers to accommodate a child in need under the ChA 1989.[223] The most common provision is ChA 1989 s20(1) which imposes a duty on local authorities to provide accommodation for:

- any child in need;
- within their area;
- who appears to require accommodation;
- as a result of:
  - there being no person who has parental responsibility for the child;
  - the child being lost;
  - the child having been abandoned; or
  - the person who has been caring for the child being prevented (whether or not permanently, and for whatever reason) from providing them with suitable accommodation or care.

9.81 In the case of *R (A) v Croydon LBC*[224] Ward LJ explained that in order to establish whether it was necessary to provide accommodation under ChA 1989 s20(1), the local authority would need to ask and answer a series of questions, which factor in the limitations on the provision of accommodation discussed at paras 9.76–9.79.

1) *Is the applicant a child?* A child is a person under the age of 18.[225] The assessment of age is discussed at paras 11.130–11.107.
2) *Is the applicant a child in need?* Generally, the question of whether or not a child is in need will require an evaluative judgment on the part of the local authority, which is one of the core functions of the assessment under ChA 1989 s17. It is for that reason that

221 *Williams v Hackney LBC* [2018] UKSC 37, [2018] 3 WLR 503 at para 47 per Baroness Hale, summarising the effect of ChA 1989 s20(9)–(10).

222 ChA 1989 s20(11).

223 See para 9.71.

224 [2008] EWCA Civ 1445, [2009] PTSR 1011 at para 75. Approved by the Supreme Court in *R (G) v Southwark LBC* [2009] UKHL 26, [2009] 1 WLR 1299 at pp1308–1310 per Baroness Hale.

225 ChA 1989 s105(1).

section 17 has been described in this chapter as the gateway to services under CA 1989 Part III. However, a child without accommodation is a child in need,[226] so there will be little to evaluate in this regard where a homeless child presents to children's services. Nevertheless, an assessment under section 17 will still be required in order to ascertain what services may be needed to safeguard and promote the child's welfare.[227]

3) *Is the child within the local authority's area?* This is a simple question of whether the child is physically present in the area. It is possible for a child to be within more than one area, for example, where they live in one area but attend school in another.[228]
4) *Does the child appear to the local authority to require accommodation?* This might be the case because the child is without accommodation entirely or is 'sofa-surfing' with friends. Or it might be because the child has 'nowhere safe to stay that night'.[229]
5) *Is that need the result of: (a) there being no person who has parental responsibility for the child; (b) the child having been lost or abandoned; or (c) the person who has been caring for the child being prevented from providing them with suitable accommodation or care?* Criteria (a) and (b) are fairly self-explanatory. The case-law emphasises that a wide construction should be given to criterion (c) 'if children are not to suffer for the shortcomings of their parents or carers'.[230] This approach was applied in the case of *R (A) v Enfield LBC*[231] where Hayden J held that a child whose parents were willing and able to accommodate her, but in circumstances where she was at risk of radicalisation, should have been accommodated under ChA 1989 s20. In addition, where criterion (c) is engaged because of a relationship breakdown between a

226 *R v Northavon District Council ex p Smith* [1994] 2 AC 402, HL at p406; *R (G) v Barnet LBC* [2003] UKHL 57, [2004] 2 AC 208 at p224; *R (G) v Southwark LBC* [2009] UKHL 26, [2009] 1 WLR 1299 at pp1308D–1308F; *R (S and J) v Haringey LBC* [2016] EWHC 2692 (Admin) at para 37; *R (U and U (children)) v Milton Keynes Council* [2017] EWHC 3050 at para 23. See para 9.17.

227 See paras 9.30–9.38 and 9.40–9.43.

228 *R (Stewart) v Wandsworth LBC, Hammersmith and Fulham LBC and Lambeth LBC* [2001] EWHC Admin 709, [2002] 1 FLR 469 at para 23 per Jack Beatson QC sitting as a deputy High Court judge. See para 9.33.

229 *Prevention of homelessness and provision of accommodation for 16 and 17 year old young people*, para 3.4.

230 *R (G) v Southwark LBC* [2009] UKHL 26, [2009] 1 WLR 1299 at para 28(5) per Baroness Hale; *R (G) v Barnet LBC* [2003] UKHL 57, [2004] 2 AC 208 at para 24 per Lord Hope.

231 [2016] EWHC 567 (Admin), [2016] HLR 33.

child and their parent(s), the fact that the child might be (partially) responsible for bringing this situation about would not justify a refusal to provide services. As Munby J remarked, in a related context, in relation to what he described as 'the problem of the uncooperative child', a 'disturbed child's unwillingness to engage with those who are trying to help is often merely a part of the overall problems which justified the local authority's statutory intervention in the first place'.[232]

6) *What are the child's wishes regarding the provision of accommodation?* These should have been identified in the course of the ChA 1989 s17 assessment,[233] if one has been completed.
7) *What consideration (having regard to the child's age and understanding) is duly to be given to those wishes?* Dyson LJ remarked in *R (Liverpool City Council) v Hillingdon LBC*[234] that 'children are often not good judges of what is in their best interests'. While this may be the case in some instances, the right of the child to express their views and have them taken into account is a fundamental one that is enshrined in UNCRC Article 12, and should not be overlooked. As recognised in Article 12, the older and more mature the child, the more weight is likely to be appropriate to attach to their views.
8) *Does any person with parental responsibility who is willing to provide accommodation for the child object to the local authority's intervention?* The issue of parental consent was discussed in depth in the case of *Williams v Hackney LBC*.[235] In practice, it is rarely an issue in cases where migrant children seek support from social services under ChA 1989 s20 as they will generally either be unaccompanied or old enough to override the parental veto.[236]
9) *If there is objection, does the person in whose favour a residence order is in force agree to the child being looked after by the local authority?*

9.82 Where questions (1)–(6) are answered in the affirmative then, unless the answers to questions (7)–(9) dictate otherwise, accommodation under ChA 1989 s20(1) must be provided. An assessment of the child's need for services under ChA 1989 s17 will also need to be

232 *R (J) v Caerphilly CBC* [2005] EWHC 586 (Admin) at para 56.
233 See paras 9.40–9.43.
234 [2009] EWCA Civ 43, [2009] BLGR 289 at para 32 quoted in *R (G) v Southwark LBC* [2009] UKHL 26, [2009] 1 WLR 1299 at para 28(7).
235 [2018] UKSC 37, [2018] 3 WLR 503 at paras 38–52 per Baroness Hale. See para 9.78.
236 ChA 1989 s20(11). See para 9.79.

undertaken, if one has not been completed already.[237] However, the completion of the assessment should not be a barrier to the provision of accommodation. The statutory guidance makes it clear that in emergency cases accommodation should be provided first and the assessment completed second:

> Where a 16 or 17 year old seeks help or is referred, and it appears that they have nowhere safe to stay that night, then children's services must secure suitable emergency accommodation for them under section 20 of the 1989 Act, whilst their needs, including their need for continuing accommodation and support, are further assessed.[238]

The duty to accommodate under Children Act 1989 s20(3)

9.83 Under ChA 1989 s20(3), local authorities are *required* to provide accommodation for any child within their area who has reached the age of 16 and whose welfare the local authority considers is likely to be seriously prejudiced if it does not provide accommodation. Since the duty to provide accommodation under ChA 1989 s20(1) will arise in the majority, if not all, cases involving children who are without accommodation, the ChA 1989 s20(3) duty tends to be of relevance in those cases where the child has accommodation available, but continued occupation of the accommodation would be detrimental to their welfare. This might be because, for example, the child would be exposed to a risk of violence, abuse or exploitation if they were to remain in occupation.

The powers to accommodate

9.84 A local authority *may* also provide accommodation:

- For any child within its area, if it considers that to do so would safeguard or promote the child's welfare.[239] This power can be exercised even if there is a person with parental responsibility for the child, who is able to provide the child with accommodation.
- For any person aged 16–20 inclusive, in a community home which takes children aged 16 and over, if the local authority considers that to do so would safeguard or promote their welfare.[240] This power is unusual in this context in that it applies to young adults as well as children.

237 See paras 9.30–9.38 and 9.40–9.43.

238 *Prevention of homelessness and provision of accommodation for 16 and 17 year old young people*, para 3.4.

239 ChA 1989 s20(4).

240 ChA 1989 s20(5).

Both of these powers are subject to the limitations described at paras 9.76–9.79.

Duties owed to looked after children

Overview

9.85 A 'looked after' child is defined as:[241]

- a child who is in the care of a local authority;[242] or
- who has been provided with accommodation by the local authority for a continuous period of more than 24 hours under any provision of the ChA 1989 save for ChA 1989 s17, s23B or s24B.

9.86 This means that a child who has been accommodated by their local authority under ChA 1989 s20 for a continuous period of more than 24 hours will be classed as a looked after child.[243]

9.87 A local authority looking after a child is under a duty to:

- safeguard and promote the child's welfare. This includes a specific duty to promote the child's educational achievement, and an officer employed by the local authority must be appointed for the purposes of discharging this aspect of the duty;[244]
- make use of the services that are provided to children cared for by their own parents, to the extent that appears reasonable;[245]
- maintain the child in other respects apart from the provision of accommodation.[246]

241 ChA 1989 s22(1)–(2); and Local Authority Social Services Act 1970 s1A and Sch 1.

242 The power to take a child into the care of a local authority, following an order of the court, is contained in ChA 1989 Part IV and lies outside of the scope of this text.

243 In *R (D) v Southwark LBC* [2007] EWCA Civ 182, [2007] 1 FLR 2181 it was suggested by Smith LJ at para 55 that 'the child is being looked after by the local authority as soon as the section 20(1) duty arises'. However, this statement has subsequently been disapproved by the Court of Appeal in two cases as being inconsistent with the terms of ChA 1989 s22. See *R (GE (Eritrea)) v SSHD and Bedford BC* [2014] EWCA Civ 1490, [2015] PTSR 854 at paras 38–40 per Christopher Clarke LJ; and *R (PC) v Hertfordshire CC* [2016] EWCA Civ 1108, [2017] 1 WLR 2153 at para 24 per Burnett LJ.

244 ChA 1989 s22(3)(a) and (3B)–(3C).

245 ChA 1989 s22(3)(b).

246 ChA 1989 s22B. The questions of where, how and with whom the child should be accommodated are discussed at paras 9.96–9.105.

9.88 Before making any decision in relation to a child whom it is looking after (or proposing to look after) a local authority, so far as is reasonably practicable, is required to ascertain the wishes and feelings of:[247]

- the child;
- the child's parents and any other person with parental responsibility for the child;
- any other person whose wishes and feelings the local authority considers to be relevant – for example, a grandparent who has been involved in the child's care.

9.89 The local authority is then required to take these wishes and feelings into account when making the decision, as well as consider the child's religious persuasion, racial origin, and cultural and linguistic background.[248] It will be readily understood how important these factors might be in making decisions about how appropriately to look after an unaccompanied migrant child who may have no family, friends or cultural ties in the UK.

The independent reviewing officer

9.90 A local authority must appoint an independent reviewing officer (IRO) in respect of every child whom it is looking after.[249] The role of the IRO is to:[250]

- monitor the performance by the local authority of its functions in relation to the child;
- participate in reviews of the child's case;[251]
- ensure that the child's wishes and feelings are given due consideration.

The person selected to perform the role of IRO must be a registered social worker with sufficient relevant experience to carry out these functions independently and with regard to the child's best interests.[252] The role of the IRO is distinct from other roles which officers of the local authority may need to perform to discharge the functions under ChA 1989 Part III.[253] For example, the IRO must

247 ChA 1989 s22(4).

248 ChA 1989 s22(5).

249 ChA 1989 s25A.

250 ChA 1989 s25B. See further Care Planning, Placement and Case Review (England) Regulations ('CPPCR(E) Regs') 2010 SI No 959 regs 36 and 45.

251 See paras 9.94–9.95.

252 CPPCR(E) Regs 2010 reg 46(1)–(2).

253 CPPCR(E) Regs 2010 reg 46(3).

not be the child's personal adviser,[254] or a person who is involved in preparing the child's care plan[255] or managing the child's case. Nor can the IRO be a person who has control over the resources allocated to the child's case.

Care planning

9.91 A local authority looking after a child must prepare a care plan for them.[256] The care plan should be based on an assessment of the services that the child needs in order to achieve or maintain a reasonable standard of health or development.[257] The care plan must include a record of:[258]

- the long-term plan for the child's upbringing;
- the arrangements made by the local authority to meet the child's needs in relation to health;[259] education and training;[260] emotional and behavioural development; identity; family and social relationships;[261] social presentation; and self-care skills;
- the placement plan for the child;[262]
- the name of the IRO responsible for the child's case;
- the wishes and feelings of the child, their parents, any person with parental responsibility for the child and any other person whom the local authority considers relevant, in relation to the plans that have been made to meet the child's needs, the placement plan and any change (or proposed change) to the care plan;

254 See paras 9.134–9.135.

255 See paras 9.91–9.95.

256 CPPCR(E) Regs 2010 regs 2(1) and 4(1).

257 CPPCR(E) Regs 2010 reg 4(1). Much of this information may already have been gathered in the course of the assessment under ChA 1989 s17. See paras 9.40–9.43.

258 CPPCR(E) Regs 2010 reg 5(1).

259 The record of the arrangements to meet the child's health needs must include the specific information referred to in CPPCR(E) Regs 2010 Sch 1 para 1. See CPPCR(E) Regs 2010 reg 5(1)(i). To facilitate this, the local authority must arrange for a registered medical practitioner to carry out an assessment of the state of the child's health. See CPPCR(E) Regs 2010 reg 7.

260 The record of the arrangements to meet the child's education and training needs must, so far as reasonably practicable, include the specific information referred to in CPPCR(E) Regs 2010 Sch 1 para 2. See CPPCR(E) Regs 2010 reg 5(1)(ii).

261 The record of the arrangements to meet the child's needs in relation to family and social relationships must include the specific information referred to in CPPCR(E) Regs 2010 Sch 1 para 3. See CPPCR(E) Regs 2010 reg 5(1)(v).

262 See paras 9.101–9.102.

- if appropriate, the fact that the child is (or may be) a victim of human trafficking;[263]
- if appropriate, the fact that the child is an 'unaccompanied asylum-seeking child' (UASC) within the meaning of the Immigration Rules,[264] or intends to make an application for asylum.

9.92 The statutory guidance *The Children Act 1989 guidance and regulations. Volume 2: care planning, placement and case review*[265] ('*Care planning and placement guidance*') emphasises that there should be 'clarity in the care plan, particularly about the desired outcomes for the child and those expected from services and other actions identified'.[266] In order to achieve the requisite level of 'clarity and transparency' the care plan should:[267]

- describe the identified developmental needs of the child and the services required to meet those needs;
- describe why a particular placement has been chosen;
- include specific, achievable, child-focused outcomes intended to safeguard and promote the welfare of the child;
- identify how progress in achieving those outcomes will be measured;
- include realistic strategies and specific actions to achieve the planned outcomes; and
- clearly identify and set out the roles and responsibilities of family members, the child's carers and practitioners.

9.93 The care plan should also include a contingency plan, in the event that the primary plan is not achievable.[268]

9.94 A local authority must keep the case of any child who it is looking after under review.[269] The first review should take place within 20 working days of the date on which the child becomes looked after.[270] The second review should be carried out within three months of the

263 See paras 11.127–11.224.
264 See paras 11.4–11.126.
265 DfE, July 2021 (originally published 31 March 2010) (www.gov.uk/government/publications/children-act-1989-care-planning-placement-and-case-review).
266 *Care planning and placement guidance*, para 2.2.
267 *Care planning and placement guidance*, para 2.29.
268 *Care planning and placement guidance*, para 2.45.
269 ChA 1989 s26; CPPCR(E) Regs 2010 reg 32(1).
270 CPPCR(E) Regs 2010 reg 33(1).

first.[271] Subsequent reviews must be carried out at intervals of not more than six months.[272] Reviews should also be carried out if:

- a significant change to the child's care plan is proposed;[273]
- the child has been persistently absent from their placement;[274]
- as a result of a visit to see the child at their placement, the local authority reaches the view that the child's welfare is not being adequately safeguarded or promoted at the placement;[275]
- the person with whom the child has been placed or, if the child has been placed in the area of another local authority, the authority in which the child has been placed, notify the local authority that they are concerned the child is at risk of harm;[276]
- the child requests a review and their IRO agrees that a review is justified;[277]
- the IRO requests a review;[278]
- it is proposed that the local authority should stop providing accommodation to the child.[279]

9.95 The review should be chaired by the IRO (providing it is reasonably practicable for them to attend), who should speak to the child in private beforehand about the matters which are to be discussed and ensure that the wishes and feelings of the child's parents (or any person with parental responsibility for them) are taken into account.[280] It is down to the IRO to ensure that a specific person is identified to implement each decision made in consequence of the review and bring any failure to implement those decisions to the attention of the local authority.[281] The statutory guidance describes the 'primary task' of the IRO as being 'to ensure that the care plan for the child fully reflects the child's needs and that the actions and outcomes set out in the plan are consistent with the local authority's legal responsibilities

271 CPPCR(E) Regs 2010 reg 33(2).
272 CPPCR(E) Regs 2010 reg 33(3).
273 CPPCR(E) Regs 2010 reg 32(2).
274 CPPCR(E) Regs 2010 reg 33(2)(aa).
275 CPPCR(E) Regs 2010 regs 30 and 33(2).
276 CPPCR(E) Regs 2010 reg 33(2)(ab).
277 CPPCR(E) Regs 2010 reg 33(2)(ac) and (4).
278 CPPCR(E) Regs 2010 reg 33(2)(a).
279 Save where the child is to be accommodated by their parents (or any person with responsibility for the child) instead.
280 CPPCR(E) Regs 2010 reg 36(1)(a)–(c).
281 CPPCR(E) Regs 2010 reg 36(1)(d).

towards the child'.[282] A written record of the review, and any decisions made in the course of the review, must be prepared and kept on the child's case record.[283]

Where, how and with whom should the child be accommodated?

9.96 A looked after child, by definition, is a child who is being accommodated by their local authority.[284] ChA 1989 Part III, read together with the CPPCR(E) Regs 2010 and the *Care planning and placement guidance*, contains a detailed framework governing where, how and with whom looked after children should be accommodated.

9.97 Under ChA 1989 s22C, a local authority looking after a child must, unless it would not be reasonably practicable or consistent with the child's welfare, make arrangements for the child to live with:[285]

- a parent;
- a person (other than a parent) who has parental responsibility for the child;
- a person with whom the child had lived prior to being taken into the care of the local authority, pursuant to a child arrangements order.[286]

9.98 The *Care planning and placement guidance* describes ChA 1989 s22C(2) as a 'rehabilitative duty' designed to reflect the principle 'that state intervention in family life should be kept to the minimum necessary to protect the child from harm'.[287] This duty does not require the local authority to provide accommodation to the parent or the person with parental responsibility in order to make such an arrangement possible. Rather, the duty is framed on the assumption that 'the person with whom the child is to be placed . . . already has accommodation which will enable the child to live with that person'.[288]

282 *Care planning and placement guidance*, para 2.107; see further paras 2.102–2.115.

283 CPPCR(E) Regs 2010 reg 38.

284 See para 9.85.

285 ChA 1989 s22C(2)–(4).

286 Within the meaning of ChA 1989 s8.

287 *Care planning and placement guidance*, para 3.2.

288 *R (G) v Barnet LBC* [2003] UKHL 57, [2004] 2 AC 208 at para 103, see also at paras 102–104 per Lord Hope in relation to the duty under ChA 1989 s23(6) which has since been superseded by the duty under ChA 1989 s22C(2). The two duties have similar effect, albeit the structure and language of the provisions are not identical. See further *R (G) v Southwark LBC* [2009] UKHL 26, [2009] 1 WLR 1299 at para 24 per Baroness Hale.

This means that where a local authority arranges for a child who has been accommodated under ChA 1989 s20 to live with a parent, or a person who has parental responsibility for them, then the child will no longer be regarded as being accommodated under ChA 1989 s20. That is because the duty to accommodate under ChA 1989 s20(1) will not be owed if a parent or person with parental responsibility is willing and able to provide the child with suitable accommodation and care.[289] In the words of Burnett LJ 'if a child has a home to go to with a family member, it cannot be said to require accommodation under section 20 of the 1989 Act'.[290] The corollary of this is that a child placed with a parent or parental responsibility will no longer meet the definition of a looked after child,[291] and the duties associated with that status will no longer be owed to them.[292]

9.99 Where the local authority is unable to arrange for a child accommodated under ChA 1989 s20 to live with a parent or a person with parental responsibility then it is required to place the child in the placement which is, in its opinion, the most appropriate of the following options:[293]

1) A placement with a relative, friend or other person connected with the child, who is also a local authority foster parent.[294] According to the statutory guidance, this is intended to reflect the principle that 'children should, wherever possible be brought up in their families and communities, if they cannot remain with their parents'.[295] Before placing a child with a local authority foster parent, the local authority must comply with various procedural requirements that are set out in CPPCR(E) Regs 2010 regs 22–25A, which involve having in place a foster care agreement with the proposed foster parent, in accordance with

289 See paras 9.78–9.79 and 9.80–9.81.

290 *R (PC) v Hertfordshire CC* [2016] EWCA Civ 1108, [2017] 1 WLR 2153 at para 13. The judge's comment here was specifically directed at the provision of accommodation under ChA 1989 s20(1). A child whose family is willing and able to provide suitable accommodation and care, but who refuses to take up that option may still be owed the duty under ChA 1989 s20(3). See para 9.83.

291 ChA 1989 s22(1); *Care planning and placement guidance*, para 3.73.

292 See paras 9.85–9.95.

293 ChA 1989 s22C(5)–(6).

294 ChA 1989 s22C(6)(a). See further *Care planning and placement guidance*, paras 3.91–3.114. The term 'local authority foster parent' is defined in ChA 1989 s105(1). See ChA 1989 s22C(12).

295 *Care planning and placement guidance*, para 3.4.

Fostering Services (England) Regulations 2011[296] reg 27(5)(b).[297] Significantly, these procedures allow the local authority temporarily to appoint a relative, friend or other person connected with the child as a local authority foster parent for a period of 16 weeks, in order to facilitate the child's placement with them, where that is adjudged to be the most appropriate placement for the child.[298] The purpose of this temporary approval is to allow time for the person with whom the child is to be placed, to have their suitability to be a local authority foster parent assessed.[299]

2) A placement with a local authority foster parent who is not a relative, friend or other person connected with the child.[300]
3) A placement in a registered children's home.[301]
4) A placement by means of 'other arrangements', in any other setting which the local authority is satisfied is suitable for the child.[302] Such placements can include care homes and family centres as well as 'semi-independent and independent settings that provide support to the older child', for example, supported accommodation services such as foyers.[303] There are restrictions on the use of 'other arrangements' which vary depending on the age of the child in question. The only types of arrangement that can be provided to children under 16 are those set out expressly in CPPCR(E) Regs 2010 reg 27A which has the effect of excluding

296 SI No 581.
297 CPPCR(E) Regs 2010 reg 22(2)(c).
298 CPPCR(E) Regs 2010 reg 24(1). See further *Care planning and placement guidance,* paras 3.97–3.114. Before making such a placement, the local authority must first carry out an assessment of the placement in accordance with CPPCR(E) Regs 2010 reg 24(2).
299 CPPCR(E) Regs 2010 reg 24(1)(b); Fostering Services (England) Regulations 2011 regs 26–27. The temporary approval may be extended in accordance with CPPCR(E) Regs 2010 reg 25 to allow for completion of the assessment and any review.
300 ChA 1989 s22C(6)(b). See further *Care planning and placement guidance,* paras 3.91–3.114.
301 ChA 1989 s22C(6)(c). See further *Care planning and placement guidance,* paras 3.115–3.118.
302 ChA 1989 s22C(6)(d); CPPCR(E) Regs 2010 reg 27. See further *Care planning and placement guidance,* paras 3.120–3.142.
303 *Care planning and placement guidance,* paras 3.124–3.125. This guidance is yet to be updated to reflect the new regulations set out at fn 305 below.

the use of supported accommodation for this age group.[304] From 28 October 2023, supported accommodation can be provided to 16/17 year olds, but only where the provider is registered with OFSTED.[305] Placements of this type may be appropriate for 'older looked after children' providing that 'the carers have the necessary competences so that the support provided by the placement enables the young person to develop the skills s/he will need to make a positive transition to greater independence in the future'. Before utilising such a placement, the local authority must take 'every step to establish that the older child's needs are matched to the services provided by the setting'.[306] Statutory guidance[307] directed at the specific needs of 16/17-year-olds reminds local authorities that it will not usually be appropriate for this group to be placed in temporary accommodation unless there is on-site support, and that 'bed and breakfast accommodation, including hotels and nightly let accommodation with shared facilities' should never be regarded as suitable.[308] In deciding whether a placement by means of other arrangements is suitable the local authority must have regard to the matters which are set out in CPPCR(E) Regs 2010 Sch 6 paras 1 and 2,[309] which include the facilities, services and support available at the accommodation, its location and affordability, and the child's views about the accommodation as well as their understanding of their rights and responsibilities and the funding arrangements in relation to the accommodation. Before placing a child in a placement of this

304 In *R (Article 39) v Secretary of State for Education* [2022] EWHC 589 (Admin) the claimant sought, unsuccessfully, to argue that the same rule should apply to 16/17-year-olds. The legislative landscape has changed since this case and supported accommodation is now subject to the regulatory regime set out at fn 305 below.

305 See Care Standards Act 2000 Pt II; the Care Standards Act 2000 (Registration) (England) Regulations 2010 SI No 2130; the Care Standards Act 2000 (Extension of the Application of Part 2 to Supported Accommodation) (England) Regulations 2022 SI No 808; and Supported Accommodation (England) Regulations 2023 SI No 416 reg 36.

306 *Care planning and placement guidance*, paras 3.120–3.127.

307 Yet to be updated to reflect the new regulations set out at fn 305 above.

308 *Prevention of homelessness and provision of accommodation for 16- and 17-year-old young people who may be homeless and/or require accommodation*, MHCLG and DfE, April 2018, paras 5.10 and 5.13, www.gov.uk/government/publications/provision-of-accommodation-for-16-and-17-year-olds-who-may-be-homeless-and-or-require-accommodation.

309 CPPCR(E) Regs 2010 reg 27(a).

type, the local authority must inform the child's IRO[310] and, unless it is not reasonably practicable, arrange for the child to visit the accommodation.[311] As a general rule, the local authority should not arrange any such placement unless that decision has been made consequent to a review[312] of the child's case.[313] However, this does not prevent the local authority from arranging such a placement if it is satisfied that it is necessary to do so as a matter of urgency in order to safeguard the child's welfare.[314]

9.100 In deciding which of these four types of placement is the most appropriate, subject to its duties under ChA 1989 s22 to safeguard and promote the child's welfare and give due consideration to the child's wishes and feelings, the local authority should:[315]

- Give preference to a placement with a relative, friend or other person connected with the child, who is also a local authority foster parent.[316] A 'relative' in this context is defined as 'a grandparent, brother, sister, uncle or aunt (whether of the full blood or half blood or by affinity), or step-parent'.[317] The concept of a 'connected' person is left undefined in the statute.[318] However, the statutory guidance explains that 'a person in this last category may be someone who knows the child in a more professional capacity such as a childminder, a teacher or a youth worker although these are not exclusive categories'.[319]
- So far as is reasonably practicable, ensure that the placement is such that it allows the child to live near their home.[320]
- So far as is reasonably practicable, ensure that the placement is such that it does not disrupt the child's education or training.[321]

310 See para 9.90.
311 CPPCR(E) Regs 2010 reg 27(b)–(c).
312 See paras 9.94–9.95.
313 ChA 1989 ss22C(6)(d) and 22D(1).
314 ChA 1989 s22D(2).
315 ChA 1989 s22C(7). Note that slightly different rules apply if the child is being considered for adoption. See ChA 1989 s22C(9A)–(9C).
316 ChA 1989 s22C(7)(a).
317 ChA 1989 s105(1).
318 By CPPCR(E) Regs 2010 reg 24(3) a person is 'connected' with a child if they are 'a relative, friend or other person connected with' the child. However, this circular definition is used in a slightly different context and adds nothing to the statute.
319 *Care planning and placement guidance*, para 3.11.
320 ChA 1989 s22C(7)(b) and (8)(a).
321 ChA 1989 s22C(7)(b) and (8)(b). See further *Care planning and placement guidance*, paras 3.15–3.20.

Additional constraints are placed on making arrangements for the placement of children at key stage four which would have the effect of disrupting their education.[322]

- So far as is reasonably practicable, ensure that the placement is such that it enables the child to live with any sibling for whom the local authority is also providing accommodation.[323]
- So far as is reasonably practicable, ensure that the placement is suitable to any particular needs which the child may have that arise from a disability.[324]
- Ensure that the placement is within the local authority's area, unless that is not reasonably practicable.[325] The procedure for the placement of a child out of area is regulated by CPPCR(E) Regs 2010 reg 11[326] which requires the decision to be approved by a nominated officer or, if the placement is not in the area of an adjoining authority, the director of children's services. The receiving local authority will need to be notified and, in some cases, consulted prior to the approval of the decision. The IRO[327] and, where appropriate, the child's relatives will also need to be consulted. Although placement within the local authority's area is intended to be the norm, the statutory guidance recognises that 'there will be circumstances where a distant placement will be the most suitable for a child, such as where the child concerned has complex treatment needs that cannot be met by services within the area of the responsible authority' or where the child requires 'an out of authority placement to ensure they can be effectively safeguarded'.[328]

9.101 Written notification of the arrangements for the child's placement should be given to the child, any parent of the child or any person with parental responsibility for the child, the IRO, and any educa-

322 See CPPCR(E) Regs 2010 reg 10.

323 ChA 1989 s22C(7)(b) and (8)(c). See further *Care planning and placement guidance*, paras 3.21–3.25.

324 ChA 1989 s22C(7)(b) and (8)(d). See further *Care planning and placement guidance*, paras 3.26–3.29.

325 ChA 1989 s22C(7)(c) and (9). See further *Care planning and placement guidance* paras 3.30–3.63.

326 Placements outside of England and Wales are regulated by CPPCR(E) Regs 2010 reg 12.

327 See para 9.90.

328 *Care planning and placement guidance*, para 3.31.

tional institution attended by the child, among others.[329] In addition, a placement plan must be prepared, setting out:[330]

- how the placement will contribute to meeting the child's needs;
- how on a day-to-day basis the child will be cared for and how the child's welfare will be safeguarded and promoted;
- any contact arrangements with the child's family;
- the arrangements made for the child's health and dental care;
- the arrangements made for the child's education and training;
- the arrangements that have been made, pursuant to ChA 1989 ss23ZA–23ZB, for either a representative of the local authority or an independent visitor to visit the child;
- the circumstances in which the placement may be terminated;[331]
- the name and contact details of the IRO,[332] any visitor who has been appointed and (if appropriate) the child's personal adviser.[333]

9.102 The placement plan should be completed before the placement is made or, where that is not reasonably practicable, within five working days of the start of the placement.[334]

9.103 Save where 'other arrangements' are made for a child to live in an unregulated setting,[335] or where a placement is arranged for a disabled child,[336] there is no express legislative requirement that the accommodation provided to the child should be 'suitable'. However, this requirement is implicit within the scheme of the legislation:

- The duty to accommodate the child under ChA 1989 s20(1)[337] arises in circumstances where the person who has been caring for the child is prevented from providing them with 'suitable' accommodation or care. In order to make up for this, the local authority

329 CPPCR(E) Regs 2010 reg 13.

330 CPPCR(E) Regs 2010 reg 9 and Sch 2 para 1. See further *Care planning and placement guidance,* paras 3.177–3.191. Where the child is placed with a local authority foster parent, in a children's home or in other arrangements, the placement plan must also include the information specified in CPPCR(E) Regs 2010 Sch 2 para 3.

331 A placement can only be terminated in accordance with the procedure under CPPCR(E) Regs 2010 reg 14. Critically, alternative arrangements will need to be made for the child's accommodation prior to termination or, where there is an immediate risk of significant harm to the child or to protect others from injury, as soon as reasonably practicable thereafter.

332 See para 9.90.

333 See paras 9.134–9.135 and 9.152–9.154.

334 CPPCR(E) Regs 2010 reg 9(2).

335 ChA 1989 s22C(6)(d); CPPCR(E) Regs 2010 reg 27(a).

336 ChA 1989 s22C(7)(b) and (8)(d).

337 See paras 9.80–9.82.

looking after the child is required to arrange for them to be accommodated in the most 'appropriate' placement available[338] and in performing this obligation the local authority is subject to a duty to safeguard and promote their welfare.[339]

- In addition, the placement plan for the child will need to set out how the placement will contribute to meeting the child's needs and how on a day-to-day basis the child will be cared for and how the child's welfare will be safeguarded and promoted.[340]
- In addition, a review of the child's case will need to be undertaken if, as a result of a visit to see the child at their placement, the local authority reaches the view that the child's welfare is not being adequately safeguarded or promoted.[341]

Taken together, the practical effect of these statutory provisions is that a local authority is required to provide suitable accommodation and any local authority which fails to do so is likely to find that it is breach of one or other of these obligations.

'Labelling' disputes

Overview

9.104 As has been discussed above, a child who has been provided with accommodation by a local authority under ChA 1989 s20 for a continuous period of more than 24 hours is categorised as a 'looked after' child, which gives rise to certain rights and entitlements.[342] In addition, a child who has been looked after by a local authority for a period of 13 weeks or more, beginning after their 14th birthday and ending after their 16th birthday, will then be entitled to a further set of duties as a 'care leaver' designed to replicate the support which might be given by a reasonable parent, to assist the child in making the transition to adulthood.[343]

9.105 This package of rights and entitlements means that the question of whether or not a child is or has been accommodated under ChA 1989 s20 is an extremely important one. As such, it is perhaps no surprise that a number of disputes over the answer to this question have come before the courts. These disputes are described here as

338 ChA 1989 s22C(5).
339 ChA 1989 s22(3)(a).
340 CPPCR(E) Regs 2010 reg 9 and Sch 2 para 1.
341 CPPCR(E) Regs 2010 reg 30 and 33(2).
342 See paras 9.85–9.89.
343 See paras 9.118–9.174.

'labelling' disputes,[344] since the issue which they raise is the correct legal label to be given to the child's accommodation arrangements. The labelling disputes have tended to fall into one of four categories:[345]

a) ChA 1989 s17 or s20?
b) Housing or children's services?
c) ChA 1989 s20 or a private arrangement?
d) Education or children's services?

Children Act 1989 s17 or s20?

9.106 The first category, which is largely (although not entirely) of historic interest, encompasses those cases where children's services have accommodated the child but assert that they have acted under ChA 1989 s17 rather than s20. It has now been established at the highest level that where the section 20 criteria were satisfied and children's services provided accommodation, then the child will have been accommodated under section 20. A local authority cannot side-step this duty by claiming to have acted under another power or duty.[346]

Housing or children's services?

9.107 The second category is where there is some dispute as to which department within a local authority has arranged for the child to be accommodated and why. In *R (M) v Hammersmith and Fulham LBC*[347] the claimant approached the housing department of Hammersmith and Fulham LBC. She was given temporary accommodation. She was never referred to children's services. After she reached the age of 18 she claimed to be owed duties as a former relevant child.[348] The House of Lords held that she ought to have been

344 This is the term used in *R (G) v Southwark LBC* [2009] UKHL 26, [2009] 1 WLR 1299 at para 9 per Baroness Hale.

345 A fifth category fell for consideration in the case of *TT v Essex CC* [2023] EWHC 826 (Admin). In that case accommodation made available to young people pursuant to contracts entered into between the local authority and a supported accommodation provider, following a referral by the local authority, was held not to be provided under CA 1989 s20. That decision, which is currently under appeal, is difficult to reconcile with the cases below.

346 See *R (G) v Southwark LBC* [2009] UKHL 26, 1 WLR 1299 at para 9 per Baroness Hale; *R (M) v Hammersmith and Fulham LBC* [2008] UKHL 14, [2008] 1 WLR 535 at para 42 per Baroness Hale; and *Prevention of homelessness and provision of accommodation for 16 and 17 year old young people*, paras 3.58–3.61 and 4.28–4.29.

347 [2008] UKHL 14, [2008] 1 WLR 535.

348 See paras 9.160–9.174.

referred to children's services, but since she had not been drawn to their attention and the local authority had not provided her with accommodation in the exercise of its social services functions under ChA 1989 s20, she had not been looked after by Hammersmith and Fulham LBC within the meaning of ChA 1989 s22 and therefore was not owed continuing duties as a care leaver.

9.108 In contrast, in *R (TG) v Lambeth LBC*[349] a 16-year-old claimant was assisted by a social worker within the Youth Offending Service (YOS) in approaching the local authority's housing department on the understanding that he was in desperate need of accommodation. He was then, ostensibly, accommodated under HA 1996 s188(1).[350] He was later found by the Court of Appeal to have been accommodated under ChA 1989 s20. The social worker in the YOS was the 'eyes and ears' of the children and families division of the Children and Young Persons Service of the authority, meaning that her actions had to be imputed to the children's services department, and that the child had been drawn to the attention of children's services as a result of which accommodation had been provided.

9.109 The cases illustrate that where a child has been accommodated, the responsibility for the provision of accommodation may be imputed to children's services in circumstances where there is not only some action by the children's services authority, but also a causal nexus between that action and the result that a child is in fact provided with accommodation.[351]

Children Act 1989 s20 or a private arrangement?

9.110 The third category deals with the situation in which accommodation is provided by a relative or friend and a dispute arises as to whether or not this amounts to a placement under ChA 1989 s20 or a private or kinship arrangement.[352] The most authoritative guidance on this situation was provided by the Court of Appeal in *R (T) v Hertfordshire CC*[353] after consideration of the earlier case-law. In that case, the

349 [2011] EWCA Civ 526, [2011] 4 All ER 453.

350 See paras 7.253–7.259.

351 *R (B) v Nottingham City Council* [2011] EWHC 2933 (Admin) at para 61 per Singh J.

352 The terms 'private' or 'kinship' arrangement are not terms of art. They are used here to describe an informal placement with friends or family which falls outside of the scope of ChA 1989 s20. They should not be confused with the term 'private fostering arrangement' which has a specific meaning set out in ChA 1989 ss66 and 105(1), that does not necessarily correspond precisely with the situations under consideration here.

353 [2016] EWCA Civ 1108, [2017] 1 WLR 2153.

court held that accommodation provided to a young person by his grandmother in circumstances where his mother had been taken into custody, did not amount to accommodation under ChA 1989 s20. Although social services had been involved in the situation and apprised of the circumstances throughout, they had done nothing to encourage, facilitate or induce the arrangement and it could not be said that they had been 'deeply involved'.[354]

9.111 In contrast, in *R (D) v Southwark LBC*,[355] the child, S, had been living with her father, RB. S told school staff that she did not wish to return home as RB had been violent toward her and asked if she could stay with RB's ex-partner, ED, instead. RB agreed to this. A representative from children's services then contacted ED and asked whether she would care for S. ED agreed to this and was told that someone from children's services would be in contact with her and that steps would be taken to offer her assistance. No such steps were taken. The Court of Appeal took the view that this amounted to a placement under ChA 1989 s20. Southwark had taken a central role in placing S with ED and had said nothing to ED to suggest that the placement was a private arrangement and that she would have to look to S's parents for support.[356]

9.112 In *R (A) v Coventry City Council*[357] the child, T, ran away from his father's home to stay with his older brother who was living with C, the mother of a friend. Social workers visited C's home and conducted an assessment in the course of which C made clear that she would be unable to look after T without assistance from children's services. The High Court held that this amounted to a placement under ChA 1989 s20 as the local authority, by its conduct, had allowed C to believe she would be provided with financial support to look after C.

9.113 In *KS v Bradford MDC*,[358] the local authority had played a 'leading role' in arranging for a child to live with his maternal grandmother, having placed the child with her and thereafter maintaining a close interest by organising home visits and multi-disciplinary meetings, among other things. The High Court held this was a ChA 1989 s20 placement and not a private arrangement.

354 *R (Cunningham) v Hertfordshire City Council* [2016] EWCA Civ 1108, [2017] 1 WLR 2153 at paras 16 and 22.

355 [2007] EWCA Civ 182, [2007] 1 FLR 2181.

356 See [2007] EWCA Civ 182, [2007] 1 FLR 2181 at paras 49–50 and 59 per Smith LJ.

357 [2009] EWHC 34 (Admin), [2009] 1 FLR 1202.

358 [2014] EWHC 11 (Admin), [2014] 3 FCR 164.

9.114 In *R (KI) v Brent LBC*,[359] a child was found to have been owed the duty under ChA 1989 s20 in circumstances where the local authority played a 'central' and 'leading' role in putting in place arrangements for him to move from supported accommodation to accommodation with his uncle.

9.115 In *Salford City Council v W*,[360] five children who had been designated as children in need by the local authority, who had been accommodated with their maternal aunt, were found not to have been owed the duty under ChA 1989 20 in circumstances where it was the children's mother who had asked her sister to care for the children and the local authority had only become aware of the move afterwards.

Education or children's services?

9.116 The fourth and final category concerns the hierarchy between accommodation provided under the ChA 1989 s20 duty and accommodation provided under EdA 1996 Part IV for children with SEN.[361] This formed the subject of the Court of Appeal decision in *R (O) v East Riding of Yorkshire Council*.[362] The child in that case, who had severe autism and ADHD and had been living at home, was provided with accommodation by his local authority under ChA 1989 s20 to provide respite for his parents. The local authority subsequently arranged for him to be accommodated in a residential school. It took the view that this placement was provided under EdA 1996 Part IV, in accordance with the child's statement of SEN and that, in arranging this placement, the duty under the ChA 1989 s20 duty had come to an end. The Court of Appeal disagreed. In 'circumstances, where the claimant's needs, social as well as educational, had driven the placement', and this had been appreciated by the local authority, it was impossible to 'regard the 1996 Act's SEN regime as supplanting rather than supporting the 1989 Act's LAC regime'.[363] The consequence of this was that the child continued to be accommodated under ChA 1989 s20 while at the residential school.

359 [2018] EWHC 1068 (Admin), (2018) 21 CCLR 294.

360 [2021] EWHC 1689 (Fam).

361 EdA 1996 Part IV now applies solely to children in Wales with SEN. In England it has been superseded by CFA 2014 Part 3.

362 [2011] EWCA Civ 196, [2012] PTSR 328.

363 *R (O) v East Riding of Yorkshire Council* [2011] EWCA Civ 196, [2012] PTSR 328 at para 117 per Rix LJ.

The discretion to assist where a local authority has failed to perform the Children Act 1989 s20 duty

9.117 In cases where a child should have been accommodated under ChA 1989 s20 but, owing to an unlawful act or omission on the part of the local authority, was not, children's services have a discretion retrospectively to treat the child or young person as if they had been looked after, thereby giving rise to the longer-term entitlements which are available to care leavers. This situation is discussed at paras 9.186–9.194.

The Children Act 1989 – the duties owed to care leavers

9.118 This section of the chapter will consider the community care services available to care leavers under ChA 1989 Part III from their local authority's children's services department. The duties owed to care leavers were the result of amendments to ChA 1989 Part III introduced by the Children (Leaving Care) Act 2000, and have been amended on a number of occasions since, most recently by the CSWA 2017.

9.119 The phrase 'care leaver', although commonly used, is not actually one which is defined (or even found) in the ChA 1989. However, it is found (although not defined) both in the statutory guidance *The Children Act 1989 guidance and regulations. Volume 3: planning transition to adulthood for care leavers*[364] ('*Transition to adulthood guidance*') and in the Care Leavers (England) Regulations ('CL(E) Regs') 2010.[365] At its broadest it might be taken to refer to any young person who has formerly been looked after, accommodated or fostered by a local authority or other such institution. More narrowly, it might be construed as referring to the specific categories of young person who are owed the duties under ChA 1989 Part III introduced by the Children (Leaving Care) Act 2000.[366] It is this latter category which this section of the chapter is concerned with, and that is the sense in which the term 'care leaver' is used here.

9.120 This latter category encompasses those who have been looked after by a local authority in England or Wales for a total period of 13 weeks or more, beginning on or after their 14th birthday and ending

364 DfE, January 2022 (www.gov.uk/government/publications/children-act-1989-transition-to-adulthood-for-care-leavers).

365 SI No 2571.

366 This reflects the definition contained in CSWA 2017 s2(7) which applies for the purposes of that Act.

on or after their 16th birthday.[367] Children who continue to be looked after, after this time, are referred to as 'eligible children'.[368] Children who cease to be looked after, after this time, are referred to as 'relevant children'.[369] A young person falling into either category will be referred to as a 'former relevant child'[370] once they reach the age of 18. Children and young people aged between 16 and 21, who have been looked after, accommodated or fostered but do not fall within one of these categories (for example, because they were not looked after for the whole 13-week period) are referred to as 'persons qualifying for advice and assistance', or 'qualifying children'.[371] All of these groups have various rights and entitlements under ChA 1989 Part III, which are described in the remainder of this section.

9.121 The legislative purpose behind these rights and entitlements is:

> . . . to ensure that a relevant or eligible child is not simply left without support the moment he reaches his 18th birthday but receives the same sort of support and guidance which children can normally expect from their own families as and when they become adults.[372]

9.122 To achieve this purpose, the local authority is cast in the role of the child or young person's 'corporate parent',[373] providing them with support 'in the same way that reasonable parents provide support for their own children',[374] in order to 'make sure that they are provided with the opportunities they need'[375] and assist them in 'making the transition from care to more independent living arrangements',[376] with the 'ultimate aim' of supporting them to 'live successful independent lives'.[377] Thus, the *Transition to adulthood guidance* states that the local authority as the corporate parent should apply the following three key principles when making decisions about care leavers:[378]

367 ChA 1989 Sch 2 para 19B(2); CPPCR(E) Regs 2010 reg 40(1). See para 9.127.
368 See paras 9.127–9.129.
369 See paras 9.136–9.140.
370 See paras 9.160–9.164.
371 ChA 1989 s24(1)–(1B).
372 *R (GE (Eritrea)) v SSHD and Bedford BC* [2014] EWCA Civ 1490, [2015] PTSR 854 at para 17 per Christopher Clarke LJ.
373 See paras 9.218–9.225.
374 *Transition to adulthood guidance*, para 3.1.
375 *Transition to adulthood guidance*, para 1.8.
376 *Transition to adulthood guidance*, para 4.1.
377 *Extending personal adviser support to all care leavers to age 25: statutory guidance for local authorities*, DfE, February 2018, para 7 (www.gov.uk/government/publications/extending-personal-adviser-support-to-age-25).
378 *Transition to adulthood guidance*, para 1.10.

- Is this good enough for my own child?
- Providing a second chance if things don't go as expected.
- Is this tailored to their individual needs, particularly if they are more vulnerable than other young people?

9.123 This legislative purpose is an important and progressive one which recognises that:

> For most young people the idea of being left unsupported at that age would be alien. They have a sense of security and know that their parents will always be there for them. Few young people ever really 'leave' the care of their parents. They may leave home, and on average do so at the age of 24, but they know that their families are only ever a phone call away and stand ready to offer financial support and advice, or a place to stay if they need it.[379]

9.124 The duties owed to care leavers are intended to make up for the fact that, for many, their families will not be just 'a phone call away' and, even if they are, they may not be in a position to offer 'financial support and advice, or a place to stay'. These duties will be of obvious importance to migrant care leavers. For example, a young person who fled the conflict in Syria as a child, leaving their family behind, will generally lack this support network. The needs of such a young person will be no less than their British counterpart. That notwithstanding, the duties and powers owed to migrant care leavers are subject to the exclusions from support contained in NIAA 2002 Sch 3 and advisers working with this cohort will need to establish whether they fall within the ambit of these exclusions in order to establish their entitlement to support.[380] Where those exclusions do apply, a care leaver over the age of 18 will only be entitled to such support as is necessary to avoid a breach of their human rights.

9.125 This means that there is inherent tension within the support regime in so far as it applies to migrant care leavers. On the one hand, local authorities are intended to step into the shoes of the 'reasonable parent', and the nature of their duties and the manner in which they choose to exercise their powers is shaped accordingly. On the other hand, the local authorities' abilities as a corporate parent to meet the needs of certain young migrant care leavers is strictly limited by their immigration status. Where NIAA 2002 Sch 3 applies, only a core minimum, if any, support will be provided. The practical

379 *Care matters: transforming the lives of children and young people in care,* Cm 6932, green paper, DfE, 2006, para 7.2 (www.gov.uk/government/publications/care-matters-transforming-the-lives-of-children-and-young-people-in-care).

380 See paras 9.195–9.217.

consequence is that the corporate parent will help some of their 'children' far more than others, hardly the actions of a reasonable parent. This inherent tension may potentially have been eased, to some extent, by the corporate parenting duty being enshrined in statute by means of CSWA 2017 s1, in force from 1 April 2018, thereby placing an increased emphasis on the need for local authorities to act in the manner of a reasonable parent and promote the best interests of the child or young person in question.[381] Putting the duty on a statutory footing will not remove the tension but it may assist local authorities by providing them with a clear set of principles to apply in situations where the tension exists.

9.126 The rights and entitlements of each category of care leaver will now be considered in turn.[382] This will be followed by a discussion of the discretion which local authorities have to confer these rights and entitlements on young people who do not qualify for them, as a consequence of an unlawful act or omission on the part of the local authority.[383]

Duties owed to eligible children

Overview

9.127 An eligible child is a child who:[384]

- is aged 16 or 17; and
- has been looked after by a local authority in England or Wales for a total period of 13 weeks or more,[385] beginning on or after their 14th birthday and ending on or after their 16th birthday.[386]

9.128 A local authority that is looking after an eligible child will owe all of the same duties to that child as would be owed to any other looked

381 See paras 9.218–9.225.

382 Further information on these rights and entitlements should be made available directly by local authorities by means of their 'local offer' to care leavers, which entails publishing information about the services described in this section of the chapter, together with any other services that may assist care leavers in, or in preparing for, adulthood and independent living: CSWA 2017 s2(1).

383 See paras 9.186–9.194.

384 ChA 1989 Sch 2 para 19B(2); CPPCR(E) Regs 2010 reg 40(1).

385 This can consist of any number of shorter periods of being looked after, providing the total amounts to 13 weeks or more. See ChA 1989 Sch 2 para 19B(2)(b).

386 The exception to this rule is where a child, who is not in the care of the local authority, has been accommodated for 13 weeks or more as a result of a series of short breaks. In this situation, where the criteria contained in CPPCR(E) Regs 2010 reg 48(2) are satisfied, the child will not be regarded as an eligible child. See ChA 1989 Sch 2 para 19B(3)(b) and CPPCR(E) Regs 2010 regs 40(2) and 48.

after child.[387] For example, a local authority will need to accommodate and maintain any eligible child whom it is looking after.[388] However, in addition to the duties which are owed to all looked after children, the local authority must:

- carry out an assessment of the eligible child's needs with a view to determining what advice, assistance and support it would be appropriate for it to provide them with under the ChA 1989 while they continue to be looked after, and after the local authority ceases to look after them;[389]
- prepare a pathway plan for the child;[390]
- arrange for the child to have a personal adviser.[391]

9.129 These steps are important because they are not only with a view to ensuring that the child's current support promotes and safeguards their welfare, but also that there is a forward-looking blueprint for how they will be supported over time as they develop. Each of these requirements will be considered in turn.

The needs assessment for the eligible child

9.130 The assessment of the eligible child's needs is to be carried out in accordance with CPPCR(E) Regs 2010 reg 42.[392] The local authority looking after the eligible child[393] must complete the assessment not more than three months after the date on which the child reaches the age of 16 or becomes an eligible child, whichever date is earlier.[394] The purpose of this is to consider the likely needs of the child after they cease to be looked after and, as such, is of critical importance in planning for the child's transition to independent living. In assessing these needs, the local authority must take account of:[395]

387 See paras 9.85–9.95.

388 ChA 1989 ss20, 22 and 22B.

389 ChA 1989 Sch 2 para 19B(1) and (4).

390 ChA 1989 Sch 2 para 19B(1) and (4).

391 ChA 1989 Sch 2 para 19C.

392 ChA 1989 Sch 2 para 19B(7); CPPCR(E) Regs 2010 reg 41(a).

393 The CPPCR(E) Regs 2010 use the term 'responsible authority' in this context (as opposed to 'local authority'), which is defined in CPPCR(E) Regs 2010 reg 2(1) as 'the local authority that looks after' the child. Although the phraseology is slightly different to that of ChA 1989 Sch 2 paras 19B–19C, the end result is the same: it is the local authority looking after the eligible child which owes the duties.

394 CPPCR(E) Regs 2010 reg 42(1).

395 CPPCR(E) Regs 2010 reg 42(2).

- the child's state of health (including their physical, emotional and mental health) and development;
- the child's continuing need for education, training or employment;
- if relevant, any needs that the child might have arising from their status as either a victim (or possible victim) of human trafficking or UASC;
- any support that will be available to the child from their parents, relatives, friends or other person connected with the child;[396]
- the child's actual and anticipated financial resources and their capacity to manage personal finances independently;
- the extent to which the child possesses the practical and other skills necessary for independent living;
- the child's need for continuing care, support and accommodation;
- the wishes and feelings of the child, the child's parents, any other person with parental responsibility, and the person with whom the child lives or who is responsible for the child at their accommodation;
- the views of: any person or educational institution that provides the child with education or training; the local authority which maintains the child's statement of SEN (if they have one); the IRO;[397] any person providing health (whether physical, emotional or mental health) or dental care to the child; the child's personal adviser; and any other person whose views the local authority considers may be relevant.

The pathway plan for the eligible child

9.131 As soon as possible after the needs assessment is completed, the local authority must prepare a pathway plan for the child.[398] This will usually be drawn up by the child's social worker.[399] The purpose of the pathway plan, in broad terms, is to set out the action that must be taken by the local authority looking after the child to ensure that they are 'provided with the services they need to enable them to achieve their aspirations and make a successful transition to adulthood'.[400]

396 See CPPCR(E) Regs 2010 regs 2(1) and 24(3); and fn 318 above for the meaning of 'connected' person.

397 See para 9.90.

398 CPPCR(E) Regs 2010 reg 43(1).

399 *Transition to adulthood guidance*, para 3.12.

400 *Transition to adulthood guidance*, para 3.5; see further paras 3.4–3.16.

9.132 The pathway plan must be prepared in accordance with CPPCR(E) Regs 2010 reg 43.[401] It must include:[402]

1) the child's care plan;[403]
2) the name of the child's personal adviser;
3) the nature and level of contact and personal support to be provided to the child, and by whom;
4) details of the accommodation the child is to occupy when they cease to be looked after;
5) the plan for the child's continuing education or training when they cease to be looked after;
6) how the local authority will assist the child in obtaining employment or other purposeful activity or occupation;
7) the support to be provided to enable the child to develop and sustain appropriate family and social relationships;
8) a programme to develop the practical and other skills the child needs to live independently;
9) the financial support to be provided to enable the child to meet accommodation and maintenance costs;
10) the child's health care needs (including any physical, emotional or mental health needs) and how they are to be met when the child ceases to be looked after;
11) the local authority's contingency plans in the event that the pathway plan ceases to be effective for any reason.

9.133 In relation to the matters set out at (3)–(11) of this list, the pathway plan must also set out the precise manner in which the local authority proposes to meet the child's needs, the date by which any action required to implement the plan will be carried out and the identity of the person responsible for that action.[404] The high level of specificity required by the CPPCR(E) Regs 2010 reflects the fact that a pathway plan is intended to contain far more than 'vague aspirations' – rather, it should be a 'detailed operational plan' that should 'spell out who does what, where and when'.[405]

401 ChA 1989 Sch 2 para 19B(7); CPPCR(E) Regs 2010 reg 41(b).

402 CPPCR(E) Regs 2010 reg 43 and Sch 8.

403 See paras 9.91–9.95.

404 CPPCR(E) Regs 2010 reg 43(2).

405 *R (J) v Caerphilly CBC* [2005] EWHC 586 (Admin) at paras 39, 45, 46 per Munby J; see paras 39–48. See further *R (A) v Lambeth LBC* [2010] EWHC 1652 (Admin) at para 21 per Kenneth Parker J; *R (A) v Lambeth LBC* [2010] EWHC 2439 (Admin) at paras 2 and 6 per Kenneth Parker J; and *R (Birara) v Hounslow LBC* [2010] EWHC 2113 (Admin) at para 54 per Dobbs J.

The personal adviser

9.134 The personal adviser who must be appointed for an eligible child is intended to be 'the focal point to ensure that care leavers are provided with the right kind of personal support'.[406] To that end, the functions of the personal adviser are to:[407]

- provide advice (including practical advice) and support;
- participate in reviews of the child's case;[408]
- liaise with the local authority looking after the child in the implementation of the pathway plan;
- coordinate the provision of services and take reasonable steps to ensure that the child makes use of such services,
- remain informed about the child's progress and well-being; and
- maintain a written record of their contacts with the child.

9.135 The role of the personal adviser has been described by one judge as being 'the advocate or representative of the child in the course of the child's dealings with the local authority'.[409] As such, the personal adviser may be an employee of the local authority, but should not be the person who undertakes the assessment, or writes or reviews the pathway plan, or the person who makes or contributes to resources decisions that affect the support received by the child.[410]

Duties owed to relevant children

Overview

9.136 A relevant child is a child who:[411]

- is aged 16 or 17;
- is no longer being looked after by any local authority in England or Wales; and
- was an eligible child before they last ceased to be looked after; or
- was detained or in hospital on their 16th birthday and immediately prior to being detained or admitted to hospital had been

406 *Transition to adulthood guidance*, para 3.18; see further paras 3.17–3.47.
407 CPPCR(E) Regs 2010 reg 44.
408 See paras 9.94–9.95.
409 *R (J) v Caerphilly CBC* [2005] EWHC 586 (Admin) at para 30 per Munby J.
410 See *R (J) v Caerphilly CBC* at paras 26–32 per Munby J; and *R (A) v Lambeth LBC* [2010] EWHC 1652 (Admin) at paras 24–41 per Kenneth Parker J.
411 ChA 1989 s23A(2)–(3); CL(E) Regs 2010 reg 3(1)–(2).

looked after by a local authority for a total period of 13 weeks or more,[412] which began on or after their 14th birthday.[413]

9.137 A child will cease to be a relevant child if they live for a continuous period of six months or more with a parent or some other person who has parental responsibility for them, save where the placement breaks down.[414]

9.138 The responsible local authority in respect of a relevant child is defined as the local authority which last looked after the child.[415] A local authority with responsibility for a relevant child is required to:

- take reasonable steps to keep in touch with the child, whether the child is within its area or not;[416]
- appoint a personal adviser for the child if it has not done so already;[417]
- carry out a needs assessment and prepare a pathway plan, if it has not done so already,[418] setting out the advice, assistance and support which it intends to provide under ChA 1989 Part III;[419]
- safeguard and promote the child's welfare;[420]
- maintain the child (unless it is satisfied that the child's welfare does not require this);[421]
- provide the child with, or maintain them in, suitable accommodation;[422]

412 This can consist of any number of shorter periods of being looked after, providing the total amounts to 13 weeks or more. See CL(E) Regs 2010 reg 3(2)(c).

413 A child who has been accommodated for 13 weeks or more as a result of a series of short breaks will not satisfy this criterion. See CL(E) Regs 2010 reg 3(3).

414 CL(E) Regs 2010 reg 3(5) and (6).

415 ChA 1989 s23A(4).

416 ChA 1989 ss23A(1) and 23B(1).

417 ChA 1989 ss23A(1) and 23B(2).

418 ChA 1989 ss23A(1) and 23B(3).

419 ChA 1989 ss23A(1), 23B(3) and 23E(1)(b).

420 CA 1989 ss23A(1) and 23B(8). Support provided by the local authority to comply with this duty may be in cash (ChA 1989 ss23A(1) and 23B(9)) and the provision of support may be subject to repayment conditions (ChA 1989 ss23B(12) and 17(7)–(9)).

421 ChA 1989 ss23A(1) and 23B(8)(a). Support may be in cash and/or subject to repayment conditions. See fn 420.

422 ChA 1989 ss23A(1) and 23B(8)(b); CL(E) Regs 2010 reg 9(2). Support may be in cash and/or subject to repayment conditions. See fn 420.

- provide assistance in order to meet the child's needs in relation to education, training or employment as provided for in the pathway plan;[423]
- consider (without delay) how to re-establish contact with any child it has lost contact with, and then take reasonable steps to do so until either it succeeds in making contact or the child ceases to be a relevant child.[424]

9.139 Before making any decision in relation to a relevant child the responsible local authority, so far as is reasonably practicable, is required to ascertain the wishes and feelings of:[425]

- the child;
- the child's parents and any other person with parental responsibility for the child;
- any other person whose wishes and feelings the local authority considers to be relevant – for example, a grandparent who has been involved in the child's care.

9.140 The responsible local authority is then required to take these wishes and feelings into account when making the decision, as well as consider the child's religious persuasion, racial origin, and cultural and linguistic background.[426]

The needs assessment for the relevant child

9.141 As has been discussed at paras 9.130–9.133, the local authority looking after an eligible child is required to carry out an assessment of their needs and then prepare a pathway plan.[427] If these duties have been complied with, then, when the child ceases to be looked after and becomes a relevant child, there will be no need to carry out a new needs assessment.[428] Instead, the responsible local authority need only keep the child's existing pathway plan under review.[429] However, where for some reason a pathway plan has not already been completed, then the local authority responsible for the relevant child must complete an assessment of the child's needs within three

423 ChA 1989 ss23A(1) and 23B(8)(c); CL(E) Regs 2010 reg 9(1). Support may be in cash and/or subject to repayment conditions. See fn 420.

424 ChA 1989 s23B(11).

425 ChA 1989 ss23B(13), 22(4).

426 ChA 1989 ss23B(13), 22(5).

427 ChA 1989 Sch 2 para 19B(4).

428 ChA 1989 s23B(3).

429 See paras 9.148–9.151.

months of the child ceasing to be looked after.[430] The needs assessment must take account of:[431]

- the child's health and development;
- the child's need for education, training or employment;
- the support available to the child from members of the child's family and other persons;
- the child's financial needs;
- the extent to which the child possesses the practical and other skills necessary for independent living;
- the child's needs for care, support and accommodation;
- the views of: the child's parents; any other person with parental responsibility; any person who on a day-to-day basis cares for or provides accommodation for the child; any educational institution attended by the child; the local authority for the area in which the child lives (where the child lives outside of the area of the relevant local authority); the child's designated teacher (where they are a registered pupil at a school); any person providing health care or treatment to the child; any person providing the child with advocacy services under ChA 1989 s26A; the child's personal adviser; and any other person whose views the responsible authority, or the child, consider may be relevant, unless it is not reasonably practicable to do so;
- if relevant, any needs that the child might have arising from their status as either a victim (or possible victim) of human trafficking or UASC.

9.142 In carrying out a needs assessment, the responsible local authority must, unless it is not reasonably practicable:[432]

- seek out, have regard to and retain a written record of the views of the child; and
- take all reasonable steps to enable the child to attend and participate in any meetings at which their case is to be considered.

9.143 Written records must be kept of the identity of the persons whose views have been sought for the purpose of carrying out the assess-

430 ChA 1989 s23B(3); CL(E) Regs 2010 reg 5(1)–(2)(a).

431 CL(E) Regs 2010 reg 5(1) and (3). The requirements are very similar to the requirements of a needs assessment for an eligible child set out in CPPCR(E) Regs 2010 reg 42(2). See para 9.130. The differences principally reflect the fact that the child is no longer looked after. For example, there is no need to seek the views of the IRO (see para 9.90) when assessing the needs of a relevant child.

432 CL(E) Regs 2010 reg 4(1) and (3).

ment, the information obtained in the course of the assessment, the deliberations at any meetings held in connection with any aspect of the assessment and the results of the assessment.[433]

9.144 After the needs assessment has been completed, the responsible local authority must provide the child with a copy as soon as practicable; and, unless it is not reasonably practicable to do so, ensure that the contents are explained to the child.[434]

The pathway plan for the relevant child

9.145 As noted in the preceding section,[435] the local authority looking after an eligible child is required to carry out an assessment of the child's needs and then prepare a pathway plan.[436] If these duties have been complied with, then, when the child ceases to be looked after and becomes a relevant child, the child's existing pathway can simply be kept under review in accordance with the principles outlined at paras 9.148–9.151. However, where for some reason a pathway plan has not already been completed then the local authority responsible for the relevant child must prepare one as soon as possible after completing the needs assessment described at paras 9.141–9.144,[437] setting out the advice, assistance and support which it intends to provide under ChA 1989 Part III.[438]

9.146 A pathway plan prepared for a relevant child must be in writing[439] and must include:[440]

- the nature and level of contact and personal support to be provided, and by whom, to the child;
- a detailed plan for the education or training of the child;
- how the responsible authority will assist the child in relation to employment or other purposeful activity or occupation;
- contingency plans for action to be taken by the responsible authority should the pathway plan for any reason cease to be effective;
- details of the accommodation the child is to occupy (including an assessment of its suitability in the light of the child's needs, and

433 CL(E) Regs 2010 reg 5(1) and (4).
434 CL(E) Regs 2010 reg 4(2).
435 See para 9.141.
436 ChA 1989 Sch 2 para 19B(4).
437 ChA 1989 s23B(3); CL(E) Regs 2010 reg 6(1).
438 ChA 1989 s23E(1)(b).
439 CL(E) Regs 2010 reg 6(4).
440 CL(E) Regs 2010 reg 6(2) and (4) and Sch 1. See further the *Transition to adulthood guidance*, paras 3.11–3.16.

details of the considerations taken into account in assessing that suitability);

- the support to be provided to enable the child to develop and sustain appropriate family and social relationships;
- a programme to develop the practical and other skills necessary for the child to live independently;
- the financial support to be provided to the child (in particular where it is to be provided to meet accommodation and maintenance needs);
- the health needs, including any mental health needs, of the child, and how they are to be met;
- details of the arrangements made by the responsible authority to meet the child's needs in relation to identity, with particular regard to the child's religious persuasion, racial origin, and cultural and linguistic background;
- whether (if relevant) the child need's arising from their status as either a victim (or possible victim) of human trafficking or an UASC, are being met.

9.147 In respect of each of these matters, the pathway plan must set out the manner in which the responsible local authority proposes to meet the needs of the child, the date by which any action required to implement any aspect of the plan will be carried out, and the identity of the person responsible for taking that action. As noted at para 9.133, the high level of specificity required of a pathway plan reflects the parliamentary intention that it should contain far more than 'vague aspirations' – rather, it should be a 'detailed operational plan' that should 'spell out who does what, where and when'.[441]

9.148 The responsible local authority must carry out a review of a relevant child's pathway plan:[442]

- if requested to do so by the child;
- if the authority or the personal adviser considers that a review is necessary;
- in any event, at intervals of not more than six months; and
- as soon as practicable after the end of the 28-day period beginning on the day on which, if applicable, the child is

441 *R (J) v Caerphilly CBC* [2005] EWHC 586 (Admin) at paras 39, 45, 46 per Munby J; see paras 39–48. See further *R (A) v Lambeth LBC* [2010] EWHC 1652 (Admin) at para 21 per Kenneth Parker J; *R (A) v Lambeth LBC* [2010] EWHC 2439 (Admin) at paras 2 and 6 per Kenneth Parker J; and *R (Birara) v Hounslow LBC* [2010] EWHC 2113 (Admin) at para 54 per Dobbs J.

442 CL(E) Regs 2010 reg 7(1)–(3).

accommodated under ChA 1989 23B(8)(b)[443] and at regular intervals of not more than three months thereafter.

9.149 The purpose of the review is to consider whether any change is necessary in relation to the various matters set out in the pathway plan.[444] To that end, the local authority carrying out the review should, to the extent it considers it appropriate to do so, seek and take account of the views of the various people who were consulted in carrying out the needs assessment.[445] The results of the review and any change to the pathway plan must then be recorded in writing.[446]

9.150 In preparing or reviewing a pathway plan, the responsible local authority must, unless it is not reasonably practicable:[447]

- seek out, have regard to and retain a written record of the views of the child; and
- take all reasonable steps to enable the child to attend and participate in any meetings at which the child's case is to be considered.

9.151 After the pathway plan or review has been completed, the responsible local authority must provide the child with a copy as soon as practicable; and, unless it is not reasonably practicable to do so, ensure that the contents are explained to the child.[448] The statutory guidance suggests that where agencies are contributing to the delivery of child's pathway plan, it will also be good practice if they are given a copy of the relevant extract from the plan relating to their contribution.[449]

The personal adviser

9.152 The role and identity of the personal adviser have been described, in the context of the duties owed to eligible children, at paras 9.134–9.135. The functions of a relevant child's personal adviser are very

443 See paras 9.155–9.159.
444 CL(E) Regs 2010 reg 7(4)(b).
445 CL(E) Regs 2010 reg 7(4)(a). See para 9.139.
446 CL(E) Regs 2010 reg 7(5).
447 CL(E) Regs 2010 reg 4(1) and (3).
448 CL(E) Regs 2010 reg 4(2).
449 *Transition to adulthood guidance*, para 3.16.

similar to those of an eligible child's personal adviser.[450] In particular, the personal adviser must:[451]

- provide advice and support to the relevant child;
- participate in the assessment and the preparation and review of the pathway plan;
- liaise with the local authority in the implementation of the pathway plan;
- coordinate the provision of appropriate services and take reasonable steps to ensure that the child makes use of them;
- remain informed about the child's progress and well-being; and
- keep a written record of contacts with, and services provided to, the child.

9.153 The main difference between these functions and those which must be carried out on behalf of an eligible child is that the relevant child's personal adviser may potentially have a more active role in the preparation and review of the pathway plan.[452] However, as discussed, at para 9.135, the personal adviser should not themself carry out the needs assessment, write the pathway plan or take sole responsibility for the review process.

9.154 In addition to the functions described above, where the relevant child is accommodated by the local authority, the personal adviser will also need to visit the child at the accommodation, within seven-days of the accommodation being provided, then again before the next review of the child's pathway plan and at intervals of not more than two months thereafter.[453] The statutory guidance emphasises that these are minimum requirements and that 'where care leavers develop problems as they assume the responsibilities of adulthood they should expect, and will require, much more frequent personal contact with their PA'.[454]

450 Note, however, that the statutory basis of the personal adviser's functions is different: the functions of the personal adviser of an 'eligible child' are set out in CPPCR(E) Regs 2010 reg 44; and the functions of the personal adviser of a 'relevant child' are set out in CL(E) Regs 2010 reg 8.

451 CL(E) Regs 2010 reg 8(1). See further the *Transition to adulthood guidance*, paras 3.17–3.47.

452 Contrast CL(E) Regs 2010 reg 8(1)(b) and (c) with CPPCR(E) Regs 2010 reg 44.

453 CL(E) Regs 2010 reg 8(2).

454 *Transition to adulthood guidance*, para 3.39.

Accommodation

9.155 A local authority with responsibility for a relevant child is required to secure suitable accommodation for the child's occupation. The local authority may choose to accommodate the child itself, or to maintain the child in accommodation[455] – for example, by arranging and paying for the accommodation on the child's behalf.[456]

9.156 'Suitable' accommodation in this context means accommodation:[457]

- which so far as reasonably practicable is suitable for the child in the light of the child's needs, including any health needs and any needs arising from any disability;
- in respect of which the local authority has satisfied itself as to the character and suitability of the landlord or other provider; and
- in respect of which the local authority has, so far as reasonably practicable, taken into account the child's wishes and feelings and education, training or employment needs.

9.157 In assessing whether accommodation is suitable, the local authority will need to have regard to:[458]

- the facilities, services and support available at the accommodation;
- the safety and state of repair of the accommodation;
- the location of the accommodation;
- the tenancy status of the accommodation;
- the financial commitments involved for the child and their affordability;
- the child's views about the accommodation;
- the child's understanding of their rights and responsibilities in relation to the accommodation;
- the child's understanding of the arrangements for funding the accommodation.

9.158 The statutory guidance advises local authorities that 'a range of semi-independent and independent accommodation options for care leavers will be required' in order to cater for the 'diverse needs of care leavers and the way in which these will change over time'.[459] The

455 ChA 1989 s23A(1) and 23B(8)(b).

456 ChA 1989 s23B(9) specifically empowers the local authority to provide cash support.

457 ChA 1989 s23B(10); CL(E) Regs 2000 reg 9(2).

458 CL(E) Regs 2010 reg 9(3) and Sch 2 paras 1 and 2. This list is not exhaustive: other relevant factors may arise on a case-by-case basis.

459 *Transition to adulthood guidance*, para 7.18.

following examples are given of the range of options that might be considered:[460]

- enabling the child to remain in the accommodation in which they lived while being looked after;
- supported lodgings;[461]
- foyers and other supported housing;[462]
- trainer flats 'where young people can "practice" living more independently without compromising their future housing options';[463]
- specialist accommodation, 'for example self-contained accommodation with personal assistance support, or therapeutic placements for young people with specific support needs such as disabilities and mental health difficulties';[464]
- independent accommodation, either in the social or private rented sector, with flexible floating support as required;[465]
- living with birth families.

9.159 Statutory guidance directed at the specific needs of 16/17-year-olds reminds local authorities that it will not usually be appropriate for this group to be placed in temporary accommodation unless there is on-site support, and that 'bed and breakfast accommodation, including hotels and nightly let accommodation with shared facilities' should never be regarded as suitable.[466] In contrast, the *Transition to adulthood guidance* adopts a slightly less prescriptive approach suggesting that 'Bed and Breakfast accommodation is not considered to be suitable other than for very exceptional emergency circumstances' and that such placements should be limited to a duration of no more than two working days.[467]

460 *Transition to adulthood guidance,* para 7.18.
461 See further *Transition to adulthood guidance,* paras 7.60–7.62.
462 See further *Transition to adulthood guidance,* paras 7.63–7.64.
463 *Transition to adulthood guidance,* para 7.18.
464 *Transition to adulthood guidance,* para 7.18.
465 See further *Transition to adulthood guidance,* paras 7.65–7.73.
466 *Prevention of homelessness and provision of accommodation for 16 and 17 year old young people,* paras 5.10 and 5.13.
467 *Transition to adulthood guidance,* para 7.12.

Duties owed to former relevant children

Overview

9.160 A 'former relevant child' is a young person who was either an eligible[468] or a relevant child[469] at the time they reached the age of 18.[470] The local authority which last looked after a former relevant child[471] will owe the child the following duties:

1) To take reasonable steps to keep in touch with the child (irrespective of whether the child is within its area or not).[472] The statutory guidance reminds local authorities that, in keeping in touch, they should respect the privacy of the former relevant child, but that they should endeavour to maintain contact 'in the same way that a reasonable parent might try to resume contact with an estranged adult child'.[473]
2) To take reasonable steps to re-establish contact if it loses touch with the child.[474]
3) To continue the appointment of the child's personal adviser.[475] The personal adviser should have been appointed before the former relevant child reached the age of 18. The role of the personal adviser is discussed at paras 9.134–9.135.[476]
4) To keep the child's pathway plan under regular review.[477] The pathway plan should have been prepared before the former relevant child reached the age of 18. Once the child reaches the age of 18 and becomes a former relevant child, the requirement is simply to keep that plan under review in accordance with the principles discussed at paras 9.148–9.151.[478] This process of review ensures that the content of the plan reflects the former relevant child's changing needs and entitlements. For example, the statutory guidance reminds local authorities that former relevant children may be eligible for mainstream welfare benefits, and

468 See paras 9.127–9.135.
469 See paras 9.136–9.159.
470 ChA 1989 s23C(1).
471 ChA 1989 ss23C(1)–(5A), read together with s23A(4).
472 ChA 1989 s23C(2)(a).
473 *Transition to adulthood guidance*, paras 4.38–4.39.
474 ChA 1989 s23C(2)(b).
475 ChA 1989 s23C(3)(a).
476 See CL(E) Regs 2010 reg 8.
477 ChA 1989 s23C(3)(b). See further *Transition to adulthood guidance*, paras 4.13–4.20.
478 CL(E) Regs 2010 regs 4 and 7.

that as they mature and develop they should be empowered to take control of the pathway planning process.[479]

5) To give assistance, to the extent that the former relevant child's welfare requires it, by contributing to expenses which the child incurs in living near the place where they are, or will be, employed or seeking employment.[480]
6) To give assistance, to the extent that the former relevant child's welfare and educational or training needs require it,[481] by contributing to expenses the child incurs in living near the place where they are, or will be, receiving education or training.[482] This may include financial contributions toward the cost of accommodation.[483] Where a local authority is providing education and training related assistance to a former relevant child who is in full-time further or higher education,[484] a secondary duty arises requiring the local authority to secure the former relevant child with vacation accommodation if the child's term-time accommodation is not available.[485]
7) To give assistance, to the extent that the former relevant child's welfare and educational or training needs require it, by making a grant to enable the child to meet expenses connected with their education or training.[486] This may include the payment of tuition fees.[487]
8) To give other assistance, to the extent that the child's welfare requires it.[488] This may be assistance in kind or, in exceptional

479 *Transition to adulthood guidance*, paras 4.7–4.12.

480 ChA 1989 ss23C(4)(a) and 24B(1). See further *Transition to adulthood guidance*, paras 5.1–5.12.

481 The purpose of this provision is to provide welfare *and* education related support (and not purely education related support) and hence the duty may be engaged, for example, for the purposes of avoiding destitution, providing it is connected with the young person's education. See *R (CVN) v Croydon LBC* [2023] EWHC 464 (Admin). This is likely to be of principal relevance in cases where the young person is aged 21 or over, and so not eligible for support under ChA 1989 s23C(4)(c) and where the NIAA 2002 Sch 3 exclusions apply. See paras 9.195–9.217.

482 ChA 1989 ss23C(4)(b) and 24B(2). See further *Transition to adulthood guidance*, paras 5.1–5.12.

483 *R (Sabiri) v Croydon LBC* [2012] EWHC 1236 (Admin).

484 Within the meaning of CL(E) Regs 2010 reg 9(4).

485 ChA 1989 ss23C(9) and 24B(5).

486 ChA 1989 ss23C(4)(b) and 24B(2). See fn 481.

487 *R (Kebede) v Newcastle City Council* [2013] EWHC 355 (Admin).

488 ChA 1989 s23C(4)(c).

circumstances, cash.[489] It may also include the provision of accommodation.[490]

9) To pay 'the relevant amount' to any former relevant child who is pursuing higher education, of at least two academic years' duration, in accordance with their pathway plan.[491] The relevant amount is currently set at £2,000.[492] It may be paid to the former relevant child as a lump sum or by instalments.[493] This payment is referred to as a 'higher education bursary'.[494] The duty to pay the higher education bursary is 'without prejudice' to the duty to contribute to the former relevant child's education and training related expenses to the extent that the child's welfare requires.[495] Where a local authority provides a former relevant child with a higher education bursary, a secondary duty arises requiring the local authority to secure the former relevant child with vacation accommodation if their term-time accommodation is not available.[496]

9.161 The provision of this support may be subject to repayment conditions.[497]

9.162 In determining the support to be provided to a former relevant child and in planning for their future, a local authority is entitled to take into account the child's immigration status.[498] The statutory guidance suggests that 'planning may initially have to be based around short term achievable goals whilst entitlement to remain in the UK is being determined'.[499]

9.163 The duties set out above subsist until the former relevant child reaches the age of 21, save where the former relevant child's pathway

489 ChA 1989 s23C(5).

490 *R (O) v Barking and Dagenham LBC* [2010] EWCA Civ 1101, [2011] 1 WLR 1283.

491 ChA 1989 s23C(5A); Children Act 1989 (Higher Education Bursary) (England) Regulations ('CA(HEB)(E) Regs') 2009 SI No 2274 reg 3.

492 CA(HEB)(E) Regs 2009 reg 2.

493 CA(HEB)(E) Regs 2009 reg 4(1).

494 CA(HEB)(E) Regs 2009 reg 2.

495 ChA 1989 s23C(5C).

496 ChA 1989 ss23C(9) and 24B(5).

497 ChA 1989 ss23C(10) and 17(7)–(9).

498 *R (Kebede) v Newcastle City Council* [2013] EWHC 355 (Admin) at para 20 per Sir Stanley Burnton; *R (Nfuni) v Solihull MBC* [2013] EWHC 3155 (Admin).

499 *Transition to adulthood guidance*, para 6.21. See also *Care of unaccompanied migrant children and child victims of modern slavery: statutory guidance for local authorities*, DfE, November 2017, paras 89–95 (www.gov.uk/government/publications/care-of-unaccompanied-and-trafficked-children).

plan sets out a programme of education or training which extends beyond then. In such a case the fifth, eighth and ninth duties will come to an end. The remaining duties will continue so long as the former relevant child continues to pursue that programme, up until the age of 25.[500] For these purposes, any interruptions in the former relevant child's pursuit of the education or training programme should be disregarded providing the local authority is satisfied that they will resume it as soon as reasonably practicable.[501]

9.164 However, the coming to an end of the duties under ChA 1989 s23C does not mean that children's services can sever all ties with the former relevant child and that the child is left entirely without support. There are two situations in which a former relevant child may be owed further duties even after the duties under ChA 1989 s23C have ended. First, where the former relevant child subsequently decides that they wish to pursue a programme of education or training. Second, while the former relevant child remains under the age of 25, if the child requests advice and support from the local authority. These two situations will be discussed in turn.

Former relevant children seeking to return to education or training[502]

9.165 A former relevant child who is under the age of 25 and who, for whatever reason, was not in a programme of education or training on or after their 21st birthday and therefore ceased receiving support, may become eligible for support once more if they start to pursue, or decide that they wish to pursue, a programme of education or training. If they inform the local authority which was last responsible for the child as a former relevant child[503] of this fact, the local authority is required to:[504]

- appoint a personal adviser;[505]
- carry out a needs assessment with a view to determining what assistance it would be appropriate to provide;[506]

500 ChA 1989 ss23C(6)–(7) and 24B(3).

501 ChA 1989 s23C(8).

502 The particular difficulties faced by former relevant children seek to pursue education or training while their immigration status is precarious and future in the UK is uncertain are discussed further at paras 11.116–11.126.

503 ChA 1989 s23CA(11).

504 ChA 1989 s23CA(1)–(5).

505 ChA 1989 s23CA(2). See CL(E) Regs 2010 reg 8; and paras 9.134–9.135 for the functions of the personal adviser.

506 ChA 1989 s23CA(3)(a).

- prepare a pathway plan setting out the advice, assistance and support which the local authority intends to provide;[507]
- give assistance, to the extent the former relevant child's educational or training needs require it, by contributing to expenses incurred by living near the place where they are, or will be, receiving education or training, or by making a grant to enable them to meet education and training related expenses.[508] The provision of such assistance to a former relevant child who is in full-time further or higher education,[509] gives rise to secondary duty which requires the local authority to secure the former relevant child with vacation accommodation if their term-time accommodation is not available.[510]

9.166 The requirements of the needs assessment and pathway plan for a relevant child are discussed at paras 9.141–9.151. The requirements of the needs assessment and pathway plan for a former relevant child in this position are similar.[511] The principal distinction is that, because the duties owed to this cohort are limited to education and training-related assistance, the needs assessment and pathway plan will be focused on the need for, and provision of, such assistance.[512] The needs assessment should be completed within three months of the former relevant child informing the local authority that they are pursuing, or wish to pursue, a programme of education or training.[513] The pathway plan should be completed as soon as reasonably practicable thereafter.[514]

9.167 The statutory guidance emphasises that in deciding whether and how to support a former relevant child under ChA 1989 s23CA 'the definition of a programme of education or training must be interpreted broadly'.[515] For example:

> . . . this might include options such as: completion of a basic skills course, so that the young person has the numeracy and literacy skills needed to compete in the jobs market; take up of a course of further

507 ChA 1989 ss23CA(3)(b) and 23E(1)(b).

508 ChA 1989 s23CA(4)–(7). See further paras 9.183–9.185. The provision of assistance may be subject to repayment conditions. See ChA 1989 ss23CA(8) and 17(7)–(9).

509 Within the meaning of CL(E) Regs 2010 reg 9(4).

510 ChA 1989 ss23CA(9) and 24B(5).

511 CL(E) Regs 2010 regs 5 and 6.

512 CL(E) Regs 2010 regs 5(5) and 6(2)(b).

513 CL(E) Regs 2010 reg 5(2)(b).

514 CL(E) Regs 2010 reg 6(1).

515 *Transition to adulthood guidance*, para 3.49.

education; take up of a university place; support to enable the young person to complete a recognised postgraduate qualification; or participation in vocational training and apprenticeships.[516]

9.168 The duties under ChA 1989 s23CA subsist so long as the former relevant child continues to pursue the programme of education or training set out in their pathway plan.[517] Interruptions in the pursuit of the programme should be disregarded providing the local authority is satisfied that the former relevant child will resume it as soon as reasonably practicable.[518]

Former relevant children under the age of 25 who have requested advice and support

9.169 A former relevant child who:

- is aged between 21 and 25;
- is, or has been, owed duties under ChA 1989 s23C;
- informs the local authority that owes, or owed, those duties that the child wishes to receive advice and support;

will be owed the duties under ChA 1989 s23CZB(3)–(6).[519] These are relatively new duties, inserted by CSWA 2017 s3 and in force from 1 April 2018, which 'enable local authorities to respond positively to requests for support from care leavers aged 21–25 who may be continuing to struggle with the transition to independence and adult life'.[520] The objective of the duties is described in the statutory guidance as being 'to protect care leavers aged 21 up to age 25 from feeling isolated, not having anybody to turn to for advice or support, or continuing to struggle with the transition to adult life'.[521] This is achieved by means of the provision of '[personal adviser] support to all care leavers towards whom the local authority had duties under section 23C of the Children Act 1989, up to age 25 – irrespective of whether they are engaged in education or training'.[522]

9.170 Specifically, under ChA 1989 s23CZB(3)–(6) the local authority is required to:

516 *Transition to adulthood guidance*, para 3.49.
517 ChA 1989 s23CA(6).
518 ChA 1989 s23CA(7).
519 ChA 1989 s23CZB(1)–(2).
520 *Extending personal adviser support to all care leavers to age 25*, para 10.
521 *Extending personal adviser support to all care leavers to age 25*, para 37.
522 *Extending personal adviser support to all care leavers to age 25*, para 2.

- provide the former relevant child with a personal adviser until the child either reaches the age of 25 or, if earlier, informs the local authority that they no longer want a personal adviser;[523]
- carry out a needs assessment;[524]
- prepare a pathway plan setting out the advice, assistance and support which the local authority intends to provide.[525]

9.171 The purpose of the needs assessment is to determine:[526]

- whether any services offered by the local authority (under the ChA 1989 or otherwise) may assist in meeting their needs; and
- if so, what advice and support it would be appropriate for the local authority to provide for the purpose of helping the former relevant child to obtain those services.

9.172 Surprisingly, the detailed statutory requirements which apply to the needs assessment and pathway planning process in respect of other care leavers[527] do not seem to apply where the needs assessment and pathway plan are carried out pursuant to ChA 1989 s23CZB.[528] The same is true in respect of the functions of the personal adviser.[529] The ChA 1989 has been amended, to the extent necessary, to provide the secretary of state with the power either to amend the CL(E) Regs 2010 so that the requirements therein in relation to needs assessment, pathway planning and personal advisers apply to the performance of the duties under ChA 1989 s23CZB, or to make equivalent regulations.[530] That power has not yet been exercised. This light touch approach to regulating the performance of the new duties would appear to allow for a degree of flexibility in the needs assessment and pathway planning process. For, example, the statutory guidance suggests that in some cases a 'full needs assessment' and a 'full pathway plan'[531] will be needed, 'covering each dimension of the young person's life'.[532] Whereas in other cases, such as where a

523 ChA 1989 s23CZB(3).

524 ChA 1989 s23CZB(4)(a).

525 ChA 1989 ss23CZB(4)(b) and 23E(1)(aa).

526 ChA 1989 s23CZB(5).

527 See paras 9.141–9.151, 9.160 and 9.166.

528 See CL(E) Regs 2010 regs 5(1) and 6(1).

529 See CL(E) Regs 2010 reg 8(1), read with the definition of personal adviser in reg 2(1).

530 See ChA 1989 ss23D(2) and 23E(1B).

531 Presumably this is a reference to a needs assessment and pathway plan complying with all of the requirements of CL(E) Regs 2010 regs 5 and 6.

532 *Extending personal adviser support to all care leavers to age 25*, paras 16–19.

former relevant child seeks advice on a single issue, a more limited assessment and plan may be warranted.[533] However, the guidance sensibly reminds local authorities that 'care leavers may in fact require support on a broader range of issues than they initially report, [and] carrying out a full needs assessment may help to identify any additional needs'.[534]

9.173 Once the needs assessment has been completed, the local authority then becomes subject to a duty to provide the advice and support that has been identified in the assessment as being appropriate to help the former relevant child access the services they need from the local authority.[535] It will be noted that, unusually, the duty under ChA 1989 s23CZB(6) is not a duty directly to provide the former relevant child with the services the child needs, rather, it is a duty to provide advice and support to help the former relevant child access those services. In this context, the statutory guidance suggests that ChA 1989 s23CZB(6) 'does not introduce additional duties on [local authorities] in relation to, for example, accommodating care leavers'.[536] However, the use of the words 'advice and support', suggests that ChA 1989 s23CZB(6) requires children's services to do far more than simply signpost the former relevant child to other statutory services. The language of ChA 1989 s23CZB(6) is plainly intended to encompass active assistance to access those services, and is broad enough to encompass the provision of interim support while this takes place. Examples are given within the statutory guidance of the provision of interim accommodation while a former relevant child is assisted to access accommodation from the housing department, and the provision of financial support while a young person is assisted to access mainstream welfare benefits.[537]

9.174 Where a former relevant child aged between 21 and 25 to whom the local authority owed, or owes, duties under ChA 1989 s23C is not receiving advice and support under s23CZB, the local authority is required to contact them as soon as possible after they reach the age of 21 and at least once every 12 months thereafter.[538] This will then

533 *Extending personal adviser support to all care leavers to age 25*, para 16.
534 *Extending personal adviser support to all care leavers to age 25*, para 16.
535 ChA 1989 s23CZB(6).
536 *Extending personal adviser support to all care leavers to age 25*, para 33.
537 *Extending personal adviser support to all care leavers to age 25*, pp11–12.
538 ChA 1989 s23CZB(7).

provide the child with the opportunity to request advice or support, if they wish.[539]

Duties owed to qualifying children and young people

9.175 Thus far, this section of the chapter has discussed what it means to be an eligible child,[540] a relevant child[541] and a former relevant child,[542] and considered the various rights and entitlements which these groups have under ChA 1989 Part III. Those rights and entitlements are intended to meet the additional needs which young people may have as a result of having spent a significant amount of time[543] in the care of, or being looked after by, a local authority. The idea is that the local authority, as the care leaver's corporate parent, should provide support to them in the same way that a reasonable parent would to their own child, in order to assist the care leaver in making the transition to adulthood.[544]

9.176 However, there will be a cohort of children and young people who have similar needs to eligible, relevant and former relevant children but who do not meet the statutory requirements to fall into one of those categories. For example, a child who has been looked after for a few days short of the 13-week period needed to qualify as an eligible child. Such a child may also need additional support in order to make the transition to adulthood and may not have a parent who is in a position to provide that support. In order to meet the needs of this cohort of care leaver, ChA 1989 s24 creates an additional category of 'person qualifying for advice and assistance' who may be entitled to support from their local authority. The statutory guidance describes this cohort a 'qualifying children' and notes that some falling within the cohort 'will be as vulnerable and have very similar needs to eligible, relevant or former relevant children'.[545]

9.177 There are two categories of 'person qualifying for advice and assistance':[546]

539 *Extending personal adviser support to all care leavers to age 25*, paras 27–32.
540 See paras 9.127–9.135.
541 See paras 9.136–9.159.
542 See paras 9.160–9.174.
543 Thirteen weeks or more, beginning on or after the child's 14th birthday and ending on or after their 16th birthday. See ChA 1989 Sch 2 para 19B(2); CPPCR(E) Regs 2010 reg 40(1); and para 9.127.
544 See paras 9.118–9.126.
545 *Transition to Adulthood guidance*, para 2.6.
546 ChA 1989 s24(1)–(1B).

1) The first category encompasses those:[547]
   - aged between 16 and 21;
   - in respect of whom a special guardianship order is in force, or was in force when they reached the age of 18; and
   - who were looked after by a local authority immediately before the special guardianship order was made.
2) The second category encompasses those who are under the age of 21 and who were looked after, accommodated or fostered[548] at any time between the ages of 16 and 18.[549]

9.178 The local authority with responsibility for a qualifying child or young person who falls within either of these categories as a result of having been looked after, is the local authority which last looked after them.[550] In any other case, the responsible local authority is the local authority in whose area the child or young person is.[551] The responsible local authority has a power, and in some cases a duty, to befriend the qualifying child or young person and provide them with general advice and assistance,[552] coupled with a more specific power to provide advice and assistance in connection with employment, education and training.[553]

9.179 Those who fall within the second category of qualifying young person as a result of having been looked after by a local authority have the benefit of an additional duty under ChA 1989 s24(4), whereby the local authority which last looked after them must take such steps as it thinks appropriate to contact the child with a view to exercising its powers and duties,[554] meaning the local authority must actively seek out the qualifying child or young person in order to try to assist them.

547 ChA 1989 s24(1A).
548 As defined at ChA 1989 s24(2).
549 ChA 1989 s24(1B).
550 ChA 1989 s24(5)(za)–(a); Special Guardianship Regulations 2005 SI No 1109 reg 22.
551 ChA 1989 s24(5)(b).
552 ChA 1989 s24A. See paras 9.180–9.182.
553 ChA 1989 s24B. See paras 9.183–9.185.
554 ChA 1989 s24(4).

Befriending, advice and assistance

9.180 The local authority with responsibility for a qualifying child or young person is required to consider whether the following conditions are satisfied in respect of the child:[555]

- that the child needs befriending, advice and assistance; and
- that the person who had been looking after the child or young person (in circumstances where the child had been accommodated or fostered by someone other than a local authority) does not have the facilities to advise or befriend them.

9.181 If these two conditions are satisfied and the qualifying child or young person is someone who was previously looked after by a local authority or accommodated by, or on behalf of, a voluntary organisation, then the local authority is under a *duty* to advise and befriend the child.[556] In any other case where these two conditions are satisfied, the local authority has a *power* to advise and befriend the child or young person.[557] In addition, in any case where these two conditions are satisfied, the local authority has a power to give the qualifying child or young person assistance.[558] That may be assistance in kind or, in exceptional cases, by way of accommodation or cash.[559] Such assistance may be provided subject to conditions as to repayment.[560]

9.182 In contrast to the duties owed to eligible children,[561] relevant children[562] and former relevant children,[563] there is no express statutory duty to carry out a needs assessment or prepare a pathway plan in respect of a qualifying child or young person. However, the statutory guidance takes the pragmatic position that 'in order to determine the extent of the support required, a core assessment may be required and the plan that follows might follow the same format as a pathway plan for a relevant or former relevant child'.[564] Such a plan should outline the support to be provided to the young person, including, if

555 ChA 1989 s24A(1)–(2).
556 ChA 1989 s24A(3)(a).
557 ChA 1989 s24A(3)(b).
558 ChA 1989 s24A(4).
559 ChA 1989 s24A(5).
560 ChA 1989 s24A(6).
561 See paras 9.127–9.135.
562 See paras 9.136–9.159.
563 See paras 9.160–9.174.
564 *Transition to adulthood guidance*, para 2.9.

necessary, any financial support and should be drawn up by a social worker or suitably qualified person.[565]

Assistance with employment, education and training

9.183 If the qualifying child or young person is someone who was previously looked after by a local authority, then the responsible local authority may also provide assistance by contributing to expenses incurred by the child or young person in living near the place where they are, or will be, employed or seeking employment.[566]

9.184 In addition, the local authority has a power to give assistance to any such qualifying child or young person by:[567]

- contributing to expenses incurred by the person in question in living near the place where they are, or will be, receiving education or training; this may include financial contributions toward the cost of accommodation;[568]
- making a grant to enable the child to meet expenses connected with their education or training; this may include the payment of tuition fees.[569]

9.185 This power subsists until the qualifying child or young person reaches the age of 25.[570] The power is supplemented by a duty to secure any qualifying child or young person who is in full-time further or higher education[571] with vacation accommodation, where their term-time accommodation is not available.[572]

The discretion to assist where a local authority has failed to perform the Children Act 1989 s20 duty

9.186 It will be apparent from the discussion in the preceding sections that the various rights and entitlements available to care leavers may be of significant importance to a young person in making the transition to adulthood. However, by definition, they are only available to those who have left care. Or, to be more precise, they only are available to those who have been looked after by a local authority in England or

565 *Transition to adulthood guidance*, para 2.9.
566 ChA 1989 s24B(1).
567 ChA 1989 s24B(2).
568 *R (Sabiri) v Croydon LBC* [2012] EWHC 1236 (Admin).
569 *R (Kebede) v Newcastle City Council* [2013] EWHC 355 (Admin).
570 ChA 1989 s24B(3)(a).
571 Within the meaning of CL(E) Regs 2010 reg 9(4). See ChA 1989 s24B(6).
572 ChA 1989 s24B(5).

Wales for a total period of 13 weeks or more, beginning on or after their 14th birthday and ending on or after their 16th birthday.[573] In some cases, disputes arise as to whether these criteria are satisfied. Generally, such disputes occur where a local authority asserts that it did not look after the young person at all, and that the child was accommodated under some other power (such as ChA 1989 s17) or by another body (such as a local housing authority) or person (such as a friend of relative). In this chapter, these disputes are described as 'labelling' disputes, since the issue which they raise is the correct legal label to be given to the child's accommodation arrangements. The principles developed by the courts for the resolution of these labelling disputes are discussed at paras 9.104–9.117. However, this class of case will often give rise to a further, associated, legal conundrum, namely, what is the position where a young person was not accommodated by children's services for the 13-week period and did not acquire leaving care rights, because of some failing on the part of the local authority?

9.187 This was the situation which fell for consideration in *R (GE (Eritrea)) v SSHD and Bedford BC*.[574] In that case, there was a dispute over the claimant's age,[575] with the result that she was accommodated by the Home Office rather than the local authority to whom she had applied as a child in need. The Court of Appeal held, assuming that she had been a child at the time she came to the attention of children's services, that she could not be deemed to have been accommodated under ChA 1989 s20. In reaching this conclusion the court took as its starting point the principles explained by Baroness Hale in *R (M) v Hammersmith and Fulham LBC*:

> It is one thing to hold that the actions of a local children's services authority should be categorised according to what they should have done rather than what they may have thought, whether at the time or in retrospect, that they were doing. It is another thing entirely to hold that the actions of a local housing authority should be categorised according to what the children's services authority should have done had the case been drawn to their attention at the time. In all of the above cases, the children's services authority did something as a result of which the child was provided with accommodation. The question was what they had done. In this case, there is no evidence that the children's services authority did anything at all. It is impossible to

573 ChA 1989 Sch 2 para 19B(2); CPPCR(E) Regs 2010 reg 40(1). See paras 9.118–9.126.

574 [2014] EWCA Civ 1490, [2015] PTSR 854.

575 See paras 11.130–11.107.

> read the words 'a child who is . . . provided with accommodation by the authority in the exercise of any functions . . . which are social services functions within the meaning of the Local Authority Social Services Act 1970 . . .' to include a child who has not been drawn to the attention of the local social services authority or provided with any accommodation or other services by that authority.[576]

Applying these principles to the facts of GE's case, it was not possible 'to attribute the accommodation of GE by UKBA/NASS to' the local authority.[577]

9.188 Although the Court of Appeal did not expressly frame it in these terms, the legal issue underpinning the decision is causation. To qualify for leaving care rights a young person must have been 'looked after' by a local authority for the requisite amount of time and this requires the child either to have been in the care of the local authority or to have been 'provided with accommodation by the authority' in the exercise of certain of its social services functions.[578] As Baroness Hale explained in the passage quoted above, in order to satisfy this criteria there needs to be some action on the part of children's services as a result of which the child is provided with accommodation. Or, to put it another way, there must be a 'causal nexus' between the action of children's services and the result that the child is provided with accommodation.[579] The point of principle which, arguably, the Court of Appeal in *R (GE (Eritrea))* did not engage with to any significant degree, is when will this causal nexus be established? What is the test to be applied? What quality of causal connection will suffice?

9.189 In a case like *R (M) v Hammersmith and Fulham LBC* it is clear, without needing to provide a definitive answer to these questions, that no sufficient causal nexus could exist because children's services in that case simply were not involved. There was no act or omission which could be attributed to them as a result of which M was accommodated. Whereas in *R (GE v Eritrea))*, there was a significant degree of involvement from children's services in the form of two age assessments. These were ultimately quashed by the High Court,[580] which found that GE was the age that she had claimed all along,

576 [2008] UKHL 14, [2008] 1 WLR 535 at para 44.

577 *R (GE (Eritrea)) v SSHD and Bedford BC* [2014] EWCA Civ 1490, [2015] PTSR 854 at para 34 per Christopher Clarke LJ.

578 ChA 1989 s22(1)(b).

579 *R (B) v Nottingham City Council* [2011] EWHC 2933 (Admin) at para 61 per Singh J.

580 *R (GE (Eritrea)) v SSHD* [2015] EWHC 1406 (Admin) upheld by the Court of Appeal in *Bedford CC v GE (Eritrea)* [2017] EWCA Civ 1521.

putting it beyond doubt that she should have been accommodated under ChA 1989 s20 when, at the age of 16, she first came to the attention of children's services and her age was first assessed. As a result of the findings of those unlawful age assessments, GE remained in immigration detention and, shortly after the second age assessment was concluded, was (by court order in the judicial review proceedings) released to Home Office accommodation. As such, there was a direct causal connection between the actions of children's services and GE being accommodated by the Home Office: 'but for' the unlawful age assessments GE would not have been accommodated by the Home Office and would instead have been accommodated under ChA 1989 s20. Why did this not constitute a sufficient causal nexus? This is difficult to answer, particularly when a sufficient nexus had been found in the labelling cases discussed at paras 9.104–9.117 like *R (D) v Southwark LBC*,[581] where children's services initial actions were more limited, or *R (TG) v Lambeth LBC*[582] where the causal connection between children's services' actions and the child being accommodated by the housing department was equally remote. The Court of Appeal in *R (GE v Eritrea))* did not provide a clear answer to these questions and it may be that, in due course, this is an issue on which further judicial guidance is needed.

9.190 However, unless and until such guidance is forthcoming, the potential for injustice is mitigated by the court's conclusion that in cases where a local authority has failed properly to discharge its duties with the effect that the ChA 1989 s20 duty was not performed, the local authority may later use its discretionary powers to make good any unlawfulness that it has committed in the past and may, in some circumstances, be obliged to do so. In particular, the court held that (dependent on the outcome of the age assessment challenge) Bedford would have a discretion to provide GE with the services which would have been provided to a former relevant child,[583] to remedy any past failing on its part.[584] The source of this discretion was not clearly explained by the court. It may be that it arises from the power to provide redress in cases of maladministration by way of 'payment' or 'other benefit' under Local Government Act 2000 s93.

581 [2007] EWCA Civ 182, [2007] 1 FLR 2181.

582 [2011] EWCA Civ 526, [2011] 4 All ER 453.

583 See paras 9.160–9.164.

584 *R (GE) (Eritrea) v SSHD and Bedford BC* [2014] EWCA Civ 1490, [2015] PTSR 854 at paras 53–55, 73 and 75 per Christopher Clarke LJ and paras 95–100 per Davis LJ.

Or it may arise from the more general power under Localism Act 2011 s1. Factors relevant to the exercise of the discretion include:[585]

- the correction of injustice;
- whether the applicant has sought or been refused interim relief;
- any 'unacceptable' delay on the part of the applicant;
- the extent to which the applicant can be regarded as blameworthy;
- the needs of the applicant;[586]
- the extent to which the local authority can be regarded as blameworthy;
- any countervailing considerations of public interest.

9.191 The principles set down in *R (GE (Eritrea))* were applied in the case of *R (A) v Enfield LBC*.[587] That case concerned a young woman who was at risk of radicalisation and who had run away from her parent's home on several occasions, including going to the Syrian/Turkish border on one occasion and Bulgaria, via Egypt, on another. Her case had been known to children's services for some time, and in November 2014 an assessment was carried out concluding that, although there were concerns about her radicalisation, she was not a child in need since her parents remained willing to accommodate her. A similar conclusion was reached following a further assessment in June 2015. Judicial review proceedings were issued in November 2015, after the claimant was arrested at Heathrow airport trying to travel to Bulgaria. In the judicial review proceedings, the claimant sought a declaration that she was a child in need and that the defendant had acted unlawfully in failing to accommodate her under ChA 1989 s20. By the time of the substantive hearing, the claimant had turned 18, meaning that the ChA 1989 s20 duty could no longer be owed,[588] and the defendant contended that the claim was academic. Hayden J allowed the claim, finding that the defendant had acted irrationally in failing to identify the claimant as a child in need. Further, the claim was not academic since the defendant

585 [2014] EWCA Civ 1490, [2015] PTSR 854 at paras 54–55 per Christopher Clarke LJ and *R (HP) v Greenwich RLBC* [2023] EWHC 744 (Admin) at paras 32–33 per Fordham J.

586 There is no legal requirement to carry out a formal needs assessment of the type discussed at paras 9.43–9.48 to identify these needs. Albeit a local authority is free to carry out such an assessment if it sees fit. See *R (HP) v Greenwich RLBC* [2023] EWHC 744 (Admin) at paras 27–29 per Fordham J.

587 [2016] EWHC 567 (Admin), [2016] HLR 33.

588 See paras 9.80–9.81 and 9.226–9.230.

retained the discretion that had been identified in *R (GE (Eritrea))* to treat the claimant as a former relevant child in order to correct the past injustice she had suffered. The judge granted declarations that the claimant was a child in need from June 2015; that the defendant had acted unlawfully in failing to accommodate her; that but for the errors of the defendant she would have been accommodated for 13 weeks and would have become a former relevant child upon turning 18; and granted an order that the defendant should consider the exercise of its discretion to treat her as a former relevant child.

9.192 The case of *R (BM) v Hackney LBC*[589] involved a refusal to re-assess the age of a young adult who had been age assessed several years previously in a process which was later admitted by the local authority to have been flawed. The court found that the local authority had erred in failing to carry out a re-assessment in light of the new material that had been provided to it. Further, although on any view the young person was now over the age of 18, the re-assessment was not academic since if she was her claimed age then, retrospectively, it could be seen that the local authority would have erred in failing to accommodate her under the ChA 1989 meaning that it would have a *R (GE (Eritrea))*-type discretion as to whether to treat her as a former relevant child.[590]

9.193 In *R (KI) v Brent LBC*[591] the court found that the local authority had unlawfully failed to consider exercising the *R (GE (Eritrea))* discretion to treat a young person as a former relevant child. The reason for the local authority's refusal was that the young person in question did not meet the statutory criteria to be treated as a former relevant child.[592] This reason, the court held, did not provide a sufficient justification for the refusal as 'self-evidently, in order to consider the exercise of the discretion the statutory criteria would not be met'.[593]

9.194 In *R (AB) v Ealing LBC*[594] the court found that a local authority had erred in law in refusing to exercise the *R (GE (Eritrea))* discretion to treat a young person as a former relevant child. The local authority had gone wrong in relying on an earlier assessment

589 [2016] EWHC 3338 (Admin).

590 See further *R (AF) v Milton Keynes Council* [2023] EWHC 163 (Admin), raising similar issues.

591 [2018] EWHC 1068 (Admin), (2018) 21 CCLR 294.

592 See paras 9.160–9.164.

593 *R (KI) v Brent LBC* [2018] EWHC 1068 (Admin), (2018) 21 CCLR 294 at para 115 per David Elvin QC sitting as a deputy High Court judge.

594 [2019] EWHC 3351 (Admin).

concluding that, at the relevant time, the young person had not been owed a duty under ChA 1989 s20. That earlier conclusion, the court found, was flawed as the decision-maker had failed to consider the ChA 1989 s20(3) criteria. The court quashed the local authority's refusal to exercise the *R (GE (Eritrea))* discretion but did not grant mandatory relief as it could not be said that there was only one result lawfully open to the defendant, in relation to whether the ChA 1989 s20(3) criteria had been met, and so it was not for the court to order 'that any reconsideration of the issue of whether the Claimant should be treated as if she were a "former relevant child" should be approached on that basis'.[595]

The Nationality, Immigration and Asylum Act 2002 s54 and Sch 3 exclusions

9.195 The availability of support under ChA 1989 Part III is circumscribed by NIAA 2002 s54 and Sch 3.[596] The effect of NIAA 2002 s54 and Sch 3 is to exclude certain categories of migrant from certain forms of state support.

Which forms of support under Children Act 1989 Part III do the Nationality, Immigration and Asylum Act 2002 Sch 3 exclusions apply to?

9.196 The particular types of support to which the exclusion applies include:[597]

- support under ChA 1989 s17;[598]
- support for former relevant children under ChA 1989 s23C;[599]

595 *R (AB) v Ealing LBC* [2019] EWHC 3351 (Admin) at paras 66–67 per Matthew Gullick sitting as a deputy High Court judge. See further *R (HP) v Greenwich RLBC* [2023] EWHC 744 (Admin) in which the refusal to exercise the discretion was quashed owing to a failure to consider new material about the young person's needs, but mandatory relief was refused as the favourable exercise of the discretion was not the 'sole justifiable outcome'.

596 As amended by Immigration and Social Security Co-ordination (EU Withdrawal) Act 2020 (Consequential, Saving, Transitional and Transitory Provisions) (EU Exit) Regulations 2020 SI No 1309 reg 13(4) and subject to the transitional modifications specified in Citizens' Rights (Application Deadline and Temporary Protection) (EU Exit) Regulations 2020 SI No 1209 reg 12(1)(k) during the grace period. See further paras 2.14–2.29.

597 NIAA 2002 Sch 3 para 1(1)(g) and (2).

598 See paras 9.12–9.69.

599 See paras 9.160–9.164.

- support for former relevant children seeking to return to education or training under ChA 1989 s23CA;[600]
- support for former relevant children under the age of 25 who have asked for advice and support, under ChA 1989 s23CZB;[601]
- support for qualifying persons under ChA 1989 ss24A and 24B.[602]

9.197 It will be noted NIAA 2002 Sch 3 para 1 does not place any restriction on the powers and duties of a local authority to accommodate children under ChA 1989 s20.[603] However, as soon as the eligible or relevant child turns 18, the Schedule 3 exclusions have the potential significantly to affect the continued role that the local authority as a corporate parent will play in their life.

Who do the Nationality, Immigration and Asylum Act 2002 Sch 3 exclusions apply to?

9.198 The exclusions in NIAA 2002 Sch 3 para 1 apply to:

1) a person, together with any dependants, who is not an EEA national but who has been granted refugee status by an EEA state other than the UK;[604]
2) a person, together with any dependants, who was (but is no longer) an asylum-seeker, who has failed to co-operate with removal directions;[605]
3) a person who is not an asylum-seeker, who is in the UK in breach of immigration laws within the meaning of British Nationality Act 1981 s50A;[606]
4) certain failed asylum-seekers with dependant children in their household, together with any dependants, who fall within the extended definition of asylum-seeker contained in NIAA 2002 s18(2),[607] and whom the secretary of state has certified as having

600 See paras 9.165–9.168.

601 See paras 9.169–9.174. ChA 1989 s23CZB was added to this list on 1 April 2018 by CSWA 2017 Sch 2 para 5 and Children and Social Work Act 2017 (Commencement No 3) Regulations 2018 SI No 346 reg 4(aa).

602 See paras 9.175–9.185.

603 See paras 9.71–9.84.

604 NIAA 2002 Sch 3 para 4.

605 NIAA 2002 Sch 3 para 6.

606 NIAA 2002 Sch 3 para 7.

607 Which provides that a person shall continue to be treated as an asylum-seeker while their household includes a dependent child who is under 18, and they do not have leave to enter or remain in the UK. This is similar, though not identical, to the extended definition of asylum-seeker contained in IAA 1999 s94(5). See paras 5.45–5.49.

failed, without reasonable excuse, to take reasonable steps to leave the UK voluntarily, or to place themselves in a position in which they are able to leave the UK.[608]

9.199 The second, third and fourth categories all invite consideration of whether a person seeking support is, or has been, an asylum-seeker. An 'asylum-seeker' in this context is a person aged 18 or over who has made a claim for asylum which has been recorded but not determined.[609] A claim for asylum means a claim that it would be contrary to the UK's obligations under the Refugee Convention or under ECHR Article 3, for the applicant to be removed from, or required to leave, the UK[610] and a claim will be regarded as determined where the secretary of state has notified the applicant of their decision and the applicant has exhausted their appeal rights.[611] The High Court has held that in order for an applicant to be regarded as an asylum-seeker for these purposes, in circumstances where the person's asylum claim has previously been rejected or withdrawn and the person has then sought to make further submissions,[612] the secretary of state needs to have accepted that those submissions amount to a fresh claim. It is only at that point, that the claim can be characterised as having been 'recorded'.[613]

9.200 The third category requires consideration of whether the person seeking support is in the UK in breach of immigration laws. This will be the case if the person:[614]

- is in the UK;
- does not have the right of abode in the UK within the meaning of Immigration Act (IA) 1971 s2;[615]
- does not have leave to enter or remain in the UK (whether or not they previously had leave);
- does not have a qualifying Common Travel Area entitlement;[616]

608 NIAA 2002 Sch 3 para 7A.

609 NIAA 2002 Sch 3 para 17(1). See further paras 5.17–5.44.

610 NIAA 2002 Sch 3 para 17(1)(b) and s18(3).

611 NIAA 2002 Sch 3 para 17(2).

612 See paras 3.42–3.43.

613 *R (Mustafa) v Kent CC* [2018] EWHC 2025 (Admin). See further the more detailed discussion of fresh claims at paras 5.23–5.28, in the context of the identical definition of asylum-seeker contained in IAA 1999 s94(1). A discussion of the compatibility of the approach of the High Court in *Mustafa* with Council Directive 2003/09/EC ('Reception Directive') can be found at paras 6.25–6.36.

614 British Nationality Act 1981 s50A(4).

615 See para 1.37.

616 As defined by British Nationality Act 1981 s50A(5).

- is not entitled to reside in the UK by virtue of any provision made under European Communities Act 1972 s2(2);[617]
- is not entitled to enter and remain in the UK, or exempt from the need for such an entitlement, by virtue of IA 1971 s8(1)–(4).[618]

9.201 Whether or not an individual is in the UK might be thought to be the most straightforward of these issues. However, this apparently simple matter is complicated by the fact that, for these purposes, a person who is physically in the UK shall nevertheless be deemed to have not entered the UK if they arrived by ship or aircraft and were either detained[619] or released on immigration bail[620] before leaving the port of disembarkation.[621] The working of this 'curious fiction',[622] whereby certain people who are within the UK are treated as if they are not, fell for consideration in the context of the exclusions contained in NIAA 2002 Sch 3 in the case of *R (AW) v Croydon LBC*.[623] One of the principal issues in that case was the scope of the second and third category of exclusion set out at para 9.198, and the relationship between the two. The claimants in that case argued that these two categories were mutually exclusive and that a failed asylum-seeker could only fall within the second category[624] and not the third.[625] The effect of this construction of the legislation would be that failed asylum-seekers could only be excluded from support under NIAA 2002 Sch 3 if they had failed to comply with removal directions. In considering this issue, Lloyd Jones J observed that:

> In this regard, it is necessary to bear in mind the distinction between those who claim asylum at the port of arrival in the United Kingdom and those who claim asylum only after having entered the United Kingdom. Miss Laing for the Secretary of State informed the court of the Secretary of State's practice in the former case. A person arriving in the United Kingdom who claims asylum at the port of arrival is normally temporarily admitted[626] to the United Kingdom. Accordingly,

617 See chapter 2.

618 Which encompass crew, diplomats, members of the armed services and other special cases.

619 Under the powers conferred by IA 1971 Sch 2 or NIAA 2002 s62.

620 Within the meaning of IA 2016 Sch 10.

621 British Nationality Act 1981 s50A(6); IA 1971 s11(1).

622 *R (AW) v Croydon LBC* [2005] EWHC 2950 (Admin), (2006) 9 CCLR 252 at para 26 per Lloyd Jones J.

623 [2005] EWHC 2950 (Admin), (2006) 9 CCLR 252 at para 18 per Lloyd Jones J.

624 NIAA 2002 Sch 3 para 6.

625 NIAA 2002 Sch 3 para 7.

626 Temporary admission has now been superseded by release on immigration bail and IA 1971 s11 has been updated to reflect that.

for the purposes of section 11 and paragraph 7 of Schedule 3 of the 2002 Act, he is deemed not to have entered the United Kingdom, by virtue of section 11(1) of the 1971 Act. If the application for asylum is unsuccessful, temporary admission is not discontinued at that point nor is it discontinued when removal directions are set. If the person is detained pending removal, temporary admission ceases at that point. However, in other cases temporary admission continues until the time set for departure. If the person does not report for the set flight, temporary admission then ceases. Consequently, a person who claims asylum at the point of arrival in the United Kingdom, who is granted temporary admission and whose claim for asylum is later determined against him will not, at that point, without more, be in the United Kingdom in breach of the immigration laws within the meaning of paragraph 7(a). By contrast, a person who has applied for asylum only after entering the United Kingdom is likely to be a person who is in the United Kingdom in breach of the immigration laws within the meaning of paragraph 7(a). For example, a person who has entered the United Kingdom unlawfully and has later applied for asylum will normally be given temporary release. He will be a person in the United Kingdom in breach of the immigration laws within the meaning of paragraph 7(a). In particular, he will not be entitled to invoke the deeming provision in section 11(1) of the 1971 Act because he has otherwise entered the United Kingdom.[627]

9.202 Viewed in this context, the judge concluded that the second and third categories of exclusion set out at para 9.198 were not mutually exclusive, and that a failed asylum-seeker could potentially fall within either or both categories.[628] The reason for having these two separate categories was not to differentiate between failed asylum-seekers and other classes of migrant. Rather, in the specific context of failed asylum-seekers, it was intended to differentiate between those who had claimed asylum at port and those who had not. As the judge noted, 'there is a clear policy in the legislation to discourage such late applications and to encourage prompt applications at the port of entry'[629] which was based on the belief that 'claims made promptly are more likely to be genuine'.[630]

627 [2005] EWHC 2950 (Admin), (2006) 9 CCLR 252 at para 18 per Lloyd Jones J.
628 At paras 8–28 per Lloyd Jones J.
629 At para 27 per Lloyd Jones J.
630 *R (Limbuela) v SSHD* [2005] UKHL 66, [2006] 1 AC 396 at para 2 per Lord Bingham, quoted in *R (AW) v Croydon LBC* [2005] EWHC 2950 (Admin), (2006) 9 CCLR 252 at para 27.

The exceptions to the Schedule 3 exclusions

9.203 The categories of excluded person set out at para 9.198 are subject to limitations. In particular, the exclusions do not prevent the provision of support to:

1) a British citizen;[631]
2) a child;[632] or
3) any person, to the extent necessary to avoid a breach of their rights under the ECHR.[633]

9.204 The first two limitations are self-explanatory. The third limitation is less so. That limitation will most typically be invoked in circumstances where the applicant for support is facing or would likely face street homelessness in the UK if support is not provided, but cannot reasonably be expected to return to their country of origin in order to avoid that plight.[634] In such circumstance, a refusal to provide support may occasion a breach of the applicant's rights under ECHR Article 3 or Article 8.[635] These issues will now be explored in turn. However, as will become apparent, the lines between these issues are not entirely clear cut. For example, there will be cases where an applicant may face a breach of their rights under ECHR Articles 3 *and* 8, if support is not provided. Equally, there will be cases where it is the risk of an ECHR Article 8 breach, which gives rise to the practical or legal obstacle that means that the individual cannot return to their country of origin.

9.205 The determination of whether support is necessary in order to avoid a breach of an individual's rights under the ECHR will, of course, necessitate an assessment of the individual's circumstances. This is typically referred to as a 'human rights assessment'. There is no prescribed form of assessment. However, the assessment will plainly need to cover all of those issues discussed at paras 9.206–9.217 that are relevant to the question of whether there will be a

631 NIAA 2002 Sch 3 para 2(1)(a).

632 NIAA 2002 Sch 3 para 2(1)(b). 'Child' means a person under the age of 18. See NIAA 2002 Sch 3 para 17(1).

633 NIAA 2002 Sch 3 para 3. The relevant rights of the ECHR are those set out in Human Rights Act 1998 s1. See NIAA 2002 Sch 3 para 17(1). See further *R (CVN) v Croydon LBC* [2023] EWHC 464 (Admin) on the extent to which the rights in question may (or may not) be affected by the purpose of the underlying statutory power which is relied on.

634 This is illustrative and should not be taken as an exhaustive statement of the circumstances in which the limitation will apply.

635 Other rights may also be relevant. See para 9.217.

breach of the individual's rights if support is not provided, and the extent to the support necessary to avoid that breach.

A practical or legal impediment to return

9.206 In *R (Kimani) v Lambeth LBC*,[636] the Court of Appeal held that NIAA 2002 Sch 3 does not mandate the provision of support in circumstances where there is no impediment to an individual returning to their country of origin:

> A State owes no duty under the Convention to provide support to foreign nationals who are permitted to enter their territory but who are in a position freely to return home. Most people who fall into this category are given leave to enter on condition that they do not have recourse to public funds.[637]

9.207 The effect of the decision in *Kimani* was considered by the Court of Appeal in *R (Clue) v Birmingham City Council*.[638] Dyson LJ explained the decision in the following terms:

> Secondly, the court seems to have been of the view that the essential question was whether it was reasonable to expect a claimant to look for sustenance or support to his home country. Thus, at [24], Lord Phillips said that the objective of Schedule 3 to the 2002 Act is to discourage classes of persons who can reasonably be expected to look to other countries for their livelihood. At [26], he said that it was not *reasonable* to expect an asylum-seeker with an outstanding claim for asylum to look to his or her home country for sustenance or support. At [40], he said that Strasbourg jurisprudence would not require this country to permit a claimant, seeking to enter the UK for family reasons, to be permitted to enter or to remain here on public support pending the resolution of his claim. Implicit in this is the proposition that it is reasonable to expect such a claimant to return to his country of origin *because the claim can be pursued from that country*. Indeed, that was the position at the time of the decision in *Kimani*. It was, therefore, reasonable to require the claimant to return pending the determination of the appeal. The same point appears from [49] where the court said that no infringement of article 8 would result from requiring the claimant to return *pending the determination of the appeal*.
>
> Thirdly, the penultimate sentence of [49] should not be misunderstood. The court said that a state owes no duty under the Convention to provide support to foreign nationals who are permitted to enter

636 [2003] EWCA Civ 1150, [2004] 1 WLR 272.

637 *R (Kimani) v Lambeth* LBC [2003] EWCA Civ 1150, [2004] 1 WLR 272 at para 49 per Lord Phillips MR.

638 [2010] EWCA Civ 460, [2011] 1 WLR 99.

their territory 'but who are in a position *freely* to return home' (emphasis added). What is meant by 'freely'? Asylum seekers who have outstanding applications for asylum clearly cannot be required to return home although, in one sense, they are 'free' to do so. Similarly, as I have said, it is implicit in the reasoning of the court that a person who it is not reasonable to require to return home is not 'free' to return home in the sense in which the court was using the word 'free'.[639]

9.208 The claimant in *Clue* was a Jamaican national whose visitor visa had expired and who remained in the UK in breach of immigration laws. Following the breakdown of her relationship with her British partner, she applied for indefinite leave to remain and sought support for herself and her four children under ChA 1989 s17(1).[640] The local authority refused to provide support, on the basis that the claimant fell within the NIAA 2002 Sch 3 para 7 exclusion,[641] and that any breach of ECHR Article 8 could be avoided by her returning to Jamaica, which the local authority was willing to fund. The High Court allowed the claimant's application for judicial review, and that decision was upheld by the Court of Appeal. Dyson LJ provided the following guidance on how local authorities should deal with an application for support from a person falling within one or other of the NIAA 2002 Sch 3 exclusions, in circumstances where they had an extant application for leave to remain:

1) When a local authority considers whether to provide assistance to a person pursuant to NIAA 2002 Sch 3 to avoid a breach of a person's rights under the ECHR, it must first decide whether NIAA 2002 Sch 3 para 6 or 7 applies.[642]
2) If NIAA 2002 Sch 3 para 6 or 7 *does* apply, the local authority must decide whether and, if so, the extent to which it is necessary to exercise a power or perform a duty for the purpose of avoiding a breach of a person's rights under the ECHR.
3) If the withholding of assistance would not cause a person to suffer from destitution amounting to a breach of their rights under the ECHR (typically Article 3[643]), the local authority's investigation ends there.
4) However, if there are no other sources of assistance which would save the person from destitution amounting to a breach of a right

639 *R (Clue) v Birmingham City Council* [2010] EWCA Civ 460, [2011] 1 WLR 99 at paras 39–40 per Dyson LJ (emphasis in original).

640 See paras 9.12–9.69.

641 See para 9.198.

642 See para 9.198.

643 See paras 9.211–9.212.

under the ECHR, then the local authority must consider whether there is an impediment to the person returning to their country of origin.

5) Where the only potential impediment is practical in nature, such as where the person concerned is unable to fund their return, it is open to the local authority to avoid a breach of the person's rights under the ECHR by arranging transport back to their country of origin.
6) Where the impediment is legal in nature, in that it is said that a breach of rights under the ECHR would occur if the person were required to return, it is necessary to distinguish between cases where the person has or has not applied for leave to remain on ECHR grounds.[644]
7) Where an application has been made to the Home Office expressly or implicitly on ECHR grounds (save in hopeless or abusive cases) the local authority cannot pre-empt the outcome of that application by refusing to provide support under the ChA 1989.
8) Where such an application has not been made, the local authority should consider for itself whether a refusal to provide support is proportionate, and if, in doing so, it is entitled to have regard to its own (lack of) resources.

9.209 This fourth step in the decision-making process – whether or not an individual faces a practical impediment to return – warrants some elaboration. A local authority may potentially exercise its general power under ChA 1989 s17(1) in order to pay for travel or accommodation to facilitate an individual's return to their country of origin, where that is necessary in order to overcome a practical impediment to return and thereby avoid a breach of their rights under the ECHR. Local authorities also have specific powers under Withholding and Withdrawal of Support (Travel Assistance and Temporary Accommodation) Regulations 2002[645] reg 3(1) and (2)[646] to assist with accommodation and travel costs of persons with dependent children,

644 See also *R (KA (Nigeria)) v Essex CC* [2013] EWHC 43 (Admin), [2013] 1 WLR 1163, a case where removal directions had not yet been set and where the failure to provide support would have deprived the claimant of her procedural right to pursue any subsequent immigration appeal.

645 SI No 3078.

646 Enacted pursuant to NIAA 2002 Sch 3 paras 8, 9 and 10.

who are subject to the NIAA 2002 Sch 3 para 4 exclusion.[647] However, there will be cases in which an individual faces a practical impediment to return which is not so easily surmountable. For example, where an essential travel document cannot be obtained despite the individual's best efforts or where they are unfit to travel for medical reasons. In such cases, the provision of support is likely to be necessary, at least in the short term, to avoid a breach of the individual's rights under the ECHR. In such cases, to adopt the language of Dyson LJ, it cannot be 'reasonable' to expect the person to look to their country of origin for support, and nor could the person fairly be characterised as being 'free' to return. Further examples of practical and legal impediments which might render it unreasonable for a person to return to their country or origin are discussed at paras 6.90–6.135.

9.210 In *R (N) v Coventry City Council*,[648] Neil Garnham QC sitting as a deputy High Court judge accepted that in a *Kimani*-type case where there is (or appears to be) no practical or legal impediment to a person's return to their country of origin, it will often make sense for a human rights assessment to be undertaken before any other community care assessment. This is because the latter assessment may be academic if the former establishes that support is not necessary in order to avoid a breach of the person's human rights. However, there will be circumstances in which this is not the case. In particular, NIAA 2002 Sch 3 does not prevent the provision of support to a child[649] and it may be necessary for such support to be provided in the short term under ChA 1989 s17(1)[650] in order to safeguard and promote the needs of a child in need.

European Convention on Human Rights Article 3

9.211 In relation to ECHR Article 3, in *R (Limbuela) v SSHD*,[651] Lord Bingham explained that:

647 See para 9.198. Under Withholding and Withdrawal of Support (Travel Assistance and Temporary Accommodation) Regulations 2002 reg 3(3) there is also a power to accommodate those with dependant children who are subject to the NIAA 2002 Sch 3 para 7 exclusion (see para 9.198) providing they have not failed to comply with removal directions. However, there is no analogous power to make travel arrangements.

648 [2008] EWHC 2786 (Admin).

649 NIAA 2002 Sch 3 para 2(1)(b).

650 See paras 9.12–9.69.

651 [2005] UKHL 66, [2006] 1 AC 396. See further the Introduction and paras 5.127–5.128 for the facts of, and background to, this decision.

> A general public duty to house the homeless or provide for the destitute cannot be spelled out of article 3. But I have no doubt that the threshold may be crossed if a late applicant with no means and no alternative sources of support, unable to support himself, is, by the deliberate action of the state, denied shelter, food or the most basic necessities of life.[652]

9.212 The Article 3 threshold, he went on to observe, would be likely to be crossed 'if there were persuasive evidence that a late applicant was obliged to sleep in the street, save perhaps for a short and foreseeably finite period, or was seriously hungry, or unable to satisfy the most basic requirements of hygiene'.[653] Where an individual is facing such destitution, then support must be provided even if the purpose of the underlying statutory provision under which support is sought is not purely avoiding destitution. The ECHR exception contained in NIAA 2002 Sch 3 para 3 refers to all 'Convention Rights',[654] and is not impliedly limited to any particular right.[655] Hence, in *R (CVN) v Croydon LBC*[656] the High Court rejected an argument that the power to provide education and welfare related support under ChA 1989 s23C(4)(b)[657] to a 21-year-old former asylum-seeker was limited to providing support to avoid a breach of ECHR Protocol 1 Article 1.[658] Although support could not be provided for the sole purpose of avoiding destitution, so long as the support was connected to the young person's educational needs it could and should be provided to avoid destitution in breach of Article 3.[659]

652 *R (Limbuela) v SSHD* [2005] UKHL 66, [2006] 1 AC 396 at para 7 per Lord Bingham.

653 [2005] UKHL 66, [2006] 1 AC 396 at para 9 per Lord Bingham. See further paras 56–63 per Lord Hope and para 78 per Baroness Hale. See *R (Humnyntskyi) v SSHD* [2020] EWHC 1912 (Admin), [2021] 1 WLR 320; *NH and others v France* App No 28820/13 [2020] ECHR 202, ECtHR; and *R (CVN) v Croydon LBC* [2023] EWHC 464 (Admin) for recent examples of cases where the Article 3 threshold was held to have been met. See further para 5.128 fn 399.

654 Meaning, the rights set out in ECHR Articles 2–12 and 14, Protocol 1 Articles 1–3, and Protocol 13 Article 1, as read with Articles 16–18: NIAA 2002 Sch 3 para 17(1); Human Rights Act 1998 s1.

655 *R (CVN) v Croydon LBC* [2023] EWHC 464 (Admin).

656 [2023] EWHC 464 (Admin).

657 See paras 9.160–9.164.

658 See para 9.217 for support to avoid a breach of ECHR Protocol 1 Article 1.

659 *R (CVN) v Croydon LBC* [2023] EWHC 464 (Admin) at para 61 per Dexter Dias KC sitting as a deputy High Court judge.

European Convention on Human Rights Article 8

9.213 As is the case for ECHR Article 3, Article 8 does not give rise to a general duty to house the homeless,[660] but is capable of giving rise to a positive obligation to provide accommodation either in circumstances where the Article 3 threshold is also met or where the welfare of children is at stake and the provision of welfare support is necessary to enable family life to continue.[661]

9.214 *R (Bernard) v Enfield LBC*[662] and *R (de Almeida) v Kensington and Chelsea RLBC*[663] provide examples of cases in which a failure to provide accommodation has been found to give rise to a breach of ECHR Article 8.[664] In the former case, it was a failure to provide suitable accommodation, as opposed to a complete failure to accommodate, which occasioned the breach. The claimant in that case was severely disabled and 'suitably adapted accommodation' was necessary 'not merely [to facilitate] the normal incidents of family life', but to secure her 'physical and psychological integrity'.[665] In the latter case, the High Court found that the local authority's refusal to provide accommodation to the claimant under National Assistance Act 1948 s21(1) to a terminally ill Portuguese national with advanced and untreatable HIV/AIDS, hepatitis C and cancer, was incompatible with his rights under ECHR Articles 3 and 8.

9.215 *R (MG (Iran)) v SSHD*[666] was another ECHR Article 8 case, involving a slightly different factual matrix. In that case, the Home Office's refusal to provide either accommodation or travel expenses in order to facilitate contact between a father and his son, who lived 130 miles away, constituted a disproportionate interference with their right to respect for family life under Article 8.

Other circumstances

9.216 The case-law in which individuals have been able to escape the strictures of NIAA 2002 Sch 3 has tended to focus on circumstances where the person has faced a breach of their rights under ECHR

660 *Wandsworth LBC v Michalak* [2002] EWCA Civ 271, [2003] 1 WLR 617 at para 18 per Brooke LJ.

661 *R (Anufrijeva) v Southwark LBC* [2003] EWCA Civ 1406, [2004] 2 WLR 603 at para 43 per Lord Woolf MR.

662 [2002] EWHC 2282 (Admin), [2003] HLR 27.

663 [2012] EWHC 1082 (Admin), (2012) 15 CCLR 318.

664 See para 5.130 fn 405 for further Article 8 cases.

665 *R (Bernard) v Enfield LBC* [2002] EWHC 2282 (Admin), [2003] HLR 27 at para 33 per Sullivan J.

666 [2015] EWHC 3142 (Admin). See paras 5.131 and 5.184.

Article 3 or 8. However, this should not be taken as suggesting that these are the only rights which may be relied on. As noted at the outset, NIAA 2002 Sch 3 para 3 requires the provision of support to the extent necessary to avoid a breach of the individual's rights under the ECHR or the EU Treaties. It is not limited to Articles 3 or 8.

9.217 For example, in the context of the ECHR, another right which may be relevant in this context is Article 4, which prohibits slavery and forced labour. This right may come into play, for example, in relation to victims of trafficking.[667] In particular, where a local authority is aware, or ought to be aware, 'of circumstances giving rise to a credible suspicion that an identified individual had been, or was at real and immediate risk of being, trafficked or exploited', the provision of support may be required in order to alleviate that risk.[668] Where education related support is sought, ECHR Protocol 1 Article 1 may also be relevant.[669]

The corporate parenting duty

9.218 Until the coming into force of the CSWA 2017, the concept of a local authority acting as a 'corporate parent' for a child of young person was one that had found occasional expression in the case-law[670] and in the statutory guidance. For example, the *Transition to adulthood guidance* provides that, as 'corporate parents, responsible authorities should provide support to care leavers in the same way that reasonable parents provide support for their own children'.[671] This quotation from the guidance is probably a fair reflection of the way in which the concept had come to be understood by local authorities, lawyers and the courts: as reflecting the idea that local authorities would sometimes need to step into the shoes of the parent of a child or young person, and support them as a reasonable parent would. However, beyond this rather loose formulation, the definition and scope of the concept were not especially well defined. Who were the

667 See paras 11.156–11.161.

668 *Rantsev v Cyprus and Russia* App No 25965/04 (2010) 51 EHRR 1, ECtHR at para 286.

669 See *R (CVN) v Croydon LBC* [2023] EWHC 464 (Admin) (discussed at para 9.212) where the High Court found it would be disproportionate (in circumstances where very limited evidence as to proportionality had been filed by the local authority) for the local authority to fail to pay for accommodation, and provide subsistence payments, under ChA 1989 s23C(4)(b) (see paras 9.160–9.164), to support a young person's continuing education.

670 For example, *Herefordshire DC v A and B* [2018] EWFC 72.

671 *Transition to adulthood guidance*, para 3.1.

children and young people in respect of whom the local authority was the corporate parent? And, as corporate parent, what exactly was it that the local authority was supposed to do for them? Did the concept of corporate parenthood impose any free-standing duties on the local authority? Or was it simply a guiding principle, influencing how it was that the local authority should exercise its powers and duties?

9.219 These questions have, to a degree, been answered by the elevation of the corporate parenting duty to a statutory footing by means of CSWA 2017 s1, in force from 1 April 2018. This duty applies to:[672]

- looked after children;[673]
- relevant children;[674]
- former relevant children aged 25 and under.[675]

9.220 In carrying out functions in respect of these children and young people, a local authority must have regard to the need:[676]

- to act in the best interests, and promote the physical and mental health and well-being, of the child or young person;
- to encourage the child or young person to express their views, wishes and feelings;
- to take into account the views, wishes and feelings of the child or young person;
- to help the child or young person gain access to, and make the best use of, services provided by the local authority and its 'relevant partners';[677]
- to promote high aspirations, and seek to secure the best outcomes, for the child or young person;
- for the child or young person to be safe, and to have stability in their home life, relationships, and education or work;
- to prepare the child or young person for adulthood and independent living.

672 CSWA 2017 s1(2).
673 See paras 9.85–9.89.
674 See paras 9.136–9.140.
675 See paras 9.160–9.164.
676 CSWA 2017 s1(1).
677 A relevant partner is one falling within the list set out in ChA 2004 s10(4), which includes the police, youth offending teams (YOTs) and educational establishments among others. See CSWA 2017 s1(3). The Home Office is not included within this list though the statutory guidance *Applying corporate parenting principles to looked-after children and care leavers*, DfE, February 2018, p13 (www.gov.uk/government/publications/applying-corporate-parenting-principles-to-looked-after-children-and-care-leavers) reminds local authorities of the importance of engaging with 'immigration services'.

9.221 The word 'functions' in CSWA 2017 s1(1) is not defined. However, it is plainly wide enough to encompass all of the various powers and duties owed to looked after children and care leavers under ChA 1989 Part III, that have been described in the foregoing sections of this chapter. Indeed, the duty goes considerably further than this. In contrast to other provisions within the CSWA 2017, it is not limited to the local authority's functions under the ChA 1989 at all.[678] The absence of any limitation indicates that the local authority must have regard to the matters set out in CSWA 2017 s1(1) when exercising *any* power, or discharging *any* duty, in relation to the child or young person.

9.222 The duty is to 'have regard' to the various matters set out in CSWA 2017 s1(1). It is not a duty to achieve a particular result. However, this does not mean that it is not capable of having an important influence on the manner in which a local authority decides to perform its functions in respect of a looked after child or a care leaver. For example, when performing functions in respect of children and young people of precarious immigration status, the duty to have regard to the need for the child or young person to have stability in their life might militate in favour of discharging the functions so as to assist the child or young person to regularise their status. This is the kind of consideration which a conscientious application of the corporate parenting principles may require to be taken into account. The underlying purpose of the corporate parenting duty is to assist in securing that looked after children and care leavers 'are not placed at significant disadvantage when compared with the support a non-looked after child or young person may receive from their family'.[679] The critical question which the statutory guidance suggests should be asked and answered by local authorities in discharging the duty is 'would this be good enough for my child?'.[680]

9.223 CSWA 2017 s1(1) may be the first statutory provision in which the legal concept of 'best interests' of the child has been incorporated into domestic legislation. The use of this language, and the sorts of factors that the local authority has to have due regard to, are plainly based on UNCRC Article 3, which requires that in all actions involving children, the best interests of the child shall be a primary consideration. As such, it might reasonably be assumed that section 1(1) is intended

678 Contrast with CSWA 2017 s2(1).

679 *Applying corporate parenting principles to looked-after children and care leavers*, para 2.3.

680 *Applying corporate parenting principles to looked-after children and care leavers*, para 1.1.

to contribute to the implementation of UNCRC Article 3, and that the principles and General Comments underpinning the application of Article 3 which are discussed at paras 11.10–11.23 will be relevant to the application and interpretation of section 1(1).

9.224 However, it should be noted that the scope of CSWA 2017 s1(1) is broader than UNCRC Article 3 in that it applies to young people aged 25 and under and not solely to children. This may be of particular significance in relation to migrant care leavers aged 18–25. As noted at para 9.125, there is an inherent tension within the support regime under ChA 1989 Part III insofar as it applies to migrant care leavers in this age bracket. There has always been an expectation that the local authority is playing the role of corporate parent to this cohort. However, the ability of local authorities to act as a reasonable parent has been restricted by NIAA 2002 Sch 3.[681] The fact that prior to the introduction of CSWA 2017 s1(1), the scope of the corporate parenting duty had only been loosely defined and understood did little to ease this tension, or assist local authorities trying to decide how to proceed in a situation where there was, or appeared to be, a conflict between what a young person's best interests require and what their immigration status permits.

9.225 Enshrining the corporate parenting duty in statute and defining it clearly does not remove this tension – but it does provide local authorities with a clear set of principles to apply, which may be of particular assistance in cases where this tension manifests itself. A local authority may be constrained by NIAA 2002 Sch 3 to providing only a minimal level of support necessary to avoid a breach of the young person's rights under the ECHR. However, it will still have a degree of discretion to exercise in deciding when, how, where and by whom such support should be provided.[682] The factors set out in CSWA 2017 s1(1) will be relevant when making the evaluative judgment as to how that discretion should be exercised. Take, for example, a 20-year-old care leaver and former UASC who has an application for leave to remain on ECHR Article 8 grounds outstanding with the Home Office. It may be the case the local authority is required only to provide the person with accommodation and subsistence pursuant to ChA 1989 s23C(4)(c) in order to avoid a breach of their rights under the ECHR, while the immigration application is decided. However, consideration of their best interests, mental well-being,

681 See paras 9.195–9.217.

682 See, by analogy, *Nzolameso v Westminster City Council* [2015] UKSC 22, [2015] HLR 22 at paras 25–27 per Baroness Hale.

wishes and feelings, and the need for stability and to promote high aspirations, as required by CSWA 2017 s1(1), might militate in favour of providing the person with accommodation close to any friends or family, in a location which allows them to continue their education and access any therapeutic provision and charitable support.

How the duties come to an end

9.226 The powers and duties described in the foregoing sections of this chapter will typically come to an end where there has been a change in circumstances meaning that the qualifying criteria which gave rise to the existence of the power or duty in the first place, are no longer satisfied. Sometimes, this will be clear-cut. For example, the ChA 1989 s20(1) duty can only be owed to a person who is under the age of 18.[683] When a child who has been accommodated under that duty reaches the age of 18, that duty will no longer be owed.[684]

9.227 In other circumstances, whether the qualifying criteria which gave rise to the duty remain satisfied will require an evaluative judgment on the part of the local authority. For example, in deciding whether a child remains 'in need' for the purposes of ChA 1989 s17(1)[685] or whether the welfare of a former relevant child continues to require the provision of 'other assistance' pursuant to ChA 1989 s23C(4)(c).[686] As a general principle, in such cases a re-assessment will be required[687] and cogent reasons provided[688] prior to any decision to bring the duty to an end.

9.228 In cases involving care leavers,[689] the ending of one duty will automatically give rise to the commencement of another. For example, the duties owed to an eligible or relevant child[690] will come to an end upon their 18th birthday, but they will be replaced instantly by the duties owed to a former relevant child,[691] reflecting their change in

683 ChA 1989 ss20(1) and 105(1).
684 This does not mean that all support should be terminated forthwith. See paras 9.229–9.230.
685 See paras 9.14–9.17.
686 See paras 9.160–9.164.
687 *R v Gloucestershire CC ex p Barry* (1997–98) 1 CCLR 7, QBD; *R (O) v East Riding of Yorkshire Council* [2011] EWCA Civ 196, [2012] PTSR 328.
688 *R (LB) v Newham LBC* [2004] EWHC 2503 (Admin) at paras 59–60 per Gibbs J.
689 See paras 9.118–9.194.
690 See paras 9.127–9.129 and 9.136–9.140.
691 See paras 9.160–9.164.

status. Alternatively, where a child has not been looked after for a sufficient period of time to be classed as an eligible or relevant child, upon ceasing to be looked after they will be eligible for the powers and duties owed to qualifying children and young people.[692]

9.229 As a general rule, in instances where accommodation has been provided, it will never be permissible for a local authority simply to terminate the placement without notice. As public bodies, local authorities must act reasonably, which will require them to give the supported person a reasonable opportunity to make alternative arrangements.[693] In *R v Newham LBC ex p Ojuri (No 5)*,[694] permission to seek judicial review of a local authority's decision to terminate accommodation provided to a father with three primary school age children with less than 24 hours' notice, was granted on the footing that it was 'strongly arguable' that the local authority had failed to discharge this obligation. The court ordered the local authority to provide accommodation for a further 28-day period, which was said to provide a reasonable opportunity for alternative arrangements to be made. Although the *Ojuri* case was only a permission decision, it is generally accepted to represent an accurate statement of the law and has been cited without demur by the High Court in a number of cases.[695]

9.230 In cases involving the termination of accommodation provided to looked after children and care leavers, more specific requirements will also apply. A local authority seeking either to terminate the placement of a looked after child or ceasing to look after a child who is not an eligible child, will in addition need to adhere to the detailed requirements set out in CPPCR(E) Regs 2010 regs 14 and 39 and the statutory guidance.[696] In respect of care leavers who are making the transition to independent living, the statutory guidance emphasises that local authorities should have in place joint protocols with relevant agencies to manage this transition and that the homelessness legislation[697] should never be used as 'a mechanism for meeting

692 See paras 9.175–9.179.

693 *R v Newham LBC ex p Ojuri (No 5)* (1999) 31 HLR 631, QBD; and *R v Secretary of State for the Environment ex p Shelter* [1997] COD 49, QBD.

694 (1999) 31 HLR 631, QBD.

695 For example, *Dacorum BC v Bucknall* [2017] EWHC 2094 (QB), [2017] HLR 40 at para 30 per Popplewell J; and *R (AM) v Havering LBC* [2015] EWHC 1004 (Admin), [2015] PTSR 1242 at para 35 per Cobb J.

696 *Care planning and placement guidance*, paras 3.64–3.68 and 5.1–5.34.

697 HA 1996 Part VII. See chapter 7.

housing needs that can be anticipated and planned for'[698] and that there should be no expectation that care leavers will be treated as homeless when their placement ends. Instead, local authority protocols should enable 'effective preparation for independence with planned, sustainable moves'.[699]

Relationship with asylum support

9.231 There are a number of situations in which an applicant, together with their household, may appear to be eligible for services under ChA 1989 Part III but may also appear to meet the criteria for the provision of support under IAA 1999 s95(1)[700] or s4(2),[701] which respectively provide for support for asylum-seekers and failed asylum-seekers. In such cases, it will be necessary to determine whether it is the local authority or the Home Office which is responsible for meeting the person's, or household's, needs. This subject is discussed in some detail at paras 5.103–5.112 and 6.141–6.153 and cross-references to the relevant sections will be made where appropriate. What follows here is a brief overview.

Asylum-seeking households with dependant children

9.232 Households comprising an asylum-seeker with dependant children will generally be the responsibility of the Home Office. This is the consequence of IAA 1999 s122(5), which precludes local authorities from providing support under ChA 1989 s17(1)[702] in circumstances where the household is entitled to support under IAA 1999 s95(1).[703] It is important to note in this context that there is an extended definition of asylum-seeker contained in IAA 1999 s94(5),[704] which encompasses certain failed asylum-seeking households. This cohort should also be eligible for support under IAA 1999 s95(1),[705] with the consequence that they would not be eligible for support under ChA 1989 s17(1). See paras 5.103–5.111 for a detailed commentary on the interplay between these legislative provisions.

698 *Transition to adulthood guidance*, para 7.74.
699 *Transition to adulthood guidance*, para 7.74; see also para 7.9.
700 See paras 5.9–5.277.
701 See paras 6.9–6.200.
702 See paras 9.12–9.69.
703 See paras 5.9–5.90.
704 See paras 5.45–5.49.
705 See paras 5.9–5.277.

Failed asylum-seeking households with dependant children

9.233 Households comprising a failed asylum-seeker with dependant children will generally be the responsibility of the local authority, save where the household falls within the extended definition of asylum-seeker contained in IAA 1999 s94(5).[706] Support under ChA 1989 s17(1)[707] should take precedence over support under IAA 1999 s4(2) even though both powers are discretionary.[708] In *R (VC) v Newcastle City Council*,[709] having examined the statutory provisions and the case-law, Munby LJ concluded that 'the legislative intent is that where section 4 and section 17 are both theoretically engaged, the more advantageous support regime under section 17 is to apply'.[710] Support under ChA 1989 s17(1) could only be refused by a local authority, or discontinued, in circumstances in which it could be shown not only that the secretary of state was able and willing to provide support under IAA 1999 s4(2) but that such support would suffice to meet the child's assessed needs. In practical terms, he observed, this rendered it 'very unlikely in the general run of such cases' that a local authority would ever be able to justify non-intervention by reliance on IAA 1999 s4(2).[711]

Unaccompanied asylum-seeking children[712]

9.234 To be regarded as an asylum-seeker for asylum support purposes, it is necessary for the applicant to be over the age of 18.[713] This means that an unaccompanied asylum-seeking child (UASC) is not, in the asylum support context, regarded as an asylum-seeker, and is therefore ineligible for asylum support.[714] Such applicants are the responsibility of their local authority under ChA 1989 Part III, and would fall to be accommodated under ChA 1989 s20.[715]

706 See paras 5.45–5.49.
707 See paras 9.12–9.69.
708 See paras 6.141–6.143.
709 [2011] EWHC 2673 (Admin), [2012] PTSR 546.
710 *R (VC) v Newcastle City Council* [2011] EWHC 2673 (Admin), [2012] PTSR 546 at para 89 per Munby LJ.
711 [2011] EWHC 2673 (Admin), [2012] PTSR 546 at paras 91–94 per Munby LJ.
712 See further paras 11.4–11.126.
713 IAA 1999 s94(1). See paras 5.17–5.18.
714 See para 5.112.
715 See paras 9.71–9.83.

Former unaccompanied asylum-seeking children and care leavers

9.235 The provision of support to former UASCs and care leavers is complicated. What support they are entitled to and from whom will depend on factors such as (if applicable) their age at the time their asylum claim was determined; whether they have acquired leaving care rights; and the status of any further submissions. As a general rule of thumb, if the young person has acquired leaving care rights, then the support regime under ChA 1989 Part III[716] takes precedence over the provision of support to asylum-seekers and failed asylum-seekers under IAA 1999 s95(1) and s4(2). Primary responsibility for this cohort lies with the local authority and not the Home Office, and in exercising its powers or performing it duties the local authority should not take into account the possibility of Home Office support.[717] However, reference should be made to the commentary at paras 6.144–6.153 where the various permutations of rights and entitlements which may be available to this cohort are discussed in detail.

Remedies

Internal complaints

Who may complain

9.236 All local authorities in England are required to have in place procedures for dealing with complaints made to them about the discharge of their functions under ChA 1989 Part III by:[718]

- any child who is being looked after by them, or who is not being looked after by them but is in need;
- the child's parent;
- any person (other than a parent) who has parental responsibility for the child;
- any local authority foster parent; and
- such other person as the local authority considers has a sufficient interest in the child's welfare to warrant their representations being considered by it.

716 See paras 9.118–9.174.

717 *R (SO) v Barking and Dagenham LBC* [2010] EWCA Civ 1101, [2011] 1 WLR 1283.

718 ChA 1989 s26(3)–(3A).

9.237 In order to facilitate the making of such complaints by children, local authorities are also required to provide advocacy services whereby assistance, including representation, is made available to those who make, or intend to make, complaints.[719]

Procedure

Making a complaint

9.238 The procedure for making and determining complaints is set out in Children Act 1989 Representations Procedure (England) Regulations ('CARP(E) Regs') 2006.[720] Each local authority must have a complaints manager, whose role is to assist in the coordination of all aspects of the complaints process.[721] A complaint may be made orally or in writing,[722] and should be handled and considered expeditiously by the local authority.[723] Generally, complaints should be lodged no longer than one year after the grounds to make the complaint arose.[724] However, local authorities have a discretion to consider a complaint made outside that timescale if they conclude that it would not have been reasonable to expect the complainant to lodge the complaint within the time limit, and that the complaint can still be dealt with fairly and effectively.[725] Complaints relating to matters which are the subject of pending or ongoing legal or disciplinary proceedings will only be considered where the local authority decides that it is possible to do so without prejudicing the conduct of the proceedings or investigation.[726]

First stage

9.239 Once the complaint has been received by the local authority, it must, as soon as possible, provide the complainant with details of the complaints procedure and information about advocacy services (where relevant), and offer them assistance and guidance on following

719 ChA 1989 s26A(1). See further *Getting the best from complaints: social care complaints and representations for children, young people and others*, DfE, September 2006, para 3.4 (www.gov.uk/government/publications/childrens-social-care-getting-the-best-from-complaints).

720 SI No 1738.

721 CARP(E) Regs 2006 reg 10(a). See further *Getting the best from complaints: social care complaints and representations for children, young people and others*, para 1.6.

722 CARP(E) Regs 2006 reg 6.

723 CARP(E) Regs 2006 reg 10(c).

724 CARP(E) Regs 2006 reg 9(1).

725 CARP(E) Regs 2006 reg 9(2).

726 CARP(E) Regs 2006 reg 8(1).

the complaints procedure.[727] Unless the local authority and the complainant agree otherwise, the first stage of the complaints process should generally be completed within ten working days, though this may be extended by the local authority for a further ten working days where it considers the complaint to be complex.[728] This stage is referred to as 'local resolution' as the local authority, at this point, does not need to involve an independent person in the consideration of the complaint.[729]

9.240 Where the local authority and the complainant have resolved matters following the first stage of the complaints process, then written details of the terms of the resolution should be provided to the complainant and their advocate (if there is one).[730] Where the complaint has not been resolved, then the complainant may request that it be escalated to the second stage of the process.[731]

Second stage

9.241 At the second stage, an independent person must be appointed to consider the complaint with the local authority.[732] Their response to the complaint should ordinarily be sent to the complainant (and any advocate) within 25 working days[733] but this may be extended by a further 40 working days where the local authority has not been able to resolve the complaint within the initial time limit.[734]

9.242 Where the complainant is dissatisfied with the outcome of the second stage, they may request that the complaint be escalated to the third and final stage.

727 CARP(E) Regs 2006 reg 11.
728 CARP(E) Regs 2006 reg 14(1) and (5).
729 CARP(E) Regs 2006 reg 14(2). See further *Getting the best from complaints: social care complaints and representations for children, young people and others*, para 3.5 on the conduct of this first stage.
730 CARP(E) Regs 2006 reg 15(1).
731 CARP(E) Regs 2006 reg 15(2). See further *Getting the best from complaints: social care complaints and representations for children, young people and others*, paras 3.6–3.8.
732 CARP(E) Regs 2006 reg 17(2)–(3) and (7).
733 CARP(E) Regs 2006 reg 17(3).
734 CARP(E) Regs 2006 reg 17(6).

Third stage

9.243 At the third and final stage, the complaint is considered by a three-person independent panel.[735] Any such request must be made within 20 working days of the complainant being notified of the outcome of the second stage complaint.[736] The review panel is required to meet within 30 working days of the request being received[737] and will consider representations from both sides and from any other person with 'sufficient interest' in the complaint to warrant their representations being taken into account.[738] The complainant is entitled to attend this meeting, together with any advocate.[739]

9.244 Following the meeting, the panel will compile a written report setting out its recommendations for the resolution of the issues raised by the complaint, which must be sent out to the parties within five working days.[740]

9.245 Within 15 working days the local authority, together with the independent person appointed at the second stage of the complaints process, must then consider the recommendations, determine what they propose to do in the light of the recommendations, and send those proposals to the complainant.[741]

9.246 Local authorities have powers of redress exercisable in cases of maladministration under Local Government Act 2000 s93 as well as more general powers under Localism Act 2011 s1 which might appropriately be exercised in such circumstances.

Complaints to the ombudsman

9.247 An applicant who has exhausted these internal complaints mechanisms, who remains unsatisfied with the outcome of their complaint, may seek to complain to the Local Government and Social Care Ombudsman (LGSCO).[742] Complaints should generally be made within 12 months from the date on which the grounds for complaint arose.

735 CARP(E) Regs 2006 regs 18(1) and 19(2)–(3). See further *Getting the best from complaints: social care complaints and representations for children, young people and others*, paras 3.9–3.19.

736 CARP(E) Regs 2006 reg 18(2).

737 CARP(E) Regs 2006 reg 19(4).

738 CARP(E) Regs 2006 reg 19(5).

739 CARP(E) Regs 2006 reg 19(6).

740 CARP(E) Regs 2006 reg 20(1)–(2).

741 CARP(E) Regs 2006 reg 20(3).

742 See: www.lgo.org.uk/make-a-complaint.

Judicial review

9.248 There will be cases in which the complaints mechanisms described above do not provide an individual with an effective remedy to a local authority's refusal or failure to comply with its duties under ChA 1989 Part III. Typically, this might be the case where urgent remedial action is needed, or where a mandatory order is required to compel the local authority to comply with its legal duties. An applicant in these circumstances is likely to need to seek judicial review. The foregoing sections of this chapter are replete with examples of such cases.

Wales – support available to children, families and care leavers under the Social Services and Well-being (Wales) Act 2014

Overview

9.249 Since 6 April 2016, the SSWB(W)A 2014 has replaced the ChA 1989 as the principal statute governing the provision of community care services to children (and their families) and care leavers in Wales. This section provides a brief overview of the powers and duties available to local authorities[743] in Wales under the SSWB(W)A 2014 which are likely to be of principal relevance to migrant children and young people. Many of these powers and duties mirror those found under ChA 1989 Part III, which are described in the foregoing sections of this chapter, and cross-references will be made where appropriate.

Social Services and Well-being Wales Act 2014 s37 – support and accommodation for children and families

9.250 Under SSWB(W)A 2014 s37, a local authority must provide care and support[744] to a child[745] if:

- the child is within the local authority's area; and
- the child has a need for care and support which meets the eligibility criteria; or

743 A local authority in this context means either a county or borough council. See SSWB(W)A 2014 s197(1).

744 Defined by the SSWB(W)A 2014 as care or support or both.

745 'Child' means a person under the age of 18. See SSWB(W)A 2014 s3(3).

- the local authority considers it necessary to meet the child's needs in order to protect them from abuse or neglect or any other harm, or a risk of abuse, neglect or other harm.

9.251 The duty under SSWB(W)A 2014 s37 is the counterpart to the duty under ChA 1989 s17(1),[746] albeit it is a specific duty which must be met if the criteria are met, rather than a target duty.[747] The duty does not apply to a child who is looked after by a local authority.[748]

9.252 In order to determine whether the duty under SSWB(W)A 2014 s37 is owed, local authorities are required to assess the needs of any child who is within their area, or is ordinarily resident within their area, who it appears may need care and support.[749] In carrying out the assessment the local authority must:[750]

- assess the developmental needs of the child;
- seek to identify the outcomes that the child, and those with parental responsibility for the child, wish to achieve;
- assess whether, and if so, to what extent, the provision of care and support, preventative services, information, advice, assistance or other matters, could contribute to the achievement of those outcomes or otherwise meet needs identified by the assessment;
- take account of any other circumstances affecting the child's well-being.

9.253 Under SSWB(W)A 2014 s38, local authorities have a power to provide care and support to a child pending the completion of the assessment. Requirements as to the training and expertise of the person carrying out the assessment and record keeping are set out in the Care and Support (Assessment) (Wales) Regulations 2015.[751]

9.254 Having carried out the assessment, the local authority will then be in a position to determine whether the child's needs meet the eligibility criteria. The eligibility criteria are contained in Care and Support (Eligibility) (Wales) Regulations ('CS(E)(W) Regs') 2015.[752] Needs will meet the eligibility criteria if:[753]

746 See paras 9.12–9.69.
747 See paras 9.22–9.29.
748 SSWB(W)A 2014 s37(6). See para 9.260.
749 SSWB(W)A 2014 s21(1)–(2).
750 SSWB(W)A 2014 s21(4).
751 SI No 1305 (W 111).
752 SI No 1578 (W 187).
753 CS(E)(W) Regs 2015 reg 4.

- the need arises from the child's physical or mental ill-health, age, disability, dependence on alcohol or drugs, or other similar circumstances, or if unmet is likely to have an adverse effect on the child's development;
- the need relates to the child's ability to carry out self-care or domestic routines; the child's ability to communicate; protection from abuse or neglect; involvement in work, education, learning or in leisure activities; maintenance or development of family or other significant personal relationships; development and maintenance of social relationships and involvement in the community; or achieving developmental goals;
- the need is one that neither the child, the child's parents nor other persons in a parental role are able to meet either alone, together or with assistance; and
- the child is unlikely to achieve one or more the outcomes identified in their assessment[754] unless the local authority provides or arranges care and support to meet the need, or enables the need to be met by making direct payments.

9.255 Having completed the assessment process and carried out the eligibility determination, a local authority has a degree of latitude in deciding how to meet the needs of a child who is owed the SSWB(W)A 2014 s37 duty. In particular, SSWB(W)A 2014 s34 provides the following examples of the way in which the child's needs may be met by a local authority:[755]

- by arranging for a person other than the local authority to provide something;
- by itself providing something;
- by providing something, or by arranging for something to be provided, to a person other than the person with needs for care and support.

9.256 This final point indicates that, as with ChA 1989 s17(1), SSWB(W)A 2014 s37 is broad enough to encompass the provision of support to a child's family, where that is necessary to meet the child's needs. Such support may include accommodation, services or cash, among other things.[756]

754 CS(E)(W) Regs 2015 reg 1(3).
755 SSWB(W)A 2014 s37(1).
756 SSWB(W)A 2014 s37(2).

9.257 The duty under SSWB(W)A 2014 s37 is subject to the restrictions on the provision of support contained in NIAA 2002 Sch 3.[757]

Social Services and Well-being Wales Act 2014 s76 – accommodation for children and the duties owed to looked after children

9.258 The counterpart to ChA 1989 s20(1)[758] is found in SSWB(W)A 2014 s76(1), which requires a local authority to provide accommodation for any child within its area who appears to require accommodation as a result of:

- there being no person who has parental responsibility for the child;
- the child being lost or having been abandoned; or
- the person who has been caring for the child being prevented (whether or not permanently, and for whatever reason) from providing the child with suitable accommodation or care.

9.259 The counterpart to ChA 1989 s20(3)[759] is found in SSWBA 2014 s76(3), which requires a local authority to provide accommodation to any child within its area who has reached the age of 16 and whose well-being the authority considers is likely to be seriously prejudiced if it does not provide the child with accommodation.

9.260 A child who is accommodated under SSWB(W)A 2014 s76 for a continuous period of more than 24 hours will be classed as a looked after child.[760] The child will then be owed the additional duties set out in SSWB(W)A 2014 ss78–85. These closely resemble the duties owed to looked after children in England which are described at paras 9.85–9.89.

9.261 The restrictions on the provision of support contained in NIAA 2002 Sch 3[761] do not apply to the duties under SSWB(W)A 2014 ss76–86.

757 NIAA 2002 Sch 3 para 1(1)(o). See paras 9.195–9.217.
758 See paras 9.80–9.82.
759 See para 9.83.
760 SSWB(W)A 2014 s74.
761 NIAA 2002 Sch 3 para 1(1)(o). See paras 9.195–9.217.

Care leavers

9.262 Various categories of young person up to the age 25 who have previously been looked after by a local authority are set out in SSWB(W)A 2014 s104. The responsible local authority[762] will owe a range of additional duties, contained in SSWB(W)A 2014 ss105–115, which include the provision of a personal adviser, a pathway plan, and may include accommodation or a contribution toward the cost of accommodation. These duties mirror the duties owed to care leavers under ChA 1989 Part III by local authorities in England – which are discussed at paras 9.118–9.174. NIAA 2002 Sch 3 applies to this cohort as it does to ChA 1989 Part III.[763]

Remedies

Internal complaint

9.263 A person aggrieved by the service they have (or have not) received from a local authority in Wales under the SSWB(W)A 2014 may lodge an internal complaint. The procedure for doing so, and the manner in which the complaint will be dealt with, are set out in SSWB(W)A 2014 Part 10 and the Social Services Complaints Procedure (Wales) Regulations 2014.[764]

Ombudsman

9.264 If the person is dissatisfied with the outcome of the complaint, then they may seek to pursue their complaint with the Public Services Ombudsman for Wales.[765]

Judicial review

9.265 In circumstances where the complaints process does not provide an adequate remedy to an error of law on the part of a local authority, an affected person may seek judicial review.

762 Determined in accordance with SSWB(W)A 2014 s104(5).
763 NIAA 2002 Sch 3 para 1(1)(o).
764 SI No 1794 (W 187).
765 See: www.ombudsman.wales.

CHAPTER 10

Healthcare for migrants

Shu Shin Luh

continued

Introduction

10.1 The National Health Service (NHS) was implemented under the National Health Service Act (NHSA) 1946 because, in words attributed to then Minister of Health Aneurin Bevan, 'illness is neither an indulgence for which people have to pay, nor an offence for which they should be penalised, but a misfortune, the cost of which should be shared by the community'. The Act of Parliament, which came into force, was amended on numerous occasions and was later consolidated in the National Health Service Act (NHSA) 2006. The NHSA 2006 is the overarching Act which governs the legal structure of the NHS, although this has been amended by the Health and Care Act 2022 which received Royal Assent on 28 April 2022, with certain provisions relevant to the structure and duties of various health bodies coming into force on 1 July 2022.

10.2 The legal framework governing the NHS has contained a provision that NHS services should be provided free of charge unless the Act expressly provided for a charge since 1946. This provision was carried over into legislation that replaced the NHSA 1946, namely the National Health Service Act (NHSA) 1977 and subsequently the NHSA 2006. Charges may be levied, in particular, by reason of a person's residence status.

10.3 The legal framework governing the NHS is complex and the duties and powers of the secretary of state, NHS England, the integrated care boards (ICBs)[1] and NHS provider trusts are many and varied. This chapter will only provide a broad overview. More extensive texts, such as *NHS law and practice* (2018) published by the Legal Action Group, provides comprehensive information about each aspect of the NHS's complex legal structure and the interrelationship between its different components, including commissioning and procurement of services. Similarly, concerning mental capacity, there are also texts including the *Court of Protection handbook*, 4th edn, Legal Action Group, 2022 which discuss the duties and powers under the Mental Capacity Act 2005 and the jurisdiction of the Court of Protection in detail.

10.4 This chapter focuses on the entitlements and limitations to access to NHS healthcare by migrants in the UK who require it for their medical conditions. It begins with an explanation of the legal

1 Integrated Care Boards replaced Clinical Commissioning Groups in the NHS in England from 1 July 2022 pursuant to section 18 of the Health and Care Act 2022.

structure of the NHS. It then examines charges for overseas visitors for the use of NHS services. Next, it discusses NHS Continuing Healthcare and NHS-funded nursing care. It then addresses the position of those migrants who may lack mental capacity, focusing specifically on the implications that their lack of mental capacity has on decision-making in respect of their access to accommodation, care and support and its interrelationship with their immigration status. Finally, the chapter discusses remedies.

Legal structure of the NHS

10.5 The Secretary of State for Health and Social Care has ultimate political responsibility for the performance of the NHS. However, and as the secretary of state is not a healthcare professional and may not have any NHS management experience, decision-making is assisted by technical and professional guidance from NHS England, and at the local level by ICBs. This section seeks to provide an overview of the key duties and powers, owed by these public bodies, that impact on access to and the provision of healthcare for migrants.

Powers and duties of the secretary of state

10.6 The primary duty of the secretary of state lies in NHSA 2006 s1, which provides that the secretary of state has a duty to 'continue the promotion of a comprehensive health service', such a service encompassing the physical and mental health of the people of England, and the prevention, diagnosis and treatment of physical and mental illness.

10.7 A like duty is imposed under NHSA 2006 s1H on NHS England.

10.8 The section 1 duty is qualified by sections 2 and 3 of the same Act. Section 2, described as a general power to provide services, gives scope to the secretary of state to decide, in the exercise of the discretion, to determine the services that 'he considers appropriate' for the purpose of discharging the section 1 duty. Section 3 is described as a 'duty as to provision of certain services' including hospital accommodation, medical services required for the diagnosis and treatment of illness, and facilities and services for the prevention of illness and the care and after-care of persons who have suffered illness. That provision leaves the secretary of state scope to exercise a degree of judgment as to the circumstances in which he or she will provide the services, by qualifying the duty to services 'to such extent as he considers it necessary to meet all reasonable requirements'.

10.9 The duty on the secretary of state under section 1 to *promote* a comprehensive health service falls short of a duty to *provide* a comprehensive health service. The duty to *promote* a comprehensive health service has limited overall legal effect because the combination of budgetary, staffing and other resource pressures on the NHS means that, in reality, a truly comprehensive health service will never exist. Thus, while the secretary of state must have this duty in mind at all times, it will not be a breach of the duty if the NHS fails to deliver a comprehensive health service. That said, as the Court of Appeal observed in *R v North and East Devon Health Authority ex p Coughlan*,[2] the section 1 duty remains an important one, and serves to remind the secretary of state that the NHS should be as comprehensive as budgets and other resources permit.

10.10 NHSA 2006 Part 1 imposes procedural duties on the secretary of state. Of most relevance to the current context is NHSA 2006 s1C, the duty to reduce health inequalities. It provides that: 'in exercising functions in relation to the health service, the Secretary of State must have regard to the need to reduce inequalities between the people of England with respect to the benefits that they can obtain from the health service'.

10.11 The wording of section 1C refers to the 'need' to 'reduce' the inequalities that presently exist with respect to the benefits that people can obtain from the health service. 'Need' and 'reduce' are both strong words, implying an added level of urgency to achieving the objective, but falling short of being an absolute requirement to do so. A key factor to which the secretary of state is obliged to have regard is the need to reduce inequalities with respect to the benefits that different people can obtain from health services. This appears to involve a recognition that health services may well be accessed by people in an unequal way, and that there is a need to reduce the inequality of benefits between different groups of people.

10.12 In *R (Pharmaceutical Services Negotiating Committee) v Secretary of State for Health*,[3] the secretary of state argued that a 'have regard' duty was a lesser form of a duty to the 'have due regard' duty under Equality Act (EqA) 2010 s149. That submission was rejected by the judge. In doing so, the judge set out what was required, at a minimum,

2 [2001] QB 213, CA at paras 24–25.

3 [2017] EWHC 1147 (Admin). The Court of Appeal's judgment ([2018] EWCA Civ 1925) did not disturb this conclusion.

by the secretary of state in the discharge of the section 1C duty given it is 'a specific need to reduce inequalities': a) first, the secretary of state needs to show that the need was recognised, and b) second, the secretary of state needs to ensure that what was proposed did not, at a minimum, cause an increase in such inequalities.

10.13 The secretary of state is additionally bound by the public sector equality duty (PSED) imposed by the EqA 2010 s149 and by the non-discrimination duties set out in that Act.

10.14 Section 149 requires the secretary of state, in the exercise of their functions in designing and implementing a regime of charging for NHS treatment, to 'have due regard to' three core equality objectives:

1) eliminate discrimination, harassment, victimisation and any other conduct that is prohibited by or under the EqA 2010;
2) advance equality of opportunity between persons who share a relevant protected characteristic and persons who do not share it;
3) foster good relations between persons who share a relevant protected characteristic and persons who do not share it.

10.15 Protected characteristics under the EqA 2010 include age, sex, and pregnancy and maternity: section 149(7). The duty to have due regard to the need to 'advance equality of opportunity' involves, at a minimum, the need to 'remove or minimise disadvantages suffered by persons who share a relevant protected characteristic that are connected to that characteristic' and 'take steps to meet the needs of persons' who share a protected characteristics that are different from those who do not share it: section 149(3).

10.16 The requirements of the section 149 duty are well rehearsed in case-law and succinctly summarised in *R (Bracking) v SSWP*.[4] Important features include:

- Equality duties are an integral and important part of the mechanisms for ensuring the fulfilment of the aims of anti-discrimination legislation.[5]
- An important evidential element in the demonstration of the discharge of the duty is the recording of the steps taken by the decision-maker in seeking to meet the statutory requirements.[6]

4 [2013] EWCA Civ 1345, [2014] Eq LR 60 at para 26.

5 *R (Elias) v Secretary of State for Defence* [2006] EWCA Civ 1293, [2006] 1 WLR 3213 at para 274.

6 *R (BAPIO Action Ltd) v SSHD* [2007] EWHC 199 (Admin) per Stanley Burnton J.

- The relevant duty is upon the minister or other decision-maker personally. What matters is what they took into account and what they knew. Thus, the minister or decision-maker cannot be taken to know what their officials know or what may have been in the minds of officials in proffering their advice.[7]
- A minister must assess the risk and extent of any adverse impact and the ways in which such risk may be eliminated before the adoption of a proposed policy and not merely as a 'rear-guard action', following a concluded decision.[8]
- The public authority decision-maker must be aware of the duty to have 'due regard' to the relevant matters.[9]
- The duty must be fulfilled before and at the time when a particular policy is being considered.
- The duty must be 'exercised in substance, with rigour, and with an open mind'. It is not a question of 'ticking boxes'; while there is no duty to make express reference to the regard paid to the relevant duty, reference to it and to the relevant criteria reduces the scope for argument.
- The duty is non-delegable.
- The duty is a continuing one.
- General regard to issues of equality is not the same as having specific regard, by way of conscious approach to the statutory criteria.[10]
- Officials reporting to or advising ministers/other public authority decision-makers, on matters material to the discharge of the duty, must not merely tell the minister/decision-maker what they want to hear but they have to be 'rigorous in both inquiring and reporting to them'.[11]
- The decision-maker must be clear precisely what the equality implications are when they put them in the balance, and they must recognise the desirability of achieving them. Provided that there has been a rigorous consideration of the duty, so that there is a proper appreciation of the potential impact of the decision on

7 *R (National Association of Health Stores) v Department of Health* [2005] EWCA Civ 154 at paras 26–27 per Sedley LJ.

8 *R (Kaur and Shah) v Ealing LBC* [2008] EWHC 2062 (Admin) at paras 23–24 per Moses LJ.

9 *R (Brown) v SSWP* [2008] EWHC 3158 (Admin) per Aitkens LJ.

10 *R (Meany) v Harlow DC* [2009] EWHC 559 (Admin) at para 84 per Davis J, approved in *R (Bailey) v Brent LBC* [2011] EWCA Civ 1586 at paras 74–75.

11 *R (Domb) v Hammersmith and Fulham LBC* [2009] EWCA Civ 941 at para 79 per Sedley LJ.

equality objectives and the desirability of promoting them, then it is for the decision-maker to decide how much weight should be given to the various factors informing the decision.[12]

10.17 The PSED under EqA 2010 s149 is a continuing duty. This extends to circumstances where the necessary evidence to inform an impact assessment is unclear or unobtainable in advance such that a decision-maker could act first but must review later.

10.18 In *R (Cushnie) v Secretary of State for Health*,[13] a claimant succeeded in establishing that the secretary of state failed to have regard to the PSED under EqA 2010 s149 when deciding not to exempt disabled failed asylum-seekers in local authority residential care from NHS charging. In finding that the secretary of state had failed to consider the equality impact of not exempting those failed asylum-seekers who are disabled, Singh J, as he then was, held that 'the purpose of the duty is to make sure that public authorities do not inadvertently overlook the impact of their decisions on relevant groups, because too often in the past they were overlooked'.

Powers and duties of NHS England

10.19 The National Health Service Commissioning Board was created by the Health and Social Care Act 2012. It is intended to act as a commissioner of specialised services and acts as a quasi-regulatory of ICBs. From 1 April 2013, the board started to refer to itself as NHS England, but the change of name does not imply any change in function. From 1 July 2022, the name change was made formal under section 1 of the Health and Care Act (HCA) 2022.

10.20 NHS England has a co-extensive duty with the secretary of state to continue the promotion in England of a comprehensive health service designed to secure improvement a) in the physical and mental health of the people of England and b) in the prevention, diagnosis, and treatment of physical and mental illness. For NHS England, this is set out in NHSA 2006 s1H.

10.21 As with the duty on the secretary of state under section 1C to reduce inequalities, NHS England has a co-extensive duty under NHSA 2006 s13G, the interpretation and application of which has been discussed above at paras 10.10–10.11 as it applies to the secretary of state. HCA 2022 s11 inserted, via a new section 13SA, a new

12 *R (Hurley and Moore) v Secretary of State for Business, Innovation and Skills* [2012] EWHC 201 (Admin) at paras 77–78 per Elias LJ.

13 [2014] EWHC 3626 (Admin).

duty under into the NHSA 2006 which requires NHS England to publish a statement describing the powers that certain NHS bodies have to collect, analyse and publish information relating to inequalities in accessing health services and in respect to the outcomes achieved for them by the provision of health services. The statement must also set out NHS England's view on how those powers should be exercised.

10.22 In December 2015, NHS England published *Guidance for NHS commissioners on equality and health inequalities legal duties,*[14] to assist decision-makers within NHS England and clinical commissioning groups (CCGs) as they were called then (now ICBs) to discharge this duty to reduce health inequalities. The introduction sets out the background for this duty as follows:

> Avoidable health inequalities are – by definition – unfair and socially unjust. A person's chance of enjoying good health and a longer life is determined by the social and economic conditions in which they are born, grow, work, live and age. These conditions also affect the way in which people look after their own health and use services throughout their life. Addressing such avoidable inequalities and moving towards a fairer distribution of good health requires a life course approach and action to be taken across the whole of society.
>
> The NHS Five Year Forward View sets out the need to address the health and wellbeing gap, preventing any further widening of health inequalities. To do so requires a move towards greater investment in health and health care where the level of deprivation is higher.
>
> The World Health Organisation (WHO) defines health inequalities as 'differences in health status or in the distribution of health determinants between different population groups'. There is clear evidence that reducing health inequalities improves life expectancy and reduces disability across the social gradient. Tackling health inequalities is therefore core to improving access to services, health outcomes, improving the quality of services and the experiences of people. It is also core to the NHS Constitution and the values and purpose of the NHS.

10.23 The guidance explains[15] that the 'have regard' duty is to be interpreted in the same way as the 'have due regard' PSED under EqA 2010 s149. This is consistent with the interpretative approach taken

14 See: www.england.nhs.uk/about/equality/equality-hub/patient-equalities-programme/legal-duties/.

15 *Guidance for NHS commissioners on equality and health inequalities legal duties*, at para 5.2.3.

by Collins J in *R (Pharmaceutical Services Negotiating Committee) v Secretary of State for Health.*[16]

10.24 The guidance goes on to explain[17] what the duty means in practice, stating that it requires the NHS England to consider:

1) the impact on inequalities as part of all decision-making processes, and keeping a record of such processes;
2) which dimensions of inequality are relevant to its work, and taking account of how inequalities could be reduced;
3) the potential impact on health inequalities and the application of the duty to its

10.25 Further comment about the impact of the duty on NHS England is set out in the guidance as follows:

> NHS England has a duty to have regard to the need to reduce inequalities between patients in access to services commissioned through its direct commissioning functions. This may involve:
>
> - Identifying health inequalities, evaluating how such inequalities might impact on people's ability to access services, and commissioning for all of the population and all needs.
> - Identifying evidence of what has previously worked in reducing inequalities in access to services and evaluating notable practice.
>
> NHS England may also consider whether:
>
> - services are universal and should reach all members of society, which may be achieved by explicitly targeting specific population groups;
> - services are commissioned on the basis of need, which may be achieved by ensuring the quantity and quality of services in deprived areas is adequate.
>
> NHS England also has a duty to have regard to the need to reduce inequalities between patients in outcomes from services commissioned through its direct commissioning functions. This involves:
>
> - Effective monitoring and evaluation that identifies health inequalities and to support action to overcome inappropriate variations in outcomes for all people.
> - Looking at how the outcome is distributed across society by area of deprivation and by different groups, rather than focusing on average outcomes for all people.
> - Considering how services can be commissioned to reduce inequalities and prevent undesirable outcomes. For example, targeting life-style factors in health and compliance with treatment, and developing key provider indicators with health inequality outcomes.

16 [2018] EWCA Civ 1925.

17 *Guidance for NHS commissioners on equality and health inequalities legal duties*, at para 5.3.2.

Many changes to address health inequalities will have a long-term impact on health outcomes, so their effectiveness may not be visible on an annual reporting basis. This should not detract from implementing such changes, if they are based upon robust evidence supporting the reduction in health inequalities.[18]

10.26 Since 2012, NHS England has been given legal and financial responsibility for commissioning the provision of healthcare across the immigration detention estate in England.[19] This is set out in further detail in a partnership agreement between the Home Office, NHS England and Public Health England. The identified priorities are:

1) better mental health assessment and treatment for detainees;
2) public health – the pro-active detection, surveillance and management of infectious diseases and suitable treatment paths;
3) to strengthen multi-agency approaches to managing detainees at serious risk of harm – better learning, process improvements, a multi-agency approach to assessment care in detention and teamwork (ACDT);
4) to align commissioning systems – including information governance.

10.27 In the Home Office-commissioned *Review into the welfare in detention of vulnerable persons* (Cm 9186, January 2016), Stephen Shaw, the appointed independent reviewer, identified a number of issues relating to the mental health needs of people in detention. In particular, he identified the absence of any clinical assessment of the level and nature of mental health concerns in immigration detention centres. He also expressed concerns about the de facto use of segregation facilities to manage detainees with a serious mental health condition. The absence of counselling and talking therapies, and the inconsistent provision of clinical specialists, including mental health nurses and occupational therapists, were of serious concern given the prevalence of mental illnesses in the detained population. Mr Shaw also considered how the absence of proper training to immigration removal centre staff and immigration caseworkers on the causes, symptoms and care of mental illness impacted on decision-making concerning immigration detention and substantive immigration application. He recommended that the Home Office, NHS England

18 *Guidance for NHS commissioners on equality and health inequalities legal duties*, at para 5.3.7.

19 National Health Service Commissioning Board and Clinical Commissioning Groups (Responsibilities and Standing Rules) Regulations 2012 SI No 2996 reg 10.

and the Department for Health develop a joint action plan to improve the provision of mental health services for those in immigration detention.

10.28 The Home Office, NHS England and the Department for Health published an *Improving mental health services in immigration detention: an action plan* in 2016 in response to the Shaw Review. In 2018, Mr Shaw carried out a further review and continued to express concerns that the Health and Justice commissioning teams in NHS England may lack the expertise or resources to undertake health needs assessments of detainee patients.

10.29 The lack of adequate healthcare in immigration removal centres was starkly exposed in the 2017 BBC Panorama programme, *Undercover: Britain's immigration secrets*, based on footage taken by a journalist going undercover as a detention custody officer, showing incidents of abuse and ill-treatment of mentally ill detainees at Brook House Immigration Removal Centre. In 2019, Medical Justice, one of the key clinical charities working with immigration detainees, published a damning report, *Failure to protect from the harm of immigration detention* which documented continued dysfunction of healthcare safeguards against the prolonged detention of vulnerable detainees. Other reports, produced by HM Inspector of Prisons, and the Independent Monitoring Board, have also identified continued failures of safeguards such as inadequate and inconsistent health screening and GP assessments and the continued use of segregation as a means of managing the mentally ill.

Powers and duties of the Integrated Care Boards

10.30 ICBs are statutory NHS bodies responsible for the planning and commissioning of healthcare services for their local area. They came into being on 1 July 2022 pursuant to NHSA 2006 s14Z25, as inserted by HCA 2022 s19. ICBs replaced CCGs, which had been created by the Health and Social Care Act 2012.[20] The policy rational behind ICBs is to secure that health services are provided in an integrated way together with Integrated Care Partnerships ('ICPs'). ICPs are statutory joint committees of the ICB and local authorities in the area.[21] It brings together a broad set of system partners to support partnership working and develop an 'integrated care strategy', a plan to address the wider health care, public health and social care needs

20 NHSA 2006 s14Z27 abolished CCGs.

21 Local Government and Public Involvement in Health Act 2007 s116ZA.

of the population. This strategy must build on local joint strategic needs assessments and health and well-being strategies and must be developed with the involvement of local communities and Healthwatch. The ICB is required to have regard to this plan when making decisions.[22]

10.31 The core function of ICBs is to assess the health needs of their local population, decide upon priorities and then commission a range of health and social care services on behalf of the local population from providers including hospitals, clinics and community health providers. NHSA 2006 s82B (as amended by HCA 2022 Sch 3) provides that ICBs are responsible to secure the provision of primary care services on behalf of NHS England. Each ICB has duties as to reducing inequalities as well under the new NHSA 2006 s14Z35. This requires an ICB, in the exercise of its functions, to (a) have regard to the need to reduce inequalities between persons with respect to their ability to access health services, and (b) reduce inequalities between patients with respect to the outcomes achieved for them by the provision of health services. There is also a new duty under NHSA 2006 s14Z37 to promote patient choices with respect to the aspects of health services provided to them.

Who can access NHS care: charges for overseas visitors

10.32 NHSA 2006 s1(4) provides that services provided by the NHS in England are, save where express enactment is made to the contrary, provided free of charge. The express power to charge for NHS healthcare treatment in respect of overseas visitors has existed since the NHSA 1977. The current regime was introduced pursuant to NHSA 2006 s17 which enables the secretary of state to make regulations for the making and recovery of charges 'in respect of such persons not ordinarily resident in Great Britain'. By section 175, the secretary of state may make regulations to specify the circumstances and services which would be the subject of charging of NHS services and persons against whom charges would be levied. By section 175(3), the secretary of state may provide that charges may be made only in such cases as may be determined in accordance with regulations.

10.33 It is important to note that NHSA 2006 s175 does not impose any obligation on the secretary of state to impose charges on those not

22 NHSA 2006 s14Z52.

ordinarily resident in the UK. However, the NHS operates in a political environment and decisions about the way it operates are made by politicians, and, driven by political leanings as much as by evidence or need. The secretary of state has exercised the power to make rules relating to overseas visitors using the NHS. Those rules have, over the years, been continually tightened by governments responding to public opinion.

10.34 The underlying policy justification for seeking to charge overseas visitors for having the benefit of NHS services is that it is a taxpayer-funded public service which works on a system of reciprocity. All taxpayers in the UK pay into the government coffers by both direct and indirect taxation and in return the same people receive NHS services. Thus, as the logic goes, those who are not UK taxpayers should not have the benefit of free NHS services. This approach was endorsed by the Court of Appeal in *R (YA) v Secretary of State for Health*,[23] which was called upon to determine whether NHS services should be made available, free of charge, to a failed asylum-seeker.[24] Ward LJ held (at para 55):

> Here the statute in need of construction is the 2006 NHS Act. As set out at [8] above, the Secretary of State's duty prescribed by section 1 is to continue the promotion in England of a comprehensive health service designed to secure improvement in the health 'of the people of England'. Note that it is the people of England, not the people in England, which suggests that the beneficiaries of this free health service are to be those with some link to England so as to be part and parcel of the fabric of the place. It connotes a legitimate connection with the country. The exclusion from this free service of non-residents and the right conferred by section 175 to charge such persons as are not ordinarily resident reinforces this notion of segregation between them and us. This strongly suggests that, as a rule, the benefits were not intended by Parliament to be bestowed on those who ought not to be here.

10.35 What was not referred to in *YA* but also a justification for the NHS charging regime is the need to deter health tourism. However, as explained at para 10.122 below, reports commissioned by the government on charging and its effects have not identified a high prevalence of health tourism, and therefore the basis for justifying the impact of charging on particular vulnerable groups.

23 [2009] EWCA Civ 225, (2009) 12 CCLR 213.

24 There are now provisions in regulations to deal with the circumstances in which failed asylum-seekers may access NHS services, considered at paras 10.100–10.105.

10.36 The present rules are set out in the National Health Service (Charges to Overseas Visitors) Regulations ('Charges Regs') 2015,[25] as amended by the National Health Service (Charges to Overseas Visitors) (Amendment) Regulations 2015[26] and the National Health Service (Charges to Overseas Visitors) (Amendment) Regulations ('Charges Amendment Regs') 2017.[27] In overview, the rules are that an 'overseas visitor'[28] will be charged for 'relevant services'[29] unless the particular service which they require is exempt,[30] or they belong to a category of persons exempt from the charging regime.[31] In circumstances where charges apply, the charge should normally be levied up front before the service is provided, save where that would prevent or delay the provision of 'an immediately necessary service' or 'an urgent service'.[32]

10.37 A discussion of the policy background is set out at para 10.119 below.

Who is an 'overseas visitor'?

10.38 Charges Regs 2015 reg 2 defines an 'overseas visitor' as 'a person not ordinarily resident in the United Kingdom'.

Meaning of 'ordinary residence'

Overview

10.39 There is no comprehensive statutory definition of the meaning of the term 'ordinary residence' for the purposes of the NHSA 2006. It is a concept which meaning has been developed by judges over many years. The words 'ordinary residence' are used in numerous statutes to define entitlement to one or more state benefits or a liability to make taxation or other payments to a state body. The words largely mean the same thing in every Act, save that for some Acts, such as the Care Act 2014, deeming provisions apply with the consequence that a person may be deemed to have one place of ordinary residence whereas for other Acts a person can have multiple places of ordinary

25 SI No 238.
26 SI No 2025.
27 SI No 756.
28 For 'overseas visitor' see paras 10.38–10.45.
29 For 'relevant services' see paras 10.56.
30 For exempt services see paras 10.55–10.87.
31 For exempt persons see paras 10.88–10.113.
32 For 'immediately necessary' and 'urgent' services see paras 10.46–10.52.

residence. Other Acts, including the NHSA 2006, use the terms 'residence', 'usual residence' and 'habitual residence'. There are clear differences in meaning between 'habitual residence' and 'ordinary residence'. However, the words 'residence', 'normally resident' and 'ordinary residence' may mean the same thing.[33] This was confirmed in *R (M) v Hammersmith and Fulham LBC* by Mitting J who held:

> There seems to me to be no perceptible difference between the three phrases, 'resident', 'ordinarily resident' and 'normally resident'. All three connote settled presence in a particular place other than under compulsion.[34]

10.40 The guidance *Overseas NHS visitors: implementing the charging regulations*[35] states[36] that a person is not ordinarily resident in the UK simply because they have British nationality; hold a British passport; are registered with a GP in the UK; have an NHS number; own property in the UK; or have paid (or are currently paying) national insurance (NI) contributions and taxes in the UK.

10.41 Rather, the test on the meaning of 'ordinary residence' is that set down by the House of Lords in *R v Barnet LBC ex p Shah*,[37] which concerned the eligibility of foreign-based students for UK student grants. Eligibility was based on an 'ordinary residence' test and the students argued successfully that once they were settled in the UK, they were ordinarily resident in the UK, and so entitled to a grant. Lord Scarman held that unless the statutory framework or legal context pointed to a different meaning, the expression 'ordinarily resident' should be taken as referring to 'a man's abode in a particular place or country which he has adopted voluntarily and for settled purposes as part of the regular order of their life for the time being, whether of short or long duration'. The issue did not depend on the identification of a person's 'real home' or on their long-term future

33 This will not always be the case. The meaning of the words will always depend on the statutory context in which they are used. For example, in the case of *Mohamed v Hammersmith and Fulham LBC* [2001] UKHL 57, [2002] 1 AC 547 (see para 10.41), in the context of the homelessness legislation, the House of Lords declined to apply the test for ordinary residence under the Education Act 1980 to normal residence under the Housing Act 1996. See at pp553A–553B per Lord Slynn. However, save where the statutory context dictates otherwise, the words may be used interchangeably.

34 *R (M) v Hammersmith and Fulham LBC* [2010] EWHC 562 (Admin) at para 25.

35 DHSC, August 2018, last updated January 2023 ('the *NHS charging guidance*').

36 See *NHS charging guidance*, para 3.5.

37 [1983] 2 AC 309, HL.

intentions or expectations but where they lived at this point in a reasonably settled manner.

10.42 A person who is detained in a mental health institution or in a prison will not acquire an ordinary residence at that institution, and so will be deemed to continue to be ordinarily resident in the place that they were prior to being detained, even if there is nowhere for them in fact to go to live at that place.[38]

10.43 It is not usually relevant how long a person has been living at their place of residence before they become ordinarily resident. If someone moves house from one place to another, giving up their former place of residence, they will instantly acquire the second place of residence as their ordinary residence.

Requirement of lawful residence

10.44 A key feature of 'ordinary residence' in a place is that the residence is required to be lawful. This element of the ordinary residence test has been extended by Immigration Act 2014 s39, which provides that the person's residence in the UK must be lawful and cannot be for a limited period of time. Therefore, people who require leave to enter or remain for a limited period of time will not be treated as individuals who are ordinarily resident within NHSA 2006 s175. However, there are provisions exempting them from NHS charging by the payment of an immigration health surcharge, discussed at paras 10.89–10.96 below.

10.45 British nationals who are ordinarily resident abroad and do not have a sufficiently settled residence in the UK to be ordinarily resident at an address in the UK will not be ordinarily resident in the UK for the purposes of NHSA 2006 s175.[39]

When should the charging regime be applied?

10.46 Charges Regs 2015 reg 3 provides that an NHS trust must only 'make and recover charges' for relevant services where it determines, having made such inquiries that it considers are reasonable in the circumstances, that an 'overseas visitor' patient is not entitled to receive relevant services free of charge. Regulation 3(1A), as inserted by the Charges Amendment Regs 2017, provides that once a relevant body determines that a person is chargeable, it 'must secure payment' for treatment – that is, up-front – before treatment is provided unless

38 *R v Mental Health Review Tribunal ex p Hall* [2000] 1 WLR 1323, CA.

39 See further *NHS charging guidance*, para 3.12.

doing so would 'prevent or delay' the provision of 'an immediately necessary service' or 'an urgent service'.

10.47 An 'immediately necessary service', as defined under Charges Regs 2015 reg 3(7), includes any treatment that the treating clinician determines the recipient needs promptly, which is life-saving, prevents a condition becoming immediately life-threatening; or prevents permanent serious damage to the recipient from occurring. The decision as to whether treatment is 'immediately necessary' is for the clinician to make.

10.48 Treatment classed as immediately necessary by the treating clinician must always be provided irrespective of whether or not the patient has been informed of, or agreed to pay, charges, and it must not be delayed or withheld to establish the patient's chargeable status or seek payment. It must be provided even when the patient has indicated that they cannot afford to pay.

10.49 Due to the severe health risks associated with conditions such as eclampsia and pre-eclampsia, and in order to protect the lives of both mother and unborn baby, all maternity services must be treated as being immediately necessary. Maternity services include all antenatal, intrapartum and postnatal services for a pregnant woman, a woman who has recently given birth and a newborn baby.

10.50 An 'urgent service' means one which 'the treating clinician determines . . . should not wait until the recipient can be reasonably expected to leave the United Kingdom'. This means that the longer a patient is expected to remain in the UK, the greater the range of their treatment needs that are likely to be regarded as urgent. If the person is unlikely to leave the UK for some time, treatment which clinicians might otherwise consider non-urgent is more likely to be considered by them as urgent.

10.51 The *NHS charging guidance* provides that factors which could inform the decision as to whether treatment can reasonably wait until the expected date by which the patient can leave the UK include:

1) the pain or disability a particular condition is causing;
2) the risk that delay might mean a more involved or expensive medical intervention being required; or
3) the likelihood of a substantial and potentially life-threatening deterioration occurring in the patient's condition if treatment is delayed until they leave the UK.

10.52 By Charges Regs 2015 reg 3A (inserted in 2017), NHS trusts are now required to record information on the overseas visitor's NHS record as to whether someone is liable to charging, and when that decision was made.

Level of NHS charges

10.53 The amount of charges to be levied on an overseas visitor for the provision of NHS services is defined by Charges Regs 2015 reg 7. The charging scheme set out in reg 7 is a mandatory one. Both NHS bodies and private providers do not have the freedom to use any other scheme to calculate the level of charges to be made to an overseas visitor.

10.54 Regulation 7(3) provides that the charge payable in respect of each relevant service provided to an overseas visitor shall be equal to the NHS tariff price for any services provided to the patient increased by 150 per cent. If the price payable for the service has been increased as a result of a Monitor approved modification under Health and Social Care Act 2012 s124, the price charged to the overseas visitor shall include that increase. However, if the ICB and the provider have negotiated a price below the national tariff under the Health and Social Care Act 2012 s116, the price charged to the overseas visitor shall be the national tariff price without the agreed reduction.[40]

NHS services exempt from charges for overseas visitors

Overview

10.55 Charges Regs 2015 Part 3 sets out a list of NHS services for which no charges can be levied, even if they are provided to overseas visitors who would otherwise be liable to pay charges under the regulations. Some of the services do not attract charges for overseas visitors because they are not 'relevant services' for the purposes of the 2015 Regs. Other services are 'relevant services', but are specifically exempt from charges.

10.56 'Relevant services' are defined in Charges Regs 2015 reg 2. They include accommodation, services or facilities which are provided, or whose provision is arranged, under the NHSA 2006, with the exception of primary medical services,[41] primary dental services,[42] primary ophthalmic services[43] or 'equivalent services which are provided, or

40 Health and Social Care Act 2012 s125.

41 Defined as medical services provided under NHSA 2006 Part 4.

42 Defined as dental services provided under NHSA 2006 Part 5.

43 Defined as ophthalmic services provided under NHSA 2006 Part 6.

whose provision is arranged, under the 2006 Act'. The latter category of services is not defined.

10.57 Apart from these identified categories of NHS services, all other NHS-funded services are 'relevant services' for the purposes of the Charges Regs 2015.

10.58 The list of exempted 'relevant services' is set out in Charges Regs 2015 reg 9. Under reg 9(1), no charge may be made or recovered in respect of relevant services provided to an overseas visitor including the following:

a) accident and emergency (A&E) services;[44]
b) services provided as part of the telephone advice line;[45]
c) family planning services;[46]
d) services provided for the diagnosis and treatment of a condition listed in Schedule 1;[47]
e) services provided for the diagnosis and treatment of sexually transmitted infections;[48]
f) services provided for the treatment of a condition caused by torture, female genital mutilation, domestic violence or sexual violence, provided that the overseas visitor has not travelled to the UK for the purpose of seeking that treatment.[49]

Accident and emergency services

10.59 The regulations contain no definition of A&E services. However, the *NHS charging guidance* provides the following explanation:

> . . . accident and emergency (A&E) services (whether provided at an A&E department or similar e.g. urgent care centre, walk-in centre or minor injuries unit) but not including services provided after the overseas visitor is accepted as an inpatient or at a follow-up outpatient appointment. So, where emergency treatment is given after admission to the hospital, e.g. intensive care or coronary care, it is chargeable to a non-exempt overseas visitor. Note that some walk-in centres provide primary care services rather than A&E-type services and overseas visitors cannot be charged for such services either because primary care services are not within the scope of the regulations.[50]

44 See paras 10.59–10.60.
45 See para 10.61.
46 See paras 10.62–10.63.
47 See paras 10. 64–10.65.
48 See para 10.66.
49 See paras 10.67–10.87.
50 *NHS charging guidance*, para 4.3.

10.60 Chapter 4 of the *NHS charging guidance* sets out a series of questions and answers, which confirm that:

1) A&E services only cover the services prior to an overseas visitor being admitted as an inpatient. Emergency services provided after a patient has been admitted as an inpatient and at outpatient appointments are chargeable.
2) A&E services includes minor eye services where they are provided as a minor injuries service similar to those within an A&E unit.
3) Charging depends upon the patient's admission status at A&E, not on their location.
4) Ambulance services are considered to be a part of A&E care and should be provided free of charge where they are part of the patient's clinical need.

Telephone advice services

10.61 Services such as 111 or out of hours telephone advice services are exempt from charges. Further, if a call is made to a GP out of hours services resulting in a visit by a GP, that is probably not a 'relevant service' because it would be an 'equivalent service' to primary care medical services. Thus no charges should be levied for such a visit if the patient is an overseas visitor.

Family planning services

10.62 Exempted family planning services are explained in the *NHS charging guidance* as including services that supply contraceptive products and devices to prevent pregnancy. However, the guidance states that termination of an established pregnancy is not a method of contraception or family planning. Termination of pregnancy will therefore be chargeable unless the overseas visitor is themself exempt from charge.

10.63 The *NHS charging guidance* explains[51] that if a person who presents seeking a termination of pregnancy and satisfies a ground under the Abortion Act 1967, cannot reasonably be expected to leave the UK before the date at which an abortion may no longer be a viable option for them, treatment should be regarded as being urgent and should not be delayed or withheld in order to establish chargeable status or seek payment. This may, for example, be the case for failed asylum-seekers or undocumented migrants who are unlikely to leave the UK in the short term, whereas in other cases, visitors may more easily be able to leave the UK within the relevant timeframe.

51 *NHS charging guidance*, para 8.11.

Services provided under NHS (Charges to Overseas Visitors) Regulations 2015 Sch 1 for diagnosis or treatment of a specified condition

10.64 Charges Regs 2015 Sch 1 sets out a list of medical conditions where there is a public health interest in ensuring that patients receive prompt medical treatment in order to protect others from the spread of the condition. This includes, for example, diphtheria, cholera, food poisoning, HIV, malaria, measles, rabies, rubella, tuberculosis, COVID-19 among a list of 35 conditions.

10.65 The *NHS charging guidance* explains that where a patient presents with tuberculosis as well as other conditions, charges should still be levied for the other conditions if they are not an exempt service. In respect of HIV, because it is a disease for which treatment is free on public health grounds, if an overseas visitor says they have forgotten to bring their antiretroviral therapy for their HIV, it should be suppled for free, subject to a limit on the amount that will last until the overseas visitor returns home or has arranged for antiretroviral therapy to be sent to them.

Services provided for the diagnosis and treatment of sexually transmitted infections

10.66 Charges Regs 2015 reg 9(1)(e) provides that no charges will be made for the diagnosis and treatment of sexually transmitted infections, the rationale being similarl to those conditions listed under Schedule 1, that there is a public health interest in ensuring prompt medical treatment to protect others from the spread of the condition.

NHS services provided to treat conditions caused by forms of violence and ill-treatment

10.67 Charges Regs 2015 reg 9(1)(f) was introduced in 2015 to exempt 'treatment of a condition **caused by** torture, female genital mutilation, domestic violence or sexual violence' (emphasis added). Regulation 8(2) provides that this includes subsequent and ongoing treatment for any condition, including chronic conditions, that 'is directly attributable' to the violence and, in the case of female genital mutilation (FGM), treatment, including any antenatal, perinatal and postpartum treatment, the need for which 'is directly attributable' to the mutilation.

10.68 The reg 9(1)(f) exemption for gender-based violence was introduced in recognition of these cohorts being amongst the 'most vulnerable' and requiring the benefit of healthcare which they would otherwise be unable to pay for: Explanatory Memorandum to the Charges Regs 2015 para 7.26. Including this exemption was 'consistent with wider government policy in respect of preventing such violence and supporting victims of violence': para 7.27.

Exemption for victims of torture

10.69 Victims of torture are exempt from charging for NHS health services where the treatment is 'caused by' torture. 'Torture' is defined in Charges Regs 2015 reg 8(1) as having the meaning given in Article 1(1) of the United Nations Convention against Torture and other Cruel and Degrading Treatment or Punishment (UNCAT). Article 1(1) of UNCAT defines torture as:

> . . . any act by which severe pain or suffering, whether physical or mental, is intentionally inflicted on a person for such purposes as obtaining from him or a third person information or a confession, punishing him for an act he or a third person has committed or is suspected of having committed, or intimidating or coercing him or a third person, or for any reason based on discrimination of any kind, when such pain or suffering is inflicted by or at the instigation of or with the consent or acquiescence of a public official or other person acting in an official capacity. It does not include pain or suffering arising only from, inherent in or incidental to lawful sanctions.

10.70 'Treatment' under reg 9(1)(f) includes 'any subsequent or on-going treatment provided to an overseas visitor for any condition, including a chronic condition' that is 'directly attributable' to the torture.

10.71 Many torture survivors will already be exempt from charges for secondary healthcare as a result of being a refugee, asylum-seeker or other category of person exempted from the charging regime.[52] This further provision for the treatment of conditions caused by torture provides some assistance to torture survivors who may not otherwise be exempt. This might include, for example, torture survivors who have made a fresh application for asylum which has not been recorded by the Home Office and are supported in the community rather than under any other provision that would lead to an exemption from charging. It may also assist torture survivors living in the UK without a regularised immigration status.

10.72 The Department of Health and Social Care (DHSC) has acknowledged that the identification of survivors of torture presents difficulties, as they may not disclose humiliating and degrading experiences of torture and ill-treatment, or may disclose this sensitive

52 See discussion at para 10.87 below.

information over a period of time as a relationship of trust develops. The *NHS charging guidance* therefore states that when determining whether treatment for an individual should be exempt from charging, NHS managers should accept:

1) confirmation from a medical professional, including a referring GP, who could identify signs and symptoms of torture and that the treatment required is attributable to this torture; or
2) confirmation from an appropriate non-governmental organisation or charity, such as the Helen Bamber Foundation or Freedom from Torture, confirming that the patient is a client of theirs and is accessing their services as a survivor of torture.

Exemptions for victims of FGM

10.73 FGM is defined for the purposes of the exemption as the excision, infibulation or other mutilation of the whole or any part of the labia majora, labia minora or clitoris, where that mutilation constituted an offence under the Female Genital Mutilation Act 2003 or would have done so if performed before the Act came into force. The exemption applies wherever and whenever the FGM took place.

10.74 'Treatment' for this purpose includes any maternity services – antenatal, perinatal and postpartum treatment – the need for which is caused by the FGM.[53] A referral from a GP, medical professional or an FGM clinic indicating that the treatment required is attributable to FGM may be used to access treatment under the exemption.

10.75 The exemption applies[54] wherever and whenever the FGM was performed, provided that the overseas visitor has not travelled to the UK for the specific purpose of seeking that treatment. Any other treatment that a person who is a victim of FGM needs that is not directly attributable to the FGM may be chargeable unless covered by another exemption.

10.76 Where FGM is identified in patients, it is now mandatory to record this in the patient's health record. Since September 2014, all acute trusts are required to provide a monthly report to the DHSC on the number of patients who have undergone FGM or who have a family history of FGM.

10.77 Health professionals in acute trusts should always update a patient's record with whatever discussions or actions have been taken. If the patient has undergone FGM, referral to a specialist FGM clinic should always be considered. If a relevant body refers a

53 Charges Regs 2015 reg 8(2)(b).

54 *NHS charging guidance*, paras 7.12–7.14.

patient to social services or the police, then this should also be recorded in the patient's health record. If a patient is identified as being at risk of FGM, then this information must be shared with the GP and health visitor, as part of safeguarding actions.

Exemption for victims of domestic violence

10.78 Until the Domestic Abuse Act 2021 introduced a statutory definition of domestic abuse, the applicable definition[55] of domestic violence for the purposes of the Charges Regs 2015 was the Home Office definition of domestic violence and abuse. This refers to:

> . . . any incident or pattern of incidents of controlling, coercive, threatening behaviour, violence or abuse between those aged 16 or over who are, or have been, intimate partners or family members12 regardless of gender or sexuality. The abuse can encompass, but is not limited to:
>
> - Psychological
> - Physical
> - Sexual
> - Financial
> - Emotional

10.79 'Controlling' behaviour is a range of acts designed to make a person subordinate and/or dependent by isolating them from sources of support, exploiting their resources and capacities for personal gain, depriving them of the means needed for independence, resistance and escape, and regulating their everyday behaviour.

10.80 'Coercive' behaviour is an act or a pattern of acts of assault, threats, humiliation and intimidation or other abuse that is used to harm, punish or frighten the victim.

10.81 Domestic Abuse Act 2021 s1 has now introduced a statutory definition of domestic abuse, which is not materially different to the non-statutory definition adopted in the *NHS charging guidance.*

10.82 Services provided for the treatment of a condition that is directly attributable to domestic violence are free to all overseas visitors provided that the overseas visitor has not travelled to the UK for the specific purpose of seeking that treatment. This will include any mental health services that are needed as a consequence of the violence.

10.83 It is often difficult to identify victims of domestic violence, particularly as victims are often in powerless and dangerous situations and may be unwilling to disclose that they are suffering in this way.

55 *NHS charging guidance,* paras 7.17–7.25.

However, where a person has disclosed previously to a medical professional that they are a victim, this may be recorded in their health record. In such cases, the overseas visitors manager at the NHS trust may be able to obtain confirmation from a medical professional (including a referring GP) who is aware of the patient's health record that the person has experienced domestic violence, and that the treatment being accessed is directly attributable to domestic violence. Otherwise, an overseas visitors manager should accept confirmation from a medical professional who could most appropriately identify signs and symptoms of domestic violence that the services being provided are directly attributable to that violence.

10.84 In the absence of confirmation from a medical professional, it is crucial that, in trying to establish if charges apply, people who may be victims of domestic violence are treated sensitively and discreetly, especially if accompanied by others who may be violent towards them. In no circumstances should documentation regarding charging (or exemption from charging) be sent to the patient that mentions domestic violence, due to the danger this might place the person in. For this reason, organisations supporting victims of domestic violence may also be reluctant to provide documentation specifying that a person is considered by them to be a victim of domestic violence. If a victim has made steps to claim legal aid because they have separated from the abusive partner/family member, they would have needed to provide documentation from a domestic violence refuge or specialist support service; this could count as evidence of entitlement to free treatment, where necessary.

10.85 The effective operation of this exemption has been criticised by non-governmental organisations (NGOs) such as Maternity Action and Doctors of the World because they have found that, in their experience, NHS trusts do not have the systems in place proactively to identify victims of such violence and do not notify patients that exemptions exist. The workability of the exemptions depends on survivors knowing the process, as well as feeling safe enough to disclose the violence to hospital staff. In 2019, Maternity Action published a research report, *A Vicious Circle: the relationship between NHS charges for maternity care, destitution and violence against women and girls.*[56] It found that according to one study of pregnant women in east London, 15 per cent reported violence during their pregnancy.

56 At: https://maternityaction.org.uk/vawg-report-december-2019/.

Of these women, just under 40 per cent reported that violence started while they were pregnant, while 30 per cent reported they had at some time suffered a miscarriage as a result. According to the seventh Confidential Enquiry into Maternal and Child Health, between 2003 and 2005, of the 295 maternal deaths reported in Saving Mothers' Lives, 70 occurred in women who had features of domestic abuse (24 per cent), and of these women, 19 were murdered. Violence against women and girls may also take the form of coercive control or reproductive coercion. It is estimated that as many as one in four pregnancies involve some form of reproductive control, be it refusal to use contraception, sabotaging of contraceptives, or not allowing the woman to access contraceptive or abortion services. In 2020, 43 per cent of women represented by Maternity Action's NHS charging team disclosed violence.

Exemptions for victims of sexual violence

10.86 'Sexual violence' refers to rape or sexual assault under the Charges Regs 2015.[57] Sexual violence may be a form of domestic violence too. When it is not, this separate exemption means that services provided for the treatment of a condition directly attributable to sexual violence are free of charge, provided that the overseas visitor has not travelled to the UK for the specific purpose of seeking that treatment. Treatment will include mental health services and maternity services needed as a consequence of sexual violence. Anyone can be a victim of rape or sexual assault, no matter what age they are or their sexuality and regardless of gender or gender identity.

10.87 If a person is a victim of rape or sexual assault, it may be recorded in their health record, in which case confirmation may be obtained from a medical professional who is aware of the patient's health record that the patient is a victim of sexual violence, and that the treatment being accessed is directly attributable to that violence. Otherwise confirmation should be accepted from a medical professional, including a referring GP, who could most appropriately identify signs and symptoms of sexual violence, that the services being provided are directly attributable to that violence. One source of referral is from a Sexual Assault Referral Centre (SARC), which provides specialist medical and forensic services. Therefore, this will be an obvious indicator that the services being accessed are as a result of sexual violence, so that treatment will be exempt from charges.

57 *NHS charging guidance*, paras 7.26–7.29.

Categories of persons exempted from NHS charging

10.88 Charges Regs 2015 Part 4 identifies categories of persons who are exempt from the payment of NHS charges despite being classified as overseas visitors. These are set out in regs 10–25. The most relevant categories for the purposes of this book are:

1) individuals who have paid or are exempt from paying the immigration health charge: reg 10;[58]
2) refugees, asylum-seekers and failed asylum-seekers and their families: reg 15;[59]
3) children looked after by the local authority: reg 15(e);[60]
4) victims of modern slavery: reg 16;[61]
5) persons detained in an NHS hospital or subject to court-ordered treatment: reg 18;[62]
6) prisoners or detainees: reg 19;[63]
7) exceptional humanitarian reasons: reg 17.[64]

Immigration health charge

Overview

10.89 Immigration Act 2014 s38 brought in provisions to enable the secretary of state to set an 'immigration health charge' (also known as the immigration health surcharge (IHS)) to be paid by anyone who makes an application for leave to enter or remain in the UK for a limited period. The secretary of state used the power to make the Immigration (Health Charge) Order ('Health Charge Order') 2015[65] which provides at art 3 that people who require leave to enter or remain in the UK and are only granted a limited period of leave are subject to the IHS. People applying for indefinite leave to remain are exempt from this requirement, although would be required to pay if they are only granted limited leave to remain notwithstanding their ILR application.

58 See paras 10.92–10.96.
59 See paras 10.97–10.105.
60 See para 10.106.
61 See paras 10.107–10.109.
62 See para 10.112.
63 See para 10.113.
64 See paras 10. 110–10.111.
65 SI No 792.

10.90 Applicants who come within the terms of the Health Charge Order 2015 still need to pay the IHS even if they have private medical insurance.

10.91 The amounts of IHS are set out in Health Charge Order 2015 Sch 1 and are reviewed and adjusted from time to time.

Persons exempt from the IHS

10.92 Health Charge Order 2015 Sch 2 sets out persons who are exempt from paying the charge. This includes:

a) visitors whose leave to enter is limited to six months or less;
b) applicants made by people who are under 18 where they are looked after by a local authority;
c) people who have made claims for asylum, humanitarian protection or leave to remain under European Convention on Human Rights (ECHR) Article 3 (prohibition of torture and inhuman or degrading treatment or punishment);
d) victims of modern slavery who have made an application for leave to remain for a reason under the Council of Europe Convention on Action against the Trafficking in Human Beings, under the Immigration Rules (HC 395) as a domestic worker who is a victim of modern slavery or human trafficking, or where the applicant has a positive Conclusive Grounds decision from the Single Competent Authority;[66]
e) people who apply for leave to remain outside the Immigration Rules with access to public funds under the Destitution Domestic Violence Concession;
f) people applying for leave to enter or remain where provision for such entry clearance or leave has been made pursuant to retained EU law obligations.

10.93 There is no general exemption from paying charges for NHS services for family members of the person who pays the IHS. Each person who wants to come to the UK is required to apply for their own visa and will have to pay the IHS as part of that application process. There is an exemption for children born to someone who pays the IHS for the first three months of their life. This is set out in Charges Regs 2015 reg 25(3). Once the child reaches the age of three months, an application needs to be made for the child to have leave to remain in the UK. The IHS will have to be paid for the child as part of that

66 A detailed discussion of the regime for the identification and support of victims of trafficking can be found at paras 11.163–11.197. Discussion about leave to remain as a victim of trafficking is at paras 1.126–1.136.

application in order for the child to be able to continue to receive NHS services without incurring charges under the Charges Regs 2015.

10.94 Health Charge Order 2015 art 8 provides that the Home Office can waive the IHS. According to the Home Office's policy on waivers,[67] waiver may be granted in all circumstances where a person is assessed to be destitute, either by virtue of being in receipt of asylum support under Immigration and Asylum Act (IAA) 1999[68] s95[69] or s4(2) or in receipt of support as a migrant family with a child 'in need' under Children Act 1989 s17.[70] Once a waiver is granted, the person would be exempt from NHS charging as if they had paid the IHS.

Consequences of paying the IHS

10.95 The effect of the IHS on the payment of NHS charges is covered in Charges Regs 2015 reg 10, which exempts anyone from NHS charges who has paid the IHS and has NHS services provided at a relevant time. The exemption does not apply to assisted conception services, that is in-vitro fertilisation (IVF) services.[71]

10.96 Regulation 10(2) provides that those who have paid the IHS or been granted a waiver/reduction of the surcharge are exempt from NHS charging, but that exemption only arises *if and when* the Home Office grants the person leave to remain. This means that for someone who is not otherwise exempt from NHS charges, while their application for leave to remain is awaiting a decision by the Home Office, they will remain chargeable. In this way, the NHS charging regime and the IHS scheme are not entirely aligned. An exemption from paying the IHS does not guarantee an exemption from NHS charging. Given the delays to decision-making by the Home Office, the waiting period before a person can potentially benefit from the exemption can be many months if not years.

Refugees and asylum-seekers

10.97 Charges Regs 2015 reg 15 provides for an exemption to NHS charging for various categories of people who have sought asylum:

67 See *Fee waivers: Human Rights-based and other specified applications*, v6.0, UK Visas and Immigration, December 2022 and its *Appendix 1: Request for Fee Waiver*.

68 See chapter 6.

69 See chapter 5.

70 See chapter 9.

71 Charges Regs 2015 reg 10(2A).

1) Under reg 15(a) and (aa), an exemption to NHS charging is provided to people who have received recognition and been granted temporary protection, asylum or humanitarian protection under the Immigration Rules. Their dependants are also exempt from NHS charging.
2) Regulation 15(b) and (ba) extend this to those who have made a claim for temporary protection, asylum or humanitarian protection under the Immigration Rules, and their dependants.
3) Regulation 15(c) and (da) exempt people who are provided with asylum support under IAA 1999 s95,[72] and their dependants.

10.98 For asylum-seekers and those who are supported under IAA 1999 s95, the exemption extends until the final determination of the asylum claim, and therefore includes the period when appeals are pending (so long as the appeal is made in-time).

10.99 Asylum-seekers supported under IAA 1999 s95 qualify for an HC2 certificate.[73] An HC2 certificate is sent by the Home Office to the applicant together with the decision to grant support under section 95. The certificate is valid for six months and will cover all dependants. The HC2 certificate entitles the applicant to free NHS prescriptions, dental treatment, wigs and fabric support, sight tests, vouchers towards the cost of glasses or contact lenses, and necessary travel costs to and from hospital for NHS treatment under the care of a consultant.

10.100 If an asylum-seeker is not supported by the Home Office, they are still eligible to register with a GP and are entitled to access all NHS services. However, they will not be issued with an HC2 certificate by the Home Office, and will need to apply for one independently using an HC1 form.

Failed asylum-seekers

10.101 In respect of failed asylum-seekers, not all of them are exempted from NHS charging. The exemption under Charges Regs 2015 reg 15(d) only applies to those who are supported under IAA 1999 s4(2) as a result of being destitute[74] (reg 15(d)(i)) or in residential care provided by the local authority under the Care Act 2014 (reg 15(d)(iii)). Eligibility for IAA 1999 s4(2) support requires the failed

72 A discussion of eligibility for support under IAA 1999 s95 is contained in chapter 5.

73 *Healthcare needs and pregnancy dispersal policy*, v3.0, Home Office.

74 A discussion of eligibility for support under IAA 1999 s4(2) is contained in chapter 6.

asylum-seeker to: a) appear to the Home Secretary to be destitute; and b) meet one or more of five prescribed conditions. Those conditions are listed in Immigration and Asylum (Provision of Accommodation to Failed Asylum Seekers) Regulations 2005[75] reg 3(2) and in effect require the person to face a legal or practical barrier to leaving the UK voluntarily. 'Destitute' is defined under IAA 1999 s95(3) as where a person: a) does not have adequate accommodation or any means of obtaining it (whether or not their other essential living needs are met); or b) they have adequate accommodation or the means of obtaining it, but cannot meet their other essential living needs.

10.102 The rationale for including failed asylum-seekers as a category of exempted persons was explained in the Impact Assessment to the National Health Service (Charges to Overseas Visitors) Regulations 2011,[76] which first introduced this exemption, and is informative of how the secretary of state had in the past sought to strike the balance between maximising cost recovery from the undocumented migrant population and the need to ensure that there were no increased health inequalities as a result of charging. As formulated, the exemption differentiated between those destitute failed asylum-seekers who have been directed to leave the UK and those who, whilst unsuccessful in the initial asylum process, 'face recognised barriers to return and on that basis qualify for support from [the Home Office]' under IAA 1999 s4(2). It was introduced to correct an 'anomalous' situation that left NHS staff in a 'difficult position in relation to charging people who are destitute and cannot leave the country' (p1). The government considered that exempting them would not only prevent health conditions 'deteriorating to the extent they need more expensive medical treatment' (p1), but would also be 'wholly consistent with this element of the government's migration and asylum policy'.[77]

10.103 In costing the inclusion of this exemption, the secretary of state took account of the following:

a) 90 per cent of charges invoiced to those in receipt of IAA 1999 s4(2) support had to be written off because they were destitute and had no prospects of being able to pay the charges;[78]

75 SI No 930.

76 SI No 1556. See also Impact Assessment No 6040: *Impact assessment of exemptions for failed asylum seekers*, March 2011.

77 *Evidence base for the 2011 impact assessment*, para 7.

78 *Evidence base for the 2011 impact assessment*, para 20.

b) charging had deterred failed asylum-seekers in receipt of IAA 1999 s4(2) support from seeking secondary healthcare, to avoid charges.[79]

10.104 As to the risk of increased demand for IAA 1999 s4(2) support to gain access to free NHS care, this was not considered by the government to be 'significant' because 'administrative hurdles to achieve section 4 [support] are significant and difficult to manipulate'.[80]

10.105 Failed asylum-seekers in receipt of local authority residential care were only included under Charges Regs reg 15(d)(iii) following a successful judicial review challenge in *R (Cushnie) v Secretary of State for Health*.[81] There, Singh J (as he then was) found that the secretary of state had failed to comply with EqA 2010 s149 (PSED) when deciding in 2011 not to exempt disabled failed asylum-seekers in local authority residential care from NHS charging. The secretary of state was found, in particular, to have failed to consider the equality impact of not exempting those failed asylum-seekers who are disabled.

Looked after children

10.106 The definition of 'looked after' is set out in Children Act 1989 s22(1). This includes a child who is subject to a care order under section 31 of the same Act or a child who is accommodated voluntarily by the local authority under section 20 of the same Act. Children who are section 20 accommodated in this context will most likely be unaccompanied children who come to the UK from overseas, often to seek asylum and humanitarian protection, and who do not have anyone in the UK with parental responsibility for them. The legal rights and entitlements of 'looked after children' who are unaccompanied and in the UK are discussed at chapter 9.

Victims of modern slavery

10.107 Charges Regs 2015 reg 16 exempts from charging all treatment provided to victims of trafficking who have either been conclusively identified as such, or who are in receipt of a positive Reasonable Grounds decision, the first stage decision in the UK's formal victim identification process, known as the National Referral Mechanism (NRM).[82]

79 *Evidence base for the 2011 impact assessment*, para 22.
80 *Evidence base for the 2011 impact assessment*, para 35.
81 [2014] EWHC 3626 (Admin), see in particular at paras 110–114.
82 See paras 11.162–11.197 for a detailed discussion of the NRM process for victim identification.

10.108 This exemption was first introduced in 2008[83] shortly before the UK was due to ratify the Council of Europe Convention on Action against Trafficking in Human Beings[84] (ECAT). The Explanatory Memorandum to the 2008 amendment explained (at para 4.2) that the exemption was necessary to 'ensure compliance with' that convention. The need for compliance was specifically linked to the ECAT obligation under Articles 12(1)(b) and 13(2) to ensure that victims have access to emergency medical treatment, and under Article 12(3), which guarantees medical treatment to victims who are lawfully resident in the UK and who do not have adequate resources and need such help (at para 7.6). The ECAT obligations do not require the victim's medical treatment to have been caused by the exploitation. This is in contrast to the limited exemption applicable to victims of torture, FGM, domestic violence and sexual violence under Charges Regs reg 9(1)(f).[85]

10.109 Again, the rationale for including this exemption is illuminating. While recognising that victims of trafficking would be able to access 'urgent' and 'immediately necessary' treatment without requiring advance payment, the secretary of state was concerned that such victims would nevertheless be 'liable for charges and pursued for any debt' after being treated and unable to avoid the debt (para 7.8 of the Explanatory Memorandum). In terms similar to the rationale for exempting failed asylum-seekers, the secretary of state noted (at paras 7.8–7.9[F4]) that:

1) Many trafficked victims will already be subject to write-offs of debts because they have no funds to pay NHS charges. Thus, including them in the exempt categories from charging 'does not necessarily increase costs for the NHS as much as it might appear, since it regularises what often happens informally anyway, reducing the stress on the victims and withdrawing the necessity for the NHS to issue fruitless bills to them'.
2) Fully exempting them for all treatment is needed to 'ensure unequivocal compliance with the CoE Convention'. Otherwise it 'risks an inadequate level of compliance in relation to healthcare provision for victims of human trafficking, meaning that the UK could not ratify the CoE Convention'.

83 National Health Service (Charges to Overseas Visitors) (Amendment) Regulations 2008 SI No 2251.

84 The UK signed the convention on 23 March 2007 and ratified the convention on 17 December 2008. It came into force in the UK on 6 April 2009.

85 See paras 10.69–10.87.

Exemption for exceptional humanitarian reasons

10.110 Charges Regs 2015 reg 17 provides that the secretary of state is entitled to designate a person exempt from NHS charging by reason of having exceptional humanitarian reasons as long as certain specific criteria are met. A determination of this designation can only be made by the secretary of state and only if the secretary of state is satisfied, in the case of the overseas visitor that:

a) the treatment sought is not available in the person's home country;
b) the necessary arrangements have been made for temporary accommodation for the person, any authorised companion and authorised child for the duration of the course of treatment; and
c) the necessary arrangements have been made for the return of that person, any authorised companion and any authorised child to their home country when the course of treatment is completed.

10.111 As the *NHS charging guidance* notes (at para 7.59), this power to exempt is unlikely to be used other than in rare circumstances, where there is a clear humanitarian imperative to do so, for example, where the UK is responsible for causing the injury needing treatment or there are humanitarian reasons for treating the person in the UK.

Persons detained in hospital or subject to court ordered treatment

10.112 This exemption set out under Charges Regs 2015 reg 18, applies to the following people:[86]

1) overseas visitors liable to be detained in a hospital under the Mental Health Act (MHA) 1983 or any other legislation authorising their detention;
2) overseas visitors received into guardianship under the MHA 1983 or subject to a community treatment order under that Act;
3) overseas visitors deprived of their liberty under Mental Capacity Act (MCA) 2005 s4A, s4B, s16 or Sch A1; and
4) overseas visitors required to submit to treatment imposed by a court order other than those set out above.

Prisoners and other detainees

10.113 Anyone detained in prison or in a young offender institution, and anyone subject to detention under immigration powers, is exempt from charges.

86 *NHS charging guidance*, para 7.62.

Write-off of NHS debt

10.114 Save in respect of the exemptions under the Charges Regs 2015, there is no means by which an NHS debt can be waived or extinguished. The secretary of state has provided no power under the 2015 Regs to *waive* a debt on consideration of individual circumstances. This is in contrast with the power to waive the IHS (including, importantly, in circumstances of destitution). Thus even in respect of treatment deemed to be immediately necessary or urgent, which must be provided irrespective of whether the person is able to pay, a charge will be raised either during the course of treatment or after it has been completed. It cannot be avoided or waived.

10.115 The only discretionary element of the regime is the limited power conferred to trusts to 'write off the debt in their accounts and not pursue it' provided for in the *NHS charging guidance* at para 13.51. At para 13.72, the guidance sets out examples for when a trust may want to 'write off' the debt, ie where:

1) the NHS chargeable patient has subsequently died and recovery from their estate is impossible; or
2) given the NHS chargeable patient's financial circumstances, it would not be cost-effective to pursue it (for example, they are a destitute illegal migrant or are genuinely without access to any funds or other resources to pay their debt); or
3) all reasonable steps have failed to recover the debt (for example, the NHS chargeable patient is untraceable or there are no further practical means of pursuing debt recovery).

10.116 Writing off a debt is only for accounting purposes and 'does not mean that the debt is waived, nor extinguished; it remains in the organisation's records and can be recovered if the patient's ability to pay changes'.[87] It remains on the NHS body's records and does not prevent the information as to the existence of the debt being notified to the Home Office. Health bodies have a duty to notify the Home Office of an unpaid NHS debt accruing for NHS treatment of at least £500 or more outstanding for more than two months. The duty to notify the Home Office of an unpaid NHS debt is set out in the DHSC guidance *Overseas chargeable patients, NHS debt and immigration rules: guidance on administration and data sharing* (March 2019) and is founded upon the power of a public authority to supply information to the Home Secretary under IAA 1999 s20.

87 *NHS charging guidance*, para 13.73.

10.117 The Home Office has a power to deny anyone with an unpaid NHS debt of £500 or more, leave to remain in the UK or an extension of their leave to enter or remain in the UK if that debt has been outstanding for more than two months. This is set out in the Immigration Rules:

1) Immigration Rules para 320(22) applies to refusal of leave to enter where there is a debt outstanding of at least £500.
2) Immigration Rules para 322(12) relates to a discretionary ground on which to refuse an application for leave to remain or an application to extend/vary leave.
3) Appendix FM paras S-LTR 4.1 and 4.5 and S-ILR 4.1 and 4.5 also deal with the same.

10.118 The rule was first brought in on 31 October 2011 (*Statement of changes in Immigration Rules*, HC 1511) and applied to unpaid debts of £1,000 and over. This was subsequently amended on 24 November 2016 (*Statement of Change in Immigration Rules*, HC 667) such that unpaid debts of £500 and over can be relied on as a ground of refusal.

Policy context of the NHS charging regime

10.119 Four 'overarching principles' of the NHS charging regime were identified by the government in the Department of Health's July 2013 *Sustaining service, ensuring fairness* consultation paper, and repeated in subsequent policy documents. They provide that the NHS system is one:

1) that ensures access for all in need so that immediately necessary treatment is available irrespective of means or status and so that no one is denied treatment necessary to prevent risks to their life or permanent health;
2) where everybody makes a fair contribution to the NHS given the pressure the system is under so as to ensure its sustainability;
3) that is workable and efficient;
4) that does not increase inequalities given the secretary of state's positive duty under NHSA 2006 s1C to reduce inequalities relating to health services; this to be achieved by ensuring the 'needs and interests of vulnerable or disadvantaged patients are protected'.

10.120 However, these governing principles cannot be properly understood without appreciating how immigration policy is 'built in' to the charging regime. This is evident from:

1) the starting presumption that all 'overseas visitors' are chargeable. See Charges Regs 2015 reg 3(1): see para 10.32 above;
2) the widely drawn definition of an 'overseas visitor' as someone not ordinarily resident in the UK (reg 2) deals at once with those seeking leave to enter the UK and therefore not presently in the UK, short-term visitors and long-term residents, the latter of whom may have lost their residence rights but who are proactively seeking to regularise their leave: see para 10.38 above;
3) the requirement on migrants to pay the IHS in order to make an immigration application and in order to access the NHS if they are granted leave to enter or remain: see para 10.89 above;[88]
4) the obligation on the NHS to inform the Home Office on any outstanding debt accruing for NHS treatment of at least £500 or more outstanding for more than two months: see para 10.116 above;
5) immigration sanctions that give the Home Office a power to deny anyone with an NHS debt of £500 or more, which has been outstanding for more than two months, leave to remain in the UK or extension of their leave to enter or remain: see para 10.117 above.

10.121 Although the secretary of state has undertaken several consultations and Equality Analyses in respect of the NHS charging regime prior to the Charges Regs 2015 being implemented and subsequently, these have not sought to evaluate the overall impact of the regime on increasing health inequalities among particularly vulnerable cohorts of migrants. This is even though avoidance of the latter is one of four overarching principles underpinning the regime.

10.122 In *R (Cushnie) v Secretary of State for Health*, the court explicitly noted the absence of consideration in the July 2013 consultation which informed the Charges Regs 2015 of the overall impact of charging or the possibility of widening exemptions to encompass more vulnerable groups.[89] Similarly, a review commissioned by the secretary of state in 2013 from Prederi Ltd (the '2013 Prederi Report') was a quantitative assessment of the scale of visitor and migrant use of the NHS and did not consider the impact of charging on vulnerable cohorts.[90] Prederi noted that the proposition that charging for NHS

88 Health Charge Order 2015 (as amended) Sch 1.

89 [2014] EWHC 3626 (Admin). See the secretary of state's evidence referred to in the *Cushnie* judgment at para 107.

90 *Quantitative assessment of visitor and migrant use of the NHS in England: Exploring the data*, October 2013.

treatment was necessary to prevent or deter health tourism was based on estimates and anecdotes and thus 'impossible to estimate with confidence'.[91]

10.123 A November 2013 Equality Analysis also failed to address the overall impact of charging on vulnerable groups with protected characteristics and did not consider whether exemptions needed to be widened to encompass particular vulnerable groups, such as pregnant women and new mothers, children 'in need' in receipt of local authority support but not in care, and victims of gender-based violence (for example, FGM, domestic abuse and sexual violence). While noting that immediately necessary treatment would not be withheld, the secretary of state did not evaluate whether the proposed new rules would increase health inequalities by deterring women and children from accessing healthcare at all, as had been suggested by respondents to the consultation.[92]

10.124 A December 2013 response to consultation identified, amongst next steps, the possibility of 'further appraisal of the case for extending exemptions to . . . potential new groups'[93] – no such appraisal was conducted at that time. There was no cost recovery analysis similar to that undertaken in 2008 and 2011 when new exemptions were created for victims of trafficking and IAA 1999 s4(2)-supported failed asylum-seekers. Instead, the secretary of state focused on the instigation of a three-year Cost Recovery Programme.

10.125 When the DHSC rolled out the Cost Recovery Programme, stakeholders, including the Royal College of Midwives and Maternity Action, were invited to be members of the department's Vulnerable Groups stakeholder group and to attend ad hoc meetings to give feedback about the NHS charging regime. At a Health Inequalities Workshop held on 10 July 2014, when stakeholders expressed specific concerns about the speed of the reforms to the charging process and the need for empirical evidence into the impact on vulnerable groups before bringing in new measures, the DHSC responded by giving a commitment to assess that impact. In particular, the DHSC told stakeholders that it would accede to the request made both by a Major Projects Authority review and the Home Affairs Select Committee that research be done on the impact of charging on vulnerable groups, including children.

91 See para 1.2.7 of the 2013 Prederi Report under the heading 'Note of Caution'. See also section 9 dealing with 'Shortcomings and limitations of the approach'.

92 See summary of responses at paras 43–45 of the government's response to the July 2013 consultation, *Sustaining services, ensuring fairness*.

93 See section 6 of the government's response to the July 2013 consultation.

10.126 The secretary of state did not honour the commitment to carry out research as to the impact of charging on vulnerable groups prior to introducing further changes to the NHS charging regime. Instead, on 5 February 2015, the secretary of state laid the Charges Regs 2015 before parliament along with an Equality Analysis which was said to have informed the changes brought in by those regulations.

10.127 The February 2015 Equality Analysis relied heavily on the 2013 Prederi Report even though Prederi had identified the absence of complete and accurate data on the undocumented migrant population as a significant limitation to any analysis. Given the absence of further and better data, the Equality Analysis was premised on 'a great deal of speculation and assumption about the numbers of visitors and short-term migrants using the NHS' (p6) and did not assess qualitatively or quantitatively the impact of charging on different demographics of migrants based on their protected characteristics.

10.128 In respect of the exemption on grounds of gender-based violence, the analysis recognised that it was more likely to benefit women, because of the 'particularly vulnerable and powerless situations that victims of such violence find themselves in' and concluded that introduction of the exemption 'is consistent with wider government policy on preventing and supporting victims of violence' and ensures victims are able to access hospital treatment in a 'safe and trusted environment'. The analysis did not consider whether reg 9(1)(f) as drafted – requiring 'causation' between the treatment and type of violence – did give full effect to wider government policy on protecting victims of violence. Neither the analysis nor the Explanatory Memorandum accompanying the Charges Regs 2015 considered whether the exemption reflected the UK's obligation under Article 20 of the Council of Europe Convention on Preventing and Combating Violence Against Women and Domestic Violence (the 'Istanbul Convention'[94]), which the government had signed on 8 June 2012 and which provided for the state to ensure victims' access to health care, facilitating their recovery from violence. This is in contrast to the approach taken in respect of victims of trafficking in 2008 by the government, when an all-round exemption from charging was seen as necessary to ensure 'unequivocal' compliance with the ECAT.[95]

10.129 In respect of maternity care, the February 2015 Equality Analysis merely noted that this was available as an immediately necessary

94 See paras 11.233–11.269.

95 See paras 10.107–10.109 above for discussion on the trafficking exemption under reg 16.

treatment which had to be provided irrespective of up-front payment. It did not address any of the available evidence on the adverse impact of not exempting maternity care from charging altogether, including significant risks of poorer health outcomes of women and babies. Such evidence was available from highly credible sources including the Royal College of Midwives, Maternity Action, consultant midwives and the Migrant Rights' Network. Nor did it revisit, still less contradict, the inequalities identified in the earlier 2011/12 Equality Analysis on Immigration Sanctions for those with unpaid debts arising from the National Health Service (Charges to Overseas Visitors) Regulations 2011, namely that:

a) pregnant women are more likely to need to access NHS hospital treatment than non-pregnant women;
b) they may also be less able to pay for treatment;
c) they are more likely to face charges during their visit to the hospital than able-bodied, non-pregnant overseas visitors;
d) they may also find it more difficult than others to pay and be more likely to face an immigration sanction, such as the reporting of a debt to the Home Office and risking their immigration applications being refused on grounds of the debt;
e) the secretary of state considered that other non-pregnant overseas visitors would be less likely to be in this position because of being less likely to need treatment and/or more able to pay and thus less likely to incur a debt in the first place.

10.130 In respect of children, the February 2015 Equality Analysis rejected a call to exempt from charging those children supported by a local authority under Children Act 1989 s17, stating that this would be 'too wide an exemption' and would 'not capture the most vulnerable children'. This conclusion assumed that section 17 support would be 'low level' (the example given was money to buy new clothes). No data or evidence-gathering had been undertaken in respect of the profile of section 17 supported children, the nature of support received or, importantly, the impact of charging on them. This is despite the absence of evidence having been known to the secretary of state since the 2013 Prederi Report, the commitment in July 2014 to undertake research into this issue and the ease with which relevant information could have been obtained from local authorities.

10.131 While the February 2015 Equality Analysis noted the difficulties faced by low- or no-income persons in paying charges, it nevertheless considered charging to be justified in respect of protected groups who 'are on low or no income', on account of the NHS's duty to provide immediately necessary or urgent care (without requiring payment up-front). The analysis did not address the feasibility of cost recovery as against this cohort, notwithstanding that the secretary of state had already noted and accepted the inefficacy of charging people who would inevitably have their debt written off, such as destitute failed asylum-seekers in receipt of IAA 1999 s4(2) support and victims of trafficking, and the deterrent effect of charging those individuals and the risks thereby posed to public health.

10.132 In December 2015, less than eight months after the Charges Regs 2015 came into force, the government held a further public consultation, *Making a fair contribution*, with a view to further extending charging, which was said to be necessary to ensure the long-term sustainability of the NHS. Proposals put forward included charges for primary medical care, for prescriptions, and for care in emergency settings and for NHS-funded care delivered outside hospitals, in the community. The Cost Recovery Impact Assessment, prepared in November 2015, acknowledged the potential for worsening access to healthcare which could affect some groups of individuals disproportionately, but justified that impact on the basis of retention of free access to GP and nurse consultation, continued provision of immediately necessary treatment irrespective of payment and maintaining exemptions from charging for vulnerable groups.[96]

10.133 Alongside the consultation, the government commissioned Prederi to conduct a further quantitative assessment in 2016 (the '2016 Prederi Report'). No national qualitative study had been undertaken to address the data gaps in respect of undocumented migrants, particularly of vulnerable groups, identified by Prederi in 2013. A continued lack of quality data and limited quantitative evidence on the health of migrants overall and the impact of charges posed difficulties for the analysis. Prederi said that data in respect of children remained 'too poor quality', making an assessment of the scale of issues hard to determine. Although Prederi extrapolated from the limited data available to conclude that the proposals would not have an overall adverse impact on the chargeable population, it highlighted particular concerns in respect of migrant children, pregnancy and maternity, and others who 'may suffer from the cumulative effect of deprivation, homelessness, poor English, illiteracy, discrimination creating further barrier to accessing health service'.[97]

96 See Section D of the *Evidence Base for the Cost Recovery Impact Assessment*, November 2015.

97 See Executive Summary of the 2016 Prederi Report under 'Findings'.

10.134 By the Charges Amendment Regs 2017, the secretary of state introduced one extension to charging which had been consulted on, for NHS services delivered in the community, and two further amendments that had not been consulted upon: the imposition of mandatory up-front charging for non-urgent care[98] and the requirement that a person's chargeable status be recorded when they sought to access NHS care.[99] Their impact and rationale were only addressed in two subsequent Equality Analyses in December 2016 and July 2017. Both of those analyses again only considered the *additional* impact of these changes on those with protected characteristics, proceeding on a (false) premise that there was no pre-existing adverse impact of charging. It was concluded that the 2017 changes would have no significant additional impact on those affected who were already chargeable, including children, largely because of the secretary of state's reliance on the exception to up-front charging for immediately necessary and urgent services as apparent mitigation.

10.135 The failure of the government to consult on the two additional amendments was challenged in *R (MP) v Secretary of State for Health and Social Care*,[100] where it was argued that those amendments were unlawful because a) they had been introduced without public consultation and b) the secretary of state had failed to discharge his duties under EqA 2010 s149 and NHSA 2006 ss1B and 1C to have due regard to certain matters, including the impact of the changes on the equality objectives in respect of protected groups, and reducing health inequalities, before making the Charges Amendment Regs 2017. The claim in *MP* was issued in October 2017. In November 2017, and apparently in direct response to the claim, it was announced that the DHSC would 'undertake a full, formal review of how these amendment regulations are implemented, and monitor delivery closely, particularly where healthcare is provided to the most vulnerable'.[101] The claim in *MP* was dismissed, partly as a result of the hastily convened review. On appeal,[102] the challenge was focused on a failure to consult on upfront charging and the recording of NHS charges under regs 3 and 3A. That challenge was also dismissed.

98 Charges Regs 2015 reg 3(1A).

99 Charges Regs 2015 reg 3A.

100 [2018] EWHC 3392 (Admin).

101 See Lord O'Shaughnessy in House of Lords, in the course of debate over the National Health Service (Charges to Overseas Visitors) (Amendment) Regulations 2017 – Motion to Regret, 16 November 2017.

102 [2020] EWCA Civ 1634.

10.136 The government confined the 'review' announced in response to *MP* to the impact of changes introduced in 2017, notably mandatory up-front charging, with a particular focus on any unintended consequences on delivery of care in the community. The review process and scope were heavily criticised by participating stakeholders for being overly narrow, for the short duration of the review period and for the limit to the stakeholders who were invited to submit evidence for the review. Some stakeholders undertook their own research and analysis of the wider impact of NHS charging on particular service users. Maternity Action published a report, *What price safe motherhood? Charging for NHS maternity care and its impact on migrant women* in September 2018, highlighting the adverse health outcomes of charging on pregnant migrant women and their children arising from the 'chilling effect' of the regime. In conjunction with the Royal College of Midwives, Maternity Action called for an end to charging for maternity services owing to the level of risk that emerged from the evidence, but that request was not acceded to. Their call was followed by a similar recommendation from the Equality and Human Rights Commission (EHRC) further to its research,[103] which similarly concluded in November 2018 that the fear of charging alone deterred women, even those exempted, from receiving antenatal care at an early stage or at all.

10.137 The analysis underlying the review and the evidence considered have not been published but a copy of the June 2018 Report on the Review, which was submitted to the minister as advice, was put in evidence in *MP* and referred to in the High Court judgment.[104] That report, which included an equality analysis, was notable in accepting that migrants affected by the 2017 amendments are more likely to be in the lower socio-economic groups, likely to remain in the UK for longer periods, and to be met with other barriers to accessing services in addition to charging (para 13). The report noted that those 'most likely to suffer detrimentally' are 'often "hard to reach" ' (para 20) but that the evidence was 'not significant' (para 16) in demonstrating that there were risks and potential detrimental impact brought on by

103 *The lived experiences of access to healthcare for people seeking and refused asylum*, Equality and Human Rights Commission, November 2018. See recommendations in a further document, *Making sure people seeking and refused asylum can access healthcare: what needs to change?*, November 2018, in which the EHRC recommended that the government should ensure 'free and full access to all family planning service and pregnancy and maternity services, regardless of immigration status'.

104 [2018] EWHC 3392 (Admin) at para 59.

the amendments. It also concluded that for longer-term migrants, most of the care they would require would be considered urgent and not subject to mandatory upfront charging (para 25).

10.138 On 20 December 2018, the Royal Colleges of Physicians, Paediatrics and Child Health, Obstetricians and Gynaecologists, and the Faculty of Public Health issued a joint statement in response to the minister's statement on the review. They strongly disputed the assessment of the absence of evidence of deterrence from treatment and characterised the Charges Amendment Regs 2017 as a 'concerning barrier to care'. They called for charging to be suspended to enable a 'full independent review' of its impact on individuals and public health to take place.

10.139 The call for a full and independent review of the whole NHS charging regime and its impact of individuals and public health, and for the suspension of charging pending review, were repeated by the British Medical Association on 11 February 2019[105] and 25 June 2019,[106] and by the Academy of Medical Royal Colleges in March 2019. The House of Commons Health and Social Care Committee also pressed the government to carry out a full and comprehensive review of the overall effect of the charging regime on vulnerable groups.[107]

10.140 In oral evidence before the Health and Social Care Committee, the Health Minister stated that 'we have kept the 2015 changes under review'.[108] When pressed on undertaking a 'thorough review' of the overall effect of the regime as a whole, the Health Minister answered that the onus was on 'local trusts . . . undertaking reviews as and when they are appropriate at the time'.[109]

105 The recommendation for a 'full and independent review' into the impact of the regulations on individual and public health was made in the British Medical Association's (BMA's) February 2019 report, *Delayed, deterred and distressed: the impact of NHS overseas charging regulations on patients and doctors who care for them*.

106 The BMA's membership voted at the Annual General Meeting to call for the suspension of the NHS charging regime and a full review of the impact of charging on individuals and public health.

107 Transcript of oral evidence session before the Health and Social Care Committee, 25 June 2019. See in particular Questions 36, 38, 39, 41 43, 45, 49, 50, 52, 54, 58 posed of the Health Minister Stephen Hammond and the Permanent Secretary of DHSC, Sir Chris Wormald.

108 See Health Minister Stephen Hammond's answer to Question 13 before the Health and Social Care Committee on 25 June 2019.

109 See Health Minister Stephen Hammond's answer to Question 37 before the Health and Social Care Committee on 25 June 2019.

10.141 On 8 July 2019, the Health Minister wrote formally to the Health and Social Care Committee declining its request for a full review to be undertaken of the overall effects of the NHS Charging regime, stating that 'the Government does not feel that it is necessary . . . at this time' but that it would consider 'emerging evidence in relation to the Charging Regulations, including the impacts on those with protected characteristics under the Public Sector Equality Duty, to ensure that they continue to deliver the policy intent'.

10.142 To date, despite repeated calls for a systems-wide review of the impact of NHS charging on migrants liable to be charged for health services, the government has not undertaken such a review.

NHS Continuing Healthcare and NHS-funded nursing care

10.143 NHS Continuing Healthcare (CHC) is a package of health and social care services, sometimes including accommodation if that is part of the patient's needs, which is to be funded by the NHS in circumstances where an individual has a 'primary health need'. The key NHS CHC provision is not found in the NHSA 2006, but in the Care Act 2014. Section 22 of the Care Act 2014 places a limit on the support that can be provided by social services authorities under the act, prohibiting support that is required to be provided under the NHSA 2006 unless: a) doing so would be merely incidental or ancillary to doing something else to meet needs under those sections; and b) the service or facility in question would be of a nature that the local authority could be expected to provide. The statutory scheme is underpinned by regulations[110] and by high level guidance, the *National Framework for NHS continuing healthcare and NHS-funded nursing care.*[111] In addition there is a 'best practice' guidance published jointly by the Association of Directors of Adult Social Services and NHS England – *Continuing healthcare: guide for health and social care practitioners: Ensuring a consistent person-centred assessment* – to facilitate dispute resolution over funding responsibility.

10.144 The detailed statutory framework and decision-making concerning NHS CHC is covered in both the *NHS law and practice*[112] and

110 National Health Service Commissioning Board and Clinical Commissioning Group (Responsibilities and Standing Rules) Regulations 2012.

111 DHSC, November 2012, last updated October 2022.

112 D Lock KC, H Gibbs *NHS law and practice,* Legal Action Group, 2018.

Community care and the law[113] books published by Legal Action Group and will not be covered in this section.

10.145 Currently NHS CHC is outside the scope of the Charges Regs 2015. This means that where it has been determined that an overseas visitor qualifies for such a package of health and care, they cannot currently be charged for it.[114]

Persons who may lack mental capacity

10.146 The law relating to mental capacity is governed by the MCA 2005. MCA 2005 s2 makes clear that capacity to make a particular decision is both 'matter'- and 'time'-specific. An assessment of a person's capacity must be based on their ability to make a specific decision at the time it needs to be made, and not their ability to make decisions in general.[115]

10.147 A person with a fluctuating condition may have capacity to take a certain decision at a certain time of day, or during a period of remission from illness, but not at other times. A person may at any particular time have capacity to take decisions about one issue but not another issue. Furthermore, in certain areas of decision-making, capacity should not be considered in broad brackets such as 'medical treatment': a person may have capacity to manage treatment for a physical health condition but not for a mental health condition.

10.148 An individual's insight into their difficulties in understanding, retaining or using information, which causes the individual to ask for assistance, is a key consideration. The greater the individual's appreciation that they have a problem on which they need advice, the more likely it is that the individual will be deemed to have the necessary capacity.

10.149 The five principles underpinning the operation of the MCA 2005, set out in section 1(2)–(6), are:

(2) A person must be assumed to have capacity unless it is established that he lacks capacity.

(3) A person is not to be treated as unable to make a decision unless all practicable steps to help him to do so have been taken without success.

(4) A person is not to be treated as unable to make a decision merely because he makes an unwise decision.

113 L Clements *Community care and the law*, Legal Action Group, 2019.
114 This is confirmed in the *NHS charging guidance* at chapter 4.
115 See Mental Capacity Act Code of Practice 2007.

(5) An act done, or decision made, under this Act for or on behalf of a person who lacks capacity must be done, or made, in his best interests.

(6) Before the act is done, or the decision is made, regard must be had to whether the purpose for which it is needed can be as effectively achieved in a way that is less restrictive of the person's rights and freedom of action.

Lack of capacity

10.150 MCA 2005 s3(1) provides that a person is 'unable to make a decision' if at the material time the person is:

a) unable to understand the information relevant to the decision;
b) unable to retain that information;
c) unable to use or weigh that information as part of the process of making the decision; or
d) unable to communicate the decision.

10.151 The information relevant to the decision will include the nature of the decision, the purpose for which it is needed, the effects of the decision, and the reasonably foreseeable consequences of a) deciding one way or the other or b) failing to make a decision: MCA 2005 s3(4). This may include the available options, any alternatives and that the person has a choice. The requirement to establish an inability to take a decision is often referred to as 'the functional test'.

10.152 MCA 2005 s2(1) provides that a lack of capacity means that at the material time the person is unable to make a decision for themself in relation to the matter because of an impairment of or a disturbance in the functioning of the mind or brain. The MCA 2005 does not define impairment and does not specifically require a diagnosis, although this requirement is often referred to as a 'diagnostic test'. The impairment or disturbance does not need to be permanent and can be temporary.

10.153 When MCA 2005 ss2(1) and 3(1) are taken together, it is clear that the fact of a person having a diagnosis of a mental disorder, for example, schizophrenia, is not sufficient in itself to establish a lack of capacity. That may be an impairment or disturbance in the functioning of the mind or brain, but it must also be shown that there is an inability to make a decision because of the identified impairment or disturbance to satisfy section 2(1).

10.154 Under MCA 2005 s3(2), when assessing a person's ability to understand, retain and use information, the information must be presented in a way that is appropriate to the person's needs and circumstances, using the most effective form of communication for that person. The inability to retain information for more than a short period is not of itself sufficient to establish a lack of capacity: MCA 2005 s3(3). The requirement is for information to be retained sufficiently long to allow the decision to be made.

10.155 There is a further and more detailed discussion on mental capacity in *Community care and the law*[116] and the *Court of Protection handbook*[117] published by Legal Action Group.

Litigation capacity

10.156 Capacity to litigate can be a different question to the questions that the MCA 2005 is concerned with. It relates to whether a person has capacity to give a lawyer instructions on the matters that concern potential and actual litigation.

10.157 It is well established that once a legal advisor reasonably entertains a doubt about a client's capacity to give proper instructions, the advisor has a professional duty to satisfy themself that the client either has or does not have capacity to give instructions.[118] Where these doubts can be resolved, there may be no need for any determination by the court: if it is established that the client has capacity, the legal representative may simply proceed to act for them; if it is established that the client lacks capacity, a litigation friend may be appointed without court order by filing and serving a certificate of suitability under Civil Procedure Rules[119] 21.5. If, however, it is not possible to determine the issue, the legal representative will be under a professional ethical duty to raise the matter with the court, regardless of any purported instructions from the client not to do so and the various other duties owed to the client, for example, confidentiality.[120]

10.158 Formally, the test of capacity to conduct proceedings will vary according to the type of court. However, as the Supreme Court has

116 L Clements *Community care and the law*, Legal Action Group, 2019.

117 Alex Ruck Keene KC (Hon) et al *Court of Protection handbook*, Legal Action Group, 2022.

118 *RP v Nottingham City Council* [2008] EWCA Civ 462 at para 99 per Wall LJ.

119 SI 1998 No 3132.

120 See for example, *McFaddens (a firm) v Platford* [2009] EWHC 126 (TCC) per HHJ Toulmin KC at para 380; see also The Law Society and The Bar Council guidance on client incapacity: *Working with clients who may lack mental capacity*, The Law Society, 5 June 2020; and *Client incapacity*, The Bar Council, February 2014, last reviewed June 2021.

made clear in *Dunhill v Burgin*,[121] there is unlikely to be any real difference whether the test is the statutory test applied under the MCA 2005 (as is applied in civil proceedings) or the common law.

10.159 The key question is set out in the judgment of Chadwick LJ in *Masterman-Lister v Brutton & Co*, and is whether 'the party to legal proceedings is capable of understanding, with the assistance of such proper explanation [in broad terms and simple language] from legal advisers and other experts as the case may require, the matters on which his consent or decision was likely to be necessary in the course of those proceedings'.[122] This test applies to the proceedings as a whole and not at each step in the conduct of the proceedings.

10.160 The test of lack of capacity to conduct proceedings is the statutory test under the MCA 2005. However, the common law principles are also helpful in applying the statutory test.

10.161 Capacity depends on time and context. The question is always whether the litigant has capacity to conduct the particular proceedings that they are involved in, and not other proceedings or their ability to make decisions in general.[123]

10.162 When assessing a client's capacity to conduct civil proceedings, think about whether the client can:

1) understand how the proceedings would be funded;
2) understand the chances of not succeeding and the risk of having to pay costs;
3) make the sort of decisions that arise in litigation;
4) give proper instructions for, and approve, the particulars of a claim, and approve a compromise.

10.163 For a client to have capacity to approve a compromise, they would need:

1) insight into the compromise;
2) an ability to instruct solicitors to advise them on it;
3) an understanding of the solicitor's advice;
4) to be able to weigh that advice before making a decision.

10.164 The Supreme Court also made clear in *Dunhill v Burgin* that the test must be applied to the claim that the party in fact has, not to the claim as formulated by their lawyers.

121 [2014] UKSC 18.
122 [2002] EWCA Civ 1889, [2003] 3 All ER 162 at para 75.
123 *Sheffield City Council v E and another* [2004] EWHC 2808 (Fam), [2005] Fam 326 per Munby J at para 38.

10.165 If the individual is a party to but lacks capacity to conduct proceedings in the county court or the High Court, a litigation friend must be appointed to give instructions and conduct the proceedings on their behalf. This is provided for under Civil Procedure Rules Part 21.

10.166 In *AM (Afghanistan) v SSHD*,[124] the Court of Appeal identified a significant lacuna in the immigration tribunal system in respect of the ability of those who require a litigation friend (whether as a vulnerable adult or as a child) to access one, including the absence of a specific rule under the Tribunal Procedure (First-tier Tribunal) (Immigration and Asylum Chamber) Rules 2014[125] to appoint a litigation friend in the immigration tribunal (although the overriding objective interpreted purposively should provide for this), and the absence of state funding for litigation friends (ie via the Official Solicitor or another public body). This issue has remained unresolved since the 2017 judgment.

Mental capacity in the context of immigration detention

10.167 There are currently no effective arrangements in place to facilitate detainees who are mentally ill or potentially lack mental capacity to be identified and to be helped to access advice and assistance on matters that impact on their immigration detention and immigration status. Whereas frequently, disputes over mental capacity arising in the community may be brought to the attention of the Court of Protection by family members, the local authority or an ICB, there is no clear mechanism for resolving such disputes under the Immigration Acts.

10.168 The absence of such arrangements was heavily criticised by the Court of Appeal in *R (VC) v SSHD*.[126] In *VC*, the Court of Appeal ruled that the failure to make reasonable adjustments to facilitate effective access to justice for the mentally ill or mentally incapacitated was a breach of EqA 2010 ss20 and 29. The Court of Appeal held (at para 161) that the burden was on the Home Secretary to show that these anticipatory duties of reasonable adjustments had been complied with. The court rejected the Home Secretary's argument that it would not be reasonable to require the secretary of state to appoint a mental health advocate (at paras 163–171), agreeing with the argument made on behalf of VC that there were several powers

124 [2017] EWCA Civ 1123.
125 SI No 2604.
126 [2018] EWCA Civ 57, [2018] 1 WLR 4781.

under which the Home Secretary could make such advocacy provision, including the Equality Act 2010 itself, IAA 1999 s153[127] and the common law. In the circumstances, the Court of Appeal concluded (at para 171) that:

> . . . the Secretary of State has not discharged the burden of proof under section 136 of the Equality Act. She has not demonstrated that she complied with her duty to make reasonable adjustments for mentally ill detainees in respect of their ability to make representations on decisions regarding their continued detention and segregation. I therefore find that she has breached this duty.

10.169 In the subsequent case of *R (ASK) v SSHD; R (MDA) v SSHD*,[128] the Court of Appeal found that the discrimination identified in *VC* had not yet been remedied, even though those co-joined cases were heard a year after the criticisms already made in *VC*. A note which the Home Secretary was directed by the Court of Appeal to file in *ASK;MDA* was rejected by the court as evidence that she had properly remedied the lacuna identified in *VC*. Hickinbottom LJ noted (at paras 244–245) that:

> ASK's case is not materially different from the cases of VC or MDA. Because of his illness, ASK suffered from a disability. It seems likely that, from time-to-time, he lacked the capacity properly to engage with the detention authorities in relation to important decisions that related to him, e.g. with regard to his continuing detention, segregation and non-transfer to hospital. In those respects, he was treated differently from those detainees who were not disabled. In breach of the PSED, the Secretary of State failed to have due regard to the duty to eliminate discrimination. Further, the duty on the Secretary of State to make reasonable adjustments having arisen, no adjustments were made and obvious adjustments (e.g. in the form of IMCA-type representation) could have been made. The burden was therefore on the Secretary of State to show he had complied with the duty to make such adjustments; and he adduced no evidence that he had even considered such adjustments and certainly no evidence that he had complied with the duty.

10.170 A similar finding was made by the Joint Committee on Human Rights (JCHR), in an inquiry into immigration detention, published on 7 February 2019. The JCHR was similarly dissatisfied with the lack of progress in remedying what was a clear failure to implement

127 This provision requires the secretary of state to make rules for the regulation and management of removal centres, including with respect to the safety, care, activities, discipline and control of detained persons.

128 [2019] EWCA Civ 1239.

procedural safeguards for the mentally ill and mentally incapacitated. The JCHR recommended (at para 84 of the report) that:

> The Government should make better provision for the identification of individuals who lack mental capacity in detention. There should be, at all times, an on-site suitably qualified expert at all IRCs able to make such assessments in accordance with mental capacity legislation. We also consider that there should be automatic provision of advocacy services in cases where individuals do not have full capacity to make decisions for themselves on account of their mental capacity to ensure that such individuals are able to participate in the legal processes to challenge their detention and make representations in respect of any immigration applications.

10.171 Notwithstanding these two Court of Appeal judgments, there remains no independent advocacy provision in place to provide an effective means by which those detainees who may lack mental capacity by reason of their mental illness or learning disability can challenge their detention, conditions of detention and treatment in detention. All the Home Office has published is Detention Services Order 04/2020: *Mental vulnerability and immigration detention*[129] but this just alerts staff in the immigration removal centres to be alive to concerns about a detainee's potential lack of mental capacity and does not provide an independent means by which the detainee could seek legal advice and assistance. The Detention Services Order is dependent on immigration removal centre staff and healthcare staff being in a position to recognise potential mental capacity issues, and take steps to identify these issues. However, even when these issues are identified, there is no procedure to refer the detainee for independent advocacy and legal advice and assistance to challenge their detention and treatment in detention, and to get advice to regularise their immigration position.

Persons subject to detention for treatment under the Mental Health Act 1983

10.172 The MHA 1983 is the primary legislative framework governing the treatment of mental health patients. It deals with detention in hospital for treatment, detention in hospital by order of a criminal court, treatment on offer while detained, and the provision of aftercare on discharge from hospital. It is beyond the scope of this chapter to discuss the detailed provisions of the MHA 1983.

129 V1.0, July 2020.

10.173 For present purposes, it is sufficient to note that migrants without regularised immigration status are not excluded from accessing treatment whilst detained in a hospital under the MHA 1983 under Nationality, Immigration and Asylum Act 2002 Sch 3. Nor are after-care services provided under MHA 1983 s117, which are aimed to reduce the risk of deterioration to a person's mental health after detention (and can include financial support and accommodation), subject to charging under the Charges Regs 2015. There is no express power in the MHA 1983 to charge for section 117 after-care services. Therefore, if there is a duty to provide such after-care services on discharge from hospital under one of the detention provisions, no charge can be levied against the person.

Remedies

NHS complaints

10.174 As with adult social care, there is a requirement for NHS bodies to have in place a formal statutory complaints process under the Local Authority Social Services and NHS Complaints Regulations 2009[130] The procedure is similar for NHS bodies as it is with local authorities. The complaints procedure to local authorities is discussed in some detail at chapter 8.

The Health Service Commissioner

10.175 The Health Service Commissioner for England is a statutory appointment under Health Service Commissioners Act (HSCA) 1993 s1. The HSCA 1993 confers on the Ombudsman a number of broad discretions, including whether to investigate a complaint in the first place, whether to discontinue an investigation, whether to investigate, notwithstanding that the complainant may have another remedy, what standard he or she shall adopt to assess whether there has been a service failure or maladministration, and what procedure for conducting an investigation is appropriate in the circumstances.

10.176 As with Local Government and Social Care Ombudsman complaints, the statutory time limit is one year, but the Ombudsman may exercise their discretion to set aside that time limit and

130 SI No 309.

investigate a complaint if he or she considers it reasonable to do so under HSCA 1993 s9(4).

10.177 The types of complaint that can be investigated by the Ombudsman are set out in HSCA 1993 s3. This includes: a) a failure in a service provided by a health service body; b) a failure of such a body to provide a service which it was a function of the body to provide, or c) maladministration connected with any other action taken by or on behalf of such a body.

10.178 A health service body can refer a complaint for investigation by the Ombudsman under HSCA 1993 s10 if a person has complained that as a consequence of a failure or maladministration, they sustained injustice or hardship.

Judicial review

10.179 There will be cases in which the complaints mechanisms described above do not provide an individual with an effective remedy to a health body's refusal or failure to exercise duties or discretions under the NHSA 2006 or other related legislation. Typically, this might be the case where urgent remedial action is needed or where a mandatory order is required to compel a health body to comply with its legal duties and powers, particularly where the need relates to treatment, discharge from hospital and the provision of after-care services, such as accommodation. An applicant in these circumstances is likely to need to seek judicial review.

CHAPTER 11

Special cases

Shu Shin Luh
with Maria Moodie

Introduction

11.1 The preceding chapters provide an examination into the legal frameworks applicable to access to and the provision of support for migrants more generally. While vulnerabilities may inevitably arise among the migrant population by virtue of the exclusions and limitations on their access to support and what they get when they are able to access support, there are particular cohorts to whom specific additional obligations are owed under international human rights treaties and domestic law and policy. The aim of this chapter is to supplement the general discussion in the preceding chapters by examining in more detail the particular issues facing these particular vulnerable cohorts of migrants, namely:

- unaccompanied children and care leavers;
- victims of human trafficking;[1] and
- victims of domestic violence.

11.2 It is not possible within the scope of this book to provide a complete analysis of the law and policy as applied to each of these vulnerable cohorts of migrants. At the time of writing, the law is also in flux, further to the UK's exit from the European Union (EU) at the end of January 2020 and the Nationality and Borders Act (NBA) 2022 and Illegal Migration Act 2023, the provisions of which affecting unaccompanied children and victims of human trafficking have not come into force in full. Chapters 1–3 provide an outline of key changes under the NBA 2022 and the legal implications of the UK's exit from the EU as the law stands at May 2023. Where relevant, this chapter will touch on specific impact on specific groups identified at para 11.1 above.

11.3 This chapter seeks to highlight the additional law and policy applicable to each of these categories as the law stands as at May 2023, and draw out key developments and common issues that practitioners are likely to come across. There are specialist materials with which practitioners may be able to consult for further explanation and discussion in respect of each of these vulnerable cohorts.[2] At the

1 References in this chapter to victims of trafficking are in line with the international definition of human trafficking. This is set out and discussed further at paras 11.131–11.145 below. The UK uses the term 'modern slavery' to describe the same, but there is no uniform definition of 'modern slavery' under international or domestic law. For the purposes of this book, the term 'victims of human trafficking' encompasses those who are victims of modern slavery as termed by the Home Office.

2 See I Wise KC et al *Children in need: local authority support for children and families*, Legal Action Group, 2013.

writing of this chapter, the government has passed further legislation which will further impact unaccompanied children and care leavers and victims of human trafficking, in the form of the Illegal Migration Act 2023. It is not possible at this time fully to appreciate the impact of those changes. It is already evident from the provisions of the Act and their statutory purpose that if and when the provisions commence, we will see further reduction of rights and protections for vulnerable migrants.

Unaccompanied children and care leavers

Introduction

11.4 Unaccompanied or separated migrant children can be some of the most vulnerable children in the UK. They may have experienced significant emotional and psychological trauma in their country of origin and on their journey to the UK. Some will have been subjected to human trafficking and exploitation. Many will have arrived in the UK without any documentation to prove their identity, nationality and age, and will face disputes over their age which will affect their rights and entitlements to care and support and which arm of the state is responsible for making these arrangements. Most, if not all, of them will require permission to remain in the UK and will inevitably need legal advice and assistance to assist them to decide what their residence entitlements are in the UK. This chapter describes this group of children as 'unaccompanied' and 'separated' in recognition of the fact that some of the children may have set off on their journey to the UK with their parents or relatives but for whatever reason became separated from them. The adults' whereabouts may or may not be known.

11.5 Almost all of the children falling in this group will be alone in an unfamiliar country, no longer able to enjoy the support or protection of their parents and relatives and may be surrounded by people unable to speak their first language. There will be some children who have relatives in the UK who may not be in a position to care for them owing to their own personal circumstances. As such, by and large, they will become the responsibility of the local authority as 'looked after children' within the meaning of Children Act (ChA) 1989 s22(1), most likely under the section 20 voluntary accommodation provision but sometimes under a section 31 care order, although there will be those who have travelled to the UK unaccompanied to reunite with relatives in the UK and whose integration gives rise to different challenges.

11.6 Chapter 9 sets out a detailed discussion of the duties and powers of local authorities toward unaccompanied children and young adults as well as toward children within their families. This section sets out the additional rights and entitlements of unaccompanied and separated children and young adults under international law and examines the key challenges facing their access to care and support in the UK.

Relevant international law

Overview

11.7 In addition to the domestic framework of the Children Acts 1989 and 2004, the following international instruments govern the rights and entitlements of migrant children in the UK:

- the UN Convention on the Rights of the Child (UNCRC);
- the Charter of Fundamental Rights of the European Union (CFEU);
- the European Union Council Directive 2004/83/EC (the 'Qualification Directive').

11.8 The EU law principles have been included into this chapter to the extent that they formed a basis for the legal analysis in recent cases. Until December 2020, the Directive was retained under European Union (Withdrawal) Act 2018 s4 but that changed with the passage of section 1 of and Schedule 1 to the Immigration and Social Security Co-ordination (EU Withdrawal) Act 2020.[3] The EU Directive on preventing and combating trafficking in human beings and protecting its victims[4] ('Anti-Trafficking Directive') has not been included in the discussion as it pertains to unaccompanied children because NBA 2022 s68 disapplies Anti-Trafficking Directive Articles 11, 13–14 and 16 concerning the provision of assistance and support to child victims of trafficking. NBA 2022 s68 came into force on 30 January 2023. But principles concerning the best interests of children

3 See discussion on the status of the Qualification Directive in domestic law at paras 3.15–3.19.

4 The full name of the Directive is Directive 2011/36/EU of the European Parliament and of the Council of 5 April 2011 on preventing and combating trafficking in human beings and protecting its victims and replacing Council Framework Decision 2002/629/JHA.

as set out in the UNCRC[5] and under Children and Social Work Act (CSWA) 2017 s1[6] will still apply to unaccompanied children.

11.9 A general discussion of the relationship between EU law and domestic immigration law is covered in chapter 2. The impact of EU law on asylum matters is discussed at paras 3.15–3.30.

UN Convention on the Rights of the Child

Relationship with domestic law

11.10 When the UK ratified the UNCRC in 1991, it entered a reservation to Article 22 of the convention, which restricted the rights of children who are subject to immigration control, including in respect of their rights to enter and remain in the UK and to their acquisition and possession of citizenship. This reservation was withdrawn in November 2008. The withdrawal of the reservation signified acceptance, in principle at least, that all children, irrespective of their immigration status, are entitled to full enjoyment of the rights and protections contained within the convention in accordance with the non-discrimination clause at Article 2.[7] The then Minister for Borders and Immigration, Phil Woolas MP, sought to minimise the significance of the withdrawal by stating that no 'additional changes to legislation, guidance or practice are currently envisaged'.[8] Many viewed this political position as a missed opportunity to remove and reform all discriminatory laws and policies pertaining to migrant children.

11.11 In preparation for the withdrawal of the reservation to the UNCRC, parliament passed UK Borders Act (UKBA) 2007 s21 as a first step to reflecting the change in the UK's position concerning the protections under the UNCRC in the immigration law context. This provision imposed an obligation on the Home Secretary to issue a Code of Practice designed to ensure that in exercising functions in the UK, the immigration authorities take appropriate steps to ensure that while children are in the UK they are safe from harm. The *UK Border Agency Code of Practice for keeping children safe from harm* was published on 16 December 2008, a month after the withdrawal of the reservation to the UNCRC was formally recorded, and came into

5 Discussed at paras 11.15–11.23.

6 Discussed at paras 11.92, 11.116 and 9.218–9.225.

7 Joint Committee on Human Rights 25th Report: Children's Rights, 13 October 2009, https://publications.parliament.uk/pa/jt200809/jtselect/jtrights/157/15708.htm.

8 Hansard, HC Debs col 825W, 24 November 2008, https://publications.parliament.uk/pa/cm200708/cmhansrd/cm081124/text/81124w0004.htm.

force on 6 January 2009.[9] The Code of Practice made explicit that 'every child does matter as much if they are subject to immigration control as if they are a British citizen' and 'the best interests of the child will be a primary consideration (although not necessarily the only consideration) when making decisions about his or her future'. The Code also stated that 'the UK Border Agency will seek to ensure that children are treated in a way that safeguards them, promotes their welfare and promotes their upbringing by their parents'. However, as a statutory instrument, the Code did not create any new or overriding duty and was not intended to interfere with the Home Office's primary functions to uphold integrity of the immigration control system through immigration laws, rules and policies. To that extent, the Code under UKBA 2007 s21 was seen as secondary to immigration control.

11.12 In 2009, the government introduced Borders, Citizenship and Immigration Act (BCIA) 2009 s55, which came into force on 2 November 2009, and placed on a statutory footing a duty on the Home Secretary, their officers and contractors, to 'make arrangements for ensuring that' immigration functions are 'discharged' in respect of children having regard 'to the need to safeguard and promote the welfare of children who are in the UK'.[10] The immigration functions include any function of the secretary of state in relation to immigration, asylum or nationality, any function conferred by or by virtue of the Immigration Acts on an immigration officer, and customs functions of the secretary of state or delegated to a customs official.

11.13 BCIA 2009 s55, in its language and purpose, goes further than that provided by UKBA 2007 s21 and the Code of Practice issued thereunder. Its intention was to place the Home Office's duty on an equivalent statutory footing to Children Act (ChA) 2004 s11.

11.14 Statutory guidance was issued in conjunction with BCIA 2009 s55 entitled *Every child matters: change for children*. This statutory guidance, issued in November 2009, has not been updated since, and the development as to the implementation of BCIA 2009 s55 has by and large been through case-law, discussed at paras 1.24–1.31 above.

Best interests of the child principle

11.15 The most important overarching provision of the UNCRC, and the one most frequently cited in case-law, is Article 3, which requires that

9 UK Borders Act 2007 (Code of Practice on Children) Order 2008 SI No 3158.

10 BCIA 2009 s55(1).

in all actions concerning children, the 'best interests of the child shall be a primary consideration'. Although the UNCRC is an unincorporated treaty and thus not directly incorporated into UK's domestic law, case-law development over the past decade has established the importance and applicability of UNCRC obligations in domestic law. See, for example, in the immigration context, *ZH (Tanzania) v SSHD*,[11] regarding the need for the impact of deportation of a parent on her children to give primary consideration to the children's best interests; and in the welfare benefits context, *R (DA and others) v SSWP*,[12] finding that a breach of UNCRC Article 3 as material to whether the differential treatment of children of lone parents in receipt of state benefits is justified; and in the housing and social care context, *Nzolameso v Westminster City Council*,[13] finding that the arrangement of accommodation and support must take account of the best interests of the affected children as a primary consideration.

11.16 The 'best interests of the child' principle has in substance become a part of UK domestic law, in the main through European Convention on Human Rights (ECHR) Article 8, with decision-makers being required to give the child's interests high priority in any decision they make,[14] although, as explained by Lord Kerr in *ZH (Tanzania)*, it is not a factor of 'limitless importance in the sense that it will prevail over all of the considerations'.[15] Thus, although it is a 'primary consideration', is not the only or paramount one that trumps other factors. How that would apply depends on the facts and circumstances of the case.

11.17 Guidance on how best interests should be approached in relation to the specific situation of migrant children was provided in General Comment No 6 (2005).[16] The analysis of the Committee on the Rights of the Child contained in its General Comments are relevant to informing the approach to be taken to interpreting the articles in the UNCRC although there is some debate in the domestic jurisprudence

11 [2011] UKSC 4, [2011] 2 AC 166.

12 [2019] UKSC 21, [2019] 1 WLR 3289.

13 [2015] UKSC 22, (2015) 18 CCLR 201.

14 *ZH (Tanzania) v SSHD* at para 33 per Lady Hale, at para 46 per Lord Kerr.

15 *ZH (Tanzania) v SSHD* at para 46 per Lord Kerr.

16 General Comment No 6 (2005): *Treatment of Unaccompanied and separated children outside their country of origin*, www2.ohchr.org/english/bodies/crc/docs/GC6.pdf.

as to the extent to which the comments are 'authoritative'.[17] as 'authoritative guidance'. The key principles in General Comment No 6 can be summarised as follows:

1) A determination of what is in the best interests of the child requires a clear and comprehensive assessment of the child's identity, including their nationality, upbringing, ethnic, cultural and linguistic background, particular vulnerabilities and protection needs.
2) The assessment process should be carried out in a friendly and safe atmosphere by qualified professionals who are trained in age- and gender-sensitive related interviewing techniques.
3) Steps such as the appointment of a competent guardian are a key procedural safeguard to ensure respect for the best interests of the unaccompanied or separated children during any immigration or administrative or judicial process.[18]

Guardianship and best interests of the child

11.18 In Scotland and Northern Ireland, there are Guardianship Services for unaccompanied or separated children. However, in England and Wales, there is no comparable scheme, thereby arguably contravening the third of the principles above. There have been repeated calls for this protection to be implemented across the UK.[19]

11.19 In England and Wales, the Modern Slavery Act (MSA) 2015 did make provision to oblige the Home Secretary to implement an Independent Child Trafficking Guardians (ICTGs) scheme.

11.20 The ICTGs scheme in England and Wales has been partially implemented. It has been rolled out in two-thirds of England and Wales. As at the writing of this chapter in March 2023, the areas where the ICTGs have been introduced include: Greater London, Surrey, Essex, West Yorkshire, Merseyside, Kent, Warwickshire, North Yorkshire, Gloucestershire and Bristol, Lancashire, Bedfordshire and Wales.

17 In *R (SG) v SSWP* [2015] UKSC 16 , (2015) 18 CCLR 215 at paras 105–106 Lord Carnwarth described the General Comments as authoritative. This was approved in *Mathieson v SSWP* [2015] UKSC 47 at para 39 per Lord Wilson and subsequently in *DA and others v SSWP*. But Lord Reed in *R (SC) v SSWP* [2021] UKSC 26 cast doubt on this.

18 See also General Comment No 12: *The right of the child to be heard*, para 124, and General Comment No 14: *The right of the child to have his or her best interests taken as a primary consideration*, para 96. See further Qualification Directive Article 30.

19 See: www.unicef.org.uk/publications/guardianship-cost-benefit-analysis/,https://www.ecpat.org.uk/specialist-support-for-trafficked-children-urgent-action-needed.

There is no timetable for when the scheme would be rolled out to the remainder of all local authorities in England and Wales

11.21 Since it was first implemented in a few select areas in 2017, the ICTGs scheme went through two reviews, an interim one in July 2018, with the final review published in May 2019. The final report of the *Independent Review of the Modern Slavery Act 2015* (the 'Independent Review') recommended a national roll-out of the ICTGs scheme, an extension of the scheme to those over 18 and up to 21–25, consistent with leaving care duties under the ChA 1989,[20] which are owed to care leavers who are victims of modern slavery. The Independent Review also recommended the removal of the current 18-month time limit, on the basis that children's needs may vary and an artificial long-stop was not helpful or consistent with a need to find a durable solution for the child. There also needed to be more effective transition to adult services. For those children who go missing, the Independent Review recommended that their cases should be kept open and continue to be discussed until the child is found. The government accepted the 'spirit of the recommendations of the Review' but did not commit to adopting the specific recommendations.[21]

Other key articles of the UNCRC

11.22 Further key provisions within the UNCRC, inextricably linked to the best interests principle, require states to provide essential support to enable a child to reach their fullest potential as well as implementing safeguards to protect the child from harm.[22] UNCRC Articles 27, 28 and 39 stipulate that *every* child has the right to a standard of living adequate to their physical, mental, spiritual, moral and social development as well as the right to education and psychological support.

11.23 Data-sharing in respect of migrants is a particularly sensitive issue and this is no different in the context of migrant children given they are often simultaneously involved with several government bodies which are responsible for their health and social welfare, their education, and their immigration status. The parameters of information-sharing in this context are thus particularly important. In November 2017, the Committee on the Rights of the Child and the Commission on the Protection of the Rights of All Migrant Workers and Members of their Families issued a joint General Comment

20 See paras 9.118–9.194.

21 *UK Government Response to the Independent Review of the Modern Slavery Act 2015*, 9 July 2019.

22 See in particular Articles 32–37 of the UNCRC requiring states to protect the child from all forms of exploitation, trafficking and harm.

No 3[23] advising on the need for states to 'implement a "firewall" and prohibit the sharing and use for immigration enforcement of the personal data collected for other purposes, such as protection, remedy, civil registration and access to services'.

EU law rights and protection for migrant children

11.24 The end of the Brexit transition or implementation period on 31 December 2020 has meant significant changes to the legal framework for immigration and asylum law in the UK. This is discussed in more detail in chapter 3. Most of the secondary EU legislation concerning examination of asylum claims has been retained under the European Union (Withdrawal) Act (EUWA) 2018 save in respect of the Dublin III Regulation concerning the EU Common Asylum System.[24]

11.25 Despite the repeal of the European Communities Act (ECA) 1972, the UK regulations which implement the key EU asylum directives, namely the Reception Directive,[25] the Procedures Directive[26] and the Qualification Directive,[27] continued to have effect in the UK after the implementation period, unless and until repealed, revoked or amended, by virtue of EUWA 2018 s2. These regulations should not be affected by the Immigration and Social Security Co-ordination (EU Withdrawal) Act 2020 discussed at para 3.19, subject to argument on this issue in the *AAA* litigation due to be heard in the Supreme Court in October 2023. The relevant regulations are:

1) the Asylum Seekers (Reception Conditions) Regulations 2005;[28]

23 Joint General Comment No 3, para 17, at https://documents-dds-ny.un.org/doc/UNDOC/GEN/G17/343/59/PDF/G1734359.pdf?OpenElement.

24 Regulation (EU) No 604/2013 of the European Parliament and of the Council of 26 June 2013 establishing the criteria and mechanisms for determining the Member State responsible for examining an application for international protection lodged in one of the Member States by a third-country national or a stateless person (recast).

25 Council Directive 2003/9/EC of 27 January 2003 laying down minimum standards for the reception of asylum seekers.

26 Council Directive 2005/85/EC of 1 December 2005 on minimum standards on procedures in Member States for granting and withdrawing refugee status.

27 Council Directive 2004/83/EC of 29 April 2004 on minimum standards for the qualification and status of third country nationals or stateless persons as refugees or as persons who otherwise need international protection and the content of the protection granted.

28 SI No 7.

2) the Refugee or Person in Need of International Protection (Qualification) Regulations 2006;[29]
3) the Asylum (Procedures) Regulations 2007.[30]

Although the NBA 2022 revokes these regulations in respect of those who make a claim for asylum on or after 28 June 2022, the regulations should continue to apply to those who arrived in the UK and made their asylum claim prior to that date subject to the Supreme Court's judgment on the issue.

11.26 Some parts of the Directives were implemented into UK law through changes to the Immigration Rules (HC 395); those rules are largely unamended. However, the provisions of the Directives themselves, where different from the UK implementation, may only be relied on where they:

1) confer directly effective rights on individuals; and
2) those rights are 'of a kind recognised by the European Court or any court or tribunal in the United Kingdom in a case decided before exit day (whether or not as an essential part of the decision in the case)': EUWA 2018 s4(2); and
3) they are not inconsistent with or otherwise capable of affecting the interpretation, application, or operation of any provision made by or under the Immigration Acts: Immigration and Social Security Co-ordination (EU Withdrawal) Act 2020 s1 and Sch 1.

This is discussed in more detail in chapter 2.

11.27 For present purposes, it is relevant to highlight the codification of the 'best interest' principle and the approach it requires the state to take in the context of the protection of refugee children. It is difficult to see that any of this is inconsistent with or otherwise capable of affecting the interpretation or operation of any provision made by or under the Immigration Acts and thus it appears arguable that they remain relevant. See, for example:

1) **the Reception Directive**, which focuses on the arrangements of care and support for people awaiting a decision on their international protection claims, requires that member states provide children in this position with social welfare support in accordance with their particular vulnerabilities;[31] access to education in

29 SI No 2525.

30 SI No 3187.

31 Reception Directive Article 17.

school or otherwise in an alternative provision;[32] access to appropriate mental health care and qualified counseling, if necessary, if they have suffered past torture or other forms of severe ill-treatment;[33] and suitable accommodation.[34] As with the UNCRC, the Directive also imposes an obligation on the state to arrange for legal guardianship for the child.[35]

2) **the Qualification Directive**, which specifically identifies the particular vulnerability and circumstances of children seeking international protection,[36] and directs member states to make decisions having regard to the 'best interests' of the child as a primary consideration.[37] In terms of support arrangements, it also requires member states to grant recognised refugee children 'full access' to education,[38] social welfare,[39] healthcare[40] and accommodation, such accommodation to be provided with regard to the child's needs and their views.[41] There is a similar provision to the UNCRC and the Reception Directive requiring the appointment of a legal guardian or representative to protect and promote the interests of the child.[42]

Key issues facing unaccompanied children and care leavers

11.28 Chapter 9 set out the key legal duties and powers owed by local authorities toward unaccompanied migrant children in terms of their rights and entitlement to care and support under ChA 1989 s20 as children and under ChA 1989 s23C as care leavers. The legal

32 Reception Directive Article 10. In the UK, the Education Act 1996 s19 makes compulsory school education for children up to the age of 16. Section 19 imposes an obligation on local authorities to make arrangements available for education other than in school if the child is unable to attend mainstream schooling. The failure to arrange suitable education for unaccompanied asylum-seeking children is unlawful, as confirmed in *R (KS) v Croydon LBC* [2010] EWHC 3391 (Admin).

33 Reception Directive Article 18.

34 Reception Directive Article 19(2).

35 Reception Directive Article 19(1).

36 Qualification Directive Article 20.

37 Qualification Directive Recital 12 and Article 20.

38 Qualification Directive Article 27.

39 Qualification Directive Article 28.

40 Qualification Directive Article 29.

41 Qualification Directive Articles 30(2)–(3) and 31.

42 Qualification Directive Article 30(1).

framework pertaining to supporting children within families under ChA 1989 s17 applies equally to unaccompanied children arriving in the UK for family reunification as it does to other migrant families supported under the same provision.

11.29 This section highlights the most common disputes that arise concerning unaccompanied migrant children's access to and provision of support, namely:

- disputes over their age preventing them from accessing support in accordance with their claimed age ('age disputes and assessments');
- inter-authority disputes over responsibility for the care and support for unaccompanied children;
- supporting separated children arriving in the UK for family reunification;
- entitlement to education and student financing for unaccompanied and other migrant children and care leavers

Age disputes and assessments

Overview

11.30 A child's age is disputed most often either when a) they present to immigration authorities to make a claim for international protection on asylum and human rights grounds or b) when they are brought to the attention of the local authority's children's services. Age disputes happen most often because unaccompanied migrant children arrive in the UK without reliable and authentic documentation to prove their age – they may have handed their documents to agents along the journey, which were then not returned to them; or they may never have had documents to prove age in the conventional sense familiar in the UK because in their country of origin they do not have similar systems of registering births and households involving documentation. Determining a person's age in these circumstances is not an easy task. Yet it is a fundamental fact both in the eyes of immigration and asylum law and social welfare law for determining how the UK will treat the person. The erroneous determination of a young person's age has significant consequences for the child's experience in the UK.

11.31 In immigration and asylum law, whether a person is a child or an adult affects the approach taken by an immigration officer to assessing the merits of an international protection claim, the young person's credibility and the safeguards to which they are entitled during the asylum determination process. Immigration Rules paras

350–352 and 352ZA–352B set out the specific procedure by which a child's asylum claim has to be assessed and when a child can be interviewed. The rules are coupled with specific guidance on how children's cases should be handled.[43] Policies determine the potential outcomes of immigration and asylum applications, with unaccompanied asylum-seeking children usually granted a period of discretionary leave to remain up until they turn 17.5 years old, even if their initial asylum claim is dismissed.[44]

11.32 Age is also relevant to the exercise of the Home Secretary's powers to detain and remove persons subject to immigration control. It is unlawful to detain an unaccompanied child under immigration powers save in a short-term holding facility where the immigration officer reasonably believes that the child will be removed from the UK, and even in such cases, the child can only be detained for a maximum of 24 hours.[45]

11.33 In respect of care and support, the fact of the child's age is the gateway eligibility criterion to the child's entitlement to care and support from the local authority under the ChA 1989. The fact of age also determines what kind of support and for how long,[46] what type of accommodation (for example, foster care, supported or independent living), and what level of education provision (for example, compulsory schooling or further education).

Assessing age

11.34 The Supreme Court held in *R (A) v Croydon LBC*[47] that age is an objective and immutable characteristic of a person's identity. There can therefore only be a right or wrong answer as to what a person's age and date of birth are. That means that although the initial dispute on age inevitably arrives from an evaluative judgment on the part of the relevant public authority that the child is not the age as claimed, the determination of age is not solely dependent on the public authority's view and may ultimately need to be decided by the courts.

43 *Children's asylum claims*, v3.0, August 2019; and *Assessing age*, v6.0, UK Visas and Immigration, 21 March 2023.

44 Immigration Rules paras 352ZC–352ZF.

45 Immigration Act (IA) 1971 Sch 2 para 18B.

46 That is, when it is that the child turns 21 or 25, as it may be, when duties owed to care leavers cease. For a more detailed discussion on leaving care provisions, see paras 9.118–9.194.

47 [2009] UKSC 8.

11.35 There is no scientific way accurately to determine a child's age. X-rays of wrists and teeth have been held to lack reliability because of the wide margin of error, but the current government is still intending to bring such methods into general use through NBA 2022 provisions.[48] The accepted approach to assessing age is known as *Merton* guidelines, named after the 2003 case of *R (B) v Merton LBC*[49] that initially outlined the applicable principles. The guidelines were subsequently developed in case-law, and the term '*Merton* compliance' has come to be a term of art, constituting a 'judge developed code, laid down in the leading case of Merton and built upon in subsequent case-law' on the requirements for a lawful and procedurally fair age assessment: *R (AB) v Kent CC*.[50] In *AAM (a child) v SSHD*,[51] the court described the term as '*shorthand for the minimum standards of fair procedure* for the carrying out of age assessments by local authorities, which have evolved out of child social work good practice and common law principles of fairness' (emphasis added).

11.36 The *Merton* guidelines have been adopted and incorporated into the *Age assessment guidance* issued by the Association of Directors of Children's Services ('*ADCS guidance*').[52] Although the *ADCS guidance* is not on a statutory footing, it was drafted by experienced social workers, and based on close collaboration between local authorities, the Home Office, health authorities, the police and a number of non-government organisations, including charities. Young people with experience of age assessments were also consulted and some of their reflections appear in the final document. In combination with the body of developing case-law, the *ADCS guidance* constitutes powerful guidance on the conduct of age assessment as well as the approach to be taken to factors relevant to assessing age.

11.37 Several court judgments have sought to provide a comprehensive statement of the *Merton* principles, but given the evolution of

48 *R (A) v Croydon LBC* [2015] UKUT 168 (IAC) at paras 11 and 85; *R (A) v Liverpool City Council* [2007] EWHC 1477 (Admin); *R (KN) v Barnet LBC* [2011] EWHC 2019 (Admin) at para 44. See also *R (Y) v Croydon LBC* [2016] EWCA Civ 398; and *R (ZM and SK) v Croydon LBC* [2016] UKUT 559 (IAC) at paras 14–35, in particular paras 77–78; and *R (AS) v Kent CC (age assessment; dental evidence)* [2017] UKUT 446 (IAC) at paras 22–120, in particular paras 83, 84, 102, 110–120.

49 [2003] EWHC 1689 (Admin).

50 [2020] EWHC 109 (Admin) at para 36 per Thornton J.

51 [2012] EWHC 2567 (QB) at para 93 per Lang J.

52 *Age assessment guidance*, Association of Directors of Children's Services, October 2015.

jurisprudence it is not easy to find a single case encapsulating all of the principles. Cases for reference include: *VS v Home Office,*[53] *MVN v Greenwich LBC*[54] and *AB v Kent CC.*[55] Drawing together the long line of case-law, the principles for assessing age can be summarised as follows, although these principles are not to be applied as a rigid checklist:[56]

1) **Age assessments should not be considered as a matter of routine in every case where a child has no documentary or other proof of their age.** It should only be carried out where 'there is reason to doubt that the individual is the age they claim'.[57]
2) **The assessment must be a holistic one and must start with an open mind, with no obligation on the child to prove their age to the assessing social workers.** Physical appearance and demeanour are notoriously unreliable factors and are not determinative of age. In particular, the courts have found limited utility in observations made by the assessing social workers of demeanour and physical appearance in the artificial surrounding of an interview.[58] The cultural, ethnic and racial context of the young person being assessed must be considered, as these may reflect in their presentation as well as their descriptions of their lives.
3) **General credibility is not to be determinative of age.** It is more likely that a young person who tells a consistent account of their life which supports their claimed age will be the age they claim to be. Conversely, young people may lie for reasons unrelated to age but related to their claims for protection or the reasons they had to leave their country of origin. For a discussion on the approach to credibility, see *MVN v Greenwich LBC*[59] (at paras 24–30).
4) **The existence of mental health disorders, trauma, cognitive or learning difficulties is also materially relevant to the approach to be adopted when assessing the credibility of a child's account and their**

53 [2014] EWHC 2483 (QB) at para 78 per Picken J.
54 [2015] EWHC 1942 (Admin) at paras 18–34 per Picken J; see in particular paras 24–30 in respect of the approach to assessing credibility of a person's account about their age and life experiences.
55 [2020] EWHC 109 (Admin) at para 21 per Thornton J.
56 *R (HAM) v Brent LBC* [2022] EWHC 1924 (Admin).
57 *Statutory guidance on the care of unaccompanied migrant children and victims of modern slavery,* Department for Education, November 2017, para 35.
58 *R (AM) v Solihull MBC (AAJR)* [2012] UKUT 118 (IAC) at para 20. See also *A v Croydon LBC; K v SSHD* [2009] EWHC 939 (Admin) at para 56.
59 [2015] EWHC 1942 (Admin).

general presentation.[60] Specialist medical input may be required in these circumstances to ensure a fair assessment process.[61]

5) **The sources of information about age will not only emanate from the child.** Other sources of information may include the views of foster carers, guardians, social care workers, advocates, teachers, support workers, and medical and mental health professionals involved in treating the child. Social workers must balance this level of insight from third parties against the limitations of their own contact with the child which has taken place during a short period of time in a formal and artificial setting.[62]
6) **The assessment must be started with an open mind,**[63] with no predisposition as to the outcome 'divorced from the information and evidence available to the local authority, to assume that an applicant is an adult, or conversely that he is a child': *B v Merton* at para 38.
7) **There is no burden of proof upon an applicant to prove their age.**[64] The corollary is that the benefit of the doubt should be applied where evidence can tip one way or the other. Where there is suspicion that the child may be a victim of trafficking, a local authority must exercise a presumption in favour of the child's claimed age pending the outcome of an age assessment.[65] This is given that it is recognised that age assessment is not a scientific process. The difficulty arises in particular in cases 'where the person concerns is approaching 18 or is only a few years over 18': *B v Merton* at para 27.

11.38 If documentary evidence exists, it may well be determinative if its provenance and authenticity can be verified. Even if that is not possible, social workers are required to engage with it and consider it in the round.[66]

11.39 As for procedure:

60 *R (T) v Enfield LBC* [2004] EWHC 2297 (Admin) at para 46.
61 *ADCS guidance*, p8.
62 *R (AM) v Solihull MBC (AAJR)* [2012] UKUT 118 (IAC) at para 20; *R (KN) v Barnet LBC* [2011] EWHC 2019 (Admin) at para 64.
63 *MVN v Greenwich LBC* [2015] EWHC 1942 (Admin) at para 21(1).
64 *AB v Kent* at para 21(4); *B v Merton* at para 38; *R (CJ) v Cardiff City Council* [2011] EWCA Civ 1590 at para 21; and *ADCS guidance*, p62.
65 Anti-Trafficking Directive Article 15, as incorporated into MSA 2015 s51.
66 *R (NA (Afghanistan)) v Croydon LBC* [2009] EWHC 2357 (Admin) at paras 6, 19 and 23. See also *SA (Kuwait) v SSHD* [2009] EWCA Civ 1157 on the approach to documentary evidence of identity. This was applied in *R (GB) v Oxfordshire CC* [2015] UKUT 429 (IAC).

1) The assessment must be conducted by two qualified and registered social workers.
2) The purpose and process of the age assessment must be clearly and fully explained to the child, as well as the implications of them being assessed as an adult. The child must be made aware that the assessment will be shared with the Home Office. It must be clear to the child that the age assessment seeks to determine their chronological age and is not an assessment of the substantive merits of the child's international protection claim as this falls outside the scope of the social workers' training and is the exclusive remit of the Home Office.
3) A suitable interpreter should be provided because of the dangers of misunderstanding when interviewing a person for whom English is not their first language;[67] this observation being made in context of a challenge to an assessment completed through a telephone interpreter. The interpreter should be provided in the correct language and dialect.[68]
4) An appropriate adult should be offered to assist the child. The purpose of an appropriate adult is to advocate on behalf of the child, represent their best interests, ensure that the child's welfare needs are met during the interview process, and challenge social workers if they feel the interview is not being conducted appropriately, for example, by asking for clarificatory questions to be asked, asking for questions to be simplified or reframed, and asking for breaks in the assessment interview where appropriate or necessary.[69]
5) Facilities such as police stations are not considered appropriate for conducting age assessments.[70] Nor is immigration detention. The Home Office's published policies[71] state that age disputed children should be given the benefit of the doubt unless their physical appearance and demeanour 'very strongly suggest' that

67 *B v Merton* at paras 52 and 55. See also *AB v Kent* at para 21(12); *R (NA (Afghanistan)) v Croydon LBC* [2009] EWHC 2357 (Admin) at para 57; and *R (AS) v Croydon LBC* [2011] EWHC 2091 (Admin) at para 19(2).

68 *ADCS guidance*, p16.

69 *ADCS guidance*, p16.

70 *ADCS guidance*, p15.

71 See *Detention: General instructions*, v2.0, January 2022, at p36; Detention Services Order 02/2019: *Care and management of post detention age claims*, January 2022.

they are 'significantly over 18',[72] and should be released into the care of the local authority pending an assessment of age.

6) Prior to a final decision on age being reached, it is imperative that the child is afforded a proper and fair opportunity to address any adverse findings and to clarify or correct any misunderstanding. It is often described in short-hand as the 'minded to' process. Misunderstandings may arise for any number of cultural, language or interpretation reasons and are not automatically indicative of a child being untruthful in their account. The child's responses and explanations must be fully taken into account as part of the final decision-making. Failure to comply with this procedural safeguard will render an age assessment unfair and unlawful.[73]
7) The child (and the child's solicitor) must be provided with a copy of the final assessment within a reasonable period of time. The decision must be properly supported by reasons.[74]

11.40 At the heart of the *Merton* guidelines is the requirement for a fair assessment, which does, to an extent, depend on the facts and circumstances of the case. The guidelines developed by case-law as to the requirements of fairness are not to be applied like a check list and the courts have warned against a 'highly technical' or 'judicialised' approach[75] to the application of the guidelines. The guidelines allow for a practical and flexible process, but with adherence to minimum standards of fairness and inquiries.

11.41 Over the years, there has been some debate in the court judgments as to whether different standards apply where local authority social workers decide to carry out an abbreviated assessment of age. In *AB v Kent CC*, the local authority defended its decision to do an assessment that lasted only 30–45 minutes, and stated that an 'abbreviated' assessment was permitted because the assessing social worker considered that it was obvious that the person was an adult, based on his physical appearance and demeanour, and between 20 and 25 years old. The judge ultimately held that Kent's abbreviated assess-

72 See *Asylum Instruction: Assessing age*, v5.0, Home Office, 14 January 2022, p12. A discussion of the Home Secretary's immigration powers is set out in chapter 1.

73 *R (FZ) v Croydon LBC* [2011] EWCA Civ 59 at paras 21, 23–25; *NA v Croydon* at paras 50–52; *Durani v SSHD and Nottingham City Council* [2013] EWHC 284 (Admin) at para 84.

74 *FZ v Croydon* at para 22.

75 *B v Merton* at para 36; *R (SB) v Kensington and Chelsea RLBC* [2022] EWHC 308 (Admin) at para 31 per Bennathan J.

ment of AB's age was not lawful because the conclusion reached by the local authority that the person was 20 to 25 years old was too close to the cut-off of 18 years for the local authority not to afford AB the benefit of the doubt.[76] However, in the course of doing so, the judge found it permissible for the local authority to carry out an abbreviated assessment and did not consider that the complaints made about the failure of certain procedural safeguards, on their own, rendered the assessment unlawful.[77]

11.42 Since then, some local authorities have adopted a practice of carrying out 'short-form' age assessments from the outset and dispensing of the provision of appropriate adults, the minded to process, sometimes, even the interpreter.[78] They have sought to justify this by relying on *AB v Kent*. It is the view of the authors that this misconstrues the effect of the *AB v Kent* judgment, and moreover, falls foul of the caution against taking an overly technical approach to age assessments.

11.43 In reality, there is no set standard of inquiry required for a lawful age assessment. In the *Merton* judgment itself, Stanley Burnton J held that[79] it would normally be necessary to take a history from the person with a view to determining whether it is true. Facts such as physical appearance and demeanour cannot be isolated completely from the question of the veracity of the applicant: appearance, behaviour and the credibility of his account are all matters that reflect on each other. As to the level of inquiry, Stanley Burnton J recognised in *B v Merton* that there may be cases where it is 'very obvious' that a person is under or over 18. In such cases, there is 'normally no need for prolonged inquiry'[80] but only 'provided safeguards of minimum standards of inquiry and of fairness are adhered to'.[81] Those 'very obvious' cases are to be distinguished from cases where the person concerned is approaching 18 or a few years over 18. Thus levels of inquiry cannot be generalised.[82]

11.44 In *AB v Kent* itself, Thornton J did not approve of short form age assessments as a type of assessment that local authorities can do at the outset. She accepted the submission made on behalf of the local

76 *AB v Kent* at para 56.
77 *AB v Kent* at para 53.
78 See *SB v Kensington and Chelsea RLBC*.
79 *B v Merton* at para 28.
80 *B v Merton* at para 27.
81 *B v Merton* at para 36.
82 *B v Merton* at para 50.

authority that there may come a point when an 'experienced' social worker has 'conducted sufficient inquiries to be confident that the person in front of them is an adult or a child' (at para 35). A view as to whether 'sufficient' inquiries have been undertaken to abbreviate the duration of an age assessment thus can only be known *after* assessing social workers commence the assessment, not before they have even begun to ask any questions.

11.45 The process by which social workers carry out those inquiries must still be fair.[83] This is consistent with the view taken in the *ADCS guidance*, which described 'short-form age assessments' as being reserved to 'rare circumstances' where it is 'very clear' that an individual is an adult well over the age of 18 such that prolonged inquiry may not be required. However, even in those rare circumstances, the *ADCS guidance* pointed out that social workers are 'still undertaking an assessment, albeit a brief one' and thus the assessment still needs to be well-reasoned and fair.[84]

11.46 A fair assessment process must, at a minimum, permit the person who is being assessed a genuine opportunity to explain their position, to answer questions that may be put to them and to respond to matters adverse to their case. What is necessary for this purpose must take account of the circumstances of the person, for example, whether an interpreter is required or whether they should be given an opportunity for an appropriate adult to be present.[85] What fairness requires depends on the facts and circumstances of the individual case. Whilst, in *HAM v Brent LBC*, the court had sympathy for the local authority's desire to have certainty as to the applicability of procedural safeguards to age assessments, and to have a check list reduced from the full *Merton* requirements that is applicable to short form assessments, the court considered taking such a prescriptive approach 'would be hostage to fortune' given fairness is 'sensitive to circumstances'.[86]

11.47 In *R (MA and HT) v Coventry City Council*[87] the court was asked to consider what minimum standards of procedural safeguards are required even when prolonged inquiries are not undertaken. In a detailed and careful judgment, Henshaw J held that the provision of

83 *SB v Kensington and Chelsea RLBC* at paras 32 and 40. See also *R (HAM) v Brent LBC* [2022] EWHC 1924 (Admin) at para 11.

84 *ADCS guidance*, p6.

85 *HAM v Brent LBC* at para 32.

86 *HAM v Brent LBC* at para 33.

87 [2022] EWHC 98 (Admin).

an appropriate adult and a minded-to process are 'necessary elements' of a fair and lawful process for assessing age in the absence of documentary evidence and given the fragility of reliance on appearance and demeanour save in obvious cases.[88] The Court of Appeal's decision in this case[89] did not overturn these findings. The appeal concerned a different question as to whether the judge applied the correct test in determining that a specific policy for detaining children at port for age assessments where the child was 'potentially clearly over 18' was unlawful. The Court of Appeal's judgment did not alter any established principles concerning age assessments. Nor did it approve the detention of children for age assessments.

Challenges to age assessments

11.48 There is currently no statutory right of appeal against an age assessment carried out by the local authority, although the reliability of an age assessment may arise in the context of an immigration appeal where age is relevant to the immigration tribunal's determination of the legal issues, most often in the context of asylum and international protection claims.

11.49 The primary remedy against a negative assessment of age is judicial review. There remains a permission filter,[90] but the substantive determination of the age dispute is a fact-finding as to the age of the putative child. Given the inexact nature of age assessments, if fresh evidence comes to light after the initial assessment, a request for a fresh age assessment may be an alternative remedy, albeit not a formal statutory remedy. A refusal on the local authority's part to carry out a fresh age assessment may be subject to judicial review.[91]

11.50 Where the age dispute cannot be resolved other than by way of judicial review, the substantive fact-finding is carried out by the Upper Tribunal (Immigration and Asylum Chamber) exercising its jurisdiction as a judicial review court under Tribunals, Enforcement and Court Act 2007 s18. The Upper Tribunal must, in the context of an age assessment challenge brought by way of judicial review, adopt an inquisitorial role, with neither party bearing the burden of proof,

88 *MA and HT v Coventry City Council* at para 109.

89 *R (MA and HT) v SSHD* [2022] EWCA Civ 1663.

90 The threshold for permission was articulated in *R (FZ) v Croydon LBC* [2011] EWCA Civ 59: whether the material before the court raises a factual case, which taken at its highest, could properly succeed in a contested factual hearing.

91 *R (BM) v Hackney LBC* [2016] EWHC 3338 (Admin).

in evaluating the available evidence to reach a decision regarding the child's date of birth.[92]

11.51 Age assessment fact-finding cases are evidentially heavy and often involve the cross-examination of witnesses in support of both the putative child's and the local authority's case, lasting for several days. Over the past decade, as the Upper Tribunal gained more experience in hearing these types of judicial reviews, it has developed a case management approach including interim case management hearings and standard directions to facilitate the progression of these cases. This has involved directions requiring the service of witness evidence early on in the proceedings post permission so that the parties are able to focus their minds on what issues are in dispute and is an opportunity, built into the directions, for the parties to meet in a roundtable with a view to exploring alternative solutions to the age dispute other than a full fact-finding hearing. Standard directions also require the applicant putative child to do a search of their social media, confirm they have done so, and disclose such material as is relevant to the fact of age. The limits of the requirement for disclosure of social media material were considered by the Upper Tribunal in *R (BG) v Hackney LBC (social media; candour; disclosure)*,[93] and guidance was set down on the approach to be taken. At first blush, these types of factual disputes which fundamentally go to a child's identity and how the child is to be supported whilst in the UK may not naturally lend themselves to mediation or alternative dispute resolution. However, many cases do achieve settlement before trial because in reality, neither party may know for certain what the child's age is in the absence of documentation and given that many cultures describe age in less precise terms than the approach taken in the UK.

11.52 Pending the age assessment judicial review, the court has the power, on an application, to grant interim relief to require a local authority to take the claimant into its care pending the determination of the outcome of age. Where a local authority had already been providing accommodation and support pending assessment, the injunction sought is prohibitory in nature, to prevent the termination of accommodation and support pending the determination of the judicial review claim. Where a local authority had refused to provide accommodation and support, the injunction sought is mandatory in nature. In either case, the court's consideration entails

92 *R (CJ) v Cardiff City Council* [2011] EWCA Civ 1590 at paras 21–23.
93 [2022] UKUT 338 (IAC).

two stages. First, the court will consider whether there is a serious issue to be tried, a test not materially different to the test for permission, that is whether the grounds of challenge are arguable. If arguable, the court moves onto the second stage, which asks where the balance of prejudice falls.

11.53 Of relevance to the balance of prejudice, the *ADCS guidance* states that 'where there is doubt about whether or not the young person is a child, the dangers inherent in treating a child as an adult are in almost all cases far greater than the dangers of taking a young adult into your care'[94] and risks are 'mitigated by the fact that they will be supervised, either closely or at least on a regular basis by those employed to support them'.[95]

11.54 The courts have also, by and large, taken the same starting point, that the risk of accommodating a child in unsuitable adult accommodation outweigh the risks – often theoretical – of accommodating a young person subsequently found to be an adult, or older than they are, with children.

11.55 In *R (BG) v Oxfordshire CC*[96] the deputy High Court judge applied the approach identified by the ADCS and granted interim relief, having considering the 'context of the best interests of the child' and the 'protective precautionary approach' of affording 'the benefit of the doubt' to a putative child.[97]

11.56 The case of *BG v Oxfordshire* has been followed and endorsed in subsequent cases, with the court coming down in favour of a precautionary protective approach to ensuing that age disputed children are not left without age appropriate support and accommodation while their age is determined.[98] In *R (NG and others) v Hillingdon LBC*[99] Lang J considered an application for interim relief brought on behalf of three age disputed children who were housed in Home Office adult asylum support hotels pending an assessment of their ages. The court considered that it was strongly arguable that their current accommodation was unsuitable and detrimental for them, taking account of the risk of dispersal and the exclusion from support under

94 *ACDS guidance*, p33.

95 *ACDS guidance*, p32.

96 [2014] EWHC 3187 (Admin).

97 *BG v Oxfordshire* at paras 31 and 39 per Michael Fordham QC (as he then was).

98 *R (Talash) v Croydon LBC* [2018] EWHC 2138 (Admin); *R (AS) v Liverpool City Council* [2020] EWHC 3531 (Admin); *R (LYB) v Kent CC* [2021] EWHC 663 (Admin); *R (AH) v Kent CC* [2021] EWHC 878 (Admin).

99 [2020] EWHC 2847 (Admin).

the ChA 1989 support.[100] The court noted that hotels are not set up to cater for children and young people; there was no evidence that staff there are DBS[101] checked; that there is a risk of abuse due to communal facilities; and there is insufficient support in place to meet the needs of putative children.

11.57 The analysis of Lang J was applied in *R (AB and others) v Brent LBC*[102] where Poole J considered three linked claims in which Brent refused to provide accommodation and support pending assessment. The three age disputed children were, instead, in Home Office hotel accommodation. The judge was concerned that whilst in such accommodation, they may be liable to be dispersed, including into detention; they were unable to access education or child health provision and received no assistance with food, hygiene or finances. They also had no access to social work support and there were no safeguarding measures in place to mitigate against risks from adult strangers with whom they were living in close proximity. The court held that on balance, the balance of prejudice fell in favour of requiring the local authority to accommodate the age disputed children, it being unreasonable to conclude that adult accommodation was suitable for them.[103]

Assessing age under the Nationality and Borders Act 2022

11.58 NBA 2022 Part 4 introduces a series of new provisions concerning age assessments, including when they are to be carried out, by whom, how they are to be conducted and what legal consequences arise. Some of provisions have been brought into force but not all. This section provides an outline of the provisions. It is not known yet how the provisions will be implemented, as the detail will be set out in regulations to be issued under NBA 2022 s53.

11.59 Part 4 applies to all 'age disputed persons' designated as someone a) who requires leave to enter or remain in the UK; and b) in relation to whom, a local authority, another public authority (to be defined in regulations) or the Home Secretary 'has insufficient evidence to be sure of their age'.

100 *NG and others v Hillingdon LBC* at para 21.
101 Disclosure and Barring Service.
102 [2021] EWHC 2843 (Admin).
103 *AB and others v Brent LBC* at paras 40–47.

When will age assessments arise?

11.60 NBA 2022 s50 sets out the circumstances in which age disputes may arise:

1) where the local authority needs to know the age of an age disputed person for the purposes of deciding whether or how to exercise any functions under relevant children's legislation[104] in relation to the person: section 50(2)(a); or
2) where the Home Secretary notifies a local authority in writing that the Home Secretary doubts that an age disputed person in relation to whom the local authority has exercised/may exercise functions under relevant children's legislation is the age that they claim (or are claimed) to be.

11.61 Where either of those two scenarios arise, a local authority 'must' do one of three things (NBA 2022 s50(3)):

1) refer the age disputed person to a designated person for an age assessment. A designated person means an official of the Home Secretary who is designated to conduct age assessments; or
2) conduct its own age assessment and inform the Home Secretary in writing of the result of its assessment, or
3) inform the Home Secretary in writing that it is satisfied the person is the age claimed (or are claimed) to be without the need for an age assessment.

11.62 It should be noted that the local authority retains the ability either to conduct its own age assessment or to decide to accept the age as claimed so long as it is reasoned. Where either the local authority conducts its own assessment or decides to accept a person as the age claimed without the need for an age assessment, the local authority must provide such evidence as the Home Secretary requires (on request by the Home Secretary) in order for the Home Secretary to consider the local authority's decision: section 50(4).

11.63 Where a local authority chooses to refer the age disputed person to a designated person for an age assessment, it is expected to provide such assistance as is reasonably required by the designated person: section 50(5). Such an age assessment, as conducted by a designated person, is *binding* on the Home Secretary and her officers exercising immigration functions, and on the local authority that has to exercise

104 'Relevant children's legislation', in relation to a local authority in England, is defined as 'any provision of or made under Part 3, 4 or 5 of the Children Act 1989 (support for children and families; care and supervision; protection of children)'. See NBA 2022 s49(3).

relevant children's legislation and where the local authority is aware of the age assessment conducted by the designated person: section 50(7).

11.64 Age assessments by a designated person (which is understood to be the National Age Assessment Board (NAAB)) may be conducted where: (section 51)

1) a public authority (as prescribed in regulations not yet issued) refers an age disputed person for one. This might arise in the context of a health authority or more likely the police or border force on a young person's arrival in the UK; or
2) the local authority has referred an age disputed person for such an assessment: section 50(1); or
3) the Home Secretary has reason to doubt a local authority's age assessment (carried out under section 50(3)(b)) or a local authority's decision not to carry out an age assessment but to accept claimed age (section 50(3)(c)).

11.65 Age assessments carried out in the circumstances set out in section 51 are binding on the Home Secretary (but appear not to be binding on the local authority).

11.66 Section 51 is particularly controversial because it gives the Home Secretary the power to overrule a local authority age assessment *for immigration purposes* (ie asylum and immigration functions (including detention) and whether to treat the person as a child for those purposes). It, however, does not bind the local authority to change its age assessment outcome or to treat the person as a different age to the age determined in the age assessment or their claimed age.

11.67 The standard of proof is a balance of probabilities (sections 50(6) and 51(4)), which is not a material change from the current standard.

11.68 How the NAAB is to be arranged, operated, supervised and monitored remains unknown and concerns have been raised about that by the ADCS, the Refugee Council and the British Association of Social Workers (BASW).

Use of scientific methods in age assessments

11.69 Powers under NBA 2022 s52 are conferred on the Home Secretary to make regulations about the use of scientific methods in age assessments, which can include use of imaging technology (section 52(2)(a)) and the analysis of saliva, cell or other samples taken from a person (section 52(2)(b)). Beyond this, the provision does not specify any further the precise scientific methods which may be used, as that will also be specified in regulations: section 52(3).

11.70 Consent is also required in order to use a scientific method as prescribed in the regulations: section 52(5). If consent is withheld, it is to be treated as 'damaging' to the age disputed person's credibility when a decision-maker is asked to decide whether to believe any statement made by or on behalf of the age disputed person that is relevant to the assessment of their age.

11.71 The use of certain scientific methods had previously been criticised heavily.

11.72 In *R (ZM and SK) v Croydon LBC*,[105] a case concerning the use of dental development and dental X-rays to determine age, the Upper Tribunal noted that whilst dental development could provide a probability that a person was older than claimed, that was not sufficient evidence in itself. This was because the evidence before the Upper Tribunal showed that there was a variance in the achievement of dental maturity across different ethnic populations. This therefore introduced a further likelihood of error, unless the individual being assessed was of the same ethnic background as the members of the reference data set. The Upper Tribunal also cautioned, in this context, against the use of statistical evidence. Material derived from a database might be of considerable use if it showed that the fact claimed was impossible or highly unlikely and it might assist in the assessment of reliability of other evidence. However, that is as far as it could go. A calculated probability of a figure over 50 per cent does not mean that a fact was provided to the civil standard.

11.73 In *R (AS) v Kent CC*,[106] the Upper Tribunal found no reason to doubt the conclusions drawn in *ZM* about the significant doubt as to the extent to which dental examinations could indicate age.

11.74 In *R (RK) v Birmingham City Council (AAJR)*,[107] a case concerning height change and measurements, the Upper Tribunal did not find that evidence about a young person's growth can be determinative of age or a weighty factor. As with the eruption of molar teeth, the most that can be said of an individual's growth in height as an indicator of chronological age is that proof of the cessation of growth tends to indicate the achievement of a physical maturity generally associated with adulthood. However, the Upper Tribunal noted that it is clear that some individuals continue to grow after they have reached the age of 18 whilst others have stopped growing before they achieve

105 [2016] UKUT 559 (IAC).
106 [2017] UKUT 446 (IAC).
107 [2013] UKUT 307 (IAC).

legal majority.[108] A similar conclusion was arrived at by the Upper Tribunal in *R (AM) v Solihull MBC (AAJR)*[109] in which it held that single measurements of height that are not charted over an extended period of time are not going to be of much assistance.

11.75 A UK Parliament POST note 666 on *The use of biological methods in asylum age assessments* (March 2022)[110] also outlines in some further detail the range of scientific methods that may be available and the concerns as to their reliability. Organisations such as the Royal College of Paediatrics and Child Health have stated that the use of radiological assessment is extremely imprecise and can only give an estimate of within two years in either direction. The British Society for Paediatric Endocrinology and Diabetes is clear that it is not possible accurately to assess a child's age based on physical examination or bone age assessments. At the time of writing, notwithstanding all of these concerns, the government intends to implement provisions of the NBA 2022 to allow for the use of scientific methods.

11.76 An additional controversial aspect of NBA 2022 s52 is the question of credibility should a person decline to consent to the use of a scientific method. That provision requires a presumption that that is damaging to credibility, but it still does fall to the assessors to determine for themselves whether and the extent to which that should bear on other evidence of age or not. As a matter of principle, it remains open to the decision-maker to consider and decide that the refusal to give consent does not alter the reliability of a specific statement relevant to age, for example, the age at which a young person went to school or the length of time they went to school. It remains open to the decision-maker to accept the credibility of such statements.

Regulations about age assessments

11.77 NBA 2022 s53 gives the Home Secretary the power to make regulations about age assessments, including about the processes to be followed, the information and evidence that must be considered and the weight to be given to it, the circumstances in which an abbreviated age assessment may be appropriate, protections or safeguarding measures for the age disputed person, and where consent is required for a specific scientific method, the process for assessing capacity to consent, for seeking consent and for recording the decision on consent.

108 *RK v Birmingham City Council* at para 46.
109 [2012] UKUT 118 (IAC) at para 17.
110 See: https://post.parliament.uk/research-briefings/post-pn-0666/.

11.78 The regulations may also include specification of the information required by the secretary of state from the local authority concerning its age assessments, and concerning decisions to accept a child's claimed age without an age assessment (under section 50(3)(b) and (c)). This may further undermine local authorities' ability to preserve autonomy over their decisions on age, although the primary legislative provisions expressly allow local authorities to carry out their own assessments and form their own views. The autonomy that a local authority has may be most relevant when it concerns appeals against decisions of age. Where age decisions are taken by a designated person, and are subject to appeal, it is not at present clear how the local authority would be able to participate, despite the potential binding nature of any outcome of appeal: section 54(5).

11.79 Draft regulations have been laid out but not yet approved by parliament, but they do not set parameters within which local authority age assessments are to be conducted that may or may not reflect the established *Merton* principles. It is difficult to see how the Home Secretary could, through regulations, legislate out procedural safeguards to ensure a fair and reliable assessment outcome, but that is a concern that has been raised by the ADCS, BASW and other organisations, including the Refugee Council and the Refugee Migrant Children's Consortium.

Age assessment appeals

11.80 NBA 2022 s54 sets out a new scheme for resolving age disputes through the courts. Where the decision-maker concludes that the child is not the age they claim to be, they may appeal that decision, instead of seeking judicial review to the Administrative Court. Rather, the appeal is to the First-Tier Tribunal (Immigration and Asylum Chamber) (FTT (IAC)).[111] Appeals must be brought within UK. If the child leaves the UK before the appeal is determined, the appeal is considered abandoned.[112]

11.81 As before, the FTT (IAC) must determine the child's age on balance of probabilities and assign them a date of birth.[113] The FTT (IAC) may consider any matter it thinks relevant, including matters the original decision-maker was not aware of and any matter that has arisen after the date of the decision appealed against.[114] FTT (IAC)

111 NBA 2022 s54(1) and (2).
112 NBA 2022 s55(3).
113 NBA 2022 s54(3).
114 NBA 2022 s54(4).

decisions are binding on the local authority and the Home Secretary, as well as his or her immigration officers in relation to immigration functions. There is a right of appeal against the FTT (IAC) decision.[115] The appeal system has not been brought into force and may be subject to amendments under the Illegal Migration Act 2023.

11.82 The child may apply to the FTT (IAC) for an order that until the appeal is finally determined, the local authority must exercise its functions under the ChA 1989 towards them on basis of their claimed age.[116]

Inter-authority disputes over support responsibilities

11.83 Inter-authority disputes over support responsibilities for migrant children and young people may arise where there is an age dispute. This is because age is relevant to determining which public authority supports the young person, the type of support and the duration of support. Where an age assessment determines that a young person is under 18 but concludes that the child is of an age older than claimed, this affects the nature of the support provided under the ChA 1989, including the type of accommodation provision and education provision (for example, whether the child is of compulsory school age and thus entitled to secondary schooling). It also affects when a child turns 18 and transitions to adulthood and whether they are entitled to ongoing support as a 'care leaver'.[117]

11.84 Where the age assessment concludes that a young person is over the age of 18, a local authority will either refuse to provide support or terminate current support because there is no statutory basis to support a lone adult under the ChA 1989. More often than not, the outcome of the age assessment is informed on the same day support is terminated or refused. It is likely to be impractical for the young person immediately to pursue a challenge to the outcome of the assessment if they disagree with it and even if there are grounds on which to bring a judicial review.

11.85 In these circumstances, the young person can be detained by the Home Office on the basis that they are treated as an adult. Where this is done without the Home Office satisfying itself as to the lawfulness of the age assessment, that would be in breach of the Home

115 NBA 2022 s55(9).
116 NBA 2022 s55(4).
117 For a detailed discussion of the support available under the ChA 1989, see chapter 9.

Office's *Assessing age* policy[118] and may give rise to a claim for false imprisonment on this basis[119] as well as if it turns out the young person was in fact a child on arrival when detained.[120] Summary age assessment pro formas should not be accepted as a general rule without inquiries being made about their reliability.[121]

11.86 In non-detained cases, if an age disputed child assessed to be over 18 has made a claim for asylum which is not subjected to Dublin III, they are frequently diverted to the Home Office to access asylum support under the Immigration and Asylum Act (IAA) 1999.[122] If the young person is not an asylum-seeker, then their only avenue to accessing support to avoid street homelessness will still be from the Home Office under Immigration Act (IA) 2016 Sch 10 para 9.[123]

11.87 The IAA 1999 s95 and IA 2016 Sch 10 accommodation schemes are both operated by the Home Office on a 'no-choice' basis. There is every possibility that a young person in receipt of Home Office accommodation and support will be dispersed out of the area of the local authority which had carried out the age assessment. Unsurprisingly, when the young person later expresses a wish to challenge the conclusion of their age assessment and obtains legal advice to do so, difficult questions arise. Should the young person direct their challenge at the original authority which first disputed their age even though they may not have spent very much time in that authority's area and have since made connections in the area in which the Home Office has dispersed them? Should they instead ask the 'host' local authority to carry out a new assessment on the basis that the previous assessment was unreliable or flawed, or alternatively because new evidence has emerged? How are they able to access support from a local authority under the ChA 1989 pending resolution of the age dispute?

11.88 There are no hard and fast rules as to which authority is responsible. Each case turns on its individual facts. Added to this, the courts have not always taken a consistent approach. In *R (Liverpool City Council) v Hillingdon LBC*,[124] the Court of Appeal held that as a

118 The version in effect at the time of writing of this chapter in March 2023 is v6.0, 21 March 2023.

119 See *VS v Home Office* [2015] EWCA Civ 1142.

120 In breach of paras 16(2A) and 18B of Schedule 2 to the IA 1971.

121 *Assessing Age*, v6.0, p34.

122 A discussion of the scheme is set out in chapter 5.

123 A discussion of the Schedule 10 powers to accommodate is set out in chapter 6.

124 [2009] EWCA Civ 43, [2009] PTSR 1067.

matter of principle, it should be the first local authority which had carried out the age assessment, the conclusion of which was subject to challenge. Similarly, in *R (HA) v Hillingdon LBC*,[125] the High Court directed that the local authority which had conducted the initial age assessment should be responsible for accommodating an age disputed child pending a substantive fact-finding hearing on their age. In *R (S) v Croydon LBC*,[126] the High Court found it unlawful for the local authority not to continue accommodating pending completion of age assessment. In all of these cases, it appears, at least on the face of the judgments, the court's conclusion was in part informed by its view that there were arguably flaws in the original assessment.

11.89 In *KA and NBV v Croydon LBC*,[127] a challenge was brought to the local authority's routine practice of terminating support and passing age disputed young people to the Home Office for dispersal without providing the young person a full age assessment. It was said that the local authority's practice significantly prejudiced the young person's right of access to support pending the resolution of the age dispute and guidance was sought from the High Court in respect of the extant responsibilities owed by a local authority which has carried out an age assessment that is disputed. The High Court held that each case turned on its own facts and individual children had alternative remedies, such as pursuing a court order for interim relief requiring support to be reinstated pending the age assessment challenge.

11.90 The Home Office and ADCS have sought to agree a dispute resolution procedure through a *Joint working guidance on age assessments* (June 2015) which set out steps to be taken when there are conflicting age assessments. Although the *Joint working guidance* was made with a view to resolving detained age disputed cases, there is no reason why it cannot be applied by analogy to non-detained cases where there is an inter-authority dispute. The procedure is as follows:

- When a local authority is requested to undertake an age assessment it must check with the Home Office whether any previous assessments have been undertaken and if so must establish whether these assessments were lawful.
- If it appears that a previous age assessment was not lawful, local authorities must collaborate and promptly agree which local authority must take responsibility for conducting the age assessment.

125 [2012] EWHC 291 (Admin).
126 [2017] EWHC 265 (Admin).
127 [2017] EWHC 1723 (Admin).

- Where the Home Office becomes aware of the existing of two conflicting age assessments, the local authorities must agree which one will take responsibility.
- If previous assessments were unlawful, the person will be given the benefit of the doubt and be treated as a child.
- If the child has moved location and new information comes to light, the original assessing local authority should be informed and an agreement reached as to which local authority will reassess age.

11.91 Where no interim relief is obtained during a judicial review challenge to an age assessment requiring the local authority to provide accommodation under ChA 1989 s20, the child can stand to lose entitlements to support under the ChA 1989 even if they are ultimately successful in their judicial review challenge. This was the case in *R (GE (Eritrea)) v SSHD and Bedford BC*.[128] There, the Court of Appeal held that if a local authority refused to accommodate a child under ChA 1989 s20(1), having wrongly assessed them as being over 18, it would be relieved of any potential statutory obligation once that child reached the age of 18. When such an error came to light, the local authority could legitimately be asked to exercise its discretion to provide some of the assistance which it would otherwise have been obliged to provide, but it would not be required to do so. While the local authority exercising its discretion (or not) may be susceptible to judicial review, the onus is on the young person to pursue such a judicial review in circumstances when the young person had done no wrong.

11.92 This decision is at odds with the established line of decisions made in favour of British children and young people who were unlawfully refused duties under the ChA 1989 owed to them by the local authority. In those cases, the courts had no hesitation to direct that the local authority accept that but for its unlawful decision, the child would have been provided with the necessary accommodation and support to accrue entitlements as a care leaver. See, for example, *R (D) v Southwark LBC*[129] and *KS v Bradford MDC*.[130] In neither of these cases was it left to the local authority to consider whether to exercise its discretion to recognise the young person should have been treated as eligible for accommodation under ChA 1989 s20 when they were still a child and therefore had that happened, the child would have acquired 'former relevant child' status. It is not clear whether the migrant status of GE and the concern over

128 [2014] EWCA Civ 1490, [2015] 1 WLR 4123. See paras 9.186–9.194.
129 [2007] EWCA Civ 182, [2007] 1 FLR 2181.
130 [2014] EWHC 11 (Admin).

resources played a part in the judges' analysis. The decision also may well now be decided differently in the light of the corporate parenting duty owed by local authorities to looked after children and care leavers under CSWA 2017 s1. At the very least, the existence of a corporate parenting duty would militate heavily in favour of exercising the *GE* discretion to treat the young person as if they had leaving care rights, because that is the kind of action that a reasonable parent may be expected to do to make up for their past mistakes.

National Transfer Scheme

11.93 It has long been the case that local authorities located near ports of entry (for example, ferry ports or airports) tend to see a larger number of unaccompanied children come into their care. In 2015, when Europe was seeing an increasing number of people crossing into and across Europe, seeking international protection, the port local authorities in the UK complained of being overwhelmed and cash-strapped, in the context of significant austerity cuts to local authority funding generally.

11.94 Against this backdrop, and with an aim of facilitating a fairer distribution across local authorities of responsibility for supporting and accommodating unaccompanied children, parliament introduced IA 2016 s69, which confers a power by which one local authority in England which has responsibilities for an unaccompanied looked after child may request that the responsibilities be transferred to another local authority in England. By IA 2016 s72, which came into force on 31 May 2016, the Home Secretary may prepare a scheme for functions of one local authority in England to become functions of another local authority in England. This has been done in an Unaccompanied Asylum Seeking Child National Transfer Scheme (NTS). The scheme only applies to unaccompanied children who have made a claim for asylum. If they have not made such a claim, they are not eligible to be included in the NTS.

11.95 When the NTS first began operating in 2016, it was based on a voluntary agreement made between local authorities in England with the objective that no local authority should be required to look after more unaccompanied minors than 0.07 per cent of the total child population. On 7 February 2018, regulations were made pursuant to IA 2016 s73, to extend the NTS to Wales, Scotland and Northern Ireland.[131]

131 Transfer of Responsibility for Relevant Children (Extension to Wales, Scotland and Northern Ireland) Regulations 2018 SI No 153.

11.96 It became apparent by the summer of 2020 that the NTS was not properly functioning when Kent County Council (CC) announced in August 2020 that it would no longer be able to take into its care any unaccompanied asylum-seeking children newly arrived into its area. The local authority attributed this difficulty to the increased number of unaccompanied children arriving at the port of Dover in Kent, and the inability of the NTS to function effectively so that responsibility for these children could be reallocated to other local authorities. The local authority made public its view that the NTS needed to be put on a mandatory basis so that other local authorities, when requested, are required to accept the transfer of unaccompanied children from requesting local authorities, such as Kent CC, which are port authorities. It is questionable whether Kent CC had any lawful power to suspend services to a particular group of children under ChA 1989 ss17 and 20 given the mandatory nature of the duty under ChA 1989 s20 where a child in the local authority's area appears to require accommodation as a result of there being no one with parental responsibility.

11.97 As a result of Kent CC's decision to close its doors to newly arrived unaccompanied children, the Home Office decided to hold the children at the Kent Intake Unit (KIU), which operates as a short-term holding detention facility. It was said by the Home Office that a non-detained area, called the Atrium, operated within the KIU and those children whose ages were not disputed were held there pending onward care arrangements.

11.98 At the same time, given the criticisms made by Kent CC of the NTS's effectiveness, the Home Office held a limited consultation between 28 August and 30 September 2020 with select organisations. The Home Office made clear, at the outset of that consultation, its strong preference for the NTS to remain voluntary as between local authorities.

11.99 In the meantime, concerns were raised about the use of the KIU to hold newly arrived unaccompanied children in circumstances where Kent CC was refusing to receive these children into its care.

11.100 HM's Inspector of Prisons (HMIP), on an unannounced inspection visit to the KIU in September 2020, found that:[132]

132 *Report on an unannounced inspection of the detention of migrants arriving in Dover in small boats, Detention facilities: Tug Haven, Kent Intake Unit, Frontier House, Yarl's Wood and Lunar House*, HMIP, 23 October 2020. See: www.justiceinspectorates.gov.uk/hmiprisons/wp-content/uploads/sites/4/2020/10/Dover-detention-facilities-web-2020_v2.pdf.

1) unaccompanied children were held overnight at the KIU with adults, often for too long, and overnight in facilities with no access to open air and little or no natural light;[133]
2) children were held on average over 17 hours (and longer than adults); 29 per cent of unaccompanied children were held for over 24 hours, and one 15 year old was held for more than 66 hours;[134]
3) according to holding room logs, 73 children had been detained in the KIU in the three months up to 31 August 2020;[135]
4) welfare interviews with children were not held until the early hours the day after their arrival and were 'perfunctory' with 'little meaningful exploration of the child's welfare';[136]
5) Kent CC's decision to suspend social services provision was a material cause of the experience of children being detained and being detained for a long time waiting for social workers to arrive from other counties.[137]

11.101 The Children's Commissioner of England also visited the KIU and her policy briefing, published in February 2021, based on the visit and on unpublished data, found that:[138]

1) Unaccompanied children were being detained at the KIU to have their identities and asylum claims registered and could 'not freely leave' during this time.
2) The average length of time a child was detained was 16 hours, which was still 'an extremely long time for children to be detained' in the KIU's 'limited facilities'.
3) The mean average also hid the fact that some children were detained for much longer period. In each month for which data was provided, one in five children were detained for over 24 hours, with the longest being 65 hours. This did not include time subsequently spent in the Atrium.
4) One in six children were moved to the Atrium in the early hours of the morning, which suggested that important interviews took place at antisocial hours in the night.

133 *HMIP October 2020 report*, paras 1.5, 1.13, 1.14.

134 *HMIP October 2020 report*, paras 1.5, 1.33, 1.34.

135 *HMIP October 2020 report*, para 1.31.

136 *HMIP October 2020 report*, para 1.32.

137 *HMIP October 2020 report*, para 1.33.

138 *Policy Briefing: Detention of unaccompanied children arriving in Kent during 2020*, www.childrenscommissioner.gov.uk/report/detention-of-unaccompanied-children-arriving-in-kent-during-2020/.

5) Children stayed in the Atrium for nearly 24 hours, with the longest waiting times being in excess of 95 hours. The significant waiting times were owing to no local authority assuming statutory caring responsibility for the child.
6) It was only after Kent CC resumed statutory caring responsibilities that children were promptly released from the KIU without much delay.

11.102 In early December 2020, Kent CC re-opened its services to newly arrived unaccompanied children although not to fully discharge its ChA 1989 duties to all unaccompanied children arriving in its area. Shortly after, the Home Office sent a letter to local authorities, informing them that there was no clear majority view on the way ahead including whether the scheme would be mandated or voluntary, and therefore the NTS would remain voluntary. This was confirmed in an announcement made in June 2021[139] by the government, although the consultation responses have never been published. The June 2021 announcement included an increase in funding for local authorities to support unaccompanied children and care leavers as an incentive to local authorities. Kent CC responded to the announcement by stating that it would again no longer be in a position to receive newly arrived unaccompanied children owing to capacity.

11.103 The Home Office responded to Kent CC's closure the second time around by commissioning hotels to house newly arrived unaccompanied asylum-seeking children. This was described as a temporary 'emergency measure' in response to Kent CC's decision.[140] But the Home Office did not explain the legal basis for commissioning hotels and requiring children to be housed there instead of in local authority care under the ChA 1989.

11.104 In late November 2021, the government announced that it would make the NTS mandatory, at least on a temporary basis. The *National Transfer Scheme protocol for unaccompanied asylum seeking children*[141] (the '*NTS protocol*') was updated to reflect this decision. The mandatory NTS rota was implemented in February 2022. The decision to make the NTS rota mandatory was unsuccessfully challenged by

139 See: www.gov.uk/government/news/changes-to-the-national-transfer-scheme.

140 Letter from Secretary of State for Education to Children England, dated 6 September 2021: https://www.childrenengland.org.uk/Handlers/Download.ashx?IDMF=db67ecec-5923-44d3-bbec-39d731c81e9b.

141 V4.0, 5 September 2022.

Medway Council.[142] The Divisional Court found that it was rational for the Home Office to exercise its power under IA 2016 s72 to make the NTS mandatory in order to ensure that the rota operated to give effect to its purpose of distributing, more fairly, the resources across local authorities in the UK required to look after unaccompanied asylum-seeking children. The Divisional Court accepted the submission made by the Home Office did not have the legal powers or duties or the skills or facilities to look after unaccompanied asylum-seeking children and that the expertise lay with local authorities.[143]

11.105 Under the *NTS protocol* (as it stands at the time of writing), the NTS operates on the basis of a rota system in which regions and nations take it in turn to assume responsibility for unaccompanied children referred into the scheme. The operation of the rota is set out in a process flow diagram at Annex A: The national rota, eligibility, referral, allocation, and transfer process. All local authorities with children's services have received a notice of the intention to direct them to comply with the NTS. There are strict parameters within which transfer can be requested by the 'entry' local authority – the local authority which first received an unaccompanied child on arrival:

1) The unaccompanied child must have made an asylum claim.
2) Those who arrive in the UK within 13 weeks of their 18th birthday are not eligible for the transfer. This is because it is not considered to be in the best interests for any child over the age of 17 years and 9 months to be referred to the NTS regardless of leaving care eligibility, as this does not provide adequate time for receiving local authorities to complete pathway planning and prepare for independence post 18th birthday.
3) An entry local authority cannot make a request for transfer unless the proportion of unaccompanied asylum-seeking children it is looking after is equal to or more than 0.1 per cent of its total child population. This is a higher threshold than the 0.07 per cent threshold that had originally applied when the NTS scheme was first implemented in 2016.
4) In respect of children whose age is disputed, but accepted to be under 18 years of age or treated as being under 18 years of age until further assessment of their age has been completed, the receiving local authority will normally conduct the age assessment. In some cases, the 'entry' local authority may agree to conduct the age assessment before referring the person into the

142 *R (Medway Council) v SSHD* [2023] EWHC 377 (Admin).
143 At para 39 per Bean LJ and Collins Rice J.

NTS. When the child is not being transferred, then the age assessment is conducted by the 'entry' local authority.[144]

5) Provided that the unaccompanied child has claimed asylum, and the entry local authority meets the 0.1 per cent threshold, a transfer request is made to the NTS team based at the Home Office, which sends this to the relevant lead for the region or nation on duty under the national rota. The relevant lead would then allocate the case to a receiving local authority within its region or nation as per its agreed local approach.
6) Even where a child is eligible to be transferred under the NTS, the decision to refer must still be made on an individualised basis, taking into account the child's 'best interests' alongside other considerations such as medical treatment; family ties; legal representation and advocacy; education; ethnic group; religious considerations; and continuity of care. Good practice notes are given in the body of the Protocol. Further guidance on the approach to considering a child's best interests and where children are found to have family members elsewhere in the UK are set out at Annexes C and D to the Protocol.
7) A referral should be made 'as soon as practicable' and ideally within two working days after the child's asylum claim has been registered. The transfer should then take place within ten working days of a referral. This is in recognition that delay may cause a child distress as they become settled in their initial placement. This timescale is a longer timescale than the original timescale of two working days for referral and transfer to be completed. It appears to have factored in administrative challenges to effecting transfer in a truncated timescale, whilst bearing in mind that it is in the child's best interests to have clarity and certainty to their care arrangements sooner rather than later.
8) In the event of any delay to transfer, based on exceptional health or other reasons, the entry and receiving local authorities are expected to agree a transfer date. Until transfer is completed, responsibility for the child's welfare remains with the entry local authority.
9) A referral request may be withdrawn if an entry local authority considers that it is no longer in the child's best interests to proceed with the transfer.

144 Annex E: Age disputes under the NTS Protocol.

11.106 Although the NTS became mandatory in February 2022, the Home Office continued to use its own commissioned hotels to accommodate unaccompanied asylum-seeking children. According to the Home Office's own data, over 4,600 unaccompanied children had been accommodated in hotels between July 2021 and January 2023.[145] At the time of writing in March 2023, this has remained the case. This is a curious position for the Home Office to take given the position it advanced before the Divisional Court in the *Medway* case as to the lack of legal powers, duties and expertise to accommodate unaccompanied asylum-seeking children. The Home Office has admitted that between July 2021 and January 2023, 440 unaccompanied children went missing, and the whereabouts of more than half of them were unknown.

11.107 The continued use of hotels has been criticised by children's rights organisations.[146] Apparently in response to questions concerning the legal powers and duties of the Home Office to accommodate unaccompanied asylum-seeking children, the government included section 16 of the Illegal Migration Act 2023, which, as drafted, confers on the Home Office a power to accommodate unaccompanied asylum-seeking children, subject to certain conditions in the provision.[147]

Support in context of family reunification

11.108 Unaccompanied minors, and in some circumstances adults, in Europe with relatives in the UK have been able, depending on their personal circumstances, to transfer their asylum claim to the UK to be reunited with family. This was provided for under the Dublin III Regulation. Concerns over the lack of an effective system to facilitate such transfer of unaccompanied child refugees from other countries in Europe to the UK came to a head in October 2016 when the French government demolished the Calais camps, where many of the children were residing. Although in the days leading up to and following the demolition of the camps, the Home Office interviewed more than a thousand children to assess whether they should be given permission to join

145 Written answer from Robert Jenrick MP, Minister for Immigration. Hansard Vol 726, 24 January 2023: https://hansard.parliament.uk/commons/2023-01-24/debates/290AF292-5D7E-411C-8FB8-A6E0F288365C/UnaccompaniedAsylum-SeekingChildren.

146 https://www.ecpat.org.uk/news/charities-call-for-action-on-children-missing-in-hotels; see also https://article39.org.uk/wp-content/uploads/2023/03/2023.03.03-Joint-Letter-to-JCHR.pdf.

147 https://bills.parliament.uk/bills/3429.

their families in the UK under the family reunion criteria in the Dublin III Regulation, more than half of the applications were rejected without much explanation. Many of these children then went missing from the French centres in which they were living.

11.109 In *R (Citizens UK) v SSHD*,[148] the Court of Appeal criticised the government for providing an 'incomplete picture' of the rationale for not giving full reasons for the rejection of the young people's applications to join their families and found that the Home Office process for dealing with the applications was 'unfair and unlawful', finding that the failures in the process were prejudicial to the children, who had no realistic prospect of challenging the rejections in the absence of reasons.

11.110 In *R (ZAT and others) v SSHD*,[149] the Upper Tribunal allowed four young claimants to travel to the UK to be reunited with relatives. The Upper Tribunal found that the terrible conditions in the so-called 'Jungle' had exacerbated the young people's poor psychological conditions, which had already suffered as a result of their experiences in their country of origin. The likely delay of almost a year at that time, in the processes for family reunification under the Dublin III Regulation would further increase the strain experienced by these young people. The court found that refusal to permit the swift entry of these four young people would interfere disproportionately with their right to family life.

11.111 The Court of Appeal allowed the secretary of state's appeal on a point of principle,[150] finding that the Upper Tribunal had erred in its approach to the test required to permit the processes and procedures of the Dublin III Regulation to be bypassed because of the right to family life under ECHR Article 8. However, it did not accept that it would never be justified for individuals to bypass the Dublin III process to apply to the Home Secretary directly to join family members in the UK, although a high hurdle must be crossed before a court would conclude such an application was justified. Although finding in favour of the Home Secretary, the Court of Appeal rejected the secretary of state's fresh evidence which had been intended to suggest that there were no obstacles to children claiming asylum and family reunion in France. It also considered that in the light of the evidence submitted by the four individuals and their families about

148 [2018] EWCA Civ 1812.

149 *R (ZAT and others) v SSHD (Article 8 ECHR: Dublin Regulation: interface: proportionality) (IJR)* [2016] UKUT 61 (IAC).

150 [2016] EWCA Civ 810.

those obstacles and in the light of their psychiatric conditions it was understandable that the tribunal had concluded that refusing to admit them until they had applied for asylum in France was a disproportionate interference with their ECHR Article 8 rights.

11.112 In the context of the Dublin III framework (which no longer applies), where the child wished to reunite with relatives in the UK, if the host state took no action to make a request to the UK so as to facilitate the transfer of the child's asylum claim to be examined in the UK, the Home Secretary was not obliged to, and indeed had no power to, ask the host state in which the child was present to make the transfer. This was the effect of the Court of Appeal's judgment in *R (RSM (Eritrea)) v SSHD*,[151] followed in *R (AM (a child)) v SSHD*.[152] In *RSM*, the court held that it would only be in an 'especially compelling' case that ECHR Article 8 considerations of family unity could prevail to permit the UK to allow for the transfer of the child to the UK and for the UK to examine the child's asylum claim, bypassing the Dublin III process.

11.113 Further to the UK's exit from the EU, there is no longer any clear route for family unification of unaccompanied asylum-seeking children in Europe or arriving in Europe wishing to join their relatives in the UK; this is in a state of uncertainty. EUWA s17 required the government to seek to negotiate an agreement with the EU. Such an agreement would aim to facilitate family reunion for unaccompanied children who have claimed asylum in the EU and have a relative in the UK (or vice versa). However, two years later, the government abolished this requirement by the introduction of an amendment under the EU (Withdrawal Agreement) Act 2020 s37. Instead, the government was only required to make a *single* policy statement to parliament 'in relation to any future arrangements' between the UK and EU about these children, within two months of the 2020 Act receiving royal assent. The Explanatory Notes to the bill when it was going through parliament do not specify why the government considers the change necessary, particularly in circumstances where the government has stated that its policy on child refugees has not changed. The policy statement was published on 16 March 2020[153] and stated the UK's 'specific commitment to seek to negotiate a

151 [2018] EWCA Civ 18.

152 [2018] EWCA Civ 1815.

153 See: www.gov.uk/government/publications/unaccompanied-asylum-seeking-children-family-reunion-policy-statement/statement-of-policy-in-relation-to-family-reunion-of-unaccompanied-children-seeking-international-protection-in-the-eu-or-the-uk.

reciprocal agreement for family reunion of unaccompanied children seeking asylum in either the EU or the UK, with specified family members in the UK or the EU, where this is the child's best interests'. It was also said that the UK's exit from the EU 'should not affect' the commitment, and that proposals had been made to the EU, although the details of these apparent proposals are not published. As matters currently stand, no agreement has been reached and there is thus no clear legal route to family reunion for separated children in Europe who have family members in the UK.

11.114 Those children who have been transferred to the UK on the basis of family reunification have normally been facilitated to do so with support from the local authority children's services department under ChA 1989 s17. Their integration has not been without challenges, particularly in terms of the adequacy of support provided to them and their relatives to integrate as a family unit in circumstances where the welfare benefits rules have not been amended to accommodate many relatives' families who are in receipt of state benefits but unable to receive the same for the unaccompanied child in view of their unresolved immigration status at the point of transfer. The legal remedies for securing adequate support to meet the needs of children transferred to the UK to reunite with their family members are discussed in paras 9.12–9.70 in the context of section 17 support under the ChA 1989.

Access to education

11.115 The UNCRC highlights the importance of access to education for children.[154] Article 2 of Protocol 1 of the ECHR confers a right to education to all children as does Article 14 of the CFEU. In the UK this is guaranteed up to the end of secondary school education, ie when a child ceases to be of compulsory school age.

Educational provision for unaccompanied migrant children

11.116 Consistent with the principles of non-discrimination, unaccompanied looked after children are entitled to access the same support in order to fulfil their educational outcomes as much as any other looked after child.[155] This is now fortified by CSWA 2017 s1, which specifically requires local authorities, in the discharge of their corporate parenting duty, to support children to achieve high aspirations in education.

154 Articles 28, 29 and 32; see also General Comment No 6, paras 41–43.

155 ChA 1989 s22(3A).

11.117 Care Planning, Placement and Case Review (England) Regulations 2010[156] reg 5 specifically requires the looked after child's care plan to include a personal education plan (PEP). Social workers, Virtual School Heads and Independent Reviewing Officers, school admission officers and special educational needs (SEN) departments should work together to ensure that appropriate education provision for the child is arranged at the same time as their placement, taking into account the specific background and needs of the child.[157]

11.118 As explained in chapter 9, when a looked after child reaches the age of 18, there are continuing duties to assist the care leaver to access education, including by the provision of funding of tuition, books, computers and other equipment.[158] It is now confirmed that in respect of relevant children over 21 years of age, the local authority has duties under ChA 1989 s23C(4)(b) also to fund accommodation if that is required for a care leaver in education.[159]

11.119 The right of migrant care leavers to access continued education on turning 18 has been subject to litigation, particularly where the care leaver's immigration status has not yet been resolved. This is because they will most likely be treated as overseas students, not eligible for student finance, and therefore require potential resources from the local authority that are greater than care leavers who are British, settled or have refugee status. Their eligibility for education support may also be subject to Nationality, Immigration and Asylum Act 2002 Sch 3, discussed in further detailed in paras 9.195–9.217.

11.120 In *R (Kebede) v Newcastle City Council*[160] the Court of Appeal considered that for migrant care leavers who are not eligible for student finance provided under a central government regime, their local authority may have duties under ChA 1989 s24B(2) to contribute (in full if necessary) to the care leavers' university tuition fees and accommodation expenses. However, the Court of Appeal accepted that the migrant care leaver's immigration status was relevant to the decision as to whether the care leaver has educational needs for which the local authority would have a duty to fund.

156 SI No 959.

157 *Care of unaccompanied migrant children and victims of modern slavery: statutory guidance for local authorities*, DfE, November 2017, para 53. See also: *Promoting the education of looked after children and previously looked after children: statutory guidance for local authorities*, DfE, February 2018, in particular, paras 13–15.

158 ChA 1989 ss23C(4)(a)–(b) and 24B.

159 See *R (Sabiri) v Croydon LBC* [2012] EWHC 1236 (Admin) at paras 50–51.

160 [2013] EWCA Civ 960.

11.121 Thus, in *R (Nfuni) v Solihull MBC*,[161] the High Court rejected a judicial review challenge to the refusal of the local authority to provide funding for a care leaver to pursue a university degree in circumstances where she had been unsuccessful in her fresh asylum claim. The claimant had not been granted an in-country right of appeal against the refusal of her fresh claim, but was in the preparatory pre-action stages of a judicial review challenge to the refusal. Notwithstanding that the local authority had decided that it was not clear whether she would be given leave to remain in the UK for the duration of her university course, and therefore she had no educational need and therefore no basis to seek funding for her university course from the local authority.

11.122 However, while immigration status is a relevant consideration, it is not determinative of whether support must be provided to a care leaver to pursue a course of education. Chapter 6b of the *Transition to adulthood statutory guidance*[162] acknowledges that claiming asylum is a complex process and sets out clear principles for how the local authority should deal with planning for this cohort of young adult care leavers.[163] In particular:

1) it directs 'dual or triple planning' which envisages a 'transitional plan during the period of uncertainty when the young person is in the United Kingdom without permanent immigration status' and a 'longer term perspective' should leave be granted (para 6.22);
2) although the guidance acknowledges that funding arrangements may be limited by uncertainty of immigration status (para 6.29), it stresses that during the period of uncertainty, the local authority is to base planning around 'short term achievable goals whilst entitlement to remain in the UK is being determined';
3) the guidance positively requires active support to be provided to the young person and does not sanction inaction (para 6.21).

11.123 Whether a migrant care leaver is eligible for continued support to access education depends, to some extent, on the facts and circumstances of the individual. Moreover, the statutory guidance rather suggests that funding of higher education is not all or nothing. Thus,

161 [2013] EWHC 3155 (Admin).

162 *The Children Act 1989 guidance and regulations. Volume 3: Planning transition to adulthood for care leavers*, DfE, January 2022 (www.gov.uk/government/publications/children-act-1989-transition-to-adulthood-for-care-leavers). For further discussion, see paras 9.118–9.194.

163 See *Transition to adulthood statutory guidance*, paras 6.20–6.25.

for example, in *R (Salih) v Kent CC,*[164] the High Court granted permission to bring a judicial review challenge to the lawfulness of a local authority's refusal to fund a university course in circumstances where the care leaver had had his fresh claim for asylum refused, but had an in-country right of appeal, which he exercised. At the time he sought funding from the local authority for his university degree, his appeal against the refusal of his claim was pending. On the facts of that case, the local authority had already agreed that the care leaver had an educational need for the area of studies that he was pursuing. The acknowledgment of a 'need' for education triggered a duty to assist under ChA 1989 s23C(4)(a) where the care leaver was otherwise unable to meet his educational need. The claimant argued that the local authority was not necessarily required to agree to fund all three years of his university degree at the outset, but, in line with chapter 6b of the statutory guidance, the local authority was required but failed to address its mind to what 'short-term achievable goals' it ought to support the young person to achieve. Thus, for example, funding could be provided on a staged basis rather than in one go. There was no evidence to suggest that supporting him to pursue a university degree was not an 'achievable goal' pending his asylum appeal, particularly in circumstances where, on the face of it, his asylum claim was not hopeless or abusive.

Access to student loans

11.124 Eligibility for student finance for higher education is governed by Education (Fees and Awards) Act 1983 ss1 and 2 (as amended). Prior to 2015, many non-British citizens needed 'settled' status – such as indefinite leave to remain – to be eligible for student finance and home fee status for universities in England. Many young people who had grown up in the UK faced a ten-year wait before they would obtain 'settled' status and before they would be able to access student finance for university. This was challenged in *R (Tigere) v Secretary of State for Business, Innovation and Skills,*[165] in which the Supreme Court held that the requirement that a person must have 'settled' status to qualify for student finance constituted unjustified discrimination in breach of ECHR Protocol 1 Article 2 (right to education) read with ECHR Article 14.

164 CO/963/2016.
165 [2015] UKSC 57.

11.125 The Education (Fees and Awards) (England) Regulations 2007[166] were amended in May 2016 to take account of the *Tigere* decision.[167] The regulations as amended introduce a 'long residency' category which permitted those who satisfied it to be eligible for student finance, namely:

1) those under 18 years of age who have lived in the UK for at least seven years preceding the first day of the course (the half-life criteria);
2) those aged 18–25 who have spent at least half of their life in the UK preceding the first day of the course (the long residence criteria).

Additionally, the young person must be ordinarily resident in England for three years before the first day of the first academic year of the course.

11.126 The qualifying long residence rules for student finance resemble Immigration Rules para 276ADE(1)(iv)–(vi) on eligibility for leave to remain on a private life, long residence basis.

Half-life/long residence criteria

Has preceding the first day of the course lived in the UK for either:

– half their life; or
– period of 20 years

Example:

A is born in Nigeria on 17 June 1998.
She came to UK, aged 7 on 24 December 2005.
She wants to start degree course in September 2016
A's age in days when she arrived in the UK = 2,747 (17/6/98 – 24/12/05)
A has been in UK for 3,904 days (24/12/05 – 1/9/16)
Conclusion: She meets the half-life test.

166 SI No 779.

167 The amendment was made pursuant to the Education (Student Fees, Awards and Support) (Amendment) Regulations 2016 SI No 584.

Three-year ordinary residence criteria

Requires three years' continuous ordinary lawful residence in England prior to start of course.
A person is ordinarily resident if they habitually, normally and lawfully reside in an area.
If they entered the UK without leave, they can only become ordinarily resident after they regularise their status.
Similarly if their leave to remain in the UK expires, their period of ordinary residence is calculated from when they next gain lawful status.

Example:

A is 19 years old. He arrived in UK as an unaccompanied asylum-seeking child (UASC) at the age of 15 in June 2013 with no leave to enter.
He is granted leave to remain to the age of 17.5 in August 2013.
He does not extend his leave after it expires in December 2015. He is in the UK with no lawful status thereafter.
Conclusion: A may have been ordinarily resident for a time before he reached the age of 17.5, but he would not have accrued the necessary three-year period before his leave expired. At that point, the clock will revert to zero. It will not begin again until he regularises his status.

Victims of human trafficking

11.127 The UK has a range of international law obligations owed to those who are or may be victims of trafficking. These are contained in:

- the Protocol to Prevent, Suppress and Punish Trafficking in Persons, Especially Women and Children, supplementing the United Nations Convention Against Transnational Organized Crime (also known as the 'Palermo Protocol');
- the Council of Europe Convention on Action against the Trafficking in Human Beings (ECAT);[168]
- ECHR Article 4.

168 The ECAT was ratified by the UK in December 2018 and came into force on 1 April 2009 in respect of the UK.

11.128 Obligations owed to victims of human trafficking are justiciable in domestic law to the extent that:

- the UK ratified the ECAT and adopted policies with a view to giving effect to obligations set out in the ECAT (discussed below);[169]
- Human Rights Act 1998 s6 requires public authorities in the UK to comply with ECHR Article 4 to identify victims of trafficking, provide protection to victims or potential victims of trafficking, and investigate crimes of human trafficking.

11.129 Until 30 January 2023, the Anti-Trafficking Directive was retained EU law to the extent of EUWA 2018 ss2 and 4. NBA 2022 s68 expressly brought this to an end on 30 January 2023. Reference is still made to the Directive to the extent that it provides context for the domestic legal framework concerning the identification and support of victims.

11.130 This chapter uses 'trafficking' to refer to victims who fall within the definition used in the UK that gives rise to the identification process under the National Referral Mechanism (NRM), the protection-based support that a victim may be provided and the immigration consequences of the identification. 'Modern slavery', which is the title of the MSA 2015, and used often as an add-on to trafficking, is a term without legal grounding in the international treaties and obligations identified in the preceding paragraph. This is a fast-evolving area of law. This section of the chapter aims to set down the base principles applicable to this cohort of migrants for reference.

Definition of trafficking

11.131 Until the NBA 2022 received royal assent, there was no domestic law definition of trafficking or modern slavery.

11.132 The ECHR does not contain a definition of human trafficking, and indeed, trafficking is not mentioned in ECHR Article 4, which prohibits slavery, servitude, and forced or compulsory labour.

11.133 'Slavery', referred to in ECHR Article 4(1) is not itself defined either, but the European Court of Human Rights relies on international instruments such as the 1926 Slavery Convention, and the 1956 Supplementary Convention on Slavery, the Slave Trade and Institutions and Practices Similar to Slavery to interpret the term 'slavery'. 'Slavery' has been broadly defined as 'the status or condition

169 *R (G and others) v SSHD* [2016] EWHC 942 (Admin).

of a person over whom any or all of the powers attached to ownership are exercised'.[170]

11.134 With regard to the concept of 'servitude', the European Court of Human Rights has held that what is prohibited under ECHR Article 4 is a 'particularly serious form of denial of freedom' and includes, 'in addition to the obligation to perform certain services for others . . . the obligation for the "serf" to live on another person's property and the impossibility of altering his condition'.[171]

11.135 The European Court of Human Rights has drawn on the International Labour Organization (ILO) conventions for its interpretation of 'forced or compulsory labour', finding that it involves physical or mental constraint, and thus is where work is exacted 'under the menace of any penalty', and performed against the will of the person concerned, that is work for which the person 'has not offered voluntarily'.[172]

11.136 As for 'human trafficking', consistent with the European Court of Human Rights' approach to using international conventions and treaties as interpretative aides, the court has held that although human trafficking is not specified within ECHR Article 4, the prohibition under the article extends to a prohibition on human trafficking.[173] The definition used is that set out in ECAT Article 4, as elaborated under Anti-Trafficking Directive Article 2.[174] This is also the definition that the UK government has adopted for the purposes of implementation of its policies on human trafficking and modern slavery.

11.137 ECAT Article 4 provides:

> 'Trafficking in human beings' shall mean **[action]** the recruitment, transportation, transfer, harbouring or receipt of persons, **by means of** the threat or use of force or other forms of coercion, of abduction, of fraud, of deception, of the abuse of power or of a position of vulnerability or of the giving or receiving of payments or benefits to achieve the consent of a person having control over another person, **for the purpose of exploitation**. Exploitation shall include, at a minimum, the exploitation of the prostitution of others or other forms of sexual

170 *Siliadin v France* App No 73316/01 (2006) 43 EHRR 16, ECtHR at para 122.

171 *Van Droogenbroeck v Belgium*, Commission's report of 9 July 1980, Series B no 44, p30, paras 78–80.

172 *Van der Mussele v Belgium* App No 8919/80 (1984) 6 EHRR 163, ECtHR at p16, para 32.

173 *Rantsev v Cyprus and Russia* App No 25965/04 (2010) 51 EHRR 1, ECtHR at paras 272–282.

174 Article 2 of the Directive explicitly recognises criminal exploitation and begging as forms of exploitation.

exploitation, forced labour or services, slavery or practices similar to slavery, servitude or the removal of organs.[175]

11.138 The ECAT comes with an Explanatory Report which elaborates on the different ingredients of the definition as well as the nature and requirements of the obligations under the convention. The key points are as follows.

11.139 Trafficking consists of three essential components: action, means and purpose.[176] It means more than mere organised movement of persons for profit.[177] The critical additional factors that distinguish trafficking from migrant smuggling are use of one of the means listed (force, deception, abuse of a situation of vulnerability and so on) throughout or at some stage in the process, and use of that means for the purpose of exploitation.

1) The '**action**' ingredient relates to 'the whole sequence of actions that leads to exploitation of the victim'[178] and it applies equally to transnational and national trafficking.
2) '**Means**' can include the use of or threat of force but also the use of fraud and deception to lead victims to believe that an attractive job awaits them rather than the intended exploitation.[179] 'Means' by way of abuse of a person's position of vulnerability includes abusing 'any situation in which the person involved has no real and acceptable alternative to submitting to the abuse'. Article 2(2) of the Anti-Trafficking Directive defines this as 'a situation in which the person concerned has no real or acceptable alternative but to submit to the abuse involved'. The vulnerability may be of any kind, whether physical, psychological, emotional, family-related, social or economic. The situation may involve insecurity or illegality of the victim's administrative status, economic dependence, or any state of hardship in which a human being is impelled to accept being exploited which reflects 'differences of degree rather than any difference in the nature of the phenomenon, which in each case can be classed as trafficking': ECAT Explanatory Report, para 83.
3) The last component, '**for the purposes of**', may be met even if actual exploitation has not taken place.[180] The categories of exploit-

175 Emphasis and insertion added.
176 ECAT Explanatory Report, paras 76–77.
177 ECAT Explanatory Report, para 77.
178 ECAT Explanatory Report, paras 78–79.
179 ECAT Explanatory Report, paras 81–83.
180 ECAT Explanatory Report, para 87.

ation as defined under the ECAT are non-exhaustive. Anti-Trafficking Directive Article 2 adopts a similar definition but adds to the forms of exploitation, exploitation for 'criminal activities' which is to be understood as the 'exploitation of a person to commit, inter alia, pick-pocketing, shop-lifting, drug trafficking and other similar activities which are subject to penalties and imply financial gain'.[181] The elaboration of the trafficking definition in the Directive reflects states' recognition of the ever-changing developments in the phenomenon of human trafficking and the need for emerging common forms of exploitation to be listed explicitly.[182] Although the Directive no longer applies as a matter of EU retained law, the government appears to accept that criminal exploitation of the sorts identified in the Directive are applicable in the domestic context.

11.140 Each of the three components of the trafficking definition must be present in respect of an adult victim for the circumstances to be considered trafficking – although the definition makes clear that the victim's apparent consent is irrelevant if the consent was obtained by one of the means of trafficking.[183] The question of consent is not simple and it is not easy to determine where free will ends and constraint begins. In trafficking, some people do not know what is in store for them while others are perfectly aware that, for example, they will be engaging in sex work. However, while someone may wish to be in employment, and possibly be willing to engage in sex work, that does not mean that they consent to be subjected to abuse of all kinds. Similarly, the fact that a woman may have agreed illegally to cross borders into the UK to work in a private household as a domestic worker, does not mean that she has consented to long hours with minimum pay and being subjected to the control of her employer.[184]

11.141 Children, defined as those under 18, are not required to meet the 'means' requirement of the trafficking definition. It is recognised by signatory states that children are a particularly vulnerable group and cannot consent to their exploitation. Prior to 30 January 2023, the *MSA 2015 statutory guidance*[185] provided that those who have been exploited as a child but who only came to the attention of the state

181 EU Anti-Trafficking Directive Recital 11.

182 EU Anti-Trafficking Directive Recital 11.

183 ECAT Article 4(b).

184 See *Hounga v Allen* [2014] UKSC 47, [2014] 1 WLR 2889.

185 *Modern Slavery Act 2015 – Statutory guidance for England and Wales*, v1.0, Home Office, March 2020 ('*MSA 2015 statutory guidance*').

when they reached 18, will be treated as if they were children for the purposes of assessing their experiences against the trafficking definition. This means that the 'means' requirement in the definition does not need to be satisfied. The current statutory guidance is silent on this issue but there is arguably no reason why this should not remain the position given the question as to whether a person has been trafficked must be determined by reference to their age at the time of the actual trafficking.

11.142 Where the age of a person subject to trafficking is uncertain, and there are reasons to believe that it is less than 18, then the person should be presumed to be a child for the purposes of protection and assistance unless and until determined otherwise. This is clear from ECAT Article 10(3). It has been incorporated as a legal principle into domestic law under MSA 2015 s51.

11.143 MSA 2015 ss1–4, which apply to England and Wales, have largely adopted the ECAT definition of trafficking, although not in a like for like form. The MSA 2015 separates out concepts of human trafficking and forced labour for the purposes of defining offences of trafficking. However, for the purposes of identification and protection of victims, the Home Office, the central government body with overall responsibility for the UK's Modern Slavery Strategy, has adopted the ECAT definition of trafficking and acknowledges the further forms of trafficking identified in the Anti-Trafficking Directive, even though this is no longer retained EU law.[186]

11.144 On 28 July 2022, the Slavery and Human Trafficking (Definition of Victim) Regulations 2022 came into force.[187] These regulations were issued pursuant to NBA 2022 s69(1):

1) Regulation 1(3) provides that 'slavery', 'servitude' and 'forced or compulsory labour' have the same meaning as they have for the purposes of ECHR Article 4.
2) Regulation 2 provides that for the purposes of NBA 2022 Part 5, a 'victim of slavery' means a person who has been subjected to slavery, servitude or forced or compulsory labour. Regulation 2(2) identifies factors that may be relevant to determining whether a person has been subjected to slavery, servitude, or forced or compulsory labour, including the person's personal circumstances such as age, family relationships, physical or mental

186 See reference to this at *Victims of modern slavery: guidance for frontline staff*, v3.0, Home Office, 18 March 2016, p23; and *Victims of modern slavery: competent authority guidance*, v7.0, Home Office, 29 April 2019, p24.

187 SI No 877.

disability or illness, that significantly impair a person's ability to protect themself from being subjected to slavery, servitude or forced or compulsory labour, and any work or services provided by the person. Consistent with ECAT Article 4(b), reg 2(3) confirms that a person's consent to any conduct alleged to show that a person had been subjected to slavery, servitude, or forced or compulsory labour is not relevant to a determination as to whether a person is a victim of slavery.

3) Regulation 3 provides that for the purposes of NBA 2022 Part 5, a 'victim of human trafficking' means a person, V, whose travel is arranged or facilitated by another person, P, using any methods mentioned in reg 3(5) with a view to the person being exploited.[188] The ways in which a person, P may arrange or facilitate V's travel, may be by recruiting V, transporting or transferring V, harbouring or receiving V, or transferring or exchanging control over V. The methods mentioned in reg 3(5) are threat or use of force or other coercive behaviour; abduction, kidnap or false imprisonment; fraud or other deception; abuse of power or a position of vulnerability; or the giving of payments or other benefits to achieve the consent of a person who has control over V. If V is a child, the method is not restricted to those mentioned in reg 3(5).
4) As for exploitation, reg 3(6) provides details of the forms of exploitation, including prostitution or sexual exploitation; slavery, servitude, or forced or compulsory labour; subjection to force, threats or deception designed to induce a person to provide services or benefits of any kind; or acts concerning organ harvesting and commercial dealings in organs and the use of live donors that are prohibited under the Human Tissue Act 2004 and Human Tissue (Scotland) Act 2006.
5) Under reg 3(8), sexual exploitation includes acts done outside the UK that would involve the commission of an offence under various sexual offences provisions in the UK if it was done in the UK.

11.145 The definitions set out in the Slavery and Human Trafficking (Definition of Victim) Regulations 2022 apply to the provisions on victim identification and support under NBA 2022 Part 5. Some of the provisions of NBA 2022 Part 5 concerning victims of trafficking

188 The regulations use 'V' to refer to the victim and 'P', the person involved in arranging or facilitating travel.

have been brought into force. To the extent that they have, they are discussed below.

Obligations to identify and support victims of trafficking

11.146 ECAT Article 1(b) explicitly cites victim protection as a primary objective and requires member states to design a comprehensive system to achieve this.[189] The systemic and individual measures have to be provided in a non-discriminatory way: Article 3. Chapter III of ECAT, entitled 'Measures to protect and promote the rights of victims, guaranteeing gender equality', sets out the core rights and obligations regarding the protection of victims.

11.147 ECAT Article 10(1) requires that state parties set up an identification process with qualified decision-makers and 'ensure' that it 'duly takes into account the special situation' of women victims and, in appropriate cases, issue residence permits to identified victims.

11.148 Identification is the gateway to the fuller benefits of protective measures set out under ECAT Chapter III and Anti-Trafficking Directive Article 11.

11.149 After a decision is taken that there are 'reasonable grounds to believe' that a person is a victim of trafficking, the person is entitled to a reflection and recovery period: ECAT Article 13. Article 13 stipulates a reflection and recovery period of a minimum of 30 days after which it is envisaged that it should be possible to complete the identification process. In the UK a minimum of 45 days is provided to a victim in these circumstances.[190]

11.150 During the recovery and period, a victim is entitled, under ECAT Article 12(1), to interim assistance and support 'at least' to meet 'standards of living capable of ensuring their subsistence', emergency medical treatment, counselling and information regarding their legal rights, and assistance to enable their rights and interests to be presented and considered in criminal proceedings.

11.151 The object of Article 12(1) is to 'assist victims in their physical, psychological and social recovery'.[191] Arrangements must be made while bearing in mind the specific nature of that aim. Thus accommodation must be 'appropriate and secure' so that victims can feel

189 See also Anti-Trafficking Directive Recital 7.

190 *Victims of modern slavery: competent authority guidance*, v7.0, p10.

191 ECAT Explanatory Report para 150.

safe from the traffickers.[192] What is appropriate 'depends on the victim's personal circumstances'. Article 11(7) of the Anti-Trafficking Directive specifically imposes a duty to have regard to victims with 'special needs' derived from pregnancy, health, disability, or a serious form of psychological, physical or sexual violence they have suffered.

11.152 After the completion of the identification process, recognised victims are entitled to be considered for a renewable residence permit under Article 14. While there is no automatic right to a residence permit, there is an obligation on the state to consider whether leave should be granted. A discussion on the approach to the grant of leave as a victim of trafficking is set out in paras 1.126–1.136 including decision-making under the new regime under NBA 2022 s65 which came into force on 30 January 2023. Under ECAT Article 14(5), the right to be considered for a residence permit is without prejudice to a victim's right to asylum, and should not be postponed or deferred because the victim has also made an asylum claim. In *R (JP and BS) v SSHD*,[193] the Home Office's practice of postponing or deferring consideration of a residence permit for a recognised victim until the asylum claim has been determined was found by the High Court to discriminate against asylum-seeking victims of trafficking in breach of Article 14 read with ECHR Article 4.

11.153 Under ECAT Article 16, even if a renewable residence permit is not granted to a recognised victim of trafficking, that victim is still entitled to a safe and dignified return to their country of origin.

11.154 A recognised victim is also entitled to access under ECAT Article 15[194] a state compensation scheme for victims if damages cannot be recovered from perpetrators. This is provided for in the UK through access to the Criminal Injuries Compensation Scheme (CICS). This is discussed further below at paras 11.220–11.224.

11.155 The completion of the identification process is necessary for progression of any criminal investigation: ECAT Articles 10(2) and 18. If there is a nexus between the person's criminal offending and their exploitation, the state may decide not to prosecute the victim. For example, production of cannabis is a criminal offence, but the person arrested for production of cannabis may have been trafficked for criminal exploitation. The police and the Crown Prosecution Service (CPS) should, in the circumstances, consider whether it is in

192 ECAT Explanatory Report para 153.

193 [2019] EWHC 3346 (Admin).

194 Article 17 of the Anti-Trafficking Directive also provided for a right to access compensation. This is discussed at paras 11.220–11.224 below in the discussion of the Criminal Injuries Compensation Scheme.

the public interest to bring a prosecution against the person, given the person is also a victim of a crime, ie human trafficking. This is known in short-hand as the 'non-punishment' provision and is set out in ECAT Article 26 and Anti-Trafficking Directive Article 8.

Human rights obligations to victims of trafficking

11.156 The obligations under the ECAT and Anti-Trafficking Directive fall to be interpreted in accordance with human rights obligations owed by the state parties to both instruments: see ECAT preamble and Article 40; and Directive Recital 33.

11.157 The European Court of Human Rights has held that ECHR Article 4 contains three main duties:[195]

1) A general duty to implement measures to combat trafficking: the 'systems duty'.
2) A duty to take all reasonable steps to protect individual victims of trafficking as soon as the state knows or ought to know of a credible suspicion that someone may be a victim of trafficking: the 'protection duty' (sometimes called the 'operational duty').
3) A duty to investigate situations of potential trafficking as soon as there is a credible suspicion of such a crime having been committed: the 'investigation duty' (sometimes called 'the procedural duty').

11.158 Relying on the ECAT and Anti-Trafficking Directive, the European Court of Human Rights has interpreted appropriate measures reasonably expected of the state under ECHR Article 4 as requiring, at a minimum, effective and prompt identification of victims[196] and support for their recovery, and assistance to aid victims in their physical, psychological and social recovery, including accommodation, subsistence, counselling, legal advice and assistance, and medical treatment.[197] It also encompasses that which is necessary to secure

195 See *R (TDT) v SSHD* [2018] EWCA Civ 1395 at para 17. See also *Rantsev v Cyprus* App No 25965/04 (2010) 51 EHRR 1, ECtHR at paras 285–288, *LE v Greece* App No 71545/12 [2016] ECHR 107, ECtHR at paras 64–68, *Chowdury v Greece* App No 21884/15 [2017] ECHR 300, ECtHR at para 110; and *SM v Croatia* App No 60561/14 (2021) 72 EHRR 1, ECtHR at paras 305–320.

196 *Rantsev v Cyprus* App No 25965/04 (2010) 51 EHRR 1, ECtHR at paras 285–288.

197 *Chowdury v Greece* at para 110; *J and others v Austria* App No 58216/12, 17 January 2017, ECtHR at para 110.

the victim's stability and rehabilitation and prevent future risks of re-trafficking: *Rantsev v Cyprus*[198] as applied in *R (TDT) v SSHD*.[199]

11.159 The state is obliged to act to investigate and protect where it is aware or ought to be aware of circumstances giving rise to a 'credible suspicion' that an individual has been or is at real and immediate risk of being trafficked or exploited.[200]

Domestic legal framework for identification and support of victims of trafficking

11.160 In domestic law, the international obligations outlined above to identify and consequently to protect victims are primarily implemented through the NRM. The explanation of the NRM is set out in the *Modern Slavery Act 2015 statutory guidance for England and Wales and non-statutory guidance for Scotland and Northern Ireland*.[201] The statutory guidance is issued under MSA 2015 s49. However, the statutory guidance is not to be taken as a complete statement on the domestic law position on the obligations concerning the identification of victims of trafficking. It needs to be read and interpreted in the light of the UK's international law obligations outlined above.

11.161 NBA 2022 Part 5 (ss58–69) contains new provisions on victim identification and support. Not all of these provisions have come into force at the time of writing in March 2023. As discussed at paras 11.142–11.143, regulations have come into force in respect of the definition of a victim applicable to these provisions. Changes to the current policy approach to victim identification and support as a result of the provisions in NBA 2022 Part 5 are identified and discussed below to the extent that they have been brought into force.

National Referral Mechanism

11.162 The structure and process of the NRM, as explained in the *MSA 2015 statutory guidance*, concentrates decision-making powers with the Single Competent Authority (SCA), which sits in the Home Office. The SCA has sole responsibility for decisions about who is a victim of trafficking or modern slavery. The approach of concentrating all decision-making with the SCA was introduced on 29 April 2019. Prior to that date, there were two designated Competent

198 App No 25965/04 (2010) 51 EHRR 1, ECtHR at para 286.

199 [2018] EWCA Civ 1395.

200 See *Rantsev* at para 286.

201 As at the time of writing, v2.10 (updated on 1 July 2022) is in operation.

Authorities within the NRM process, the UK Visa and Immigration (UKVI) based in the Home Office, responsible for decisions on victim identification concerning victims and potential victims who are subject to immigration control, and the National Crime Agency (NCA), responsible for decisions on victim identification concerning victims and potential victims who are European nationals. Decisions on grants of residence permits to victims of trafficking are made by a separate department within the Home Office.

11.163 The stages of the NRM are in brief as follows, and discussed further below:

1) A referral has to be made by a designated First Responder, the list of which is set out in the statutory guidance (paras 11.165–11.169).
2) A first-stage decision is made, to answer the question: are there reasonable grounds to believe that the person is a victim of trafficking? (the 'Reasonable Grounds' stage). If there are reasonable grounds, the victim is afforded a 45-day 'reflection and recovery' period during which no final decision on victim status will be made, although evidence-gathering may be carried out (paras 11.170–11.176).
3) A second-stage decision is made, to answer the question: is the person a victim of trafficking? (the 'Conclusive Grounds' stage) (paras 11.177–11.178). Recognised victims will be assessed for their eligibility for a residence permit to remain in the UK. Residence permits are discussed at chapter 1 at paras 1.126–1.136.

11.164 NBA 2022 ss58–69 will affect certain people who have experienced human trafficking, slavery, servitude, or forced or compulsory labour, although it does not make changes to the basic structure of the NRM. On 30 January 2023, certain of these provisions were brought into force, namely, sections 60–65 and 68–69. The changes are discussed below where relevant to the stage of decision-making.

Making a referral into the NRM

11.165 A referral has to be made on behalf of a victim of trafficking by a designated First Responder in order to trigger the formal identification process set out in the NRM. The Home Office's *Guidance to frontline staff* sets out a list of designated First Responders, which includes most statutory agencies (for example, the police, health authorities, prisons, social services and the Home Office) as well as certain approved non-governmental organisations. Oddly, the CPS is not a designated First Responder even though potential victims may come to its attention during the course of a criminal prosecution, and the CPS has a detailed policy on what steps prosecutors should take when it comes to their attention that a criminal defendant may be a victim of trafficking.

11.166 The referral is made to the SCA, based in the Home Office, and only the SCA can determine victim status. It is relevant to note that neither the ECAT nor the Anti-Trafficking Directive mandate such a structured process for victim identification. ECAT Article 10 refers to the state needing to ensure that decisions on victim identification are made by competent authorities, but does not require the creation of a single 'Competent Authority' office. Rather it appears to envisage that there may be different authorities of the state who would have people trained and qualified to make victim identification decisions, and who would co-operate with one another. Having a single Competent Authority, with decision-making concentrated with one central government department, is an invention of the UK.

11.167 There is no minimum number of indicators of trafficking which must be present in order for an NRM referral to be made to the SCA. The indicators can be personal to the individual and based on their account of their experiences, behavioural, circumstantial or situational factors (for example, if the person was found in a brothel or a cannabis farm), or based on objective evidence showing that the individual fits the profile of a victim of trafficking. Indeed, the European Court of Human Rights, under ECHR Article 4, does not approach identification in a mechanical way. The duty to identify is triggered where there is a 'credible suspicion' that a person may have been trafficked or at a real and immediate risk of trafficking. Therefore, the fact that a person may not have actually been exploited should not bar that person from being identified and recognised as a victim of trafficking.

11.168 In the context of European Court of Human Rights decisions, a state is expected to act in compliance with ECHR Article 4 'as soon as' the state is aware or ought to be aware of circumstances giving rise to a 'credible suspicion' that a person has been or is at real and immediate risk of being trafficked or exploited. This threshold may arise, as in *Rantsev v Cyprus and Russia*[202] where there was objective evidence that cabaret artiste visas were being used in Cyprus to traffick women from other countries for the purposes of sexual exploitation. It was not necessary for the individual victim to prove her personal circumstances constituted trafficking for there to be a 'credible suspicion'. The threshold was deliberately low because it is

202 App No 29965/04 (2010) 51 EHRR 1, ECtHR.

precautionary in nature and is the threshold triggering an investigation and precautionary protective steps.

11.169 In the domestic context, the Court of Appeal in *R (TDT) v SSHD*[203] took a similar view, finding that it is possible for generic evidence showing that a person falls into a class known to be particularly vulnerable to being trafficked to constitute a credible suspicion triggering the duty to identify under ECHR Article 4, and a domestic law obligation to investigate the circumstances and act to protect the potential victim. The investigation may take the form of an NRM referral, but the Court of Appeal held that the credible suspicion could also mean that the person's circumstances meet the 'Reasonable Grounds' threshold. The Court of Appeal noted that the staged approach taken in the NRM is a domestic policy decision, and not required under either ECAT Article 10 or ECHR Article 4. In *TDT*, the generic evidence was of a high incidence of young Vietnamese males being trafficked to the UK and being subject to criminal exploitation, farming cannabis.

The Reasonable Grounds decision

11.170 The SCA must act promptly on receipt of the referral to determine whether there are reasonable grounds to believe that a person is a victim of trafficking. The statutory guidance provides that this should be done within five working days of receipt of the referral.

11.171 What constitutes 'reasonable grounds to believe' is not defined in primary legislation. The statutory guidance defines 'reasonable grounds to believe' as meaning 'I suspect but cannot prove'. This, the Court of Appeal in *TDT v SSHD* held,[204] is a low threshold, equivalent to the 'credible suspicion' threshold formulated by the European Court as the trigger for the positive obligation under Article 4 ECHR to take measures to protect a victim.[205] In *R (Minh) v SSHD*,[206] the High Court provided helpful guidance as follows:

1) The Reasonable Grounds decision is intended to do no more than act as an initial filter to a fuller, conclusive decision.[207] The question is not whether, subjectively, the decision-maker thinks the person is a victim. Nor should decision-making, on an objective

203 [2018] EWCA Civ 1395 at para 48 per Underhill LJ. See further paras 11.170–11.173 for a discussion of the 'Reasonable Grounds' threshold.
204 *TDT v SSHD* at para 37.
205 See *Rantsev v Cyprus* at para 286.
206 [2015] EWHC 1725 (Admin).
207 *Minh* at 74.

basis, be elevated to a detailed summary determination of the ultimate credibility of the case advanced.[208]

2) There could be both reasonable grounds upon which a reasonable person could believe that a person could be a victim of trafficking and reasonable grounds for belief that they might not be. That may be so in circumstances where there are inconsistencies or gaps in the evidence but reasons such as potential psychological problems to explain these gaps. Where this arises, the question as to 'reasonable grounds to believe' must be answered in the affirmative.[209]
3) Provided there are reasonable grounds for belief, then the question of whether there are also reasonable grounds for disbelief is irrelevant. The question of whether the grounds for disbelief outweigh the grounds for belief is one for the next stage after the reflection and recovery period and if necessary after additional inquiries.[210]
4) Although credibility is relevant to the existence or otherwise of 'reasonable grounds', a decision-maker does not have to (and may be unable to) form a concluded view at the 'reasonable grounds' stage as to whether the victim is being truthful. There may be many reasons why the victim may not be able to provide detailed information or recall facts accurately that may relate to trauma of the experience, shame, mistrust of authorities or other factors.[211] In the Reasonable Grounds context, the decision for the Competent Authority is not whether the grounds for claiming to be a victim of trafficking are necessarily true, but only whether they and all the information available to the Competent Authority are sufficient to constitute reasonable grounds to trigger a requirement of further inquiry before the state can be rationally satisfied that it does not have any positive obligations towards the individual.[212]

11.172 NBA 2022 s60 amends MSA 2015 s49, the provision concerning the content of statutory guidance about identifying and supporting victims. It directs that the guidance sets out the factors that indicate a person 'is' a victim of slavery or human trafficking instead of the

208 *Minh* at paras 71 and 74.

209 *Minh* at para 70.

210 *Minh* at para 70.

211 *Minh* at para 75. This is also acknowledged in the *Competent Authority guidance* at pp70–72.

212 *Minh* at para 80.

factors that indicate a person 'may be' a victim. Whereas previously the guidance directed identification on whether there are reasonable grounds to believe that someone 'may be' a victim, the amendment directs decision-makers to address whether there are reasonable grounds to believe that someone 'is' a victim. It also directs that the threshold for Conclusive Grounds decisions as to whether a person is a victim of slavery or trafficking is the balance of probabilities.

11.173 It may appear, on the face of it, that the amendment under section 60 raises the thresholds for a Reasonable Grounds and a Conclusive Grounds decision. However, as the Explanatory Notes to the section states, the amendment is to bring the language of MSA 2015 s49 in line with ECAT Article 10 and the European Court of Human Rights case-law, both of which direct that the question to ask at the Reasonable Grounds/credible suspicion stage, is whether there are reasonable grounds to believe that a person *is* a victim. The use of 'may be a victim' referred to in MSA 2015 s49 appeared to have been unintentional slippage of the drafting. There is nothing in the Explanatory Notes to MSA 2015 s49 or in the Hansard debates about the provision to suggest that parliament had intended, by the use of 'may be a victim', to lower the threshold below that used in international law.

11.174 The victim's entitlement to assistance and support for recovery[213] is now set out in statute under NBA 2022 s64. Until 30 January 2023, if that decision was positive, the victim was given a minimum of 45 days of recovery and reflection. After 30 January 2023, NBA 2022 s61 was brought into force. It put on a statutory footing the entitlement of a person with a positive Reasonable Grounds decision to a minimum period of recovery and reflection. The recovery period extends to the day on which the Conclusive Grounds decision is made. The victim cannot be removed during this period. The statutory minimum for the recovery period has been shortened to 30 days, and is subject to the application of disqualification provisions under NBA 2022 s63.[214]

11.175 During this reflection and recovery period, the Home Office is expected to make the necessary inquiries for a full evaluation to decide if the person is a victim of human trafficking on a balance of probabilities.[215] If the decision is a negative one, there is, at present,

213 For a discussion on the support a victim can receive during the reflection and recovery period, see paras 11.198–11.216.

214 Disqualification is discussed at paras 11.179–11.185.

215 *MSA 2015 statutory guidance*, paras 7.10 14.134-4.136.

no statutory right of appeal against the decision to an immigration tribunal. The primary remedy is a judicial review. There is also the possibility of requesting reconsideration of the decision if flaws in the decision-making can be identified or alternatively further evidence has emerged which warrants the decision being reconsidered. See further paras 11.196–11.197 below.

11.176 Further to NBA 2022 s62 coming into force on 30 January 2023, a person with a positive Reasonable Grounds decision may not be able to benefit from an additional period of recovery and reflection following a second positive Reasonable Grounds decision for a different set of circumstances of trafficking if those circumstances occurred prior to the first positive decision. There is a discretion to grant an additional recovery period of time. Detailed guidance on the approach to be taken by the decision-maker is set out in the *MSA 2015 statutory guidance.*[216] Children (those under 18 at the time of the second Reasonable Grounds decision) are exempt from the additional recovery period provision.[217]

The Conclusive Grounds decision

11.177 A Conclusive Grounds decision may be made as soon as the reflection and recovery period ends,[218] but in practice there are significant delays to the making of a Conclusive Grounds decision.[219] It is at this stage where there will be a closer scrutiny of the available evidence obtained in the course of the SCA's inquiries. The sources of evidence are not limited to that of the victim and can and should be drawn from support organisations, health professionals, police and social care professionals where they are involved. Objective country evidence of patterns of trafficking as well as medical evidence (such as scarring, psychiatric and psychological evidence) must be taken into account where available. If there are grounds to disbelieve a person is a victim, established rules of procedural fairness require the SCA to give the victim an opportunity to know what these

216 *MSA 2015 statutory guidance*, paras 14.86–14.117. See in particular the decision-making framework set out after para 14.114.

217 *MSA 2015 statutory guidance*, para 14.117.

218 *MSA 2015 statutory guidance*, para 14.128.

219 The statistics as to the time it takes for a Conclusive Grounds decision to be made are not published. The most recent available statistics, at the time of writing, are those contained in the case of *R (EOG) v SSHD* [2020] EWHC 3310 (Admin) at para 26.

grounds are and to clarify or correct any misunderstanding and provide any additional evidence if available.[220]

11.178 NBA 2022 s60(4) confirms in statute that the threshold for a Conclusive Grounds decision is the 'balance of probabilities'. This is consistent with the decision of the Court of Appeal in *MN and IXU v SSHD*.[221]

Public order disqualification

11.179 One of the provisions that came into force on 30 January 2023 is NBA 2023 s63, entitled 'Identified potential victims etc: disqualification from protection'. By this section, the SCA may determine a post-Reasonable Grounds decision that a person is disqualified from protection and support where either (1) they are a 'threat to public order', or (2) they have claimed to be a victim of trafficking 'in bad faith'. NBA 2022 s63 does not explain what 'bad faith' means.

11.180 NBA 2023 s63(3) sets out a non-exhaustive list of circumstances in which a person is a 'threat to public order' and therefore disqualified from support as a victim. The list includes people involved in or suspected of being involved in serious offences such as terrorism, murder, manslaughter and other serious offences listed in MSA 2015 Sch 4, people who have been deprived of citizenship where it is conducive to the public good, and people who otherwise pose a risk to UK national security. But the list also includes a person who is 'a foreign criminal' within the meaning of UKBA 2007 s32(1), that is a person who has received a custodial sentence of 12 months or more. This is a category of persons who can be convicted of far lower-level offences than the other serious crimes included in NBA 2022 s63(3), For example, a victim of trafficking convicted for his role in cannabis production or a victim who was sex-trafficked to the UK on a false document and convicted of possession of such a document could be caught by this provision.

11.181 The Explanatory Notes to NBA 2022 s63[222] suggest that the provision puts on a statutory footing ECAT Article 13(3), which provides that state parties are not bound to afford a reflection and recovery period to a victim with a positive Reasonable Grounds decision 'if grounds of public order prevent it or if it is found that victim status is being claimed improperly'.

220 See by analogy, *R (FZ) v Croydon LBC* [2011] EWCA Civ 59 at para 21.
221 [2020] EWCA Civ 1746.
222 Explanatory Notes to NBA 2022 s63 at para 622.

11.182 NBA 2022 s63(2) provides that where a person is disqualified under section 63(1), they are not barred from being removed even though ordinarily a positive Reasonable Grounds decision serves as a bar to removal pending the completion of the NRM process. Furthermore, by NBA 2022 s63(2)(b), the person will not be considered for a grant of limited leave to remain under NBA 2022 s65.

11.183 It is not clear on the face of NBA 2022 s63 whether the whole NRM decision-making process is suspended in the light of the disqualification, such that no Conclusive Grounds decision is made. That is not spelt out in NBA 2022 s63(2) but the *MSA 2015 statutory guidance* issued further to this provision coming into force states that if a Conclusive Grounds decision has not yet been made, it will not be made.[223] Although the Explanatory Notes to NBA 2022 s63 state that the provision seeks to implement ECAT Article 13(3), neither Article 13 nor Article 10, the main article on victim identification, provide for the cessation of victim identification on grounds of public order or because the claim was improperly claimed. The earlier version of the *MSA 2015 statutory guidance* provided that a negative Conclusive Grounds decision or the refusal of leave could be made on public order grounds or a refusal of leave on a case-by-case basis. This seems more in line with the ECAT provisions.

11.184 Also not stated on the face of NBA 2022 s63 is whether the statutory defence to a criminal charge can be raised under MSA 2015 s45 in cases where the victim is subject to a public order disqualification. This becomes an issue of concern particularly in cases where a victim has been prosecuted for a crime which is connected to their criminal exploitation. The Court of Appeal (Criminal Division) in *R v Joseph*[224] had highlighted the importance of the statutory defence to prosecution in cases like this.

11.185 At the time when the bill was going through parliament, the Joint Committee on Human Rights had expressed serious concerns about the effect of NBA 2022 s63, stating that excluding certain victims from protection increases the likelihood that their cases will not be adequately investigated or prosecuted. This is likely to mean that action will not be taken against organised gangs exploiting these victims of slavery or human trafficking, creating a loophole for people responsible for exploiting people in slavery and human trafficking to

223 *MSA 2015 statutory guidance*, para 14.236.
224 [2017] EWCA Crim 36.

evade investigation and prosecution by targeting those with a criminal past.[225]

NRM decision-making

11.186 The *MSA 2015 statutory guidance* sets out detailed guidance on the approach to be taken to assessing the credibility of a victim, which must be set against the context of known vulnerabilities of victims, including the impact of trauma affecting memory, ability to recall events and details, and ability to provide a coherent narrative account.

11.187 It is well recognised that children experience trafficking differently to adults. The *MSA 2015 statutory guidance* acknowledges that children may not know or be able to label their experience as abuse or exploitation, and often relate their experiences in an inconsistent way or with obvious errors.[226] The guidance also notes the particular features of unequal power dynamics in child trafficking, particularly the use of grooming and the presence of 'Stockholm syndrome' (where victims create an inappropriate emotional or psychological attachment to their controller). The Competent Authority guidance cross refers to the Department for Education's *Child sexual exploitation* guide to recognise that victims of child sexual exploitation may have been abused as well as having been provided with what they perceive to be demonstrations of love and affection, treats, and protection. The existence of the latter does not mean that they have not been exploited. Further detailed guidance issued by the Home Office in the context of assessing credibility in asylum claims can analogously be applied in the present context.[227]

11.188 Although the onus is on the SCA to make inquiries and gather the evidence, in practice the bulk of information and evidence about the victim's narrative and their circumstances are produced by the victim with assistance of legal representatives. There has been an inadvertent and erroneous shift on to the victim to demonstrate that they meet the three components of the trafficking definition.

11.189 As with asylum claims, Conclusive Grounds decisions on trafficked victim status often turn on the credibility of the account of the victim. The *MSA 2015 statutory guidance* sets out some guidance on the approach to credibility at Annex E but this does not sufficiently encompass the approach that the SCA is to take to assess the evidence and the credibility of a person's account. The guidance contrasts

225 Joint Human Rights Committee, *Legislative Scrutiny: Nationality and Borders Bill (Part 5) – Modern Slavery*, HC 964, at para 53.

226 *MSA 2015 statutory guidance*, section 9, which deals with child victims.

227 *Asylum policy instruction on assessing credibility and refugee status*, v9.0, 9 January 2015.

with the more detailed guidance in the asylum context concerning assessments of credibility of both adults and children, having regard to their accounts of traumatic past experiences.

11.190 In *MN and IXU v SSHD*,[228] the Court of Appeal criticised the guidance given to Home Office caseworkers deciding trafficking claims for using the term 'mitigating circumstances'. The court held that this inappropriate phraseology not only echoed criminal proceedings but also encouraged caseworkers to fall into the error of first identifying the defects in the account of a putative victim and then trying to decide whether they can be excused for reasons of the kind given in the guidance. The court considered this 'over-mechanistic' and not reflecting the real nature of the exercise on assessing credibility. What is really asked of the decision-maker is to assess the core account of the victim, to consider whether there are aspects that are incoherent or inconsistent or have been disclosed belatedly, alongside evidence which may explain those aspects.

11.191 It is worth quoting the relevant passage in the judgment in full to understand the Court of Appeal's warning on the approach to credibility:

> The term 'credibility' is used a good deal in the context both of asylum appeals and of decisions whether a person is a victim of trafficking, and we have detected a tendency to treat it as having some special technical meaning. But in truth it connotes no more than whether the applicant's account is to be believed. In making that assessment the decision-maker will have to take account all factors that may bear on that question. Likewise the term 'plausibility' is not a term of art. To say that a particular account, or element in that account, is implausible is simply to say that it seems to the decision-maker to be inherently surprising, or the kind of thing that you would not normally expect to happen; and such an assessment will obviously feed in to the overall assessment of credibility, though the weight to be given to it will depend on the degree of unlikelihood and how confident the decision-maker can be about it. Perhaps both points are too obvious to need making; but if terms are used too regularly they sometimes get in the way of the process of common sense decision-making.[229]

11.192 As for the use of experts' report in context of credibility assessments, the Court of Appeal in *MN and IXU v SSHD* held (at para 121) that:

1) The decision whether the account given by a putative victim is in the essential respects truthful has to be taken by the tribunal or

228 [2020] EWCA Civ 1746.
229 *MN and IXU v SSHD* at para 127.

SCA decision-maker on the totality of the evidence, viewed holistically.

2) Where a doctor's opinion, properly understood, goes no further than a finding of 'mere consistency' with the applicant's account it is neutral on the question whether that account is truthful.
3) However, it is open to a doctor to express an opinion to the effect that their findings are positively supportive of the truthfulness of an applicant's account (ie an opinion going beyond 'mere consistency'); and where they do so that opinion should in principle be taken into account. Such an opinion may be based on physical findings (such as especially characteristic scarring). However, it may also be based on an assessment of the applicant's reported symptoms, including symptoms of mental ill-health, and/or of their overall presentation and history. There is no rule that doctors are prevented by their professional role from considering critically the truthfulness of what they are told. A doctor's assessment of the truthfulness of the applicant may be of particular value.
4) The weight to be given to any such expression of opinion will depend on the circumstances of the particular case. It can never be determinative, and the decision-maker will have to decide in each case to what extent its value has to be discounted if at all.
5) One factor bearing on the weight to be given to an expression of opinion by a doctor that the applicant's reported symptoms support their case that they were persecuted or trafficked (as the case may be) is whether there are other possible causes of those symptoms. If the expert has not considered that question, that does not mean the value of the expert's opinion is extinguished. It may diminish the value that can be put on their opinion, but the extent to which that is so will depend on the likelihood of such other causes operating in the particular case and producing the symptoms in question.

Other impacts of the Nationality and Borders Act 2022 on victim identification

11.193 NBA 2022 s58 gives the Home Secretary the power to serve a slavery or trafficking information notice (STIN) on a person who has made a protection and human rights claim. The STIN is a notice requiring the recipient to provide the Home Secretary (and the competent authority specified in the notice) with any information that may be relevant for the purposes of making a Reasonable Grounds or Conclusive Grounds decision in relation to the recipient. The STIN will specify a date by which a response is required. If a person is late in responding to the STIN, that is, the response is provided on or after the specified date in the STIN, then under NBA 2022 s58(5) the person must also provide a statement explaining why the information relevant to the making of a Reasonable Grounds or Conclusive Grounds decision could not be provided before the specified date. NBA 2022 s59(2) directs that the Home Secretary 'must' take account, 'as damaging the person's credibility' late compliance with an STIN in cases concerning adults (those who are 18 years old or over) unless there are good reasons why the information was provided late.

11.194 These two provisions place a significant burden on the individual to self-identify as a victim, to understand what information may be considered relevant and to provide full disclosure at the initial stage. This may be at a time when the victim has not had any access to legal advice and assistance. These provisions also ignore the recognised barriers that victims face to disclosure. Paragraph 13.18 of the *MSA 2015 statutory guidance* acknowledges that victims' disclosures of historic events are often delayed due to an unwillingness to self-identify or due to the impact of trauma, particularly post-traumatic stress disorder. Trauma may affect a victim's ability to recall facts or may affect the coherence of the victim's recounting of past difficulties experiences. Although the *MSA 2015 statutory guidance* recognises that this is why a recovery period is so important, the provisions concerning STIN do not properly reflect this recognition. These provisions have not yet come into force but it is already evident that they are likely to have a punitive effect on victims' ability to be identified and access protection.

Challenges to NRM decision-making

11.195 Negative decisions, either of there being no reasonable grounds to believe that a person is or has been trafficked or no conclusive grounds to believe the same, can be challenged by way of judicial review on conventional judicial review grounds. As the question of whether a person is trafficked engages fundamental rights under ECHR Article 4, the court should apply anxious scrutiny to the review of the negative decision: *R (SF (St Lucia)) v SSHD*.[230] This means that the court needs to be satisfied that the decisions: 'show by their reasoning that every factor which might tell in favour of an applicant has been properly taken into account. The greater the likely

230 [2015] EWHC 2705 (Admin).

impact of a decision on the rights of the person affected, the greater the detailed justification and explanation which will be expected'.[231]

11.196 The alternative to a judicial review is a request to the SCA for the decision to be reconsidered. Prior to November 2019, the Home Office's reconsideration policy, contained in the Competent Authority guidance, provided that reconsideration requests could only be made by the designated First Responder who had made the original NRM referral on behalf of the victim. Lawyers and other professionals involved in supporting the victim could not do so and the guidance provided for their requests to be summarily rejected on the basis that they were not a designated First Responder regardless of the underlying merits of the reconsideration request. This was successfully challenged in *R (DS) v SSHD*[232] and declared to be unlawful for contravening the obligation to identify victims correctly under the ECAT and Anti-Trafficking Directive, and for being procedurally unfair and a fettering of the common law discretion to reopen decisions. The Home Secretary agreed to disapply the policy and to inform its caseworkers of the outcome of the case and its implications.

11.197 The *MSA 2015 statutory guidance* now has a section that addresses the circumstances in which a victim may seek reconsideration of the Reasonable Grounds or Conclusive Grounds decision. This can now be done by the victim, or with the support of their Support Provider or First Responder, but it can also be a lawyer. See further details at paras 14.216–14.230 of the *MSA 2015 statutory guidance*.

Support regime for victims of trafficking

11.198 The *MSA 2015 statutory guidance* confirms the UK's obligation to provide victims with support pursuant to ECAT Article 12 during the reflection and recovery period but provides no specifics. The guidance provides limited information concerning the support that victims are entitled to and that their needs are to be determined by a recovery needs assessment, but with very little direction on how that assessment is to be conducted by support workers contracted by the Home Office through the Adult Modern Slavery Victim Care Contract (AMSVCC).

11.199 The detail on the nature and extent of support is likely to be contained in the AMSVCC although there is no way of verifying this

231 *R (FM) v SSHD* [2015] EWHC 844 (Admin) at para 30, quoting *R (YH (Iraq)) v SSHD* [2010] EWCA Civ 116 at para 24.

232 [2019] EWHC 3046 (Admin).

because the AMSVCC is not a public document. Since 2011, the main contractor for the Adult Victims of Modern Slavery (AVMS) contract has been the Salvation Army, which in turn subcontracts with other charities ('NRM Support Providers') to deliver the actual support to victims.

11.200 Broadly speaking, support under the NRM consists of safe house accommodation, weekly subsistence money for meeting basic living needs, allocated key work support, access to primary care treatment and some counselling provision. Support is normally accessed after a positive 'Reasonable Grounds' decision, although the *MSA 2015 statutory guidance* provides the possibility of an individual being able to access the support prior to a 'Reasonable Grounds' decision.[233]

11.201 There is, however, no guidance comparable to the Care Act 2014 statutory guidance[234] or the ChA 1989 assessment framework[235] to assist NRM Support Providers to assess the needs of victims assigned to their care so that support provisions are matched according to victim need. There are no publicly available standards of care for victims of trafficking and no minimum qualifications for support staff tasked with providing support through the AVMSCC to victims. The combination of an absence of assessment guidance and a lack of qualification standard for support staff means there are inconsistencies in the approach to the provision of support for victims of trafficking or slavery, dependant on the experience and knowledge of the support workers providing direct support on the ground to the victim.

11.202 The absence of guidance was criticised by the High Court in *R (K) v SSHD*[236] as unlawful. The absence of an inspection regime to check the quality of care and support provided to victims of trafficking was also criticised by the National Audit Office.[237] In 2015, the Human Trafficking Foundation published a set of Trafficking Survivor Care Standards, with the purpose of filling the gap left by the government's inaction. These were endorsed by the Independent Anti-Slavery Commissioner[238] and were updated in 2018,[239] with the

233 *MSA 2015 statutory guidance*, para 8.2 and Annex F.

234 See paras 8.33–8.70.

235 See paras 9.40–9.43, 9.130 and 9.141–9.144.

236 [2018] EWHC 2951 (Admin).

237 *Reducing modern slavery*, National Audit Office, HC 630 Session 2017–2019, 15 December 2017.

238 The Independent Anti-Slavery Commissioner was established under MSA 2015 s40. Its general functions are set out in section 41.

239 See: www.antislaverycommissioner.co.uk/media/1235/slavery-and-trafficking-survivor-care-standards.pdf.

government announcing its commitment to adopt these Standards as a 'minimum standard for victim support'.[240] However, as stated in para 11.199 above, as the AMSVCC and its terms have not been made public and therefore, it is not known whether the government has fulfilled its commitment to incorporating these care standards into the contract.

11.203 In May 2022, the Care Quality Commission (CQC) published a framework for inspecting safe-houses and outreach services which support victims of trafficking. No inspection report has yet been published at the time of writing.

Accommodation

11.204 Under the current AVMSCC, NRM Support Providers are subcontracted to provide safe house accommodation. It is not known how many safe house placements there are, or how the contracted numbers of placements are determined by the Home Office, as this information is not published. Similarly, there is no published information about how safe house placements are allocated. Anecdotally, it is widely believed to operate on a 'no choice basis', dependent only on where there is available appropriate accommodation, similar to how the asylum support regime operates[241] except there are no clear policies for how to deal with cases where there are particular needs and concerns which require a specific type or location of accommodation.

11.205 One of the consequences of the lack of publicly available standards of care for victims of trafficking is that there are no clear standards for safe house accommodation, and no consistency as to the quality and arrangements across the different safe houses. What is available at each safe house depends on what a given NRM Support Provider subcontracted under the AVMS can offer. This is in contrast even with asylum support accommodation, where the contracts between the Home Office and accommodation providers set down certain minimum standards for the room arrangements and facilities. There are also concerns related to the adequacy of skill sets within a particular safe house to deal with the complex needs of particular victims of trafficking because, as discussed above, there are no minimum qualifications required to be a support worker at a

240 See announcement by Sarah Newton MP, Parliamentary Under-Secretary of State for the Home Department in Hansard HC Debs vol 630 col 512, 26 October 2017.

241 See paras 5.169–5.184.

safe house or be a part of an outreach service, or specialist requirements to work with victims of trafficking. Placements also do not appear to be based on any considered needs assessment in contrast with the adult social care regime under the Care Act 2014 or the structured framework for placement arrangements for children under ChA 1989 s20.

11.206 There have been challenges brought to the termination of safe house accommodation to particularly vulnerable victims of trafficking on the basis that their needs, which may be associated with an underlying disability or mental ill-health, are too high for the safe house to cope with, or their behaviour has resulted in their eviction. Although there has yet to be a reported case on the approach taken to termination of accommodation in these contexts, the fact that these issues arise suggests there may be structural problems in the NRM arrangements for safe house accommodation. It may be that such problems are attributable to the lack of any structured and directed individualised needs assessment underpinning the management and allocation of accommodation.

11.207 The *MSA 2015 statutory guidance* strongly suggests that asylum-seeking victims should be accommodated under the IAA 1999[242] unless they have specific needs over and above asylum accommodation.[243] The problem is the lack of a standardised needs assessment framework and lack of consistency in qualification and experience among support workers tasked with the needs assessment. The diversion of victims away from safe house accommodation is of concern and arguably unlawful. Both ECAT Article 12(1) and Anti-Trafficking Directive Article 11(5) state the assistance and support measures may include the provision of 'appropriate and safe accommodation'. This applies to *all* victims, and is not dependent on the immigration application they may have pending separate from the NRM trafficking inquiry. Article 11(7) of the Directive requires member states, like the UK, to pay attention to victims with 'special needs' and make arrangement for assistance addressing those needs. Nothing can be drawn from the trafficking obligations to support a general assumption that by virtue of having made an asylum claim, a victim of trafficking should be expected to access accommodation through the asylum support scheme. Particularly as asylum support accommodation under the IAA 1999 is not designed specifically to

242 A detailed discussion of sections 95 and 4(2) support under the IAA 1999 is given in paras 5.9–5.281 and 6.9–6.200.

243 *MSA 2015 statutory guidance*, para 15.13.

meet the special needs with which victims of trafficking present and, in practice, is frequently of a poor standard.[244] A similar approach taken by the Home Office in respect of subsistence levels was held to be unlawful, in breach of the UK's ECHR Article 4 obligations and to discriminate unlawfully against asylum-seeking victims. For a discussion of that case, *R (K) v SSHD*, see para 11.211 below.

Essential living needs

11.208 Subsistence is intended, under ECAT Article 12 and Anti-Trafficking Directive Article 11(5), to be capable of meeting the victims' 'standards of living'. The arrangements under the AVMSCC are complicated and depend on the type of accommodation that the victim is in, whether the victim is pregnant, has dependant children, and the age of those children, and whether the victim is eligible and receives asylum support or universal credit.

11.209 In addition to weekly subsistence, victims of trafficking within the NRM may receive support in kind and finance, as is necessary, for transport and attending appointments with health professionals. However, similar concerns arise in the absence of any structured assessment of the particular needs of the victim and the absence of clear guidance on how the nature and level of support is determined.

11.210 In March 2018, the government sought to cut the weekly subsistence amounts due to asylum-seeking victims of trafficking to the base level of asylum support, removing the top-up payment, specifically meant to cover additional recovery needs that victims have. In the policy announcement, the government sought to explain that this was because victims receiving NRM support are 'in a comparable situation to those awaiting their immigration decision . . . there is no clear justification' to give them more than asylum-seekers.[245] Prior to the policy announcement, asylum-seeking victims of trafficking received a total of £65 per week, which included £37.75 per week, the rate they were entitled to under IAA 1999 s95 or s4(2) depending on which they were eligible for, plus a weekly 'top-up' to meet their victim-specific recovery needs. The cut, in effect, removed the 'top-up' from asylum-seeking victims, but not from other victims who were non-asylum-seekers.

244 See paras 5.154–5.168 on standards of asylum support accommodation.

245 See announcement made on 26 October 2017 by the Minister for Crime, Safeguarding and Vulnerability, Sarah Newton MP, cited in *R (K) v SSHD* [2018] EWHC 2951 (Admin) at para 17.

11.211 The subsistence cut was successfully challenged by way of judicial review in *R (K) v SSHD*[246] by two victims affected by the cuts as being in breach of the government's trafficking obligations under the Anti-Trafficking Directive, the ECAT and ECHR Article 4, and being unlawfully discriminatory for treating asylum-seeking victims less favourably than those who have not claimed asylum. In a short but cutting judgment, Mostyn J rejected the government's statement that there was 'no clear justification' to give victims of trafficking more subsistence than asylum-seekers. He held that in the context of trafficking obligations, 'subsistence' is intended to contribute to the victim's recovery.[247] This was, he found, clear from the more 'expansive view' of subsistence set out in Article 11 and Recital 18 of the Directive than that which is needed to avoid destitution in the context of the IAA 1999.[248] The High Court quashed the decision to cut asylum-seeking victims' weekly subsistence and ordered the Home Office to repay those asylum-seeking victims whose subsistence was cut the sums cut from 1 March to 7 November 2018.[249] The Home Office published a scheme on 17 January 2019 to enable the back-payments to be processed in all affected cases.

11.212 The current rates payable to victims and any child dependant are reviewed over time, and therefore reference should be made to the *MSA 2015 statutory guidance* for the most current rates applicable at the relevant time.

Health care

11.213 Victims of trafficking are entitled to NHS healthcare free of charge once they have received a positive Reasonable Grounds decision.[250] The exemption from charging was first introduced in 2008[251] further to the commitment made by the UK government to ratify the ECAT.[252] This was in acknowledgment of the fact that many victims will be without funds to pay any NHS charges that they may have

246 [2018] EWHC 2951 (Admin).

247 *K v SSHD* at para 26.

248 *K v SSHD* at paras 24–30.

249 See order annexed to the judgment in *K v SSHD* accessible on the British and Irish Legal Information Institute (BAILII) website (www.bailii.org).

250 See National Health Service (Charges to Overseas Visitors) Regulations 2015 SI No 238 reg 16.

251 See National Health Service (Charges to Overseas Visitors) (Amendment) Regulations 2008 SI No 2251 reg 2.

252 See Explanatory Memorandum to the NHS (Charges to Overseas Visitors) 2008 Regulations, paras 4.1–4.3.

incurred or will incur and it is unlikely that any charges can effectively be recovered from them. Accordingly, even though the ECAT itself does not impose on the state an obligation to provide healthcare free of charge to victims, including those who are undergoing the identification process, the government took the view that exempting victims from being charged would ensure full compliance with the protective obligations owed by the UK under the ECAT to victims of trafficking and would reduce the 'stress on the victims'. It would, according to the government, also obviate the need for the NHS to issue 'fruitless bills' which are unlikely to be recoverable.[253] In 2015, further amendments were introduced in the regulations on NHS charging so that NHS trusts are prohibited from raising invoices or recovering NHS charges for treatment that victims received prior to being identified and are required to refund victims who had previously paid the charges invoiced to them prior to identification as a victim.[254]

11.214 Although ECAT Article 12(1) and Anti-Trafficking Directive Article 11(5) envisage that the assistance and support provided to victims of trafficking will include access to psychological assistance, there does not appear, from information available in the public domain, that any additional funding has been made available through the NHS to ensure that victims of trafficking are able to access psychological assistance as a matter of course. It is unlikely that this will be remedied under any new AVMS contract. More often than not, victims in receipt of NRM support will often be referred for counselling from charitable organisations because the waiting lists for specialist NHS provision are too long and exceed the time period that a victim spends in the reflection and recovery period.

Access to legal services

11.215 Under ECAT Article 12(1)(d), assistance and support to victims should include access to 'counselling and information, in particular as regards their legal rights and the services available to them, in a language that they can understand'. The government has made provision for legal aid to be available to victims of trafficking under Legal Aid, Sentencing and Punishment of Offenders Act 2012 (LASPO) Sch 1 Part 1 paras 32 and 32A in the following ways:

253 See Explanatory Memorandum to the NHS (Charges to Overseas Visitors) 2008 Regulations paras 7.7–7.9.

254 See National Health Service (Charges to Overseas Visitors) Regulations 2015 reg 6.

1) Victims are entitled to legal aid funding, subject to a means and merits test, for an application for leave to enter or remain in the UK as soon as they have received a 'Reasonable Grounds' decision.[255] This is irrespective of whether a formal application for leave to remain has been made.[256] This is in recognition of the Home Office's policy of automatically considering whether to grant a residence permit further to making a Conclusive Grounds decision.
2) Victims are entitled to legal aid, subject to a means and merits test, to bring a claim for compensation arising in connection with their trafficking or exploitation.[257]

11.216 Legal aid funding is not available to a victim as of right to seek legal advice and assistance prior to a 'Reasonable Grounds' decision being made,[258] but exceptional funding may be available under LASPO s10.

Support after the NRM

11.217 ECAT Article 12 does not stipulate a specified time when the obligation on member states to provide specialist assistance and support to victims of trafficking comes to an end, and certainly does not state that it should end once the identification process has been completed and the state accepts that their circumstances meet the definition of trafficking. In the UK, however, the government has long treated the NRM as a self-contained and discrete system directed at identification and support pending identification.

11.218 Victims of trafficking who are granted a residence permit or otherwise secure leave to remain will normally be granted leave to remain without any restriction to their ability to access public funds. They will therefore be entitled to access mainstream benefits,[259]

255 LASPO Sch 1 Part 1 paras 32(1) and 32A(1).

256 This was confirmed further to litigation brought in April 2018 challenging the Legal Aid Agency's (LAA's) refusal to grant funding where the immigration application for leave to remain is part of the automatic consideration of a residence permit within the NRM. See news item 'Legal aid and immigration advice for victims of modern slavery', 30 April 2018, accessed from the Anti-Trafficking and Labour Exploitation Unit website, https://atleu.org.uk/.

257 LASPO Sch 1 Part 1 paras 32(2), (3) and 32A(2), (3).

258 *R (Gudanaviciene) v Immigration and Asylum First Tier Tribunal* [2017] EWCA Civ 352.

259 See further details on welfare benefits in chapter 4.

housing[260] and social care,[261] subject to the same eligibility criteria as others who are not restricted from accessing public funds. Victims of trafficking are not considered to be automatically in 'priority need' for accommodation for the purposes of the homelessness legislation under the Housing Act 1996, but may be found to have such a need if they are assessed as being vulnerable.[262] In assessing whether they are vulnerable, a housing authority ought to take into account advice from specialist agencies involved with the victim (such as the NRM Support Provider). The *Homelessness code of guidance for local authorities*[263] acknowledges that many victims will suffer from poor mental health and often lack support structures in the area in which they are residing. If they are threatened with homelessness or are homeless, the code recognises that this significantly increases their risk of being re-trafficked or exposed to further exploitation.[264]

11.219 Victims of trafficking who are recognised by way of a positive 'Conclusive Grounds' decision but who have not been granted a residence permit are, subject to assessment, entitled to continued support under the NRM support arrangements. Prior to July 2019, the government had imposed a 45-day time limit on continued support under the NRM after a positive 'Conclusive Grounds' decision.[265] This was challenged by two victims of trafficking[266] as being incompatible with ECAT Article 12, which requires support to be provided by reference to an individual victim's needs rather than by reference to how long they have been supported. The Home Office conceded prior to a substantive hearing that that support should not be delimited by time alone. In September 2019, the Home Office published new guidance, *Recovery needs assessments*, v1.0, establishing a process for considering the need for continued support post-Conclusive Grounds decision. This was incorporated into the current version of the *MSA 2015 statutory guidance.*

260 See further details on housing and homelessness in chapter 7.

261 See further details on eligibility for adult social care in chapter 8.

262 See Housing Act 1996 s189(1)(c); and *Homelessness code of guidance for local authorities*, para 25.17.

263 Department for Levelling Up, Housing and Communities, February 2018, last updated January 2023.

264 *Homelessness code of guidance*, para 25.17. See also paras 7.136–7.151 for further details on assessments of vulnerability under the Housing Act 1996.

265 Prior to October 2018, the post-NRM support period was 14 days.

266 *R (NN and LP) v SSHD* CO/1040/2019, CO/1039/2019.

Criminal Injuries Compensation Scheme

11.220 Under ECAT Article 15(4) and Anti-Trafficking Directive Article 17 it is envisaged that victims of trafficking may also be able to access a state compensation scheme for money that will assist them in their continued recovery from their past experiences of trafficking. In the UK, provision has been made for this under the CICS, a statutory scheme made under the Criminal Injuries Compensation Act 1995. Eligibility for compensation as a victim of trafficking is based on the following criteria:[267]

1) The applicant has sustained a criminal injury which is directly attributable to their being a direct victim of a crime of violence[268] committed in Great Britain or a place specified under the rules of the scheme.[269]
2) The applicant has been referred to the NRM and conclusively identified as a victim of trafficking or has claimed asylum and been granted asylum or human rights protection or temporary protection on human rights grounds.[270]

11.221 Applications for criminal injuries compensation must be 'as soon as reasonably practicable' after the incident giving rise to the injury and in any event within two years after the date of the incident.[271] In respect of children, the time period starts after they reach their 18th birthday.[272]

11.222 Victims of trafficking who have unspent criminal convictions which resulted in a custodial sentence or a community order would not be granted an award even if they meet the other criteria.[273] This was subject to an unsuccessful challenge by way of judicial review in *A and B v Criminal Injuries Compensation Authority and Secretary of State for Justice*[274] on grounds that the rule preventing victims with certain unspent convictions from getting criminal injuries compensation discriminated against those victims in breach of ECHR Article 14 read with ECHR Article 4. The Supreme Court rejected the argument that the rule discriminated against *all* victims of trafficking on

267 See the CICS 2012 (as amended).
268 CICS, para 4.
269 CICS, para 8 and Annex C.
270 CICS, paras 13, 15 and 16.
271 CICS, para 87.
272 CICS, para 88.
273 CICS, para 26 and Annex D.
274 [2021] UKSC 27.

the facts of that claim because the offence of human trafficking to which the appellants were subjected did not bear a nexus with the crime for which they were convicted, and also rejected the argument that victims of trafficking with relevant unspent convictions ought to have been treated the same as those who do not have relevant unspent convictions. It weighed heavily on the court's mind that the CICS had been approved by parliament further to debate and that it sought to address the question of compensation for victims of crimes of violence against the backdrop of limited resources. The evidence for consideration of the question of justification by the court under ECHR Article 14 was limited to that which was contained in the government's consultation document and summary of consultees' responses provided in July 2012 (nearly a decade ago). The Supreme Court left open the question as to whether the position was different for victims of trafficking whose criminal conviction arose in relation to their trafficking circumstances.

11.223 Applications for criminal injuries compensation have also been rejected in some cases because the Criminal Injuries Compensation Authority does not always accept that, as a matter of principle, the act of trafficking constitutes a crime of violence. This frequently arises in difficult cases where the exploitation was committed by means of psychological threats and coercion which leave no scars and are difficult to show. Such an approach jars with the universal acceptance in international law of trafficking as an abhorrent crime.

11.224 There have been further reports of applications for compensation being rejected in the absence of any criminal investigation or prosecution, even though this is not a prerequisite to the right of effective access to a state compensation scheme under either ECAT Article 15(4) or Anti-Trafficking Directive Article 17.

Victims of domestic violence

11.225 Both men and women can experience domestic abuse, but research and statistics show that women are overwhelming more likely to suffer from it.[275] Research has also shown that migrant women are

275 *Domestic abuse: findings from the Crime Survey for England and Wales: year ending March 2018*, Office for National Statistics.

considerably more likely to experience sustained and repeated forms of abuse at the hands of multiple perpetrators.[276]

11.226 The UK is a signatory to international treaties which seek to combat violence against women and girls and to address domestic abuse as a crime and a scourge of society. The two main treaties relevant to this topic are the UN Convention on the Elimination of all Forms of Discrimination against Women (CEDAW); and the Council of Europe Convention on Preventing and Combatting Violence Against Women and Domestic Violence, also known as the 'Istanbul Convention'.

Convention on Elimination of All Forms of Discrimination against Women

11.227 The CEDAW was adopted in 1979 by the UN General Assembly and ratified by the UK on 7 April 1986. The CEDAW defines discrimination against women as follows in Article 1:

> . . . any distinction, exclusion or restriction made on the basis of sex which has the effect or purpose of impairing or nullifying the recognition, enjoyment or exercise by women, irrespective of their marital status, on a basis of equality of men and women, of human rights and fundamental freedoms in the political, economic, social, cultural, civil or any other field.

11.228 The CEDAW requires state parties to 'pursue all appropriate means and without delay a policy of eliminating discrimination against women' and to that end undertake to implement measures to ensure women's full enjoyment of human rights on an equal basis by:

- eradicating stereotyped roles for women and men;
- ensuring women's equal participation in public life;
- establishing measures that ensure equality before the law;
- eliminating discrimination in employment.

11.229 Article 13 specifically requires state parties to 'take all appropriate measures to eliminate discrimination in other areas of economic and social life in order to ensure, on a basis of equality of men and

276 See 'Protection for all: The Domestic Abuse Bill and migrant women', Southall Black Sisters, 2019; K Smith, C Miles, 'Nowhere to Turn: Findings from the first year of the No Women Turned Away Project', Women's Aid, 2017. See also S Anitha, 'No recourse, no support: state policy and practice towards South Asian women facing domestic violence in the UK' (2010) 40(2) *British Journal of Social Work* 462–479; and ' "No Recourse" No Safety: The Government's failure to protect women from violence', Amnesty UK, March 2008.

women, the same rights, in particular . . . the right to family benefits'.

11.230 The UN last examined how well the UK is implementing the CEDAW in February 2019 and published its recommendations in March 2019. These included:

- incorporating the CEDAW into domestic law and creating a national mechanism to oversee its implementation;
- ensuring women's rights are protected during the process of withdrawing from the EU;
- ratifying the Istanbul Convention, and taking all necessary steps to protect women and girls from gender-based violence;
- assessing the impact of public spending, tax and welfare reforms on women's rights, and taking action to reduce and resolve any negative effects;
- ensuring that legal aid and representation is available especially to women who are asylum-seekers, from ethnic minority backgrounds, or victims of gender-based violence and of trafficking, recognising that they are often disproportionately disadvantaged, particularly in the areas of immigration, housing and welfare benefits law; and
- taking measures to end or impose a time limit on immigration detention of migrant women and enable asylum-seeking and refugee women to gain access to appropriate housing and employment.

11.231 As an unincorporated treaty, the CEDAW has no direct effect in domestic law. However, the CEDAW has been relied on to determine the scope of human rights obligations under the ECHR: see *Opuz v Turkey*,[277] an ECHR Articles 2 and 14 case involving a complaint of failure to protect from domestic violence. The court relied in part on the CEDAW in determining the scope of Article 14.[278] The importance of this interpretative approach was highlighted in *Neulinger v Switzerland*[279] by the Grand Chamber (at para 131):

> The Convention cannot be interpreted in a vacuum but must be interpreted in harmony with the general principles of international law. Account should be taken . . . of 'any relevant rules of international law applicable in the relations between the parties', and in particular the rules concerning the international protection of human rights . . .

277 App No 33401/02 (2010) 50 EHRR 28, ECtHR.

278 See *Opuz v Turkey* paras 185–187.

279 App No 41615/07 (2012) 54 EHRR 31, ECtHR.

11.232 This approach has been adopted in domestic case-law. UN treaties such as the CEDAW, the UNCRC and the UN Convention on the Rights of Persons with Disabilities (UNCRPD), have been relied to illuminate the approach to justification of differential treatment under Article 14.[280]

Istanbul Convention

11.233 The Istanbul Convention was adopted on 11 May 2011. The UK signed the Convention on 8 June 2012. The UK has not yet ratified it, but the government has committed to do so. In a parliamentary debate on UN International Day for the Elimination of Violence against Women, Sarah Newton MP, then the Parliamentary Under Secretary for the Home Office, stated, when asked that: 'I am proud that we signed that convention and I know that we will ratify it. I want to assure Members that the lack of ratification is not stopping us doing anything; we are already complying with every single aspect of that convention.'[281] The same was repeated a week later by Brandon Lewis, Minister for Policing and the Fire Service.[282] The bold statement as to the full compliance of the UK with the Istanbul Convention is untested and conflicts with immigration policies, formulated in context of the 'hostile environment', which create gaps in protection for migrant women who are victims of domestic abuse and subject to immigration control.

11.234 The Istanbul Convention is premised on the following core principles:

1) Violence against women is both a violation of human rights and a form of discrimination against women.
2) The state must refrain from acts of violence against women.
3) Where the violence or risk of violence emanates from private individuals (for example, rape or other sexual assaults, slavery and human trafficking, female genital mutilation (FGM), forced marriage, domestic violence etc) the state must take the necessary legislative and other measures to prevent and investigate acts of violence perpetrated against women.

280 See, for example, *Burnip v Birmingham City Council* [2012] EWCA Civ 629, [2013] PTSR 117 in respect of the UNCRDP; *R (SG) v SSWP* [2015] UKSC 16 in respect of the CEDAW and UNCRC.

281 Sarah Newton MP, Parliamentary Under-Secretary for the Home Office, Hansard HC Debs col 437, 8 December 2016.

282 Brandon Lewis, Minister for Policing and the Fire Service, Hansard HC Debs col 1110, 16 December 2016.

4) The state must also take the necessary legislative and other measures to protect victims from any further acts of violence, including from being re-victimised.

11.235 As a human rights instrument, the Istanbul Convention recognises the gendered nature of domestic violence and the need for legislative and other measures to include a gender perspective to state implementation of legislative and other measures in the fulfilment of the obligations under the Convention: see preamble and Articles 2(2) and 6. The Convention emphasises a non-discrimination and inclusive approach; this can be seen by:

1) Article 3(f), which defines 'women' as inclusive of girls under the age of 18.
2) Article 4(3), which requires the provisions of the Convention to be secured without discrimination on any ground including an explicit ground of discrimination based on 'migrant or refugee status'.
3) Article 18(1) requires legislative or other measures to protect '*all* victims' from any further acts of violence. Measures taken to protect women from violence should avoid secondary victimisation, address the specific needs of vulnerable persons, and be aimed at the empowerment and economic independence of women victims of violence.
4) Article 20 requires states to take measures to ensure that victims have access to services, including health and social services, housing, financial assistance, and education/training, to facilitate their recovery from violence.

11.236 The inclusion under the Istanbul Convention of non-discrimination on grounds of 'migrant or refugee status' is an important addition to the familiar list of grounds contained in ECHR Article 14. This is in recognition that women of ethnic minority origin more frequently are victims of multiple discrimination and migrant and refugee women, in particular, are frequently unable to access much needed support services by reason of their residence status. The wider grounds of discrimination recognised in the Istanbul Convention reflect its status as a modern day human rights treaty and exemplifies the continued progressive evolution of human rights instruments.

11.237 The progressive nature of the Istanbul Convention is also reflected in it being a treaty which addresses not only domestic violence but also violence against women. It defines the two concepts as follows:

1) 'Violence against women' is understood as a violation of human rights and a form of discrimination against women and shall mean all acts of gender-based violence that result in, or are likely to result in, physical, sexual, psychological or economic harm or suffering to women, including threats of such acts, coercion or arbitrary deprivation of liberty, whether occurring in public or in private life: Article 3(a).
2) 'Domestic violence' shall mean all acts of physical, sexual, psychological or economic violence that occur within the family or domestic unit or between former or current spouses or partners, whether or not the perpetrator shares or has shared the same residence with the victim: Article 3(b).

11.238 Article 59 introduces the possibility of granting 'autonomous residence status' to migrant women victims who depend on their abuser for their residence permit 'in the event of the dissolution of the marriage or relationship' and 'particularly difficult circumstances'. States '*shall* issue' a renewable residence permit to victims in one of two situations (or both):

1) when the competent authority considers that their stay is necessary owing to their personal situation;
2) where the competent authority considers that their stay is necessary for the purpose of their co-operation with the competent authorities in investigation or criminal proceedings.

The particular conditions relating to the granting and duration of the autonomous residence permit are established by internal law.

11.239 States are also required to adopt measures for victims of forced marriage who have lost their residence status in the country where they usually reside by helping them to re-obtain it. Furthermore, states must adopt a gender-sensitive approach when considering whether to grant refugee status and international protection. Article 60 goes on to impose obligations to recognise gender-based violence against women as:

1) a form of persecution under the meaning of the Refugee Convention; and
2) a form of harm that requires specific protection measures.

11.240 Articles 18–28 of the Istanbul Convention set out obligations owed by states concerning protection and support for victims of domestic violence.

- Article 18 imposes a general obligation on the state to take legislative or other measures for the protection of *all* victims within their territory from any further acts of violence.

- Article 20 imposes a duty on states to take the necessary legislative or other measures to ensure that victims have access to services facilitating their recovery from violence. These include services such as legal and psychological counselling, financial assistance, housing, education, training, and assistance in finding employment.
- Article 22 imposes an obligation on states to provide or arrange for immediate, short- and long-term specialist support services to any victim.
- Article 23 imposes an obligation on the state to provide for the set-up of appropriate, easily accessible shelters in sufficient numbers to provide safe accommodation for, and to reach out pro-actively to, victims, especially women and their children.

11.241 The support duties imposed under the Convention are in recognition of victims' needs for adequate protection from further violence, for support and assistance to overcome the multiple consequences of such violence, and to rebuild their lives.[283]

Domestic application of international obligations

11.242 Although the UK signed the Istanbul Convention in June 2012, it has not yet ratified the Convention. The government has said that amendments to domestic law – to take extra-territorial jurisdiction over a range of offences – are necessary before the Convention can be ratified.[284] The government has also, however, said that the 'UK already complies with the vast majority of the Convention's articles through its comprehensive work to protect women and girls'.[285]

11.243 The Preventing and Combating Violence Against Women and Domestic Violence (Ratification of Convention) Act 2017, which came into force in June 2017, imposed a duty upon the Secretary of State for the Home Department (SSHD) to provide annual reports to parliament in order to report on the progress made towards ratification. Two such annual reports have been published and laid before parliament.

283 *Explanatory Report to the Istanbul Convention*, para 110.

284 PQ 26764 on implementing the Istanbul Convention, answered 22 February 2016, available at: www.parliament.uk/written-questions-answers-statements/written-question/commons/2016-02-10/26764.

285 PQ 10888 on ratifying the Istanbul Convention, answered 22 February 2016 available at: www.parliament.uk/written-questions-answers-statements/written-question/commons/2015-10-09/10888.

11.244 In respect of immigration and the position of migrant women, the government stated in its November 2017 report[286] that it was committed to ensuring that the UK asylum process is gender-sensitive. It also referred to the availability of the Destitute Domestic Violence Concession (DDVC) to migrant spouses of permanent UK residents who are fleeing domestic violence. Such spouses may be granted a period of leave of three months in order to make an application for indefinite leave to remain (ILR) under the Immigration Rules. The subsequent October 2018 report[287] was silent on any further steps toward strengthening the government's commitment to protecting the position of migrant women who suffer from or are fleeing domestic violence.

11.245 Separately in March 2018, the government launched a consultation seeking views on both legislative proposals for a draft Domestic Abuse Bill and a package of practical actions. The full consultation document proposed, inter alia, the introduction of a statutory definition of domestic abuse; the creation of a new domestic abuse protection notice (DAPN) to be issued by the police; a new domestic abuse protection order (DAPO) to be available to the courts in a wide range of circumstances; a Domestic Abuse Commission; and putting the Domestic Violence Disclosure Scheme into law.

11.246 The consultation and the progress reports published under the 2017 Act did not consider or grapple with the potential gaps and inadequacies in the existing domestic law and policy framework which primarily, but not solely, relate to the immigration laws and policies necessary to fulfil the UK's obligations under the Istanbul Convention.

11.247 The Domestic Abuse Bill, presented to parliament in July 2019, did not address these gaps, focusing predominantly on enhancing prosecution and criminal prevention measures. Although important in their own right, these measures were subject to criticism on the

286 *Ratification of the Council of Europe Convention on Combating Violence Against Women and Domestic Violence (Istanbul Convention), Report on Progress,* Home Office, November 2017, available at: https://assets.publishing.service.gov.uk/government/uploads/system/uploads/attachment_data/file/656561/CCS207_CCS1017309396-1_HO_Istanbul_Convention_report_WEB_ACCESSIBLE.PDF.

287 *Ratification of the Council of Europe Convention on Combating Violence Against Women and Domestic Violence (Istanbul Convention), 2018 Report on Progress,* Home Office, October 2017, available at https://assets.publishing.service.gov.uk/government/uploads/system/uploads/attachment_data/file/752315/CCS207_CCS0918513168-001_Domestic_Violence_Istanbul_Convention_2018_Accessible__002_.pdf.

basis that they were not accompanied by a robust victim support framework. The announcement of the December 2019 general election brought the bill to a rapid end. However, the reinstatement of a draft Domestic Abuse Bill was included in the Queen's Speech later that month, which subsequently became law in the form of the Domestic Abuse Act (DAA) 2021, which came into force in April 2021. The Act introduces a broad statutory definition of domestic abuse (see DAA 2021 s1) intended to promote a cross-governmental consistency of approach to the issue, and creates the role of Domestic Abuse Commissioner whose role, under DAA 2021 s7, involves encouraging best practice in dealing with domestic abuse and monitoring the provision of services, among other things. But, in the main, the DAA 2021, like the consultation that preceded it, is focused on enhancing prosecution and criminal prevention measures and does little to address the potential gaps and inadequacies highlighted at para 11.233 relating to immigration law and policy and the implementation of the Istanbul Convention in this regard.

11.248 Like the CEDAW, the Istanbul Convention is an unincorporated treaty, but one which is an important interpretative tool for a clearer understanding of human rights obligations and policy objectives in the protection of victims of domestic abuse victims, which do not have direct effect in domestic law. The interpretative approach outlined in *R (SG) v SSWP*,[288] cited above in respect of the legal reach of the UNCRC and CEDAW,[289] applies equally to the Istanbul Convention, particularly given the government's clear belief that the UK is already in full compliance with the Convention and commitment to ratifying it formally.

Access to support for victims of domestic abuse

Access to accommodation and subsistence support

11.249 The rest of this section illustrates that the nature and level of support to which a person is entitled from the state is heavily dependent on their particular immigration status, and in relation to a number of areas of support[290] there is a presumption that migrants are prima facie excluded save for particular categories which are explicitly

288 [2015] UKSC 16.

289 See paras 11.10–11.32 for a discussion of the UNCRC and paras 11.227–11.232 for a discussion of the CEDAW.

290 For example, eligibility for homelessness assistance and the allocation of social housing, which proceed on the basis that those from outside the EEA will be ineligible unless they fall within a prescribed category. See chapter 7.

carved out and legislated for. Crucially, 'victims of domestic violence and abuse' is not in and of itself a category of persons exempt from the presumption against providing support to migrants. Thus, migrant women who are victims of domestic abuse, who require leave to remain but do not have it, will not have recourse to 'public funds', such as income support or universal credit.[291]

11.250 If they require other forms of support, such as community care services[292] (their need for which may have arisen precisely because they are ineligible for public funds), along with their dependants, and they have no claim for asylum, they will be subject to human rights assessments under NIAA 2002 Sch 3[293] for the purposes of determining whether they are eligible for support.

11.251 As for those victims of domestic abuse who are seeking asylum, if they are eligible for asylum support[294] they can make a request for accommodation to be arranged away from their abusive partner using the *Allocation of accommodation policy*.[295] The risks posed to them and the impact on their children will fall to be considered on a case-by-case basis. No legal aid is available to access advice and assistance to advance a request for accommodation away from the abusive partner, but in major dispersal areas where asylum support accommodation is located, there may be charities which are able to assist.

11.252 If the abusive partner was a dependent on the victim's asylum support claim, the victim can make a request in writing for the dependent to be removed: see the *Dependants on an asylum support application* policy, section 4.[296] The removal of the abusive partner would necessarily lead to an adjustment in the level of financial support received to reflect the reduction in people on the application. It is also possible that the accommodation that had been provided is no longer appropriate.

11.253 If the victim is a dependent on the abusive partner's asylum support application, they can also make a request to be removed from the main applicant's asylum support application. The power under IAA 1999 s95(1) can be exercised to provide asylum support to

291 The full list of public funds may be found in Immigration Rules para 6. See further para 1.166.

292 See chapters 8 and 9.

293 The operation of Schedule 3 to the NIAA 2002 is discussed at paragraphs 9.195–9.217.

294 See paras 5.9–5.281.

295 *Allocation of asylum accommodation policy (accessible)*, UKVI, updated December 2022.

296 *Dependants on an asylum support application policy*, v8.0, Home Office.

a dependent of an asylum-seeker separate from the asylum-seeker.[297] Thus a dependent who is subject to domestic violence can conceivably be provided with asylum support separate from their abusive partner. The Home Office's policy *Domestic abuse: responding to reports of domestic abuse from asylum seekers*[298] stresses the need to take immediate steps to ensure that a victim and any children are transferred to alternative accommodation that is safe and secure, save where the victim wishes to remain, in which case consideration must be given to relocating the perpetrator.[299] In addition, accommodation providers should consider referring the victim and their dependent children to a refuge, the cost of which will be met by the Home Office, or consulting with the local authority about the appropriate action to take.[300] Any report of domestic violence must be acted upon, with a presumption that the victim should be believed.[301]

11.254 Asylum Seekers (Reception Conditions) Regulations 2005 (as amended) reg 4 requires the SSHD to take account of the special needs of an asylum-seeker or their family member who is a vulnerable person when providing or considering whether to provide support under IAA 1999 s95(1).[302] For the purposes of this regulation, a vulnerable person is defined as: a minor; a disabled person; an elderly person; a pregnant woman; a lone parent with a minor child; or a person who has been subjected to torture, rape or other serious forms of psychological, physical or sexual violence, who has had an individual evaluation of their situation that confirms that they have special needs. There is no obligation on the Home Office to carry out or arrange for the carrying out of an individual evaluation of a

297 The power under IAA s95(1) applies to destitute asylum-seekers *or* their dependants. The categories of dependants are set out in IAA 1999 s94(1) and Asylum Support Regulations 2000 SI No 704 reg 2(4). A number of these categories, such as spouse or child under the age of 18, do not require cohabitation for a relationship of dependency to exist. Other categories do require cohabitation but only at the point the application is made and not necessarily on a continuous basis thereafter. See further paras 5.50–5.56.

298 *Domestic abuse: responding to reports of domestic abuse from asylum seekers*, v2.0, Home Office. January 2022.

299 *Domestic abuse: responding to reports of domestic abuse from asylum seekers*, v2.0, pp10 and 11.

300 *Domestic abuse: responding to reports of domestic abuse from asylum seekers*, v2.0, p11.

301 *Domestic abuse: responding to reports of domestic abuse from asylum seekers*, v2.0, p10.

302 See further para 5.143.

person's situation to determine whether such special needs exist. The evidential onus is on the vulnerable person.

11.255 In all likelihood, where a victim leaves their abusive partner, they will no longer wish to remain dependent on their partner. It is inevitable that, unless they make their own free-standing asylum claim or another immigration application, they are unlikely to be able to remain on IAA 1999 s95 support as a dependent of their abusive partner. The Home Office is thus likely to discontinue support to them under section 95(1).

11.256 If the victim has dependent children, any decision to discontinue must have proper regard to the need to safeguard and promote the welfare of the children under BCIA 2009 s55. Account also needs to be taken of the impact of the decision on the family, particularly if it is known that the family is destitute but for the provision of IAA 1999 s95(1) support.

11.257 The Home Office's *Policy Bulletin 70* makes clear that before any action is taken to begin the process to discontinue support, the Home Office case worker should liaise with the relevant local authority, notifying it that the Home Office plans to discontinue support from the family, and request that the local authority provides alternative support. If the local authority makes an offer of support (most likely under ChA 1989 s17), then IAA 1999 s95 support is to be discontinued as soon as the family transfers in local authority care. If the local authority refuses to provide support, the provision of asylum support is to be maintained until the local authority provides support.

11.258 Access to local authority support is precarious unless the victim is able to pursue an immigration application of sorts, particularly if the victim ceases to be a dependent not only on their partner's asylum support claim but also on their partner's asylum claim. Unless the victim regularises their immigration position, the victim and their children will likely be caught by the exclusionary provisions of NIAA 2002 Sch 3, which is discussed in detail at paras 5.9–5.281. Furthermore, support under the ChA 1989 is not directed at the needs of a victim who has suffered domestic violence – it is directed at meeting the needs of the child: see ChA 1989 s17(1) and (6), discussed in detail at paras 9.12–9.69. While the victim's needs may be met indirectly by virtue of them being the carer of the child(ren), that is not the main aim of ChA 1989 s17.

11.259 Moreover, the decision to support is based on a needs assessment; the process often puts victims and their children under intense scrutiny. There have been reports of local authorities offering to support only the children, by taking them into care, instead of supporting the family as a whole, causing a separation of the children from their primary carer. Local authorities are also known to obtain credit checks, and require bank statements and information about the victim's extended support network, if any. Victims who have fled domestic violence often will not have any documentation on them because of the circumstances in which they have left. They may also have had no knowledge of the family's finances because the perpetrator controlled that information. Extended family and friends who may have offered support to the victim and their children may be reluctant to provide evidence of their support to social services. All of these issues pose challenges to a victim of domestic violence seeking local authority support.[303] Thus for victims with children who may be able to access support under the ChA 1989, there remain significant protection barriers to their being able to leave their abusive relationships and/or access support to facilitate their recovery, all because of their immigration status, specifically because they cannot avail themselves of the destitute domestic violence (DDV) concession and to access recourse to public funds.

11.260 If the victim does not have dependent children, the discontinuance decision still needs to take into account the potential special needs that the victim has under Asylum Seekers (Reception Conditions) Regulations 2005 (as amended) reg 4. The difficulty is, however, that there is no obvious mainstream provision of support that is a substitute for asylum support for a lone woman comparable to ChA 1989 s17.

11.261 The Care Act 2014 imposes an eligibility threshold based on assessed needs for care and support, those being met only if the individual is unable to meet certain prescribed outcomes under the Care and Support (Eligibility Criteria) Regulations 2015.[304] It is not a set of eligibility criteria that is directed toward addressing the needs of victims of domestic violence. Furthermore, the victim is likely to be caught by Care Act 2014 s21, which precludes a local authority from meeting the needs for care and support of an adult to whom IAA 1999 s115 applies and whose needs for care and support arise because they are destitute or because of the physical effects or anticipated

303 See *R (MN) v Hackney LBC* [2013] EWHC 1205 (Admin) and *R (N) v Newham LBC* [2013] EWHC 2475 (Admin) in which the courts found that where the parent(s) were not forthcoming with information necessary to establish whether a child was in need, the local authority acted lawfully in refusing to provide support to the family. See also R (*O*) *v Lambeth LBC* [2016] EWHC 937 (Admin).

304 SI No 313.

physical effects of being destitute. NIAA 2002 Sch 3 (for which see paras 9.195–9.217) also operates to impose a prima facie exclusion from such mainstream support. Although Care Act 2014 s42 imposes a duty on local authorities to make safeguarding inquiries, there is no primary legislative provision that obliges local authorities to provide support to the person subjected to a safeguarding inquiry. Local safeguarding policies may direct consideration of interim support but this is by no means guaranteed.

Access to healthcare

11.262 In respect of access to health, the National Health Service (Charges to Overseas Visitors) Regulations ('Charges Regs') 2015[305] (discussed in chapter 10) seek to charge all 'overseas visitors' for secondary healthcare services, with non-urgent care subject to upfront charging. There is a limited exemption for victims of domestic abuse victims under Charges Regs 2015 (as amended) reg 9(1)(f) for 'the treatment of a condition *caused by* torture; female genital mutilation, domestic violence or sexual violence'. This includes subsequent and ongoing treatment for any condition, including chronic conditions, that 'is directly attributable' to the violence and, in the case of FGM, treatment, including any antenatal, perinatal and postpartum treatment, the need for which 'is directly attributable' to the mutilation: reg 8(2).

11.263 According to the Explanatory Memorandum to the Charges Regs 2015,[306] the reg 9(1)(f) exemption for gender-based violence was introduced in recognition of these cohorts being amongst the 'most vulnerable' and requiring the benefit of healthcare which they would otherwise be unable to pay for. Including this exemption was 'consistent with wider government policy in respect of preventing such violence and supporting victims of violence': Explanatory Memorandum para 7.27. An Equality Analysis completed in February 2015 also stated that the exemption was needed to ensure victims of gender-based violence, including FGM, are able to access hospital treatment in 'a safe and trusted environment'.

11.264 There is nothing in the Explanatory Memorandum or the Equality Analysis that explains the rationale behind limiting the charging exemption to treatment 'caused by' the specific gender-based violence. Neither document considered or addressed whether or how the exemption meets the UK's obligation under Istanbul Convention

305 SI No 238.

306 Explanatory Memorandum to the Charges Regs 2015 para 7.26.

Article 20 which provides for the state to ensure victims' access to health care, facilitating their recovery from violence. This is in contrast to the approach taken in respect of victims of trafficking under Charging Regs reg 16, who are similarly recognised to be vulnerable but who are *fully* exempt from charges for all treatment, regardless of whether it is directly attributable to the trafficking. The difference of treatment is hard to understand and has been subject to criticism by the Royal College of Midwives and by national charities such as Maternity Action.

Access to benefits

11.265 A detailed discussion of the overall welfare benefits framework is contained in chapter 4. For those victims of domestic abuse who have recourse to public funds, the benefits system has specific provisions directed at addressing, to some extent, the challenges they face:

1) Victims who have applied for a DDV concession[307] will get leave outside the rules for up to three months. They can claim benefits during this period of time while their substantive DVILR application is under consideration.
2) Those in receipt of housing benefit are permitted to be temporarily absent from their home through fear of domestic violence and abuse. If the victim intends to return to their former home, they can receive housing benefits for both the former home and their temporary accommodation for up to 52 weeks.
3) Those in receipt of jobseeker's allowance (JSA) can have a break from jobseeking and work preparation requirements for up to 13 weeks, split into two parts, an initial four-week period starting on the day the victim informs Jobcentre Plus that they have been threatened with or subject to domestic violence or abuse, and an extension from four to 13 weeks on production of supporting evidence. This would only apply to those already receiving JSA, not those who are new applicants.
4) This similarly applies to universal credit recipients who are victims of domestic violence. They get a 13-week break from the work-related requirements providing that the domestic abuse occurred within the previous six months, the victim no longer

307 See paras 1.118–1.125.

lives with the abuser and evidence is produced within a month of the date on which it was first informed to their work coach.[308]

5) The seven waiting days that are applied to new universal credit claims will not apply to victims of domestic violence in the six months prior to making a claim.
6) Universal credit payments may also be split so that the alleged abuser does not retain the whole payment of universal credit, through an alternative payment arrangement. However, this is only granted in 'very exceptional circumstances'.[309]
7) Certain accommodation is exempt from the benefit cap, including refuges, hostels and managed properties under certain conditions.
8) Discretionary housing payments (DHPs) may be available to victims of domestic violence to top up the shortfall left by the benefits cap or other welfare reforms.

11.266 Although the welfare benefits system does acknowledge the need for special protection for victims of domestic violence, some of these key safeguards are undermined by welfare reforms which have had a disproportionate impact on women more generally, such as the benefits cap, which imposes an overall cap on the total amount in benefits that 'workless' working-age people can receive, even if their full entitlement to benefits would otherwise be higher.[310] It works via a reduction in housing benefit or, if applicable, the housing cost element of universal credit. By Welfare Reform and Work Act 2016 ss8 and 9, the annual cap is £20,000 per annum (£384.62 per week) for families (couples without children, couples with children and lone parents) across England, Scotland and Wales, apart from Greater London where the limit is set at £23,000 for families (£442.31 per week).[311]

11.267 The effect of the benefits cap on single parent families, a large proportion of which will be led by women, is stark. It is well known that women fleeing domestic abuse will often leave without their

308 See further details about universal credit and domestic abuse in the report of the House of Lords Work and Pensions Committee published on 18 July 2018, available at: https://publications.parliament.uk/pa/cm201719/cmselect/cmworpen/1166/1166.pdf.

309 See: https://assets.publishing.service.gov.uk/government/uploads/system/uploads/attachment_data/file/747989/personal-budgeting-support-and-alternative-payment-arrangements.pdf.

310 This was first introduced by regulations made under Welfare Reform Act 2012 ss96 and 97.

311 The level for a single housing benefits claimant is £13,400 per annum outside Greater London, and £15,410 per annum in Greater London.

belongings, and that to ensure their safety they often have to leave the area that they live in, their homes, support networks and, in certain cases, their jobs. In many cases this will leave them in urgent need of welfare support to help them rebuild their lives in safety. The benefits cap adds a potential additional barrier to women trying to flee an abusive relationship who may be forced to choose between their safety and being pushed into poverty. Shelter's research has shown that the benefit cap leaves capped single-parent families with children in a position where their monthly income after housing costs put them below the relative poverty line. This puts a parent in an invidious position of having to choose between feeding and meeting the basic needs of their children, and paying their rent on a consistent basis. It also puts the family at real risk of homelessness and eviction.[312] However, the courts have stated that the impact of the cap on single parent families, a majority of whom are women, does not discriminate unlawfully.[313]

11.268 Thus even a woman who is eligible for public funds (including via the DDV concession) may be faced with trying to meet her and her children's housing and living needs while under the cap unless she is someone who is already in employment and/or can find employment with ease. This is unlikely to be realistic for those who are granted leave outside the rules under the DDV Concession given the extremely short duration of three months.

11.269 The additional barriers to access to support without specific provisions of assistance directed at supporting victims of domestic violence include the general shortage of affordable housing and the reluctance of landlords to rent to benefits claimants.[314]

312 See Shelter's evidence to the Work and Pensions Committee's inquiry into the benefit cap, available at: http://data.parliament.uk/writtenevidence/committeeevidence.svc/evidencedocument/work-and-pensions-committee/benefit-cap/written/89483.html.

313 *R (DA and others) v SSWP* [2019] UKSC 21.

314 See research carried out by Shelter in *Stop DSS Discrimination: Ending Prejudice against renters of housing benefits*, 2018, available at: https://england.shelter.org.uk/__data/assets/pdf_file/0009/1581687/Stop_DSS_Discrimination_-_Ending_prejudice_against_renters_on_housing_benefit.pdf.

Index